THE OXFORD HANDBOOK OF

UNITED NATIONS TREATIES

THE OXFORD HANDBOOK OF

UNITED NATIONS TREATIES

Edited by

SIMON CHESTERMAN,

DAVID M. MALONE,

and

SANTIAGO VILLALPANDO

with

ALEXANDRA IVANOVIC

OXFORD
UNIVERSITY PRESS

OXFORD
UNIVERSITY PRESS

Oxford University Press is a department of the University of Oxford. It furthers the University's objective of excellence in research, scholarship, and education by publishing worldwide. Oxford is a registered trade mark of Oxford University Press in the UK and certain other countries.

Published in the United States of America by Oxford University Press
198 Madison Avenue, New York, NY 10016, United States of America.

Library of Congress Cataloging-in-Publication Data
Names: Chesterman, Simon, editor. | Malone, David, 1954– editor. |
Villalpando, Santiago, editor.
Title: The Oxford handbook of United Nations treaties/edited by
Simon Chesterman, David M. Malone & Santiago Villalpando.
Description: Oxford [UK]; New York: Oxford University Press, [2019] |
Includes bibliographical references and index.
Identifiers: LCCN 2018045227 | ISBN 9780190947842 ((hardback): alk. paper)
Subjects: LCSH: United Nations—Treaty-making power. | United Nations.
Charter. | Treaties. | International agencies.
Classification: LCC KZ4992.7 .O94 2019 | DDC 341.3/7—dc23
LC record available at
https://lccn.loc.gov/2018045227

1 3 5 7 9 8 6 4 2

Printed by Sheridan Books, Inc., United States of America

Foreword by the UN Secretary-General

Treaties are the building blocks of the international rule of law. For the United Nations, they have been a vital means of living up to the promises of its Charter—which is, of course, a treaty itself. To maintain peace and security, States have concluded treaties in the areas of disarmament, dispute settlement, the fight against terrorism, and the peaceful uses of outer space. To develop friendly relations among nations and achieve international cooperation, they have elaborated complex treaty regimes on human rights, labor relations, drugs and crime, environmental protection, trade and development, health, culture, science and education, transport, and communications.

Over seven decades, the United Nations system has produced hundreds of multilateral treaties, with detailed mechanisms of implementation and a complex network of institutional structures. Countless studies have examined the treaty regimes in specific areas of international relations. Library shelves are filled with books on the institutional underpinning of multilateral cooperation and its effectiveness in responding to the demands of the international community. What has been missing is a cross-cutting assessment of how the United Nations system has contributed, through its multilateral treaty-making activity, to the purposes and principles laid down in the Charter.

This *Handbook*, edited by Simon Chesterman, David M. Malone, and Santiago Villalpando, gathers the writings of a select group of authors from different perspectives: diplomats and international civil servants involved in treaty negotiations or working to implement them, scholars and experts analyzing those agreements in theory and in practice. The diversity of these contributions is a vivid reflection of the breadth and depth of United Nations treaty-making. Together, they tell the story of how United Nations treaties have evolved from the ideals of the Charter in 1945 to the ambitious goals of the 2030 Agenda for Sustainable Development.

When I took my oath of office in 2016, I noted that today's paradox is that, despite greater connectivity, societies are becoming more fragmented. In the end, however, the links that bind the human family come down to the values enshrined in the Charter: peace, justice, respect, human rights, tolerance and solidarity. These values find their expression in the treaties negotiated under the auspices of the United Nations, an endeavor to which this volume gives the scholarly attention it deserves.

António Guterres
Secretary-General of the United Nations

Foreword

For delegates taking part in the 1945 San Francisco Conference, it was clear that the Charter of the United Nations (UN) was a historic document. Its ambition was to build a new international system, founded on the rule of law. From their inception, the UN Organization and its specialized agencies—at different speeds and through different procedures—pursued that ambition through treaty-making, which today embraces almost every aspect of international affairs.

Assessing the contribution that the UN system has made, through its treaty-making, to our contemporary world is a daunting task. It demands remarkable attention to detail: each treaty regime—in human rights, environmental protection, disarmament, etc.—has its own individual features, complex treaty-making techniques, and detailed implementation mechanisms. To truly understand their scope and significance, one needs to examine thoroughly each of these regimes separately, taking into account the background of negotiations and their influence on the practice of states. But, at the same time, this task requires an all-embracing view of the multilateral treaty framework as a whole. In assessing the impact of a multilateral regime on international relations, consideration needs to be given to its interactions with other treaty regimes, how institutions have engaged in a dialogue to achieve their common goals, and how they have influenced each other's treaty-making practices.

In their introduction, the Editors of this volume advance the argument that the UN's greatest contribution to humankind might properly be thought of as a process—in other words, that the UN has permitted a major shift in the normative structure of international law that has expanded the range and depth of subjects covered by treaties. They show how the UN has served as a flexible forum of treaty negotiation, which has taken advantage of the institutional strengths of the system, as well as an effective vehicle for implementation, to ensure that treaty regimes are followed up in practice. They demonstrate how this has transformed the landscape of international law, in its evolution from bilateralism to multilateralism.

The present Oxford Handbook on UN Treaties is an invaluable addition to scholarship in this field. The Editors were uniquely positioned to initiate this endeavor. Their combined expertise draws from their long-standing involvement in diplomatic circles and international organizations, as well as their impressive scholarly production covering a multitude of topics of international law. But an enterprise of this magnitude is necessarily a collective one, since it requires a detailed examination of many treaty regimes. And the Editors have been able to call upon an extraordinary group of contributors, which includes judges of international tribunals, experienced diplomats and international officials, and distinguished scholars in law and other social sciences, as well as younger voices from practice and academia. The result is 34 chapters, which individually offer insightful descriptions of specific regimes or thematic issues, but together form a remarkable mosaic that will allow readers to make their own assessment of the contribution of UN treaty-making to international relations.

The first part of the volume, entitled "Evolution," provides a historical and systemic overview of how the activity of the UN system has developed in the area of treaty-making. This part traces the evolution of UN treaty-making means and objectives from the Charter into the various treaty regimes, but also offers a fascinating dialogue between scholars offering a theoretical analysis of major trends and practitioners who can assess those same trends from their firsthand involvement in the UN system.

The second part, entitled "Practice," provides an in-depth examination of specific treaty regimes, structured in four main areas: international peace and security, economic and social development, human rights, and international law. Each contribution identifies the major UN treaties in the area and describes the background of their negotiation; it also examines the main aspects of the relevant treaty regime and assesses its impact on international relations, as well as avenues of future development. In many cases, authors are leading authorities in their field, often with personal experience on the topic. An interesting feature of the volume is that, in some cases, the main contribution on a specific topic is supplemented with a "practitioner reflection" in which a person involved in the practical aspects of the treaty regime provides a unique inside view of negotiations.

Finally, the third part, entitled "Technique," addresses certain practical matters relating to the building of the international treaty framework. Chapters examine patterns in the negotiation of multilateral treaties, the participation of international organizations and other nonstate actors in the multilateral treaty process, the depositary role played by the Secretary-General with regard to multilateral treaties, and the lessons learned from the significant body of treaties and international agreements registered under Article 102 of the Charter. These chapters bring us back to a more hands-on perspective of UN treaty-making, showing major trends in legal techniques.

The Editors invited all contributors to an "Authors Meeting," which was held in Greentree, not far from the United Nations Headquarters in New York, early in the process of drafting, in April 2017. That gathering offered an opportunity for contributors to share their preliminary thoughts on this *Handbook* and exchange views on possible approaches to its topic. More importantly, the meeting, which I joined, created a sense of community in this collective endeavor—something apparent in reading the pages of this volume.

Like the subject matter it addresses, this *Handbook* shows how diversity may engender unity and coherence. I commend the book to anyone interested in understanding how international law has contributed to world order and prosperity, and how the UN and its specialized agencies have helped draft and implement the growing number of documents grouped here, fittingly, as "United Nations treaties."

Miguel de Serpa Soares
United Nations Legal Counsel and Under-Secretary-General
for Legal Affairs

Acknowledgments

Books such as this are rarely the product of a few hands. We have many people to thank. Financial support was provided by the United Nations University and the National University of Singapore Faculty of Law. The Greentree Foundation allowed us the use of their wonderful facilities in Long Island, NY, to convene an authors' retreat. This enabled our many scholars and practitioners to exchange ideas in person, engendering a rich set of interactions that we hope has been transferred to the page. We are also very grateful for the in-kind support provided by the UN Office of Legal Affairs.

Preparing the manuscript for publication was a herculean effort that would not have been possible without additional research support. Thank you especially to Sheiffa Safi (in Singapore) and Jonathan Agar (in New York).

The editors have been greatly helped by several individuals, above all Alexandra Ivanovic (of the UN University), herself a law graduate and lecturer, who marshaled this complex project to conclusion—cajoling, encouraging, and ultimately succeeding in extracting from our terrific authors the high-quality chapters of which they were capable. The UN University's Office team in New York, headed by James Cockayne, himself also with a legal background and much published, together with Alexandra Cerquone, made possible the author meeting at the Greentree Estate mentioned above. We are very grateful to them all.

David Malone warmly thanks the Council of the UN University for encouraging his own research work.

Thank you also to Blake Ratcliff, John Louth, and their colleagues at Oxford University Press for believing in the project from the outset and sticking with it to conclusion.

Insofar as the volume has merit, it is due to the hard work of all these people. Any deficiencies can be attributed to the editors themselves.

Santiago Villalpando and David Malone record here that the views expressed within the volume, including its introduction, reflect not the UN's or UNESCO's position on the issues involved, but, where relevant, their own opinions.

Simon Chesterman, David M. Malone, Santiago Villalpando
March 2019

Note to Readers

Table of Contents

PART II PRACTICE—SCHOLARLY AND PRACTITIONER ACCOUNTS OF UN TREATY-MAKING

PART III TECHNIQUE—INNOVATION IN TREATY-MAKING AT THE UNITED NATIONS

List of Contributors

Hirad Abtahi is the Legal Adviser, Head of the Legal and Enforcement Unit, Presidency at the International Criminal Court

Jonathan Agar is a Legal Officer with the UN Office of Legal Affairs

Davinia Aziz is Senior State Counsel in the International Affairs Division, Attorney-General's Chambers, Singapore

David Bewley-Taylor is Professor of International Relations and Public Policy at Swansea University

Pierre Bodeau-Livinec is Professor of Public Law at the University Paris Nanterre

Alan Boyle is Emeritus Professor of Public International Law at the University of Edinburgh

Gian Luca Burci is Adjunct Professor at the Graduate Institute of International and Development Studies Geneva

Roberto Cassar is a LLM (cum laude) in Advanced Studies in Air and Space Law, International Institute of Air and Space Law at Leiden University

Hilary Charlesworth is a Melbourne Laureate Professor at Melbourne Law School and a Distinguished Professor at the Australian National University

Simon Chesterman is Dean and Professor at the National University of Singapore Faculty of Law

Jane Connors is the United Nations Victims' Rights Advocate and former International Advocacy Director Law and Policy at Amnesty International. Her contribution was written before she entered into her current role

Marie-Claire Cordonier Segger is Senior Director of the Centre for International Sustainable Development Law, Full Professor of International Law at the University of Waterloo, and an LCIL and CEENRG Fellow at the University of Cambridge

Sanderijn Duquet is a Belgian diplomat and an Associate Research Fellow, Leuven Centre for Global Governance Studies, University of Leuven

Malgosia Fitzmaurice is Professor of Public International Law, Department of Law at the Queen Mary University of London

Giorgio Gaja is a Judge at the International Court of Justice

Guy S. Goodwin-Gill is Professor of Law and Acting Director, Andrew & Renata Kaldor Centre for International Refugee Law at the University of New South Wales, and Emeritus Fellow of All Souls College, University of Oxford

Alexandra Harrington is Lead Counsel for Governance & Intergenerational Justice at the Centre for International Sustainable Development Law

Corina Heri is a postdoctoral researcher at the Amsterdam Centre for International Law at the University of Amsterdam

Arancha Hinojal-Oyarbide is a Legal Officer in the Treaty Section at the UN Office of Legal Affairs

Alexandra Ivanovic is a qualified Australian solicitor and mediator, and the Senior Manager in the Office of the Rector at the United Nations University, where she also teaches a post-graduate course on Law and Practice of the United Nations

Martin Jelsma is the Drugs and Democracy Programme Director at the Transnational Institute Amsterdam and a Senior Research Associate at Swansea University

Sam Johnston is a Senior Fellow, Faculty of Law at the University of Melbourne

Ian Johnstone is Dean *ad interim* and Professor of International Law at the Fletcher School of Law and Diplomacy at Tufts University

Helen Keller is a Judge at the European Court of Human Rights and Professor of Public Law, European and Public International Law at the University of Zurich

Barry Kellman is Professor of Law at the DePaul College of Law, DePaul University

Philippe Kirsch is a former Judge and first President of the International Criminal Court

Jan Klabbers is a Professor of International Law at the University of Helsinki

Pierre Klein is a Professor of International Law, Centre of International Law, Université libre de Bruxelles

Tommy Koh is Ambassador-At-Large at the Ministry of Foreign Affairs, Singapore and Professor of Law at the National University of Singapore

Edward Kwakwa is Senior Director, Department for Traditional Knowledge and Global Challenges at the World Intellectual Property Organization

David M. Malone is Rector of the United Nations University and UN Under-Secretary-General

Tanja Masson-Zwaan is Assistant Professor and Deputy Director of the International Institute of Air and Space Law at Leiden University

Stephen Mathias is Assistant Secretary-General for Legal Affairs at the UN Office of Legal Affairs

Makane Moïse Mbengue is Professor of International Law at the University of Geneva Law School

Christel Mobech is a Human Rights Officer with the UN High Commissioner for Human Rights and a former Associate Legal Officer in the Treaty Section at the UN Office of Legal Affairs

Corinne Montineri is a Legal Officer in the International Trade Law Division at the UN Commission on International Trade Law

A. Rohan Perera is the Permanent Representative of Sri Lanka to the United Nations

George P. Politakis is the Legal Adviser of the International Labour Office

Daniël Prins is Chief of the Conventional Arms Branch at the UN Office for Disarmament Affairs

Bertrand G. Ramcharan is a Former Acting High Commissioner for Human Rights and Under-Secretary-General and Professor at The Graduate Institute, Geneva

Shirley V. Scott is Professor and Head of the School of Humanities and Social Sciences at UNSW Canberra

Tullio Scovazzi is Professor of International Law at the University of Milano-Bicocca

Alison See is a Justices' Law Clerk at the Supreme Court of Singapore

Christian J. Tams is Professor of International Law at the University of Glasgow and an Academic Member of the Matrix Chambers, London

Yoshifumi Tanaka is Professor of International Law, Faculty of Law at the University of Copenhagen

Allyn Taylor is an Affiliate Professor of Law at the University of Washington

Santiago Villalpando is Legal Adviser of the United Nations Educational, Scientific and Cultural Organization and former Chief of the Treaty Section at the UN Office of Legal Affairs

Philippa Webb is Reader (Associate Professor) in Public International Law, The Dickson Poon School of Law at King's College London

Michael Wood is a barrister and Member of the International Law Commission

Jan Wouters is Professor of International Law and International Organizations and Director of the Leuven Centre for Global Governance Studies—Institute for International Law at the University of Leuven

Lionel Yee is a Deputy Attorney-General of Singapore

Salvatore Zappalà is Professor of International Law at the University of Catania

INTRODUCTION TO THE OXFORD HANDBOOK OF UNITED NATIONS TREATIES

SIMON CHESTERMAN, DAVID M. MALONE, AND SANTIAGO VILLALPANDO*

As scholars of the United Nations (UN) we are sometimes asked—or ask ourselves—what has been the UN's greatest contribution to humankind? There is a tendency to attempt to answer such questions by reference to an outcome achieved—improvements in health and economic development, for example—or avoided, such as the absence of a global war or use of weapons of mass destruction. This book makes the argument that the greatest contribution might be more properly thought of as a *process*. In particular, the UN has been part of a major shift in the normative structure of international law that has expanded the range and depth of subjects covered by treaties.

In *Modern Treaty Law and Practice*, Anthony Aust—a former UK Foreign Office lawyer who devoted much of his career to treaty-making—reminds us that treaty-making dates back to early antiquity.[1] By 1914, around 8,000 treaties were in force, covering topics from border delimitation to trade. Most of these treaties were bilateral, though the nineteenth century witnessed the new phenomenon of multilateralism, notably in the founding documents of the first international organizations recognizable as such. The interwar period increased treaty-making activity, with the League of Nations registering almost 5,000 treaties, most of them bilateral, while also spearheading the adoption of several multilateral conventions.[2]

* The authors are responsible for the choice and the presentation of the facts contained in the article and for the opinions expressed therein, which are not necessarily those of UNESCO and do not commit the Organization.

1 Anthony Aust, *Modern Treaty Law and Practice* (3rd edn, CUP 2013) 1.

2 See also Duncan B Hollis, *Oxford Guide to Treaties* (OUP 2012).

Yet it seems indisputable that the most radical changes in quantity and quality of treaties took place after 1945. Since the adoption of the Charter, more than 70,000 treaties have been registered with the UN Secretariat, and treaty-making activity continues at an unrelenting pace, with an average of 250 treaties and treaty actions—ratifications, accessions, withdrawals—registered every month. Multilateral conventions now cover topics ranging from human rights to drugs and crime, from trade and development to the governance of outer space.

Many (though certainly not all) of these treaties were adopted under the auspices of the UN. A rich literature analyzes the various treaties, but a study on the auspices themselves—the contribution of the UN as a forum and as an institution—has lagged. What is missing is a detailed examination of how the UN itself has contributed, through its multilateral treaty-making activity, to the development of international law. This Introduction briefly surveys how that role has evolved, from serving primarily as the place at which treaties are negotiated to being one of the vehicles for implementing that which has been agreed. In doing so, the UN has reflected and contributed to a larger transformation as international law moved from bilateralism to multilateralism.

1 A Forum for Negotiation

By proclaiming the determination of the peoples of the United Nations "to establish conditions under which justice and respect of the obligations arising from treaties and other sources of international law can be maintained," the preamble of the Charter suggests the important role that treaties might play in the new postwar order. Despite such ambitious rhetoric, however, the operative provisions do not specify how this objective is to be achieved.[3] The General Assembly is to have a role in "encouraging the progressive development of international law and its codification," and the Economic and Social Council (ECOSOC) is empowered to prepare draft conventions,[4] but the Charter is silent on how these mandates are to be fulfilled.

This is reflected in the general landscape of multilateral treaties adopted under the auspices of the UN system, as described in this *Handbook*.

Texts, for example, do not follow any established template. The features of a UN treaty—preambular language, overall structure, implementing mechanisms, final clauses—vary widely from one area to the other. As various chapters in this *Handbook* show, negotiators typically rely more on precedent in their area of expertise than across the UN system. It is not infrequent, therefore, for wheels to be reinvented, notably on technical treaty issues, even when solutions have been tried and tested in other fields.

[3] In the words of the International Court of Justice, the preambular parts of the Charter "constitute the moral and political basis for the specific legal provisions thereafter set out," but "do not…in themselves amount to rules of law." *South-West Africa Cases* [1966] ICJ Rep 6, 34, para 50.

[4] UN Charter, respectively art 13(1)(a) and 62(3).

Treaty-making processes also diverge. Who initiates the process? Typically, it is an initiative of one or more governments, but a treaty-making process may be initiated by an intergovernmental organ, an expert body, the UN Secretariat itself, or an outside entity such as an intergovernmental or nongovernmental organization. Who prepares the first draft? Sometimes this may be the entity driving the process; sometimes the role is entrusted to an expert body, a committee or working group, or even to the Secretariat. Where do negotiations take place? This *Handbook* describes a myriad of conferences, assemblies, commissions, committees, subcommittees, meetings and working groups, involving varying types of representation. What rules, if any, govern negotiations? If conducted within established bodies, such as the main committees of the General Assembly or ECOSOC, the rules of procedure of those bodies apply. Conferences and ad hoc committees must adopt their own rules of procedure—though there are perilous examples of negotiations proceeding without even agreement on those. How long should negotiations take? The UN often appears impervious to deadlines—some treaties taking decades to adopt, in the process shifting between forums or hibernating, while others race to conclusion in mere years. Assuming there is an agreement, who adopts the final document? For some treaties this may be the General Assembly, through a resolution; for others it may be a diplomatic conference or a regional entity.

Predictably, the results of these diverse methods have been inconsistent. In some areas, such as labor, long-standing practices of the International Labour Organization (which predated the UN) have seen a steady stream of treaties. In others, such as human rights, an early burst of activity became bogged down by politics, but eventually flourished in later decades. In still others, such as environmental law, the UN has been a late bloomer.

On a closer look, however, the fact that the UN system did not reduce treaty-making to a cookie-cutter template model has been instrumental in the UN's impressive multilateral treaty production since the adoption of the Charter. The variety of possible forums and the flexibility of procedures has allowed negotiating processes to be adapted to the needs and concerns of states in each area of international law. When background research and legal expertise is required, the UN is able to create subsidiary expert bodies, as in the case of the codification of international law. When the complexity and sensitivity of issues requires political creativity, the UN can establish ad hoc committees enabling negotiators to convene in different configurations that may facilitate agreement.

The UN has also placed at the states' disposal a suite of services to facilitate multilateral treaty negotiations. These include logistical amenities (conference rooms, technological equipment), conference support (documentation, translations, interpretation), secretariat services (including legal advice), established rules of procedure (on credentials, voting majorities), and working methods (working groups, informal consultations, and so on). Use of these services can be cost-effective, especially because governments generally maintain stable national representation in the main UN headquarters locations, and is a major factor in explaining why multilateral treaty-making has been so successful in the framework of the UN system.

Over time, a degree of consistency has emerged within subfields. Most human rights treaties, for example, are negotiated within the institutional framework of the UN.

Initial work takes place in the Human Rights Council (or its predecessor, the Commission on Human Rights) and presented as a General Assembly resolution. A non-binding declaration is adopted first, defining basic principles and gathering acceptance, followed by treaty negotiations properly speaking. Implementation relies on monitoring by expert committees that review state reports and receive communications. Environmental treaties, by contrast, are negotiated in an ad hoc forum—typically an intergovernmental negotiating committee, followed by a diplomatic conference. Implementing mechanisms rely on the work of a conference of the parties, and there may be flexibility to specify the obligations of states at a later stage or adapt them to new realities. Such treaties may take the form of a main convention, which is followed by protocols or includes annexes subject to a more flexible amendment regime.

Furthermore, cross-fertilization has expanded across different fields of treaty-making, thanks to the UN's technical assistance role. An illustration of this phenomenon is the depositary function entrusted to the Secretary-General for around 600 multilateral treaties concluded under the auspices of the Organization, which permits a harmonious interpretation of final clauses and the sharing of best practices across different fields of treaty-making. In the case of reservations, for example, the Secretary-General's discharge of his depositary functions for all UN treaties[5] allowed for the rapid crystallization of a novel legal regime, which was then codified in the 1969 Vienna Convention on the Law of Treaties. Sometimes the assistance offered goes significantly beyond technique. The use of a framework convention followed by a protocol in the area of tobacco control, for example, was suggested to negotiators by the World Health Organization (WHO) secretariat—inspired by the experience of environmental treaties. Similarly, implementation mechanisms used in the conventions on transnational organized crime and corruption bear strong resemblance to models found in environmental treaties. The centralized advice of the UN Office of Legal Affairs on procedural matters also contributes to the consistent formulation and application of rules of procedure used in the various treaty-making processes—for example in areas such as accreditation, voting, or adoption.

It is by providing a reliable, yet flexible, forum of negotiation that the UN has been able to make such a substantial contribution to the building of a solid multilateral treaty-framework.

2 A Vehicle for Implementation

Treaties can be strictly normative in their aims, but often their follow-up, in one form or another, requires organized implementation by an actor or several actors whose commitment is to the purposes of the treaty rather than to the objectives of this or that

[5] In line with the International Court of Justice (ICJ)'s 1951 advisory opinion on *Reservations to the Genocide Convention*, as instructed by General Assembly resolutions 598 (VI) and 1452 (XIV).

government. This reality has kept the regional and universal systems of international organizations growing steadily, until quite recently, with responsibilities being added to existing institutions or new secretariats and other forms of intergovernmental architecture accreting at a significant rate.

Some international treaty regimes have, from the outset, been created with follow-up provisions—though member states may try to resist the creeping expansion of institutional bureaucracy. The Conference on Security and Cooperation in Europe (CSCE), and its successor in 1995, the Organization for Security and Cooperation in Europe (OSCE), are good examples of the restraints imposed by member states. The OSCE has selected specialized staff for its monitoring and observation activities, but these draw on rosters of potentially available experts rather than the OSCE burdening itself with many tenured full-time employees. Most of the implementing architecture of multilateral treaties has inclined toward expansion—at times headlong expansion—with the extreme being the mutation of the 1951 European Steel and Coal Community into what was renamed the European Union in 1993. The growth of implementing machinery is not simply the result of bureaucracies seeking to expand, however. More often, it is driven by the complexity of the tasks entrusted to them. In many cases, efforts to check expansion runs in direct contrast to the material and political support needed to fulfill such mandates.

Follow-up mechanisms are essential because widespread ratification does not mean widespread compliance. This need not mean the threat of sanctions or punishment; sometimes merely monitoring compliance is enough. Through national legislative processes and evolving custom, "compliance pull," of which Thomas M. Franck wrote so eloquently, has produced impressive results in many parts of the world.[6] When states derogate from their obligations under these agreements, they are rarely proud of it. They tend to plead special circumstances, national or regional preferences at variance with some of the provisions involved, or imply that they are honoring the spirit of treaties while adapting their terms to contemporary times or exigencies. Merely inviting states to report on their own activities without threat of sanction can thereby encourage compliance.

Given the enthusiasm with which some states ratify treaties, it is easy to underestimate the importance of ensuring adequate resources are devoted to implementation. This is not a problem limited to developing countries. The UN Convention against Illicit Traffic in Narcotic Drugs and Psychotropic Substances of 1988, which entered into force with much fanfare a mere two years later, focused, among many other things, on the risks of diversion of precursor chemicals for the manufacture of some of these drugs. While recognizing that developing countries sometimes lack the resources necessary for serious implementation of such undertakings, industrialized countries might have been expected to take their provisions quite seriously, given the ravages that narcotic drugs were inflicting on many of their societies. Yet the Canadian government discovered,

[6] Thomas M Franck, *The Power of Legitimacy among Nations* (OUP 1990).

15 years after ratifying the treaty and with narcotic use on the rise, that it had only three inspectors to monitor compliance across the entire country.[7]

This volume brings the implementation challenge into focus, in particular, through its three mutually reinforcing chapters on the UN's major human rights agreements. Several of those agreements included provisions for UN monitoring of implementation, including optional protocols under which states could bind themselves more stringently to UN oversight through expert committees. When the number and ambition of the treaties escalates and proliferates, however, it risks overwhelming the implementation mechanisms. Our authors report expert committees falling behind on workloads, while governments and some UN officials have suggested the need for consolidation. The mismatch between the admirable objectives of many treaties and the implementation capacity of ratifying states has received too little attention in polite legal circles, in part because the parts of government involved in negotiation are discrete from those that oversee implementation, and in part because foreign ministers get more press coverage signing new treaties than bureaucrats tasked with implementing old ones.

3 From Bilateralism to Multilateralism

The UN is more than a place in which treaties are negotiated and an actor that takes part in their implementation, however. Its existence and its role are part of a larger transformation in the structure of international law more generally.

International law in the first half of the twentieth century relied heavily upon bilateral, contractual agreements between states. The "international community," such as it was, acted through states that enjoyed a monopoly over legal status at the international level. These states, to be sure, did not always reflect domestic legitimacy—the colonial project was still underway, and race and sex were grounds in many of those states for disenfranchisement.

By the middle of the century, however, the aftermath of the Second World War saw a transformation in attitudes toward multilateralism. One indication of this was in the name of the international organization created in the hope of preventing such a global conflagration from ever recurring. The term "United Nations" was first used in a declaration signed by 26 of the Allied states in January 1942. A year later, as the tide of war was turning, US President Franklin D. Roosevelt observed in his 1943 New Year's Day message that "the United Nations are passing from the defensive to the offensive." By the time the UN Charter was signed in San Francisco on June 26, 1945 the plural had been replaced by the singular: it became common to refer not to what the United Nations as a group of states *were* doing, but what the United Nations as an institution *was* doing. In this way, an alliance against common foes became an organization with common goals.

[7] Confidential interview with Canadian senior official, March 5, 2008.

The achievement of those goals was explicitly tied to the possibility of multilateral treaty-making. The Charter repeatedly stressed the importance of international law and mandated the General Assembly to encourage its progressive development and codification.[8] From the outset, the Assembly approached this function with the "broadest possible interpretation"—including but not limited to the roles played by the International Law Commission (ILC), the Sixth Committee, and the UN Commission on International Trade Law (UNCITRAL).[9] In addition, by establishing itself as the presumptive depository of treaties, the UN further promoted the conclusion and publication of international agreements.[10]

Not surprisingly, this led to significant growth in the number of treaties concluded and the subjects covered.

The most striking shift was the move to multilateralism.[11] In Chapter 34, Jonathan Agar and Christel Mobech note three periods in treaty-making. The first, lasting from the end of the Second World War into the 1960s, saw an annual average of 70 multilateral treaties concluded. Between 1962 and 1976, this rose to 95 treaties per year with an all-time high of 121 treaties in 1967. After that period, the number appears to have declined.

That decline runs counter to much exuberant commentary in the post–Cold War era and at the turn of the millennium, some of which appeared to assume that international law as measured by treaties was growing—and would continue to grow—indefinitely.[12] Joost Pauwelyn, Ramses Wessel, and Jan Wouters note that for the second half of the twentieth century the number of multilateral treaties deposited at the United Nations per decade was around 35 and never dropped below 34. From 2000 to 2010, however, it dropped to 20. They posit a "stagnation hypothesis," due in part to a turn to informality in international lawmaking processes.[13]

Without disputing the importance of informal and nontraditional processes—whether they be the forces of transgovernmental networks,[14] global administrative law,[15] a new constitutionalism,[16] or economic forces[17]—pronouncements of the death of multilateral treaty-making appear to be greatly exaggerated.

[8] UN Charter, art 13(1)(a).

[9] Carl-August Fleischhauer and Bruno Simma, "Article 13" in Bruno Simma et al (eds), *The Charter of the United Nations: A Commentary* (3rd edn, OUP 2012) 526–27.

[10] UN Charter, art 102.

[11] See Bruno Simma, "From Bilateralism to Community Interest in International Law" (1994) 250(IV) Recueil des cours 217.

[12] See, eg, José Alvarez, "The New Treaty Makers" (2002) 25 BC Int'l & Comp L Rev 213, 216.

[13] See Joost Pauwelyn, Ramses A Wessel, and Jan Wouters, "When Structures Become Shackles: Stagnation and Dynamics in International Lawmaking" (2014) 25(3) EJIL 733. See also Richard Collins, *The Institutional Problem in Modern International Law* (Hart Publishing 2016).

[14] See, eg, Anne-Marie Slaughter, *A New World Order* (Princeton University Press 2004).

[15] See, eg, Simon Chesterman, "Globalization Rules: Accountability, Power, and the Prospects for Global Administrative Law" (2008) 14 Global Governance 39.

[16] See, eg, Nicholas Tsagourias (ed), *Transnational Constitutionalism: International and European Perspectives* (CUP 2007).

[17] See generally Chris Brummer, *Minilateralism: How Trade Alliances, Soft Law, and Financial Engineering Are Redefining Economic Statecraft* (CUP 2014).

Indeed, one factor in the reduced number of new multilateral treaties is that in some areas the major thematic issues have essentially been covered. In the field of human rights, for example, of the nine core human rights treaties, seven date from 1990 or earlier. Another relevant factor is the increased recourse to more flexible techniques of multilateral treaty-making. The traditional monolithic conception of the multilateral treaty—set in stone for future generations—is replaced by regimes in which the core treaty is supplemented by optional protocols (a phenomenon that we often see in the area of human rights), or regimes in which the initial convention only sets a framework that is later completed by further protocols, schedules, or nationally determined contributions. Furthermore, the amendment of the treaty (or its annexes), which was a rare occurrence in the early twentieth century, is today considered an efficient means to adapt the multilateral regime to the changing needs of the international community, while maintaining its institutional structures: the 2016 Kigali amendment to the Montreal Protocol, by which parties committed to reduce the emission of hydrofluorocarbons, is a case in point. In this context, it is also noteworthy that, while the number of new *treaties* has declined, the number of treaty *actions* has continued to increase in the last 20 years. Agar and Mobech conclude that this may suggest that attention is moving from developing new substantive law in multilateral treaties to broadening support for those treaties that already exist.[18] Similarly, Alan Boyle points out in Chapter 6 that soft-law processes do indeed play a larger role in international affairs, but that this is complementary rather than exclusionary to the role played by traditional treaties.

Another indicator of the ongoing relevance of multilateral treaties—despite the prevalence of less formal processes—is the clear preference in some areas for the treaty form. The 2015 Paris Agreement (on climate change), for example, could have been adopted as a non-binding instrument. Instead, member states adopted it as a treaty, reflecting both the importance of the subject matter as well as the fact that the field of environmental law is far from saturated in terms of binding treaty obligations—a point made clear in Chapter 10 by Marie-Claire Cordonier Segger and Alexandra Harrington. Indeed, the conventional form continues to present distinct advantages, both at the international level (for the creation of implementation and dispute settlement mechanisms, for example) and at the domestic level (to gather political commitment and support for the adoption of legislation allowing the national implementation of international obligations), as well as outside from the strict domain of law (for example, to obtain international aid for national implementation).

International law, like most of human activity, rarely falls into neat categories. It would be a mistake to suggest that the twentieth century was marked by a paradigm shift from bilateralism to multilateralism, as it would be to assume that the twenty-first century is seeing a shift from multilateralism to informalism.[19] On the contrary, bilateral,

[18] Cf Pauwelyn, Wessel, and Wouters (n 13) 739–41.

[19] Cf JHH Weiler, "The Geology of International Law: Governance, Democracy and Legitimacy" (2004) 64 Heidelberg J Intl L 547.

multilateral, and informal normative activity coexist and interact. Similarly, it is not the claim of this volume that the UN alone is responsible for the increase in treaty-making through the latter part of the previous century. The more modest argument of this book is that the UN reflected demand and supply: demand in the need to build a new global order and "establish conditions under which justice and respect for the obligations arising from treaties and other sources of international law can be maintained," supply on the part of states willing to exercise their sovereignty to create regimes and other organizations in support of that end.

In doing so, the UN offered itself initially as a forum for negotiation—a "centre for harmonizing the actions of nations." It quickly also became an important actor in its own right, moving from facilitating agreement between states to supporting and monitoring the implementation of the agreements reached. Though the UN was never intended to serve as a global government, in this way it contributed to the emergence of meaningful global governance and a world ordered—albeit imperfectly—under law.

4 Overview of the Volume

The objective in producing this *Handbook* is to explore these major ideas of how the UN has contributed to the development of international law through its multilateral treaty-making activity. We gathered a diverse group of authors from different fields, including academics and practitioners, lawyers and specialists from other social sciences (international relations, history, science), professionals with an established reputation in the field, and younger researchers and diplomats involved in the negotiation of multilateral treaties and scholars with a broader view on the issues involved. We are grateful to all of those who accepted the challenge, sharing their knowledge and experience in the different areas that we proposed.

The volume provides unique insight to UN treaty-making activity. Through the thematic and technical parts, it also offers a lens through which to view challenges lying ahead and the possibilities and limitations of the Organization. A key benefit of this approach is that it provides an opportunity for exchange of ideas between specialists in different fields, with a view to promoting the cross-fertilization of legal concepts and methods. The various chapters are grouped into three Parts, focusing on evolution, practice, and technique.

4.1 Evolution

The volume begins with a historical and theoretical overview of how the activity of the UN has evolved in the area of treaty-making, tracing the manner in which treaties have been used as a tool for the pursuit of the goals of the UN Charter and how they have become a factor of change in international affairs.

Chapter 1 by Ian Johnstone examines the Charter and its evolution over more than seven decades of practice. The Charter itself is, of course, a treaty. Yet it has long been suggested that the Charter also embodies elements of a constitution.[20] Johnstone argues that a third lens, relational contract theory, offers insights into how the Charter has been interpreted over time, as well as the role that the UN has come to play as a venue for and an actor in treaty-making.

Shirley Scott offers a survey of international relations scholarship in Chapter 2, focusing on the literature most relevant to multilateral treaty-making. Reflecting the long and puzzling divide between international law and international relations, many of the categories of analysis used by the two disciplines do not match. Nevertheless, work on norm dynamics and regimes in particular suggests the possible benefits of greater interaction in the future. More recent scholarship on the decline of the liberal order echoes warnings of a crisis of multilateralism; what is telling here is that much of the crisis appears to be self-inflicted by the West and may in fact be welcomed by many of those traditionally excluded by the ancien régime.

In Chapter 3, Stephen Mathias presents an insider's view of UN treaty-making processes. His contribution highlights the various ways in which the Secretariat participates in the treaty-making process—by preparing technical and substantial reports in the pre-initiation study phase, contributing to the formulation of treaty provisions, advising on rules of procedure, and even assisting in many ways in the post-adoption phase (through dissemination, technical assistance, depositary functions, and so on). He also reflects on the extensive UN practice in concluding bilateral treaties with states and other intergovernmental organizations, for example in the area of peacekeeping, which in his view may be seen as constituting in some sense a multilateral regime.

In Chapter 4, Christian Tams examines how treaties are used in general to pursue the objectives of the UN Charter. In doing so, he draws important and illuminating distinctions between the manner in which the Charter first operated in 1945 and how it operates today, as well as between the contributions of treaties in pursuit of distinct Charter objectives outlined in Article 1(3)—maintaining peace and security, developing friendly relations, and fostering international cooperation. Two significant conclusions are that treaties tend to be most important where provisions in the Charter resemble a framework agreement in need of elaboration, but that the significance of treaties has been shaped more by practice than by the strict text of the founding document.

Giorgio Gaja offers, in Chapter 5, a reflection on the transformative effect of the UN's role in the codification and progressive development of international law. At the end of the Second World War, the general part of international law consisted of customary rules; today, codification conventions have substantially changed the situation. His contribution examines the circumstances in which such codification conventions have been adopted, distinguishing the cases in which these conventions reflect customary rules from those in which it is the customary rules that have aligned to codification

[20] See Thomas M Franck, "Is the UN Charter a Constitution?" in Jochen Abr Frowein et al (eds), *Verhandeln für den Frieden—Negotiating for Peace: Liber Amicorum Tono Eitel* (Springer 2003).

conventions. While Gaja notes that recent trends at the UN may suggest that the season of codification conventions is over, he maintains there is no reason to abandon recourse to hard law instruments when the circumstances so require.

Treaties are not, of course, the only means of normative development pursued under the auspices of the United Nations. Alan Boyle discusses the choice of "soft" as opposed to "hard" treaty law in Chapter 6, sometimes preferable because it allows states to adopt common positions without formal obligation, it is more flexible, it may avoid domestic barriers to implementation, and it may enable swifter action without the requirement for a given treaty to enter into force. An example is in the field of human rights, where most of the current treaty regime is traceable back to soft-law instruments, such as the Universal Declaration.

4.2 Practice

Part II offers thematic studies of some of the different treaty regimes that the UN has developed in key areas of international relations. These studies highlight the differences and similarities of approach to multilateral cooperation in given issue areas, encouraging a comparative perspective on the work of the Organization in its various areas of activity. This section includes contributions that trace the procedural history of major UN multilateral treaties, as well as their contribution to the development of international law. Selected studies are paired with separate commentaries by practitioners—in most cases officials involved in the negotiations themselves, either as representatives of member states or working for the Secretariat—analyzing the relevant negotiations or difficulties encountered in the national implementation of international regimes.

The first area of practice is international peace and security.

In Chapter 7 on UN weapons control, that embraces arms control, nonproliferation, and disarmament, Barry Kellman highlights some of the inherent difficulties facing negotiators. These include the speed of technological and political developments, which may outpace drafters. As a result, the regime that exists developed sporadically, in response to emerging threats rather than unfolding some grand strategy. The outlawing of chemical and biological weapons might be a highpoint in this context (although contemporary breaches of that law are very worrying), while the stuttering nuclear nonproliferation regime serves a reminder of the fragility of apparent success in this area.

Daniël Prins offers a practitioner reflection on this topic, drawing on his experiences in the UN working on arms control and disarmament. He describes the strengths of UN treaty-making processes, but also the improvisational, at times contingent, nature of some of its processes and participants. This makes for an unpredictable—at times, unmanageable—process. Occasional national disinterest, limited preparation by delegations, the enduring need for informal talks to achieve real progress, individual skill gaps, and communication errors can all inhibit progress. Yet the ostensibly chaotic process conceals the spirited and profoundly creative nature of UN treaty-making, marked by the conceptual and linguistic ingenuity and resourcefulness of individual players.

Chapter 8 by Pierre Klein turns to the long but fraught efforts to counter terrorism. Various attempts at a comprehensive treaty have failed, often because of disputes over the precise meaning of that term. More success has been had in sectoral conventions that criminalize specific acts, requiring states to prosecute or extradite those accused of committing them. Work on a draft comprehensive convention began in 2000, but obstacles remain in terms of its scope—in particular, the extent to which it should cover acts by states and national liberation groups.

Rohan Perera then offers a practitioner reflection on terrorism, elaborating on the fault lines that have developed within the UN between those advocating prevention and punishment of terrorism and those emphasizing the need to address its underlying causes. He highlights the different negotiating positions of various groups over the years, in particular the current efforts to bridge the divide through a carefully worded definition of terrorism, or clear demarcation of the scope of application of the proposed comprehensive convention. These efforts also reflect a move from a "piecemeal" to a "package" approach to negotiations at the UN.

As noted by Tanja Masson-Zwaan and Roberto Cassar in Chapter 9, the UN has also played a major role in elaborating an entirely new field of international law relating to peace and security, namely the law of outer space. Competition between the two Cold War superpowers triggered the geopolitical conditions for the establishment, in the framework of the UN, of a Committee on the Peaceful Uses of Outer Space, which proposed, first, the adoption by the General Assembly of a Declaration of Legal Principles in 1963, and then the conclusion of a treaty, which was to become the Magna Carta of space law, the 1967 Outer Space Treaty. Since then, four additional treaties have been adopted under the auspices of the UN elaborating on the basic principles enshrined in the Outer Space Treaty, but in more recent years states, while still working in the UN framework, rather prefer to explore soft-law solutions.

The second area of practice is economic and social development.

Marie-Claire Cordonier Segger and Alexandra Harrington examine the UN treaties on the global environment and on environmental sustainability in Chapter 10. The global challenges contrast starkly with the fragmented nature of national and international governance in response. The Sustainable Development Goals (SDGs) provide an accretive framework for addressing interlocked risks to both sustainability and development, but pitfalls for implementation abound. This is evidenced by the continuing tough international negotiations over implementation of the Paris Agreement on climate change due to enter into effect in 2020—despite considerable triumphalism at the time of its adoption in December 2016.

Like the extensive human rights treaty system, the groundbreaking treaties negotiated under the umbrella of the International Labour Organization, one of the oldest and most interestingly structured agencies of the UN family, can also fall victim to systems overload or anxiety over the lack of internal compliance monitoring and enforcement capacity within states. George Politakis, in Chapter 11 on labor, discusses these and other challenges relating to multilateral treaty-making, partially explaining the smaller number of ratifications for some recent ILO treaties.

A new focus on women's equality and specific rights flowing from adoption of the human rights Covenants in 1966 and their coming into force in 1976 was altogether exciting within the UN system. Hilary Charlesworth in her Chapter 12 discusses this area of UN treaty-making and follow-up, stressing both its achievements and limitations, some of them inevitably linked to uneven implementation. Importantly, this chapter highlights the paradox, and ensuing normative tension, of having one strand of treaties with provisions aimed at eradicating differences in the treatment of women, with another strand calling for their differential treatment based on the particularity of women's lives.

David Bewley-Taylor and Martin Jelsma discuss in Chapter 13 the efforts to tackle the interrelated problems of drugs and crime. Early efforts tended to focus on suppression of illicit drugs, planting the seeds of conflict with modern human rights and health policies today. The difficulty of amending or updating those treaties has led to a surprising range of unilateral actions on the part of states. The more recent treaties on organized crime suggest the benefits of having periodic conferences of the parties (COPs), though ongoing differences over concepts such as "organized crime" have led to implementation challenges in that regime also.

Makane Moïse Mbengue's Chapter 14 may at first glance seem an odd inclusion in this volume. The UN Conference on Trade and Development (UNCTAD) was first a conference and then a regular forum, underpinned by a secretariat whose work on international investment policies and patterns was widely hailed. But it did not arise from a treaty, although the Commodities agreement treaties (tin, coffee, and so on) have been negotiated at conferences convened by it. Rather, its work complemented that of the General Agreement on Tariffs and Trade (GATT) and the World Trade Organization (WTO) (each established by treaty), and served as a source of alternative views incubated within and championed by developing countries. In spite of the system of preferences for developing country access to industrialized country markets, Mbengue makes a strong case that the GATT, and, to a lesser degree, the WTO, have mostly served the interests of the strongest trading powers (including those from the developing world), while all too often neglecting those of the poorest countries. This serves as a reminder of why the UN, its agencies, funds, and programs have always been particularly important to developing countries and sometimes shunned on economic issues by forum-shopping powerful ones looking for an accommodating climate rather than a confrontational one.

Culture and science both fall under the purview of the UN Educational, Scientific and Cultural Organization (UNESCO), but present different challenges from the perspective of treaty-making. As pointed out by Tullio Scovazzi in Chapter 15, the UN interest in cultural matters stems from the inherent relationship between peace and culture, which is set forth in the preamble of the UNESCO Constitution, and the recognition of culture as a general interest of the international community as a whole. This has resulted in a number of UNESCO treaties addressing cultural concerns from different angles, such as the protection of cultural property in the event of armed conflict, international movements of cultural property, world cultural heritage, underwater cultural heritage, intangible cultural heritage, and cultural diversity.

On the other hand, as Sam Johnston demonstrates in Chapter 16, even in the absence of science treaties, scientific discoveries and concerns have played a significant role in triggering or supporting UN treaty-making efforts in a wide variety of areas, including the law of the sea, the preservation of the ozone layer, biological diversity, climate change, and health. Johnston examines in detail the role that science plays in the treaty-making process, and the contribution of UN treaties in promoting access to existing science and supporting research and development, as well as how UN treaties have managed the threats posed by science. His contribution also warns us to remain attentive at the increasing politicization of science and its limitations.

The area of health presents a curious anomaly in the world of UN treaties. As Allyn Taylor explains in Chapter 17, the scope of international legal cooperation in public health was, until recently, highly limited. While the establishment of the World Health Organization (WHO) marked the commitment of the UN system to this field, it traditionally neglected international legislative strategies to promote its global public policies. The expansion of international health law is tied with the protection of human rights, as enshrined in UN treaties, but treaty-making remains an exception in this field, which is mainly governed by other regulatory tools, most notably WHO's international health regulations.

Gian Luca Burci's practitioner's reflection offers a unique insider's perspective on the only multilateral treaties that have been adopted in the field of global health in recent years, namely the Framework Convention on Tobacco Control and its Protocol to Eliminate Illicit Trade in Tobacco Products. He vividly explains the rationale that led to the adoption of the model of a framework convention, the initial ambivalence of many countries toward the topic, and the unfolding of the negotiations. His study highlights a number of factors that affected the dynamics of the negotiation, such as the composition of the delegations, the relevance of regional positions, and the broad range of topics covered that required wide expertise, but ultimately shows the value of the compromise that emerged and the success of the initiative. A question remains as to whether this experiment will remain isolated or whether treaty-making may provide avenues for the further development of health law.

Intellectual property (IP) is one of the fastest changing areas of legal practice, a fact that might suggest its incompatibility with the notoriously ponderous methods of international lawmaking. Nevertheless, as Edward Kwakwa shows in Chapter 18, the World Intellectual Property Organization (WIPO) has long used precisely such methods to create binding obligations. To be sure, non-treaty processes are becoming more significant in this field, but treaties remain vitally important, with several more on the horizon. In part, this is due to the World Trade Organization's inclusion of IP within the multilateral trading system, establishing a direct link between protection of IP rights and economic development.

The third area of practice is human rights.

Three chapters examine initiatives flowing from the Universal Declaration on Human Rights. They represent a tremendous normative success, but also highlight the challenges of follow-up and implementation. Echoing other sections of the book, there is a disjunction between what negotiators *say*, and what the UN and its member states are able to *do*.

Jane Connors in Chapter 19 addresses the human rights treaty body systems, which include many expert committees, staff dedicated to liaising with member states, and mechanisms for complaint and response. She notes an important contradiction: on the one hand, member states are resistant to rationalizing an overstretched set of treaty bodies; on the other, the same member states have signaled a reluctance to increase the financial resources available to the High Commissioner to service these bodies. Something will need to change in how these responsibilities are handled within the UN.

Bertrand G. Ramcharan, a totemic figure in the world's human rights pantheon, contributes a wide-ranging Chapter 20 on the two Covenants of 1966 that, with the Universal Declaration, form the cornerstone of the UN human rights normative architecture. He suggests that national follow-up machinery for challenges arising within societies on implementation of Covenants be revisited as a means of promoting more systematic follow-up. And he suggests that identifying implementation problems may not be sufficient—rather, he recommends that attention to overarching national policies might be a more efficient way of proceeding along with addressing systemically important individual cases (and by implication leaving aside repetitive ones or ones of lesser significance).

Helen Keller and Corina Heri take a deep dive into two expert Committees that monitor compliance with the Covenants in Chapter 21. In one case, that includes entertaining complaints with respect to state compliance from individuals against governments having ratified the Optional Protocol of the Covenant on Civil and Political Rights. This Committee (known as the Human Rights Committee) has, through its decisions on individual cases, influenced administrative approaches by member states to implementing the Covenant and created a meaningful body of jurisprudence flowing from cases brought by individuals. At the same time, the Committee also struggles with workload, exacerbated by limited administrative and analytical support for its important work. Such problems contrast with resistance by member states to efforts to develop similar accountability mechanisms with respect to economic, social, and cultural rights.

In his survey of conventions relating to refugees and stateless persons, Guy Goodwin-Gill argues in Chapter 22 that the UN regime has been successful in many individual cases as well as transformative in terms of global norms. He notes the pressures currently facing the refugee "system" created by large numbers of migrants, many of whom can lay credible claim to refugee status, from the Middle East and Africa into Europe. (In fact, earlier and contemporary global migration flows and those within Africa and Asia, for example, dwarf this politically sensitive but not uniquely massive phenomenon involving Europe—however keenly it is experienced within that continent.) Some critics argue that refugees should be encouraged to remain in the neighborhoods of their countries of origin, where jobs might be found for them.[21] Unfortunately, examples of this being attempted in countries such as Jordan are inconclusive at best for now.

[21] For example, see Paul Collier, Exodus: *How Migration Is Changing Our World* (OUP 2013). By 2016 he was arguing that immigration should be "slowed" down and war-affected migrants looked after locally rather than offered refugee status, which he and some others see as outdated and counterproductive.

The UN was created to "save succeeding generations from the scourge of war" and so it is unsurprising that it became a focal point for discussion of rules criminalizing recourse to war and the excesses that accompany it, as well as new means to protect human dignity outside of international armed conflict. As Salvatore Zappalà shows in Chapter 23, early movement on the Genocide Convention soon stalled with the Cold War. The end of that conflict and the tragedy of Yugoslavia led the Security Council to create ad hoc tribunals in the 1990s, laying the foundation for the Rome Statute of the International Criminal Court (ICC) in 1998. The ICC and the UN remain closely connected, creating both opportunities and challenges.

In their accompanying practitioner reflection, Hirad Abtahi and Philippe Kirsch situate the development of international criminal law in the context of the truly international courts, such as the tribunals and the ICC, as well as the various experiments with hybrid tribunals from Cambodia to Sierra Leone and Lebanon. Practice has taken the form of experiments with form and process, but there has been evidence of the UN as a forum helping to institutionalize knowledge about international criminal law and capitalize on the universal membership of the UN to offer these tribunals a degree of legitimacy that might otherwise have been lacking.

The final area of practice is in relation to international law itself.

One of the UN's most important contributions has been to the laws that determine how treaties are concluded, interpreted, and applied. As Malgosia Fitzmaurice shows in Chapter 24, the universality of the UN and its permanence made possible the slow and deliberate work of elaborating principles that were eventually put to states in the form of the Vienna Convention on the Law of Treaties (VCLT). Other key instruments address questions such as state succession and treaties entered into with international organizations, while ongoing work of the ILC addresses reservations and the impact of armed conflict.

In his practitioner reflection, Lionel Yee describes how the process of interpreting a treaty may begin well before it is concluded. Negotiators may choose to insert provisions that favor a particular understanding of an obligation, even if the result is ambiguity in the final text. On occasion, side agreements or joint statements may be used. The VCLT is reasonably clear on how to handle most such provisions, but difficulties may arise when side agreements are vague as to their binding nature or are kept confidential.

Another key contribution of the UN is the Convention on the Law of the Sea (UNCLOS). In Chapter 25, Yoshifumi Tanaka traces its history back to early efforts in the twentieth century to address the competing interests of coastal states. One of the important transformations in the regime governing the high seas reflects the larger transformation in international law emphasized by this book: the shift from law reconciling individual competing interests to law helping to safeguard shared community interests.

That shift features also in Tommy Koh's practitioner's reflection on the negotiations that led to UNCLOS. A number of unusual features helped nudge parties toward agreement. These included a "package deal" approach and the discouragement of voting until the final stages, the long duration of the negotiations and encouragement of interest groups that cut across traditional political affiliations, and the use of informal private negotiating groups and groups of experts. Perhaps the most unusual aspect was that the conference began without a draft text, and that preparation of the single negotiating text was delegated to the chairs.

The Conventions on the Privileges and Immunities of the United Nations and Its Specialized Agencies were among the first ones to be negotiated in the framework of the UN. In describing the procedural history of these Conventions, in Chapter 26, Davinia Aziz and Alison See thus discover the very first steps of the UN treaty-making processes. They highlight the emergence of certain working methods (such as the use of legal and policy background materials and the adoption of a multistage process with small negotiating groups), as well as conceptual innovations (such as the multilateral format to address the issue of privileges and immunities, and the shift from diplomatic to functional immunity). The various roles assumed by the UN with respect to these conventions (setting for the debates, active driver of the negotiations, subject matter of legal regulation) explain the specificities of this convention in terms of treaty structure and functioning, for example with respect to reservations.

The area of diplomatic and consular relations has provided fertile ground for as many as five conventions adopted by the UN as part of its codification mandate. In Chapter 27, Sanderijn Duquet and Jan Wouters explore the reasons that the UN engaged in the codification of this topic as a priority, and place the negotiations in their legal and geopolitical context. Procedurally, the five conventions adopted in this area share similarities in their preparatory phase (with the initial work of the ILC), but adopted different approaches for the intergovernmental negotiation (in three cases, this took place in a diplomatic conference; in two others within the Sixth Committee of the General Assembly). Duquet and Wouters assess the success of these conventions, taking into account not only the number of ratifications, but also the level of compliance among their parties, which they consider through certain landmark judicial cases.

The UN contribution in the area of international commercial arbitration stems from the work of the Commission on International Trade Law (UNCITRAL). In Chapter 28, Corinne Montineri examines the two multilateral treaties that UNCITRAL has produced in this field. As she notes, the 1958 Convention on the Recognition and Enforcement of Foreign Arbitral Awards responded to calls for the respect of arbitration agreements and the enforcement of arbitral awards that had been voiced as early as in the 1920s, and it contains several major breakthroughs in this area. Nevertheless, UNCITRAL did not choose to resort again to a multilateral treaty to regulate commercial arbitration for another half a century. The Convention on Transparency in Treaty-Based Investor-State Arbitration, which was adopted in 2014, aims at extending the application of UNCITRAL's Transparency Rules to the more than 3,000 bilateral investment treaties concluded prior to 2014, thus bringing greater efficiency and coherence to the system. Despite being separated in time, both of these multilateral treaties were negotiated in a government-led and inclusive process, involving all relevant stakeholders, thus achieving a delicate balance between competing interests and principles. Furthermore, UNICTRAL has resorted to creative means to ensure their implementation.

As Pierre Bodeau-Livinec observes in Chapter 29, given the reluctance shown by the UN in crystallizing into treaty form the topic of international responsibility, it may appear paradoxical to include a chapter devoted to this topic in our *Handbook*. His contribution clearly shows, however, that an examination of the debate on the ILC Articles on State Responsibility and the Responsibility of International Organizations sheds some light on the potential added value of UN treaties in the formation and further development of international law. Bodeau-Livinec offers an insightful description of how the discussion on the outcome of these codifications evolved within the ILC itself, leading to a final recommendation that favored a non-binding text in the short term and to an indecisive debate in the General Assembly, which continues to date. His contribution helpfully ponders what is at stake in this debate and explores available procedural options for the conclusion of a hard law instrument on international responsibility. As he notes, the ILC texts have sufficiently stood the test of time to provide a solid basis for states to explore the unchartered territories of a possible convention.

4.3 Technique

The final part of the volume offers cross-cutting analysis of technical developments in treaty-making promoted in the framework of the United Nations. More than mere diplomatic craftsmanship, these developments have brought about innovations in the conduct of multilateral negotiations and international treaty law.

In Chapter 30, Michael Wood examines the diversity of treaty-making techniques used in the framework of UN negotiation. He briefly describes several specific UN negotiating processes to illustrate that these techniques are inherently flexible, before proposing some reflections from a negotiator's point of view. He highlights three important decisions for negotiators. First, the preliminary determination whether it is necessary to regulate the issue by treaty and when it is the appropriate to start negotiations. Second, the need to ensure advance preparation through the elaboration of a draft text for discussion, which may require the intervention of an expert body such as the ILC. Third, the determination of the most suitable forum to conduct the negotiations, which should take into account the working methods, practices, and "atmosphere" of the available options.

In Chapter 31, Philippa Webb writes on the participation of nonstate actors in multilateral negotiating processes. In some cases, nonstate actors have been the lead. For example, the Convention on the Prohibition of the Use, Stockpiling, Production and Transfer of Anti-Personnel Mines and on Their Destruction of 1997 (known as the Ottawa Treaty) was spearheaded by an international nongovernmental organization (NGO) working alongside the Canadian government. This earned the International Campaign to Ban Landmines a Nobel Peace Prize in 1997, a feat repeated two decades later by the International Campaign to Ban Nuclear Weapons (ICAN). States remain the key actors in the negotiations of treaties, but they are not impervious to pressure from their publics and others to take action on perceived threats that treaties could constructively address.

Nonstate actors, for their part, benefit from greater flexibility and low operating costs, as well as typically being more media savvy.

In addressing the participation of international organizations in the multilateral treaty framework, Jan Klabbers focuses his attention in Chapter 32 on the specific case of the European Union, noting that it remains the only entity that, in actual practice, currently responds to the description of a "regional economic integration organization" used in several UN treaties. His contribution explores the logic of opening UN treaties to participation by the European Union, both from the UN and the Union's perspective. He then identifies several possible modes of participation, which may include full membership in the treaty-making organization, observer status in such an organization, participation in formal or informal groups, and participation in treaties concluded under the auspices of the UN. Finally, Klabbers examines in detail the intricacies of the European experiences in participating to UN treaties.

In Chapter 33, Jonathan Agar and Christel Mobech address how the UN has promoted transparency in the international treaty framework through the registration and publication of treaties pursuant to Article 102 of the Charter. From the origins of this provision (which date back to the inception of the League of Nations) to its operationalization, Agar and Mobech retrieve the ideals that have inspired this centennial endeavour and the challenges it has faced. But their contribution goes beyond, by providing a unique thematic and statistical analysis of data from the United Nations treaty database, revealing global trends in treaty-making and recurrent practical issues relating to the law of treaties.

Finally, in Chapter 34, Arancha Hinojal-Oyarbide examines the important role played by the Secretary-General as depositary of the hundreds of multilateral treaties concluded in the framework of the UN. The Secretary-General's depositary practice has greatly evolved in recent years, a phenomenon not always reported in the legal literature. Her contribution describes in detail some of these recent developments, for example with respect to the provision of legal advice in negotiations and the interpretation of final clauses, participation and entry into force, amendments, or withdrawal.

Overall, the volume provides a unique opportunity to discover—or rediscover—the enormous diversity of UN treaty-making activity since 1945. From a comparative reading of these detailed examinations of the various facets of the UN work in the field of treaties, readers can also trace a larger narrative of missed opportunities and surprise successes, major breakthroughs and recurring challenges, outcomes already obtained and ideals still pursued. Most of all, what emerges is the manner in which these efforts have contributed to achieving the aims of the UN—aims once paraphrased by Secretary-General Dag Hammarskjöld as being, if not to take humanity to heaven, at least to save it from hell.

PART I

EVOLUTION—UN TREATY-MAKING IN PRACTICE AND IN THEORY

CHAPTER 1

THE UN CHARTER AND ITS EVOLUTION

IAN JOHNSTONE

THIS chapter seeks to answer two questions: What type of legal instrument is the United Nations Charter, and why has the UN come to play such a central role in treaty-making? I draw on relational contract theory to answer both. My central claim is that the Charter is neither an ordinary treaty nor a global constitution, but something in-between. It is a legal instrument that structures a long-term relationship among UN member states and as such provides the normative and procedural context within which many multilateral treaties are made.

The chapter begins with an explanation of relational contract theory and how it illuminates the nature of the UN Charter. A section on interpretation of the Charter as a "living tree" follows. The third section looks at the UN as both a venue for and actor in treaty-making. The chapter concludes with reflections on where this is heading. If the strength of a "relational" treaty depends in part on the desire of the parties to preserve the relationship it embodies, do the current challenges to the UN and multilateralism generally put the viability of the Charter in jeopardy?

1 The Charter as a Relational Contract

The UN Charter is not an ordinary treaty. It has certain constitution-like features that distinguish it from most other treaties.[1] Foremost among them is the primacy principle embodied in Article 103, which holds that in the event of a conflict between obligations

[1] Simon Chesterman, Ian Johnstone, and David Malone, *Law and Practice of the United Nations: Documents and Commentary* (2nd edn OUP 2016) xxxiii–xxxix. For other scholars who explore the "constitutional" nature of the UN Charter, see Bardo Fassbender, *The United Nations Charter as the*

under the UN Charter and those under any other agreement, the Charter trumps. Second, like most national constitutions, amending the Charter is difficult—requiring the approval of a supermajority in the General Assembly, including all five permanent members of the Security Council. A third feature is that the Charter spells out the division of competencies among the constituent parts of the organization. Moreover, some of its core articles are "constitutive rules" of the international system—rules that do not simply regulate the conduct of states, but give structure to the international system.[2] The principle of sovereign equality, the prohibition against the use of force, and respect for the obligations that arise from treaties (pacta sunt servanda) are amongst these rules.

While the Charter has certain constitution-like features and is the constitutive act for the United Nations, it is not a global constitution. To begin with, even its constitutional elements are more limited than the above account suggests. By its terms, Article 103 applies only to other "agreements," not customary law or general principles. Amendment is difficult, but that is not a defining feature of all constitutions nor is it true only of constitutional documents. Indeed, most treaties require a consensus to be amended, whereas a qualified majority vote is enough for the Charter. It spells out the division of powers among organs, but those powers are quite limited with only the Security Council possessing supranational authority. Finally, while the constitutive rules provide a structure for the international legal system (based on state sovereignty), a true constitution governs a single polity—in democratic theory, a *demos*. International society is not a single polity.

The Charter, therefore, falls somewhere between an ordinary treaty and a constitution. This gray area is hard to define, but an analogy to relational contracts is instructive. Relational contract theory (RCT) emerged in the United States in the 1970s as an alternative to classical contract theory. Classical theory sees a contract as essentially a transaction between two entities, in which one asset is exchanged for another (typically money for a good or service). An archetypal transactional or "discrete" contract is the purchase of a tank of gasoline on a highway far from home. Relational contracts are not a single exchange but rather seek to structure a long-term relationship. Collective bargaining agreements between unions and management are a good example. Franchise agreements are another. Some have characterized marriages in that way.[3] Moreover the relational nature of the contract has two dimensions. As noted, it provides the structure or framework for a long-term relationship. At the same time, the contract itself is embedded in a broader context of existing legal and social norms.[4] No contract is purely one or the other. Even buying a tank of gasoline assumes a set of background

Constitution of the International Community (Martinus Nijhoff 2009); Pierre-Marc Dupuy, "The Constitutional Dimension of the UN Charter Revisited," (1997) 1 *Max Planck Yearbook of United Nations Law* xix; Michael Doyle "Dialectics of a Global Constitution: The Struggle over the UN Charter" (2012) 18 European Journal of International Relations 601.

[2] On the concept of "constitutive rules", see John Searle, *The Construction of Social Reality* (Free Press 1995).

[3] Elizabeth Scott and Robert E Scott, "Marriage as a Relational Contract" (1998) 84 Virginia LR 1225.

[4] James W Fox, "Relational Contract Theory and Democratic Citizenship" (2003) 54 Case Western Reserve LR 1, 10–16.

norms—for example, the exchange value of money, and government rules on the quality of the gas and accuracy of the pumps. However, certain types of contracts fall closer to one end of the spectrum than the other.

Treaties can be conceived along a similar spectrum, with the UN Charter falling at the "relational" end.[5] Ian MacNeil, the originator of RCT, states, "contract can only be understood as a complex interaction between self-interest and social solidarity."[6] The mere act of entering into a contract is a social act—evidence that one is participating in society and its conventions. By analogy, the UN can be seen as embodying a complex interaction between national interests and global solidarity. While the UN was created to be a truly universal organization, covering all areas of international activity and giving all member states the chance to collaborate with each other, it is fundamentally an intergovernmental organization where states pursue national interests. Moreover, the structure ensures that the security interests of the five permanent members of the Security Council cannot be compromised.

More specifically, the UN Charter is like a relational contract in four ways.[7] First, it structures an enduring relationship among member states but does not spell out in detail the terms of that relationship. Most important provisions of the Charter are open-textured, with many contingencies not provided for. Tacitly, the parties have committed to cooperate with each other over time—filling in some of the gaps and managing the disputes and tensions that are bound to arise.

Second, consistent with RCT, the Charter implicates stakeholders other than the direct parties. When the UN was founded, although not every state in the world was a member, every state would be affected by decisions taken there. Article 2(6) even stipulates that nonmembers should be pressured to act in accordance with the Charter's principles. Moreover, parties to the Charter are the governments of the world yet it is signed in the name of "we the peoples." It includes provisions on human rights and self-determination, which challenge governmental authority. This does not alter the intergovernmental nature of the UN, but it does suggest that people as well as governments are stakeholders in what the UN does.

Third, the Charter has been and should be interpreted broadly in light of changing circumstances. Because not every contingency is explicitly covered and because there are stakeholders other than the founders, proper interpretation requires looking beyond

[5] Elsewhere I have argued that peace agreements in the aftermath of civil wars are like relational contracts. Ian Johnstone, "Managing Consent in Contemporary Peace Operations" (2011) 18 International Peacekeeping 160; see also Bart Smit Duijzentkunst and Sophia Dawkins, "Arbitrary Peace? Consent Management in International Arbitration" (2015) 26 EJIL 139. On the application of relational contract theory to other areas of international law, see Edwin Smith "Understanding Dynamic Obligations" (1991) 64 Southern California LR 1549; Jared Wessel, "Relational Contract Theory and Treaty Interpretation: End-Game Treaties v. Dynamic Obligation" (2004) 60 NYU Annual Survey of American Law 149.

[6] IR MacNeil, *The New Social Contract: An Inquiry into Modern Contractual Relations* (Yale University Press 1980) 94–98.

[7] These characteristics of relational contracts draw on the writings of leading domestic contract scholars: MacNeil (n 6); Scott and Scott (n 3); Fox, supra n. 4; and Charles Goetz and Robert Scott, "Principles of Relational Contracts" (1981) 67 Virginia LR 1089.

the "four corners of the page." This is true of any treaty, whose terms are to be read "in their context and in the light of [the treaty's] object and purpose."[8] Being on the far end of the transactional-relational spectrum, it is especially true of the UN Charter.

Fourth, interpretation, implementation, and enforcement of the Charter tend not to occur through adjudication but through diplomatic and discursive interaction among its members. The International Court of Justice (ICJ) settles some disputes and offers Advisory Opinions but disputes over the meaning of Articles 2(4), 2(7), 39, 51, 99, and other key provisions rarely get settled in courts. RCT downplays judicial settlement because constant litigation can undermine the relationship the "contract" is meant to preserve. (Consider a marriage.) The threat of adjudication is valuable because it can level the playing field between unequal states, but an expectation that every dispute will be settled through adjudication can be a disincentive to negotiate and compromise.

Of course, there are limits to the relational contract analogy. Domestic contracts (relational or otherwise) are usually between two parties only. The UN Charter and all treaties negotiated in the UN are multilateral. This raises questions about whether the Charter should be viewed as a contract at all, but if one does accept the contract analogy, it suggests that RCT is more illuminating than classical contract theory. A more telling limit to the analogy is the fact that the background legal and social norms are much thinner at the international level than in well-functioning states. The interdependence among states that is embodied in the UN Charter is subverted by power asymmetries that are more pronounced than for most relational contracts.

Despite those limitations, viewing the Charter as a relational contract can be instructive. It helps to explain and justify the evolution of the Charter through dynamic interpretation, as well as prominent features of ICJ jurisprudence such as the implied powers doctrine. It also sheds light on why the UN became a venue for and actor in treaty-making, and what are the implications of that for the development of treaty law. In sum, the UN Charter is both a relational contract in itself and is the embodiment of the relationship in which other multilateral treaties are negotiated, adopted, and implemented.

2 The Evolving Charter

In this section, I will first consider *who* interprets the UN Charter, highlighting the fact that it is rarely the ICJ. Interpretation more often occurs through a discursive process primarily amongst states but also nonstate actors, typically in response to incidents or through the implementation of programmatic activities. I will then discuss *how* the Charter has been interpreted as a living instrument, with examples from the field of peace and security. This section concludes with insights about Charter interpretation that can be drawn from RCT.

[8] Vienna Convention on the Law of Treaties, Article 31(1).

2.1 Who Interprets the Charter?

At the UN Conference on International Organizations it was decided that, as a general matter, "each United Nations organ interprets such parts of the Charter as are applicable to its functions."[9] The General Assembly, Security Council, ECOSOC, and all specialized agencies can request the ICJ to provide an Advisory Opinion on Charter interpretation. States can also submit a dispute to the ICJ that may require it to interpret Charter provisions. But otherwise, each organ decides for itself what the Charter means in respect of the functions it performs. An important implication of the UN Conference is that the ICJ was not given the power of judicial review over decisions by the political organs. It is not difficult to understand why. Doing so would have run the risk that the ICJ could constrain the ability of member states to perform what were essentially political functions, especially in the Security Council. Interpreting the Charter was seen as a political rather than legal exercise.

The US Constitution does not give the Supreme Court the power of judicial review either, but the Supreme Court asserted such authority in the famous case of *Marbury v. Madison*. The ICJ has not had its *Marbury* moment, but there have been some cases in which it hinted that it might assume that power, notably the *Lockerbie* and *Bosnia Genocide* cases.[10] Neither case proceeded to the merits, but some scholars—based on their readings of the preliminary rulings and statements of some of the judges—felt the court left the door open to judicial review.[11] José Alvarez doubts the ICJ will ever do so, but claims it engaged in an "expressive mode of review."[12] The Court in its advisory opinions and contentious cases can and often must comment on Council action, perhaps critically, short of a finding that it exceeded its competence. In a sort of dialogue with the Council, some of the judges in the *Lockerbie* case sent signals or "warnings" to exercise care not to undermine basic legal rights in how it goes about its functions.[13]

Even more interestingly, the European Court of Justice (ECJ) has engaged in indirect judicial review of the Council. In a series of decisions in the famous *Kadi* case, the Court of First Instance (now General Court) and the ECJ ruled that EU regulations imposing sanctions on individuals associated with the Taliban and al-Qaeda violated fundamental human rights, in particular due process rights.[14] Eventually the Security Council

[9] UNCIO Doc. 933, IV/2/42(2), p 7.

[10] *Questions of Interpretation and Application of the 1971 Montreal Convention arising from the Aerial Incident at Lockerbie (Libyan Arab Jamahiriya v. United States of America)* (Provisional Measures) [1992] ICJ Rep 114; *Case Concerning Application of the Convention on the Prevention and Punishment of the Crime of Genocide (Bosnia and Herzegovina v Serbia and Montenegro)* (Provisional Measures) [1993] ICJ Rep 325.

[11] Thomas Franck, "The Powers of Appreciation: Who Is the Ultimate Guardian of UN Legality?" (1992) 86 AJIL 519.

[12] José Alvarez, "Judging the Security Council" (1996) 90 AJIL 1, 28.

[13] Alvarez (n 12) 4, 30.

[14] *Kadi v Council and Commission* [2005] ECR II-3649 (Court of First Instance of the European Communities, 21 September 2005); *Kadi and Al Barakaat International Foundation v. Council and Commission* [2008] ECR I-6351 (European Court of Justice, 3 September 2008); *Kadi v.* Commission

introduced new procedural protections for those placed on the sanctions list. The Council never explicitly acknowledged that it was responding to the ECJ ruling (and that of multiple national courts), but its actions were an indirect response to what was, in effect, indirect judicial review.

This dialogue with the Council about the limits of its powers is not restricted to courts. The UN General Assembly, the Secretary-General, and senior UN officials such as the High Commissioner for Human Rights may also send signals. Individual and groups of states can as well. Thus, members of the Organization of African Unity collectively rebelled against the sanctions imposed on Libya that became the subject of the *Lockerbie* proceedings.[15]

2.2 Interpretation in Practice

It is not difficult to find examples of how the Charter has been interpreted as a "living tree." It dates back to the earliest days of the United Nations and found expression in the implied powers doctrine. In the *Reparations* case, the ICJ decided that the UN could bring an international claim on behalf of one of its agents who suffered injuries in the performance of his duties. The Court applied the so-called "functional limitation test": "Under international law, the Organization must be deemed to have those powers which, though not expressly provided by the Charter, are conferred upon it by necessary implication as being essential to the performance of its duties."[16] It decided that the UN must often rely on agents to carry out missions, and since those missions are often dangerous and politically sensitive, the UN must have the right to bring a claim on the agent's behalf in order that the functions may be carried out efficiently and without interference.

Following that logic, the UN has engaged in numerous activities that are not explicitly provided for in the Charter and were not contemplated in 1945. The term "peacekeeping," for example, does not appear anywhere in the UN Charter. Yet, based on an expansive reading of Chapter VI, the Security Council established small observer missions on the India-Pakistan border and in the Middle East in the 1940s. In 1956, the General Assembly established the first armed peacekeeping mission on the Sinai Peninsula in the aftermath of the Suez Canal crisis. Today, peace operations deployed under Chapters VI, VII, or both have become the signature activity of the UN. It is the result of constructive interpretation of the broad powers conferred on the Council and General Assembly when it became apparent that the collective security scheme embodied in the Charter could not function as intended. That scheme depended on unanimity among the

[2-10] ECR II-5177 (European General Court, 30 September 2010); *European Commission and Others v. Kadi* [2010] (European Court of Justice, 18 July 2013).

[15] For an analysis of the OAU action in terms of the Council's legitimacy, see Ian Hurd, *After Hegemony: Legitimacy and Power in the UN Security Council* (Princeton University Press 2007) ch VI.

[16] *Reparations for Injuries Suffered in the Service of the United Nations (Advisory Opinion)* [1949] ICJ Rep 174.

permanent members of the Security Council and their willingness to put forces on standby for UN-authorized military action, based on "special agreements" pursuant to Article 43. The superpower rivalry meant no such agreements were ever reached.

Based on Article 99 of the UN Charter, the Secretary-General has engaged in fact-finding and good offices without an explicit mandate from the UN's political organs. Early in his term, Trygve Lie sent a commission of inquiry to investigate alleged infiltration across Greece's northern frontier. He said to the Security Council at the time that he hoped the Council would understand that he reserved the right to make such inquiries as he deemed necessary in order to know whether a matter should be brought to its attention.[17] The Council agreed, and since then there has been little question that fact-finding initiated by the Secretary-General falls within the authority of Article 99. Dag Hammarskjold took matters a step further by engaging in personal diplomacy to secure the release of American aircrew imprisoned in Beijing in 1955. In 1958, he augmented the UN observer group in Lebanon on his own initiative. Afterward he said to the Council, "Were you to disapprove, I would of course accept the limits of your judgement."[18] The Secretary-General's actions represented an expansive interpretation of Article 99, leaving it to the Council to rein him in if it disapproved of his judgment. It did not.

In the post–Cold War era, the Security Council has acted in a quasi-legislative manner—first by creating ad hoc criminal tribunals in the former Yugoslavia and Rwanda in 1992 and 1994 respectively,[19] then by imposing far-reaching obligations on all member states in the field of counterterrorism.[20] The Council has also delegated substantial law-making powers to its subsidiary organs. For example, the international transitional administrations established for Kosovo and East Timor in 1999 were granted full legislative and executive authority within the territories they governed for a transitional period, and other peace operations have been given more limited executive powers, such as the power of arrest. The Council has acted in a quasi-judicial manner by declaring Iraq to be liable for damages caused during its 1990 invasion of Kuwait, and then demarcating the border between the two states.[21] Under Article 42, it has imposed asset freezes and travel bans on individuals,[22] sparking the indirect back and forth between the Council and ECJ described earlier.

The Council has employed a broad reading of "threat to the peace" within the meaning of Article 39 to authorize humanitarian intervention. This began (ambiguously) in

[17] Thomas Franck and Georg Nolte, "The Good Offices Function of the UN Secretary-General" in Adam Roberts and Benedict Kingsbury (eds), *United Nations, Divided World: The UN's Roles in International Relations* (2nd edn, OUP 1993) 143, 176.

[18] Franck and Nolte (n 17) 176. See also Brian Urquhart, *Hammarskjold* (Knopf 1972).

[19] UNSC Res 827 (25 May 1993) UN Doc S/RES/827; UNSC Res 955 (8 November 1994) UN Doc S/RES/955.

[20] UNSC Res 1373 (28 September 2001) UN Doc S/RES/1373; UNSC Res 1540 (28 April 2004) UN Doc S/RES/1540; UNSC Res 2178 (24 September 2014) UN Doc S/RES/2178.

[21] UNSC Res 687 (3 April 1991) UN Doc S/RES/687.

[22] The 1267 targeted sanctions regime on the Taliban, later expanded to anyone associated with the Taliban and al-Qaeda, is the best known. UNSC Res 1267 (15 October 1999) UN Doc S/RES/1267. See also UNSC Res 2253 (17 December 2015) UN Doc S/RES/2253.

Northern Iraq in 1991 and was followed through a series of cases in the 1990s from Somalia, to Bosnia, Haiti, and Sierra Leone. None of these was a pure case of humanitarian intervention, but in all of them the Security Council authorized military action in part for humanitarian purposes. The 1999 intervention in Kosovo was not explicitly authorized by the Security Council, but the military action in Libya 12 years later was.[23] In that same year in Côte d'Ivoire, the Council reaffirmed a protection-of-civilians mandate that was used by a UN peace operation and French forces as the legal basis for robust military action to help install democratically elected president Alassane Ouatarra in power.

Article 51 has been interpreted broadly to extend well beyond military aggression by one state against another.[24] Thus, in 2001, it was invoked by the United States to justify military action in Afghanistan in response to the terrorist attacks of September 11, 2001. This was a stretch of the concept of self-defense in three respects. First, it was invoked against a nonstate actor (al-Qaeda).[25] Second, the US deemed supporting and harboring the perpetrators to be enough to make the Taliban government complicit in the terrorist acts. This is a more relaxed standard than the *Nicaragua* case, which would attribute conduct of insurgents to a neighboring state only if they were "sent by or on behalf of" that state. Third, in exercising its right of self-defense, the United States and its allies changed the regime that was in power in Afghanistan. While the Taliban was not widely recognized by the outside world as the country's legitimate authority—its representatives were never allowed to occupy the seat in the UN, for example—it was in control of 90 percent of Afghan territory. While lawyers may argue about whether the military action violated Article 51, the international community as a whole seems to have accepted the US government's position.[26]

Finally, as Rosalyn Higgins pointed out many years ago, the Article 2(7) line between matters of international concern and those that are "essentially within the domestic jurisdiction" of a state has shifted.[27] Consider the UN's peace-building operations and democracy-promoting activities. These are undertaken with the consent of the host

[23] UNSC Res 1973 (17 March 2011) UN Doc S/RES/1973.

[24] Christine Gray, *International Law and the Use of Force* (3rd edn, OUP 2008).

[25] In the *Nicaragua case*, the International Court of Justice implied that self-defense can only be exercised against *states* who commit an "armed attack"—not nonstate actors. *Military and Paramilitary Activities in and against Nicaragua (Nicaragua v United States)* (Merits) [1986] ICJ Rep 14. The ICJ reiterated that position in *Legal Consequences of the Construction of the Wall in Occupied Palestinian Territory* (Advisory Opinion) [2004] ICJ General List No 131. It then retreated somewhat in *Armed Activities on the Territory of the Congo (Democratic Republic of Congo v Uganda)* [2005] ICJ General List No 116.

[26] Evidence that the US position was accepted includes: UNSC Res 1368 (12 September 2001) UN Doc S/RES/1368, preamble; NATO's invocation of Article 5, Statement of Secretary-General Lord Robertson, 2 October 2001, reprinted in 41 ILM 1267; OAS statement, "Terrorist threat to the Americas," Resolution adopted at the 24th meeting of the Consultations of Ministers of Foreign Affairs, Washington DC, 21 September 2001, DOC OEA/Ser.F/II.24 RC.24/Res.1/01. Other evidence includes the number of participants in Operation Enduring Freedom.

[27] Rosalyn Higgins, *Problems and Process: International Law and How We Use It* (Clarendon Press 1994).

government and therefore arguably not "intervention," but nevertheless demonstrate that our understanding of Article 2(7) has evolved. Such evolution has occurred primarily through the practices of the UN rather than judicial interpretation.

2.3 Charter Interpretation and Relational Contract Theory

How does relational contract theory help to understand the developments described above?

First, RCT illustrates the relational rather than transactional nature of the UN Charter. Most of the discourse occurred not in courts, but through the practices of the UN and the interaction among state and—to a lesser extent—nonstate actors. Even when courts rendered judgments on the issues in dispute, it often played out as dialogue rather than binding and enforceable dispute settlement.

Second, it is clear that the Charter has been interpreted dynamically to accommodate new threats, challenges, and opportunities without requiring Charter amendment. There have been many developments—one might even say deviations from strict Charter terms—since 1945. But equally important, these developments occurred within the normative context embodied by the UN Charter. The meaning of its terms may have been expanded, but the Charter remained the foundation for the practice and discourse around that practice. In other words, the rules were stretched and bent, but they were not ignored or torn up.

Third, dynamic interpretation of the UN Charter is not a game played among equals. If anything, treating the Charter as a "living tree" rather than a multiparty transaction with clearly spelled-out rights and obligations benefits the more powerful. Powerful states often prefer vague law, enabling them to set the terms of the discourse and present plausible interpretations that advance their interests, which weaker states have trouble resisting. Violations of hard precise law are more easily branded as such in the court of international governmental and public opinion, imposing reputational costs if nothing else. This is why some critical legal theorists regret the creative interpretation of open-textured norms and call for a return to formalism.[28]

3 UN Treaty-Making

As noted previously, the UN Charter provides the normative and procedural context within which many multilateral treaties are negotiated and implemented. So, for example, negotiating a UN counterterrorism convention that impinged on fundamental human

[28] See for example Marti Koskenniemi, *Gentle Civilizer of Nations: The Rise and Fall of International Law 1870–1960* (CUP 2002); Jean d'Aspremont, *Formalism and the Sources of International Law: A Theory of the Ascertainment of Legal Rules* (OUP 2011).

rights would face substantial resistance. Similarly, seeking to deprive nongovernmental organizations any access to treaty negotiations in a UN setting would go against long-standing practice, dating back at least to the United Nations Conference on the Human Environment in Stockholm, 1972. These norms and practices may or may not have roots in Charter language, but in either case they emerged and evolved as UN member states interacted with each other, in effect defining the nature of the relationship amongst them. Obviously, subgroups within the UN have tighter bonds than the membership as a whole. Although there is no "global identity" that binds all UN member states together, this does not prevent a set of shared assumptions, expectations, and understandings from emerging over time.[29] Even if these shared expectations and understandings have not been fully internalized by all states, they do impact the ability of the UN to function as both a venue and actor in the negotiation, interpretation, and implementation of treaties. The impact is often positive, though as noted at the end of this section, it can also be negative.

3.1 The United Nations as a Venue

The UN was not conceived as being a legislative body. Other than the Security Council, UN intergovernmental organs do not have the power to make binding decisions other than on internal matters, such as the budget and elections. There is strong language in the Charter about respect for international law but, beyond Article 1(4), which lists "harmonizing the actions of states" as a purpose of the organization; and Article 62(3), which empowers ECOSOC to submit draft conventions to the General Assembly, there is little about creating new law. Yet, the General Assembly and its subsidiary organs have become important venues for adopting multilateral treaties. RCT helps to explain why.

First, the purposes and principles of the UN are set out in rather broad terms in the Charter. Thus, while the promotion of human rights is one of the objectives listed in Articles 1 and 55, all the Charter asks of member states is "to pledge themselves to take joint and separate action" to achieve that purpose (Article 56). A rationale for human rights treaty-making is to give effect to that open-ended pledge. The UN did so first by adopting the Universal Declaration of Human Rights (not a treaty), whose terms were later codified in the two International Covenants both negotiated and adopted in the Human Rights Commission. Today, there is a dense web of human rights treaties negotiated in the UN, many of which are overseen by UN treaty bodies.

[29] Drawing on Habermas's notion of a common lifeworld, this argument has been made by Ian Johnstone, "Security Council Deliberations: The Power of the Better Argument" (2003) 14 EJIL 437; Corneliu Bjola, "Legitimate Use of Force in International Politics: A Communicative Action Perspective" (2005) 11 *European Journal of International Relations* 266, 279; Ingo Venzke, "Is Interpretation in International Law a Game?" in Andrea Bianchi, Daniel Peat, and Matthew Windsor (eds), Interpretation in International Law (OUP 2015) 352; Rene Provost, "*Interpretation in International Law* as a Transcultural Project" in Andrea Bianchi, Daniel Peat, and Matthew Windsor (eds), *Interpretation in International Law* (OUP 2015) 290.

Second, the UN has been a convenient place to meet the demand for new law, for reasons captured by neoliberal institutionalism.[30] According to the theory, international institutions facilitate cooperation among states for several reasons: they lower transaction costs, not least by providing the physical infrastructure for multilateral negotiations; they enable states to learn about each other's interests and preferences; they enhance transparency by facilitating the flow of information; and they create opportunities for linkages and mutually beneficial trade-offs among issues. In sum, states find it easier to negotiate and bargain with each other in settings where they have a preexisting relationship, rather than starting from scratch in an ad hoc conference. Of course, other factors may militate against using the UN as a venue. For example, in UN settings all states have the right to participate in the negotiations. Some issues do not lend themselves to negotiations among 193 states and have achieved more progress in other fora, such as the Ottawa Land Mines Convention.

Third, multilateral treaties are a mechanism for *managing* the fragile relationship among the UN's member states. To use an analogy from treaty practice, the UN Charter is akin to a framework convention and the treaties negotiated under its auspices are like protocols. Following on points one and two above, the Charter establishes the normative and procedural parameters for how to manage that relationship, with the details worked out organically over time. Sometimes that crystallizes into treaties, as was the case with the human rights covenants; sometimes not, as with the stalled efforts to adopt a comprehensive convention on terrorism.

Fourth, the UN system offers multiple fora for negotiations: the General Assembly, ECOSOC, the various funds and programs (such as UN Environment Programme (UNEP)), and the specialized agencies (such as the International Labour Organization (ILO) and WHO). For the General Assembly and its subsidiary organs, the steps in the treaty-making process are relatively standard: producing an initial draft, negotiating, adopting, signing (with or without reservations), and then ratifying it by the requisite number of states. There are interesting variations on this standard process in some of the specialized agencies. For example, all ILO members—including those who vote against a labor convention—are obliged to bring the treaty to the attention of competent domestic authorities for appropriate action. If action is not taken, members must report that back to the ILO with an explanation. This is designed to put pressure on members to reject a treaty only for good reasons.[31]

These variations create the possibility of forum shopping, with all the implications—positive and negative—associated with that. One benefit is that different kinds of expertise reside in the secretariats of different organizations. It makes sense to negotiate labor treaties in the ILO, health treaties in the WHO, treaties on cultural heritage in UNESCO, etc. On the other hand, the dynamics within those organizations may push some states

[30] The seminal work on neoliberal institutionalism is Robert Keohane, *After Hegemony: Cooperation and Discord in the World Political Economy* (Princeton University Press 1984).

[31] Fredric Kirgis, "Specialized Law-Making Processes," in Christopher Joyner (ed), *The United Nations and International Law* (CUP 1997) 65, 68. See also Jose Alvarez, *International Organizations as Lawmakers* (OUP 2006) 331–36.

to seek other fora where they are more likely to achieve preferred outcomes. Thus, some environmental treaties are negotiated in UNEP; many are not.

3.2 The United Nations as an Actor

What does it mean to call any organization an actor as opposed to venue? To begin with, supranational powers make an IO an actor, because some members can be bound by decisions they did not vote for. The EU has such powers, as does the Security Council of the UN. In terms of treaty-making, most IOs do not have supranational power (not even the EU), but there are a few interesting exceptions. The constituent instruments of at least two specialized agencies can be amended by qualified majority vote: the Statute of the IAEA (International Atomic Energy Agency) (by two-thirds majority) and the Articles of Agreement of the IMF (International Monetary Fund) (by three-fifths of its members who have 85 percent of the weighted voting power). For the United States, the IMF procedure is inconsequential because the United States has 17 percent of the voting share; for other members, the IMF can "act" on them in this way.

Another actor-like feature of an IO is when secretariat officials, experts, and nongovernmental organizations play an influential role in treaty-making. The quasi-official International Law Commission plays a large role preparing treaties. Senior officials of the UN are often instrumental in producing treaty drafts. Increasingly, nongovernmental organizations participate in negotiations, not in a voting capacity, but with independent influence. Constituent parts of the UN can be a focal point for the coalescence of these nongovernmental actors. The Montreal Protocol on Substances that Deplete the Ozone Layer illustrates this point. A resolution was appended to the Vienna Convention for the Protection of the Ozone Layer empowering UNEP to convene working group negotiations for a Protocol. These working groups were composed of not only government representatives, but also scientists, industry representatives, nongovernmental activists, and other experts. Under the charismatic leadership of then Executive Director Mostafa Tolba, this gave UNEP leverage to force the agenda in the face of lingering opposition to chlorofluorocarbon (CFC) controls. More recently, it facilitated the adoption of the Kigali Amendment on hydrofluorocarbons, a substance that replaced CFCs as a refrigerant in household appliances which contributes to global warming.

Third, UN system entities are actors in interpreting, monitoring, and overseeing the implementation of treaties. Like the Charter itself, UN treaties often become the subject of interpretative disputes. There are various mechanisms for providing authoritative interpretation, starting with but not restricted to the ICJ. Ten treaty bodies interpret the main human rights treaties, as do the Human Rights Council and its thematic and country rapporteurs. Even if the reports, opinions, and decisions of these entities are not binding, they can be an influential source of guidance. The General Comments of UN treaty committees, for example, are considered to be authoritative interpretations of the treaties they monitor. Similarly, the "views" of the human rights committees in dealing with individual complaints are often followed in practice. The ILO Office and associated experts play a similar role for the labor conventions. By clarifying the law, interpretation has the effect of promoting compliance.[32] When it gives content to vague provisions or fills gaps in a treaty, interpretation is a form of lawmaking.

Finally, many UN entities contribute to the development of treaty law through operational activities. This can be in the form of technical assistance to help states fulfill their obligations under a treaty—for example, assistance the UNHCR provides for states to comply with the Refugee Convention. The programmatic activities of IOs may also be a way of implementing imprecise treaty norms, causing them to harden as a result.[33] Thus electoral assistance and monitoring activities by the UN have given content to the right to political participation. Arguably, UNICEF programs have done the same for child rights, WHO programs for the right to health, and the World Food Program for the right to food. Again, to the extent that these activities lead to the "hardening" of treaty norms, they are a form of lawmaking.[34]

3.3 UN Treaty-Making and Relational Contract Theory

How does relational contract theory help to explain the features of UN law-making described above?

First, multilateral treaties adopted through interaction among UN member states can sustain or even deepen the relationship embodied in the UN Charter. This happens in various ways. The treaties help to achieve broad Charter goals such as peace, human rights, and economic and social cooperation. Mechanisms for interpretation and oversight help manage the relationship without resort to judicial dispute settlement. Operational activities by UN agencies not only implement the treaties, but also fill gaps and give content to imprecise treaty norms.

Second, UN processes tend to be relatively inclusive—accounting for the interests of a wide range of stakeholders. All members of the UN have the right to participate in the negotiation of treaties. UN officials and experts can help to assess and balance the competing interests of states involved. Nongovernmental actors and representatives of civil society can speak for voices that might not otherwise be heard, or at least can sound the alarm when their interests are being ignored. If global civil society has the chance to

[32] The "management model" of compliance posits that noncompliance is often the result of lack of clarity, not a lack of will to comply. See Abram Chayes and Antonia Chayes, *The New Sovereignty: Compliance with International Regulatory Agreements* (Harvard University Press 1995) 10–13.

[33] Ian Johnstone, "Law-Making through the Operational Activities of International Organizations" (2008) 40 George Washington International LR 87.

[34] On the spectrum of soft to hard law, see Kenneth Abbot, Robert Keohane, Andrew Moravcsik, Anne-Marie Slaughter, and Duncan Snidal, "The Concept of Legalization" in Judith Goldstein et al (eds), *Legalization and World Politics* (MIT Press 2001) 17–35. For skeptical views on whether "soft law" exists at all, see Prosper Weil, "Towards Relative Normativity in International Law" (1983) 77 AJIL 413; Jan Klabbers, "The Redundancy of Soft Law" (1996) 65 Nordic JIL 167.

witness, question, and critique what the UN does—whether directly or in the court of public opinion—that creates an incentive for those within the institution to refrain from behavior that will attract criticism.[35] While far from a fully inclusive deliberative setting, the UN does reasonably well compared to most other institutions.

Third—and this is a downside of treaty-making in the UN—managing the relationship among 193 states with widely diverse interests can inhibit agreement on anything but the lowest common denominator. The difficulty of global negotiations creates an incentive to move away from universal, multilateral treaty-making to more flexible and efficient arrangements—what has been called "plurilateralism,"[36] "minilateralism,"[37] or "the new multilateralism."[38] Security Council quasi-legislating is an illustration. The resurgence of regionalism in Africa and Asia is another. New development and financial institutions such as the Asian Infrastructure Investment Bank and BRICS Development Bank are a third. Non-binding arrangements among groups of states, such as G-20 agreements on the global economy and the Proliferation Security Initiative are also manifestations of plurilateralism. Arguably, the populist challenge against multilateral institutions generally is a dimension of this phenomenon, with Brexit as Exhibit A.

4 Conclusion

It is tempting to conclude that the challenge to global institutions means the United Nations and treaty-making under its auspices are past their prime. If the Charter is indeed a relational contract, these challenges reflect a loss of faith in that contract. Anxiety about the future of the UN is driven in part by its perceived inability to cope with phenomena such as terrorism, cyberattacks, the diffusion of technology, and the pace of socioeconomic change. As an inter-governmental organization composed of 193 states and rigid decision-making processes, it may no longer be fit for purpose. However, a fundamental tenet of relational contract theory is that the viability of the relational contract depends heavily on the desire of the parties to preserve that relationship. The UN has proven to be a resilient institution despite the dramatic changes that have occurred since it was founded in 1945. Through the Cold War, decolonization era,

[35] Buchanan and Keohane call this a "transnational civil society channel of accountability." Allan Buchanan and Robert Keohane, "The Legitimacy of Global Governance Institutions" (2006) 20 Ethics and International Affairs 405, 430. See also Ian Johnstone, *The Power of Deliberation: International Law, Politics and Organizations* (OUP 2011) 209–12.

[36] Anthony Aust (2000). *Modern Treaty Law and Practice* (Cambridge: Cambridge University Press) p. 112.

[37] Miles Kahler, "Multilateralism with Small and Large Numbers" (1992) 46 International Organization 681–708; Moses Naim, "Minilateralism: The Magic Number to Get Real International Action" Foreign Policy (June 21, 2009).

[38] Stewart Patrick, "The New 'New Multilateralism': Minilateral Cooperation but at What Cost?" (2015) 1(2) Global Summitry 115. See also, Richard Haas, 'The Case for Messy Multilateralism', *Financial Times*, January 2, 2010.

unipolarity at the end of the Cold War, and rise of intrastate conflict and terrorism since then, the UN faced many challenges—including some that seemed existential. Yet it survives. The Organization is again being put to the test by deep geopolitical fissures and nationalist sentiment. If history is any guide, the web of relationships embodied in the UN Charter and UN treaties is resilient enough to pass this test too.

CHAPTER 2

TREATY-MAKING IN INTERNATIONAL ORGANIZATIONS

international relations theory

SHIRLEY V. SCOTT*

The United Nations is inextricably intertwined with the contemporary system of international law. As a result, the reawakening of interest in international law within the field of international relations (IR) over the last two decades has generated a considerable body of IR literature of some relevance to understanding UN treaty-making. The UN's role in facilitating treaty-making has consolidated a shift from bilateral to multilateral treaties and the increased use of multilateral treaties as policy tools, with a vastly thickened, and broadened, web of international law as a consequence. This chapter engages with some key bodies of IR scholarship that offer insights regarding UN treaty-making. It is noteworthy that only some of this literature has the multilateral treaty as its object of analysis. Far more common is for the IR discipline to devise its own units of analysis, without necessarily linking those units explicitly to legal categories.

The first body of literature with which the chapter engages is that on norm dynamics. Here the unit of analysis is at a sub-treaty level; within this scholarship, the conclusion of a multilateral treaty is a success point in the global acceptance and dissemination of a norm as a standard of behavior. Second, we will move to the supra-treaty level and the literature that views treaties in the context of international institutions and organizations. Here the unit of analysis has for several decades been the regime, of which a multilateral treaty or treaties are generally a component. More recently attention has been directed to "regime complexes." A third section considers the relevance for understanding UN treaty-making of more recent IR literature on the decline of the liberal international order.

* I would like to acknowledge the valuable research assistance of Roberta C Andrade.

1 UN Treaties as the Institutionalization of Norms

In political terms, the conclusion of a multilateral treaty serves to institutionalize a previously emergent norm. Norms have been the subject of a considerable body of IR scholarship over the last two decades. A norm has typically been defined as "a standard of appropriate behaviour for actors with a given identity";[1] the term "norm" has been used to encompass a wide variety of types of ideas

> of varying degrees of abstraction and specification with respect to fundamental values, organizing principles or standardized procedures that resonate across many states and global actors, having gained support in multiple forums including official policies, laws, treaties or agreements.[2]

What is in this literature referred to as a norm is likely to be embedded in a multilateral treaty as one of the substantive provisions, albeit that as a treaty provision it will probably be more precisely and narrowly defined than might be the norm. Thus, the norm of no first-use of force is embedded in Article 2(4) of the UN Charter, and the norm against child soldiers in articles 1–4 of the Optional Protocol to the Convention on the Rights of the Child on the involvement of children in armed conflict.

The particular contribution of the norm literature to our understanding of UN treaty-making is its directing our attention to the non-legal as well as legal pathways by which ideas emerge and carry political weight, and to how those norms are diffused, by whom, and with what effect. Researching the genesis of global norms helpfully directs our attention to the prehistory of a treaty, and to the complex interplay between legal and other forms of norms. This is valuable insofar as the success or effectiveness of a treaty is dependent to a considerable extent on how well the treaty meets the shared goals to which it had been a response. The study of norms has also enabled us to better understand the political functioning of treaties once in place. A norm may continue to meet with resistance even after it has been embedded in a treaty; it may nevertheless spread, evolve, or merge with other norms.

The first wave of literature on norm dynamics focused on the "life cycle" of norms. The seminal study by Finnemore and Sikkink introduced the term "norm entrepreneur" to refer to those who set out to alter the normative status quo and hence—from the perspective of our interest here—who exert influence during treaty pre-negotiations and

[1] Martha Finnemore and Kathryn Sikkink, "International Norm Dynamics and Political Change" (1998) 52 Intl Org 887, 891.

[2] Mona Lena Krook and Jacqui True, "Rethinking the Life Cycles of International Norms: The United Nations and the Global Promotion of Gender Equality" (2010) 18 Eur J Intl Rel 103, 103–04. See also Antje Wiener, "Enacting Meaning-in-Use: Qualitative Research on Norms and International Relations" (2009) 35 Rev Intl Stud 175, 183ff.

formal negotiations.[3] The early norm entrepreneur literature tended to assume that it was the West that introduced new and progressive norms and that then sought to convince the rest of the world of the appropriateness of those norms and to disseminate those norms around the globe. The general assumption was that new norms were always liberal and an improvement on what had existed previously. Finnemore and Sikkink explained that once key leaders had accepted the new norm, a process of cascade ensued.[4]

More recently, norm theorists have questioned several aspects of the early norm literature, including the idea of norms "trickling" down from a treaty to the local level, the static view of norm content, and just whose norms we are investigating. Krook and True proposed that norms be conceived of as processes,[5] and there has been a turn to highlight the agency of the South.[6] According to Acharya, key concepts of postwar governance—including human development, responsible sovereignty, and sustainable development—have been deeply influenced by ideas from the postcolonial world.[7] This resonates with the revisionist literature on human rights. Steven Jensen's book on *The Making of International Human Rights* establishes the importance of the Global South in the global human rights phenomenon.[8] Whereas most historians have emphasized the 1940s and 1970s, when Western activists and states had most influence, Jensen illuminated the role of Jamaica, Liberia, Ghana, and the Philippines in the 1960s postcolonial moment in putting forward a human rights agenda, which he regards as having transformed the norms of the international community.[9]

According to Stuenkel, the assumption that the West is the source of progressive norms has led to the unhelpful equation of the Responsibility to Protect (R2P) norm with the West (or North) and an anti-R2P position with the Global South, which in turn suggests that Brazil's leadership of discussion on strengthening R2P was obstructionist.[10] The influence of non-Western states on global norms and UN treaty-making is set to increase with the shifting distribution of power, as captured in the concept of an "idea-shift."[11] In the language of norm theorists, BRICs states in particular are no longer simply "norm takers" but norm shapers, shakers, contesters, and defenders.[12]

Much of the very considerable norms literature has a rather unsophisticated understanding of international law per se, if it has a view at all, tending toward perceiving

[3] Finnemore and Sikkink (n 1). [4] ibid. [5] Krook and True (n 2).

[6] Eric Helleiner, "Southern Pioneers of International Development" (2014) 20 Global Gov 375.

[7] Amitav Acharya, "'Idea-Shift': How Ideas from the Rest Are Reshaping Global Order" (2016) 37 Third World Q 1156.

[8] Steven LB Jensen, *The Making of International Human Rights: The 1960s, Decolonization, and the Reconstruction of Global Values* (CUP 2016).

[9] Jensen (n 8). See also Kathryn Sikkink, "Latin American Countries as Norm Protagonists of the Idea of International Human Rights" (2014) 20 Global Gov 389.

[10] Oliver Stuenkel, "Brazil and R2P: A Case of Agency and Norm Entrepreneurship in the Global South" (2016) 30 Intl Rel 375.

[11] Acharya, "'Idea-Shift'" (n 7).

[12] Sikina Jinnah, "Makers, Takers, Shakers, Shapers: Emerging Economies and Normative Engagement in Climate Governance" (2017) 23 Global Gov 285.

multilateral treaties as simple norm repositories and implicitly assuming a norm to have been accepted by the international community once it has been successfully placed into such a repository. To the extent that norms tend to be embedded in the early substantive provisions of a treaty and may be integral to its object and purpose, this may be a valid assumption. Yet most international lawyers would likely assume that the degree to which a norm has "arrived" depends on a variety of factors other than the conclusion of a multilateral treaty. These factors might include rates of ratification, entry into force, reservations, relationship with other treaties, dissemination via domestic legal systems, and so on.

Whaling affords a useful example. Although many regard the anti-whaling norm as the dominant (political) norm, it has never been universally accepted or embedded in international law. The International Convention for the Regulation of Whaling was designed to regulate the whaling industry, conserving whale stocks to the extent necessary to preserve the industry as opposed to protecting whales as an end in itself. Those now promoting a norm of sustainable whaling may be regarded as norm entrepreneurs. While this places those who oppose the concept of sustainable whaling as promoted by Japan as "antipreneurs," that is unlikely to be how they self-identify.[13] The ongoing assumption that it is the West that generates and disseminates norms means that those opposed to *any* lethal whaling do not see themselves as opponents of a new, or at least reworked, norm designed to reconcile the institutionalized norms in the Whaling Convention with the norms of environmentalism. Rather, they perceive themselves as working to strengthen and fully universalize a progressive, anti-whaling norm, against long-standing opposition. Despite the terms of the Convention, the decision in the *Whaling* Case[14] could be read as serving to reinforce the prevailing (political) norm against commercial whaling,[15] illuminating the political significance of the work of the International Law Commission on subsequent agreements and subsequent practice in relation to interpretation of treaties.[16]

Norm theorists have contributed some counterintuitive findings to our understanding of the dynamics at play, both prior to, and following the conclusion of, a multilateral treaty. Risse, Ropp, and Sikkink demonstrated, for example, that even though a state might have ratified a treaty without fully embracing its embedded norms, human rights NGOs and others may then engage in advocacy work with the state concerned, using the treaty obligations as a normative benchmark, to bring about change over time.[17]

[13] Shirley V Scott and Lucia Oriana, "Resisting Japan's Promotion of a Norm of Sustainable Whaling" in Alan Bloomfield and Shirley V Scott (eds), *Norm Antipreneurs and the Politics of Resistance to Global Normative Change* (Routledge 2016).

[14] *Whaling in the Antarctic (Australia v Japan: New Zealand intervening)* (Judgment) [2014] ICJ Rep (31 March 2014).

[15] Shirley V Scott and Lucia Oriana, "Whaling in the Antarctic (Australia v. Japan: New Zealand intervening) Judgment of 31 March 2014: A Decisive Victory—but for Whom?" (2014) 29 IJMCL 547, 557.

[16] International Law Commission, "Summaries of the Work of the International Law Commission" (16 February 2017) <http://legal.un.org/ilc/summaries/1_11.shtml> accessed March 8, 2018.

[17] Thomas Risse, Stephen C Ropp, and Kathryn Sikkink (eds), The Power of Human Rights: International Norms and Domestic Change (CUP 1999).

This raises the further question as to the potential impact of a norm embedded in a multilateral treaty on nonstate parties. For example, given that no Nuclear Weapon State is likely to ratify the 2017 Treaty on the Prohibition of Nuclear Weapons, its potential efficacy would, from a legal perspective, at first glance appear low. In strict legal terms, the treaty imposes no obligations on nonparties. Viewed through the lens shared by many norm theorists and civil society campaigners, however, a norm embedded in a treaty may over time influence states not yet party to the treaty; over the mid- to longer-term, the norm may impact the choices even of nonparty nuclear weapons states. Norms may spread, for example, through the "socialization" of policymakers interacting in international organizations.[18]

This reinforces the insight that multilateral treaties do not serve to disseminate norms simply through a process of treaty ratification and implementation via domestic legal systems. There may also be a bottom-up transfer, such that analytical attention is validly directed to the local. Norm theorists are taking increasing interest in the interpretation of norms both to suit local needs and as a sophisticated form of resistance. Acharya has demonstrated that local actors create rules with a view to preserving their autonomy from domination by more powerful central actors, which he refers to as norm subsidiarity.[19] Variation in acceptance of two Association of Southeast Asian Nations (ASEAN) norms can best be explained in terms of local agents reconstructing the foreign norms to ensure a better fit with prior local norms.[20] Such research reveals both a multidirectional spread of norms and multi-agent complexity.

If the object of analysis is the norm as opposed to a treaty per se, it becomes apparent that norms may often spread transnationally—for example through city network interactions—with no treaty involved in the process.[21] Of the three types of norms described by Antje Wiener in her theory of norm contestation, only fundamental norms at the macro level, such as "human rights" or "democracy," notable for their wide moral and ethical reach, are likely to be negotiated by representatives of government at the macro level of governance and stipulated by treaties.[22] Despite the claims by IR constructivists that, in contradistinction to their disciplinary forebears, they take ideas seriously, it is arguably only with recent norm scholarship and exploration of how non-Western, non-rising, states are influencing ideas, that IR is truly embracing norms and ideas as forms of power and influence in their own right. The assumption that ideas,

[18] Adam Bower, *Norms without the Great Powers: International Law and Changing Social Standards in World Politics* (OUP 2017). See also Robert L Brown, "The Causes and Effects of International Treaties" (2016) 131 PSQ 597, 619: "While the negotiation of treaties results in increasing dissimilarity and worsening conflicts of interest, socialization occurs after treaties enter into force."

[19] Amitav Acharya, "Norm Subsidiarity and Regional Orders: Sovereignty, Regionalism, and Rule-Making in the Third World" (2011) 55 Intl Stud Q 95.

[20] Amitav Acharya, "How Ideas Spread: Whose Norms Matter? Norm Localization and Institutional Change in Asian Regionallism" (2004) 58 Intl Org 239.

[21] Laura Reidel, "Beyond a State-Centric Perspective on Norm Change: A Multilevel Governance Analysis of the Retreat from Multiculturalism" (2015) 21 Global Gov 317.

[22] Antje Wiener, "A Theory of Contestation—A Concise Summary of Its Argument and Concepts" (2017) 49 Polity 109.

rules, and norms are mere reflections and extensions of material forms of power exercised by dominant states underpinned IR's previous long-standing neglect of multilateral treaties on the basis that they were unlikely to be of any independent moment in world politics.

2 UN Treaties as the Creation of Regimes

A second body of IR scholarship with implications for our understanding of UN treaty-making, which predates that on norms, has "regimes" as its object of analysis. The term "regime" has been used in IR since the 1980s in a manner complementary to that in law; whereas lawyers typically use the term "regime" to refer to the body of law addressing the subject matter at hand, IR scholars use the term more broadly to refer to a process of international cooperation of which norms, principles, and processes are integral. In the classic book on international regimes, Stephen Krasner defined a regime as the "principles, norms, rules and decision-making processes around which actor expectations converge in a given issue area."[23] One or more multilateral treaties are typically integral to this process of cooperation, even though the term "treaty" featured rarely in the literature for at least the first decade. During that period, regime theory investigated several interrelated questions including why and how international regimes come into existence, the extent to which they are independent of the exogenous forces that form them, their impact on state behavior, and their long-term effects on national and international politics.[24] There is now some overlap between the norms and regime literature, including in their research questions.

The question of the necessity of hegemonic leadership in the creation of regimes and of the independence of regimes if the distribution of power subsequently changes, has been an enduring concern of regime theorists.[25] As our engagement with the norm literature above would suggest, such baldly crafted research questions may obscure the subtleties of practice. In any literal sense, it is now clear that the international community has been able to create a number of significant multilateral treaties absent US support, even if concluding a new multilateral treaty is unlikely to be an end in itself. In fact, research suggests that states that are powerful and independent from the United States are more likely to ratify a treaty when the United States does not lead.[26]

[23] Stephen D Krasner (ed), *International Regimes* (Cornell University Press 1983), 1.

[24] Marc A Levy, Oran R Young, and Michael Zürn, "The Study of International Regimes" (1995) 1 Eur J Intl Rel 267, 268–69.

[25] Michael C Webb and Stephen D Krasner, "Hegemonic Stability Theory: An Empirical Assessment" (1989) 15 Rev Intl Stud 183. This theme continues in the norms literature: see Bower (n 18).

[26] Karolina M Milewicz and Duncan Snidal, "Cooperation by Treaty: The Role of Multilateral Powers" (2016) 70 Intl Org 823.

US ratification of multilateral treaties is a fraught issue. The United States does not idly ratify a treaty if it does not intend to comply with the provisions of the treaty, and treaty ratification requires the consent of two-thirds of the Senate. Hegemonic United States therefore found itself in the double bind of being criticized for non-ratification of, for example, the UN Convention on the Law of the Sea, while at the same time acknowledging that it was bound by the vast majority of the treaty's provisions through customary international law. This is not a case of non-respect for international law but of taking international law seriously even to the extent of suffering reputational damage as a consequence.

Considerable speculation as to whether China would take a proactive role in the further development of the system of international law is gradually being rendered superfluous through China's own actions, including its lead in negotiating the Articles of Agreement for the Asian Infrastructure Investment Bank and its enthusiasm to negotiate a treaty to prevent the weaponization of space.[27] On the other hand, the growing influence of China and other BRICS states means that the Global South is far less likely than in the past to adopt a common position in multilateral treaty negotiations. Stokes, Giang, and Selin found that divergence in the positions of China and India during negotiation of the Minamata Convention on Mercury was due to domestic resources and regulatory politics, development constraints, and domestic scientific and technological capacity.[28]

Compliance has been a perennial subject of enquiry within the regime literature, in part so as to demonstrate international law's effects on state behavior.[29] Why, for example, do states join treaty regimes, particularly those from which they obtain few obvious direct benefits while accepting significant constraints on their behavior? In the case of human rights, Hathaway concluded that states with a robust domestic rule of law might be more likely than states with weaker domestic institutions but similar rights records to shy away from committing to international treaties precisely because commitment will be consequential.[30] In fact, the United States has a record of not agreeing to any human rights treaty provisions not already provided for by US law. According to Kenneth Roth, Justice Department lawyers "comb through [every human rights treaty] looking for any requirement that in their view might be more protective of US citizens' rights than pre-existing US law."[31] Where any such provision is found, "a reservation, declaration,

[27] The United States has taken the attitude that such a treaty is unnecessary. See Jeffrey Lantis, "To Boldly Go Where No Country Has Gone Before: US Norm Antipreneurism and the Weaponization of Outer Space" in Alan Bloomfield and Shirley V Scott (eds), *Norm Antipreneurs and the Politics of Resistance to Global Normative Change* (Routlege 2016).

[28] Leah C Stokes, Amanda Giang, and Noelle E Selin, "Splitting the South: China and India's Divergence in International Environmental Negotiations" (2016) 16 Global Envtl Pol 12.

[29] Beth A Simmons, "Treaty Compliance and Violation" (2010) 13 Ann Rev Pol Sci 273.

[30] Oona A Hathaway, "Why Do Countries Commit to Human Rights Treaties?" (2007) 51 J Conflict Res 588. And more recently, see Wayne Sandholtz, "Domestic Law and Human Rights Treaty Commitments: The Convention against Torture" (2017) 16 JHR 25.

[31] Kenneth Roth, "The Charade of US Ratification of International Human Rights Treaties" (2000) 1 Chic JIL 347, 347.

or understanding is drafted to negate the additional rights protection. These qualifications are then submitted to the Senate as part of the ratification package."[32]

Perhaps the most significant contribution of regime theory to our understanding of treaty-making by international organizations has been its search for the ingredients of regime "effectiveness," generally understood as the degree to which the regime achieves its goals—preventing dangerous anthropogenic climate change, for example. Enhancing compliance is a useful first step; in his study of the international regime controlling international oil pollution, Mitchell found that compliance was higher when integrated compliance systems increased transparency, provided for potent and credible sanctions, reduced implementation costs for governments by building on existing infrastructures, and prevented, rather than merely deterred, violations.[33]

This is a research field in which scholars have turned to quantitative methods in an effort to generate precise findings. They have nevertheless encountered "evidentiary hurdles" and "highly contested" methodological issues in seeking to establish that any changes in behavior are due to the independent influence of the treaty as opposed to merely reflecting state preferences.[34] Multiple large-scale quantitative studies of regime effectiveness have yielded the rather underwhelming conclusion that "regimes do matter."[35] One is reminded of Koskenniemi's warning of the dangers of reductionism and scientism associated with empiricism; "since expert systems are no less indeterminate than law, this move only institutionalizes an anti-political, technical mindset."[36]

Compliance is an inadequate conceptual tool for studying the political functioning of multilateral treaties, not only in respect of state behavior but in understanding effectiveness, most fundamentally because if a regime has been badly designed in the first place it may not achieve its objectives even if all states are fully compliant.[37] Beyond compliance, specific factors likely to contribute to the effectiveness of environmental regimes have been identified as including a sense of fairness regarding the major provisions and the availability of resources to build capacity if and as required by states parties.[38]

[32] ibid.

[33] Ronald B Mitchell, "Regime Design Matters: Intentional Oil Pollution and Treaty Compliance" (1994) 48 Intl Org 425.

[34] Beth A Simmons and Daniel J Hopkins, "The Constraining Power of International Treaties: Theory and Methods" (2005) 99 Am Pol Sci Rev 623.

[35] See, for example, Helmut Breitmeier, Arild Underdal, and Oran R Young, "The Effectiveness of International Environmental Regimes: Comparing and Contrasting Findings from Quantitative Research" (2011) 13 Intl Stud Rev 579.

[36] Martti Koskenniemi, "Constitutionalism as Mindset: Reflections on Kantian Themes about International Law and International Relations" (2007) 8 Theo Inq L 9, 30.

[37] George W Downs, David M Rocke, and Peter N Barsoom, "Is the Good News about Compliance Good News about Cooperation?" (1996) 50 Intl Org 379.

[38] Oran R Young, "The Effectiveness of International Environmental Regimes: What Do We Know; What Do We Need to Know; How Can We Find Out?" [2010] Unpublished Manuscript 1, 7. <https://groups.nceas.ucsb.edu/sustainability-science/2010%20weekly-sessions/session-92013-11.08.2010-institutions-for-managing-human-environment-systems/supplemental-readings-from-moderator-discussant-william-clark-harvard-univ/Young%202010%20Environmental%20Governance.pdf accessed March 8, 2018.

There are some parallels here to those factors to which a "negotiation practitioner" attributed the success of the Ozone Depletion regime. These included: that the science was very clear, that it had the support of industry, that the United States had effectively trialed the regime at a domestic level, that key individuals were fully committed to achieving the treaty, that it included special provisions for developing countries, and that the regime once established held regular meetings and made adjustments to the Montreal Protocol as the issue evolved.[39] And yet, after being at the forefront of research on regime effectiveness for many years, Oran Young cautioned that the success of environmental regimes is highly sensitive to contextual factors such that an "arrangement that works perfectly well in one setting may fall flat in another setting."[40]

More recently, and using a large data set and game theoretic framework, Koremenos has asked related but slightly different questions about institutional design. She has demonstrated the manner in which the nature of the cooperation problems at the negotiating table correlate with specific design features of multilateral treaties, including rules governing duration, monitoring, punishments, disputes, and withdrawal.[41] To take but two examples: "under conditions of high uncertainty about the consequences of international cooperation" any international agreement that enters into force will be of finite duration; furthermore, the extent to which one side lacks confidence that the other side will comply determines whether monitoring is delegated to a third party or the treaty provides only for self-reporting.[42]

Meanwhile the tradition of qualitative regime analysis, in particular that which focuses on interaction amongst regimes,[43] continues through research on regime complexes. A regime complex is a network of distinct regimes.[44] To view the climate regime, for example, solely in terms of a set of nested regimes is, from this perspective, inadequate; the structural and interest diversity inherent in the contemporary world has given rise to a more fragmented array of regulatory regimes.[45] Climate governance should not be seen solely in terms of inter-state arrangements but necessitates consideration of "transnational institutions, standards, financing arrangements, and programs."[46] The diagrammatic portrayal of the climate change complex as presented by Keohane and Victor includes "UN legal regimes" as but one of 13 components.[47]

[39] Elliot Benedick, "Perspectives of a Negotiation Practitioner" in Gunnar Sjöstedt (ed), *International Environmental Negotiation* (Sage 1993), 234.

[40] Oran R Young, "Effectiveness of International Environmental Regimes: Existing Knowledge, Cutting-Edge Themes, and Research Strategies" (2011) 108 PNAS 19853, 19855.

[41] Barbara Koremenos, *The Continent of International Law: Explaining Agreement Design* (CUP 2016).

[42] ibid 16–17.

[43] See, eg, Arild Underdal and Oran R Young (eds), *Regime Consequences: Methodological Challenges and Research Strategies* (Springer 2004).

[44] Young, "Effectiveness" (n 41) 19856.

[45] Robert O Keohane and David G Victor, "The Regime Complex for Climate Change" (2011) 9 Perspectives on Politics 7.

[46] Kenneth W Abbot, "The Transnational Regime Complex for Climate Change" (2012) 30 Envt & Plan C: Govt & Policy 571.

[47] Keohane and Victor (n 45) 10.

Notably, it is relegated to the far-left corner rather than appearing center stage, portrayed as of no more importance to the regime complex overall than bilateral initiatives or subnational action.

Viewing climate governance through the prism of the regime complex offers the opportunity to recognize the importance of transnational institutions, standards, financing arrangements, and programs. Responsibility for creating rules is now shared amongst multiple organizations with diverse memberships operating at different scales; it is also decentralized, with most organizations having been created from the bottom up with little central coordination.[48] According to Lesage and Van de Graaf, international organizations seem to be particularly adept at managing regime complexes, although this has not always been true of the United Nations.[49]

Betts has utilized the regime complex concept in order to demonstrate that it is no longer adequate to speak of a stand-alone refugee regime. According to Betts there are, rather, many institutions with implications for refugee protection, whether they reinforce, contradict, or even undermine the core refugee treaties.[50] Here there are synergies with the international law concern with fragmentation. Scholars of regime complexes have identified dynamics different to those at play in stand-alone legal regimes; "the lack of legal consistency that flows from differing and overlapping rules pushes states to seek resolutions and to negotiate broad rules. At times, states also create strategic inconsistency as they seek to jolt rules in one or another direction."[51] Laura Gómez-Mera referred to the "spaghetti bowl" of regional trade, economic, environmental, energy, and security agreements in the Americas, finding that the resulting fragmentation and rule ambiguity exacerbated implementation and compliance problems, facilitated more powerful states exploiting self-seeking cross-institutional strategies, and undermined regional cohesion and solidarity.[52]

3 UN Treaties and the Decline of the Liberal Order?

Seven decades after the creation of the United Nations, states that had hitherto been peripheral to the postwar order are seeking to renegotiate their role within that order. Key global treaty regimes have been blocked or, through the passage of time and

[48] Abbot (n 46) 571.

[49] Dries Lesage and Thijs Van de Graaf, "Thriving in Complexity? The OECD System's Role in Energy and Taxation" (2013) 19 Global Gov 83.

[50] Alexander Betts, "The Refugee Regime Complex" (2012) 29 Refugee Surv Q 12.

[51] Kal Raustiala and David G Victor, "The Regime Complex for Plant Genetic Resources" (2004) 58 Intl Org 277, 306.

[52] Laura Gómez-Mera, "International Regime Complexity and Regional Governance: Evidence from the Americas" (2015) 21 Global Gov 19.

changing configurations of power, fallen out of step with the structures of world politics. The United States is marginal to important recent multilateral treaties; even where new multilateral treaties are established on a global scale, they do not necessarily serve to mediate interests but, as in the case of the Paris Agreement, leave this to subsequent processes. In the case of the Iran nuclear agreement, what was of sufficient political moment to be labeled a treaty was instead referred to as a "deal."

The literature on this "crisis of multilateralism"[53] takes as its object of enquiry not the norm, or the governance system, but the sum of multilateral treaties and associated governance systems with the United Nations at its heart—sometimes referred to as the liberal international order. Here, the perennial IR question as to whether an international institution has agency independent of the power configuration within which it was derived, has become the focus of study. Can, or will, the liberal international order, with the United Nations at its core, survive the relative decline of the United States and rise of other states that do not share a rule-of-law heritage?

G. John Ikenberry has been a long-term champion of the affirmative, and for a number of years it was certainly the case that even if the Republican-dominated Senate blocked many treaty ratifications, US officials were able to develop strategies by which to continue to act multilaterally in an approach David Kaye referred to as "stealth multilateralism."[54] As recently as 2014, Ikenberry wrote of the "enduring power of the liberal order."[55] Under the administration of President Trump, even Ikenberry has become less sanguine and his language increasingly forthright. According to Ikenberry in 2017, the greatest threat to the liberal international order is not from rising states but from the United States itself; the United States has begun to "sabotage" the order it created. "Across ancient and modern eras, orders built by great powers have come and gone—but they have usually ended in murder, not suicide."[56]

4 Conclusion

It is over a decade since international lawyer Jan Klabbers noted that whenever he "wish[ed] to learn something about the world around [him], no matter how international the topic, [he] rarely grasp[ed] for international relations scholarship."[57]

[53] G John Ikenberry, "The Future of Multilateralism: Governing the World in a Post-hegemonic Era" (2015) 16 Jap J Pol Sci 399. See also Edward Newman, *A Crisis of Global Institutions? Multilateralism and International Security* (Routledge 2007).

[54] David Kaye, "Stealth Multilateralism: U.S. Foreign Policy without Treaties – or the Senate" (2013) 92 Foreign Affairs 113, 115.

[55] G John Ikenberry, "The Illusion of Geopolitics: The Enduring Power of the Liberal Order" (2014) 93 Foreign Affairs 80.

[56] G John Ikenberry, "The Plot against American Foreign Policy: Can the Liberal Order Survive?" (2017) 96 Foreign Affairs 2.

[57] Jan Klabbers, "The Relative Autonomy of International Law or the Forgotten Politics of Interdisciplinarity" (2004) 1 JILIR 35, 43.

IR research has since then become more relevant for international lawyers, even if it often requires some translation. From a legal perspective, the early norms literature was rather simplistic; norms were taken at face value, international history was assumed to consist of never-ending progress, and the "other" was the passive recipient of Western progressivism. Its promise seemed no greater than that of regime theory, with its disappointingly nebulous internal debates and rather inconsequential findings. Koremenos's identification of links between the nature of the cooperation challenges faced by treaty negotiators and the final clauses of the ensuing treaties was a notable methodological achievement. Nevertheless, the fact that negotiators had not needed that knowledge in order to bring about the treaties in the first place somewhat limited the "real world" significance of the scholarly breakthrough.

Norm theorists are increasingly building into their analysis the sophistication required to do justice to the complexity of the multilateral treaty-making phenomenon. They are also being forced to adapt to a more complicated "multiplex" world, the characteristics of which include "a proliferation of transnational challenges and a diffusion of ideas, actors, and processes of global governance."[58] Perhaps surprisingly, this growing sophistication in the analysis of ideas has revealed that taking international law as a starting point for global intellectual history would be less valid than it might previously have seemed. The Responsibility to Protect (R2P), for example, has been an enduring subject of norm analysis, despite its arguably weak importance in establishing new legal obligations. Understanding the politics of international law, and multilateral treaties in particular, can only be enriched by an even greater maturity and sophistication of IR scholarship, inclusive of the literature on norms.

Many lawyers might assume that the proliferation of multilateral treaties under UN auspices has been ineluctably positive. One of the challenges posed by norms scholarship is that the UN system, and by extension the treaties it has generated, "functions paradoxically as a symbol of both global solidarity and global injustice."[59] We may be experiencing a decisive moment in the evolution of the great UN experiment and its associated multilateral treaty-making project. While liberal institutionalist scholars might lament the apparent demise of the US-led order to which the complex web of UN treaties has been so integral, their sentiment may not be universally shared.

[58] Amitav Acharya, "The Future of Global Governance: Fragmentation May Be Inevitable and Creative" (2016) 22 Global Gov 453, 454.

[59] Acharya, "'Idea-Shift'" (n 7) 1157.

CHAPTER 3

TREATY-MAKING AT THE UNITED NATIONS

the view from the secretariat

STEPHEN MATHIAS*

BEGINNING in the mid-1970s, the General Assembly conducted a review of multilateral treaty-making in the United Nations and other international organizations and fora.[1] In 1985, the materials generated in the course of this review were published in a volume in the United Nations Legislative Series entitled "Review of the Multilateral Treaty-Making Process,"[2] which included a 1980 Report of the Secretary-General on that subject,[3] observations of governments and international organizations, and detailed information on the "techniques and procedures used in the formulation of multilateral treaties by various United Nations organs and offices, the specialized and related agencies, and other international organizations."[4] This volume remains of substantial interest today.

In the Report of the Secretary-General included in the volume, it is observed that at that time some 200 multilateral treaties had been concluded within the United Nations since its founding[5] (today the number is around 600),[6] and that "[a]n examination of the various procedures previously or currently employed within the United Nations to prepare these treaties discloses extensive diversity."[7] It is further observed that "[a]mong the significant bases on which these procedures can be differentiated is the extent to

* The views expressed are personal. I acknowledge the assistance of Gabrielle Goettsche-Wanli, Arnold Pronto, Jenny Clift, Santiago Villalpando, Trevor Chimimba, Tomoko Iwata, Charlotte Salpin, and Fanny Marie Schaus.

1 "Review of Multilateral Treaty-Making Process" (1980) UN Doc ST/LEG/SER.B/21 at 1 (hereinafter "Review").

2 ibid 1.

3 Report of the Secretary-General, "Review of the Multilateral Treaty-Making Process" (1980) UN Doc A/35/312 and Corr.1 (hereinafter "SG Report").

4 Review 1.

5 Review 16.

6 UN Treaty Section website, at <https://treaties.un.org> accessed January 19, 2019.

7 Review 16.

which they are established and structured or ad hoc in nature, the extent to which they involve expert and representative bodies, and the extent of the involvement of the General Assembly."[8] Finally it is noted that "[s]eemingly the only generalization possible is that multilateral treaty-making in the United Nations is almost always (except for some regional or specialized instruments of a most restrictive nature) a multistage process."[9]

That was the essence of the view from the Secretariat in 1980. Is it any different today?

As an initial matter, it must be noted that no single UN official is in a position to provide a comprehensive view of UN treaty-making at any given moment. Indeed, it would be difficult for a single official even to state with authority how many treaty-making exercises are underway at some stage and in some sense under the auspices of the United Nations at a given moment. The United Nations is a large and decentralized, not to say fragmented, institution, and it may be only in the last stages that the fact that a negotiation is taking place becomes widely known outside the forum within which it is being discussed. The Secretariat, while conceptually and legally a single entity working under the direction of the Secretary-General, is substantively and operationally a collection of different departments and offices that, in their treaty-making functions, may have little contact with one another. The view from the Secretariat on this issue would, in fact, be many views, and this diversity of entities involved in the treaty-making process can be seen, at least to some extent, as part of the "institutional design" of the Charter.

Moreover, the conceptually distinct phases of determining whether to negotiate a legally binding international legal instrument and then negotiating it may, in practice, bleed into each other, so that a process that at one stage does not appear to have been part of a treaty-making process may at a later point be seen to have been part of one.

The Office of Legal Affairs of the United Nations nonetheless provides a perch from which a reasonable assessment of some aspects of UN treaty-making at the present time may be assessed. This is because the Office of Legal Affairs, headed by the Under-Secretary-General for Legal Affairs, the UN Legal Counsel, comprises six entities—four divisions, an office, and a section, in UN administrative parlance—all but one of which play distinct but important roles that, when taken together, illuminate the current practices.

Some general observations are possible. Multilateral treaty-making at the United Nations remains extensively diverse. There is no single process or forum within the UN for negotiating a treaty; there are a wide variety of processes and fora. Even considering only three of the more notable treaties negotiated within the broader UN framework in recent years—the Arms Trade Treaty, the Paris Agreement, and the Treaty on the Prohibition of Nuclear Weapons—it is clear that the treaty-making processes used remain diverse and, to a certain extent, ad hoc. Within specific thematic areas, a particular approach may be followed. A strikingly different approach may be used in another thematic area. It is possible that this diversity is of even a broader range than it was in 1980, as the number of actors and entities engaged in an increased number and kind of processes has expanded. In addition, a variation in practice might be observed over

[8] ibid.
[9] Review 17.

time. It has been noted, for example, that in recent years it is less common than it once was for a topic to proceed from consideration by the International Law Commission through the Sixth Committee of the General Assembly to final form as a multilateral convention.[10] Nonetheless, the significant bases of differentiation identified in the Secretary-General's 1980 Report—established process or ad hoc, expert and representative participation, role of the General Assembly—continue to provide a meaningful way to distinguish among the processes. Even the sole generalization in the 1980 Report concerning a multistage process appears to have stood the test of time.[11]

What is the cause of this diversity of processes and fora? From a Secretariat perspective, the answer is both clear and incomplete. This is the way that member states have decided, in their various resolutions and decisions in various bodies, to structure the treaty-making processes. As we shall see, in some cases the Secretary-General may be asked for options as to how to proceed, or the Secretariat may have other opportunities to influence the process, but the decision is ultimately taken by member states through the intergovernmental process.

Why do they resort to such a variety of mechanisms? This is the aspect of the analysis that may be regarded as incomplete. Some of the variation no doubt has to do with the complexity of the subject matter or of the instrument being negotiated. Some international agreements are of a general character, and the process of their negotiation is straightforward. The number of pages may be in the single digits and the undertakings may be easily stated and agreed. Other agreements may be in a highly specialized or technical area or may include hundreds of pages of complex provisions. The negotiating processes in such cases may mirror this complexity. These factors are not sufficient, however, to explain the diversity of practice that has in fact emerged and been sustained.

The diversity in the multilateral treaty-making process has given rise to criticism in some quarters, which, in fact, led to the 1980 Report of the Secretary-General quoted previously. The Foreign Minister of Australia, one of the states that proposed a review, addressed the General Assembly at its 31st session in the following terms:

> The ways in which we approach multilateral treaty-making are varied, chancy, frequently experimental and often inefficient. They place great burdens upon the Governments of Member States, especially upon the developing countries, and it is open to question whether the community could not find more economical and efficient methods of drafting conventions.[12]

[10] See Michael Wood's Chapter 30.

[11] One possible exception to the "multistage process" is the Treaty on the Prohibition of Nuclear Weapons, which was adopted on July 7, 2017, at the Conference to negotiate a legally binding instrument to prohibit nuclear weapons, leading toward their total elimination. This Conference held two meetings, between March 27–31 and July 15–July 7, 2017 (and a one-day organizational meeting), but there was no preparatory committee, ad hoc working group, or expert group in which a draft was initially prepared or discussed. The Treaty also did not go to the General Assembly for adoption, as everything was done by the Conference itself.

[12] See Rationale for the Review of the Multilateral Treaty-Making Process (Review 7).

There was specific criticism by some states of the negotiations that formed part of the Third United Nations Conference on the Law of the Sea:

> [O]ne may refer to the experimental and not always satisfactory way in which the treatment of the law of the sea has developed in the last decade.... The process of negotiation has been far from simple and has been marked by a degree of improvisation (some of it imaginative and possibly of long-term value, but some of it not), which has been time-consuming and has led only to results which are as yet incomplete.[13]

Other states participating in the review process saw the problem more as a matter of the number of treaty-making processes rather than the processes themselves. Written comments submitted by Austria set forth this view as follows:

> It would... be deceiving to attribute existing problems solely or even mainly to deficiencies in the treaty-making procedure and, hence, to expect that they would disappear with a revision of the latter. The problems originate primarily in the international community's unrestrained appetite for new international instruments, which it then has problems digesting nationally. Only the setting of priorities and the concurrent reduction of the yearly output could provide a remedy to that unsatisfactory situation. It would, therefore, seem advisable for the General Assembly to include this aspect into its future considerations.[14]

The 1985 volume included useful summaries of the treaty-making processes prepared by various UN entities, including the International Law Commission, the Office of Legal Affairs, the Secretariat of the Third United Nations Conference on the Law of the Sea, and the United Nations Conference on International Trade Law (UNCITRAL).[15]

In the end, the review yielded little in the way of reform. The diversity of processes remains prevalent, although it has not given rise to an intergovernmental review process as was the case in the 1970s and early 1980s. Nor should such diversity necessarily be construed as a negative phenomenon, given that many, if not most, differences in procedure and approaches are simply a function of the varying complexity of the topics being dealt with, as well as of the differences among the entities within which treaties are initiated and negotiated.

1 The Secretariat Role in the Treaty-Making Process

The Secretariat role in contemporary treaty-making processes varies widely. In some negotiations of multilateral instruments, the substantive aspects of the negotiations are entirely in the hands of the potential future parties of the potential instrument, and

[13] ibid 9. [14] ibid 43. [15] ibid 177–384.

the role of the Secretariat may be limited to processing the paperwork and providing procedural advice on the conduct of the negotiations and, at a later stage, giving advice on final clauses. In other such negotiations, the Secretariat may be assigned a larger role, such as preparing a conference paper or a draft instrument.

The Secretary-General's 1980 Report identifies five stages in the multilateral treaty-making process: Initiation of Treaty-Making, Formulation of Multilateral Treaties, Adoption of Multilateral Treaties, Post-Adoption Concerns, and Supplementing and Updating Treaties.[16] In the following discussion, the role of the Secretariat at each of these stages will be considered on the basis of the roles played in recent processes by the various entities within the Office of Legal Affairs: the Codification Division, the Division for Ocean Affairs and the Law of the Sea (DOALOS), the International Trade Law Division, the Office of the Legal Counsel, and the Treaty Section.

2 Initiation of Treaty-Making

The 1980 Report identifies four aspects of the initiation process: proposal, pre-initiation study, formal initiation of treaty-making, and decision as to type of instrument.[17] It has already been observed that the treaty-making process is a member-state-led process, and that is also the case at this initial stage (while acknowledging that individual experts chosen by member states may play a large role in initiating some processes). The Secretariat may, however, play a vital role, particularly in the pre-initiation study phase, when requested to do so by member states (or the experts chosen by them). This work may consist of the performance of Secretariat functions for the body considering the initiation of a treaty-making process as well as the preparation of pre-initiation studies and reports on technical or substantive issues before the body.

The Secretary-General's Bulletin setting forth the organization of the Office of Legal Affairs provides that among the core functions of the Codification Division are:

> [p]roviding substantive secretariat services to the Sixth Committee of the General Assembly, the International Law Commission, ... and other bodies of the United Nations, as well as diplomatic conferences, in the progressive development of international law and its codification; [and]
>
> [c]onducting research and preparing analytical legal and policy papers and background studies on various topics of public international law that have been selected or are considered for codification or progressive development.[18]

The Codification Division regularly performs these functions, frequently at the pre-initiation phase, and, in particular, often provides reports informing member states

[16] Review 23–37. [17] ibid 24–26.

[18] Secretary-General's bulletin, "Organization of the Office of Legal Affairs" UN Doc ST/SGB/2008/13 (hereinafter "SGB") 5.

about substantive or technical issues, generally at the request of the International Law Commission or the Sixth Committee of the General Assembly.

With respect to the Division's assistance to the International Law Commission, the Report of the Secretary-General entitled "Assistance to Special Rapporteurs of the International Law Commission"[19] is of particular interest, as it provides extensive detail concerning the assistance provided by the Codification Division to special rapporteurs and to the Commission more generally.

An example of a successful outcome stemming from the support provided by the Division came in 2016, with the completion by the Commission of its work on the draft articles on the protection of persons in the event of disasters, intended for adoption as a treaty, which was undertaken following a 2006 recommendation by the Codification Division (in its capacity as Secretariat of the Commission) that the topic was ripe for codification, including by means of adoption of a multilateral treaty.[20]

With respect to its assistance to the Sixth Committee, an interesting example of the current activity of the Codification Division at the pre-initiation stage involves the articles on the responsibility of states for internationally wrongful acts. These articles already have a long and interesting history, which has been treated elsewhere and is beyond the scope of this chapter.[21] The key point for present purposes is that, while the Commission completed its work on the articles in 2001, the General Assembly has not yet decided on the question of whether a convention on the responsibility of states for internationally wrongful acts should be developed on the basis of the articles.

In the context of pre-initiation studies on this topic, it is noteworthy that in its most recent resolution,[22] the Assembly requests two substantive documents from the Secretariat and holds open the possibility of requesting a third at a future session. First, the Secretary-General is requested to prepare a technical report listing in tabular form references to the articles in a compilation previously prepared by the Secretariat. Second, the Secretary-General is asked to update the compilation. Finally, the Assembly

> [a]knowledges the possibility of requesting, at its seventy-fourth session [2019], the Secretary-General to provide the General Assembly with information on all procedural options regarding possible action on the basis of the articles, without prejudice to the question whether such possible action is appropriate.

The range of the reports mentioned—a compilation, a technical study, and a presentation of procedural options—illustrates the range of studies that may be requested of the Secretariat at the pre-initiation phase.

[19] Report of the Secretary-General, "Assistance to Special Rapporteurs of the International Law Commission" UN Doc A/64/283.

[20] ILC, "Report of the International Law Commission on the Work of its 58th Session" (May 1–June 9 and July 3–August 11, 2006) UN Doc A/61/10, annex III.

[21] See the Pierre Bodeau-Livinec's Chapter 29. See also J Crawford, *The International Law Commission's Articles on State Responsibility: Introduction, Text and Commentaries* (CUP 2000) 1–60.

[22] A/RES/71/133 of December 13, 2016.

Other recent examples of the preparation of reports by the Codification Division in support of potential treaty-making activity under consideration in the Sixth Committee arose in the context of the topics of criminal accountability of United Nations officials and experts on mission and of universal jurisdiction. With respect to the criminal accountability topic, in 2007, the Secretariat provided a "Note by the Secretariat"[23] to the General Assembly, which set forth specific recommendations of both short-term and long-term measures, including adoption of a convention, with a view to addressing issues relating to the exercise of jurisdiction in cases involving alleged criminal activity by UN officials and experts. With respect to universal jurisdiction, the Codification Division in 2011, in response to a request of the General Assembly contained in a report of the Sixth Committee on the item,[24] prepared, on an informal basis, for the working group established to consider the scope and application of the principle of universal jurisdiction, two reports, one a compilation of multilateral and other instruments relevant to the item[25] and the other a compilation of excerpts from decisions of international tribunals.[26]

The DOALOS provides similar assistance to states at the pre-initiation phase for matters falling within its mandate. The Secretary-General's Bulletin provides that among the core functions of the Division are

> [p]roviding advice, studies, assistance and research and information on the application of the United Nations Convention on the Law of the Sea (the Convention) and related Agreements, on oceans and the law of the sea issues of a general nature and on specific developments relating to the research and legal regime for the oceans; and
>
> [p]roviding substantive servicing to the General Assembly [and other Oceans-related meetings and bodies].[27]

The Secretary-General's bulletin has been complemented by later resolutions of the General Assembly, which have designated DOALOS as secretariat of additional processes.[28]

DOALOS's work in recent years on the issue of conservation and sustainable use of marine biological diversity beyond areas of national jurisdiction is illustrative of its engagement at the pre-initiation stage.

[23] A//62/329.

[24] Note by the Secretary-General, Ensuring the Accountability of United Nations Staff and Experts on Mission with respect to Criminal Acts Committed in Peacekeeping Operations, forwarding the Report of the Group of Legal Experts on Ensuring the Accountability of United Nations Staff and Experts on Mission with respect to Criminal Acts Committed in Peacekeeping Operations (UN Doc A/60/980). See also the Report of the Adviser to the Secretary-General on Sexual Exploitation and Abuse by United Nations Peacekeeping Personnel (UN Doc A/59/710) ("the Zeid report," which provided an analysis of the problem of sexual exploitation and abuse by United Nations peacekeeping personnel.

[25] UN Doc A/C.6/66/EG.3/INF.1 (unpublished).

[26] UN Doc A/C.6/66/WG.3/INF.2 (unpublished).

[27] SGB 5–6.

[28] See, eg, UNGA Res 65/37A.

In 2015, the General Assembly decided "to develop an international legally binding instrument under the United Nations Convention on the Law of the Sea on the conservation and sustainable use of marine biological diversity of areas beyond national jurisdiction."[29] This decision—the formal initiation of the treaty-making process—followed more than a decade of activity regarding the question of conservation and sustainable use of marine biological diversity beyond areas of national jurisdiction, beginning with the Assembly's establishment of an Ad Hoc Open-ended Working Group to study issues relating the subject in its resolution 59/24 in 2004.

The Working Group met for nine sessions from 2006 through 2015. All of those meetings were supported by DOALOS. DOALOS prepared the four reports of the Secretary-General that served as a background for the work of the Working Group. Those reports addressed the scientific, technical, economic, legal, environmental, and socioeconomic aspects of the issue.[30]

The activities of the International Trade Law Division within its substantive area of expertise are similar. The Secretary-General's bulletin lists as among its core functions providing substantive secretariat services to UNCITRAL and related bodies and conferences, preparing drafts of, inter alia, international conventions, and conducting research and preparing studies and policy papers on aspects of international trade law.[31]

A Guide to UNCITRAL prepared by the Division elaborates to some extent on the Bulletin, noting that

> the Secretariat undertakes a variety of different tasks, which includes preparation of studies, reports, and draft texts on topics that are being considered for future inclusion in the work programme .... In preparing its work, the secretariat may seek the assistance of outside experts from different legal traditions, conducting ad hoc consultations with individuals or convening meetings of groups of experts in a particular field, as required. Such groups have included academics, practicing lawyers, judges, bankers, arbitrators and members of various international, regional and professional organizations.[32]

The drafting of the United Nations Convention on the Assignment of Receivables in International Trade (New York, 2001) was preceded by the preparation of three reports, which ultimately led to the Commission entrusting a Working Group with preparation of a uniform law on assignment of receivables financing.[33] This same approach was

[29] UNGA Res 69/292 (June 19, 2015) op para 1.

[30] See UN Doc A/60/63/Add.1 (taken note of in UNGA Res 60/30, para 78); A/62/66/Add.2 (taken note of in UNGA Res 62/215, para 104); A/64/66/Add.2 (taken note of in UNGA Res 64/71, para.147); and A/66/70 (mentioned in the preamble of UNGA Res 66/231).

[31] SGB 7.

[32] "A Guide to UNCITRAL," available at <www.uncitral.org> accessed January 19, 2019.

[33] See Explanatory Note by the UNCITRAL Secretariat on the United Nations Convention on the Assignment of Receivables in International Trade, footnote 1, UN publication, Sales No. E.04.V.14; ISBN 92-1-133588-4.

taken with the United Nations Convention on Independent Guarantees and Stand-by Letters of Credit (New York, 1995).[34]

3 Formulation of Multilateral Treaties

The 1980 Report discusses as distinct aspects of the formulation stage the initial draft; negotiations, consultations with governments and others, drafting committees, languages, final clauses, records and commentaries, and conflicts with other treaties.[35] For the purposes of this chapter, and with the objective of illustrating in particular the role of the Secretariat, it seems best to focus on two main points: the Secretariat's contribution to the formulation of the substance of the multilateral instrument and its role with respect to the negotiating process.

It has already been noted that the core functions of the Codification Division, DOALOS, and the International Trade Law Division all include serving as the substantive secretariat for meetings of intergovernmental bodies that may engage in treaty-making, and that all also have the mandate to prepare studies and reports to inform the substantive work of these bodies. It can be added under this heading, with respect to the Codification Division, that its core functions specifically include: "[a]ssisting in the preparation of drafts of international conventions and other forms of legal instruments on subjects of public international law and commentaries explaining various provisions of the legal instruments."[36] Similarly, the International Trade Law Division has the function of preparing drafts of conventions.[37]

As to DOALOS, we have already noted that, in resolution 69/292, the General Assembly decided to develop an international legally binding instrument under the United Nations Convention on the Law of the Sea on the conservation and sustainable use of marine biological diversity of areas beyond national jurisdiction. In this same resolution, the Assembly decided, prior to holding an intergovernmental conference, to establish a preparatory committee to make substantive recommendations to the Assembly on the elements of a draft text of an internationally binding instrument. In that regard, the Assembly requested the Secretary-General "to provide the preparatory committee with the necessary assistance for the performance of its work, including secretariat services and the provision of essential background information and relevant documents, and to arrange for support to be provided by the Division for Ocean Affairs and the Law of the Sea of the Office of Legal Affairs of the Secretariat."[38] The preparatory

[34] See Explanatory Note by the UNICTRAL Secretariat on the United Nations Convention on Independent Guarantees and Stand-by Letters of Credit, footnote 1, UN publication, Sales No. E.97.V.12, ISBN 92-1-133525-6.

[35] Review 27–33.

[36] SGB 5.

[37] See the text at (n 34).

[38] UNGA Res 69/262, op para 6.

committee met for two sessions of 10 working days each in 2016 and 2017.[39] DOALOS provided substantive support to the presiding officer by preparing initial drafts of various non-papers, including a Chair's non-paper containing indicative suggestions of clusters of issues and questions to assist further discussions and two Chair's non-papers on elements of a draft of an international legally binding instrument under UNCLOS on the basis of contributions received from delegations.[40]

In December 2017, the General Assembly decided "to convene an intergovernmental conference, under the auspices of the United Nations, to consider the recommendations of the Preparatory Committee on the elements and to elaborate the text of an international legally binding instrument under the United Nations Convention on the Law of the Sea on the conservation and sustainable use of marine biological diversity of areas beyond national jurisdiction, with a view to developing the instrument as soon as possible."[41] The Assembly requested the Secretary-General "to provide the conference with the necessary assistance for the performance of its work, including secretariat services and the provision of essential background information and relevant documents, and to arrange for support to be provided by the Division of Ocean Affairs and the Law of the Sea of the Office of Legal Affairs of the Secretariat."[42]

On several occasions, substantive initial preparation of an UNCITRAL treaty has been undertaken by the International Trade Law Division in consultation with expert, and it has then been taken up by a Working Group for further negotiation and development, including for example, the United Nations Convention on the Use of Electronic Communications in International Contracts (New York, 2005) and the United Nations Convention on Contracts for the International Carriage of Goods Wholly or Partly by Sea (New York, 2008).

From the foregoing, it is clear that the Secretariat can and does, when invited by states, play a substantive role in the development of treaty texts.

It is also important to note the role of the Secretariat in the procedural aspects of the negotiating process.

In this regard, while the Codification Division, DOALOS, and the International Trade Law Division each perform this function as part of their secretariat functions relating to the intergovernmental bodies they service, it is relevant to note that an additional entity within the Office of Legal Affairs, the Office of the Legal Counsel, has as one of its core functions as defined in the Secretary General's Bulletin: "[p]reparing draft rules of procedure and advising United Nations organs and conferences on the conduct of business."[43]

[39] UNGA Res 69/292.

[40] See Report of the Preparatory Committee established by General Assembly resolution 69/292: Development of an International Legally Binding Instrument under the United Nations Convention on the Law of the Sea on the Conservation and Sustainable Use of Marine Biological Diversity of Areas Beyond National Jurisdiction, UN Doc A/AC.287/2017/PC.4/2, paras. 21, 26, 32. The non-papers are available from the website of DOALOS at <www.un.org/depts/los/biodiversity/prepcom.htm>.

[41] UNGA Res 72/249 (24 December 2017), op para 1.

[42] ibid op para 22.

[43] SGB 4.

Frequently in the same resolution that initiates the treaty-making process, or, failing that, in a follow-up resolution, the initiating body will define certain aspects of the negotiating process. There are various options at this stage, and further options for how aspects of the process not finalized at this time will be resolved subsequently. For a process that is intended to be concluded by a UN conference convened under the auspices of the General Assembly, the issues would typically be dealt with in a "modalities" resolution. One fundamental issue to be addressed at an early stage is who can participate in the negotiations and on what basis. Is full (voting) participation limited to UN member states, or is the "Vienna Formula," also permitting members of the specialized agencies to participate; or an "All States" model, permitting the participation of all states, to apply? How should the European Union participate? What should be the role of observers, and what entities are permitted to act as observers? What should be the role of civil society? What credentialing process should be used for nonstate participants?

The participation issue was particularly important during the period before the United Nations became a nearly universal organization, when many states could be part of the treaty-making process only if the modality for participation was expanded beyond UN members. Even in the current period, however, the issue can be significant. Application of the Vienna Formula in UN conferences permits the Holy See, the State of Palestine, the Cook Islands, and Niue to participate on an equal basis with member states. (Participation in the meetings of parties of specific conventions depends, of course, on which entities have become parties to the instrument in question.)

Even following the adoption of a modalities resolution, the question of which entities can participate in negotiations is not always clear. In connection with the negotiations of the Convention on the Prohibition of Nuclear Weapons, for example, the Secretariat understood from the modalities resolution that the General Assembly had intended the conference to be convened on a member-state basis, but the preparatory body for the conference itself decided that the Vienna Formula should apply.[44] In a number of recent conferences, the issue of which international bodies would be permitted to act as observers gave rise to some controversy. The Secretariat's consistent advice to member states on these issues is that the modalities resolution should be as clear as possible to prevent problems at a later stage.

Once issues relating to participation are addressed, other procedural or technical issues may arise during the run-up to or at the diplomatic conference. The issue of which rules of procedure will apply at a conference has been addressed in various ways.[45]

[44] "Rules of Procedure of the United Nations Conference to Negotiate a Legally Binding Instrument to Prohibit Nuclear Weapons, Leading towards Their Total Elimination" UN Doc A/CONF.229/2017/5.

[45] For the UN Conference to negotiate a legally binding instrument to prohibit nuclear weapons, the "modalities" resolution provides "that the Conference shall convene in New York, under the rules of procedure of the General Assembly unless otherwise agreed by the Conference" (UNGA Res 71/258, op para 10). The Conference then went on to adopt its own rules of procedure (UN Doc A/CONF.229/2017/5). For the UN Conference on the Arms Trade Treaty, the "modalities" resolution was silent, but did provide for the establishment of "a fifth session of the Preparatory Committee in 2012 . . . to decide on all relevant procedural matters, including the composition of the Bureau, the draft agenda and the submission of

While the rules are particularly vital on the question of voting (as will be discussed in the next section), they also address other matters, such as credentials and speaking. Drafting committees are used in many conferences, and will be supported by the Secretariat as requested, but the roles they play differ greatly from conference to conference depending on the rules applied.

At any stage, but often arising nearer to the conclusion of the negotiations, questions may arise concerning the final clauses of the draft treaty and the entity that will serve as depositary. For treaties negotiated under the auspices of the UN, OLA's Treaty Section will take a leading role in working with negotiating parties on these issues.[46] This role is formalized in the Secretary-General's Bulletin on the procedures to be followed by UN departments, offices, and regional commissions with regard to treaties and international agreements. This bulletin also requires UN entities to submit to the Office of Legal Affairs the draft texts of multilateral treaties to be deposited with the Secretary-General for review and comment prior to finalization.[47]

documents for the United Nations Conference on the Arms Trade Treaty" (UNGA Res 64/48, op para 8). The Fifth Preparatory Committee recommended, for adoption by the Conference, draft provisional rules of procedure (see UN Doc A/CONF.217/L.1). For the UN Diplomatic Conference of Plenipotentiaries on the Establishment of an International Criminal Court, there was nothing in the "modalities" resolution for the Conference (UNGA Res 51/207) or in the resolution establishing the Preparatory Committee (UNGA Res 50/46) concerning procedural matters. However, the Preparatory Committee recommended to the Conference draft rules of procedure for the Conference. For the UN Conference on Straddling Fish Stocks and Highly Migratory Fish Stocks, the "modalities" resolution requested "the Secretary-General to prepare draft rules of procedure for the consideration of the conference at its organizational session" (UNGA Res 47/192, op para 8). For the Intergovernmental Negotiating Committee for a Framework Convention on Climate Change (INC), the "modalities" resolution requested the head of the ad hoc secretariat to prepare draft rules of procedure for consideration by the INC at its first session (UNGA Res 45/212, op para 23). For the Conference of the Plenipotentiaries on the Minamata Convention on Mercury and the Intergovernmental Negotiating Committee to Prepare a Global Legally Binding Instrument on Mercury, there was nothing in the decision adopted at the 25th session of the Governing Council of the UN Environment Programme and Global Ministerial Environment Forum in 2009, where the delegates agreed to develop a legally binding agreement on mercury and requested the Executive Director of the UN Environment Programme to convene the negotiations. The draft rules of procedure prepared by the Secretariat were considered by the ad hoc open-ended working group to prepare for the INC, which then agreed to recommend that the Committee adopt those rules, as amended by the working group with regard to the number of members of the Bureau (UN Doc UNEP(DTIE)/Hg/INC.1/3). The INC then adopted the rules at its first session. The Conference had before it the rules of procedure of the INC, and the Conference agreed to apply the rules of procedure of the INC mutatis mutandis to its proceedings. (see Final Act, UN Doc UNEP(DTIE)/Hg/CONF/4). This is similar to the process followed for the Rotterdam Convention on Prior Informed Consent Procedure for Certain Hazardous Chemicals and Pesticides in International Trade, which was organized jointly by UNEP and FAO.

[46] See Arancha Hinojal-Oyarbide's Chapter 34.

[47] Secretary-General's bulletin, "Procedures to Be Followed by the Departments, Offices and Regional Commissions of the United Nations with regard to Treaties and International Agreements" UN Doc ST/SGB/2001/7.

4 Adoption of Multilateral Treaties

The 1980 Report discusses organs, special procedural rules, and voting majorities under this heading.[48] In practice, it remains the case that procedures relating to voting, or, in the alternative, adoption by consensus, remain the key issue necessitating Secretariat involvement at this stage.

Pursuant to the modalities resolution or to the rules of procedure, the question of adoption of the instrument will be addressed. In some cases, such as the Arms Trade Treaty conference, voting is not permitted by the applicable rules.[49] In the case of instruments negotiated in the UNFCCC (United Nations Framework Convention on Climate Change) process, voting is not permitted because the draft rules have not been formally adopted.[50] In both cases, negotiations instead proceeded on the basis of consensus. Within the UN context, the meaning of consensus is relatively clear: it is an alternative to voting, not a form of voting, pursuant to which a measure will be regarded as adopted if no participant (for this purpose, an entity eligible to vote) formally objects to the measure.[51] Other rules have provided that every effort should be made to reach consensus, which has been interpreted to mean that, if consensus cannot be reached, a vote can be held.[52]

The issue became a critical one at the Arms Trade Treaty conference. As noted, the rules provided that all decisions on substantive matters were to be made by consensus.[53] When the treaty text was presented on the final evening of the conference, there was a

[48] Review 33–35.

[49] UN Doc. A/CONF.217/L.1.

[50] "Draft Rules of Procedure of the Conference of the Parties" UN Doc FCCC/CP/1996/2.

[51] "Use of the Term 'Consensus' in United Nations practice" (1974) UNJYB 163; "Meaning of consent in the practice of the United Nations" (1987) UNJYB 174.

[52] See, eg, Note by the Secretariat, "Information Note on the Draft Provision Rules of Procedure" UN Doc A/CONF.224/PC(I)/INF.5.

[53] The Rules of Procedure for the ATT Conference (UN Doc A/CONF.217/L.1) provided as follows:

> Substantive work
>
> Rule 33
>
> The Conference shall take its decisions and consider the text of the Treaty by consensus, in accordance with General Assembly resolution 64/48;
>
> Procedural matters
>
> Rule 34
>
> 1. The Conference shall make every effort to ensure that all its decisions on matters of procedure are taken by consensus.
>
> 2. Except as otherwise provided in these rules, decisions of the Conference on all matters of procedure shall be taken by a two-thirds majority of the representatives present and voting, only when the President decides that efforts to reach a consensus have been exhausted.

formal objection, and the text could not be adopted.[54] The text was then presented to the General Assembly a few days later, and adopted by the Assembly by a recorded vote.[55]

5 Post-adoption Concerns

The Secretary-General's 1980 Report addresses this stage by examining the facilitation of acceptance of treaties by states following their adoption, including by ensuring that the method of formulating treaties has been inclusive.[56] This section of the report then also focused on the follow-up on state action following adoption. Under the first point, it considers the admission of reservations. While this remains an important issue with respect to the acceptance of treaties, it falls outside the scope of this chapter.

It is decidedly within the scope of this chapter to highlight the fact that the Codification Division, DOALOS, the International Trade Law Division, and the Treaty Section all have specific mandates to publicize the work taking place within their respective fields of activity and do so on an ongoing basis. This can involve the delivery of capacity-building activities, through which awareness can be raised amongst states and concerned entities with regard to recent developments in the relevant area of international law, and their participation in relevant multilateral treaties may be promoted.

With respect to the International Trade Law Division, the Secretary-General's bulletin includes as a core function "[d]eveloping and implementing a technical assistance programme to promote the work of the United Nations Commission on International Trade Law and the use and adoption of the legislative and non-legislative texts it has developed to further the progressive harmonization and modernization of private law."[57] Among the relevant activities in which ITLD has engaged pursuant to this mandate was assisting Fiji to accede to the UN Convention on Contracts for the International Sale of Goods (Vienna, 1980) and to the UN Convention on the Use of Electronic Communications in International Contracts (New York, 2005).[58]

The Codification Division has also, on occasion, been mandated to undertake a number of post-adoption tasks. For example, the Final Act of the Rome Conference on the Establishment of the International Criminal Court established a preparatory process involving the negotiation of a number of ancillary texts and putting into place a range of

3. If the question arises as to whether a matter is one of procedure or of substance, the President of the Conference shall rule on the question. An appeal against this ruling shall be put to the vote immediately, and the President's ruling shall stand unless overruled by a majority of the representatives present and voting.

4. If a vote is equally divided, the proposal or motion shall be regarded as rejected.

[54] "Report of the Final United Nations Conference on the Arms Trade Treaty" (2 April 2013) UN Doc A/CONF.217/2013/2, para 15.

[55] UNGA Res 67/234 B (2 April 2013).

[56] Review 35–36.

[57] SGB 7.

[58] See, eg, Technical Assistance and Cooperation, Note by the Secretariat, UN Doc A/CN.9/905, (18 April 2017) paras. 23, 28, and 46).

practical arrangements needed for the establishment of the court. The Codification Division, as the Secretariat of the Rome Conference, also served as both the substantive and technical Secretariat for the post-Rome process up until and including the inaugural session of the Assembly of States Parties of the ICC.

In the case of the Treaty Section, the area of post-adoption activity is particularly broad, as it is the sole office that discharges the depositary functions of the Secretary-General, which can include the interpretation and application of final clauses and the settlement of several issues that may arise with respect to such issues as entry into force, ratifications, amendments, and corrections.[59]

It should be noted that the Under-Secretary-General for Legal Affairs, the UN Legal Counsel, also takes an active role in encouraging states to consider joining multilateral treaty regimes, primarily through the annual Treaty Event organized during the high-level segment of the General Assembly.[60]

6 Supplementing and Updating Treaties

The 1980 Report discussed under this heading the fact that a number of organs and organizations had commented

> that the modern age requires the conclusion of more and more treaties in technical and other fields where the conditions to which the treaty is addressed or the nature of the obligations to be undertaken may change relatively rapidly. For this purpose, the normal purpose of changing multilateral treaties, by concluding what is in effect a new treaty among the States parties to the original instrument is too slow, involved and uncertain a process. Consequently, many organizations have developed special devices to facilitate the adjustment of treaty provisions.[61]

This development remains of note in some important contexts. For example, there has been an increased use of technical annexes in multilateral treaty regimes, particularly those in the field of the environment and transport, which have been used to allow states parties to rapidly amend and add to the technical content of such agreements without recourse to formal and cumbersome treaty amendment mechanisms.[62]

[59] See the Arancha Hinojal-Oyarbide's Chapter 34.

[60] The concept and practice of the annual Treaty Events take root in the Secretary-General's Millennium report (UN Doc A/54/2000) to the General Assembly where he stated the need to provide "special facilities for the Heads of States or Government to add their signatures to any treaty or convention of which the Secretary-General is the depositary." See UN Treaty Section website for more information.

[61] Review 36.

[62] See **Chapter 10** in this *Handbook*.

7 Other Treaty-Related Activities of the Secretariat

If one includes among "treaty-making exercises" not only multilateral treaty-making among mainly states but also bilateral treaty-making between the United Nations and states or other intergovernmental organizations, one would need to take into account an extensive and wide-ranging practice that has so far not received much public attention from scholars, notwithstanding that on occasion it has been of some importance in the broader context of international relations. It can be asked in this regard whether a series of bilateral agreements following a common model can itself be seen as constituting in some sense a multilateral regime and whether the development of a multilateral regime of this character may on occasion obviate the need for the negotiation of a single multilateral instrument.

In addition to the work of the Secretariat in facilitating the negotiation of multilateral treaties, the Secretariat plays a leading role in the negotiation of bilateral international agreements with member states or other intergovernmental organizations in support of its mandated activities. In the Office of the Legal Counsel, for example, such agreements are negotiated and finalized across the range of the Office's activities.

In the peacekeeping area, the negotiation of Status of Forces Agreements (SOFAs) with Host States on the basis of a General Assembly-endorsed text[63] updated to take account of more recent practice is well known, but peacekeeping missions also frequently require the negotiation of Transit Agreements[64] with neighboring states. On the force generation side of things, of course, the UN must also enter into agreements with Troop and Police Contributing Countries.[65] For Special Political Missions (not including military forces), Status of Mission Agreements (SOMAs), based on the model SOFA as updated, must be negotiated with the Host State, and Transit Agreements with neighboring states are also frequently required.

[63] For a listing of bilateral treaties negotiated by OLA, see Repertory of United Nations Practice, Suppl No. 9 (1995–1999), vol 6 (Articles 104 and 105). The supplements for Article 104 and 105 are available at <http://legal.un.org/repertory/art104_105.shtml>.

[64] See, eg, the Agreement between the United Nations and the Government of the Republic of Benin concerning the status of the United Nations Multidimensional Integrated Stabilization Mission in Mali (MINUSMA) in the territory of the Republic of Benin (8 February 2017) available at <https://treaties.un.org>; and the Exchange of letters constituting an agreement between the United Nations and the Government of the Republic of the Niger concerning the activities carried out in the Republic of the Niger by the United Nations Multidimensional Integrated Stabilization Mission in Mali (MINUSMA) (24 January 2017) available at <https://treaties.un.org>.

[65] For the model Memorandum of Understanding see UN Doc A/C.5/66/8, Chapter 9. See also for example the Memorandum of Understanding between the United Nations and the Government of the Republic of Maldives concerning contributions to the United Nations standby arrangements system (28 May 2014) available at <https://treaties.un.org>; and the Memorandum of Understanding between the United Nations and the Government of Romania contributing resources to the United Nations Special Police Unit in Kosovo (11 February 2002) 2421 UNTS 293.

Agreements between the UN and other intergovernmental organizations may be of a general or specific nature. For example, in 2016, the UN and the International Organization for Migration, pursuant to mandates from their respective intergovernmental policy bodies, negotiated a Relationship Agreement deepening the ties between the two organizations.[66] Similar agreements have also been reached with the International Tribunal for the Law of the Sea[67] and the International Seabed Authority.[68] Agreements of a more specific character were negotiated between the UN and the Organization for the Prohibition of Chemical Weapons (OPCW) at various times in recent years to implement decisions of the Security Council and the Executive Council of the OPCW with respect to various tasks to be jointly carried out relating to chemical weapons in Syria.[69]

The UN has also entered into agreements with Sierra Leone,[70] Cambodia,[71] and Lebanon,[72] as authorized by the Security Council or the General Assembly, to create hybrid international criminal courts of various types. It has entered into a Relationship

[66] Agreement concerning the Relationship between the United Nations and the International Organization for Migration (19 September 2016) available at <https://treaties.un.org>.

[67] Agreement on cooperation and relationship between the United Nations and the International Tribunal for the Law of the Sea (18 December 1997) 2000 UNTS 467.

[68] Agreement concerning the relationship between the United Nations and the International Seabed Authority (14 March 1997) 1967 UNTS 256.

[69] Agreement concerning the relationship between the United Nations and the Organisation for the Prohibition of Chemical Weapons (17 October 2000) 2160 UNTS 209; See also Supplementary Arrangement concerning the implementation of Article II (2)(C) of the Relationship Agreement between the United Nations and the Organisation for the Prohibition of Chemical Weapons (20 September 2012); Supplementary Arrangement concerning cooperation between the United Nations and the Organisation for the Prohibition of Chemical Weapons for the implementation of the OPCW Executive Council decision EC-M-33/DEC.1 and United Nations Security Council resolution 2118 (2013) relating to the elimination of Syrian chemical weapons (16 October 2013); Supplementary Arrangement pursuant to Article XIV of the Agreement concerning the relationship between the United Nations and the Organisation for the Prohibition of Chemical Weapons (5 May 2014); Supplementary Arrangement concerning the implementation of the United Nations Security Council Resolution 2235 (2015) between the United Nations and the Organisation for the Prohibition of Chemical Weapons (20 November 2015) all available at <https://treaties.un.org>.

[70] Agreement between the United Nations and the Government of Sierra Leone on the establishment of a Special Court for Sierra Leone (16 January 2002) 2178 UNTS 137; Agreement between the United Nations and the Government of Sierra Leone on the establishment of a Residual Special Court for Sierra Leone (11 August 2010) 2871 UNTS 333.

[71] Agreement between the United Nations and the Royal Government of Cambodia concerning the prosecution under Cambodian law of crimes committed during the period of Democratic Kampuchea (6 June 2003) 2329 UNTS 117; Supplementary Agreement between the United Nations and the Royal Government of Cambodia ancillary to the Agreement between the United Nations and the Royal Government of Cambodia concerning the prosecution under Cambodian law of crimes committed during the period of Democratic Kampuchea, regarding utilities, facilities and services (14 March 2006) 2363 UNTS 578; Supplementary Agreement between the United Nations and the Royal Government of Cambodia ancillary to the Agreement between the United Nations and the Royal Government of Cambodia concerning the prosecution under Cambodian law of crimes committed during the period of Democratic Kampuchea, regarding safety and security arrangements (14 March 2006) 2363 UNTS 553.

[72] Agreement between the United Nations and the Lebanese Republic on the establishment of a Special Tribunal for Lebanon (6 February 2007) 2461 UNTS 257.

Agreement with the International Criminal Court making possible ongoing cooperation with that Court on a reimbursable basis.[73]

It has also entered into Host Country Agreements with many states relating either to a permanent UN presence in those states or the holding there of a UN conference or other temporary activity.[74]

Many of these bilateral agreements are based on a model text or contain provisions of a similar nature, with the result that the agreements taken together can be seen as establishing a quasi-multilateral regime, albeit one constituted on the basis of a series of bilateral instruments.

8 Conclusion

The Secretariat in general, and, within their mandates, the various parts of the Office of Legal Affairs, in particular, support member states on both substantive and procedural aspects of the multilateral treaty-making process at all stages of that process. Recent examples illustrate the range of this support, from the preparation of highly specialized reports and drafts within a Secretariat entity's particular substantive expertise to more generalized support of a secretariat nature.

The Secretariat will in any given case seek to perform at a high level of professionalism the role that it is given, and seeks to be prepared in all cases to perform additional tasks if it is requested to do so, all with the objective of facilitating the efforts of the negotiating parties to reach a successful outcome.

[73] Relationship Agreement between the United Nations and the International Criminal Court (4 October 2004) 2283 UNTS 195.

[74] See, eg, Agreement between the United Nations and the Government of India relating to the establishment of the subregional office for South and South-West Asia of the United Nations Economic and Social Commission for Asia and the Pacific (13 March 2012) 2824 UNTS X; Agreement between the United Nations and the Government of Denmark relating to the Headquarters and Other Offices in Copenhagen of the United Nations for Project Services (13 December 2007) 2486 UNTS 89; Agreement between the Federative Republic of Brazil and the United Nations regarding the arrangements for the 2015 Internet Governance Forum Meeting (28 October 2015) available at <https://treaties.un.org>.

CHAPTER 4

THE ROLE OF TREATIES IN PURSUING THE OBJECTIVES OF THE UN CHARTER

CHRISTIAN J. TAMS

TREATIES are a central building block of the UN legal order. Agreements prepared under the auspices of the United Nations, or with UN involvement, are ubiquitous; the Organization itself is also party to a significant number of treaties. A diverse category, "United Nations treaties"[1] are an instrument of choice for the Organization and its member states and cover large parts of the "continent of international law."[2] Indeed, the UN has described "the establishment of a comprehensive and robust multilateral treaty framework" as one of its "major contributions . . . to an international order based on the rule of law."[3]

What is true for the United Nations at large seems to have particular significance for the objectives set out in the UN Charter: these need to be implemented and effectuated, and treaties, especially multilateral ones with wide membership—"workhorses of community interest," in Bruno Simma's popular phrase[4]—can help achieve that aim. And yet a closer look at the role of treaties in pursuing the objectives of the Charter reveals important nuances. While crucial to the attainment of some of the Charter's objectives, treaties play a lesser role in relation to others. While they implement decisions taken or foreshadowed in the Charter, they also develop the Charter's normative programme. The role of treaties in pursuing the objectives of the UN Charter, in other words, varies

[1] The term is used here to describe international agreements governed by international law, to which the UN is either a party, or whose elaboration it has influenced. For more on the term see the Introduction to this *Handbook*.

[2] cf Barbara Koremenos, *The Continent of International Law: Explaining Agreement Design* (CUP 2016).

[3] See United Nations, *2015 Treaty Event: Seventy Years of Multilateral Treaty Making at the United Nations* (United Nations 2015) iii.

[4] Bruno Simma, "From Bilateralism to Community Interest in International Law" (1994) 250(IV) Recueil des cours 217, 322.

significantly—and it varies along two axes: between "text" and "practice," and between the different Charter objectives: the relevance of treaties is "sector-specific."

The variable role of treaties is at the heart of the present contribution. Unlike many other contributions to this *Handbook*, it does not address treaties in any particular area, but focuses on their relevance as a category. This requires a rather broad-brush treatment—one that cannot do justice to the intricacies of treaty practice in particular fields, and that is based on two basic distinctions. First, the contribution distinguishes between the initial Charter scheme as reflected in the text of 1945 and the subsequent application and adaptation of that scheme in the UN's practice. Second, seeking to highlight differences and commonalities between the different Charter objectives, it proceeds on the basis of the popular division between three fields of UN activities,[5] *viz.* those aimed at (1) maintaining international peace and security, (2) developing friendly relations between states on the basis of equality and international law, and (3) fostering international cooperation in solving international problems of a social, economic, and humanitarian character. Both distinctions are open to challenge, of course. There is, for example, significant overlap between "peace and security," "friendly relations," and "international cooperation" in the UN's activity; and the allocation of particular activities to one of the three Charter objectives often remains discretionary. What is more, the evolutionary character of the Charter, recognized from the beginning, blurs the lines between initial text and subsequent practice.[6] That said, in a *Handbook* offering many detailed analyses of the UN's treaty practice in particular fields of international law, a broad-brush, perhaps even schematic, treatment, may be defensible: it can provide a bird's-eye view on the role of treaties, encourage an engagement with the text of the Charter (including sections that receive little attention today), and help assess to what extent the Charter framework for treaty-making has been adapted in practice.

1 The Charter and Treaties

The text of the Charter offers a convenient starting-point for the inquiry. Precisely because so much of the UN's work is shaped by decades of pragmatic adaptation to

[5] This division follows the formulation of Article 1, paras 1–3 of the Charter. See further Benedetto Conforti and Carlo Focarelli, *The Law and Practice of the United Nations* (5th edn, Brill/Nijhoff 2010) 7-8; Franz Cede, "The Purposes and Principles of the United Nations" in Cede and Lilly Sucharipa-Behrmann (eds), *The United Nations: Law and Practice* (Kluwer 2001) 11; Rüdiger Wolfrum, in Bruno Simma et al (eds), *The Charter of the United Nations. A Commentary* (3rd edn, OUP 2012), Art 1 MN 7.

[6] As anticipated by Brierly in 1946, the Charter shares the characteristic feature of "[c]onstitutions [which] always have to be interpreted and applied, and in the process they are overlaid with precedents and conventions which change them after a time into something very different from what anyone, with only the original text before him, could possibly have foreseen": James L Brierly, "The Covenant and the Charter" 23 BYIL 83 (1946). Through Article 31(3)(a) and (b) VCLT (recognizing the role of subsequent agreements and subsequent practice as relevant means of treaty interpretation), a dynamic perspective in inscribed into the regime of treaty interpretation.

ever-changing circumstances, the Charter text deserves to be taken seriously—and studied as a constituent document. Such a study, it is submitted, yields three important insights into the role of treaties in pursuing Charter objectives: (1) the Charter does not set out a master plan for how the UN should use treaties; (2) a number of provisions, however, explicitly require or encourage recourse to treaties in pursuit of UN objectives; and (3) beyond express references, the Charter offers hints at the relative relevance of treaties as a means of pursuing the different Charter objectives. These three points are explored in turn.

1.1 No Master Plan

Given the significance of treaties to the UN's daily practice, the first point may come as a surprise: the Charter has relatively little to say on the subject of treaties. The overall impression, when perusing the Charter text for "treaty markers," is in fact rather underwhelming. Few of the Charter's provisions address treaties specifically. "Treaty" or equivalent terms ("agreement" and the like) appear no more than 10 times, and then often only as a reference to preexisting arrangements.[7] The most prominent reference, in the Preamble, is not to treaty-making as such, but to the establishment of "conditions under which justice and respect for the obligations derived from *treaties* and other sources of international law can be maintained."[8] Most other references are found in the remoter parts of the Charter, which, for better or worse, most contemporary commentators choose not to explore.

Beyond the express references, in what it says and what it leaves out, the Charter is rather unsystematic in its treatment of treaties. Of course, the drafters knew very well that the Charter's objectives would need to be filled with meaning through subsequent action—and that agreement on treaties would be one way of concretizing vague commitments. In Article 62, they translated this conviction into a normative agenda: paragraph 3 of the provision—added late in the day during the San Francisco debates[9]—encourages ECOSOC to "prepare draft conventions for submission to the General Assembly, with respect to matters falling within its competence." But in the broader Charter scheme, this conscious attempt to task one UN organ with the concretization of law relating to one of the Charter objectives remains exceptional. Provisions other than Article 62 are more guarded. Article 13 (to take the most prominent) reflects the drafters'

[7] Namely in the Preamble, in Article 13, Article 43 (taken up in Articles 45 and 106), Article 53, Article 62, Article 63 (together with Article 57), Article 77 (taken up in Articles 80–85), Article 92, Article 102, and Article 103.

[8] Significantly, an Egyptian proposal to include among the purposes of the UN a reference to the "determination, definition, codification and development of the rules of international law and international morality" (UNCIO III, 453) (which would have emphasized the importance of developing international law for the Organization as a whole) was not adopted.

[9] See Ruth B Russell and Jeannette E Muther, *A History of the United Nations Charter: The Role of the United States 1940–1945* (Brookings Institute 1958) 796.

desire to keep the General Assembly involved in "the progressive development of international law and its codification." Unlike Article 62, it is not tied to any of the UN's objectives, and purposefully restricts the Assembly's role to "initiat[ing] studies and mak[ing] recommendations." The Charter, in other words, does not lay down a general program for pursuing Charter objectives through treaty-making: there is no Charter equivalent to the sections on institutional lawmaking of many other constitutions of international organizations. To illustrate (and illustration may be required, as the point is hardly ever made), no provision of the Charter expressly states that the UN can pursue its goals through the adoption of "conventions and agreements"—in the way the FAO, UNESCO, ILO, the EU, and various other organizations are explicitly empowered to do.[10] Still less does the Charter facilitate such treaty-making process by moving away from the principle of state consent, which—unlike the constituent documents of ICAO (International Civil Aviation Organization), the WHO, and others[11]—the Charter preserves.[12] All things considered, given its status as the founding document of an Organization that counts "the establishment of a comprehensive and robust multilateral treaty framework" among its "major contributions . . . to an international order based on the rule of law,"[13] the Charter is rather haphazard in its approach to treaties.

1.2 Express References

Even in the absence of a master plan, the Charter of course mentions treaties here and there. But express references are few and far between, and hardly ever attract the attention of commentators. A handful of examples suffice to illustrate the point and to highlight the function that the Charter's express clauses assign to treaties:

1.2.1 *Treaties Enabling UN Action*

First, a number of Charter provisions refer to treaties as a prerequisite for UN action in pursuit of Charter objectives. Articles 57 and 63 are illustrative: they envisage the adoption of treaties as a means of bringing preexisting special agencies in the social,

[10] *Pars pro toto*, see Art XIV(1) of the FAO Constitution, which provides: "The Conference may, by a two-thirds majority of the votes cast and in conformity with rules adopted by the Conference, approve and submit to Member Nations conventions and agreements concerning questions relating to food and agriculture." See also George P. Politakis's Chapter [11] and Tullio Scovazzi's Chapter [15] in this *Handbook*.

[11] As Alvarez notes, these permit some form of secondary lawmaking "with strings attached": José L. *International Organizations as Law-Makers* (OUP 2006) 331.

[12] Alvarez (n 11), 274; Carl-August Fleischauer in Simma et al (n 5), Art. 13 MN 4 and 9 (noting that "[a] t the San Francisco Conference, all attempts to give the GA any power to establish the content of international law with binding force were rejected"). Whether the Security Council has over time acquired some form of legislative power is much discussed; the Charter text does not reflect such a competence.

[13] See (n 3).

economic, and humanitarian fields into a "special [institutional] relationship" with the new world organization. Similarly, Article 77 prescribes "which territories will be brought under the [newly created] trusteeship system and under what terms." Not least to accommodate concerns of administering powers, the Charter thus very clearly accepted that "territories would only be placed under trusteeship following explicit consent."[14] In both instances, "enabling treaties" were required to activate particular aspects of the UN's program for development and friendly relations; they were necessary to unlock the UN's potential—as an umbrella organization integrating the work of older specialized agencies and as a supervisor of trust territories taken over from the League.

1.2.2 *Treaties Effectuating UN Action*

In other provisions, the Charter views treaties as a means of rendering UN action more effective. Article 43 is the most significant of these, and, by some distance, the most specific Charter provision addressing treaties. It requires states to "negotiat[e] as soon as possible on the initiative of the Security Council" special agreements for the establishment of a UN peace enforcement force, available "to the Security Council, on its call"[15]—a "cornerston[e] of the new, centralized, system of collective security"[16] devised by the drafters. Of an entirely different character,[17] but structurally not dissimilar, is the function of special agreements and treaty-based compromissory clauses in the sense of Article 36(1) of the Statute of the International Court of Justice (ICJ):[18] such clauses are not indispensable to the exercise of the Court's jurisdiction (which can also be based on matching unilateral declarations under the optional clause, preexisting commitments transferred to the ICJ, or conduct[19]). However, they increase the range of matters over which the Court can exercise jurisdiction and in that sense render the UN's regime of peaceful dispute resolution more effective.

All this suggests that treaties were on the drafters' minds as they formulated the UN's program of action. At the same time, the brief review reinforces the sense of haphazardness in the Charter's approach to treaties: explicit references to treaties are rather "all over the place"; treaties are envisaged in diverse and typically discrete contexts, but (with the exception of Article 62, paragraph 3) not integrated into any overarching plan of implementing the Charter's objectives.

[14] As noted by Dietrich Rausching, in Simma et al (n 5), Art. 77 MN 1. The ICJ in essence accepted this construction in its advisory opinion on the *International Status of South West Africa* [1952] ICJ Rep 128.

[15] See paras 3 and 1 of Article 43.

[16] Nico Krisch in Simma et al (n 5), Art. 43 MN 1.

[17] Different not only because the context varies, but also because compromissory clauses are found in treaties concluded between states, without any UN involvement as a party.

[18] According to the provision, the Court has jurisdiction to decide in "all cases which the parties refer to it and all matters specially provided for... treaties and conventions in force."

[19] See Article 36, para 2, and Article 37, para 5 of the ICJ Statute. The ICJ Handbook prepared by the Court's Registry, gives a succinct overview over the Court's jurisdictional regime: see *The International Court of Justice: Handbook* (6th edn, United Nations 2014), 34 et seq.

1.3 Implicit References

In the absence of a master plan, and with express references rather all over the place, the main "takeaway" as to the role of treaties is *implicit* in the Charter. The point has been hinted at in the introduction, but deserves to be explored: Contrary to what the succinct listing in the Preamble and Chapter I might suggest, in which the UN's objectives appear in neat succession, the Charter is very uneven in regulating them. Not only are the objectives different in scope—with "peace and security" at least somewhat focused, and "development of friendly relations" open-ended. More importantly, the Charter's text offers very different levels of guidance as to how the different objectives should be construed. Adapting terms borrowed from constitutional law discourse (without necessarily accepting constitutional readings), the Charter could be said to oscillate between comprehensive regulation and mere institutional arrangement; in terms used in treaty-making practice, certain parts of the Charter contain fully fledged rules, others are in the form of a mere framework agreement waiting to be filled with meaning. The Charter's geometry, in other words, is highly variable. This can be illustrated by reference to different sectors of UN activity.

1.3.1 *International Peace and Security*

With respect to one objective, the maintenance of international peace and security, Charter provisions themselves offer a significant amount of normative guidance. Fundamental normative decisions that define the core of the UN's "peace and security architecture" are taken in the Charter itself. To list but the most prominent: Article 2(4) bans the threat or use of force in international relations between UN member states. Article 51 explicitly preserves the right to use force in self-defense, as do Articles 53 and 107 for forcible measures against "enemy states." Most important, Chapter VII (in line with Chapter VIII) establishes a mechanism for dealing collectively with breaches of, and threats to, international peace. While the terms are left undefined, the Charter does define the trigger points that permit collective action for the maintenance of international peace and security. When looking beyond this core, the Charter also offers some guidance on how conditions conducive to the maintenance of peace and security can be brought about—namely by encouraging "plans for the establishment of a system for the regulation of armaments,"[20] and by putting in place the procedures of Chapter VI and the establishment of the ICJ as a forum for the peaceful settlement of disputes. In other words, in relation to questions of peace and security, the Charter comes closest to being a fully fledged treaty: while certainly not comprehensive, the Charter itself lays down a normative program for the implementation of the UN's "purpose of all purposes."[21]

[20] Article 26 of the Charter.

[21] See Rüdiger Wolfrum, in Simma et al (n 5), Art 1 MN 5; Mohammed Bedjaoui, "L'humanité en quête de paix et de développement (II)" (2006) 325 Recueil des cours 9, 378 ("but des buts").

1.3.2 *Friendly Relations between States*

By contrast, the Charter rules relating to the other two objectives listed comparatively vague. The Charter contains little more than starting points for the development of friendly relations between states: alongside the ban on force (which of course is vital), it enshrines the principle of sovereign equality of its members, which in turn is accompanied by a (rather nebulous) prohibition against intervention. Yet quite how international relations should become "more friendly," the Charter does not state—hence Article 1, paragraph 2 has rightly been described as an "all inclusive"[22] encouragement to do *something*. The Charter's main normative contribution concerns what might be viewed as a preliminary aspect: Article 1(2) clarifies that friendly relations are to be based on the principle of "equal rights and self-determination of peoples"; this "was meant to underline that no hierarchy existed between the various peoples."[23] However, it is only in relation to trust territories (as opposed to colonies) that the Charter implemented that principle with any measure of specificity.

1.3.3 *International Cooperation*

Insofar as the Charter seeks to facilitate international cooperation in solving international problems of a social, economic, and humanitarian character, it is similarly vague; in fact, its language remains largely aspirational. In comparison with Article 1(2), the encouragement "to do something" is slightly more targeted but hardly more determinate. Articles 55 and 56 encourage the UN and its members to take "joint and separate action" to "create conditions of stability and well-being," but do so in hortatory language. As in the case of Trust Territories, the Charter's main contribution is to establish a process and a forum (in this case: ECOSOC), and to encourage the Organization to integrate (or "take over") preexisting institutions active in the social, economic, and humanitarian fields. Put differently, while expressing (in the words of the Preamble) a "determin[ation] . . . to employ the [newly created] international machinery for the promotion of social and economic advancement of all peoples," the Charter left the decision on how it should be employed to UN practice.

This variable geometry affects the potential role of treaties as a means of giving meaning to Charter objectives. The basic point is straightforward: where key normative decisions are taken within the Charter itself (as in relation to peace and security), treaties and other forms of subsequent conduct may be useful, but not strictly required. By contrast, where the Charter resembles a framework agreement, some subsequent action is required to unlock the Charter's potential. Haphazard as it is in addressing treaties, the Charter typically does not specify whether such subsequent action ought to take the form of treaties, resolutions, statements, pledges, or other forms of conduct. Without any follow-up action, however, the Charter objectives would remain hollow; one might therefore expect treaties to play a relatively more significant role.

[22] Conforti/Focarelli (n 5) 8.

[23] Rüdiger Wolfrum, in Simma et al (n 5) Art 1 MN 24.

2 Treaties in UN Practice

So, what have the UN and its member states made of the Charter regulation of treaties? Detailed answers to this question are to be found in the chapters comprising Parts II and III of this *Handbook*; these offer accounts of how UN treaties since 1945 have (or have not) shaped particular fields of international law. The subsequent sections can do no more than sketch out some of the key trends and developments. They do so in three steps that loosely follow the three lines of thought developed in the preceding section—by inquiring whether a master plan for the use of practice has emerged in practice, asking what has become of the Charter's express references to treaties, and assessing the extent to which the Charter's variable geometry has impacted the practice of treaty-making.

2.1 No Master Plan but Proliferation

2.1.1 *A Gigantic Network of Treaties*

The first point to be made in relation to the UN's treaty practice is to note just how much there is. The absence of a Charter master plan has clearly not prevented the UN from embracing treaties as a preferred instrument for realizing its objectives. The UN is party to well over 1,500 treaties.[24] Irrespective of its involvement as a party, the UN regularly instigates and facilitates treaty-making—perhaps it is indeed today's "principal promoter of international law-making":[25] the web of multilateral treaties prepared under UN auspices has been described as a "dense web of normativity"[26] and a "gigantic network... regulating all major international activities";[27] the smooth operation and development of this network has become an important part of the UN's work; and the VCLT's recognition of "treaties as... a means of developing peaceful co-operation among nations"[28] one of the leitmotifs of the Organization in the "age of treaties."[29]

[24] See Philippa Webb, "Treaties and International Organizations: Uneasy Analogies" in Christian J Tams, Antonios Tzanakopoulos, and Andreas Zimmermann (eds), *Research Handbook on the Law of Treaties* (Edward Elgar 2014) 567.

[25] Alan Boyle and Christine Chinkin, *The Making of International Law* (OUP 2007) 108.

[26] Dirk Pulkowski, "Structural Paradigms of International Law" in Tomer Broude and Yudal Shany (eds.), *The Shifting Allocation of Authority in International Law: Considering Sovereignty, Supremacy and Subsidiarity* (Hart 2008) 51, 60.

[27] Roy Lee, "Multilateral Treaty-Making and Negotiation Techniques: An Appraisal" in Bin Cheng and ED Brown (eds), *Contemporary Problems of International Law: Essays in Honour of Georg Schwarzenberger on His 80th Birthday* (Stevens 1988) 158.

[28] Preamble, Vienna Convention on the Law of Treaties (adopted 23 May 1969, entered into force 27 January 1980) 1155 UNTS 331.

[29] Ulf Linderfalk, *On the Interpretation of Treaties: The Modern International Law as Expressed in the 1969 Vienna Convention on the Law of Treaties* (Springer 2007) 1.

2.1.2 *Diverse Processes of Treaty-Making*

All this seems to suggest a break with the Charter's relatively cautious approach—but there is much continuity, too. For the massive resort to treaties has not followed any overarching design: institutional practices have emerged and routines been established,[30] but overall, UN treaties have spread through rank growth, not careful cultivation. As will be explored below, treaties dominate certain fields of international law, but have a lesser role in others.[31] More importantly, at least for present purposes, the making of treaties has not followed any standard approach: a bewildering array of treaty-makers has engaged in highly diverse processes of treaty-making. The ILC, an expert body and the most prominent agency through which the General Assembly has sought to "initiate studies and make recommendations" for the codification and progressive development of international law, has been influential in areas broadly considered to belong to the field of general international law (itself not clearly demarcated).[32] But it clearly has no monopoly, and the more one looks into specialized fields of international law, the more heterogeneous the range of actors and processes becomes.[33] ECOSOC has made ample use of its power, under Article 62(3), to draw up draft conventions. UNCITRAL was established to address (private law) aspects of international trade law and has come to "own" this field over the course of the past half century. While different standing committees of the General Assembly have initiated treaty-making processes, the Sixth (Legal) Committee has over time assumed a significant role, partly as the ILC's controller and interlocutor, partly on its own initiative. To add complexity, in the latter case, the Sixth Committee has typically acted through ad hoc committees set up to draft a particular treaty, among them antiterrorism conventions and the Special Missions conventions.[34] In areas of concerted lawmaking efforts, more stable structures have over time emerged and taken a lead: COPUOS in relation to space law; UNCLOS in relation to the law of the sea; UNCTAD in relation to commodities agreements; UNEP in relation to international environmental law.[35]

[30] The Secretariat's *Review of the Multilateral Treaty-Making Process* provides a comprehensive account: see UN Doc. ST/LEG/SER.B/21 (1985).

[31] See Section 2.3 of this chapter.

[32] Core areas of cross-cutting relevance—the law of treaties, diplomatic and consular relations, the law of the sea, state responsibility (the latter not regulated by treaty)—have been a focus of the ILC's work; however, the Commission does not shy away from engaging with specialized fields, as witnessed by its recent work on crimes against humanity and the protection of the atmosphere.

[33] The following summary draws on accounts by Paul C Szasz, "General Law-Making Processes" in Christopher C Joyner (ed), *The United Nations and International Law* (CUP 1997) 27; Fred L Kirgis, "Specialized Law-Making Processes," ibid. 65; and Fleischauer, in Simma et al (n 5), Art. 13 MN 12–94.

[34] For details see Fleischauer, in Simma et al (n 5), Article 13 MN 51–53: "The method of establishing special committees for the preparation of important legal texts and instruments has been resorted to by the Sixth Committee with increasing regularity." The "special committee process" has also been used for the drafting of important General Assembly resolutions, among them the Friendly Relations Declaration or the Definition of Aggression (both of which are mentioned below).

[35] See Chapter [14] by Makane Mbengue in this *Handbook*.

While all of these bodies have had some involvement in treaty-making, their precise roles have differed from one treaty to another; in this respect too, pragmatism and ad hockery dominate. The 1948 Genocide Convention and the 1958 New York Convention, for example, both emanated from within ECOSOC—but one was adopted (and opened for signature) by the General Assembly, the other based on drafts prepared by the International Chamber of Commerce and negotiated at a diplomatic conference. ILC texts also have fared very differently: some were transformed into draft treaties almost "lock, stock, and barrel"; others diluted; still others buried (as ILC projects) and then resuscitated in specialized working groups.[36]

2.1.3 *Treaty-Making within Specialized Agencies*

If all this suggests a deliberate lack of centralization, one should bear in mind that the illustrations given so far all refer to activities of the institutions belonging to the core of the UN system. Once specialized agencies are taken into account, processes and complexities multiply: most specialized agencies have their own processes of treaty-making, and some of them, as noted above, are serious about facilitating secondary lawmaking by qualifying requirements of strict state consent. As a result, centers of treaty-making have emerged on the margins of the UN system: in ICAO, in the ILO, in UNESCO, in WIPO, etc.[37]—to the point where significant coordination efforts are required to avoid duplication and delimit fields of activity.[38] Finally, and unsurprisingly, the role of the UN and its different agencies in the diverse, fragmented lawmaking processes has varied. With respect to some treaties, the UN has been there from start to finish: providing direction, expertise, and political support. With respect to others, the UN has been no more than the forum for the coordination of inter-state negotiation processes: useful perhaps, and convenient no doubt—but without real influence.

The main trend, then, has been one of "fragmentation of international law-making" processes.[39] Treaties have come to play a huge role in the UN's activities, perhaps more than could have been anticipated in 1945. Yet with respect to none of the relevant indicators just referred to—spread of treaties, actors, treaty-making processes, and the relative influence of the UN's role in them—does practice reveal any clear pattern or systematic approach. Quite to the contrary, the massive growth of treaties has been

[36] The 2004 Immunities Convention is an example of the latter type: stalled as an ILC project, it was revived by a working group and then finalized by an ad hoc committee set up by the General Assembly: for details see Gerhard Hafner, "Historical Introduction" in Roger O'Keefe and Christian J Tams (eds), *The United Nations Convention on Jurisdictional Immunities of States and Their Property: A Commentary* (OUP 2013) 1.

[37] Some of these lawmaking efforts, as reflected in the subsequent chapters, have had a transformative effect on international law in its specialized fields.

[38] To give but one example, as noted by Röben, "[w]ith the approval of the GA, ECOSOC has requested the ILO to continue to prepare international conventions within its area of competence": see Volker Röben, in Simma et al (n 5), Article 62 MN 32 (his footnote 39), *citing the Repertory of Practice* III 287, para 34.

[39] Boyle/Chinkin (n 25), 124.

possible precisely because it has not been forced into a rigid masterplan. In this respect, practice has made use of the Charter's flexibility.

2.2 Practice Pursuant to Express Charter Clauses

Moving from the general to the particular, in working toward "the establishment of a comprehensive and robust... treaty framework,"[40] the UN has made use of Charter provisions expressly mandating or encouraging the adoption of treaties. ECOSOC-sponsored treaties prepared pursuant to Article 62(3) have been mentioned already. By the same token, the Charter's "enabling clauses" were quickly used: agreements concluded in 1946 and 1947 were finalized relatively smoothly,[41] transforming League mandates into UN trust territories,[42] from which status they eventually moved on to independence.[43] The integration of specialized agencies into the UN system was a more protracted process, as existing organizations sought to preserve autonomy. However, the more significant ones (among them the ILO, ICAO, IBRD, IMF, and WHO) soon entered into inter-institutional agreements, and by the 1970s, nearly all of the older international organizations had been absorbed into the UN system through treaties agreed pursuant to Article 63(1) of the Charter.[44]

Insofar as the Charter envisages resort to treaties as a means of rendering UN action more effective, the picture is mixed. Over the decades, the UN has encouraged states to agree on treaties permitting recourse to "its" court, the ICJ, under Article 36, paragraph 1 of the ICJ Statute. Compromissory clauses in bilateral and multilateral treaties, permitting the unilateral recourse to the ICJ, have been the main[45] focus of that endeavor:[46] the UN's efforts in this respect have met with increasing resistance, as larger numbers of states have become wary of binding dispute resolution by the ICJ. However, the UN has

[40] See (n 3).

[41] For details see Andriy Y Melnyk, "United Nations Trusteeship System" in *Max Planck Encyclopaedia of Public International Law* (<www.mpepil.com>), para 10.

[42] Where no treaty could be agreed, as with respect to South West Africa, the UN asserted a right to terminate mandates unilaterally through UN GA action; this course of action was accepted by the ICJ in the *Namibia* opinion: see *Legal Consequences for States of the Continued Presence of South Africa in Namibia, International Court of Justice* [1971] ICJ Rep 16.

[43] Thus depriving the Trusteeship Council of its purpose: As anticipated by Trygvie Lie at the Council's opening session, its "full success, incidentally, [was to] put this organ out of existence": Trusteeship Council 4th Meeting [28 March 1947] TCOR 1st Session 58, 79.

[44] Meng gives details: see Werner Meng in Simma et al (n 5), Article 57 MN 34.

[45] Special agreements referring ongoing disputes to the ICJ—the other type of treaty mentioned in Article 36, paragraph 1—have remained relatively rare, and the UN's role in them typically limited. The Secretary-General's however established a Trust Fund to assist states in meeting expenses of ICJ proceedings brought by special agreement: see UN Doc. A/47/444 for details.

[46] For details see Christian J Tams, "The Continued Relevance of Compromissory Clauses as a Source of ICJ Jurisdiction" in Thomas Giegerich (ed), *A Wiser Century? Judicial Dispute Settlement, Disarmament and the Laws of War 100 Years after the Second Hague Peace Conference* (Duncker & Humblot 2009) 461.

persevered, and the different treaties envisaged in Article 36(1) of the ICJ Statute remain central to the Court's exercise of jurisdiction.[47]

By contrast, in the collective security field, the UN's efforts to fill an explicit treaty clause with concrete meaning have remained unsuccessful. Notwithstanding the clear language of Article 43, no state has "undertake[n] to make available to the Security Council, on its call..., armed forces... necessary for the purpose of maintaining international peace and security." Even during the 1990s, when the military dimension of Chapter VII was rediscovered, the Security Council restricted itself to *authorizing* measures, without interfering with member state control over troops.[48] Treaties have, of course, been used to ensure the rapid deployability of peacekeepers, and more recently for standby arrangements.[49] However, these are meagre substitutes for the ambitious, treaty-based scheme anticipated by Article 43. Practice, in other words, has ignored the Charter's most detailed provision on treaties.

The brief survey reflects the diversity of Charter provisions explicitly envisaging the conclusion of treaties, as well as the dominance of prudential and pragmatic considerations guiding member states and UN organs. While typically the Charter's normative impulses have been translated into some form of treaty action, the sobering experience with Article 43 agreements demonstrates the limits of ambitious Charter designs. This, too, illustrates how much the Charter is a living instrument, which through constant interpretation and (non-)application "change[s]... after a time into something very different from what anyone, with only the original text before him, could possibly have foreseen."[50]

2.3 The Charter's Variable Geometry: Three Pen Pictures

If the text of the Charter is an unreliable guide, can the UN's treaty practice be explained by reference to the variable geometry of the Charter's regulatory scheme? As noted above,[51] the Charter regulates its different objectives differently. It defines one of the UN's objectives ("peace and security") with greater specificity than the two others ("friendly relations" and "international cooperation"). At the same time, outside the explicit references just discussed, the Charter does not prejudge whether action in pursuit of the Charter objectives should take the form of treaties, or whether some other form of follow-up action would be more suitable. Under these circumstances, the decision

[47] The *ICJ Handbook* puts the number of such compromissory clauses at 400 and lists prominent examples: see (n 19), at 38–39.

[48] As Nico Krisch observes, "in contrast to the centralized Charter model, [the authorization practice] leaves to the member states the decision as to whether, to which degree, and how long to participate in measures of collective security": in Simma et al (n 5), Art. 42 MN 10. Attempts to revive the Article 43 system, for example in the *Agenda for Peace*, were short-lived (UN Doc. A/47/277, at para 43); even during the heyday of robust UN peace enforcement during the 1990s, ad hoc arrangements proved too appealing.

[49] On all this, see Adam Roberts, "Proposals for UN Standing Forces: A Critical History" in Vaughan Lowe et al (eds), *The United Nations Security Council and War* (OUP 2008) 99.

[50] Cf Brierly (n 6). [51] See Section 1.3 of this chapter.

for or against the elaboration of treaties is a matter of judgment, predilection, and prudence: one that, in the ongoing process of translating Charter objectives into UN action, requires constant reconsideration.

As is clear from the preceding discussion, over the course of the Organization's 70-year history, member states and UN organs have taken innumerable small decisions in favor of treaties: what appears to contemporary observers as a "dense web"[52] of treaty rules is the result of a decades-long process of weaving. At the same time, an exclusive focus on treaties risks overlooking the fact that, more often than not, member states and UN organs prefer other means of pursuing Charter objectives (resolutions, statements, and other non-binding mechanisms) or, indeed, choose to remain passive. The detailed accounts in Parts II and III of this *Handbook* assess the relative significance of treaties—as compared to other forms of follow-up action—in relation to the UN's main fields of activity. The remainder of the present contribution is an attempt to step back from the detail: it offers three "pen pictures" of the role of treaties in relation to the three Charter objectives—sketchy, no doubt, and incomplete, but hopefully helpful as an attempt to highlight essentials.

2.3.1 *Peace and Security: The Dominance of Institutional Practice*

So, what is the role of treaties in relation to the UN's attempts to maintain international peace and security? When stepping back from the details, it seems safe to say that treaties have not dominated UN practice. This is partly due to the fact that, as set out above, the UN Charter's regulation in this field is relatively more detailed than in other areas. But more than that, it also reflects a preference among member states and UN organs for giving meaning to the Charter's objective through means other than treaties. As a result of both factors, treaties are relevant, but have a lesser role than in relation to other objectives.

More specifically, the core of the Charter collective security regime has mainly been interpreted and concretized through the subsequent practice of UN organs: Security Council resolutions have shaped the contemporary, broad understanding of the notion of "threats to peace" in the sense of Article 39.[53] The Security Council's practice has been key to operationalizing the system: rather than entering into agreements in the sense of Article 43, the Council has authorized member state action; more recently, it has begun to unlock the potential of Chapter VIII on regional organizations.[54] The UN's long-standing efforts to reach agreement on the notion of "aggression" culminated in the adoption of a General Assembly resolution, not a treaty.[55] Resolutions of both organs,[56] as well as

[52] Pulkowski (n 26).

[53] Krisch retraces the main steps in the development: in Simma et al (n 5), Art 39 MN 12–39.

[54] See Section 2.2 of this chapter. On regional enforcement action, seeChristian Walter in Simma et al (n 5), Introduction to Chapter VIII, MN 20–34.

[55] UNGA Res 3314 (XXIX) (14 December 1974) UN Doc A/RES/3314.

[56] In addition to the Definition of Aggression (last fn) see, eg, GA Res 42/22; SC Res 1368; SC Res 1373.

diplomatic international practice and international decisions[57] (but less so treaties), contain vital pointers to the construction of the Charter's "cornerstone rule,"[58] the prohibition against the use of force.

None of this is to say that treaties do not matter in the field of peace and security: of course they do, and the subsequent chapters reflect that. Treaties notably have been a preferred means of establishing conditions that are conducive to the maintenance of peace and security—through regulating disarmament, through limiting recourse to certain types of weaponry, through formalizing alliances and defense pacts, by ensuring nonproliferation, and more recently by harnessing state power to combat threats emanating from nonstate actors.[59] Yet even in these areas, treaty prescriptions have been supplemented by Security Council action, which since the turn of the century has occasionally taken the form of quasi-legislative action.[60] The first pen picture emerging from these sketches shows treaties as relevant instruments of maintaining peace and security, but not as primary tools used by the UN.

2.3.2 *Friendly Relations: A Patchwork of Treaties*

The second and third pen pictures differ. They do so necessarily because the objectives themselves are so extremely broad; this is turn has affected the role of treaties in the UN's practice since 1945. Insofar as the Charter seeks to ensure the "develop[ment] [of] friendly relations between states on the basis of equality and international law," it has prompted much treaty-making action, notably aimed at spelling out legal requirements for "international relations" to be considered "friendly." Treaties adopted in pursuit of this second, and broadest, of UN objectives are numerous and extremely diverse. Areas of successful codification through treaty-making include the law of the sea and outer space; international aviation, shipping and other forms of cross-border transport, and the regulation of international sales, to name but a few.[61] To these substantive branches of international relations, one should add treaties concluded with a view to "oiling the wheels" of international relations: such as those aimed at standardizing treaty-making practices, or facilitating diplomatic and consular relations or international cooperation against transnational crime.[62] Perhaps unavoidably, given the open-endedness of this particular Charter objective, treaties agreed to develop friendly relations between states, while numerous, resemble a patchwork. The absence of a master plan is felt

[57] See Christine Gray, "The International Court of Justice and the Use of Force" in Christian J Tams and James Sloan (eds), *The Development of International Law by the International Court of Justice* (OUP 2013) 237.

[58] *Armed Activities case* [2005] ICJ Rep 168, para 14.

[59] See chapter [7] by Barry Kellman and chapter [8] by Pierre Klein in this *Handbook*.

[60] See UNSC Res 1373 (28 September 2001) UN Doc S/RES/1373 and UNSC Res 1530 (11 March 2004) UN Doc S/RES/1530 for the two most prominent examples.

[61] See the chapters by Tanja Masson-Zwaan and Robert Cassar [9], Yoshifumi Tanaka [25], and Corinne Montineri [28] in this *Handbook*.

[62] See the chapters by Malgosia Fitzmaurice [24], Davinia Aziz and Alison See [36], Martin Jelsma and David Bewley-Taylor [13], and Sanderijn Duquet and Jan Wouters [27] in this *Handbook*.

acutely here: immunities are gradually addressed,[63] while jurisdiction remains largely uncodified; there are a number of general "treaties on treaties,"[64] but none on responsibility (including responsibility for treaty breaches). Despite many treaties regulating aspects of international relations between states, international treaties since 1945 do not yield a generally accepted definition of statehood.[65] Blank spots remain, in other words; but in the ongoing "regularization" of international relations, treaties are a primary tool.

Curiously, at the metalevel, things look somewhat different. Whereas treaties have proved essential to the development of (vital and marginal) *aspects* of international relations, the most relevant document spelling out "an irreducible core of principles"[66] on which friendly relations ought to be based was purposefully not adopted as a treaty: the Friendly Relations Declaration—"something close to a constitutional document" and a "manifesto"[67] for good conduct in the family of states—was elaborated within the General Assembly and passed as a consensus resolution.[68] The same is true for the Manila Declaration[69]—international law's "manifesto" for peaceful dispute resolution—and the milestones in the UN's struggle against colonialism: in its attempt to overcome the most obvious obstacle to state equality, the Organization relied on the persuasive force of a General Assembly resolution, not the binding force of a treaty.[70] Here, as elsewhere, decision by the main political organ has been the most significant impulse for UN action.

2.3.3 *International Cooperation: A Charter Objective Kissed Awake by Treaties?*

It is in relation to the third of the Charter's objectives that treaties have arguably been most influential. In the UN's practice since 1945, international cooperation to address problems of an economic, social, cultural, or humanitarian character has emerged as a central challenge; and treaties have been a crucial part of the international response. In the social and humanitarian fields in particular, treaties have "kissed awake" the third Charter objective and given it concrete meaning. The "age of (human) rights"[71] may have begun with a General Assembly resolution,[72] but it is now an age of human

[63] See the 2004 UN Convention on Jurisdictional Immunities of States and Their Property for the most ambitious codification effort—which so far has attracted few ratifications.

[64] Namely the two Vienna Conventions (or three, if the one on succession in included). See chapter [24] by Malgosia Fitzmaurice in this *Handbook*. cf Richard D Kearney and Robert E Dalton, "The Treaty on Treaties" (1970) 64 AJIL 495.

[65] Hence continued references to the (regional) Montevideo Convention of 1934: LNTS 165, 19.

[66] Vaughan Lowe, *International Law* (OUP 2007) 100.

[67] ibid.

[68] Declaration on Principles of International Law concerning Friendly Relations and Co-operation among States, UNGA Res 2625 (XXV) (24 October 1970).

[69] Manila Declaration on the Peaceful Settlement of International Disputes, UNGA Res 37/10 (15 November 1982).

[70] Declaration on the Granting of Independence to Colonial Countries and Peoples, UNGA Res 1514 (XV) (14 Dec 1960) (adopted by 89 votes to none; 9 abstentions).

[71] cf Louis Henkin, *The Age of Rights* (Columbia University Press 1990).

[72] See Universal Declaration of Human Rights, UNGA Res 217 A (III) (10 December 1948).

rights *treaties*.[73] Specialized agencies such as the ILO, the WHO, and UNESCO have relied heavily on treaties to shape the rules in their fields.[74] Treaties have been equally vital as the UN has sought to adapt to new challenges such as environmental degradation, climate change, and (after a hiatus) international criminal justice.[75] Here—as in relation to other Charter objectives—additional blind spots remain. High-profile UN initiatives seeking to shape international economic relations have typically taken the form of resolutions.[76] International economic law has been "treatified," but largely[77] outside the United Nations—under the aegis of the WTO or on the basis of bilateral arrangements for the promotion of cross-border investments.[78] In the more recent UN initiatives in the social and economic field (the Millennium Development Goals (MDGs) and their successors, the Sustainable Development Goals (SDGs), treaties play a rather limited role: human rights treaties serve as building blocks, but drives by successive UN secretaries-general to ensure that "development... forms the centre of the UN's work"[79] has not (yet) resulted in significant treaty-making projects.

3 Conclusion

The three pen pictures just offered highlight differences in the relative significance of treaties as a means of pursuing Charter objectives. At one level, they can be said to reflect the differences in the Charter's regulatory scheme. Where the Charter resembles a framework agreement, treaties have concretized and developed its normative program; where it defines objectives with some degree of precision, treaties have not been used to the same extent. Member states and UN organs have not, however, had their hands tied: they have pragmatically made use of treaties to advance the Charter's program in some areas, but often opted to avoid treaty-making. Indeed, the preceding analysis suggests

[73] Human rights feature prominently in most general accounts of UN lawmaking: see, eg, Alvarez (n 11), 274: "Whole areas of modern international law, including human rights, would be unimaginable without treaties concluded under IO auspices." Tellingly, Part II of the present *Handbook* devotes five chapters to them (while treating "Labour" and "Women" as a specialized areas).

[74] See the chapters by George P. Politakis [11], Allyn Taylor [17], and Tullio Scovazzi [15] in this *Handbook*.

[75] See the chapters by Cordonier Segger and Alexandra Harrington [10] and Salvatore Zappalà [23] in this *Handbook*.

[76] See notably the General Assembly's (largely unsuccessful) attempts to lay the foundations for a "New International Economic Order' and to formulate a "Charter of Economic Rights and Duties of States": UNGA Res 3201 (S-VI) (1 May 1974) and UNGA Res 3281 (XXIX) (12 December 1974)

[77] Specialized agencies have, of course, elaborated treaties addressing aspects of international trade: see notably the UNCTAD Commodity Agreements discussed in Chapter 14 by Makane Mbengue in this *Handbook*.

[78] While WTO and the UN have agreed on an inter-institutional arrangement, the former is not a specialized agency of the latter. As regards investment law, UNCTAD has come to play an influential advisory role, but for a long time resisted the move toward bilateral investment treaties.

[79] See, eg, "Taking Oath of Office, António Guterres pledges to work for peace, development and a reformed United Nations" *UN News Centre* (12 December 2016).

that the Charter hardly ever seeks to tie or force member state hands—and where it attempted to do so, as with respect to Article 43, it has been ignored.

The Charter is, then, haphazard in its approach to treaties, which are hardly mentioned explicitly, and whose role is not defined systematically. The drafter's surprising caution means that the role of treaties in pursuing UN objectives is primarily shaped by practice rather than the Charter text. In seven decades of UN practice, treaties have sprawled: in the absence of a Charter master plan, they have grown into a "gigantic network"[80] covering large parts of the continent of international law, but the landscape is as uneven as it is diverse.

80 Lee (n 27).

CHAPTER 5

THE PLACE OF TREATIES IN THE CODIFICATION AND PROGRESSIVE DEVELOPMENT OF INTERNATIONAL LAW

GIORGIO GAJA

At the end of World War Two, notwithstanding the existence of a large number of multilateral and bilateral treaties, the general part of international law mainly consisted of rules of customary law. The situation has changed mostly because several treaties that have been concluded have either replaced customary rules or influenced their current content. Some of these treaties are generally referred to as codification conventions.

The term "codification" attributed to a treaty conveys the idea that it contains a statement of rules previously existing in an unwritten form. However, the change from an unwritten rule to a written treaty inevitably implies some innovation. Moreover, treaties that are defined as codification conventions often contain provisions that cover matters not previously regulated or that supplement or specify existing rules. These provisions are more clearly innovative and regarded as being per se part of the "progressive development of international law," following the terminology of Article 13, paragraph 1 (a) of the United Nations Charter.

The United Nations Convention on the Law of the Sea provides a striking example of this phenomenon. While several of its provisions have been considered by the International Court of Justice as reflecting customary rules,[1] there are many provisions

[1] Among the many examples, one may refer to the treatment of the "definition of an island embodied in Article 121, paragraph 1, as part of customary international law" (*Territorial and Maritime Dispute Case (Nicaragua v. Colombia)* [2012] ICJ Rep 674, para 139).

in the Convention that add precisions or cover new ground, such as most of those included in Part XI, concerning "The Area."

In furtherance of the task that the United Nations Charter gave to the General Assembly of "encouraging the progressive development of international law and its codification," resolution 174 (II), which established the International Law Commission [hereinafter sometimes referred to as the Commission], included the following definitions:

> In the following articles the expression "progressive development of international law" is used for convenience as meaning the preparation of draft conventions on subjects which have not yet been regulated by international law or in regard to which the law has not yet been sufficiently developed in the practice of States. Similarly, the expression "codification of international law" is used for convenience as meaning the more precise formulation and systematization of rules of international law in fields where there already has been extensive State practice, precedent and doctrine.

These definitions have attracted criticism.[2] Between the two situations described in the resolution there appears to be a wide gray area, where practice may be "sufficiently developed" but less than "extensive." Moreover, the description of "codification" as "the more precise formulation and systematization of rules of international law" appears to be restrictive, while the "preparation of draft conventions" is too general a description for defining progressive development.

As was observed,[3] "the difference between codification and development, if it exists at all, is one of degree rather than kind." There is in fact a continuum between progressive development and codification, and it may often be difficult to ascertain which characterization is more appropriate. This explains why the International Law Commission has not attempted to base its work on that distinction. It has instead followed the same procedure for all topics, even if its Statute envisaged the appointment of a special rapporteur only for the case of progressive development, and has generally made no distinction among the draft articles it adopted according to whether they pertain to codification or progressive development.

Already in 1956, the Commission stated that:

> In preparing its rules on the law of the sea, the Commission has become convinced that, in this domain at any rate, the distinction established in the statute between these two activities can hardly be maintained. Not only may there be wide differences of opinion as to whether a subject is already "sufficiently developed in practice", but also several of the provisions adopted by the Commission, based on "recognized

[2] The most famous critical opinion was voiced by Hersch Lauterpacht, "Codification and Development of International Law," in Elihu Lauterpacht (ed.), *International Law. Collected Papers. Volume 2: The Law of Peace* (CUP 1975) 271, 276–77, and 286.

[3] Robert Y Jennings, "The Progress of International Law" (1958) 34 British YB of Intl L 345.

> principles of international law", have been framed in such a way as to place them in the "progressive development" category. Although it tried at first to specify which articles fell into one and which into the other category, the Commission has had to abandon the attempt, as several do not belong to either.[4]

Forty years on, the Commission similarly stated that it:

> [...] has inevitably proceeded on the basis of a composite idea of "codification and progressive development". In other words, its work has involved the elaboration of multilateral texts on general subjects of concern to all or many States, such texts seeking both to reflect accepted principles of regulation, and to provide such detail, particularity and further development of the ideas as may be required.[5]

1 Recourse to Codification Conventions

Codification of international law may be pursued by various methods. The United Nations is usually involved, but does not necessarily have a role. When the United Nations intends to promote codification, the International Law Commission is often entrusted with preliminary work, but this is not always the case. For technical matters and for subjects of significant political import, the Commission is often not considered the suitable forum for such a work and therefore is not involved.[6] Here one can refer again, as an example, to the United Nations Convention on the Law of the Sea, the preparation of which did not involve the Commission, although the preamble of the Convention describes its object as "the codification and progressive development of the law of the sea" and four codification conventions had been previously adopted on the basis of the preparatory work of the Commission.

The main choice is whether to pursue codification through a non-binding text or seek the adoption of a treaty, which would bind the states that accept it once it enters into force. The resolution of the General Assembly that adopted the Statute of the International Law Commission (resolution 174 (II) referred to above) envisaged three possibilities that the Commission may recommend to the General Assembly: "tak[ing] note of or adopt[ing] the [Commission's] report by resolution," "recommend[ing] the draft to Members with a view to the conclusion of a convention," or "convok[ing] a conference to conclude a convention." The emphasis in the Statute is on the adoption of a treaty.

[4] 1956-II YBILC 255–6, para 26.

[5] 1996-II(2) YBILC 86, para 157.

[6] See for instance Hisashi Owada, "Presentation," in *Making Better International Law: The International Law Commission at 50* (United Nations 1998) 70–72, and Yves Daudet, "Les méthodes et pratiques de la codification: Rapport général," in: Société française de droit international, *Colloque d'Aix-en-Provence, La codification du droit international* (Pedone 1999) 143–45.

The adoption of codification conventions has been for many years the principal aim pursued by the General Assembly in this regard. In certain cases, when the matter did not seem important enough to warrant the convening of a conference, the General Assembly has adopted a codification convention directly, on the basis of the draft articles submitted by the Commission. The alternative to the adoption of a convention, which has become more frequent in recent years, is that the General Assembly endorses to some extent the statement of rules drafted by the Commission.

One of the advantages of concluding a codification convention is that it gives states first an opportunity to discuss the rules before these are adopted and then to express their will to accept the text through the political institutions empowered to conclude treaties for the state. This method was perceived as particularly significant for newly independent states, which had not been able to influence the content of customary rules. As the International Law Commission noted when it decided in 1962 to prepare draft articles on the law of treaties "capable of serving as a basis for a multilateral convention":

> [...] the codification of the law of treaties through a multilateral convention would give all new States the opportunity to participate directly in the formulation of the law if they so wished; and their participation in the work of codification appears to the Commission to be extremely desirable in order that the law of treaties may be placed upon the widest and most secure foundations.[7]

The position of the states that accept a codification convention with regard to the rules therein contained becomes clear and facilitates the application of these rules.

However, the advantages described above come at a cost.

First of all, there is the eventuality that a conference is convened but that a codification convention is not adopted or leads to results that many states consider unsatisfactory.[8] This could occur in particular when some aspects of the subject matter are controversial, for instance with regard to certain issues relating to the responsibility of states for internationally wrongful acts. It may then be preferable, as the Commission suggested in 2001, to keep, at least for some time, the articles drafted by the Commission as a non-binding text,[9] which the General Assembly recommended to the attention of member states, and let the draft articles enjoy the authoritativeness that they have acquired,[10] rather than run the risk that a failure of a codification conference would undermine the value of the draft articles.

[7] 1962-II YBILC 160, para 17. This point was emphasized by Roberto Ago, "La codification du droit international et les problèmes de sa réalisation" in *Recueil d'études de droit international en hommage à Paul Guggenheim* (Faculté de droit de l'Université de Genève 1963) 95–97.

[8] See in particular Roberto Ago, "Nouvelles réflexions sur la codification du droit international" (1988) 92 Revue Générale de Droit International Public 539, and in Yoram Dinstein (ed), *International Law at a Time of Perplexity: Essays in Honour of Shabtai Rosenne* (Martinus Nijhoff 1989) 28.

[9] 2001-II(2) YBILC 25, paras 72–73. The General Assembly endorsed this solution in its resolution 56/83.

[10] Arthur Watts, "Codification and Progressive Development of International Law" in *Max Planck Encyclopedia of Public International Law* <http://opil.ouplaw.com/home/epil>, para 31.

When a codification convention is adopted, whether by an international conference or by the General Assembly directly, practice has shown that acceptance of the convention is often slow, and sometimes even very slow. As the International Court of Justice [sometimes referred to hereinafter as the Court] noted in the *North Sea Continental Shelf* cases, this may be due to "factors other than active disapproval of the convention concerned."[11] It is more likely that the delay in ratification finds a reason in the limited interest that states have in regulating the subject matter or, in some cases, in the reluctance of states to commit themselves to the acceptance of rules the implications of which are not easily predictable.

It has been suggested that the General Assembly should seek to hasten the process by recommending that member states take action within a certain deadline, either by ratifying a codification convention or by explaining their reasons for delaying ratification or for not ratifying.[12] However, should the General Assembly make recommendations of this or similar nature, it is unlikely that many states would respond by outlining their position.

Moreover, the limited number of ratifications of codification conventions that have entered into force raises problems concerning the relations between these conventions and customary rules. In relation to states that are not parties, the applicable rules are likely to be customary rules. If the content of the latter is not affected by the codification convention, there may be inconsistencies that could give rise to non-compliance with a state's obligations under the convention or customary rules. As was noted by an author who presided over two codification conferences, codification conventions have the potential to be "rather divisive and confuse the already precarious state of the law."[13] However, as we shall consider in the following paragraphs, the relevance of codification conventions does not solely depend on their role in governing relations between their states parties.[14]

Under the law of treaties, states parties to a codification convention are bound by the rules in the convention with regard to the other states parties to the same convention. Customary rules may nevertheless still be applicable in the same relations. For instance, in the case concerning *United States Diplomatic and Consular Staff in Tehran*, the International Court of Justice noted that, notwithstanding the entry into force of the Vienna Conventions on Diplomatic and Consular Relations between the states parties to the dispute, their obligations were "not merely contractual obligations established by the Vienna Conventions of 1961 and 1963, but also obligations under general international law."[15] In the *Military and Paramilitary Activities in and against Nicaragua* case the Court found that "[p]rinciples such as those of the non-use of force, non-intervention,

[11] [1969] ICJ Rep 42, para 73.

[12] Ago, "La codification du droit international et les problèmes de sa réalisation" (n 7) 123.

[13] Karl Zemanek, "Codification of International Law: Salvation or Dead End?" in *International Law at the Time of Its Codification. Essays in Honour of Roberto Ago* (Giuffrè 1987) 600.

[14] As was expressed by Mark E Villiger (*Customary International Law and Treaties* (2nd edn, Martinus Nijhoff 1997) 144), "the text will always remain a code."

[15] [1980] ICJ Rep 31, para 62.

respect for the independence and territorial integrity of States, and the freedom of navigation" were still applicable. The Court said:

> The fact that the above-mentioned principles, recognized as such, have been codified or embodied in multilateral conventions does not mean that they cease to exist and to apply as principles of customary law, even as regards countries that are parties to such conventions.[16]

Whether a treaty displaces a customary rule in the relations between the states who are parties generally appears to be a matter of interpretation of the relevant treaty. When a codification convention is inconsistent with a previously existing customary rule, one would have to assume that the convention prevails. However, there may be cases in which the formation of treaty rules may not be sufficient to replace customary rules, because the codification convention can regulate a matter only if it leads to the formation of higher rules. This is the case with the rules on the validity of treaties, which make sense only if they are viewed as situated at a level higher than treaties. Therefore, rules in a codification convention on the validity of treaties, such as those contained in the Vienna Convention on the Law of Treaties, are only significant if they give rise to corresponding rules of higher law.

2 Codification Conventions Reflecting Customary Rules

At least some provisions included in a codification convention are expected to reflect previously existing rules of customary international law. They do so only to a certain extent because, as noted above, the formulation in writing and the added precisions in the convention inevitably imply some modification of the customary rules.

It is clear that if—as does the Geneva Convention on the High Seas—the codification convention itself states in the preamble that the Convention articles are "generally declaratory of established principles of international law," there is a strong indication that, in the view of the states parties to the Convention, at least certain articles in the Convention embody customary rules. The same attitude may be attributed to those states that did not ratify the Convention, but voted in favor of the adoption of the preamble. The fact of signing the Convention may also show some measure of agreement with the statement included in the preamble. However, the statement leaves open the question of which provisions of the convention are to be considered as declaratory of "established principles."

[16] [1984] ICJ Rep 424, para 73.

In any event, most codification conventions do not contain statements concerning their relation with customary rules. In the *North Sea Continental Shelf* cases, the International Court of Justice examined whether the provision of the Geneva Convention on the Continental Shelf on the delimitation of the continental shelf between adjacent states represented a "consecration" of a customary rule, in other words the embodiment of a preexisting customary rule. The Court considered in general terms the relations between codification conventions and customary rules. It adopted what appeared to be, also in light of the conclusion reached with regard to the specific provision, a restrictive view in assessing whether a provision in a codification convention could reflect a customary rule. The Court concluded that:

> [...] the Geneva Convention did not embody or crystallize any pre-existent or emergent rule of customary law, according to which the delimitation of continental shelf areas between adjacent States must, unless the Parties otherwise agree, be carried out on an equidistance-special circumstances basis.[17]

One of the criteria that the Court used to reach this conclusion was based on the attitude of the proponents of the provision. The Court referred to the fact that:

> the principle of equidistance, as it now figures in Article 6 of the Convention, was proposed by the Commission with considerable hesitation, somewhat on an experimental basis, at most *de lege ferenda*, and not at all *de lege lata* or as an emerging rule of customary international law.[18]

The Court gave further consideration in later decisions to the circumstances of the adoption of a rule in a codification convention. In its advisory opinion on the *Legal Consequences for States of the Continued Presence of South Africa in Namibia* the Court noted that:

> The rules laid down in the Vienna Convention on the Law of Treaties concerning termination of a treaty relationship on account of breach (adopted without a dissenting vote) may in many respects be considered as a codification of existing customary law on the subject.[19]

[17] [1969] ICJ Rep 41, para 69. By crystallization the judgment refers to a form of alignment of the customary rule with the provision in the codification convention, which will be discussed in the next paragraph. The quoted passage leaves a strange impression given the conclusions that the more recent jurisprudence of the Court reached with regard to the delimitation of the continental shelf and the exclusive economic zone. In the case concerning the *Land and Maritime Boundary between Cameroon and Nigeria*, the Court noted that the method to be followed "is very similar to the equidistance/special circumstances method applicable in delimitation of the territorial sea" ([2002] ICJ Rep 441, para 288).

[18] [1969] ICJ Rep 38, para 62.

[19] [1971] ICJ Rep 47, para 94.

In the *Delimitation of the Maritime Boundary in the Gulf of Maine Area* case, the Chamber of the Court similarly referred to the circumstance that:

> certain provisions of the Convention [on the Law of the Sea], concerning the continental shelf and the exclusive economic zone, which may, in fact, be relevant to the present case, were adopted without any objections.[20]

For the Court, the absence of objections showed that the states participating in the adoption of the codification convention agreed with the relevant provisions. However, the attitude of these states may have various explanations that do not necessarily lead to the conclusion that the provision reflects a customary rule.[21] Similarly, the fact that a certain provision is controversial does not necessarily mean that it is considered innovative. The divergent views of states may find their origin in a variety of positions with regard to the actual content of the existing customary rule.

In its judgment in the *North Sea Continental Shelf* cases, the Court also gave weight to the fact that, according to the Geneva Convention on the Continental Shelf, the provision concerning the delimitation of the continental shelf between adjacent states could be the object of a reservation. In the view of the Court, this indicated that the provision could not reflect a customary rule:

> [...] for, speaking generally, it is a characteristic of purely conventional rules and obligations that, in regard to them, some faculty of making unilateral reservation may, within certain limits, be admitted.[22]

The argument is not fully persuasive. The possibility that states parties to a convention may make reservations to a certain provision does not imply per se that the relevant provision does not correspond to a customary rule.[23] By making a reservation a state may only wish to exclude being subjected to the treaty regime with regard to the obligations under a certain rule.

In its later jurisprudence, the Court has not elaborated further methodological approaches to ascertaining whether a codification convention embodies a customary rule. However, it has reached conclusions, often in the affirmative, without discussing the circumstances that it had outlined as relevant in the *North Sea Continental Shelf* cases.

In many cases, the Court has not provided reasons for its conclusion that the content of the customary rule corresponds to that of a provision in the codification convention. For instance, in the passage quoted above of its advisory opinion on the *Legal Consequences for States of the Continued Presence of South Africa in Namibia*, the Court noted that the rule in the Vienna Convention on the Law of Treaties on termination of a

[20] [1984] ICJ Rep 294, para 94.

[21] This point was made by Gennadiĭ M. Danilenko, *Law-Making in the International Community* (Martinus Nijhoff 1993) 150–51.

[22] [1969] ICJ Rep 38, para 63.

[23] See the dissenting opinion of Judge Morelli, [1969] ICJ Rep 198, para 1.

treaty relationship on account of breach "may in many respects be considered as a codification of existing customary law on the subject."[24] In this and several other decisions, the Court's analysis has not been prompted by the need to assess whether a provision in the codification convention was innovative in relation to the previously existent customary rule. The adoption of the codification convention has rather been viewed by the Court as an indication of the content of the applicable rules of customary international law.

3 The Alignment of Customary Rules with Codification Conventions

When a rule set out in a codification convention is substantively innovative in relation to previously existing customary rules, the divergence may be overcome through a development of international custom.

In the *North Sea Continental Shelf* cases the Court devoted much attention to the argument submitted by Denmark and the Netherlands to the effect that the provision in the Geneva Convention on the delimitation of the continental shelf between adjacent states, while innovative, "crystallized" customary law as a consequence of the attitude taken by states in the codification process.[25] According to this argument, the agreement reached within the codification conference on the criteria for delimiting the continental shelf provoked a change in the content of the customary rules, which became aligned with the provision in the Geneva Convention. The term "crystallization" is a metaphor referring to the consolidation of an emerging rule stated in a codification convention.

The Court dealt with this argument in conjunction with the argument that the provision in the convention embodied customary rules. It noted that Articles 1 to 3 of the Geneva Convention on the Continental Shelf "were [...] regarded as reflecting, or as crystallizing, received or at least emergent rules of customary international law relative to the continental shelf."[26] It concluded that, on the contrary, no crystallization had occurred with regard to the provision on the delimitation of continental shelves between adjacent states.

The impact that a codification convention may have on customary rules is not restricted to the phase of the adoption of the convention. It may well be that the factors involved in this process take a little longer and that therefore there is not an immediate crystallization of an emerging rule. Even if the Court devoted separate sections of its judgment in the *North Sea Continental Shelf* cases to the alignment at time of adoption and the later alignment,[27] the phenomenon appears to be the same and involves the same factors. In either case, a state not party to the codification convention would become bound by a rule of customary international law reflecting a provision in the convention.

[24] [1971] ICJ Rep 47, para 94.
[25] [1969] ICJ Rep 38, para 61.
[26] Ibid 39, para 63.
[27] Ibid 38–40, paras 61 ff., and 40–45, paras 70 ff.

Article 38 of the Vienna Convention on the Law of Treaties deals with both aspects when it states that "[n]othing in articles 34 to 37 [on treaties and third States] precludes a rule set forth in a treaty from becoming binding upon a third State as a customary rule of international law, recognized as such." This provision was meant to apply in particular to codification conventions. It does not set any requirements for a matching customary rule to arise. Notwithstanding the wording of Article 38, the customary rule would bind not only third states, but also states parties to the codification convention in their relation to third states and possibly also between themselves.[28]

As the Court recalled in the *North Sea Continental Shelf* cases, for a customary rule to become aligned with the provision in a codification convention, the latter should be treated:

> [...] as a norm-creating provision which has constituted the foundation of, or has generated a rule which, while only conventional or contractual in its origin, has since passed into the general *corpus* of international law, and is now accepted as such by the *opinio juris*, so as to have become binding even for countries which have never, and do not, become parties to the Convention.[29]

The general requirements for a customary rule to arise or be modified apply. The practice of states not parties to the codification convention and of states parties in relation to third states are equally relevant.

One element that has been considered significant is the number of states that have accepted the convention. Should most states become parties to a codification convention on a certain matter, there would be little scope for applying customary rules on that matter. Unless some states take a critical attitude toward the rules expressed in the codification convention, the limited practice involving states that are not parties to the convention is likely to be affected by those rules. The wide acceptance of new rules included in a codification convention may determine a change in the attitude of states. This seems to be the case with respect to diplomatic relations that are not governed by the Vienna Convention on Diplomatic Relations, which is a codification convention that has attained nearly universal participation. While quite a few of the provisions in that Convention were innovative at the time of its adoption, it has become progressively more difficult to find elements of *opinio juris* and state practice that reaffirm the customary rules that were previously in existence.

In its judgment in the *North Sea Continental Shelf* cases the Court noted that:

> [...] it might be that, even without the passage of any considerable period of time, a very widespread and representative participation in the convention might suffice of itself, provided it included that of States whose interests were specially affected.[30]

[28] This point was made in my commentary on Article 38 in Olivier Corten and Pierre Klein (eds.), *The Vienna Conventions on the Law of Treaties* (OUP 2011) 953.

[29] [1969] ICJ Rep 41, para 71.

[30] Ibid 42, para 73.

The attitude of "States whose interests [are] specially affected" may well be relevant for certain multilateral treaties whose practical significance depends on the participation of the main stakeholders. One could assume that, when a convention is intended to govern some specific relations mainly concerning certain states, the attitude of those states is particularly important. However, with regard to a codification convention that aspires to become universal, no state can be appropriately defined as "specially affected" in relation to the convention.

If, on the contrary, there are only a few ratifications or accessions to a codification convention, the impact of this convention on customary law is likely to be limited. However, the number of ratifications and accessions is not necessarily decisive. There may be reasons for a state to delay or withhold ratification or accession, which do not necessarily reflect a negative attitude toward all or some of the provisions included in the convention.

In the *North Sea Continental Shelf* cases, the Court also put an emphasis on state practice when assessing whether an alignment has taken place between customary rules and the provisions included in a codification convention:

> an indispensable requirement would be that within the period in question, short though it might be, State practice, including that of States whose interests are specially affected, should have been both extensive and virtually uniform in the sense of the provision invoked; - and should moreover have occurred in such a way as to show a general recognition that a rule of law or legal obligation is involved.[31]

Leaving aside the question of the possible existence of states whose interests are specially affected, what needs to be considered is the state practice that is not governed by the codification convention, including the practice of states parties in their relations with third states.[32] In the passage quoted above, the Court seems to consider requirements with respect to practice that are more stringent than what is generally considered sufficient for a customary rule to arise. However, there is no reason to apply in that case a different standard from the one that is generally adopted for assessing the existence of a rule of customary international law.

When the Court asserts that a customary rule is embodied in a provision of a codification convention, it generally omits to specify whether this is the result of a change in the customary rule. The question may be only of theoretical importance, but in certain cases it could lead to a retrospective application of a customary rule. This may in turn raise the question whether a breach of an international obligation under that rule could

[31] Ibid 43, para 74.

[32] However, in the *North Sea Continental Shelf* cases the Court seems to have discarded the attitude of states parties to the codification convention because they were "presumably, so far as they were concerned, acting actually or potentially in the application of the Convention" ([1969] ICJ Rep 43, para 76).

have occurred. According to Article 13 of the Articles on Responsibility of States for Internationally Wrongful Acts:

> An act of a State does not constitute a breach of an international obligation unless the State is bound by the obligation in question at the time the act occurs.[33]

This provision is meant to apply equally to breaches of obligations under rules of customary international law.

4 Codification Conventions in a Changing Context

Over time, codification conventions may become obsolete or need to be updated. This may, or may not, occur in parallel with changes affecting customary rules.

An evolution of customary rules may lead to a divergence between those rules and provisions in a codification convention. This may even occur in cases where those provisions had originally embodied customary rules or had subsequently become aligned with them. The new customary rules that have arisen after the adoption of the codification convention would be likely to apply also in the relations between states parties and would then prevail over the provisions in the convention.

Should customary rules evolve in such a fashion, the need may arise for the codification to be modified, which would require a new treaty to be concluded. However, this process would likely require a long period of time. A state may then wish to free itself of its obligations under the codification convention. If the convention includes a denunciation clause, the fact that states make use of that clause would provide evidence that, in the view of the denouncing states, the convention needs to be overhauled. In its advisory opinion on the *Legality of the Threat or Use of Nuclear Weapons*, the Court considered the reverse case, arguing that the fact that a denunciation clause in "codification instruments" of international humanitarian law had not been used was an indication of the existence of "a corpus of treaty rules the great majority of which had already become customary."[34] The Court implied that the use of the denunciation clause may, on the contrary, negatively affect the existence of customary rules that have a content corresponding to the provisions in the convention. This would seem to depend on the reasons, if any, given by the denouncing state or attributable to it.

Most codification conventions do not contain clauses providing for their denunciation. When Senegal denounced in 1971 the Geneva Conventions on Fishing and Conservation of the Living Resources of the High Seas and on the Territorial Sea and the

[33] 2001-II(2) YBILC 57.

[34] [1996] ICJ Rep 258, para 82.

Contiguous Zone,[35] which contain no such clause, the United Kingdom objected that "those Conventions are not susceptible to unilateral denunciation by a State which is a party to them."[36] It would be difficult to argue that a state party's right of denunciation is "implied by the nature of the treaty," as required by Article 56, paragraph 1 (b) of the Vienna Convention on the Law of Treaties for denouncing, or withdrawing from, a treaty containing no provision regarding termination, denunciation, or withdrawal. On the other hand, termination or suspension of a codification convention could be based on reasons specifically allowed by the law of treaties, such as the occurrence of a fundamental change of circumstances.[37]

5 Concluding Remarks

Not all the subjects of international law lend themselves to the adoption of a codification convention. The same remark may apply to some of the subjects that the International Law Commission has chosen to examine. Even if a codification convention would be appropriate, when the Commission, or for that matter a working group established by the General Assembly, submits a draft treaty, the General Assembly may not pursue the path toward a codification convention. The most likely obstacle is that there are some political reasons, especially diverging views on certain key parts of the text. What the General Assembly now often does in this case is to recommend the text to the attention of states and indicate that it may reconsider the issue of promoting a convention at a future session.

In recent years, the General Assembly's choice of not promoting a codification convention has become more frequent. The last codification convention—the United Nations Convention on Jurisdictional Immunities of States and Their Property—was adopted in 2004 by resolution 59/38. Reluctance in proceeding toward a codification convention may have been enhanced by the limited success of some recent conventions, which have not entered into force because the required number of ratifications has not been reached and which have also had little influence on state practice.

This current trend may suggest that the season of codification conventions is over. However, there is no good reason for abandoning recourse to an instrument that has significantly contributed to the development of international law in several areas. When the subject matter of a text lends itself to being regulated by a treaty and there is a broad consensus on the basic elements of the draft, a codification convention should still be regarded as the most efficient way for obtaining a change in international law: between the states parties to the convention, when the convention enters into force for them, but also more widely for the international community when consequential modifications are likely to affect international customary law at the universal level.

35 781 UNTS 332.
36 854 UNTS 214.
37 See Watts (n 10), para 20.

CHAPTER 6

THE CHOICE OF A TREATY

hard law versus soft law

ALAN BOYLE*

In the modern world, treaties are not only a source of obligations between the parties. Many of the more important multilateral treaties have become lawmaking instruments—codifying existing law, creating new law, and establishing widely accepted norms and principles applicable to all or the large majority of states. But if the use of multilateral treaties for lawmaking purposes has undoubtedly been refined since 1945, other developments now supplement "the only and sadly overworked instrument with which international society is equipped."[1] At one end of the spectrum, soft-law instruments play a noticeably larger role than before. At the other, the UN Security Council's forays into international lawmaking provide another indicator that there are alternatives to multilateral treaty-making.[2] As we will see, it is no longer true that "law-making by treaty is the only organized procedure for the conscious, rational positioning of legal rules, at least at the universal level."[3]

This chapter begins by examining the political considerations that may encourage states to pursue "soft" rather than "hard" legal commitments, before examining the legal consequences of that decision. A third section considers specific fields in which member states have chosen to follow the path of soft law: declaratory lawmaking, codification

* Emeritus Professor of Public International Law, University of Edinburgh; barrister, Essex Court Chambers, London. This chapter draws upon the author's previous work on the subject, most notably his chapter in Malcolm Evans (ed), *International Law* (5th edn, OUP 2018) and ch 5 of Alan Boyle and Christine Chinkin, *The Making of International Law* (OUP 2007).

[1] Arnold D McNair, "The Functions and Differing Legal Character of Treaties" (1930) 11 BYIL 101.

[2] See UNSC resolutions 687, 1373 and 1540; Paul Szasz, "The Security Council Starts Legislating" (2002) 96 AJIL 901–05.

[3] Christian Tomuschat, "Obligations Arising for States without or against Their Will" in The Hague Academy of International Law, *Collected Courses of the Hague Academy of International Law* (1993) 241 Recueil des cours 239.

and progressive development, facilitating treaty negotiation, interpretation of treaties, and subsidiary rules and standards.

1 Treaties or Soft Law?

The literature identifies at least four reasons why soft law instruments represent an alternative to lawmaking by treaty.[4] First, it may be easier to reach agreement when the form is non-binding. Its great advantage over a treaty is that, as occasion demands, it can enable states to take on commitments that they otherwise would not, or to formulate them in a more precise and detailed form that could not at that point be agreed in a treaty. The soft-law approach thus allows states to tackle a problem collectively at a time when they do not want to shackle their freedom of action. Their legal commitments, and the consequences of any noncompliance, are more limited. In this context soft law has been a useful instrument for developing international law in relatively new fields such as human rights or environmental protection.

Second, soft-law instruments are more flexible. They will normally be easier to supplement, amend, or replace than treaties, since all that is required is the adoption of a new resolution by the relevant international institution.[5] The important point is that soft law is often relied on to provide the detailed technical rules and standards required to implement international regulatory regimes concerned with safety, pollution, resource conservation, and so on. Because they are often based on expert advice and may need to change frequently to reflect changes in policy or in the underlying science, there is little point putting these rules and standards into the text of a treaty.

Third, it may be easier for some states to adhere to non-binding instruments because they can avoid the domestic treaty ratification process and perhaps escape democratic accountability for the policy to which they have agreed. In this context the benefits of soft law are essentially domestic and constitutional in character. Of course, this very feature may also make it comparably harder to implement such policies if public funding, legislation, or public support are necessary. As a new government may also find it easier to repudiate soft-law commitments, other governments may wish to be careful about relying on them.

Last, soft-law instruments may provide more immediate evidence of international consensus on an agreed text than a treaty whose impact is qualified by reservations and the need to wait for ratification and entry into force. Codification of the law of state

4 For a detailed examination see Christine Chinkin, "The Challenge of Soft Law: Development and Change in International Law" (1989) 38 ICLQ 850; Kenneth Abbott and Duncan Snidal, "Hard and Soft Law in International Governance" (2000) 54 Int Org 421; Hartmut Hillgenberg, "A Fresh Look at Soft Law" (1999) 10 EJIL 499; Hanspeter Neuhold, "The Inadequacy of Law-Making by International Treaties: 'Soft Law' as an Alternative?" in Rüdiger Wolfrum and Volker Roben (eds), *Developments of International Law in Treaty Making* (Heidelberg, 2010) 40.

5 Anthony Aust, "The Theory and Practice of Informal International Instruments" (1986) ICLQ 787, 791.

responsibility in the form of a General Assembly resolution reflects the advantages of a soft-law form that, in this context, is viewed by many states and the International Law Commission (ILC) as sufficient for the purpose.[6]

Soft law has obvious limitations, however. A treaty may be perceived as more authoritative; this is one reason the ILC has generally preferred to pursue codification by treaty rather than soft law, although its practice in recent years has evolved.[7] Treaties may carry greater weight than soft-law instruments insofar as they become part of national law on ratification, or because they indicate a stronger commitment to the norms and principles in question. A treaty gives each party a credible assurance that its terms will be complied with in good faith, and that some remedy exists if they are not.[8] Litigation, resort to noncompliance procedures, state responsibility, termination or suspension of the treaty, and countermeasures are all potentially available when one party breaches its treaty obligations. Soft law provides no such assurance for other interested states unless some form of noncompliance procedure has been specifically agreed upon.[9] A multilateral treaty serves, above all, to stabilize the policies and principles it promotes across the community of states; soft law will not achieve that objective. Thus, the argument for using a treaty is strongest when binding commitments are necessarily required or where an existing treaty regime has to be changed or replaced. For example, the adoption of an international regulatory regime on climate change or the creation of an international criminal court with jurisdiction to try international crimes could only be effected by legally binding treaties that committed the parties to taking the necessary measures and establishing the required institutions. Only a new treaty—the 1982 UN Convention on the Law of the Sea—could have rewritten the law of the sea because the existing treaty law had to be amended or overridden, and new institutions had to be created. Soft law could not have achieved these goals.

Even for new law, however, non-binding instruments may be useful if they can generate widespread and consistent state practice and/or provide evidence of *opinio juris* in support of a customary rule. There are good examples of UN General Assembly resolutions and intergovernmental declarations potentially having this effect in the *Nicaragua Case*,[10] the *Nuclear Weapons Advisory Opinion*,[11] and the *Western Sahara Advisory Opinion*.[12] It is noteworthy that no international tribunal has ever found the mere act of voting for such resolutions to constitute the state practice necessary to create a customary rule. But then neither does the mere act of becoming party to a treaty.[13]

What all of this suggests is that the non-binding form of a soft-law instrument is of relatively limited relevance in the context of international lawmaking. Treaties do not

[6] See Section 3.2 in this chapter. [7] See Section 3.2 in this chapter.

[8] See in particular Kenneth Abbott and Duncan Snidal, "Hard and Soft Law in International Governance" (2000) 54 Int Org 421, 427; Kal Raustiala, "Form and Substance in International Agreements" (2005) 99 AJIL 581; Andrew T. Guzman, "The Design of International Agreements" (2005) 16 EJIL 579.

[9] There are examples: see Dinah Shelton (ed), *Commitment and Compliance: The Role of Non-binding Norms in the International Legal System* (OUP 2000).

[10] [1986] ICJ Rep 14. [11] [1996] ICJ Rep 226. [12] [1975] ICJ Rep 12.

[13] See *North Sea Continental Shelf Cases* [1969] ICJ Rep 3 at [24]–[38], [47]–[56], [60]–[81]; *Paramilitary Activities Case in Nicaragua Case* [1986] ICJ Rep 14 at [172]–[186].

generate or codify customary law because of their binding form but because they either influence state practice and provide evidence of *opinio juris* for new or emerging rules, or because they afford good evidence of what the existing law is.[14] In many cases the potential effect of non-binding soft-law instruments is no different. Both treaties and soft-law instruments can be vehicles for focusing consensus on rules and principles, and for mobilizing a consistent, general response on the part of states. In this context the assumption that treaties are necessarily more authoritative is misplaced. To take only one example, the 1992 Rio Declaration on Environment and Development both codifies existing international law and aspires to develop new law. It is not obvious that a treaty with the same provisions would carry greater weight or achieve its objectives any more successfully. On the contrary, it is quite possible that such a treaty would, several years later, still have far from universal participation whereas the 1992 Declaration secured immediate consensus support, with such authority as that implies.[15]

At the same time, if we explore this example a little further it seems clear that other Rio and post-Rio agreements, such as the Conventions on Climate Change, Biological Diversity and Desertification, and the Agreement on Straddling and Highly Migratory Fish Stocks could only be in treaty form because of the political need for a clearly binding commitment on the part of states, their inter-relationship with other treaties, and their institutional and dispute settlement provisions. For all these reasons, incorporation in a treaty was the right option, if only for symbolic reasons. For quite different reasons the same can be said about the ILC articles on state immunity. Only adoption as a treaty would facilitate the necessary changes in national law for those states where treaties are part of national law.

2 What Do We Mean by "Soft Law"?

"Soft law" has a range of possible meanings.[16] From a lawmaking perspective it is simply a convenient description for a variety of non-binding, normatively worded instruments used in contemporary international relations by states and international organizations. Examples include UN conference declarations; appropriately worded resolutions and declarations adopted by the UN General Assembly, or one of its subsidiary organs or specialized agencies; or codes of conduct, guidelines, and principles adopted by any of these UN organs. The proposition is <u>not</u> that non-binding declarations or resolutions of the General Assembly or any other soft-law instrument are law per se, but that, inter alia,

[14] *North Sea Continental Shelf Cases*, ICJ Rep 3; *Nuclear Weapons Advisory Opinion* [1996] ICJ Rep 226.

[15] See Alan Boyle and Catherine Redgwell, *International Law and the Environment* (4th edn, OUP 2019) ch 3; Jorge Viñuales (ed), *The Rio Declaration on Environment and Development: A Commentary* (OUP 2015) ch 1.

[16] See generally Richard R Baxter, "International Law in 'Her Infinite Variety'" (1980) 29 ICLQ 549; Chinkin (n 4); Pierre-Marie Dupuy, "Soft Law and the International Law of the Environment" (1991) 12 Mich JIL 420; Hartmut Hillgenberg, "A Fresh Look at Soft Law" (1999) 10 EJIL 499.

if drafted in normative terms they may be evidence of existing law,[17] or formative of the *opinio juris* or state practice that generates new law.[18] Widespread acceptance of soft-law instruments will tend to legitimize conduct and make the legality of opposing positions harder to sustain.[19] Brownlie refers in this context to the "decisive catalytic effect" of certain UNGA resolutions.[20] Other soft-law instruments are significant because they codify or assist in the development and application of general international law,[21] or because they are the first step in a negotiating process eventually leading to the conclusion of a multilateral treaty.[22] Soft-law instruments may acquire binding legal character as elements of a treaty-based regulatory regime,[23] or constitute "a subsequent agreement between the parties regarding the interpretation of a treaty or the application of its provisions."[24]

Moreover, it is possible for states to adopt soft-law general principles with the intention that international institutions, courts, and states should apply them when relevant. Such general principles do not have to create rules of customary law to have legal effect. Rather, their importance derives principally from the influence they can exert on the interpretation, application, and development of other rules of law.[25] Soft-law declarations such as the 1992 Rio Declaration on Environment and Development or the 1948 Universal Declaration of Human Rights will have to be taken into account insofar as they articulate general principles agreed by consensus.[26] The point is not confined to treaty interpretation, however. General principles of this kind may also influence the interpretation and application of customary law.[27]

The recognition that non-binding soft-law instruments may have legally significant effects does not entail rewriting the law of treaties or expanding the sources of international law; still less does it require us to engage in the "deformalization of the ascertainment of international legal rules."[28] To argue otherwise is to miss the point. The point is that treaties, soft law, general principles, and custom interact and supplement each

[17] *Legality of the Threat or Use of Nuclear Weapons* (Advisory Opinion) [1996] ICJ Rep 226, paras 68–73; *Texaco v Libya* (1977) 53 ILR 389.

[18] *Western Sahara* (Advisory Opinion) [1975] ICJ Rep 3 at [48]–[74] and Judge Dillard at [120]–[123]; *Paramilitary Activities in Nicaragua Case* [1986] ICJ Rep 14 at [172]–[209].

[19] See Chinkin (n 4).

[20] Ian Brownlie, "The Legal Status of Natural Resources" (1970) 162 Recueil des cours 261.

[21] *Gabčíkovo-Nagymaros Case* [1997] ICJ Rep 7, para 140; *Texaco v Libya* (1977) 53 ILR 389.

[22] See Section 3 of this chapter.

[23] Eg, under the 1982 UN Convention on the Law of the Sea, Articles 210–211, or the 1994 Nuclear Safety Convention, on which see later in this chapter.

[24] Vienna Convention on the Law of Treaties 1969, Article 31(3)(a).

[25] See, eg, the influence of the precautionary principle in the drafting and interpretation of environmental agreements: see 1992 Rio Declaration on Environment and Development, Principle 15; *Pulp Mills on the River Uruguay Case* [2010] ICJ Rep 14, para 164; *Advisory Opinion on Activities in the Area*, ITLOS Reports (2011), para 131; and Boyle and Redgwell (n 15) ch 3, section 6.

[26] See Section 3.1 in this chapter.

[27] See, eg, the ICJ's references to sustainable development in the *Gabčíkovo-Nagymaros Dam Case* [1997] ICJ Rep 7, para 140; *Pulp Mills on the River Uruguay Case (Interim Measures)*, 2006 ICJ Rep 113, para 80; *Pulp Mills on the River Uruguay Case* (Merits) [2010] ICJ Rep 14, paras 177 and 184.

[28] Argued by Jean D'Aspremont, *Formalism and the Sources of International Law* (OUP 2011) 129.

other. What matters is to understand that there is an interaction, even when the instrument itself is formally non-binding.

An alternative view of soft law focuses on the contrast between "rules," involving clear and reasonably specific commitments that are in this sense hard law, and "norms" or "principles," which, being more open-textured or general in their content and wording, can thus be seen as soft even when contained in a binding treaty.[29] This form of soft law typifies the often broadly framed powers of many international organisations, including the UN.[30] But in the context of this study, we are not concerned with soft law in this sense, but only with its non-binding form.

3 Soft Law in UN Practice

The UN has pioneered the use of soft law, most obviously through the adoption of General Assembly resolutions that, inter alia, interpret and amplify the UN Charter, codify and progressively develop international law, provide evidence of *opinio juris* on new norms and principles, or legitimize state practice.[31] Judge Higgins has observed that "the passing of binding decisions is not the only way in which law development occurs. Legal consequences can also flow from acts which are not, in the formal sense, 'binding'. And, further, law is developed by a variety of non-legislative acts which do not seek to secure, in any direct sense, 'compliance' from Assembly members."[32] What those consequences are will depend on the context and the purposes for which a soft-law instrument is adopted. The following examples illustrate these points.

3.1 Declaratory Lawmaking

Some soft-law instruments serve declaratory law-making purposes. The UN has made particular use of declarations in order to set forth normative principles in new or developing areas of international law.[33] The Universal Declaration on Human Rights (UDHR)

[29] See Prosper Weil, "Towards Relative Normativity in International Law?" (1983) 77 AJIL 413; Ulrich Fastenrath, "Relative Normativity in International Law" (1993) 4 EJIL 305; Chinkin (n 4); Lavanya Rajamani, "The 2015 Paris Agreement: Interplay between Hard, Soft and Non-obligations" (2016) 28 J Env L 337.

[30] Eg, the references to human rights and self-determination of peoples in Articles 1, 55 and 73 of the UN Charter. See further Jose Alvarez, *International Organizations as Law-Makers* (OUP 2005) 597–600.

[31] Literature on the legal effect of UNGA resolutions is extensive, but see in particular Blain Sloan, "General Assembly Resolutions Revisited" (1987) 58 BYBIL 39.

[32] Rosalyn Higgins, *Problems and Process: International Law and How We Use It* (OUP 1995) 24.

[33] In UN practice a "declaration" is used in preference to a "resolution" when "principles of great and lasting importance are being enunciated." See UN Doc E/CN.4/L.610 (1962).

and the Rio Declaration on Environment and Development represent two of the General Assembly's most significant soft-law contributions in this category.

3.1.1 *The* 1948 *Universal Declaration of Human Rights*

In the human rights context, UN declarations have been used almost since the inception of the UN itself. The key instruments nearly all began in soft-law form but are now incorporated in the multilateral treaties that today form the corpus of international human rights law. Once that transformation was achieved the declarations themselves ceased in most cases to have any further relevance. The one exception is the first and most important: the Universal Declaration of Human Rights.

The Universal Declaration was the earliest internationally endorsed statement of what UN member states regarded as human rights.[34] In the words of the chair of the Human Rights Commission, "It is not a treaty; it is not an international agreement. It is not and does not purport to be a statement of law or of legal obligation."[35] It is plainly soft; but is it in any sense law? Yes, in at least two, possibly three, senses. First, it represents a common understanding by UN member states of the human rights provisions of the UN Charter.[36] As such it is relevant to the interpretation of the Charter and development of human rights law by the UN. Second, some of its provisions express "general principles of law" recognized as sources of international law by Article 38(1)(c) of the Statute of the ICJ.[37] As such they can be taken into account and applied by courts. The right of access to justice is one example of such principles.[38] A third, but more contested view, is that, whatever its initial status, the UDHR has created a customary international law of human rights.[39] Even if this is not true of the whole declaration, some of its provisions have undoubtedly become customary international law, including freedom from genocide, slavery, and torture.[40]

Moreover, regardless of the status of the declaration itself or of the rights it sets forth, it has provided the essential negotiating foundation for the UN's two principal human rights treaties, the International Covenants on Civil and Political Rights, and on Economic, Social and Cultural Rights. The negotiations lasted 18 years and they resulted in the creation of two distinct categories of human rights, formulated differently and with different compliance machinery, but the core principles were those laid down in 1948.

[34] UNGA Res 217A (III). Forty-eight states voted in favor; none against; 8 abstained.

[35] Quoted in Marjorie M Whiteman, *Digest of International Law* 55 (USGPO, 1963). The chair was Eleanor Roosevelt.

[36] UN Charter, Articles 1(3), 55, 56, 62, and 76. See Hurst Hannum, "The Status of the Universal Declaration of Human Rights in National and International Law" (1995–1996) 25 Georgia J Int & Comp L 287.

[37] Theodor Meron, *Human Rights and Humanitarian Norms as Customary Law* (OUP 1991) 88–89.

[38] See *Golder v United Kingdom* (1975) 1 *EHRR* 524.

[39] Hannum (n 36); Louis Sohn, "The New International Law: Protection of the Rights of Individuals Rather than States" (1982) 32 Am ULR 1, 17, but compare the more nuanced position in Meron (n 37) 82–90.

[40] See *Obligation to Prosecute or Extradite Case* [2012] ICJ Rep 422, para 99; *Bosnian Genocide Case* [2007] ICJ Rep 43, para 161.

Not all states are parties to the UN Covenants, however, and it is in that context that the UDHR remains relevant in contemporary international law.

Aspirational declarations on human rights do not necessarily have normative effect or lead to treaty negotiations.[41] As one commentator has observed: "[a]t the time of their adoption most UN resolutions on human rights are promotional rather than restatements or reaffirmations of legal norms. However, to suggest that they do not contribute to law-making is to underestimate the impact of 'merely' moral or political statements in the area of human rights."[42]

Since 1948, UN lawmaking in the human rights field has largely followed the same pattern: first a declaration is adopted, then a treaty is negotiated.[43] In some cases the treaty follows within a few years (e.g., the 1965 Convention on the Elimination of All Forms of Racial Discrimination); in others it has taken 30 years (e.g., 1989 Convention on the Rights of the Child) for negotiations on a binding instrument to be concluded.

3.1.2 *The* 1992 *Rio Declaration on Environment and Development*

The Rio Declaration on Environment and Development,[44] adopted by consensus at the UN Conference on Environment and Development in 1992, remains the most significant universally endorsed statement of general rights and obligations of states affecting the environment. Despite its apparently soft-law status it should not be underestimated. The Declaration is in part a restatement of existing customary law on transboundary matters, partly an endorsement of new or developing principles of law concerned with protection of the global environment, and partly a statement of policies and ideals set out more fully in Agenda 21 (the program of action for tackling environmental problems also adopted by the Conference, and whose implementation has led to further lawmaking).

This does not mean that the Declaration itself is binding law. Its value, like certain other soft-law declarations, is evidential: it tells us what states believe the law to be in certain cases, or in others what they would like it to become or how they want it to develop. The Declaration's legal significance can therefore only be properly appreciated in conjunction with an examination of the preexisting customary law and the subsequent development of state practice, further treaties, protocols, regulations, and judicial decisions. The Declaration has had significant impact in all of these areas of lawmaking; many of the principles have been referred to by the ILC in support of its codification of

41 See, eg, the 1993 Vienna Declaration and Programme of Action on Human Rights, and other examples quoted in Christopher Joyner (ed), *The United Nations and International Law* (CUP 1997) 146–47.

42 Joyner (n 41) 147.

43 See, eg, 1959 Declaration on the Rights of the Child, UNGA Res. 1386 (XIV); 1963 Declaration on the Elimination of Racial Discrimination, UNGA Res. 1904 (XVIII); 1967 Declaration on the Elimination of Discrimination Against Women, UNGA Res. 2263 (XXII); 1973 Declaration Against Torture, UNGA Res. 3059 (XXVIII).

44 See Jorge Viñuales (ed), *The Rio Declaration on Environment and Development: A Commentary* (OUP 2015).

the law relating to transboundary harm,[45] and it appears to be one of the "great number of instruments" setting out norms of international environmental law to which the ICJ referred in the *Gabčíkovo-Nagymaros Dam Case*, and on which the Court also relied explicitly in its *Nuclear Weapons Advisory Opinion*.[46]

Two factors give the Rio Declaration significant authority and influence in the articulation and development of contemporary international law relating to the environment. First, many of its carefully drafted terms are capable of being and were intended to be norm-creating or to lay down the parameters for further development of the law.[47] These commitments were reaffirmed by the Rio+20 Conference and the UNGA in 2012.[48] Second, the Declaration's 27 principles represent something of a "package deal"—negotiated by consensus, rather like the 1982 UNCLOS,[49] and must be read as a whole.[50] Some of its provisions thus reflect the interests of developed states, while others were more strongly supported by developing states. For the first time it was possible to point to a truly international agreement on some core principles of law and policy concerning environmental protection, sustainable development, and their interrelationship. These principles have clearly influenced the subsequent development of the customary and conventional law of the environment.[51]

3.2 Codification and Progressive Development

Some soft-law instruments are intended more to codify and progressively develop existing law than to create new law, but it is of course difficult to do one without also doing the other, so the difference between this group and the previous one is largely one of degree. Even on the most conservative view, "[i]f a resolution purports to be declaratory of international law, if it is adopted unanimously (or virtually so, qualitatively as well as quantitatively) or by consensus, and if it corresponds to State practice, it may be declaratory of international law."[52]

[45] The commentaries to the 2001 Articles on Transboundary Harm and the 2006 Principles on the Allocation of Loss draw upon Principles 2, 7, 10, 11, 13, 15, 16, 17, 18, and 19. See *ILC Report* (2001) GAOR A/56/10; id (2006) GAOR A/61/10, paras 51–67.

[46] [1996] ICJ Rep 226, paras 29–30, and see also dissenting opinions of Judges Weeramantry and Palmer in the *Request for an Examination of the Situation* [1995] ICJ Rep 288. See also *Iron Rhine Arbitration*, PCA (2005) para 59; *Kishenganga Arbitration* (Partial Award), PCA (2013) para 449.

[47] See UNGA Res. 47/190 and 191 (1992) and 48/190 (1993).

[48] See "The Future We Want", UNGA Res. 66/288 (2012) and annex.

[49] On the package deal consensus character of the 3rd UN Conference on the Law of the Sea see Hugo Caminos and Michael Molitor, "Progressive Development of International Law and the Package Deal" (1985) 79 AJIL 871. On the Rio negotiations see Ilona Porras in Philippe Sands (ed), *Greening International Law* (The New Press 1993), 20.

[50] Porras (n 49) 20.

[51] See Boyle and Redgwell (n 15) ch 3.

[52] Judge Schwebel in *Advisory Opinion on the Legality of the Threat or Use of Nuclear Weapons* [1996] ICJ Rep 226. See also *Texaco v Libya*, 53 ILR (1977) 389.

The UN General Assembly resolution on the law of state responsibility is a good example.[53] Although views within the ILC and the UN 6th Committee on the eventual form of the ILC draft articles were divided, both bodies recommended that the UNGA "take note" of the draft articles, in the expectation that in this form they would "exert an influence on the crystallization of the law of State responsibility through application by international courts and tribunals and State practice," deferring for later a decision on whether to proceed with a codification treaty.[54] Much of it was already existing law or had become accepted as law during the process of codification, a conclusion that international courts have done nothing to dispel.[55]

Why has this topic been treated differently from almost all its predecessors? It cannot be said that the state responsibility articles are unsuited to adoption in the form of a multilateral treaty; on the contrary they are drafted as if in treaty form. An UNGA resolution may in this case be more effective than a treaty for two reasons. First, a treaty runs the risk of securing only a relatively small number of parties. The Commission's work on the law of treaties is among its most successful and authoritative codifications, but it is difficult to suggest that this owes much to the Vienna Convention's treaty status, or to the number of states parties. Second, referring the draft articles to a diplomatic conference might reopen debates on a text that already rests on a delicate compromise between differing views.[56] It would thus be better for states simply to endorse a consensus in the Commission and then argue about the status of the rules in their dealings with each other and in litigation. In this case, the form of the articles is more significant for what it tells us about the process of international lawmaking than about the nature or legal status of the rules themselves.

If we look at the more recent work of the ILC, it can be seen that the multilateral treaty is no longer the Commission's preferred instrument for the codification of international law. Although Articles 17 and 23 of the Statute of the Commission refer expressly to the conclusion of conventions, other possibilities are left open. Since 2001 soft-law outcomes have increasingly been used.[57] Even the re-examination of the law and practice on reservations to treaties has concluded with the adoption of soft-law guidelines.[58] Guidelines can be expressed differently from treaty articles. Their purpose is more practical, and they do not create binding commitments or amend the earlier Vienna Conventions, although they may help interpret them or simply disseminate a better

[53] UNGA Res 56/83 (2001).

[54] James Crawford and Simon Olleson, "The Continuing Debate on a UN Convention on State Responsibility" (2005) 54 ICLQ 959.

[55] *Gabčíkovo-Nagymaros Dam Case* [1997] ICJ Rep 7. See James Crawford (ed), *The International Law Commission's Articles on State Responsibility: Introduction, Text and Commentaries* (CUP 2002) 1–60.

[56] Crawford and Olleson (n 54) 961; Martti Koskenniemi, "Solidarity Measures: State Responsibility as a New International Order" (2001) 72 BYIL 337, 341.

[57] On the comparative advantages of different forms see Crawford (n 55) 58–60.

[58] ILC, Guide to Practice on Reservations to Treaties, 63rd session (2011), GAOR A/66/10/Add.1.

understanding of the law. Other ILC topics have continued this trend, including fragmentation of international law[59] and identification of customary law.[60] The Commission's 2015 report includes five topics whose outcome will take the form of guidelines, conclusions, or principles, one report whose content is intended to provide guidance, and only four that will lead to draft articles being adopted.[61]

One important feature of the treaty as an instrument of codification is that states have significant input into the treaty negotiations and have sometimes made substantial changes to ILC drafts.[62] This renegotiation does not necessarily happen when the UN General Assembly simply adopts or takes note of a declaration of principles drafted by the Commission. A treaty basis may also be required when creating new international organizations or institutions, such as the International Criminal Court, or for dispute settlement provisions. Finally, for some states, ratified treaties become part of their national law, and adoption of a text in this form becomes a convenient way of changing national law. The latter point explains why these states ultimately favored adoption of a treaty on the law of state immunity, rather than a simple declaration.

Nevertheless, except for topics where the main objective is to harmonize national laws or to establish institutions, it is of secondary importance whether codification takes the form of a treaty, or a non-binding declaration or guidelines. There are advantages and disadvantages to both forms, but they need to be assessed in their particular context and not in general or dogmatic terms.

3.3 Facilitating Treaty Negotiation

Some non-binding soft-law instruments are significant because they are the first step in a process eventually leading to conclusion of a multilateral treaty. The non-binding Universal Declaration of Human Rights was adopted long before agreement on the 1966 Covenants became possible, but it was always intended by the Human Rights Commission that further binding agreements would follow. Other examples are numerous, but they include General Assembly resolutions on outer space,[63] the deep seabed,[64]

[59] ILC, Fragmentation of International Law: Report of the Study Group, 58th session (2006), GAOR A/CN.4/L.682.

[60] ILC Report, 68th session (2016), GAOR A/71/10, ch V.

[61] ILC Report, 67th session (2015), GAOR A/70/10.

[62] Eg, the 1969 Vienna Convention on the Law of Treaties and the 1997 International Convention on the Non-navigational Uses of International Watercourses.

[63] UNGA Res 1962 (XVIII): 1963 Declaration of Legal Principles Governing the Activities of States in the Exploration and Use of Outer Space.

[64] 1970 Declaration of Principles Governing the Sea Bed and Ocean Floor and Subsoil Thereof Beyond the Limits of National Jurisdiction, UNGA Res 2749 (XXV).

and climate change[65]—all of which are now reflected in the relevant multilateral treaties.[66] Non-binding IAEA Guidelines[67] formed the basis for the rapid adoption of the 1986 Convention on Early Notification of a Nuclear Accident following the Chernobyl accident, UNEP Goals and Principles on Environmental Impact Assessment[68] were subsequently incorporated in the 1991 ECE Convention on Environmental Impact Assessment in a Transboundary Context, and UNEP's Guidelines on Land-based Sources of Marine Pollution[69] provided a model for regional treaties.[70]

If UNGA resolutions are not law, and are meant to be replaced by treaties,[71] why adopt them at all? If we take the resolutions on outer space as an example, apart from practical considerations of simplicity and speed of adoption as compared to treaties, the importance of resort to the UNGA or other UN agencies lies in the collective affirmation that is thereby provided for negotiated rules and principles otherwise only impliedly asserted by state practice, if at all. The resolutions provided both a record of what all states believed the relevant rules on use of outer space should be, and evidence of *opinio juris* demonstrating the lawmaking significance of their earlier practice when the first spacecraft were launched.

In those circumstances it would be safe for space states to proceed on the assumption that there would be no opposition to activities conducted in conformity with the principles endorsed by the resolutions. That these principles were subsequently reaffirmed in treaty form shows both the value of soft-law precedents as a prelude to later agreement on a more detailed international regime and the preference for treaties as a means of stabilizing the law within an appropriate institutional framework once the views and practice of states are settled. This may suggest a perception that soft law is too fragile an instrument to sustain the long-term regulation of common areas such as space or the deep seabed,[72] but it is certainly an effective starting point when states need reassurance before commencing novel and previously unregulated activities.

3.4 Interpretation of Treaties

Treaties take time to replace or amend, and the attempt to do so can result in an awkward and overlapping network of old and new obligations between different sets of parties.

65 1988 Resolution on Protection of Global Climate for Present and Future Generations of Mankind, UNGA Res 43/53.

66 Respectively the 1967 Convention on Outer Space; 1982 UN Convention on the Law of the Sea, Part XI; 1992 UN Framework Convention on Climate Change.

67 IAEA/INFCIRC/321 (1985).

68 UNEP/GC14/25 (1987).

69 UNEP/WG.120/3 (1985).

70 See, eg, 1990 Kuwait Protocol for the Protection of the Marine Environment Against Marine Pollution from Land-based Sources.

71 See now the 1967 Outer Space Treaty and the 1979 Moon Treaty.

72 The USSR had from the start argued in favor of a treaty; Cheng surmises that it agreed to the adoption of a resolution out of concern that any treaty might be vetoed by the US Senate. See Bin Cheng, "United Nations Resolutions on Outer Space: 'Instant' Customary Law?" (1965) 5 Indian J Int L 23, 31, reprinted in Bin Cheng (ed), *International Law Teaching and Practice* (Stevens 1982) 237.

One of the better examples of the confused state of the law that sometimes results from repeated treaty revisions is the 1929 Warsaw Convention Relating to International Carriage by Air.[73] Provided the parties are in agreement, a soft-law resolution, recommendation, or decision can perform the function of interpreting and amplifying a more general treaty text without the need for formal amendment of the treaty.

There are well-known instances of General Assembly resolutions interpreting and applying the UN Charter, including those dealing with decolonization or the use of force.[74] The ILC commentary to what is now Article 31(3)(a) of the Vienna Convention on the Law of Treaties notes that "... an agreement as to the interpretation of a provision reached after the conclusion of the treaty represents an authentic interpretation by the parties which must be read into the treaty for purposes of its interpretation."[75] That agreement does not have to be binding. The ICJ has acknowledged the relevance of soft-law instruments for the interpretation of treaty provisions.[76] Provided they are adopted by consensus, they may constitute either a subsequent agreement on interpretation of the treaty or subsequent practice pursuant to Articles 31(3)(a) and (b) respectively.[77] If the parties subsequently wish to add to or change their previous interpretation or practice they are free to do so by the simple expedient of adopting another resolution. However, there are limits to this possibility. Soft-law resolutions cannot change the object and purpose of a treaty nor can they formally amend it.[78]

Environmental soft law is quite often used to give hard content to the open-textured terms of environmental treaties.[79] UNEP's Goals and Principles of Environmental Impact Assessment[80] have provided guidance for international courts faced with the task of interpreting and applying treaty provisions that mandate the EIA without specifying either the content or the process in any detail.[81] In the *Pulp Mills Case*, for example, Argentina and Uruguay referred the court to the 1992 Rio Declaration on Environment

[73] Richard Gardiner, "Revising the Law of Carriage by Air: Mechanisms in Treaties and Contract" (1998) 47 ICLQ 278.

[74] 1960 Declaration on the Granting of Independence to Colonial Countries and Peoples, UNGA Res. 1514 (XV); 1970 Declaration on Principles of International law Concerning Friendly Relations and Co-operation Among States in Accordance with the Charter of the United Nations, UNGA Res.2625 (XXV). See *Western Sahara, Advisory Opinion* [1975] ICJ Rep 12; *Paramilitary Activities in Nicaragua* [1986] ICJ Rep 14.

[75] ILC, "The Law of Treaties," commentary to Article 27, at para (14), in Arthur Watts, *The ILC 1949–98* (OUP 1999) vol II, 689.

[76] See *Kasikili/Sedudu Island Case* [1999] ICJ Rep 1075–1076, paras 47–51 and the case law cited at para 50. See also Preliminary conclusions by the Chairman of the Study Group on the subject of Treaties over Time, ILC, Report on the work of its sixty-third session (2011), GAOR, Supp No 10 (A/66/10), 281–84.

[77] *Whaling in the Antarctic Case* [2014] ICJ Rep 226, paras 46, 83.

[78] ibid, para 56.

[79] See Paolo Contini and Peter Sand, "Methods to Expedite Environment Protection: International Ecostandards" (1972) 66 AJIL 37; Daniel Bodansky, "Rules vs Standards in International Environmental Law" (2004) 98 Proc AmSIL 275.

[80] UNEP Governing Council decision 14/25 (1987), endorsed by UNGA Res 42/184 (1987).

[81] See *Pulp Mills on the River Uruguay Case* [2010] ICJ Rep 14, paras 203–219; *Advisory Opinion on the Obligations of States Sponsoring Activities in the Area,* 2011 ITLOS, paras 141–150. See also *Border Activities/San Juan River Cases* [2015] ICJ Rep, paras 104 and 153.

and Development, UNEP's 1987 Goals and Principles of Environmental Impact Assessment, and the ILC's 2002 Draft Articles on Prevention of Transboundary Harm. The Court noted that the UNEP Goals and Principles on EIA constitute guidance issued by an "international technical body" and therefore have to be taken into account under Article 41 of the Statute of the River Uruguay.[82] The Court made no specific reference to the ILC draft articles or to the Rio Declaration, but its judgment affirms the legal status of the relevant provisions of both texts.

The advantages of regulating environmental risks in this way are that the detailed rules and standards can easily be changed or strengthened as scientific understanding develops or as political priorities change. They could of course be adopted in treaty form, using easily amended annexes to provide flexibility,[83] but the parties may prefer a more cautious option. It was a resolution of the parties to the Montreal Protocol to the Ozone Convention that first set out the terms of the noncompliance procedure provided for in the Protocol.[84] The procedure was subsequently revised, and once states had become comfortable with the idea, it was then incorporated by amendment as an annex in the Protocol, showing again how non-binding soft law can be transformed into binding form.

3.5 Subsidiary Rules and Standards

Despite their importance as modern instruments of international lawmaking, treaties have the obvious disadvantage that, like all written law, they will become obsolete unless some mechanisms exist to ensure the possibility of subsequent modification and evolution. Moreover, as we noted earlier, some treaties are deliberately expressed in broad or general terms that deprive them of the character of "hard law" in any meaningful sense.[85] Agreements of this kind need to be fleshed out in detail through the addition of protocols, annexes, additional agreements, or soft-law instruments.[86] Because of the ease with which they can be adopted and replaced, soft-law instruments are particularly useful for this purpose.

Sometimes binding force is conferred on soft-law instruments by incorporating them into the terms of a treaty by implied reference. The 1982 UN Convention on the Law of the Sea makes use of this technique, impliedly incorporating recommendations and resolutions of IMO as "generally accepted rules and standards established through

[82] At para 205.

[83] See, eg, the procedures for adopting and amending protocols, annexes, and appendices set out in Article 16 (f) and (g) of the 1973/78 MARPOL Convention.

[84] Decision II/5, UNEP/OzL.Pro/WG.3/2/2, Annex III (1990).

[85] Richard R Baxter, "International Law in 'Her Infinite Variety'" (1980) 29 ICLQ 549–66.

[86] For example, the 1973/78 MARPOL Convention, the 1985 Ozone Convention and the 1992 Climate Change Convention all provide for the adoption of annexes and protocols containing more detailed rules.

the competent international organisation or general diplomatic conference."[87] Thus, although IMO has no general power under its constitution to adopt binding resolutions, UNCLOS may indirectly render some of these resolutions obligatory.

The same is true of IAEA soft law. In performing its nuclear regulatory role, the IAEA has made particular use of formally non-binding standards through its nuclear safety codes and principles.[88] These generally represent an authoritative technical and political consensus, approved by the Board of Governors or General Conference of the Agency. The preamble to the 1994 Nuclear Safety Convention recognizes that internationally formulated safety guidelines "can provide guidance on contemporary means of achieving a high level of safety." Despite their soft-law status, they are directly relevant to interpreting the phrase "appropriate steps" used throughout the 1994 Nuclear Safety Convention to express the general obligation of due diligence.[89] However, in order to further strengthen the nuclear safety regime, the 1994 Convention and the 1997 Joint Convention on the Safety of Spent Fuel and Radioactive Waste Management now incorporate in binding treaty articles the main elements of IAEA's safety standards for nuclear installations, radioactive waste management, and radiation protection, including most of its former Code of Practice on the Transboundary Movement of Radioactive Waste. These various agreements have significantly strengthened the legal force of IAEA standards and, in conjunction with the remaining soft-law standards, have created a more convincing legal framework for the international regulation of nuclear risks. They exemplify how soft law and treaties can interact in a complex regulatory framework.

FAO has also made use of a mixture of hard- and soft-law instruments to promote implementation of the fisheries provisions of the 1982 UNCLOS. The 1993 Agreement to Promote Compliance with Conservation Measures on the High Seas is a binding treaty, but it forms an integral part of the non-binding 1995 Code of Conduct on Responsible Fishing, which is itself further implemented by other measures including the 2001 Plan of Action on Illegal, Unreported and Unregulated Fishing (also a soft-law instrument). Negotiated in the same manner as treaties, and adopted by consensus in FAO,[90] these non-binding "voluntary instruments" are aimed at regional fisheries organizations and the fishing industry as well as states, but in part they also reiterate, interpret, and amplify relevant provisions of UNCLOS and the 1995 UN Fish Stocks Agreement. The 1993

[87] See articles 208–211. On the variety of meanings attributed to the phrase "generally accepted," see Erik J Molenaar, *Coastal State Jurisdiction over Vessel-Source Pollution* (Kluwer 1998) ch 5. For the status of IMO and ILO conventions as "generally accepted international standards" see Mario Valenzuela, in Alfred HA Soons (ed), *Implementation of the Law of the Sea Convention through International Institutions* (Noordwijk aan Zee 1990) 187, and more cautiously, Bernard H Oxman, "The Duty to Respect Generally Accepted International Standards" (1991–1992) 24 NYUJILP 109.

[88] See Boyle and Redgwell (n 15) ch 9.

[89] The preamble to the Nuclear Safety Convention recognizes that internationally formulated safety guidelines "can provide guidance on contemporary means of achieving a high level of safety."

[90] However, some states expressed significant reservations when adopting the Plan of Action: see FAO, *Rept of the Committee on Fisheries*, 24th Session (2001).

Agreement and the 1995 Code were negotiated in parallel with the Fish Stocks Agreement, and all three "can be viewed as a package of measures that reinforce and complement each other."[91] The choice of soft-law instruments can partly be explained by the opposition of some states to binding agreements. Another reason, however, is that they are aimed at regional fisheries organizations and the fishing industry as well as states, and contain some elements that are unlikely to find their way into treaty form. They are also easier to amend or replace than treaties, requiring simply the adoption of another instrument.

These examples all point to the conclusion that the non-binding force of UN soft law can be overstated. In many of the above examples states are not free to disregard applicable soft law: even when not incorporated directly into a treaty, it may represent an agreed understanding of the terms of the treaty or reflect the subsequent practice of the parties to a treaty. Thus, although of themselves these instruments may not be legally binding, their interaction with related treaties can transform their legal status into something more.

4 Conclusion

This short survey points to several conclusions. First, the functions of soft law in the international legal system—and in UN practice—are diverse, but it would be wrong to see the choice of instrument—treaty or soft law—in either/or terms. Non-binding soft law sometimes presents alternatives to lawmaking by treaty; at other times it complements and amplifies treaties, while also providing different ways of understanding the legal effect of different kinds of treaties. But it is inconceivable that modern treaty regimes or international organizations such as the UN could function successfully without resort to soft law.

Second, there are no particular areas of international law where soft law is uniquely appropriate, or uniquely inappropriate. UN practice demonstrates that soft law has perhaps been more significant in the evolution of newer areas of international law, such as human rights, outer space, and environmental protection, and rather less important in international economic law, international criminal law, or the law of the sea, where the legal foundations already existed. That tells us only that soft law is in these instances a lawmaking tool—a means to an end, not an end in itself. It does not tell us that some areas of international law are in some sense "softer" than others.

Third, in deciding whether to use a treaty or a soft-law instrument, or both, much will depend on what is proposed and the context. If the issue involves no more than reaching preliminary agreement pending eventual incorporation in a treaty, the codification and progressive development of existing law, or the interpretation or application of a treaty

[91] G Moore, "The Code of Conduct for Responsible Fisheries" in Ellen Hey (ed), *Developments in International Fisheries Law* (Kluwer 1999) 91–92.

or other rule of law, there is no necessity to go further than soft law. Similarly, in the context of a global or regional regulatory regime, the detailed subsidiary rules and standards do not need to be in treaty form; by virtue of Article 31(3) of the VCLT they are no less binding but are much easier to amend or replace when they are in the form of soft law.

Fourth, the main advantage of adopting rules and principles in soft law form is that the process is simpler, faster, and potentially more inclusive. Once adopted, no ratification is necessary. Whether soft-law instruments have the same effect as a treaty, or any legal effect at all, will depend on the particular instrument and its relationship to customary international law and to specific treaties. But we should not assume that rules adopted in soft-law form are necessarily soft in their legal effects.

Finally, choosing soft-law forms over treaties does not diminish the need for negotiation or consensus. On the contrary, while treaties, protocols, or implementing agreements may limp into force with only partial participation, adopting soft-law principles without consensus support has little, if any, impact on the lawmaking process. That is why they are rarely the product of majority voting. It is also why the voting record for UNGA (UN General Assembly) resolutions matters.

Soft law is not the paradox portrayed in some of the literature. It is the product of an increasingly sophisticated legal system. It needs to be understood, not simply dismissed as something that is not law.

PART II

PRACTICE—SCHOLARLY AND PRACTITIONER ACCOUNTS OF UN TREATY-MAKING

A. INTERNATIONAL PEACE AND SECURITY

CHAPTER 7A

UNITED NATIONS WEAPONS CONTROL TREATIES

BARRY KELLMAN

WEAPONS control[1] was born neither from precedent nor principle but from necessity. Three decades of the most relentless slaughter in human history (1914–1945) brought forth weapons that could wipe out many millions, if not all humanity, in an hour. The new discipline of weapons control emerged from this existential crisis, for if the challenge of controlling weapons was not and is not met, all other human aspirations would be vaporized, poisoned, sickened, or decimated.

The early US-USSR nuclear arms control arrangements (the Hot Line agreements and bans on nuclear testing) were designed to prevent reckless or ill-formed escalation to nuclear holocaust. Later bilateral agreements focused on capping nuclear weapons numbers and characteristics. These agreements highlighted the imperative of "verifiability" as adversaries could manage risks only if they could be certain of each other's adherence to negotiated commitments.

The inevitable spread of weapons technologies and the escalation of regional conflict, however, compelled a global approach sensitive to states' asymmetrical interests, with multilateral institutions that could verify states' compliance with detailed commitments and that could offer dispute resolution mechanisms to ameliorate potential flashpoints for conflict. In recent decades, the threat of criminals' and terrorists' acquisition of exceedingly lethal weapons evoked the need for inter-state cooperation and legal assistance to prevent access to weapons-critical materials and to intercept attacks—a critical priority to this day. To address these dangers, multilateral arrangements were imperative, negotiated and supervised by the United Nations.

[1] The term "weapons control" is used here as inclusive of efforts to restrain the quality and quantity of weapons ("arms control"), to limit the spread of weapons ("nonproliferation"), and to eliminate or dismantle weapons ("disarmament"). The term "weapons control" is also inclusive of formal treaties as well as various types of less formal arrangements.

Weapons control treaties signify that, in a dangerous and anarchic world, security can be enhanced by substituting multilateral agreements for unconstrained procurement, deployment, and transfer of weapons. Most commentators agree that the development and implementation of these treaties has contributed significantly to global security during the past half century, albeit the precise measure of that contribution is unquantifiable.

This chapter focuses on four aspects of weapons control: (1) nonproliferation of nuclear weapons, (2) eradication of chemical and biological weapons, (3) prohibition of unique inhumane weapons, and (4) restriction of the trade in conventional weapons.

1 Nuclear Weapons Nonproliferation

Preventing use of nuclear weapons has been and is humanity's most essential imperative. Nuclear weapons nonproliferation is a pillar of this imperative because the potential spread of nuclear weapons inherently renders strategic threats and conflict more intractable and complicates pursuit of a world free from the risk of absolute annihilation.

The United Nations' role in promoting nuclear nonproliferation treaties manifests two cardinal aspects of weapons control. First, international institutions have a pivotal role in implementing and verifying compliance with treaty commitments. Second is the value of incrementally building a control framework through successively reinforcing treaties.

1.1 The Nuclear Nonproliferation Treaty (NPT)

The foundation for all efforts to curtail the spread of nuclear weapons is the Nuclear Nonproliferation Treaty (NPT),[2] which is based on complementary "bargains." The five states that tested a nuclear device prior to 1967 (the Nuclear Weapons States (NWS)) are entitled to retain nuclear weapons subject to the Article VI obligation to negotiate cessation of the nuclear arms race and pursue global disarmament. All other NPT states parties (the non-nuclear weapons states (NNWS)) may share the benefits of peaceful nuclear power applications but may not receive, manufacture, or otherwise acquire nuclear explosive devices, directly or indirectly. Accordingly, the NWS must share the benefits of peaceful application of nuclear power for civilian purposes, and must not assist, encourage, or induce any NNWS in acquiring nuclear weapons.

According to the United Nations' Statement of Principles issued in the NPT drafting process, the Treaty "should be void of any loop-holes which might permit nuclear or

[2] Treaty on the Non-proliferation of Nuclear Weapons (opened for signature 12 June 1968) 729 UNTS 161 (NPT).

non-nuclear powers to proliferate, directly or indirectly, nuclear weapons in any form."[3] The International Atomic Energy Agency (IAEA), formed long before negotiation of the NPT, was assigned authority to implement safeguards, including declarations and on-site inspections, for NNWS' peaceful nuclear activities for the purpose of deterring diversion of nuclear material for military applications. Under the IAEA's Statute, if a state refuses to grant access to the IAEA for the purpose of carrying out safeguards, the IAEA Board has legal authority to not confirm that there has been no diversion due to the state's refusal to consent to inspections, and, ultimately, report that State's noncompliance to the Security Council.[4] The IAEA Statute and comprehensive safeguards agreements set out the circumstances in which a noncompliance finding should be reached and reported to the Security Council. By correlating compliance with safeguards with "verification" of each NNWS' peaceful nuclear intentions, safeguards serve to transfer questions of compliance with nonproliferation obligations from national military officials to international authorities—a profoundly significant advance of international law.[5]

Yet, the shortcomings of the NPT must be acknowledged. The few NPT non-nuclear weapons states that have pursued a weapons capability, notably Iraq, Iran, and North Korea, exposed a critical flaw in safeguards by developing nuclear weapons programs altogether outside, and thus hidden, from detection. In response, the IAEA approved "complementary" or "extended" access inspections of nuclear and nuclear-related activities.[6] Despite objections to the IAEA's authority to undertake such inspections, Iraq's program came to an end due to Security Council-mandated-inspections, and Iran's program was the subject of the Iran Deal,[7] unanimously approved by the Security Council,[8] which significantly empowered the IAEA to monitor Iran's compliance.

1.2 Protection of Nuclear Material

The Convention on the Physical Protection of Nuclear Material (CCP)[9] addresses the dangers posed by states or non-state actors gaining access to loose or diverted nuclear

[3] United Nations General Assembly (UNGA) Res 2028 (XX) (19 November 1965) UN Doc A/6014 para 2(a).

[4] The Statute of the International Atomic Energy Agency (approved 26 October 1956; entered into force 29 July 1957) 276 UNTS 3. Article III(B)(4) provides: "... if in connexion with the activities of the Agency there should arise questions that are within the competence of the Security Council, the Agency shall notify the Security Council, as the organ bearing the main responsibility for the maintenance of international peace and security."

[5] See generally Barry Kellman, "Enforcing Nuclear Non-Proliferation—The Role of Verification" in Jonathan L. Black-Branch and Dieter Fleck (eds), *Nuclear Non-proliferation in International Law* (MC Asser Press 2016).

[6] Model Protocol Additional to the Agreement(s) Between State(s) and The International Atomic Energy Agency for The Application of Safeguards (September 1997) INFCIRC/540.

[7] Joint Comprehensive Plan of Action (signed at Vienna on 14 July), Relating to the Nuclear Program of Iran, HR 3461, 114th Cong (2015).

[8] United Nations Security Council (UNSC) Res 2231 (20 July 2015) UN Doc S/RES/2231.

[9] Convention on the Physical Protection of Nuclear Material (signed 3 March 1980) TIAS 11080, 1456 UNTS 101.

material to make a crude nuclear weapon or a dirty bomb.[10] States parties agree to protect nuclear material in storage and in international transport by implementing special oversight measures and requiring that all recipient and transfer states abide by such measures. States parties must also cooperate in the recovery of lost or stolen nuclear materials. To prevent, detect, and punish the unlawful taking of such materials, states parties must enact laws to: (1) criminalize acts related to unauthorized transfers, theft, or fraudulent receipt of nuclear material as well as threats to use nuclear material to cause injury or property damage; and (2) to assure prosecution or extradition of offenders.

1.3 Banning Nuclear Weapons Tests

A widely accepted premise of nuclear arms control, going back to the 1960s, is that states seeking to develop nuclear weapons will need to undertake testing of a nuclear device in order to ensure mastery of the many technological challenges associated with nuclear weapons; a ban on nuclear testing renders it more difficult for a state to develop nuclear weapons. Following agreement on indefinite extension of the NPT in 1995, the Conference on Disarmament negotiated a draft Comprehensive Test Ban Treaty (CTBT),[11] but it failed to gain the requisite consensus. In 1996, the UN General Assembly approved a ban on nuclear weapons tests or other nuclear explosions (but not simulated or computer-generated tests). The Treaty creates the International Monitoring System (IMS) and calls for establishment of monitoring stations to detect seismic activity and radioactive materials related to nuclear detonations. The Comprehensive Nuclear Test Ban Treaty Organization (CTBTO) oversees the IMS.[12]

1.4 Regional Bans on Nuclear Weapons

Banning nuclear weapons from certain regions serves to restrict the NWS from deploying weapons into areas belonging to the global commons and diminishes risks that NNWS will respond to regional tensions by acquiring nuclear weapons. Moreover, a number of the treaties establishing nuclear weapons free zones also authorize specialized regional organizations to supervise compliance, reinforcing the IAEA's efficacy.

[10] See generally Barry Kellman, with David S. Gualtier, "Barricading The Nuclear Window: A Legal Regime to Curtail Nuclear Smuggling" [1996] U Ill L Rev 667.

[11] Comprehensive Nuclear Test-Ban Treaty (adopted 10 September 1996) 35 ILM 1439.

[12] In 2016, the U.N. Security Council adopted UNSC Res 2310 (23 September 2016) UN Doc. S/RES/2310 (2016), by a vote of 14 in favor to none against, with 1 abstention (Egypt). The Resolution emphasized "the vital importance and urgency of achieving the early entry into force of the Treaty" and "calls upon all States to refrain from conducting any nuclear-weapon test explosion or any other nuclear explosion and to maintain their moratoria in this regard." The Council encouraged all state signatories to promote the instrument's universality, affirming that its early entry into force would help enhance international peace and security.

The Outer Space Treaty[13] prohibits the placing in earth orbit of any objects carrying nuclear weapons or any other kinds of weapon of mass destruction as well as the installation of such weapons on celestial bodies. This prohibition does not ban nuclear-armed missiles that traverse space without entering into orbit, nor does it restrict ground-based anti-satellite weapons.

The Antarctic Treaty[14] more broadly prohibits any military measures on Antarctica, including establishment of military bases, carrying out military maneuvers or nuclear tests, and disposal of radioactive wastes. Compliance with these prohibitions may be verified that extends to all "stations, installations and equipment... all ships and aircraft or points of discharging or embarking cargoes or personnel in Antarctica."

The Seabed Treaty[15] prohibits states parties from emplacing on the seabed and the ocean floor any nuclear weapons or other types of weapon of mass destruction, or any launching installations, storage, or testing facilities. However, the Treaty does not prohibit emplacement of nuclear weapons on the seabed beneath its 12-mile seabed zone. States parties may verify the activities of other states parties through observation by national technical means, and doubts about compliance may be referred to the Security Council following efforts to resolve those doubts through consultation and cooperation.

In addition to treaties barring nuclear weapons from global commons areas, neighboring states have agreed to declare their region free of nuclear weapons.[16] As these states have not had nuclear weapons, these agreements have not required disarmament but have preserved the non-nuclear status of their regions—an important step in stabilizing regions where proximity has often bred conflict, and where spiraling tensions can impel acquisition of nuclear weapons. By mutually agreeing to forswear nuclear weapons, states signify a willingness to promote regional diplomacy and cooperation in the development and use of peaceful nuclear energy. While these agreements have been separately negotiated through regional processes, the United Nations has encouraged the process by promulgating standards for such zones.[17] However, recurring and arduous efforts to establish a Middle East nuclear-weapons-free-zone have been an abject failure.

[13] Treaty on Principles Governing the Activities of States in the Exploration and Use of Outer Space, including the Moon and Other Celestial Bodies (opened for signature 27 January 1967) 18 UST 2410, 610 UNTS 205.

[14] Antarctic Treaty (signed 1 December 1959) 12 UST 794, 402 UNTS 71.

[15] Treaty on the Prohibition of the Emplacement of Nuclear Weapons and Other Weapons of Mass Destruction on the Seabed and the Ocean Floor, and in the Subsoil Thereof (signed 11 February 1971) 955 UNTS 115.

[16] Treaty for the Prohibition of Nuclear Weapons in Latin America (signed 14 February 1967) 6 ILM 521, 634 UNTS 281 (1969) (Treaty of Tlatelolco); The South Pacific Nuclear Free Zone Treaty (opened for signature 6 August 1985) 24 ILM 1440 (1986) (Treaty of Rarotonga); Treaty on the Southeast Asia Nuclear Weapon-Free Zone (opened for signature 15 December 1995) 35 ILM. 635 (1996) (Bangkok Treaty); The African Nuclear-Weapon-Free Zone Treaty, (opened for signature 11 April 1996) 35 ILM 698 (1996) (Treaty of Pelindaba); Treaty on a Nuclear-Weapon-Free Zone in Central Asia (opened for signature 8 September 2006) UNGA Res 61/88 (18 December 2006) UN Doc A/RES/61/88 (Treaty of Semipalatinsk).

[17] See United Nations Group of Governmental Experts on Regional Disarmament "Study on All Aspects of Regional Disarmament" (1980) UN Doc A/35/416, and UNGA Res 45/58 (4 December 1990) UN Doc A/RES/45/58.

1.5 Recent Initiatives for Nuclear Weapons Nonproliferation and Elimination

Recent United Nations' efforts to advance multilateral nuclear disarmament are deserving of acknowledgment, even though their legal and political significance, at the time of this writing, is unclear. In 2009, the Security Council called upon all states to create the conditions for a world without nuclear weapons. Furthermore, the Conference on Disarmament should negotiate a Treaty banning the production of fissile material for nuclear weapons or other nuclear explosive devices.[18]

In 2016, the Open-Ended Working Group issued its Report "Taking Forward Multilateral Nuclear Disarmament Negotiations" highlighting measures to: reduce and eliminate the risk of accidental, mistaken, unauthorized, or intentional nuclear weapon detonations; additional measures to increase awareness and understanding of the complexity of and interrelationship between the wide range of humanitarian consequences that would result from any nuclear detonation; and other measures that could contribute to taking forward multilateral nuclear disarmament negotiations. The Report further recommended pursuit of "elaborate concrete effective legal measures, legal provisions and norms that will need to be concluded to attain and maintain a world without nuclear weapons."[19]

Most recently, the UNGA adopted the Treaty on the Prohibition of Nuclear Weapons,[20] outlawing nuclear weapons use, threat of use, testing, development, production, possession, transfer, and stationing in a different country. For nuclear-armed nations that choose to join, the treaty outlines a process for destroying stockpiles and enforcing the countries' promise to remain free of nuclear weapons. While all five NPT nuclear weapons states refused to participate in negotiation of the Treaty and have expressly avowed their intention to not sign it, its proponents urge that it will help delegitimize nuclear weapons and strengthen the legal and political norm against their use.[21]

1.6 Summary of Nuclear Nonproliferation Treaties

When the NPT entered into force, there was widespread concern that as many as 30 states would have nuclear weapons by the end of the twentieth century. Such concerns have not materialized. Various states were alleged to have pursued but later abandoned

[18] UNSC Res 1887 (24 September 2009) UN Doc S/RES/1887.

[19] UNGA "Report of the Open-Ended Working Group taking forward multilateral nuclear disarmament negotiations" (2016) UN Doc A/71/371.

[20] Treaty on the Prohibition of Nuclear Weapons (signed 20 September 2017) Chapter XXVI: Disarmament—No. 9 United Nations Treaty Collection. The Treaty was adopted by a vote of 122 countries in favor, 1 opposed (Netherlands), and 1 abstention (Singapore).

[21] For a thorough discussion of "delegitimatization" as part of a strategy to eliminate nuclear weapons, see Nicholas Edward Ritchie, "Pathways to Nuclear Disarmament: Delegitimizing Nuclear Violence" (2016) <http://eprints.whiterose.ac.uk/100665/3/2016_May_OEWG_paper_RITCHIE_5.pdf>.

capabilities for making nuclear weapons. For the vast majority of NNWS subject to safeguards, the nuclear nonproliferation regime has strongly reinforced mutual confidence that security is best pursued without nuclear weapons, enabling devotion of scarce resources to less cataclysmic priorities.

To be fair, however, long-sought objectives of the nonproliferation regime have stalled. Most significant has been the failure to achieve an international agreement to halt or at least restrain the production of fissile material for nuclear weapons or other explosive devices. The UN General Assembly has long made such an agreement a priority as a step toward permanent nonproliferation and eventual nuclear weapons disarmament. But consensus on a fissile material cutoff treaty has not yet been attained.

The larger nonproliferation danger has involved four states not parties to the NPT: India,[22] Israel, North Korea (which was a state party but withdrew from the NPT), and Pakistan. These four states demonstrate the fundamental weakness of UN weapons control treaties: any state can refuse to consent and thereby avoid any legal accountability, leaving humanity with only political and economic options to deal with proliferators.

2 Chem-Bio Disarmament and Nonproliferation

Chemical and biological weapons are traditionally grouped with nuclear weapons as "weapons of mass destruction," but there are important differences. More accurately, chem-bio weapons do not destroy structures but are very effective for indiscriminately killing people, especially unprotected civilians in crowded urban areas. In comparison to nuclear weapons, chem-bio weapons are easier to produce with widely available industrial and scientific materials. Chemical weapons have a long history of use, beginning in World War I and more recently by Iraq under Hussein, by Syria under Assad, and by the Aum Shinrikyo cult. Biological weapons have been developed and deployed by states but not used; their most infamous use was by a nonstate actor in 2001.

The Geneva Protocol of 1925[23] prohibited the first use of chem-bio weapons in international armed conflict but did not ban the production or deployment of such weapons or their use in retaliation for another state's use. The Protocol's shortcomings were addressed first by the Biological Weapons Convention (BWC)[24] and later by the

[22] There have been discussions to amend the NPT to enable India to join as a nuclear weapons state. See A. Vinod Kuma "Reforming the NPT to Include India" (May 1, 2010), Bulletin of the Atomic Scientists <https://thebulletin.org/reforming-npt-include-india>.

[23] Geneva Protocol for Prohibition of the Use in War of Asphyxiating, Poisonous or Other Gases, and of Bacteriological Methods of Warfare (signed 17 June 1925, entered into force 8 February 1928) 26 UST 461, TIAS No 8061.

[24] Convention on the Prohibition of the Development, Production, and Stockpiling of Bacteriological (Biological) and Toxin Weapons, Feb. 25, 1972, 11 I.LM. 309, T.I.A.S. No. 8062, 1013 U.M.T.S. 163 (entered into force Mar. 26, 1975).

Chemical Weapons Convention (CWC).[25] Both Conventions, in contrast to the NPT, are nondiscriminatory; no state party may develop, deploy, or use these weapons, and states that had stockpiles must destroy them. Yet, the BWC and the CWC are very different: the BWC is very brief, setting forth a normative prohibition but without any verification system or any institutional capacity for enforcement; the CWC is by far the lengthiest weapons control treaty, with an exceptionally detailed verification system supervised by the Organization for the Prohibition of Chemical Weapons (OPCW).

2.1 The Biological Weapons Convention (BWC)

Following the bilateral US-USSR decision to abandon their biological weapons programs, the Conference of the Committee on Disarmament (CCD) drafted the BWC, ensconcing into international law, for the first time, a prohibition against an entire class of weapons. No state party may develop, produce, stockpile, or otherwise acquire or retain microbial or other biological agents or toxics that have no justification for prophylactic, protective, or other peaceful purposes. Each state party must safely destroy or divert to peaceful purposes all of its agents, weapons, equipment, and means of delivery. States parties must not develop or acquire biological weapons, but nothing in the BWC restricts research activities, production of biological agents, or testing of biological agents.

Because lethal biological agents have important medical and scientific applications, their possession is prohibited only if the possessor intends to use them as weapons. Although the possessor's intentions might be easily determined after an attack or if biological agents are deployed in munitions, determining a possessor's intentions may be difficult before such obvious signals are manifest. Significantly, biological agents are self-replicating; a small quantity can, in short order, be the seed of a full-blown weapons program.[26]

The BWC, in sharp contrast to the NPT and the CWC, does not specify any verification modalities. Despite revelation of enormous BW stockpiles in the former Soviet Union and in Iraq, efforts to develop a compliance and verification regime failed to materialize in the face of concerns that verification modalities to address nonproliferation of biological weapons would consume substantial resources without effectively assuring that states were not developing BW.

In the face of global opprobrium attached to biological weapons and their limited military value, no state has an overt BW program, nor are there widespread allegations of covert programs. Of far greater concern is the possible development of lethal biological agents by terrorists or criminals.[27] The BWC obligates states parties to "take any necessary

[25] The Convention on the Prohibition of the Development, Production, Stockpiling and Use of Chemical Weapons and on Their Destruction (signed 13 January 1993, entered into force 29 April 1997) 32 ILM 800.

[26] See generally Barry Kellman, *Bioviolence: Preventing Biological Terrorism and Crime* (CUP 2007).

[27] See Barry Kellman, "An International Criminal Law Approach to BioTerrorism" (2002) 25 Harv J L & Pub Pol'y 721.

measures to prohibit and prevent the development...of the agents" for disallowed purposes. However, few states took any significant steps in response to this obligation before the 2001 anthrax attacks in the United States. Since then, efforts to strengthen criminalization of biological weapons development by non-state actors have advanced outside the framework of the BWC.[28]

2.2 The Chemical Weapons Convention (CWC)

Like the BWC, the CWC demands eradication of an entire category of weapons. No state party may use chemical weapons or engage in preparations for such use. It is also prohibited to develop, otherwise acquire, stockpile, or transfer them or assist anyone to engage in prohibited conduct. Existing chemical weapons stockpiles and production facilities must be declared and destroyed according to specified timetables. Each state party may produce and use toxic chemicals only for legitimate commercial or other peaceful purposes.

The CWC establishes a new independent international body, the Organization for the Prohibition of Chemical Weapons (OPCW), empowered to monitor states parties' chemical capabilities and activities and, more broadly, to supervise all aspects of CWC compliance. The OPCW, unlike the IAEA, is not an organ of the United Nations, authorized to make determinations of noncompliance and to impose such sanctions or collective measures as it deems appropriate. The OPCW may bring cases of particular gravity to the Security Council.

In profound contrast to the BWC, the CWC establishes the most far-reaching verification system of all weapons control treaties. Precursor chemicals that could be made into weapons are listed on three "schedules" corresponding to the ease of making a prohibited chemical weapon. On Schedule 1 are chemicals weapons agents or their immediate precursors; states parties may produce them only in very limited quantities. Schedules 2 and 3 list lethal chemicals that have legitimate industrial purposes. States parties are subject to extensive record-keeping and reporting requirements concerning the use, production, and transfer of listed chemicals. Hundreds of private sector enterprises, operating thousands of chemical facilities, must keep records and report their activities to their national governments.

Each state party's declared chemical facilities are subject to "routine" inspections to verify the accuracy of declared information. The number, intensity, and duration of these inspections vary according to the risk to the objectives of the CWC posed by the chemicals at the facility and the activities carried out there. Notably, OPCW inspectors have broader, albeit limited, powers than IAEA inspectors. The CWC also provides for "challenge" pursuant to request by a state party if it has doubts about another state party's compliance. These inspections can happen anywhere and may not be refused by the inspected state.

[28] See, eg, The Interpol Bioterrorism Prevention Programme <https://www.interpol.int/Crime-areas/CBRNE/Bioterrorism> accessed January 21, 2019.

The CWC's focus on private chemical enterprises is due to the simple fact such enterprises produce and control almost all the materials and equipment to make chemical weapons. Thus, by requiring detailed declarations and inspections of each state party's chemical production and trade activities, the CWC represents a significant departure from other efforts to control weapons—notably the NPT—that focus exclusively on state military's weapons production and deployment activities without significantly impacting the rights and interests of private citizens. Because of these impacts, implementation of the CWC has required many states parties to harmonize their CWC compliance obligations with their legal protections against disclosure of confidential business information and unwarranted intrusion of privately owned facilities.[29]

Finally, Article VII of the CWC requires each state party to enact penal legislation to prohibit persons within its jurisdiction from undertaking any activity prohibited to a state party. Moreover, each state party must provide other states parties with the "appropriate form of legal assistance" to investigate suspected CWC violations. Because of threats posed by terrorists and criminals who can far more readily access lethal chemicals than weapons-usable nuclear or biological materials, states must authorize the dedication of law enforcement resources to enforce restraints on the traffic and misuse of chemicals. This extension of weapons control into patrolling, policing, and prosecuting non-state criminality is an unprecedented advance of international law.

It should be noted that the efficacy of the CWC in addressing the use of CW by a state party against its own citizens has been called sharply into question by Russia's vetoes of Security Council resolutions concerning Syria's chemical weapons.[30] Syria's use of CW is the most blatant proof that no weapons control treaty, not even one as detailed as the CWC, can be effectively enforced absent the Security Council's willingness to investigate and perhaps to take action with regard to treaty breaches.

3 Controlling Conventional Weapons Transfers

Despite the fact that conventional arms have taken more lives than all unconventional weapons cumulative, the control of conventional weapons has been neglected because of the broad acceptance of nations' asserted right to have well-armed forces. UN initiatives in this context have not focused on disarmament but on eradicating illicit trafficking in

[29] See Barry Kellman, "The Advent of International Chemical Regulation: The Chemical Weapons Convention Implementation Act" (1999) 25 J Leg 117.

[30] These vetoes include, most recently, draft resolution S/2017/315, which would have opened an investigation into the April 4, 2017, chemical gas attack in Syria; draft resolution S/2017/884, which would have renewed the mandate of the Organization for the Prohibition of Chemical Weapons-United Nations Joint Investigative Mechanism (JIM) for one year; and draft resolution S/2017/970, which would have allowed for further discussions among Council members to consider the future of the JIM.

conventional arms and establishing human rights standards that nations should apply to their authorized arms transfers.

In 2001, the UNGA adopted the Firearms Protocol (FP)[31] to the United Nations Convention against Transnational Organized Crime, calling upon states to criminalize firearms trafficking. The same year, the General Assembly adopted the non-binding *Programme of Action to Prevent, Combat and Eradicate the Illicit Trade in Small Arms and Light Weapons in All Its Aspects* (the PoA) to develop and implement public awareness and confidence-building programs with regard to the consequences of illicitly traded small arms in conflict and post-conflict situations. It recommends that states enact laws to control the production of small arms and their export, import, transit, or retransfer. States are also advised to take legal action against persons and entities engaged in the illicit small weapons trade.

The General Assembly adopted the International Tracing Instrument (ITI)[32] as the basis of a standardized system to improve capacities for tracing a weapon to its source and thereby hold its supplier accountable. The ITT is strengthened by the Interpol International Weapons and Explosives Tracing System (IWETS) as well as by regional initiatives to curtail arms transfers to recipients that use conventional weapons to commit gross human rights violations.

In 2013, the General Assembly adopted the Arms Trade Treaty (ATT)[33] by a supermajority after consensus in the Conference on Disarmament proved unachievable (154 votes in favor to 3 against). The ATT establishes high common standards for regulating the conventional arms trade and for preventing and eradicating the illicit trade in conventional arms, and it propounds two important sets of international obligations. First, states must not transfer conventional weapons in violation of (1) Security Council arms embargoes, (2) if they are used to commit grave international crimes, or (3) if they pose an overriding risk of contributing to violations of human rights or humanitarian law. Second, states must implement legal measures to prevent wrongful diversion of conventional weapons, in other words to combat weapons trafficking.

3.1 Prohibited Conventional Weapons Transfers

The ATT prohibits weapons transfers that violate Security Council embargoes. Accordingly, a state is responsible if weapons from its jurisdiction are transferred to a

[31] UNGA Res 55/255 (8 June 2001) "Protocol against the Illicit Manufacturing of and Trafficking in Firearms, Their Parts and Components and Ammunition, supplementing the United Nations Convention against Transnational Organized Crime (May 31, 2001)" UN Doc A/RES/55/255. See generally: <http://www.unodc.org/unodc/en/firearms-protocol/the-firearms-protocol.html>. UNGA "Report of the Ad Hoc Committee on the Elaboration of a Convention against Transnational Organized Crime on the work of its first to eleventh sessions" (2 November 2000) UN Doc A/55/383.

[32] UNGA Res 58/241 (9 January 2004) UN Doc A/58/241; UNGA "Report of the Open-ended Working Group to Negotiate an International Instrument to Enable States to Identify and Trace, in a Timely and Reliable Manner, Illicit Small Arms and Light Weapons" (27 June 2005) UN Doc A/60/88.

[33] The Arms Trade Treaty (adopted 2 April 2013), UNGA Res 67/234B (11 June 2013) UN Doc 67/234B.

Security-Council-embargoed recipient. Before the ATT, the Security Council's arms embargoes were matters of exclusively political responsibility. After the ATT, a state must consider that prohibited weapons transfers from its jurisdiction are, pursuant to the treaty, its legal responsibility.

Even more far-reaching is the prohibition against transferring arms knowing that they will be used to commit grave international crimes including genocide, crimes against humanity, and war crimes. The ATT's *knowledge* criterion is satisfied whether knowledge stems from the official's own information or information that is publicly available or is brought to the official's attention by an NGO, or even if the circumstances of the transaction are sufficiently unusual to put reasonable officials on notice of a suspicious purpose for a particular transfer. Asserting legal responsibility for supplying weapons used to commit grave international crimes means that to authorize such transfers is to commit an international wrong, and weapons-transferring states are at risk of violating the ATT if authorized transfers of weapons are used horrifically.

The ATT's broadest requirement is that states shall assess all conventional weapons transfers to determine if there is an overriding risk that the weapons will contribute to violations of international human rights or humanitarian law, or to breaches of treaties against terrorism and transnational organized crime. Each state must consider the implications of each weapons transfer and must refuse to export weapons that it determines might pose an overriding risk of proscribed violations. Put negatively, under the ATT, an exporting state cannot deny its legal responsibility for its weapons transfers because, under its export controls, it did not enquire about the risk that the recipient of the exported weapons will use them to violate international law. The defense of willful blindness is no longer available.

3.2 Preventing Diversion

Diversion of conventional weapons—transferring them without official authorization—is estimated to account for as much as 20 percent of all conventional weapons transactions. Global criminal smuggling networks, using flexible routing systems where their shipments can be kept secret and where law enforcement capacities are least challenging, operate in a gray zone of legality. Because such weapons distribution networks are segmented among many states, no one state may have jurisdiction over or responsibility for the criminal enterprise as a whole, and dedication of law enforcement resources to stopping the enterprise often has been seen as a low priority.

The ATT's provisions for combating illicit weapons networks do not cut new ground from the principles promulgated by the FP and the United Nations Programme of Action. More important is that it reinforces the commitment to combating the illicit conventional weapons trade as a matter of humanity-wide interest. It underscores the precept that to stanch the illicit trade in conventional weapons requires enabling law enforcers to detect, interdict, and prosecute incidents of illicit weapons trafficking.[34] Thus, the

[34] See generally B Kellman, "Controlling the Arms Trade: One Important Stride for Humankind" (2013) Fordham Int'l LJ 37.

ATT specifies that when a state party detects a diversion of transferred conventional weapons, it shall take "appropriate measures" to address that diversion through investigation and law enforcement. And states must share information regarding illicit activities and actors in order to prevent and eradicate diversion of conventional arms. The United Nations has established the UN Trust Facility Supporting Cooperation on Arms Regulation (UNSCAR) to work in conjunction with the UN Office of Drugs and Crime, other UN offices, a host of international and regional organizations and NGOs—all seeking to strengthen legal capacities for ensuring that only peaceful and lawfully authorized people have conventional arms.

The ATT should not be viewed as the last initiative in this area. but more aptly as building upon a foundation of hard treaties, soft international guidelines, and webs of interactive commitments that are enhancing law's incremental victory over weaponized violence. Yet, it is undeniable that since the ATT's approval, ongoing arms transfers to several conflict and armed-violence situations around the world are playing an acutely destabilizing role, sustaining and accelerating the misuse of conventional arms.[35]

4 Strengthening IHL Prohibitions on Weapons That Cause Indiscriminate or Unnecessary Harm

International humanitarian law mandates that the use of weapons must be limited to what is necessary and proportional to achieve a military objective. Accordingly, it has long been prohibited to inflict injuries upon noncombatants that are not incidental to military operations or through the use of indiscriminate weapons. Also prohibited are weapons that cause cruel or inhumane suffering. These normative prohibitions support much of weapons control, including chem-bio weapons control discussed previously.

4.1 Convention on the Use of Certain Conventional Weapons (the Inhumane Weapons Convention)

The Inhumane Weapons Convention (CCW)[36] is an umbrella treaty to limit the use of certain weapons considered particularly inhumane. Protocol I prohibits use of any

[35] See Control Arms Secretariat, "Arms Trade Treaty Monitor 2017" (11 September 2017) <http://armstreatymonitor.org/en/wp-content/uploads/2017/09/EN-ATT_Monitor-Report-2017_ONLINE-1.pdf>.

[36] Convention on Prohibitions or Restrictions on the Use of Certain Conventional Weapons Which May Be Deemed to Be Excessively Injurious or to Have Indiscriminate Effects (concluded 10 October 1980, entered into force 2 December 1983) 19 ILM 1523.

weapon that causes injury by fragments too small for X-ray detection in the human body, thereby complicating medical treatment. Protocol II restricts use of mines, booby traps, and other devices in order to curtail civilian casualties caused by these devices during and after hostilities. Such devices may not be used against civilian populations or used indiscriminately so as to cause injuries that are excessive in relation to the anticipated military advantage. Remotely delivered mines are banned unless their location can be accurately recorded or if a neutralizing or self-destruct mechanism can render the mines harmless when they no longer serve their intended military purpose. Protocol III protects civilians from being the direct target of attack from incendiary weapons—weapons that are designed to set fire to objects or to cause burn injury to persons through flame action, heat, or a combination thereof, produced by a chemical reaction of a substance delivered on the target.

4.2 The Mine Ban Treaty

The Mine Ban Treaty[37] prohibits the use, stockpiling, production, and transfer of antipersonnel mines. The Treaty does not cover anti-vehicle or other static explosive devices. States parties must cease production and development of antipersonnel mines and destroy their stockpile of such mines within four years of ratification; each state party should clear all of its mined areas within 10 years of ratification. Moreover, states parties are required to provide assistance to mine victims. Although the Treaty contains no verification mechanisms, several "transparency measures" are mandated, including a requirement that each state party submit a detailed report on compliance-related matters to the Depository, the UN Secretary-General, within 180 days of the treaty's entry into force and annual reports on their implementation activities. Provision is also made for fact-finding missions to clarify any doubts as to a state party's compliance with the treaty. Perhaps the Mine Treaty's most notable accomplishment has been the identification of cleansing of older mine fields, significantly reducing the human toll to innocent persons after the conclusion of conflict.

The process through which the Mine Ban Treaty was negotiated and entered into force deserves attention. In 1996, diplomatic efforts to strengthen the CCW Protocol II failed for lack of consensus, despite widespread support. Thereupon, the UN General Assembly resolved that states should vigorously pursue an international agreement to ban antipersonnel landmines. The Canadian government organized a meeting of pro-ban states outside the formal treaty review process, initiating the "Ottawa Process" and thereby sidestepping the requirement of consensus. The next year, 121 states signed the Treaty, and it entered into force in 1999.

[37] Convention on the Prohibition of the Use, Stockpiling, Production and Transfer of Anti-Personnel Mines and on their Destruction (concluded 18 September 1997), 2056 UNTS 241.

4.3 The Convention on Cluster Munitions

A similar negotiation process led to the Cluster Munitions Convention,[38] which prohibits all use, production, stockpiling, and transfer of cluster munitions—bombs, rockets, and artillery shells that disperse small submunitions over broad areas. Many submunitions fail to explode initially; later, non-combatants might mishandle them causing death or injury. The Convention does not mandate a total ban. Indeed, states may develop cluster munitions that do not cause indiscriminate area effects and the risks posed by unexploded submunitions. Meanwhile, each state party must destroy its stockpile of prohibited cluster munitions within eight years of entry into force, and must clear and destroy remnants located in munition-contaminated areas under its jurisdiction and control within 10 years of becoming a state party. Victims of cluster munitions are entitled to receive medical care, rehabilitation, and psychological support. Like the Mine Ban Treaty, states parties must submit annual reports on their implementation activities to the United Nations Secretary-General.

5 Conclusion

Over the last half century, multilateral weapons control evolved without precedent or foundational principle, not so much a designed series of progressive strategies as much as episodic attempts to curb threats that the spread of lethal technologies could, and too often have, led to unacceptable death and destruction. These treaties were achieved through the United Nations or with its support, albeit negotiated through various processes and promulgating disparate precepts and mechanisms. These weapons control treaties have woven a lattice of norms that undergird international security and thereby have helped nations prevent the types of cataclysm that devastated the first half of the nineteenth century and threatened to end humanity altogether in the last 70 years. As the UN efforts to control weapons have become increasingly intermeshed and complex, methodologies have developed with established institutions and stipulated procedures that influence virtually every state's military choices, significantly enhancing global security. Cumulatively, these treaties serve to lower the risk of war, reduce war's devastation should it begin, and curtail the enormous financial drain of procuring and stockpiling weapons.

It is fair to say that weapons control cannot decisively respond to the conditions that engender war such as conflicts over territory, ideological disagreements, racism and ethnic hatred, strife over access to resources, etc. More modestly viewed, the treaties discussed in this chapter have helped curb proliferation of uniquely dangerous or inhumane weapons, and they have helped stabilize consensus that particular types of weapons

[38] Convention on Cluster Munitions (adopted 30 May 2008), CCM/77, Dublin Diplomatic Conference for the Adoption of a Convention on Cluster Munitions.

should not be militarily deployed. These treaties have enabled humanity to stanch the inherent tendency of employing advancing technologies to make and use more powerful weapons. By significantly contributing to capping centuries of accelerating violence and by restraining how escalating fears of an adversary's weapons can accelerate political friction into armed conflict, these treaties have contributed to building a more secure world order, thereby enabling diplomacy and other processes to help address more deep-rooted social conditions. Indeed, without these treaties, all other peaceful pursuits might not have a chance.

Yet, while these treaties have curtailed the use and proliferation of certain types of weapons, the threat of their use remains, and indeed may be worsening. The entrenched rules of treaty-making allow a few states to avoid widely accepted obligations, retard progress, and rearouse fears that all weapons control efforts will turn to ash. And, looking forward, emerging technologies will soon enable pursuit of a virtually infinite array of weapons types that do not readily fit within the ambit of existing treaties and are therefore unconstrained.

The United Nations deserves considerable credit for the fact that, as of 2017, so much progress in controlling weapons has been made. The achievements of the United Nations in controlling weapons deserve respect. Unquestionably, the careful pronouncement of detailed norms concerning many types of weapons in the possession of many different persons and entities is profoundly progressive. It is perhaps the greatest achievement of these treaties to have fostered trust among the vast majority of states and their populations with regard to lethal weapons, enabling maturation of innumerable initiatives for promoting peace. Nevertheless, it cannot be denied that there are disconnects between the pronouncement of weapons constraints and enforcement of obligations against avowedly recalcitrant states. The current condition of international law makes it difficult to hold accountable states that reject application of these treaties' constraints to them. The continuous, even escalating assertion of "sovereign prerogatives" corrodes pursuit of global de-weaponization and undermines world peace.

Perhaps even more important is that emerging technologies bode weapons that could diminish the threat or reality of armed violence, or could escalate the risks of armed violence, or both. Looking forward, how the United Nations oversees diverse technological domains—for example. outer space, cyberspace, nanotechnology, materials synthesis—will be critical to control of weapons. It is commendable that the United Nations, supported by the world's great universities and institutes, is undertaking studies and enabling vibrant debates about the risks of specific types of weapons. However, there are larger questions about how technological advances should be broadly managed to dampen and constrain armed violence. Tomorrow's weapons control challenges must appreciate yesterday's challenges, but should not replicate, in either process or substance, yesterday's responses to past challenges. The future of UN efforts to control weapons will depend not only on promoting compliance with existing obligations, but also on creating new strategies for addressing emerging capabilities for committing violence. It would be lamentable if succeeding generations pay the price of the United Nations failing to confront tomorrow's threats.

CHAPTER 7B

CREATING FROM CHAOS

practitioner reflections on multilateral treaty-making

DANIËL PRINS*

UNITED Nations treaties come about in formal settings in which heads of delegation read out prepared official statements laced with diplomatic niceties while taking care to avoid—where possible—mention of raw national interests. Once a treaty is agreed, the next step is a solemn signing ceremony that starts the clock ticking toward entry into force. Once ratified by enough states, the treaty will underpin a regime of conferences of states parties, during which the treaty text can only be altered through an elaborate procedure.

At first glance, all this ritual and formality assert that UN processes are governed by predictability, professionalism, and time-tested practice. But from my vantage point, often at the podium of the conference room and also when in the smaller negotiation settings, the treaty-making process seems inherently messy and deeply improvisational. The profound unruliness beneath the veil of stiff behavior originates in the dominance of national sovereignty, which limits any conference president's attempt at firm process management. Meanwhile, many key discussions take place in informal settings beyond the official meeting, as the formal plenary sessions do not lend themselves to dealmaking. Marking the whole is frequent lack of substantive and procedural expertise, usually among quite a number of the delegations, from all continents. Moreover, time pressures grow more acute in the closing days of any treaty-making process.

1 Sovereignty and Consensus

Although national legislation and international treaties are both considered "law," the contrast between their geneses is stark. National lawmaking involves deliberation and the wordsmithing of watertight written formulations that allow for the least possible

* The author is Chief of the Conventional Arms Branch at the UN Office for Disarmament Affairs. He was secretary-general of the 2012 and 2013 United Nations conferences on the Arms Trade Treaty.

margin of interpretation (unless constructive ambiguity is deliberately inserted). Terms are vetted and double-checked, sentences scrutinized and reviewed until they unequivocally reflect what the legislators intend to convey; parliamentarians debate, committees adjudicate, and high offices of state review successive drafts before legislation is adopted. And although the bill may contain compromise language hammered out between parliamentary and other factions, it is the parliamentary vote that separates those in favor of the bill from those against it.

In contrast, multilateral treaty-making is untidy and anarchic. Under the Westphalian arrangement of sovereign states, accession to multilateral treaties remains a national decision. But those advocating a new globally binding code will aim for it to be accepted, as a matter of principle, by as many of the world's nations as possible. They will sacrifice a great deal to make their new norm a universal one. In practice, and contrary to lawmaking by majority, the disagreements between stakeholders (which always exist) need to be bridged *within* the text, because a vote—which would have shown the fault lines between diverse stakeholders—is supposed to be avoided.

This implies that those countries unenthusiastic about the purpose of the proposed treaty or its specific terms enjoy considerable opportunities for mischief and can hold the process ransom for extended periods. As a consequence, conference negotiations can quickly degenerate into exhaustive rounds aimed at identifying elements of compromise. Meanwhile, the legal quality and grammatical clarity of the draft text often suffer: key provisions may fail to garner agreement and will have to be dropped; concepts are frequently diluted with additions of weasel words such as "where appropriate" or "if feasible." Sometimes constructive ambiguity is the only way forward to save a key idea. And, in the end, signatories can disassociate themselves from specific unwanted commitments even when they ratify by expressing "reservations."

As well, in the daily practice of conference diplomacy, delegates often make it clear that they represent sovereign states and as such do not necessarily feel compelled to abide by meeting rules the moment they deem these inconvenient. Time limits on interventions or deadlines for submitting text proposals are often disregarded, as representatives insist their national viewpoints cannot be curtailed. The chairperson, who is supposed to bring some order to the deliberations, remains in practice at the mercy of delegations.

Sometimes national positions cannot be bridged, and the negotiations collapse. Discussions on a legally binding international regulation of anti-vehicle mines during the early 2000s serve as an example of how multilateral talks dissolved when far-apart positions could not be drawn under one narrative. Delivering humanitarian aid is often hampered by such mines. During negotiations, those in favor of a new international instrument asserted that adequate mine clearance requires mines to be detectable, that is, that they be produced containing at least some metal parts. In addition, to diminish civilian casualties, they advocated that these devices should be able to self-deactivate, preventing them from threatening civilians after the cessation of hostilities. But a number of countries producing this weaponry considered their non-detectability a military advantage and saw any requirement to introduce a self-deactivation mechanism as cost-prohibitive. They thus maintained that a legally binding instrument on such mines was "premature."[1] Negotiations ceased when it became obvious to the initiators that the draft text had become devoid of any significant measure beyond voluntary national regulation.

Under the consensus principle, naysayers rule as kings. To try keeping them on board is time-consuming and a constant threat to the quality of the end product.

2 Informality

UN treaty negotiations form intriguing material for anthropologists. Hundreds of delegates—fully aware they serve their national tribes foremost—come together for a multi-week group process in which they are expected to interact intensely in order to forge an outcome binding their respective constituencies to new policy.

The great scholar of diplomatic history and practice, Ernest Satow, asserted that diplomacy is "the application of intelligence and tact to the conduct of official relations,"[2] underscoring how crucial an international negotiator's character and skills are for a state's effective participation in conference diplomacy.[3] Mostly, a government's instructions ("from capital") to its representatives provide the outline of national objectives. But the final treaty text is shaped by individual displays of tactical acumen, rhetorical ability, tenacity, nerve, and a creative understanding of how internationally agreed procedures can work best for the national interest.

Nevertheless, even the most professional and persuasive of conference participants will find the UN a challenging venue in which to convince others to change their positions. The organization's rules-based setting initially provides a shared sense of procedural predictability, which can, to a degree, shield from brazen power play by dominant nations. But sitting behind a country nameplate in the official plenary meetings inhibits delegates from forming relationships needed to build acceptance for their ideas. This explains why experienced representatives are keen to constantly develop pockets of informality within the formal framework, in which they can build the trust needed for recognition of at least some of their priorities.

For those delegates aiming to create informal meeting situations where partnerships can be built, perhaps yielding only a single paragraph, the first step is to get acquainted with a good number of the conference participants. The diversity in cultural backgrounds, languages, political systems, and economic development makes that a challenge, as does

1 The *United Nations Disarmament Yearbook 2006*, vol 31, 115.

2 Ernest Satow, *A Guide to Diplomatic Practice* (Calcutta: Longmans, Green and Co,1917), quoted in Bhagevatula S Murty, *The International Law of Diplomacy. The Diplomatic Instrument and World Public Order* (Springer Netherlands 1989) 1.

3 See also Tom Fletcher, *The Naked Diplomat* (Harper Collins 2017) 102: "(T)he most important diplomatic skills can be distilled to tact, curiosity, courage and the ability to get on with anyone and eat anything."

the sheer number of participants. Permanent delegation staff struggle to maintain collegial bonds with the other 200-odd delegations, up to a third of whom annually rotate away from the UN. And those joining the conference as experts from capitals have had even less opportunity to build a working relationship with the majority of international colleagues. Clearly, a UN treaty conference—with its interpersonal unfamiliarity and cultural miscellany—is anything but an ideal setting for trade-offs, with very particular skill sets and personal networks of connection needed for effective multilateral negotiating.

To forge coalitions that add value, a delegation needs to look beyond its country's longer-standing strategic partnerships. In this setting it might be better to downplay those well-established bonds, as these only emphasize group affiliation, whereas it could pay to display a more open interest in the topic. To champion the broadest common global good, one's ad hoc coalition would preferably be cross-regional. Such outreach is an intricate affair. The potential partner country or countries need to be convinced of the returns from committing to a passing partnership as against its longer-term strategic environment: the certainties of being embedded in, for example, the African Union, the League of Arab States, ASEAN, or NATO.

The president of a conference may also seek opportunities for informality, in particular to move discussion away from listening to the well-known official positions while the clock is ticking. When negotiations became difficult during the 2012 Conference on the Arms Trade Treaty at UN headquarters in New York, the presiding ambassador asked me if the UN Secretariat could set up a makeshift meeting space for informal discussions among a hundred or so delegates *outside* of the conference chamber but inside the UN premises—preferably a UN lounge area.

Despite the difficulties involved in setting this up, including those of inconvenience to other UN delegates, altered security arrangements, and costs estimated at over $60,000, we understood the astuteness of this request. The president had deemed the customary "formal informal" setting in a 600-seat meeting room not informal enough: it was also the vast size of the room, the elevated massive desk visually separating the president from the delegates, and the country nameplates implying that the president may not personally know those requesting the floor, which could inhibit frank exchange. In the improvised negotiation space we were able to establish, a chair was provided for the conference president not behind but beside a small table (with UN Secretariat staff nearby), so that he could interact with those present more conversationally. This alternative choreography functioned for days, and allowed the treaty to take further shape.

Although informality is vital for making progress in treaty-making conferences, one should be aware that quite a number of participants may *not* proactively pursue the encountering of foreign colleagues. Some delegates represent governments that are for their own reasons not interested in the progress that a majority of states advocate. Their task is more oriented to damage limitation than toward facilitating creative ways forward. Others may not engage due to the absence of a national position. Or instructions may have not reached the delegation: for quite some countries a smooth chain of communications between government entities and the state's permanent representation at the UN is a daily challenge. Alternatively, limited language skills or a lack of negotiating expertise can contribute to a sense of intimidation by the conference setting. On the whole, the energetic search for informal bonding which some delegations display, may be met by a more detached approach by others.

Those delegates from countries in favor of a new treaty who are able to shift seamlessly between the formal and the informal, mostly are the ones who dominate negotiations. On the formal side, they find ways to use the rules of procedure to their benefit, as well as displaying a keen sense of optimal timing for key interventions in open debate. And when informality is required, they will have already established the personal contacts needed to cultivate empathy and understanding, recognizing the value of being on civilized terms even with their most committed opponents.

The frequent switch from formal to informal negotiations in multilateral treaty negotiations adds to the sense of unpredictability and chaos, sometimes helpfully, sometimes not. And the disarray is exacerbated by the sometimes surprisingly limited expertise of participants combined with the relentless time pressure toward the end of a conference.

3 Skills and Means

Regarding the resources available to national delegations, quantitative as well as qualitative factors play a role. For treaty negotiations—more consequential for domestic politics than most other UN meetings—various countries add experts from their capitals to their team of resident diplomats: from sectoral experts and legal professionals to roving ambassadors and parliamentarians. In particular legal experts are often the only ones with knowledge of precedent and of the wide array of possible textual options. They can make a significant difference in effectiveness and influence during negotiations, as only a few generalist diplomats have prior experience with negotiating multilateral treaty texts.

Thus, the quality rather than the size of a delegation matters most. Intrinsic to this is how well a country can prepare its negotiators for the high-pressure, bazaar-like environment of treaty conferences. Are civil servants recruited on the basis of merit? Do they have good knowledge of the subject matter? And are they aware that it is their mastery of the multilateral process, even more than the subject matter, that will yield results for their government?

Of course, effective multilateralism is not only a matter of individual competencies. Effective governments provide comprehensive instructions taking into account the interests of all relevant government agencies, while allowing their diplomats negotiating leeway. They view their delegation as capable enough that it can be trusted to explore avenues that have not yet been thought of, and to follow up on new developments in ways congruent with the national interest. The confidence of one's capital is of particular value in the feverish days close to the conference's finishing line when it becomes progressively more unrealistic to obtain new instructions from "back home" in a timely manner. But numerous national systems do not encourage diplomatic initiative and agency within their own workforce. Having limited room for maneuvering, such delegations can play only a marginal role in the gestation of a treaty.

4 Time Pressure

Conferences are costly. A multilateral meeting at the UN comes with a price tag easily exceeding $50,000 per day, paid by assessed contributions. Flying in and accommodating one's national delegation adds to the costs for each country. Those governments not keenly interested in the topic, as well as those who owe the largest shares of the UN budget, often resist proposals for lengthy negotiation conferences. The alternative of rich countries picking up the conference costs outside of the regular UN budget is not broadly supported, as it opens the way to an international agenda mainly set by those nations eager to highlight favorite causes and able to pay for them. Extending the debates into the nights and the weekends was largely banned decades ago, because of the exorbitant costs involved (including interpretation into multiple languages). All in all, time set aside for negotiations is kept to a minimum, resulting in severe time pressures during the final laps of a conference.

However, extending its duration would never fully solve the messiness of a treaty conference's endgame. Progress in negotiations is inevitably slow, because the urgency is never shared by all, and because uncomfortable showdowns are postponed. Endgames of treaty negotiations grow into a confused scramble for agreement by the last Friday of the conference regardless of their duration.

Another complicating element in this chaotic rush toward the finish, is the use of the UN's six official languages. Successive drafts of the treaty text are circulated in translation, but in the final days and hours of the process, when the chairperson may churn out a barrage of new formulations for the most contested paragraphs, top-quality, faultless on-the-spot translation becomes an impossibility. At this point, the English version typically is taken, temporarily and unofficially, as the sole authoritative version. But formal adoption of the treaty at the conference's end needs to be carried out in all six languages, however unpolished some of those versions may be.

After a treaty's adoption within the UN, inaccuracies in the rushed translations need to be ironed out, in order for the treaty's six language versions to be accepted as equally authoritative. The presiding ambassador overseeing adoption usually has no mandate to continue that task; therefore, it falls to the UN Secretariat to tie up post-adoption loose ends. In the case of the Arms Trade Treaty, this task fell to my unit within the Office for Disarmament Affairs.

The first post-adoption step was the final polishing of the English text, whereby UN editors screened it, proposing corrected terminology, grammar, syntax, and punctuation. My office only accepted those text improvements that did not alter the meaning of a sentence.

This can sometimes result in the survival of a linguistically questionable formulation. Consider the superfluous comma in this sentence from the ATT's Article 13.1 on national reporting: "Reports shall be made available, and distributed to States Parties by the Secretariat." During the endgame of negotiations, we had advised the President to *insert* this comma. The punctuation allowed for an interpretation of the paragraph that would otherwise have been impossible. Without the comma, the future ATT Secretariat would not have had a mandate to make national reports public. The comma introduced sequencing of two distinct propositions: first to make the national reports (publicly) available, and subsequently to distribute them to the authorities of ATT States Parties. In the post-adoption editorial process this comma—never needed from a syntax point of view—survived, because the wordsmithing *and* the editing need to serve the objectives of the process, not complicate or vitiate them.

After the English version was completed the others were tackled. Obviously, translating is not a binary process of replacing terms from one language with those of identical meaning in the other five. To translate is to interpret. And where there is room for interpretation, there is room for maneuvering. In diplomacy this means that some delegations will see the translation process, even after adoption of the treaty, as a continued opportunity to further their interests.

Official UN regulations basically skip over this issue. The practice is that "a comparison of the authentic texts precedes the physical work of collating the articles, arranging their layout and checking the texts."[4] But how is this undertaken? Who is involved?

In the case of the ATT, having concluded the editing of the English version, an invitation was then sent to all permanent delegations to attend translation comparison meetings. A separate meeting was held for each of the six languages, with all countries welcome in each discussion. Only a few delegates showed up.

Nevertheless, linguistically different versions can prove highly relevant politically. In 1967, UN Security Council Resolution 242 had mentioned Israeli withdrawal "from occupied territories"—not necessarily meaning all territory. Leaving out the definite article "the" was a conscious choice of the British drafters of the resolution, as it would leave room for further negotiations.[5] The French version mentioned "retrait des territoires occupés" ("from *the* territories"), which basically meant all of them. "When the French text appeared, the British and American governments raised the matter at once with the United Nations Secretariat, and with the French government, only to be told that the French language offered no other solution for the problem.... [N]one of the people involved could think of a more accurate French translation."[6]

[4] United Nations "Summary of Practice of the Secretary-General as Depositary of Multilateral Treaties. Prepared by the Treaty Section of the Office of Legal Affairs" (New York, 1999) UN Doc ST/LEG/7/Rev.1, para 40 p 11.

[5] Lord Caradon et al, *UN Security Council Resolution 242—A Case Study in Diplomatic Ambiguity* (Georgetown University 1981); Dean Rusk, *As I Saw It* ([Norton 1990) 389.

[6] Eugene V Rostow, "The Illegality of the Arab Attack on Israel of October 6, 1973" (1975) 69(2) The Am J Intl Law 69 (2) 272, 285.

The Arms Trade Treaty also had a number of translation issues with potential or real political significance, showing that the case of the above-mentioned Security Council resolution was likely far from unique. The best example may have been the Russian translation of Article 6. The article prohibits an exporting country from authorizing an arms transfer if it "has knowledge" at the time of authorization that these weapons will be used in the commission of war crimes.

Russian negotiators asserted that in Russian, "knowledge" could be translated in two ways. If the Russian text would use "izvestno," it would merely mean "information." Would an outcry from an NGO count as "knowledge," forcing the government to refuse an export license? Would a local newspaper article be enough to prohibit a deal? Better to use "dostovernym znaniyem," which would be a translation of "knowledge" truly conveying a sense of factual solidity.

The Russian delegation had brought this up during the last days of treaty negotiations, in the plenary meeting. No one had objected. The Russian-language draft treaty text was changed to that effect.

When a week later the treaty was adopted, and the process of comparing translations started, some permanent representations asserted that the Russian translation of "knowledge," when translated back into English, would read "credible knowledge." The agreed English version did not include the "credible"—so shouldn't only the last word from "dostovernym znaniyem" be retained? But the Russian delegation explained that in Russian the two words go hand in hand to explain "knowledge," and it underscored that this interpretation had gone unchallenged during negotiations. The Russian translation was not changed.

Earlier, the significance of the comma in Article 13.1 was mentioned, permitting an interpretation that the ATT Secretariat can make national reports public. To confuse matters further, this comma never found its way into some language versions, as comma usage differs across languages. This leaves us with a curious situation: the UN treaty text is equally authentic in all six languages, which means a state party can correctly insist that the official language version of its choice is valid—but other states can do the same for the versions they prefer.

Translations provide wiggling room. A treaty's translations correction process constitutes a little-known post-factum extension of the negotiations, at which points may still be scored by countries unhappy with some of the treaty's agreed formulations.

5 Wrapping Up

The chaotic manner in which multilateral treaties are produced is a surprise to many first-time observers. The main cause of the unsettling conditions of negotiation is the overriding importance for most states of their national sovereignty, resulting in representatives taking care of domestic interests foremost. Finding shared common ground may be widely admired as a principle, but treaty-making is in practice pursued as a function of state concerns.

Bringing complete order to this process is not possible. Disinterest in the topic within some governments, limited preparation by delegations, the enduring need for informal talks in order to make real progress, individual skill gaps, constant communication errors between delegations and their capitals, and restrictions on time and resources prevent the process from playing out in a well-planned, methodical way.

From the messiness of it all, there is, however, a cardinal takeaway: treaty-making may be seen on the surface as a ceremonial and bureaucratic procedure, but its nervous system is playful, spirited, and profoundly creative. As UN conferences do not follow a linear, predictable process toward their outcome, the quality of the end result depends largely on the conceptual and linguistic ingenuity, and resourcefulness, of individual players—including those serving the negotiations as their secretariat.

CHAPTER 8A

TERRORISM

PIERRE KLEIN

TREATIES have been a recurrent tool to which states have had recourse in their efforts to combat terrorism at the international level, but with mixed success. The first attempt was extremely ambitious. In 1937, a convention for the prevention and punishment of terrorism was adopted under the auspices of the League of Nations. It sought to criminalize terrorism globally, supplemented by another convention that provided mechanisms for prosecuting terrorists before an international criminal court. The project proved to be a failure; the treaties never came into force, ratified only by a single state.

In the aftermath of the Second World War, states opted for a more modest (and more focused) approach, with the development of so-called sectional conventions, covering specific areas then affected by activities characterized as "terrorist." These, too, are typical instruments of international criminal law, criminalizing certain conducts on the one hand and providing for their prosecution, on the other. Several of them were drafted and adopted under the auspices of the United Nations, but a significant number were also adopted under the auspices of specialized agencies (notably the International Civil Aviation Organization and the International Maritime Organization).

This chapter will focus on the former. It will first examine the role played by UN political organs—mostly the General Assembly—in the adoption of these conventions and in the development of a UN treaty-based system for the fight against terrorism. The contents of "sectional" conventions and the duties they create for states parties shall then be analyzed. Finally, an account will be given of attempts at establishing a more comprehensive regime for the prevention and punishment of terrorism within the UN.

1 The General Assembly

As international treaties, the conventions adopted under the auspices of the UN are first and foremost the product of state action and may not be equated with institutional acts adopted *by* an international organization.[1] They are negotiated by states and come into

[1] For more on this, see, eg, Philippe Sands and Pierre Klein, *Bowett's Law of International Institutions* (6th edn, Sweet & Maxwell 2009) 280ff.

effect only upon ratification by states, following the same procedures as are applicable to any other international treaty. This is not to say, however, that the elaboration process of some of these instruments—notably the most recent—has not been characterized by a clearly "institutional" dimension. Two such institutional aspects may be pointed out here: what could be termed the "pre-normative role" assumed in certain areas by the UN General Assembly on the one hand, and the creation of structures tasked with the preparation—and sometimes the drafting—of some instruments, on the other.

The UN General Assembly has been dealing with the issue of terrorism since the 1970s. While its early involvement was mostly focused on the causes of international terrorism, it started to deal more specifically with actions required from states in order to fight terrorism as from the mid-1990's.[2] Resolution 51/210 of 1996, in particular, emerges as a significant milestone in that respect. Entitled "Measures to eliminate international terrorism", it provided that states should:

> accelerate research and development regarding methods of detection of explosives and other harmful substances that can cause death or injury [and] undertake consultations on the development of standards for marking explosives in order to identify their origin in post-blast investigations [...][3]

or should take "appropriate domestic measures" to "prevent and counteract [...] the financing of terrorists and terrorist organizations."[4] And, in more general terms, the Declaration appended to the resolution provided that:

> States are encouraged, when concluding or applying extradition agreements, not to regard as political offences excluded from the scope of those agreements offences connected with terrorism which endanger or represent a physical threat to the safety and security of persons, whatever the motives which may be invoked to justify them.[5]

By inviting states to take measures against the use of explosives for terrorist purposes or against the financing of terrorism, the General Assembly obviously paved the way for the preparation and adoption of the two treaties that were to deal specifically with these issues shortly thereafter.[6] As for the exclusion of the "political offense" exception to extradition when it comes to acts of terrorism, it found its way in all the conventions

[2] See, eg, Pierre Klein, "Le droit international à l'épreuve du terrorisme" in *Collected Courses of the Hague Academy*, vol 321, 310ff.

[3] A/RES/51/210 of 17 December 1996, para 3(b).

[4] A/RES/51/210 of 17 December 1996, para 3(f).

[5] Para 6 of the "Declaration to Supplement the 1994 Declaration on Measures to Eliminate International Terrorism," appended to the resolution.

[6] 1997 Convention for the Suppression of Terrorist Bombings and 1999 Convention for the Suppression of the Financing of Terrorism respectively.

later adopted under the auspices of the UN in this area.[7] To that extent, it certainly does not seem excessive to identify the Assembly's role as "pre-normative."

This is fully in line with the Assembly's function, under the UN Charter, to encourage "the progressive development of international law and its codification."[8] It stands in stark contrast with what has often been described as the interference of the UN Security Council in the traditional norm-making process when it adopted Resolution 1373 (2001) a few years later. The Security Council indeed incorporated numerous provisions of the 1999 Convention for the Suppression of the Financing of Terrorism in Resolution 1373 (2001), which was adopted under Chapter VII. This had the effect of making these provisions instantly binding for all member states, whether they were parties to the 1999 Convention or not. For many observers, this amounted to the exercise of truly "legislative" powers by the Council, in the sense that the scope of the resolution was not limited to a particular situation or in time and the obligations flowing from the resolution were enunciated in general and abstract terms.[9] Such acts go beyond the provisions and spirit of the UN Charter, since the Security Council's role was never conceived as that of an international lawmaker.[10] This however did not prevent the Council from making further use of such powers on later occasions—although exceptionally, and always in the context of the fight against terrorism.[11] In comparison with the normative role thus played by the Security Council in this area, the involvement of the Assembly in the normative process that led to the adoption of several conventions aimed at combating terrorism certainly proved less controversial.

Further evidence of the discrete role of the Assembly is seen in a second aspect of the action it undertook: the creation of specific structures aimed at stimulating and facilitating the normative process. Hence, in Resolution 51/210, the Assembly not only assumed the "pre-normative" role referred to earlier, but it also decided to establish an ad hoc committee. The committee's mandate included the preparation of a convention for the suppression of terrorist bombings and, subsequently, of a convention for the suppression of acts of nuclear terrorism.[12] Such mandate was thereafter extended to the elaboration of a draft convention on the suppression of terrorist financing[13] and of a comprehensive convention on international terrorism.[14] While the elaboration of the latter instrument gave rise to serious difficulties,[15] the ad hoc committee most effectively carried out its mandate and played a decisive role in the swift elaboration of the three "sectional" conventions that have just been mentioned.

[7] See Section 2.2 of this chapter.

[8] Charter of the United Nations, Article 13(1)(a).

[9] See, eg, Pierre-Marie Dupuy, "La Communauté internationale et le terrorisme" in SFDI, *Les nouvelles menaces contre la paix et la sécurité internationales* (Pedone 2004) 36; J Alcaide Fernandez, "La 'guerra contra el terrorismo': un 'OPA hostil' al derecho de la communidad internacional?" [2001] Revista Espanola de Derecho Internacional 297.

[10] See, eg, Jochen A Frowein and Nico Krisch, "Comment to Article 39" in Bruno Simma (ed), *The Charter of the United Nations—A Commentary* (2nd edn, OUP 2002) 709.

[11] See in particular Resolution 1540 (2004) (weapons of mass destruction) and 2178 (2014) (foreign fighters).

[12] A/RES/51/210 of 17 December 1996, para 9.

[13] A/RES/53/108 of 8 December 1998, para 11.

[14] A/RES/54/110 of 9 December 1999, para 12.

[15] See Section 3 of this chapter.

2 "Sectional" Conventions

Like most treaties dealing with international criminal matters, the conventions adopted under the auspices of the UN to counter terrorism follow the same basic structure: they criminalize specific activities or conducts (states must define these as criminal offenses in their domestic legal order); they establish the jurisdiction of domestic courts and tribunals for the prosecution of such activities or conducts; and they ensure that punishment is made possible by cooperation between states (including by the means of extradition).

The various aspects of the regime thus established by these conventions shall be examined in turn, with a focus on the criminalized acts, the obligations incumbent upon states parties, and, ultimately, on the scope of the conventions.

2.1 Criminalized Acts

Significant developments may be observed over time as far as the acts being criminalized are concerned, following to a large extent the evolution of methods used by terrorists or terrorist groups. In that sense, it may be said that the elaboration of the conventional framework to counter terrorism has most often been reactive, even though more preventive actions were also taken on some occasions—the 2005 Convention for the Suppression of Acts of Nuclear Terrorism being a prime example. However, it should be noted at the outset that the terrorist dimension of the activities that were criminalized in the conventions was initially merely alluded to (hence, a reference is made to "international terrorism" in the preamble of the 1979 Convention Against the Taking of Hostages, but none in the definition of the offense itself in Article 1) or altogether absent (this is particularly visible in the conventions adopted under the auspices of ICAO (International Civil Aviation Organization) and IMO (International Maritime Organization)). It was, in other words, not an element of the offense and those treaties could equally have been applicable in situations where mere "ordinary" criminal activities were at stake. As far as the treaties adopted under the auspices of the UN are concerned, the focus on acts of terrorism became more explicit only later on (from 1997 onward).

The protection of means of transportation quickly emerged as a main concern following a string of hijackings and other attacks carried out since the 1960s by terrorist groups against airplanes and—later—ships. This led to the adoption of several sectional conventions aimed at criminalizing such activities, under the auspices of two UN specialized agencies—the ICAO and the IMO.[16] These however do not come within the

[16] ICAO: 1963 Convention on Offences and Certain other Acts Committed Aboard Aircrafts, 704 UNTS 219 (amended by a 2014 Protocol; not yet in force as of January 10, 2019); 1970 Convention for the suppression of the unlawful seizure of aircrafts, 860 UNTS 105; 1971 Convention for the Suppression of Unlawful Acts against the Safety of Civil Aviation, 974 UNTS 178 (and 2010 Supplementary Protocol);

scope of this analysis and shall not be detailed here. It may simply be said that these instruments display the same structure as the one described earlier, and that the early conventions adopted under ICAO largely provided the pattern for conventions that were later adopted under the auspices of the UN to counter international terrorism.

Within the UN itself, attention first focused on the protection of state representatives, with the adoption of the 1973 Convention on the Prevention and Punishment of Crimes against Internationally Protected Persons, including Diplomatic Agents.[17] This instrument criminalizes various acts of violence against representatives of states or of intergovernmental organizations, without making reference to the particular terrorist dimension of such acts.[18] The focus was later extended to the protection of individuals, irrespective of a possible official capacity, with the adoption in 1979 of the—abovementioned—Convention against the Taking of Hostages.[19] Here too, as noted previously, the offense is defined without any express reference to terrorist activities, but it is nonetheless worth mentioning that the convention specifically targeted the taking of hostages "in order to compel [...] a State, an intergovernmental international organization, a natural or juridical person or a group of persons, to do or to abstain from doing any act."[20] This introduces a notion of coercion that will resurface in later instruments as an element of definition of terrorist activities. Under both conventions, attempts to commit the criminalized acts, or participation in such acts, are also included in the scope of the offense.

As exposed earlier, it is not before close to another 20 years that the production of international conventions aimed at countering terrorism received a new impetus within the UN. The late 1990s to early 2000s proved to be a most productive period in that regard, with the adoption of no less than three such conventions. But while the adoption of the 1997 Convention for the Suppression of Terrorist Bombings[21] has undeniably been prompted by the fact that "terrorist attacks by the means of explosives [...] have become increasingly widespread"—as its preamble expresses it—it is still remarkable that it criminalizes the use of explosive devices under particular circumstances and conditions without any specific reference to the terrorist dimension of such acts, or to the intention of the perpetrators (in particular, provoking fear among a civilian population or compelling a state or an international organization to do or abstain from doing something, which emerge in other conventions as elements of definition of terrorist

1988 Protocol for the Suppression of Unlawful Acts at Airports serving International Civil Aviation, 1589 UNTS 474; 2010 Convention on the Suppression of Unlawful Acts Relating to International Civil Aviation (ICAO Doc. 9960).

IMO: 1988 Convention on the Suppression of Unlawful Acts against the Safety of Maritime Navigation and Protocol on the Suppression of Unlawful Acts against the Safety of Fixed Platforms Located on the Continental Shelf (and 2005 Protocols), 1678 UNTS 201.

17 1035 UNTS 167; in force 20 February 1977; 180 states parties as of 10 January 2019.

18 Article 2 of the Convention.

19 1316 UNTS 204; in force 3 June 1983; 176 states parties as of 10 January 2019.

20 Article 1 of the Convention.

21 2149 UNTS 256; in force 23 May 2001, 170 states parties as of 10 January 2019;] see generally Samuel M. Witten, "The International Convention for the Suppression of Terrorist Bombing" (1998) 92 AJIL 774ff.

activities). The "terrorist dimension" of the offense is merely evidenced by other elements of the convention (its title and abovementioned preambular paragraph, in particular). It could therefore be argued that this instrument could also be applicable in situations where the acts it criminalizes are committed without any relation to terrorist activities. The same could arguably be said—in spite, here too, of its very title—of the 2005 Convention for the Suppression of Acts of Nuclear Terrorism.[22]

This approach was obviously not possible in the 1999 Convention for the Suppression of the Financing of Terrorism,[23] where a nexus with terrorist activities was clearly necessary, since it was only when they contributed to such activities that financial operations were to be made illegal. Article 2 thus criminalizes the provision or collection of funds "with the intention that they should be used or in the knowledge that they are to be used" in order to carry out any

> act intended to cause death or serious bodily injury to a civilian, or to any other person not taking an active part in the hostilities in a situation of armed conflict, when the purpose of such act, by its nature or context, is to intimidate a population or to compel a government or an international organization to do or to abstain from doing any act.

One may find here the two elements that constitute the major components of most definitions of terrorist offenses: causing—or intending to cause—serious material damage on the one hand (although this is limited here to physical damage and does not extend to damages to property or infrastructures) and doing so with a specific intent (provoking fear or coercing a state or an international organization), on the other hand. Here again, a number of behaviors that are closely related to the offense of financing of terrorism are also criminalized. This includes the attempt to commit the offense,[24] the participation in the offense as an accomplice, the organization or direction of such activities, or the contribution to the commission of the offense.[25]

2.2 Obligations on States Parties

Whereas the specific object of the various conventions examined here is very different, all are conceived following a similar structure. While these treaties are first and foremost instruments of international criminal law, aimed at ensuring the punishment of the offenses they define, they also emphasize the duty of states parties to undertake actions that would contribute to the prevention of the activities at stake.

[22] 2220 UNTS 89; in force 7 July 2007, 114 states parties as of 10 January 2019.

[23] 2178 UNTS 197; in force 10 April 2002, 188 states parties as of 10 January 2019; see generally Ilias Bantekas, "The International Law of Terrorist Financing" (2003) 97 AJIL 315–33.

[24] Article 2(4).

[25] Article 2(5)(a), (b), (c) respectively.

2.2.1 *Prevention*

Obligations of prevention are provided for in all of the conventions adopted under the auspices of the UN to counter terrorism. These obligations take different forms. They include, for instance, the transfer of information concerning the preparation of the offenses mentioned in the conventions, and the prohibition of illegal activities of persons or groups that are likely to be involved in the preparation of acts criminalized under the conventions.[26] Obligations of prevention are even more significant under the 1999 Convention for the Suppression of the Financing of Terrorism, where they include a number of measures to be taken by states parties in relation to the functioning of financial institutions and the control of financial transactions.[27] Such obligations of prevention are grounded in the basic duty of due diligence, whose importance has often been recalled by UN organs in the specific area of the fight against terrorism.[28]

But beyond this, the conventions adopted under the auspices of the UN to counter terrorism organize a regime aimed at ensuring the maximum efficacy of punishment of the acts they criminalize, through prosecution or extradition.

2.2.2 *Prosecution*

As far as prosecution is concerned, the conventions may be said to organize a "division of labor" between international law and domestic legal orders. Indeed, while international law provides the basis for criminalization, with the identification and definition of the offenses, the prosecution and punishment of these offenses is to take place in the framework of domestic legal orders. The first obligation of states, when they become parties to any of the instruments examined here, will therefore be to adapt, to the extent necessary, their domestic legislation. They will do so by ensuring that the offenses identified in the conventions become criminal offenses under domestic law, on the one hand, and are liable to prosecution before national courts and tribunal, on the other.[29] Jurisdictional grounds have been multiplied in order to maximize possibilities of prosecution. The most striking illustration of this is probably to be found in the 2005 Convention for the Suppression of Nuclear Terrorism, which provides for no less than nine such different grounds. Some are mandatory: a state party has to establish jurisdiction when the offense is committed on its territory, on board a vessel flying the flag of that state or a plane registered under the laws of that state, or by one of its nationals.[30]

[26] See Article 4 of the 1997 Convention against the Taking of Hostages, Article 15 of the 1997 Convention for the Suppression of Terrorist Bombings; see also Article 8 of the 2005 Convention for the Suppression of Nuclear Terrorism, providing for the protection of radioactive materials.

[27] Article 18.

[28] See, eg, A/RES/51/210, para 3; A/RES/69/127, paras 5–6; S/RES/1373 (2001), para 3.

[29] Logically, the conventions also provide for the prior obligation of states parties to investigate information that an offense set forth in the conventions "has been committed or is being committed in the territory of a state party or that a person who has committed or who is alleged to have committed such an offense may be present in [their] territory" and to take appropriate measures "to ensure that person's presence for the purpose of prosecution or extradition" (2005 Convention for the suppression of nuclear terrorism, Article 10(1) and (2)).

[30] Article 9(1).

Others are optional: a state may establish jurisdiction when the offense is committed against one of its nationals, against its state or government facilities abroad, by a stateless persons who resides usually on its territory, when the offense is aimed at compelling it to do or abstain from doing something, or has been committed on board an aircraft operated by the government of that state.[31] This is an addition to the (mandatory) exercise of universal jurisdiction, when the alleged perpetrator of the offense is present on the state's territory and is not to be extradited,[32] and to the possibility for the state party to prosecute "in accordance with its national law."[33]

A remarkable characteristic of this system—very similar versions of which are present in the other UN conventions—is the absence of hierarchy or priorities among the jurisdictional grounds thus established. A possible adverse consequence of this could of course be the apparition of conflicts between different states claiming to exercise jurisdiction in relation to a particular alleged offender, on the basis of different jurisdictional grounds. This is very much the problem the International Court of Justice was faced with in the *Lockerbie* case, where Libya (on the basis of the nationality of the alleged offenders), the United States (where the plane that was blown up over the Scottish village of Lockerbie was registered), and the United Kingdom (in the airspace of which the event took place and on the territory of which it caused further victims) all claimed to have a title to exercise jurisdiction over the alleged offenders.[34] While the treaty whose application was at stake—the 1971 Montreal Convention for the Suppression of Unlawful Acts against the Safety of Civil Aviation—had been adopted under the auspices of ICAO rather than the UN, a similar scenario may undoubtedly arise under any of the conventions discussed here. It is only through a negotiated settlement between the parties to that dispute that a most original solution, not foreseen in the Montreal Convention—a trial before a Scottish court sitting in the Netherlands—could ultimately be agreed upon. It should also be noted that the coexistence of so many different jurisdictional grounds entails a risk of double jeopardy (i.e., the successive or simultaneous prosecution of the same person for the same facts in different fora), since the *non bis in idem* principle is not enshrined in the UN conventions. Practice however shows that such conflicts constitute—by very far—the exception rather than the rule, first and foremost due to the fact that sectional conventions are rarely applied by domestic courts.

It may also be observed that while these instruments put a strong emphasis on the obligation to prosecute, they do not say much about penalties. This is due to a large extent to divergences among states, in particular as far as the application of the death penalty is concerned.[35] The UN conventions therefore simply provide that the offenses

[31] Article 9(2). [32] Article 9(4). [33] Article 9(5).

[34] See *Questions of Interpretation and Application of the 1971 Montreal Convention arising from the Aerial Incident at Lockerbie (Libyan Arab Jamahiriya v. United Kingdom and Libyan Arab Jamahiriya v. United States)*, [1998] ICJ Rep 9 and 115 respectively; see also S Shubber, "The Destruction of Aircraft in Flight over Scotland and Niger: The Questions of Jurisdiction and Extradition under International Law" (1995) BYIL 246ff.

[35] See Gilbert Guillaume, "Terrorisme et droit international" (1989) 215 Collected Courses of the Hague Academy 328.

they identify must be made "punishable by appropriate penalties which take into account the grave nature of these offences,"[36] leaving thereby a significant margin of appreciation to states parties.

Finally, states parties also undertake to ensure that criminal acts coming within the scope of the conventions "are under no circumstances justifiable by considerations of a political, philosophical, ideological, racial, ethnic, religious or other similar nature."[37] This is clearly in line with the approach favored by the Assembly since the early 1990s, which consisted in dealing with terrorism without making reference to the underlying causes of the phenomenon and with a strong concern to reject any justification for such acts.[38]

It is worth noting that since the end of the 1970s, conventions emphasize the rights of individuals prosecuted based on the domestic law of the state concerned[39] and later, in addition thereto, on international law.[40] In the same vein, they also make mention of the right to consular protection of the alleged perpetrators of acts criminalized by the conventions when these persons are taken into custody for the purpose of prosecution or extradition.[41]

2.2.3 *Extradition*

As typical treaties of international criminal law, the conventions examined here are based on a key principle: when the conditions set forth in the treaty are met, states parties incur an alternative obligation. They have to either prosecute or extradite the alleged offender, in accordance with the principle *aut judicare aut dedere*.

The regime established by the conventions in this respect is quite complex and is aimed, once again, at maximizing the possibilities for prosecution. If an extradition treaty exists between the two states concerned, the offense is automatically deemed to be included in the list of offenses provided for by the bilateral extradition treaty.[42] If no extradition treaty exists between both states and the existence of such a treaty is, under the domestic law of the requested state, a condition for extradition, the latter may consider the multilateral convention to constitute such a treaty.[43] Finally, if no extradition treaty is required, then the requested state is bound to accept extradition for the offense considered, in accordance with its domestic legislation.[44]

[36] 1999 Convention for the Suppression of the Financing of Terrorism, Article 4 (b); 2005 Convention for the Suppression of Nuclear Terrorism, Article 5(b).

[37] 1997 Convention for the Suppression of Terrorist Bombings, Article 5; 1999 Convention for the Suppression of the Financing of Terrorism, Article 6.

[38] See, eg, A/RES/51/210, para 2; A/RES/69/127, para 4.

[39] 1979 Convention for the Suppression of the Taking of Hostages, Article 8(2).

[40] 1997 Convention for the Suppression of Terrorist Bombings, Article 14; 1999 Convention for the Suppression of the Financing of Terrorism, Article 17.

[41] 1979 Convention for the Suppression of the Taking of Hostages, Article 6(3); 2005 Convention for the Suppression of Acts of Nuclear Terrorism, Article 10(3).

[42] 2005 Convention for the Suppression of Acts of Nuclear Terrorism, Article 13(1).

[43] 2005 Convention for the Suppression of Acts of Nuclear Terrorism, Article 13(2).

[44] 2005 Convention for the Suppression of Acts of Nuclear Terrorism, Article 13(3).

The 1997, 1999, and 2005 conventions provide that the provisions of existing extradition treaties may under no circumstances constitute an obstacle to extradition, such provisions being "deemed to be modified as between State Parties to the extent that they are incompatible with th[e] Convention."[45] In the same spirit, the more recent conventions also provide that it will be impossible to invoke any political exception to extradition. According to Article 11 of the 1997 Convention for the Suppression of Terrorist Bombings, for instance,

> None of the offences set forth in [the Convention] shall be regarded for the purposes of extradition or mutual legal assistance, as a political offence or as an offence connected with a political offence or as an offence inspired by political motives. Accordingly, a request for extradition or for mutual legal assistance based on such an offence may not be refused on the sole ground that it concerns a political offence or an offence connected with a political offence or an offence inspired by political motives.

These are typical examples of the "Belgian clause," also known as "*clause d'attentat*."[46] Such provisions aim at "depoliticizing" offenses that are obviously eminently political (and again avoid obstacles to extradition and, ultimately, punishment).

This is however counterbalanced to a certain extent by the inclusion in the same conventions of "French clauses," according to which extradition may be refused if the request is obviously motivated by the will to prosecute and punish a person for political, racial, or religious reasons, or on grounds of nationality or ethnicity.[47] While such provisions ("Belgian" and "French" clauses) may at first sight be seen as difficult to reconcile, a closer examination confirms that they are not contradictory. The "Belgian clause" indeed ensures that the requested state will not be able to invoke the political character of the act as a motive to refuse extradition (or legal assistance). This is clearly a reflection of the concern that has been repeatedly expressed by states, as from the early 1990s, to reject any possible justification to acts of terrorism.[48] The "French clause," on the other hand, merely aims at ensuring that an extradition request will not be granted if it is based

[45] 1979 Convention for the Suppression of the Taking of Hostages, Article 9(2); 1997 Convention for the Suppression of Terrorist Bombings, Article 9(5).

[46] Note however that, obviously animated by the will to ensure the perpetuation of such possibilities to deny extradition, Belgium (of all states...) made a reservation in respect of Article 11 of the 1997 Convention upon ratification. According to that reservation, Belgium, "[i]n exceptional circumstances," "reserve[d] the right to refuse extradition or mutual legal assistance in respect of any offence set forth in article 2 which it considers to be a political offence or as an offence connected with a political offence or as an offence inspired by political motive." This was met by a significant number of objections from other states parties (such as Canada, Germany; Italy, Spain, the United Kingdom, or the United States), which deemed the reservation to be contrary to the object and purpose of the convention, and Belgium ultimately withdrew its reservation in 2008.

[47] 1979 Convention for the Suppression of the Taking of Hostages, Article 9(1); 1997, Article 12, 1999, Article 15, 2005 Convention for the Suppression of Acts of Nuclear Terrorism, Article 16.

[48] See, eg, the Declaration on Measures to Eliminate International Terrorism annexed to General Assembly Resolution 49/60 of 9 December 1994.

upon motives that go beyond—or are foreign to—the prosecution and punishment for acts that have been criminalized by these conventions. Such provisions are fully consistent with the above-mentioned concern for the protection of human rights reflected in other parts of the conventions.

All in all, the conventions adopted under the auspices of the UN to counter terrorism may be said to establish a very effective regime for the criminalization and prosecution of the acts or activities they are dealing with. However, it remains to be seen to which extent their efficacy may possibly be limited by the scope of application of these treaties.

2.3 Scope of Application and Exclusions

The first such limitation flows from the fact that the conventions only apply in situations characterized by an international element.[49] Quite logically, if no such element is present and the situation is merely internal to a state, there is no reason (or grounds) for the application of international norms.[50]

More significantly, the conventions examined here also exclude from their scope of application acts committed in the context of an armed conflict, which are to be governed by the specific body of rules applicable in such situations, that is, international humanitarian law.[51] While this exclusion was formulated in general terms in the 1979 Convention for the Suppression of the Taking of Hostages, it became more specific from 1997 onward with the indication that the "activities *of armed forces* during an armed conflict [...] are not governed by th[e] Convention[s]."[52] It may be noted, on the one hand, that the terms are still rather broad. In particular, the exclusion is not limited to activities of the armed forces of a state—or to international armed conflicts—and may encompass those of other groups (nonstate actors), provided the latter meet the criteria set out in the relevant instruments of international humanitarian law.[53] But, on the other, these terms are also restrictive in the sense that the exclusion applies only to activities of armed forces and not to those of other persons, groups, or entities that do not qualify as such but could nevertheless be involved in a situation of armed conflict. A provision to the same effect was included in the 2005 Convention for the Suppression of Nuclear Terrorism,[54] although not without giving rise to some controversy.[55]

[49] 1979 Convention for the Suppression of the Taking of Hostages, Article 13; Article 3 of the 1997, 1999, and 2005 conventions.

[50] It may however be noted that such limitation has for some time now been absent from resolutions of the UN Security Council dealing with terrorism, which refer to "terrorism in all its forms and manifestations [as] one of the most serious threats to peace and security" (see for instance S/RES/1904 (2009), 2nd preambular paragraph).

[51] 1979 Convention for the Suppression of the Taking of Hostages, Article 12.

[52] 1997 Convention for the Suppression of the Financing of Terrorism, Article 19(2) (emphasis added).

[53] See in particular Article 1(1) of the Second Additional Protocol to the Geneva Conventions.

[54] Article 4(2).

[55] See Report of the Ad Hoc Committee established by General Assembly resolution 51/210 of 17 December 1996, Seventh session (31 March–2 April 2003), UN Doc A/58/37, Annex II, B, paras 3–7.

The 1997 and 2005 conventions went further and also excluded from their scope of application the "activities undertaken by military forces of a state in the exercise of their official duties, inasmuch as they are governed by other rules of international law."[56] This certainly appears much more debatable, in view of the very different consequences attached to the perpetration of an act that may come within the material scope of application of these conventions when such an act is committed in a situation of armed conflict (and governed by international humanitarian law) on the one hand, and outside of such situations (when the activities of the armed forces of a state are governed by "other rules of international law"), on the other hand. In the first case indeed, the law of armed conflicts specifically prohibits the use of terrorism as a method of warfare (both in international and non-international armed conflicts)[57] and provides (in the case of international armed conflicts) that the commission of such acts will entail the criminal responsibility of their authors.[58] Such is not the case for acts committed in situations other than armed conflicts. While the activities of the armed forces of a state in such situations will indeed be "governed by other rules of international law" (such as rules for the protection of human rights, in particular), these very generally do not provide for the criminal responsibility of the authors of breaches. This carries very significant consequences.

Indeed, provisions such as Article 19 of the 1997 Convention make it impossible to ever characterize as acts of terrorism the use of explosive devices by the armed forces of a state outside a situation of armed conflict (even if it was used as a means to intimidate a civilian population or a group) and, by doing so, shield the authors of such acts from the application of the mechanisms of repression established by the Convention. To take but one example, had the 1997 Convention been in force then, the sinking of Greenpeace's *Rainbow Warrior* in the port of Auckland by agents of the French secret services in 1985 could not have been considered as an act of terrorism within the scope of the Convention and could not have been prosecuted on that basis. By avoiding the characterization of such acts as acts of terrorism, states obviously aim at avoiding the stigmatization that such a characterization inevitably carries with it. This concern is even more apparent when one considers the rather extensive interpretations of the term "military forces of a state" put forth by some states parties. Germany, for instance, declared upon signature that it understood "that, for the purposes of this Convention, the term 'military forces of a state' also covers police forces." Along the same lines, Israel declared that "the term 'military forces of a state' includes police and security forces operating pursuant to the internal law of the State of Israel" and that "the Convention does not apply to civilians who direct or organize the official activities of military forces of a state." Singapore and the United States made declarations to the same effect. These declarations did not give rise to any opposition or objections.

[56] 1997, Article 19(2); 2005, Article 4(2).

[57] See Article 33 of the Fourth Geneva Convention, Article 51(2) of the First Additional Protocol, Article 13(2) of the Second Additional Protocol.

[58] See Article 147 of the Fourth Geneva Convention, Article 85 of the First Additional Protocol.

Such exclusion clauses thus mark a significant shift in the way terrorism has been dealt with within the UN. While the phenomenon was initially mainly—if not exclusively—considered under the prism of state—or state-sponsored—terrorism, the emphasis is now put almost exclusively on acts of terrorism committed by private persons or groups. This only confirms the classical observation according to which the use of the term "terrorism" is a convenient way to dismiss and stigmatize specific acts or activities: acts of terror are always those committed by "others."[59]

Other declarations made by states parties to the 1997 Convention—albeit with a very different content and concern—lead to the same conclusion. One may in particular mention in that respect the declaration made by Pakistan when it became a party to the convention:

> The Government of the Islamic Republic of Pakistan declares that nothing in this Convention shall be applicable to struggles, including armed struggle, for the realization of right of self-determination launched against any alien or foreign occupation or domination, in accordance with the rules of international law. This interpretation is consistent with Article 53 of the Vienna Convention on the Law of Treaties 1969 which provides that an agreement or treaty concluded in conflict with an existing *jus cogen* or peremptory norm of international law is void and, the right of self-determination is universally recognized as *a jus cogen*.[60]

Here again, the concern is clearly to avoid the stigmatization ensuing from the characterization of some acts or activities as acts of terrorism; in this case when acts that would normally come within the material scope of application of the convention are committed in the context of "struggles [...] for the realization of right of self-determination launched against any alien or foreign occupation or domination." In contrast with the above-mentioned declarations relating to the "armed forces of a state," however, the declaration made by Pakistan was met with objections from many other states parties, who believed that the declaration was contrary to the object and purpose of the convention.[61] Such positions are certainly consistent with the well-established trend—already referred to earlier—to treat terrorist acts as such, independently of their motivations and causes. They reflect a clear choice not to call into question the principle of equality of belligerents, according to which the rules governing armed conflicts (*ius in bello*) apply in a uniform manner to all parties to the conflict, irrespective of the (il)legality of their position in regard of the rules governing the use of force in international law (*jus contra bellum*). To put it otherwise, in this area, the end may never justify the means, and the fact that an act coming within the material scope of application of the 1997 Convention

[59] See, eg, Antonio Remiro Brotons, "Terrorismo, mantenimiento de la paz y nuevo orden" [2001] Revista Espanola de Derecho Internacional 167.

[60] Available at https://treaties.un.org/Pages/ViewDetails.aspx?src=TREATY&mtdsg_no=XVIII-9&chapter=18&clang=_en (last accessed on 10 January 2019).

[61] See, eg, the objections formulated by Australia, Austria, Canada, Denmark, Finland, France, Germany, India, Ireland, Israel, Italy, Japan, Moldova, the Netherlands, New Zealand, Norway, Poland, Russia, Spain, Sweden, the United Kingdom, and the United States.

is committed in the context of a struggle for self-determination will never exclude the application of the regime established by the Convention.

These thorny questions relating to the scope of application of some of the conventions adopted under the auspices of the UN to counter terrorism remain at the core of the negotiations on the Comprehensive Convention on International Terrorism, to which we shall now turn.

3 A "Comprehensive" Approach

States have for a long time focused their efforts to counter terrorist activities through the adoption of international treaties on the sectional approach described in the previous section. Higher ambitions were however expressed at the end of the 1990s, when the ad hoc Committee established by the General Assembly in Resolution 51/210 was tasked with the elaboration of a draft Comprehensive Convention on International Terrorism.[62] That instrument is meant to cover acts that do not necessarily come within the realm of the existing (sectional) conventions—such as acts of cyberterrorism, for instance. It is however not intended to replace the sectional conventions, but rather to supplement them—a fact that is highlighted by the precedence given to these instruments in the draft Comprehensive Convention.[63]

Progress in the elaboration of the draft Comprehensive Convention however proved to be significantly slower than had been the case for the three other sectional conventions prepared by the ad hoc Committee. Indeed, while work on the draft Comprehensive Convention began in 2000, it was not before 2013 that an almost complete draft could be tabled by the Bureau of the Committee. The Committee did not meet since then and at the time of this writing, the draft Comprehensive Convention very much remains a work in progress, for reasons that shall be exposed in the following paragraphs.

The draft Convention, as it presently stands, includes a proposed definition of terrorism as such, for the first time at the universal level. Draft Article 2 (1) indeed provides that:

> Any person commits an offence within the meaning of the present Convention if that person, by any means, unlawfully and intentionally, causes:
>
> (a) Death or serious bodily injury to any person; or
>
> (b) Serious damage to public or private property, including a place of public use, a State or government facility, a public transportation system, an infrastructure facility or to the environment; or

[62] A/RES/54/110 of 9 December 1999, para 12.

[63] See Article 4[2bis] of the draft comprehensive convention, as reproduced in the Report of the Ad Hoc Committee established by General Assembly resolution 51/210 of 17 December 1996, Sixteenth Session, doc. A/68/37, at p. 7.

(c) Damage to property, places, facilities or systems referred to in paragraph1 (b) of the present article resulting or likely to result in major economic loss,

when the purpose of the conduct, by its nature or context, is to intimidate a population, or to compel a Government or an international organization to do or to abstain from doing any act.

This definition obviously draws on the elements used in the 1999 Convention to identify the offense of terrorism financing[64]—which have in turn inspired the definitions of terrorism that may be found in subsequent regional instruments.[65] Here again, two main elements of the offense emerge: a material component (causing death, serious injuries, or serious damages) and a subjective component (the intent to intimidate a population or coerce a government or an international organization). The draft definition actually appears rather broad, and one may wonder whether this could lead to abuse in the application of the (future) Convention by some states. As the definition presently stands, indeed, it could for instance be applied in the context of judicial proceedings against foreign activists who took an active part in demonstrations against a public infrastructure project (attempting thereby to "compel a government" to abstain from doing an act) in the context of which "serious damages" might have been caused to public or private property. Such an interpretation may appear far-fetched, but it should be kept in mind that some states have been keen to promote rather broad definitions of "terrorism" in the past.[66] Be that as it may, such concerns do not appear to have been voiced within the ad hoc Committee or its Bureau. Discussions and controversies rather concerned the scope of application of the future Convention.

Before we turn to these, however, a few words should be said about the content of the draft Comprehensive Convention. It should be noted in that respect that, as was the case for the sectional conventions examined earlier, the Comprehensive Convention will be applicable only in situations characterized by an international element, and that it criminalizes not only terrorist acts as such, but also related acts (complicity in, organization of, and contribution to acts identified as terrorism).[67] Beyond this, the draft Convention provides for the same overall mechanism as sectional conventions: states parties will be required to criminalize the acts and activities identified in the convention,[68] to establish jurisdiction for the offenses set forth therein,[69] to take measures to prevent the perpetration

64 See Section 2.1 of this chapter.

65 See in particular the EU framework decision of 2002 (2002/475/JHA), as replaced by the directive of 23 February 2017 (available at http://data.consilium.europa.eu/doc/document/PE-53-2016-INIT/en/pdf) and the 2005 Convention on the Prevention of Terrorism adopted under the auspices of the Council of Europe (CETS, nr 196).

66 To take but one example, one may refer to the characterization by the Russian Federation of certain activities of Greenpeace's ship *Arctic Sunrise* as acts of terrorism (see the arbitral award of 14 August 2015 in the case of the *Arctic Sunrise (Kingdom of the Netherlands v. Russian Federation)*, eg, paras 93ff.).

67 Draft Article 5[3] and draft Article 2(4) respectively.

68 Draft Article 6[4].

69 No less than 10 different grounds for establishing jurisdiction (some mandatory, others optional) are envisaged in draft Article 8[6].

of acts of terrorism,[70] and to initiate prosecution against persons suspected of having committed such offenses if they do not extradite them, in conformity with the *aut dedere aut judicare* principle.[71]

As mentioned earlier, the main stumbling blocks in the negotiation process are related to the scope of application of the future convention. Two main issues have emerged in that regard: to which extent would that instrument be applicable to the acts of the armed forces of a state, on the one hand, and to those of national liberation movements on the other hand.

As far as the first of these issues is concerned, two different approaches have crystallized. The first one, proposed by the Bureau, is merely a reiteration of the exclusion clauses enshrined in the 1997 and 2005 Conventions, according to which the regime established by the treaty will not be applicable to activities of armed forces during an armed conflict, on the one hand, and to activities of "the military forces of a state in the exercise of their official duties, inasmuch as they are governed by other rules of international law," on the other.[72] It has been mentioned earlier that while the inclusion of such clauses in the 1997 Convention did not appear problematic, it gave rise to more serious discussions before being included in the 2005 Convention for the Suppression of Nuclear Terrorism.[73] Similar problems resurfaced during the negotiating process of the draft Comprehensive Convention, regarding, in particular, the clause concerning the activities of the armed forces of a state outside of situations of armed conflict. The member states of the Organization of the Islamic Conference (OIC) thus put forward a proposal to draft that clause in a slightly different manner, by providing that:

> [t]he activities undertaken by the military forces of a State in the exercise of their official duties, inasmuch as they are in conformity with international law, are not governed by this Convention.[74]

This version of the clause—similar to the wording of the declaration made by Egypt upon ratification of the Convention for the Suppression of Terrorist Bombings[75]—thus leads to a rather different result, in the sense that activities of the armed forces of a state would be excluded from the scope of the Convention only inasmuch as they are *in conformity with* (and not only *governed by*) international law. One may however wonder whether such exclusion would have any practical impact, since it is not easy to identify acts of the armed forces of a state that would be in conformity with international law and

[70] Draft Article 10[8]. [71] Draft Articles 13[11] and 19[17].

[72] See Article 3[18] proposed by the Bureau for discussion, as reproduced in the Report of the Ad Hoc Committee established by General Assembly resolution 51/210 of 17 December 1996, Sixteenth Session, doc. A/68/37, at p. 16.

[73] See Section 2.3 of this chapter.

[74] Article 3[18](3) as proposed by the member states of the Organization of the Islamic Conference, as reproduced in the Report of the Ad Hoc Committee established by General Assembly resolution 51/210 of 17 December 1996, Sixteenth Session, UN Doc A/68/37, 19.

[75] The text of the Egyptian declaration is available at <https://treaties.un.org/Pages/ViewDetails.aspx?src=TREATY&mtdsg_no=XVIII-9&chapter=18&clang=_en#EndDec> accessed January 10, 2019).

would nevertheless come within the scope of the Comprehensive Convention if such exclusionary clause was absent. But such a formulation would at least have the merit of not preventing the application of the Comprehensive Convention to members of the armed forces of a state whenever they are involved in the perpetration of acts that meet the criteria set out in Article 2 of the draft, in situations other than armed conflicts.

During negotiations, various states also expressed the concern that the future Comprehensive Convention should clearly distinguish between acts of terrorism and the "legitimate struggle of peoples under colonial or alien domination and foreign occupation in the exercise of their right to self-determination."[76] Such concerns prompted, here too, member states of the OIC to propose an alternative drafting of the exclusionary clause relating to situations of armed conflicts:

> The activities of the parties during an armed conflict, including in situations of foreign occupation, as those terms are understood under international humanitarian law, which are governed by that law, are not governed by this Convention.[77]

This certainly represents a departure from the position taken by Pakistan in its declaration concerning the Convention on the Suppression of Terrorist Bombings,[78] to the extent that the OIC proposal does not amount to the exclusion of any characterization of acts of national liberation movements as acts of terrorism for the sole reason that they were committed in the context of a struggle for self-determination. But here too, the practical difference between the OIC draft and that of the Bureau actually appears limited. It has been explained earlier that the term "armed forces" encompasses both the armed forces of a state and other groups involved in armed conflicts, provided that they meet the criteria set out in the relevant instruments of international humanitarian law. And since wars of national liberation are equated with international armed conflicts under Article 1 of the First Additional Protocol to the Geneva Conventions (First Additional Protocol), both proposals (from the Bureau and from the OIC) are actually quite similar in substance. It should however be kept in mind that some states maintain a firm opposition to the First Additional Protocol, precisely because of the assimilation of war of national liberation to international armed conflicts. When this is taken into account, the difference between both proposals becomes more apparent and explains why the member states of the OIC deemed it necessary to make a more explicit reference in their proposal to "situations of foreign occupation." But this also explains why the drafting of this clause remains a point of contention between (groups of) states involved in the negotiating process.

[76] As recalled in the informal summary prepared by the Chair on the exchange of views during the plenary debate and the informal consultations, *in* Report of the Ad Hoc Committee established by General Assembly resolution 51/210 of 17 December 1996, Sixteenth Session, UN Doc A/68/37, 20, para 4.

[77] Text of draft Article 18[3](2), as proposed by the member states of the Organization of the Islamic Conference, Report of the Ad Hoc Committee (n 76) 19.

[78] See Section 2.3 of this chapter.

4 Conclusion

At this juncture, the deadlock within the ad hoc Committee remains obvious. In December 2016, the General Assembly recommended that the Sixth Committee "establish a working group with a view to finalizing the process on the draft comprehensive convention on international terrorism."[79] It remains to be seen whether the consensus that proved so elusive so far will be reached any time soon in this new context. It may simply be emphasized at this stage that these ongoing debates are reflective of persistent divisions within the international society, even in an area that has been identified as one of its most important priorities for the last two decades.

[79] A/RES/71/151, 13 December 2016, para 24.

CHAPTER 8B

TERRORISM

practitioner reflection

A. ROHAN PERERA

FROM an historical perspective, multilateral efforts to deal with the phenomenon of terrorism can be traced back to the 1930s, when political assassinations spread across the Balkans. In 1934, the League of Nations became seized of the issue of international terrorism when terrorist attacks were directed against high-profile political figures such as the King of Yugoslavia, in France, as well as the assassination of the Austrian Chancellor and the French Minister of Foreign Affairs.

From the contemporary perspective of UN treaty-making practice concerning terrorism, it is noteworthy that the initiatives taken in the League of Nations led to the adoption of two Conventions in 1937: the Convention on the Prevention and Punishment of Terrorism and the Convention on the Creation of an International Criminal Court.[1] Although they failed to enter into force, these two conventions could be regarded as forerunners to contemporary initiatives taken by the United Nations to formulate an international normative framework of treaty obligations to combat the current manifestations of terrorism.

The importance of the Convention for the Prevention and Punishment of Terrorism was that it contained the legal elements for a definition of the term "terrorism."[2] This is significant because agreement on the meaning of "terrorism" has eluded the international community up to the present day and remains the subject of deep controversy.

A second factor which is of relevance to current initiatives on terrorism is that it was possible at the time to adopt an accompanying Convention for the establishment of an

[1] Convention for the Prevention and Punishment of Terrorism (adopted 16 November 1937, never entered into force), (1938) 19 League of Nations Official Journal 23; Convention for the Creation of An International Criminal Court (adopted 16 November 1937, never entered into force), (1936) League of Nations Official Journal, Special Supplement No 156.

[2] See Article II of the Convention which states "[a]ll criminal acts directed against a state and intended or calculated to create a state of terror in the minds of particular persons or a group of persons or the general public."

International Criminal Court vested with jurisdiction to bring to trial offenders who commit terrorist crimes, as defined in the first Convention. This provides a sharp contrast to the outcome of the efforts made at the 1998 Rome Conference when the Statute of the International Criminal Court was adopted, where efforts to include within the Statute terrorist crimes as "most serious crimes of concern to the International Community as a whole" and defined in existing Conventions, proved to be unsuccessful.

These factors provide an important historical perspective in a discussion on the current UN Treaty Practice relating to terrorism.

1 UN TREATY-MAKING

The debates within the United Nations Ad Hoc Committee on Measures to Prevent International Terrorism (AHC), which was first constituted in the 1970s, reflect the divergence of political attitudes and perceptions that dominated the issue of combating terrorism. Key political factors triggering the approach of some members of the international community at the time were the then on-going national liberation struggles in Southern Africa and the activities of liberation movements against foreign occupation in the Middle East, in particular, the question of occupied territories in Palestine.

Against this political backdrop, the group of non-aligned (NAM) countries sought to place emphasis on the need to address the underlying causes of terrorism, in any United Nations initiative on the subject of terrorism.

Consequent to the Munich Olympic Massacre of 1972, the Federal Republic of Germany took the initiative to introduce in the General Assembly an item entitled "Measures to prevent International Terrorism which endangers or takes innocent human lives or jeopardizes fundamental freedoms." The original German draft resolution under this item was amended subsequently at the insistence of the NAM. General Assembly Resolution 3034 as adopted read:

> 'Measures to prevent international terrorism which endangers or takes innocent human lives or jeopardizes fundamental freedoms, and study of the underlying causes of those forms of terrorism and acts of violence which lies in misery, frustration, grievance and despair and cause some people to sacrifice human lives, including their own, in an attempt to effect radical changes'.[3]

The mandate thus given to the UN AHC constituted a careful balance, taking due account of the positions of different political groupings: one emphasizing the need for effective measures to prevent and combat acts of terrorism, the other emphasizing the need to address the underlying root causes that lead to acts of terrorism.

[3] See GA Res 3034 (XXVII) (18 December 1972). Also Report of the Ad-hoc Committee (AHC) on International Terrorism, GAOR, 28th Session, Suppl No 28 (A/9028).

2 Sectoral approach

Given the divisive political debates that dominated the treatment of the subject in the United Nations, the international community opted to adopt what has since come to be known as the "sectoral" or "piece-meal" approach in the formulation of legal norms to combat terrorism. It followed the precedent set in the early conventions in the 1960s and early 1970s on the suppression of aerial hijacking, such as the Tokyo, Hague, and Montreal Conventions on offences against aircraft.[4] This was followed by a series of specific conventions each dealing with a crime involving indiscriminate violence, which was most likely to be committed by terrorists. Examples of these were the Convention on the Prevention and Punishment of Crimes against Internationally Protected Persons, including Diplomatic Agents (1973)[5], Convention against the Taking of Hostages (1979)[6], and the Convention for the Suppression of Unlawful Acts against the Safety of Maritime Navigation (1988).[7]

The core legal regime under these sectoral conventions, which were essentially law enforcement instruments, imposed an obligation on state parties to either "extradite or prosecute" an offender—*aut dedere aut judicare*—to ensure denial of safe haven to an offender in the territory of any state party. Accordingly, the state party in the territory of which an alleged offender is present, if it does not extradite that person to a state seeking his or her extradition, is obliged to submit the case without undue delay to its competent authorities for purpose of prosecution, without any exception whatsoever; the fundamental rationale underlying the regime being that no terrorist offender should find safe haven in the territory of any state party.[8]

With a view to achieving the objectives of an "extradite or prosecute" regime, the Sectoral Conventions provided a common architecture.

First, states parties are obliged to criminalize, under their domestic laws, the specific acts falling within the scope of the Conventions and to make these offences punishable by providing for appropriate penalties which take into account the grave nature of such offences.

[4] Convention on Offences and Certain Other Acts Committed on Board Aircraft (adopted 14 September 1963); Convention for the Suppression of Unlawful Seizure of Aircraft (adopted 16 December 1970); Convention for the Suppression of Unlawful Acts against the Safety of Civil Aviation (adopted 23 September 1971).

[5] Convention on the Prevention and Punishment of Crimes against Internationally Protected Persons, including Diplomatic Agents, Annexed to GA Res 3166 (XVII) (14 December 1973).

[6] International Convention against the Taking of Hostages (adopted 17 December 1979), UN Doc A/34/146.

[7] Convention for the Suppression of Unlawful Acts against the Safety of Maritime Navigation, 1678 UNTS 221, 27 ILM 668 (1988).

[8] On the "extradite or prosecute" regime under the sectoral Conventions, see A Rohan Perera, *International Terrorism: Initiatives to Combat Terrorism and the Development of Principles of International Law* (Vikas 1997) 174.

Secondly, in order to make the "extradite or prosecute" regime under the Conventions effective, states parties are obliged to establish jurisdiction over the acts in question, in a wide ranging number of situations. Extending beyond the traditional and more limited grounds for the exercise of criminal jurisdiction, such as territoriality and nationality, the domestic courts of states parties are required to exercise jurisdiction, *inter alia*, when the alleged offender is present on its territory, irrespective of the place where the crime was committed or the nationality of the offender/victim. This is to ensure the effective prosecution of a terrorist offender, where a request for extradition is not granted.[9]

The "extradite or prosecute" regime is also complemented by wide-ranging provisions designed to facilitate extradition arrangements and, particularly, by rendering of mutual legal assistance amongst states parties. Accordingly, in the absence of existing bilateral extradition treaties, provision is made enabling the states parties to ~~at their discretion~~, treat the Conventions, at their discretion ~~deem the Conventions~~ as the legal basis for extradition in respect of the offences set forth in the Conventions. Further, the "Convention Offences" would also be deemed to be extraditable offences in existing bilateral treaties between states parties to the Conventions.

These provisions are designed to ensure that an extradition request would not fail due to the absence of a treaty or due to any legal uncertainty as to whether a Convention offence constitutes an "extraditable offence" under the domestic extradition law of a state party.

Thus, collectively, these provisions give effect to the underlying rationale of the "extradite or prosecute" regime in the Sectoral Conventions—that no terrorist offender should find safe haven in the territory of any state. They are premised on the assumption that, as the number of states parties to these Conventions grow, this will have the effect of casting the safety net wider, and, consequently reducing the possible escape routes open to an offender.

3 Contemporary threats

In the late 1990s the world witnessed a series of terrorist attacks through the use of bombs, other explosive devices, and harmful substances such as Sarin gas, targeting public buildings and transportation and other facilities, causing death or injury to civilians, and extensive damage to public property.

The unprecedented nature of these attacks, which were to later culminate with the events in the United States on 9/11, led to a growing international consensus in favour of adopting collective measures to deal with such new forms and manifestations of terrorism. Related to the aspect of terrorist bombings was also the growing realization that terrorist groups sustain their campaign of terror by a continuous flow of funds through a complex network of fund-raising operations spread throughout the world.

[9] On the nature of jurisdiction under the Conventions, see Perera (n 8) 174.

Against the background of these developments, the UN General Assembly decided in 1997 to re-constitute the Ad Hoc Committee (AHC) on Measures to Eliminate International Terrorism. The mandate given to the AHC required it to elaborate, as a matter of priority, an International Convention for the suppression of terrorist bombings, addressing specifically the need to criminalize the indiscriminate use of bombs and explosives targeting public buildings and facilities, including public transportation systems.[10]

3.1 International Convention for the Suppression of Terrorist Bombings

The negotiations on the conclusion of an International Convention on the Suppression of Terrorist Bombings[11] brought to surface several key issues that cut across the negotiations that were to follow on several other anti-terrorism instruments, including the ongoing negotiations on a Comprehensive Convention on International Terrorism (CCIT).

The negotiations in the AHC were initially confronted with what is commonly referred to as the "definitional issue." Nevertheless, it needs mention that it was also possible during the negotiations to successfully reach agreement on an innovative element, by way of "an exception to the political offences exception" relating to extradition.[12] By treating the offence of terrorist bombings as defined in the Convention as a "non-political" offence for purposes of extradition, the Convention sought to ensure that a normal defence available to a fugitive offender under the general extradition law, to plead that an act was committed in furtherance of a political motivation in order to preclude extradition, could not be invoked in respect of extradition proceedings under the Terrorist Bombings Convention. The Convention, by recognizing that where there is recourse to indiscriminate violence targeting innocent civilians a defence that would be available under the general extradition law would not be available in respect of terrorist bombing offences, set an important precedent for the Conventions that were to follow and contributed to a progressive development of the law.

Although precedent existed in the European Convention on the Suppression of Terrorism[13], this was the first instance that the application of the "political offences exception" was expressly excluded in a law-enforcement instrument negotiated within the United Nations.

The negotiations regarding this provision were not altogether an easy one. Steeped in liberal thinking, the "political offence exception" sought to recognize that "circumstances

[10] UN Doc A/RES/51/210 (17 December 1996).

[11] International Convention for the Suppression of Terrorist Bombings (adopted 15 December 1997), UN Doc A/RES/52/164.

[12] Art 11.

[13] European Convention on the Suppression of Terrorism (adopted 27 January 1977, entered into force 4 August 1978) 15 ILM 1272.

may exist under which in the interest of free expression of political dissent, acts which might normally be the cause for extradition should be exempted from the extradition process."[14]

After much discussion, during which human rights considerations were in the forefront of the deliberations, the "exception to the political offences exception" was successful in attracting a consensus, however, only after it was counter-balanced by a provision which came to be regarded as the "non-persecution" safeguard. The latter provision stipulated that the obligation to extradite would not arise if the requested state has substantial grounds for believing that the request for extradition has been made for the purpose of prosecuting or punishing a person on account of his race, religion, nationality or political opinion, or that that person's position may be prejudiced for any of those reasons.[15]

Thus the package comprised a combination of provisions related to the serious nature of the offence (the exception to the political offence exception), balanced with a provision relating to the motivation of the state in seeking extradition, the "non-persecution safeguard." The "non-persecution safeguard" well established under the general law of extradition, inspired by human rights considerations, sought to afford protection to those persons with respect to whom it could legitimately be established that the requesting state is proceeding for "reasons other than the enforcement of the Criminal Law."[16]

However, there were two critical issues that arose in the context of these negotiations that have had an impact on the subsequent instruments negotiated before the AHC. First, the question of incorporating a provision that would exclude acts of military forces of states (that may involve the use of bombs, explosives and similar devices) from the scope of the Convention. Secondly, the question of excluding acts of national liberation movements committed in the course of struggles against foreign occupation, on the other.

Western and European states with military enforcement capability were strongly committed to maintaining a provision relating to the official activities of state military forces, on the basis that such activities would be within the scope of official duties of such military forces and should not be subject to any form of exercise of jurisdiction by foreign courts or tribunals. At the early stages of the negotiations, the US made it clear that it was essential that a specific exemption was accorded to military forces of states in respect of actions taken pursuant to self-defence, law enforcement, evacuation, and peacekeeping operations.

In an informal Working Paper circulated by the US, the rationale for their position on this issue was explained as follows:

> Under the Convention, alleged offenders are subject to universal criminal jurisdiction with a mandatory 'prosecute or extradite' requirement. By including State action within the Convention's scope, military forces of any State would be at risk throughout the world, and at any time, of being arrested to answer charges related to their official conduct. This cannot be a rational conclusion to this negotiation.

[14] See also, *Schtraks v the Government of Israel* [1967] UKHL 33 ILR 332.

[15] Article 12.

[16] See reasoning in *Schtraks* (n 14).

> In this connection, in so far as conduct in violation of international humanitarian law is concerned, State military forces would in no way be exempted from existing law concerning grave breaches.[17]

These concerns were also shared by other West European states, such as the United Kingdom.

In the context of this proposal, the negotiations were thereafter confronted with counter-proposals, mainly by the Organization of Islamic Cooperation (OIC) group as well as key members of the NAM Group. The position articulated by these countries sought a similar exemption in respect of acts of "armed forces" of entities other than states, which are engaged in national liberation struggles and against situations of foreign occupation in particular. These countries also sought to limit the scope of any exemption being accorded to military forces of states by confining such exception only to activities "as are in accordance with international law, in particular, international humanitarian law."

The stage was thus set to find a compromise to address these contending considerations, which came to be known as the "definitional issue" and were fraught with both legal and political complexities.

The approach adopted by the Coordinators and the Bureau of the AHC and the Working Group in addressing the "definitional issue" was to carefully delineate the specific "legal regimes" that would be applicable to such specific situations, rather than attempting to exclude "specific acts" from the scope of the Convention.[18]

The compromise, which finally emerged as a package after protracted negotiations, comprised a preambular provision and an operative article (Art 19). The preambular paragraph states:

> Noting that the activities of military forces are governed by rules of international law outside the framework of this Convention and that the exclusion of certain actions from the coverage of this Convention does not condone or make lawful otherwise unlawful acts, or preclude prosecution under other laws.

Article 19 of the Convention provided:

1. Nothing in this Convention shall affect other rights, obligations and responsibilities of States and individuals under international law, in particular the purposes and principles of the Charter of the United Nations and international humanitarian law.

[17] Informal "Non-Paper" circulated by the US in the Ad Hoc Committee (October 1997); see further A Rohan Perera, "Reviewing the UN Conventions on Terrorism: Towards a Comprehensive Terrorism Convention" in C Fignaut, J Wouters, F Naert (eds), *Legal Instruments in the Fight against International Terrorism: A Transatlantic Dialogue* (Martinus Nijhoff 2004). The US position was consistent with their approach on the Statute of the International Criminal Court that was being negotiated.

[18] This was in contrast to the approach adopted in some regional and other instruments, such as the OIC Convention on Combatting International Terrorism, which sought to exclude acts committed by national liberations movements from the generic term, "terrorism."

2. The activities of armed forces during an armed conflict, as these terms are understood under international humanitarian law, which are governed by that law, are not governed by this Convention, and the activities undertaken by military forces of a State in the exercise of their official duties, inasmuch as they are governed by other rules of international law, are not governed by this Convention.

The above formulation represented an attempt to carefully balance the contending considerations involved.

Article 19 represents a "savings clause"—clarifying that there is already in existence a distinct body of international law governing responsibility of "armed forces" during an armed conflict as well as activities of military forces of states. The preambular paragraph addresses concerns that had been expressed during the negotiations of possible impunity that could arise through these exclusions, by making it clear that exclusion accorded to activities of "military forces" in no way condones unlawful acts or preclude persecution under other applicable laws. It is also important to note that Article 19(2) seeks to address in its first limb, "activities of armed forces" in its widest sense (including both state and non-state actors) and in the second limb, the activities of "military forces of states." This distinction acquires a particular importance in the context of the negotiations on the CCIT that were to follow.[19]

3.2 International Convention for the Suppression of Financing of Terrorism

The successful adoption of the Terrorist Bombings Convention was followed by the negotiations on a draft International Convention for the Suppression of Financing of Terrorism.

The objective of the Convention was to provide a comprehensive legal framework to oblige states to take necessary measures to prevent and counteract the financing of terrorists and terrorist organizations—whether such financing is direct or indirect, for instance, through front organizations "which also have or claim to have charitable, social or cultural goals."[20]

The draft text was based on the "extradite or prosecute" regime that had formed the core of the precedent sectoral conventions. There were, however, two noteworthy elements that were successfully negotiated. First, the Convention criminalized the specific act of "financing"—irrespective of whether the funds were actually used to carry out an offence covered by the Convention—making "financing" of terrorism an independent offence. Secondly, it reinforced the existing sectoral Conventions by making it

[19] See section 3.4.

[20] International Convention for the Suppression of the Financing of Terrorism (adopted 9 December 1999, entered into force 10 April 2002).

an offence to wilfully and unlawfully finance to commit any act which constitutes an offence within the scope of and defined in one of the treaties listed in an annex.

In contrast to the precedent Conventions, taking into account the complexities of financial transactions, the Terrorist Financing Convention also contained detailed provisions, imposing obligations on states of a very specific nature—the monitoring and controlling of trans-border financial activities. These provisions require banks and other financial institutions within states to adopt strict regulatory measures with a view to countering terrorist financing through illegal financial flows. Accordingly, states are required to cooperate in the prevention of terrorist financing offences by requiring their financial institutions and other professions involved in financial transactions to take effective measures for the "identification of their usual or occasional customers as well as customers in whose interest accounts are opened", to pay special attention to unusual or suspicious transactions, and to report all transactions suspected of stemming from criminal activities'.[21]

Given the nature of the subject matter of the Convention and its focus on the technicalities on curbing trans-frontier financial flows, the issue of a carve-out in respect of acts committed in the course of armed conflict, while not dominating the negotiations to the same extent as in the case of the Terrorist Bombing Convention, did figure in the negotiations. The solution was found in the operational definition found in Article 2, which read:

> Any other action intended to cause death or serious bodily injury to a civilian, or any other person not taking an active part in hostilities in a situation of armed conflict, when the purpose of such act, by its nature or context, is to intimidate a population, or to compel a government or an international organization to do or to abstain from doing any act.

Thus, causing death or serious bodily injury to a person taking an active part in hostilities in situations of armed conflict is carved out of the scope of the Convention, and left to be dealt with by the applicable law in such situations.

As referred to below, the issue of "carve-outs" from the Convention's scope was raised in the negotiations which followed, namely the draft Nuclear Terrorism Convention (NTC) and the draft CCIT.

Entry into force of the Terrorist Financing Convention was accelerated by the adoption of SC Resolution 1373 in the aftermath of the events in the US on 9/11. Drawing largely from the provisions of the Terrorist Financing Convention, that resolution prohibited financing for terrorist purposes and constituted a binding obligation under Chapter VII of the UN Charter.

[21] These provisions were influenced by similar measures being taken by the Financial Action Task Force (FATF) under the auspices of the World Bank.

3.3 International Convention for the Suppression of Acts of Nuclear Terrorism

The core issue of delineating the precise scope of a convention through the incorporation of an "exclusion clause" came into sharp focus once again in the context of the negotiations on the International Convention on the Suppression of Acts of Nuclear Terrorism[22] (NTC). The issue specifically arose when the Organization of the Islamic Conference (OIC) and key NAM countries took the position that, since nuclear material and nuclear reactors are in the possession or control of states, the draft Convention should clearly address the question of state responsibility for the use of nuclear weapons or nuclear material.

States opposed to this approach—mainly the West European and Others Group (WEOG)—responded that the issue should be addressed only in the context of disarmament negotiations and not in the context of negotiations on a legal instrument on suppression of terrorism. These states argued that the position of the OIC countries tended to overlook the fact that, in legal instruments in the field of suppression of terrorism, the focus has always been the question of individual criminal responsibility for terrorist activities—in this instance, the threat of nuclear material falling into unlawful hands and their possible use by non-state entities. Accordingly, it was pointed out that the legal regime under these conventions consistently focused on the question of individual criminal responsibility, carefully excluding the question of state responsibility (which was regulated by other principles of international law).

Thus, the option before the Ad Hoc Committee in working towards a consensus was to follow the precedent of the Terrorist Bombings Convention, clearly recognizing that other legal regimes apply to the specific situations envisaged, such as the Principles of State Responsibility.

After several years of negotiations, a compromise was reached. Concerns regarding activities of military forces of states and state responsibility were addressed through a package of proposals both in the preambular part of the Convention as well as in Article 4. Thus, the final preambular paragraph provides;

> Noting that the activities of military forces of States are governed by rules of international law outside of the framework of this Convention and that the exclusion of certain actions from the coverage of this Convention does not condone or make lawful otherwise unlawful acts, or preclude prosecution under other laws.

Article 4, following the precedent of the Terrorist Bombings Convention, is essentially a "savings clause" or a "choice-of-law" provision, preserving the applicability of existing legal regimes with regard to "activities of armed forces during an armed conflict" as well as "activities undertaken by military forces of a State in the exercise of their official duties." The article also contains in sub-paragraph 4 an additional provision addressing

[22] International Convention on the Suppression of Acts of Nuclear Terrorism (adopted 13 April 2005), 2445 UNTS 89.

specifically the question of the legality of the use or threat of use of nuclear weapons by states, through a "carve-out":

> This Convention does not address, nor can it be interpreted as addressing, in any way, the issue of the legality of the use or threat of use of nuclear weapons by States.

This provision was included with the objective of providing interpretative clarity. The draft Nuclear Terrorism Convention was thus concluded following the approach of carefully defining the precise scope of application of the Convention and carving out the other applicable legal regimes—an approach that was first resorted to in negotiating the Terrorist Bombings Convention.

However, the Group of OIC countries went on record that the acceptance of a compromise on the Draft Nuclear Terrorism Convention on the above basis should not prejudice their position on the negotiations of the draft Comprehensive Convention on International Terrorism, which was also pending before the Ad Hoc Committee at the time.

3.4 Draft Comprehensive Convention on International Terrorism

The negotiations on the CCIT, therefore, had to contend from the outset with the issue that was being consistently pursued by the OIC within the work of the Ad-hoc Committee: that the Convention should contain a definition of the generic term "terrorism" that unequivocally distinguishes terrorism from the "legitimate struggle of all peoples under foreign occupation in the exercise of their right to self-determination." Other states, primarily those from the WEOG, objected to the OIC's proposal as presented by Malaysia.[23] This objection was on the basis that the Comprehensive Convention was not the proper instrument for addressing the question of "peoples" legitimate struggle' that should necessarily be dealt with within the context of international humanitarian law. It was contended that the objective of the Draft Convention was to further develop international rules concerning individual criminal responsibility for terrorist acts, not covered under existing Sectoral Conventions, and to enable the perpetrators to be brought to justice. During the CCIT negotiation process, following the broad approach followed in precedent Conventions, the Coordinator and Bureau proceeded to discuss the issue—not in the context of a generic definition of the term "terrorism", but in the context of the scope of application of the Convention. It was possible to reach a broad understanding on this approach, when members of the OIC Group agreed to participate on the basis of this proposal, without prejudice to the proposal they had tabled and on the understanding that "nothing is agreed until everything is agreed."[24]

[23] Proposal submitted by Malaysia on behalf of the OIC Group, A/57/37, Annex IV, UN Doc A/68/37.

[24] See Report of the Ad Hoc Committee established by GA Res 51/210 (17 December 1996), UN Doc A/68/37, Annex I, note (a).

There were two positions to be addressed by the Coordinator and that had to be reconciled. First, the position of the OIC states to include a generic definition of the term "terrorism" and affirm that the armed struggle of the peoples under foreign occupation, aggression, colonialism and so on, aimed at achieving the right of self-determination, cannot be considered as a terrorist crime coming within the scope of the Convention. Secondly, a related issue that had to be addressed was the objection of this group to the inclusion of a provision in the negotiating text, as insisted upon by the US and other Western states, designed to exclude the activities of military forces of states in the exercise of their official duties from the scope of the Convention.

On the other hand, the position of a large number of delegations, including the sponsor state India, Latin America, and the EU, was that this issue should be addressed from the perspective of a limitation of the field of application of the Convention rather than attempting exclusions from a definition of terrorist acts. This position was consistent with the precedent set by the Terrorist Bombings Convention and the Nuclear Terrorism Convention.

In fact, the negotiating text presented by the sponsor state India contained language stating that the "activities of armed forces during an armed conflict", as those terms were understood under international law, were governed by that law and not by the Convention. The delegations who supported this latter approach also stressed that the same approach was applicable to the official activities of the military forces of states, outside the context of an armed conflict, inasmuch as these activities were governed by other rules of international law.

The negotiations, therefore, proceeded on the basis of the draft Article 18 presented by the Coordinator (later adopted by the Bureau).[25] Referred to as the "exclusion" article, the purpose of Article 18 was to demarcate the areas of application of the Convention and point to the different legal regimes that governed each situation.

In light of these divergent and different positions, the challenge for the negotiators was to shift the focus of the negotiations away from the "definitional issue" and to address the concerns that were being raised in the context of the scope of application of the CCIT.

Accordingly, negotiations proceeded on the basis of the compromise package which was designed to meet these divergent concerns. The package, which provided for a "carve-out" of the other applicable legal regimes, sought to avoid the risk of going down the politically sensitive path of attempting to draw a distinction between acts of terrorism and acts committed during an armed struggle for national liberation.

At the meeting of the Working Group on Measures to Eliminate International Terrorism convened during the 65th Session of the General Assembly in 2002, the Coordinator circulated a text, containing the elements of a possible compromise,

[25] See Report of the Ad Hoc Committee (n 24) Annex II.

for discussion. This text was further refined in 2009 to meet the lingering concerns of delegations and was presented by the Bureau for discussion:[26]

> *Preamble*
>
> Noting that the activities of military forces of States are governed by rules of international law outside the framework of the present convention, and that the exclusion of certain actions from the coverage of the present Convention does not condone or make lawful otherwise unlawful acts or preclude prosecution under other laws...
>
> *Article 3 [previously Article 18]*
>
> 1. Nothing in the present Convention shall affect other rights, obligations and responsibilities of States, peoples and individuals under international law, in particular the purposes and principles of the Charter of the United Nations and international humanitarian law;
>
> 2. The activities of armed forces during armed conflict, as those terms are understood under international humanitarian law, which are governed by that law, are not governed by the present Convention;
>
> 3. The activities undertaken by the military forces of a State in the exercise of their official duties, inasmuch as they are governed by other rules of international law, are not governed by the present Convention;
>
> 4. Nothing in the present article condones or makes lawful otherwise unlawful acts, nor precludes prosecution under other laws; acts which would amount to an offence as defined in article 2 of the present Convention remain punishable under such laws;
>
> 5. The present Convention is without prejudice to the rules of international law applicable in armed conflict, in particular those rules applicable to acts lawful under international humanitarian law'.

The "Compromise Package" presented by the Coordinator recognizes that the draft CCIT, once adopted, would not operate in a vacuum but alongside other applicable legal regimes. It thereby sought to preserve the integrity of such other legal regimes and sought to assuage any concern that the CCIT would have the effect of overriding any such regime.

Paragraph (I) of the Coordinator's proposal, set out above, contains the overarching principles that underpin what would be excluded from the draft CCIT's scope. An important element in this paragraph was that it included an explicit reference to the "right of peoples" which is a significant addition to the general "carve-out" language contained in precedent sectoral conventions. This term seeks to address concerns relating to the rights of peoples to self-determination, articulated by the OIC in the course of the negotiations.

The core element of the Coordinator's proposal is the carve-out in respect of International Humanitarian Law (IHL) that is applicable in situations of armed conflict.

[26] See Text relating to the Preamble and Article 3 [18] of the Drat Comprehensive Convention proposed by the Bureau for discussion. Report of the Ad Hoc Committee (n 24) Annex II.

The essence of Paragraphs 2 and 5, read together, is to make it explicit that acts committed by "armed forces" (covering both state and non-state actors) in situations of armed conflict will be governed by IHL, as the "*lex specialis*" applicable in such situations, and would therefore be outside the scope of the CCIT. By thus seeking to preserve the integrity of IHL through this "carve-out" or "choice of law" provision, the Coordinator's proposal seeks to address concerns that were expressed during the negotiations—that the CCIT could have a criminalizing effect on acts that are not prohibited under international humanitarian law (eg: killing or injuring an enemy combatant). It was contended by those expressing this concern that the "conflation" between IHL and counter-terrorism laws could have the effect of jeopardizing the protection of acts considered not unlawful under IHL, by providing an additional layer of criminality under the rubric of counter terrorism laws.[27]

Paragraph 3 of the Coordinator's proposal addresses concerns expressed by the US and other Western European states that acts of "military forces" of states in peacetime should be outside the scope of the Convention, and should not be criminalized under the CCIT. By stipulating that activities undertaken by the military forces of a state are not governed by the CCIT, "inasmuch as" they are governed by other rules of international law, this provision points to the applicability of principles of international law relating to state responsibility, use of force, and applicable provisions of human rights law. In addressing the issue of "state terrorism", the approach of the Coordinator, keeping with the overall rationale of the proposal, is that other fields of law continue to apply to such situations. It is understood that such fields of law include the UN Charter, international humanitarian law, international criminal law (such as the crime of aggression, crimes against humanity), and the rules relating to internationally wrongful acts, which are considered to adequately cover the obligations of states in situations where acts of violence are committed by states or their agents acting on behalf of the states.[28]

In order to allay possible concerns of impunity that could be said to arise from the exclusionary elements, the proposal makes clear in the preambular paragraph and in Paragraph 4 that the exclusion of certain acts from the scope of the CCIT will not lead to impunity in respect of such acts, if these acts are unlawful and punishable under other applicable rules of international law.

While a broad degree of convergence had been attracted towards the Coordinator's text and delegations continue to be engaged in the negotiations based on that text, a key sticking point that has held up a consensus being reached on the CCIT so far has been the position of OIC Members aimed at broadening the notion of "armed forces during a conflict" through the use of the term "parties during a conflict."

[27] See International Committee of the Red Cross, International Humanitarian Law and the Challenges of Contemporary Armed Conflicts: Report of the 31st International Conference of the Red Cross and Red Crescent (2011) 48–53.

[28] The CCIT text refines the parallel text on the Terrorist Bombings Convention by dealing with "activities of armed forces" in situations of armed conflict and "acts of military forces" of states in times of peace in two separate paragraphs, and injects a greater degree of clarity. Paragraph 2 is sufficiently broad to cover both state and non-state actors and paragraph 3 specifically applies to "acts of military forces" of states.

The effect of this proposal, which broadens the language, is that activities of armed groups that do not correspond to the definition of the term "armed forces" under IHL could also be exempted from the scope of the Convention.

Such a widening of covered categories is not acceptable to other states, particularly, the US and West European states. Further, OIC states also sought to qualify the term "armed conflict" in Paragraph 2 by the inclusion of an express reference to the phrase "including in situations of foreign occupation." They further insisted that, with regard to the exception accorded to activities of military forces of states (referred to in Paragraph 3 of the text), the phrase "official duties of the military forces of states" be qualified by the term "inasmuch as they are in *conformity* with international law" (rather than the phrase contained in the proposal "inasmuch as they are *governed* by other rules of international law"). It is these concerns that have held up the reaching of a consensus on the CCIT to this date.

4 Conclusion

While a consensus still eludes the negotiation process of the CCIT, discussions have proceeded on the key outstanding issue of the scope of the Convention based on the Coordinator's proposal and upon the text of the earlier conventions. Delegations have been engaged in negotiations based on this approach, appreciating that this is the best option of reaching the shared goal of achieving a consensus. An aspect that has consistently been emphasized by the Bureau concerning the Coordinator's proposal is that the text represents a carefully nuanced and delicately balanced package which must be viewed by delegations as an integrated whole, and that a "pick and choose" approach would unravel the package and defeat the very purpose of the exercise. This view has also been articulated by states supporting the approach adopted by the Bureau.

Another aspect that has been emphasized by the Bureau is that some element of constructive ambiguity would be necessary in order to provide an element of flexibility of interpretation and to garner a general consensus. Views have been expressed that the text should not be over-prescriptive, since issues that arise in the interpretation and the application of the Convention would ultimately have to be determined by the domestic courts or tribunals. In contrast, some delegations, however, have sought to inject a very high degree of specificity to the language, being wary of over expansive interpretation by domestic courts or tribunals.

The Chair of the Working Group has also presented the elements of a draft resolution that could possibly accompany the adoption of the CCIT, as a further measure towards assuaging lingering concerns that remain and to be considered as part of an overall compromise package.[29]

[29] See Report of the Ad Hoc Committee (n 24), Annex III, Informal Summary prepared by the Chair, on the exchange of views during the plenary debate and the Informal Consultations, para 34.

The proposed elements of the draft resolution addresses the issue of state terrorism, *inter alia*, by confirming the duty of states to refrain from organizing, instigating, assisting or participating in acts of civil strife or terrorist acts in another state; and recalls, *inter alia*, the Declaration of Principles of International Law concerning Friendly Relations and Cooperation among States (GA Res. 2625) (XXV) and reaffirms the importance of maintaining the integrity of IHL in the context of combatting international terrorism. Towards this end, the draft text reiterates that states must ensure that any measure taken to combat terrorism complies with their obligations under international law, in particular, international human rights law, international refugee law, and IHL.

The draft resolution seeks to provide an additional measure of comfort to delegations in respect of diverse concerns expressed, and supplements the elements presented in the Coordinator's proposal which could not be accommodated within the text of the Convention. The device of the accompanying resolution is a time-tested method resorted to in the context of negotiations in the UN's treaty-making practice and serves as an interpretative tool in understanding and applying the provisions of a Convention.

CHAPTER 9

THE PEACEFUL USES OF OUTER SPACE

TANJA MASSON-ZWAAN*
AND ROBERTO CASSAR**

THIS chapter addresses the context in which the law of outer space has evolved under the auspices of the United Nations (UN), and indicates how the most fundamental legal instrument relating to outer space—the "Treaty on Principles Governing the Activities of States in the Exploration and Use of Outer Space, including the Moon and Other Celestial Bodies"—was formulated and adopted. Further, this chapter provides a brief overview of the key aspects of the UN legal regime for space activities, and indicates its effectiveness over time. The chapter concludes with an assessment of the robustness of this regime in view of future developments and new activities in the highly dynamic field of space exploration and use. To this end, it will be argued that the drafters of the UN space treaties demonstrated great wisdom, vision, and craftsmanship when creating this legal regime that has stood the test of time, despite the challenges it has faced and will continue to face as the privatization and commercialization of space activity increase and necessitate a further evolution of its constituent rules.

The law of outer space primarily lays down what is, and what is not permitted when using and exploring outer space. Space law is composed of hard law and soft law; it

* Asst. Professor and Deputy Director, International Institute of Air and Space Law, Leiden University. President Emerita, International Institute of Space Law.

** LLM (cum laude) in Advanced Studies in Air and Space Law, International Institute of Air and Space Law, Leiden University.

The authors would like to thank Ambassador Eugeniusz Wyzner, former chairman of the Legal Subcommittee of COPUOS, for reviewing the chapter and for providing invaluable insights on the treaty-making processes of space law.

includes instruments containing legally binding obligations (i.e., "hard" law),[1] as well as non-legally-binding instruments used to express preferences, rather than obligations, that states should act or refrain from acting in a specific manner (i.e., "soft" law).[2] The present chapter mainly focuses on the evolution of the former, as it is comprised of treaties, whereas the evolution of the latter shall only be mentioned in passing.

Before analyzing the *evolution* of hard space law, the *genesis* of space law, set amidst the Cold War and the creation of the UN, will be contextualized. Accordingly, the analysis begins in September 1945.

1 The Geopolitical Context of the Genesis of Space Law

At the end of World War II, a vacuum of power engulfed Europe and separated the two great powers of the time: the United States of America and the Union of Soviet Socialist Republics (USSR).

As history goes on to prove, it was impossible for these two powers to fill this vacuum without bruising each other's interests.[3] Conceivably the most fundamental disagreement between the United States and the USSR was whether capitalism or socialism was the best socioeconomic system to attain modernity.[4] So strong was this ideological conflict that it not only percolated through the global political arena,[5] but morphed over time into a military one as both powers began to acquire and expand stockpiles of nuclear weapons capable of destroying humanity as a whole.[6] Although the international landscape was thus dominated by an intensely bipolar structure of world power that in its own right yielded a form of stability and predictability, this came at the enormous price of a risk of nuclear war.[7]

This risk reached even more distressing heights some 10 years into the Cold War, specifically on October 4, 1957, for on that day, by successfully launching the first artificial satellite "Sputnik I" into outer space, the USSR demonstrated that it possessed

[1] Kenneth W Abbott and Duncan Snidal, "Hard and Soft Law in International Governance" (2000) 54 Intl Org 421.

[2] Alan Boyle and Christine Chinkin, *The Making of International Law* (OUP 2007) 212; Joseph Gold, *Interpretation: The IMF and International Law* (Kluwer 1996) 301.

[3] John Lewis Gaddis, *We Now Know: Rethinking Cold War History* (Clarendon 1997) 11.

[4] Naoko Shibusawa, "Ideology, Culture, and the Cold War" in Richard H Immerman and Petra Goedde (eds), *The Oxford Handbook of the Cold War* (OUP 2013) 32, 41.

[5] Allen Lynch, *The Soviet Study of International Relations* (CUP 1987) 95.

[6] Akira Iriye, "Historicizing the Cold War" in Immerman and Goedde (n 4) 15, 21.

[7] Douglas A Ross, "Multilateralizing the Nuclear Disarmament Process: Next Steps after the START Agreement" in Edward McWhinney, Douglas Ross, Grigory Tunkin, and Vladlen Vereshchetin (eds), *From Coexistence to Cooperation: International Law and Organization in the Post-Cold War Era* (Martinus Nijhoff 1991) 62.

the ability to launch intercontinental ballistic missiles and deliver nuclear warheads to anywhere on earth.[8] In doing so, the USSR brought about a paradigm shift in the invulnerability of the United States. While throughout most of its history the latter had not needed to worry much about the security of its land owing to its geographical separation by the oceans from direct threats,[9] this illusion of its territorial inaccessibility was abruptly dispelled with the launch of "Sputnik I".[10]

Reverting at this juncture to the wake of World War II, we can shift our focus from the unfolding of the Cold War to the synchronous establishment of a new legal world order in lieu of the failed League of Nations.[11] This new organization, eventually named the "United Nations," was to symbolize the birth of a new world wherein peace would be effectively safeguarded.[12] The purpose of the UN, therefore, was none other than world peace.[13]

From the above account it follows quite unsurprisingly that, less than six weeks after the launch of "Sputnik I" and its exacerbation of the specter of nuclear war, the UN General Assembly emphasised the urgency of decreasing the danger of war,[14] and took the stance that outer space should be used *exclusively* for peaceful purposes.[15] This, eventually, not only led to the regulation of an entirely new domain—outer space—whose characteristics and possibilities were hardly known at the time, but it also made the law of outer space quite unlike that of any other area ever regulated under UN auspices, signaling the creation of a new branch of public international law.

Months later, during the first quarter of 1958, the United States and the USSR followed suit: in January, US president Eisenhower suggested in a letter to USSR premier Bulganin that their nations should both agree to use outer space for peaceful purposes only;[16] in March, the USSR submitted a provisional agenda item for consideration by the General Assembly wherein it proposed that outer space should not be used for military purposes.[17]

[8] Richard Pipes, *U.S.-Soviet Relations in the Era of Détente* (Westview 1981) 141–42; John Prados, "Cold War Intelligence History" in Immerman & Goedde (n 4) 414, 425.

[9] John Lewis Gaddis, *The Cold War: A New History* (Penguin 2005) 15.

[10] B Artemov, "O Sovetsko-Amerikanskikh Otnosheniakh" (1958) 11 Mirovaia Ekonomika I Mezhdunarodnye Otnosheniia 15, 22; as cited in William Zimmerman, *Soviet Perspectives on International Relations, 1956–1967* (Princeton University Press 1973) 172.

[11] Franz Cede, "Historical Introduction" in Franz Cede and Lilly Sucharipa-Behrmann, *The United Nations: Law and Practice* (Kluwer Law International 2001) 3, 5–6.

[12] Evan Luard, *A History of the United Nations: Volume 1: The Years of Western Domination, 1945–1955* (Macmillan Press 1982) 17.

[13] Hans Kelsen, *The Law of the United Nations: A Critical Analysis of Its Fundamental Problems* (Praeger 1950) 19.

[14] UNGA Res 1148 (XII) (14 November 1957), preambular para. 2.

[15] ibid para 1(f) (emphasis added).

[16] Letter by Dwight D Eisenhower to Nikolai Bulganin (12 January 1958) reprinted in (1958) 38 Department of State Bulletin (USA) 122, 126.

[17] "Union of Soviet Socialist Republics: Request for the Inclusion of an Item in the Provisional Agenda of the Thirteenth Session" (17 March 1958) A/3818; reprinted in GAOR 13th Session Annexes, Agenda Item 60 1.

Although from this rather brief course of events it may be deduced that there was indeed an understanding between the United States and the USSR that some regulation of the use of outer space was required and that such regulation should be dealt with within the newly established UN,[18] this understanding ought not however eclipse the fact that the two powers disagreed over *how* such regulation was to be achieved.

On the one hand, in a draft resolution to the First Committee of the General Assembly,[19] the USSR proposed the establishment of a UN agency for international cooperation in the study of cosmic space.[20] On the other, in a separate draft resolution to the same Committee, the United States and 19 additional states counterproposed the establishment by the General Assembly of an ad hoc committee on the peaceful uses of outer space.[21]

Pursuant to the counterproposal of the latter, the USSR revised its draft resolution and abandoned the idea of a UN agency,[22] suggesting instead the establishment of a UN committee for cooperation in the study of outer space for peaceful purposes, and a preparatory group thereof consisting of representatives of several states.[23] The United States and its 19 allies, all of whom objected to the revised USSR suggestion on the ground that the component states of the proposed preparatory group were either Soviet satellites or unfriendly neutral states,[24] responded by revising their own draft resolution and counter-suggesting that their proposed ad hoc committee consist of a set of different states.[25]

[18] Stephan Hobe, "Historical Background" in Stephan Hobe, Bernhard Schmidt-Tedd & Kai-Uwe Schrogl (eds), *Cologne Commentary on Space Law: Volume 1* (Carl Heymanns Verlag 2009) 4.

[19] This draft resolution was submitted to the First Committee since, in September, the UNGA had referred to it a single "Question of Peaceful Use of Outer Space" for consideration and report; Howard J Taubenfeld, "Consideration at the United Nations of the Status of Outer Space" (1959) 53(2) American Journal of International Law (hereafter AJIL) 400.

[20] "Union of Soviet Socialist Republics: Draft Resolution" (7 November 1958) A/C.1/L.219 reprinted in GAOR 13th Session Annexes, Agenda Item 60 4, 4–5. Note that the USSR had already proposed the establishment of such a UN agency in March when it submitted the provisional agenda item for consideration by the UNGA; "Union of Soviet Socialist Republics: Request for the Inclusion of an Item in the Provisional Agenda of the Thirteenth Session" (17 March 1958) A/3818 reprinted in GAOR 13th Session Annexes, Agenda Item 60 1, 3.

[21] "Australia, Belgium, Bolivia, Canada, Denmark, France, Guatemala, Ireland, Italy, Japan, Nepal, Netherlands, New Zealand, Sweden, Turkey, Union of South Africa, United Kingdom of Great Britain and Northern Ireland, United States of America, Uruguay and Venezuela: Draft Resolution" (13 November 1958) A/C.1/L.220 reprinted in GAOR 13th Session Annexes, Agenda Item 60 5, 5–6.

[22] Philip C Jessup & Howard J Taubenfeld, *Controls for Outer Space and the Antarctic Analogy* (Columbia University Press 1959) 255.

[23] The representatives proposed were those of the USSR, the United States, the United Kingdom (UK), France, India, Czechoslovakia, Poland, Romania, the United Arab Republic (UAR), Sweden and Argentina; "Union of Soviet Socialist Republics: Revised Draft Resolution" (18 November 1958) A/C.1/L.219/Rev.1 reprinted in GAOR 13th Session Annexes, Agenda Item 60 5.

[24] Jessup and Taubenfeld (n 22) 256.

[25] The states suggested were Argentina, Australia, Belgium, Brazil, Canada, Czechoslovakia, France, India, Iran, Italy, Japan, Mexico, Poland, Sweden, the USSR, the UAR, the UK and the United States; A/C.1/L.220/Rev.1 as cited in "Report of the First Committee" (28 November 1958) UN Doc A/4009 reprinted in GAOR 13th Session Annexes, Agenda Item 60 6, 7.

Evidently, a compromise on the composition and permanence of the proposed UN committee was unattainable.[26] Thus, the USSR withdrew its draft resolution, arguing that it had been submitted as a basis for a *unanimous* decision without which it would not be put to a vote.[27] With this withdrawal, the path for the revised resolution of the United States and its allies was cleared, allowing it to be adopted as a whole by 54 votes to 9 with 18 abstentions.[28]

Ultimately and albeit over Soviet bloc dissent,[29] the General Assembly adopted a resolution[30] whereby, in recognizing the common aim that outer space should be used exclusively for peaceful purposes, and in considering that international cooperation in the study and utilization of outer space for peaceful purposes will promote the strengthening of friendly relations among peoples,[31] it established an Ad Hoc Committee on the Peaceful Uses of Outer Space.[32] The Committee on the Peaceful Uses of Outer Space, or COPUOS, was born.

2 The Advent of Space Law

The establishment of COPUOS marks an important milestone in the regulation of the use and exploration of outer space for, by growing over time into *the* forum for international cooperation in the peaceful uses of outer space,[33] this Committee catalyzed the advent of space law. With its initial task, this Ad Hoc Committee sought to determine, inter alia, the nature of the legal problems that could arise in the conduct of space activities.[34] When this was completed, in the summer of 1959,[35] COPUOS presented a report[36] to the General Assembly containing a multitude of considerations.

One of these considerations suggested that:

> [Because] countries throughout the world proceeded on the premise of the permissibility of the launching and flight of space vehicles which were launched, regardless

[26] Taubenfeld (n 19) 402.

[27] "Report of the First Committee" (28 November 1958) A/4009 reprinted in GAOR 13th Session Annexes, Agenda Item 60 6, 8 (emphasis added).

[28] ibid 8.

[29] Philip C Jessup & Howard J Taubenfeld, "The United Nations Ad Hoc Committee on the Peaceful Uses of Outer Space" (1959) 53(4) AJIL 877.

[30] UNGA Res 1348 (XIII) (13 December 1958).

[31] ibid preambular para 1; 8. [32] ibid para 1.

[33] Nandasiri Jasentuliyana, *International Space Law and the United Nations* (Kluwer 1999) 21 (emphasis added).

[34] UNGA Res 1348 (XIII) (n 30) para 1(d).

[35] C Wilfred Jenks, *Space Law* (Stevens & Sons 1965) 52–53. This task was completed notwithstanding the refusal of the USSR, Poland, and Czechoslovakia (as well as India and the UAR) to participate; Myres S McDougal, Harold D Lasswell, and Ivan A Vlasic, *Law and Public Order in Space* (Yale University Press 1963) 210. In this regard it is to be stated that India and the UAR presumably kept a distance in order to avoid involvement in what may have appeared to be a "Cold War" dispute; Jessup and Taubenfeld (n 29) 877.

[36] COPUOS "Report of the *Ad Hoc* Committee on the Peaceful Uses of Outer Space" (25 June 1959) A/4141.

> of what territory they passed "over" during the course of their flight through outer space [...], there may have been initiated the recognition or establishment of a generally accepted rule to the effect that, in principle, outer space is, on conditions of equality, freely available for exploration and use by *all* in accordance with existing or future international law or agreements.[37]

Thus, in a legal-first, COPUOS pronounced the unique feature of the "freedom" of outer space[38] -a proposition that went unchallenged by all states.[39] Following its consideration of this report, toward the end of 1959 the General Assembly decided to convert the Committee from ad hoc to permanent.[40] With this now permanent status, COPUOS set out to regulate activities conducted in outer space so as to prevent and avoid the development of haphazard practices dictated by national interests.[41]

COPUOS presented the fruit of its first negotiations to the General Assembly two years later.[42] In its report, COPUOS reiterated and elaborated upon the previous legal consideration of the Ad Hoc Committee that outer space was a res communis.[43] It further formulated two principles of utmost importance, which were sanctioned by the General Assembly in its resolution 1721 (XVI), namely (1) that outer space and celestial bodies, unlike newly discovered continents and seas on earth, are not subject to national appropriation and are free for exploration and use by all states, and (2) that international law, including the Charter of the United Nations, applies to outer space and celestial bodies.[44] These principles are in fact so important that, apart from serving as the foundation upon which contemporary space law is erected,[45] they reverberate in contemporary space law itself.[46]

In the following years, COPUOS continued its institutional consolidation with the establishment of two subsidiary organs in 1962, namely its Legal Subcommittee and its Scientific and Technical Subcommittee.[47] This was followed by an even more remarkable

[37] ibid 23 para 9 (emphasis added).

[38] Walter A McDougall, *The Heavens and the Earth: A Political History of the Space Age* (Basic Books 1985) 192.

[39] The "freedom" of outer space also went unchallenged by those states that had refused to participate since, although they refused to endorse the report of COPUOS, this refusal was directed against the composition of COPUOS rather than the results of its deliberations, meaning in turn that this refusal should not be interpreted as implying rejection of the "freedom" principle; McDougal, Lasswell, and Vlasic (n 35) 211.

[40] UNGA Res 1472 A (XIV) (12 December 1959) para 1.

[41] "Era infatti urgente evitare lo sviluppo di pratiche dettate esclusivamente da interessi nazionali"; Sergio Marchisio, "Il Diritto delle Attività Spaziali nell'Era della Cooperazione" in Antonello Folco Biagini & Mariano Bizzarri (eds), *Spazio. Scenari di Collaborazione: Note di Diritto Internazionale* (Passigli Editori 2013) 12.

[42] See UNGA Res 1721 (XVI) (20 December 1961).

[43] Supra (n 37). For more on the res communis nature of outer space see Steven Freeland and Ram Jakhu, "Article II" in Hobe et al (n 18) 46.

[44] UNGA Res 1721 A (XVI), para 1.

[45] Hobe et al (n 18) 12.

[46] Jenks (n 35) 54–55; Katrin Nyman-Metcalf, "Space for the Benefit of Mankind? New Developments and Old Problems" (2009) 34 Annals of Air and Space Law (hereafter AASL) 621, 624.

[47] Sergio Marchisio, "The Evolutionary Stages of the Legal Subcommittee of the United Nations Committee on the Peaceful Uses of Outer Space (COPUOS)" (2005) 31 J Space Law 219, 223.

accomplishment when COPUOS submitted, for consideration by the General Assembly, a draft Declaration of Legal Principles Governing the Activities of States in the Exploration and Uses of Outer Spaces.[48] This declaration (hereinafter the "Declaration of Legal Principles") was adopted by the General Assembly under resolution 1962 (XVIII)[49] and it represents a fundamental step in the codification of space law.[50]

By galvanizing the two principles pronounced in resolution 1721 (XVI) and enshrining a further seven,[51] the Declaration of Legal Principles was the first significant document articulating legal principles on the conduct of activities in outer space.[52] One of the seven additional principles however stands out significantly, especially in terms of the currently increasing privatization and commercialization of space activities. This addition is paragraph 6 of the Declaration of Legal Principles, which provides that states shall bear international responsibility for national activities in outer space, including those by nongovernmental entities, and that activities of nongovernmental entities in outer space shall require authorization and continuing supervision by the state concerned.[53]

Resolution 1962 (XVIII), which embodies the cardinal early normative framework for space activities,[54] is thus "the first chapter in the book of space law."[55]

2.1 The Evolution of Hard Space Law

Notwithstanding the swift pace at which COPUOS progressed in its nascent stages, its work appeared to hit a plateau in the three years following the adoption of the Declaration of Legal Principles. As the then-Chairman of the Legal Subcommittee stated during its fifth session toward the end of 1966, "in [those three years] little progress had been made towards ensuring that outer space was used for [the] advancement [of man] and not for his destruction."[56]

48 Vladimir Kopal, "United Nations and the Progressive Development of International Space Law" (1996) 7 Finnish Yearbook of International Law 1, 7; Martin Menter, "The Developing Law for Outer Space" (1967) 53 ABA J 703.

49 UNGA Res 1962 (XVIII) (13 December 1963).

50 "Cette Résolution marque une étape fondamentale dans la codification du droit de l'espace"; Armand D Roth, *La Prohibition de l'Appropration et les Régimes d'Accès aux Espaces Extra-Terrestres* (Presses Universitaires de France 1992) 47.

51 UNGA Res 1962 (XVIII). Note that it is paragraphs 2–4 of this resolution that galvanize the two principles proclaimed in resolution 1721 (XVI).

52 Karin Traunmüller, "The 'Declaration of Legal Principles Governing the Activities of States in the Exploration of Outer Space': The Starting Point for the United Nations' Law of Outer Space" in Irmgard Marboe (ed), *Soft Law in Outer Space: The Function of Non-binding Norms in International Space Law* (Böhlau 2012) 145; Fabio Tronchetti, *The Exploitation of Natural Resources of the Moon and Other Celestial Bodies: A Proposal for a Legal Regime* (Martinus Nijhoff 2009) 16.

53 UNGA Res 1962 (XVIII) (n 49) para 6.

54 Hobe et al (n 18) 13.

55 Bin Cheng, "United Nations Resolutions on Outer Space: 'Instant' International Customary Law?" (1965) 5 Indian J. Int. Law 23.

56 COPUOS LSC "Summary Record of the Fifty-Seventh Meeting" (20 October 1966) A/AC.105/C.2/SR.57 2–3; Bin Cheng, *Studies in International Space Law* (Clarendon 1999) 216.

Yet, less than half a year later and barely 10 years after the decision was made to regulate this new domain of human endeavour, COPUOS presented to the General Assembly a treaty that the latter unanimously commended,[57] and that eventually became known as the Magna Carta of space law:[58] the "Treaty on Principles Governing the Activities of States in the Exploration and Use of Outer Space, including the Moon and Other Celestial Bodies" (the "Outer Space Treaty" or OST).[59]

The rationale behind the OST was to crystallize the legal principles set forth in resolution 1962 (XVIII) for, although the latter was adopted unanimously[60] and although states, in principle, were and are to respect it by virtue of the maxim *venire contra factum proprium non valet*,[61] being a resolution, it could not be deemed legally binding.[62]

The OST rectified precisely this weakness, and with virtually all of its provisions, except Article IV, being already agreed upon in the Declaration of Legal Principles,[63] it expanded the latter into a *binding* legal framework for the exploration and use of outer space.[64]

Prior to analyzing how the negotiations evolved from that day onward, it is vital to mention that they were successful first and foremost by virtue of the then-Chairman of the LSC of COPUOS: Judge Manfred Lachs. It is beyond any doubt that the United States and the USSR reached a compromise and eventual agreement on the OST thanks to his diplomatic skills and legal brilliance, making him, in his own right, as much a father of this treaty as the states that negotiated it.[65]

[57] UNGA Res 2222 (XXI) (19 December 1966).

[58] Stephan Hobe, "Outer Space as the Province of Mankind—An Assessment of 40 Years of Development" (2007) 50 Proceedings of the International Institute of Space Law (hereafter PIISL) 442; Francis Lyall and Paul B Larsen, *Space Law: A Treatise* (2nd edn, Routledge 2018) 49.

[59] Treaty on Principles Governing the Activities of States in the Exploration and Use of Outer Space, including the Moon and Other Celestial Bodies (adopted 19 December 1966, entered into force 10 October 1967) 610 UNTS 205. As at January 1, 2018, the OST has been ratified by 107 states and signed by another 23 states; COPUOS LSC "Status of International Agreements relating to activities in outer space as at 1 January 2018" (9 April 2018) A/AC.105/C.2/2018/CRP.3 10.

[60] James Crawford, *Brownlie's Principles of Public International Law* (OUP 2012) 42, fn 143.

[61] "'To come against one's own fact (is not allowed).' A maxim of customary international law meaning that one may not set one's self in contradiction to one's own previous conduct" Aaron X Fellmeth and Maurice Horwitz, *Guide to Latin in International Law* (OUP 2009) 290.

[62] Alex Meyer, "Der Weltraumvertrag" (1967) 16 Zeitschrift für Luft- und Weltraumrecht (hereafter ZLW) 65, 69; UN Office of Legal Affairs "Use of the Terms 'Declaration' and 'Recommendation'" (2 April 1962) E/CN.4/L.610 1–2; Cheng (n 56) 133.

[63] Bin Cheng, "The 1967 Outer Space Treaty: Thirtieth Anniversary" (1998) 23 Air and Space Law 156.

[64] ibid; Bin Cheng, "Outer Void Space: The Reason for this Neologism in Space Law" (1999) Australian Intl Law J 1, 4.

[65] See the chapter about Manfred Lachs's contributions to the field of space law by Francis Lyall in Stephan Hobe (ed), *Pioneers of Space Law* (Nijhoff 2013), 193–209. Among Manfred Lachs's many writings in the field, special mention should be made of his excellent book *The Law of Outer Space, an Experience in Contemporary Law-Making* (Sijthoff 1973, republished by the IISL, Nijhoff 2010) and his course *The International Law of Outer Space* at The Hague Academy of International Law, Recueil des Cours (1964-III) 1–114.

2.2 Negotiating the Outer Space Treaty

Set amidst the Cold War, it comes as no surprise that the OST was the product of negotiations between the two major players thereof: the United States and the USSR. These negotiations in fact began on May 11, 1966, nearly three months after the landing of the Soviet "Luna IX" on the moon.[66]

On that day, the United States proposed to the USSR an outline of 12 points, which, the former opined, were to be included in a treaty governing the exploration of the moon and other celestial bodies.[67] Swift in its reply, on May 30, the USSR requested the inclusion of the item "Conclusion of an international agreement on legal principles governing the activities of States in the exploration and conquest of the Moon and other celestial bodies" in the agenda of the 21st session of the General Assembly.[68]

Accordingly, the USSR submitted the text of a draft treaty on June 16, 1966,[69] in light of which the United States submitted the text of its own draft treaty that same day.[70] Juxtaposing the draft of the USSR with that of the United States, a clear difference between the two emanates. The Soviet draft was intended as a general treaty on principles governing the activities of states in the exploration and use of outer space, including the moon and other celestial bodies,[71] and thus may be regarded as a direct implementation of the Declaration of Legal Principles.[72] The US draft had its scope limited to the moon and other celestial bodies,[73] and rather than attempting to convert resolution 1721 (XVI) and the Declaration of Legal Principles into hard law, it represented more of an adaptation of these resolutions to the special circumstances of the moon and other celestial bodies.[74]

[66] Cheng, (n 56) 220. Note that negotiations between the United States and the USSR had already been undertaken with regard to the Declaration of Legal Principles. For instance, in negotiating this resolution, the United States and USSR reached a compromise on whether private activities in outer space could be allowed, with the former being in favor and the latter against. For more on the matter see Jenks (n 35) 210–12.

[67] "Letter dated 16 June 1966 from the Permanent Representative of the United States of America addressed to the Chairman of the Committee on the Peaceful Uses of Outer Space" (17 June 1966) A/Ac.105/32. The 12 points were namely: freedom of exploration, non-appropriation, freedom of and cooperation in scientific investigations, reporting of findings, open access to all areas, non-militarization, jurisdiction of the launching state, ownership of objects launched into space, mutual assistance among astronauts, avoidance of harmful contamination, settlement of disputes, and final clauses; ibid 1-2.

[68] "Union of Soviet Socialist Republics: request for the inclusion of an item in the provisional agenda item of the twenty-first century" (31 May 1966) A/6341.

[69] "Letter dated 16 June 1966 from the Permanent Representative of the Union of Soviet Socialist Republics to the United Nations Addressed to the Secretary-General" (16 June 1966) A/6352.

[70] "Draft Treaty Governing the Exploration of the Moon and Other Celestial Bodies: Letter dated 16 June 1966 from the Permanent Representative of the United States of America addressed to the Chairman of the Committee on the Peaceful Uses of Outer Space" (17 June 1966) A/AC.105/32.

[71] Paul G Dembling and Daniel M Arons, "The Evolution of the Outer Space Treaty" (1967) 33 J Air Law and Commerce 419, 428.

[72] Cheng (n 56) 221. [73] Dembling and Arons (n 71) 428. [74] Cheng (n 56) 221.

Thus, at the opening of the fifth session of the Legal Subcommittee, on July 12, 1966, the debate revolved around two drafts of a rather different nature, and although it soon became clear that the overwhelming majority of states were in favor of the USSR draft, substantial support was also found for many of the novel features included in the US draft.[75]

The general debate ended in a spirit of cooperation between the United States and the USSR, with each declaring its readiness to consider the possibility of incorporating in its draft those features that appeared in the proposal of the other.[76] By way of example, the United States not only agreed to enlarge the scope of the treaty to apply to celestial bodies *and* outer space,[77] but also indicated its general preparedness to accept all proposals in the draft of the USSR that incorporated the terms of previous General Assembly resolutions on outer space.[78] Likewise, the USSR not only accepted the principles of freedom of, and international cooperation in scientific investigations contained in the draft of the United States,[79] but also demonstrated readiness to accept the proposal of the United States of free access to all installations on celestial bodies.[80]

As a result, agreement was reached quite smoothly on what consequently became the first nine articles of the treaty, even though insofar as the substantive articles of the treaty were concerned, agreement had yet to be reached on several facets.[81] One of these facets that proved to be a major stumbling block for the treaty as a whole was the Soviet proposal that each contracting state must grant equal rights, subsequently limited to equal facilities for tracking space objects, to all other contracting states engaged in the exploration of outer space.[82] When the Legal Subcommittee resumed its fifth session on September 12, 1966, it became clear that its members, bar those in the Soviet bloc, were generally unwilling to agree to the equivalent of an unconditional "most-favoured nation clause" on tracking facilities.[83] This seemed problematic since the USSR made it clear that it regarded this provision a sine qua non of the treaty; without an agreement on this article, the USSR was not prepared to take the treaty further.[84]

No further progress had been made by the time COPUOS reconvened on September 19, 1966.[85] However, on September 22, the United States informed the USSR that, if the latter truly desired to provide for tracking coverage from US territory, it was prepared to discuss with Soviet representatives the technical and other requirements involved with a view to reaching some mutually beneficial agreement.[86] Consequently, on October 4, the USSR submitted a revised draft of its treaty, the terms of which show that it had

[75] ibid.

[76] COPUOS LSC "Summary Record of the Sixty-Second Meeting" (24 October 1966) A/AC.105/C.2/SR.62 10–12.

[77] COPUOS LSC "Summary Record of the Sixty-Third Meeting" (20 October 1966) A/AC.105/C.2/SR.63 2–3 (emphasis added).

[78] Cheng (n 56) 222.

[79] COPUOS LSC "Summary Record of the Sixty-Third Meeting" (n 77) 4–5.

[80] ibid.

[81] Cheng (n 56) 222.

[82] ibid 222–23; Dembling and Arons (n 71) 442.

[83] Cheng (n 56) 223.

[84] ibid.

[85] Dembling and Arons (n 71) 444.

[86] UN, First Committee of the General Assembly "Twenty-First Session" (22 September 1966) A/PV.1412 41.

reached a compromise with the United States on tracking facilities,[87] along with agreement on several other facets such as the preamble, the use of military equipment, and the conditions governing visits to installations on celestial bodies.[88]

With this progress, minor formalistic issues were creased out and, on December 8, complete agreement was achieved.[89] The agreed text was submitted to the First Committee of the General Assembly on December 15,[90] which adopted it without objection on December 17.[91] Ultimately, the treaty was opened for signature on January 27, 1967, and came into force on October 10, 1967.

2.3 Beyond the Outer Space Treaty

Now that we have seen how the OST was brought to life, it is possible to provide some insight on its substance. Insight can be also provided on the substance of the four other treaties that followed the Magna Carta of space law, which, along with their predecessor, form the hard law regime of outer space.

Composed of 13 substantive articles,[92] the OST lays down *the* fundamental legal rules on the use and exploration of outer space. While Articles I, II, and III of the OST expand upon what by then had become rather clear principles of space law–that is, the principles that the use and exploration of outer space shall be the province of all mankind, that any sovereign or territorial claims in outer space are prohibited, and that space activities shall not violate international law, including the UN Charter–its subsequent provisions articulate an array of diverse and often innovative principles.

Key among these other articles is Article IV, which, although far less celebrated than the previous three, provides the principle that the moon and other celestial bodies are to be used exclusively for peaceful purposes.[93] The importance of this principle cannot be stressed enough: were it not for this principle, it is plausible that, by now, weapons would have been warehoused in outer space, with earth being their primary target. It is therefore by virtue of Article IV that life on earth has been able to flow on in relative peace.

[87] Cheng (n 56) 224. [88] ibid. [89] ibid.

[90] "International Co-operation in the Peaceful Uses of Outer Space: Report of the Committee on the Peaceful Uses of Outer Space" (15 December 1966) A/AC.1/L.396; "International Co-operation in the Peaceful Uses of Outer Space: Report of the Committee on the Peaceful Uses of Outer Space" (15 December 1966) A/AC.1/L.396/Add.1; "International Co-operation in the Peaceful Uses of Outer Space: Report of the Committee on the Peaceful Uses of Outer Space" (15 December 1966) A/AC.1/L.396/Add.2.

[91] UN, First Committee of the General Assembly "Twenty-First Session" (17 December 1966) A/AC.1/SR.1493 445, para 86.

[92] Articles XIV to XVI of the OST only deal with certain non-substantive formalities; Carl Q Christol, *Modern International Law of Outer Space* (Pergamon Press 1982) 49.

[93] Note that the term "peaceful purposes" poses some difficulty as to its true meaning; Julia Neumann, "An Interpretation of the Outer Space Treaty after 40 Years" (2007) 50 PIISL 431, 437. This notwithstanding, state practice over the years has generally supported the view that "peaceful purposes" means "non-aggressive purposes"; therefore, although space objects have been used extensively to support military operations here on earth, weapons per se have never actually been deployed in outer space; Space Security Index 2004, "Chapter 2: Space Security Laws, Policies, and Doctrines" (2005) 30(2) AASL 343, 346.

Over and above Articles I, II, III, and IV, the other articles of the OST inter alia provide that states are internationally responsible for governmental and private activities in outer space,[94] that states are liable for damages caused by space objects they launch,[95] and that states retain jurisdiction and control over the space objects they register.[96]

Although the OST was a momentous leap in the evolution of space law, in view of the broadness of its legal rules it soon came to be seen as requiring further elaboration,[97] and to this end four more treaties were negotiated under the auspices of the UN. These four subsequent treaties did not deviate from the OST; mostly, they served to elaborate on the basic principles enshrined within it so much so that they could be considered as a lex specialis thereof. However, a unique and new feature that was introduced in these four treaties is the possibility for intergovernmental organizations to declare their acceptance of the rights and obligations under them, and indeed, several of such organizations[98] have done so for the first three treaties addressed in this section.

The first of these additional treaties was the Agreement on the Rescue of Astronauts, the Return of Astronauts and the Return of Objects Launched into Outer Space (the "Rescue Agreement"), adopted on December 19, 1967.[99] This treaty is an earth-oriented instrument as it provides that a state that learns that either an astronaut, or a space object, has landed anywhere on earth other than in the territory of another state, shall notify the launching authority and the Secretary-General of the UN of that landing,[100] and shall help return the astronaut or space object safely to the launching authority.[101]

Following this treaty came the Convention on International Liability for Damage Caused by Space Objects (the "Liability Convention") of November 29, 1971,[102] which was crafted so as to build upon the principle of liability held within Article VII of the OST.[103] In achieving this, the Liability Convention provides that a "launching State"[104]

[94] OST (n 59) art VI. [95] ibid art VII. [96] ibid art VIII.

[97] Frans von der Dunk, "International Space Law" in Frans von der Dunk and Fabio Tronchetti (eds), *Handbook of Space Law* (Edward Elgar 2015) 39.

[98] These IGOs are the European Organization for the Exploitation of Meteorological Satellites (EUMETSAT) and the European Space Agency (ESA) for the first three treaties hereunder addressed, the European Telecommunications Satellite Organization (EUTELSAT) for the second and the third, and the Intersputnik International Organization of Space Communications for the third treaty only.

[99] Agreement on the Rescue of Astronauts, the Return of Astronauts and the Return of Objects Launched into Outer Space (adopted 19 December 1967, entered into force 3 December 1968) 672 UNTS 119. As at January 1, 2018, the Rescue Agreement has been ratified by 96 states, signed by 23 states, and 2 international organizations have deposited a declaration of acceptance of its rights and obligations; COPUOS LSC (n 59).

[100] Rescue Agreement arts 1 and 5. [101] ibid arts 2 to 5.

[102] Convention on International Liability for Damage Caused by Space Objects (adopted 29 November 1971, entered into force 1 September 1972) 961 UNTS 187. As at January 1, 2018, the Liability Convention has been ratified by 95 states, while 19 states have signed it and 3 international organizations have deposited a declaration of acceptance of its rights and obligations; COPUOS LSC (n 59).

[103] von der Dunk and Tronchetti (n 97) 82.

[104] A "launching State" is defined as "a State that launches or procures the launch of a space object; a State from whose territory or facility a space object is launched"; Liability Convention (n 102) art I(c).

is absolutely liable to pay compensation for damages caused by its "space object"[105] on the surface of earth or to aircraft in flight.[106] Furthermore, a state is liable to pay compensation if its space object causes "damage"[107] elsewhere than on the surface of the earth to a space object, or persons or property on-board it, due to the fault of persons for whom it, as a state, is responsible.[108]

The third treaty following the OST was the Convention on Registration of Objects Launched into Outer Space (the "Registration Convention"), adopted on November 12, 1974.[109] This treaty refined the registration principle contained in Article VIII of the OST by establishing, at its core, a dual system of registration of objects launched into outer space.[110] Thus, the Registration Convention first provides that a "launching State"[111] is to maintain a registry of space objects and enter on it a space object that it has launched into earth orbit or beyond,[112] then it further creates a UN Registry that fundamentally serves the same purpose.[113]

Last, the Agreement Governing the Activities of States on the Moon and Other Celestial Bodies (the "Moon Agreement") was adopted on December 5, 1979.[114] The majority of this treaty, like the three previous ones, reiterates certain well-established principles such as that the moon shall be used exclusively for peaceful purposes,[115] and that the exploration of the moon shall be the province of all mankind.[116] Nevertheless, this treaty goes beyond the Magna Carta of space law by addressing not only the "use" and "exploration" of the moon, but also the "exploitation" of its natural resources. It is impossible to overlook the fact that, in doing so, the Moon Agreement is much less successful than its predecessors.[117] This stems from its classification of the moon and

105 A "space object" is defined as "[including] component parts of a space object as well as its launch vehicle and parts thereof"; ibid art I(d). In this regard, it is acknowledged that this description is effectively a non-definition since it is (clearly) circular and difficult to interpret; Stephan Hobe, "International Space Law in Its First Half Century" (2006) 49 PIISL 373, 375; Henry R Hertzfeld, "A Roadmap for a Sustainable Space Law Regime" (2012) 55 PIISL 299, 303.

106 Liability Convention (n 102) art II.

107 "Damage" is defined as "loss of life, personal injury, or other impairment of health, or, loss of or damage to property of States or of persons, natural or juridical, or property of international intergovernmental organisations"; ibid art I(a).

108 ibid art III.

109 Convention on Registration of Objects Launched into Outer Space (adopted 12 November 1974, entered into force 15 September 1976) 1023 UNTS 15. As at January 1, 2018, the Registration Convention has been ratified by 67 states, signed by 3 states, and 4 international organizations have deposited a declaration of acceptance of its rights and obligations; COPUOS LSC (n 59).

110 Fabio Tronchetti, *Fundamentals of Space Law and Policy* (Springer 2013) 12; Hobe (n 105) 375.

111 A "launching State" is defined as "a State that launches or procures the launch of a space object; a State from whose territory or facility a space object is launched"; Registration Convention (n 109) art I(a).

112 Registration Convention art II.

113 ibid art III; Cheng, (n 56) 159.

114 Agreement Governing the Activities of States on the Moon and Other Celestial Bodies (adopted 5 December 1979, entered into force 11 July 1984) 1363 UNTS 3. As at January 1, 2018, the Moon Agreement has been ratified by 17 states and signed by 4 states; COPUOS LSC "Status of International Agreements relating to activities in outer space as at 1 January 2017" (n 59).

115 Moon Agreement art 3(1).

116 ibid art 4(1).

117 Stephan Hobe, "The Moon Agreement—Let's Use the Chance!" (2010) 59 Zeitschrift für Luft- und Weltraumrecht (hereafter ZLW) 372.

the natural resources thereof as "the common heritage of mankind,"[118] a concept derived from the law of the sea, even though the Moon Agreement specifies that this term should "find its expression in [its] provisions."[119] Suffice it to say that the concept of common heritage of mankind in the Moon Agreement has led to much debate and disagreement, especially in recent years with the prospect of commercially harvesting space resources having become more realistic.[120] Consequently, the limited role that the Moon Agreement has played thus far is not likely to change, despite its unanimous adoption by the General Assembly.

3 The Future of Hard Space Law

After the Moon Agreement of 1979, no new space treaties were adopted under the auspices of the UN, and thus the dynamic phase of treaty-making came to an end. The lack of new treaties could be attributed to a lack of political will among states, sometimes referred to as "treaty fatigue/congestion" also seen in other areas of international law.[121]

Instead, there was a return to declaring legal principles in the form of UN General Assembly resolutions, leading to a number of new "soft law" instruments. However, as one of the early Chairs of COPUOS recently put it:

> [...] while the first of these resolutions, in particular resolution 1962 (XVIII) of 13 December 1963, had the objective to launch the process of international cooperation in space and thus create a basis for a space legislation process later, now the establishment of a number of sets of principles by UN General Assembly resolutions had to regulate more special and more technical categories of space activities. In this way the sets of principles elaborated and adopted by the General Assembly included

[118] Moon Agreement (n 114) art 11(1).

[119] ibid.

[120] Stephan Hobe, Peter Stubbe, and Fabio Tronchetti, "Historical Background and Context" in Stephan Hobe, Bernhard Schmidt-Tedd, and Kai-Uwe Schrogl (eds), *Cologne Commentary on Space Law: Volume 2* (Carl Heymanns Verlag 2013) 336. Note that art 11(7)(d) of the Moon Agreement requires an "equitable sharing" by all states parties in the benefits derived from the exploited natural resources of the moon. This constitutes the most controversial idea, if not also the greatest deterrent, of the said treaty; Ram Jakhu, Steven Freeland, Stephan Hobe and Fabio Tronchetti, "Article 11 (Common Heritage of Mankind/International Regime)" in Hobe et al supra 398.

[121] Edith Brown Weiss, "International Environmental Law: Contemporary Issues and the Emergence of a New World Order" (1993) 81 Georgetown LJ 675, 697. Note that the essence of treaty congestion lies in the appearance of too much law, too fast; Donald K Anton, "'Treaty Congestion' in Contemporary International Environmental Law" in Shawkat Alam, Jahid Hossain Bhuiyan, Tareq MR Chowdhury, and Erika J Techera (eds), *Routledge Handbook of International Environmental Law* (3rd edn, Routledge 2015) 652. Note further that, although EB Weiss originally coined the concept of "treaty congestion" in terms of international environmental law, this concept can be equally applied to public international law in general; Joost Pauwelyn, Ramses A Wessel, and Jan Wouters, "When Structures Become Shackles: Stagnation and Dynamics in International Lawmaking" (2014) 25 Eur. J Intl Law 733,739.

> principles governing television broadcasting (1982), remote sensing of the earth from space (1986), the use of nuclear power sources in outer space (1992) and a Declaration on international cooperation for the benefit and in the interest of all states, taking into particular account the needs of developing countries (1996).[122]

A third wave of General Assembly resolutions adopted in the early part of the twenty-first century have addressed certain concepts contained in the treaties, such as the concept of the launching state,[123] the practice of states in registering space objects,[124] and the adoption of national legislation to implement the obligation to authorize and supervise activities by nongovernmental entities.[125] Interestingly, however, each of these resolutions contains a preambular paragraph stating that nothing in the resolution constitutes an authoritative interpretation of, or proposed amendment to, any of the UN treaties on outer space.

While it makes sense, of course, that a soft-law instrument such as a UN General Assembly resolution cannot be considered as treaty interpretation unless its specific intent and purpose was to serve as such, in the absence of jurisprudence by, for instance, the International Court of Justice, this is also somewhat regrettable. Nonetheless, the resolutions provide useful insight in the opinio juris of states, and could, if accompanied by state practice, be seen as evidence of customary law.[126]

The question of how effective and influential the UN treaty regime has been over time is a valid one, as is the question whether that regime can address future challenges and accommodate all legal issues raised by recent developments, for the landscape is changing swiftly. An increasing number of private entities, including start-ups and universities, are entering the field of space activity, and more and more emerging space nations, in seeking to achieve their space ambitions, request membership of COPUOS to participate in its rule-making activities, consequently making its consensus process exponentially more complex.

Space technology progresses at rapid speed, and revolutionary, new space endeavors enter the scene, such as the deployment of large constellations of very small satellites, private human launches to the edge of space, and space resource mining on the moon or asteroids. The legal aspects of these new activities are not explicitly addressed in the treaties, and additional clarification and elaboration of the basic principles contained therein is needed.

122 Peter Jankowitsch, "The Outer Space Treaty: Its First Fifty Years" (2017) 60 PIISL 3, 7–8. The four resolutions mentioned by Jankowitsch respectively are: UNGA Res 37/92 (10 December 1982); UNGA Res 41/65 (3 December 1986); UNGA Res 47/68 (14 December 1992); UNGA Res 51/122 (13 December 1996).

123 UNGA Res 59/115 (10 December 2004).

124 UNGA Res 62/101 (17 December 2007).

125 UNGA Res 68/74 (11 December 2013).

126 *North Sea Continental Shelf (Germany v Denmark/Netherlands)* (Merits) [1969] ICJ Rep 3, 43–44; *Continental Shelf (Libyan Arab Jamahiriya v Malta)* (Merits) [1985] ICJ Rep 13, 29; *Case Concerning Military and Paramilitary Activities in and against Nicaragua (Nicaragua v USA)* (Merits) [1986] ICJ Rep 14, 97.

Be that as it may, the UN space treaties remain fully applicable and valid even after 50 years: a small number of states ratify the space treaties each year, no state has ever withdrawn from them, there have been no violations of the main legal tenets of peaceful space cooperation, and amendments have never been proposed. Challenges posed by the new playing field can, to some extent, be addressed by means of national space legislation designed to keep private activities in line with the treaty provisions, as well as by bilateral or multilateral agreements. The risk, however, is that commercial interests, rather than global ones, may prevail.[127]

Arguably, issues that affect humankind as a whole require global solutions to be agreed under the auspices of the UN. The long-term sustainability of space activities is a good example of an issue that affects all actors and that requires such a global solution, ideally in the form of a hard law instrument such as a treaty. Interestingly, however, this topic is not included on the agenda of the Legal Subcommittee of COPUOS, but is dealt with in the Scientific and Technical Subcommittee.[128] Furthermore, the process is cumbersome and fraught with political interests, and full agreement has not yet been reached. These points can be seen as further illustrations of the reluctance of states to accept new legally binding rules, and of their preference for soft-law solutions, even if the latter are still to have a global scope, and are still to be achieved within COPUOS and under the auspices of the UN.[129]

4 Conclusion

To date, the UN has played a major role in elaborating an entirely new field of international law applicable to activities in the new dimension of outer space. These rules have stood the test of time and have ensured peaceful cooperation among states in outer space, despite a geopolitical setting characterized by extreme tension. Fifty years later,

[127] The recently adopted national legislations on commercial space mining in the United States and Luxembourg may serve as an example. Even though these laws were justified by the need to provide clarity and legal certainty to an emerging new industry, and both laws explicitly state the intent not to violate international space law, not all states approve this process. For an analysis, see for instance Tanja Masson-Zwaan and Neta Palkovitz, "Regulation of Space Resource Rights: Meeting the Needs of States and Private Parties" (2017) 35 Questions Intl Law 5.

[128] In 2010, the Working Group on the Long-term Sustainability of Outer Space Activities was established in the Scientific and Technical Subcommittee. Its objectives include identifying areas of concern, proposing measures to enhance sustainability, and producing voluntary guidelines to reduce risks to long-term sustainability. Thematic areas include, inter alia, space debris, space situational awareness, space weather and regulatory regimes, and guidance for actors. In June 2016 a first set of guidelines was agreed (COPUOS "Report of the Committee on the Peaceful Uses of Outer Space" (8 June 2016) A/71/20 Annex), and in 2018, consensus was reached on a preamble and nine additional guidelines; "Report of the Scientific and Technical Sub-committee on its Fifty-Fifth Session" (14 February 2018) A/AC.105/1167, Annex III; see also COPUOS "Report of the Committee on the Peaceful Uses of Outer Space" (20 June 2018) A/73/20. This notwithstanding, the Working Group was unable to refer the said preamble and guidelines to the General Assembly.

[129] Jankowitsch (n 122) 10.

the scene has changed dramatically, both in terms of actors involved and emerging opportunities. In response, the UN must reassess its role in regulating this new phase of space activity.

The relevance of newly emerging topics is acknowledged by COPUOS, while they also gradually find their way onto the Legal Subcommittee. For instance, new items addressing space traffic management and small satellites,[130] and the governance of the use, exploration, and exploitation of space resources[131] were included in the agenda of the Legal Subcommittee, respectively in 2015 and 2016. It is also encouraging that COPUOS cooperates efficiently with other UN bodies, thus recognizing the interdisciplinary nature of space activities. By way of example, a booklet on "Guidance on Space Object Registration and Frequency Management for Small and Very Small Satellites"[132] was recently developed in cooperation with the International Telecommunication Union. Likewise, the Office of Outer Space Affairs (the secretariat of COPUOS) cooperates with the International Civil Aviation Organization with regard to the regulation of commercial space flight.[133]

A number of states have expressed the concern that the role of the UN as a forum for space lawmaking may be reduced in the future, given, for instance, the emergence of national legislation addressing topics of universal concern.[134] A fruitful opportunity with which COPUOS reaffirmed its unique role in international space lawmaking arrived in the form of the "UNISPACE+50" session,[135] held in June 2018. This event was constructed around seven "Thematic Priorities," one of which was titled "Legal Regime of Outer Space and Global Space Governance: Current and Future Perspectives." Another indication that states are determined to uphold the pivotal role of the UN in the field of space lawmaking is the resolution adopted by the General Assembly, in the form of a "Declaration," on the fiftieth anniversary of the OST.[136] With this Declaration, the

[130] UNOOSA, "Space Traffic Management and Small Satellites: New Topics to Be Included in the United Nations International Space Law Discussions" (24 April 2015) UNIS/OS/449 <http://www.unoosa.org/oosa/en/informationfor/media/2015-unis-os-449.html> accessed March 12, 2019.

[131] UNIS, "Utilization of Space Resources to Be Included In United Nations International Space Law Discussions" (19 April 2016) UNIS/OS/464 <http://www.unis.unvienna.org/unis/en/pressrels/2016/unisos464.html> accessed March 12, 2019.

[132] UNOOSA & ITU, "Guidance on Space Object Registration and Frequency Management for Small and Very Small Satellites" (1 April 2015) <http://www.unoosa.org/documents/pdf/psa/bsti/2015_Handout-on-Small-SatellitesE.pdf> accessed March 12, 2019.

[133] ICAO, "Space Transportation" <https://www4.icao.int/space> accessed March 12, 2019.

[134] See, eg, "Report of the Legal Sub-committee on its Fifty-Sixth Session" (18 April 2017) A/AC.105/1122 9, paras 44 and 45.

[135] See UNOOSA, "Fifty Years since the First United Nations Conference on the Exploration and Peaceful Uses of Outer Space (1968–2018): UNISPACE+50" <http://www.unoosa.org/oosa/en/ourwork/unispaceplus50/index.html> accessed March 12, 2019.

[136] UNGA Res 72/78 (14 December 2017). Although the adoption of this resolution is positive, it was "hidden" in a package of 38 resolutions and 2 decisions, meaning that the UN General Assembly missed out on a rare opportunity to bring to the forefront the importance of the OST and space law as a whole; UN, "General Assembly Adopts 38 Resolutions, 2 Decisions from Fourth Committee, Including Texts on Decolonization, Israeli-Palestinian Issues" (*UN*, 7 December 2017) <https://www.un.org/press/en/2017/ga11987.doc.htm> accessed March 12, 2019.

member states of the UN "reaffirm the fundamental role played by the treaty" and are "convinced that it will continue to provide an indispensable framework for the conduct of outer space activities."[137]

The UN will certainly continue to play a major role in the formulation of new international space law, although it might be in the form of soft law. Much will depend on the political will of states to reach consensus. The tendency toward increased adherence to the five UN space treaties, and the efforts of states to reach international agreement, even if non-legally binding, on new issues of universal interest are encouraging in this respect.

[137] UNGA Res 72/78 (14 December 2017) (n 136) paras 4–5.

B. ECONOMIC AND SOCIAL DEVELOPMENT

CHAPTER 10

ENVIRONMENT AND SUSTAINABLE DEVELOPMENT

MARIE-CLAIRE CORDONIER SEGGER AND ALEXANDRA HARRINGTON*

THE ecological systems of our planet are interconnected, across earth, water, and air. Environmental challenges, and also opportunities for more sustainable development, often extend beyond the sovereign boundaries of states. International problems, accords, and disputes on the environment and on sustainable development have been identified, negotiated, adopted, implemented, resolved, and refined for centuries, as documented in international law scholarship.[1] In recent decades, however, scientific information on the drivers and scope of global environment and development problems has become more certain.[2] At the same time, fragmented domestic environment and development policy efforts have demonstrably failed to address increasing risks on many levels. International consensus has emerged on the need to deliver more sustainable development

* Full Professor of Law, School of Environment, Entrepreneurship & Development (SEED), University of Waterloo; Senior Director, Centre for International Sustainable Development Law (CISDL); Senior Advisor/Fellow, Centre for Environment, Energy & Natural Resources Governance (CEENRG) and Lauterpatcht Centre for International Law (LCIL), University of Cambridge; & Executive Secretary, UN Framework Convention on Climate Change Climate Law & Governance Initiative (CLGI). Warmest thanks and acknowledgments are extended for the insights and contributions of Dr. Alexandra Harrington, Lead Counsel for Governance & Intergenerational Justice, CISDL; & Fulbright Canada Research Chair in Global Governance, Balsillie School of International Affairs, Canada.

[1] See, eg, Patricia W Birnie, Alan E Boyle, and Catherine Redgwell, *International Law & the Environment* (3rd edn, OUP 2009); Philippe Sands, *Principles of International Environmental Law* (3rd edn, CUP 2012); Marie-Claire Cordonier Segger and Ashfaq Khalfan, *Sustainable Development Law: Principles, Practices & Prospects* (OUP 2004).

[2] See United Nations Environment Programme (UNEP) "Global Environment Outlook 5: Environment for the Future We Want" (2012); Intergovernmental Panel on Climate Change (IPCC) "Climate Change 2014: Synthesis Report. Contribution of Working Groups I, II and III to the Fifth Assessment Report of the Intergovernmental Panel on Climate Change" (Geneva 2015).

worldwide, even as it becomes increasingly apparent that much greater collaboration is required to achieve global goals in many areas.

In this context, international treaty-making has intensified.[3] For international accords on the environment and on sustainable development, during recent decades of intensive treaty negotiations and implementation efforts, all actors involved have relied on the UN at each step of the way. The role of the UN in treaty-making on the environment and on sustainable development has been significant, substantial, and indeed, almost ubiquitous in many instances. The UN's involvement supports the formal negotiators representing interested coalitions of states, and also the broader epistemic communities—the networks of state and nonstate actors involved in problem-solving and collaboration related to the object and purpose of the treaties. From transboundary problem identification and scientific collaboration; to the facilitation of negotiations and eventual consensus; to the promotion of ratification and implementation; to the establishment and operation of financial instruments; to support for capacity-building, public education, and participation; to the peaceful dispute settlement, compliance, and transparency (monitoring, reporting, and verification) efforts that then "interactionally" refine the regimes themselves, the UN has guided and supported the emergence of international law on the environment and sustainable development.[4]

The myriad and interconnected processes that the UN chaperones in these fields also contribute to achieving the objectives of the UN Charter itself, including efforts to realize the global Sustainable Development Goals (SDGs), which were adopted by the UN in 2015 to chart an international cooperation agenda forward to 2030.[5]

Several waves of environmental treaties have been negotiated over recent decades to establish and refine international structures for cooperation. International regimes, sometimes linking several international treaties and instruments, seek to address interrelated "clusters" of environmental problems as their object. For the purposes of this chapter, such environmental treaties can be clustered (non-exhaustively) as addressing objects such as: (1) the conservation and recovery of nature, biodiversity, and wildlife; (2) the protection of clean freshwater systems and wetlands; (3) the sound management of chemicals, air pollutants, and hazardous substances; (4) the protection of the world's oceans and marine resources; and (5) the global response to atmospheric threats such as anthropogenic climate change and the destruction of the ozone layer.[6] While this chapter

[3] Birnie, Boyle, and Redgwell (n 1); Sands (n 1); Cordonier, Segger, and Khalfan (n 2).

[4] Jutta Brunnee and Stephen J Toope, "Interactional International Law" [2011] 3 International Theory 307; Marie-Claire Cordonier Segger, "Advancing the Paris Agreement on Climate Change for Sustainable Development" (2016) 5(2) Cambridge J Intl and Comp L 38; Carol A Petsonk, "The Role of the United Nations Environment Programme (UNEP) in the Development of International Law" (1990) 5 Am Univ Intl L Rev 351; Laurence D Mee, "The Role of UNEP and UNDP in Multilateral Environmental Agreements" (2005) 5(3) Intl Environmental Agreements: Politics, Law and Economics 227.

[5] UN General Assembly (UNGA) "Transforming Our World: The 2030 Agenda for Sustainable Development" (25 September 2015) UN Doc A/70/L.1.

[6] See Governing Council of the United Nations Environment Programme "Fourth Programme for the Development and Periodic Review of Environmental Law" (27 October 2008) UN Doc UNEP/GC/25/INF/15.

focuses mainly on the key multilateral environmental agreements brokered by the United Nations, many bilateral and regional environmental accords have also been agreed, seeking to address more localized aspects of these and other challenges.

At the same time (and in several instances, quid pro quo), international law and policy commitments have been made to promote more sustainable development, not just in developing countries but across all regions of the world.[7] International instruments and accords on sustainable development include many environmental treaties, but also accords on human rights and social development, and agreements on trade, investment, and other economic cooperation.[8] Inter-state efforts are intensifying to promote more sustainable use of natural resources such as renewable energy, water, soil, seeds and plants, forests, genetic resources, marine resources including fisheries, and minerals. There are efforts to support more sustainable development in social sectors such as health and education, and in economic sectors such as transport, infrastructure, tourism, information and communications technology, and bioprospecting.[9]

In this light, this chapter considers the UN contributions to treaty-making *in practice* on the environment and sustainable development. It begins with a brief survey of the crafting and "clustering" of multilateral environmental agreements as international responses to emerging global environmental problems. Specifically, the chapter considers the role of the UN in this process, focusing on successive waves of treaty-making over recent decades. It suggests that the UN has played a very important role in negotiations in this field, and continues to serve as a crucial and valuable actor in the implementation and refinement of these treaties and the broader problem-based clusters, in spite of very limited resources.

The interrelationships between myriad international instruments across environmental, economic, and social spheres seeking to promote more sustainable development are also highlighted in this chapter. The chapter identifies, as illustrative examples, several key treaties that address a selection of the SDGs, leading to a concluding consideration of how international accords in this field are, in turn, contributing to the UN Charter. Indeed, it suggests, without the UN-facilitated treaties, many SDGs could be considered "hollow," dependent on voluntary collaborations, and devoid of reliable regimes to achieve their targets. Not all relationships are equally integrated, and fragmentation, duplication, and even unintended overlapping of obligations or conflicts can exist. However, as international governance becomes more sophisticated and complex, these interrelated instruments can be negotiated, implemented, and interactionally refined across multiple nested levels. To this end, the chapter argues, adoption of the SDGs may support greater coherence across the UN system.

[7] See, eg, Marie-Claire Cordonier Segger and HE Judge CG Weeramantry (eds), *Sustainable Development Principles in the Decisions of International Courts and Tribunals* (Routledge, 2017); Nico Schrijver, Freidl Weiss, and Bruno Simma, *International Law and Sustainable Development: Principles and Practices* (Martinus Nijhoff 2004); Elisabeth Burgi Nonanomi, *Sustainable Development in International Law Making and Trade: International Food Governance and Trade in Agriculture* (Edward Elgar 2015).

[8] Cordonier, Segger, and Khalfan (n 2).

[9] ibid.

1 Problem-Based Clusters of Multilateral Environmental Agreements (MEAs)

In recent decades, facilitated by the UN primarily through UN-Environment, there has been a significant strengthening of international environmental governance (IEG). Even before the creation of the UN Environment Programme (UNEP, or since 2016, UN-Environment) in 1972, many international organizations, policy instruments, financing mechanisms, rules, procedures, and norms were mobilized to facilitate and regulate the processes of global environmental protection. As UN-Environment explains, the international community has adopted over 500 Multilateral Environmental Agreements (MEAs), around 25 of which are truly global in nature; created a series of environmental funds including Global Environment Facility (GEF); and given mandates to more than 40 UN and other intergovernmental bodies to address environmental issues.[10] For analysis, MEA regimes can be clustered around key global problems, where substantive cooperative inter-regime bonds exist to facilitate more efficient, coordinated, and effective action.[11] In each cluster, as mentioned previously, it can be argued that the role of the UN has been key, not just in consensus-building and treaty-making, but also in scientific collaboration, ratification and compliance promotion, financing, capacity-building, public education and participation, dispute settlement, and transparency.

1.1 Global Response to the Threat of Climate Change, Desertification, and Ozone Layer Destruction

The UN's support for the negotiation, implementation, and strengthening of the regime surrounding the 1992 UN Framework Convention on Climate Change (UNFCCC)[12] has been deeply influential in shaping global response to climate change. The UNFCCC itself has been important not only for its principles and the framework for scientific collaboration that was established under its auspices, but also for the instruments for cooperation established through the 1987 Kyoto Protocol and the 2015 Paris Agreement.[13] An annual conference of the parties (CoPs) has grown from about 500 delegates to over

[10] UN-Environment, International Environmental Governance (UNEP, 2017) online: <1https://www.unenvironment.org/annualreport/2015/en/environmental-governance.html>.

[11] See Konrad von Moltke, "On Clustering International Environmental Agreements" (IISD 2001).

[12] United Nations Framework Convention on Climate Change (UNFCCC) (adopted 9 May 1992, entered into force 21 March 1994) 1771 UNTS 107.

[13] Kyoto Protocol to the United Nations Framework Convention on Climate Change (adopted 11 December 1997, entered into force 16 February 2005) 2303 UNTS 148; Paris Agreement (adopted 12 December 2015, entered into force 4 November 2016).

25,000 parties and observers in the Paris UNFCCC CoP21, supported by a network of domestic national authorities that have steadily gained in expertise and influence. To support these party-led processes, UNFCCC Secretariat facilitates technical and scientific collaboration, gathers crucial information from state parties and observers, and facilitates transparent monitoring and reporting on progress, encouraging higher ambition to address climate mitigation, adaptation/resilience and financing, raising public awareness, and promoting collaboration for compliance. Though the slow nature of inter-state negotiations has raised questions, the CoPs provide an important meeting point for inter-party coalitions and activities, including for least-developed parties, such as the most highly climate vulnerable countries, to participate in the regime. CoPs also serve to engage a vast array of observers and other non-state actors, including subnational authorities, cities, firms, academic institutions, and civil society organizations, to develop collaborations within the treaty framework, launching initiatives and actions to support the implementation and monitoring of the treaty. UN-Environment, UNDP (United Nations Development Programme), and other agencies have played crucial roles in the regime. They facilitate scientific cooperation and monitoring endeavors on climate change including the Inter-Governmental Panel on Climate Change itself, provide expertise and guidance for the drafting and implementation of Nationally Determined Contributions under the Paris Agreement, build capacity and broker compromises, and assist access to the Global Environment Facility and the Green Climate Fund, among other contributions.

In addition, the UN system plays an essential organizational and implementation role in the treaty regime for the protection of the common global atmosphere. The Vienna Convention on the Protection of the Ozone Layer, enacted in 1985 and subsequently updated and subject to additional protocols, was established to resolve a significant environmental challenge (the depletion of the ozone layer), based on scientific collaboration facilitated by UN-Environment and other UN instruments.[14] It creates general obligations for states to engage in inter-state cooperation to understand the impacts of ozone depletion on human health, requiring states to translate these findings into national and international legal regimes to prevent ozone depletion and address its effects.[15] To ensure coordination and cooperation, the Vienna Convention provides for CoPs that are, in application, administered by UN-Environment.[16] Indeed, the Vienna Convention is overseen and supported overall by the Ozone Secretariat, which exists within the parameters of UN-Environment.[17]

[14] Vienna Convention on the Protection of the Ozone Layer (open for signature 22 March 1985, entered into force 22 September 1988) 1513 UNTS 293, preamble. See also Osamu Yoshida, *The International Legal Regime for the Protection of the Stratospheric Ozone Layer: International Law, International Regimes, and Sustainable Development* (Martinus Nijhoff 2001); Petsonk (n 5); Cesare PR Romano, "Ozone Layer Depletion" in CPR Romano, *Conventions, Treaties and Other Responses to Global Issues II* (UNESCO 2009).

[15] Vienna Convention on the Protection of the Ozone Layer (n 14) arts 1–4.

[16] ibid art 6.

[17] ibid art 7.

Under the Vienna Convention, the Montreal Protocol on Substances that Deplete the Ozone Layer has been enacted to control identified substances that cause damage to the ozone layer.[18] In the Montreal Protocol, state parties agree to regulate their trade of certain ozone-depleting substances with each other and also with non-state parties to the Protocol.[19] It establishes an intergovernmental compliance mechanism to facilitate transparency and capacity for treaty implementation, linked to a financing mechanism that is supported by UN-Environment and the UNDP, among others.[20] The Montreal Protocol is overseen by the Ozone Secretariat, falling under the rubric of UN-Environment, and its implementation is guided by an annual Meeting of the Parties (MoPs).[21] As a result of work conducted across several MoPs, with significant support from UN-Environment and others, in 2016 the Kigali Amendment to the Montreal Protocol was established.[22] The Kigali Amendment focuses on the reduction of emissions of hydrofluorocarbons (HFCs) by developed and developing states, with the assistance from the Multilateral Fund that is financed in large part through UN agencies.[23]

Further, in 1994, the UN Convention to Combat Desertification in those Countries Experiencing Serious Drought and/or Desertification, Particularly in Africa (UNCCD)[24] was approved by the international community. The UNCCD requires that states parties incorporate drought and desertification planning and mitigation in their policies and laws, and that states that are particularly vulnerable to these threats receive assistance from the international community in doing so.[25] A significant portion of the UNCCD's obligations centers on the creation and implementation of a National Action Programme "to identify the factors contributing to desertification and practical measures necessary to combat desertification and mitigate the effects of drought."[26] States parties examine the contributions of the government, individuals, communities, and other entities, such as nongovernmental organizations, to action on desertification and drought, and are mandated by the treaty to take these into account when generating policy.[27] Further, the UNCCD requires that there be a periodic review of the National Action Programmes by a designated UNCCD committee in order to promote transparency and ensure their

[18] See generally Montreal Protocol on Substances that Deplete the Ozone Layer (Montreal Protocol) (concluded 16 September 1987, entered into force 1 January 1989) 1522 UNTS 3; 26 ILM 1550. See also Oscar Casswell-Laird, "International Environmental Agreements: Does Montreal Have Lessons for Kyoto?" (2008) IPS Working Paper 3/2008; David W. Fahey, "The Montreal Protection Protocol of Ozone and Climate" (2013) 14 Theoretical Inquiries L 21.

[19] See Montreal Protocol (n 18)arts 4, 4A.

[20] ibid art 10. See Yoshida (n 14); Cesare PR Romano, "Ozone Layer Depletion" in Gabriela Maria Kutting (ed), *Conventions, Treaties and Other Responses to Global Issues* vol II (UNESCO 2009).

[21] Montreal Protocol (n 18) arts 11–12; Fahey (n 18).

[22] Kigali Amendment to the Montreal Protocol on Substances that Deplete the Ozone Layer (15 October 2016).

[23] ibid.

[24] UN Convention to Combat Desertification in those Countries Experiencing Serious Drought and/or Desertification, Particularly in Africa (adopted 7 June 1994, entered into force on 26 December 1996) 1954 UNTS 3.

[25] ibid. [26] ibid art 10.

[27] UN Convention to Combat Desertification (n 24) art 10.

proper implementation.[28] The UN has played an important role in facilitating these reviews, and following up to address capacity and other gaps identified in the process.

In essence, several essential elements of the international law to address environmental problems have been generated under the auspices of the UNFCCC and subsequent CoPs.[29] Throughout the UNFCCC Paris Agreement, UNCCD and Montreal Protocol treaty-negotiations processes, the UN played a key role in convening legal and technical experts, and in building negotiator capacity and consensus, to address newly appearing challenges in a guided setting geared toward producing meaningful results. Through the UNCCD, the UN has also supported the negotiation and implementation of local and regional action plans, under the treaty, to try to increase resilience among communities and groups of countries. For climate change, desertification, and ozone depletion, a high-water mark is being set in openness and transparency of international law and treaty-making, through the work of the UNFCCC Secretariat, UN-Environment, and others.[30]

In these regimes, the UN fosters the emergence of carefully constructed, intricate regimes and legal instruments, particularly through its efforts to ensure that all parties and observers can participate in the treaty-making and refinement process. Indeed, the platforms created for negotiations in the UNFCCC and UNCCD systems give a voice to key states that are often excluded, due to capacity and financing concerns, from international proceedings, such as African and Small Island Development States. Not only has this promoted greater equity, it can also ensure more balanced treaties and instruments that can be implemented in ways that include and benefit a greater number of parties in addressing a global problem. A key example of this is the primacy of place given to Small Island Developing States in climate negotiations under the UNFCCC, with the designation of Fiji as the host of the 2017 UNFCCC CoP23.[31] It is this iterative reinforcement that, perhaps, is the most valuable aspect of UN involvement in many of these treaties.

1.2 Chemicals, Wastes, and Transboundary Air Pollutants

The negotiation of the Convention on Persistent Organic Pollutants (Stockholm Convention)[32] was heavily informed by the scientific consensus facilitated by UN-Environment (then UNEP) and its partners, including the environmental departments of many countries, on the harm caused by persistent organic pollutants to

[28] See generally ibid.

[29] See United Nations Framework Convention on Climate Change (adopted 9 May 1992, entered into force 21 March 1994) 1771 UNTS 107.

[30] Cordonier Segger (n 5). See also generally Sébastien Duyck, Sébastien Jodoin, and Katherine Lofts (eds), *Public Participation and Climate Governance Working Paper Series* (CISDL 2015).

[31] UNFCCC Secretariat, Meet the Hosts (2017) <https://unfccc.int/process/conferences/un-climate-change-conference-november-2017/about/meet-the-conference-hosts>.

[32] Stockholm Convention on Persistent Organic Pollutants (adopted 22 May 2001, entered into force 17 May 2004) 2256 UNTS 119.

individuals and the world community. In light of the broad-based threat posed by persistent organic pollutants, the Stockholm Convention provides for extensive public education and awareness activities by states parties, as well as requiring the states parties to report their measures for compliance to the governance entity established under the Stockholm Convention.[33] Additionally, the Stockholm Convention establishes procedures for review of its effectiveness and implementation at a global level, ensuring that the public has the ability to access these findings openly.[34] This treaty operates together with the 1989 Basel Convention on the Control of Transboundary Movements of Hazardous Wastes and their Disposal,[35] which was designed to reduce the movements of hazardous wastes between nations, especially from developed to least-developed states, and to minimize the quantities and toxicity of wastes generated, ensuring the environmentally sound management close to their sources. It also operates, as a triumvirate, with the 1998 Rotterdam Convention on the Prior Informed Convention Procedure for Certain Hazardous Chemicals and Pesticides,[36] which establishes shared responsibilities in relation to the importation of hazardous chemicals, by promoting open exchange of information, and ensuring exporters use proper labeling and directions on safe handling, inform purchases of known restrictions, and respect any bans. The role of the UN, particularly UN-Environment, has been crucial in bringing together the scientific evidence, and galvanizing negotiations for all three agreements, throughout the long years of consensus-building and detailed technical negotiations. This "cluster" is perhaps one of the most coherent, due in part to collaborations fostered by parties through UN-Environment. Indeed, in 2012, after an intensively negotiated process, the Secretariats of the Basel and Stockholm Conventions, together with the UN-Environment part of the Rotterdam Convention Secretariat, merged into a single UN-Environment supported Secretariat with a matrix structure to serve all three treaties.

As further refinements to these efforts, the international community, with significant assistance from UN-Environment, crafted the Minamata Convention on Mercury[37] in 2013, seeking to address the threat of mercury to society and to future generations. The Minamata Convention includes prohibitions and restrictions on the use of mercury generally and particularly in manufacturing settings as well as mercury disposal at the industrial level.[38] States parties are required to provide citizens with information on mercury and its hazards.[39] As in the UNFCCC Paris Agreement and the Montreal Protocol, the treaty oversight system includes an intergovernmental Implementation

[33] ibid arts 10, 15. [34] ibid art 16.

[35] Basel Convention on the Control of Transboundary Movements of Hazardous Wastes and their Disposal (adopted 22 March 1989, entered into force 5 May 1992) 1673 UNTS 57.

[36] Rotterdam Convention on the Prior Informed Convention Procedure for Certain Hazardous Chemicals and Pesticides (adopted 10 September 1998, entered into force 24 February 2004) 2244 UNTS 337.

[37] Minamata Convention on Mercury (adopted 10 October 2013, entered into force 16 August 2017).

[38] ibid. [39] ibid art 18.

and Compliance Committee, which is tasked with reviewing states parties' compliance efforts, and addressing questions regarding implementation from states parties.[40]

In terms of air pollutants, the 1997 Convention on Environmental Impact Assessment in a Transboundary Context (Espoo Convention)[41] and its 2003 Kiev Protocol[42] are also important instruments. While the Espoo Convention relates to potential impacts in fields other than air pollution, it also plays an important role in promoting the use of environmental impact assessments—which can promote scientific collaboration, transparency, and public participation—in addressing air pollution, chemicals, and other challenges.[43] Included in the enforcement mechanisms for the Espoo Convention is a Compliance Review system that allows other states to bring complaints regarding state party noncompliance to an organizational oversight body and nonstate actors to provide information on issues of concern as well.[44] This review system, like others mentioned previously, is facilitated and supported by UN-Environment, and also by the UNECE.

1.3 Biodiversity, Wildlife, and Species at Risk

To attempt to address increasingly serious global problems of human-induced aquatic and terrestrial species loss and related habitat degradation, a mix of policy action plans and binding treaty instruments have been adopted by the international community. In this cluster of challenges, key instruments include the 1992 Convention on Biological Diversity (CBD),[45] its protocols and several well-known, traditional treaties that seek to protect migratory species, conserve wetlands, and address international trade in endangered species.

The CBD, originally called the UN Convention on Biological Diversity, has relied to varying degrees on UN support and engagement at different moments throughout its development as a treaty regime, and the relationships continue to evolve. The CBD regime works through expert technical theme-based committees and working groups, bringing together guidance and support of the parties through their national focal points to share science and knowledge, agree on policies and guidelines, exchange experiences, and report on implementation. Under the CBD, drawing on these technical exchanges, the 2000 Cartagena Protocol on Biosafety to the Convention on Biological

[40] ibid art 15.

[41] Convention on Environmental Impact Assessment in a Transboundary Context (Espoo Convention) (adopted 5 February 1991, entered into force 10 September 1997) 1989 UNTS 309.

[42] Protocol on Strategic Environmental Assessment to the Convention on Environmental Impact Assessment in a Transboundary Context (Kiev Protocol) (adopted 21 May 2003, entered into force 11 July 2010).

[43] Espoo Convention (n 41).

[44] Espoo Convention Implementation Committee, Structure and Functions of the Implementation Committee, and Procedures for Review of Compliance and Consolidated Operating Rules (2011).

[45] United Nations Convention on Biological Diversity (adopted 5 June 1992, entered into force 29 December 1993) 1760 UNTS 79.

Diversity[46] was negotiated to govern the movements of living modified organisms (LMOs), through reporting requirements to support adequate biosafety measures, opening space for states to adopt precautionary approaches.[47] UN-Environment, with funds from the Global Environmental Facility (GEF), were able to support the adoption and implementation of the Protocol, including by providing technical support to develop national policy and regulatory frameworks for implementation in over 120 countries. This regime has developed iteratively. When the UN (particularly UN-Environment) provided technical support to less-developed parties, this built confidence to ratify the Protocol and secured greater participation in the regime. Participation led to identification of further areas of consensus, and in 2010, the Nagoya–Kuala Lumpur Supplementary Protocol on Liability and Redress,[48] which addresses LMO damage response measures, was set in place. Similarly, building on the Bonn Guidelines, parties and indigenous groups with high levels of biodiversity were able, with UN technical support, to press for further negotiations, resulting in a 2010 Nagoya Protocol on Access to Genetic Resources and the Fair and Equitable Sharing of Benefits Arising from their Utilization.[49] The Protocol seeks to provide a more secure framework for access and benefit-sharing in relation to genetic resources, promoting more predictable access conditions, rules, and procedures; fair and equitable mutually agreed terms for benefit-sharing for parties and knowledge-holders; and recognizing traditional knowledge.[50] Over several years, supported by the CBD Secretariat, UN-Environment and others, an Action Plan was negotiated to set a common global agenda on biodiversity, resulting in the Aichi Targets.[51] While the new accords have been welcomed by many, and the active engagement of UN technical and legal experts was overall highly successful, the maturing of the regime also led to reconsideration of the relationship. Over time, the role of the UN in the CBD changed, with decisions by the parties that the CBD would need to work more independently across intergovernmental systems, conducting its own relations with states and other international organizations. To respect this new relationship, the UN now demonstrates considerable flexibility toward its modalities of interlinkages with CBD, and the support it can provide to parties that request assistance for treaty implementation.

[46] Cartagena Protocol on Biosafety to the Convention on Biological Diversity (adopted 29 January 2000, entered into force 11 September 2003) 2226 UNTS 208.

[47] Cartagena Protocol (n 46); see Marie-Claire Cordonier-Segger and Frederic Perron-Welch (eds), *Legal Aspects of Implementing the Biosafety Protocol* (CUP 2013).

[48] Nagoya—Kuala Lumpur Supplementary Protocol on Liability and Redress to the Cartagena Protocol on Biodiversity (adopted 15 October 2010, entered into force 5 March 2018) UN Doc No. UNEP/CBD/BS/COP-MOP/5/17.

[49] Nagoya Protocol on Access to Genetic Resources and the Fair and Equitable Sharing of Benefits Arising from their Utilization to the Convention on Biological Diversity (adopted 29 October 2010, entered into force 2014) UN Doc No. UNEP/CBD/COP/DEC/X/1.

[50] ibid.

[51] Jorge Cabrera-Medaglia, Frederic Perron-Welch, and Olivier Rukundo, "Overview of National and Regional Measures on Access to Genetic Resources and Benefit-Sharing" (CBD/CISDL 2011).

In recognition of the specific threats to particular species and the impact of illegal wildlife trade on the decline of species at risk, the international community continued to collaborate through the mature yet dynamic Convention on International Trade in Endangered Species of Wild Flora and Fauna (CITES) in 1973.[52] Together with the International Union for the Conservation of Nature (IUCN), other international organizations, and civil society groups, the UN has proven instrumental in bringing parties together for the implementation of CITES, and these vital roles are included in the treaty terms and requirements. For instance, the CITES Secretariat is supported by UN-Environment, which provides the essential mechanisms and structure for governance of the Convention's implementation.[53] In addition, an important implementation project of the CITES, TRAFFIC (Trade Records Analysis of Flora and Fauna in Commerce), is co-located and works in tandem with the UN-Environment's World Conservation Monitoring Centre. Together with the 1979 Bonn Convention on the Conservation of Migratory Species of Wild Animals,[54] these treaties provide a global platform for the conservation of terrestrial, marine, and avian migratory species, and their habitats, throughout their ranges.[55] Essential to the CMS is a state-based commitment to protecting migratory species through scientific research, legal protections, and policy coordination and innovation.[56] Through the CMS, parties regulate these activities, also encouraging and facilitating the creation of additional, more tailored agreements on specific migratory species.[57] The CMS treaty also operates directly under the aegis of UN-Environment, with the CMS Secretariat supported by UN-Environment, and senior CMS staff often appointed from their ranks.[58] In sum, the role of the UN, particularly UN-Environment, has been essential to support the negotiation, implementation, and reporting requirements of the major international accords for biodiversity conservation and sustainable use. As parties' needs have evolved over time, particularly among different developing country parties, and subject to the collective will of each treaty bodies, this role has grown but changed, and it will likely continue to do so.

[52] Convention on International Trade in Endangered Species of Wild Flora and Fauna (CITES) (adopted 3 March 1973, entered into force 1 July 1975). See also Christine Fuchs, "Convention on International Trade in Endangered Species of Wild Flora and Fauna (CITES) – Conservation Efforts Undermine the Legality Principle" (2008) 9 German LJ 1565; John Lanchbery, "The Convention on International Trade in Endangered Species of Wild Flora and Fauna (CITES): Responding to Calls for Action from Other Nature Conservation Regimes" in Sebastian Oberthur and Thomas Gehring (eds), *Institutional Interaction in Global Environmental Governance: Synergy and Conflict among International and EU Policies* (MIT Press 2006); John L Garrison, "The Convention on International Trade in Endangered Species of Wild Flora and Fauna (CITES) and the Debate Over Sustainable Use" (1994–1995) 12 Pace Environmental LR 301.

[53] CITES, (n 52) at art XII.

[54] Convention on the Conservation of Migratory Species of Wild Animals (CMS/Bonn Convention) (adopted 1979, entered into force 1 November 1983).

[55] See Richard Caddell, "Convention on Migratory Species of Wild Animals" (2012) 22 YB Intl Environmental L 273; Cyril De Klemm, "Migratory Species in International Law" [1989] 29 Natural Resources J 935; Robert A Johnson et al, "Climate Change and Migratory Species" BTO Research Report 414 (2005).

[56] CMS (n 54). [57] ibid art V. [58] ibid art IX.

1.4 Protection of Transboundary Freshwater Systems and Wetlands

To address problems of global and transboundary freshwater management and wetlands, the UN has also taken on a special role, including through its regional commissions. For instance, the negotiations for the Convention on the Protection and Use of Transboundary Watercourses and International Lakes,[59] also known as the Water Convention, which seeks to improve national attempts and measures for protection and management of transboundary surface waters and groundwaters, were supported by the United Nations Economic Commission for Europe (UNECE). The regional UN support takes a fit-to-purpose approach to both the regional water management problems and the jurisdictions involved in finding solutions, as the treaty takes a decidedly local/regional watershed approach, obliging parties to cooperate and create joint bodies to manage shared watercourses and lakes, issues that occur mainly on the regional level.[60] To assist in the facilitation of these goals, the Convention Implementation Committee was established as part of the governance structure, and is supported by the UN through measures such as monitoring and assistance with compliance of UNECE instruments.[61] The work of this more recent Water Convention builds on the long-standing efforts of the UN Convention on the Law of the Non-navigational Uses of International Watercourses,[62] which established an initial framework for collaboration by providing protections for a number of watercourse areas, and also establishing requirements for notice of potentially damaging activities. Also included in the Convention terms are requirements regarding the protection, preservation, and management of watercourse resources domestically and as a matter of international conduct.[63] As a product and part of the UN structure, working closely with UN-Water, two conventions that are administered under the auspices of the UNECE—the New York Convention and the Geneva Water Convention—are built into the structure of the UN for implementation, and supported by its staff and expertise, as well as its convening powers.[64]

International cooperation on transboundary water sources, including wetlands, is also facilitated by the venerable 1971 Convention on Wetlands of International Importance

[59] Convention on the Protection and Use of Transboundary Watercourses and International Lakes (adopted 17 March 1992, entered into force 6 October 1996) 1936 UNTS 269.

[60] ibid.

[61] UN Economic and Social Council (ECOSOC)/Economic Commission for Europe (UNECE) "Addendum" to "Report of the Meeting of the Parties on its sixth session: Decisions and vision for the future of the Convention: Decision VI/1 Support to implementation and compliance" (19 September 2013) UN Doc. ECE/MP.WAT/37/Add.2.

[62] Convention on the Law of the Non-navigational Uses of International Watercourses (adopted 21 May 1997, entered into force 17 August 2014); Convention on the Protection and Use of Transboundary Watercourse (n 60) pt II.

[63] Convention on the Protection and Use of Transboundary Watercourse (n 60) pt III.

[64] Stephen McCaffrey, "The UN Convention on the Law of the Non-navigational Uses of International Watercourses: Prospects and Pitfalls" World Bank Technical Paper (1998).

especially as Waterfowl Habitat,[65] known as the Ramsar Convention, which seeks to conserve water and land areas of great importance for biodiversity and aquatic systems, addressing biodiversity concerns, and also freshwater and marine resources.[66] The Ramsar Convention, in some ways, provided a template for and gives an important place to intergovernmental collaborative scientific research and international advisory missions. The treaty also encourages domestic and international legislative activities, and policy coordination as part of a concerted treaty regime.[67] With a Secretariat affiliated and co-located with the IUCN, the Ramsar Convention is nonetheless supported by the UN entities that are part of its membership structure. For instance, alongside "International Organization Partners" (IOPs), these actors host projects to implement the Convention, and share information on initiatives that can help to achieve the goals of the Convention.

1.5 Protection of the World's Oceans and Marine Resources

The preeminent source of international law on the world's oceans is well-recognized as the UN Convention on the Law of the Sea (UNCLOS),[68] in which the UN has played a preeminent role from facilitation of negotiations to support for implementation and refinement, including stable settlement of disputes.[69] The well-established UNCLOS regime, with a strong dispute settlement mechanism through a special International Tribunal on the Law of the Sea (ITLOS), touches on all manner of oceanic regulations, including part II that addresses conservation and resource management. As existing literature extensively covers, within the UNCLOS context, states parties are required to provide protections for resources in the high seas and to provide for their enforcement.[70] This requirement has been raised to support parties' arguments before the ITLOS, and through decisions of the ITLOS, environmental protection and sustainable development have been incorporated into the UNCLOS regime, and taken into account. In this way, the UNCLOS dispute settlement regime has fostered greater transparency and modernisation of the treaty, contributing to the interactional development of the broader global system of maritime conservation.

In addition, the international community recognized the specific protection needs of straddling stocks in the United Nations Agreement for the Implementation of the Provisions of the United Nations Convention on the Law of the Sea of 10 December 1982 relating to the Conservation and Management of Straddling Fish Stocks and Highly

[65] Convention on Wetlands of International Importance especially as Waterfowl Habitat (Ramsar Convention) (adopted 2 February 1971) 996 UNTS 245.

[66] See Daniel Navid, "The International Law of Migratory Species: The Ramsar Convention" (1989) 29 Natural Resources Journal 1001; GVT Matthews, *The Ramsar Convention on Wetlands: Its History and Development* (Ramsar Convention Bureau, 1993).

[67] Navid, Ramsar Convention (n 66).

[68] United Nations Convention on the Law of the Sea (adopted 10 December 1992, entered into force 16 November 1994) 1833 UNTS 3, pt VII sect 2.

[69] ibid. For a more comprehensive analysis, see the chapter in this *Handbook* on law of the sea.

[70] United Nations Convention on the Law of the Sea (n. 68).

Migratory Fish Stocks.[71] The Straddling Stocks Agreement incorporates many aspects of sustainable development law and practice, such as the precautionary approach, into the regulation of these forms of fish species and the scientific and legal systems that govern them at the domestic and international levels.[72] As part of the UNCLOS, the Straddling Stocks Agreement also forms part of the overall UN system, which assists in the facilitation of periodic review meetings regarding its terms, their implementation, and additional issues that need to be addressed within the Agreement's context. The role of the UN in these treaties is discussed in greater detail elsewhere in this volume.

1.6 Regional and Bilateral Environmental Innovations

As discussed previously, the UN has played a very important role in the making, implementation, and interactional refinement of key multilateral treaties to facilitate international collaboration on global environmental challenges, in several key clusters of interlinked problems. Environmental issues are not always global, however, and at the regional and bilateral levels, significant innovations are occurring to help resolve more local problems.

In a very direct manner, UN regional commissions have played an important role. For instance, the UNECE has a history of treaty regimes relating to long-range transboundary air pollution, beginning with the 1979 Convention on Long-Range Transboundary Air Pollution itself.[73] Fundamental to the Convention is the network of information exchange and consultation for research and monitoring of air pollution levels and associated technologies.[74] It also established the Cooperative Programme for the Monitoring and Evaluation of the Long-Range Transmission of Air Pollutants in Europe, which fostered additional mechanisms for consultation and the creation of a regional method for combatting the issues associated with pollution.[75] This Convention set the stage for the subsequent Espoo Convention and international treaty regimes addressing climate change and air pollution. In addition, it should be noted that the UNECE's Aarhus Convention on Access to Information, Public Participation in Decision Participation in Decision-Making and Access to Justice creates a system through which citizens are

[71] United Nations Agreement for the Implementation of the Provisions of the United Nations Convention on the Law of the Sea of 10 December 1982 relating to the Conservation and Management of Straddling Fish Stocks and Highly Migratory Fish Stocks (Straddling Stocks Agreement) (adopted 4 August 1995, entered into force 11 December 2001); Colin Warbrick, Dominic McGoldrick, and DH Anderson, "The Straddling Stocks Agreement of 1995 – An Initial Assessment" (1996) 45 Intl. & Comp LQ 463; David A Bolton, "Strengthening the Law of the Sea: The New Agreement on Straddling Fish Stocks and Highly Migratory Fish Stocks" (1996) 27 Ocean Dev& Intl L125. But see Lawrence Juda, "The 1995 United Nations Agreement on Straddling Fish Stocks and Highly Migratory Fish Stocks: A Critique" (1997) 28 Ocean Dev & Intl L 147.

[72] Straddling Stocks Agreement (n 71) at arts 5, 6.

[73] Convention on Long-Range Transboundary Air Pollution (adopted 13 November 1979, entered into force 16 March 1983) 1302 UNTS 217.

[74] See ibid. [75] ibid art 9.

entitled to greater means of information sharing, transparency, and participation in matters that are particularly impactful, such as environment and climate.[76] Indeed, the Convention's drafters specifically noted the essential link between access to information, participation, and climate governance, stressing that "improved access to information and public participation in decision-making enhance the quality and the implementation of decisions, contribute to public awareness of environmental issues, give the public the opportunity to express its concerns and enable public authorities to take due account of such concerns."[77] The Aarhus Convention continues to receive extensive support from the UNECE and, in connection with this, assisted in the negotiation of the 2009 Kiev Protocol on Pollutant Release and Transfer Registers. This Protocol requires that national registers for both pollutant release and transfer be created and maintained so as to ensure an informed population.[78] As part of the Kiev Protocol regime, an International Pollutant Release and Transfer Registers (PRTR) Coordinating Group was established to allow for coordination and dialogue among governments, nongovernmental organizations, and international organizations on these topics.[79] Such mechanisms, supported in their technical design and practice by all UN regional commissions where they can be relevant, have since become more common in domestic and regional environmental law. Similarly, the African Union began working to control transportation and management of hazardous wastes in the early 1990s. The Basel Convention on the Control of Transboundary Movements of Hazardous Wastes and Their Disposal supports the ability of regional and other entities to create more intensive agreements where appropriate,[80] and within this framework, the African Union promulgated the Bamako Convention on the Ban of the Import into Africa and the Control of Transboundary Movement and Management of Hazardous Wastes within Africa.[81] While the Basel Convention's terms are more wide-ranging, as is its application, its work is influenced by the regional practices typified in the Bamako Convention in terms of understanding the issues as they apply to states that receive significant amounts of hazardous wastes, and the regional accord operates within the framework of the global.

Further, in an indirect manner, treaty arrangements adopted in transboundary contexts, or regionally, can also serve as first steps for global cooperation or iteratively, can assist in implementing multilateral accords. They are both an opportunity to test instruments and rules that if successful, can be picked up by the UN or others, and

[76] Convention on Access to Information, Public Participation in Decision-Making and Access to Justice (Aarhus Convention) (adopted 25 June 1998, entered into force 30 October 2001) 2161 UNTS 447.

[77] ibid preamble.

[78] Protocol on Pollutant Release and Transfer Registers (adopted 21 May 2003, entered into force 8 October 2009) 2629 UNTS 119.

[79] International Pollutant Release and Transfer Register Coordinating Group, "Terms of Reference" (2009).

[80] Basel Convention on the Control of Transboundary Movements of Hazardous Wastes and Their Disposal (adopted 22 March 1989, entered into force 5 May 1992) 1673 UNTS 57, art 16.

[81] Bamako Convention on the Ban of the Import into Africa and the Control of Transboundary Movement and Management of Hazardous Wastes within Africa (adopted 30 January 1991, entered into force 22 April 1998) 2101 UNTS 177.

eventually adopted globally, and a global framework for regional treaties, which are often facilitated by the UN. For instance, concerns about air pollution, particularly transboundary haze generated as a result of forest and other fires, led the Association of South East Asian Nations (ASEAN) and its member states to craft the ASEAN Agreement on Transboundary Haze Pollution[82] to address transboundary haze in the region.[83] It seeks to balance the rights of member states to exploit their natural resources while developing in ways that respect environmental law,[84] and is supported by a Co-ordinating Centre for Transboundary Haze Pollution Control, which seeks coordinated management of fires and other disasters, as well as prevention and monitoring efforts.[85] Its prevention and monitoring solutions, if successful, might be considered to support implementation of the UNFCCC Paris Agreement internationally. Iteratively, as a second example, in 1986, Caribbean states and associated regions ratified the Convention for the Protection and Development of the Marine Environment in the Wider Caribbean Region in order to facilitate broad-based cooperation between states parties and to provide for a follow-up mechanism.[86] This Convention has been influential in designing protections for the regions throughout its existence, and supports the implementation of the CBD.[87] The Convention has also generated measures that supplement the CBD's goals and protections, for example through the Specially Protected Areas and Wildlife Protocol.[88]

2 The UN Role in Treaty-Making to Address Environmental Problems

Treaty regimes, particularly those focused on understanding and resolving quickly changing environmental problems, often develop interactionally, building on the foundations of intergovernmental and also independent scientific collaboration mechanisms, to generate new and innovative solutions to persistent and emerging issues on

[82] ASEAN Agreement on Transboundary Haze Pollution (adopted 10 June 2002, entered into force 25 November 2003).

[83] ibid art 2. [84] ibid art 3(1).

[85] ASEAN Agreement on Transboundary Haze Pollution (n 83) art 5.

[86] Convention for the Protection and Development of the Marine Environment in the Wider Caribbean Region (Cartagena Convention) (adopted on 24 March 1983, entered into force on 11 October 1986) 1506 UNTS 157.

[87] ibid.

[88] Protocol Concerning Specially Protected Areas and Wildlife to the Convention for the Protection and Development of the Marine Environment of the Wider Caribbean Region (adopted 18 January 1990, entered into force 17 June 2000) 2180 UNTS 101.

the international scale.[89] This tendency has been fostered by the mission and framework of the United Nations itself, including its expert staff, and the leadership of the treaty regimes that are established to address some of the most difficult environmental challenges. In a direct and central manner, the United Nations has played a crucial role in advancing international cooperation to address environmental problems. The UN's involvement supports states and coalitions of like-minded states, and also the work of broader epistemic communities in supporting treaty negotiation and implementation.

Through problem identification and scientific collaboration; facilitation of negotiations and eventual consensus; encouragement for ratification; provision of technical support for implementation; establishment and operation of financial instruments; compliance procedures; peaceful dispute resolution; assistance with capacity-building, public education, and participation; and also through transparency (monitoring, reporting, and verification) efforts that then "interactionally" help to refine the regimes themselves, the UN has guided and supported the emergence of international law on the environment and sustainable development.[90]

On transboundary problem identification and scientific collaboration, for instance, the UN can assist in coordinating international scientific scans and studies, or providing independent and relatively neutral summaries and compilations of scientific data. Often, in environmental matters, it is a question of sounding the alarm on problems. Data is shared with state decision-makers, and in certain instances, becomes the platform for states and nonstate actors to reach consensus on environmental problems and work to address them together. In some cases, the UN has also supported efforts to "fail forward" into cooperative instruments to address them.[91]

As another example, support from the UN has been crucial in the establishment of effective and reliable financial bodies to support activities agreed in international treaties, and therefore, also compliance. Increasingly complex financial mechanisms are being established as states and others start to invest more deeply in addressing environmental problems, and the UN has played a significant role in making this possible. For instance, the UN supported the creation of the Global Environment Facility as recommended by the UN Conference on Environment and Development in 1992, and contributes to its work, with both UNDP and UN-Environment as implementing agencies.[92]

[89] Lon L. Fuller, "Human Interaction and the Law"(1969) Am J Jurisprudence 1; Jutta Brunnee and Stephen J Toope, "Interactional Legal Theory, the International Rule of Law, and Global Constitutionalism" in Anthony F Lang and Antje Wiener (eds), *Handbook on Global Constitutionalism* (Edward Elgar, 2017); Marie-Claire Cordonier Segger, "Sustainability, Global Justice, and the Law: The Contributions of Hon. Justice Charles Doherty Gonthier" (2010) 55 McGill LJ 337. See also Anne-Marie Slaughter, "Liberal International Relations Theory and International Economic Law," (1995) 10 Am Univ L Rev 717; Edith Brown Weiss, "International Environmental Law: Contemporary Issues and the Emergence of a New World Order" (1993) 81 Georgetown LJ 675.

[90] Petsonk (n 4); Mee (n 4).

[91] Petsonk (n 4), Mee (n 4), Bolton (n 71).

[92] Charlotte Streck, "The Global Environment Facility—A Role Model for International Governance?" (2001) 1(2) Global Environmental Politics 71; Frank Biermann and Bernd Siebenhüner (eds), *Managers of Global Change: The Influence of International Environmental Bureaucracies* (MIT Press 2009).

Similarly, new methods of financing for clean development and renewable energy have been tested under the UNFCCC through the Kyoto Protocol, and are now included through a sustainable development mechanism in the Paris Agreement.[93] Through its programs and treaty secretariats, the UN supports the design and implementation of these funds to implement the law, convening and facilitating the engagement of states that guide and contribute to the funds, and providing guidance to ensure adherence to agreed principles, rules, and procedures.

As a further example, the UN supports states in resolving disputes on treaty interpretation peacefully, both through the inclusion of dispute settlement provisions in the accords, and through the encouragement of their appropriate use. Dispute settlement mechanisms, particularly references to the International Court of Justice, the International Tribunal on the Law of the Sea, and others, are customarily entrenched in treaty regimes. The awards and decisions of these bodies not only resolve disputes that might otherwise further degrade the contested areas, but also assist states to understand their binding obligations and principles, interpreting the treaty law with an independent and respected voice. UN-Environment, through a highly motivated Law Division,[94] has assisted states in complying with their treaty obligations, providing analysis, technical knowledge, and training on MEA obligations, and by hosting forums for judges and officials to discuss new developments in international law that affect environmental protection.

Transparent reporting, monitoring, and verification practices have also become more common in international law, having arguably been piloted by the UN and states parties to the treaties discussed herein. For instance, with UN technical support, the adoption of operational information-sharing arrangements, such as regular peer-reviewed monitoring, reporting, and verification (MRV) systems, public online databases, and clearinghouses for information-sharing have engaged states and nonstate actors in the international community in treaty implementation.[95] By encouraging greater transparency in the treaty negotiation and implementation process, in part through the provision of important national information, the UN has advanced international law and procedure. Presently, regular submission of "national communications" has become nearly a standard obligation for states under treaties on the environment, generating an increase in transparency and greater compliance with agreed state reporting practices.[96] The transparent information exchange has made it possible for parties to better understand the likely risks and impacts of harmful practices or inaction, building political will over time, strengthening their resolve to follow through on the implementation of their treaty obligations, and assisting with the prioritization of their investments.

[93] See Paris Agreement (2015).

[94] UN-Environment,InforMEA https://e-learning.informea.org/ accessed January 01, 2019.

[95] See Vienna Convention on the Protection of the Ozone Layer (n 14) art 5; Minamata Convention (n 37) art 17; Convention on Migratory Species (n 55) art V; UN Convention on the Law of the Non-navigational Uses of International Watercourses (n 62) art 9.

[96] See Minamata Convention (n 37) art 19; Espoo Convention (n 41) Appx II; Convention on Biological Diversity (n 45) art 26; Convention on the Protection and Use of Transboundary Watercourses and International Lakes (n 59) arts 4, 5.

Treaty regimes on the environment rely upon public participation, education, and dissemination of information to generate awareness, ownership, and support for their work on all levels, and the UN assists in this process. In the treaties, parties commit to promote public participation within their decision-making regimes, for instance through the granting of observer status to nongovernmental organizations with an interest in the subject matter, encouraging multilateral engagement of stakeholders in a manner similar to the observer status granted to ECOSOC-accredited organizations at the UN. Public access to information through technology and media is generating new potentials for meaningful public participation and engagement.[97] International and national registries are being routinely encouraged, serving to increase citizen knowledge and awareness of science, law, and other developments related to the treaty's subject matter.[98] Across the UN, many agencies also work to provide independent, accessible information in relation to the objectives and obligations of the accords. This public engagement in turn supports states' efforts to comply with treaty obligations, encouraging partners and stakeholders to contribute to the treaty.

These important efforts to foster interactional mechanisms constitute an innovation attributable to the UN system. However, despite many positive aspects, recent increases in the complexity and numbers of international treaties in the field of the environment are presenting important challenges, particularly for coherent, effective treaty implementation across a broad cross section of parties to the agreements. This is perhaps unsurprising, given the need to bring together key treaty-bodies that have been created in different eras and circumstances, even if through a common UN-based system. Indeed, each challenge presents unique opportunities to further strengthen and develop the environmental aspects of a broader international legal system that is both supported and facilitated by the UN, in support of global policy goals.

Fragmented, overlapping, incoherent, or even contradictory priorities with limited resources have become an important obstacle for progress in implementing any treaty, and this is particularly clear in the environmental arena. In some cases, treaty obligations under one regime appear to encourage actions that overlap with, or even obviate, the efforts of countries under other accords. Such overlaps, particularly where environmental and other development concerns are all at stake, can be difficult to manage.[99] For the UN, ensuring that all actors are working toward similar goals can become crucial, to avoid instructions that are impossible to carry out or worse, conflict, rendering one set of treaty priorities impossible to achieve purely through lack of coordination. This could be the case, for example, where requirements of trade and investment liberalization disciplines appear to overlap or even discourage environment and sustainable development treaty implementation.

A further challenge occurs when a state, particularly a major power, decides or threatens to withdraw from the treaty regime, trailing broken commitments. While the UN,

[97] Duyck, Jodoin, and Lofts (n 30).

[98] Montreal Protocol on Substances that Deplete the Ozone Layer (n 18) art 9; Minamata Convention (n 37) at art 18; CBD (n 46) at art 13.

[99] Cordonier Segger and Khalfan (n 1).

as a neutral body, only has a certain role to play in addressing such challenges to a treaty regime, other states will often rally to oppose and repudiate the decision, and can act collaboratively limit the effects of such a defection. As an illustrative example, after being deeply engaged in negotiations, gaining many concessions, and committing to provide strong support, in 2017 following an administration change the United States announced an intention to withdraw from the UNFCCC Paris Agreement. Rather than causing the downfall of the Paris Agreement as US leaders had predicted, the international response was strong repudiation and rallying of a broad swath of states, all expressing their renewed determination to implement and respect the Paris Agreement.

Further, treaty regimes themselves can be constructed to ensure greater resilience, for instance, by providing time for other states to accommodate the (often temporary) loss of a partner. Such provisions are found in the successful Montreal Protocol to the Vienna Convention on the Protection of the Ozone Layer, which encourages parties to join or rejoin the regime by excluding them temporarily from global markets if they continue to permit the use of ozone-depleting substances. Indeed, states are increasingly negotiating long-term and relatively sophisticated instruments that create new entities to administer collaboration.[100] Such compliance measures, reporting obligations, financial commitments, withdrawal arrangements, and capacity-building elements, together with other mechanisms, seek to support implementation of the accords even in the instance of broken promises.

While such a role for the UN is typical of many multilateral environmental agreements that have been negotiated to address particular environmental problems, it also applies more broadly to treaties that seek to promote sustainable development solutions. Indeed, the need for coherent commitments to commonly agreed solutions across the UN system became particularly evident in 2012, with calls for a universal framework for collaboration on the world's shared environment, economic, and social priorities, mobilizing parties, the UN system, and other partners around a set of common targets and objectives for decades to come.

3 UN Treaty-Making to Promote Sustainable Development Solutions

The UN works to ensure that its member states, the grand majority of which are developing countries, can meaningfully and accountably participate in international efforts to address global environmental problems. States have sovereignty over natural resources, and are vested with authority to regulate development activities that can drive or cumulatively

[100] See Montreal Protocol on Substances that Deplete the Ozone Layer (n 18) art 10; UNFCCC (n 12) art 11; CBD (n 45)] arts 2, 21; Nagoya Protocol (n 49) art 25; Cartagena Protocol (n 46) art 28.

exacerbate environmental problems.[101] In many cases, international efforts to address problems will fail without broad-based cooperation. Especially in developing countries, viable solutions are needed to secure sustainable livelihoods for people. In addition to providing for nature conservation and environmental protection, many multilateral environmental accords also aim to promote more sustainable development. From a pragmatic viewpoint, such sustainable development provisions are important. Global environmental problem-solving is otherwise unlikely to be prioritized, particularly in democratic developing countries with many communities living below poverty lines, and governance systems that are accountable to citizens. UN decision-makers are aware of these pressures, and have sought for years to ensure that treaty promises on sustainable development can be achieved on the ground.

Global commitment to sustainable development, in international policy debates and in laws, have crystallized over recent decades.[102] As scientific cooperation, technological advances, and globalization continues to link economies, ecosystems, and people in more fundamentally important and impactful ways, it has become clear that social, economic, and environmental challenges will not be resolved without significant effort to deliver sustainable development, worldwide.[103] Sustainable development solutions are being sought in international trade and investment treaties, in international human rights instruments, and also in multilateral environmental agreements.[104] Indeed, sustainable development has joined the lexicon of crucial objectives in environmental agreements, such as protecting the environment, preventing pollution, and preserving endangered species. Through these treaties and other international consensus-building processes, often led by the UN in collaboration with expert institutions, sustainable development principles have been recognized over time. As explained in the 2002 International Law Association New Delhi Declaration Principles of International Law on Sustainable Development, states are increasingly recognizing the importance of key norms—such as the need to ensure that natural resources are used sustainably,

[101] Nico Schrijver, *Sovereignty over Natural Resources: Balancing Rights and Duties* (CUP 2007).

[102] Cordonier Segger (n 4).

[103] See Amartya Sen, *Development as Freedom* (OUP 1999); Paul Collier, "Democracy, Development and Conflict" (2008) 6 J European Economic Assn 531; Jeffrey D Sachs, "From Millennium Development Goals to Sustainable Development Goals" (2012) 379(9832) The Lancet 2206.

[104] See Nico Schrijver, "Advancements in the Principles of International Law on Sustainable Development" in Marie-Claire Cordonier Segger and CG Weeramantry (eds), *Sustainable Development Principles in the Decisions of International Courts and Tribunals, 1992–2012* (Routledge 2017) 99–102 (providing an overview of the ways that sustainable development principles have been incorporated into and operationalized by international treaty regimes and tribunals); Duncan French, "The Sofia Guiding Statements on Sustainable Development Principles in the Decisions of International Tribunals," in Cordonier, Segger, and Weeramantry, supra 177–84 (noting the ways that sustainable development has been incorporated into the juridical activities of international bodies convened under the auspices of UN associated and influenced treaty regimes); Marie-Claire Cordonier Segger, Alexandra Harrington, and FJ Condon, "Judicial Deliberations and Process on Sustainable Development" in Cordonier Segger and Weeramantry supra 814–24 (discussing the ways in which various treaty regime entities, including multilateral environmental agreements, have incorporated sustainable development into frameworks that were facilitated and endorsed by the UN and associated entities).

to support greater equity and the eradication of poverty, to respect common but differentiated responsibilities, to adopt a precautionary approach, to promote public participation and access to justice, to ensure good governance, and to facilitate integration of environmental and social concerns into economic decisions. Such principles may well already be shaping their collaborations for sustainable development.[105]

Discerned by leading international experts over a decade of analysis, the ILA New Delhi Principles are identified across the spectrum of international law, from binding multilateral treaty regimes to international tribunal decisions. These principles are increasingly being incorporated into international treaty regimes. One notable example is the Paris Agreement, which reflects the importance of promoting public participation, integration, common but differentiated responsibilities, intergenerational equity, and other sustainable development principles.[106] As a second example, commitments to equity and the protection of natural resources also feature prominently in the 2004 International Treaty on Plant Genetic Resources for Food and Agriculture, which seeks to balance the needs of the farmers and farming communities with the needs of the states and international community in order to promote fairness and equality of access.[107]

Across international courts, the International Court of Justice has taken account of principles of good governance and precaution in such seminal decisions as the *Costa Rica v. Nicaragua* territorial dispute cases.[108] These principles have also helped the World Trade Organization's Dispute Settlement Body to render decisions,[109] as has the principle that economic policies must integrate environmental and social considerations.[110] In the context of human rights, the ILA Principles have also been incorporated in the intergovernmental findings of the UN Human Rights Council and the Committee on the Rights of the Child,[111] as well as at the regional level in the African Court of Human

[105] International Law Association New Delhi Declaration Principles of International Law on Sustainable Development (2002).

[106] Paris Agreement (n 93) at art 2.

[107] International Treaty on Plant Genetic Resources for Food and Agriculture (adopted 2 November 2011, entered into force 29 June 2004) 2400 UNTS 303.

[108] See Jorge Cabrera-Medaglia and Miguel Saldivia-Olave, "Sustainable Development Law Principles in the Costa Rica v Nicaragua Territorial Disputes" in Cordonier, Segger, and Weeramantry (n 104) at 262–65 (suggesting that key sustainable development principles such as the states' duties to ensure the sustainable use of natural resources, good governance, polluter pays, and prevention are key in the ICJ's opinion).

[109] J Hepburn, "The Principles of Good Governance in WTO Disputes" in Cordonier, Segger, and Weeramantry (n 104) 386–396 (discussing the ways in which principles of sustainable development such as transparency, due process, and the duty to give reasons have acted as guiding forces in the generation and application of WTO law as applied to trade disputes between member states).

[110] Henning Grosse Ruse-Khan, "The Principle of Integration in WTO/TRIPS Jurisprudence" in Cordonier Segger and Weeramantry (n 104) 399–402 (providing a discussion of the ways in which integration links sustainable development and legal practice at the WTO level).

[111] Stephanie Safdi and Sebastien Jodoin, "The Principles of Sustainable Development in the Practice of UN Human Rights Bodies" in Cordonier, Segger, and Weeramantry (n 104) 447–51 (establishing the ways in which UN-based human rights systems and treaty regimes have implemented sustainable development principles).

and Peoples' Rights,[112] the Inter-American Court of Human Rights,[113] and the European Court of Human Rights.[114] In essence, sustainable development, in international law, is reflected through a variety of instruments, with key roles being played by the UN, together with many other intergovernmental agencies and actors. The opportunity for progress has never been greater, alongside the risk of fragmentation, duplication, and dispersal of wasted effort.

Negotiated over several years following the 2012 United Nations Conference on Sustainable Development, as the successor to the 2000 Millennium Development Goals, the UN-sponsored Sustainable Development Goals (SDGs) offer a unique opportunity for states and stakeholders to collectively collaborate in an integrated manner on key environmental, social, and economic development priorities, worldwide. [115] As a common framework to minimize fragmentation and duplication, to encourage and channel cooperation efforts, and to facilitate joint monitoring and reporting on progress, the SDGs offer many advantages. A collection of 17 global, universal goals and 169 targets, addressing diverse policy priorities including poverty, hunger, health, education, gender, water and sanitation, clean energy, employment, infrastructure, consumption and production, climate change, marine life, and terrestrial life among others, are relevant to all countries and communities.[116] Further, while the SDGs themselves may be considered aspirational, as CISDL and UN-Environment legal research has demonstrated, each SDG is supported by an array of binding international treaty law, which sets instruments in place to support collaboration to achieve key targets.[117]

The role of the UN in the international treaties that respond to the environmental aspects of these SDGs have been discussed previously. In particular, to achieve SDG 13—Climate Action, the treaties noted earlier, as global responses to the threat of climate change, desertification, and ozone layer destruction are directly relevant. To achieve elements of SDG 3—Good Health and Wellbeing, and SDG 12—Responsible Consumption and Production, the treaties on pollution, including chemicals, wastes, and transboundary air pollutants, provide important tools. To achieve SDG 15—Life on Land, the treaties

[112] Hennie Strydom, "Sustainable Development Controversies in the African Commission on Human and Peoples' Rights" in Cordonier, Segger, and Weeramantry (n 5) 472–90 (using two key cases from the African Court of Human and Peoples' Rights to demonstrate the importance of sustainable development principles in the Court's juridical practices).

[113] Alexandra Keenan, "Sustainable Development Priorities in the Inter-American Human Rights System" in Cordonier, Segger, and Weeramantry (n 5) at 496–509 (describing the ways in which sustainable development principles have been incorporated into the jurisprudence of the Inter-American Court of Human Rights in regard to indigenous communities).

[114] Armelle Gouritin, "Sustainable Development Principles in the European Court of Human Rights" in Cordonier, Segger, and Weeramantry (n 105) at 516–25 (discussing the European Court of Human Rights' usage of the fair balance requirement).

[115] United Nations General Assembly (UNGA) Res 70 (21 October 2015) UN Doc A/RES/70/1, Sustainable Development Goals (2015).

[116] ibid.

[117] Marie-Claire Cordonier Segger and Elizabeth Mrema (eds), "Sustainable Development Goals (SDGs): Contributions of International Law, Policy and Governance" Series of 10 Legal Issues Papers (UNEP/CISDL 2016).

that focus on biodiversity, wildlife, and species at risk are crucial international instruments. To deliver on key environmental aspects of SDG 6—Clean Water and Sanitation, the treaties surveyed for their contributions to the protection of transboundary freshwater systems and wetlands are key, although international human rights instruments also support the human right to water and sanitation.[118] The UN and its partners play a key role in both the environmental and the human rights aspects of delivering this SDG.[119] Further, in order to achieve SDG 14—Life Below Water, the global treaties to ensure protection of the world's oceans and marine resources establish frameworks for collaboration, although accords governing regional seas and other instruments are also highly relevant.

For other SDGs, including SDG 1—No Poverty, SDG 4—Quality Education, SDG 5—Gender Equality, and SDG 7—Affordable and Clean Energy, among others, there are further clusters of other relevant UN treaties, all of which aim to secure more sustainable development. In each of these policy areas, the UN plays a vital role in engaging states in negotiations, in developing the broader treaty regimes, and in supporting implementation and interactionally, refinement of the regimes themselves. In essence, clusters of international treaty regimes address the subject matter of each SDG, and hold sustainable development as part of their object and purpose. The broader collaborative regimes that surround these treaties, it can be argued, also provide pathways to support the Charter of the United Nations as a whole.

In the final part of this chapter, a few illustrative examples are offered that explain this view, noting that for the UN, all support for the making (and constant remaking) of international law, may also be part of a broader mission to build coherent and cooperative frameworks for sustainable development.

To support sustainable development, the crucial SDG 1—No Poverty must be achieved. Key UN human rights treaties and their associated regimes, such as the International Covenant on Civil and Political Rights and the International Covenant on Economic, Social and Cultural Rights,[120] play important roles in efforts to eradicate poverty.[121] Nearly all international accords that touch on the environment and development include commitments to poverty eradication, and seek to facilitate sustainable ways to end poverty.[122]

[118] See United Nations Committee on Economic, Social and Cultural Rights "General Comment No. 15: The right to water" (20 January 2003) UN Doc E/C 12/2002/11; UN Human Rights Council Resolution 15/9 (6 October 2010) UN Doc A/HRC/RES/15/9; UNGA Res 68/157 (12 February 2014) UN Doc A/RES/68/157; UNGA Res 70/169 (22 February 2016) UN Doc A/RES/169.

[119] See Freedom-Kai Phillips, Cameron A. Miles, Ashfaq Khalfan, and Maria Leichner Reynal, "SDG 6 on Ensuring Water and Sanitation for All: Contributions of International Law, Policy and Governance" Legal Issue Paper (UNEP & CISDL 2016).

[120] See Sumudu Atapattu, "International Human Rights and Poverty Law in Sustainable Development" in Cordonier, Segger, and Khalfan (n 1) 319; UNGA Res 41 Declaration on the Right to Development (4 December 1986) UN Doc A/RES/41/128.

[121] See International Covenant on Civil and Political Rights (ICCPR) (adopted 16 December 1966, entered into force 23 March 1976) 999 UNTS 17; International Covenant on Economic, Social and Cultural Rights (ICESCR) (adopted 16 December 1966, entered into force 3 January 1976) 993 UNTS 3.

[122] See Sumudu Atapattu and Sean S Fraser, "SDG 1 on Ending Poverty in All Its Forms: Contributions of International Law, Policy and Governance," Legal Issue Paper (UNEP & CISDL 2016).

For instance, to achieve SDG 3—Good Health and Well-Being, progress is needed in many areas, ranging from maternal and child mortality to tuberculosis to non-communicable diseases to illness stemming from air pollution.[123] Global efforts to improve health fall broadly within the purview of the World Health Organization and its associated treaty efforts, such as a Global Convention on Tobacco,[124] but are also supported by UN treaties such as the Convention on the Rights of Persons with Disabilities,[125] which are discussed elsewhere in this volume. Further, the Minamata Convention stresses the health impacts of mercury pollution, and links health and environmental concerns.[126] Relevant instruments equally include human rights treaties such as the ICESCR, the CRC, and CEDAW.[127] The role of the UN in these accords is discussed elsewhere in this volume, but among others, they directly address the targets established in SDG 3,[128] and are part of international law on sustainable development. Through such accords and other efforts, the UN, in collaboration with many actors worldwide, plays a key role to achieve SDG 3 on Good Health and Well-Being.[129]

As another example, efforts to achieve SDG 4—Quality Education are furthered through the efforts of states to respect their obligations under the UN Convention on the Rights of the Child and the associated Committee on the Rights of the Child.[130] By committing to further public awareness and environmental education, and by taking into account the rights and needs of future generations, many environmental treaties mentioned earlier support SDG 4. The role of the UN in the creation and implementation of these conventions and associated regimes has been important in the past, and continues to be significant.[131] SDG 4 identifies many key facets to secure quality education, such as ensuring equality of access to education for boys and girls, access to free education for boys and girls through established levels, literacy for children and adults, the ability of those with disabilities to access and partake in education in their communities, and the

[123] See SDG 3.

[124] See World Health Organization Framework Convention on Tobacco Control (adopted 21 May 2003, entered into force 27 February 2005) 2302 UNTS 166.

[125] Convention on the Rights of Persons with Disabilities (CRPD) (adopted on 13 December 2006, entered into force 3 May 2008) 2515 UNTS 3.

[126] See generally Minamata Convention (n 37).

[127] See ICESCR (1966) (n 121); Convention on the Rights of the Child (CRC) (adopted 20 November 1989, entered into force 2 September 1990) 1577 UNTS 3; Convention on the Elimination of All Forms of Discrimination Against Women (CEDAW) (adopted 18 December 1979, entered into force 3 September 1981) 1249 UNTS 1.

[128] Maya Prabhu and Stephanie Blakely, "SDG 3 on Ensuring Healthy Lives and Promoting Well-Being for All at All Ages: Contributions of International Law, Policy and Governance" Issue Brief (UNEP & CISDL 2016).

[129] Kent Buse and Sarah Hawkes, "Health in the Sustainable Development Goals: Ready for a Paradigm Shift?" (2015) Globalization and Health 11(13); UN Committee on Economic, Social and Cultural Rights (CESCR), "General Comment No. 14: The Right to the Highest Attainable Standard of Health (Art. 12 of the Covenant)" (11 August 2000) UN Doc E/C.12/2000/4.

[130] See CRC (n 127).

[131] See Claire Fenton-Glynn and Pamela Towela-Sambo, "SDG 4 on Ensuring Inclusive and Equitable Quality Education: Contributions of International Law, Policy and Governance" Legal Issue Paper (UNEP & CISDL 2016).

supply of qualified teachers.[132] Alongside the CRC and the ICESCR, accords such as CEDAW and the Disabilities Convention, discussed elsewhere in this volume, play a crucial role.[133] In building, through education for sustainable development and for global citizenship, an educated international population, the UN, including for instance the UNESCO and UNICEF, play a crucial role in achieving SDG 4 and all other SDGs.[134]

As an additional example, to achieve SDG 5—Gender Equality, the UN, its member states, and its partners aim to ensure that women and girls can be free from gender-based and associated violence in conflict and in daily life, as well as providing for full access to participation in society for women, including for governance and economic spheres.[135] SDG 5 rallies and recognizes the efforts of the UN and its partners to achieve the CEDAW, the CRC, and the ICESCR, and also environmental accords that explicitly commit to foster the education and involvement of citizens, such as the Espoo Convention and the Paris Agreement.[136] Efforts of the UN, including through technical assistance and direct engagement, have been essential for the negotiation and implementation of such accords to support SDG 5.[137]

As one further example, there are also international treaties that support efforts to achieve SDG 7—Affordable and Clean Energy. For instance, the Energy Charter Treaty offers methods of encouraging sustainability in energy use and production, leading to an overall increase in sustainable production of goods across sectors.[138] At the same time, by seeking to ensure that there is individual access to clean energy at the global level, SDG 7 acts as a way of furthering essential protections contained in the ICESCR and the CRC, such as the ability of children to attend school in diverse conditions.[139] Trade and investment agreements, which increasingly seek to promote renewables and other forms of clean energy technologies, can also play a role, and in some instances, UN agencies such as UNCTAD can assist in ensuring that developing countries can understand and participate in these negotiations,[140] as is discussed elsewhere in this volume.

In conclusion, although the SDGs are aspirational in nature, they are supported by significant and entrenched treaty regimes that are capable of both assisting in their

[132] See SDG 4.

[133] See ICESCR (n 121); CRC (n 127); CEDAW (n 127); CRPD (n 125).

[134] May Miller-Dawkins, "Global Goals and International Agreements: Lessons for the Design of the Sustainable Development Goals" ODI Working Paper 402, Overseas Development Institute November 2014 <http://www.odi.org/sites/odi.org.uk/files/odi-assets/publications-opinion-files/9295.pdf>; Transparency International, "2015 and Beyond: The Governance Solution for Development" Working Paper 01/2013; UNESCO, "Education for All Movement and Report" (UNESCO 2015) <https://en.unesco.org/gem-report/report/2015/education-all-2000-2015-achievements-and-challenges> accessed January 01, 2019.

[135] See SDG 5.

[136] See CEDAW (n 127); CRC (n 127); ICESCR (n 121); Espoo Convention (n 41).

[137] See Alexandra Harrington and William B. Shipley, "SDG 5 on Gender Equality: Contributions of International Law, Policy and Governance" Legal Issue Paper (UNEP & CISDL 2016).

[138] See Energy Charter Treaty (adopted 17 December 1994, entered into force 16 April 1998) 2080 UNTS 95.

[139] See ICESCR (n 121); CRC (n 127).

[140] See Stuart Bruce and Sean S. Stephenson, "SDG 7 on Sustainable Energy for All: Contributions of International Law, Policy and Governance" Legal Issue Paper (UNEP & CISDL 2016).

implementation and growing to meet the needs of the SDGs. These treaty regimes can be viewed as setting baselines for the interpretation and implementation of many SDG commitments. The engagement of the UN, as facilitator of the SDG drafting process, and in its role, across all programs and agencies, to help states to achieve the SDGs, has been crucial, and continues to be significant in efforts to gather, coordinate, and support intergovernmental cooperation on each SDG.

4 Contributions of International Law on the Environment and Sustainable Development toward Achieving the UN Charter

In conclusion, this chapter has argued that international treaty regimes to address environmental problems, and for sustainable development more broadly, are facilitated and supported by the UN from inception to implementation to improvement, interactionally. These treaties in turn support and promote the objects of the UN Charter, including through their role in facilitating the achievement of the global SDGs.

Building from the successes and failures of the Millennium Development Goals, the process of developing the SDGs was facilitated by the UN to bring about a broad global consensus on the future global sustainable development agenda. With inputs and commitments from governments, civil society, nongovernmental organizations, the private sector, and the public, the SDGs were drafted and adopted. For each SDG, epistemic communities and nonstate actors have engaged and been strengthened, building cross-sectoral understanding supported, in part, by UN-facilitated stakeholder participation in the 1992 Rio Earth Summit, the 1997 UN General Assembly Special Session on Sustainable Development, the 2002 Johannesburg World Summit on Sustainable Development, and the 2012 United Nations Conference on Sustainable Development, among other global consensus-building processes.[141]

From a history rooted in limited, sector-specific, science-based specialist environmental problem-solving, international environmental treaty regimes have joined, and been recognized as, an integral pillar of international law on sustainable development. Practice and scholarship supports the growing acceptance of theories of interactional regime development supported by epistemic communities, and as the recent SDGs demonstrate, there is every reason to believe that this trend will continue in the future. Examples such as the Paris Agreement and the Minamata Convention demonstrate clearly the role of the UN in supporting both the purposes and obligations of specific treaty regimes, and the broader SDGs that these accords, in turn contribute toward.

[141] Cordonier, Segger, and Khalfan (n 1), Cordonier, Segger, and Weeramantry (n 105).

This review concludes that within the ambit of international society and international organizations, the UN is a unique entity in which such discussions and information-sharing can take place due to its overall identity, ability to convene the whole of the international community through the weight of its name, ability to facilitate and support discussions and meetings in which all aspects of public and private society can engage in meaningful dialogue, ability to build the capacity necessary to implement treaty terms and engage with treaty mechanisms, and ability to resolve disputes on the environment and sustainable development in a well-respected forum. Each of these abilities is essential to the treaty negotiation and implementation process, and together they lend a special presence to UN involvement in these processes that cannot be replicated in other organizations or entities.

International treaty-making processes have been essential in the development and adoption of the SDGs, and the interactional process of implementation, which includes strengthening the accords and their instruments through peace negotiation and refinement of the treaty terms themselves, will be equally vital for the meaningful achievement. At present, the international community faces challenges regarding the implementation of sustainability, particularly from fragmentation and incoherence among multiple efforts on one hand, and growing trends of intolerance and parochialist populism that risks defeating the scant efforts of key countries on the other. The fragile yet complex, interdependent, and increasingly binding webs of international law shall be essential to forge any common future for humanity. Coherent governance shall be particularly crucial to resolve increasingly urgent environmental and natural resources management threats. As states and their nonstate partners struggle to build and implement, by consensus, increasingly complex systems of rules and actions, across uncertain science and diverse societies, treaties can do a world of good.

This chapter has highlighted emerging trends in international collaborations, including transboundary ecosystem management, partnerships with civil society, different levels of government and the private sector, green economy financial measures and investment incentives, and many forms of dispute resolution and consensus-building. These measures, among others, are furthered and made more meaningful as a result of UN involvement in the treaty negotiation and implementation process. In essence, while weak and imperfect, the efforts of states through their environmental treaty regimes to address emerging challenges, and the ever-increasing contributions of these and other international accords toward achieving the world's broader Sustainable Development Goals, remain positive signs. Political oscillations of large economies shaped by interests vested in unsustainable development may continue to occur. However, the potential for coherence and cooperation through international law has deep roots. With our only planet and all its people at stake—these roots must prove strong enough to support the structures that are necessary for our common future.

CHAPTER 11

THE ILO'S STANDARD-SETTING

the first one hundred years

GEORGE P. POLITAKIS*

The International Labour Organization (ILO) was created in 1919 as part of the Paris Peace Treaty, based on sentiments of humanity, a clear understanding of the importance of social justice in securing international peace, the world's economic interdependence, and the need to harmonize working conditions in countries competing for markets. Having become in 1946 the first UN specialized agency, the ILO has a unique tripartite structure that brings together government, employer, and worker representatives from its 187 member states with a view to adopting international labor standards and elaborating policies and programs that ensure all parts of society prosperity and progress. Given an equal voice within the Organization's governance organs, the tripartite constituents exemplify the conditions necessary for the development of effective and universally applicable standards for labor and social protection.

1 Origins and Purpose of International Labor Standards

In its 100-year-old history, the core activity of the International Labour Organization has been and still remains the drawing up of international labor instruments in the form of international treaties, called international labor Conventions, and of soft instruments

* George P Politakis is the Legal Adviser of the International Labour Office. The views expressed herein are those of the author and do not necessarily reflect the views of the International Labour Organization.

known as international labor Recommendations.[1] Together, these normative texts are commonly referred to as international labor standards. To date, the ILO *corpus juris*, metaphorically dubbed "international labour Code,"[2] comprises 400 instruments, including 189 Conventions, six Protocols, and 205 Recommendations.[3] International labor standards address a wide variety of issues around workers' protection and labor rights and are currently classified in the following 22 thematic categories: freedom of association, collective bargaining, and industrial relations; forced labor; elimination of child labor; equality of opportunity and treatment; tripartite consultation; labor administration and inspection; employment policy and promotion; vocational guidance and training; employment security; wages; working time; occupational safety and health; social security; maternity protection; social policy; migrant workers; HIV and AIDS; seafarers; fishers; dockworkers; indigenous and tribal peoples; and specific categories of workers.

Conventions are instruments open to ratification by member states, thus creating legal obligations; they set out binding provisions implying state accountability for not applying them and regular control of their effective implementation by the supervisory organs of the Organization. Recommendations are non-binding instruments, giving guidance as to policy, legislation, and practice.[4] Most standard-setting exercises have resulted in the adoption of a Convention supplemented by a Recommendation, which was nonetheless not the original intention of the drafters of the ILO Constitution.

[1] See Ernest Mahaim, "The Historical and Social Importance of International Labor Legislation" in James Shotwell (ed), *The Origins of the International Labor Organization* (Columbia University Press 1934) vol I, 3–18; Georges Scelle, *L'Organisation internationale du Travail et le B.I.T.* (M Rivière 1930) 18–37; JF McMahon, "The Legislative Techniques of the International Labour Organization" (1965–1966) 41 BYIL L 1–16.

[2] See C Wilfred Jenks, "The Corpus Juris of Social Justice" in *Law, Freedom and Welfare* (Stevens & Sons 1963) 101–36; Nicolas Valticos, "Fifty Years of Standard-Setting Activities by the International Labour Organisation" (1969) 100 Intl Labour Rev 201–37.

[3] As at January 15, 2019, ILO conventions had received a total of 8,139 ratifications. Ten states have ratified 100 Conventions or more, 59 have ratified between 50 and 100 Conventions, 79 have ratified between 20 and 50 Conventions, and 43 states fewer than 20 Conventions. The average number of ratifications by region is 68 in Europe, 48 in the Americas, 33 in Africa, and 22 in Asia. The eight core Conventions relating to fundamental workers' rights near universal acceptance with 144 states having ratified all of them and another 15 states having ratified seven of the eight. The most widely ratified among the fundamental Conventions is Convention No.182 concerning worst forms of child labor with 182 ratifications; among the governance Conventions, Convention No.81 concerning labor inspection with 146 ratifications; and among the technical Conventions, Convention No.14 concerning weekly rest with 120 ratifications. More detailed information on ratification status are available at www.ilo.org/normlex.

[4] To date, the ILO has adopted 81 stand-alone Recommendations; the remaining 124 recommendations have been adopted together with a corresponding international labor Convention and are meant to be read in conjunction with that Convention. For more on the role of international labor recommendations, see Francis Maupain, "International Labor Organization Recommendations and Similar Instruments" in Dinah Shelton (ed), *Commitment and Compliance—The Role of Non-binding Norms in the International Legal System* (OUP 2003) 372–93; Georges P Politakis and Kroum Markov, "Les recommandations internationales du travail: instruments mal exploités ou maillon faible du système normatif?" in Jean-Claude Javillier and Bernard Gernigon (eds), *Les normes internationales du travail: un patrimoine pour l'avenir—Mélanges en l'honneur de Nicolas Valticos* (International Labour Office 2004) 497–525.

It is worth recalling that the founding fathers of the Organization had initially considered the possibility of adopting only international labor Conventions, which once adopted by the Conference by a two-thirds majority would become within one year automatically applicable to all member states. According to another proposal, Conventions adopted by a two-thirds majority vote would be considered tacitly ratified by member states except for those whose national parliament would expressly object within one year. A third proposal consisted in limiting the power of the Conference to communicating any adopted text—in the form of recommendation—to the competent authorities of member states for appropriate action, legislative or otherwise. The current system, as reflected in Article 19 of the ILO Constitution, is a compromise solution based on these three proposals. Accordingly, the ratification of an international labor Convention is neither mandatory nor tacit, while an international labor Recommendation is a second-best option where the complexity of a question or the differences among states render the adoption of a Convention very difficult.[5]

As conceived by the drafters of Part XIII of the Paris Peace Treaty of 1919, which later became the ILO Constitution, the Organization was founded with the aim of contributing to international peace through the promotion of social justice and conditions of fair competition among states. To achieve its noble objectives, the Organization was designed to rely mainly on the setting of global benchmarks for admissible labor conditions. Based on the premise that "the failure of any nation to adopt humane conditions of labour is an obstacle in the way of other nations which desire to improve the conditions in their own countries," the Preamble of the ILO Constitution calls for urgent action with respect to working hours, the provision of a living wage, social security, the protection of children, migrant workers, the recognition of freedom of association, and the principle of equal remuneration for work of equal value. As for the Philadelphia Declaration of 1944 concerning the aims and purposes of the Organization—now an integral part of the ILO Constitution—it extended the scope of action of the Organization by recognizing its obligation to work for the achievement of full employment, fair wage policies and a minimum living wage, effective recognition of the right to collective bargaining, adequate protection for the life and health of workers, child welfare and maternity protection, and equality of educational opportunity. Two more recent declarations, the 1998 Declaration on Fundamental Principles and Rights at Work and the 2008 Declaration on Social Justice for a Fair Globalization, have since recast the social justice mission of the ILO, which is now encapsulated in the concept of a "decent work agenda" and the promotion of four strategic objectives, namely employment, social protection, social dialogue, and fundamental principles and rights at work.[6]

International labor standards are adopted by a two-thirds majority vote by the International Labour Conference, which brings together annually tripartite delegations from all member states. The text of Conventions and Recommendations is negotiated and

[5] For more, see Scelle (n 1) 164–72.

[6] See Anne Trebilcock, "From Social Justice to Decent Work: Is the Shift in the ILO Significant for International Law?" (2008) 2 Select Proceedings of the European Society of Intl L 697–716.

voted upon by representatives of governments and employers' and workers' organizations. Once adopted, the text is authenticated by the President and the Secretary-General of the Conference and not by plenipotentiaries as would have been the case at an intergovernmental conference.

International labor Conventions seek to foster change in the social legislation of all countries and therefore set minimum standards representing a compromise between the ideal and average existing practice. Their value and effectiveness ultimately depend on how balanced and appropriate that compromise is since setting the bar utopianly high or unambitiously low would only favor the status quo and hinder progress. Another general characteristic is that the body of international labor standards is not immutable but essentially a living set of principles and rules that may be adapted and revised according to constantly evolving realities.

2 The Standard-Setting Process

The process that ultimately leads to the adoption of international labor standards formally starts with the placing of an item on the agenda of the international labor Conference, which is drawn by the Governing Body after consideration of proposals made by the Office. Before placing a question for possible standard-setting on the Conference agenda, the Governing Body usually convenes a tripartite meeting of experts to elucidate the main problems that need to be addressed and to set the parameters for possible normative action.

The examination of the standard-setting item by the Conference proceeds at two successive annual sessions; hence the procedure is known as the "double discussion" procedure.[7] The process is initiated with the preparation by the Office of a law and practice report, which offers an overview of the state of affairs globally and includes a questionnaire seeking the views of the tripartite constituents on the scope and content of desirable standards on the question under examination. On the basis of the replies, a report is drafted to serve as the basis of the first Conference discussion. This discussion proceeds within an ad hoc tripartite technical committee, with the three groups having equal voting power, and results in the adoption of proposed conclusions. Based on the outcome of the first discussion, the Office prepares a draft convention or recommendation, as the case may be, and communicates it to the member states for their comments. In the light of the observations, the Office introduces any necessary amendments to the draft text, which is then submitted to the Conference for the second and final discussion.

[7] In case of special circumstances, the Governing Body may decide to refer an item to the Conference for a single discussion only. Although the procedure for preparing the draft text through tripartite consultations, preparatory reports, and questionnaires is the same, the timeline for the adoption of the instrument is practically half of that of a double discussion. Single discussions were last used last for the adoption of the Seafarers' Identity Documents Convention (Revised), 2003 (No.185) and the Protocol of 2014 to the Forced Labour Convention 1930.

This is again held within a technical committee that negotiates and finalizes the provisions of the draft instrument before it is put to a vote at the Conference plenary. To be adopted, international labor Conventions and Recommendations need a two-thirds majority of the delegates attending the Conference and entitled to vote.

As regards their entry into force, the vast majority of Conventions provide that they take effect, initially, 12 months after the date on which the ratifications of two members have been registered, and thereafter, 12 months after the registration date of each subsequent ratification. This is a quasi-standard clause inserted in Conventions adopted since 1928. Conventions adopted in the period 1919–1926 entered into force on the date of the second ratification while Conventions adopted in 1927 entered into force 90 days from the date of registration of the second ratification. Exceptionally, the 12-month period may be shortened to 6 months. Regarding the number of ratifications, certain technical Conventions require a higher number of ratifications for their entry into force.[8]

With respect to denunciation, Conventions usually provide that denunciation is permitted within a one-year interval—known as the "denunciation window"—from the expiration of successive periods of 10 (or, less frequently, 5) years from the date on which these Conventions first came into force. A distinction is often made between genuine or "pure" denunciations, which involve the unilateral termination of the acceptance of the obligations of a Convention without the simultaneous acceptance of any related obligations, and "automatic" denunciations, which are the direct consequence of the ratification of revising more up-to-date Conventions on the same subject in accordance with the explicit provisions to that effect of the revised Conventions. Withdrawing unilaterally from a ratified Convention is politically sensitive, and therefore pure denunciations are far less common than automatic ones.[9]

3 Controlling Features of International Labor Conventions

3.1 A Hybrid Legal Nature

The unique conditions under which international labor Conventions are negotiated and adopted by the Conference have given rise to an extensive debate about their legislative

[8] For instance, the Maritime Labour Convention, 2006 (MLC, 2006) required ratifications of at least 30 Members with a total share in the world gross tonnage of ships of at least 33 per cent and the Work in Fishing Convention, 2007 (No.188) required ten ratifications, including eight from coastal States.

[9] In the last ten years, for instance, there have been 698 ipso jure denunciations due to ratification of more up-to-date Conventions and only 40 spontaneous denunciations for reasons unrelated to the ratification of more up-to-date Conventions.

(*traités lois*) or contractual (*traités contrats*) legal nature.[10] For those who viewed the Conference as an international legislative assembly, international labor Conventions are true legislative acts to which member states accede through the process of ratification, and they lack any transactional character since they are not based on reciprocal concessions or an exchange of benefits which characterize contracts.[11] For others, international labor Conventions are in reality legal acts reflecting contractual engagements among states, which once ratified, become the property of those states,[12] and besides, the Conference lacks a direct legislative power as it can only adopt "draft Conventions."[13]

The doctrinal debate around the legal nature of international labor Conventions assumed all its practical significance in relation to the question of revision of standards and the powers of the Conference in this respect. The question arose in 1928–1929 as the first Conventions adopted in 1919 expressly provided that 10 years after their entry into force the Conference should consider the need for possible revision.[14] If Conventions were to be regarded as legislative acts, the Conference would naturally be competent to abrogate Conventions it had previously adopted. If, on the contrary, they were seen as contracts concluded inter partes, the Conference would have no authority to put an end to their legal existence. From a practical point of view, if a revising Convention adopted by the Conference abrogated the revised one, there would a be a real risk of retrogression and a possible vacuum in protective coverage as there would be no guarantee that states parties to the abrogated Convention would become parties to the newly adopted standard. In contrast, should the Conference be deprived of the power to abrogate, all revising Conventions would necessarily coexist, with revised ones creating parallel legal regimes.

In the event, the "contractual theory" prevailed and epitomized ILO's legal orthodoxy for several decades. As for the solution to the problem of revision, it took the form of a new final clause providing that any revising Convention, once entered into force, would close the revised instrument to further ratification, and that the ratification of a revising Convention by a member state would ipso jure involve the denunciation of the revised one. The quarrel over the legislative or contractual nature of international labor

[10] See C Wilfred Jenks, "Some Characteristics of International Labour Conventions" (1935) 13 Canadian Bar Rev 448–62; Anne Trebilcock, "International Labour Organization" in Michael Bowman and Dino Kritsiotis (eds), *Conceptual and Contextual Perspectives on the Modern Law of Treaties* (CUP 2018) 848–80.

[11] Scelle (n 1) 179–85.

[12] See Jean Morellet, "Un type original de traités : Les conventions internationales du travail" (1938) Revue critique de droit international 1–21; HC Oersted, "La question de la révision des conventions internationales du travail" (1931) Nordisk Tidsskrift for International Ret 3–20.

[13] In fact, Article 19(1) of the Constitution, as originally drafted, provided that the Conference would determine whether proposals should take the form of a recommendation or "of a draft international convention for ratification by the Members." The word "draft" was deleted by the constitutional amendment of 1946.

[14] See Ernest Mahaim, "Quelques questions de droit au sujet des conventions internationales du travail" (1929) 20 Revue internationale du Travail 807–38; CH Dillon, *International Labor Conventions—Their Interpretation and Revision* (University of North Carolina Press 1942) 88–120.

Conventions was finally put to rest in 1997 following the adoption of a constitutional amendment that would authorize the Conference, acting upon the recommendation of the Governing Body, to abrogate Conventions in force if it considered that they are obsolete and no longer contribute to the attainment of the objectives of the Organization.[15]

3.2 Inadmissibility of Reservations

Probably the most singular aspect of the tripartite structure of the Organization from an international treaty law perspective is the prohibition of ratifying an international labor Convention subject to reservations. The principle of inadmissibility of reservations has been clearly spelled out since the early days of the Organization as a direct consequence of the full participation of nongovernmental representatives in all the stages of the elaboration and adoption of international labor standards.

In 1921, in response to a request for clarification by the government of India as to whether it would be permissible to ratify the Minimum Age (Industry) Convention, 1919 (No. 5) fixing the minimum age for admission of children to industrial employment subject to a reservation concerning factory workers, the Office explained its position as follows:

> The new procedure in the negotiation of the labour Conventions initiated by the creation of the International Labour Conference brings into the field of negotiation other interested parties than the governments concerned, namely, representatives of organisations of employers and workers. Since these representatives are parties in the negotiation of the Convention for which the Conference as a whole is responsible, it would seem that they should also have the opportunity of giving their acquiescence to a reservation (...) These arguments would appear to indicate conclusively that the procedure of ratification with reservations was not contemplated by the authors of the Treaty and would, if instituted, gravely damage the efficiency of the machinery set up by Part XIII of the Treaty of Versailles.[16]

The principle of inadmissibility of reservations was reaffirmed in the written statement submitted to the International Court of Justice (ICJ) in the context of the advisory

[15] See Francis Maupain, "Une révolution tranquille dans le droit des traités: L'abrogation des conventions internationales du Travail obsolètes" (1996) 42 Annuaire français de droit international 629–35; Francis Maupain, "The ILO's Standard-Setting Action: International Legislation or Treaty Law?" in V Gowlland-Debbas (ed), *Multilateral Treaty-Making* (Springer 2000) 129–35.

[16] See International Labour Conference, Record of Proceedings (3rd Session 1921) vol II, 1046. Likewise, in an Office memorandum submitted to the League of Nations in 1926, it was indicated that "the rights which the treaties have conferred on non-governmental interests in regard to the adoption of international labour Conventions would be overruled if the consent of governments alone could suffice to modify the substance and detract from the effect of the Conventions"; League of Nations Official Journal (July 1927) 883.

opinion on the question of reservations to the Convention on the Prevention and Punishment of the Crime of Genocide, which read in part:

> The Constitution of the International Labour Organization, grants to employers' and workers' organizations rights to invoke, and to initiate procedures in connexion with the application of, the provisions of conventions, and gives their representatives an important place in the international organs entrusted with the supervision of such application, and the individual conventions provide for consultation with such organisations in connexion with the application of a wide range of provisions leaving certain matters to national discretion; the purpose of all these provisions would be completely frustrated by the acceptance of reservations in regard to which governments alone had been consulted and, in the absence of any special procedure provided for in conventions for examining and deciding upon the acceptability of reservations, the only procedure by which the necessary consent of non-governmental elements could be validly obtained would be that of the adoption by the International Labour Conference of a revising convention incorporating the effect of the reservation.[17]

It is now well-entrenched in ILO constitutional theory and practice that no government is allowed to depart unilaterally from a text that is the outcome of tripartite negotiations as this would run counter to key values and seriously weaken the credibility of the entire system of standards. As it has been observed, the ILO "has been the staunchest advocate of the absolute integrity of the Convention as negotiated and finally adopted, ... The result is that a State is forced to make a choice; either the entire package of obligations must be accepted or the state will not be permitted to ratify."[18] Accordingly, the Director-General in the exercise of depositary functions refuses to register ratifications accompanied by reservations.

[17] *Reservations to the Convention on the Prevention and Punishment of the Crime of Genocide* (Written Statements 14 December 1950) 235–36. In 1968, in a statement made at the UN Vienna Conference on the Law of Treaties, Wilfred Jenks explained why the procedural arrangements concerning reservations embodied in the draft provisions of the Vienna Convention would be entirely inapplicable to the ILO by reason of its tripartite character:

> Great flexibility is of course necessary in the application of certain international labour Conventions to widely varying circumstances, but the provisions regarded by the collective judgment of the International Labour Conference as wise and necessary for this purpose are embodied in the terms of the Conventions and, if they prove inadequate for the purpose, are subject to revision by the Conference at any time in accordance with its regular procedures. Any other approach would destroy the international labour code as a code of common standards; Ybk Intl L Commission (2000) vol II, 173.

[18] W Paul Gormley, "The Modification of Multilateral Conventions by Means of Negotiated Reservations and Other Alternatives: A Comparative Study of the ILO and Council of Europe" (1970) 39 Fordham L Rev 65. On a more general level, it was noted that "it is the new role of employers' and workers' organizations and representatives both in the formulation and in supervising the application of international labour Conventions, which has so altered the nature of the international legislative process as to make it necessary to reconsider, in respect of international labour Conventions, the substance of the ordinary rules of treaty law"; see C Wilfred Jenks, "The Significance for International Law of the Tripartite Character of the International Labour Organisation" (1937) 22 Transactions of the Grotius Society 14.

In contrast, conditional ratifications and interpretative declarations are permissible. A conditional ratification consists in declaring that the ratification of a Convention will only take effect if and when the ratifications of a certain number of other countries have been registered.[19] Interpretative declarations do not intend to exclude or modify the scope of obligations arising from a Convention but simply to put on record the member state's understanding of a particular provision. In registering a ratification accompanied by an interpretative declaration, the ILO Director-General generally indicates that the understanding does not in any way qualify the acceptance by the member concerned of the obligation to make effective the provisions of the Convention, but simply constitutes a formal record of the interpretation that the member attaches to the Convention.[20] Similarly, making use of flexibility clauses specifically provided for in certain Conventions raises no legal objections as these clauses aim at promoting ratification and adaptability to national circumstances.[21]

3.3 Need for Flexibility

International labor standards aspire to universal application and need therefore to be flexible. The need to draft standards so that they are easily adaptable to the divergent socioeconomic and developmental conditions in member states is reflected in Article 19(3) of the Constitution that requires consideration to be given to the situation of countries in which climatic conditions, the imperfect development of industrial organization, or other special circumstances call for modifications to be proposed to accommodate the needs of such countries. Although this provision was initially interpreted narrowly to mean that a convention should expressly name the countries concerned

[19] For instance, in 1927, the United Kingdom filed a conditional ratification of Convention No. 21 subject to the receipt and registration of formal ratifications without reservations of the Convention by France, Germany, Italy, the Netherlands, Norway, and Spain while in 1929 and 1932 similar conditional ratifications of the same Convention were filed by Sweden and France. It soon became apparent, however, that an extensive use of conditional ratifications—although not legally objectionable—could undermine the Organization's efforts for social progress. As the Director-General's report noted in 1924, "it appears an abuse of the practice to make ratification dependent on the ratification of an excessive number of States. The result of such action would be simple to paralyse the whole work of ratification and to render impotent the whole machinery created by Part XIII"; International Labour Conference, Record of Proceedings, (6th Session 1924) vol II, 764. The practice of conditional ratifications has since fallen into desuetude.

[20] The use of interpretative declarations or understandings remains fairly limited; recent instances include the interpretative declarations attached to the ratification of the Indigenous and Tribal Peoples Convention, 1989 (No. 169) by Denmark in 1996; the Worst Forms of Child Labour Convention, 1999 (No. 182) by the United States in 1999; and the Labour Relations (Public Service) Convention, 1978 (No. 151) by Brazil in 2010.

[21] The view has been expressed, however, that to the extent that flexibility clauses seek to modify the scope of certain provisions, they are in reality reservations, and therefore it would the more precise to refer to the inadmissibility only of those reservations not expressly authorized by international labor Conventions; see Guido Raimondi, "Réserves et conventions internationals du travail" in Javillier and Gernigon (n 4) 528. See also Gormley (n 18) 68.

and set out differentiated standards applicable to them,[22] it later served as the basis for developing a wealth of practical solutions to ensure widespread acceptance and effective implementation of international labor standards. Among the numerous methods ensuring flexibility, some conventions contain optional parts that ratifying states may accept at a later date; others define the scope in such way that governments have some latitude as regards the categories of persons or economic sectors to be covered by the convention; in yet other instances, conventions permit the progressive implementation of standards or use flexible expressions to qualify certain requirements.[23] Despite the many advantages flexibility clauses offer, it is widely acknowledged that an excessive use of such clauses could defeat the very purpose of standard-setting, or as Wilfred Jenks has observed, "flexibility is not an end in itself; the maximum of flexibility is secured by the absence of any international standard."[24]

4 Constitutional Theory and Practice on Interpretation of International Labor Conventions

The need to prevent interpretation questions from undermining the uniform application of labor standards has been a key concern since the early days of the Organization. The constitutional provisions on the "judicial" settlement of interpretation disputes attest to the importance attached to the authoritative determination of any difficulties arising from the text of conventions.[25] Article 37(1) of the ILO Constitution provides, in fact, for the compulsory jurisdiction of the ICJ for deciding "any question or dispute" relating to the interpretation of the Constitution or of any international labor Convention adopted by member states pursuant to the provisions of the Constitution, whereas article 37(2) provides for the establishment of an internal tribunal for the expeditious settlement of

[22] For instance, the Hours of Work (Industry) Convention, 1919 (No.1) contained modified standards and conditions for seven countries explicitly mentioned.

[23] For more on the different types of flexibility clauses in international labor instruments, see McMahon (n 1) 31–68; Jean-Michel Servais, "Flexibility and Rigidity in International Labour Standards" (1986) 125 Intl Labour Rev 193–208; Georges P. Politakis, "Deconstructing Flexibility in International Labour Conventions" in Javillier and Gernigon (n 4) 463–96.

[24] C Wilfred Jenks, "ILO Standards: Are They Obsolete, Premature, Marginal or Important?" in *Social Policy in a Changing World: The ILO Response—Speeches by W. Jenks)* (International Labour Office 1976) 92. In the words of another scholar, "it all depends on what is meant by flexibility. It goes without saying that the provisions of standards must be flexible enough to be applied to a variety of countries and situations. However, if what is proposed is to make their wording so loose as to render them inoperative, it would then amount to betraying the Organization's mandate, which is to bring about a real improvement in working and living conditions"; Nicolas Valticos, "The ILO: A Retrospective and Future View" (1996) 135 Intl Labour Rev 477.

[25] See Dillon (n 14) 121–64.

disputes relating to the interpretation of international labor Conventions based on the understanding that not all questions are critical or complex so as to merit referral to the ICJ, and that probably a more flexible method at a lower level would be desirable.

In its early years, the ILO had recourse to the advisory function of the Permanent Court of International Justice (PCIJ) on six occasions between 1922 and 1932. Five of the six cases concerned the interpretation of the Constitution, and only one referred to the interpretation of an international labor Convention.[26] No use of the advisory jurisdiction of the ICJ has been made thus far,[27] while the idea of setting up an in-house tribunal for the rapid settlement of interpretation disputes has never been followed up beyond the level of preliminary studies.[28] The possibility of having recourse to ICJ advisory proceedings for the purpose of obtaining an authoritative interpretation of a Convention was last considered in 2014 with respect to the Freedom of Association and Protection of the Right to Organise Convention, 1948 (No. 87) and the right to strike. Following a profound disagreement between the employers' and the workers' groups on this issue, which threatened the ILO supervisory system with paralysis,[29] the ILO Governing Body considered taking action under Article 37 by either referring the matter to the ICJ or setting up a tribunal. Although a strong body of opinion favored a "constitutional" solution under Article 37, the Governing Body decided in March 2015 not to pursue the matter any further in view of perceived uncertainties around an ICJ ruling on the one hand and the lengthiness of establishing an in-house tribunal on the other.[30] Regrettable though it may seem from the point of view of legal certainty and security, this situation confirms the chronic diffidence of tripartite constituents of making use of the sole methods of

[26] The advisory opinion of November 15, 1932, concerned the Night Work (Women) Convention, 1919 (No. 4) and led to its revision.

[27] The question of seeking an advisory opinion from the ICJ was raised in 2006 in relation to the observance by Myanmar of the Forced Labour Convention, 1930 (No. 29) but concerned the consequences of Myanmar's noncompliance with the conclusions of the Commission of Inquiry rather than an interpretation of the provisions of the Convention; see International Labour Conference, Record of Proceedings, Provisional Record 3-2 (95th Session 2006) 11 and GB.298/5, paras 139–141. In another instance, the Committee of independent Experts monitoring the application of ratified Conventions, in examining the application of Convention No. 87 by the United Kingdom, had suggested that the ICJ "might more appropriately be requested to provide an opinion under the relevant provisions of the Constitution"; International Labour Conference, Report III (Part 4A) (71st Session 1985) 194.

[28] Possible action for the implementation of Article 37(2) was considered between 1993 and 2002 and again in 2008–2009, but no decision was taken; see GB.256/SC/2/2.

[29] See Francis Maupain, "The ILO Supervisory System: A Model in Crisis?" (2013) 10 Intl Organizations L Rev 117–65; L Swepston, "Crisis in the ILO Supervisory System: Dispute over the Right to Strike" (2013) 29 Intl J of Comparative L and Industrial Relations 199–218; Janice R Bellace, "The ILO and the Right to Strike" (2014) 153 Intl Labour Rev 29–70; Keith D Ewing, "Myth and Reality of the Right to Strike as a Fundamental Labour Right" (2013) 29 Intl J of Comparative Labour L and Industrial Relations 145–66; Paul A Mackay, "The Right to Strike" (2014) 38 New Zealand J of Employment Relations 58–70.

[30] See GB.322/INS/5 and GB.323/INS/5. With specific reference to the reluctance to seek an advisory opinion from the ICJ, this seems to stem from the instinctive skepticism toward an external mechanism that constituents cannot control but also from what is perceived as relative inexperience of ICJ judges in labor law matters.

interpretation expressly provided for in the Constitution and their preference for maintaining the status quo.[31]

The unique tripartite character of the Organization has a marked impact on the principles of interpretation applicable to international labor instruments. Whereas the customary rule of treaty interpretation crystallized in Article 31 of the 1969 Vienna Convention on the Law of Treaties elevates the agreement or the intention of the parties to a decisive criterion for determining the context in which a treaty must be interpreted, in the case of international labor Conventions it is not the intention of the states parties that needs to be established but rather the intention of the Conference in its tripartite composition.

Nothing attests better to the need to establish the intention of the tripartite drafters when interpreting the provisions of international labor Conventions than the practice of the PCIJ to permit international employers' and workers' organizations to submit information in relation to advisory proceedings concerning the ILO in the period 1922–1932 despite the clear provision in the Court's Statute limiting the possibility of presenting written or oral statements to states and, upon the Court's invitation, international organizations. The Court evidently took the view that it would not be possible to determine the intention of the Conference composed of both governmental and non-governmental representatives if it were to ignore the specificity of the Organization and invite only states to furnish information. As the Court's President had put it at the time, "practice had created a precedent of admitting great industrial organizations, whether of workers or of employers, which would be difficult to exclude owing to their very great importance, although admittedly these great organizations were at any rate indirectly recognized as constituting elements of the ILO."[32]

In addition, unlike Article 32 of the Vienna Convention, which provides that the preparatory work may only be used as supplementary means of interpretation, the Office practice has recourse to the preparatory work leading up to the adoption of international labor Conventions as a primary means of interpretation, and is often referred to in order to demonstrate the meaning of a provision, and not only to confirm the meaning resulting from the use of other rules of interpretation or to determine the meaning when the application of those rules leaves the meaning ambiguous.

It is recalled that Article 5 of the Vienna Convention recognizes that the application of the Convention to treaties that are adopted within an international organization shall be subject to any relevant rules of the organization. Speaking before the UN

[31] In the view of a former ILO legal adviser, it is not only regrettable that the sidelining of judicial means of settlement of interpretation disputes would now seem confirmed but that it would indeed be worrying if this situation reflected the sentiment that problems of interpretation of international labor conventions did not merit the inconvenience of a judicial process and could rather be resolved through some accommodating "negotiated uncertainty"; see Francis Maupain, "L'interprétation des conventions internationales du travail" in René-Jean Dupuy (ed), *Mélanges en l'honneur de Nicolas Valticos—Droit et justice* (Pedone 1999) 583.

[32] Cited in Yaël Ronen, "Participation of Non-state Actors in ICJ Proceedings" (2012) 11 The Law and Practice of Intl Courts and Tribunals 88.

Conference on the Law of Treaties in April 1968, Wilfred Jenks defended the principle that conventions adopted within an international organization may be subject to a *lex specialis* in these words:

> There are cases in which an organisation has special rules and a well-established body of practice governing an important group of conventions which create a body of international obligations in respect of these conventions more coherent, more stable and, in certain respects, better adapted to the requirements of the situation than would or could be secured by applying the necessarily more flexible provisions of the general law. Our special interest in the matter in the International Labour Organization is that we have responsibilities in connection with 128 international labour Conventions which have now received over 3,340 ratifications distributed over 115 member States and some further 1,200 declarations of application in respect of other territories. This widespread network of obligations is governed by the provisions of the ILO Constitution and by a well-established body of practice which has been tested by almost fifty years of experience and has created a solid foundation for the discharge by the International. Labour Organization of the responsibilities entrusted to it by its member States.[33]

Notwithstanding Article 37 of the Constitution, which seems relegated at present to an inactive status, "interpretative functions" have been exercised in practice by the Office and the supervisory organs of the Organization. In the case of informal opinions of the Office, interpretation is solicited by a government or an employers' or workers' organization and takes the form of administrative clarifications or guidance, whereas in the case of supervisory organs interpretation is incidental to the exercise of supervisory responsibilities. Yet, as explained later in the chapter, the practical explanations of the Office or the incidental views of the supervisory organs are at best working solutions to fill the gaps and settle day-to-day difficulties of interpretation, but cannot offer authoritative and definitive settlement of controversies concerning the meaning to be given to the provisions of a Convention.

As regards Office unofficial interpretations, they have always been considered part of administrative assistance that governments of member states could expect to receive from the ILO secretariat, subject to the understanding that the Constitution does not confer upon it any special competence to interpret international labor Conventions.[34] In most cases, questions are asked prior to the ratification of a Convention and concern its scope of application or the exact meaning of a particular term. Office opinions seek principally to establish the drafters' intention and the context in which a specific provision was introduced in an international labor Convention by tracing its negotiating history—hence the importance of detailed minutes of Conference proceedings,

[33] United Nations "Official Records of the First session of the UN Conference on the Law of Treaties" (26 March–24 May 1968) UN Doc A/CONF.39/11, 36.

[34] C Wilfred Jenks, "The Interpretation of International Labour Conventions by the International Labour Office" (1939) 20 BYIL 132–41.

including the amendment process.[35] Until 2002, unofficial interpretations of the Office were communicated to the Governing Body and published in the Official Bulletin—147 in total—but this practice has since been discontinued, with the exception of selected opinions concerning the Maritime Labour Convention, 2006 (MLC, 2006) which have been compiled and published in the form of frequently asked questions. Although highly valued as a practical and efficient advisory service, informal opinions remain of a purely administrative nature, and are without prejudice to the views of the ILO supervisory bodies. It is generally recognized that informal opinions derive their authority from the quality of the analysis they contain but have no binding legal effect.[36]

The ILO bodies responsible for the supervision of the application of ratified Conventions, and in particular the Committee of independent experts on the application of Conventions and Recommendations, have also had to decide on questions of interpretation in the course of fulfilling their supervisory functions. While recognizing that its terms of reference do not require it to give definitive interpretations of international labor Conventions, the Committee of Experts has indicated on several occasions that the examination of the meaning of the provisions of Conventions is necessarily an integral part of the evaluation of the application of Conventions, that its mandate logically and inevitably requires an assessment that involves a degree of interpretation, and that insofar as its views are not contradicted by the ICJ, they are to be considered as valid and generally recognized.[37] Over the past five years, the interpretative function of the Committee of Experts has been the subject of significant controversy, with part of the ILO constituency considering that the Committee of Experts has overstepped its mandate.[38]

[35] The Office has consistently made it clear that it must restrict itself to providing governments that so request with indications that may clarify the meaning of particular provisions of a Convention, taking account of any elements emerging from the preparatory work; see GB.221/19/1. Similarly, under the Office circular of 1987, in drawing up replies to interpretation requests, account should be taken principally of "the preparatory work which preceded the adoption of the Convention, in particular the various reports submitted to the Conference and the reports of the Conference Committees."

[36] Maupain (n 31) 570. Others suggest, however, that continuous, unchallenged practice has established the Office as the principal organ for rendering authoritative opinions concerning the interpretation of international labor standards and that those opinions, once communicated to the Governing Body and published in the Official Bulletin, are tacitly accepted and presumed binding; see McMahon (n 1) 90, 99; Ebere Osieke, *Constitutional Law and Practice in the International Labour Organisation* (Springer 1985) 207–10; Nicolas Valticos, "Labour Law - International Sources and Institutional Aspects" (1978) 15 Intl Encyclopedia of Comp L 10.

[37] See International Labour Conference, Report III (Part 1A) (100th Session 2011) 9; International Labour Conference, Report III (Part 1A) (102nd Session 2013) 12.

[38] The controversy centered around the Committee of Experts' position that although not expressly provided for in Convention No. 87, the right to strike is an intrinsic corollary of the right to organize protected by that Convention and one of the essential means available to workers and their organizations for the promotion and protection of their economic and social interests. For more, see Claire La Hovary, "The ILO's Supervisory Bodies' Soft Law Jurisprudence" in Adelle Blackett and Anne Trebilcock (eds), *Research Handbook on Transnational Labour Law* (Edward Elgar 2015) 316–28.

5 Review of Standards and Abrogation of Obsolete Conventions

In view of the proliferation of standards and the constant evolution of the world of work, there is a need to carry out from time to time a review of the entire body of standards with a view to assessing their continued relevance. Such review has been undertaken by the Governing Body at regular intervals, in 1979, 1987, and again in the period 1995–2002.[39] In these exercises and due to the absence of a constitutional basis for abrogating obsolete instruments, the Governing Body limited itself to proposing second-best arrangements aimed at containing the administrative implications of such instruments without however affecting their legal status. In 1985, for instance, the Ventejol working party suggested that 20 instruments that it had identified as having lost their relevance should be described as "dormant," while in 1996 the Cartier working party labeled 29 Conventions that no longer corresponded to current needs as "shelved." The identification by the Governing Body of a series of outdated instruments led eventually to a discussion on the possible abrogation of these instruments, which resulted in the adoption in 1997 of a constitutional amendment.

The effect of the abrogation within the meaning of the new paragraph 9 of article 19 of the ILO Constitution is to eliminate definitively all legal effects arising out of the Convention between the Organization and its members. An abrogated Convention is removed from the ILO's body of standards, and as a result, members having ratified that Convention are no longer obliged to submit reports under Article 22 of the Constitution, and are no longer subject to representations (Article 24) and complaints (Article 26) for alleged nonobservance of its provisions. For their part, the ILO supervisory bodies are not required to examine the implementation of the abrogated Convention while the Office ceases all relevant activities, including the publication of the text of the Convention and the official information regarding its ratification status. Conventions that are not in force (i.e., those that have never entered into force for lack of sufficient ratifications or those that are no longer in force due to denunciations) and Recommendations can be withdrawn under exactly the same conditions as those applicable to the abrogation of Conventions. As the Conference by virtue of its Standing Orders could withdraw outdated instruments irrespective of the entry into force of the 1997 constitutional amendment, it has already proceeded to the withdrawal of five Conventions and 36 Recommendations.

The 1997 amendment entered into force in October 2015 upon having been ratified by two-thirds of member states, including 5 of the 10 states of chief industrial importance, as required under Article 36 of the ILO Constitution. It empowers the International Labour Conference acting on a proposal of the Governing Body and by a majority of

[39] See ILO Official Bulletin (Vol LXII 1979 Series A, special issue); ILO Official Bulletin (Vol LXX 1987 Series A, special issue); GB.283/LILS/WP/PRS/1/2.

two-thirds of the votes cast by the delegates present, to abrogate any Convention if it appears that the Convention has lost its purpose or that it no longer makes a useful contribution to attaining the objectives of the Organization. The rationale underlying the constitutional amendment is that maintaining obsolete Conventions in force is damaging to the credibility of ILO's body of standards as a global reference and that by concentrating its action to up-to-date instruments, the Organization would reinforce the relevance, impact, and coherence of standards. In June 2017, the Conference abrogated for the first time four Conventions in force while another six Conventions were abrogated by the Conference in June 2018.[40]

The entry into force of the 1997 constitutional amendment coincided with the initiation of the Standards Review Mechanism (SRM) process and the establishment by the Governing Body of the SRM Tripartite Working Group, which is responsible for reviewing on a more permanent basis the existing body of standards and making recommendations to the Governing Body on their status. The SRM Working Group was established in March 2015 to contribute to "the overall objective of the Standards Review Mechanism to ensure that the ILO has a clear, robust and up-to-date body of international labour standards that respond to the changing patterns of the world of work for the purpose of protecting workers and taking into account the needs of sustainable enterprises." According to its terms of reference, the SRM Working Group is mandated to "review the international labour standards with a view to making recommendations to the Governing Body on: (a) the status of the standards examined, including up-to-date standards, standards in need of revision, outdated standards, and possible other classifications; (b) the identification of gaps in coverage, including those requiring new standards; (c) practical and time-bound follow-up action, as appropriate." The SRM Working Group has already held four meetings and has formulated its first recommendations, which have led to the abrogation or withdrawal of nine instruments in 2018 and could result in the abrogation or withdrawal of another 32 instruments by 2024.[41]

6 Supervision of Application of International Labor Standards

The system of monitoring the application of ratified Conventions has been pioneering in its inception and highly prolific in its operation. Being the fruit of a "process of empirical response to growing needs and opportunities" based on an "ILO tradition

[40] Among the obsolete Conventions already abrogated, are Conventions overtaken by social developments and modern thinking (for instance Conventions prohibiting the night work of women in industry or regulating the recruitment of indigenous workers in dependent territories) or Conventions referring to situations that virtually no longer exist (for instance, the employment of trimmers and stokers or the transport conditions of migrant workers by boat).

[41] GB.325/LILS/3; GB.326/LILS/3/2; GB.328/LILS/2/1; GB.328/INS/3(Add.); GB.331/INS/2 (Add.); GB.334/LILS/2(Rev.); GB.334/LILS/3.

of bold and cautious innovation,"[42] the system is articulated around two complementary procedures: a standard examination of periodical reports communicated by governments and ad hoc supervision triggered by the submission of complaints.[43]

The constitutional obligation arising out of the adoption of international labor Conventions is submission, that is, the obligation to submit the text of the Convention one year from its adoption to the competent national authorities (e.g., Parliament or other legislative body) for the enactment of legislation or other action, whereas the obligation arising out of ratification is regular reporting. A first detailed report is due one year after the entry into force of the Convention for the country concerned while subsequent reports are requested periodically either on a two-year or on a five-year basis. These reports, together with any comments formulated by employers' and worker' organizations, represent the main channel through which the ILO supervisory bodies collect the necessary information that enables them to evaluate the legislative conformity of implementing legislation and its effective application in practice.

The regular system of supervision is carried out by the Committee of independent Experts on the application of Conventions and Recommendations and the Conference Committee on the Application of Standards and is based on the reporting requirements set out in the ILO Constitution. The Committee of Experts, which was not foreseen by the Constitution but was set up in 1927 on the basis of a Conference resolution, comprises 20 members appointed by the Governing Body and serving in their personal capacity based on the principles of independence, impartiality, and objectivity. It meets once a year and adopts its report that contains individual observations and direct requests addressed to member states. Its task consists in assessing the legislative conformity of implementing legislation and the practical application of a ratified Convention based on documentary evidence.[44]

The Conference Committee is a standing tripartite committee, which reviews and debates at each annual session of the Conference a limited number of cases of noncompliance among those contained in the report of the Committee of Experts. Based on the oral, and sometimes written explanations of the government concerned, the Committee

[42] C Wilfred Jenks, *Social Justice in the Law of Nations—The ILO Impact after fifty years* (OUP 1970) 42.

[43] Among the numerous studies on the ILO supervisory system, see Nicolas Valticos, "Un sytsème de contrôle international: la mise en oeuvre des conventions internationals du travail" (1968) 123 Receuil des Cours de l'Académie de Droit International 311–407; Nicolas Valticos, "L'évolution du système de contrôle de l'Organisation internationale du Travail" in *International Law at the Time of Its Codification—Essays in Honour of Roberto Ago* (Giuffrè 1987) vol II, 505–21; Nicolas Valticos, "Once More about the ILO System of Supervision: In What Respect Is It Still a Model?" in *Towards More Effective Supervision by International Organizations—Essays in Honour of Henry G Schermers* (Springer 1994) vol I, 99–113; E Landy, *The Effectiveness of International Supervision—Thirty Years of ILO Experience* (Stevens & Sons 1966).

[44] Over the past five years, the Committee has formulated 3,117 observations (or an average of 623 observations per year) and 6,598 direct requests (or an average of 1,320 direct requests per year) in respect of the application of ratified Conventions. In addition to those country-specific comments, the Committee prepares annually a general survey on a particular Convention or group of Conventions on the basis of reports requested from all member states whether or not they have ratified the Convention or Conventions concerned.

adopts conclusions that seek to ensure the government's follow-up action to rectify discrepancies by offering assistance while at the same time maintaining the situation under the scrutiny of the supervisory bodies.

The ILO Constitution also provides for special procedures, activated on an adversarial basis, in the event of nonobservance of ratified Conventions. These contentious proceedings may take the form of either complaints—filed by any member state, the Governing Body of its own motion, or by a delegate to the Conference—or representations that may be made by an employers' or workers' organization on the ground that a member state contravenes the requirements of a Convention to which it is a party.

Under the complaints procedure, the Governing Body may appoint a Commission of Inquiry to establish the facts and draw up recommendations. The government concerned must indicate within three months whether it accepts the Commission's recommendations or whether it proposes to refer the complaint to the ICJ, whose decision shall be final.[45] As for representations, if found receivable, they are examined in the first place by an ad hoc tripartite committee of three members that submits its conclusions and recommendations to the Governing Body for adoption.[46]

Particular reference should be made to the special machinery in the field of freedom of association, which was set up in 1950, and empowers governments or employers' and workers' organizations to file complaints with the Committee on Freedom of Association—composed of nine members of the Governing Body and an independent Chairperson.[47]

Despite its intrinsic qualities, the system of supervision of international labor Conventions faces multiple challenges. Enhancing the real impact of the various supervisory procedures and managing effectively the ever-expanding workload generated by the relevant bodies are two of the main concerns. With respect to impact, evaluating the effectiveness of the action undertaken by the various supervisory bodies in terms of concrete and measurable advancement of workers' protection at the national level is a rather elusive task. It is often suggested that the practical results obtained by the supervisory machinery may be measured by analyzing "cases of progress" identified by the Committee of Experts, or situations where legislative changes are noted "with satisfaction,"[48] but this is inevitably an approximation as not all positive developments, which may be directly or indirectly attributable to the operation of the ILO supervisory machinery, produce immediate results or are readily recognized as such.

[45] To date, a total of 36 complaints have been filed and a Commission of Inquiry has been appointed on 14 occasions.

[46] To date, a total of 178 representations have been submitted of which 48 are within the past 10 years.

[47] To date, the Committee on Freedom of Association has dealt with over 3,270 cases and has developed a comprehensive body of principles covering all aspects of freedom of association and the right to organize. Notably, the Committee can consider complaints against a country irrespective of whether it has ratified Conventions Nos. 87 or 98.

[48] See Eric Gravel and Chloé Charbonneau-Jobin, *The Committee of Experts on the Application of Conventions and Recommendations: Its Dynamic and Impact* (International Labour Office 2003).

As regards the workload, the sheer volume of the reports communicated by member states but also limitations in resources and the working methods of the Committee of Experts, in particular as regards the length and degree of technical detail of comments, render the functioning of the Committee increasingly cumbersome to the point that some question its sustainability. It is indicative that the Committee of Experts receives typically 65 percent of the reports due each year and manages to examine approximately 65 percent of the reports received, which implies that in a near future the Committee will not be in a position to process two-thirds of its workload. Several commentators have drawn attention to the risks associated with the current situation and the pressing need for practical solutions.[49]

As part of the seven initiatives launched by the ILO Director-General in 2013 and now being implemented in advance of the ILO's centenary year in 2019, the Standards Initiative aims at consolidating a tripartite consensus on an authoritative supervisory system. Among the areas identified for possible improvements are the streamlining of reporting and the clarification of the respective role and mandate of the various supervisory bodies in order to enhance complementarity and eliminate unnecessary overlap.

7 Concluding Remarks

On the eve of the ILO's centenary, the system of international labor standards remains the backbone of the work of the Organization for the promotion of social justice and decent work globally. Unique in many respects, not least because of the tripartite constituency that drafts and adopts them, international labor Conventions represent by far the most comprehensive and integrated body of international treaties in the area of socioeconomic human rights.[50] Often praised as the ILO's crown jewel, international labor Conventions and the supervisory system that oversees their application, have paved the way in many respects for international lawmaking and international supervision, and still remain a model among international organizations.[51] Fundamental principles and rights at

[49] See, for instance, Francis Maupain, "Une Rolls Royce en mal de revision—L'efficacité du système de supervision de l'OIT à l'approche de son centenaire" (2010) 114 Revue générale du droit international public 465–99; E Gravel, "Les mécanismes de contrôle de l'OIT: bilan de leur efficacité et perspectives d'avenir" in Javillier and Gernigon (n 4) 3–9; WR Simpson, "Standard-Setting and Supervision: A System in Difficulty" in Javillier and Gernigon (n 4) 47–73.

[50] To the extent that the ratification rate is a measure of the relevance of international labor Conventions, in the period January 2018 to January 2019, 47 new ratifications were registered, including 4 ratifications of fundamental Conventions, 5 ratifications of the 2014 Protocol to the Forced Labour Convention, 6 of the occupational safety and health Conventions, and 7 of the Maritime Labour Convention, 2006.

[51] See, for instance, Kari Tapiola, "The ILO System of Regular Supervision of the Application of Conventions and Recommendations: A Lasting Paradigm" in Georges P Politakis (ed), *Protecting Labour Rights as Human Rights: Present and Future of International Supervision—Proceedings of the International Colloquium on the 80th Anniversary of the ILO Committee of Experts on the Application of Conventions and Recommendations, Geneva, 24–25 November 2006* (International Labour Office 2007) 29–36.

work are today largely echoed in instruments such as the Global Compact, the OECD Guidelines on Multinational Enterprises, and the UN Guidelines on Principles on Business and Human Rights. Labor clauses requiring compliance with ILO core standards feature prominently in a growing number of free trade agreements,[52] and ILO Conventions are directly referred to by courts, both nationally and internationally.[53]

The system of ILO standards remains nonetheless perfectible.[54] International labor conventions have not always elicited broad support; some remained poorly ratified or have fallen into obsolescence, while others had only a limited impact due to their fragmented or over-prescriptive character. Conscious of the need for improvement, the Organization has engaged and currently pursues a holistic review process aiming at enhancing the visibility, coherence, and impact of international labor standards. Among the key challenges calling for innovative and credible responses are the identification and abrogation of outdated instruments without creating gaps in protection; the experimentation of soft-law techniques to induce change without undermining the regulatory function of standards; the adaptation of tripartite deliberations on standard-setting items to the reduced duration of the annual Conference while preserving the quality and intensity of the preparatory work; the facilitation of the revision of standards through accelerated amendment processes; the activation of constitutional provisions for the authoritative resolution of interpretation disputes, including through the setting up of a special in-house tribunal; and the rationalization of the working methods of the supervisory organs, including the adoption of rules of procedure.

Certainly, the challenges are significant and require vision and audacity but the ILO has never shied away from its responsibilities. The collective wisdom and legal ingenuity that the tripartite constituents have shown in the course of the ILO's first hundred years of existence are the most solid asset and source of inspiration to guide the way forward. Often compared to a Sisyphean task, the ILO's standard-setting action is a never-ending process as it is meant to follow the incessant transformations of the world of work and adapt to new needs. Symptomatic as this may be of an endeavor in pursuit of an ideal, the relevance of international labor standards will continue to depend on how effectively they translate the human aspiration to decent life into an adequately protective and reasonably flexible set of rules.

[52] See, for instance, *Social Dimensions of Free Trade Agreements* (International Labour Office 2013).

[53] See, for instance, Franz C. Ebert and Martin Oelz, *Bridging the Gap between Labour Rights And Human Rights: The Role of ILO Law in Regional Human Rights Courts* (International Institute for Labour Studies 2012); Xavier Beaudonnet, "L'utilisation des sources universelles du droit international du travail par les juridictions internes" (2005) *Bulletin de droit comparé du travail et de la sécurité sociale* 43–84.

[54] See Francis Maupain, "ILO Normative Action in Its Second Century: Escaping the Double Bind?" in Blackett and Trebilcock (n 38) 301–15.

CHAPTER 12

WOMEN

HILARY CHARLESWORTH[*]

THE designation of the category of "women" as the subject of United Nations treaties raises some thorny questions. There is, for example, no chapter in this *Handbook* labeled as dealing with "men." Indeed, the only other chapter specifically addressing a category of humans is that on "Refugees and Stateless Persons," a group defined technically by what has happened to its members. The focus on women as a class implies that there is a commonality among women at the global level, a claim over which there is intense theoretical dispute.

The large and almost universal state membership of the UN has particular implications for treaties relating to women. The lives and roles of women are critical to the organization of the state and to accounts of its identity. Women, particularly as mothers, are regarded as the repository of many national and cultural values.[1] The negotiation and supervision of treaties relating to women have thus been the battleground for contests between principles of universality and deference to cultural and religious norms. Another relevant aspect of the composition of the UN is that, historically, few women delegates have represented states in UN bodies, even fewer have been selected to lead UN agencies, and the UN Secretariat has made glacial progress in appointing women at senior levels.[2] For this reason, women's organizations and

* Thanks to Michael McArdle and Athena Nguyen for their kind assistance with this chapter.

[1] Jan Jindy Pettman, *Worlding Women: A Feminist International Politics* (Routledge 1996) 48–52.

[2] In January 2018, after 70 years of campaigns by women's organizations, the UN Secretary-General announced that "gender parity" had been achieved at the senior management level: see Michelle Milford Morse, "Milestone at the UN: Gender Parity in the UN's Leadership" (United Nations Foundation, 26 January 2016) <unfoundationblog.org/milestone-un-gender-parity-un-leadership/> accessed April 28, 2018. UN Women has however estimated that, on current trends, the UN will only achieve gender parity throughout the UN Secretariat by 2039: UN Women, "Trends and Projections for Gender Parity: UN Secretariat" (UN Women, December 2015) <www.unwomen.org/-/media/headquarters/attachments/sections/how%20we%20work/unsystemcoordination/data/secretariat/projections/un-secretariat.pdf?la=en&vs=1318> accessed April 28, 2018. In areas such as the Department of Peacekeeping Operations, current trends suggest that it will take until 2182 to achieve gender parity: UN Women, "Trends and Projections for Gender Parity: DPKO" (UN Women, December 2015)

civil society have played a critical role in ensuring that women's voices have been heard in the UN.[3]

This chapter offers an overview of UN approaches to women's lives in legal instruments. It begins by describing the engagement of women's organizations with international institutions before the founding of the UN in 1945, and then moves to UN treaties dealing with women. Its focus is the major UN treaty in this area, the 1979 Convention on the Elimination of All Forms of Discrimination Against Women (CEDAW).[4]

UN treaty activity raises the question of the strategic value of creating special regimes for women's lives. The French revolutionary Olympe de Gouges summarized this dilemma in 1788 by identifying the paradox for feminists of, on the one hand, insisting that differences between women and men should be irrelevant in claiming political rights; while, on the other hand, acting in the name of the category of women, thus bolstering the idea of difference.[5] This paradox is well illustrated in the international sphere.

1 Women and the International Sphere

Women's groups have long seen the international arena as a hopeful site for their campaigns, transcending the conservatism of national systems. A series of International Congresses of Women, held in various countries starting from 1878, promoted women's equality. Some focused on women's right to vote, but others made broader claims about women's rights.[6] The 1915 Women's Congress, held in The Hague, emphasized women's critical role in ending international conflict and adopted proposals aimed at ending the Great War.[7]

The League of Nations became a repository of hope for national and international women's movements. British feminist Vera Brittain wrote that "the time has now come to move from the national to the international sphere, and to endeavour to obtain by international agreement what national legislation has failed to accomplish."[8] International

<http://www.unwomen.org/-/media/headquarters/attachments/sections/how%20we%20work/unsystemcoordination/data/secretariat/projections/dpko.pdf?la=en&vs=631> accessed April 28, 2018.

[3] Charlotte Bunch, "Women and Gender" in Thomas G Weiss and Sam Daws (eds), *The Oxford Handbook on the United Nations* (OUP 2008) 496.

[4] Convention on the Elimination of All Forms of Discrimination Against Women (opened for signature 18 December 1979, entered into force 3 September 1981) 1249 UNTS 13 (CEDAW).

[5] Joan Wallach Scott, *Only Paradoxes to Offer: French Feminists and the Rights of Man* (Harvard University Press 1997) 22.

[6] Laura Beers, "Advocating for a Feminist Internationalism between the Wars" in Glenda Sluga and Carolyn James (eds), *Women, Diplomacy and International Politics since 1500* (Routledge 2016) 202, 203–04.

[7] See International Congress of Women, *Report of the International Congress of Women: The Hague—The Netherlands, April 28th to May 1st, 1915* (Women's Peace Party 1915) 11–17.

[8] Quoted in Carol Miller, "'Geneva—the Key to Equality': Inter-war Feminists and the League of Nations" (1994) 3 Women's History Rev 219, 221.

women's organizations sent delegates to the 1919 Paris Peace Conference and advocated for the representation of women in all aspects of the League's operations. They also urged the League to address issues relating to women, such as trafficking, equal political rights, and health and education.[9] The partial success of this lobbying was reflected in provisions in the Covenant of the League stating that all positions in the League "shall be open equally to men and women"[10] and referring to conditions of women's work and trafficking in women as part of the League's work.[11] In some respects, women's engagement with the League served to legitimize European imperial interests. For example, Susan Pedersen has argued that the presence of a woman on the nine-member Permanent Mandates Commission operated to give a sense that the mandate system was based on education and tutelage, rather than coercion. Calls for self-determination by mandate populations could be deflected by insistence on social progress, steered by a womanly sensibility.[12]

Later, feminists believed that the League's support might counter moves against women's rights prompted by the 1930s Depression and the spread of nationalist conservative movements.[13] A significant expression of faith in the capacity of international organizations to alleviate women's inequality at the national level was a campaign for the League to adopt an equal rights treaty in the 1920s and 1930s. A draft treaty, proposed by the American feminist Alice Paul in 1926, contained a single operative clause: states parties agreed that, on ratification of the treaty, "men and women shall have Equal Rights throughout the [ratifying state's] territory subject to their respective jurisdictions."[14] This initiative caused dissension among international women's groups. Its proponents viewed the treaty as an antidote to the restrictive approach to the regulation of women's work taken in some national jurisdictions and by the International Labour Organization (ILO), discussed later on in this chapter. Other women's groups supported protective treaties to support working women's social roles as mothers and wives and saw an equal rights treaty as a threat.[15]

While the equal rights treaty campaign ultimately failed, the work of the League of Nations elevated the status of women from a purely national to an international issue. Prodded by transnational women's organizations during the 1930s,[16] the League secretariat began to amass information on women's social and legal situations and the Legal Committee of the League Assembly instituted an inquiry into the comparative status of women in 1937.[17] This prompted the Assembly to launch a major inquiry of its own into the legal status of women throughout the world later that year, at least in part to forestall

[9] Leila J Rupp, *Worlds of Women: The Making of an International Women's Movement* (Princeton University Press 1997) 210–17.

[10] Covenant of the League of Nations art 7.

[11] ibid art 23.

[12] Susan Pedersen, "Metaphors of the Schoolroom: Women Working the Mandates System of the League of Nations" (2008) 66 History Workshop J 188, 192.

[13] See Miller (n 8).

[14] Quoted in ibid 220–21.

[15] ibid 222–24, 233–24.

[16] The membership of these organizations, such as the International Alliance of Women and the World's Young Women's Christian Association, included women's groups from Europe, Latin America, and the United States.

[17] Miller (n 8) 236–37.

moves to adopt some form of equal rights treaty. In any event, this inquiry by a committee of experts was truncated by the start of the Second World War in 1939.[18] The League also adopted a number of specific treaties to deal with concerns relating to women. These included slavery[19] and trafficking in women and children.[20] Women's groups hoped that the League would address the vexed issue of the nationality of married women, but they were left disappointed by discriminatory provisions on the topic in the 1930 Convention on Certain Questions relating to the Conflict of Nationality Law.[21] After a spirited campaign against the Convention, a Liaison Committee of Women's International Organisations was formed to engage with the League Assembly on the issue of equal nationality rights.[22] Again, the demise of the League left this concern unresolved.

The ILO, established in the same year as the League, was also a site of considerable activity relating to women. Starting in 1919, it adopted a series of conventions protecting working women, including the Night Work Convention (1919),[23] the Childbirth Convention (1919),[24] and the Lead Paint Convention (1921).[25] These instruments were not cast in the language of rights, and their aim was primarily protective of ideals about womanhood, such as women's physical weakness and vulnerability outside their families.[26] As noted previously, women's groups were deeply divided on the value of these treaties. Some supported them as crucial for working women, while others were concerned that such treaties in fact restricted women's right to work.[27] Indeed, the protective cast of the ILO activity was an impetus for the drafting of the Equal Rights Treaty.

At the San Francisco conference in 1945, a few women delegates, mainly from Asia and the Americas, along with nongovernmental organizations (NGOs), lobbied for the inclusion of a reference to "the equal rights of men and women" in the Preamble to the UN Charter as well as to nondiscrimination on the basis of sex with respect to human

[18] See Committee for the Study of the Legal Status of Women, "Report on the Progress of the Enquiry (Adopted on January 10th, 1939)" (Doc C.59.M.21, League of Nations, 23 January 1939).

[19] *Convention to Suppress the Slave Trade and Slavery* (adopted 25 September 1926, entered into force 9 March 1927) 60 LNTS 253.

[20] International Convention or the Suppression of the Traffic in Women and Children (opened for signature 30 September 1921, entered into force 24 April 1950) 53 UNTS 39; International Convention for the Suppression of the Traffic in Women of Full Age (opened for signature 11 October 1933, entered into force 24 August 1934) 150 LNTS 431.

[21] Convention on Certain Questions relating to the Conflict of Nationality Laws (opened for signature 12 April 1930, entered into force 1 July 1937) 179 LNTS 89 arts 8–11.

[22] Miller (n 8) 227–28.

[23] Convention concerning Employment of Women during the Night (adopted 28 November 1919, entered into force 13 June 1921) ILO Convention No 4 (Night Work (Women) Convention).

[24] Convention concerning the Employment of Women Before and After Childbirth (adopted 29 November 1919, entered into force 13 June 1921) ILO Convention No 3.

[25] Convention concerning the Use of White Lead in Painting (adopted 19 November 1921, entered into force 31 August 1923) ILO Convention No 13.

[26] The instruments, however, also contemplated some economic considerations trumping the protection. For example, in the case of the Night Work Convention, women were able to work at night in cases of force majeure, and when dealing with rapidly deteriorating materials: Night Work (Women) Convention (n 23) art 4.

[27] See Miller (n 8).

rights in defining one of the purposes of the UN.[28] This group was also successful in including Article 8 in the UN Charter, which provides that the UN "shall place no restrictions on the eligibility of men and women to participate in any capacity and under conditions of equality" in its work, echoing the spirit of Article 7 of the Covenant of the League.

Olympe de Gouges's dilemma emerged in debates about the institutional location of women's rights in the UN. In 1946, the Commission on the Status of Women (CSW) was established as a subsidiary body of the Commission on Human Rights (CHR). After much lobbying by NGOs and women delegates to avoid women being relegated to a "queue" of human rights issues, CSW became an independent body reporting directly to the United Nations Economic and Social Council (ECOSOC) in 1947.[29] It has been an important institution in promoting the drafting of treaties dealing with women's rights, although the resources allocated to it have been a fraction of those enjoyed by the CHR, now replaced by the Human Rights Council.[30]

The most substantial galvanization of UN activity relating to women came with the declaration of a UN Decade for Women (1976–1985) and four World Conferences on women held in Mexico City (1975), Copenhagen (1980), Nairobi (1985), and Beijing (1995). Women also used international summits on the environment (Rio), human rights (Vienna), and development (Cairo) in the 1990s to obtain recognition of women's rights. All these intergovernmental events were accompanied by parallel NGO conferences, and both the official and unofficial activity generated a cornucopia of debates, declarations, and blueprints for the future.[31] The UN Decade and World Conferences created an awareness of the potential of the UN to support women's movements, while also exposing divisions between feminists from the Global North and the Global South. Feminists from the Global North tended to emphasize individual rights for women, such as the rights to nondiscrimination in the workplace and to reproductive choice, while feminists from the South focused on economic and social rights, and inequalities between states caused by the international economic order.[32] The World Conferences also revealed the capacity of coalitions of states and other actors to curtail the definition of women's rights on the basis of claims to religious observance and culture.[33] The failure to hold a World Conference on women in the two decades since the Beijing Conference reflects concerns that the normative advances made in these forums could be wound

[28] Charter of the United Nations art 1.3.

[29] Hilkka Pietila, "Engendering the Global Agenda: The Story of Women and the United Nations" (Development Dossier, UN NGLS, 2002) 13–14.

[30] Laura Reanda, "The Commission on the Status of Women" in Philip Alston (ed), *The United Nations and Human Rights: A Critical Appraisal* (OUP 1992) 265, 267.

[31] Bunch (n 3) 499–500; Christine Chinkin and Marsha A. Freeman, "Introduction" in Marsha A. Freeman, Christine Chinkin, and Beate Rudolph (eds), *The UN Convention on the Elimination of All Forms of Discrimination Against Women: A Commentary* (OUP 2012) 1, 6 [hereinafter Freeman, Chinkin, and Rudolph].

[32] Chilla Bulbeck, *One World Women's Movement* (Pluto Press 1988).

[33] Hilary Charlesworth, "Women as Sherpas: Are Global Summits Useful for Women?" (1996) 22 Feminist Studies 537.

back by coalitions of states pursuing conservative religious agendas, as illustrated by debates in the UN Human Rights Council.

2 UN Instruments Relating to Women

Prompted by civil society and the energy of particular women civil servants and diplomats, the UN, and in particular the CSW, has been active in developing normative standards to respond to the disadvantaged position of women across the globe. A series of treaties adopted in the early years of the life of the UN addressed discrimination against women in certain areas of public life. The purpose of the Convention on the Political Rights of Women (1952) was the implementation of the UN Charter's preambular commitment to equality of rights for men and women. This brief instrument, with just three operative paragraphs, provides for treatment of women on equal terms with men with respect to voting rights,[34] election to all publicly elected bodies,[35] and the holding of public office and the exercise of public functions.[36] The Convention on the Nationality of Married Women (1957)[37] deals with married women's rights with respect to nationality, although in a qualified manner, avoiding the language of nondiscrimination and equality. The Convention on Consent to Marriage, Minimum Age for Marriage and Registration of Marriages (1962)[38] elaborates modestly on Article 16 of the Universal Declaration of Human Rights (1948),[39] again without reference to women's equality. It calls for full and free consent of both parties to a marriage, and for states to specify a minimum age for marriage and to register marriages. None of these treaties provide mechanisms for international scrutiny of states parties' compliance.

Another focus of UN activity has been the protection of women from particular forms of harm, specifically in sexual matters. For example, the UN continued the interest of the League of Nations in regulating the trafficking of and prostitution by women. The Convention for the Suppression of the Traffic in Persons and of the Exploitation of the Prostitution of Others (1949)[40] applies to both women and men, although it regards women and girls as more vulnerable. The Convention linked the prostitution industry, wherever it occurs, with trafficking, or the forcible movement of people across borders.

[34] Convention on the Political Rights of Women (opened for signature 20 December 1952, entered into force 7 July 1954) 193 UNTS 135 art I.

[35] ibid art II.

[36] ibid art III.

[37] Convention on the Nationality of Married Women (opened for signature 20 February 1957, entered into force 11 August 1958) 309 UNTS 65.

[38] Convention on Consent to Marriage, Minimum Age for Marriage and Registration of Marriages (opened for signature 10 December 1962, entered into force 9 December 1964) 521 UNTS 231.

[39] Universal Declaration of Human Rights (adopted 10 December 1948) UNGA Res 217 A(III) (UDHR).

[40] Convention for the Suppression of the Traffic in Persons and of the Exploitation of the Prostitution of Others (opened for signature 21 March 1950, entered into force 25 July 1951) 96 UNTS 271.

Its compliance mechanisms were weak and were widely disregarded. Half a century later, the Protocol to Prevent, Suppress and Punish Trafficking in Persons, Especially Women and Children,[41] known as the Palermo Protocol, was adopted to supplement the United Nations Convention against Transnational Organized Crime (2003).[42] Feminist activists and scholars have had mixed reactions to UN initiatives on trafficking, which is generally associated with forced prostitution. The Palermo Protocol, for example, was welcomed by women's groups who regarded all types of prostitution, whether coerced or voluntary, as a form of slavery; it was equally criticized by those who understood prostitution as a legitimate form of labor. The latter group argued for a distinction between forced and voluntary prostitution, and rejected the notion of women engaged in prostitution as victims.[43]

The UN has also paid considerable attention to the situation of women in armed conflict. An early intervention in this area is the General Assembly's Declaration on the Protection of Women and Children in Emergency and Armed Conflict (1974).[44] The Declaration applies principles of international humanitarian law that protect civilian populations in international armed conflicts to struggles for self-determination and independence. It prohibits attacks on civilian populations, particularly women and children. The Resolution presents women and children as a unified category of people who are "defenceless" and "the most vulnerable members of the population." The linkage of women and children in this context reinforces the image of women as not only innately weak but also as the primary caregivers whose importance is linked to their capacity to give birth. These patterns remain evident in the "Women, Peace and Security" agenda of the UN Security Council. Its founding resolution, UNSC Resolution 1325 (2000),[45] emphasizes the "special needs" of women and children in times of conflict, while also invoking the language of equality in calling for women to be involved in negotiating peace. Later Security Council resolutions on women depict women in conflict zones as particularly susceptible to sexual violence, requiring protection, rather than as potential agents in shaping their own futures.[46] As discussed further later on in this chapter, the UN human rights system has taken a different approach to violence against women.[47]

[41] Protocol to Prevent, Suppress and Punish Trafficking in Persons, Especially Women and Children, Supplementing the United Nations Convention Against Transnational Organized Crime (opened for signature 15 November 2000, entered into force 25 December 2003) 2237 UNTS 319.

[42] United Nations Convention Against Transnational Organized Crime (opened for signature 15 November 2000, entered into force 29 September 2003) 2225 UNTS 209.

[43] For a discussion of the controversies surrounding the drafting of the Palermo Protocol see Gabrielle Simm, "Negotiating the United Nations Trafficking Protocol: Feminist Debates" (2004) 23 Australian YBIL 135.

[44] UNGA Res 3318(XXIX) (14 December 1974) UN Doc A/RES/3318(XXIX).

[45] UNSC Resolution 1325 (2000) UN Doc S/RES/1325.

[46] See, eg, UNSCR Res 1820 (19 June 2008) UN Doc S/RES/1820; UNSC Res 1888 (30 September 2009) UN Doc S/RES/1888; UNSC Res 1889 (5 October 2009) UN Doc S/RES/1889; 1960 (16 December 2010) UN Doc S/RES/1960; UNSC Res 2106 (24 June 2013) UN Doc S/RES/2106; UNSC Res 2242 (13 October 2015) UN Doc S/RES/2242.

[47] For an analysis of the different approaches taken by CEDAW and the Security Council to violence against women during armed conflict see Hilary Charlesworth and Christine Chinkin, "An Alien's

The principle of nondiscrimination on the basis of sex is contained in a number of generally applicable UN human rights instruments and treaties. The Universal Declaration of Human Rights (UDHR), adopted by the UN General Assembly in 1948, assures that the rights and freedoms it contains apply to everyone "without distinction of any kind, such as... sex...."[48] Article 7 recognizes equality before the law and the right to equal protection of the law without discrimination, but does not refer specifically to women. The two UN general human rights treaties, the 1966 International Covenant on Economic, Social and Cultural Rights (ICESCR) and the 1966 International Covenant on Civil and Political Rights (ICCPR), both commit states parties to respect and ensure the rights recognized by the treaties "without distinction of any kind, such as... sex"[49] and "to ensure the equal right of men and women" to the rights they contain.[50] Article 26 of the ICCPR repeats in effect the language of the UDHR's Article 7, but adds the requirement that national laws must prohibit any discrimination and "guarantee to all persons equal and effective protection against discrimination on any ground such as... sex...." Other human rights treaties include parallel provisions.[51]

Discrimination against women generally first became the subject of a formal UN instrument with the General Assembly's adoption of a Declaration on the Elimination of Discrimination against Women in 1967.[52] This resolution was initiated by third world and socialist states[53] and declared discrimination against women to be an offense against human dignity.[54] It called on states "to establish adequate legal protection for equal rights of men and women."[55] The momentum generated by the 1975 Mexico World Conference on Women and the subsequent UN Decade for Women encouraged the translation of the Declaration into the Convention on the Elimination of all Forms of Discrimination against Women (CEDAW), adopted in 1979.[56] Another influential document in the drafting of CEDAW was the 1965 International Convention on the Elimination of Racial Discrimination (ICERD),[57] particularly the definition of discrimination, discussed later on in this chapter.

CEDAW is the central node of UN activity with respect to women. It offers a broad account of discrimination in Article 1 as:

Review of Women and Armed Conflict" in Dale Stephens and Paul Babie (eds), *Imagining Law: Essays in Conversation with Judith Gardam* (University of Adelaide Press 2016) 171; Catherine O'Rourke and Aisling Swaine "CEDAW and the Security Council: Enhancing Women's Rights in Conflict"(2018) 67 ICLQ 167.

48 UDHR (n 39) art 2.

49 International Covenant on Civil and Political Rights (adopted 16 December 1966, entered into force 23 March 1976) 999 UNTS 171 (ICCPR) art 2.1. See also International Covenant on Economic, Social and Cultural Rights (opened for signature 16 December 1966, entered into force 3 January 1976) 993 UNTS 3 (ICESCR) art 2.2: "without discrimination of any kind as to... sex."

50 ICESCR (n 49) art 3; ICCPR (n 49) art 3.

51 See, eg, Convention on the Rights of the Child (opened for signature 20 November 1989, entered into force 2 September 1990) 1577 UNTS 3 art 2.

52 UNGA Res 2263 (XXII) (7 November 1967). 53 Chinkin and Freeman (n 31) 5.

54 UNGA Res 2263 (XXI) (n 52) art 1. 55 ibid art 2. 56 CEDAW (n 4).

57 International Convention on the Elimination of All Forms of Racial Discrimination (opened for signature 21 December 1965, entered into force 4 January 1969) 660 UNTS 195 (ICERD).

> any distinction, exclusion or restriction made on the basis of sex which has the effect or purpose of impairing or nullifying the recognition, enjoyment or exercise by women, irrespective of their marital status, on a basis of equality of men and women, of human rights and fundamental freedoms in the political, economic, social, cultural, civil or any other field.[58]

Notable here is the focus on discrimination affecting women, rather than discrimination on the basis of sex, which would apply to both women and men. During the drafting of CEDAW, some states advocated for a treaty aimed at eliminating sex discrimination generally, but they were in a distinct minority. Most states accepted that there was a deep asymmetry in the positions of women and men, and sought to address this.[59] Another feature of the definition is its coverage of direct and indirect discrimination through its attention to the "effect or purpose" of actions. It is concerned with both procedural and substantive equality for women.

Article 1, as most of CEDAW's descriptions of specific rights, refers to "a basis of equality of men and women" as the critical measure of nondiscrimination, suggesting that male lives are the appropriate comparator for women. Scholars have argued however that Article 1 indeed supports a notion of "transformative" equality, going beyond preventing discrimination to undertake an ambitious positive program to achieve equality. Andrew Byrnes, for example, sees transformative equality "embodied in the text and spirit of the Convention."[60] It is particularly evident in Article 3, requiring states parties to take positive measures to "ensure the full development and advancement of women"; in Article 5, discussed later in this section, which calls for the modification of social and cultural practices; and in Article 11's prohibition of discrimination against women in employment on the basis of marriage and maternity.[61] The CEDAW Committee has endorsed the notion of transformative equality,[62] which demands much more than simply allowing women entry into a male-defined world, and requires a transformation of social structures that rest on male domination. This entails not only institutional change, but also action to achieve a radical redistribution of resources and power in society. Sandra Fredman suggests that transformative equality involves "a dismantling of the public-private divide and a reconstruction of the public world so that child-care and parenting are seen as valued common responsibilities of both parents and the community." Such measures, she argues, are the basis of women being able to reach their capabilities and to fully express their choices in society.[63]

[58] CEDAW (n 4) art 1.

[59] Andrew Byrnes, "Article 1" in Freeman, Chinkin, and Rudolph (n 31), 52.

[60] ibid 56.

[61] Frances Raday, "Article 11" in Freeman, Chinkin, and Rudolph (n 31), 304–05.

[62] See, eg, CEDAW Committee, General Recommendation 25 (2004) para 10.

[63] Sandra Fredman, "Beyond the Dichotomy of Formal and Substantive Equality: Towards a New Definition of Human Rights" in Ineke Boerefijn, Fons Coomans, Jenny Goldschmidt, Rikki Holtmaat, and Ria Wolleswinkel (eds), *Temporary Special Measures: Accelerating De Facto Equality of Women under Article 4(1) UN Convention on the Elimination of All Forms of Discrimination Against Women* (Intersentia 2003) 111, 115.

The definition of discrimination in CEDAW closely tracks that of ICERD.[64] One distinction between the two treaties is in the final words of the definition: in ICERD these are "any other field of public life,"[65] while in CEDAW they are "civil or any other field." CEDAW thus extends ICERD's focus on discrimination in public life to acknowledge the problem that discrimination against women occurs not only in the public sphere, but also in the private sphere.[66] Article 16, for example, applies the prohibition of discrimination against women to "all matters relating to marriage and family relations," including with respect to choosing a spouse, family planning, choice of family name and occupation, and disposition of property.

CEDAW's ambitious obligations of implementation are set out in Article 2. States parties undertake to include "the principle of the equality of men and women" in their national legal systems and to "ensure... the practical realisation of this principle."[67] Article 2 also requires states to eliminate discrimination against women through legal and other "appropriate measures." Such measures include the adoption of temporary special measures.[68]

The Convention covers a wide range of areas where states parties must work to eliminate discrimination against women including political and public life,[69] international organizations,[70] education,[71] employment,[72] healthcare,[73] financial credit,[74] cultural life,[75] the rural sector,[76] and the law.[77] Many observers have celebrated CEDAW for its broad coverage, particularly its attention to women's civil and political rights as well as their economic, social, and cultural rights. Because of this, the treaty has been termed "an international bill of rights for women."[78] Radhika Coomaraswamy has referred to the "unique" form of this treaty in its attempt to transform state practice rather than simply codifying it.[79] A striking example of this is Article 5(a), which calls on states parties to take "all appropriate measures... [t]o modify the social and cultural patterns of conduct of men and women, with a view to achieving the elimination of prejudices and... practices which are based on the idea of the inferiority or the superiority of either of the sexes or on stereotyped roles for men and women."[80] Article 5(b) requires parties to ensure that maternity is understood as a social function, and that men and women

[64] ICERD (n 57) art 1.1: racial discrimination means "any distinction, exclusion, restriction or preference based on race, colour, descent, or national or ethnic origin which has the purpose or effect of nullifying or impairing the recognition, enjoyment or exercise, on an equal footing, of human rights and fundamental freedoms in the political, economic, social, cultural or any other field of public life."

[65] ibid. [66] Byrnes (n 58) 57. [67] CEDAW (n 4) art 2(a).

[68] ibid art 4. See CEDAW Committee (n 62) para 30; CEDAW Committee General Recommendation 28 (16 December 2010) paras 9, 20, 37(d).

[69] CEDAW (n 4) art 7. [70] ibid art 8. [71] ibid art 10. [72] ibid art 11.

[73] ibid art 12. [74] ibid art 13(b). [75] ibid art 13(c). [76] ibid art 14.

[77] ibid art 15.

[78] Boutros Boutros-Ghali, "Introduction" in United Nations (ed), *The United Nations and the Advancement of Women, 1945–1995* (United Nations Department of Public Information 1996) 5.

[79] Radhika Coomaraswamy, "Women and Children: The Cutting Edge of International Law" (2015) 30 Am Univ Intl L Rev 1.

[80] CEDAW (n 4) art 5(a).

have common responsibilities with respect to the upbringing and development of children.[81] These are far-reaching measures have a clearly transformative agenda.

Article 28 of CEDAW contemplates reservations to the treaty, following general international law by excluding those that are "incompatible with [its] object and purpose."[82] In 2018, almost a third of the 189 states parties had entered reservations or declarations in relation to one or more provisions. Many of these relate to Article 29(1), which grants the International Court of Justice jurisdiction over disputes relating to the implementation of the Convention. A significant number of reservations, however, are based on assertions of culture and religion, so broad as to call their compatibility with CEDAW's object and purpose into question.[83] One example is the statement of Malaysia:

> The Government of Malaysia declares that Malaysia's accession is subject to the understanding that the provisions of the Convention do not conflict with the provisions of the Islamic Sharia' law and the Federal Constitution of Malaysia.[84]

The subordination of treaty obligations to religious law is also found in many reservations from Islamic countries, such as Brunei, Mauritania, Morocco, Oman, Saudi Arabia, and Tunisia. Other reservations, such as that of Pakistan, make treaty observance subject to the provisions of national constitutions, which often contain religious commitments.[85] Algeria has entered a reservation to Article 2, making CEDAW obligations subject to the Algerian Family Code.[86] Other examples of religious reservations include those of Israel, which are designed to preserve the autonomy of religious communities: for example, allowing them not to appoint female judges to religious courts.[87]

Claims that obligations imposed by CEDAW are subject to national cultural dictates are common. For example, Monaco's reservations include the statement that its CEDAW obligations have no impact on Monaco's laws relating to succession to the throne, which give men priority over women.[88] Monaco does not accept CEDAW's injunction to prevent discrimination in public life in the context of allowing women to serve in its police force, nor does it accept the obligation to treat women and men in the same way with respect to nationality laws, or equal rights in the choice of a family name. It also resists the application of CEDAW to its social security laws:

> The Principality of Monaco reserves the right to continue to apply its social security laws which, in certain circumstances, envisage the payment of certain benefits to the head of the household who . . . is presumed to be the husband.[89]

[81] ibid art 5(b). [82] ibid art 28.

[83] The text of the reservations is available at the website of the United Nations Treaty Collection: United Nations "Status of the Convention on the Elimination of All Forms of Discrimination Against Women" (*United Nations Treaty Collection*, 29 April 2018) https://treaties.un.org/Pages/ViewDetails.aspx?src=IND&mtdsg_no=IV-8&chapter=4&lang=en> accessed April 30, 2018.

[84] ibid "Malaysia." [85] ibid "Pakistan." [86] ibid "Algeria."

[87] ibid "Israel." [88] ibid "Monaco." [89] ibid.

Niger's extensive list of reservations states that many CEDAW provisions are contrary to existing customs and practices:

> The Government of the Republic of the Niger expresses reservations with regard to article 2, paragraphs (d) and (f), concerning the taking of all appropriate measures to abolish all customs and practices which constitute discrimination against women, particularly in respect of succession.
>
> The Government of the Republic of the Niger expresses reservations with regard to the modification of social and cultural patterns of conduct of men and women [in Article 5, paragraph (a)].[90]

India's Declaration provides:

> i) With regard to articles 5 (a) and 16 (1) of the Convention on the Elimination of All Forms of Discrimination Against Women, the Government of the Republic of India declares that it shall abide by and ensure these provisions in conformity with its policy of non-interference in the personal affairs of any Community without its initiative and consent.[91]

The provisions of CEDAW that have attracted many cultural, traditional, or religious objections are Article 2 (containing the implementation obligations in the treaty), Article 9 (dealing with equality between women and men in changing or retaining nationality and with respect to the nationality of their children), and Article 16 (setting out rights in marriage and in relation to the family).[92]

Reservations to CEDAW are often cast in broad terms, obscuring the nature of the reserving state's obligations. The references to Islamic sharia law, cited previously, add a particular uncertainty because of the range of views among Islamic scholars as to the content and rules of sharia and the appropriate mode of scriptural interpretation.[93] Most states parties have been reluctant to object to even sweeping reservations, but a small group of states have regularly made formal objections to some reservations.[94] This relies on observant foreign offices, because the objections must be lodged within a year of the reservation being made. It is almost exclusively European countries who are active on this front, particularly the Nordic countries.[95] The Committee on the Elimination of Discrimination against Women has also probed reserving states on this issue.[96] Although the process of objecting to reservations has little legal impact,[97] pressure to withdraw reservations can sometimes be effective. For example, a range of states have withdrawn reservations to Article 9 on nationality, Malaysia reduced the extensive list of

90 ibid "Niger." 91 ibid "India." 92 See, eg, Iraq's reservation: ibid "Iraq."

93 Jane Connors, "Article 28" in Freeman, Chinkin, and Rudolph (n 31) 569.

94 The text of objections to the reservations is available at the website of the United Nations Treaty Collection: see United Nations (n 83).

95 Exceptions include Canada and Mexico. 96 See the account in Connors (n 93) 581–91.

97 See Vienna Convention on the Law of Treaties (opened for signature 23 May 1969, entered into force 27 January 1980) 1155 UNTS 331 art 21.

provisions in relation to which it made reservations in 2010 and in 2011, and Morocco withdrew its reservations to Article 16, which made that provision subject to the dictates of sharia law. But overall, few reservations that are justified on the basis of culture, tradition, or religion have been withdrawn.[98]

CEDAW follows the pattern of UN human rights treaties in providing for an expert committee to monitor treaty implementation. Article 17 establishes the Committee on the Elimination of Discrimination against Women, consisting of 23 members elected for four-year terms.[99] The Committee first convened in 1982. Almost all its members since that time have been women, a striking contrast with the other UN human rights treaty bodies whose membership is dominated by men.[100] Although Committee members are elected as experts, rather than as state representatives, the first years of the Committee's work were marked by Cold-War-inspired political tensions.[101] The Committee however has evolved into a productive and creative body, developing jurisprudence on women's rights to respond to systematic violations of women's rights. It has adopted a series of General Recommendations, elaborating and developing the provisions of CEDAW.

The Committee has also played a constructive role in amplifying the general language of the Convention to cover issues that are not explicitly addressed by it. A good example is the issue of violence against women, absent from both the Declaration and the Convention text, reflecting the limited contemporary understandings of the prevalence or significance of such violence and the belief that it was not a matter of international concern, but one of domestic criminal regulation.[102] During the 1980s, civil society groups launched campaigns drawing attention to violence against women as an international issue[103] and the UN eventually took this up.[104] In 1992, the Committee adopted General Recommendation 19 on violence against women.[105] The Recommendation presents violence against women as both a cause and a consequence of inequality between women and men, and identifies such violence as a form of discrimination on the basis of sex, affecting women's enjoyment of human rights and freedoms equally with men. The rights-based approach departs from approaches to violence that emphasize women's

[98] Connors (n 93) 595. [99] CEDAW (n 4) art 17.

[100] For example, in April 2018, 17 out of 18 members of the Committee on the Rights of Persons with Disabilities, 7 out of 10 members of the Committee on Enforced Disappearances, and 11 of 14 members of the Committee on Migrant Workers, are men: OHCHR, "Members of the Committee on the Rights of Persons with Disabilities" (*OHCHR*, 2018) http://www.ohchr.org/EN/HRBodies/CRPD/Pages/Membership.aspx accessed April 30, 2018; OHCHR, "Members of the Committee on Enforced Disappearances" (*OHCHR*, 2018) www.ohchr.org/EN/HRBodies/CED/Pages/Membership.aspx accessed April 30, 2018; OHCHR, "Members of the Committee on Migrant Workers" (*OHCHR*, 2018) <http://www.ohchr.org/EN/HRBodies/CMW/Pages/Membership.aspx accessed April 30, 2018.

[101] Elizabeth Evatt, "Finding a Voice for Women's Rights: The Early Years of CEDAW" (2002) 34 Geo Wash Intl L Rev 515, 520.

[102] Christine Chinkin, "Violence against Women" in Freeman, Chinkin, and Rudolph (n 31) 444–45.

[103] See Charlotte Bunch, "Women's Rights as Human Rights: Towards a Re-vision of Human Rights" (1990) 12 Hum Rights Q 486.

[104] See, eg, UNGA Res 45/114 (14 December 1990) UN Doc A/RES/45/114.

[105] CEDAW Committee General Recommendation 19 (1992).

victimhood,[106] for example the Security Council's Women, Peace and Security agenda, referred to previously.[107] The Recommendation offers a broad account of violence, including both physical and mental harm and suffering, and calls on states parties to prevent, investigate, punish, and make reparation for violence against women in both public and private spheres. It articulates a state's duty of due diligence in dealing with the behavior of nonstate actors, drawing on the jurisprudence of the Inter-American Court of Human Rights.[108]

The Committee's inclusion of violence against women within the remit of CEDAW prompted a cascade of activity in other parts of the UN system. The following year the UN General Assembly adopted a Declaration on the Elimination of Violence against Women, taking the issue of general application beyond the treaty system.[109] The Declaration views violence against women as "a manifestation of historically unequal power relations between men and women,"[110] and, following the CEDAW Committee, presents it as a violation of women's human rights. In 1994, the UN Commission on Human Rights appointed a Special Rapporteur on the causes and consequences of violence against women, a mandate that has produced far-reaching and influential documentation and analysis.[111] The 1995 Beijing Declaration and Platform for Action designated violence against women as one of its 10 areas of critical concern, and three regional systems have adopted treaties on this issue.[112] The CEDAW Committee updated General Recommendation 19 in 2017.[113] General Recommendation 35 identifies the structural basis of violence against women as "the ideology of men's entitlement and privilege over women."[114] It acknowledges the array of contexts in which violence occurs, including actions by both state and nonstate actors,[115] as well as the ways that diverse factors such as culture, tradition, and austerity economics contribute to impunity for violence against women.[116]

Initially, international monitoring of CEDAW relied on state reporting to the CEDAW Committee alone. After a lengthy campaign to strengthen the monitoring system, the UN General Assembly adopted an Optional Protocol in 1999. This provides a right

[106] Chinkin (n 102) 451.

[107] UNSC Resolution 1325 (2000) UN Doc S/RES/1325.

[108] *Velásquez Rodriguez Case*, Judgment of July 29, 1988, Inter-American Court of Human Rights Series C No 4 (29 July 1988).

[109] UNGA Res 48/104 (20 December 1993) UN Doc A/RES/48/104.

[110] ibid Preamble.

[111] UNCHR Res 1994/45 (4 March 1994) UN Doc E/CN.4/RES/1994/45.

[112] Inter-American Convention on the Prevention, Punishment and Eradication of Violence Against Women" (opened for signature 9 June 1994, entered into force 5 March 1995) (Convention of Belém do Pará); Council of Europe Convention on Preventing and Combating Violence Against Women and Domestic Violence (opened for signature 11 May 2011, entered into force 1 August 2014) CETS No 210; Protocol to the African Charter on Human and Peoples' Rights on the Rights of Women in Africa (opened for signature 11 July 2003, entered into force 25 November 2005) OAU Doc CAB/LEG/66.6.

[113] CEDAW Committee General Recommendation 35 (14 July 2017) updating CEDAW Committee General Recommendation 19 (1992).

[114] ibid para 19.

[115] CEDAW Committee General Recommendation 35 (14 July 2017) (n 114) para 20.

[116] ibid para 7.

of individual communication to the Committee about a violation by a state party of rights protected by CEDAW, once all domestic remedies have been exhausted,[117] as well as a Committee-initiated inquiry procedure in the case of "grave or systematic violations" by a state party.[118] Unlike other human rights treaties, such as the ICCPR and CERD, there is no possibility of complaints by one state against another for breaches of the Convention. The Optional Protocol came into force quickly, in 2000, but its potential has been rarely exploited. By June 2014, just 66 cases had been registered; 40 cases had been concluded, with 17 found inadmissible, and views adopted by the Committee in 16 cases, 15 of which found a violation of CEDAW. Twenty-six cases were pending.[119] The infrequent recourse to the complaint procedure is the result of many circumstances, including lack of knowledge, the complexity and slowness of the process, and the lack of enforcement mechanisms for the Committee's views.[120] Many of the Committee's decisions under the Optional Protocol include claims that states have failed to provide women with adequate protection from violence and claims of harm to reproductive health.[121]

International and national human rights groups have successfully invoked the Optional Protocol's Article 8 inquiry procedure in a series of cases. In all cases, the Committee has found that there had been "grave and systematic violations" of the Convention and called on the relevant states to remedy the abuses. The cases include an epidemic of violence against women in the town of Ciudad Juárez in Mexico perpetrated mainly by nonstate actors, but supported by the passivity of law enforcement authorities;[122] Canada's failure to take action on the disproportionately high levels of violence suffered by Aboriginal women and girls;[123] the restriction of access to contraceptives in Manila in the Philippines;[124] and Northern Ireland's criminalization of abortion.[125]

117 Optional Protocol to the Convention on the Elimination of All Forms of Discrimination Against Women (opened for signature 6 October 1999, entered into force 22 December 2000) 2131 UNTS 83 arts 1, 4.

118 ibid art 8.

119 Latest figures available on OHCHR website: See OHCHR, "Committee on the Elimination of Discrimination Against Women: Statistical Survey on Individual Complaints" (*OHCHR*, 2014) www.ohchr.org/EN/HRBodies/CEDAW/Pages/CEDAWIndex.aspx accessed April 30, 2018.

120 Connors (n 93) 618.

121 See, eg, CEDAW Committee, "Communication No 24/2009" (2015) UN Doc CEDAW/C/61/D/24/2009; CEDAW Committee, "Communication No 4/2004" (2006) UN Doc CEDAW/C/36/D/4/2004.

122 CEDAW Committee, "Report on Mexico Produced by the Committee on the Elimination of Discrimination Against Women under Article 8 of the Optional Protocol to the Convention, and Reply from the Government of Mexico" (27 January 2005) UN Doc CEDAW/C/2005/OP.8/Mexico.

123 CEDAW Committee, "Report of the Inquiry Concerning Canada of the Committee on the Elimination of Discrimination Against Women under Article 8 of the Optional Protocol to the Convention" (30 March 2015) UN Doc. CEDAW/C/OP.8/CAN/1.

124 CEDAW Committee, "Summary of the Inquiry Concerning the Philippines under Article 8 of the Optional Protocol to the Convention on the Elimination of Discrimination Against Women" (22 April 2015) UN Doc CEDAW/C/OP.8/PHL/1.

125 CEDAW Committee, "Report of the Inquiry Concerning the United Kingdom of Great Britain and Northern Ireland of the Committee on the Elimination of Discrimination Against Women under Article 8 of the Optional Protocol to the Convention" (19 July 2017) UN Doc. CEDAW/C/OP.8/GBR/1.

The most significant impact of CEDAW has been at national and local levels. It has been the basis for legislation in many countries, as well as a resource in domestic litigation.[126] Civil society groups have invoked CEDAW's principles in campaigns for women's rights, while often changing their meanings to adjust to local contexts, a process Sally Engle Merry has described as "vernacularization."[127] In a study of the appropriation and adaptation of CEDAW in China, India, Peru, and the United States, Peggy Levitt and Sally Merry show how vernacularization is affected by local cultural histories and geographies, the contents of the relevant "global women's rights packages," who the agents of vernacularization were and how they worked, and the way that the relevant human rights ideas were framed.[128]

3 Conclusion

UN treaties on women nicely illustrate Olympe de Gouges's paradox that feminism dismisses the relevance of physical differences between women and men in asserting claims to human rights, while relying on the category of women and their differential treatment to ground its politics. One strand of provisions in UN treaties aims to eradicate differences in the treatment of women, compared to men. Another strand has sought to recognize the particularity of women's lives, calling for special treatment and often endorsing a rather limited notion of womanhood in the process. These two strands coexist and are regularly included in the same treaty, even though they can be in normative tension. The treaties do not generally acknowledge differences among women, presenting women as an omnibus category facing common problems. The CEDAW Committee, however, has shown some awareness of intersectionality, or the experience of discrimination on the basis of multiple, intersecting, identities, in its General Recommendations.[129]

Complex international coalitions of states and other actors have formed to resist the expansion of women's rights. On one side there is pressure from the international community and cosmopolitan elites to become a party to international legal instruments setting universal standards, such as CEDAW; indeed, Sally Engle Merry has described ratification of human rights treaties as "the coin of admission" to the category

[126] Christopher McCrudden, "Why Do National Court Judges Refer to Human Rights Treaties? A Comparative International Law Analysis of CEDAW" (2015) 109 AJIL 534.

[127] See Sally Engle Merry, *Human Rights and Gender Violence: Translating International Law into Local Justice* (University of Chicago Press 2006). See also Catherine O'Rourke, "Advocating Abortion Rights in Northern Ireland: Local and Global Tensions" (2016) 25 Social & Legal Studies 716.

[128] See Peggy Levitt and Sally Engle Merry, "Vernacularization on the Ground: Local Uses of Global Women's Rights in Peru, China, India and the United States" (2009) 9 Global Networks 441.

[129] See, eg, CEDAW Committee General Recommendation 27 (16 December 2010) para 13; CEDAW Committee General Recommendation 28 (16 December 2010) para 18.

of "civilized" states.[130] On the other side, there is often stronger pressure to placate domestic constituencies by protecting particular versions of local tradition and culture. The pattern of reservations to CEDAW illustrates the contest between catalogues of women's rights and claims to "culture," "tradition," and "religion." This is also evident in the UN Human Rights Council's debates on "traditional values" and its ongoing resolutions on the role of the family.[131] Invocations of the categories of culture and tradition at the international level pay no attention to the politics of culture: questions such as whose practices are enshrined in the particular culture at issue, and who benefits from these claims.

UN treaties and activities on women reflect these political pressures, but CEDAW in particular also manifests a transformative edge. Its text offers the possibility of translation and creative development to respond to the realities of women's varied lives.

[130] Sally Engle Merry, "Human Rights Law as a Path to International Justice: The Case of the Women's Convention" in Marie-Bénédicte Dembour and Tobias Kelly (eds), *Paths to International Justice: Social and Legal Perspectives* (CUP 2007) 161, 163.

[131] See, eg, UN HRC Res 32/23 (18 July 2016) UN Doc A/HRC/RES/32/23.

CHAPTER 13

DRUGS AND CRIME

DAVID BEWLEY-TAYLOR
AND MARTIN JELSMA*

THE increasingly complex and transnational nature of various types of criminal activity are well known. The same cannot be said for some of the UN treaties established to counter them. This chapter is concerned with the relatively little-known convention framework focusing on the traditionally connected issues of drugs and crime. Comprising two related and reinforcing treaty-based regimes (in the case of drugs, dating back to the early years of the twentieth century), the underpinning conventions are the product of the international community's multilateral legal response to perceived areas of increasing concern. With both contemporary regimes operating under the auspices of the UN—and with high levels of adherence—they can be considered global with considerable, although varied and not always positive, reach and impact. Moreover, as will be discussed here, diverging views among parties on how to deal with illicit drug markets has over recent years generated substantial tensions not only within the drug control system itself, but also between that system and other parts of the UN, most notably regarding human rights and health principles and norms. While this is the case, the drug control treaties' remarkable resistance to structural change and modernization has led to the use of unusual legal procedures and dubious unilateral decision-making processes: processes that have a potential effect beyond the confines of the UN's international drug control agenda.

The legal structures examined in this chapter currently comprise five separate, open, binding—though non-self-executing—instruments: three strongly interlinked drug control treaties, the 1961 Single Convention on Narcotic Drugs as amended by the 1972 Protocol ("the 1961 or Single Convention"), the 1971 Convention on Psychotropic Substances ("the 1971 Convention"), the 1988 Convention against Illicit Traffic in Narcotic Drugs and Psychotropic Substances ("the 1988 Convention"), the more recent 2000 Convention against Transnational Organized Crime (UNTOC or "Palermo Convention"), the Protocols Thereto (on human trafficking and firearms), and the 2003 Convention against Corruption (UNCAC).

* Thanks go to Prof Neil Boister for his comments on an earlier draft. Any errors of fact or interpretation remain with the authors.

All examples of what are known as "suppression" conventions, these instruments are mostly operated through the Vienna-based part of the UN system. Governance and policymaking roles are fulfilled by two UN Economic and Social Council (ECOSOC) functional commissions: the Commission on Narcotic Drugs (CND), and the Commission on Crime Prevention and Criminal Justice (CCPCJ) established in 1946 and 1992 respectively. Oversight and monitoring of the drug control treaties are performed by the International Narcotics Control Board (INCB or "Board"), established in its current incarnation in 1968 by the Single Convention, while the crime conventions use a more politically representative mechanism: Conferences of the Parties (COPs) of the conventions. The UN Office on Drugs and Crime (UNODC), an umbrella organ that administers both the UN's anti-drugs and counter-crime activities, is mandated to, in various ways, "assist Member States in their struggle against illicit drugs, crime and terrorism."[1] The notable exception to the bodies located in Vienna is the Geneva-based World Health Organization (WHO). This holds specific treaty mandates under the 1961 and 1971 conventions regarding the scheduling of substances under international control.

Having traced the evolution and expanding scope of, as well as the growing tensions within, the international drug control regime, the chapter moves on to examine the development of the transnational organized crime and corruption regime and assessments thereof. It concludes by looking to the future with a discussion of some of the available options to "unfreeze" the drug control treaties, including what lessons might be learned from the mechanisms within their sister crime control conventions.

1 The International Drug Control Regime

The overarching goal of the international drug control regime, as expressed in the preamble of the Single Convention, is to safeguard the "health and welfare" of humankind. In so doing it applies a dual imperative: to ensure an adequate supply of controlled pharmaceuticals for the licit market—including WHO-listed essential medicines—and at the same time prevent the non-scientific and non-medical production, supply, and use of narcotic and psychotropic substances. Within this context, the system has been developed on two interconnected tenets. First, a deeply held belief that the best way to protect health and reduce what has become known simply and somewhat vaguely as the "world drug problem" and the harms associated with it is to minimize the scale of—and ultimately eliminate—the illicit market. Second, that this can be achieved through a reliance on prohibition-oriented and supply-side-dominated measures. In this way, and while permitting some deviation from its authoritative norm, the regime has successfully

[1] See "About UNODC" (*United Nations Office on Drugs and Crime*) < https://www.unodc.org/unodc/en/about-unodc/index.html?ref=menutop> accessed February 9, 2018.

generated a powerful prohibitionist expectancy in relation to how its members approach the non-medical and non-scientific use of substances scheduled or listed in the UN drug control conventions. Indeed, with the proscription of certain activities at its core, the UN control system can be legitimately termed the "global drug prohibition regime."[2]

It has been noted that international drug control "is now the centrepiece of transnational criminal law."[3] Yet, the origins of the UN drug control regime predate even the League of Nations, with the first International Opium Convention adopted in 1912. Several more of what can be regarded as foundational treaties were negotiated during the period between the First and Second World Wars. These primarily focused on imposing regulatory controls (licensing, import, and export certification) on the licit international trade in pharmaceutical products derived from opium, coca, and cannabis, to prevent their diversion—or "leakage"—to the expanding gray and black markets for non-medical use. This was especially so in the United States and Europe—markets that were in many ways the product of attempts to create a clearly defined licit trade. Cultivation of the plants and traditional uses—a mix of medicinal, ceremonial, and social uses—in the major producing countries of the raw materials were basically left to the discretion of national legislation. A first multilateral attempt in 1936 to make non-licensed production and trafficking of drugs an international crime subject to penal sanctions was only signed by 13 countries.

Following the Second World War, the functions and drug control apparatus of the League of Nations were transferred to the United Nations. This required several immediate amendments to the existing treaties, and these were laid down in the 1946 Lake Success Protocol—the first UN legal instrument in the field of drug control. A year later, the recently formed ECOSOC adopted a resolution on the "Simplification of Existing International Instruments on Narcotic Drugs" requesting the UN Secretary-General "to begin work on the drafting of a new single convention" to replace the earlier treaties.[4] After long negotiations and three drafts between 1950 and 1958, this process culminated in 1961 with a plenipotentiary conference and the adoption of the Single Convention on Narcotic Drugs, still in force today as the bedrock of the international drug control regime. However, beyond "tidying up" the system and consolidating the key features of the prewar treaties, the Single Convention also brought about significant change to the regime.[5]

The ECOSOC resolution had specified that the new convention also needed to "include provisions for the limitation of the production of narcotic raw materials." And indeed the Single Convention extended existing controls to include the cultivation of

[2] Ethan A Nadelmann, "Global Prohibition Regimes: The Evolution of Norms in International Society" (1990) 44(4) Intl Org 479–526.

[3] Neil Boister, *An Introduction to Transnational Criminal Law* (OUP, 2012) 50.

[4] ECOSOC, Resolutions of 3 August 1948, *D, Simplification of Existing International Instruments on Narcotic Drugs*, in Resolutions adopted by the Economic and Social Council during its seventh session from 19 July to 29 August 1948, United Nations, Geneva, 48.

[5] For a detailed discussion see David Bewley-Taylor and Martin Jelsma, "Regime Change: Re-visiting the 1961 Single Convention on Narcotic Drugs" (2012) 23 Intl J Drug Policy 72–81.

plants grown as raw material for the production of narcotic drugs, and required the gradual abolition of all the widespread "quasi-medical" and traditional uses of opium, coca leaf, and cannabis. Moreover, in the words of Neil Boister, "if the Convention regulated any particular form of conduct the Convention was designed to get the parties to criminalize any failure to comply with that regulation."[6] A control regime with a more prohibitionist orientation was thus established—limiting the production, trade, and significantly, via provisions on possession, use of narcotic drugs strictly to medical and scientific purposes. Despite this shift, the 1961 Convention was not deemed strict enough by the United States, a state long involved in the effort for international drug control. As in other issue areas Washington, DC, had exploited its geopolitical position after the Second World War to initiate the process toward a consolidating convention. Yet amidst complicated bureaucratic infighting that included parallel work for ratification of the particularly strict 1953 Opium Protocol, which came into force in 1962 only to be superseded by the 1961 instrument when it came into force two years later,[7] the United States was dissatisfied with the outcomes of the treaty negotiations. When in 1967 it finally acceded to the Single Convention, moves were immediately made to amend and tighten the regime.[8]

1.1 Expanding the Scope of the Regime

To be sure, the original 1948 ideal of having a unified "single" convention was quickly abandoned when parallel negotiations began for both an amending protocol and a separate convention to extend controls to psychoactive drugs appearing on the black market that were not covered by the 1961 Convention. Following a plenipotentiary conference in Geneva to consider an extensive list of amendments, the 1972 Protocol amending the Single Convention brought about adjustments, including a strengthened mandate of the INCB as the treaty body to monitor state compliance. Following provisions within the 1971 Convention, it also drew attention to the need to provide treatment and alternatives to penal sanctions for drug users. While modeled closely on the Single Convention, the 1971 Convention on Psychotropic Substances itself established looser controls for a variety of mostly synthetic drugs (such as amphetamines, barbiturates, benzodiazepines) than those in the earlier instrument since they were considered too restrictive for the pharmaceutical industry: an industry based predominantly within those Western states that remained dominant within the CND and negotiations at the

[6] Neil Boister, *Penal Aspects of the UN Drug Conventions* (Kluwer 2001) 75.

[7] William B McAllister, *Drug Diplomacy in the Twentieth Century: An International History* (Routledge 2000) 179–84, 202–04; and David R Bewley-Taylor, *The United States and Drug Control, 1909–1997* (Pinter 1999) 92–93.

[8] Nelson G Gross and G Jonathan Greenwald, "The 1972 Narcotics Protocol" [1973] Contemporary Drug Problems 122; Vladimir Kušević, "Drug Abuse Control and International Treaties" (1977) 7(1) J Drug Issues 35. Also see Kevin Fisher, "Trends in Extraterritorial Narcotics Control: Slamming the Stable Door after the Horse Has Bolted" (1984) 16 NYUJILP 361; and McAllister (n 7) 236–37.

Vienna plenipotentiary conference. Significantly, the 1971 Convention also departed again from the control logic behind the Single Convention that plants and precursors required similar controls as the extracted alkaloids. Consequently, and contrary to the zero-tolerance regime imposed for "narcotic drugs," the 1971 Convention explicitly respected legal space within domestic legislation for the use of hallucinogenic plants containing "psychotropic substances" in religious ceremonies and traditions.

The 1961 and 1971 conventions were relatively effective in limiting the leakage of controlled substances from licit production and trade to the illicit market. That said, they did very little to prevent the emergence of the large-scale *illicit* production and trade that had developed in response to the control regime. This reality provided the rationale for drafting the 1988 Convention against Illicit Traffic in Narcotic Drugs and Psychotropic Substances, a third instrument specifically designed to combat the rapidly expanding illicit trade, including that controlled by increasingly powerful Colombian drug trafficking organizations. As the UN Commentary to the 1988 Convention notes, the treaty deviates from the earlier drug conventions by requiring parties to "legislate as necessary to establish a modern criminal code of criminal offences relating to various aspects of illicit trafficking and ensure that such activities are dealt with as serious offences by each State's judiciary and prosecutorial authorities."[9]

As such, the 1988 Convention, adopted at a plenipotentiary conference in Vienna, significantly extended the scope of measures against trafficking, introduced provisions to control money laundering and seize the assets of drug traffickers, allowed for the extradition of major traffickers, and facilitated international legal cooperation.[10] For one commentator, in the years prior to the UNTOC, the 1988 Convention went so far as to serve as an extradition treaty "for those without separate agreements in place."[11] Significantly, it also requires states parties to establish as a criminal offense the cultivation and possession for personal use, though with the escape clause that the obligation was "[s]ubject to its constitutional principles and the basic concepts of its legal system." This, along with several interpretative ambiguities within the drug control conventions—including a lack of clear definition on "medical and scientific" drug use—allows for significant room to maneuver at the national level and the pursuit of policies that deviate from punitive-prohibition. Such flexibility, however, is finite with clear parameters laid down vis-à-vis the object and purpose of the treaties, and obligations under the Vienna Convention on the Law of Treaties.

Complementing the three hard law instruments, the regime has also continued to adjust to some extent to changing circumstances and views of member states via a series

[9] United Nations, *Commentary on the United Nations Convention Against Illicit Traffic in Narcotic Drugs and Psychotropic Substances*: Done at Vienna on 20 December 1988, E/CN.7/590 (New York: United Nations, 1998), 48, Section 3.1.

[10] David P Stewart, "Internationalizing the War on Drugs: The UN Convention Against Illicit Traffic in Narcotic Drugs and Psychotropic Substances" (1990) 18(3) Denver JILP 387–404; David Bewley-Taylor and Michael Woodiwiss, *The Global Fix: The Construction of a Global Enforcement Regime* (TNI Briefing Series 2005).

[11] CarrieLyn B Guymon, "International Legal Mechanisms for Combatting Transnational Organized Crime" (2000) 18 Berkley JIL 53, 96.

of consensus-drafted soft-law declarations and documents. These relate to periodic high-level meetings beyond the standard annual CND sessions in Vienna (and associated General Assembly, CND and ECOSOC resolutions[12]), including three United Nations General Assembly Special Sessions (UNGASS) on the "world drug problem" in 1990, 1998, and 2016. The language in those political declarations demonstrate a slow but steady trend away from the most controversial aspects of the zero-tolerance "war on drugs" approach, introducing cautionary principles derived from the human rights and development discourse.[13]

While this is the case, taken together, the three conventions have established a framework of mandatory minimum norms significantly impacting national drug laws around the world and harmonizing basic features of a criminal law approach to the drugs issue. Today, the drug control treaties are among the most widely adhered to of all UN conventions—possessing near universal acceptance among member states. As of February 2019, the 1961 (as amended), 1971, and 1988 Conventions could boast 186, 184 and 190 parties respectively. Although not self-executing, a combination of factors has ensured—though to varying degrees across member states—substantial influence at the domestic level. Among these is a combination of the framing of the drug issue as a "serious evil" for "mankind" [14] and the UN's benevolent image and associated normative expectations.[15] Moreover, beyond a "naming and shaming" process operating predominantly through the INCB to leverage its limited formal powers of sanction,[16] the regime has also benefited from the United States' long-standing role in policing the system. While operating without an international mandate,[17] this process is intimately connected to the US Foreign Assistant Act, the Foreign Relations Authorization Act, and the consequent unilateral identification of states deemed to have "failed demonstrably... to make substantial efforts" to adhere to international counternarcotic agreements, particularly the 1988 Convention. The resulting "Presidential Determination," what for many years was called "de-certification" can, depending on US "vital interests," result in

[12] See for example <https://www.unodc.org/unodc/en/commissions/CND/Resolutions_Decisions/Resolutions-Decisions_1970-1979.html> accessed January 18, 2019.

[13] As with hard law, however, there often remains a disconnect between high-order language at the UN and policy practice within the boundaries of parties. Jamie Bridge et al, "Edging Forward: How the UN's Language on Drugs Has Advanced since 1990," Briefing Paper, International Drug Policy Consortium, Transnational Institute, Global Drug Policy Observatory; Swansea University (September 2017) <http://fileserver.idpc.net/library/Edging-Forward_FINAL.pdf> accessed February 9, 2018.

[14] See Preamble of Single Convention. Christopher Hobson, "Challenging "Evil": Continuity and Change in the Drug Prohibition Regime" (2014) 51(4) Intl Politics 534; Julia Buxton, "The Historical Foundations of the Narcotic Drug Control Regime" (World Bank Policy Research Paper series, Washington DC, 2008) 70–71; Rick Lines, " "Deliver Us from Evil"? – The Single Convention on Narcotic Drugs, 50 Years On" (2010) 1 Intl J Human Rights and Drug Policy 3.

[15] David R Bewley-Taylor, *International Drug Control Consensus Fractured* (CUP 2012).

[16] On naming and shaming see HR Friman, "Behind the Curtain: Naming and Shaming in International Drug Control" in HR Friman (ed), *The Politics of Leverage in International Relations: Name, Shame and Sanction* (Macmillan 2015) 143–64.

[17] Boister (n 3) 60.

loss of US economic aid.[18] Within this environment, there is much to be said for the view that the "prohibitionist nature of international drug control has been accepted in an uncontested way since drug control fell under UN auspices."[19] Further, the implementation of the 1988 Convention led to the tightening of national drug laws and the introduction of harsher sentences for drug law offenses—a shift that did much to facilitate a "war on drugs" approach characterized by mass incarceration and military involvement in anti-drug operations in many parts of the world. As one commentator notes, "whether drug supply and use for non-medical purposes would be far more widespread and would constitute a far greater menace to the whole world without international drug control remains speculation. It is clear that the cost of suppression using draconian provisions adopted in the 'spirit of the conventions' is high."[20] Richard Vogler and Shahrzad Fouladvand go further, claiming that, although the treaties are impressive in terms of participation, "it is fair to say that their operation has been an almost unmitigated failure, producing consequences directly opposite to those envisaged."[21]

1.2 Growing Tensions: From Soft Defection to Recalibration and Breach

With this in mind, and amidst improving understanding—particularly since the era when most states became parties to the Single Convention—of both the relative harms of currently internationally scheduled substances and the outcomes of market interventions designed to control them, the last 20 years or so have seen a growing number of parties adjust their relationship to the treaty system. This has taken place via what can be termed "soft defection."[22] Rather than quitting the regime, a gradually expanding group of countries, initially primarily in Europe and later in Latin America and elsewhere, have used the embedded escape clauses and interpretative space within the treaties to deviate from the prohibitive expectancy at its core and implement a range of health-oriented harm reduction measures and various forms of decriminalization and depenalization of the possession of drugs for personal use. With a growing awareness of the linkages between drug policy, public health, and human rights,[23] increasing dissatisfaction with

[18] See, eg, United States Department of State, Bureau for International Narcotics and Law Enforcement Affairs, *International Narcotics Control Strategy Report* (March 2017) vol 1 (Drug and Chemical Control), 2 <https://www.state.gov/documents/organization/268025.pdf> accessed February 9, 2018.

[19] Neil Boister, "Waltzing on the Vienna Consensus on Drug Control? Tensions in the International System for the Control of Drugs" (2016) 29 Leiden JIL 389–409.

[20] Boister (n 3) 61.

[21] Richard Vogler and Shahrzad Fouladvand, "The Convention against Illicit Traffic in Narcotic Drugs and Psychotropic Substances 1988 and the Global War on Drugs" in Pierre Hauck and Sven Peterke (eds), *International Law and Transnational Organised Crime* (OUP 2016) 107.

[22] Bewley-Taylor (n 15).

[23] D Barrett and M Nowak, "The United Nations and Drug Policy: Towards a Human Rights Based Approach" in A Constantinides and N Zaikos (eds), The *Diversity of International Law: Essays in Honour of Professor Kalliopi K. Koufa* (Brill 2009) 449–78 and P Hunt, *Human Rights, Health and Harm Reduction: States' Amnesia and Parallel Universes* (International Harm Reduction Association 2008) 9.

the structure and operation of some aspects of the regime also stems from its role in creating and sustaining the global crisis of inadequate access to essential medicines controlled under the drug conventions,[24] as well as creating obstacles to the implementation of effective evidence and rights-based treatment interventions and harm reduction strategies against the HIV epidemic. Injecting drug use, it should be recalled, is the principle vector for the spread of HIV outside sub-Saharan Africa. The resulting increasingly heterogeneous policy landscape has led some commentators to observe that "it is fair to say that no international convention regime has been interpreted in such widely different ways by states parties."[25]

That said, the basic imperative and architecture of the treaty regime to impose a repressive approach has proven difficult to challenge, change, or even to discuss in UN fora. Despite an increasingly persuasive evidence base,[26] a significant number of states, increasingly important among them being the Russian Federation, have retained faith in a zero-tolerance law enforcement dominated approach to dealing with illicit drug markets and continue to support it at the international level. In addition to the position of some states within the CND, the Vienna-based specialized UN entities have in particular traditionally been staunch defenders of the treaty regime, almost immune to questions or doubts raised about its effectiveness or collateral damage; the latter identified by the UNODC Executive Director in 2008 as "unintended consequences."[27] In recent years, however, there has been a marked institutional change in the understanding of how to best achieve the regime's core dual goal, with, among other things, the WHO, INCB, and UNODC acknowledging that overemphasizing punitive measures to reduce demand and supply has hampered access to controlled drugs for medicinal purposes.

As the issue of international drug control has increasingly seeped beyond the Vienna silo, several problems with system-wide coherence and fragmentation of international law have been identified by—among others—the High Commissioner for Human Rights, especially as conceptualizations of human rights have developed.[28] The UNODC and more recently the INCB have gone through changes regarding their positions and performance. More active involvement from other parts of the UN system, most notably in the 2016 UNGASS process, has shown a capacity to move the UN drug control debate toward the overarching principles of human rights protection, sustainable development, and peace and security. The consensus-driven political negotiations at the CND, however,

[24] N Burke-Shyne et al, "How Drug Control Policy and Practice Undermine Access to Controlled Medicines" (2017) 19(1) Health and Human Rights J 237–52.

[25] Vogler and Shahrzad (n 21) 120.

[26] T Babor et al, *Drug Policy and the Public Good* (OUP 2010).

[27] AM Costa, Making Drug Control "Fit for Purpose": Building on the UNGASS Decade, Statement of the Executive Director of the United Nations Office on Drugs and Crime, 2008.

[28] See Statement by Zeid Ra'ad Al Hussein, United Nations High Commissioner for Human Rights, Round Table 3: Cross-cutting issues—drugs and human rights, youth, women, children and communities, 30th Special Session on the World Drug Problem, General Assembly, 20 April 2016.

still present obstacles for open discussion. A good argument can be made that there remains a need to address the flaws in and inconsistencies between not just the drug control treaties themselves, but also the growing tension between the regime and other UN instruments. Further, in terms of system-wide initiatives, serious discussion is required regarding genuine harmonization of UN drug control efforts with the 2030 Agenda for Sustainable Development.[29]

Normative shifts deriving from soft law, treaty interpretation, and subsequent practice must be acknowledged. Yet treaty "flexibility" can only be stretched so far, with, in the face of changing circumstances, hard-law treaty structures themselves displaying remarkable resilience to change. As such, when moving to formally correct via treaty amendment what is widely regarded to be a historical error reflecting inherent cultural bias within the Single Convention, Bolivia was faced with a problematic nexus of politics and procedure. The INCB itself had already in 1994 pointed out the "conflict between the provisions of the 1961 Convention and the views and legislation of countries where the use of the coca leaf is legal"[30] and stressed the urgency to "resolve such long-standing ambiguities, which have been undermining the conventions."[31] Bolivian attempts in 2009 to reconcile its national constitution with its international obligations regarding coca leaf chewing culminated in recourse to a rarely used and controversial practice deployed in the "absence of alternative paths to resolve legal conflicts":[32] withdrawal and reaccession with a reservation.[33] More recently, within admittedly different political contexts, both Uruguay and the United States resorted to "untidy legal justifications"[34] to deflect criticism of the adoption within their borders—in the United States at the state level—of the legalization of cannabis for recreational use. This policy choice was in many ways driven by a concern for public health and a reduction in drug-related criminality, but nonetheless is inconsistent with the provisions of the 1961 and 1988

[29] David R Bewley-Taylor and Martin Jelsma, *UNGASS 2016: A Broken or B-r-o-a-d Consensus: UN Summit Cannot Hide Growing Divergence in the Global Drug Policy Landscape,* Transnational Institute-Global Drug Policy Observatory (Swansea University), Drug Policy Briefing, No 45, June 2016 <http://www.swansea.ac.uk/gdpo/projectpages/ungass/> accessed February 9, 2018.

[30] E/INCB/1994/1, *Report of the International Narcotics Control Board for 1994*, United Nations, New York, 1995, 4.

[31] E/INCB/1994/1/Supp.1, *Effectiveness of the international drug control treaties, Supplement to the Report of the International Narcotics Control Board for 1994*, United Nations, New York, 1995, 11.

[32] Transnational Institute, "Bolivia Wins a Rightful Victory on the Coca Leaf: Creates Positive Example for Modernizing the UN Drug Conventions" (2013) <https://www.tni.org/en/article/bolivia-wins-a-rightful-victory-on-the-coca-leaf-0> accessed February 9, 2018.

[33] C.N.829.2011.TREATIES-28 (Depositary Notification), *Communication Plurinational State of Bolivia*, Single Convention on Narcotic Drugs, 1961, as Amended by the Protocol Amending the Single Convention on Narcotic Drugs, 1961, 10 January 2012.

[34] David Bewley-Taylor, T Blickman, and Martin Jelsma, *The Rise and Decline of Cannabis Prohibition: The History of Cannabis in the UN Drug Control System and Options for Reform* (Transnational Institute-Global Drug Policy Observatory, Amsterdam/Swansea, March 2014) 68.

Conventions.[35] The Board pointed this out in clear terms when Canada recently decided to make the same choice: "the limitation of the use of drugs to medical and scientific purposes is a fundamental principle that lies at the heart of the international drug control framework, to which no exception is possible and which gives no room for flexibility."[36] The inability of the control apparatus to even consider recalibration in response to the shifting perspectives of treaty parties and improvements in knowledge go some way to help explain why the regime has been described as "Jurassic" with its underpinning drug conventions "so stubbornly resistant to change compared to other treaty systems" that they almost seem ' "frozen in time.' "[37]

Indeed, while the international drug control regime relies predominantly on the INCB—a body dating back to treaties in 1925 and 1931—for its monitoring functions, other international treaty regimes often have more responsive and built-in monitoring and evaluation organs, such as COPs and related bodies, to review implementation problems encountered by the parties. This is particularly so for Multilateral Environmental Agreements,[38] but, as noted previously, is also the case for the UN's crime control treaties. The three drug control conventions lack such a regularized review mechanism to enable structural evolution and modernization of the system over time. The 1988 Convention is also an exceptional case of a UN treaty that does not have any monitoring or review mechanism because the INCB mandate was limited to the precursor control regime established under Article 12. In contrast to its broader mandate under the 1961 and 1971 conventions, the INCB was not charged to perform any monitoring duties regarding the rest of the 1988 Convention. According to the treaty commentary, this was "no doubt because of the very different character" of the 1988 Convention, "dealing as it does with matters of criminal law and its enforcement that go beyond the scope of the earlier conventions into areas touching more closely on the sovereignty and jurisdiction of States."[39] And it is to broader issues of criminal law that we now turn.

[35] Lord Carlile of Berriew and Sarah Clarke, *Legal Opinion Commissioned by All-Party Parliamentary Group for Drug Policy Reform*, London, December 2013 and David Bewley-Taylor and Martin Jelsma, *The UN Drug Control Conventions: The Limits of Latitude*, Transnational Institute-International Drug Policy Consortium, Series on Legislative Reform of Drug Policies, Nr. 18, March 2012. For research into treaty flexibility predating the current debates around cannabis but that reach the same conclusion see N Dorn and A Jamieson, *Room for Manoeuvre: Overview of Comparative Legal Research into National Drug Law of France, Germany, Italy, Spain, the Netherlands and Sweden and Their Relationship to Three International Drugs Conventions* (Drugscope 2000) and B De Ruyver et al, *Multidisciplinary Drug Policies and the UN Drug Treaties* (Institute for International Research on Criminal Policy 2002).

[36] E/INCB/2016/1, *Report of the International Narcotics Control Board for 2016*, United Nations, New York, 2017, 31.

[37] *International Law and Drug Policy Reform*. Report of a GDPO/ICHRDP/TNI/WOLA Expert Seminar, Washington DC, October 17–18, 2014, 34–35.

[38] S Schiele, *Evolution of International Environmental Regimes: The Case of Climate Change* (CUP 2014) 39–44.

[39] United Nations, *Commentary on the United Nations Convention Against Illicit Traffic in Narcotic Drugs and Psychotropic Substances*: Done at Vienna on 20 December 1988, E/CN.7/590 (New York: United Nations, 1998) 374, Section 22.2.

2 The Transnational Organized Crime and Corruption Regime

2.1 The UN and Transnational Organized Crime

With some countries, notably the United States, having put in place national legislation to deal with organized criminality as early as the 1970s, moves to address its transnational dimensions through the UN were inspired by the success of negotiations for the 1988 Convention. Supporters of a global multilateral treaty to suppress organized crime argued not unreasonably that "criminal organizations that operate transnationally do so beyond the control of any one state" and that this demanded a "coordinated international response."[40] It is also fair to say that the end of the Cold War elevated what was seen to be an increasingly pressing threat to security higher up the diplomatic agendas of many member states, including recognition at the General Assembly in 1990.[41] Within this environment, the first significant step toward a UN instrument was taken at the World Ministerial conference on Organized Crime in Naples in 1994, where a Political Declaration called for more effectual international cooperation on the issue and recommended a treaty. Taking the lead, Poland put the development of such a convention on the UN General Assembly (UNGA) agenda in 1996 and submitted a preliminary draft text. This was developed through the work of several expert and working groups and an Ad Hoc Committee to produce a draft convention and three protocols addressing illegal trafficking in migrants, illicit manufacturing of and trafficking in firearms and ammunition, and trafficking in women and children.[42] Reflecting its close relationship to the 1988 Convention, CarrieLyn Guymon pointed out in 2000 how the working groups improved upon the Polish draft by "incorporating more directly some of the language from the UN Drug Convention and elaborating on measures for cooperation between law enforcement agencies."[43] It can also be argued that beyond technical borrowings from the 1988 Convention, the UNTOC also benefits to some extent from the same UN engendered benevolent aura as all the drug control conventions.

Following these meetings, a conference was held in Palermo, Sicily (symbolically the home of the Italian Mafia), where delegates negotiated the UN Convention against Transnational Organized Crime and Protocols Thereto. Regarded as "one of the most

[40] Boister (n 3) 78.

[41] Martin Jelsma, "UNGASS 2016: Prospects for Treaty Reform and UN System-Wide Coherence on Drug Policy" (2016) J Drug Policy Analysis <https://doi.org/10.1515/jdpa-2015-0021.>

[42] On the drafting process see Andreas Schloenhardt, "Transnational Organized Crime" in Neil Boister and RJ Currie, *Routledge Handbook of Transnational Criminal Law* (Routledge 2015) 409–33; Guymon (n 11); D McClean, *Transnational Organized Crime: A Commentary on the UN Convention and Its Protocols* (OUP 2007); Neil Boister, "The UN Convention Against Transnational Organized Crime" in P Hauk and S Peterke (eds), *International Law and Transnational Organised Crime* (OUP 2016) 126–49.

[43] Guymon (n 11) 96.

important developments in international criminal law"[44] and marking "a turning point in the commitment of the community of states to cooperate against transnational organized crime"[45], the UNTOC was adopted in 2000 and entered into force in 2003. As of July 2018, it has 189 parties with 147, 156, and 173 parties to its supplementing protocols respectively. As laid out in Article 1, the UNTOC's purpose is to "promote co-operation to prevent and combat transnational organized crime more effectively." This is to be achieved through "legislative harmonization and more effective suppression" and crucially, "while remaining within the bounds of human rights safeguards."[46] Among its many provisions, key areas of focus are corruption and money laundering, with articles relating to the latter developing those within the 1988 Convention. Importantly, as Boister points out, the Convention's "elaborate framework for cooperation... is so extensive that it suggests that cooperation rather than criminalization is the main subject matter of the UNTOC."[47] As with the relationship between hard law of the drug control treaties and various soft-law declarations, the UNTOC is among the crime conventions supplemented by the outcomes of high-level UN meetings. In this case, these are the quinquennial United Nations Congresses on Crime Prevention and Justice. Dating back to 1955; the latest was held in Doha in April 2015.

Acknowledging some resistance to idea of a convention from some states concerned by potential definitional problems, the relative alacrity with which negotiations were completed and the UNTOC brought into effect thereafter reflected widespread agreement around the need for an instrument with a specific focus on transnational organized crime. Yet, the speed with which the convention was born hides the perhaps inevitable failure of states to reach a consensus around a legal definition of the slippery concept of "organized crime." Consequently, the UNTOC is directed instead at the involvement of organized criminal groups in serious crimes. This has led to criticism that a combination of Article 2 concerning "definitions"[48] and other somewhat vague aspects of the Convention (for example Article 5, "Criminalization of participation in an organized criminal group") leaves too much discretion to parties.[49] That said, it can also be argued that, as in other issue areas such as drugs, some flexibility to take into account local conditions is beneficial and was necessary to ensure the widespread buy-in necessary for an effective multilateral instrument. The resulting low definitional thresholds, as Boister points out, "makes for broad suppression not precise denunciation."[50] In a similar fashion to the UN drug control treaties, the UNTOC has also been criticized for acting as a vehicle for the internationalization of a flawed US approach in dealing with organized crime.[51]

[44] G Kemp, "The United Nations Convention Against Transnational Organized Crime: A Milestone in International Criminal Law" (2001) 14 South African J Crim Justice 152.

[45] V Militello, "Participation in an Organized Criminal Group as International Offence" in H-J Albrecht and C Fijnaut (eds), *The Containment of Transnational Organized Crime: Comments on the UN Convention of December 2000* (Freiburg im Breisgau 2002) 97.

[46] Boister (n 42) 127. [47] ibid.

[48] A Orlova and J Moore, "'Umbrellas' or 'Building Blocks?': Defining International Terrorism and Transnational Organized Crime in International Law" (2005) 27(2) Houston JIL 283.

[49] Schloenhardt (n 42) 42. [50] Boister (n 3) 86.

[51] M Woodiwiss, *Double Crossed: The Failure of Organized Crime Control* (Pluto Press 2017) 224–29.

Nevertheless, while certainly of significance, the influence of the Convention is arguably less than its companions in the realm of drug policy. The cause of what can be seen as patchy legislative activity and implementation and a consequent "middling" impact lies with the instrument's lack of definitional clarity. It has been argued that some states are reluctant to engage with the instrument because "there is little in the UNTOC concept to fix on, to legislate and train around—because the concept is largely content free"—a problem that as with other hard-law instruments may derive from the reliance on the "level of knowledge" at the time of construction.[52] The inchoate state of the UNTOC review mechanism means that a systematic evaluation of the treaty and its Protocols as initially promised is not currently possible.[53] Yet, there is a feeling that, more than 15 years after its adoption, the "UNTOC's aims of promoting cooperation to prevent and combat transnational organized crime more effectively have not been fully realized." Boister identifies the fact that the 2015 Doha Declaration, for example, calls on states parties to implement and make more effective use of the UNTOC.[54] Struggles around the establishment of a review system, despite—as we shall see—the existence of a mechanism within the UNCAC suggests the ongoing reticence of many states to engage with the UNTOC.

2.2 UN Efforts against Corruption

Although both the 1988 Convention and the UNTOC contain provisions on the issue, the UNCAC is the first binding global agreement on corruption. John Hatchard noted in 2014 that "the past 20 years have seen unprecedented global efforts aimed at combating corrupt practices."[55] Indeed, growing awareness of the issue and appreciation that states were unable to deal with it effectively on their own led to the development of several multilateral agreements in the late 1990s aimed exclusively at suppressing corruption. These included treaties under the auspices of the Organization of American States, the Organization for Economic Cooperation and Development, and the European Union. Further, as with moves to establish the UNTOC, the end of the Cold War also changed the way corrupt practices in some countries, including lucrative trading partners within the global south, were perceived. The fall of the Berlin Wall and increasing globalization "altered the economic and political framework in which corruption could be ignored or tolerated for so long."[56]

[52] Boister, "The UN Convention" (n 42) 148.

[53] See: CTOC/COP/WG.8/2016/2, Conference of the Parties to the United Nations Convention Against Transnational Organized Crime, *Report on the meeting to explore all options regarding an appropriate and effective review mechanism for the United Nations Convention against Transnational Organized Crime and the Protocols thereto, held in Vienna on 6 and 7 June 2016*, 10 June 2016.

[54] Boister (n 42) 127–28.

[55] J Hatchard, "Criminalizing Corruption" in Boister and Currie, *Routledge Handbook* (n 42) 347.

[56] Michael Kubiciel and Anna Cornelia Rink, "The United Nations Convention Against Corruption and Its Criminal Law Provisions" in Pierre Hauk and Sven Peterke (eds), *International Law and Transnational Organised Crime* (OUP 2016) 220.

While there had been unsuccessful attempts to get corruption on to its agenda in the 1970s,[57] it was also not until the 1990s that focused discussions took place at the UN. This came with the special session on corruption held at the Ninth UN Congress on the Prevention of Crime and Treatment of Offenders in 1995, the original title of the current Congresses on Crime Prevention and Criminal Justice. The following year, the UNGA adopted a Declaration against Corruption and Bribery in International Commercial Transactions, and pressure grew for a "multilateral treaty of global scope targeting both private and public corruption."[58] Provisions for the criminalization of corruption in Article 8 of the UNTOC "hardened" these obligations to some extent, but they were not considered "extensive enough."[59] Although this was the case, according to Philippa Webb, the existing multilateral agreements "not only indicated the key areas of concern, but also helped build the necessary consensus to commence negotiations" on a treaty through the UN.[60] Within this context, a 2000 UNGA declaration recognized that an effective legal instrument against corruption, independent of the UNTOC, was desirable and led to the establishment of an Ad Hoc Committee for negotiations in Vienna. Following this, an Open-Ended Expert group was established and asked to prepare draft terms of reference for negotiation. Another UNGA resolution then requested the Ad Hoc Committee to adopt a comprehensive and multidisciplinary approach, with the resulting text negotiated at seven sessions of the Committee between January 2002 and October 2003. The process culminated at a conference in Merida, Mexico, in December 2003. Here the Convention was signed by 95 states with the mood marked by "high expectations and intense optimism" surrounding "the latest addition to multilateral initiatives against corruption."[61] Indeed, the Convention's preamble highlights several motivating concerns, including corruption's potential to threaten "political stability and sustainable development." As of June 2018, there were 186 parties to the UNCAC.

Beyond building upon the earlier instruments to raise the issue to a global level through the UN, the Convention's contribution lies in the fact that it includes provisions for the criminalization of a broader range of activities than the previous instruments. A core aim in this regard is to add certainty to national responses to corruption across states and ensure that the behavior is treated the same in all jurisdictions. However, more than simply a criminal law convention, the UNCAC also includes specialized law enforcement provisions and articles focusing on international cooperation, asset recovery, money laundering, technical support, information exchange, and the prevention of corruption. Importantly, it does not introduce a generic definition of corruption. Rather, as with the other conventions on the issue, it criminalizes various forms of corruption. Nonetheless, the UNCAC contains the "broadest list of criminal obligations of any of

[57] M Bukovansky, "The Hollowness of Anti-corruption Discourse" (May 2006) 13(2) Rev Intl Political Economy 186.

[58] Boister (n 3) 94.

[59] ibid.

[60] P Webb, "The United Nations Convention Against Corruption: Global Achievement or Missed Opportunity" (2005) 8(1) J Intl Economic L 192.

[61] ibid 205.

the corruption conventions, designed to suppress every form of corruption," including, for example, the bribery of national and foreign public officials.[62]

As with the UNTOC, the UNCAC has been criticized in terms of implementation and impact. It has been noted how despite the existence of the Convention and other instruments, prosecutions for corruption within states parties remain low. For Cecily Rose, the UNCAC's "limited capacity to influence domestic legal systems" owes much to its "inclusion of a large number of non-mandatory criminalization provisions, and otherwise vague and imprecise norms."[63] She goes on to stress: "despite the Convention's binding status, global reach... and relative comprehensiveness, the language of its provisions diminishes its potential to contribute to international anti-corruption efforts by penetrating domestic legal systems."[64] From this perspective, the "UNCAC's provisions have not been designed to ensure" that the instrument "will influence domestic legal systems by bringing about implementation and enforcement of its criminalization provisions." In fact, it has been "designed to allow states parties great leeway in determining the extent to which the treaty will influence their legal systems."[65] In a familiar dynamic within multilateral negotiations, the stringency of provisions had to be balanced with the need for engagement from a wide range of nation-states; each with their own specific national interests. This situation led Rose to conclude that in the creation of international anticorruption norms negotiated under the auspices of the UN, effectiveness was sacrificed for inclusiveness.[66] It can also be argued that the UNCAC's resulting limited effectiveness is compounded by an inherent paradox within the Convention's area of concern. As Hatchard notes, "the need for political will to combat corruption, and the fact that those called upon to make the necessary decisions to so are often the very actors who benefit most from the status quo, means that taking action at the national level is often problematic."[67]

Such weaknesses remain an ongoing concern despite the option with the UNCAC, provided for by the COP, of a review mechanism "to assist in the effective implementation of the Convention." Inclusion of the clause that the mechanism can be implemented if the COP "deems it necessary" (Article 63 (7)) as well as a lack of timelines and concrete commitments, has led Webb to go so far as to argue that the Convention might be a *lex simulata:* "a legislative exercise that produces a statutory instrument apparently operable, but one that neither the prescribers, those charged with its administration, nor the putative target audience ever intend to be applied."[68] Indeed, while the Convention's Implementation Review Mechanism (IRM), created by the third session of the COP in 2009,[69] is both innovative and still evolving, it certainly reveals the complexities

[62] Boister (n 3) 94.

[63] Cecily Rose, *International Anti-corruption Norms: Their Creation and Influence on Domestic Legal Systems* (OUP 2015) 12.

[64] ibid 97. [65] ibid 99.

[66] ibid 217. [67] Hatchard (n 55) 362.

[68] Webb (n 60) 221. Also see PX Delany, "Transnational Corruption: Regulation across Borders" (2007) 47(2) Virginia JIL 414.

[69] "Implementation Review Mechanism" (*United Nations Office on Drugs and Crime*) <http://www.unodc.org/unodc/en/corruption/implementation-review-mechanism.html> accessed February 9, 2018.

surrounding a system to review state action relative to treaty obligations; particularly where this includes both self-assessment and crucially peer review.[70] The sensitivities of the review process help to explain not only why it was such a controversial issue during negotiations for the UNCAC itself but also—and despite support within the CCPCJ[71]—why progress vis-à-vis the IRM remains tentative. For Michael Kubiciel and Anna Cornelia Rink, so far, the UNCAC remains the "peak of global anti-corruption development." Yet, they continue, "it is now necessary to climb to the next, and even higher, mountain: the thorough, successful implementation of these laws."[72]

3 Conclusion

The UN treaty-based regimes for drug and crime control share some characteristics, but also significant differences. In terms of similarities, as in other issue areas of transnational concern, both sets of conventions are predicated on a degree of flexibility within their provisions. This is essential for the construction of any multinational regime requiring engagement by significant numbers of states that, while in general agreement on the issue, have varying concerns regarding specific details and obligations. How this reality plays out for both regimes, however, is different. For crime control, a lack of definitional clarity on key concepts, for example "organized crime," "transnational," and "corruption," has led to legitimate criticism regarding ineffective and limited implementation. Meanwhile, it is possible to argue that for international drug control, flexibility and interpretative space have been essential in sustaining a regime where there is growing dissatisfaction with the dominant control philosophy among parties to the current conventions—instruments that, it should be recalled, have their foundations in a group of treaties dating from 1912. Indeed, considering advances in knowledge, not only about relative harm of substances under control but also the effectiveness—or otherwise—of a range of market interventions, it is fair to argue that many aspects of the drug conventions are now antiquated. It is also important to acknowledge that while there may be increasing rhetorical reference to the need for drug policy to be designed and implemented in line with human rights norms, there remains a disconnect between high order soft-law declarations and practice within many member states. Reflecting systemic dissonance on the issue, this pattern is also replicated to a certain extent in the approach to drug control in Vienna and other parts of the UN system, including Geneva. Within this context and the resultant tensions within the drug control regime, and

[70] See CAC/COSP/IRG/2016/12, Conference of the States Parties to the United Nations Convention against Corruption, *Good practices and experiences of, and relevant measures taken by, States parties after the completion of the country reviews, including information related to technical assistance*, 20 September 2016.

[71] United Nations, *Commission on Crime Prevention and Criminal Justice, Report on the twenty-fifth session* (11 December 2015 and 23–27 May 2016), Economic and Social Council, Official Records, 2016, Supplement No. 10, E/2016/30-E/CN.15/2016/13, 43.

[72] Kubiciel and Rink (n 56) 237.

despite INCB recent claims that the treaties do not require modernization,[73] there are growing calls for member states to at least consider some form of treaty revision.

How such a process might be managed reveals other significant differences between the regimes. Unlike the crime conventions that contain inbuilt COPs—allowing for regular discussion of issues relating to implementation, interpretation, additional protocols and, if necessary, amendments—the drug conventions lack formal comprehensive review mechanisms and thereby the ability to evolve over time by adapting to new realities. It is plausible to suggest that this structural shortcoming has contributed to recourse to extraordinary procedures and "untidy legal justifications" as states struggle to reconcile domestic circumstances to international obligations under the drug control treaties. Indeed, while flexibility is essential, it is finite. Although politically attractive, recent attempts to argue that regulated cannabis markets are permissible within the current boundaries of the conventions risk undermining international law in general and diminishing the UN's effectiveness and credibility in a range of issue areas beyond drug policy. In an era of ever-increasing interconnectedness, complexity, and conflict, international law remains an important part of the structure of international society, especially for weaker states and citizens therein.[74] For the drug control regime in particular, an inability to undergo a process of recalibration may lead to irrelevance as more countries resort to dubious unilateral reinterpretations.

Admittedly, such an approach is in many ways appealing. Substantial amendment proposals that follow existing procedures are likely to encounter significant opposition and are relatively easily blocked even by a small minority of states. Consequently, other options that do not require consensus or majority support but operate within the confines of international law merit serious exploration. Innovative approaches include rescheduling of specific substances based on a WHO recommendation; denunciation and readherence with a new reservation, as applied by Bolivia in relation to coca chewing; and inter se modification among a group of like-minded states.[75] Amidst current debates about relieving the tensions around cannabis, consideration could also be given to other

[73] International Narcotics Control Board, *Report of the International Narcotics Control Board for 2016* (United Nations 2017) iii. Interestingly, this is in contrast to the position stated within the Board's 1994 Supplement. For example, then the INCB noted that it was "determined not to shy away from highlighting, where necessary, the shortcomings of the present system." E/INCB/1994/1/Supp.1, *Effectiveness of the international drug control treaties, Supplement to the Report of the International Narcotics Control Board for 1994* (United Nations 1995) iv.

[74] A Watts, "The Importance of International Law" in Michael Byers (ed), *The Role of Law in International Politics: Essays in International Relations and International Law* (OUP 2001) 16.

[75] On this point see K Odendahl, who notes that "due to the conflicting interests prevailing at an international level, amendments of multilateral treaties, especially amendments of treaties with a large number of parties, prove to be an extremely difficult and cumbersome process; sometimes, an amendment seems even impossible. It may thus happen that some of the States Parties wish to modify the treaty as between themselves alone". Also see N Boister and M Jelsma, "*Inter se* Modification of the UN Drug Control Conventions. An exploration of Its Applicability to Legitimise the Legal Regulation of Cannabis Markets" (2018) 20 Int Community Law Rev 457–494; K Odendahl, "Article 41: Agreements to Modify Multilateral Treaties between Certain of the Parties only" in Oliver Dörr and Kirsten Schmalenbach (eds), *Vienna Convention on the Law of Treaties: A Commentary* (Springer 2012) 719.

wider-ranging structural changes that would allow for a "multi-speed" approach to drug control.[76] This is particularly the case since tensions within the drug control regime around treaty breach are unlikely to end with cannabis. Among other suggestions,[77] states might consider incorporating a COP structure within the drug control regime. Bringing it into line with other treaty regimes, including those focusing on crime, could be the first stage in the evolution of an apparatus to allow for systemic modernization. As the debates and negotiations around the review mechanisms within the still-evolving crime conventions reveal, COPs should not be seen as a silver bullet. Nonetheless, the provision of a high-level forum for discussion has the potential to thaw and modernize the currently frozen drug control conventions.

[76] Boister (n 19) 409.

[77] See, eg, B Riedel, "I'd Like to Make a Reservation: Bolivian Coca Control and Why the United Nations Should Amend the Single Convention on Narcotic Drugs" (2016–2017) 49 George Washington ILR 711.

CHAPTER 14

TRADE AND DEVELOPMENT

MAKANE MOÏSE MBENGUE

> Peace is the natural effect of Trade.
> Charles De Montesquieu

The establishment of a new world order in the aftermath of the Second World War (WWII) was premised on a greater understanding among the various nations of the world. In particular, the interdependence of commercial interests between civilized nations—including those that had recently gained their independence—was seen as a viable foundation for peace. It was this realization that had led to the need for a coordinated multilateral system for managing and regulating trade. The organization best positioned in 1945 to achieve this economic, political, and societal cohesion in the service of peace was the United Nations (UN).

However, despite the UN's critical role in the development of a wide range of treaties in many fields of international relations (human rights, environment, health, etc.), it was curiously marginalized in its early foray into the trade and development spheres. Indeed, the International Trade Organization (ITO) conceptualized during the 1944 Bretton Woods conference collapsed in 1950 following efforts to establish it alongside the International Monetary Fund (IMF) and the International Bank for Reconstruction and Development (IBRD) within the UN system. The IMF and IBRD today remain loosely framed within the UN system (albeit with unique governance structures), and indeed are more inclined than in the past to identify with wider UN initiatives such as the 2015 Sustainable Development Goals.

Given that the present chapter appears within a handbook on UN treaties, it is helpful to recognize at the outset that none of the key instruments in the field of trade and development are UN treaties. Rather, the key multilateral treaties and organizations concerning trade have been either regional or non-UN multilateral conventional instruments. Yet a discussion of the UN's direct and indirect influence over multilateral consideration of and action on global trade finds a natural place within this volume, not least because of the work of the continuing UN Conference on Trade and Development (UNCTAD). Initially convened in 1964, UNCTAD's permanent secretariat has since established an authoritative role in related areas of international economic affairs, such as under international investment law.

The UN's contribution toward the emergence of a multilateral trading system is often underappreciated, sometimes even in theory. This is perhaps because of the evolution of international trade law as an independent species of jurisprudence largely regulated today by the World Trade Organization (WTO). However, the UN has exerted a direct and pervasive influence on the shape of the multilateral trading "system" today, notably through the advocacy of developing countries and their allies and friends. The UN has from the adoption of its Charter had a mandate to consider (and indeed has considered) the whole range of economic problems inherent in the development process.[1]

The checkered history of the UN's failures and successes is worth consideration because it highlights the overwhelming preference of developing countries (still today the vast majority of countries) for the UN to host discussions on trade and related treaty-making. This preference has often gone unreciprocated by the developed world. For example, since the 1950s, the United States has generally opposed centering any treaty and decision-making process on major economic and financial issues at the UN.

This chapter aims to provide an account of how the UN's participation in this history has influenced international trade relations. The chapter first examines the emergence of a multilateral trading "system" in the aftermath of WWII, and the role played by the UN therein. Thereafter, the chapter examines the events leading up to the conception of the ITO, its planned structure, and its failure to take off. This is assessed from the perspective of developing countries, many of whom were not yet fully or even partially decolonized at the time, and who were bitterly disappointed in their hopes for an inclusive model of international economic and social development. Given that many countries considered UNCTAD as a surrogate for the aborted ITO, the chapter then discusses the emergence of UNCTAD, and its structure, role, and contribution to the multilateral trading system. The chapter then examines UNCTAD's interplay with the General Agreement on Tariffs and Trade (GATT) process and secretariat, and its role in helping the GATT to evolve into an organization that could respond to developing nations' calls for inclusion and fairness. In its final substantive section, the chapter focuses on the evolution of the GATT into the more ambitious WTO established in January 1995, and the subtle ways in which the UN has played a role in the progressive direction that WTO jurisprudence has taken.

[1] Joseph A Greenwald, "UNCTAD and GATT as Instruments for the Development of Trade Policy" (1967) 61 Am Soc'y Intl Proc 155, 162.

1 The Founding of the Multilateral Trading System

The multilateral trading system as we know it today emerged from many earlier developments running in parallel with each other. In the aftermath of WWII, the architects of the postwar order were very much focused on economic rehabilitation and reconstruction, but overwhelmingly reflected the interests of developed countries. One may recall in this context that India, one of the first European colonies to attain independence, did not do so until 1947. The trickle of decolonization during the first 10 years after WWII soon developed into a flood, such that the number of states in the "Global South" predominated within the community of nations by 1964, even though many of these were comparatively small. These newly independent countries increasingly raised in global forums (such as the UN) issues that industrialized countries had not been prepared to engage with at an early stage, and that communist states had mainly championed at a rhetorical level: seeking to address the inequality and poverty that plagued them and contesting inequalities at the international level.

Whereas these different groups of countries aspired to the common ideal of economic development through sustained growth, they diverged considerably on the means of achieving this shared goal. Indeed, from the GATT's entry into force in 1948 (after attaining only 23 signatures upon adoption in October 1947) until the end of the Cold War around 1990, the leading industrialized countries of the West significantly and increasingly preferred a multilateral framework for international trade that excluded Eastern bloc countries.

Even from the early stages of WWII, the allied powers had already begun to plan for peace.[2] They shared a strong conviction that the mutually destructive and discriminatory trade and economic policies of the 1930s should never again be allowed to undermine the international economy, thereby threatening peace.[3] This concern was so important to them that in 1941, off the coast of Newfoundland, Prime Minister Churchill and President Roosevelt met in secret to discuss the principle of multilateralism as the cornerstone of a new postwar global economic system.[4] They pledged commitment to a new international order that would give weight to improving the well-being and employment prospects of all.[5] Principle 4 of the Atlantic Charter embodied the endeavor of both the United States and the UK "with due respect for their existing obligations, to

[2] Daniel Drache, "The Short but Significant Life of the International Trade Organization: Lessons for Our Time" (November 2000) CSGR Working Paper No. 62/00, Centre for the Study of Globalisation and Regionalisation (CSGR), University of Warwick.

[3] ibid.

[4] ibid. Reference to the joint declaration issued by the United States and United Kingdom on 14 August 1941, commonly referred to as the "Atlantic Charter." Atlantic Charter 14 August 1941, The Avalon Project, Yale Law Lillian Goldman Law Library, <http://avalon.law.yale.edu/wwii/atlantic.asp> accessed April 8, 2018.

[5] ibid.

further the enjoyment by all States, great or small, victor or vanquished, of access, on equal terms, to the trade and to the raw materials of the world which are needed for their economic prosperity."

This solemn pledge was doubtless the first irrevocable step toward encouraging other governments to organize their external trade internationally, most readily through multilateral arrangements.[6] This meeting provided the foundation for the creation of the UN (already referred to as such by the two men).[7]

The motivation behind these leaders' approach to a new postwar order was their focus on economic cooperation, rather than the punitive approach to the losing powers of the First World War that had proven so disastrous, paving the way for the rise of nationalist dictators such as Hitler.[8] This emphasis on economic factors that led to the 1944 Bretton Woods conference would presage the 1945 San Francisco conference to discuss and adopt the UN Charter.[9] The IMF was charged with overseeing a system of fixed exchange rates centered on the US dollar and a gold standard. It served as a forum for consultation and cooperation and a provider of short-term financial assistance to countries experiencing temporary deficits in their balance of payments. The IBRD was responsible for providing financial assistance for the reconstruction of war-ravaged nations and thereafter the economic development of less advanced countries.[10]

The next identifiable step to organize international economic relations took place on February 18, 1946, when the UN Economic and Social Council (ECOSOC) passed a resolution[11] calling for an International Conference on Trade and Development.[12]

[6] ibid.

[7] The Atlantic Charter included the following as goals for the postwar world: no territorial aggrandizement, no territorial change made against the wishes of the people, self-determination, restoration of self-determination to those deprived of it, reduction of trade restrictions, global cooperation to secure better economic and social conditions for all, freedom from fear and want, freedom of the seas, and abandonment of the use of force. Adherents to the Atlantic Charter signed the *Declaration by United Nations* on 1 January 1942, which became the basis for the UN.

[8] See John Maynard Keynes, *The Economic Consequences of the Peace* (Routledge 2003). Keynes saw the Versailles Peace Treaty as establishing a sort of "Cartighinian" peace, and emphasized the following: "The power to become habituated to his surroundings is a marked characteristic of mankind. Very few of us realize with conviction the intensely, unusual, complicated, unreliable, temporary nature of the economic organisation by which Western Europe has lived for the last half century. We assume some of the most peculiar and temporary of our late advantages as natural, permanent, and to be depended on, and we lay our plans accordingly. On this sandy and false foundation we scheme for social improvement and dress our political platforms, pursue our animosities and particular ambitions, and feel ourselves with enough margin in hand to foster, not assuage, civil conflict in the European family."

[9] United Nations Monetary and Financial Conference, July 1944 at Bretton Woods, New Hampshire, United States of America.

[10] Bretton Woods—GATT, 1941–1947, Milestones: 1935–1947, Office of the Historian, United States of America Department of State, <https://history.state.gov/milestones/1937-1945/bretton-woods> accessed April 4, 2018.

[11] Final act and Related Documents, United Nations Conference on Trade and Employment held at Havana, Cuba, from November 21, 1947 to March 24, 1948, <https://www.wto.org/english/docs_e/legal_e/havana_e.pdf> accessed April 4, 2018; Peter Neumann, "The Relationship between GATT and the United Nations" (1970) 3 Cornell Intl LJ 63,78.

[12] Neumann (n 11).

In accordance with the resolution, ECOSOC appointed members to a Preparatory Committee and defined its mandate.[13] At its second session in Geneva on April 19, 1947, the Preparatory Committee initiated negotiations toward the substantial reduction of tariffs and other trade barriers and aimed to eliminate trade preferences on a reciprocal and mutually advantageous basis.[14] This drive toward the reduction of trade barriers supported the objectives of the Bretton Woods Agreement.[15]

In light of the international situation today, it is interesting to note that while the world community was able to establish the above institutions to coordinate and underpin global growth with relative ease, an agreement on international trade proved difficult primarily because of US opposition.[16] It was only after UN negotiations held from April to October 1947 that the foundation of this new world trade order was established with the signing of the GATT on October 30, 1947.[17]

The GATT's formation was the first major multilateral effort to establish a system of rules that would regulate international trade. Early on, the GATT featured two main provisions. The most important requirement was that each contracting party must confer most-favoured nation treatment (MFN) on every other contracting party.[18] This meant that all contracting parties had to be treated equally with respect to tariffs.[19] It excluded from its provisions the special tariffs among members of the British Commonwealth and of customs unions. It also permitted tariffs if their removal would cause serious injury to domestic producers. Second, the GATT prohibited restrictions on the number of imports and exports. It provided exceptions for situations involving surpluses of agricultural products, instances of a contracting party needing to protect its balance of payments because its foreign exchange reserves were low, and instances of developing countries needing to protect fledgling industries. In addition, countries could restrict trade for reasons of national security.

Yet the reduction of tariff barriers was not itself the principal economic challenge facing the postwar world. In fact, the improvement of labour standards, the special needs of developing countries, and the codification and advancement of human rights were beginning to be viewed as equally urgent. The postwar global community had begun to recognize the value of the concept of inclusion, along with minimum normative standards to which the UN membership could subscribe, abandoning hitherto narrow economic approaches. Indeed, on economic issues, the world community was driven to view economic progress, free of ideology, as a key goal, thus helping to generate

[13] ibid. [14] ibid.

[15] Kimberly Amadeo, "GATT: Purpose, History, Pros, Cons: How GATT Saved the World," The Balance (Updated 22 September 2018) <https://www.thebalance.com/gatt-purpose-history-pros-cons-3305578> accessed January 16, 2018.

[16] ibid. Amadeo (n 15).

[17] 17General Agreement on Tariffs and Trade 1947 (adopted 30 October 1947, entered into force 1 January 1948) 55 UNTS 187, 194, 196, 198, 200 https://www.wto.org/english/docs_e/legal_e/gatt47.pdf accessed April 4, 2018.

[18] Amadeo (n 15). [19] ibid.

support for a balance between market forces and the democratic aspirations of people across the world.[20]

Within the UN, most countries understood that if trade liberalization was to be achieved in a manner that was inclusive of all interests, a new set of multilaterally sanctioned principles would be required.[21] It flowed from this understanding that the objectives of sustainable economic development and trade liberalization could not be served solely by the IMF and IBRD. It was in the expression of this realization that a tentative mandate for the International Trade Organization (ITO) was articulated when the United Nations Conference on Trade and Development (UNCTAD) was convened in Havana between late 1947 and early 1948, and resulted in the conclusion of the Havana Charter.[22] As its provisions were unfortunately not ratified by the required number of national legislatures, however, the ITO would prove stillborn.[23]

2 The UN and the Aborted Attempt to Establish the International Trade Organization (ITO)

Interestingly, the ITO was not aimed at removing all non-tariff barriers to trade.[24] This reflected an acceptance that countries needed to (and still need to) employ restrictions from time to time to address a range of problems, such as the balance of payment deficits and the promotion of development.[25] Rather, the framers of the Havana Charter had concentrated on prohibition of practices that could contribute to an uneven playing field, biased against a competitor as a result of deliberate government measures.

In fact, the ITO project was seen as a step toward answering some of the most pressing concerns of developing countries in the face of the GATT's emergence. When this project collapsed in 1950, developing and soon-to-be-independent countries were notably disappointed.[26]

[20] <IBT>Drache (n 2)</IBT>. Drache states that one of the most forceful advocates of the need to steer trade away from liberal ideology came unexpectedly from *The Economist*, a vocal and persistent champion of laissez-faire free trade.

[21] ibid.

[22] Final Act of the United Nations Conference on Trade and Employment (Havana Charter), signed by 56 countries participating in the said conference that took place in Havana, Cuba.

[23] The most serious opposition arose in the US Congress, even though the US government had been one of the driving forces in drafting the text. In 1950, Washington announced that it would not seek congressional ratification of the Havana Charter, thus rendering the ITO effectively dead.

[24] Drache (n 2).

[25] ibid. Also refer to R Miskell, "Antecedents of the ITO Charter and Their Relevance for the Uruguay Rounds" (Spring 1992) 14 Northern Ill ULR 323:2.

[26] <IBT>Miskell (n 25)</IBT>. It is important to note, however, that among the original 23 signatories of the GATT were several important developing countries, including Brazil, Chile, China, India, and Pakistan, as well as some smaller ones such as Burma, Ceylon (now Sri Lanka), Cuba, Lebanon, and

The UNCTAD 16 years later resulted in part from a growing call from developing countries that trade ought to serve explicit employment goals.[27] By then, developing countries constituted a majority at the UN and were able to muster much more influence collectively. Mass unemployment had become a scourge of the interwar period, encouraging extreme politics in Europe. At least in theory, employment issues should have also been important for industrialized countries. Indeed, several of the major economic thinkers of the 1930s and 1940s, such as John Maynard Keynes,[28] Joan Robinson,[29] and James Meade,[30] had highlighted the centrality of employment issues to economic stability and growth.

Advocates of this view began at this time to articulate that workers' rights must be an integral part of any trade and commercial policy.[31] It was increasingly felt that investors ought to receive their due, but not to the exclusion of other concerns: hence the quest to create an organization that could find a middle ground in this and other matters. The ITO was conceived to address this pressing concern, which could have easily been overshadowed by pure economic liberalization favoring the interests of the United States and the UK.[32]

The Havana Charter was designed to complement the IMF and the World Bank, and aimed to bolster public authority while complimenting the opening of markets.[33] It included detailed rules, not only on the "staples of trade" such as tariffs, quotas, exchange controls, and state monopolies, but also on a host of other matters. In addition, the Charter contained rules on restrictive business practices, intergovernmental commodity

Syria—a reasonable showing of developing country support for the Agreement. This chapter should not be taken to imply that developing countries opposed GATT either in 1947 or subsequently. Rather, such countries wanted a number of their specific concerns addressed in ways that the GATT was not designed to do.

[27] ibid. Also refer to R Sidelesky, *John Maynard Keynes: The Economist as Saviour 1927–1937* (Allan Lane 1994).

[28] Sidelesky (n 27); Drache (n 2) argues that the international demand problem of modern economics had pushed Keynes toward his General Theory. It had convinced him that a new social and political agenda was needed to ensure the stability of the international economy once the war ended.

[29] Drache (n 2) As a testament to the above view, Robinson, the dean of Cambridge radical economic thought, began her influential book, *Introduction to the Theory of Employment* (which had been reprinted seven times by the 1950s) with these eponymous words: "*The modern economic system fails to provide employment continuously for those who desire to work* . . . ."

[30] ibid. In fact, Drache (n 2) notes that Meade, winner of the 1977 Nobel Prize for economics, had recast modern trade theory to "cover the domestic aspects of economic policies designed for the maintenance of full employment" in order to achieve a socially desirable distribution of income and property. He advocated enlarging domestic and international demand with a policy of employment at home and an international policy of nondiscriminatory trade as desirable objectives in and of themselves. Reference to JM Meade, *The Theory of International Economic Policy: The Balance of Payments* (OUP 1951).

[31] Meade (n 30).

[32] Lance A Compa, "Labor Rights and Labor Standards in International Trade" (1993) <https://digitalcommons.ilr.cornell.edu/articles/341/> accessed April 4, 2018. See also Havana Charter for an International Trade Organization (1948) U.S. Department of State Pub. No. 3206; Steve Charnovitz, "The Influence of International Labour Standards on the World Trading Regime: A Historical Overview" (September–October 1987) 126 Intl Labor Rev 5 565–81.

[33] Drache (n 2).

agreements, industrial stabilization, and international investment, as well as non-tariff barriers. It also set out the terms and conditions for exceptions from targeted obligations for reasons of economic development.[34]

The Havana Charter recognized the appropriateness of including labour standards in a trade agreement.[35] More specifically, it recognized that there were links among core standards and trade, foreign direct investment, and employment.[36] Interestingly, it also included a provision that mandated the International Labour Organization (ILO) and ITO to cooperate with each other in matters of common interest.[37] Its most interesting feature, however, was to provide for unfair labour conditions to be subject to nullification and impairment complaints within the ITO's dispute settlement procedures.[38]

In the interests of regulation, the ITO's jurisdictional scope included power to make recommendations and to promote agreements "*to facilitate an equitable distribution of skills, arts, technology, materials and equipment to assure just and equitable treatment for the enterprise, skills, capital, arts and technology brought from one Member country to another*" and to "*avoid double taxation*."[39] Interestingly, members were permitted to take safeguard "*actions within the provisions of the charter,*" should other members fail to comply with these commitments.[40]

For developing countries, new ground was broken with respect to price volatility, which had commonly affected production and trade in primary commodities.[41] Both developing and industrialized countries agreed to establish procedures for temporary intergovernmental commodity agreements based on regulation of price and production (though excluding buffer stocks).[42] The aim was to bring price and revenue stability to primary producers and consumers. At the time, this provision was trailblazing.[43]

[34] These include balance-of-payments difficulties, the need to prevent injury to domestic producers, and the right to form customs unions and free trade areas.

[35] The ITO Charter did not lay out a core group of labor standards, but it did supply a potentially important institutional mechanism within the ITO for members and its Executive Board to consider such issues.

[36] Article 7.1 stated that "*the Members recognize that unfair labour conditions, particularly in production for export, create difficulties in international trade*. . ." See also Drache (n 2).

[37] Article 7.2. See also Drache (n 2).

[38] Drache (n 2). Specific references appear in Charter Articles 94 and 95.

[39] Drache (n 2). See also S Piccioto, "Global, Liberalization, Regulation" (Warwick University 1998). In fact, the Charter included a chapter requiring states to prevent enterprises from engaging in practices restraining competition, limiting access to markets, or fostering monopolistic control, and it set up a procedure for investigating and reporting on specific complaints about such practices.

[40] Drache (n 2). The crucial clause in favor of full employment policy concerned lifting the ban on quantitative restrictions. This was an innovative provision, even if it remained a solution of last resort. Under the Charter, a member state targeted for retaliation was free to withdraw from the ITO within 60 days (arts. 6, 21, 75, 93–95). Another group of trade norms and principles was also addressed under the category of "special circumstances" (i.e., when a country could not implement the principles of the Charter due to a "*drastic and sudden change in existing trade practise*").

[41] Such as products from mining and agriculture.

[42] For specifics refer to the Havana Charter, Chapter 6.

[43] ibid. Havana Charter, Chapter 6. The collapse of primary products had affected all countries severely in the interwar period, and the Charter attempted to provide a practical alternative that would

In relation to investment, the Havana Charter implicitly recognized the right of expropriation of host countries and entitled them to impose specific measures on foreign direct investment (FDI). A nuanced approach was adopted, to accommodate the aspirations of developing countries, whereby it was acknowledged that host countries could take any "*appropriate important measures*" to prevent FDI from interfering in their domestic policy. Furthermore, the host country's right of nationalization was implicitly recognized, and payment of compensation as a remedy was acknowledged.[44] These special provisions to promote economic development were designed "*particularly for those countries which (were) in the early stage of industrial development*."[45]

This discussion has sought to demonstrate how the spirit of the Havana Charter came to be seen as partly at odds with the traditional view of laissez-faire economic policy that was in vogue in the United States at that time. However, this departure from pure commercial interests and profit is not hard to understand. The Havana Charter intentionally adopted a blend of Keynesian demand principles, to provide a mutually acceptable basis for freer trade between developed and developing nations. This was seen as the most potent answer to the new challenges of development and decolonization.[46] Unfortunately, it was this aspect of the Havana Charter that led to its demise.

3 The Demise of the ITO and the Birth of UNCTAD: UNCTAD and Its Impact on Multilateral Trade

While the GATT itself had notably contained no explicit provisions regarding developing countries, their concerns were intended to be assuaged by the structure and powers of the ITO, as foreseen in the Havana Charter. However, the latter's failure to take off stymied these efforts, leading developing countries to start raising concerns about the inclusiveness of international trade.[47]

permit and encourage marketing boards and other market-limiting institutions. In addition, special provisions were designed to guarantee support for the agricultural sector through subsidies and quantitative restrictions.

44 Havana Charter, Article 12.

45 Havana Charter, Chapter 3. Furthermore, at the insistence of developing countries, this principle was given a very broad reading so as to include tariff preferences, quantitative restrictions, and limitation of investor rights.

46 Havana Charter, Chapter 3 (n 45). Also see WA Brown Jr, "The United States and the Restoration of World Trade. An Analysis and Appraisal of the ITO Charter and the General Agreement on Tariffs and Trade" (1950) Washington, DC: The Brookings Institution.

47 Constantine Michalopoulos, "Trade and Developments in the GATT and WTO: The Role of Special and Differential Treatment for Developing Countries" (28 February 2000) Working Draft <https://www.wto.org/english/tratop_e/devel_e/sem01_e/costa_e.doc> accessed April 4, 2018.

These concerns were spurred by the belief that sustainable increases in income and output could only be brought about through increased industrialization.[48] This was seen as a very tall order because of then-prevailing patterns of international specialization.[49] It was this specific concern that thereafter guided the strategy developed by the international community to favor inclusiveness in multilateral trade.[50] The 1954-1955 GATT review session was the first occasion on which provisions were adopted to address the needs of developing countries as a group within the GATT. Agreement was reached on three main provisions, two of which related to Article XVIII.[51] In 1961, the GATT adopted a declaration on the "Promotion of Trade of Less-developed Countries," which inter alia called for preferences in market access for developing countries not covered by existing preferential tariff systems (such as the Commonwealth preferences) or by subsequently established preferences in customs unions or free trade areas.[52] This was the first mention in the GATT of what would later become the Generalized System of Preferences (GSP) for developing countries.

Despite the above, pressure remained because developing countries still felt that their trade concerns were not being effectively addressed in the GATT. Indeed, this pressure built toward additional institutional arrangements to deal explicitly with the interlinkages of trade and development. Arising from a substantive international meeting, UNCTAD was established in 1964 as a permanent secretariat to underpin and provide analysis and documentation for UN discussions on these topics.

The birth of UNCTAD as an institution was emblematic of the struggles between developed and developing countries to assert control over international trade.[53] When the ITO failed to crystallize, the economic issues were addressed at two levels.

[48] ibid.

[49] Developing countries specialized mostly in raw materials and primary commodity exports, characterized by low price and income elasticities of demand, as well as considerable price volatility; while they were dependent on imports for manufacturing, capital goods, and intermediate inputs for investment and industrialization. They believed that liberal trade policies would stymie the development of infant industries, while the continued dependence on primary commodity and raw materials exports would result in volatile export earnings and deteriorating terms of trade. See also R Prebisch, "The Economic Development of Latin America and Its Principal Problems, UN ECLA, Santiago" (1950) United Nations Department of Economic Affairs, Lake Success, New York, 43.

[50] Michalopoulos (n 47). Throughout this period, developing countries sought to emphasize the uniqueness of their development problems and challenges and the need to be treated differently and more favorably in the GATT, in part by being permitted not to liberalize their own trade and in part by being extended preferential access to developed country markets.

[51] ibid. The Article XVIII (B) revision allowed countries at "an early stage of their development" to adopt quantitative restrictions on imports whenever monetary reserves were deemed to be inadequate relative to the country's long-term development strategy. Article XVIII (C) was revised to allow for the imposition of trade restrictions (both tariffs and quantitative restrictions) to support infant industries with a view to raising living standards. The granting of a right of veto to certain affected contracting parties was deleted, making the imposition of quantitative restrictions easier. Refer to GATT Basic Instruments and Documents (BISD) (1954), 3rd Supplement, Geneva.

[52] Michalopoulos (n 47).

[53] Gautam Rohidekar, "UNCTAD and International Trade-The Forgotten Link" (1997) 9 Student Advoc. 104, 107.

The negotiations on tariff concessions were taken up under the GATT. Other issues were taken up within other institutions.[54] The ensuing frustrations, on the part of developing countries, led to many (essentially political) attempts to form the ideal institution to take responsibility for these issues, ultimately leading to the formation of UNCTAD as well as the creation of, the Trade and Development Board (TDB), which counted 55 members.[55] UNCTAD gradually became the main institution through which developing countries tried to pursue their international trade agenda for some decades.

An understanding of this process, and the institutionalization of UNCTAD as "*continuing machinery*" through its permanent secretariat, reveals how the UN reinserted itself into the sphere of multilateral trade.[56] The Conference's Final Act contains no legal rights or obligations, but authorizes the conclusion of particular agreements having binding effect.[57] Trade policy is but one of UNCTAD's spheres of interest. It is seized of a wide range of policies that bear on the problems of economic development, and its analytical work on international investment flows and policy is widely considered authoritative. Its membership is open to members of the UN, and various international agencies contribute to it.

UNCTAD came to be viewed as a permanent member of the group of UN institutions, today seated within the UN's Chief Executives Board (CEB).[58] The fact that UNCTAD was mandated to report directly to the General Assembly rather than through ECOSOC, in which developing countries did not yet have a voting majority, proved to be advantageous.[59] The developing countries viewed UNCTAD as a means to circumvent developed countries' control of the international financial institutions, a privilege that was ensured through weighted voting and that remains in place today. UNCTAD has moreover contributed significantly to the UN's role in developing successive waves of guiding principles for sustainable development, such as the 2001 Millennium Development Goals and the 2015 Sustainable Development Goals. The TDB is, through its recommendations, able to propose resolutions that the General Assembly often adopts.[60] UNCTAD's own institutional development has involved various committees (for example, on Commodities, Manufactures, Invisibles and Financing, and Shipping) and informal working groups over the years.[61]

One way in which UNCTAD had a substantial impact on the evolution of the multilateral trading system was in the emergence of the G77.[62] A major consequence of the

[54] ibid. See also Gavin Corea, *Encyclopedia of Public International Law* (1980) vol 5, 301. He notes that, regarding the effects on the stated institutions, "*Nor did they satisfy the aspirations of the growing number of developing states for an organisation which would address itself to these questions of trade and development of particular importance to* them."

[55] Rohidekar (n 53). [56] Greenwald (n 1). [57] ibid. The same remains true today.

[58] L Joseph Love, "Latin America, UNCTAD, and the Postwar Trading System" (2001) <https://www.iatp.org/sites/default/files/Latin_America_UNCTAD_and_the_Postwar_Trading_S.pdf> accessed April 4, 2018.

[59] Rohidekar (n 53). [60] ibid. [61] ibid.

[62] ibid. A leading authority notes that the G77 holds meetings at the ministerial level prior to each session of UNCTAD in order to reach agreement on an agenda and common strategy. See also Love (n 58).

emergence of this group has been the de facto institutionalization of the group system of negotiation within UNCTAD. This allows for interaction between rich and poor countries on the principle of equality of vote weighting, as decision-making is mostly based on consensus procedures rather than "one country, one vote."[63]

An example of UNCTAD's early effectiveness was the substantive amendment of the GATT to include a Part IV on "Trade and Development," containing three new articles.[64] These articles expanded particular GATT structures and activities: the GATT Committee on Trade and Development and its various subsidiaries, the GATT's initiation of trade and aid studies, and (perhaps most important of all) the GATT International Trade Centre. The latter began operating in May 1964 (during the conference establishing UNCTAD), and now implements Article XXXVIII of Part IV, which helps meet developing countries' needs by providing a market information service, a publications program, training in export promotion, and trade promotion advisory services.

Furthermore, in 1968, developing countries succeeded in establishing a GSP under the auspices of UNCTAD.[65] The system was established on a voluntary basis, and the developed countries were not legally bound under the GATT to accept it. However, a GATT waiver from MFN obligations was granted in 1971, initially for a period of 10 years (GATT, 1972), along with another waiver allowing developing countries to grant preferences among themselves.[66]

Apart from the above, there have been other ways in which the UNCTAD has been instrumental in shaping the course of the multilateral trading "system" to become more inclusive of the interests of developing countries. The 1974 UN Convention on a Code of Conduct for Liner Conferences is a prime example.[67] This treaty relates to the international regulation of ocean shipping. Developing countries had expressed interest in participating in the open cargo shipping industry. The United States had always opposed such a Code of Conduct,[68] and the treaty was adopted only when the European Economic Community (EEC) led the way.[69] No amount of pressure by developing countries had been effective until the EEC entered the picture.[70]

[63] Rohidekar (n 53). In fact, developing countries use the permanent secretariat of UNCTAD to produce statistics, collect data, and generate arguments supportive of third world claims, at times contradicting the views of the staff of economic organizations such as GATT, the IMF, and the World Bank and thereby giving the third world a rich and reasoned basis on which to challenge the positions of developed countries.

[64] Greenwald (n 1). See articles XXXVI, XXXVII, and XXXVIII.

[65] Michalopoulos (n 47). The United States withdrew, perhaps temporarily, from the WTO successor to this system when Congress allowed it to lapse in 2017. In March 2018, a House of Representatives draft bill sought to authorize its renewal for three years, as its principles continue to be supported by a significant number of members of Congress. Its ultimate fate is unknown at the time of this writing. Some of President Trump's decisions have taken the GSP into favorable account.

[66] ibid. [67] Rohidekar (n 53).

[68] ibid. The United States, viewing this as a threat to its own powerful shipping sector, objected on the basis that by allowing quotas, the Code was incompatible with the US policy of free competition, and that freight rates were to be fixed by an independent authority at a level as low as feasible from a commercial point of view.

[69] ibid. [70] ibid.

Moreover, UNCTAD has enabled the conclusion of many other important multilateral agreements that have helped strengthen international trade.[71] These include three important instruments adopted in 1980: the UN Convention on International Multimodal Transport, the Multilaterally Agreed Equitable Principles and Rules for the Control of Restrictive Business Practices, and the Agreement Establishing the Common Fund for Commodities. By far the most ambitious legal instrument that UNCTAD has promoted is the 1974 Charter of Economic Rights and Duties of States, a precursor to the so-called New International Economic Order. Noteworthy was Article 14 of the Charter, which stated:

> Every State has the duty to co-operate in promoting a steady and increasing expansion and liberalization of world trade and an improvement in the welfare and living standards of all peoples, in particular those of developing countries. Accordingly, all States should co-operate, *inter alia*, towards the progressive dismantling of obstacles to trade and the improvement of the international framework for the conduct of world trade and, to these ends, co-ordinated efforts shall be made to solve in an equitable way the trade problems of all countries, taking into account the specific trade problems of the developing countries. In this connexion, States shall take measures aimed at securing additional benefits for the international trade of developing countries so as to achieve a substantial increase in their foreign exchange earnings, the diversification of their exports, the acceleration of the rate of growth of their trade, taking into account their development needs, an improvement in the possibilities for these countries to participate in the expansion of world trade and a balance more favourable to developing countries in the sharing of the advantages resulting from this expansion, through, in the largest possible measure, a substantial improvement in the conditions of access for the products of interest to the developing countries and, wherever appropriate, measures designed to attain stable, equitable and remunerative prices for primary products.

Acceptance of the Charter nevertheless proved elusive after its proponents ran headlong into what Sylvia Ostry, the Canadian economist, defined as Ronald Thatcherism: the powerful alliance of economically conservative US and UK leaders at the 1981 Cancun North-South Summit.[72]

4 The UN and the GATT/WTO: A Continuous Interplay

Though preceding pages have documented progress in achieving improvements in international trade arrangements for developing countries since 1947, the playing field remained far from level, and breakthroughs since the early 1980s have been few and

[71] These agreements are all the result of the work of specific committees.

[72] New International Economic Order. For Sylvia Ostry on the derailment of the NIEO, see <www.g8.utoronto.ca/scholar/ostry1990/ost3.htm> accessed April 4, 2018.

far between. This has been due primarily to the relatively limited participation of developing nations in the GATT process of negotiating concessions, further exacerbating their frustration.[73]

Earlier work by developing countries under the auspices of the UN had laid the foundation for renewed efforts under the GATT, resulting in the 1979 adoption of the Enabling Clause.[74] The Clause established the principle of differential and more favourable treatment, reciprocity, and fuller participation of developing countries.[75] It provided a stronger legal basis for the special and differential treatment of developing countries within the rules of the multilateral trading system, albeit in permissive terms. Specifically, the Clause transformed the 10-year waivers for the GSP and trade preferences among developing countries into permanent waivers.[76]

While the UN's contributions to treaties governing multilateral trade are noteworthy, they are not the only reflections of the UN's influence in this area. That influence has also guided the evolution of jurisprudence under contemporary trade treaties. This is due to potential conflicts between international trade law and other fields of international law. The UN has been helpful in reconciling opposing logics and viewpoint, which has furthered the cause of the multilateral trading system.

The GATT was overtaken by the success of the Uruguay Round of negotiations, which laid the groundwork for the creation in 1995 of the WTO (the establishment of which had been agreed in 1993). Yet the GATT lives on in the form of a body of rules, rights, and obligations that continue to serve as the foundation of the multilateral trading system. From 1948 until 1993, the GATT's purview and membership had grown dramatically.[77] During this period, the GATT sponsored eight trade rounds wherein member nations agreed to reduce trade barriers.

By the late 1980s, a growing number of nations had decided that the GATT could better serve global trade expansion if it were to become a formal international organization.[78] They pressed for negotiations to formalize the GATT as a more powerful and ambitious

[73] Michalopoulos (n 47). See also RE Hudec, *Developing Countries in the GATT Legal System* (Gower 1987); R. Kemper, "The Tokyo Round: Results and Implications for Developing Countries" (1980) World Bank Staff Working Paper No. 372, Washington DC.

[74] Hudec (n 73)

[75] ibid. See also GATT (1980) BISD 26th Supplement, Geneva. It provided for: (1) the preferential market access of developing countries to developed country markets on a non-reciprocal, nondiscriminatory basis; (2) "*more favourable*" treatment for developing countries in other GATT rules dealing with non-tariff barriers; (3) the introduction of preferential trade regimes among developing countries; and (4) the special treatment of least developed countries in the context of specific measures for developing countries.

[76] The Clause did not create any new legally binding obligations for developed-country members. Rather, it made possible the introduction of preferential and non-reciprocal market access schemes, leaving the extent of preferences and level of reciprocity to the discretion of each country. Thus, the Enabling Clause was a summation, rather than an extension, of the efforts made since 1954 to address the concerns of developing countries within the multilateral trading system.

[77] By 1994, the GATT counted 128 contracting parties.

[78] In the *1988 Omnibus Trade and Competitiveness Act*, the US Congress explicitly called for more effective trade dispute settlement mechanisms.

organization. Today, the WTO provides a permanent arena for member governments to address international trade issues and oversees the implementation of the trade agreements negotiated during the Uruguay Round of trade talks.

The WTO is not simply the GATT transformed into a more formal international organization. It covers many additional actions, activities, and assets, including subsidies, intellectual property, food safety, and other policies that were once solely the subject of national governments. The WTO also is endowed with strong dispute settlement mechanisms.

However, despite all of this structural formality, the WTO was established without the means to always adequately address non-trade issues, such as environmental issues that had been gradually gaining awareness throughout the world, especially in developing countries. The Preamble to the Agreement Establishing the World Trade Organization ("WTO Agreement")[79] recognizes that trade is not an end in itself, but rather that sustained economic growth must be pursued in ways that encourage sustainable development and protection of the environment. Nevertheless, WTO practice until now has not always been supportive of this avowed principle.[80]

The WTO has attracted increased attacks by environmentalists all over the world, who believe that its rules have been invoked to undermine environmental protection. The sustained nature of these attacks and the inability of the international trade community (generally in favor of freer trade) and environmentalists to find common ground, or even to discuss their differences, suggests that their antagonism runs deeper than a mere disagreement over policy. Environmentalists regard the environment as immeasurably more important than the transaction of trade, which they view simply as financially driven.[81] Additionally, they are impatient with arguments that environmental regulations should be sensitive to cost-benefit calculations and should conform to international trade rules. On the other hand, those favoring free trade view environmentalists as woolly-headed and animated by an anti-business bias. These radically different perspectives have generated intense debate, but there has been little, if any, progress toward a meeting of minds. It is on this divide that the UN has served as a bridge between these two seemingly irreconcilable sets of convictions. One of the best examples of such a "bridging effect" of the UN is the famous 1992 Rio Declaration on Environment and Development that was adopted during the United Nations Conference on Environment and Development and whose Principle 12 states as follows:

> States should cooperate to promote a supportive and open international economic system that would lead to economic growth and sustainable development in all countries, to better address the problems of environmental degradation. Trade policy measures for environmental purposes should not constitute a means of arbitrary or

[79] Marrakesh Agreement Establishing the World Trade Organization, preamble (December 15, 1993) 33 I.L.M. 15, 15.

[80] Bruce Neuling, "The *Shrimp-Turtle* Case: Implications for Article XX of GATT and the Trade and Environment Debate" (1999) 22 Lop LA. Int'l & Comp L Rev 1.

[81] ibid.

> unjustifiable discrimination or a disguised restriction on international trade. Unilateral actions to deal with environmental challenges outside the jurisdiction of the importing country should be avoided. Environmental measures addressing transboundary or global environmental problems should, as far as possible, be based on an international consensus.

The biggest clashes between trade and the environment have related to environmental policies/measures affecting GATT 1994 Articles I, II, and XI and other provisions of the WTO's founding agreement (which imported the GATT 1947 main provisions).[82] Article XX on General Exceptions lays out a number of specific circumstances under which WTO parties may be exempted from WTO rules.[83] Two of these are relevant for environmental protection, which are as follows:

> Subject to the requirement that such measures are not applied in a manner which would constitute a means of arbitrary or unjustifiable discrimination between countries where the same conditions prevail, or a disguised restriction on international trade, nothing in this Agreement shall be construed to prevent the adoption or enforcement by any contracting party of measures:...(b) necessary to protect human, animal or plant life or health;...[or] (g) relating to the conservation of exhaustible natural resources if such measures are made effective in conjunction with restrictions on domestic production or consumption;....[84]

While the negotiating history of Article XX may indicate that Article XX was not intended to shield environmental measures from basic GATT disciplines,[85] arguments to the contrary add complexity to the situation.[86] Furthermore, the application of the

[82] ibid. [83] ibid. See also GATT art. XX. [84] GATT art. XX.

[85] ibid. Article XX(b) is based on a proposal by the United States and the UK, which included an exception for measures "necessary to protect human, animal or plant life or health"—a common formula in numerous pre-GATT commercial treaties. This was later modified but then abandoned because Article XX's preamble accomplished the same purpose. There was no avowal of an environmental purpose during the limited debate on Article XX(b), and the term "sanitary" was commonly used to characterize this Article. It is likely the negotiators intended only to exempt national regulations designed to keep out unsafe food, block the importation of products bearing pests, and so forth. Article XX(g) language was discussed in terms of export, rather than import, restrictions, and the conserved natural resource was typically described as a "raw material" or "mineral." "Exhaustible" natural resource apparently meant stock resources, such as oil, in contrast to renewable or flow resources, such as plants or animals. The proposal was ultimately adopted with the deletion of the words "taken pursuant to international agreements." Arguably, GATT negotiators intended to specifically exempt national regulations aimed at conserving resources, such as minerals or oil, by prohibiting their exportation, as long as domestic conservation measures were also applied.

[86] Steve Charnovitz, "Exploring the Environmental Exceptions in GATT Article XX" (1991) 25 J World Trade 37, 38–47, for example, argues that environmental provisions were already in existence in various laws and treaties at the time GATT was negotiated (such as a 1911 treaty to ban imports of seal skins to protect and preserve seals and sea otters), and that GATT should be construed in a manner consistent with them. Charnovitz argues that no GATT delegation contended that these preexisting laws and treaties were to be overridden by GATT. It is, however, possible that GATT negotiators were unaware of

1969 Vienna Convention on the Law of Treaties[87] renders the negotiating history of Article XX irrelevant insofar as the terms used in Article XX(b) and (g) are nontechnical and reasonably clear, and can be related to the object and purpose of GATT in an intelligible way to support measures that could go far beyond traditional sanitary and quarantine measures to conserve nonliving resources.[88] However, the question of whether paragraphs (b) and (g) were written for exclusively non-environmental reasons is still debatable, as the phraseology does not lend itself smoothly to environmental goals. Such a clear dichotomy of ideologies rendered the disputes between WTO members inevitable as the profile of environmental issues continued to rise over subsequent decades.

The situation was further exacerbated by initial jurisprudence during the 1990s, which proved a constant source of disappointment to environmentalists and served to reinforce their suspicion that "trade bureaucrats" were incapable of taking a broad view of the relationship between environmental protection and the world trading system. The *Thai-Cigarettes*[89] and *Tuna-Dolphin I*[90] served as landmarks in the trade and environment debate. Probably more than any other event prior to the implementation of the North American Free Trade Agreement (NAFTA), the *Tuna-Dolphin I* case mobilized environmental nongovernmental organizations (NGOs) to oppose GATT.[91] Environmentalists objected not only to the dispute settlement Panel's conclusions, but also to the restrictive way in which the Panel interpreted Article XX. It was perceived as a clear warning that trade considerations would invariably trump environmental protection under the GATT. The fact that the related second case brought by the European Communities against the US (*Tuna-Dolphin II*)[92] met the same fate did not assuage this perception. Both decisions enraged environmentalists.

Matters came to a head with the first environmental case decided after the establishment of the WTO, *United States-Standards for Reformulated and Conventional Gasoline (Reformulated Gas)*, which pitted the United States against Venezuela and Brazil.

these treaties and laws and if so, then the question of making room for measures to protect the environment was never an issue during the negotiations. This interpretation is plausible because no reference to these laws and treaties appears in the negotiating record, and the environment was not a major public issue at the time. Also Neuling (n 81).

[87] According to the Vienna Convention, Article 31, "*[a] treaty shall be interpreted in good faith in accordance with the ordinary meaning to be given to the terms of the treaty in their context and in the light of its object and purpose.*" Article 32 states: "*Recourse may be had to supplementary means of interpretation, including the preparatory work of the treaty and the circumstances of its conclusion... to determine the meaning when the interpretation according to [A]rticle 31: (a) leaves the meaning ambiguous or obscure; or (b) leads to a result which is manifestly absurd or unreasonable.*" See also Neuling (n 80).

[88] Neuling (n 80).

[89] *Thailand-Restrictions on Importation of and Internal Taxes on Cigarettes* (adopted November 7, 1990) GATT B.I.S.D. 37th Supp. at 200.

[90] *United States-Restrictions on Imports of Tuna* (Aug. 16 1991, not adopted) GAIT B.I.S.D. (39th Supp.) at 1.

[91] ibid.

[92] *GATT Dispute Panel Report on U.S. Restrictions on Import of Tuna* (June 16 1994) 33 I.L.M. 839.

The latter members alleged that the United States had been instituting unfair restrictions on import of their oil under the guise of new environmental standards.[93]

The emerging legal picture from these decisions was not supportive of those championing environmental protection.[94] A restrictive interpretation of the "life or health" exception in paragraph (b) was being adopted. Additionally, serious restrictions were placed on the extraterritorial application of environmental measures.[95] Discriminatory measures designed to simplify environmental enforcement might be unjustified if alternative diplomatic solutions are not first explored.[96]

All of these decisions were leading many environmentalists around the world to worry that adequate protection of the environment was not possible within the existing framework of the WTO. It is in this context that the UN's work on environmental protection became more prominent and constructive. Perhaps related to this, the decision of the Appellate Body of the WTO in *Shrimp-Turtle*[97] introduced a healthy reconciliation between the opposing ideologies.

The Panel Report had favored an unusually restrictive interpretation of the contents of paragraphs (b) and (g) of Article XX by making them first subject to requirements of the *Chapeau.*[98] The Panel held that Article XX allowed WTO members to derogate from their GATT obligations only if they did so without undermining the WTO multilateral trading system:[99] any measure that undermines the system would constitute an abuse of that system and would violate Article XX.[100]

However, the Appellate Body declined to adopt the Panel's approach. While the Appellate Body rejected the United States' case on the grounds that the measures adopted by the United States were discriminatory insofar as they were "*rigid and unbending,*"[101] it nevertheless took a significant step toward enhancing the scope of the terms used in Article XX(g), reflecting its preference for an interpretation in tune with the evolving priorities of the international community as reflected in several UN environmental treaties. The Appellate Body found that Article XX(g) is not limited to the conservation of mineral or nonliving natural resources.[102] It held "*that 'exhaustible' natural resources and 'renewable' natural resources are mutually exclusive.... Living resources are just as 'finite' as petroleum, iron ore and other non-living resources.*"[103]

Interestingly, this conclusion was not based on an analysis of the paragraph's negotiating history, or a careful exegesis of its language in the context of Article XX. Instead, the

[93] *World Trade Organization: Report of the Panel in United States-Standards for Reformulated and Conventional Gasoline* (January 29, 1996) 35 I.L.M. 274. See also *World Trade Organization Appellate Body: Report of the Appellate Body in United States-Standards for Reformulated and Conventional Gasoline* (May 20 1996) 35 I.L.M. 603.

[94] Neuling (n 80). [95] ibid. [96] ibid.

[97] *World Trade Organization: United States-Import Prohibition of Certain Shrimp and Shrimp Products* (October 12, 1998) 38 I.L.M. 118 [hereinafter *Appellate Body Report I]; World Trade Organization: United States-Import Prohibition of Certain Shrimp and Shrimp Products* (May 15, 1998) 37 I.L.M. 832 [hereinafter *Dispute Panel Report I].*

[98] Dispute Panel Report I 844. [99] ibid. 849–50. See also Neuling (n 80).

[100] ibid. 849. [101] *Appellate Body Report I* (n 97) 156–68.

[102] Neuling (n 80). [103] *Appellate Body Report I* (n 97) 154.

Appellate Body considered that Article XX(g) had to be read in an evolutive manner, in particular taking into account new international norms, such as those included in UN treaties[104]:

> The words of Article XX(g), "exhaustible natural resources," were actually crafted more than 50 years ago. They must be read by a treaty interpreter in light of contemporary concerns of the community of nations about the protection and conservation of the environment... [T]he generic term "natural resources" in Article XX(g) is not "static" in its content or reference but is rather "by definition, evolutionary."[105]

Importantly, the Appellate Body emphasized the objective of "sustainable development"—which was launched by the 1992 United Nations Conference on Environment and Development—as explicitly acknowledged in the Preamble to the WTO Agreement.[106] It drew inspiration from the UN Convention on the Law of the Sea[107] and other UN instruments such as the UN Convention on Biological Diversity and Agenda 21 of the United Nations Conference on Environment and Development to conclude that the words "exhaustible natural resources" include both living and nonliving resources.

It is, thus, apparent that the UN—through its extensive work on environmental problems, and by developing and supporting treaties that addressed some of the major environmental challenges facing mankind—has at many levels counterbalanced restrictive interpretations of what GATT/WTO texts can mean in a significantly changing world. The UN, in serving as a platform for subsequent agreements in the environmental, health, and other fields, has inevitably qualified aging understandings of what constitutes an appropriate multilateral framework for trade. The Appellate Body's decision in *Shrimp-Turtle* reinforced a strong sense that as time moves on, so must interpretation of treaty law in many cases.[108]

5 Conclusion

The American economist Walter Black famously stated, "*[P]rotectionism is a misnomer. The only people protected by tariffs, quotas and trade restrictions are those engaged in uneconomic and wasteful activity. Free trade is the only philosophy compatible with international peace and prosperity.*" There is no doubt that in an ideal (if utopian) world, this philosophy could reign supreme. Unfortunately, our reality is inequality between countries, and between the relative influence of large corporations (and their national champions)

[104] ibid. Neuling (n. 80).
[105] *Appellate Body Report I* (n 97) 154–55.
[106] ibid 156. Neuling (n 80).
[107] Article 56, UN Convention on the Law of the Sea (December 10, 1982) U.N. Doc. A/Conf.62/122.
[108] ibid. *Appellate Body Report I* (n 97) 154–155.

and that of poorer nations. While we can certainly aspire to this standard, existing realities predispose countries and other actors in international trade to infringe upon it.

The "good opinion of mankind," as Thomas Jefferson noted, moves the world. That opinion has evolved considerably since WWII, and the creation of the WTO—doubtless more sensitive to a range of opinion around the world than was the GATT—has helped to update multilateral trade arrangements to reflect a new understanding of emerging concerns relating to problems undiscussed in 1946–1947.

However, status quo power fights back. The failure of the Doha round of WTO negotiations in Bali in 2013—a fate already clear from kinetic disagreements in Geneva in 2008—suggests that tensions between developing and industrialized countries remain lively within the international community.[109] The entire round has underscored a disconnect among varying political perceptions of how the modern reality of multisectoral trade and value chains increasingly combining goods and services can be governed multilaterally.[110] A great source of grievance for the developing world has been the perceived inability of the developed world to extend the benefit of market access or differential treatment to still-developing countries, in ways that would have led to their greater inclusion in multilateral trade.[111]

Deadlock in the Doha Round introduced what could be an extended period of uncertainty and disappointment, particularly in the developing world, with respect to the suddenly more fragile multilateral trade regime. Harking back to the early days of the UN, developing countries moreover experience the deadlock as a betrayal of the UN's initial promise and ideals.

Such circumstances only reinforce the relevance of the UN as a forum in which global opinion can truly be reflected, whereas the specialized world of multilateral trade arrangements has too often marginalized views from much of the world. The UN can serve as a platform from where a truly representative path to multilateral trade, inclusive of all aspirations, can be charted.

Primary examples of what the UN can achieve are the various International Commodity Agreements (ICAs) entered into between countries of varying regions through the efforts of UNCTAD. While all current ICAs are administrative in nature, they serve as a valuable forum for producer-consumer cooperation and consultations, market transparency, development projects, and sources of statistics.[112] These ICAs represent an attempt to offset acute price instabilities, which result in precipitous price rises and declines adversely affecting developing countries. For example, the International Coffee

[109] Frederik Erixon, "After the Bali Agreement: Lessons from the Doha Round for the WTO's Post-Bali Agenda" (2014) Policy Brief No. 2/2014, European Centre for International Political Economy <https://ecipe.org/wp-content/uploads/2014/12/PB02.pdf> accessed April 4, 2018.

[110] ibid. [111] ibid.

[112] Nishant Raj, "What Is the Role of UNCTAD in International Commodity Agreements?" <http://www.shareyouressays.com/knowledge/what-is-the-role-of-unctad-in-international-commodity-agreements/114420> accessed April 4, 2018. For a complete list of all ICAs, refer to <http://www.fao.org/fileadmin/templates/est/CCP/oewg/International_Commodity_Organisations_.pdf> accessed April 4, 2018.

Agreement[113] is believed to have had some effect in stabilizing world coffee prices, particularly since 1964, with the adoption of adjustable quotas that can be changed in light of price pressures.[114] It may also have succeeded in achieving higher export earnings for coffee-producing countries than they would have attained without the agreement.[115] Likewise, in April 2005, the International Agreement on Olive Oil and Table Olives was successfully renegotiated under the UN Olive Oil Conference.[116] Moreover, in January 2006, the fourth part of the UN Conference for the Negotiation of a Successor Agreement to the International Tropical Timber Agreement, 1994 resulted in the adoption of the 2006 International Tropical Agreement.[117]

Such concrete evidence of the UN's relevance and influence on trade and development—sometimes direct and sometimes subtle—reinforces its standing, particularly in developing countries. The UN continues to act as an inspiration in this respect. The ethos of sustainable development, based on inclusiveness and reciprocity and widely accepted and supported around the world, confirms this proposition.

[113] International Coffee Agreement 2007 (entered into force on 2 February 2011) <http://www.ico.org/documents/ica2007e.pdf> accessed April 4, 2018.

[114] Vernon L Sorenson, "Trade and International Commodity Programs," (1968) Michigan State University <https://ageconsearch.umn.edu/bitstream/17862/1/ar680085.pdf> accessed April 4, 2018.

[115] ibid. [116] Raj (n 112). [117] ibid.

CHAPTER 15

CULTURE

TULLIO SCOVAZZI

THE treaties of global scope concluded to date in the field of culture[1] aim at bringing two fundamental messages. First, culture contributes to the maintenance of peace. Second, the protection and promotion of culture is a general interest of the international community as a whole.

As outlined in Article 1, paragraph 2, of the Charter, one of the purposes of the United Nations is to achieve international cooperation in solving international problems of cultural character. The United Nations is furthermore required, under Article 55 of the Charter, to promote, inter alia, international cultural and educational cooperation, with a view to the creation of conditions of stability and well-being that are necessary for peaceful and friendly relations among nations based on respect for the principle of equal rights and self-determination of peoples.[2] The drafters of the Charter agreed that the mandate of the United Nations, established primarily for maintaining international peace and security, should also include those conditions—economic, social, and cultural—that are necessary to the existence of a viable peace.[3]

Most of the world treaties in the field of culture have been concluded within the framework of the United Nations Educational Scientific and Cultural Organization

[1] The references given hereunder are limited to a few volumes of general character: Barbara T. Hoffman (ed), *Art and Cultural Heritage. Law, Policy and Practice* (CUP 2006); Abdulqawi Yusuf (ed), *Standard-Setting in UNESCO* (UNESCO-Martinus Nijhoff 2007); James AR Nafziger and Tullio Scovazzi (eds), *The Cultural Heritage of Mankind* (Martinus Nijhoff 2008); James AR Nafgizer and Ann M Nicgorski, (eds), *Cultural Heritage Issues: The Legacy of Conquest, Colonization, and Commerce* (Martinus Nijhoff 2009); Toshiyuki Kono (ed), *The Impact of Uniform Laws on the Protection of Cultural Heritage and the Preservation of Cultural Heritage in the 21st Century* (Martinus Nijhoff 2010); Silvia Borelli and Federico Lenzerini (eds), *Cultural Heritage, Cultural Rights, Cultural Diversity* (Martinus Nijhoff 2012); Francesco Francioni and James Gordley (eds), *Enforcing International Cultural Heritage Law* (OUP 2013).

[2] See also art 13, para 1 *b*; art 55; art 57, para 1, and art 73, *a*. The words "cultural" or "culture" appear five times in the UN Charter.

[3] See Leland M Goodrich and Edward Hambro, *Charter of the United Nations—Commentary and Documents* (Stevens & Sons 1949) 319.

(UNESCO), an international organization linked to the United Nations by a relationship agreement (UN specialized agency), concluded in 1946.

1 The Concept of Cultural Heritage

The Constitution of UNESCO, adopted in 1945, provides, in its Article I, paragraph 1, that the purpose of this specialized agency is to contribute to peace and security by promoting collaboration among the nations through education, science, and culture in order to further universal respect for justice, the rule of law, human rights, and fundamental freedoms. The close relationship between peace and culture is clearly set forth in the preamble of the UNESCO Constitution, whereby states parties declare

> That since wars begin in the minds of men, it is in the minds of men that the defences of peace must be constructed;
>
> That ignorance of each other's ways and lives has been a common cause, throughout the history of mankind, of that suspicion and mistrust between the peoples of the world through which their differences have all too often broken into war; [...]
>
> That a peace based exclusively upon the political and economic arrangements of governments would not be a peace which could secure the unanimous, lasting and sincere support of the peoples of the world, and that the peace must therefore be founded, if it is not to fail, upon the intellectual and moral solidarity of mankind.

The concept of "cultural heritage" can be understood in many different meanings. To realize its purposes, UNESCO is called upon, inter alia, to maintain, increase, and diffuse knowledge "by assuring the conservation and protection of the world's inheritance of books, works of art and monuments of history and science, and recommending to the nations concerned the necessary international conventions" (Article I, paragraph 2(*c*), UNESCO Constitution). However, at the World Conference on Cultural Policies, convened by UNESCO and held at Mexico City in 1982, states agreed to give the concept of cultural heritage a quite broader meaning, as the expression of the spirituality and creativity of men and peoples:

> The cultural heritage of a people includes the works of its artists, architects, musicians, writers and scientists and also the work of anonymous artists, expressions of the people's spirituality, and the body of values which give meaning to life. It includes both tangible and intangible works through which the creativity of that people finds expression: languages, rites, beliefs, historic places and monuments, literature, works of art, archives and libraries" (paragraph 23 of the Mexico City Declaration on Cultural Policies).[4]

[4] At the World Conference on Cultural Policies "delegates found agreement in understanding culture not in the restricted sense of *belles-lettres*, the fine arts, literature and philosophy, but as the totality of the distinctive and specific features of the ways of thinking and organizing the lives of every individual and every community" (*From Ideas to Actions—70 Years of UNESCO* (UNESCO 2015) 111).

The adoption in the first years of the twenty-first century of three new cultural conventions within the framework of UNESCO is a sign of a continued trend toward widening the concept of cultural heritage.[5]

Besides its intrinsic value, as the expression of spirituality and creativity, cultural heritage has also an economic dimension. It offers important opportunities for generating sustainable development, including through cultural activities and tourism. It may be difficult to strike a fair balance between the intrinsic and the economic aspects of cultural heritage. For instance, it has been remarked that commercialization of elements of the intangible cultural heritage[6] is not a priori a disqualifying factor, highlighting the vital role of this heritage as a factor of economic development in some communities. However, as excessive commercialization could distort traditional cultural customs or expressions, it is necessary that such processes remain under the control of the communities that create and transmit the heritage and not of private companies.[7]

Both the high participation of states in most of the UNESCO cultural treaties and international practice in general confirm that many of the provisions included in them have today become part of customary international law.[8] Despite the political vicissitudes that have affected UNESCO in recent years,[9] the continued importance of its mandate and achievements in the area of treaty-making in the cultural field remains undoubted.

2 The Protection of Cultural Heritage during Conflicts

The Convention for the Protection of Cultural Property in the Event of Armed Conflict, adopted in The Hague in 1954 ("the 1954 Convention")[10] is the first treaty relating to cultural heritage concluded within the framework of UNESCO. In the preamble of the

[5] The concept is even broader if the International Convention against Doping in Sport (Paris, 2005) is considered. Sport is seen in this convention "as a means to promote education, health, development and peace" (preamble).

[6] For this kind of heritage see para 3.4 of this Chapter.

[7] UNESCO, Subsidiary Body for the Examination of Nominations to the Representative List of the Intangible Cultural Heritage of Humanity, Report by the Rapporteur, doc. ITH/09/4.COM/CONF.209/INF.6 (26 August 2009) 6.

[8] As it has been remarked by Francesco Francioni ("The Evolving Framework for the Protection of Cultural Heritage in International Law" in Borelli and Lenzerini (n 1) 25), the current framework of the international protection of cultural heritage "is constituted largely of treaty law and to a smaller extent of soft law instruments mostly adopted within UNESCO. However, based on careful examination of international practice, it can be argued that some general principles have formed, or are in process of being formed, as part of general international law with regard to the obligation to respect and protect cultural heritage of significant importance."

[9] UNESCO was the first United Nations agency to admit the State of Palestine (31 October 2011). "Unfortunately, the decision to admit Palestine as a member with full rights triggered a major financial crisis at UNESCO as the United States decided to withhold its contributions" (*From Ideas* (n. 4) 207). In 2017, the United States notified its decision to withdraw from UNESCO, taking effect on December 31, 2018.

[10] 133 states are today (January 2019) parties to the 1954 Convention.

1954 Convention, the parties recognize that cultural property has suffered grave damage during recent armed conflicts and that, because of the developments in the technique of warfare, it is in increasing danger of destruction. They also emphasize that the preservation of the cultural heritage is of great importance for all peoples of the world and declare themselves convinced "that damage to cultural property belonging to any people whatsoever means damage to the cultural heritage of all mankind, since each people makes its contribution to the culture of the world."

The 1954 Convention requires states parties to refrain from acts of hostility directed against cultural properties and from any use of such properties for purposes that are likely to expose them to destruction or damage in the event of armed conflict. Any form of theft, pillage, misappropriation, and vandalism of cultural property is prohibited. The First Protocol, which was adopted on the same day as the Convention,[11] prohibits the export of cultural properties from an occupied territory and binds parties to return such properties at the close of hostilities in the event that they have been exported.

The obligation to refrain from any act of hostility directed against cultural property may be waived only in cases where military necessity imperatively requires such a waiver. Special protection is granted to a limited number of refuges intended to shelter movable cultural property in the event of armed conflict and of centers containing monuments and other immovable cultural property of very great importance, provided that they have been entered in the International Register of Cultural Property under Special Protection, held by UNESCO. States parties are required to ensure the immunity of cultural property under special protection from any act of hostility. Such immunity may be withdrawn only in exceptional cases of unavoidable military necessity, and only for such time as that necessity continues. Moreover, an even stronger protection—although not amounting to absolute immunity from acts of warfare—is granted to properties that have been included in the List of Cultural Property under Enhanced Protection, as established under the Second Protocol (The Hague, 1999)[12] to the 1954 Convention. The conceptual nuances between "protection," "special protection," and "enhanced protection" show the inherent difficulties encountered in any attempt to find a balance between the needs of cultural heritage, on one hand, and those of so-called military necessity, on the other.

The customary obligation to return cultural properties that have been removed as a consequence of conflicts[13] has been confirmed by the United Nations Security Council. Under resolution 1483 (2003) of 22 May 2003, the Council decided that all member states were bound to

[11] 110 States are today parties to the First Protocol.

[12] Today 82 states are parties to the Second Protocol, which was concluded "considering that the rules governing the protection of cultural property in the event of armed conflict should reflect developments in international law."

[13] This obligation finds a solid basis in the Regulations concerning the Laws and Customs on Land, annexed to the Fourth Hague Convention (1907); the treaties of peace adopted after World War II; the fourth Geneva Convention on the protection of civilian persons in time of war (1949); and in several elements of international practice.

> take appropriate steps to facilitate the safe return to Iraqi institutions of Iraqi cultural property and other items of archaeological, historical, cultural, rare scientific, and religious importance illegally removed from the Iraq National Museum, the National Library, and other locations in Iraq since the adoption of Resolution 661 (1990) of 6 August 1990 [...)] (para. 7).

Such an obligation was restated and enlarged by resolution 2199 (2015) of 12 February 2015, whereby the Security Council also noted with concern

> that ISIL [the Islamic State in Iraq and the Levant], ANF [the Al-Nusrah Front] and other individuals, groups, undertakings and entities associated with Al-Qaida, are generating income from engaging directly or indirectly in the looting and smuggling of cultural heritage items from archaeological sites, museums, libraries, archives, and other sites in Iraq and Syria, which is being used to support their recruitment efforts and strengthen their operational capability to organize and carry out terrorist attacks (para. 16).

Recently, under resolution 2347 (2017) of 24 March 2017, the Council took a further step, by pointing out the existence of a vicious circle. It explicitly stated that the destruction and looting of cultural properties, besides being a likely consequence of war, can also be in itself a cause of war. The Council emphasized

> that the unlawful destruction of cultural heritage, and the looting and smuggling of cultural property in the event of armed conflicts, notably by terrorist groups, and the attempt to deny historical roots and cultural diversity in this context can fuel and exacerbate conflict and hamper post-conflict national reconciliation, thereby undermining the security, stability, governance, social, economic and cultural development of affected States (preamble).

The first two above-mentioned Security Council resolutions were adopted under Chapter VII of the Charter (action with respect to threats to the peace, breaches of the peace, and acts of aggression).

3 Culture as a General Interest of the International Community

Besides the 1954 Convention, the other UNESCO cultural treaties are also based on the assumption that the protection and promotion of cultural properties is not only an obligation for the state in whose territory they are located, as they represent its history and identity, but also represents a general interest of the international community as a whole. Through the adoption of these treaties, which are described hereinafter, states parties have recognized culture as a common heritage of humankind.

3.1 International Movements of Cultural Properties

The preamble of the Convention on the Means of Prohibiting and Preventing the Illicit Import, Export and Transfer of Ownership of Cultural Property (Paris, 1970)[14] recalls that, in order to avert the dangers posed by theft, clandestine excavation, and illicit export of cultural properties, "it is essential for every State to become increasingly alive to the moral obligations to respect its own cultural heritage and that of all nations."

The 1970 Convention stresses that "cultural property constitutes one of the basic elements of civilization and national culture, and that its true value can be appreciated only in relation to the fullest possible information regarding its origin, history and traditional setting" (preamble). As was pointed out as early as the end of the eighteenth century by Quatremère de Quincy, to remove one element from its original cultural context could be the equivalent of destroying it ("diviser, c'est détruire").[15] This is particularly evident for archaeological properties, as their looting implies the destruction of the site, the loss of information, and the dispersion of irreplaceable and finite artifacts. For instance, when an object is stolen from a tomb, not only can it be damaged forever, but the site is also disrupted. Even where the object is taken away intact, it is uprooted from the context in which it belongs, losing its identity and real meaning. The other objects in the same setting, which have been left by the looters either deliberately or by chance, also lose their original significance, as it becomes impossible to reconstruct the whole context that has been altered in its true composition.

However, it seems that the substantive part of the 1970 Convention does not correspond to the ambitious objectives set forth in its preamble. The obligations of the importing state do not match those of the exporting state. While the latter is bound to prohibit the export of cultural objects not accompanied by an export certificate, the former is not required to prohibit the import of such objects if not accompanied by such a certificate. The obligation to return cultural objects is limited to those that have been stolen from museums or similar institutions, without covering cases where private individuals or entities have been the victims of the crime. The return is also subject to payment of just compensation to an innocent purchaser or to a person who has valid title to the property (Article 7, *b*, ii). Illegally excavated archaeological objects appear to be excluded from the application of the 1970 Convention, as states parties are bound to take appropriate steps to recover and return cultural objects stolen from a museum or a religious or secular public monument or similar institution in another state party, "provided that such property is documented as appertaining to the inventory of that institution." But there are no inventories underground.

[14] 138 states, including both states of origin and states of destination of cultural properties, are today parties to this Convention.

[15] Antoine Quatremère de Quincy, *Lettres sur le préjudice qu'occasionneroient aux arts et à la science, le déplacement des monumens de l'art de l'Italie, le démembrement de ses écoles, et la spoliation de ses collections, galeries, musées, etc.* (Rome 1815; published for the first time in 1796).

To date, attempts to improve and update the 1970 Convention have produced no results.[16]

The 1970 Convention is complemented by the UNIDROIT Convention on Stolen or Illegally Exported Cultural Objects (Rome, 1995)[17] which primarily deals with the private law aspects of illegal movements of cultural properties. The UNIDROIT Convention represents a more advanced instrument, providing enhanced protection to the interests of the original owners of removed cultural properties. For instance, Article 4, paragraph 1 of this Convention stipulates that the possessor of a stolen cultural object required to return it shall be entitled, at the time of its restitution, to payment of fair and reasonable compensation only if he neither knew nor ought reasonably to have known that the object was stolen, and can prove that he exercised due diligence when acquiring the object.[18] However, the UNIDROIT convention has so far been ratified by only a limited number of states.[19]

In cases not covered by the relevant conventions, including those where the movement of cultural properties has taken place before the entry into force of any treaty applicable to the states involved, present international practice shows that an evolutionary trend is developing in customary international law.[20] According to this trend, claims relating to the return of removed cultural properties should be addressed by the states concerned in order to achieve an equitable solution, taking into account all the relevant circumstances, such as, inter alia:

- the factors surrounding the removal of the cultural property from the state of origin, in particular the legality of the removal under the law of the state of origin or the substantive injustice of the removal in the light of ethical principles;
- the importance of the cultural property for the state of origin, in particular its emblematic character;
- the harm to the integrity of the cultural context from which the cultural property was removed;

[16] Notable for their advanced character are the Operational Guidelines for the implementation of the 1970 Convention, adopted by consensus in 2015 by the Meeting of States Parties. They not only aim "to strengthen and facilitate the implementation of the Convention," but are also intended "to identify ways and means to further the achievement of the goals of the Convention through strengthened international cooperation." In fact, the Guidelines provide advanced interpretations to the most important provisions of the 1970 Convention. However, they do not have a binding character.

[17] The Convention was negotiated within the framework of the International Institute for the Unification of Private Law.

[18] Under Article 4, paragraph 4, "in determining whether the possessor exercised due diligence, regard shall be had to all the circumstances of the acquisition, including the character of the parties, the price paid, whether the possessor consulted any reasonably accessible register of stolen cultural objects, and any other relevant information and documentation which it could reasonably have obtained, and whether the possessor consulted accessible agencies or took any other step that a reasonable person would have taken in the circumstances."

[19] 45 states are today parties to this Convention.

[20] For some instances see Tullio Scovazzi, "'Diviser c'est détruire": Ethical Principles and Legal Rules in the Field of Return of Cultural Property" (2011) *Rivista di Diritto Internazionale* 341.

- the amount of time since the cultural property was removed from the state of origin;
- the appreciation for and the care used to preserve the cultural property by the state of destination;
- the state of origin's commitment to care for the preservation of the cultural property if it is returned to it.

3.2 World Cultural Heritage

According to the preamble of the Convention Concerning the Protection of the World Cultural and Natural Heritage (Paris, 1972),[21] "the deterioration or disappearance of any item of the cultural or natural heritage constitutes a harmful impoverishment of the heritage of all the nations of the world." For this reason, "in view of the magnitude and gravity of the new dangers threatening them, it is incumbent on the international community as a whole to participate in the protection of the cultural and natural heritage of outstanding universal value, by the granting of collective assistance which, although not taking the place of action by the State concerned, will serve as an effective complement thereto."

The 1972 Convention applies to both cultural and the natural heritage. The former is defined for the purposes of this instrument as including only immovable properties, such as monuments,[22] groups of buildings,[23] and sites.[24]

The 1972 Convention has an exclusive character, insofar as it applies to properties that have an "outstanding universal value." As pointed out in the Operational Guidelines for its implementation, the 1972 Convention "is not intended to ensure the protection of all properties of great interest, importance or value, but only for a select list of the most outstanding of these from an international viewpoint" (Op. Guid. 52). The concept of outstanding universal value is defined as "cultural and/or natural significance which is so exceptional as to transcend national boundaries and to be of common importance for present and future generations of all humanity" (Op. Guid. 49).

The 1972 Convention sets forth two lists, namely the World Heritage List and the List of World Heritage in Danger. On the basis of a decision of the World Heritage Committee,[25] properties of "outstanding universal value" can be entered on either of the

[21] Hereinafter: 1972 Convention. 193 states are today parties to it.

[22] Defined as "architectural works, works of monumental sculpture and painting, elements or structures of an archaeological nature, inscriptions, cave dwellings and combinations of features, which are of outstanding universal value from the point of view of history, art or science" (art 1).

[23] Defined as "groups of separate or connected buildings which, because of their architecture, their homogeneity or their place in the landscape, are of outstanding universal value from the point of view of history, art or science" (art 1).

[24] Defined as "works of man or the combined works of nature and of man, and areas including archaeological sites which are of outstanding universal value from the historical, aesthetic, ethnological or anthropological points of view" (art 1).

[25] The World Heritage Committee, which has been established by the 1972 Convention, is composed of 21 states parties.

two lists if they meet a number of criteria established by the World Heritage Committee,[26] comply with the conditions of authenticity and integrity, and have an adequate protection and management system. The properties that may be entered on the List of World Heritage in Danger are those threatened by serious and specific dangers, such as "the threat of disappearance caused by accelerated deterioration, large-scale public or private projects or rapid urban or tourist development projects; destruction caused by changes in the use or ownership of the land; major alterations due to unknown causes; abandonment for any reason whatsoever; the outbreak or the threat of an armed conflict; calamities and cataclysms; serious fires, earthquakes, landslides; volcanic eruptions; changes in water level, floods, and tidal waves" (Article 11, paragraph 4). The 1972 Convention has established a World Heritage Fund to be used for purposes determined by the World Heritage Committee, with priority given to those properties included in the List of World Heritage in Danger.

To date (January 2019), 1,092 properties have been entered on the lists (845 cultural, 209 natural, and 38 mixed), 54 of which are on the List of World Heritage in Danger. As the records of its activities shows, the World Heritage Committee faces a significant challenge in establishing and maintaining a World Heritage List that is adequately representative, balanced, and credible.

The 1972 Convention seeks to achieve a balance between the interest of individual states and the interest of humankind. On the one hand, the inclusion of a property in the World Heritage List requires the consent of the state on the territory of which it is located (Article 11, paragraph. 4). On the other, the inclusion of a property on the List of the World Heritage in Danger and the removal of it from either of the two lists can be decided by the World Heritage Committee even without the consent of the territorial state. In particular, the removal from the World Heritage List can be seen as a moral sanction in cases where it is the consequence of a deliberate action by the state concerned affecting the outstanding universal value of the property. So far, the World Heritage Committee removed two properties from the World Heritage List, namely the natural property "Arabian Oryx Sanctuary" (Oman), in 2007, due to the reduction of the size of the protected area by 90 percent, as well as the cultural property "Dresden Elbe Valley" (Germany), in 2009, due to the construction of a four-lane bridge within it.

The World Heritage Committee monitors the actions taken by states parties in application of the 1972 Convention and the state of the conservation of listed properties through the review of periodic reports that states parties are required to submit. A special process of so-called reactive monitoring is also provided for in the Operational Guidelines.[27]

It should be noted that the listing of a property in the World Heritage List may also have an effect on the gravity of the sentences imposed on individuals for war crimes in international criminal proceedings. This was the case of Miodrag Jokić and Pavle Strugar, convicted by the International Criminal Tribunal for the former Yugoslavia for

[26] See Op Guid 77. [27] See ibid 169–76.

the bombing of the Old City of Dubrovnik in Croatia,[28] and of Ahmad Al Faqi Al Mahdi, convicted by the International Criminal Court for the destruction of mausoleums in Timbuktu in Mali.[29]

3.3 The Underwater Cultural Heritage

The Convention on the Protection of the Underwater Cultural Heritage (Paris, 2001) ("the 2001 Convention") acknowledges in its preamble the importance of underwater cultural heritage as an integral part of the cultural heritage of humanity, and a particularly important element in the history of peoples, nations, and their relations with each other. It follows that the responsibility of preserving and protecting this heritage rests with all states.

The 2001 Convention sets forth a legal framework for the prevention of the looting of properties, which, if located beyond the 12-mile limit of the territorial sea, can be the result of the application of the traditional regime of freedom of the high seas. The key challenge in this regard stems from a provision (Article 303, paragraph 3) in the United Nations Convention on the Law of the Sea (Montego Bay, 1982) which, at least in the English official text, subjects the duty to protect objects of an archaeological and historical nature found at sea to "the law of salvage and other rules of admiralty." In a number of common law countries, and in particular in the United States, admiralty law has been enlarged by court decisions to cover also activities related to ships that have been lost for hundreds or thousands of years, together with their cargo. In particular, the law of salvage gives the salvor a lien (or right in rem) over the wreck, and the law of finds allows a person who discovers a wreck that has been abandoned to become its owner. This in practice corresponds to a first-come-first-served approach that only plays in favor of the commercial interest of private treasure hunters, and neither ensures the preservation of the heritage for the benefit of humankind nor takes into consideration the special position of states that have a link with that heritage.

With the aim of preventing the looting of the heritage, the 2001 Convention provides, in general terms, that states parties are bound to "preserve underwater cultural heritage for the benefit of humanity" (Article 2, paragraph 3) and that "underwater cultural heritage shall not be commercially exploited" (Article 2, paragraph 7), as this is fundamentally incompatible with the protection and proper management of it (Rule 2 of the Annex). In order to facilitate decision-making on how best to protect the heritage, the 2001 Convention sets forth a procedural mechanism that seeks to ensure cooperation among those states with a verifiable link to the heritage, involving three steps (reporting, consultations, and urgent measures).

[28] *Prosecutor v Jokić* (Sentencing Judgment) IT-01-42/1-S, T Ch I (18 March 2004) and *Prosecutor v Jokić* (Judgment on Sentencing Appeal) IT-01-42/1-A, App Ch (30 August 2005); *Prosecutor v Strugar* (Judgment) IT-01-42-T, T Ch II (31 January 2005) and *Prosecutor v Strugar* (Judgment) IT-01-42-A, App Ch (17 July 2008).

[29] *Prosecutor v. Al Mahdi* (Judgment and Sentence) ICC-01-/12-01/15, Tr Ch VIII (27 September 2016).

Regrettably, the message of cooperation for the protection of an endangered cultural heritage coming from the 2001 Convention is not yet shared by a sufficiently high number of states.[30]

3.4 The Intangible Cultural Heritage

The Convention for the Safeguarding of the Intangible Cultural Heritage (Paris, 2003)[31] was negotiated to fill a gap within the UNESCO legal instruments in this field and aims in particular at placing due emphasis on an aspect of cultural heritage that, although not as "tangible" as buildings or natural sites, is equally important "as a mainspring of cultural diversity and a guarantee of sustainable development" and deserves to be safeguarded in the "general interest to humanity" (preamble). The heritage addressed here is that of "the practices, representations, expressions, knowledge, skills—as well as the instruments, objects, artefacts and cultural spaces associated therewith—that communities, groups and, in some cases, individuals recognize as part of their cultural heritage" (Article 2, paragraph 1). It is manifested in a number of domains, such as oral traditions and expressions, including language as a vehicle of the intangible cultural heritage, performing arts, social practices, rituals and festive events, knowledge and practices concerning nature and the universe, and traditional craftsmanship (Article 2, paragraph 2).

The parties to the 2003 Convention recognize that the processes of globalization and social transformation, while creating conditions for renewed dialogue among communities, "also give rise, as does the phenomenon of intolerance, to grave threats of deterioration, disappearance and destruction of the intangible cultural heritage" (preamble). Apart from its cultural dimension, the intangible cultural heritage also involves other fundamental values, such as the respect of human rights of the communities that create, maintain, and transmit the heritage, especially those of indigenous peoples and minority groups, and the preservation of the natural environment. It is important to recall that the 2003 Convention takes into consideration solely the heritage that "is compatible with existing international human rights instruments, as well as with the requirements of mutual respect among communities, groups and individuals, and of sustainable development" (Article 2, paragraph 1).[32]

The 2003 Convention establishes two lists, namely the Representative List of the Intangible Cultural Heritage of Humanity and the List of Intangible Cultural Heritage in Need of Urgent Safeguarding. A third list is also drawn up to include the national, subregional, and regional programs, projects, and activities for the safeguarding of the heritage that best reflect the principles and objectives of the 2003 Convention (so-called "best practices"). The Intergovernmental Committee for the Safeguarding of the Intangible Cultural Heritage is established under the 2003 Convention with responsibility

[30] The 2001 Convention is today in force for 60 states.

[31] Hereinafter: 2003 Convention. It is today in force for 178 states.

[32] Obviously practices, such as female genital mutilation, however traditional they might be, cannot be protected under the Convention.

for examining the proposals submitted by states parties for addition to the lists. The Committee has so far entered 508 elements in the lists (429 in the representative list, 59 in the urgent safeguarding list, and 20 in the best practices list).

The social and evolving character of intangible cultural heritage gives rise to complex questions. For instance, it may be asked to what extent activities of recreation, reinterpretation, or revitalization of such heritage are not admissible because they result in changes in its substance. Natural transformation does not mean artificial alteration, even though many variations can be found between one extreme and the other.[33]

During the negotiations for the 2003 Convention it was agreed that the crucial question of the relationship between intangible cultural heritage and intellectual property rights falls within the mandate of the World Intellectual Property Organization (WIPO).[34] However, the way in which the main intellectual property rights have been conceived and formulated in national legislation and international instruments seems to be in conflict with many of the peculiarities of the intangible cultural heritage and with the needs of the communities that create and transmit such heritage, especially the indigenous communities.[35] For instance, the requirement of novelty under intellectual property law cannot apply to most of the manifestations of intangible heritage that are based on the transmission of practices and knowledge from generation to generation. The granting of intellectual property rights to a specific person seems equally inappropriate for cultural manifestations that are often expressed in a collective way and are considered by the practitioners themselves as belonging to a whole community. The temporary limits of the rights granted to the holder of a patent do not comply with the permanent character of a heritage that often has deep social or religious roots and is not intended to fall into the public domain after the expiration of a given time. Furthermore, the cost itself of obtaining a patent may discourage traditional holders of intangible cultural heritage from initiating the relevant procedures.

3.5 Cultural Diversity

The Convention on the Protection and Promotion of the Diversity of Cultural Expressions (Paris, 2005) ("the 2005 Convention")[36] starts from the assumption that "cultural diversity

[33] Very interesting is the element "Gule Wamkulu," inscribed in the Representative List by Malawi, Mozambique, and Zambia. It is a dance where, in a rather unexpected manner and as a clear demonstration of the passing of time, the dancers wear costumes and masks representing wild animals, spirits of the dead, and slave traders, as well as motorcycles and helicopters.

[34] Article 3, paragraph b, clearly provides that nothing in the Convention may be interpreted as affecting the rights and obligations of states parties deriving from any international instrument relating to intellectual property rights or to the use of biological and ecological resources to which they are parties.

[35] According to the Model Provisions for National Laws on the Protection of Expressions of Folklore against Illicit Exploitation and Other Prejudicial Actions, adopted in 1982 by UNESCO and WIPO, there is a need for protection of such expressions against "(i) use without authorization; (ii) violation of the obligation to indicate the sources of folklore expressions; (iii) misleading the public by distributing counterfeit objects as folklore creations, and (iv) the public use of distorted or mutilated folklore creations in a manner prejudicial to the cultural interests of the community concerned."

[36] The 2005 Convention is today in force for 145 states.

forms a common heritage of humanity and should be cherished and preserved for the benefit of all" and that "cultural diversity creates a rich and varied world, which increases the range of choices and nurtures human capacities and values, and therefore is a mainspring for sustainable development for communities, peoples and nations" (preamble). The process of globalization, while facilitating the rapid development of information and communication technologies and affording unprecedented conditions for enhanced interaction between cultures, also represents "a challenge for cultural diversity, namely in view of risks of imbalances between rich and poor countries." For these reasons, states parties to the 2005 Convention recognize "the need to take measures to protect the diversity of cultural expressions, including their contents, especially in situations where cultural expressions may be threatened by the possibility of extinction or serious impairment."

According to Article 4, paragraph 1 of the 2005 Convention, "cultural diversity" refers to the manifold ways in which the cultures of groups and societies find expressions that are passed on within and among groups and societies. Cultural diversity is made manifest not only through the varied ways in which the cultural heritage of humanity is expressed, augmented, and transmitted, but also through diverse modes of artistic creation, production, dissemination, distribution, and enjoyment, whatever the means and technologies used.

The 2005 Convention tries to strike a balance between the two main "souls" of cultural expressions. They must not be treated as solely having a commercial value,[37] as they also have a cultural nature, conveying identities, values, and meanings. If there are special situations where cultural expressions on the territory of a state party are at risk of extinction, under serious threat, or otherwise in need of urgent safeguarding, the state concerned is allowed to take all appropriate measures to protect and preserve such cultural expressions (Article 8). Whether this provision is compatible with the obligations arising from treaties promoting the free movement of goods and services is open to debate. Article 20 addresses the thorny issue of the relationship between the 2005 Convention and other treaties, and is based on the criteria of mutual supportiveness, complementarity, and non-subordination. However, the lack of clarity of this provision has been criticized by some states:

> Under the provisions of the convention as drafted, any State, in the name of cultural diversity, might invoke the ambiguous provisions of this convention to try to assert a right to erect trade barriers to goods or services that are deemed to be cultural expressions. That term, "cultural expressions", has never been clearly defined and therefore is open to wide misinterpretation. Such protectionism would be detrimental to the free exchange of ideas and images. It could also impair the world trading system and hurt exporters of all countries.[38]

[37] The commercial character of cultural activities, goods, and services explains why the European Union was an active participant in the negotiations for the 2005 Convention, which is open to the accession also by regional economic integration organizations.

[38] Statement of 17 October 2005 by the United States representative, Mrs. Oliver, quoted in Scovazzi, "La notion de patrimoine culturel de l'humanité dans les instruments internationaux" in Nafgizer and Scovazzi (n 1) 113.

4 Concluding Remarks

Some gaps can be identified among the subject matters covered by the treaties of world scale of application so far adopted within the framework of UNESCO. For instance, no convention has been negotiated with respect to the preservation of languages in danger of disappearance.[39] In other areas, where the adoption of a treaty has not proven feasible, soft-law instruments have been adopted within UNESCO. This is the case of the Declaration concerning the Intentional Destruction of Cultural Heritage, adopted in 2003 by the UNESCO General Conference. It recalls the tragic destruction of the Buddhas of Bamiyan, Afghanistan, which affected the international community as a whole.

As regards intentional destruction of cultural property, there is an evident gap and inconsistency in the list of crimes of the individual provided for under the 1998 Rome Statute of the International Criminal Court. It is not clear why "intentionally directing attacks against buildings dedicated to religion, education, art, science or charitable purposes, historic monuments, hospitals and places where the sick and wounded are collected, provided they are not military objectives" is established as a war crime (Article 8, paragraph 2, *b*, ix, and Article 8, para. 2, *e*, iv),[40] while the widespread or systematic destruction of cultural properties in time of peace is not considered as a crime against humanity.

It should also be noted that at least two instruments, namely the above-mentioned UNIDROIT Convention[41] and 2001 Convention,[42] have not yet received the sufficiently widespread acceptance from states that they would deserve.

But these challenges should not obscure two fundamental messages to be drawn, in a clear and coherent manner, from the mandates and activities of the United Nations and UNESCO in the field of culture, as reflected in the treaties of global scope adopted within the framework of UNESCO. First, culture contributes to the maintenance of peace. Second, the protection and promotion of culture is a general interest of the international community as a whole.

[39] However, the 2005 Convention applies in general also to languages, as a manifestation of cultural diversity.

[40] The two provisions respectively cover conflicts of an international character and conflicts not of an international character. Their wording is taken from Article 27 of the Annex to the Convention with respect to the Laws and Customs of War on Land (The Hague, 1899). In fact, this wording needs today some updating.

[41] This Chapter, para 3.1.

[42] Ibid para 3.3.

CHAPTER 16

THE PRACTICE OF UN TREATY-MAKING CONCERNING SCIENCE

SAM JOHNSTON

SCIENCE has long played an important role in international affairs. Throughout the Cold War, scientific organizations were essential conduits for informal discussion of nuclear issues between the United States and the Soviet Union. Today, science offers alternative channels of engagement for countries facing political challenges.[1]

The importance of science in international affairs has reflected its importance in society more generally. The information and communication revolution of the last couple of decades is but one of many significant impacts science has had on society recently.

Another measure of this growing impact is the shift from tangible assets or physical capital to intangible assets or scientific, intellectual, or knowledge-based capital. For example, corporate assets in the S&P 500, which were 95 percent tangible assets and 5 percent intangible assets in 1978, had become 20 percent tangible assets and 80 percent intangible assets by 2010.[2]

Science is also becoming more internationalized. The United Kingdom's Royal Society estimates that over 35 percent of all scientific articles were internationally coauthored in 2011, up from 25 percent in 1996.[3] According to the United States National Science Foundation, between 2004 and 2014, the percentage of publications with authors from multiple countries rose from 30 percent to 35 percent.[4]

[1] Royal Society, *New Frontiers in Science Diplomacy, Navigating the Changing Balance of Power* (Royal Society 2010); Paul Arthur Berkman, Michael A Lang, David WH Walton, and Oran R Young, *Science diplomacy: Antarctica, and the Governance of International Spaces* (Smithsonian Institution Scholarly Press 2011); and http://ec.europa.eu/research/iscp/index.cfm?pg=iran accessed January 18, 2019.

[2] Cate Elsten and Nick Hill, "Intangible Asset Market Value Study?" (2017) 52 Les Nouvelles—J Licensing Executives Soc'y, available at <https://ssrn.com/abstract=3009783> and Ocean Tomo, LLC, "Annual Study of Intangible Asset Market Value from Ocean Tomo, LLC," available at http://www.oceantomo.com/2015/03/04/2015-intangible-asset-market-value-study/ accessed January 18, 2019.

[3] Royal Society (n 1).

[4] See <https://www.nsf.gov/statistics/2018/nsf18300/overview.htm> accessed January 18, 2019.

Science and technology feature prominently in the Sustainable Development Goals (SDGs). There are 17 SDGs that group together 169 targets, 15 of which explicitly refer to "science" and "technology," and another 34 relate to issues that are largely technologically or scientifically orientated. There are also significant scientific and technological dimensions to the other remaining 120 targets. The 48 targets that are most closely related to science and technology relate to three goals: (1) developing science and technology, (2) promoting access to science and technology, and (3) developing global effective innovation systems. The General Assembly launched the United Nations (UN) interagency task team on science, technology, and innovation for the SDGs to "promote coordination, coherence and cooperation within the UN system on science, technology and innovation-related matters, enhancing synergy and efficiency, in particular to enhance capacity-building initiatives." The *Global Sustainable Development Report* aims to strengthen the science-policy interface and provide a strong evidence-based instrument to support policymakers to achieve the SDGs.

The increasing importance, reach, and complexity of science demand that the regular tools, techniques, and tactics of international diplomacy, policy, and law be adapted to this new global context.

The UN's treaty-making provides the standards and frameworks within which these tools and techniques can be used. This chapter considers how the UN has contributed, through its multilateral-treaty-making activity, to the promotion of science and, vice versa, how science has influenced the treaty-making process.

As it is not an established field of international law a few words about the scope of this chapter are necessary.

The term "science" is used in this chapter in a broad way, including not only the study of the natural or physical world, but also of social, cultural, and economic facts. For the purposes of this chapter however, science does not include technology, despite the two concepts being closely related and very often treated together in UN treaties.

Science affects all aspects of modern day life and so the topic is as vast as the work of the UN. Consequently, this short chapter does not seek to provide a comprehensive analysis of the topic but only to highlight some of the key issues.

1 The History of Science in UN Treaty-Making

While science was not explicitly mentioned[5] in the UN Charter, it nevertheless was seen as a specific and important goal of many of the early UN agencies, such as the United Nations Food and Agricultural Organization (FAO), the United Nations Educational,

[5] Albeit reference is made to "scientific purposes" in Article 73(d) of the Charter relating to the Declaration regarding non-self-governing territories.

Scientific and Cultural Organization, International Civil Aviation Organization, the World Health Organization (WHO), the World Meteorological Organization (WMO), the International Atomic Energy Agency, and the International Maritime Organization, which is reflected in the treaties that establish these agencies.

The prominence of science in the work of the UN is also evident in its treaty-making. The 1958 Conventions on the Law of the Sea[6] contained many provisions promoting the role of science.[7]

The Declaration of Legal Principles Governing the Activities of States in the Exploration and Uses of Outer Space[8] and the five treaties on outer space stress as a fundamental notion of the law of outer space that it should be reserved for peaceful purposes—the most important one being science—and promoting international cooperation, in particular in the scientific field.

The promotion of science was also a major aim of the 1982 United Nations Convention on the Law of the Sea. Its preamble identifies the objective to "promote the peaceful uses of the seas and oceans . . . and the study, protection and preservation of the marine environment." The discovery of manganese nodules in the deep seabed was a catalyst for the establishment of the legal regime governing the Area.[9] Marine science provides essential data for the implementation of many of the key features of the Convention, such as the fishery regime's concepts of maximum sustainable yield and total allowable catch, as well as the delimitation of boundaries and the outer limits of the continental shelf beyond 200 nautical miles.[10]

A significant milestone in the importance of science in UN treaty-making is the response to the scientific discovery of the damage being done to the ozone layer, which will be further examined hereinafter.[11] Three other treaties, adopted in 1992 (the Convention on Biological Diversity (CBD), the UN Framework Convention on Climate Change (UNFCCC), and the Convention to Combat Desertification) were also shaped by science and contain commitments to using and promoting science.

Climate change and the UNFCCC is perhaps the most important UN treaty that has been influenced by, and in turn has influenced, science. Negotiations were marked from the very beginning by the contribution from science. The work of the Intergovernmental Panel on Climate Change (IPCC), established in 1988 by UN Environmental Programme and the WMO, has been marked by an increasing recognition of the fundamental inputs

[6] The Convention on the Territorial Sea and the Contiguous Zone (CTS), the Convention on the High Seas (CHS), the Convention on Fishing and Conservation of the Living Resources of the High Seas (CFCLR), the Convention on the Continental Shelf (CCS), and the Optional Protocol of Signature concerning the Compulsory Settlement of Disputes (OPSD).

[7] See, eg, art 7(2). [8] UNGA Res 1962 (13 December 1963).

[9] Donald R Rothwell and Tim Stephens, *The International Law of the Sea* (2nd edn, Hart 2016) and Yoshifumi Tanaka, *The International Law of the Sea* (2nd edn, CUP 2015).

[10] Rothwell and Stephens (n 9).

[11] K Madhava Sarma and Stephen O Andersen, "Science and Diplomacy: Montreal Protocol on Substances That Deplete the Ozone Layer" in PA Berkman, MA Lang, DWH Walton, and OR Young (eds), *Science Diplomacy: Antarctica, Science, and the Governance of International Spaces* (Smithsonian Scholarly Press 2011) 123–33.

from science. Its five assessment reports benefit from the contributions of thousands of scientists from all regions and provide a basis for intergovernmental negotiations. The international authority of the IPCC in this field has also been recognized through its receipt of the Nobel Peace Prize in 2007.

This institutional history shows that science has played an important role in the UN. The UN has also adopted a wide variety of mechanisms and approaches to promote science and use it to address many of the most pressing issues it faces. Virtually every UN treaty adopted since the 1970s recognizes the importance of science and contains provisions calling for its use and development.

2 Science and UN Treaties

Comprehensively detailing such a wide-ranging relationship as the one between science and UN treaties is not possible within the confines of this chapter. There are, however, a number of recognized key aspects to this relationship that illustrate systemic issues and challenges the UN faces in using and contributing to science.

2.1 Scientific-Based Treaty-Making

Science contributes to successful treaty-making in a number of ways. Treaties based on scientific facts tend to be more successful as they can more effectively identify and respond to real issues and problems.[12] Science has a facilitative effect on treaty development. Science can be used to identify a problem, develop a common starting point, and narrow the scope of the negotiations and treaty.[13] It can also help with developments by identifying potential solutions[14] of facilitating action by allowing policymakers to reframe questions of burden and equity. For example, policymakers may claim that science demonstrates the need for an unpopular decision that will entail short-term cost for long-term gains.[15]

As a result, many UN treaties are adopted in response to new science, are shaped fundamentally by science, and contain provisions calling for the further use of science.

UN treaties have developed considerable experience and sophistication in ensuring that science is delivered in a useful manner to the policymaking processes and that it is used appropriately. The range of mechanisms is as numerous as the treaties adopted

[12] Timothy Meyer, "Institutions and Expertise: The Role of Science in Climate Change Lawmaking" in Cinnamon P Carlarne, Kevin R Gray, and Richard Tarasofsky (eds), *The Oxford Handbook of International Climate Change Law* (OUP 2016) 442–462.

[13] ibid 2016. [14] ibid. [15] ibid.

under the auspices of the UN. Framework conventions with various types of amendment procedures, standing or permanent subsidiary bodies, scientific advisory bodies, assessment processes, periodic reporting, relationships with scientific organizations, clearing house mechanisms, intersessional platforms, rosters of experts, and science expertise on the delegations are some of the more common techniques. Over recent years even dispute settlement processes have become a means for clarifying scientific concepts in a particular treaty. Decisions such as the International Court of Justice's judgment in the *Whaling* Case,[16] the International Tribunal for the Law of the Sea's judgment in the *Bluefin Tuna* case,[17] or the advisory opinion on *Responsibilities and obligations of States sponsoring persons and entities with respect to activities in the Area*, and the *South China Sea* arbitral award are examples where the relevant body incorporated science considerations in its reasoning.[18]

One area in which science has been very important for the UN treaty-making process is the regime for the protection of the atmosphere. It has played a key role in each of the key treaties in this area, as will be described hereinafter.

2.1.1 *Ozone Regime*

The protection of the ozone layer is widely recognized as the most successful example of a UN treaty regime responding to science. However, the success of this response belies the controversy and complexity surrounding the issue at the time of the negotiation of the regime in the 1980s, which included: scientific uncertainty, no evidence of harmful effects, potentially high costs, widespread use of ozone-depleting substances (ODSs), the opposition of some of the largest companies in the world, unequal contribution and capacity, and a global problem that required global participation.[19]

The regime centers around the 1985 Vienna Convention for the Protection of the Ozone Layer (the Vienna Convention) and the 1987 Montreal Protocol on Substances That Deplete the Ozone Layer (the Montreal Protocol). Both treaties have been universally ratified, the first treaties to reach universal participation in the history of the United Nations.

[16] Margaret Young and Sebastián Rioseco Sullivan, "Evolution through the Duty to Cooperate: Implications of the *Whaling* Case at the International Court of Justice" (2015) 16 Melbourne J Intl L 311; Donald K Anton, Timo Koivurova, and Anastasia Telesetsky, "ICJ's Decision in Australia v Japan: Giving Up the Spear or Refining the Scientific Design?" (2014) 45(4) Ocean Dev and Intl L 328.

[17] Natalie Klein, "Litigation over Marine Resources: Lessons for Law of the Sea, International Dispute Settlement and International Environmental Law" (2009) 28 Australian YBIL 131.

[18] Tim Stephens and Donald R Rothwell, "The LOSC Framework for Maritime Jurisdiction and Enforcement 30 Years On" (2012) 27 Intl J Marine & Coastal L 701; Rosemary Rayfuse, "The Future of Compulsory Dispute Settlement under the Law of the Sea Convention" (2005) 36 Victoria Univ of Wellington L Rev 683.

[19] R Benedick, *Ozone Diplomacy* (1991) xii, an insider's account of the negotiations of the Montreal Protocol (see also the second edition, 1998); K Litfin, *Ozone Discourses: Science and Politics in Global Environmental Cooperation* (CUP, 1994) and EA Parson, *Protecting the Ozone Layer Science and Strategy* (OUP 2003).

The Assessment Panels, established by Article 6 of the Montreal Protocol, have been the main mechanism for incorporating science into the regime. There are three different Panels at the moment, which carry out periodic assessments every four years (the first of which was published in 1989 and the latest in 2018). The Scientific Assessment Panel, consisting of hundreds of top scientists from around the world, assesses the status of the depletion of the ozone layer and relevant atmospheric science issues. Any emerging scientific issue of importance is brought to the attention of the Parties by the Co-Chairs for consideration at the Meetings of the Parties. The Technology and Economic Assessment Panel provides technical information related to the alternative technologies that have been investigated and employed to make it possible to virtually eliminate use of ODSs. The Environmental Effects Assessment Panel assesses the various effects of ozone layer depletion.

The 1985 Vienna Convention contained no commitments to reduce the use of ODSs, and the Montreal Protocol only contained limited commitments. However, from 1990, there was a rapid increase in the commitments of Parties. These were developed through five amendments to the Protocol (adopted in London (1990), Copenhagen (1992), Montreal (1997), Beijing (1999), and Kigali (2016)), and 13 Adjustments of the Annexes of the Protocol. Amendments are used for important changes to the Protocol and require ratification by a number of parties before they enter into force, while Adjustments are used to adjust commitments with respect to ODSs already covered by the Protocol and enter into force automatically unless a Party expressly notifies it is opting out. This treaty regime, as adapted and strengthened to meet scientific challenges, has led to the phaseout of 99 percent of ODSs and the first signs of recovery of the ozone layer.

The framework approach and its flexible opt-in and opt-out mechanisms of adjustment allows incorporation of science rapidly into the usually slow and cumbersome UN treaty-making process.

Another lesson of the Montreal Protocol is the role of the scientists and, over time, diplomats who develop a high level of expertise through their active involvement in the process. The emergence of an epistemic community of atmospheric scientists and diplomats played a primary role in gathering information, disseminating it to governments and ODS manufacturers, and helping them formulate international, domestic, and industry policies regarding ODS consumption and production. This core group has been widely recognized as contributing to the timing and stringency of ODS regulations through a combination of strategies ranging from the persuasion of individuals and the capture of the negotiating process. They also ensured that the underlying science was known to, and influenced, the policymaking process. By influencing the actions of the United States and DuPont, the largest producer of ODS, the epistemic community developed the political context or enabling environment of the negotiations.[20]

[20] P Haas, "Banning Chlorofluorocarbons: Epistemic Community Efforts to Protect Stratospheric Ozone," (1992) 46 Intl Org 187.

2.1.2 *UNFCCC*

Science has played a key role in identifying, shaping, and influencing the UN's effort to tackle climate change, which is widely recognized as one of the greatest threats to peace, security, and development.[21]

The UNFCCC, the Kyoto Protocol, and the Paris Agreement identify the need for an effective and progressive response to the urgent threat of climate change on the basis of the best available scientific knowledge. For example, the UNFCCC calls on Parties: to promote and cooperate in research, systematic observation, and the development of data archives, including through exchange of information; to support programs, networks, and organizations; and to improve the capacities of developing countries (Articles 4(g) and (e), and 5). The preamble to the Paris Agreement identifies the need for an effective and progressive response to the urgent threat of climate change on the basis of the best available scientific knowledge.

Article 9 of the UNFCCC establishes a subsidiary body for scientific and technological advice (SBSTA), which is one of two permanent subsidiary bodies to the Convention. It supports the work of the Conference of the Parties (COP) through the provision of timely information and advice on relevant scientific and technological. The SBSTA itself though is a largely political process that provides negotiated recommendations to the COP on scientific matters.

Through their national communications, the UNFCCC Parties report on their national and cooperative research activities and their contributions to climate science, as well as emerging research needs and priorities.

While the IPCC predates the UNFCCC, it has been the most influential direct mechanism for the incorporation of science in the UNFCCC regime. It has a well-established role in the Convention process in communicating scientific information through its assessment reports, special reports, and technical papers; assessing the scientific literature; and providing vital scientific information to the process.

Article 21(2) of the UNFCCC also provides that the secretariat "will cooperate closely" with the IPCC "to ensure that the Panel can respond to the need for objective scientific and technical advice."

Cooperation with the IPCC has been further defined and strengthened by several COP decisions. In 1995, COP 1 invited the UNFCCC subsidiary bodies, particularly the SBSTA, to submit proposals for future cooperation with the IPCC.[22] This resulted in the establishment, in the same year, of an informal group—the Joint Working Group (JWG) of the SBSTA and the IPCC—that meets regularly to ensure coordination and exchange information on the activities of the two bodies. The JWG is composed of the SBSTA and IPCC Chairs, other presiding officers of the UNFCCC and IPCC, and secretariat members.

[21] Philippe Sands and Jacqueline Peel, *Principles of International and Environmental Law* (4th edn CUP, 2018) Chapter 8, and T Skodvin, *Structure and Agent in Scientific Diplomacy on Climate Change* (Kluwer Academic 2000).

[22] See decision 6/CP.1 The subsidiary bodies established by the Convention.

The IPCC is best known for its comprehensive assessment reports, which are widely recognized as the most credible sources of information on climate change. The First Assessment Report in 1990 helped launch negotiations on the Convention.[23] The 1995 Second Assessment Report, in particular its statement that "the balance of evidence suggests . . . a discernible human influence on global climate," stimulated many governments into intensifying negotiations on what was to become the Kyoto Protocol.[24] The 2007 Fourth Assessment Report provided the scientific foundation for the Marrakech Accords, which were critical to operationalizing the Kyoto Protocol.[25] The 2014 Fifth Assessment Report informed the negotiations and policy formulation toward the Paris Agreement.[26] The sixth assessment due in 2020 is seen as a critical input to the review and development of Parties' commitments under the Paris Agreement.

The IPCC also produces shorter special reports and technical papers on specific issues, some of them at the request of the COP or the SBSTA. For example, in 2000, the IPCC issued a Special Report on Land Use, Land-Use Change and Forestry, which served as an input into negotiations on the rules for this sector under the Kyoto Protocol.[27]

Through its Task Force on Greenhouse Gas Inventories, the IPCC carries out work on methodologies for estimating and reporting greenhouse gas emissions. The IPCC 2006 Revised Guidelines for National Greenhouse Gas Inventories, for example, are used by all Parties to prepare their annual emission inventories. In addition, the IPCC has developed guidance to help Parties deal with data uncertainties and support the use of good practices in managing emission inventories.[28]

2.1.3 *Influence of Science on the Treaty-Making Process*

Assessing the actual influence of science on UN treaty-making is a challenging task and more of an art than a science. It is an issue that political scientists and international relations scholars have been researching and analyzing for decades, addressing topics such as "when does power listen to truth."[29] Scholars are increasingly skeptical about the

[23] See <https://unfccc.int/topics/science/workstreams/cooperation-with-the-ipcc/background-cooperation-with-the-ipcc> accessed January 18, 2019.

[24] See <https://unfccc.int/topics/science/workstreams/cooperation-with-the-ipcc/background-cooperation-with-the-ipcc> accessed January 18, 2019.

[25] See <https://unfccc.int/topics/science/workstreams/cooperation-with-the-ipcc/background-cooperation-with-the-ipcc> accessed January 18, 2019.

[26] See <https://unfccc.int/topics/science/workstreams/cooperation-with-the-ipcc/background-cooperation-with-the-ipcc> accessed January 18, 2019.

[27] See <https://unfccc.int/topics/science/workstreams/cooperation-with-the-ipcc/background-cooperation-with-the-ipcc> accessed January 18, 2019.

[28] See <https://unfccc.int/topics/science/workstreams/cooperation-with-the-ipcc/background-cooperation-with-the-ipcc> accessed January 18, 2019.

[29] Aaron Wildavsky, *Speaking Truth to Power: The Art and Craft of Policy Analysis* (Little, Brown 1979); Peter M Haas, *Epistemic Communities, Constructivism, and International Environmental Politics* (Routledge 2015); S Boehmer-Christiansen, "Uncertainty in the Service of Science: Between Science Politics and the Politics of Power" in G Fermann (ed), *International Politics of Climate Change* (Scandinavian University Press 1997); S Andresen, L Walkte, and GK Rosendal, "The Precautionary

influence that science has on the policymaking process, whether scientists are capable of developing truth, and whether power ever listens to them anyway. Indeed, many scholars seem to be surprised by the occasions when science does have a demonstrable impact on the policymaking process.

Part of the problem is that most UN treaties address issues that are inherently political or economic in nature, and there are few, if any, examples in which science is the overriding or predominant influence. Even with the ozone regime, it is hard to assess the extent to which governments and the UN were influenced by science or the lobbying by big chemical companies whose patents over ODS were expiring: markets diminishing through domestic regulatory action in the United States and who had an interest in phasing out old ODS technology to speed up the introduction of a new and more expensive generation of ODS technology. The interests of these companies were therefore very much aligned with the rapid development of the treaty.[30]

Further complicating any assessment is the experience where conclusive science has not been a necessary condition for collective action. The decision of the 1987 North Sea Conference to adopt very stringent and ambitious targets to reduce pollution, even though the scientific message was very far from conclusive on the basis of the precautionary principle, is one well-known example in environmental spheres.[31] The 1982 International Whaling Commission moratorium on commercial whaling, even though its Scientific Committee gave no such recommendation, is another.[32]

Nevertheless, the institutional relationship between the treaty and the relevant scientific advisory mechanism is a significant treaty-making issue. Each UN treaty has a different structure, even closely related treaties such as the Montreal Protocol (where the main scientific assessment processes are established under the Protocol itself) and the UNFCCC (where the IPCC is an independent entity). The institutional balance between control and relevance, on the one hand, and independence and objectivity, on the other, is critical for ensuring a strong relationship between science and treaties. Science generated by treaty processes is controlled by governments and therefore relevant to the treaty, but it is viewed as being less independent, credible, and authoritative. Integrity is needed to ensure that the scientific input is politically, economically, and socially objective. Yet, treaty-generated mandates and guidance are necessary so that scientists are aware of the needs of policymakers. Treaty-generated science further ensures that the enabling or receiving environment—the decision-making body of

Principle: Knowledge Counts but Power Decides," in R Cooney and B Dickson (eds), *Biodiversity and the Precautionary Principle: Risk and Uncertainty in Conservation and Sustainable Use* (Earthscan 2005) 39, and A Underdal, "The Politics of Science in International Resource Management: A Summary," in S Andresen and W Ostreng (eds), *International Resource Management* (Belhaven Press 1989) 253.

30 David Hunter, James Salzman, and Durwood Zaelke, *International Environmental Law and Policy* (4th edn, Foundation Press 2011), chapter 10, section III, 566–605.

31 D Freestone and T IJlstra, "The North Sea: Perspectives on Regional Environmental Cooperation," special issue of *International Journal of Coastal and Estuarine Law* (Graham and Trotman 1990).

32 Meyer (n 12); Young (n 16), and S Andresen, "The International Whaling Commission: More Failure than Success?," E Miles et al, *Explaining Environmental Regime Effectiveness* (MIT Press 2002) 379.

the treaty—is not only aware of the science but also has a responsibility to respond to the science. The lack of influence that the UNEP's Global Biodiversity Assessment had on the CBD, which was not mandated by the treaty, is a stark example of the importance of this responsibility to respond.

The IPCC has been criticized along both these lines, with some questioning the legitimacy of its process, and others its relevance and impact.[33]

Independence and relevance serve different functions for different parties. For many countries, the independence of science is a feature that boosts its credibility and utility. Other countries tend to perceive so-called "independent science" to be science done by and for the countries that commissioned it. The more marginal their role in science, the more critical they tend to be of science. These perceptions are no doubted amplified by politicization of science in many countries recently, especially in the United States, the United Kingdom, and Australia.

An illustration of these tensions can be seen even in preeminent UN scientific processes, such as the IPCC, which relies predominantly on English language sources. Other science or what the IPCC calls "marginalised knowledge systems," which even includes Spanish and French climate change science and knowledge, let alone more marginalized knowledge such as indigenous peoples' knowledges systems, are not adequately represented or reflected in the IPCC's work. As a result, over recent years there has been increasing criticism about the authority and credibility of IPCC work, and serious, although relatively unsuccessful, attempts by the IPCC to develop mechanisms to access these "marginalised knowledge systems."[34]

The Intergovernmental Platform on Biodiversity and Ecosystem Services provides a platform for interaction and cooperation among more than 40 science organizations, UN programs, specialized agencies, and several UN treaties, such as the CBD and Convention on the Conservation of Migratory Species of Wild Animals, and has put enormous effort into drawing on a wide range of knowledge systems, in particular those of indigenous peoples, but so far, the results have been disappointing.

Another aspect of the problems faced in broadening knowledge systems is that the social, economic, and legal sciences tend to be more qualitative, subjective, and value laden, thereby undermining the acceptability or "credibility" of those sciences. Problems over risk assessment illustrate the limitations of science when addressing more value-laden issues such as precaution. As a result, serious questions have been raised about the neutrality of all science.

[33] PM Haas and C Stevens "Organized Science, Usable Knowledge, and Environmental Governance," in R Lidskog and G Sundqvist (eds), *Governing the Air: The Dynamics of Science, Policy, and Citizen Interaction* (MIT Press, 2011); K Hasselman and T Barker "The Stern Review and the IPCC Fourth MIT Press, 2008; Assessment Report: Implications for Interaction between Policymakers and Climate Experts: An Editorial Essay," 2008 89 *Climatic Change* 219; and James D Ford, Laura Cameron, Jennifer Rubis, Michelle Maillet, Douglas Nakashima, Ashlee Cunsolo Willox, and Tristan Pearce, "Including Indigenous Knowledge and Experience In IPCC Assessment Reports" (2016) 6 *Nature Climate Change* 349.

[34] Ford et al (n 33).

Modern science is also becoming more complex and multidisciplinary, and achieving scientific consensus, even for the more quantitative sciences, is increasingly challenging. Smoking and tobacco control, climate change, and genetically modified organisms all provide examples in which progress in the negotiation, conclusion, or implementation of UN treaties has been slowed, even stymied, by subjective or biased science.[35]

Another issue is the increasing complexity of the range of issues and actors involved in UN treaties. For example, in 2017 at the 23rd session of the UNFCCC COP there were over 16,000 participants representing nearly 2,000 different organizations. These included lobby groups, think tanks, companies, industry umbrellas, radical activists, and religious groups. The UNFCCC seeks all their input without making any meaningful assessment of their expertise or qualification. In this more complex diverse world, science is losing its influence.

In conclusion, science has played a significant catalytic role in many UN treaties. Yet as science becomes more successful and influential it is increasingly scrutinized, more politicized, and less certain. Moreover, as UN treaties become more open and complex, science is increasingly being crowded out and becoming less influential. This politicization undermines the influence of science on UN treaties and allows other factors to become dominant. For example, it allows countries to prioritize economic interests over environmental ones, which is what has happened with the withdrawal of Canada and Japan from the Kyoto Protocol and the United States' threatened withdrawal from the Paris Agreement.

2.2 Promoting Access to Existing Science

Many UN treaties contain provisions calling for better access for developing states to science and technologies. The typical approach is based around science and technology needs assessments and on capacity-building. Cutting-edge approaches are moving to a more dynamic arrangement geared toward: fostering public-private partnerships, promoting innovation, catalyzing the use of technology roadmaps or action plans, responding to developing country requests on matters related to technology transfer, and facilitating joint research and development activities.

Examples of this role in UN treaties include the work of World Intellectual Property Organisation (WIPO) and the WHO.

The whole purpose of the WIPO patent system is to publish science and allow access to that science. This remains one of the most successful areas of UN treaty-making dealing

[35] Kevin Trenberth, "More Knowledge, Less Certainty," (2010) 4 Nature Reports Climate Change 20, available at https://www.nature.com/articles/climate.2010.06; D Henderson, "The Climate Change Debate Today: COP15, the CRU Affair, and the Basis for Policy" (2010) 21(3) Energy and Environment 279, and SB Capstick and NF Pidgeon, "What Is Climate Change Scepticism? Examination of the Concept Using a Mixed Methods Study of the UK Public" (2014) 24 Global Environmental Change 389.

with science. WIPO uses, and in most cases has pioneered, many of the cutting-edge approaches listed previously.[36]

The WHO international health standards are another example of UN treaty-making contributing to science.[37] One interesting example is the WHO's Pandemic Influenza Preparedness Framework to improve pandemic influenza preparedness and response and strengthen the protection against the influenza pandemic by improving and strengthening the WHO Global Influenza Surveillance and Response System (WHO GISRS). It established a global, fair, transparent, equitable, and efficient system for the sharing of information on H5N1 and other influenza viruses with human pandemic potential, and also promoted access to vaccines and sharing of other benefits.

2.3 Promoting Science

Many UN treaties contain provisions calling for the promotion of science, research, and development. These provisions typically call on parties to exchange information, cooperate, and assist one another with resources and expertise.[38] Few, if any, of them mandate the provision of financial support for the implementation of these provisions. Consequently, their impact on the work of the science is limited, with domestic priorities and budgets being much more important.

One important contribution, albeit not well acknowledged, is the extent to which meetings of UN treaty bodies, such as governing bodies (e.g., COPs) or subsidiary bodies (e.g., the SBSTA), provide venues for science exchange and collaboration. The UNFCCC COPs have become scientific conferences in their own right with more than 830 applications to host satellite events at COP 23 in 2017.

UN treaties have also provided the framework to support and promote science in relation to the management of global commons, in the face of intense political tensions between states.

A key legal tension in this area is balancing the need for retaining and promoting free access to science and information, which underpins the traditional approach, with the increasing need to share benefits equitably in the face of rising commercialization of global commons, as these become more accessible and economically valuable.

For example, the use of outer space has until recently been restricted to government-sponsored exploration. This is changing with the emergence of private satellites, paying tourists, and the mining of helium or plutonium from asteroids or the moon. Serious concerns emerge about space debris and challenges with regard to the allocation of orbits. The general regime under UN treaties on outer space is based upon free use and a

[36] Its effectiveness is covered in Chapter 18 in this *Handbook* on intellectual property.

[37] Their effectiveness is covered in Chapters 17A and 17B in this *Handbook* on health.

[38] See, eg, CBD arts 12, 17, and 18.

prohibition of claims to sovereignty by individual states. However, increasing private sector interest is creating a need for these basic principles to be developed.[39]

A similar phenomenon is noticeable in the framework of the International Treaty on Plant Genetic Resources for Food and Agriculture (ITPGRFA). Traditionally, genetic resources in the agricultural sector were openly shared and moved around the globe. They were treated like public goods, or a global commons, with the 1983 FAO International Undertaking on Plant Genetic Resources for Food and Agriculture being "based on the universally accepted principle that plant genetic resources are a heritage of mankind and consequently should be available without restriction."

An increasing proportion of these genetic resources have been subject to various forms of ownership, as a result of advances in science, technology, and the expansion of property rights, particularly plant variety rights and patents supported by developments under the International Union for the Protection of New Varieties of Plants and the World Trade Organisation (WTO) trade-related intellectual property agreements. As a response to this privatization, the UN has tried to maintain the public nature and open access of plant genetic resources. The center of these efforts is the ITPGRFA, which recognizes that plant genetic resources for food and agriculture are the "common concern of all countries" and establishes a multilateral system for 64 of the most important crops, included in Annex I of the Treaty. Under this multilateral system, Parties agree to provide each other with facilitated access to resources that are "under the management and control" of national governments and "in the public domain," for the purposes of training, research, and breeding for food and agriculture. This system aims at maintaining global food security, and benefits science as well. It is also being considered as a model for other types of global commons genetic resources under threat, such as those of the high seas or Antarctica.

UNCLOS ensures that the high seas and the seabed beyond national jurisdictions or deep seabed (the Area) are managed for peaceful purposes, including the practice of science.[40] It also recognizes marine scientific research (MSR) as a freedom of the high seas and contains provisions protecting this freedom in the exclusive economic zone (EEZ) and the continental shelf. Historically, the regime of MSR was akin to a freedom of the high seas. Part XIII of UNCLOS, due to the demands from developing countries, changed this significantly by balancing the freedom of MSR and the recognition of the interests of coastal states, with the freedom being seen as a prerequisite to developing MSR.

This balance is an evolving and dynamic one. MSR is not defined in the Convention, despite several proposals that were made for a definition during the negotiations. It is therefore often difficult to distinguish MSR from exploration of natural resources in practice, which is a modern manifestation of the "pure"/"applied" distinction that

[39] A more detailed analysis of these treaties is provided in chapter 9 of this *Handbook* on peaceful uses of outer space.

[40] The effectiveness of these measures and the challenges they face is addressed in Chapters 25A and 25B in this *Handbook* on law of the sea.

caused problems in the first years of the UN.[41] The distinction between MSR and other activities is also ambiguous and has been the source of disputes with regard to coastal state jurisdiction over marine survey activities in the EEZ, in particular between China and the United States.[42] The legality of hydrographic and military survey activities in the EEZ of another state is a particularly contentious issue. While the United States advocates the freedom of such surveys in the EEZ of a third state as MSR, China takes the position that it is entitled to regulate such activities in its EEZ.[43] So far, the question remains open.

Another example of this problem is whether geoengineering experiments involving the fertilization of the sea with iron to increase plankton and thereby increase absorption of carbon dioxide by the ocean is MSR or rather an activity that involves depositing material covered by the London Dumping Convention. Parties have responded to this by developing amendments to the London Protocol, which outline in some detail what is research and what is a prohibited activity, with the distinction essentially being drawn between pure and applied or commercial science.[44]

These types of legal tensions around MSR are escalating and threaten to undermine the role of MSR, the ability of UNCLOS to promote science, and, ultimately, UNCLOS itself.

2.4 Dangerous Scientific Substances and Risk Management

UN treaties on the protection against the threats of dangerous substances promote science by ensuring its safety and providing it with a social licence to operate. Science also has a pivotal role in determining what is "dangerous" and what measures are legal under these treaties.

UN treaties in this area include: the Nuclear Safety Convention, the Basel Convention on the Control of Transboundary Movements of Hazardous Wastes and their Disposal, the Rotterdam Convention on the Prior Informed Consent Procedure for Certain Hazardous Chemicals and Pesticides in International Trade, and the Stockholm Convention on Persistent Organic Pollutants addressing hazardous substances; and the Cartagena Protocol on Biosafety, the International Plant Protection Convention, and the FAO's *Codex Alimentarius* in the field of biosafety.

The approaches adopted for each of these areas are highly technical, elaborate, and detailed, usually centred around the provision of prior informed consent by the receiving country and involving both a heavy reliance on science as a key determinate or input and controversy as to how that input should be made and relied upon.

[41] Rothwell and Stephens (n 9). [42] ibid. [43] Tanaka (n 9).

[44] IMO Guidance and Amendments under the London Convention/Protocol, available at <http://www.imo.org/en/OurWork/Environment/LCLP/EmergingIssues/geoengineering/Pages/default.aspx> accessed January 18, 2019 and Grant Wilson, "Murky Waters: Ambiguous International Law for Ocean Fertilization and Other Geoengineering" (2014) 49 Tex Intl LJ 507.

The Cartagena Protocol on Biosafety illustrates these points. Its operational provisions focus largely on the processes of decision-making by Parties regarding the import of Living Modified Organisms (LMOs). Article 15 requires that decisions regarding the import of LMOs for intentional introduction into the environment be taken in accordance with a risk assessment. Annex III provides more detailed guidance on the application of risk assessments, including some general principles such as the need for them to be carried out in a scientifically sound and transparent manner, taking into account expert advice and relevant international guidelines. Articles 10 and 11 also provide that, when making a decision as to whether to allow import of an LMO, "[l]ack of scientific certainty due to insufficient relevant scientific information and knowledge regarding the extent of the potential adverse effects of a living modified organism . . . , taking also into account risks to human health, shall not prevent that Party from taking a decision."[45]

A critical aspect of the relationship between science and policymakers is the confusion about how a decision can be simultaneously based on risk assessment and precaution. Risk assessment refers to the determination of quantitative or qualitative estimate of risk related to a well-defined situation and a recognized threat (also called hazard). Precaution to a measure taken in advance to prevent something dangerous from happening.

One source of confusion about the roles of risk assessment and precaution stems from the mandate given to risk assessors. Usually, risk assessors are scientists with expertise in relevant disciplines, which allows them to characterize risks based on available scientific information. However, inevitably, decision-makers also ask for the advice of risk assessors on appropriate risk-management actions, and may even ask for their advice on the acceptability of risks. For example, Annex III on Risk Assessment in the Cartagena Protocol contains the following text as part of the methodology of risk assessment (paragraph 8e): "A recommendation as to whether or not the risks are acceptable or manageable, including, where necessary, identification of strategies to manage these risks." Risk assessors are entirely capable of commenting on whether risks can be managed. However, their role in determining the acceptability of risks is less clear. Formally, such value judgments are the realm of decision-makers. However, in practice, the link between risk assessment and decision-making is usually complex, based on an iterative relationship that involves a continuing dialogue between risk assessors (who must communicate complicated and uncertain information to decision-makers) and decision-makers (who must inform risk assessors about what type of information is needed), as well as dialogue with the public and stakeholders affected by the decision. Partly due to the nature of this process, in many regulatory systems the scientists responsible for risk assessment are often given some responsibility for decision-making as well. Risk assessors are inevitably involved in the broader decision-making process in one way or another. Still, their primary role is assessment, and the Protocol's language clearly asks only for a "recommendation" from risk assessors on the acceptability of risks.

[45] Ryan Hill, Sam Johnston, and Cyrie Sendashonga "Risk Assessment and Precaution in the Biosafety Protocol" (2004) 13 (3) RECIEL 263.

Another source of confusion about the compatibility of risk assessment and precaution is the misunderstanding that decisions based on risk assessment cannot reflect value judgments. Decision-makers inevitably base their decisions in part on their values or risk attitudes, or those of the constituencies they represent. Two different decision-makers, faced with the same decision, may make different choices because one is less willing than the other to accept the risks.

Differences were clearly evident during the negotiations of the Protocol and the WTO *GMO Case*, where the governance cultures of the opposing groups contributed significantly to different understandings of the need for, and the role of, the Protocol. On the one hand, the Miami Group (comprising the United States, Canada, Argentina, Australia, Uruguay, and Chile) believed that the precautionary approach might not lead to decisions based on sound science. They were concerned that it could be applied in an arbitrary manner, and could lead to distortions of trade. On the other hand, the European Union and other governments could not understand the reluctance of the Miami Group to accept rules that would allow a prudent approach to this new technology. This debate was in part a reflection of the different cultures of risk assessment that existed in each country. For example, the type of risk assessment favored by the United States is a highly formalized and adversarial method that is to the greatest possible extent based on quantitative data. This process has evolved in response to a regulatory environment in which decisions based on ambiguous scientific findings are liable to be contested in court. Most other countries do not have such a complex and adversarial system of governance.[46]

It is important that the UN and governments recognize such differences as legitimate. Insistence upon, or careless translation of, one approach to risk management will not resolve deep-seated cultural differences regarding risk management of new technologies. In fact, attempts to harmonize these differences out of existence are liable to be resisted as attacks on types of governance rather than a dispute about science.

3 Conclusion

The United Nations has contributed, through its multilateral treaty-making activity, to the promotion of science and, vice versa, science has influenced the treaty-making process.

This relationship centers around four main issues, namely scientific influence in the treaty-making process, promoting access to existing science, supporting research, and managing the threats posed by science.

[46] Sands and Peel (n 21) ch. 10; Jacqueline Peel, *Science and Risk Regulation in International Law* (CUP 2010) 305; Helmut Gaugitsch, "Under the Cartagena Protocol on Biosafety—Where Is the Roadmap for Risk Assessment Taking Us?" (2015) 3 Frontiers in Bioengineering and Biotechnology, 212, and M. Geistfeld, "Reconciling Cost-Benefit Analysis with the Principle That Safety Matters More than Money" (2001) 76 New York Univ L Rev 114, 176.

Science will continue to play an important role in shaping any UN treaty that responds to new and emerging areas such as managing new technologies including nanotechnologies, synthetic biology, or artificial intelligence;[47] protecting biodiversity of the high seas;[48] guarding against new forms of pollution such as microplastics[49] or space debris;[50] managing new uses of the environment, such as deep seabed or outer-space tourism;[51] or protecting against new threats, such as cyberwarfare and security. Given the global nature of these issues, the role of the UN will inevitably be central, and there have been calls for new UN treaties to be negotiated on all these issues.

If UN treaty-making is to maintain a strong relationship with science and an evidentiary-based treaty-making process, the UN's activities and treaties will need to respond to the challenges highlighted, such as resolving the tensions that exist between pure and applied science; maintaining science's role as a peaceful activity in the global commons; ensuring that scientific input is not lost among the increasing complex and crowded nature of treaty-making; ensuring that science is more inclusive, holistic, and balanced; and improving its relevance while retaining its credibility.

A recurring theme is the increasing politicization of science and the need to understand its limitations. It is troubling that science has never before been so necessary, while being so contested. Failures of science in predicting and managing threats from climate change, epidemics, and nuclear disasters have revealed the uncertainties underlying many of its areas of practice and has demonstrated the critical role that social, economic, and institutional expectations play. Recognizing that science is not neutral or objective is an important step in addressing the key shortcomings facing the role of science in UN treaties. Determining what measures need to be taken to balance social and economic influences is another important side of this challenge. Reconciling these enduring challenges will be increasingly important in all areas where UN treaty-making processes and science intersect, and necessary if UN treaty-making is to remain founded on scientific and evidentiary-based policymaking.

[47] Elen Stokes and Diana M. Bowman, "Back to the Future of Regulating New Technologies: The Cases of Nanotechnologies and Synthetic Biology" (2012) 2 Eur J Risk Reg 235.

[48] Dire Tladi, "The Proposed Implementing Agreement: Options for Coherence and Consistency in the Establishment of Protected Areas beyond National Jurisdiction" (2015) 30 Intl J Marine and Coastal L 654.

[49] PJ Kershaw and CM Rochman, (eds), *Sources, Fate and Effects of Microplastics in the Marine Environment: Part Two of a Global Assessment*, IMO/FAO/UNESCO-IOC/UNIDO/WMO/IAEA/UN/UNEP/UNDP The Joint Group of Experts on Scientific Aspects of Marine Protection (GESAMP No. 93, 2016).

[50] Lawrence Li, "Space Debris Mitigation as an International Law Obligation" (2015) 17(3) Intl Community L Rev 297.

[51] Dirk HR Spennemann, "Extreme Cultural Tourism from Antarctica to the Moon" (2007) 34(4) Annals Tourism Research 898.

CHAPTER 17A

HEALTH

ALLYN L. TAYLOR

THE evolution of United Nations (UN) treaties in the domain of public health over the last two decades is one of the most significant developments in public international law. Traditionally, public health was viewed as a realm of almost exclusive national jurisdiction, and multilateral cooperation was restricted to discrete areas. Public health law today remains predominantly domestic and national, but the field of international health law is extant and extending. Through the codification of binding international legal standards that regulate interstate behavior and national conduct as well as the creation of other global norms that influence state actions, the UN system has contributed to the evolution of the field of international health law.

This chapter provides an overview of the contribution of UN treaties and other international legal instruments in this evolving field. It examines its historical origins and the factors contributing to its contemporary evolution, as well as the contribution of UN organizations to the codification efforts in this realm. Finally, the role of the World Health Organization (WHO) in the contemporary development of international health law is considered in connection with examples of lawmaking with important public health implications.

1 The Evolution of International Health Law

Although public health is one of the earliest fields of international legal cooperation and one of the first domains in which an intergovernmental organization was created, the scope of international legal cooperation in public health was, until recently, highly limited.

Disease has been the unwelcome traveling companion of international commerce throughout history, and international public health cooperation from the beginning was as concerned with facilitating trade as with protecting public health. The functions of the early international health organizations of the nineteenth and twentieth centuries (such as the *Conseil supérieur de santé* of Constantinople or the *Office International d'Hygiène Publique*) centered on combating infectious and communicable diseases and preventing their spread across international boundaries.[1]

With a focus limited to international communicable disease control, public health remained a relatively neglected field of international legal concern throughout most of the twentieth century. The WHO, established in 1948 as the UN specialized agency in the field of health, stood out as unique in that it neglected the use of international legislative strategies to promote its global public policies. WHO member states also paid little attention to the potential contribution of international law in advancing global health.

Nevertheless, the long-standing historical connection between international law and communicable disease control pointed to the larger role that UN treaty-making could serve in future health diplomacy.[2] In the last couple of decades, a number of recent and interconnected developments have expanded the field of international health law under UN auspices.

2 Globalization and the Expanding Domain of International Health Law

It is widely recognized that globalization is contributing to the expansion of international health law. Although increasing global integration is not an entirely new phenomenon, contemporary globalization has had an unprecedented impact on global public health and is creating new and increasingly difficult governance needs and health policymaking challenges. Globalization has contributed to the rapid decline in the practical capacity of sovereign states to address public health challenges through unilateral action alone and expanded the need for health governance structures that transcend traditional and increasingly inadequate national approaches.

Globalization can be broadly understood as a process characterized by changes in a range of social spheres including economic, political, technological, cultural, and environmental. These processes of global change are restructuring human societies, ushering in new patterns of health and disease and reshaping the broad determinants of health. The globalization of trade, travel, communication, migration, information, and lifestyles has obscured the traditional distinction between national and global health. Increasingly

[1] Charles O. Pannenberg, *A New International Health Order: An Inquiry into International Relations of World Health and Medical Care* (Sijthoff and Noordhoff 1979).

[2] For a historical analysis of WHO's limited contribution to international health lawmaking, see generally Allyn Taylor, "Making the World Health Organization Work: A Legal Framework for Universal Access to the Conditions for Health" (1992) 18 Am J L & Med 301. For an examination of the potential role of international law global health diplomacy, see Allyn Taylor "Governing the Globalization of Public Health" (2004) 32 J L Med & Ethics 500.

human activities have profound health consequences for people in all parts of the world, and no country can insulate itself from the effects. Members of the world's community are interdependent and reliant on one another for health security.

The spread of infectious diseases in an interdependent world is to be expected, given increased human migration, congregation, and trade, but globalization has presented other myriad health risks that were not as predictable and are gaining the attention of national political leaders. For example, non-communicable diseases (NCDs), the burden of which was once felt disproportionately in high-income countries, are now the major cause of death and disability worldwide, increasingly affecting people from resource-poor countries.

Globalization also profoundly affects healthcare services in multiple ways. International trade and intellectual property laws limit the ability of low- and middle-income countries to ensure access to essential drugs and vaccines (such as antiretroviral medications). At the same time, through recruitment practices and the "push and pull" of market forces, doctors and nurses are migrating to high-income states, leaving low-income states without adequate human resources needed for well-functioning healthcare systems.

Conventional international law has received new prominence as a mechanism or a tool that can be used by states to facilitate multilateral cooperation in this era of globalization. Globalization has increased the need for new, formalized frameworks for international cooperation, including treaties, to address emerging global health threats. For instance, the dynamics of globalization have created fertile global breeding conditions for the cross-border spread of emerging threats to health, such as weapons of mass destruction (including bioterrorism), emerging and re-emerging infectious diseases, antimicrobial resistance, and the vectors of non-communicable diseases (including tobacco, alcohol, and obesity). Some of these health threats have been the subject of codification efforts within the UN system while others have been under active discussion as possible topics of new global regulatory initiatives.

3 Health and Human Rights Treaties

The evolution of international law in the domain of health is very much tied to the protection and promotion of human rights related to physical and mental integrity. The preamble to the WHO Constitution, the first international expression of the right to health, declares that "[t]he enjoyment of the right of the highest attainable standard of health is one of the fundamental rights of every human being without distinction or race, religion, political belief, economic or social condition." The principal international legal basis for the right to health is found in the core human rights instruments promulgated under the auspices of the UN, particularly the 1966 International Covenant on Economic, Social and Cultural Rights.

Read in conjunction with Article 2, Article 12 of the Covenant, the most significant binding legal expression of the right to health, provides, among other things, that each state "undertakes to take steps," to the maximum extent of its available resources and with a view toward progressive achievement, toward "the highest attainable standards of physical and mental health of all individuals, without discrimination." Beyond this broad formulation, however, Article 12 is replete with ambiguity, neither defining "health" nor the particular state obligations necessary to realize the right to health.

In 2000, the Committee on Economic, Social and Cultural Rights adopted General Comment 14, a detailed explanatory commentary on the right to health under Article 12 of the Covenant. This General Comment sets forth that the right to health is not simply a right to be healthy, but rather a robust human right extending to access to healthcare services and to the underlying determinants of health, including an access to safe water and adequate sanitation, occupational health and environmental conditions, and health-related education and information. Although highly influential, the legal significance of General Comment 14 remains controversial.

The strong connection between health and human rights has only recently received significant attention. A number of emerging global concerns, including HIV and women's health issues, including rape and other forms of violence against women, brought this intrinsic connection to the forefront of international policy concern beginning in the late 1980s and early1990s. Of particular importance was a pioneering human rights approach to the global HIV pandemic adopted by WHO in the late 1980s, which compelled governments to be publicly accountable on an international stage for their actions against persons living with HIV. This innovative global political approach to public health issues highlighted for the very first time the underlying legal responsibility of governments to protect and promote the health of their populations.

The domain of health and human rights has expanded significantly under the auspices of UN agencies and organs, and other international organizations. Specific international legal instruments addressing the rights of particular groups, such as persons with HIV, women, children, migrant workers, and refugees have been adopted. An example is the 2006 Convention on the Rights of Persons with Disabilities, adopted by the UN General Assembly, by which states commit to "provide persons with disabilities with the same range, quality and standard of free or affordable health care and programmes as provided to other persons, including in the area of sexual and reproductive health and population-based public health programmes" (Article 25). Ratifying States also agree to "provide those health services needed by persons with disabilities specifically because of their disabilities, including early identification and intervention as appropriate, and services designed to minimize and prevent further disabilities, including among children and older persons."

Globalization also contributes to the further elaboration of international legal instruments in the realm of health and human rights. Widespread recognition of growing inequalities in health status and differential access to medical advances in rich and poor states has expanded interest in the relationship between social and economic rights and health. Of particular concern is the impact of international intellectual property protection under the World Trade Organization (WTO) Trade Related Aspects of Intellectual Property (TRIPs) Agreement in restricting access to essential medicines in low-income countries. The unprecedented human catastrophe posed by HIV led the international community to adopt a number of non-binding resolutions at the UN General Assembly, the former United Nations Commission on Human Rights, and the WHO specifying the relationship among HIV/AIDS, human rights, and access to medicines. In June 2013, the UN Human Rights Council adopted a Resolution 23/14, broadly recognizing that access to medicines is one of the fundamental elements in achieving progressively the full realization of the right of everyone to the enjoyment of the highest attainable standard of physical and mental health.

4 Linkage and the Scope of International Health Law

The expanding domain of international health law can be understood, in part, as a product of enhanced appreciation of the linkage of health to other legal issues. Global health is increasingly understood to be a central component of other international legal regimes, including labor law, environmental law, biotechnology, human rights, arms control, and international trade. A fascinating illustration is the linkage of public health law and international drug control law under the 1961 UN Single Convention on Narcotic Drugs. The twin aims of this Convention are to control the use and trafficking of substances with abuse potential while assuring the availability of these drugs for scientific and medical purposes. Ensuring an appropriate balance between these twin aims has been a critical challenge for the institutions involved in international drug control, including the UN Commission on Narcotic Drugs, the UN International Narcotics Control Board, the UN Drug Control Programme, and the WHO. In the last decade debate within the UN drug bodies has focused upon expanding access to opioid medications to patients in need without increasing the risk of diversion to illicit channels to, most recently, increasing national and subnational efforts to regulate and even legalize cannabis in contravention of the UN drug conventions.[3]

The evolution of the concept of human security provides another interesting example of this development. The traditional understanding of human security has come under increasing pressure in recent years, with growing support for a comprehensive approach that addresses the wide-ranging factors impacting upon the vulnerability of people. The WHO's 2005 International Health Regulations (IHR) have been at the epicenter of this discussion.[4] The new IHR underscore, the strong interconnection between public health and security. The Regulations establish legal commitments, which are clearly

[3] Allyn Taylor, "Addressing the Global Tragedy of Needless Pain: Rethinking the Single Convention on Narcotic Drugs" (2007) 35 J L, Medicine & Ethics 557.

[4] The National Academy of Medicine, Commission on Global Health, "The Neglected Dimension of Global Security: A Framework to Counter Infectious Disease Crises" (2016) at <http://nam.edu/wp-content/uploads/2016/01/Neglected-Dimension-of-Global-Security.pdf> accessed January 6, 2018.

designed to apply to releases of biological, chemical, and radiological events, both accidental and deliberate. Recent disease outbreaks, epidemics, natural disasters, and other health emergencies have reinforced the linkage between global health and security. For example, the recent Ebola outbreak revitalized discussions of global health security through a range of proposals for reframing global health governance to strengthen the global health security regime.[5]

5 The Role of United Nations in the International Lawmaking Process

International health law is largely treaty-based, and most international treaty-making today is conducted under the auspices of international organizations. In recent years, there has been a significant increase in the number of international organizations active in the domain of health. Within the UN system, institutions with significant involvement in the health sector include specialized agencies, such as the WHO, the Food and Agriculture Organization (FAO), and the World Bank, as well as funds and programs, such as UNICEF, UNEP, UNDP, and UNFPA. For example, international organizations in the UN system have served as centers for codification and debate of treaties focused on food safety and human health. FAO has adopted treaties and other international instruments related to protection of agriculture, genetic resources, and fisheries. For example, the International Plant Protection Convention sets standards for the safe international movement of plants and plant products to prevent the spread of plant pests and diseases, and the International Treaty on Plant Genetic Resources for Food and Agriculture, designed to be in harmony with the UN Convention on Biological Diversity, is focused on supporting sustainable agriculture and global food security. The latter 2004 treaty establishes a mechanism for governments, farmers, research institutes, and agro-industries to work together by pooling their genetic resources and sharing the benefits derived from their use.

As a further example, UNEP has also led codification efforts of several multilateral chemical conventions with important human health implications, including the Basel Convention on the Control of Transboundary Movements of Hazardous Wastes and their Disposal, the Rotterdam Convention on the Prior Informed Consent Procedure for Certain Hazardous Chemicals and Pesticides in International Trade, or the Stockholm Convention on Persistent Organic Pollutants.

Today, there is considerable jurisdictional overlap in the field of international health lawmaking. In the absence of an umbrella organization to manage lawmaking efforts, the proliferation of international organizations with overlapping authority and ambitions is increasingly creating the risk of institutional overload and inconsistent standard-setting.

[5] Ilona Kickbush, *Governing the Global Health Security Domain*, Global Health Programme Working Paper No. 12 (2016) 3.

Rising institutional density is also contributing to expanded use of forum shopping in international health. A host of factors may shape the choice of the negotiating forum, including differences in composition, jurisdiction, decision-making procedures, or working methods. As discussed by Lawrence Helfer, in some cases forum shopping is aimed at gaining a single favorable agreement, while in others it is part of an iterative long-term strategy aimed at "broadening the policy spaces within which relevant decisions are made." International relations scholars have sought to distinguish this broader strategy of forum shopping by defining it as "regime shifting."[6]

An important example of potential "regime shifting" in global health revolves around intellectual property and access to medicines, a topic of fierce political and legal battles in the international community. The TRIPS Agreement ushered in a new era of powerful international intellectual property law that has had a critical impact on access to medicines, particularly in low-income countries. It is also at the core of a wave of international legal instruments and processes seeking to redefine the law of intellectual property. Its impact in impeding drug development capacity and access to medicines in developing countries has received considerable public attention during the last few decades. Concern has arisen particularly in the context of global access to HIV antiretroviral medications in low-income nations. According to UNAIDS, in 2016, only 54 percent of the world's population with HIV had access to care or treatment with life-saving antiretrovirals.

Dissatisfaction with the TRIPS Agreement and shifting power bases at the WTO has led those who support stronger and weaker intellectual property protections in search of alternative and more favorable venues to promulgate treaties and other legal instruments. For example, since 2005, some countries, along with nongovernmental organizations, have undertaken efforts to initiate the development of a proposed treaty on medical research and development under the auspices of the WHO. While efforts to shift the codification debate to the WHO have thus far stalled, other global health actors have undertaken steps to establish more robust intellectual property protections than provided by the TRIPS Agreement elsewhere. Most well known are the so-called "TRIPS-plus" bilateral and multilateral agreements that establish intellectual property rights and obligations that are more stringent than required under the TRIPS Agreement. Furthermore, a range of global standard-setting initiatives act below the level of formal international law, through global networks of international regulators, including best practice standards for custom authorities established by the World Customs Organization, which also cooperates with Interpol and the Universal Postal Union to strengthen the enforcement of intellectual property law.

This regime-shifting battle is symptomatic of the overall challenge of securing development of and access to essential medicines for emerging economies and developing nations, taking into account that one-third of the world's population lacks access to basic medicines. An increasingly significant related legal challenge is the issue of patent protection for repurposed medicines. The process of reusing previously patented

[6] Lawrence Helfer, "Regime Shifting: The Trips Agreement and the New Dynamic of Intellectual Property Lawmaking" (2004) 29 Yale J Intl L 1, 12.

medicines is expanding as an avenue for providing cost-effective and timely access to drugs in low- and middle-income countries. Granting another patent on a known product for a newly discovered use or form adds an additional layer of exclusive rights on the same chemical entity, although only for the new use. The TRIPS Agreement is silent on this issue. Debate on the patentability of repurposed drugs is being taken up in national and international venues, and there is to date no commonly accepted international legal practice. Finding the delicate balance among health, trade, and intellectual property policies to sustain innovation and ensure widespread access to life-saving technologies is one of the primary public policy challenges of our time.

The emerging strategy of regime shifting in global health lawmaking may also point to broader trends in the international health lawmaking arena. Recent dissatisfaction with the WHO is leading some stakeholders in search of alternative forums for international health law codification, both within and outside of the UN system. An important example of this phenomenon is the international community response to the contemporary global threat of counterfeit medicines. The global challenge of international trafficking in counterfeit medicines, including substandard, defective, and adulterated medicines, has underscored the interconnections among international health law, customs law, criminal law, and trade law. It further led, in the late 2000s, to expanding support for an international legal instrument under WHO auspices,[7] but, despite years of debate, the World Health Assembly (WHA) did not achieve consensus on adopting such a legal instrument. Eventually, the Council of Europe adopted the first international treaty on counterfeit medicines, the Medicrime Convention, which is open not only to the member states of the Council of Europe but also, under certain conditions, to nonmember states. The Convention, which entered into force in 2016, provides a framework for national and international cooperation, as well as for coordination at the national level.

States also produce a wide variety of non-binding international instruments that can have an important impact on state behavior. For example, the WTO Doha Declaration on Trade and Public Health is widely considered to have advanced global understanding and, perhaps, action on trade and health matters, particularly in relation to access to essential medicines, even though its legal significance is unclear. Another well-known example is the 1981 WHO Code of Marketing Breastmilk Substitutes, which was designed to protect and promote breastfeeding through the provision of adequate information on appropriate infant feeding and the regulation of the marketing of breast milk substitutes, bottles, and teats. Additional WHA resolutions adopted over the years have further defined and strengthened the Code and, according to UNICEF, as of 2016 over 84 countries have adopted legislation implementing all or part of it. Yet another example is the legal framework established by the 2001 UN General Assembly Special Session Declaration of Commitment on HIV/AIDS and the monitoring mechanism mandated under its auspices and two other subsequent General Assembly resolutions.

7 A Attaran et al, "How to Achieve International Action on Falsified and Substandard Medicines" (2012) 345 BMJ 7381.

6 Examples of World Health Organization International Lawmaking

The WHO has wide-ranging responsibilities to address global public health concerns based upon responsibilities assigned by its Constitution and by its affiliation with the UN. The structure of the relationship between the WHO and the UN is grounded in the Charter. Article 55 describes the goals that the UN has pledged to promote among its members, including solutions to international economic, social, health, and related problems. As the UN specialized agency with the constitutional directive to act as "directing and co-ordinating authority" on international health work, the WHO has the cardinal legal responsibility to fulfil the aims of the Charter with respect to health.

The WHO's broad authority to serve as a platform for international health lawmaking is expressly established by the terms of its Constitution. Article 19 specifies that the WHA, the WHO's legislative body composed of all of its member states, "shall have the authority to adopt conventions or agreements with respect to any matter within the competence of the Organization." Article 1 provides that the objective of WHO "shall be the attainment by all peoples of the highest possible level of health." The broad scope of this mandate vests the organization with the legal authority to serve as a platform for conventions and agreements that potentially address all aspects of national and global public health, as long as advancing human health is the primary objective of such instruments.

However, the WHO has only recently used this broad legal authority to develop conventions to protect global health. The negotiation and adoption of the 2003 Framework Convention on Tobacco Control (FCTC), WHO's first convention, was heralded by many as the sign of a more robust lawmaking role for the organization, but the WHO has undergone severe financial and political challenges and has been in the process of instituting a reform agenda since 2011. The splintering of the WHO's political and financial capacity is contributing to the process of forum shopping in global health governance described previously.

6.1 The Framework Convention on Tobacco Control

The author initiated the idea of a framework convention on tobacco control in the early 1990s and was the WHO senior legal adviser throughout the negotiations and adoption of the treaty.[8] The FCTC was envisioned as a mechanism to promote national public

[8] A detailed first account discussion of the origins of the FCTC and its negotiations are described in: Ruth Roemer, Allyn Taylor, and Jean Lariviere, "The Origins of the Framework Convention on Tobacco Control" (2005) 95 Am J Pub H 936; Allyn Taylor, "Global Health Law: International Law and Public Health Policy" in Stella Quah (ed), *International Encyclopedia of Public Health* (Elsevier 2017); Allyn Taylor, "An International Regulatory Strategy for Global Tobacco Control" (1996) 21 Yale J Int'l L 257 at <http://digitalcommons.law.yale.edu/cgi/viewcontent.cgi?article=1032&context=yjil> accessed December 17, 2017). See also the chapter 17B by Gian Luca Burci in this *Handbook*.

health interventions and multilateral cooperation on aspects of tobacco control that transcend national boundaries.

The choice of tobacco control as the WHO's first treaty enterprise continues to surprise observers. Lawmaking in any context is not just about a single idea, decision or event, but about a constellation of factors and the advocacy of many key actors that come together to create a window of opportunity to shift an issue on the political agenda. In the case of tobacco control, a historic combination of circumstances came together to make the time "ripe" for tobacco lawmaking following the initiation of the idea in the early 1990s. At some level, the WHO's first international lawmaking venture can be understood, of course, within the context of the broader social and political forces operating in the international system at the end of the twentieth century, including the rise of health on the foreign policy agenda of states. But specific contextual factors also included the global problem of tobacco consumption itself and the surrounding political circumstances.

First, by the mid-late 1990s, there was increasing recognition within the WHA of the need for innovative strategies, including potentially legal mechanisms, to protect population health. For over 20 years, the WHA, which then predominantly consisted of Ministers of Health, had adopted resolutions on tobacco and health that had little or no impact on domestic policy. At the same time, the global burden of tobacco consumption and accompanying disease and death was spiralling and rapidly spreading from high-income to low-income countries worldwide. At the time of the negotiations of the FCTC, it was estimated that 5.4 million people were dying annually from tobacco-related diseases, two-thirds of whom lived in high-income states. However, the epidemic was spreading rapidly to low-income states. The WHO predicted that, by 2030, 8 million people would die annually from tobacco-related diseases with 80 percent of those deaths occurring in low-income countries if the epidemic was left unchecked. A second key factor was the globalization of the epidemic. It was not simply that people were smoking and using other tobacco products everywhere, but the epidemic was being spread and reinforced by factors that transcended national boundaries, including advertising and illicit trade. Overall, the globalization of the epidemic was restricting the capacity of sovereign nations to advance tobacco control through domestic legislation alone, making international coordination an essential complement to domestic efforts. Finally, a key rationale behind the initiation of treaty idea was that tobacco consumption was highly sensitive to regulatory interventions: similar types of regulatory strategies had been used successfully in countries around the world at all stages of development. This makes international lawmaking for tobacco control very different and potentially much more effective than some other proposed treaties to address global health problems, such as alcohol and obesity.

In addition, a number of endogenous and exogenous political factors contributed to making the time ripe for international tobacco control lawmaking. First, the WHO's traditional organizational culture and historical resistance to lawmaking strategies evolved under the leadership of its new Director-General in the late 1990s, Dr. Gro Harlem Brundtland. Exogenously, the 1990s also witnessed the evolution of the global political environment and support for effective regulation of the tobacco industry, nationally and internationally. Widespread litigation against the tobacco industry in the United States led to the release of a treasure trove of internal industry documents that revealed that the industry had long known and concealed the addictive and lethal qualities of cigarettes. This led to a seismic shift in public and policymakers' willingness to hold the tobacco industry accountable through national and international regulation. Economic factors also fueled support for the treaty. In the late 1990s, the World Bank released a groundbreaking report, *The Economics of Tobacco Control,* that evidenced that, apart from Malawi and Zimbabwe, tobacco production and sales was a net economic loss for most countries. This report proved to be a crucial factor in building the support of finance ministers and, in turn, foreign ministers for the FCTC negotiations. Finally, an important endogenous political factor contributing to the success of the negotiations was what I have observed as the "failure of the tobacco industry to take the negotiations seriously"—that is, until the legal process was too advanced to derail through political interference without direct legal action by the WHA.

Formally negotiated between 1999 and 2003 in six rounds open to all WHO member states, the FCTC was adopted by the WHA in May 2003 and entered into force in February 2005. The final text of the Convention cuts across a wide range of tobacco control topics, including advertising, production, smuggling and counterfeit cigarettes, warning labels, clean indoor air policies, and health education. As of January 2019 181 countries have ratified the FCTC making it one of the most widely subscribed to treaties in the history of the UN.

The WHO's first lawmaking venture was an important learning exercise that holds lessons for future negotiations. Elsewhere this author has identified important limitations of the negotiation process and the FCTC itself. However, it is important to identify some of the FCTC's critical key successes as a lawmaking exercise. First, the FCTC put tobacco control on the permanent agenda of states. As mentioned previously, in the late 1990s, the WHA primarily consisted of health ministers, who rarely had the authority or capacity to implement commitments made at the WHA domestically. The FCTC raised tobacco control commitments to the level of international legal obligations. The commitments established by the FCTC include procedural as well as substantive ones, including the legal obligation to establish a national coordinating mechanism on tobacco control and cooperate internationally. Second, by raising the political profile of tobacco control, the FCTC process also served as a launch for expansive multisectoral cooperation, including attracting new partners, such as foundations (i.e., the Bloomberg Foundation) and the health and human rights communities. Third, the now biannual meeting of the FCTC Conference of the Parties ensures that tobacco control and the FCTC stays on the agenda of states. By keeping states parties focused on tobacco control through these biannual meetings, the FCTC is generating new legal responses, as shown by the adoption in 2013 of the Protocol to Eliminate Illicit Trade in Tobacco Products.

Fourth, most observers agree that the FCTC has been effective, to some degree, in strengthening the global political environment for tobacco control. However, it is impossible to fully document the impact of the Convention in advancing legislative and policy change in many countries. Many of the FCTC commitments are quite broad, and while the treaty process does include a monitoring mechanism, it remains largely undeveloped. Fifth, the FCTC has been successfully used by states to counter industry threats to tobacco control efforts, and courts have applied it as a legal obligation of states when national law has been challenged by the tobacco industry.

6.2 International Health Regulations

In another lawmaking initiative, on May 23, 2005, the WHA adopted the new International Health Regulations (IHR). The IHR, first adopted in 1951 and last modified in 1981, were designed to provide an effective framework for addressing the international spread of disease while ensuring minimum interference with world traffic. However, they were ineffective in ensuring national action and global cooperation to stop the spread of disease. They only applied to a highly narrow subset of infectious diseases, and were routinely ignored by states. The magnitude of the global impact of catastrophic appearances of new infectious diseases and the virulent re-emergence of old contagions during the 1980s and 1990s underscored the irrelevancy of the old IHR and initiated global interest in securing more effective international cooperation to control infectious diseases.

Although the IHR revision process had been underway since 1995, the negotiations were galvanized by the well-publicized global threats of severe acute respiratory syndrome (SARS) in late 2002 and 2003, and outbreaks of both human (H3N2) and avian (H5N1) influenza less than a year later. The new IHR adopted in 2005 are an important example of the linkage of traditionally distinct subject matters for the protection of global public health. They bring together under one treaty intertwined concerns of public health, security, international trade, and human rights. The IHR include 66 articles divided into 10 parts, as well as nine annexes, expanding the scope of disease coverage, incorporating human rights principles, and instituting demanding obligations for state surveillance and response.

The IHR were adopted pursuant to Article 21 of the WHO's Constitution, a unique lawmaking device in the international system. According to Article 22, regulations adopted under Article 21 are subject to a contracting-out procedure designed to simplify and expedite the lawmaking process. Regulations come into force automatically for all WHO member states, unless they notify the Director-General of any rejection or reservations. The WHO Constitution severely circumscribes the scope of this simplified lawmaking process by limiting the scope of the regulatory authority under Article 21 to traditional public health concerns. In the case of the new IHR, WHO member states that do not opt out are legally required to update policy and law to comport with the provisions of the new instrument. The IHR core capacities required of countries are to detect, assess, report, and respond to public health risks and emergencies of national and international concern. However, progress toward implementing the core capacity provisions of the instrument have been slow at the country level, and the WHA has extended the deadlines for implementation. Significantly, the IHR do not include any financial mechanism to assist states that lack capacity to implement the broad public health system and reporting obligations of the instrument.

Although the new IHR are widely recognized as a significant improvement from the old Regulations, their effectiveness has suffered from the WHO's inability to coordinate stakeholders and from states' noncompliance and lack of implementation capacity. The emergency provisions of the new IHR have been invoked only four times since their entry into force, each time raising criticisms. The Organization, member states, and the Regulations themselves faced considerable criticism during the outbreak of Ebola in 2013 in West Africa and, ultimately, the UN led the global response to this epidemic. The Ebola outbreak, along with the HIN1 2009 outbreak and the Zika virus in 2014, evidence that the global community is not prepared to respond to global health emergencies. In the wake of the flawed response to these outbreaks, commentators have called for major reforms to prevent future disasters and repair the global system for outbreak prevention and response.[9]

6.3 Global Code of Practice on the International Recruitment of Health Personnel

The loss of highly skilled personnel has been a central concern of low-income countries for the last half century. In the context of health personnel, the global workforce shortage and the inequitable distribution of workers among and within nations has expanded in the last few decades and has now reached crisis proportions. The WHO Global Code of Practice on the International Recruitment of Health Personnel, adopted by consensus by the WHA in 2010, marks the first time that the world community has considered and sought to respect critical and, at times, conflicting issues in this realm, including human rights issues.[10] It also reflects the increasing significance of non-binding instruments in contemporary global health governance. It is only the second instrument of its kind adopted by the WHA since the 1981 WHO Code of Marketing Breastmilk Substitutes. In 2015, the WHO held its first formal review of the nature and significance of the Code, finding that while it was highly relevant for global health, it was not yet widely significant in global practice due, in part, to a lack of national and international resources devoted to its implementation.

[9] Suri Moon et al, "Will Ebola Change the Game for the Next Pandemic: Ten Essential Reforms before the Next Pandemic: The Report of the Harvard: LSHTM Panel on the Global Response to Ebola" (2015) 386 The Lancet 2204. See also Lawrence Gostin and Rebecca Katz, "The International Health Regulations: The Governing Framework for Global Health Security" (2016) 94 Milbank Q 264.

[10] Allyn Taylor and Ibadat Dhillon, "The WHO Global Code of Practice on the International Recruitment of Health Personnel" (2011) 1 Global H. Governance 24 at <http://cdrwww.who.int/workforcealliance/14.pdf>.

6.4 Pandemic Influenza Preparedness Framework

An interesting example of a recent non-binding international legal instrument in communicable disease control is the Pandemic Influenza Preparedness (PIP) Framework adopted as a WHA resolution in 2011. The PIP Framework was designed to address the controversy that erupted in 2007 when Indonesia refused to share samples of influenza A (H_5N_1) with WHO collaborating centers, in part because of concerns that its population would not receive a fair share of the benefits of any vaccine developed. The IHR do not address the thorny issue of access to vaccines and other medications in the context of influenza pandemics. The PIP Framework attempts to begin to resolve the controversy. Article 2 sets forth the objective to improve pandemic preparedness and response systems with a benefit-sharing system for influenza viruses that have human pandemic potential, and access to vaccines and other benefits including antiviral medications. Viewed as an international legal instrument, the PIP Framework has several interesting features. Although adopted as a WHA resolution, it is a hybrid instrument that includes contractual instruments (designated as Standard Material Transfer Agreements) and other mechanisms designed to legally bind members of the WHO's Global Influenza Sharing Network and pharmaceutical companies involved in the production of vaccines. While recognized as an innovative instrument in global health governance, the PIP Framework suffers from some notable defects. While it advances a purported equitable benefit-sharing arrangement, the scope of benefits to low-income nations is in many respects limited. Furthermore, its narrow scope implies that it only applies to influenza viruses with human pandemic potential and excludes not only seasonal influenza, but also a host of non-influenza pathogens with dangerous global impacts such as MERS, Ebola, and the Zika virus. Finally, it suffers from a lack of sustainable financing.

7 Conclusion

This is an era of significant change in health policy. Over the last two decades, public health has emerged as an issue central to virtually all areas of multilateralism, ranging from arms control to security to human rights to trade. However, major health concerns ranging from the control of non-communicable diseases to mental health to injuries are not regulated at the international level. In this new era of global health governance, international law may have an important role to play in promoting and coordinating international cooperation and national action on an increasing range of global public health concerns.

The effective design, management, and implementation of international law will be one of the major challenges for global health governance in this century. However, there are conflicting trends. The rise of nativism in some states suggests that it may be difficult to achieve multilateral consensus and action on social issues in the near future unless such issues are directly framed as security concerns. It is also unclear at this point what impact the Trump administration's disengagement from the international community will have on international lawmaking in the near future. As Harold Koh has pointed out, some like-minded countries may strategically leverage international legal cooperation as a countermeasure. The impact of these political changes on concerns such as health has yet to be determined. At the same time, recent developments in international health law and diplomacy have led to increasing calls for international lawmaking in an expanding number of areas related to public health.

The perceived success of the FCTC has inspired calls for the codification of new international legal instruments in multiple realms of public health. In the last decade, there has been a proliferation of proposals for new binding instruments in global health from states, civil society, and academics, which are explicitly modeled upon the FCTC's framework convention/protocol approach. Such proposals have included, among others, framework conventions on alcohol control, obesity, biotechnology, nanotechnology, occupational safety and health, health worker migration, global health, and infectious diseases.

Unfortunately, widespread enthusiasm for new lawmaking has not always been accompanied by sound legal and political analysis. The rising demand for treaties may reflect, in part, their perceived credibility and the widely held view that non-binding instruments are weak and ineffective. However, international law is not an appropriate policy instrument for all global health problems. Given the substantial limitations of international law and the international legislative process, careful consideration should be given to the selection of global health concerns and the construction of legal regimes in future international health lawmaking enterprises in the future. To this end, the FCTC holds important lessons for future lawmaking endeavors. Among other lessons, the FCTC process evidences that context matters—just because a topic appears to be a global health concern does not evidence (1) if there is political will for collective action, or (2) if the topic is a good fit for global lawmaking. The FCTC legal process was propelled by a variety of political, economic, and social circumstances. Tobacco control was also distinctively well-suited for an international regulatory framework because worldwide consumption among adults and children is highly sensitive to similar types of regulatory strategies.

When the FCTC was adopted in 2003, observers widely predicted that the global community was entering into a new era of international health law in which multilateral treaty-making would emerge as a central function of the WHO. To date, this has not been the case. This is partially due to the fact that other organizations within the UN system are addressing global health concerns, and some international health lawmaking topics are splintering off to organizations outside of the UN system, including at the regional level. In addition, given the contemporary challenges of multilateralism and challenges facing the WHO, we are unlikely to see significant expansion of lawmaking under WHO auspices in the foreseeable future. Somewhat surprisingly, this outcome may, in fact, herald an evolution in global health diplomacy.

It is increasingly recognized that the challenges of global governance demand faster and more flexible approaches to international cooperation than can be provided by traditional and heavily legalized strategies. In other realms of international concern, ranging from the environment to arms control, the world community is increasingly turning to the creation of non-binding international norms, which have important strengths and limitations as international legal tools. In the case of tobacco control, one of the key arguments behind the treaty initiative was the fact that a binding instrument was needed to raise the political profile of the public health concern. Much has changed in the 25 years since the FCTC was initiated. As observed in the negotiations of the WHO Global Code of Practice on the International Recruitment of Health Personnel, as health has risen on the foreign policy agenda of states the character of state delegations to the WHA has transformed and there has been a maturing or a deepening of diplomatic capacity of states to engage in global health negotiations at the WHO and domestic policy transformation at home. The transformation of global health on the foreign policy agenda of states and the WHA suggests the potential for greater flexibility in international legal responses to contemporary global health challenges.

It is beyond the scope of this chapter to discuss in detail the advantages and disadvantages of binding versus non-binding approaches to future global health governance within the UN system. Policymakers, however, must give high priority to identifying if and how legal strategies, binding and non-binding, can contribute to the agenda in future international health cooperation, including the major challenges that plague many low-income nations. Each case must be carefully evaluated on the merits. Effectively managed and implemented, the wider use of binding and non-binding international legal instruments in this century may contribute to controlling the global risks and threats to health associated with globalization and, perhaps, assist the global community to take advantage of the opportunities to equitably improve world health that have been afforded by global change.

CHAPTER 17B

HEALTH

practitioner comment

GIAN LUCA BURCI

THIS commentary will give an account of the author's considerations arising from his participation—first as a Legal Officer in the Office of the Legal Counsel of World Health Organization (WHO) and later as the Legal Counsel—in the negotiation and implementation of the Framework Convention for Tobacco Control (FCTC). Some of those considerations reflect his firsthand experiences gathered in the negotiation and internal meetings in the Secretariat. Consequently, it will not always be possible to support them through documentary references.

Even though a broad overview of WHO's normative functions is provided in the previous chapter of this *Handbook*,[1] it is useful to recall briefly the apparent contradiction between the emphasis in WHO's Constitution on the normative authority of the organization and its historical hesitation in exercising that authority. Such shyness is symptomatic of the lack of a substantial body of international law dedicated primarily to the protection and promotion of health.[2] While the reasons for such a development are beyond the scope of this commentary, the point to be stressed here is that a significant number of other international legal regimes are also addressing health protection concerns and have a direct or indirect impact on individual and public health. Maximizing health outcomes requires therefore a careful assessment of the implications of applicable international rules, in particular with regard to investment and trade law that tend to constrain and limit the national authority necessary to regulate in the public interest. This was precisely one of the concerns that FCTC negotiators had to grapple with and that is being tested at the implementation stage through trade and investment litigation against tobacco control measures.[3]

[1] See chapter 17A by Allyn Taylor in the *Handbook*.

[2] Lawrence O Gostin and Devi Sridhar, "Global Health and the Law" (2014) 370 New England J Med 1732.

[3] See, eg, the 2016 award whereby an arbitral panel convened by ICSID has found in favor of Uruguay in a dispute initiated by Philip Morris International against various tobacco control measures implemented by Uruguay (International Centre for the Settlement of Investment Disputes *Philip Morris Brands SARL v. Oriental Republic of Uruguay* (Award) (8 July 2016), ICSID Case No. ARB/10/7.

1 Rationale for a Framework Convention

WHO had been supporting national tobacco control programs at a technical level since the 1970s, with mixed results. Throughout the 1990s, the economic liberalization and deregulation embodied by the WTO agreements and the explosion of investment agreements contributed to the availability of cheap and unregulated tobacco products and was used by the tobacco industry to thwart public health regulations. It became increasingly evident that such a pervasive legal framework, and the perceived uniqueness of tobacco as a lawful product that kills half of its users when consumed as intended, required a dedicated legal approach to try to "carve out" or distinguish its regulation from general rules of international economic law. Two more considerations created a unique political momentum in favor of an aggressive regulatory approach: the discrediting of the tobacco industry, weakened by scandals and lawsuits that disclosed its manipulative practices and portrayed it as devoid of any social legitimacy; and the strong and charismatic leadership of newly elected Director-General Gro Harlem Brundtland, who declared tobacco control as one of her main priorities. After a number of exploratory studies by the Secretariat (including a pioneering feasibility analysis by Professor Allyn Taylor),[4] the World Health Assembly launched a "pre-negotiation exercise" in 1999, and then negotiations in 2000. The FCTC was negotiated by a dedicated Intergovernmental Negotiating Body (INB) and was eventually adopted by the 56th World Health Assembly in May 2003. The Convention entered into force on February 27, 2005, and had 181 parties as of January 2019.

The proposal to develop a "framework convention" following the pattern of environmental agreements came from the Secretariat as a compromise between a recommendatory instrument and a detailed and prescriptive single convention. The model of a general convention, containing broad principles and establishing an institutional framework that would subsequently work toward more detailed obligations in the form of protocols or annexes, was strongly advocated by the Secretariat as the sole effective approach. The main stated reason for such an approach was the heterogeneous nature of the regulatory measures concerned—from taxation to advertising, from smoking in public places to illicit trade—the predictable resistance of countries with strong tobacco interests, and the sheer diversity of positions and interests. As a consequence, it was felt that the negotiation of a single prescriptive instrument would have been too difficult and may have undermined the existing momentum. Negotiating an initial convention containing broad principles and establishing an institutional framework was therefore largely based on considerations of political expedience.

Given the groundbreaking nature of the instrument, the initial ambivalence of many countries, and the mobilization of the tobacco industry against it, the WHO Legal

[4] Allyn L Taylor and Ruth Roemer, "International Strategy for Tobacco Control," WHO/PSA/96.6 (1996).

Counsel was concerned that an irreversible decision at an early stage toward a framework instrument rather than a self-contained detailed treaty could lead to a worst-case outcome: the adoption of a weak convention for the ostensible reason to enable participation by the largest possible number of states, followed by obstacles arising in the negotiation of strong protocols. There were concerns that the strong bias within WHO in favor of consensus decision-making would increase the negotiating leverage of countries determined to avoid strong obligations and pay lip service to the cause of tobacco control.

The latter concerns were proven unfounded, since the final text of the FCTC contains several detailed provisions on key issues, such as packaging and labeling (Article 11); advertising, promotion and sponsorship (Article 13); and sales to and by minors (Article 16). The argument that a framework convention "lacked something" to produce meaningful effects is further countered by the requirement that even the general provisions of the Convention be interpreted in the light of its object, purpose, and principles.[5] On the other hand, it is true that the framework convention approach has resulted in unexpected difficulties in negotiating the protocol on illicit trade in tobacco products (so far the only protocol concluded under the FCTC) and in securing the required number of ratifications needed for this protocol to enter into force.[6] This approach also gave rise to some challenging discussions during the FCTC negotiations on issues such as whether protocols could be adopted before the conclusion of the convention itself, and possible priority topics.[7] In a way, all this was the consequence of transferring the framework convention approach in environmental conventions—where it is justified by the need to develop detailed obligations in the light of evolving scientific consensus—to the realm of health—where it was rather used to create a legal and policy space allowing for progressive agreement on a variety of regulatory issues largely supported by available evidence and science.

A final challenge, which was voiced informally at the outset of the negotiations, was whether the WHO had constitutional authority to adopt a framework convention on tobacco control, since the measures under discussion were largely of an economic and commercial nature, and had no immediate relation to the Organization's public health mandate. That argument echoed the refusal by the International Court of Justice, in 1996, to render an advisory opinion on the World Health Assembly's question regarding the legality of the use of nuclear weapons.[8] At the time, the Court evoked for the first time a "principle of speciality" to assess whether requests by specialized agencies touched on "legal questions arising within the scope of their activities" under Article 96

[5] Jonathan Liberman, "The Power of the WHO FCTC: Understanding Its Legal Status and Weight" in Andrew Mitchell and Tania Voon (eds), *The Global Tobacco Epidemic and the Law* (Edward Elgar 2014).

[6] Protocol to Eliminate Illicit Trade in Tobacco Products, (2013) 52 ILM 365. The Protocol only entered into force on September 25, 2018, after having reached the 40 required ratifications.

[7] "Possible subjects of initial protocols" (Report of the Secretariat) (15 February 2000) A/FCTC/WG2/4.

[8] *Legality of the Use by a State of Nuclear Weapons in Armed Conflict* (Advisory Opinion) [1996] ICJ Rep 66.

of the Charter of the United Nations, and the Court concluded that the WHO's request did not meet that test.[9] Those questions, however, did not escalate into a formal challenge, and the rebuff by the Court just a few years before did not stand in the way of an overwhelming political determination to treat tobacco as a health rather than an economic issue.

2 Negotiation of the Convention

One of the main factors that determined the dynamics of the negotiation, as well as the final text of the Convention, was the lack of experience and familiarity with treaty-making both in the Secretariat and among member states, which are usually represented within the WHO by their ministries of health. Such inexperience manifested itself in a number of ways.

As mentioned previously, WHO member states were initially reluctant to commit themselves to negotiating an unprecedented legal instrument simply on the basis of feasibility studies and proposals made by the Secretariat. For this reason, the World Health Assembly in 1999 decided to establish an unusual "pre-negotiation" phase to discuss the main elements of a possible framework convention, as well as the process that should be followed for its negotiation, before any final decision was made to move to the stage of a proper negotiation.[10] While the dividing line between a general discussion and a negotiation may be artificial, that initial step enabled delegations to familiarize themselves with the treaty-making process and the Secretariat to advocate for what it considered to be the essential measures that should be included in the future convention.

A second factor that affected the dynamics of the negotiation was that, in the initially stages, delegations were strongly representing health protection concerns rather than commercial or political ones. Even though officials from foreign and trade ministries were present from the outset, delegations were clearly not familiar with international trade rules and complex regulatory questions. This inevitably led to a number of misunderstandings and questionable proposals on the more technical and normative elements of the text. Moreover, ministry of health officials maintained an uncompromising stance on certain issues, which they could not accept weakening since this would be considered as an abandonment of the very reason for negotiating a treaty on tobacco control. It follows that public health imperatives initially prevailed over the need to reach compromises to achieve an agreed text.

[9] Laurence Boisson de Chazournes and Philippe Sands (eds), *International Law, the International Court of Justice and Nuclear Weapons* (CUP 1999).

[10] WHO (Resolution of the World Health Assembly) "Towards a WHO framework convention on tobacco control" (24 May 1999) WHA52.18

Negotiations were also sometimes complicated by the alignment of certain groups of states (notably, African states or the members of the European Union) along regional positions, which could not be changed without further agreement within the group. That initial stance was used by more recalcitrant delegations, who exploited the limited negotiating space and filled the text with equally extreme counterproposals. This led to a chaotic rolling text, which was only overtaken by a compromise text proposed by the Chairman at the fifth and next-to-last session.[11] The last two negotiating sessions aimed therefore at salvaging what looked like a jeopardized exercise and saw a number of painful compromises—for example, differentiated obligations to eliminate or restrict tobacco advertising, promotion, and sponsorship under Article 13. Negotiators strived, in particular, to meet the concerns of a sceptical US government. A nonnegotiable request to allow for reservations, which was made by the United States taking into account the attitude of its Senate in giving advice and consent to the ratification of treaties, was rejected so as not to affect an already weakened text. The United States eventually signed the Convention, but has not ratified it.

Some of the foregoing sociological and practical considerations explain the challenges experienced in the negotiation of the protocol on illicit trade. The content of the negotiating text, developed on the basis of an initial expert study, covered a broad number of complex regulatory measures, from the tracking and tracing of tobacco products throughout the supply chain to the licensing of economic operators, and from law enforcement to international cooperation in areas such as extradition and mutual legal assistance. The expertise necessary to master such a broad range of topics was absent or insufficient in many delegations, again leading to confusing discussions and questionable compromises. One example is the lack, in Article 14, paragraph 2, of an exhaustive list of criminal offenses, which would have been valuable to ensure a consistent application of the double criminality test as required in many extradition treaties; every party is instead free to establish its own list among the offenses provided in paragraph 1. Moreover, after much uncertainty, negotiators decided to reproduce almost *verbatim* entire articles of the United Nations Convention on Transnational Organized Crime instead of simply relying on their applicability to most significant illicit trade activities, thus creating potential difficulties in deciding which instrument is to be applied in case of overlaps or inconsistencies. A sobering and unexpected lesson was the realization that regulating the tobacco supply chain would be difficult without the cooperation of the tobacco industry, an anathema for the tobacco control community that has excluded any form of consultation or even contact with the industry. This led to considerable soul-searching, including among the nongovernmental organizations supporting the FCTC process,[12] as well as to the exclusion of tobacco product counterfeiting from the scope of the protocol when it became clear that the industry would have been the net

[11] WHO, "New Chair's text of a framework convention on tobacco control" (25 June 2002) A/FCTC/INB5/2.

[12] Jonathan Liberman, "Combating Counterfeit Medicines and Illicit Trade In Tobacco Products: Minefields in Global Health Governance" (2012) 40(2) JL Med Ethics 326.

beneficiary of its inclusion. The very fact that Philip Morris International issued a congratulatory press release upon the adoption of the protocol, and that its website strongly supports it, created unease among negotiators and health advocates who felt that an instrument aimed at weakening the tobacco industry (accused of being complicit in the illicit trade of large quantities of cigarettes) was being used by the industry to position itself as a legitimate partner in the fight against contraband.

3 Building a Normative Framework

In keeping with the framework convention approach, the FCTC established a Conference of the Parties (COP) with broad powers of coordination, direction, and review (Article 23). It also envisaged in general terms the adoption of protocols (Article 33) and annexes (Article 29) and foreshadowed the adoption of guidelines for the implementation of demand-reduction measures (Article 7). An immediate priority of the COP was precisely to further the normative development of the FCTC through the adoption of guidelines and an early decision to launch negotiation of the first protocol.

The adoption of eight guidelines on nine FCTC articles (as of January 2019) is one of the most significant achievements of the COP and an important development in assisting parties in the design and implementation of robust tobacco control policies. Guidelines have been adopted on eight articles concerning demand reduction measures as well as on Article 5, paragraph 3, aimed at protecting parties from the undue influence of the tobacco industry.[13] Guidelines are adopted by consensus after an elaborate preparatory process involving as many parties as feasible and following a template adopted by the first session of the COP.[14] Albeit not legally binding, guidelines spell out the normative content of FCTC articles; build on previous legislation, international regulation, and evidence; guide parties in the design of their own implementation measures; and represent a subsequent agreement regarding the interpretation of the treaty under Article 31, paragraph 3(a) of the Vienna Convention on the Law of Treaties. The importance of the guidelines in increasing the impact of the FCTC at country level cannot be underestimated, including by clarifying the scope and implications even of vaguer FCTC provisions, such as Article 6 on taxation. It is also significant that FCTC guidelines, as an authoritative statement on evidence-based measures necessary to reduce tobacco consumption, have gained evidentiary and normative force under other international legal regimes, notably on trade and investment. For example, the Partial Guidelines on Articles 9 and 10—contents of tobacco products and regulation of tobacco product disclosures, respectively—have been referred to by the Panel established under

[13] The text of the guidelines is available at <www.who.int/fctc/treaty_instruments/adopted/en/> accessed September 30, 2017.

[14] "Elaboration of guidelines for implementation of the Convention" (17 February 2006) FCTC/COP1(15), available at <http://apps.who.int/gb/fctc/PDF/cop1/cop1_06_cd_decisionsdocumentsauxiliaires-en.pdf> accessed September 30, 2017.

the WTO dispute settlement procedures in the *United States—Clove Cigarettes* case, even though neither the United States nor the claimant in the case, Indonesia, were parties to the FCTC.[15]

As noted previously, the implementation of the FCTC must be viewed against the background of the deep-seated hostility of the tobacco control community against the tobacco industry and its declared intent not only to tighten tobacco regulation but most importantly to ideally "destroy" the industry and through that achieve a "tobacco-free world." In this connection, the COP used the rather generic language of Article 5, paragraph 3[16] to develop a far-reaching guideline that aims at strictly limiting contacts between FCTC parties and the tobacco industry, treating the latter as a special case that should be disenfranchised and not supported in view of the health effects of its products. The guidelines also seek to ensure that FCTC parties implement strict limitations on contacts with the tobacco industry while avoiding conflicts of interest or agreed voluntary measures instead of enforceable regulation.[17] The guidelines create particular predicaments for those parties where the tobacco industry is owned partly or entirely by governments that should "ensure that the setting and implementing of tobacco control policy are separated from overseeing or managing tobacco industry."[18]

Article 5, paragraph 3, was also used as an unorthodox interpreting tool to exclude the public from otherwise open meetings at the COP or during the negotiation of the protocol, once it was realized that representatives of tobacco companies were observing the proceedings from the public gallery. Initially, the rules of procedure of the COP only foresaw meetings to be fully public or restricted (i.e., with the sole presence of parties and the secretariat). However, upon the advice of the Legal Counsel, parties relied on Article 5, paragraph 3 to read into the rule the possibility of excluding the public (including the media) from otherwise open meetings. The rules of procedure were amended in 2014 by including a third category of meetings that explicitly excludes the public while allowing participation of the parties and accredited observers.[19] A more controversial measure was proposed by the secretariat at the seventh session of the COP, in 2016, whereby all representatives would have had to fill out conflict-of-interest declarations and representatives of parties affiliated with the tobacco industry could have been refused accreditation.[20] These proposals, which would have arguably deviated from the

[15] WTO, *United States—Measures Affecting the Production and Sale of Clove Cigarettes—Report of the Panel*, (2 September 2011) WT/DS406/R, 7.5.

[16] "In setting and implementing their public health policies with respect to tobacco control, Parties shall act to protect these policies from commercial and other vested interests of the tobacco industry in accordance with national law."

[17] "Guidelines for implementation of Article 5.3—Protection of public health policies with respect to tobacco control from commercial and other vested interests of the tobacco industry" (22 November 2008) FCTC/COP3(7).

[18] ibid 8, Recommendation 8.2.

[19] "Amendment to the Rules of Procedure of the Conference of the Parties to the WHO FCTC" (18 October 2014) FCTC/COP6(24).

[20] "Maximizing transparency of Parties' delegations, intergovernmental organizations, nongovernmental organizations and civil society groups during sessions of the COP and meetings of its subsidiary bodies" (Report by the Convention Secretariat) (13 July 2016) FCTC/COP/7/30.

sovereign right of a state to appoint its own representatives at international conferences, were eventually not adopted, but are emblematic of the unique mindset surrounding tobacco control.

4 Conclusions

The FCTC undoubtedly represents a major breakthrough in international health law, in particular for the regulation of the risk factors of non-communicable diseases, which have become the highest cause of death worldwide.[21] The momentum created by the FCTC and by the revision of the International Health Regulations in 2005 raised expectations that the WHO had finally discovered international law as an effective tool for the discharge of its mandate. The narrative of "framework convention" has captured the imagination of politicians and health advocates; a number of framework conventions have been proposed by scholars and governments, ranging from an ambitious "framework convention on global health"[22] to a framework convention on pharmaceutical innovation[23] to conventions on alcohol control, non-communicable diseases, pharmaceutical research and development, falsification of medical products, and anti-microbial resistance.[24] Some of those proposals share the same rationale as the FCTC in favor of a normative approach, dealing with market and economic issues otherwise falling within the scope of potentially health-unfriendly legal regimes. New dedicated treaties would limit the applicability of those regimes and signal the credibility of the international political commitment in support of the right to health and the provision of global public goods.

It is striking, however, that none of those proposals have been seriously discussed within the WHO, and that the public health community continues to show a strong bias in favor of non-binding regulatory instruments. Exploring the reasons for this apparently irreversible trend is beyond the scope of this commentary, but it raises legitimate questions as to whether there is legal and political space for new health treaties or whether the FCTC will remain a fortunate exception, brought about by an unrepeatable conjunction of historical, social, and personal factors.

[21] Lawrence O Gostin, *Global Health Law* (Harvard University Press 2014) 383–411.

[22] Lawrence O Gostin, "Meeting Basic Survival Needs of the World's Least Healthy People: Toward a Framework Convention on Global Health," (2004) 96 Geo LJ 331.

[23] Xavier Seuba, "Submission from Global Health Law Committee of the International Law Association" (submission to the United Nations Secretary-General's High-Level Panel on Access to Medicines, 22 February 2016) <http://www.unsgaccessmeds.org/inbox/2016/2/22/contributionxavier-seubaon-behalf-of-global-health-law-committee-of-the-international-law-association?rq=seuba> accessed September 29, 2017.

[24] S Hoffman, JA Rottingen, and J Frenk, "Assessing Proposals for New Global Health Treaties: An Analytic Framework" (2015), 105 AJPH 1523.

CHAPTER 18

INTELLECTUAL PROPERTY

EDWARD KWAKWA

INTELLECTUAL property (IP) law is one of the most rapidly changing areas of legal practice, both nationally and internationally. This is partly due to the mobility and global application of innovation, ideas, and creative works, especially in the digital age. The global IP regime requires a method of norm-creation that is flexible enough to adapt to a dynamic, fast-paced, and technologically driven area of law. In this regard, it is imperative that IP law remains current and responsive to market concerns.

That imperative, on its face, may seem hindered by the traditional methods of rule-making in international law. Yet in the specific area of IP, the World Intellectual Property Organization (WIPO), a specialized agency of the United Nations, has long used precisely those methods to create treaties under its auspices. Unlike many other areas of international law, soft-law initiatives are rarely used in the IP arena.

Indeed, despite talk of the waning of multilateralism, the multilateral IP system does not seem to have succumbed to that depressing development. On the contrary, there is an impressive array of IP treaties adopted in just the last few years. In 2012, for example, the member states of WIPO adopted the Beijing Treaty on Audiovisual Performances.[1] They also concluded, in 2013, the Marrakesh Treaty to Facilitate Access to Published Works for Persons Who Are Blind, Visually Impaired or Otherwise Print Disabled.[2]

[1] The Beijing Treaty on Audiovisual Performances was adopted on June 24, 2012. It deals with the intellectual property rights of performers in audiovisual performances. See Beijing Treaty on Audiovisual Performances, WIPO Publ. No. 228E.

[2] The Marrakesh Treaty is the first treaty ever that is devoted exclusively to creating limitations and exceptions to copyright law. This could be seen as a deviation from the traditional tenets of copyright law. It is instructive to note, however, that the treaty entered into force only three years after its adoption. This makes it one of the IP (indeed, one of the multilateral, not just IP), treaties that has entered into force in the shortest amount of time. For the provisions of the Marrakesh Treaty, see Marrakesh Treaty to Facilitate Access to Published Works for Persons Who Are Blind, Visually Impaired, or Otherwise Print Disabled, WIPO Publ. No. 218E.

In 2015, they adopted the Geneva Act of the Lisbon Agreement on Appellations of Origin and Geographical Indications.[3]

Despite the ongoing importance of multilateral treaties, the IP system now also uses a broad range of instruments of international cooperation, confirming the perception that many practical advances can be achieved without a treaty. Examples of such instruments are WIPO's global databases, practical services such as the WIPO Centralized Access to Search and Examination (WIPO CASE), and the WIPO Digital Access Service (WIPO DAS), as well as a number of public-private partnerships, the most prominent of which are WIPO Re: Search[4] and the Accessible Books Consortium.[5] All these initiatives and platforms function extremely well, yet their establishment did not require a treaty.

Over the years, WIPO has used the convening power of its status as a Specialized Agency of the United Nations to act as a forum through which its member states adopt IP treaties. More recently, WIPO has also used its technical expertise in intellectual property to advance multilateral cooperation in the field of intellectual property law through non-treaty means of multilateralism. Against this background, this chapter will first discuss the historical and political forces that have shaped the IP system today. It will describe the international IP arena, including the establishment, development, and role of WIPO. It will then discuss the politics of the IP system. The third section of the chapter will review actual norm-setting, through treaty-making, in the IP field, while the fourth section will describe some of the new and innovative means of non-treaty forms of international cooperation in the IP arena.

[3] Geneva Act of the Lisbon Agreement on Appellations of Origin and Geographical Indications, WIPO Publ. No. 239E. The Geneva Act of the Lisbon Agreement was adopted on May 21, 2015. However, it has yet to enter into force. Although it will enter into force after ratification or accession by five states, only two states (Cambodia and Cote d'Ivoire) have acceded so far. This may be attributable to the several hurdles that were faced in the run-up to the adoption of this Treaty. See generally Marcus Hopperger and Matthijs Geuze, "Negotiators Modernize International System for Registering Geographical Indications," at <https://www.wipo.int/wipo_magazine/en/2015/03/article_0001.html.> accessed March 8, 2018.

[4] WIPO Re:Search catalyzes the development of medical products for neglected tropical diseases, malaria and tuberculosis through innovative research partnerships and knowledge sharing. It was established by WIPO in 2011, in collaboration with BIO Ventures for Global Health (BVGH), and with the active participation of several of the world's leading pharmaceutical companies and other private and public sector organizations. See generally <http://www.wipo.int/research/en> accessed February 4, 2018.

[5] The Accessible Books Consortium (ABC) aims to increase the number of books worldwide in accessible format—such as braille, audio, and large print—and to make them available to people who are blind, have low vision, or are otherwise print disabled. The ABC is a multi-stakeholder partnership, comprising WIPO, organizations that serve people with print disabilities, and organizations representing publishers and authors. See generally <https://www.accessiblebooksconsortium.org/portal/en/index/html> accessed February 4, 2018.

1 A Brief History

The Convention Establishing the World Intellectual Property Organization (the WIPO Convention) was signed in 1967, and entered into force in 1970.[6] WIPO's origins predate the WIPO Convention to 1883 and 1886, the years in which the Paris Convention for the Protection of Industrial Property and the Berne Convention for the Protection of Literary and Artistic Works were adopted.[7]

WIPO is dedicated to developing a balanced and accessible IP system that rewards creativity, stimulates innovation, and contributes to economic development while safeguarding the public interest. It is responsible for promoting the protection of IP throughout the world, and for the administration of various multilateral treaties that address the legal and administrative aspects of IP. The Secretariat of WIPO comprises about 1,300 staff members from some 120 countries. The budget of the Organization for the 2018–2019 biennium is approximately US$900 million.[8]

WIPO is largely self-financing. The Organization generates almost 90 percent of its income from fees paid by private sector users of the international registration services provided by the WIPO Secretariat.[9] Less than 5 percent of the Organization's income is received from its 191 member states,[10] and the remaining income comes from the sale of WIPO publications, fees related to the arbitration and mediation services provided by WIPO, and interest earnings.[11]

[6] Convention Establishing the World Intellectual Property Organization, July 14, 1967, 21 U.S.T. 1770, 828 U.N.T.S. 3 (last amended Sept. 28, 1979). For a detailed account of the history of WIPO, see generally World Intellectual Property Organization, *Introduction to Intellectual Property: Theory and Practice* (2nd edn, Kluwer, 2017); see also Carolyn Deere Birkbeck, *The World Intellectual Property Organization (WIPO)* (Edward Elgar, 2016).

[7] Paris Convention for the Protection of Industrial Property, Mar. 20, 1883, 21 U.S.T. 1538, 828 U.N.T.S. 305 (last revised July 14, 1967) [hereinafter Paris Convention]; Berne Convention for the Protection of Literary and Artistic Works, Sept. 9, 1886, 828 U.N.T.S. 221 (last revised July 24, 1971) [hereinafter Berne Convention].

[8] Program and Budget 2018–2019, WIPO Doc. A/57/6, <https://www.wipo.int/export/sites/www/about-wipo/en/budget/pdf/budget_2018_2019.pdf.> (Sept. 26, 2017), accessed February 4, 2018.

[9] Some of the WIPO Treaties relating to patents, trademarks, and industrial designs ensure that a single international registration or filing will have effect in any of the designated or relevant member states. The WIPO secretariat's services under these treaties aim at simplifying and reducing the cost of making individual or à la carte applications or filings in each country in which protection for a given IP right is sought. General information is available at http://www.wipo.int/about-wipo/en, accessed February 4, 2018.

[10] It is recalled that there are three WIPO member states that are not UN member states (Cook Islands, Holy See, and Niue), and five UN member states that are not WIPO member states (Micronesia, Nauru, Palau, Solomon Islands, and South Sudan).

[11] WIPO does not have a system of weighted voting. Each member state belongs to 1 of 14 contribution classes, but their rights remain the same, irrespective of the contribution class to which they belong. The effect of the contribution system is that unlike the United Nations, for example, where the United States pays some 22 percent of the organization's regular budget, at WIPO the United States pays less than

In 1974, WIPO became a Specialized Agency of the UN by signing the Agreement between the United Nations and the World Intellectual Property Organization.[12] That Agreement recognized WIPO as "a specialized agency... responsible for... promoting creative intellectual activity and for facilitating the transfer of technology related to industrial property to the developing countries in order to accelerate economic, social and cultural development."[13]

The need for cooperation and coordination between the UN system and WIPO was obvious. To be sure, the rights of "authors" of "scientific, literary and artistic productions" had been recognized in the UN's 1966 International Covenant on Economic, Social and Cultural Rights. The objectives of WIPO, as enshrined in its mandate, included promoting international respect for those rights and the practical need to promote the orderly diffusion of works of the mind, the more efficient and rapid transfer of technology, the international exchange of culture, and the development of international trade law. WIPO's work was therefore seen as an integral part of the UN's efforts to accelerate economic and social development. As stated by a consultant who wrote a report on relations between the UN and WIPO, "[g]reater awareness of this fact on the part of peoples and governments is needed, and the closer WIPO's association with the UN system—with its almost universal membership, its innumerable meetings in all parts of the world, its access to governments and to the public—the more effectively is that awareness likely to be enhanced and extended."[14]

IP has clearly moved to a stage where most economies, not just the largest ones, have explicitly recognized its indispensable role in their economic future. IP is increasingly important because of its interface with global issues such as public health, climate change, biodiversity, food security, and human rights. While this has meant that IP has become less esoteric, the IP system has also become more politicized.

1 percent of the operating budget of the organization. The five largest contributing countries (France, Germany, Japan, United Kingdom, and United States) each contribute less than 1 percent of the organization's budget.

[12] See Agreement between the United Nations and the World Intellectual Property Organization, WIPO Publ. No. 111 (WIPO 1975).

[13] ibid art 1.

[14] See WIPO-UN Relationship, A Study Prepared by Martin Hill, WIPO Doc. WO/CC/III/2 (July 10, 1972). In the Report, Hill also pointed out that "WIPO has major interests in common with the International Labour Organisation (ILO) and the United Nations Educational, Scientific and Cultural Organization (UNESCO), particularly in respect of employees' inventions, the rights of performers and the protection of producers of phonograms and broadcasting organizations. WIPO and UNESCO are both concerned with copyright, each separately administering a multilateral convention, assembling and publishing information in this field, and rendering technical assistance to their member States. WIPO, along with UNESCO and the International Telecommunication Union (ITU), is also involved in the problems of communication by satellite. As regards the International Atomic Energy Agency (IAEA), cooperation with WIPO has been established in relation to the search and retrieval of information contained in patent documents relating to peaceful applications of nuclear energy." ibid, para 13.

2 Politics

While the subject of international IP is, by definition, technical in nature, the IP system has not been immune from the politics of the international system. Historically, IP connoted issues relating to patents, trademarks, industrial designs, copyright, and geographical indications—of interest only to technical IP experts. Today, however, IP is also seen as embracing matters of development, sustainable development goals, access to medicine, and so on. Tensions underlying some of these questions have led to a schism between the general position of developed countries, on the one hand, and developing countries, on the other. To characterize the positions very broadly, debates on IP matters in all relevant fora in the last several years generally trend toward developed countries insisting that we maintain the traditional practice of protecting IP rights per se, and developing countries insisting that we protect IP rights only in such a manner as to ensure that other important social and economic goals are attained.

A few examples illustrate the problem. In 2016, for example, the UN Secretary-General's High Level Panel on Access to Medicines released its report.[15] While most developed countries reacted with skepticism to the High Level Panel's Report, most developing countries welcomed its conclusions.[16]

[15] The High Level Panel (HLP) on Access to Medicines was convened by then UN Secretary-General Ban Ki Moon in November 2015 "to review and assess proposals and recommend solutions for remedying the policy incoherence between the justifiable rights of inventors, international human rights law, trade rules and public health in the context of health technologies." The HLP was cochaired by Ruth Dreifuss, former president of Switzerland, and Festus Mogae, former president of Botswana. See Report of the United Nations Secretary-General's High-Level Panel on Access to Medicines (September 2016).

[16] See, eg, Doc. IP/C/M/83/Add.1, paras 618–624 (Meeting of WTO TRIPs Council Nov. 8–9, 2016, US government arguing in the WTO TRIPs Council that it was "deeply disappointed by the report which detracts from, rather than advances... critical objectives," and that the HLP "has now concluded its work and missed a key opportunity to provide practical observations regarding the complex issues surrounding access to medicines. The report instead offers only a narrow perspective on a subset of those issues and articulates divisive policies that, if implemented, could severely undermine the innovation critical for the development of medicines and health technologies as well as private sector, university and government-funded research." See also ibid paras 631–642 (European Union arguing in the WTO TRIPs Council that "due to its limited mandate, the High-Level Panel has focused its proposals exclusively on addressing an alleged conflict between a research and development model that partially relies on IPRs and the possibility of providing affordable medicines. In doing so, it has missed an opportunity to advance more balanced, comprehensive and workable solutions to the problem of access to health. The Commission would also highlight that no conclusions could be reached with the support by all Members of the Panel, as demonstrated by the dissenting opinions attached to [the HLP] Report, which are no less than nine." cf, see ibid paras. 590–596 (government of Brazil, explaining to the TRIPs Council the rationale behind the HLP's recommendations, and asserting the need for the TRIPs Council to pay due attention to the issues and recommendations raised by the HLP"; see also ibid paras. 597–602 (government of South Africa, summarizing the various issues raised in the HLP Report, and concluding that the Report "is a rich repository and reference document which we intend to use as a reference point to conduct further discussion in the TRIPs Council regarding issues that are pertinent and relevant to its mandate.")

A second example is the ongoing debates at the World Trade Organization (WTO) in respect of the relationship between the TRIPS Agreement and the Convention on Biological Diversity (CBD). Most developing countries take the position that the TRIPs Agreement should be amended to introduce a mandatory disclosure requirement in patent applications.[17] Most developed countries, by contrast, take the position that there is no inconsistency between the TRIPs Agreement and the CBD.[18] While the debates are not always along a North/South divide, it seems fair to conclude that the differences in position are related to countries' levels of development.

As detailed later on in the chapter, the differences in position have also permeated treaty-making discussions in the IP arena.

3 Treaty-Making

The international IP system remains one of the areas of law in which norm-setting through the treaty method is at its most prolific. This section will discuss this trend, which is at variance with the generally slow pace of treaty-making in other areas of international law.

Treaty-making in the IP field is rich with examples. Indeed, WIPO currently administers some 26 treaties in IP.[19] In the adoption of all 26 treaties, the practice was normally as follows: the establishment of a Committee of Experts, whose deliberations, normally

[17] See, eg, Statement by India, TRIPS Council meeting on October 19–20, 2017 (arguing for the amendment to include a new article 29bis for disclosure of origin of genetic resources and/or associated traditional knowledge, as a "mandatory disclosure requirement in patent applications to include disclosure of origin and evidence of prior informed consent and access and benefit sharing, would, in addition to combating bio-piracy, further strengthen the credibility of the patent system by facilitating assessment of the novelty and inventiveness criteria." See Doc. IP/C/M/87/Add.1 (7 February 2018) 12; see also Statement by Haiti on behalf of the LDC Group (arguing that "the TRIPS Agreement should be amended to include a provision making it mandatory to disclose the origin of genetic resources and traditional knowledge when filing a patent application," and that "LDCs are rich in terms of biodiversity and traditional knowledge. They are often victims of bio-piracy. Therefore, the disclosure of the origin of genetic resources and traditional knowledge would allow for these dishonest practices to be combatted effectively, and facilitate the sharing of the benefits gained from the exploitation of such resources." Doc. IP/C/M/87/Add.1 (7 February 2018) 9.

[18] See, eg, Statement by Japan, TRIPs Council meeting on October 19–20, 2017 (arguing that Japan "is firmly convinced that the disclosure requirement would discourage industries from conducting research and development activities on biological materials overseas," and that "the disclosure requirement is not an adequate means for dealing with such misappropriation, so therefore, we have to avoid including it in the intellectual property system." Doc. IP/C/M/87/Add.1 (7 February 2018) 10; see also Statement by Canada, TRIPs Council meeting on October 19–20, 2017 (arguing that "Canada continues to firmly believe that the TRIPs Agreement and the CBD are complementary and that there is therefore no need to amend the TRIPs Agreement in this regard." Doc. IP/C/M/87/Add.1 (7 February 2018) 10.

[19] Some of these treaties were adopted by the predecessor organization of WIPO, the United International Bureaux for the Protection of Intellectual Property—best known by its French acronym, BIRPI. The figure 26 excludes the 27th treaty listed on the table. While that treaty, the Treaty on Intellectual Property in Respect of Integrated Circuits, had its substantive provisions incorporated into

over several years, would be followed by a meeting of a so-called preparatory committee for purposes of deciding on venue, rules of procedure for a conference, and other administrative and final provisions of the treaty, before the actual convening of a diplomatic conference to adopt the treaty in question.[20]

In short, treaty-making in the IP field, as in most other areas of law, has been slow and time-consuming.[21] It is noteworthy that, in addition to being slow and time-consuming, treaties are only binding on those states that ratify or accede to them. Some treaties may never enter into force, notwithstanding the considerable human and financial resources expended on their drafting, negotiation, and adoption. The Washington Treaty on the Protection of Intellectual Property in Respect of Integrated Circuits,[22] for example, was adopted in 1989 after more than five years of negotiations. Almost 30 years after its adoption, the Treaty has been ratified by only one country and acceded to by two others.[23]

The various IP treaties have generally had differentiated administrative and final clauses. For example, as detailed in Table 18.1, the median range for number of ratifications or accessions needed for a WIPO treaty to enter into force is just over nine years. This number is, as in any other area of international law, a function of various variables, including the particular provisions at play in the treaty, the delegates who participated in the negotiation of the treaty's provisions, and other factors dictating one or the other preference.

The procedural as well as the substantive issues at play during the negotiations for the IP treaties outlined previously have also varied. They have ranged from detailed deliberations on what substantive IP protections should be granted, to more recent debates on how best to incorporate development-related issues of concern, in particular, to the developing countries.[24]

WTO's TRIPs Agreement, the Treaty never entered into force at WIPO. It is therefore not included in WIPO's count of 26 IP-administered treaties.

[20] See generally Edward Kwakwa, "Some Comments on Rulemaking at the World Intellectual Property Organization" (2002) Duke J Comp & Intl L 179–182.

[21] On other drawbacks of the treaty-making method, see generally ibid 181–83.

[22] Treaty on the Protection of Intellectual Property in Respect of Integrated Circuits, WIPO Publ No. 202E.

[23] These are Egypt, and Bosnia Herzegovina and Saint Lucia respectively. The Treaty is due to enter into force after the deposit of five instruments of ratification or accession. See art 16(1).

[24] To give just two examples from some of the more recent WIPO treaties: a. The Beijing Treaty on Audiovisual Performances of 2012 makes express reference to the Development Agenda as follows: "Recalling the importance of the Development Agenda recommendations, adopted in 2007 by the General Assembly of the Convention Establishing the World Intellectual Property Organization (WIPO) [sic], which aim to ensure that development considerations form an integral part of the Organization's work, ... Recognizing the need to introduce new international rules in order to provide adequate solutions to the questions raised by economic, social, cultural and technological developments, ..." See Beijing Treaty, Preamble, para 2; and b. The Marrakesh Treaty similarly makes express reference to the WIPO Development Agenda by "[r]ecalling the importance of the Development Agenda recommendations, adopted in 2007 by the General Assembly of the World Intellectual Property Organization (WIPO), which aim to ensure that development considerations form an integral part of the Organization's work." See Marrakesh Agreement, Preamble, para 11.

TABLE 18.1. Treaties administered by the World Intellectual Property Organization

	Treaty	Ratifications or accessions for entry into force
1	Convention Establishing the World Intellectual Property Organization	10
2	Paris Convention for the Protection of Industrial Property	10
3	Berne Convention for the Protection of Literary and Artistic Works	5
4	Madrid Agreement for the Repression of False or Deceptive Indications of Source on Goods	2
5	Madrid Agreement Concerning the International Registration of Marks	5
6	Protocol Relating to the Madrid Agreement Concerning the International Registration of Marks	4
7	Hague Agreement Concerning the International Registration of Industrial Designs	6
8	Nice Agreement Concerning the International Classification of Goods and Services for the Purposes of the Registration of Marks	6
9	Lisbon Agreement for the Protection of Appellations of Origin and their International Registration	5
10	International Convention for the Protection of Performers, Producers of Phonograms and Broadcasting Organizations	6
11	Locarno Agreement Establishing an International Classification for Industrial Designs	5
12	Patent Cooperation Treaty	8
13	Strasbourg Agreement Concerning the International Patent Classification	[complicated calculation]
14	Convention for the Protection of Producers of Phonograms Against Unauthorized Duplication of their Phonograms	5
15	Vienna Agreement Establishing an International Classification of the Figurative Elements of Marks	5
16	Convention Relating to the Distribution of Programme-Carrying Signals Transmitted by Satellite	5
17	Budapest Treaty on the International Recognition of the Deposit of Microorganisms for the Purposes of Patent Procedure	5
18	Nairobi Treaty on the Protection of the Olympic Symbol	3
19	Trademark Law Treaty	5
20	WIPO Copyright Treaty	30
21	WIPO Performances and Phonograms Treaty	30
22	Patent Law Treaty	10
23	Singapore Treaty on the Law of Trademarks	10
24	Marrakesh Treaty to Facilitate Access to Published Works for Persons who are Blind, Visually Impaired or Otherwise Print Disabled	20

	Treaty	Ratifications or accessions for entry into force
25	Beijing Treaty on Audiovisual Performances	30
26	Geneva Act of the Lisbon Agreement on Appellations of Origin and Geographical Indications	5
27	Treaty on Intellectual Property in Respect of Integrated Circuits	5

Treaty-making in the IP field has remained relatively active, especially in respect of those subject matters deemed uncontroversial. Examples are the 2012 Beijing Treaty on Audiovisual Performances, and the 2013 Marrakesh Treaty to Facilitate Access to Published Works for Persons Who Are Blind, Visually Impaired or Otherwise Print Disabled. Another reason treaty-making in the IP field has remained active could be the perception that IP law needs to evolve or change rapidly, in order to adapt to rapid changes in technology and know-how. In addition, it seems likely that the technical nature of IP is such that it calls for clear and transparent rules to specify its regulatory provisions. A treaty naturally provides the most transparent and specific form of regulation.

While WIPO has been the predominant actor in IP treaty-making, there are other non-UN entities that have played a role in treaty-making in the IP field. It is, however, instructive to note that there are only two multilateral IP treaties that are not WIPO-administered. These are the WTO Agreement on Trade-Related Aspects of Intellectual Property Rights,[25] and the UN Educational, Scientific and Cultural Organization's (UNESCO) Universal Copyright Convention.[26] There are several other regional or plurilateral, not to mention bilateral, IP treaties in force. Prominent examples are: the International Convention for the Protection of New Varieties of Plants,[27] the European Patent Convention,[28] the various treaties administered by the African Regional Intellectual Property Organization (ARIPO),[29] and the African Intellectual Property Organization (OAPI).[30]

[25] WTO's multilateral framework includes the well-known Agreement on Trade-Related Aspects of Intellectual Property Rights (TRIPs). See Agreement on Trade-Related Aspects of Intellectual Property Rights, 15 April 1994, Marrakesh Agreement Establishing the World Trade Organization, Annex 1C, Legal Instruments—Results of the Uruguay Round, Vol. 31, 33 I.L.M. 81 (1994).

[26] "UNESCO Universal Copyright Convention 1954," <http://portal.unesco.org/en/ev.php-URL_ID=15381&URL_DO=DO_TOPIC&URL_Section=201.html> accessed February 3, 2018.

[27] International Convention for the Protection of New Varieties of Plants, 1961 (revised March 19, 1991), UPOV Publ. No. 221E.

[28] The European Patent Convention is a multilateral or regional IP treaty instituting the European Patent Organisation and providing an autonomous legal system through which European patents are granted.

[29] Example, the Swakopmund Protocol on the Protection of Traditional Knowledge and Expressions of Folklore. For other treaties administered by ARIPO, see generally www.wipo.int/wipolex/en/profile.jsp?code=ARIPO> accessed February 18, 2018.

[30] The African Intellectual Property Organization (OAPI) is a French-speaking African regional IP organization that was established by the Bangui Agreement Relating to the Creation of an African

It is worth noting, though, that WIPO still plays a significant role or part even in treaties that were not adopted under the auspices of the United Nations. In the case of the TRIPs Agreement, for example, TRIPs incorporates, by reference, the substantive provisions of as many as four WIPO-administered treaties.[31] WIPO also happens to be the only organization that is expressly mentioned in the Preamble to TRIPs.[32] WIPO has also played an active role whenever IP treaties have been adopted in other regional or plurilateral contexts.[33]

In summary, the United Nations, through its Specialized Agency WIPO, is clearly an indispensable player in the negotiation, establishment, and implementation of the multilateral IP framework that exists today.

4 Non-treaty Means of International Cooperation

While the treaty-making method remains the predominant form of norm-setting and international cooperation in the IP field, it is important to recall that there also exist other new and innovative forms of international collaboration that do not necessarily entail treaty-making or norm-setting. As stated at the outset, the treaty-making method has certain disadvantages when it comes to international collaboration and multilateralism in IP. As a result, the international community is increasingly resorting to non-treaty means of international cooperation and certain soft-law methods of multilateralism. A few such examples from WIPO's practice in the last decade will illustrate the point.

In 2011, WIPO, in collaboration with BIO Ventures for Global Health (BVGH), and with the active participation of the world's leading pharmaceutical companies and other private and public sector research organizations, established WIPO Re:Search. It is "a consortium through which public and private sector organizations around the world share valuable intellectual property and expertise with the global health research community. The aim is to promote the development of new drugs, vaccines, and diagnostics in the fight against neglected tropical diseases, malaria, and

Intellectual Property Organization, Constituting a Revision of the Agreement Relating to the Creation of an African and Malagasy Office of Industrial Property (March 2, 1977). See <www.oapi.int> accessed February 18, 2018.

[31] These are: the Paris Convention (n 7); the Berne Convention (n 7); the International Convention for the Protection of Performers, Producers of Phonograms and Broadcasting Organizations (the Rome Convention (1961)); and the Treaty on Intellectual Property in Respect of Integrated Circuits (1989).

[32] "Desiring to establish a mutually supportive relationship between the WTO and the World Intellectual Property Organization (referred to in this Agreement as 'WIPO') as well as other international organizations." See Preamble to TRIPs Agreement.

[33] Notable recent exceptions are the Anti-Counterfeiting and Trade Agreement (ACTA), in which WIPO played no role whatsoever.

tuberculosis."[34] The Accessible Books Consortium (ABC) is another multi-stakeholder partnership led by WIPO, including organizations that represent people with print disabilities, libraries for the blind, standards bodies, and entities representing authors, publishers, and collective management organizations. It aims to "increase the number of books worldwide in accessible formats—such as braille, audio, e-text, large print—and to make them available to people who are blind, have low vision or are otherwise print disabled."[35]

In addition to the examples shown previously, there are several non-treaty forms of international cooperation in the IP field, including soft-law mechanisms and instruments.[36]

Given the disadvantages associated with the treaty-making method, and given the increasing need for quick and responsive methods of multilateral cooperation in the IP field, it seems clear that the IP system needs to adopt non-treaty means of norm-setting or international cooperation. It seems likely that such non-treaty means will increasingly be used in the IP multilateral cooperation framework.

5 Conclusion

Ongoing discussions at WIPO suggest that there may be as many as three new treaties adopted under WIPO's auspices in the next few years.[37] It seems reasonable to conclude that in the foreseeable future, treaty-making as a method, and WIPO as a venue, will

[34] See <http://www.wipo.int/cooperation/en/multi_stakeholder_platforms> accessed February 18, 2018.

[35] See <http://www.accessiblebooksconsortium.org/portal/en/index.html> accessed February 18, 2018. Other examples of non-treaty international collaboration mechanisms include WIPO GREEN, "an interactive marketplace that promotes innovation and diffusion of green technologies by connecting technology and service providers with those seeking innovative solutions." See http://www.wipo.int/cooperation/en/multi_stakeholder_platforms/ accessed February 18, 2018.

[36] Specific soft-law initiatives at WIPO are: the 1999 Resolution Concerning Provisions on the Protection of Well Known Marks, aimed at clarifying and supplementing existing international protection of well-known marks, under the Paris Convention and the TRIPs Agreement (see WIPO Doc. No. A/34/13 (August 4, 1999, available at <http://www.wipo.int/edocs/pubdocs/en/marks/833/pub833.pdf> accessed February 18, 2018; the 2000 Recommendation Concerning Trademark Licenses, which seeks to simplify and harmonize procedures relating to the recordal of trademark licenses (see WIPO Doc. No. A/35/10 (July 26, 2000), available at <http://www.wipo.int/edocs/pubdocs/en/marks/835/pub835.pdf> accessed February 18, 2018; and the 2001 Recommendation Concerning Provisions on the Protection of Marks, and Other Industrial Property Rights in Signs, on the Internet, which seeks to make all rights in distinctive signs that are of a territorial nature internet-compatible, particularly trademarks, trade names, and geographical indications. See WIPO Doc. No. A/36/8 (June 18, 2001), available at <http://www.wipo.int/edocs/pubdocs/en/marks/845/pub845.pdf> accessed February 18, 2018. These soft-law initiatives do not seem to have gained traction, and the treaty-making method has continued to predominate in IP norm-making.

[37] These are; i. The Design Law Treaty, a potential new international treaty that would aim at the establishment of a dynamic and predictable legal framework for the simplification and harmonization of industrial law formalities and procedures set by national/regional offices; ii. The Broadcasting Treaty,

remain the predominant means through which norm-setting in international IP law is carried out. Its role as a Specialized Agency of the UN has significantly aided WIPO's efforts in this regard, by virtue of WIPO's mandate, as elaborated in the Convention Establishing the World Intellectual Property Organization, and as further enunciated in the UN-WIPO Specialized Agency Agreement, which entrenched WIPO's role in the promotion of IP, transfer of technology, and other related socioeconomic development.

Nevertheless, some of the drawbacks that have depressed treaty-making in other areas are clearly affecting the IP regime. For this reason, it is likely that non-treaty methods of international collaboration will continue to emerge and proliferate in the coming years.

In conclusion, IP law has gained increasing resonance in the international system. This may be largely attributable to the WTO's introduction of IP in the multilateral trading system, which has cemented the direct links between IP, on the one hand, and socioeconomic development, on the other hand. Given the advantages as well as the drawbacks of the treaty method, it may be concluded that the multilateral system of cooperation in IP will continue to be enhanced through a combination of treaty and non-treaty forms of collaboration.

which would aim to protect broadcasting organizations' program-carrying signals from theft or other forms of unauthorized misappropriation; and iii. A treaty or an international legal instrument that will ensure the effective protection of traditional knowledge, traditional cultural expressions, and genetic resources.

C. HUMAN RIGHTS

CHAPTER 19

THE HUMAN RIGHTS TREATY BODY SYSTEM

JANE CONNORS

When the United Nations Economic and Social Council created the Commission on Human Rights (CHR) in 1946[1] it instructed it to prepare proposals on an international bill of rights. The CHR chose to formulate a draft declaration, accompanied by a covenant and a report on means of implementation, which were transmitted to the ECOSOC and then the United Nations General Assembly (UNGA). The Assembly adopted the Universal Declaration of Human Rights on December 10, 1948; it also requested the ECOSOC to ask the CHR to prepare a draft covenant on human rights, and measures of implementation, and to examine the rights to petition.[2] The Commission devoted itself to this work from 1949, but it took the General Assembly until 1966 to approve the International Covenants on Civil and Political Rights (ICCPR) and Economic, Social and Cultural Rights (ICESCR). One year earlier, in 1965, the Assembly adopted the International Convention on the Elimination of Racial Discrimination (ICERD). Since then, a further six "core" UN human rights treaties have been adopted, as have substantive and procedural protocols, with most negotiated in the CHR and its replacement the Human Rights Council. All UN member and observer states are party to at least one of these treaties, while the majority has accepted four or more. In line with its articles 42 and 43 on accession or confirmation by regional integration organizations, the Convention on the Rights of Persons with Disabilities (CRPD) has also been accepted by the European Union.[3]

[1] UN Economic and Social Council (ECOSOC) Res 5(I) (16 February 1946) UN Doc E/Res/5(I).

[2] UN General Assembly (UNGA) "Draft International Covenants on Human Rights: Annotation prepared by the Secretary-General" (1 July 1955) UN Doc A/2929, Chapter I, paras 1–9.

[3] See UN Treaties Collection "Multilateral Treaties Deposited with the Secretary-General: Chapter IV: Human Rights for information on the status of acceptance, reservations and declarations" <https://treaties.un.org/Pages/Treaties.aspx?id=4&subid=A&clang=_en> accessed January 17, 2019.

A "human rights treaty body," comprising between 10 and 23 independent experts, is established to examine the progress made by states parties in the implementation of the guarantees set out in each of the treaties and their related substantive protocols. A 25-member treaty body also implements the mandates created by the Optional Protocol to the Convention against Torture.[4]

This chapter provides an overview of these bodies, including their composition and the tools they have to encourage states parties to implement their treaty obligations fully. It traces the development of their working methods and interface with stakeholders, such as UN entities and civil society. In so doing, it highlights the fact that each has approached its treaty as a living document, thereby expanding the individual treaty body's competence and influence so that, among other things, newer treaties codify improvements made by the treaty bodies overseeing treaties adopted and established earlier. The chapter also touches on the many initiatives that have been launched to strengthen the treaty bodies and create a dynamic and coherent human rights treaty body system.

1 Composition

With the exception of the members of the Committee on Economic, Social and Cultural Rights, treaty body experts are elected at biennial meetings of states parties to the instruments.[5] Experts are nominated by states parties, but serve in their personal capacity and are not subject to instruction from any state. Each works pro bono and is not an employee of the UN. They serve a four-year term and, except in the case of the Subcommittee on the Prevention of Torture (SPT), the CRPD and the Committee on Enforced Disappearances (CED) whose members are eligible for consecutive re-election once, there is no limit on the number of terms they may serve. Indeed, some members have served for long uninterrupted periods, while others have been re-elected after a break or have been elected as a member of another human rights treaty body.

The treaties call for members to be of high moral standing and competence in the field addressed by the instrument.[6] In electing experts, states parties are called on to give consideration to equitable geographic distribution and the representation of the different forms of civilization and legal systems. Some treaties indicate that legal or similar experience

[4] See Table "The UN human rights treaties and the human rights treaty bodies" in Section 2 of this chapter.

[5] This Committee is established by ECOSOC Res 1985/17 (28 May 1985) UN Doc E/RES/1985/17. Its members are elected by ECOSOC member states. Unlike other treaty bodies, membership is subject to strict regional distribution. The UNGA has recommended that consideration be given to replacing this procedure with elections by states parties to the ICESCR, while preserving the requirements set out by ECOSOC: UNGA Res 68/268 (21 April 2014) UN Doc A/RES/68/268, para 11.

[6] Article 5, para 2 of the Optional Protocol to the Convention against Torture and Other Cruel, Inhuman or Degrading Treatment or Punishment requires experts to have "proven professional experience in the field of administration of justice, in particular criminal law, prison or police administration, or in the various fields relevant to the treatment of persons deprived of their liberty."

should be borne in mind. Paying "due account" to balanced gender representation is suggested in recent treaties, and the CRPD also refers to desirability of the inclusion of persons with disabilities. The strength of each treaty body depends on the quality and independence of its experts, and this has been a perennial preoccupation of states, civil society, and treaty body members. State officials, including ambassadors, are amongst the members of treaty bodies, and this is often cited as a factor that compromises that member's independence, or, at the very least, engenders a perception of lack of independence. Additionally, equitable geographical representation is sometimes not achieved, an issue that has attracted the attention of the General Assembly, which has discussed promotion of equitable geographical distribution in the membership of the human rights treaty bodies, most recently at its 72nd session in 2017.[7] Gender balance in the membership of the treaty bodies has also been a challenge, as with the exception of the Committee on the Elimination of Discrimination against Women, to which only six men have been elected since its inaugural session in 1982, treaty body members are predominantly male.[8]

Various strategies have been introduced by individual treaty bodies to bolster the appearance of independence and impartiality of their members, including precluding members from participating in activities that concern their countries of nationality. In 2012, the meeting of the chairs of the human rights treaty bodies, which constitutes the treaty bodies' coordination mechanism, adopted the Addis Ababa guidelines on the independence and impartiality of members of the human rights treaty bodies, which systematize these strategies on the basis of best practice, as well as encouraging states parties to ensure that independent, expert, and diverse candidates are elected.[9] Implementation of the guidelines, which are not mandatory, by each treaty body will buttress the independence and diversity of members. Complementary measures have also been suggested by the UN Office of the High Commissioner for Human Rights,[10] which is responsible for the provision of technical and substantive support to all human

[7] UNGA "Report of the Secretary-General: promotion of equitable geographical distribution in the membership of the human rights treaty bodies" (4 August 2017) UN Doc A/72/284 provides comprehensive information on the membership of the treaty bodies as of August 4, 2017. On December 19, 2017, the General Assembly adopted A/RES/72/174 on the issue following a recorded vote.

[8] The 2016 CRPD election where no woman was successful was particularly criticized, especially as this resulted in a committee of 1 woman and 17 men: <www.unwomen.org/en/news/stories/2016/6/committee-on-the-rights-of-persons-with-disabilities>accessed January 17, 2019.

The Committee itself expressed dismay at its composition in a statement adopted at its 17th session from March 29 to April 12, 2017. The gender balance in the membership of treaty bodies as of August 4, 2017 is described in A/72/284 (n 7) paras 23–24.

[9] UNGA "Note by the Secretary-General: Implementation of human rights instruments: Report of the chairpersons of human rights treaty bodies on their twenty-fourth meeting" (2 August 2012) UN Doc A/67/222, Annex I.

[10] Office of the United Nations High Commissioner for Human Rights (OHCHR) "Strengthening the United Nations Human Rights Treaty Body System: A report by the United Nations High Commissioner for Human Rights, Navanethem Pillay" (26 June 2012) UN Doc A/66/860, Section 4.4, para 75–79. The OHCHR also produced a "Handbook for Human Rights Treaty Body Members" (New York and Geneva 2015) HR/PUB/15/2 designed to assist treatybody members to understand their responsibilities, especially in respect of independence.

rights treaty bodies, and civil society, but sustained advocacy with states parties is required to ensure these ideas are implemented.

2 Competence

Each treaty body overseeing a core treaty is invested with various capacities aimed at assisting states parties to implement their treaty obligations. These include: consideration of states parties' reports, the formulation of general comments, the conduct of communications procedures and inquiries, and early warning and urgent action procedures.

2.1 Reporting

States parties to each core UN human rights treaty undertake to report regularly on their implementation of the treaty.[11] In general, initial reports must be submitted to the relevant treaty body within one or two years of the treaty entering into force for the state concerned. Thereafter, periodic reports[12] are due in accordance with the provisions of the treaty or the established practice of the treaty body. Most treaties also allow committees to call for reports at any time, but this power is rarely used.[13]

All treaty bodies have issued detailed reporting guidelines on the form and content of initial and periodic reports.[14] In general, states parties are to submit a "treaty specific document" outlining the legal, administrative, and judicial measures taken to give effect to the treaty obligations and any difficulties they may have encountered. States are also to submit a "common core document" to all the treaty bodies to which they report, which they are encouraged to keep updated, setting out the general domestic legal and constitutional framework for the protection of human rights and information on implementation of substantive treaty provisions that are common to all, or several, treaties. The reporting guidelines urge states to provide concrete examples of implementation, and not focus exclusively on the constitutional and legal framework.

Reports are prepared at the national level, usually under the direction of a lead ministry or an inter-ministerial committee. The UN High Commissioner for Human Rights

[11] "Note by the Secretariat: Compliance by States parties with their reporting obligations to international human rights treaty bodies" (23 March 2018) UN Doc HRI/MC/2018/2 paras 1–5.

[12] CPED, art. 29 only requires a report on implementation two years after the entry into force for the state concerned; it may request further information on implementation at any time.

[13] The most recent example is the request to the government of Myanmar by the Committee on the Elimination of Discrimination against Women made at its 68th session that an exceptional report on the situation of women and girls from northern Rakhine State be submitted by May 2018: <http://www.ohchr.org/EN/NewsEvents/Pages/DisplayNews.aspx?NewsID=22459&LangID=E> accessed January 17, 2019.

[14] See the webpages of each treaty body at <http://www.ohchr.org/EN/HRBodies/Pages/HumanRightsBodies.aspx> accessed January 17, 2019.

encourages each state to establish a national reporting and coordination mechanism to systematize preparation of reports and facilitate national consultations and follow-up.[15]

2.1.1 The UN Human Rights Treaties and the Human Rights Treaty Bodies

Instrument	Treaty body
International Convention on the Elimination of Racial Discrimination (ICERD)	Committee on the Elimination of Racial Discrimination (18 members)
International Covenant on Civil and Political Rights (ICCPR)	Human Rights Committee (18 members)
First Optional Protocol to the ICCPR (ICCPR-OP1)	Human Rights Committee
Second Optional Protocol to the ICCPR on the Abolition of the Death Penalty (ICCPR-OP2)	Human Rights Committee
International Covenant on Economic, Social and Cultural Rights (ICESCR)	Committee on Economic, Social and Cultural Rights (18 members)
Optional Protocol to the ICESCR (ICESCR-OP)	Committee on Economic, Social and Cultural Rights
Convention against Torture and Other Forms of Cruel, Inhuman and Degrading Treatment (UNCAT)	Committee against Torture (10 members)
Optional Protocol to UNCAT (UNCAT-OP)	Subcommittee on Prevention of Torture (25 members)
Convention on the Elimination of All Forms of Discrimination against Women (CEDAW)	Committee on the Elimination of Discrimination against Women (23 members)
Optional Protocol to CEDAW (CEDAW-OP)	Committee on the Elimination of Discrimination against Women
Convention on the Rights of the Child (CRC)	Committee on the Rights of the Child (18 members)
Optional Protocol on Sale of Children, Child Prostitution and Child Pornography	Committee on the Rights of the Child
Optional Protocol on Children in Armed Conflict	Committee on the Rights of the Child
Optional Protocol to the Convention on the Rights of the Child on a Communications Procedure (CRC-OP3)	Committee on the Rights of the Child
International Convention on the Rights of Migrant Workers and their Families (ICRMW)	Committee on the Rights of Migrant Workers (14 members)
Convention on the Rights of Persons with Disabilities (CRPD)	Committee on the Rights of Persons with Disabilities (18 members)
Optional Protocol to the CRPD (CRPD-OP)	Committee on the Rights of Persons with Disabilities
International Convention for the Protection of all Persons from Enforced Disappearance (CPED)	Committee on Enforced Disappearances (10 members)

15 OHCHR "National Mechanisms on Reporting and Follow-up: A Practical Guide to Effective State Engagement with International Human Rights Mechanisms" (New York and Geneva 2016) HRI/PUB/16/1.

There is usually a delay in the consideration of the report as most treaty bodies have many reports awaiting examination;[16] thus they review the report in a pre-sessional working group, which convenes one or two sessions prior to the session at which the plenary will consider the report, to adopt a "list of issues and questions" that allows for updates. The list is based on all available information, including that provided by UN entities and civil society, such as nongovernmental organizations and national human rights institutions (NHRIs), and the state is asked to respond in writing well before the plenary consideration. In 2007, the Committee against Torture adopted an optional reporting procedure, whereby if the state party agrees, the Committee prepares lists of issues *prior* to the submission of the report, which are based on all available information, and the response of the state party, together with the common core document, constitutes the its report. The UNGA has encouraged the treaty bodies to offer this "simplified reporting procedure" to states parties,[17] and currently all treaty bodies invite states to use this approach with respect to *periodic* reports. The Committee on the Elimination of Racial Discrimination and the Committee against Torture also offer this option to states with long overdue *initial* reports.[18]

Consideration of reports takes place in public meetings, with the relevant treaty body engaging in what is termed "constructive dialogue" with representatives of the reporting state, sometimes participating through video technology. After the public consideration, which typically lasts six hours, the relevant committee adopts "concluding observations," designed to provide the state with concrete guidance on strengthening implementation of the treaty. Accordingly, although reference is made to positive developments, the primary focus is on areas of concern and recommendations for action. Concluding observations, which the UNGA indicates should be short, targeted, specific, pragmatic, and as implementable as possible, so that the state party may follow up,[19] have become more operational over the years.

Treaty bodies require information on implementation of previous recommendations to be included in the next periodic report, and all, except the Committee on the Rights of the Child, have developed procedures for follow-up to concluding observations, whereby states are invited to report back within one or two years on follow-up action. Most have appointed a Special Rapporteur/s or Coordinator/s for follow-up who is/are in regular contact with states parties. Where follow-up information is deficient or not forthcoming despite reminders, this mechanism can organize meetings with government representatives to survey possible follow-up action and urge the state party to

16 See UNGA "Report of the Secretary-General: Status of the Human Rights Treaty Body System" (18 July 2016) UN Doc A/71/118 paras 29–35 and Annex VIII, for an indication of the backlog of reports awaiting review on December 31, 2015.

17 UNGA Res 68/268 (21 April 2014) UN Doc A/RES/68/268.

18 "Status of Human Rights Treaty Body System" (n 16) Annex XIV. The advantages of the simplified reporting procedure are outlined in: "Note by the Secretariat: Simplified Reporting Procedure" (14 April 2014) UN Doc HRI/MC/2014/4.

19 See UNGA Res 68/268. "Note by the Secretary-General: Implementation of human rights instruments: report of the Chairs of the human rights treaty bodies on their twenty-sixth meeting" (11 August 2014) UN Doc A/69/285 Annex II.

implement the committee's recommendations. Some of the treaty bodies that have developed follow-up procedures grade states on progress made, and most report on the status of follow-up in a chapter of reports and on their web pages.[20]

Reporting to the treaty bodies can be a challenge for states parties, particularly those that have ratified most or all of the core instruments. Indeed, as of December 1, 2017, 578 reports relating to 160 states parties to be submitted to the human rights treaty bodies were overdue.[21] The reports of some states are more than a decade overdue, and some may have never submitted a report. States that experience difficulties with the reporting procedures may seek technical assistance from the OHCHR, which has conducted many reporting workshops for states, often in partnership with other organizations and/or NGOs.

Where states fail to submit reports despite repeated reminders, the relevant treaty body may initiate a process, sometimes referred to as the "review procedure," of consideration of the state's implementation in the absence of a report. The state party is notified of the intention of the treaty body to proceed with a review in the absence of a report; if it submits a report, or indicates that one will be submitted, the review procedure is suspended. If no response is received, the treaty body may formulate a list of issues and questions for the state party and invite a state delegation to attend a nominated session. Concluding observations are formulated on the basis of the dialogue with the state party and other information. Although states are actively encouraged to send a delegation, if no response is received the treaty body will conduct the review in its absence. Examination of the state's performance by the treaty body takes place in public session on the basis of existing information from relevant stakeholders, and the concluding observations are adopted and transmitted to the state concerned. The review procedure is used in exceptional cases only, although since October 2010 the Human Rights Committee has examined at least one state party each session in this way. In most cases, notification by a committee that it intends to consider a state in the absence of a report results in the state agreeing to present the overdue report within an agreed deadline.

2.2 General Comments/Recommendations

All treaty bodies, with the exception of the Sub-Committee for the Prevention of Torture, issue "general comments." In the case of the Committee on the Elimination of Racial Discrimination and the Committee on the Elimination of Discrimination against Women, in line with the language of their treaties, these are termed "general recommendations." These documents, which are addressed to states parties as a whole, are adopted

[20] "Note by the Secretariat: Procedures of the human rights treaty bodies for following up on concluding observations, decisions and views" (8 May 2017) UN Doc HRI/MC/2017/4 Part III paras 5–49; 2–14. See also "Note by the Secretariat: Expert meeting on follow-up to treaty body recommendations" (21 March 2018) UN Doc HRI/MC/2018/CRP.2.

[21] "Note by the Secretariat: Compliance by States parties with their reporting obligations to international human rights treaty bodies" (n 11).

through a consultative, inclusive, and transparent process.[22] The comments or recommendations, which may be formulated jointly by one or more committees,[23] are drafted rigorously and adopted by consensus. They provide authoritative guidance on the general treaty obligations of states parties or set out how the treaty body interprets the scope of the substantive provisions of their treaty. General comments and recommendations frequently deal with wider thematic or cross-cutting issues, such as the role of NHRIs, the obligations of states during states of emergency, gender-based violence against women, or gender-related dimensions of racial discrimination. While not legally binding, these documents are considered by individual committees to constitute its jurisprudence. Some have had influence on the development of human rights law at the international and regional levels. They have also been referenced in laws, policies, and programs in states parties and formed the basis of civil society advocacy and interventions. States and complainants in litigation and other complaints procedures also invoke these texts, and, increasingly, they are cited by international, regional, and national courts in their judgments.[24]

Often the elaboration of general comments/recommendations includes the organization of a day of general discussion or thematic debate, but these may also be convened to discuss issues of general concern or provide guidance to states parties. In general, these allow for broad participation, but some treaty bodies convene closed thematic discussions with invited experts. [25]

In addition to general comments/recommendations, some treaty bodies adopt "suggestions" and "decisions" that usually relate to procedural matters, and, particularly recently, "statements" or "open letters," which can be adopted jointly by several treaty bodies or with other human rights mechanisms. The human rights treaty body chairpersons also issue statements on behalf of all human rights treaty bodies, frequently on UN processes, such as the Sustainable Development Goals.[26] The Committee on the

[22] UNGA "Note by the Secretary-General: Implementation of human rights instruments: Report of the Chairs of the human rights treaty bodies on their twenty-seventh meeting" (7 August 2015) UN Doc A/70/302 para 91.

[23] UN Convention on the Elimination of All Forms of Discrimination against Women, Convention on the Rights of the Child "Joint general recommendation 31 of the Committee on the Elimination of Discrimination against Women/ general comment 18 of the Committee on the Rights of the Child on harmful practices"(14 November 2014) UN Doc CEDAW/C/GC/31-CRC/C/GC/18 is the first example of this.

[24] See Advisory Opinion relating to the Administrative Tribunal of the International Labour Organization on a complaint filed against the International Fund for Agricultural Development [2012] ICJ Rep 10; Case Concerning Ahmadou Sadio Diallo (Republic of Guinea v Democratic Republic of Congo) [2010] ICJ Rep 639; *Secretary of Security v Sakthevel Prabakar* [2005] 1 HKLRD 289 (Hong Kong Court of Final Appeal); *Vishaka v State of Rajasthan* (1997) 6 SCC 241 (Supreme Court of India); *Opuz v Turkey* (9 June 2009) ECHR 3340/02; *Gonzàlez v Mexico* (16 November 2009) Inter-American Court of Human Rights Series C; *Government of the RSA et al v Grootboom* (11) BCLR 1169 (Judgement of 4 October 2000).

[25] "Note by the Secretariat: Other activities of the human rights treaty bodies and participation of stakeholders in the human rights treaty body process" (22 April 2013) UN Doc HRI/MC/2013/3 paras 19–20.

[26] "Joint statement of the treaty body chairpersons on human rights and the post-2015 development agenda: Note by the Secretariat: Report of the Chairs of the Human Rights Treaty Bodies on their twenty-seventh Meeting" (7 August 2015) UN Doc A/70/302 Annex I.

Rights of the Child also has the power to recommend to the General Assembly that it request the Secretary-General to undertake studies on specific issues relating to the rights of the child.[27] Pursuant to this, studies have been conducted on the impact of children of armed conflict and violence against children, both of which led to the establishment of special representatives of the Secretary-General on the topic. At the time of this writing, a study on children deprived of their liberty was ongoing.[28]

2.3 Complaints Procedures

The ability to consider claims that human rights have been violated is an important part of the protection function of the human rights treaties bodies. The ICCPR-OP1, ICESCR-OP, UNCAT, ICERD, ICRMW, CPED, and CRC-OP3 provide that a state party may complain to the relevant treaty body that another state party is not fulfilling its treaty obligations where, except in the case of ICERD, both the states concerned have accepted this competence.[29] These inter-state complaints mechanisms had not been used until 2018 when three such complaints were submitted to CERD.[30]

All but one of the treaty bodies that support the core human rights treaties implement optional individual complaints procedures. These procedures allow individuals or groups of individuals to complain that a state party has violated its obligations under the relevant treaty or substantive protocols to that treaty. As these procedures are optional, states must accept the competence of the relevant committee to receive individual complaints, before they can be accessed. The ICRMW provides for such a procedure, but it has not been accepted by the required number of states for the Committee to start receiving communications.[31]

The procedure for the examination of individual complaints is generally characterized as "quasi-judicial." It is written and confidential; oral hearings are rare. Complainants do not need to be supported by legal representation, but this is advisable; however, there is no UN system of legal aid to help with this.

Complaints are prescreened as to their compatibility with the provisions of the relevant treaty and fulfilment of basic admissibility requirements by the OHCHR. A treaty body member designated as Special Rapporteur for New Communications, or a Working Group, decides on the registration of complaints and issues instructions on how to proceed with new cases. Once formally registered, the complaint is normally transmitted to

[27] CRC art 45(c). [28] Relevant material up to July 1, 2018 is reflected in this chapter.

[29] ICCPR, art 41; ICESCR-OP, art 10; UNCAT, art 21; ICERD, arts 11–13; ICRMW, art 76; CPED, art 32; CRC-OP3, art 12. These procedures should be distinguished from the provisions relating to disputes between two states parties in respect of interpretation or application of the treaty found in ICERD, CEDAW, ICRMW, and CPED that have been invoked on rare occasions.

[30] "Press release: Committee on the Elimination of Racial Discrimination concludes its ninety-fifth session" (11 May 2018) <https://www.ohchr.org/EN/NewsEvents/Pages/DisplayNews.aspx?NewsID=23079&LangID=E>

[31] Ten acceptances are required before this procedure can start to function: ICRMW, art 77(8).

the respondent state party for observations. Deadlines for observations vary according to the treaty and the practice of each committee, but states usually have six months to submit observations on both the admissibility and merits of a communication. The state party's observations are sent to the complainant for comments, who also has a set deadline in which to respond. If a state party fails to respond to a complaint, the relevant treaty body usually bases its assessment of the situation on the facts as submitted by the complainant, provided they are properly substantiated. A state party may request that the treaty body examine the admissibility of the communication separately from the merits should it believe that the communication is inadmissible. The state must set out the reasons for its view. In such circumstances the complainant is given the opportunity to respond to the claims of inadmissibility and it is up to the treaty body to decide whether to consider the admissibility and merits of the communication separately.

Treaty bodies may issue interim measures of protection in situations of particular urgency, which require immediate action to prevent irreparable harm to the complainant. These are often issued in death penalty, life-threatening, and deportation or extradition cases.[32] The vast majority of states parties complies with such requests. The Human Rights Committee and the Committee against Torture also issue requests for "provisional measures of protection." These differ from interim measures as they indicate explicitly that they may be reviewed, at the request of the state, in light of information and comments received from it and further comments, if any, from the complainant. Treaty bodies regard compliance with interim measures requests as inherent in a state party's treaty obligations, and any failure to comply with them a serious breach thereof.[33]

Decisions on admissibility are adopted either by the Committee plenary or a working group. The Committees examine a number of admissibility criteria, which are set out in the constituent instruments.[34] First, the complainant must show that he or she is a "victim" of a violation of provisions of the instrument he or she invokes. The complainant must be personally affected by the impugned state action. General claims by groups or an individual not affected by the alleged violation ("*actio popularis*") are not permissible. However, complaints may be brought by third parties on behalf of individuals provided they have given their written consent or are unable to do so.

Second, the complaint must relate to events that occurred *after* the entry into force of the complaint mechanism for the state party concerned (admissibility *ratione temporis*), unless these continue to produce effects after the date of its entry into force that constitute a violation of the relevant treaty.

[32] Human Rights Committee, "Rules of Procedure of the Human Rights Committee" (11 January 2012) UN Doc CCPR/C/3/Rev 10, Rule 92; Committee against Torture, "Rules of Procedure of the Committee against Torture (1 September 2014) UN Doc CAT/C/3/Rev 6 Rule 114;); Committee on the Elimination of Racial Discrimination, "Rules of Procedure, of the Committee on the Elimination of Racial Discrimination" (1986) CERD/C/35/Rev. 3, Rule 94(3). Explicit powers to request interim measures are included in the CEDAW-OP, CRPD-OP, CPED, ICESCR-OP, and CRC-OP.

[33] See *Piandiong v The Philippines*, CCPR/C/70/D/869/1999 (19 October 2000) para 5.2; *Uteev v Uzbekistan* CCPR/D/91/D/1150/(26 October 2007) para 5.2.

[34] The criteria are set out in the ICCPR-OP1; CERD, art 14; UNCAT, art 22; CEDAW-OP; CPRD-OP; CPED, art 31; CRC-OP, art 7; ICESCR-OP, art 3.

Third, the complaint must relate to rights that are protected by the instrument invoked by the complainant (admissibility *ratione materiae*).

Fourth, the same matter must not have been examined by the treaty body concerned or by another international investigation or settlement procedure, such as the European Court of Human Rights, the Inter-American Court of Human Rights, or the African Commission on Human and Peoples' Rights, or be undergoing examination by such a procedure. In regard to ICCPR-OP1 and CPED, only those cases that are being examined by such a procedure *at the same time* as the communication to the UN treaty body will be excluded.

Fifth, the complainant must have exhausted all available domestic remedies. This means that, in principle, the highest court of the state party concerned must have considered and dismissed the case before a treaty body may consider it. The rule does not apply if the pursuit of domestic remedies has been "unreasonably prolonged." This is an assessment made on a case-by-case basis. Such remedies must not only be available, but also *effective*, thereby offering a reasonable prospect of actual redress.

Finally, the complaint must be compatible with the rights in the treaty concerned, must be well founded, and may not constitute an abuse of the right to petition.

Complaints that do not fulfill these criteria will be declared inadmissible, and such decisions are final. The Optional Protocol to the International Covenant on Economic, Social and Cultural Rights adds another layer by allowing the Committee to decline to consider a claim that does not reveal that the author has suffered a clear disadvantage, unless the relevant committee considers the communication raises a serious issue of general importance.[35]

Complaints declared admissible are referred to the state party for its observations on the merits, if it has not provided these earlier. Once these are provided and the complainant has been given a reasonable opportunity to comment on these observations, or the deadline for submission has expired, the treaty body will examine the merits of the case.

The CESCR-OP and CRC-OP provide that their respective committees shall make available their good offices to the parties with a view to reaching a friendly settlement of the matter of the communication. An agreement on a friendly settlement terminates consideration of the communication.

Treaty bodies generally adopt decisions on complaints—called "views" or "opinions"—by consensus. The decisions include measures to be taken by the state if a violation is found, which will usually include steps to provide individual relief and broader recommendations to strengthen implementation of the treaty more generally.[36] Often those experts who do not share the opinion of the majority append individual (dissenting or concurring) opinions to the final decisions. This does not undermine the authority of the decision.

Views are not legally binding and thus cannot be enforced. However, in its General Comment 33, the Human Rights Committee stated that although its views are non-binding

[35] ICESCR-OP, art 4. [36] UN Doc HRI/MC/2017/4 (n 20) paras 52 and 53.

they "exhibit some important characteristics of a judicial decision."[37] The Committee also stated that its views are an authoritative interpretation of the ICCPR by a body entrusted by states parties to give such interpretations, and, as such, the principle of good faith regarding treaty obligations requires that states cooperate with the Committee and inform it of action taken to implement its views. All of the treaty bodies monitor and encourage implementation of their decisions on individual complaints, and six have formal follow-up procedures usually administered by "Special Rapporteurs on follow-up on views" who are in regular contact with states parties. All of the committees adopt follow-up decisions based on an analysis of information provided by states parties and/or complainants, and some grade the state party's level of compliance with their views.[38] The annual reports of the treaty bodies to the General Assembly include a chapter in which follow-up to views is detailed, while all follow-up information provided by the parties to a case is, in principle, public.

Many states parties pay compensation to victims, even though some indicate they do so not as a matter of legal obligation, but ex gratia. Others have released individuals detained or imprisoned arbitrarily, or commuted death sentences. Legislation that makes decisions of treaty bodies enforceable at the national level is rare. Some states challenge the findings of the treaty body concerned. However, the fact that all treaty bodies that decide complaints have instituted, and largely aligned, their follow-up on views mechanisms has improved the level of compliance with recommendations.

For many years, the treaty bodies developed their jurisprudence under these procedures independently from each other, and without reference to regional human rights mechanisms or national tribunals. This raised the possibility of conflicting interpretations of substantively very similar, if not identical, provisions of international or regional human rights instruments. More recently, comparative analyses of jurisprudence prepared by the OHCHR and others have helped treaty bodies to keep abreast of relevant developments in regional and national tribunals. The treaty bodies now take into account the relevant jurisprudence of regional courts and national tribunals when seized of complex or novel legal issues. So also, the regional mechanisms (for example, the European Court of Human Rights and the Inter-American Court of Human Rights)[39] and some national tribunals regularly rely on, or cite, treaty body jurisprudence. This contributes to the emergence of substantively consistent human rights jurisprudence.

2.4 Inquiries

The Committee against Torture; the Committee on the Elimination of Discrimination against Women; the Committee on Economic, Social and Cultural Rights; the Committee

[37] HRC "General Comment 33: The Obligations of States Parties under the Optional Protocol to the International Covenant on Civil and Political Rights" (5 November 2008) UN Doc CCPR/C/GC/33 para 11.

[38] UN Doc HRI/MC/2017/4 (n 20) paras 50–59.

[39] Eg *González (Claudia) et al. ("Cotton Field") v Mexico*, IACtHR Series C No 205 (16 November 2009); *Opuz v Turkey* (2010) 50 EHRR 28.

on the Rights of Persons with Disabilities; and the Committee on the Rights of the Child may initiate inquiries upon receipt of reliable, well-founded indications of serious, grave, or systematic violations of the respective conventions by a state party. Inquiries may only be conducted in relation to states that recognize the competence of the relevant committee to conduct them, and the cooperation of the state party is required throughout. Once a state has consented to an inquiry, the relevant committee may urgently designate one or several members to undertake a confidential inquiry and report back. Where this is warranted and the state party consents, this may include a visit to the state. The findings of the members are examined by the whole committee and transmitted to the state party with appropriate recommendations. Confidentiality is the hallmark of the inquiry procedure, but findings are usually disclosed in some form after dialogue with the state party at the end of each inquiry. The Committee against Torture has published the results of its inquiries on Brazil, Egypt (two), Lebanon, Mexico, Nepal, Peru, Sri Lanka, Turkey, and the former Yugoslavia; the Committee on the Elimination of Discrimination against Women, the results of inquiries on Canada, Mexico, the Philippines, and the United Kingdom of Great Britain and Northern Ireland (UK); and the Committee on the Rights of Persons with Disabilities, the results of inquiries on the UK and Spain.

A similar inquiry procedure is created by article 33 CPED, which allows the Committee on Enforced Disappearance to request that one or more of its members visit a state party where it receives reliable information indicating a serious violation of the Convention. States parties do not have to have recognized the competence of the Committee for it to request a visit, although consultation with the state and agreement are required before the visit, as is collaboration in respect of its modalities and conduct.

The UNCAT-OP creates a novel preventative inquiry mechanism. It establishes a system of complementary regular visits to places of detention conducted by both independent international and national bodies. UNCAT-OP's two-pillar approach relies on an international body, the Subcommittee on Prevention of Torture, and "national preventive mechanisms" (NPMs)—national bodies that must be established by each state party within one year of entry into force of the UNCAT-OP for the relevant state. NPMs should have unrestricted access to all places of detention and all relevant information about the treatment and conditions of detention of individuals deprived of liberty. In order to discharge its mandate to advise states on national mechanisms and supervise their work, the Subcommittee should have the same level of unrestricted access as the NPMs. Since the beginning of its activities in 2007, the Subcommittee has conducted over 60 visits, including regular visits to states parties, follow-up visits, and visits to advise NPMs.

2.5 Early Warning and Urgent Action

The competence and working methods of human rights treaty bodies are not well suited to provision of early warning of impending violations or engaging in urgent action.

Nonetheless, in 1993 the Committee on the Elimination of Racial Discrimination (CERD) introduced an early warning procedure to prevent situations in states parties developing into conflict. It also created an urgent action procedure to respond to problems requiring immediate attention to prevent or limit the scale or number of serious violations of the International Convention on the Elimination of All Forms of Racial Discrimination. These procedures, which are managed by a five-member working group, may be initiated by the Committee itself or other interested parties. Decisions, statements, and letters to states parties adopted pursuant to these procedures are uploaded on the Committee's web page.[40] The CRPD working methods envisage similar competence.[41]

The CERD and CRPD procedures grow out of the reporting competence. In contrast, the CPED explicitly invests its Committee with two innovative methods of dealing with urgent or severe violations of the CPED. First, article 30 provides it may request urgent action that a disappeared person be sought and found. By June 2017, 497 urgent actions had been registered.[42] Second, having sought information from the state concerned, article 34 enables the Committee to bring to the attention of the UNGA through the Secretary-General well-founded indications that enforced disappearance is being practiced on a widespread or systematic basis by a state party.

2.6 Stakeholder Engagement

An important feature of the human rights treaty body system is the contribution that stakeholders, including nongovernmental organizations (NGOs), national human rights institutions, UN entities, and other human rights mechanisms make. Indeed, the advocacy of civil society has often inspired the development of human rights treaties, while it and UN entities have participated in their negotiations.

Although explicit provision on interaction with NGOs appears only in the CRC, CRPD, and the International Convention on the Rights of All Migrant Workers and Members of their Families, all treaty bodies have developed procedures in this context. In terms of the reporting process, all emphasize the importance of cooperation with NGOs, whether national or international, and the positive role NGOs can play at the domestic level in follow-up activities. In addition, most treaty bodies have instituted formal mechanisms for consultations with NGOs.[43] NGOs, frequently coordinated by coalitions,

[40] <www.ohchr.org/EN/HRBodies/CERD/Pages/EarlyWarningProcedure.aspx>

[41] Convention on the Rights of Persons with Disabilities (CRPD) "Working methods of the Committee on the Rights of Persons with Disabilities adopted at its fifth session" (2 September 2011) UN Doc CRPD/C/54 paras 26–29.

[42] Press release "Committee in Enforced Disappearances closes its fourteenth session" (1 June 2018) indicates that the Committee is preparing an analytical study on the procedure <www.https://ohchr.org/EN/NewsEvents/Pages/Display/News.aspx?NewsID=23169&ID=E>.

[43] See OHCHR "Working with the United Nations Human Rights Programme: A Handbook for Civil Society" (New York and Geneva 2008) <http://www.ohchr.org/EN/AboutUs/Pages/CivilSociety.aspx>; see also UN Doc HRI/MC/2013/3 (n 26) paras 37–42.

often submit "alternative," "parallel," or "shadow" reports to treaty bodies, which analyze, and often challenge, the content of the state party's report. Many treaty body members rely on NGO information, which is also provided orally to pre-sessional working groups as they draw up the lists of issues and questions and via briefings to the plenary, when preparing the constructive dialogue with the state party. NGOs are also involved in the process of elaborating general comments/recommendations. They may advocate that the relevant treaty body address a particular theme through such a document, and are invited to participate in discussions with committees during their preparation. Detailed written submissions and comments on developing drafts, which are available on the web pages of the relevant committees, are also provided by NGOs. Civil society, including NGOs, have been instrumental in the initiation of individual petitions, including by representing victims of alleged violations; they also submit amicus briefs in this context. In addition, NGO information has frequently instigated treaty body inquiries.

Treaty bodies interact with NHRIs, and some have adopted guidelines on their relationship.[44] In June 2017, the 29th meeting of the chairs of the human rights treaty bodies adopted detailed recommendations, informed by their discussions with the Global Alliance of National Human Rights Institutions, on treaty body interface with NHRIs, and in all areas of their work.[45] If implemented, the role of NHRIs in treaty body processes will be significantly strengthened.

Specialized agencies and other entities of the UN system, including UN Country Teams (UNCTs), also interact with treaty bodies, with this interaction being envisaged in the terms of some treaties and in the rules of procedure of most committees. Many have also developed relationships with other bodies such as the Inter-parliamentary Union. CPED mandates consultation of CED with other treaty bodies, in particular the Human Rights Committee, to ensure consistency,[46] and CED meets formally with that Committee and informally with others. The Optional Protocol to the Convention against Torture and Other Cruel, Inhuman or Degrading Treatment or Punishment provides for the Subcommittee on the Prevention of Torture to present a public annual report on its activities to the Committee against Torture,[47] and that both Committees hold at least one of their sessions simultaneously each year.[48] Beyond this, collaboration amongst and between committees is ad hoc and uneven. Similarly, interaction with other human rights mechanisms, such as the special procedures of the Human Rights Council and regional human rights mechanisms, is unsystematic. Exceptionally, the CPED mandates the CED to cooperate with relevant special procedures.[49]

[44] "Note by the Secretariat: Common Approach to engagement with national human rights institutions" (9 June 2017) UN Doc HRI/MC/2017/3.

[45] UNGA "Note by the Secretary-General: Implementation of Human Rights Instruments: Report of the Chairs of the human rights treaty bodies on their twenty-ninth meeting" (20 July 2017) UN Doc A/72/177 paras 45–47.

[46] CPED art 28 para 2.

[47] UNCAT-OP art 16 para 3.

[48] UNCAT-OP art 10 para 3.

[49] CPED art 28 para 1.

3 Strengthening the Human Rights Treaty Body System

The treaty bodies have continuously sought to improve their effectiveness. However, they face challenges, many related to the fact that their number has expanded significantly, but ad hoc, and they have developed their working methods to achieve the greatest impact on the promotion and protection of human rights to a large extent independently. While welcome, the broad acceptance of the human rights treaties by states has multiplied their tasks. Although they have sought to streamline and align their working methods and practices, there are differences in approach, despite their similar competence, including in the preparation of lists of issues, the procedure for the examination of reports, processes for formulating general recommendations, and the involvement of stakeholders in their work.

Since 1984, the chairs of each treaty body have met formally to discuss issues of common concern, in particular working methods and common approaches to thematic issues, such as reprisals against those who seek to interact with them, to enhance the effectiveness of the treaty body system as a whole. These meetings, which are now held annually and whose reports are transmitted to the General Assembly, are usually held in Geneva, but have been held in Brussels, Addis Ababa, New York, and Costa Rica in order to bring the treaty bodies closer to the site of implementation and strengthen links among international and regional mechanisms and institutions and stakeholders. On occasion, informal meetings are convened to deepen their work. Harmonization of the human rights treaty body system has been an issue since the chairs' first meeting. It has been the subject of many UN reports, as well as academic commentary, and gained greater prominence as the system has become more overstretched.[50]

In 2002, the UN Secretary-General identified modernization of the UN treaty system as a crucial element in the UN goal to promote and protect human rights. He called on the treaty bodies to craft a more coordinated approach to their activities by standardizing their reporting requirements and allowing states parties to produce a *single report* summarizing their compliance with the full range of treaties to which they are a party.[51] The idea of a single report was not supported by the treaty bodies and many other stakeholders, but the treaty bodies were amenable to standardizing their reporting requirements. In 2005, Louise Arbour, then the High Commissioner for Human Rights, made a bold proposal for treaty body reform when she called for discussions on proposals for a unified treaty system and the replacement of the existing treaty bodies by a single, unified,

[50] <https://www.ohchr.org/EN/HRBodies/HRTD/Pages/TBStrengthening.aspx> accessed January 17, 2019.

[51] UNGA "Report of the Secretary-General: Strengthening of the United Nations: An Agenda for Further Change" (9 September 2002) UN Doc A/57/387 paras 52–54.

standing treaty body.[52] The OHCHR prepared a concept paper, which was discussed widely.[53] A majority of stakeholders—many states parties, most treaty body experts, and numerous NGOs—was wary of the proposal. Many considered that the establishment of such a body would jeopardize, and perhaps undermine, the specificity of approach of the respective treaty bodies and the human rights treaties themselves. Some were concerned that this might be the first step toward the establishment of an international human rights court. Others considered that the creation of a single body merging all treaty body activities was politically unrealistic, but some form of unification, such as a single body for examination of complaints, might be feasible.

Succeeding high commissioners have not pursued High Commissioner Arbour's proposal. In 2009, the then High Commissioner Navi Pillay launched a process of reflection on ways to strengthen the treaty body system based on the premise that the legal parameters of the treaties should not be altered. Around 20 consultations involving states, treaty body experts, UN entities, NHRIs, academics, and civil society were organized by OHCHR. There was broad support for this multi-stakeholder process, but in 2011 some states expressed the view that states must play the primary role in any discussions relating to the treaty body system. As a result, in early 2012, the UNGA adopted a resolution requesting its President to launch an intergovernmental process on strengthening and enhancing the effective functioning of the human rights treaty body system.[54] This process was initiated in July 2012, one month after the High Commissioner published a report setting out her vision for the future of the system.[55]

The intergovernmental process concluded in April 2014 with the adoption of UNGA resolution 68/268 on strengthening and enhancing the effective functioning of the human rights treaty body system.[56] The lengthy resolution reaffirms the independence of the treaty bodies and their members, but encourages them to align their methodology and harmonize their working methods. In so doing, however, they must pay attention to the views of states, and no new obligations for states should be created. The treaty bodies are encouraged to enhance the role of their chairs in relation to procedural matters, and there should be strengthened interaction between states parties and the chairs during their annual meetings so that these meetings constitute a forum where all issues, including

[52] Plan of Action submitted by the High Commissioner for Human Rights: Annex to UNGA "Report of the Secretary-General: In Larger Freedom: Towards Development, Security and Human Rights for All" (26 May 2006) UN Doc A/59/2005/Add.3.

[53] "Report by the Secretariat: Concept Paper on the High Commissioner's Proposal for a Unified Standing Treaty Body" (22 March 2006) UN Doc HRI/MC/2006/2.

[54] UNGA Res 66/254 (23 February 2012) UN Doc A/RES/66/254. The resolution was introduced by Russia and adopted with 85 states voting in favor, none against, and 66 abstaining.

[55] OHCHR "Strengthening the United Nations Human Rights Treaty Body System" (n 10). For a discussion of the report see: Suzanne Egan, "Strengthening the United Nations Human Rights Treaty Body System" (2013) Human Rights L Rev 13(2) 209.

[56] UNGA Res 68/268. See Christen Broecker and Michael O'Flaherty, "The Outcome of the General Assembly's Treaty Body Strengthening Process: An Important Milestone on a Longer Journey" (June 2014) Universal Rights Group Policy Brief.

those related to the independence and impartiality of treaty bodies, can be raised constructively. Efficiency strategies are promoted. These include: combining overdue reports to eliminate the backlog of outstanding reporting obligations; establishing word limits for documents produced by states parties, other stakeholders, and the treaty bodies themselves; and limiting treaty body working languages and translation of summary records. In order to enhance accessibility and visibility of the treaty bodies, they are encouraged to webcast their public meetings, and the Secretary-General is requested to make the system accessible to persons with disabilities to ensure their full and effective participation. To enable wider participation in the reporting process, the OHCHR is requested to facilitate participation of members of its delegations via videoconferencing, and states are encouraged to provide voluntary funds to facilitate the engagement of states parties, particularly those without representation in Geneva, with the treaty body system. Recommendations are made to sustain and strengthen the independence and impartiality of treaty body members, and all acts of intimidation and reprisals against individuals and groups contributing to the work of human rights treaty bodies are condemned. At the heart of the resolution, however, is the allocation of increased meeting time to the human rights treaty bodies, determined on the basis of a formula based on their workload in 2014, to be reviewed biennially. This is mirrored by a capacity-building program, including the deployment of dedicated officers in the OHCHR's regional offices, to support states parties in implementing their treaty obligations.

Full implementation of GA Resolution 68/268 began on January 1, 2015. The Secretary-General reports on progress made to the UNGA on a biennial basis: the first report was considered by the Assembly in 2016,[57] and the second will be submitted to its 73rd session in 2018.[58] The UNGA will review the state of the human rights treaty body system in 2020, including the measures taken in line with resolution 68/268 to ensure their sustainability, and, if appropriate, decide on further action to strengthen and enhance the effective functioning of the system. Discussions have begun on possible further action, including in the framework of an academic platform project on the 2020 review established by the Geneva Academy, which issued a report entitled "Optimizing the UN Treaty Body System" in May 2018.[59]

[57] UNGA "Report of the Secretary-General: Status of the human rights treaty body system" (18 July 2016) UN Doc A/71/118.

[58] UNGA "Report of the Secretary-General: Status of the human rights treaty body system" (6 August 2018) UN Doc A/73/309; On December 4, 2017, the Office of the High Commissioner for Human Rights circulated a questionnaire to states on implementation of resolution 68/268: <http://www.ohchr.org/Documents/HRBodies/TB/TBS/Biennal/QuestionnaireStates_en4dec17.doc>.

[59] <https://geneva-academy.ch/policy-studies/research-projects-and-policy-studies/un-treaty-body-review-2020>.

4 Conclusion

The activities of the human rights treaty bodies have developed in scope and sophistication since the first such body, the Committee on the Elimination of Racial Discrimination, began its work in 1970. Reporting and other functions are being increasingly aligned[60] to assist states parties with multiple reporting obligations, while the quality, specificity, and usability of concluding observations have gradually improved, making it possible for states parties and others to follow-up on recommendations meaningfully. Follow-up procedures have helped to keep those states parties that display little or no political will to implement treaty body recommendations engaged. In terms of individual complaints, the jurisprudence emanating from such procedures has improved substantively and qualitatively over the years. Follow-up to decisions of the treaty bodies has also improved, with an increasing number of states granting appropriate remedies following a finding of a violation. Importantly, the treaty body system has inspired positive changes in countries, afforded some victims with access to justice and redress for violations, and provided the context for the creation of strong stakeholder engagement in its work.

Despite these achievements, the treaty bodies continue to face challenges. All face severe human and financial resource constraints, which compromise their capacity to comply with the many expectations of states and individuals. Many states parties fail to meet their reporting obligations in a timely fashion; there is a backlog of reports to be considered, and, in the case of some treaty bodes, pending individual complaints and inquiry requests. The non-binding nature of treaty body decisions is a concern, and follow-up procedures that encourage domestic implementation of decisions require strengthening.

Measures pursuant to GA Resolution 68/268, and High Commissioner Pillay's report, which aim to create a holistic and harmonized functioning of the treaty body system should be intensified. This is particularly important given the resistance to rationalizing existing treaty bodies, manifested most recently by the decision of states parties to the International Convention for the Protection of All Persons from Forced Disappearances, to continue its Committee rather than to transfer its functions to another treaty body, an option envisaged in the treaty.[61] The likely adoption of new treaties with related implementation mechanisms must also be considered. Notably, while it is often said that the age of human rights standard-setting has passed and implementation is the focus, processes that may lead to new instruments on the human rights of older persons,[62]

[60] "Note by the Secretariat: Identifying progress achieved in aligning the working methods and practices of the treaty bodies" (23 March 2018) UN Doc HRI/MC/2018/3.

[61] This decision was made pursuant to CPED, art 27, by a Conference of states parties of the CPED convened on December 19, 2016.

[62] UNGA Res 65/182 (21 December 2010) UN Doc A/RES/65/812.

the regulation of private military and security companies,[63] and the activities of transnational corporations and other business enterprises[64] are underway.

Alignment of working methods, cooperation among human rights treaty bodies, and capacity-building of states are essential and desirable, but will not address the underlying challenges that arise from the existence of nine human rights treaty bodies enjoying similar competence, and another exercising a preventive function, whose treaties enjoy wide acceptance. These can be met only if sufficient and realistic financial and human resources are allocated to the system. In the long term, however, profound structural change, perhaps along the lines of High Commissioner Arbour's proposal, is needed.

It is to be hoped that this proposal and other innovative and imaginative ideas to deepen the system's influence, while not weakening its independence that guarantees its protection for individuals, will be discussed constructively and candidly during the lead-up to the UNGA's review of the system in 2020.

[63] HR Council Res 15/26 (7 October 2010) UN Doc A/HRC/RES/15/26.
[64] HR Council Res 26/9 (26 June 2014) UN Doc A/HRC/RES/26/9.

CHAPTER 20

THE COVENANTS

BERTRAND G. RAMCHARAN

THE International Covenant on Civil and Political Rights (ICCPR) and the International Covenant on Economic, Social and Cultural Rights (ICESCR) were adopted in 1966 to take forward, in binding form for their states parties, the inspirational human rights principles of the Universal Declaration of Human Rights (UDHR) adopted 18 years earlier, in 1948. Together, these instruments were considered by the Commission on Human Rights to be the International Bill of Rights, which, alongside the United Nations Charter, would be the foundations of a new international order grounded in human dignity and freedom.

In 2016, on the occasion of the 50th anniversary of the adoption of the Covenants, United Nations (UN) Secretary-General Ban Ki-moon reminded the world that the Covenants provided a vision for a peaceful and prosperous world emerging from the Second World War. That vision, he thought, was still relevant today, and the aim must therefore be greater respect and stronger implementation of the Covenants over the next 50 years. He linked the Covenants with the UN's 2030 Agenda that he thought provided the international community with a blueprint by which it could strengthen implementation. At the same time, the Covenants, in turn, could anchor the 2030 Agenda in Treaty Law: "The Sustainable Development Goals and the Covenants are clearly [mutually] reinforcing."[1]

A Joint Statement by the Human Rights Committee (HRC) and the Committee on Economic, Social and Cultural Rights (CESCR), "The International Covenants on Human Rights: 50 Years On," recognized that "The adoption of the two Covenants was accompanied by great hopes." It assessed that "During the Years to follow, the ideal of human rights has continued to guide States, international and regional organizations, as well as social movements and people world-wide." "And the achievements", it added, "are not meagre."[2] The statement continued: "Their influence on national constitutions has led to

[1] UN Secretary-General "Commemorative Event to Mark the 50th Anniversary of the Two Covenants. Remarks by the Secretary-General" (19 October 2016) United Nations General Assembly.

[2] UN Human Rights Committee (HRC) and the UN Committee on Economic, Social and Cultural Rights (CESCR) "The International Covenants on Human Rights: 50 Years On: Joint Statement by the

the emergence of a common understanding of human rights across regions and allowed collective learning across jurisdictions, guided by the same ideals. The Covenants have decisively contributed to the emergence of a common universal language of human rights and offered a protection shield to millions of people world-wide."[3]

A protection shield worldwide?

The 2016/17 *Annual Report* of Amnesty International gives cause for sobering reflection on this.[4] As the Committees themselves recognized, "However, progress has not always been smooth. Genocides have been committed over the last 50 years; terrorism has resulted in very serious human rights violations, and some of the measures taken to counter it have put civil liberties at risk. The global financial and economic crisis that began in 2008 led the Governments of many countries to cut down on resources available to meet basic human needs to the detriment of progress in the enjoyment of social, economic and cultural rights."

In an optimistic spirit, the two Committees declared that in the fulfilment of their mandates, they would continue to uphold the ideals of the Universal Declaration of Human Rights. In their endeavors, the members of the two Committees would also seek to uphold those ideals. The task undoubtedly remains a daunting one. As the Committees themselves recognized: "All rights require remedies, otherwise they are only words on paper. All rights must be guaranteed, without discrimination, either formal or *de facto*. All rights impose immediate obligations on States, although it may take time for some elements to be implemented fully. All rights are mutually supportive—civil and political rights and economic, social and cultural rights reinforce each other."[5]

Unfortunately, even as gross human rights violations proliferate worldwide, the international normative order is manifestly under challenge by countries as powerful as China, Russia, and even the United States, not to mention myriad states of varying political, philosophical, religious, and legal persuasions worldwide. States have been using their voting majorities in bodies such as the UN General Assembly (UNGA) to impose controls on the operations of the human rights treaty bodies.[6] General Assembly resolution 68/268 called upon the treaty bodies "to set a limit on the number of questions posed, focusing on areas seen as priority issues..."[7] One might ask where that leaves the exercise of conscience by the experts on human rights treaty bodies.

Human Rights Committee and the Committee on Economic, Social and Cultural Rights" (17 November 2016) UN doc. CCPR/C/2016/1 – E/C.12/2016/3.

[3] Ibid.

[4] Amnesty International, Annual Report 2016–2017: The State of the World's Human Rights (Amnesty International Ltd 2017).

[5] HRC and CESCR "The International Covenants on Human Rights: 50 Years On" (n 2) para 10.

[6] See, eg, UNGA Res 268 "Strengthening and enhancing the effective functioning of the human rights treaty body system" (9 April 2014) UN Doc A/RES/68/268.

[7] ibid para 16. See also Christen Broecker and Michael O'Flaherty, "The Outcome of the General Assembly's Treaty Body Strengthening Process. An Important Milestone on a Longer Journey" (2014) Policy Brief, Universal Rights Group <http://www.universal-rights.org/urg-policy-reports/the-outcome-of-the-general-assemblys-treaty-body-strengthening-process-an-important-milestone-on-a-longer-journey/> accessed March 12, 2017.

Mindful of the foregoing, what approach should the international lawyer take in a presentation of the Covenants for a Handbook on UN Treaties? We would suggest that the approach be threefold: insistence on the legal obligations of states parties to the Covenants, while placing the Covenants in the context of broader United Nations efforts such as the Sustainable Development Goals, and bearing in mind the need for modernized approaches to the implementation of the Covenants.

The need for modernized approaches is particularly important as one looks to the future. The UN High Commissioner for Human Rights, Prince Zeid Ra'ad Al Hussein, in a lecture on the occasion of the 50th anniversary of the adoption of the Covenants, offered some significant suggestions for future reform. He stated: "My overall concern regarding the future of the Covenants is how we can ensure better **implementation on the ground.** I am nagged by a sense that a formalized ballet of international diplomacy requires various Excellencies to bow and nod to international conventions, in a ritual that is often utterly divorced from the real world."[8]

"The Covenants need to be applied," the High Commissioner added, and pointed out that in many countries there is no actionable framework of laws and policies to apply economic and social rights as rights—and no mechanisms of accountability to ensure that decision-makers protect them. The High Commissioner asked: "How can we bring the Human Rights Committee and the Committee on Economic, Social and Cultural Rights closer, so that we more convincingly support the indivisibility of the Covenants?" "Could the two Committees consider reports together? Could one body consider petitions under both Covenants—or even under all treaties? What other options are there to strengthen the monitoring of the Covenants"?[9]

Then, a document on the working methods of the Human Rights Committee consulted on the website of the Office of the High Commissioner for Human Rights (OHCHR), states the following on "Early-warning measures and urgent procedures":

> In the 1990s the Committee requested that several States facing serious difficulties in the implementation of Covenant rights (Bosnia and Herzegovina, Croatia, Federal Republic of Yugoslavia, Burundi, Angola, Haiti, Rwanda and Nigeria) either present their overdue initial/periodic report without delay or prepare *ad hoc* reports on specific issues. Only Bosnia and Herzegovina, Croatia and the Federal Republic of Yugoslavia reacted to this initiative and submitted *ad hoc* reports. In March 2004, the Committee's Bureau discussed the possibilities of reviving the urgent procedure/*ad hoc* report procedure.[10]

[8] UN High Commissioner Zeid Ra'ad Al Hussein, "Closing Keynote Remarks at the AHRI Human Rights Research Conference: 50 Years of the Two UN Human Rights Covenants: Legacies and Prospects" (2016) Peter Baehr Lecture. Emphasis in original.

[9] ibid.

[10] OHCHR "Human Rights Committee: Working Methods" (2017) <http://www.ohchr.org/EN/HRbodies/CCPR/Pages/WorkingMethods.aspx> accessed March 12, 2017.

In the meantime, the earth turned on, its citizens bearing the brunt of violence in large numbers. The question that immediately arises for reflection is whether the early warning and preventive approaches of the two Committees should not become more pronounced.[11]

In what follows, we shall refer briefly to the adoption of the Covenants, trace some significant features of their interpretation and application, look briefly at the salient jurisprudence of the Human Rights Committee, and revisit a significant proposal for backup national machinery made at the time of the adoption of the Covenants but which was deferred, never to be revisited again. It may be time to do so now.

1 Adoption and Assessment

The international covenants were adopted and opened for signature and ratification on December 16, 1966. Ten years later in 1976, they entered into force. Reading the records of the General Assembly when the Covenants were adopted, one sees that the assembled delegates felt they were doing something truly historic. "There is no doubt," the Philippines' delegate commented, "that the International Covenants on Human Rights will constitute, after they enter into force, one of the most important documents adopted by our Organization. . . ."[12]

Presciently, however, the representative of Israel cautioned at the time, "The United Nations can project great ideas more easily than it can convert them into reality."[13] Fifty years later, the task of converting the Covenants into reality remains a formidable one. Ratification is still not universal and important states are still to do so. There is much of value that has come out from the two Committees established to follow up on the implementation of the covenants: the Human Rights Committee established under the civil and political covenant and the Committee on Economic, Social and Cultural Rights established under the economic, social, and cultural covenant. The Committees' consideration of reports and of petitions, their drawing up of recommendations for individual states parties, their general comments,[14] and the human rights jurisprudence built up, especially by the Human Rights Committee, are valuable parts of the normative and jurisprudential human rights architecture of the world and have great potential to make the world a better place if governments accept them in good faith.

Unfortunately, however, the record of national implementation is uneven and the state of respect of human rights is distressing, with numerous gross violations of human rights in numerous countries worldwide. Respect for human rights is adversely affected by widespread poverty, conflicts, terrorism, inequality, poor governance, gross violations,

[11] See generally, Bertrand G. Ramcharan, *Preventive Human Rights Strategies* (Routledge 2010).

[12] UNGA Official Records (16 December 1966) Twenty-First Session, UN Doc A/PV 1495 para 164.

[13] ibid para 139.

[14] All General Comments are available on the OHCHR website related to the treaty bodies: http://www.ohchr.org/EN/HRBodies/Pages/TreatyBodies.aspx.

and increasingly by climate change. International and regional organs are struggling to cope with the challenges of endemic gross violations of human rights.

2 Substantive Content

The substantive articles of the ICCPR provide for protection of the right to life (article 6) and lay down that no one shall be subjected to torture or to cruel, inhuman, or degrading treatment or punishment (article 7); that no one shall be held in slavery; that slavery and the slave trade shall be prohibited; and that no one shall be held in servitude or required to perform compulsory labor (article 8); that no one shall be subjected to arbitrary arrest or detention (article 9); that all persons deprived of their liberty shall be treated with humanity (article 10); and that no one shall be imprisoned merely on the ground of inability to fulfill a contractual obligation (article 11).

The Covenant further provides for freedom of movement and freedom to choose a residence (article 12), and for limitations to be placed on the expulsion of aliens lawfully in the territory of a state party (article 13). They make provision in considerable detail for equality before the courts and tribunals and for guarantees in criminal and civil procedure (article 14). They also provide for the prohibition of retroactive criminal legislation (article 15), lay down the right of everyone to recognition everywhere as a person before the law (article 16), and call for the prohibition of arbitrary or unlawful interference with an individual's privacy, family, home, or correspondence (article 17).

The Covenant goes on to provide for protection of the right to freedom of thought, conscience, and religion (article 18) and to freedom of expression (article 19). The Covenant calls for the prohibition by law of any propaganda for war and of any advocacy of national, racial, or religious hatred that constitutes an incitement to discrimination, hostility, or violence (article 20). It recognizes the right of peaceful assembly (article 21) and the right to freedom of association (article 22). It also recognizes the right of men and women of marriageable age to marry and to found a family, and the principle of equality of rights and responsibilities of spouses, during marriage and at its dissolution (article 23). The Covenant lays down measures to protect the rights of children (article 24), and recognizes the right of every citizen to take part in the government of his or her country (article 25). It provides that all persons are equal before the law and are entitled to the equal protection of the law (article 26). Finally, the Covenant provides measures for the protection of members of such ethnic, religious, or linguistic minorities as may exist in the territories of states parties to the Covenant (article 27).

The substantive articles of the ICESCR recognize the right to work (article 6); the right to enjoyment of just and favorable conditions of work (article 7); the right to form and join trade unions (article 8); the right to social security, including social insurance (article 9); the right of the family, mothers, children, and young persons to the widest possible protection and assistance (article 10); the right to an adequate standard of living (article 11); the right to the enjoyment of the highest attainable standard of physical and mental health (article 12); the right to education (articles 13 and 14); and the right to take part in cultural life (article 15).

3 Obligations of State Parties

General Comment No. 31 adopted by the Human Rights Committee on May 26, 2004, is a superb statement on the obligations of states parties to the Covenants. A state party, the Committee declared, must respect and ensure the rights in the Covenant to anyone within its power or effective control. The obligations in the Covenant in general and under Article 2 in particular are binding on every state party as a whole. All branches of government (executive, legislative, and judicial), and other public or governmental authorities, at whatever level—national, regional, or local—are in a position to engage the responsibility of the state party.[15] (CCPR 2004).

States parties must adopt legislative, judicial, administrative, educative, and other appropriate measures in order to fulfill their legal obligations. It is important to raise levels of awareness about the Covenants not only among public officials and state agents but also among the population at large.

The positive obligations on states parties to ensure Covenant rights will only be discharged if individuals are protected by the state not just against violations of Covenant rights by its agents, but also against acts committed by private persons or entities that would impair the enjoyment of Covenant rights insofar as they are amenable to application between private persons or entities.

States parties are required to respect and to ensure the Covenant rights to all persons who may be within their territory and to all persons subject to their jurisdiction. This means that a state party must respect and ensure the rights laid down in the Covenant to anyone within the power or effective control of that state party, even if not situated within the territory of the state party.

The Covenant applies also in situations of armed conflict to which the rules of international humanitarian law are applicable. While, in respect of certain Covenant rights, more specific rules of international humanitarian law may be especially relevant for the purposes of the interpretation of Covenant rights, both spheres of law are complementary, not mutually exclusive.

Article 2, paragraph 2 of the Covenant requires that states parties take the necessary steps to give effect to the Covenant rights in the domestic order. It follows that, unless the Covenant's rights are already protected by their domestic law or practices, states parties are required on ratification to make such changes to domestic laws and practices as are necessary to ensure their conformity with the Covenant. Where there are inconsistencies between domestic law and the Covenant, article 2 requires that the domestic law or practice be changed to meet the standards required by the Covenant's substantive guarantees.

[15] HRC "General comment no. 31 [80], The nature of the general legal obligation imposed on States Parties to the Covenant" (26 May 2004) UN Doc CCPR/C/21/Rev.1/Add.13.

The requirement under Article 2, paragraph 2, to take steps to give effect to the Covenant rights is unqualified and of immediate effect. A failure to comply with this obligation cannot be justified by reference to political, social, cultural, or economic considerations within the state.

Article 2, paragraph 3, requires that in addition to effective protection of Covenant rights states parties must ensure that individuals also have accessible and effective remedies to vindicate those rights. Such remedies should be appropriately adapted so as to take account of the special vulnerability of certain categories of person, including, in particular, children. The Covenant attaches importance to states parties establishing appropriate judicial and administrative mechanisms for addressing claims of rights violations under domestic law.

Article 2, paragraph 3 of the Covenant requires that states parties make reparation to individuals whose Covenant rights have been violated. Without reparation to individuals whose Covenant rights have been violated, the obligation to provide an effective remedy, which is central to the efficacy of Article 2, is not fulfilled.

In general, the purposes of the Covenant would be defeated without an obligation integral to article 2 to take measures to prevent the recurrence of a violation of the Covenant. Accordingly, it has been a frequent practice of the Human Rights Committee, in its consideration of individual petitions under the Optional Protocol, to include in its Views the need for measures, beyond a victim-specific remedy, to be taken to avoid recurrence of the type of violation in question. Such measures may require changes in the state party's laws or practices.

Where investigations reveal violations of certain Covenant rights, states parties must ensure that those responsible are brought to justice. The right to an effective remedy may in certain circumstances require states parties to provide for and implement provisional or interim measures to avoid continuing violations and to endeavor to repair at the earliest possible opportunity any harm that may have been caused by such violations.

4 National Implementation

Just prior to the General Assembly's adoption of the Covenants the Jamaican delegate, Ambassador Egerton Richardson, recalled an earlier Jamaican proposal that an additional article should be added to this Covenant providing that each state party to the Covenant would undertake to establish a national commission on human rights within its territory. The exact nature of the proposal and the precise functions that the commissions would be established to discharge had been set out in the proposed article.

The Jamaican Permanent Representative read the proposal into the record:

> 1. Each State Party undertakes to establish or designate in accordance with its constitutional processes a National Commission on Human Rights or another appropriate institution which shall perform throughout the territories under its jurisdiction the functions set out in this article:

> (a) It shall study and keep under review the status of the legislation, judicial decisions and administrative arrangements for the protection of the rights recognized in this Covenant and shall prepare and submit to the Head of State and the appropriate authorities of the Government an annual report on the progress made during each year in giving effect to the provisions of this Covenant;
>
> (b) It may also advise the Government on any question referred to it by the Government in regard to the protection of the rights recognized in this Covenant;
>
> (c) Copies of the report referred to in sub-paragraph (a) of this article shall be transmitted to the Human Rights Committee established under article 27 of this Covenant. The Committee may communicate to the Governments concerned its confidential comments of a general character on the report thus submitted....[16]

This proposal is one that could usefully be reverted to in the future.[17]

Both the Human Rights Committee and the Committee on Economic, Social and Cultural Rights have given guidance on the issue of national implementation. The Human Rights Committee, in General Comment No. 3 (1981), drew the attention of states parties to the fact that the obligation under the Covenant is not confined to the respect of human rights, but that states parties have also undertaken to ensure the enjoyment of these rights to all individuals under their jurisdiction. This aspect called for specific activities by the states parties to enable individuals to enjoy their rights. In principle this obligation relates to all rights set forth in the Covenant.

The Committee on Economic, Social and Cultural Rights, in its General Comment No. 10, adopted on December 3, 1998, considered it essential that national human rights institutions give full attention to economic, social, and cultural rights in all of the relevant activities of these institutions. It drew up the following indicative list of the types of activities that could be, and in some instances already had been, undertaken by national institutions in relation to these rights: the promotion of educational and informational programs; the scrutinizing of existing laws and administrative acts as well as draft bills and other proposals to ensure that they are consistent with the requirements of the Covenant on Economic, Social and Cultural Rights; providing technical advice, or undertaking surveys in relation to economic, social and cultural rights; the identification of national level benchmarks; conducting research and inquiries designed to ascertain the extent to which particular economic, social, and cultural rights are being realized, either within the state as a whole or in areas or in relation to communities of particular vulnerability; and examining complaints alleging violations of applicable economic, social, and cultural rights standards within the state.

[16] UNGA "Report of the Third Committee" (13 December 1966) UN Doc. A/6546, para 557. The earlier proposal is contained in UN Doc A/C.3/L.1407, submitted at the 1436th meeting of the Third Committee.

[17] ibid paras 557, 621.

5 The Reporting Obligation

The Committee on Economic, Social and Cultural Rights has given superb guidance on the objectives of reporting systems. A first objective is to ensure that a comprehensive review is undertaken with respect to national legislation, administrative rules and procedures, and practices in an effort to ensure the fullest possible conformity with the Covenant. Such a review might, for example, be undertaken in conjunction with each of the relevant national ministries or other authorities responsible for policymaking and implementation in the different fields covered by the Covenant.

A second objective is to ensure that the state party monitors the actual situation with respect to each of the rights on a regular basis and is thus aware of the extent to which the various rights are, or are not, being enjoyed by all individuals within its territory or under its jurisdiction. A third objective of the reporting process is to enable the government to demonstrate that principled policymaking has been undertaken in order to provide the basis for the elaboration of clearly stated and carefully targeted policies, including the establishment of priorities that reflect the provisions of the Covenant.

A fourth objective of the reporting process is to facilitate public scrutiny of government policies with respect to economic, social, and cultural rights and to encourage the involvement of the various economic, social, and cultural sectors of society in the formulation, implementation, and review of the relevant policies. A fifth objective is to provide a basis on which the state party itself, as well as the Committee, can effectively evaluate the extent to which progress has been made toward the realization of the obligations contained in the Covenant. For this purpose, it may be useful for states to identify benchmarks or goals against which their performance in a given area can be assessed.

A sixth objective is to enable the state party itself to develop a better understanding of the problems and shortcomings encountered in efforts to realize progressively the full range of economic, social, and cultural rights. For this reason, it is essential that states parties report in detail on the "factors and difficulties" inhibiting such realization. This process of identification and recognition of the relevant difficulties then provides the framework within which more appropriate policies can be revised.

A seventh objective is to enable the Committee and the states parties as a whole to facilitate the exchange of information among states and to develop a better understanding of the common problems faced by states parties and a fuller appreciation of the type of measures that might be taken to promote effective realization of each of the rights contained in the Covenant. This part of the process also enables the Committee on Economic, Social and Cultural Rights to identify the most appropriate means by which the international community might assist states, in accordance with articles 22 and 23 of the Covenant.[18]

[18] CESCR "General Comment No. 1: Reporting by States Parties" (1 January 1989).

6 Emergency Measures

In its General Comment 29, the Human Rights Committee elaborated on the meaning of article 4 of the ICCPR dealing with emergency measures. The Committee began by observing that article 4 of the Covenant was of paramount importance for the system of protection for human rights under the Covenant.[19] (CCPR 2001) It underlined that measures derogating from the provisions of the Covenant must be of an exceptional, temporary nature. Before a state moves to invoke article 4, two fundamental conditions must be met: the situation must amount to a public emergency threatening the life of the nation, and the state party must have officially proclaimed a state of emergency. The latter requirement was essential for the maintenance of the principle of legality and rule of law at times when they were most needed. When proclaiming a state of emergency with consequences that could entail derogation from any provision of the Covenants, states must act within their constitutional and other provisions of law that govern such proclamation and the exercise of emergency powers.

A fundamental requirement for any measure derogating from the Covenant is that such measures be limited to the extent strictly required by the exigencies of the situation. Derogation from some Covenant obligations in emergency situations is distinct from restrictions or limitations allowed even in normal times under several provisions of the Covenant. The obligation to limit any derogations to those strictly required by the exigencies of the situation reflected the principle of proportionality common to derogation and limitation powers. This condition requires that states parties provide careful justification not only for their decision to proclaim a state of emergency but also for any specific measures based on such a proclamation. The fact that some of the provisions of the Covenant have been listed in article 4 (para. 2) as not being subject to derogation does not mean that other articles in the Covenant may be subjected to derogations at will, even where a threat to the life of the nation exists.

In assessing the scope of legitimate derogation from the Covenant, one criterion can, in the view of the Human Rights Committee, be found in the definition of certain human rights violations as crimes against humanity. If action conducted under the authority of a state constitutes a basis for individual criminal responsibility for a crime against humanity by the persons involved in that action, article 4 of the Covenant cannot be used as justification that a state of emergency exempted the state in question from its responsibility in relation to the same conduct. The recent codification of crimes against humanity, for jurisdictional purposes, in the Rome Statute of the International Criminal Court is of relevance to the interpretation of article 4 of the Covenant.

The Human Rights Committee has emphasized that the notification by states parties should include full information about the measures takes and a clear explanation of the reasons for them, with full documentation attached regarding their law. Additional

[19] HRC "General Comment No. 29: Article 4: Derogations during a State of Emergency" (31 August 2001) UN Doc CCPR/C/21/Rev.1/Add.11.

notifications are required if the state party subsequently takes further measures under article 4, for instance by extending the duration of a state of emergency. The requirement of immediate notification applies equally in relation to the termination of derogation.

7 Jurisprudence

The Human Rights Committee has dramatically influenced the human rights jurisprudence of the world. The Human Rights Committee is in the process of humanizing sovereignty. It insists that governments are not at liberty to act as they see fit but must conform to international human rights standards. Of equal significance, the Human Rights Committee has held, in the landmark case of *Savadi and others v. Belgium* (2008), that the foremost UN organ, the Security Council, must comply with international human rights norms when its actions affect individuals. In that case, Belgium argued that it was shielded from scrutiny because it was acting to implement a Security Council resolution. "No," the Committee replied; Belgium must comply with its human rights obligations, which took precedence. The Security Council cannot act in breach of human rights.

Among the legal precepts developed by the Human Rights Committee are the following:

- Governments are legally bound to take reasonable and appropriate measures to protect people within their jurisdiction or control.
- The law must strictly control and limit the circumstances in which a person may be deprived of his or her life by the authorities of the state.
- A state, by invoking the existence of exceptional circumstances, cannot evade the obligations it has undertaken under international human rights law by ratifying the Covenant.
- A situation in which the functions and competences of the judiciary and the executive are not clearly distinguishable or where the executive is able to control or direct the judiciary is incompatible with the notion of an independent and impartial judiciary.
- Governments are under a legal obligation to ensure that remedies for violations are effective. Expedition and effectiveness are particularly important in the adjudication of cases involving torture.
- Where violations have occurred, governments must take measures to ensure that similar violations do not take place in the future.
- Governments should take specific and effective measures to prevent the disappearance of individuals and establish effective facilities and procedures to investigate thoroughly, by an appropriate and impartial body, cases of missing and disappeared persons.
- Being subjected to incommunicado detention in an unknown location constitutes cruel and inhuman treatment.

- Women and men are entitled to equal treatment in the application of laws.
- The Committee has made landmark contributions in the area of state responsibility for violations of human rights.[20] (Mavromatis 2009)

In its general comment No. 6 (16) adopted at its 378th meeting on July 27, 1982, the Human Rights Committee observed that the right to life enunciated in the first paragraph of article 6 of the International Covenant on Civil and Political Rights is the supreme right from which no derogation is permitted even in time of public emergency. The same right to life is enshrined in article 3 of the Universal Declaration of Human Rights. It is basic to all human rights. The Committee also observed that it is the supreme duty of states to prevent wars. War and other acts of mass violence continue to be a scourge of humanity and take the lives of thousands of innocent human beings every year.

In general comment No. 14 (23) adopted at its 23rd session in 1984, the Human Rights Committee stated that the designing, testing, manufacture, possession, and deployment of nuclear weapons are among the greatest threats to the right to life that confront mankind today. This threat is compounded by the danger that the actual use of such weapons may be brought about, not only in the event of war, but even through human or mechanical error or failure. Furthermore, the very existence and gravity of this threat generates a climate of suspicion and fear between states, which is in itself antagonistic to the promotion of universal respect for and observance of human rights and fundamental freedoms in accordance with the Charter of the United Nations and the International Covenants on Human Rights.

The production, testing, possession, deployment, and use of nuclear weapons should be prohibited and recognized as crimes against humanity. The Committee accordingly, in the interest of mankind, calls upon all states, whether parties to the Covenant or not, to take urgent steps, unilaterally and by agreement, to rid the world of this menace.

8 Remedies

The Human Rights Committee, in its General Comment No. 31 adopted on March 29, 2004, provided the following guidance on the issue of remedies:

> 15. Article 2, paragraph 3, requires that in addition to effective protection of Covenant rights States parties must ensure that individuals also have accessible and effective remedies to vindicate those rights. Such remedies should be appropriately adapted so as to take account of the special vulnerability of certain categories of person, including, in particular, children. The Committee attaches importance to States parties establishing appropriate judicial and administrative mechanisms for addressing claims of

[20] Andreas Mavromatis, "Foreword" in Jakob Th. Möller and Alfred de Zayas, *United Nations Human Rights Committee Case Law 1977–2008* (N.P. Engel, 2009) xix–xxi.

> rights violations under domestic law. The Committee notes that the enjoyment of the rights recognized under the Covenant can be effectively assured by the judiciary in many different ways, including direct applicability of the Covenant, application of comparable constitutional or other provisions of law, or the interpretive effect of the Covenant in the application of national law. Administrative mechanisms are particularly required to give effect to the general obligation to investigate allegations of violations promptly, thoroughly and effectively through independent and impartial bodies. National human rights institutions, endowed with appropriate powers, can contribute to this end. A failure by a State party to investigate allegations of violations could in and of itself give rise to a separate breach of the Covenant. Cessation of an ongoing violation is an essential element of the right to an effective remedy.[21]

The Committee on Economic, Social and Cultural Rights has taken the view that:

> The right to an effective remedy need not be interpreted as always requiring a judicial remedy. Administrative remedies will, in many cases, be adequate and those living within the jurisdiction of a State party have a legitimate expectation, based on the principle of good faith, that all administrative authorities will take account of the requirements of the Covenant in their decision-making. Any such administrative remedies should be accessible, affordable, timely and effective. An ultimate right of judicial appeal from administrative procedures of this type would also often be appropriate. By the same token, there are some obligations, such as (but by no means limited to) those concerning non-discrimination in relation to which the provision of some form of judicial remedy would seem indispensable in order to satisfy the requirements of the Covenant. In other words, whenever a Covenant right cannot be made fully effective without some role for the judiciary, judicial remedies are necessary.[22]

9 Suggestions for Improvement

Prof. Yogesh Tyagi, who has spent decades, starting with his doctoral thesis, studying the Human Rights Committee, and who has written a leading study on it, concludes his book with various suggestions for improvements. These include: increasing ratifications, enhancing cooperation with the Committee, improving the process of selecting members of the Committee, providing more staff, increasing interactions with other human rights bodies, meeting more often, extending advisory services, monitoring emergency measures more closely, developing cooperation with specialized agencies, developing a larger constituency of support for the Committee, drawing more upon NGOs, helping

[21] HRC "General comment no. 31 [80]" (n 15) para 15.

[22] CESCR "General Comment No. 9: The domestic application of the Covenant" (3 December 1998) UN Doc E/C.12/1998/24 para 9.

in the deployment of preventive diplomacy, interpreting its mandate liberally and invoking its powers to improve its effectiveness, and contributing to the evolution of equitable mechanisms for establishing its own accountability.[23]

Prof. Manisuli Ssenyonjo, who has written one of the leading books, *Economic, Social and Cultural Rights in International Law*, now in its second edition, comments that the Concluding Observations of the Committee on Economic, Social and Cultural Rights (ESCR) following its consideration of state reports, "do not have a section that deals expressly, in-depth and consistently with the "violations of the Covenant." Only rarely has the Committee expressly referred to a violation of the Covenant.... The finding of a violation is a form of condemnation by a treaty body that a state is not complying with its international human rights obligations...."[24] Perhaps this need might be partially met by the ESCR Committee as it considers petitions under the Optional Protocol to the Covenant and delivers its views thereon.

10 Conclusion

This chapter confirms that the International Covenants are central treaties in the constitutional architecture of international order. The treaty implementation bodies, the Human Rights Committee and the Committee on Economic, Social and Cultural Rights, have established a solid body of practice in considering state reports, in offering comments and recommendations to individual governments, and in drawing up general comments, as well as through their human rights jurisprudence.

The task of the two Committees in the future will be, as previously, to continue to uphold and articulate the validity of the norms of the two covenants and to promote cooperation for their implementation inside states parties. This represents work for the future of humanity grounded in international human rights norms.

The process set in motion by General Assembly resolution 68/268 of 9 April 2014 on the future of the treaty-body system raises profound legal and policy issues of concern. As a matter of law, the role of a supervisory body is to watch over whether a state party is giving effect to its obligations of conduct or of results under a particular treaty. Can this be replaced by general promotional approaches rooted in "the principle of cooperation and genuine dialogue" mentioned in the General Assembly's resolution? The principal human rights treaties were all adopted in response to serious gross violations being experienced worldwide. So far, the response by member states to many of the continuing violations has been disappointing and does little to counter individual impunity and the refusal of many governments to assume full accountability for rights violations.

[23] Yogesh Tyagi, *The UN Human Rights Committee. Practice and Procedure* (CUP 2011).

[24] Manisuli Ssenyonjo, *Economic, Social and Cultural Rights in International Law* (2nd edn, Hart 2016) 41.

Finally, there is room for reflection on modernized approaches to the implementation of the Covenants. The treaty bodies would be well advised to pay more attention to urgent, preventive measures in the future.

As regards the International Covenant on Civil and Political Rights, the Jamaican proposal shelved at the time of the drafting of the Covenants for the establishment of national implementation machinery, which we recalled previously, could usefully be revisited. Over time, it can make quite a difference.[25]

When it comes to the International Covenant on Economic, Social and Cultural Rights, one wonders whether the Committee on Economic, Social and Cultural Rights, in its interactions with states parties, might prioritize the identification of situations of the poorest sections of the population and those facing the greatest risks to their survival. The Committee, based on information provided by a state party, supplemented by information gathered from other reliable sources, might discuss with the state party its policies and allocations of resources to relieve the plight of such populations. The Committee could also pay attention to policies that could help prevent such situations from arising. The Committee might propose to a state party, when it considers that this could be helpful, a visit by one or more of its members or by a qualified international expert.

Following its consideration of situations involving the poorest and the most vulnerable, the Committee might formulate recommendations for the consideration of the state party as well as by relevant international organizations. Based on its work in studying the plight of the poorest and the most vulnerable people, the Committee could submit to the Economic and Social Council for its consideration and that of the General Assembly, every five years, a global report on the plight of the poorest and of those most at risk.

The future implementation of the Covenants should respect their provisions in law and in practice. Gross violations of human rights should not be met with velvet gloves. And new, modernized approaches to implementation can be developed.

[25] See also Helen Keller and Geir Ulfstein, *UN Human Rights Treaty Bodies: Law and Legitimacy* (CUP 2012); Bertrand G. Ramcharan, *The Fundamentals of International Human Rights Treaty Law* (Martinus Nijhoff 2009).

CHAPTER 21

THE COMMITTEES ON HUMAN RIGHTS AND ECONOMIC, SOCIAL AND CULTURAL RIGHTS

HELEN KELLER AND CORINA HERI*

THIS contribution explores the work of the two quasi-judicial treaty-based human rights bodies created under the International Covenant on Civil and Political Rights (ICCPR)[1] and the International Covenant on Economic, Social and Cultural Rights (ICESCR),[2] respectively. At first glance, a chapter on these two bodies, the UN Human Rights Committee (HRC) and the UN Committee on Economic, Social and Cultural Rights (CESCR), may seem to be amiss in a volume about the contribution of the UN to international treaty-making: these bodies, which are tasked with interpreting their respective covenants, are not actors in but products of the treaty-making process. However, this impression is easily corrected when recalling the nature of human rights treaties, and taking into account the extensive contributions that these bodies have made to treaty development and implementation, which are essential aspects of the covenants' significance post-ratification. Together, the Universal Declaration of Human Rights[3] and the two binding human rights covenants are only two of the three limbs of the

* Helen Keller is a Judge at the European Court of Human Rights, a former member of the UN Human Rights Committee and Professor of Public International Law, European Law, and Constitutional Law at the University of Zurich. Corina Heri is a postdoctoral researcher at the Amsterdam Centre for International Law, University of Amsterdam. Both authors' views and statements as expressed in this contribution are strictly personal.

[1] International Covenant on Civil and Political Rights (adopted 16 December 1966, entered into force 23 March 1976) 999 UNTS 171.

[2] International Covenant on Economic, Social and Cultural Rights (adopted 16 December 1966, entered into force 3 January 1976) 993 UNTS 3.

[3] Universal Declaration of Human Rights (adopted 10 December 1948) UNGA Res 217 A(III) (10 December 1948) UN Doc A/RES/3/217A.

International Bill of Human Rights: the third limb, which consists of international measures of implementation, is provided by the two committees.[4] Indeed, creating supervisory mechanisms for the covenants, and enforcement "with teeth," turned out to be the most challenging aspect of creating the International Bill of Human Rights.[5]

In this regard, and in order to evaluate the "success" of treaty-making, it is useful and relevant to consider the measures of implementation as provided by bodies such as the two committees and the advancement of norms and raising of standards brought about by them. This chapter will accordingly draw on the committees' work through the state reporting procedures, their General Comments, and the Views issued as part of the individual complaint mechanisms by both bodies in order to determine the impact of the committees' work on the wider system of human rights law. The scope of this analysis will not, however, allow a holistic commentary on developments under individual covenant rights; this is available elsewhere.[6] Instead, the analysis will seek to pinpoint some key examples of the committees' impact on the conceptual framework of human rights. In this regard, it must be noted that the "influence," "effect," "success," or "impact" of the committees' work can be understood in a multitude of ways and is difficult to measure. The present chapter cannot offer thorough insight into the heterogeneous domestic reactions to and reception of the committees' findings or provide a detailed exploration of the committees' authority to issue binding interpretations of the underlying covenants.[7] Instead, the aim here is to create an understanding, albeit necessarily incomplete, of the ways in which the UN, in the form of these two bodies, transcends the role of a passive forum for negotiation to engage in a dialogue with states and provide concrete guidance and expertise to states and other actors related to the human rights field.

1 The Committees' Monitoring Work

To preface the remainder of this chapter, the present section will briefly explore the three main mechanisms through which the committees fulfill their functions. This will provide a basis for exploring how the two bodies' work has contributed to the development of

[4] See ECOSOC (UN Economic and Social Council) Res 5(I) (16 February 1946) UN Doc E/RES/5(I); Maya Hertig Randall, "The History of the Covenants: Looking Back Half a Century and Beyond" in Daniel Moeckli, Helen Keller, and Corina Heri (eds), *The Human Rights Covenants at 50* (OUP 2018) (hereafter Hertig Randall, "History").

[5] Hertig Randall, "History" (n 4) 23–24, with further references.

[6] Compare, on the CESCR, Ben Saul, David Kinley, and Jacqueline Mowbray, *The International Covenant on Economic, Social and Cultural Rights: Commentary, Cases, and Materials* (OUP 2014), and on the HRC, Sarah Joseph and Melissa Castan, *The International Covenant on Civil and Political Rights: Cases, Materials, and Commentary* (3rd edn, OUP 2013).

[7] On this, compare also Samantha Besson, "The Influence of the Two Covenants on States Parties across Regions: Lessons for the Role of Comparative Law and of Regions in International Human Rights Law" in Daniel Moeckli, Helen Keller, and Corina Heri (eds), *The Human Rights Covenants at 50* (OUP 2018) (hereafter Besson, "Influence").

international human rights law. Of course, the committees may affect the development of international law beyond their monitoring work—thus, for example, HRC members met with then High Commissioner for Human Rights Louise Arbour to discuss her proposals for the reform the UN human rights system[8]—but the focus here will be on the committees' work as monitoring bodies made up of independent experts.

The three main methods of the committees' work are the state reporting procedure, through which the committees engage with the states parties to the covenants in order to ensure accountability and stimulate a human-rights-related dialogue; the committees' General Comments, which allow them to consolidate and clarify their guidance; and the individual complaints mechanisms, through which they provide individuals with access to justice for specific claims. The inter-state complaints mechanisms provided for under article 10 of the Optional Protocol to the ICESCR and articles 41–43 ICCPR will not be discussed further here, as they had never been used as of the time of this writing.

1.1 The State Reporting Procedure

Under article 40 ICCPR and article 16 ICESCR, states are obligated to submit reports on the measures adopted in order to give effect to covenant rights and the progress made as concerns the enjoyment of those rights in their jurisdictions. Receiving and responding to state reports in the form of concluding observations was originally the mainstay of the committees' work. In the case of the HRC, the monitoring mechanism established in 1966 provided for mandatory state reporting complemented by optional individual and inter-state complaint procedures, and under the ICESCR, mandatory reporting to ECOSOC was the only implementation measure upon which states could agree.[9] The submission of periodic reports by states concerning their performance of covenant requirements was thus originally the only way in which the two committees could engage directly with all states' compliance with their obligations under the covenants. Even after the creation of the independent CESCR in 1985 and with the developments regarding individual complaint mechanisms, state reporting continues to play a hugely influential role by allowing an ongoing dialogue between individual governments and the committees.[10]

1.2 General Comments

The General Comments elaborated by both committees provide states—along with additional interested parties, including other human rights bodies and scholars—with consolidated guidance. This guidance is convincing, in part, because of its consultative

[8] HRC "Summary Record (Partial) of the 2296th Meeting" (26 July 2005) UN Doc CCPR/C/SR.2296.

[9] Hertig Randall, "History" (n 4) 23–24.

[10] For more on this function, see Yogesh Tyagi, *The UN Human Rights Committee: Practice and Procedure* (CUP 2011), 151–324.

elaboration.[11] The General Comments draw on the experience that the committees have gained in evaluating states' periodic reports, and their purpose is to make this expertise available to all states, to draw attention to widespread problems, to suggest improvements to the reporting procedure, and to stimulate all actors involved in the realization of the relevant human rights.[12]

1.3 Individual Complaints

The individual complaints mechanisms under the twin covenants allow individuals to seize the committees with complaints relating to respect for their covenant rights. Complaints brought by individuals and the resulting Views of the committees concretize the requirements of the covenants in the individual case. The Views are not legally binding on states, and their authority, like that of all of the committees' work, is not free of controversy, especially where the CESCR is concerned.[13] However, the involved states' implementation of the recommended measures is monitored and the committees' Views, beyond the individual case, also represent a source of guidance for third-party states and other actors.

As concerns the individual complaints procedure, the HRC is by far the most active UN human rights treaty body. As of early 2018, it had received more than 3,162 communications regarding 92 States parties.[14] Indeed, the HRC spends a considerable portion of its time—particularly in the context of pre-session meetings—on individual applications. Thus, its ordinary sessions are preceded by a pre-session of about one week's duration during which the individual rapporteurs, who are in charge of three or four specific individual communications each, deliberate with those half-dozen other members of the Committee in attendance. This significantly reduces the amount of time that the HRC spends on individual cases in its regular sessions, as the outcome of individual communications procedures has already largely been discussed by this time and the draft Views have been prepared. Nonetheless, the individual complaints mechanism takes up one-third of the HRC's regular sessions. By contrast, the CESCR, which lacked its own

[11] On the participation of nongovernmental organizations in the elaboration of General Comments, see Patrick Mutzenberg, "NGOs: Essential Actors for Embedding the Covenants in the National Context" in Daniel Moeckli, Helen Keller, and Corina Heri (eds), *The Human Rights Covenants at 50* (OUP 2018).

[12] See CESCR "Introduction: The Purpose of General Comments" (24 February 1989) UN Doc E/1989/22, annex III at 87 in "Note by the Secretariat, Compilation of General Comments and General Recommendations Adopted by Human Rights Treaty Bodies" (12 May 2003) UN Doc HRI\GEN\1\Rev.6, 8. See, on this topic, Helen Keller and Leena Grover, "General Comments of the Human Rights Committee and Their Legitimacy" in Helen Keller and Geir Ulfstein (eds), *UN Human Rights Treaty Bodies: Law and Legitimacy* (CUP 2012).

[13] Compare the statement by the US government that "there is no suggestion [in the ICESCR] that the Committee is empowered to render authoritative interpretations of the treaty or identify new non-treaty obligations of States" (United States Government, "Observations by the United States of America on 'The Right to Health, Fact Sheet No 31"' <www.state.gov/documents/organization/138850.pdf> accessed August 22, 2017, para 17 (hereafter USA, "Observations")).

[14] UNGA "Annual Report of the Human Rights Committee 2017" (18 July 2018) UN Doc A/73/40.

independent monitoring body until 1985 and which did not receive the competence to examine individual complaints until the Optional Protocol to the ICESCR entered into force in 2013, lags behind in this regard: as of early 2019, the CESCR had reached a decision on the admissibility or the merits of 16 cases, and received a total of 47 further pending communications.[15] However, in some sense, the very existence of an individual complaint procedure before this body is a noteworthy development: the idea of justiciable economic, social, and cultural (ESC) rights represents a significant improvement of the protection of those rights, and was a political impossibility at the time of the ICESCR's drafting. Indeed, textually, the ICESCR even lacks the clause contained in article 2(3)(a) ICCPR that binds states to "ensure that any person whose rights or freedoms as herein recognized are violated shall have an effective remedy."[16]

2 Contribution to the Conceptual Framework of Human Rights

The discussion in Section 1 has shown that the committees are set up to contribute to the development of international law—in the sense of transcending the idea of a UN that provides a purely passive forum for negotiation—through their very existence as bodies of independent experts who are not state representatives. How the committees concretely contribute to the conceptual framework of human rights law through their work will be the subject of the present section. Given space constraints, however, this chapter will not provide a commentary on all of the committees' findings over the years. Instead, this section will focus particularly on ways in which the committees have affected the concept and understanding of rights through their work.

2.1 Contributions by the UN Human Rights Committee

2.1.1 *Contribution to the Substance of Rights*

The HRC has led advances in a number of fields as far as the substance of rights is concerned, as shown by the many references to its work made by other human rights bodies,[17] and has been unafraid to tackle politically polarizing issues. For example, its

[15] Cf the jurisprudence database of the UN High Commissioner on Human Rights <http://juris.ohchr.org/> accessed January 18, 2019. For pending communications, see the Table of Pending Cases <https://www.ohchr.org/EN/HRBodies/CESCR/Pages/PendingCases.aspx> accessed January 18, 2019.

[16] See Hertig Randall, "History" (n 4) 19.

[17] Compare, for the ECtHR, *Bayatyan v Armenia* ECHR 2011, paras 59–64, or *Al-Dulimi and Montana Management Inc v Switzerland* ECHR 2016, paras 66–69. For the Inter-American Court of Human Rights, see *Case of the Saramaka People v Suriname* (Preliminary Objections, Merits, Reparations, and Costs) Inter-American Court of Human Rights Series C No 172 (28 November 2007), paras 94, 98, and 130.

finding in the *Toonen v Australia* case that the ICCPR's nondiscrimination provision also applies to discrimination on the basis of sexual orientation represented a significant advance for the area of LGBTQ rights.[18] In those landmark Views, in 1994, the HRC found that the sodomy laws in place in Tasmania at the time were incompatible with the ICCPR.[19] Another set of influential findings, made by the HRC in the early 1990s, concerned the factors that may render detention arbitrary.[20]

In the religious freedom context, three cases brought against France by Sikh applicants who had been refused permission to wear their turbans in different situations bear mention.[21] These cases were notably discussed in academic circles given that they diverged from the more restrictive case law of the European Court of Human Rights (ECtHR).[22] In other regards, too, the HRC has provided a counterpoint to the Strasbourg Court; for example, the HRC has definitively rejected[23] the concept of a margin of appreciation, which is used extensively in Strasbourg,[24] and has re-examined cases previously brought before the ECtHR, to very different results.[25] Thus, in 2013, the HRC considered a case that had previously been declared manifestly ill-founded by a three-judge Committee of the ECtHR because it did not reveal an appearance of an ECHR violation.[26] The HRC, by contrast, found a violation of article 7 ICCPR, the prohibition of torture and cruel, inhuman, or degrading treatment or punishment.[27]

The HRC has also played a part in the ongoing process to provide adequate protection and access to a remedy to individuals included on sanctions lists under Security Council Resolutions, making one of the first findings by a human rights body that the inclusion of individuals on such a list had violated their rights.[28] Another example is the HRC's

[18] *Toonen v Australia* (1994) 5 Selected Decisions of the Human Rights Committee 133.

[19] Ibid.

[20] Compare, for example, *Womah Mukong v Cameroon* (1994) 5 Selected Decisions of the Human Rights Committee 86, para 9.8, as cited in Inter-American Court of Human Rights, *Case of Chaparro Álvarez and Lapo Íñiguez v Ecuador* (Preliminary Objections, Merits, Reparations, and Costs) Inter-American Court of Human Rights Series C No 170 (21 November 2007), para 92, or *A v Australia* (1997) 6 Selected Decisions of the Human Rights Committee 89, cited in ECtHR, *Saadi v the United Kingdom* ECHR 2008, paras 31–32.

[21] *Ranjit Singh v France* (HRC, 27 September 2011) UN Doc CCPR/C/102/D/1876/2009; *Bikramjit Singh v France* (HRC, 4 February 2013) UN Doc CCPR/C/106/D/1852/2008; *Mann Singh v France* (HRC, 19 July 2013) UN Doc CCPR/C/108/D/1928/2010.

[22] See *Mann Singh v France* App no 24479/07 (ECHR, 13 November 2008); as discussed in Emmanuelle Bribosia, Gabrielle Caceres, and Isabelle Rorive, "Les signes religieux au coeur d'un bras de fer: la saga Singh" (2014) 98 Revue trimestrielle des droits de l'homme 495.

[23] HRC "General Comment 34" in "Note by the Secretariat, Compilation of General Comments and General Recommendations adopted by Human Rights Treaty Bodies" (2008) HRI/GEN/1/Rev.9 (vol I), para 36.

[24] On the ECtHR's margin of appreciation, see George Letsas, "Two Concepts of the Margin of Appreciation" (2006) 26 Oxford J L Studies 705.

[25] *María Cruz Achabal Puertas v Spain* (HRC, 27 March 2013) UN Doc CCPR/C/107/D/1945/2010, as discussed in Janneke Gerards, "Inadmissibility Decisions of the European Court of Human Rights: A Critique of the Lack of Reasoning" (2014) 14 Human Rights L Rev 148.

[26] *Achabal Puertas v Spain* (ECtHR, 13 May 2008), paras 7.2. and 7.3.

[27] HRC, *María Cruz Achabal Puertas v Spain* (n 25).

[28] *Sayadi and Vinck v Belgium* (HRC, 22 October 2008) UN Doc CCPR/C/94/D/1472/2006.

approach to conscientious objection; in this context, too, the HRC took a trendsetting role, as one of the first international bodies to recognize the right to conscientiously object to the performance of military service.[29]

The HRC has also played a part in shaping how human rights are understood beyond the context of a specific right, for example as concerns the existence of positive and procedural obligations or the permissibility of limiting rights. Thus, the HRC was a forerunner in recognizing the existence of positive obligations, for example in the context of the right to life,[30] detention,[31] or, in the nondiscrimination context, by recognizing the need for "affirmative action designed to ensure the positive enjoyment of rights."[32] In addition, the HRC has derived procedural obligations from the rights enshrined in the ICCPR.[33] Furthermore, in deciding the cases that come before it, and in its General Comments, the HRC has also addressed the permissibility of limiting ICCPR rights. In this regard, it has often taken a strong rights-protective approach, for example limiting the weight given to state security or public order considerations.[34]

2.1.2 *Contribution to Treaty Law*

Beyond the substance of rights, too, the HRC has made important contributions to the development of human rights law and of international law more generally. One area in which the HRC has made significant headway concerns the permissibility of state reservations to ICCPR rights[35]—although it has, of course, not been the only body concerned with these issues.[36] Thus, in its General Comment 24, the HRC established that it had the power to determine whether reservations entered by states are compatible with the

[29] *Yoon and Choi v the Republic of Korea* (2007) 9 Selected Decisions of the Human Rights Committee 218. See, on this, Jeremy K Kessler, "The Invention of a Human Right: Conscientious Objection at the United Nations, 1947–2011" (2013) 44 Columbia Human Rights L Rev 753; Hitomi Takemura, *International Human Right to Conscientious Objection to Military Service and Individual Duties to Disobey Manifestly Illegal Orders* (Springer 2009), especially 56–61, 68–80.

[30] See *Lantsova v the Russian Federation* (HRC, 22 October 2002) UN Doc CCPR/C/74/D/763/1997, para 9.2.

[31] See *Deidrick v Jamaica* (HRC, 9 April 1998) UN Doc CCPR/C/62/D/619/1995, para 7.6; HRC "General Comment 21" in "Note by the Secretariat, Compilation of General Comments and General Recommendations adopted by Human Rights Treaty Bodies" (2008) HRI/GEN/1/Rev.9 (vol I), para 3.

[32] HRC "General Comment 4" in "Note by the Secretariat, Compilation of General Comments and General Recommendations adopted by Human Rights Treaty Bodies" (2008) HRI/GEN/1/Rev.9 (vol I), para 2.

[33] Compare *Mulezi v Democratic Republic of the Congo* (HRC, 8 July 2004) UN Doc CCPR/C/81/D/962/2001, para 7; Carazo María Pía, "Enhancing Human Rights Protection through Procedure: Procedural Rights and Guarantees Derived from Substantial Norms in Human Rights Treaties" in Russell A Miller and Rebecca M Bratspies (eds), *Progress in International Law* (Brill 2008).

[34] On state security, see *Kim v Republic of Korea* (1999) 6 Selected Decisions of the Human Rights Committee 110. On public order, see the religious freedom cases mentioned previously (*Ranjit Singh*, *Bikramjit Singh*, and *Mann Singh v France* (n 21)).

[35] HRC "General Comment 24" in "Note by the Secretariat, Compilation of General Comments and General Recommendations adopted by Human Rights Treaty Bodies" (2008) HRI/GEN/1/Rev.9 (vol I).

[36] Compare, for example, ECtHR, *Belilos v Switzerland* (1988) Series A no 132, paras 50–60.

ICCPR's object and purpose, and effectively to invalidate those that are not.[37] In particular, it found that reservations or declarations impeding the application of certain "supportive guarantees" in the ICCPR that are "essential to its object and purpose," such as the right to an effective remedy, are always invalid.[38] The General Comment did not sit well with all states, some of which accused the HRC of going "much too far" in this regard, with its approach allegedly running "contrary to the Covenant scheme and international law."[39] However, the Committee has proven resolute, declaring some reservations and interpretive declarations to the ICCPR to be incompatible with the Covenant and therefore severable.[40] This position lends support to the idea that human rights treaties are "special" as opposed to "ordinary" treaties between states.[41]

In 1998, the UN was faced with another interesting issue, and one that had theretofore not yet been explored by an international adjudicator: whether states parties can denounce human rights treaties that do not expressly provide for denunciation. When North Korea attempted to denounce the ICCPR in 1997,[42] the HRC drafted a General Comment that took a clear stance on the continuity of states' obligations, stating that the ICCPR cannot be denounced by the states parties given the absence of an intention on the part of the drafters to allow denunciation, and that "[t]he rights enshrined in the Covenant belong to the people living in the territory of the State party. [O]nce the people are accorded the protection of the rights under the Covenant, such protection devolves with territory and continues to belong to them, notwithstanding change in government of the State party, including dismemberment in more than one State or State succession or any subsequent action of the State party designed to divest them of the rights guaranteed by the Covenant."[43]

The HRC has also taken an increasingly broad approach to the application of the ICCPR, considering that the Covenant may find extraterritorial application where states have "power or effective control" over individuals outside of their own territory.[44] This represents an expansive interpretation of article 2(1) ICCPR, which limits a state's

[37] HRC "General Comment 24" (n 35) para 18. [38] Ibid, para 11.

[39] HRC "Observations on General Comment No 24 (52)" in "Report of the Human Rights Committee" (4 February 1996) UN Doc A/50/40 (vol 1) (supp) Annex VI, 126, 126–27.

[40] HRC "Concluding Observations on the Third and Fourth Periodic Reports of Egypt" (28 November 2002) UN Doc CCPR/CO/76/EGY, para 5; HRC "Concluding Observations on the Initial Periodic Report of Kuwait" (27 July 2000) UN Doc CCPR/CO/69/KWT, para 4; *Kennedy v Trinidad and Tobago* (1999) 7 Selected Decisions of the Human Rights Committee 5. See also Frédéric Mégret, "Nature of Obligations" in Daniel Moeckli, Sangeeta Shah, and Sandesh Sivakumaran (eds), *International Human Rights Law* (3rd edn, OUP 2018), 95–97 (hereafter Mégret, "Nature of Obligations").

[41] See Mégret, "Nature of Obligations" (n 40).

[42] UN Secretary General, "Notification by the Democratic People's Republic of Korea" (1997) UN Doc C/N/467/1997.

[43] HRC "General Comment 26" in "Note by the Secretariat, Compilation of General Comments and General Recommendations adopted by Human Rights Treaty Bodies" (2008) HRI/GEN/1/Rev.9 (vol I), *passim*.

[44] HRC "General Comment 31" in "Note by the Secretariat, Compilation of General Comments and General Recommendations adopted by Human Rights Treaty Bodies" (2008) HRI/GEN/1/Rev.9 (vol I), para 10.

obligations to "all individuals within its territory and subject to its jurisdiction." Applying this approach, the HRC has found, for example, that the United States of America must respect the ICCPR in its extraterritorial detention camps,[45] and that Israel bears responsibility for rights abuses in the Occupied Territories, including the Gaza Strip.[46] In 2015, the HRC also noted that, where the interception of communications outside of a state's national territory is concerned, the state must continue to respect the right to privacy enshrined in article 17 ICCPR.[47] While this finding seems to have had little impact on the US approach to foreign surveillance,[48] the HRC's stance on the matter has been gaining traction, and will likely have a significant influence on future debates in this regard.[49]

2.2 The UN Committee on Economic, Social, and Cultural Rights

The CESCR has been in existence for a shorter time than the HRC: its first session was only held in 1987. Since then, its often groundbreaking work has had a particular impact on the conceptual understanding of ESC rights, and thus of human rights overall. Indeed, the "renaissance" of economic, social, and cultural rights in past decades has been credited to the work of the CESCR, through its general comments and concluding observations on state reports, which have been described as "influential and catalytic" in concretizing the conceptual framework of these rights.[50]

[45] HRC "Concluding Observations on the Combined Second and Third Periodic Reports of the United States of America" (18 December 2006) UN Doc CCPR/C/USA/CO/3/Rev.1.

[46] HRC "Concluding Observations on the Third Periodic Report of Israel" (3 September 2010) UN Doc CCPR/C/ISR/CO/3, para 5. See also Sarah Joseph and Sam Dipnall, "Scope of Application" in Daniel Moeckli, Sangeeta Shah, and Sandesh Sivakumaran (eds), *International Human Rights Law* (3rd edn, OUP 2018), 124–125.

[47] HRC "Concluding Observations on the Seventh Periodic Report of the United Kingdom of Great Britain and Northern Ireland" (17 August 2015) UN Doc CCPR/C/GBR/CO/7, para 24; Gerald L Neuman, "Has the Human Rights Committee Extended Its Reach?" (*Just Security*, 29 July 2015) <www.justsecurity.org/25022/human-rights-committee-extended-reach> accessed August 22, 2017.

[48] In that it does not seem to have had any direct and decisive influence on domestic policy, for example on the draft "USA Rights Act" (HR 4124, introduced to the US House of Representatives on October 25, 2017).

[49] Cf United Nations High Commissioner for Human Rights "The Right to Privacy in the Digital Age" (30 June 2014) UN Doc A/HRC/27/37; Marko Milanović, "Human Rights Treaties and Foreign Surveillance: Privacy in the Digital Age" (2015) 56 Harv. Intl L J 81, *passim*; Francesca Bignami and Giorgio Resta, "Human Rights Extraterritoriality: The Right to Privacy and National Security Surveillance" in Eyal Benvenisti and Georg Nolte (eds), *Community Interests across International Law* (OUP 2018).

[50] Malcolm Langford and Jeff A King, "Committee on Economic, Social and Cultural Rights: Past, Present and Future" in Malcolm Langford (ed), *Social Rights Jurisprudence: Emerging Trends in International and Comparative Law* (CUP 2008), 477 (hereafter Langford and King, "CESCR").

2.2.1 *Contribution to the Development of Specific Rights*

Since its inception, the CESCR has recognized a number of rights implied in the ICESCR. Thus, for example, in 2003, it issued a General Comment through which it recognized that the right to an adequate standard of living as enshrined in article 11(1) ICESCR, which does not explicitly contain a right to water, "was not intended to be exhaustive. The right to water clearly falls within the category of guarantees essential for securing an adequate standard of living, particularly since it is one of the most fundamental conditions for survival."[51] This is not the only example of the Committee's identification of implied rights. Thus, like other human rights bodies,[52] the CESCR has taken an inclusive approach to the proscribed grounds of discrimination covered by the ICESCR, finding that disability—to which there is no explicit reference anywhere in the Covenant—falls under article 2(2) ICESCR.[53]

In addition to identifying implied rights, the CESCR has also fleshed out those rights contained in the ICESCR. In this regard, its guidance is often highly ambitious; however, despite its tendency to evoke controversy, in many cases, this also means that its findings are likely to be considered convincing by other actors in the human rights field. As concerns the right to health, for example, the CESCR identified four essential elements of that right—namely availability, accessibility, acceptability, and quality of health facilities, goods, and services, or the AAAQ criteria—in its General Comment 14, and provided states with guidance about what each element requires.[54] These findings were later taken up by the OHCHR and the World Health Organization in a joint fact sheet,[55] and have become prominent criteria for judging the acceptability of healthcare provision. This widespread adoption of the CESCR's approach evidences the level of authority accorded to its findings; at the same time, the reaction of the government of the United States—which is not a party to the ICESCR—to the fact sheet took a decidedly less respectful view of the Committee's authority to interpret the ICESCR or the right to health.[56]

The CESCR has also played a role, although perhaps not always a leading one,[57] in drawing attention to the impacts that austerity measures adopted after financial and economic crises, especially the 2008 financial crisis, have had on ESC rights. As concerns

[51] CESCR "General Comment 15" in "Note by the Secretariat, Compilation of General Comments and General Recommendations adopted by Human Rights Treaty Bodies" (2008) HRI/GEN/1/Rev.9 (vol I), para 3.

[52] One example being the HRC, and the approach it took in *Toonen* (n 18).

[53] CESCR "General Comment 5" in "Note by the Secretariat, Compilation of General Comments and General Recommendations adopted by Human Rights Treaty Bodies" (2008) HRI/GEN/1/Rev.9 (vol I), para 5. See, on this, Langford and King, "CESCR" (n 50), 480.

[54] CESCR "General Comment 14" in "Note by the Secretariat, Compilation of General Comments and General Recommendations adopted by Human Rights Treaty Bodies" (2008) HRI/GEN/1/Rev.9 (vol I).

[55] OHCHR and the World Health Organization, "The Right to Health: Factsheet No 31" (UN 2008).

[56] USA, "Observations" (n 13), para 17.

[57] See Christine Kaufmann, "The Covenants and Financial Crises" in Daniel Moeckli, Helen Keller, and Corina Heri (eds), *The Human Rights Covenants at 50* (OUP 2018), 313 and 316.

Greece, for example, the Committee has noted the "severe impact" of austerity[58] and called on the state to take its ESC rights obligations into account in negotiations with international financial institutions and to review its policies to ensure a progressive waiver of austerity measures and ensure the effective protection of Covenant rights as the economy recovers.[59] The CESCR has furthermore called for human rights impact assessments by both borrowing and lending states, admonishing the lenders to "ensure that they do not impose obligations on borrowing States that would lead them to adopt retrogressive measures in violation of their obligations under the Covenant."[60]

2.2.2 *Contribution to Human Rights Law Overall*

Beyond its interpretation and development of individual rights in the ICESCR, the CESCR has also contributed immensely to the understanding and framework of ESC rights in more general terms. Thus, for example, the triad of obligations adopted by the Committee—namely the obligations to respect, to protect, and to fulfill human rights, which the CESCR has used since its General Comment 12[61]—has helped to shape the way in which ESC rights and human rights in general are understood. This idea of differentiated obligations, such as the HRC's approach to reservations, indicates an understanding of human rights as a "special" regime.[62]

In addition, and perhaps even more notably, the CESCR pioneered the idea of states' obligation to use all available resources to satisfy their minimum core obligations as a matter of priority.[63] In the realm of ESC rights, where the idea of progressive realization forms a well-worn refrain and no right to an effective remedy is guaranteed by the text of the ICESCR,[64] this represents a revolution.[65] Through the obligation to take steps to realize ESC rights, the prohibition of retrogressive measures even in times of austerity, and the distinction between immediate and progressive obligations,[66] the work of the CESCR has managed to make ESC rights concrete, applicable in practice, and—since the entry into force of the Optional Protocol—even justiciable.

[58] CESCR "Concluding Observations on the Second Periodic Report of Greece" (9 October 2015) UN Doc E/C.12/GRC/CO/2, para 7.

[59] Ibid, para 8.

[60] CESCR "Public Debt, Austerity Measures and the International Covenant on Economic, Social and Cultural Rights" (22 July 2016) UN Doc E/C.12/2016/1, paras 10 and 11.

[61] As noted by Eibe Riedel, Gilles Giacca, and Christophe Golay, "The Development of Economic, Social and Cultural Rights in International Law" in Eibe Riedel, Gilles Giacca, and Christophe Golay (eds), *Economic, Social, and Cultural Rights: Contemporary Issues and Challenges* (OUP 2014), 18ff, referring to CESCR "General Comment 12" in "Note by the Secretariat, Compilation of General Comments and General Recommendations adopted by Human Rights Treaty Bodies" (2008) HRI/GEN/1/Rev.9 (vol I).

[62] See Mégret, "Nature of Obligations" (n 40).

[63] CESCR "General Comment 3" in "Note by the Secretariat, Compilation of General Comments and General Recommendations adopted by Human Rights Treaty Bodies" (2008) HRI/GEN/1/Rev.9 (vol I), para 10; Manisuli Ssenyonjo, *Economic, Social and Cultural Rights in International Law* (Hart 2009), 65–68 (hereafter Ssenyonjo, *ESCR*).

[64] Contrast art 2(3)(a) ICCPR, as noted in Hertig Randall, "History" (n 4), 19.

[65] See Mahon Claire, "Progress at the Front: The Draft Optional Protocol to the International Covenant on Economic, Social and Cultural Rights" (2008) 8 Human Rights L Rev 617.

[66] Compare Langford and King, "CESCR" (n 50).

Furthermore, like the HRC, the CESCR has been faced with the question of the extraterritorial effect of its Covenant. In this context, it has accepted that there can be extraterritorial effect of certain state obligations, for example the obligation to respect the right of access to health in other countries and to provide aid in order to contribute to the fulfillment of ESC rights abroad,[67] and the obligation to abstain from participating in decisions of intergovernmental bodies where these would undermine ESC rights.[68]

Last but not least, the CESCR has engaged with states' obligations in the context of business activities, establishing in its General Comment 24 that, under certain circumstances, states may be held directly responsible for the activities of corporate actors. It also held that states have a range of specific obligations when it comes to business activities, including an obligation to conduct human rights impact assessments prior to concluding trade or investment treaties and an obligation to enshrine the corporate responsibility to exercise human rights due diligence in domestic law.[69]

3 Issues and the Committees' "Influence"

As shown previously, the HRC and the CESCR have made impressive contributions to how the rights in the ICCPR and ICESCR, respectively, are understood. However, an analysis of this "influence" would not be complete without touching on at least some of the issues and problems facing the committees in their work and their ability to act as a guiding force in the evolution of human rights law. First, it is necessary to mention that the committees continue to struggle with a number of problems that impact their work. These problems are either shared (such as delays in the submission of state reports, the "silo" approach that isolates the work of the various UN human rights treaty bodies from each other, problems of coherence and reasoning within the work of the individual bodies, difficulties in securing proportionate representation of different legal systems and cultures, and issues of non-reporting, compliance, and follow-up) or specific to one of the bodies (such as the backlog facing the HRC, or the particularly acute resistance to the idea of the justiciability of ESC rights or to the legitimacy of the CESCR to interpret those rights).

[67] CESCR "General Comment 14" (n 54), para 39; Ssenyonjo, *ESCR* (n 63).

[68] Compare CESCR, "Concluding Observations on the Second Periodic Report of Belgium" (1 December 2000) UN Doc E/C.12/1/Add.54, para 31; Ssenyonjo, *ESCR* (n 63), 73; Coomans Fons, "Application of the International Covenant on Economic, Social and Cultural Rights in the Framework of International Organisations" in Armin von Bogdandy and Wolfrum Rüdiger (eds), 11 *Max Planck Yearbook of United Nations Law* (Brill 2011). Cf also Christian Courtis and Magdalena Sepúlveda, "Are Extra-Territorial Obligations Reviewable under the Optional Protocol to the ICESCR?" (2009) 27 Nordisk Tidsskrift for Menneskerettigheter 54.

[69] CESCR "General Comment 24" (10 August 2017) UN Doc E/C.12/GC/24.

Ultimately, many of these problems can be traced to the fact that the findings of the committees, which do not bind states, are heavily dependent on state cooperation—as concerns the submission of periodic reports, but also regarding the implementation of the committees' guidance and indirectly the provision of adequate funding and support to enable the committees to do their work. States' willingness to comply with their reporting obligations and with the requirements imposed by the committees' practice is variable, but as a whole certainly far from perfect. The heterogeneity of responses to committee guidance can be attributed to a variety of sources, including differences in legal and political culture, the domestic institutional framework, the existence of judicial remedies and relevant legislation on the national plane, and the existence of regional human rights systems.[70]

In some instances, failure to engage with the guidance of the committees can also be ascribed to the inadequate diffusion of information in a state—this is particularly acute at the grass-roots level, if the committees' guidance is not translated into local languages—or to the persistent failure of states to submit their periodic reports on time and to thus allow for a dialogue with the committees.[71] In the latter regard, the Universal Periodic Review procedure may help to engage reticent states to some extent, and even encourage human rights dialogues among individual states in a region, even though the recommendations made in this context may again go unimplemented.[72] A number of other reforms have been posited that could continue to improve this process, including tailoring reporting burdens and granting the committees access to more resources.[73] Samantha Besson has, in a recent comparison of regional approaches to the two covenants, argued that these measures should also include improving the dissemination of information, ensuring proportionate representation and adequate consideration for moral and religious pluralism in the committees, and creating new tools to pressure reticent states to comply with their reporting obligations.[74]

4 Conclusion

The level of engagement demonstrated by the CESCR and the HRC provides an answer to the question posed by the editors of this volume about the extent to which the UN's role transcends that of a passive forum or venue for negotiation. Through their very existence as bodies of independent experts who do not represent their native states,

[70] Besson, "Influence" (n 7), 261–62.

[71] Yogesh Tyagi, "Influence of the ICCPR in Asia" in Daniel Moeckli, Helen Keller, and Corina Heri (eds), *The Human Rights Covenants at 50* (OUP 2018), 203–5.

[72] Ibid.

[73] Cf Felice D Gaer, "The Institutional Future of the Covenants: A World Court for Human Rights" in Daniel Moeckli, Helen Keller, and Corina Heri (eds), *The Human Rights Covenants at 50* (OUP 2018), footnote 77 (hereafter Gaer, "World Court") 339–42.

[74] See Besson, "Influence" (n 7), 262, and also Gaer, "World Court" (n 72).

the committees have made and continue to make a valuable contribution to the development of international law. Beyond this, and although their power to authoritatively interpret the underlying instruments has been contested, the two committees have nonetheless managed to play a formative role for the understanding of covenant rights and states parties' responsibilities under these instruments. Furthermore, the two committees have helped to shape the "special" regime applicable to human rights treaties, one in which certain reservations made by states are considered severable by treaty bodies and state obligations are seen as continuous because of the "special" nature of human rights as compared to other international legal obligations.

CHAPTER 22

UNITED NATIONS TREATY-MAKING

refugees and stateless persons

GUY S. GOODWIN-GILL

IN the 25 years between the appointment of the first League of Nations High Commissioner for Refugees and the first UN General Assembly resolution on refugees, the world changed.[1] For the League, the refugee and the stateless person were virtually indistinguishable, but they were also anomalous, being individuals effectively without the protection of their state of nationality and hence, in the doctrine of the day, the responsibility of none. The general view then was that everyone should have a nationality, but only one nationality,[2] and that international law provided no remedy for the stateless.[3]

The 1917 revolution in Russia and the subsequent denationalization of Russian refugees challenged many of the premises then underlying the system of the law of nations, even as the League and voluntary organizations sought to grapple with the humanitarian dimension. The government of Czechoslovakia underlined the need for international protection, "in connection with... passports, certificates of identity, and all other documents

[1] Fridtjof Nansen accepted the invitation of the Council of the League of Nations to act as High Commissioner for Russian Refugees on September 1, 1921: "Russian Refugees. Acceptance by Dr Nansen of the Post of High Commissioner," LoN doc C.337. M.239. 1921, 2 LoN OJ 1006, 1027 (1921). The UN General Assembly (UNGA) unanimously adopted resolution 8(I), "Question of refugees," on February 12, 1946.

[2] cf Convention on Certain Questions relating to the Conflict of Nationality Laws (adopted 12 April 1930, entered into force 1 July 1937) 179 LNTS 89, Preamble: "it is in the general interest of the international community to secure that all its members should recognise that *every person should have a nationality* and should have *one nationality*..." (emphasis added). See also *Dickson Car Wheel Company (U.S.A.) v. United Mexican States* (July 1931) IV *Reports of International Arbitral Awards* 669, 678: "A State... does not commit an international delinquency in inflicting an injury upon an individual lacking nationality, and consequently, no State is empowered to intervene or complain on his behalf either before or after the injury."

[3] *Dickson Car Wheel Company Case* (n 2) 678, citing Oppenheim, *International Law.*

bearing on legal status," and that all those recognizing the government of the Soviets, "will have to find some uniform method of protecting non-Bolshevik refugees."[4] Gustave Ador, President of the International Committee of the Red Cross, appealed for political action and leadership from the League, precisely because of the limits of a purely humanitarian response.[5]

As the first High Commissioner for Refugees, Fridtjof Nansen's mandate was to address the legal protection gap—to define the legal status of refugees, organize their repatriation or allocation to other states, find them productive employment, and, together with private voluntary organizations, provide for their relief.[6] From the very start, it was accepted that while repatriation might be in order, no compulsion or indirect pressure was to be employed; both the League and the ICRC accepted that if refugees were to return to Russia, this would need to be accompanied by "assurances of the most elementary security and the prospects of conditions, at least as favourable as those under which they are now living."[7]

In 1946, the UN General Assembly recognized at once and unanimously that the refugee problem was international in scope and nature, and that no state alone should be expected to bear sole responsibility.[8] Resolution 8(I) set in motion the UN's first program of response to the immediate needs of those displaced by the Second World War, and then for those caught up by later political developments to which they were opposed. Out of this experience emerged the framework of the current refugee regime, the Office of the United Nations High Commissioner for Refugees, and the 1951 Convention relating to the Status of Refugees. Apart from the 1967 Protocol, which effectively removed both the time and geographical limitations on the scope of the 1951 Convention, this structure remains formally unchanged. No other international instrument has emerged in the past 50 years, despite increasing numbers of refugees traveling farther and farther

[4] "Russian Refugees." Summary of the Documents received by the Secretariat on this subject since the 12th Session of the Council. LoN doc C 126 M 72.1921 (16 June 1921), 2 LoN OJ 485, 491–93 (1921); Further Communications, completing Council Document No C. 126(a) M 72(a). 1921, VII (1 August 1921), 2 LoN OJ 1006 (1921).

[5] Letter and Memorandum from the President of the Comité International de la Croix-Rouge, M. Gustave Ador, to the President of the Council of the League of Nations, dated 20 February 1921, in "The Question of the Russian Refugees," 2 LoN OJ 225, 227–29 (1921).

[6] "The Question of the Russian Refugees," Report by M Hanotaux, French Representative, and adopted by the Council on June 27, 1921, LoN doc C.133(b) M 131. 1921. VII; 2 LoN OJ 7558 (1921); "Russian Refugees," Report by Dr Nansen, LoN doc C.602. M 360. 1922 (2 September 1922); "Refugee Questions," Memorandum by Dr Fridtjof Nansen, LoN doc C.553. 1924. XIII; 23 LoN OJ, Spec Supp 144 (25 September 1924).

[7] "Russian Refugees," Letter from the International Red Cross Committee (Gustave Ador), 15 June 1921, LoN doc C 132 M 73. 1921 (18 June 1921); "Russian Refugees: Report by Dr Nansen," LoN doc C 602.1922 (31 August 1922) 3–4 on possible repatriation; Report by Dr Nansen, LoN doc C.473.1923 (recording interventions to prevent expulsion, and including views of the Advisory Committee of Private Organisations); see also Katy Long, *The Point of No Return: Refugees, Rights, and Repatriation* (OUP 2013) 44–78.

[8] It would be another 70 years before the General Assembly was to recognize that international migration was no different: UNGA res 71/1 "New York Declaration on Refugees and Migrants" (19 September 2016) para 11: "We acknowledge a shared responsibility to manage large movements of refugees and migrants in a humane, sensitive, compassionate and people-centred manner."

in search of refuge, the protracted and intractable nature of displacement, the lack of formal "distribution" mechanisms, whether in relation to people or financial responsibility, the institutionalisation of protection rights at the individual level, and the complexity of causes and drivers.

Meanwhile, the situation of stateless persons and the challenge to reduce or eliminate statelessness, which engaged the UN at the technical level during the 1950s, has received renewed attention, by reason both of the intrinsic denial of rights that statelessness entails, and of the common causal link between lack of protection and displacement.[9]

In different times and different political circumstances, both the League and the UN saw themselves as institutionally responsible, in some measure, for refugees, stateless persons, and the unprotected. That responsibility, which could be characterized as "political," or "legal," or "international," was expressed both within the organizations and by the representatives of States. General Assembly resolutions today repeatedly confirm that the primary responsibility for protection rests with states themselves. What is particularly significant for the purposes of UN treaty-making in this field, however, is the close engagement of the relevant international institutions in driving legal developments, in supervising the application of conventions, in advocating for the protection of individual refugees and stateless persons, and in simultaneously working with states at the operational level, where "subsequent practice" can and does develop.

1 The Refugee Treaties

In the push for a new refugee treaty in the 1940s, the UN maintained continuity of practice, drawing on what the League had done and attempted from 1920 to 1940.[10] Under Nansen's leadership, the task of "identifying" refugees and improving their legal status was pursued, not by treaty in the strict, formal sense, but by agreements and "arrangements" with generally non-binding content; the measures adopted in 1922, 1926, and 1928 were thus framed as conference resolutions embodying a series of recommendations.[11] The 1922 Arrangement, for example, *recommended* the issuance of certificates of

[9] Nick Cheesman, "How in Myanmar 'National Races' Came to Surpass Citizenship and Exclude Rohingya" (2017) 47 J Contemporary Asia 461, 461–68; see also Mukul Kesavan, "Murderous Majorities," reviewing Azeem Ibrahim, *The Rohingyas: Inside Myanmar's Genocide* (rev'd and updated edn, Hurst 2018) and Melissa Crouch (ed), *Islam and the State in Myanmar: Muslim-Buddhist Relations and the Politics of Belonging* (OUP 2016); (January 18, 2018) 65 The New York Review of Books 37–40.

[10] See Charter of the United Nations (adopted 26 June 1945, entered into force 24 October 1945) art 1(3), which includes among the purposes of the UN, "To achieve international cooperation in solving international problems of an economic, social, cultural, or humanitarian character, and in promoting and encouraging respect for human rights and for fundamental freedoms for all without distinction. . . ."

[11] Arrangement of 5 July 1922 with respect to the Issue of Certificates of Identity to Russian Refugees, 13 LNTS 355 (1922 Arrangement); Arrangement of 12 May 1926 relating to the Issue of Identity Certificates to Russian and Armenian Refugees, supplementing and amending the previous Arrangements dated July 5, 1922, and May 31, 1924, 89 LNTS 2004; Arrangement of 30 June 1928 relating to the Legal Status of Russian and Armenian Refugees, 89 LNTS 2005 (1928 Arrangement relating to the Legal Status of

identity to Russian refugees (a model was set out in the Schedule), and in due course some 53 states signed on to this practice.[12] Later series of recommendations were not so effective in attracting signatures and improving the legal status of refugees, and during the 1930s, attempts were made to translate the informal, discretionary practices of the previous decade into formal obligations; although a number of texts were agreed to, however, they were not widely ratified.[13]

During the first session of the Commission on Human Rights in July 1947, the situation of stateless persons came up incidentally. The Drafting Committee on an International Bill of Human Rights had before it Article 32—the precursor to Article 15 UDHR48—submitted by René Cassin. It provided not only for a right to a nationality, but also that "It is the duty of the United Nations and Member States to prevent statelessness as being inconsistent with human rights and the interests of the human community."[14] At its second session in December 1947, the Commission adopted a resolution on stateless persons, expressing its wish that the UN recommend to states that they conclude conventions on nationality; and that the UN give early consideration to the legal status of "persons who do not enjoy the protection of any government," and as regards "their legal and social protection and their documentation."[15]

In 1948, the Economic and Social Council (ECOSOC) asked the Secretary-General to prepare a study on the protection of "stateless persons" and, taking account of relevant national legislation, conventions, and agreements, to recommend whether a new convention was called for.[16] The *Study* came down firmly in favor of a convention.[17]

Russian and Armenian Refugees); Arrangement of 30 June 1928 concerning the extension to other categories of refugees of certain measures taken in favour of Russian and Armenian Refugees, 89 LNTS 2006.

[12] 1922 Arrangement (n 11). See also UNHCR, "Background paper submitted by UNHCR to the Colloquium on the development in the law of refugees with particular reference to the 1951 Convention and the Statute of the Office of the United Nations High Commissioner for Refugees," Villa Serbelloni Bellagio (Italy), 21–28 April 1965, doc MHCR/23/05 (1965) 14–17 (Bellagio Background Paper).

[13] 1933 Convention relating to the International Status of Refugees, 159 LNTS 3663; 1936 Provisional Arrangement concerning the Status of Refugees coming from Germany, 171 LNTS 3952; 1938 Convention concerning the Status of Refugees coming from Germany 192 LNTS 4461; 1939 Additional Protocol to the 1936 Provisional Arrangement and to the 1938 Convention concerning the Status of Refugees coming from Germany, 193 LNTS 4634.

[14] Commission on Human Rights, Drafting Committee on an International Bill of Human Rights, First Session, "Report of the Drafting Committee to the Commission on Human Rights" (1 July 1947) UN doc E/CN.4/21 21.

[15] "Report of the Commission on Human Rights: Second Session" (17 December 1947) UN doc E/600; Commission on Human Rights, Second Session, "Report of the Working Party on an International Convention on Human Rights" (11 December 1947) UN doc E/CN.4/56.

[16] ECOSOC res 116 (VI) "Report of the Second Session of the Commission on Human Rights" (1 and 2 March 1948) "D. Stateless persons". The *Study* understood the phrase "stateless persons" also as including the general class of refugees (those stateless de facto): United Nations, *A Study of Statelessness* (August 1949) UN doc E/1112–E/112/Add.1 8–10.

[17] *A Study of Statelessness* (n 16) 72–74. It was suggested that a convention might be drafted either by the Secretary-General in consultation with the Director General of the International Refugee Organization, or by an ad hoc committee appointed by the Council.

Certain measures to improve the legal status of refugees in fact necessitated legal agreement, such as the issue and acceptance of a document that might serve as a passport. In addition, a convention might avoid any state's apprehensions about taking the first step to improve the situation of refugees, while also mitigating the "politicisation" of action in favor of refugees.[18] League practice suggested that some measures were more likely to be incorporated into national law if made the subject of specific treaty provisions, rather than being left simply as recommendations.[19] Moreover,

> A general convention is a lasting international structure; being open to the accession of States which have not signed it, it encourages Governments to associate themselves with the work of their forerunners; even if those Governments are not in a position to accede to it, such a convention sometimes exerts a direct influence on the administrative and legal practice of their countries.[20]

ECOSOC took note of the *Study* and appointed an ad hoc Committee of 13 government representatives to consider whether a revised and consolidated convention was desirable and, if so, to prepare a draft.[21] Not surprisingly, the Committee also favored a convention as the most effective solution, and advised the Council that, given the urgency of the situation, "and the responsibility of the United Nations in this field," it would focus on *refugees*, leaving non-refugee stateless persons for later consideration.[22] So from having had a first, broad understanding of the general class of the "unprotected," the UN now moved to a narrower focus on the refugee who, in East-West relations, had begun to acquire both humanitarian and political significance.[23]

[18] *A Study of Statelessness* (n 16) 63–64; also "*Ad Hoc* Committee on Statelessness and Related Problems. Status of refugees and stateless persons. Memorandum by the Secretary-General" (3 January 1950) UN doc E/AC.32/2, 5–6.

[19] The *Study* referred to the "non-implementation" of recommendations included in the 1928 Arrangement relating to the Legal Status of Russian and Armenian Refugees (n 11), by contrast with provisions contained in later treaties. The 1928 recommendations were intended to clarify the issue of legal status and proposed various services to be provided by the High Commissioner, including "[c]ertifying the identity and the position of the refugees," and "[r]ecommending" individual refugees with a view to their obtaining visas, residence, and so forth: at section 1(a)–(f).

[20] *A Study of Statelessness* (n 16) 64.

[21] Representatives of 11 states took part: Belgium, Brazil, Canada, China, Denmark, France, Israel, Turkey, United Kingdom, United States, and Venezuela. The east/west split having entrenched itself after the first, short bout of unanimity on refugees in February 1946, none of the "Soviet bloc" states participated. See further Guy S. Goodwin-Gill, "The Politics of Refugee Protection" (2008) 27 Refugee Survey Q 8.

[22] "Report of the *Ad Hoc* Committee on Statelessness and Related Problems" (17 February 1950) UN doc E/1618, E/AC.32/5; ECOSOC Social Committee: UN docs E/AC.7/SR.156 (14 August 1950) – E/AC.7/SR.169 (23 August 1950).

[23] These politics also necessarily affected the first 30 or so years of UN and member state practice, which in turn generated a critique of the international refugee regime for its "exilic bias." See GJL Coles, "The Human Rights Approach to the Solution of the Refugee Problem: A Theoretical and Practical Enquiry," in Alan E Nash (ed), *Human Rights and the Protection of Refugees under International Law* (Canadian Human Rights Foundation/The Institute for Research on Public Policy 1988) 209.

The Ad Hoc Committee on Statelessness and Related Problems submitted its report in February 1950.[24] ECOSOC followed up with a composite resolution in August of that year, returned the draft for further review, prior to its being considered by the General Assembly, and finalized the Preamble and refugee definition. In December, the General Assembly decided to convene a Conference of Plenipotentiaries to finalize the Convention and a Protocol on stateless persons.[25]

The Conference met in Geneva from July 2 to 25, 1951 and took as its basis for discussion the Ad hoc Committee's draft, save that the Preamble was that adopted by the Economic and Social Council, while Article 1 was as recommended by the General Assembly and annexed to Resolution 429(V). On adopting the final text, the Conference also unanimously adopted a Final Act, including five recommendations covering travel documents, family unity, nongovernmental organizations, asylum, and application of the Convention beyond its contractual scope.[26]

2 The 1967 Protocol Relating to the Status of Refugees

The recommendation as legal technique emerged again in the background documentation for the 1965 Bellagio Colloquium that prepared the ground for the 1967 Protocol relating to the Status of Refugees.[27] The problem lay in the limiting dateline in the 1951 Convention's refugee definition, so that only those with a well-founded fear of persecution by reason of events occurring before January 1, 1951 could qualify.[28] This had led to new refugee groups being without Convention protection, and to a growing disjuncture between the Convention scheme and the mandate of the High Commissioner, whose Statute contained neither temporal nor geographical limits.[29] Recommendation E of the Final Act of the Convention expressed the hope that states would apply the Convention beyond its contractual scope, but as UNHCR noted, international rather than national action was required, particularly if the benefits of Convention status were to have

[24] "Report of the *Ad Hoc* Committee on Statelessness and Related Problems" (n 22).

[25] UNGA res 429(V) (14 December 1950).

[26] Convention relating to the Status of Refugees (adopted 28 July 1951, entered into force 22 April 1954) 189 UNTS 137 (1951 Convention). The Protocol on Stateless Persons was left for another day; see further in Section 3.1 of this chapter.

[27] The "Colloquium on Legal Aspects of Refugee Problems," which met in Bellagio, Italy, from April 21 to April 28, 1965, was organized by the Carnegie Endowment for International Peace with the support of the Swiss government, and brought together prominent legal experts from 13 countries.

[28] 1951 Convention, art 1A(2). An optional clause allowed states to narrow their obligations still farther, by reference to events occurring "in Europe."

[29] Statute of the Office of the United Nations High Commissioner for Refugees, para 6, annexed to UNGA res 428(V) (14 December 1950) (UNHCR Statute).

extraterritorial effect.[30] The answer might have been to seek revision of the Convention under Article 45, with a request to the Secretary-General followed by the General Assembly thereafter recommending what steps, if any, should be taken. The disadvantage here was that any discussion in the General Assembly would necessarily include states that were not party to the Convention and might have no interest in the issues.[31]

In UNHCR's view,[32] a legally binding instrument was needed, not a recommendation or resolution, and a new convention or formal revision would be too lengthy. It was therefore proposed that a protocol extending the scope of the Convention be drafted, to be adopted directly by states parties to the 1951 Convention without prior discussion in the General Assembly.[33]

The High Commissioner duly reported to the Thirteenth Session of the Executive Committee on the Colloquium's recommendations as to how the Convention might be adapted to changed circumstances and to the fact that the refugee problem was now recognized as "universal" and of "indefinite duration."[34] A draft was also put to the Executive Committee, indicating that the Protocol should also be open to states not party to the Convention. The possibility of geographical limitations was rejected on principle, the object and purpose of the Protocol being to extend the scope of protection,[35] but reservations to the article on dispute settlement were generally accepted as likely to encourage accession. The idea that Contracting States might be permitted to suspend application of the extended treaty in "exceptional circumstances" was also considered but, while this might encourage accession, many states were concerned that any such provision could be subject to unilateral abuse.

The following year, after seeking the comments of states parties and Executive Committee members and noting their generally favorable response at its Fourteenth and Fifteenth Sessions,[36] the High Commissioner requested ECOSOC to submit the draft Protocol to the General Assembly as an addendum to UNHCR's Annual Report.[37]

[30] UNHCR, "Bellagio Background Paper" (n 12) paras 8–9, 123–24, 127.

[31] ibid paras 129–30. As noted previously, the refugee issue was also highly politicized.

[32] cf UNHCR Statute, para 8: "The High Commissioner shall provide for the protection of refugees falling under the competence of his Office by: (a) Promoting the conclusion and ratification of international conventions for the protection of refugees, supervising their application and proposing amendments thereto…"

[33] "If general agreement cannot be reached by all States Parties…at least some progress could be achieved by the adoption of a Protocol by a limited number of them…with the possibility of others acceding at a later date." UNHCR, "Bellagio Background Paper" (n 12) para 131.

[34] UN High Commissioner for Refugees (UNHCR) "Colloquium on the legal aspects of refugee problems: Note by the High Commissioner" (5 May 1965) UN doc A/AC.96/INF.40.

[35] Existing geographical reservations could be continued, although states were encouraged to withdraw them.

[36] Executive Committee of the Programme of the UNHCR, "Report of the 14th Session," (October 1965) UN doc A/AC.96/313, para 33; "Report of the 15th Session" (May 1966) UN doc A/AC.96/334, paras 25, 26; see also UN doc A/AC.96/INF.59 (12 May 1966).

[37] UNHCR "Proposed measures to extend the personal scope of the Convention on the Status of Refugees of 28 July 1951" (Submitted by the High Commissioner in accordance with paragraph 5(b) of UNGA res 1166 (XII) (26 November 1957)) (12 October 1966) UN doc A/AC.96/346. This somewhat

The draft included minor editorial and procedural changes, but as the Executive Committee had recommended, now contained no provision on suspension in exceptional circumstances.[38] On December 16, 1966, the General Assembly duly took note of the Protocol and requested the Secretary-General to transmit it to states with a view to their accession.[39] Although none opposed adoption of the resolution, 15 states abstained, as they had done also in the Third Committee.[40] No formal vote was counted in the General Assembly, but it is reasonable to infer that had the General Assembly been directly involved in revision of the 1951 Convention, the task would have been considerably harder, particularly given the politics of the day. As it was, within less than 10 months, the Protocol received the necessary six ratifications and entered into force on October 4, 1967.[41]

3 The Stateless Persons and Statelessness Treaties

3.1 The 1954 Convention Relating to the Status of Stateless Persons

As already noted, in December 1947 the Commission on Human Rights urged the UN to give early consideration to the legal status of "persons who do not enjoy the protection of any government."[42] The Economic and Social Council in turn recognized that interim

oblique reference invokes the terms of reference of the UNHCR Executive Committee, which is "To advise the High Commissioner, at his request, in the exercise of his function under the Statute of his Office."

[38] UNHCR "Proposed measures to extend the personal scope of the Convention on the Status of Refugees of 28 July 1951" (n 37) Annex I (summary of replies from governments); and Annex II (revised text of Draft Protocol).

[39] UNGA res 2198(XXI) (16 December 1966) (adopted 91-0-15); UN General Assembly Official Records (UNGAOR), 21st Sess, 1495th Mtg, 16 December 1966. See also ECOSOC res 1186(XLI) (18 November 1966); "Addendum to the Report of the High Commissioner for Refugees," UNGAOR, 21st Sess, Supp No 11A, (1967) UN doc A/6311/Rev.1/Add.1; UNGA "Report of the United Nations High Commissioner for Refugees. Report of the Third Committee" (13 December 1966) UN doc A/6586.

[40] Bulgaria, Burundi, Byelorussian Soviet Socialist Republic, Cuba, Czechoslovakia, Hungary, India, Mexico, Mongolia, Poland, Romania, Rwanda, Thailand, Ukrainian Soviet Socialist Republic, and Union of Soviet Socialist Republics.

[41] Protocol relating to the Status of Refugees (adopted 31 January 1967, entered into force 4 October 1967) 606 UNTS 267. The Protocol is often referred to as "amending" the 1951 Convention, but it is an independent instrument that can be ratified or acceded to by a state without becoming a party to the Convention. Under article I, Parties to the Protocol simply undertake to apply articles 2 to 34 of the Convention to refugees defined in article 1 thereof, as if the dateline were omitted. Cape Verde, Swaziland, the United States, and Venezuela have acceded only to the Protocol, while Madagascar, Monaco, Namibia, and St Vincent & the Grenadines are party only to the Convention (and Congo, Madagascar, Monaco, and Turkey have retained the geographical limitation).

[42] "Report of the Commission on Human Rights: Second Session" (n 15); Commission on Human Rights, Second Session, "Report of the Working Party on an International Convention on Human Rights" (n 15).

measures to afford protection were called for, to be followed by joint and separate action by states in cooperation with the UN, "to ensure that everyone shall have an effective right to a nationality."[43]

What was needed first was to improve the status of "stateless persons," and second, to eliminate statelessness. For "receiving countries," such persons were an anomaly, possessing "no definite legal status and without protection." For the stateless themselves, their abnormal position might reduce their "social value," and destroy "self-confidence." In the organizing world of the late 1940s, status was required, together with international agreement on freedom of movement, residence, and settlement; the exercise of trades or professions; education; relief; and social security. Most important of all, the stateless needed protection, and that was best achieved by providing identity documents, consular services, and legal status. Thus, the better protection of stateless person was to be secured by offering them the *status* of stateless person. At the same time, the phenomenon of "technical," as opposed to refugee, statelessness, was to be eliminated by appropriate agreement: harmonization of nationality legislation, restrictions on deprivation of nationality as a penalty, better regulation of territorial settlements, and reduction of existing numbers through the facilitation of naturalization.[44]

The Ad Hoc Committee on Statelessness and Related Problems met twice in New York in 1950. At the very beginning, the French representative isolated two distinct issues in an approach that quickly became the majority view: the status of refugees, on the one hand, and the problems related to the legal status of stateless persons, on the other. A draft convention on the first was urgently required, but the elimination of statelessness was basically different: "rather a continuing concern of the world community than an acute situation which required immediate remedial measures." Among the two categories of stateless persons, those who were also refugees were in need, hence the special urgency of their plight; but the same could not be said for non-refugee stateless persons. The US representative agreed and pressed for separate treatment; the draft convention should be limited and "should not be based upon a confusion between the humanitarian problem of the refugees and the primarily legal problem of stateless persons."[45] Other representatives were less sure, noting the similarities between refugees and stateless persons, the lack of legal protection, and the need for similar entitlements. The British representative also emphasized the necessity to distinguish measures to eliminate statelessness and measures taken to protect existing stateless persons until such time as their position had been regularized.[46]

[43] ECOSOC res 116 (VI) (n 16) "D. Stateless persons."

[44] *Study on Statelessness* (n 16) Section V.

[45] Ad Hoc Committee on Statelessness and Related Problems, "Summary Record of the Second Meeting" (26 January 1950) UN doc E/AC.32/SR.2, paras 6–8, 15, 18; Ad Hoc Committee on Statelessness and Related Problems, "Summary Record of the Third Meeting" (26 January 1950) UN doc E/AC.32/SR.3, paras 22, 28.

[46] Ad Hoc Committee on Statelessness and Related Problems, "Summary Record of the Second Meeting" (n 45) para 20; Ad Hoc Committee on Statelessness and Related Problems, "Summary Record of the Third Meeting" (n 45) para 24.

In the event, and as noted previously, the Ad Hoc Committee decided to focus upon the refugee, strictly so called, and in its report to ECOSOC, it simply proposed an additional protocol on stateless persons, under which states might agree to apply the refugee convention, mutatis mutandis, to stateless persons to whom it did not otherwise apply.[47]

In a composite resolution adopted a year later, ECOSOC expressed its view that reducing the numbers of the stateless and eliminating causes could not be achieved except through cooperation and the adoption of international conventions.[48] It recommended that states make provision for the avoidance of statelessness on the occasion of any territorial transfer, and that they "examine sympathetically" naturalization applications by habitually resident stateless persons, if necessary, reviewing also their nationality laws so as to reduce statelessness arising by operation of law. The Council saw that the International Law Commission was to take up the question of nationality, and urged it to draft the instrument or instruments necessary for the elimination of statelessness.

As noted already, the July 1951 Conference of Plenipotentiaries met in Geneva to complete the draft refugee convention *and* the draft protocol on stateless persons;[49] however, having adopted the Refugee Convention, it decided to take no decision on the draft protocol, referring it back to the appropriate organs of the United Nations for more detailed study.[50] In February 1952, the General Assembly deferred the draft protocol for lack of time,[51] but later requested the Secretary-General to seek the views of governments as to which provisions of the Refugee Convention they would be prepared to apply to stateless persons.[52] A further United Nations Conference then convened in New York[53] and adopted the 1954 Convention relating to the Status of Stateless Persons, an independent convention being preferred to the draft protocol initially proposed by the Ad Hoc Committee in 1950.[54] In many respects, the content of the 1954 Convention parallels that of the Refugee Convention with regard to standards of treatment. Certain refugee-specific protections are excluded, however, such as non-penalization for illegal entry and non-refoulement, while Article 1 defines a stateless person as "a person who is not considered a national by any State under the operation of its law."[55]

47 See "Report of the *Ad Hoc* Committee on Statelessness and Related Problems" (n 22) Annex III. Measures to eliminate statelessness received even less attention, being dealt with in a Danish proposal: at Annex V.

48 ECOSOC res 319 (XI) "Refugees and stateless persons" (11 and 16 August 1950).

49 UNGA res 429(V) (14 December 1950). The draft protocol on stateless persons appears in *Report* of the Ad Hoc Committee on Refugees and Stateless Persons, Second Session, UN doc E/1850, Annex II; the Committee had been renamed in the interim.

50 1951 Convention, Final Act, Part III.

51 UNGA res 538 (VI) "Assistance to and protection of refugees" (2 February 1952); UNGA res 539 (VI) "Draft Protocol relating to the Status of Stateless Persons" (4 February 1952).

52 UNGA res 629 (VII) "Draft protocol relating to the status of stateless persons" (6 November 1952).

53 ECOSOC res 526 A (XVII) (26 April 1954).

54 Convention relating to the Status of Stateless Persons (adopted 28 September 1954, entered into force 8 June 1960) 360 UNTS 117 (1954 Convention). As of March 2019, 91 states were party to the 1954 Convention.

55 This definition was proposed by the UN Secretariat, drawing on the words of Manley O Hudson, the International Law Commission's Special Rapporteur, in his first report on "Nationality, including

UNHCR was present as a nonvoting participant in the New York Conference, where one further notable omission from the new treaty regime was that of a supervisory body with functions similar to those under Article 35 of the Refugee Convention. Paul Weis was the UNHCR Legal Adviser at the time and, writing on the occasion of the entry into force of the Stateless Persons Convention, he thought that this was because, notwithstanding some prevalent sense of stateless persons as "not protected," there was then simply no equivalent agency in existence.[56] He regretted this, along with the fact that the 1954 Convention did not include de facto stateless persons[57]—the gap may have been narrowed, but unprotected persons remained outside the scope of the Convention and of any competent agency.[58] This was one, perhaps unintended, effect of the bifurcation of the unprotected that occurred in the Ad Hoc Committee, when political "urgency" was attached to the refugee.[59]

Although stateless persons within the 1954 Convention lacked a protecting agency as such, nationality and the issue of statelessness could and did arise in the refugee context, both for UNHCR and for states. The stateless refugee is specifically mentioned in Article 1A(2) of the 1951 Convention, while inquiries into nationality can also be required when determining the availability of protection, such that refugee status was not called for.

At the institutional level, however, it was some time before the stateless and statelessness were recognized formally as a matter within UNHCR's mandate. Not surprisingly, the human rights dimension—the right to a nationality in Article 15 of the 1948 Universal Declaration and later instruments—played a role here. For example, in its 1987 "Note on Refugee Children,"[60] UNHCR called attention to the risk of statelessness arising from the non-registration of births, and the Executive Committee expressed its concern in that year's general conclusion.[61] The following year, UNHCR's "Note on International Protection" gave particular prominence to statelessness, while recognizing the complex issues involved, and its own limited role and capacity, but also the breadth of its humanitarian mandate.[62] The General Assembly that year also expressly noted "the close connection between the problem of refugees and stateless persons," and invited states

Statelessness" (21 February 1952) UN doc A/CN.4/50, 17. Whether the Special Rapporteur was intending to define stateless persons as such, as opposed to distinguishing those stateless de jure from those stateless de facto, is a moot point.

[56] Paul Weis, "The Convention Relating to the Status of Stateless Persons" (1961) 10 Intl & Comp L Q 255, 260.

[57] De facto stateless persons still retain the formal link of nationality, but are effectively denied or without protection: Weis (n 56) 262. The Final Acts of both the 1954 and 1961 Conventions nevertheless contain certain recommendations as to their treatment.

[58] Weis (n 56) 264.

[59] See text to notes 22–23.

[60] UNHCR, "Note on Refugee Children," doc EC/SCP/46 (31 August 1987) para 25.

[61] Executive Committee, "Report of the 38th Session" (12 October 1987) UN doc A/AC.96/702, para 205(f)–(g).

[62] UNHCR, "Note on International Protection" (15 August 1988) UN doc A/AC.96/713, paras 59–69; see also "Report of the Working Group on Solutions and Protection" (12 August 1991) Doc EC/SCP/64 para 52; "Stateless Persons: A Discussion Note" (1 April 1992) Doc EC/SCP/1992/CRP.4; "Report of the Standing Committee on International Protection" (7 July 1992) Doc EC/SCP/70; "Note on International Protection" (7 September 1994) UN doc A/AC.96/830, paras 60, 66.

actively to explore and promote measures favorable to stateless persons in accordance with international law.[63]

In its 1992 conclusion on international protection, the Executive Committee recognized the absence of an international body with a general mandate for stateless persons, and called on UNHCR to continue its efforts on their behalf.[64] In 1995, UNHCR reported at length on what it was doing for the stateless,[65] following up on the Executive Committee's call the previous year to strengthen its efforts.[66] The Executive Committee then adopted a conclusion on the prevention and reduction of statelessness and the protection of stateless persons, encouraging UNHCR to continue its activities "as part of its statutory function of providing international protection."[67] This was endorsed by the General Assembly, particularly from a "preventive" perspective, but also with formal recognition of stateless persons as part of UNHCR's "statutory function of providing international protection," in addition to the specific role entrusted to it in relation to the 1961 Convention.[68]

With its general mandate confirmed across the broad field of protection and the reduction and elimination of statelessness,[69] UNHCR created a Statelessness Unit in 2005,[70] and has since engaged with states on the framing or amendment of nationality legislation, initiated the ambitious **#IBelong** campaign with the goal of eradicating statelessness by 2024,[71] actively and successfully promoted increased participation by states in the basic treaties,[72] issued guidelines for states, and recommended the adoption of procedures for the identification of stateless persons so that they can receive protection and be treated consistently with international law.[73]

[63] UNGA res 43/117 "Office of the United Nations High Commissioner for Refugees" (8 December 1988) para 9.

[64] Executive Committee, "Report of the 43rd Session" (15 October 1992) UN doc A/AC.96/804, para 21(y).

[65] "Note on Current UNHCR Activities on Behalf of Stateless Persons," doc EC/1995/SCP/CRP.6; "Report of the Sub-Committee on International Protection" (17 October 1995) UN doc A/AC.96/858, paras 21–27.

[66] Executive Committee, "Report of the 45th Session" (11 October 1994) UN doc A/AC.96/839, para 19(ee).

[67] Executive Committee, "Report of the 46th Session" (23 October 1995) UN doc A/AC.96/860, para 20.

[68] UNGA res 50/152 "Office of the United Nations High Commissioner for Refugees" (21 December 1995), Preamble, operative paras 14, 15, 16.

[69] Matthew Seet, "The Origins of UNHCR's Global Mandate on Statelessness" (2016) 28 Intl J Refugee L 7; Kate Darling, "Protection of Stateless Persons in International Asylum and Refugee Law" (2009) 21 Intl J Refugee L 742.

[70] See also the comprehensive Executive Committee Conclusion no 106 (LVII) on the Identification, Prevention and Reduction of Statelessness and Protection of Stateless Persons: "Report of 56th Session" (10 October 2006) UN doc A/AC.96/1035, para 18.

[71] See <http://www.unhcr.org/ibelong/> accessed April 9, 2018.

[72] By March 2019, the 1961 Convention had attracted 73 ratifications (up from 38 in June 2011).

[73] Three sets of guidelines originally issued in 2012 have now been replaced; see UNHCR *Handbook on Protection of Stateless Persons under the 1954 Convention relating to the Status of Stateless Persons* (2014) <http://www.refworld.org/docid/53b676aa4.html> accessed April 17, 2018. For an example of a national procedure, see "Stateless" (GOV.UK) <https://www.gov.uk/browse/visas-immigration/stateless> accessed April 9, 2018; see also UK Home Office, "Asylum Policy Instruction. Statelessness and applications for leave to remain" (18 February 2016). The UN itself has recognized the cross-cutting

3.2 The 1961 Convention on the Reduction of Statelessness

In July 1951, apparently responding to the "technical aspects" of statelessness, the International Law Commission appointed Manley O Hudson, a US lawyer and former judge of the Permanent Court of International Justice, as Special Rapporteur for the study of nationality.[74] At the Commission's first substantive meeting the following year, Hudson submitted papers dealing with nationality in general, the nationality of married persons, and statelessness.[75] The first paper, intended to be partly historical and partly analytical, noted the common linkage between nationality and allegiance to a state, and also that the uniformity of nationality laws seemed "to indicate a consensus of opinion of States that conferment of nationality at birth has to be based on either, on *jus soli* or on *jus sanguinis*, or on a combination of these principles." Whether the revealed usage went to the point of obligation was an open question, however, while in the matter of naturalization—the conferment of nationality after birth—no rules of international law could be deduced, other than that there should be a personal or territorial link between the state and the individual concerned.[76]

Hudson noted that statelessness could arise at birth, because of the inconsistent operation of the principles of *jus soli* and *jus sanguinis*; and later, because of conflicting national laws, voluntary acts of the individual, unilateral acts by the state, and territorial changes. Statelessness was "undesirable" from the perspective of orderly international relations, for every individual should be "attributed to some State"; and it was also undesirable for the individual, because of its "precariousness." Reducing or eliminating statelessness therefore meant focusing on causes, which seemed to suggest that the answer lay in the adoption of two rules: (1) If no other nationality is acquired at birth, the individual should acquire the nationality of the state in whose territory he or she is born; and (2) loss of nationality after birth should be conditional on the acquisition of another nationality. However, the Special Rapporteur did not consider that states were prepared to accept these principles at the time.[77]

At its sixth session in 1954, the Commission reviewed the observations of governments, many of which simply reiterated their view that the proposed texts were incompatible

nature of statelessness, and the Secretary-General has issued guidance notes on the ways in which it has an impact on UN agencies: see "Guidance Note of the Secretary-General. The United Nations and Statelessness" (June 2011) <http://www.refworld.org/docid/4e11d5092.html> accessed April 9, 2018. Also, the Human Rights Council has adopted a number of resolutions dealing with children's right to a nationality and arbitrary deprivation: "Right to a Nationality and Statelessness" (United Nations Human Rights: Office of the High Commissioner) <http://www.ohchr.org/EN/Issues/Pages/Nationality.aspx> accessed April 9, 2018.

[74] *Yearbook of the International Law Commission 1951*, vol I, 133rd mtg, paras 1–12, 418–419; *Yearbook of the International Law Commission 1952*, vol II, paras 5, 4.

[75] "Nationality, Including Statelessness: Report by Manley O. Hudson, Special Rapporteur," UN doc A/CN.4/50, in *Yearbook of the International Law Commission 1952*, vol II, 3.

[76] *Yearbook of the International Law Commission 1952*, vol II, 7–8.

[77] *Yearbook of the International Law Commission 1952*, vol II, 19–22. Considerations "of a political nature" inclined the Special Rapporteur to refrain from making concrete proposals.

with existing legislation.[78] The Commission redrafted some of the articles, adopted final drafts of the two conventions, and submitted them to the General Assembly,[79] while indicating that this body should consider which of the two drafts it preferred—that on *elimination*, which imposed stricter obligations, or that with the more modest aim of simply *reducing* statelessness.[80]

The United Nations Conference on the Elimination or Reduction of Statelessness[81] met first in Geneva from March 24–April 18, 1959, and again in New York from August 15 to August 28, 1961. The Conference decided to use the draft convention on the *reduction* of statelessness as the basis for discussion, and focused on provisions aimed at reducing statelessness at birth. Once again, fundamental differences were revealed between states that favored the principle of *jus soli* and those that opted for *jus sanguinis*. Whereas endorsement and acceptance of the former would have stopped many instances of original statelessness at the source, consensus was missing and the final compromise combined elements of both principles. Equally divisive was the issue of deprivation of nationality, a facility defended by many states as essential to their vital interests;[82] this lack of agreement necessitated the second session, at which the final text of the Convention on the Reduction of Statelessness was duly adopted.[83]

At one time, the International Law Commission had favored the idea of both a protecting agency for stateless persons, and a tribunal to decide upon their claims. Neither suggestion found much favor with states, which opted instead for the establishment of a body within the framework of the United Nations, "to which a person claiming the benefit of (the) Convention may apply for the examination of (the) claim and for assistance in presenting it to the appropriate authority."[84] On the eve of the entry into force of the 1961 Convention in December 1975, the General Assembly requested UNHCR to undertake the functions foreseen in Article 11 on a provisional basis,[85] and two years later,

[78] The Commission did not consider this decisive: "If Governments adopted the principle of the elimination, or at least the reduction, of statelessness in the future, they should be prepared to introduce the necessary amendments in their legislation": "Report of the International Law Commission to the General Assembly," UN doc A/2693 in *Yearbook of the International Law Commission 1954*, vol II, paras 12, 141.

[79] *Yearbook of the International Law Commission 1954*, vol I, paras 3–52.

[80] *Yearbook of the International Law Commission 1954*, vol II (A/2693, para. 14).

[81] UNGA res 896 (IX) (4 December 1954).

[82] United Nations Conference on the Elimination or Reduction of Future Statelessness "Note by the Secretary-General with Annex containing observations by Governments on Deprivation of Nationality" (9 June 1961); UN doc A/CONF.9/10; "Additional observations by Governments on Deprivation of Nationality" (5 July 1961) UN doc A/CONF.9/10/Add.1; "Observation by the Government of Sweden on Deprivation of Nationality" (19 July 1961) UN doc A/CONF.9/10/Add.2; "Observation by the Government of Ceylon on Deprivation of Nationality" (24 July 1961) UN doc A/CONF.9/10/Add.3.

[83] Convention on the Reduction of Statelessness (adopted 30 August 1961, entered into force 13 December 1975) 989 UNTS 175.

[84] ibid arts 11, 20(2).

[85] UNGA res 3274 (XXIX) "Question of the establishment, in accordance with the Convention on the Reduction of Statelessness, of a body to which persons claiming the benefit of the Convention may apply" (10 December 1974).

it asked UNHCR to continue to perform these functions, which were carried out "without any financial implications for the United Nations."[86]

4 International Protection: Treaty Interpretation, Application and Development

The League of Nations identified the refugee problem by reference to the lack of that protection which an individual abroad ought normally to expect from the diplomatic services of his or her country of nationality. Although the notion has evolved,[87] protection then was synonymous with diplomatic protection, and the League and the High Commissioner sought to make up for that deficiency, not just rhetorically or textually, but in a practical sense, including by intervening with governments to prevent forcible repatriation.[88] Initially, the challenge was to secure a sufficient legal status for refugees, understood as the provision or validation of documents, such as passports or certificates of identity, but the range of "legal and social disabilities" arising from the refugee's situation was not so limited. The Arrangement of 30 June 1928, for example, listed six different "services" that the High Commissioner was recommended to render, ranging from "Certifying the identity and the position of the refugees," to "Recommending the individual refugee to the competent authorities, particularly with a view to his obtaining visas, permits to reside in the country, admission to schools, libraries, etc."[89]

"Legal and political protection" was intended to relieve the refugee of the "disabilities" resulting from his or her "peculiar status," reflected in the inability, either to return home or to access the protection ordinarily available through consular or diplomatic services.[90] As a contemporaneous report from the International Refugee Organization (IRO) noted, these disabilities would extend to the conditions of residence, international travel, and legal status.[91] Looking to the future, the IRO referred to the views of several European states that a possible future High Commissioner for Refugees "would be entrusted with the task of keeping in touch with the question of refugees and stateless persons throughout the world, of promoting international conventions defining the status of refugees, of enquiring into specific situations, of receiving and examining

86 UNGA res 31/36 (30 November 1976).

87 Antonio Fortin, "The Meaning of 'Protection" in the Refugee Definition' (2000) 12 Intl J Refugee L 548.

88 Although the term non-refoulement was not then in use; see text to note 7 above.

89 1928 Arrangement relating to the Legal Status of Russian and Armenian Refugees (n 11) art 1(a)–(f).

90 "Refugees and Stateless Persons: Report of the Secretary-General" (6 October 1949) UN doc A/C.3/527, paras 19–20.

91 ECOSOC "Refugees. Communication from the International Refugee Organization" (11 July 1949) UN doc E/1392, 12–14.

complaints and of making recommendations," and of ensuring "that this protection was international in character."[92]

The UN Secretary-General in turn thought that a distinction might need to be drawn between refugees as a class or in large groups, and those protection functions that related to individual refugees. He proposed a broad range of activities, including promoting the wider application of present and future conventions; consulting with governments so as to facilitate the application of conventions, including suggesting appropriate legislative and administrative measures;[93] reporting on the implementation of conventions;[94] proposing new conventions; making a "continuous survey of all aspects of the refugee problem," and bringing to the notice of the UN any future situations appearing to require urgent attention;[95] issuing certificates of identity and related documents to refugees,[96] which in turn would require decisions in individual cases, including whether refugees had valid objections to returning to their countries of origin;[97] and acting in the interests of refugees before national authorities.[98]

4.1 The Office of the United Nations High Commissioner for Refugees

After extensive discussions in the Third Committee, the General Assembly moved to replace the IRO with a subsidiary organ (under Article 22 of the UN Charter), and by resolution 428(V), it decided to set up the Office of the United Nations High Commissioner for Refugees (UNHCR) with effect from January 1, 1951,[99] initially for three years. The High Commissioner's mandate was regularly renewed thereafter for five-year periods until 2003, when the General Assembly decided "to continue the Office until the refugee problem is solved."[100]

Paragraph 1 of the UNHCR Statute identifies the High Commissioner's primary responsibility as being to provide "international protection" to refugees and to seek "permanent solutions for the problem of refugees" by assisting governments to facilitate voluntary repatriation, local asylum, or third-country resettlement. Paragraph 8 of the Statute mentions many, though not all, of the protection activities undertaken in the past, while UNHCR's involvement in individual cases, as opposed to just the

92 ibid 5. The IRO noted that its protection activities included assisting illegal entrants, preventing forcible repatriation, expulsion and deportation, securing travel documents, promoting protection generally (for example, in the Commission on Human Rights on the right of asylum, and through encouraging the inclusion of special provisions on refugees in the 1949 Geneva Conventions on the laws of war and in ILO agreements): ibid 16–35.

93 ibid para 25.

94 ibid para 27.

95 ibid para 33.

96 ibid paras 34–36.

97 ECOSOC "Refugees. Communication from the International Refugee Organization" (n 91) para 36.

98 ibid paras 37–38. See also the list of IRO activities in "Refugees. Communication from the International Refugee Organization" (n 91) 15–20.

99 See (n 29).

100 UNGA res 58/153 (24 February 2004) UN doc A/RES/58/153 para 9.

"groups and categories" referred to in paragraph 2, has evolved consistently with earlier practice, but also interstitially, as a frequently integral part of its work with states and governmental authorities.

States parties to the 1951 Convention/1967 Protocol recognize the High Commissioner's duty "to supervise the application" of their provisions, and undertake to cooperate.[101] However, in contrast with the oversight mechanisms established under treaties such as the 1966 International Covenant on Civil and Political Rights, the 1984 United Nations Convention against Torture, and the 1989 Convention on the Rights of the Child, UNHCR is not formally competent, either to review national reports or to decide individual or inter-state complaints. The precise nature of the obligation of states under the 1951 Convention/1967 Protocol is not immediately clear, although together with the statutory role entrusted to UNHCR by the General Assembly, it is enough to give the Office a sufficient legal interest (*locus standi*) in relation to states' implementation of their obligations under the Convention and Protocol. States do not accept that UNHCR has the authority to lay down binding interpretations of these instruments, but its positions generally on the law or specifically on particular refugee problems are required to be considered in good faith.

This combination of activities, together with UNHCR's *operational* role in relation to material assistance,[102] no less than the determination of refugee status,[103] has ensured that the UN remains an integral part of the international refugee regime, at the policy level, in protection in individual cases, in the implementation of treaties, and in the progressive development of international refugee law. Although not a treaty supervisory body in the sense generally understood today, UNHCR's operational and collaborative role with governments, and with civil society, means that it is often well placed to influence national protection institutions, even if its primary protection responsibility can lead it into confrontation with governments over the refugee status of individuals, or the treatment generally of refugees and asylum seekers; here, its role straddles, as it were, the interpretation/application divide.

The "success" of the 1951 Convention/1967 Protocol can be gauged generally,[104] or at the national level, when individuals seek asylum. Here, effectiveness is highly contingent

[101] 1951 Convention, art 35; 1967 Protocol, art II; UNHCR Statute, para 8(a). See also Guy S Goodwin-Gill, "The Search for the One, True Meaning...", in Guy S Goodwin-Gill & Hélène Lambert (eds), *The Limits of Transnational Law: Refugee Law, Policy Harmonization and Judicial Dialogue in the European Union* (CUP 2010).

[102] In practice, the links are extensive. UNHCR's staff of 10,500-plus operate, and interoperate with states at the official level, in 130 countries worldwide.

[103] UNHCR is relied on by many states to determine refugee status, both as a "delegated" function in states lacking the necessary national infrastructure, and within the context of resettlement programs. UNHCR also engages with national refugee status determination procedures, for example, as a member or observer on decision-making bodies, or through formal advice, for example, as intervener or amicus curiae.

[104] The two treaties continue to be recognized as the foundation of the international refugee protection regime; see, for example, UNGA res 71/1 "New York Declaration for Refugees and Migrants" (3 October 2016) UN doc A/RES/71/1, para 65.

on the extent to which key international principles, such as non-refoulement and the refugee definition, have been incorporated into domestic legal systems that otherwise tend to prioritize sovereign control of borders over and against any who, like the refugee or the stateless person, claim benefit of an exception. Implementation, in turn, may depend on the place of international law in the constitutional system, and of the readiness of courts, in particular, to control legislative and executive powers. Over the past 40 years or so, national legal systems have seen increased "judicialization" of refugee protection and of human rights at large, although states have also pushed back, seeking to limit the scope of protection obligations for fear that they may be defeated by numbers. A permanent tension necessarily exists, therefore, between states bound by obligations, on the one hand, and the UNHCR charged with its supervisory responsibility, on the other.

Certainly, states have turned to UNHCR for guidance in the application of the 1951 and 1954 Conventions,[105] while UNHCR itself has sought to expand the protection envelope through guidelines on pressing legal issues, such as the protection of children, or the meaning of terms, such as social group, or the framing of national legislation.[106] Where the Office has employed a rigorous methodology, factored in relevant and reasoned jurisprudence from a variety of national jurisdictions, and been sensitive to the direction of international law at large, then its guidelines have undoubtedly contributed to moving the goal of protection forward,[107] even as states have remained reluctant to countenance any further change in the basic instruments.[108] In the highly securitized world of the early twenty-first century, where massive displacements continue, refugee situations are increasingly protracted, and where inequality and destitution compete with conflict and persecution as drivers of the movement of people between states, long-standing deficiencies in the international protection regime have become only too obvious.

As described previously, the UNHCR successfully employed a combination of non-UN and UN institutions and mechanisms to revise the 1951 Convention without going

[105] On the background to the UNHCR *Handbook on Procedures and Criteria for Determining Refugee Status*, see GS Goodwin-Gill, "The Search for the One, True Meaning. . . ." (n 101) 209–13.

[106] See UNHCR, *Handbook and Guidelines on Procedures and Criteria for Determining Refugee Status under the 1951 Convention and the 1967 Protocol Relating to the Status of Refugees*, HCR/1P/4/ENG/REV. 3 (1979, reissued December 2011). See also UNHCR *Handbook on Protection of Stateless Persons under the 1954 Convention relating to the Status of Stateless Persons* (2014) (n 73); UNHCR and OSCE, *Handbook on Statelessness in the OSCE Area: International Standards and Good Practices*, (2017) <http://www.refworld.org/docid/58b81c404.html> accessed April 17, 2018.

[107] cf GS Goodwin-Gill, "The Dynamic of International Refugee Law" (2013) 25 Intl J Refugee L 651, 657–61.

[108] Within the treaty framework, there is plenty of scope for the emergence and consolidation of doctrine (who is a refugee?). Practice also confirms, more generally, that the UN's concern for the unprotected has contributed to the expansion of UNHCR's institutional mandate beyond the literal terms of its 1950 Statute, to include refugees from conflict, the internally displaced, stateless persons, and statelessness. While such institutional developments work no direct effect on the obligations of states, the symbiotic relationship linking operations to principle and the practice of states is significant in the dynamic of international refugee law.

through the formal procedural requirements, and a majority of member states were able to bring the 1967 Protocol onto the General Assembly's agenda. It was not so successful when, 10 years later, it sought to promote a Convention on Territorial Asylum.

Article 14(1) of the 1948 Universal Declaration on Human Rights proclaims the right of everyone "to seek and to enjoy in other countries asylum from persecution," and its final, equivocal wording, omitting any reference to the right to be granted asylum, was a compromise between states that saw this form of protection as but one aspect of their territorial sovereignty, and those that urged that an individual right to asylum be recognized, as well as the involvement or responsibility of the United Nations.[109] The issue did not go away after 1948, however, but remained very much alive, first as the drafting of the human rights covenants got underway in the 1950s, and then separately, in the work of the International Law Commission, the Third Committee, and the Sixth Committee.[110]

In 1967, the text of the "Draft Declaration on Territorial Asylum" came before the Sixth Committee,[111] where it was generally accepted as a compromise, but still "a well-balanced consensus." The Committee unanimously recommended the draft to the General Assembly;[112] while the Declaration was not binding, "if it achieved its purpose of serving as a guide for State practice, it might eventually, through the unification of such practice, lead to the establishment of new customary rules of international law creating new obligations for States."[113] Others stressed that it should be seen as a "transitional step," leading in the future to the adoption of binding rules in an international convention.[114] After brief examination, the General Assembly unanimously adopted the Declaration on Territorial Asylum on December 14, 1967, while noting also the work of codification being undertaken by the International Law Commission (ILC).[115]

Although the ILC had always been somewhat wary of the asylum topic, not least because of the politicization of the refugee question in a time of cold war, UNHCR seems to have been encouraged to take up the possibility of a convention. The first draft was thus proposed, not by the ILC, but by a group of experts meeting in 1971 and 1972 under the auspices of the Carnegie Endowment for International Peace, in consultation with UNHCR.[116] This was discussed in the Third Committee in 1972; the High Commissioner consulted with governments, many of which appeared to favor a convention; and the General Assembly decided that the text should be reviewed by a UN Group of Experts.

[109] In 1957, for example, France proposed a declaration on asylum to the Commission on Human Rights, and suggested that responsibility for granting asylum should lie "with the international community as represented by the United Nations": UN doc E/CN.4/L.454/Rev.1.

[110] For further details, see G S Goodwin-Gill, "Introductory Note: The Declaration on Territorial Asylum, 1967" <http://legal.un.org/avl/ha/dta/dta.html> accessed April 9, 2018.

[111] UNGAOR, 22nd Session, Sixth Committee, 983rd, 984th, 986th and 989th Meetings, 26, 30, 31 October and 2 November 1967.

[112] UNGA "Draft Declaration on Territorial Asylum: Report of the Sixth Committee," UN doc A/6912 (30 November 1967) para 1.

[113] ibid para 14. [114] ibid para 16.

[115] UNGA res 2312 (XXII) "Declaration on Territorial Asylum" (14 December 1967).

[116] The Carnegie Endowment had also organized the 1965 Bellagio Colloquium, which led to the 1967 Protocol; see (n 27).

The General Assembly then asked the Secretary-General, in consultation with the High Commissioner, to convene a conference on territorial asylum in early 1977[117]—a conference that is generally considered a failure where little if anything was achieved.[118]

For many states, the idea of an individual right to be granted asylum was a step too far, just as it had been when Article 14(1) of the Universal Declaration of Human Rights was drafted. Although the right has advanced at the regional level, for example, within the EU Charter of Fundamental Rights and consequentially to the jurisprudence of the European Court of Human Rights, it continues to be resisted at the universal level, even as states generally recognize and accept the strong normative principle of non-refoulement.

States also continue to support the 1951 Convention and the 1967 Protocol, and to endorse the activities of UNHCR. On the 50th anniversary of the Convention, states parties unanimously adopted a Declaration reaffirming "the fundamental importance of UNHCR as the multilateral institution with the mandate to provide international protection to refugees and to promote durable solutions," recalling the obligations of states parties to cooperate with UNHCR in the exercise of its functions, and urging all states to consider what may be required to strengthen implementation, and to ensure closer cooperation between states parties and UNHCR to facilitate it's supervisory responsibilities.[119]

On the basis of the Declaration, UNHCR initiated the "Global Consultations on International Protection," which were intended to "provoke both reflection and action to revitalize the 1951 Convention framework and to equip States better to address the challenges in a spirit of dialogue and cooperation."[120] This consultative process, bringing in a wide range of concerns and recommendations, is widely credited with having reinvigorated protection discourse after the doldrums of the 1990s.[121] In particular, it gave impetus to the guidelines project, by way of which UNHCR has been able to contribute to the promotion of an interpretative approach to key Convention terms rooted

[117] UNGA res 3456 (XXX) "Elaboration of a draft Convention on Territorial Asylum" (9 December 1975).

[118] See generally Atle Grahl-Madsen, *Territorial Asylum* (Almquist & Wicksell International 1980); Paul Weis, "The United Nations Declaration on Territorial Asylum" (1969) 7 Can YB Intl L 92; Paul Weis, "The Draft Convention on Territorial Asylum" (1979) 50 Brit YB Intl L 176. Notwithstanding a recommendation from the conference at its final session, the Third Committee has since declined to submit any proposal for its reconvening. The ILC appears to have taken advantage of the conference, which allowed it to conclude that the "Right of Asylum," first selected for codification in 1949 by the Commission and then referred to it again by the General Assembly in 1959, "did not appear to require active consideration by the Commission in the near future...": "Report of the International Law Commission on the work of its twenty-ninth session: 9 May–29 July 1977," UN doc A/32/10, in *Yearbook of the International Law Commission 1977*, vol II, Part Two, para 109, 129–30; it is no longer in the ILC's work program.

[119] The Ministerial Meeting of States Parties was organized jointly by Switzerland and UNHCR on December 12–13, 2001: see "Declaration of States Parties to the 1951 Convention and or its 1967 Protocol Relating to the Status of Refugees," doc HCR/MMSP/2001/09 (16 January 2002) paras 8, 9.

[120] "Agenda for Protection" (26 June 2002) UN doc A/AC.96/965/Add.1, endorsed by the Executive Committee, "Report of the Fifty-Third Session of the Executive Committee of the High Commissioner's Programme" (8 October 2002) UN doc A/AC.96/973, para 21.

[121] See Erika Feller, Volker Türk, and Frances Nicholson (eds), *Refugee Protection in International Law: UNHCR's Global Consultations on International Protection* (CUP 2003).

in the principle of protection. Since 2002, some 13 guidelines have been issued, in addition to guidance specific to particular refugee situations.[122] UNHCR has also actively participated in litigation, where permitted, either as an "intervener" or through amicus curiae briefs. When carefully framed and oriented to achievable goals, such interventions can contribute to the progressive development of protection, although domestic legislation may restrict interpretative impact, and words themselves are limited in scope and meaning.[123]

Other concerns, central to the functioning overall of the refugee regime, have proven more elusive. In 1950, when proposing draft articles to the Ad Hoc Committee,[124] the Secretary-General noted that the regime would stand or fall on the basis of international cooperation. He urged states to work with countries of refuge so as to lighten the burden,[125] but also to undertake to admit a certain number of refugees. Both proposals were rejected, with the result that no clear rules regulate either the apportionment of responsibility for individual refugee claimants[126] or the "operationalization" of that international cooperation which is required if the refugee problem is to be solved.

4.2 Looking Ahead

In recent years, the international refugee regime has been confronted with the double impact of a globalized and securitized world, in which the numbers of those displaced or otherwise on the move show little sign of diminishing, the related businesses of people smuggling and trafficking appear to be thriving, and states veer between stumbling compliance with international law and arbitrary policy and practice, while the protection of both refugees and migrants is in jeopardy. In an effort to bring about better responsiveness, and increased cooperation and predictability in the face of large-scale movements of refugees and migrants, the UN Secretary-General took the initiative in 2016, not to propose a new treaty, but rather to sketch out the idea of new global commitments.[127] Later that year, the General Assembly unanimously adopted the New York Declaration on Refugees and Migrants, in which it endorsed the existing international law framework

[122] See <http://www.refworld.org/rsd.html> accessed April 9, 2018.

[123] cf the contrasting response of UK courts to arguments for the "progressive" interpretation of "particular social group," on the one hand, and the scope of article 1C(5), on the other: Goodwin-Gill, "The Search for the One, True Meaning..." (n 101).

[124] See "*Ad hoc* Committee on Statelessness and Related Problems. Status of refugees and stateless persons. Memorandum by the Secretary-General" (n 18) 11, 22–23.

[125] In its 1949 memorandum to the ECOSOC, the IRO remarked that refugees' lack of freedom of movement was a serious obstacle to their "even distribution over the world," and prejudiced countries that, because of their geographic position, bore the brunt of refugee movements: "Refugees. Communication from the International Refugee Organization" (n 91) para 12.

[126] For example, when the claimant may have transited through various states before lodging a claim.

[127] UNGA "In safety and dignity: addressing large movements of refugees and migrants. Report of the Secretary-General" (21 April 2016) UN doc A/70/59.

of refugee protection, and proposed the negotiation and agreement of two global compacts, one on refugees and one on safe, orderly, and regular migration.[128]

In some respects, this approach recalls that employed by the League of Nations in the 1920s, with reliance being placed on what is hoped to be best practice and on the goodwill and good faith of states concerned, but without any new obligations.[129] Better response mechanisms to large-scale movements of refugees and migrants could certainly serve the interests of states, for example, through removing or mitigating the necessity for secondary movements driven by insecurity, impoverishment and lack of education and livelihood opportunities, and by introducing better "management" overall into the movements of people. A wholly comprehensive response, if that is ever attainable in an unequal world, will need to address "root causes," by mediating and preventing conflict, and by getting to grips with under-development. Absent such an all-encompassing approach, refugees, the stateless, and the displaced at large will have to rely on the still incomplete protection regime built up over nearly one hundred years of international law and practice.

Since its founding in 1945, the United Nations has played a major role in the drafting, finalization, and implementation of the treaties and other instruments on refugees, stateless persons, and statelessness described previously, and in keeping the issues on an ever-expanding international agenda. In this, it has continued that practice of the League of Nations, which found the institution and its member states as seeing themselves "responsible" for those without or denied the protection of their home or any state. The legal regime is far from perfect, not least because those in search of refuge or who are without a nationality both touch on core sovereignty issues. With regard to refugees and stateless persons, however, that treaty base is commonly combined with the work of an operational and supervisory body responsible, not only for providing international protection, but also for assisting governments in the search for solutions.

As a subsidiary organ of the General Assembly, UNHCR enjoys substantial autonomy under its Statute and its mandate, but it also has a "representative" dimension so far as states' interests are engaged by the 102-member Executive Committee of the High Commissioner's Programme.[130] In addition, although the Executive Committee allows

[128] UNGA res 71/1 "New York Declaration on Refugees and Migrants" (n 8). UNHCR was entrusted with the responsibility of leading a multi-stakeholder consultative process, piloting the Comprehensive Refugee Response Framework (CRRF – Annex I), and presenting a model and program of action to the General Assembly for consideration and possible adoption in September 2018. The International Organization for Migration, a non-UN agency just recently brought into a "closer relationship" with the UN (UNGA res 70/296 "Agreement concerning the Relationship between the United Nations and the International Organization for Migration" (25 July 2016)), was requested to work with the UN and the Special Rapporteur on International Migration in drawing up the global compact on migration.

[129] UNGA res 71/280 "Modalities for the intergovernmental negotiations of the global compact for safe, orderly and regular migration" (6 April 2017) para 2, nevertheless refers to "actionable commitments," which are linked in turn to means for implementation, follow-up, and review.

[130] The Executive Committee of the High Commissioner's Programme succeeded earlier advisory bodies and was set up by ECOSOC, further to UNGA res 1166 (XII) (26 November 1957); see ECOSOC res 672 (XXV) (30 April 1958). As of 2018, it had 102 members.

for some civil society involvement by nongovernmental organizations having consultative status, UNHCR's field presence ensures regular contact and exchange with national and international voluntary agencies, and with the "sub-national" host communities that are commonly at the forefront of reception and protection for the displaced. Moreover, its mandate for and on behalf of individual refugees and stateless persons means that operations and doctrine should stay rooted in the everyday needs of those in search of refuge, status, and protection. In that sense, and with due regard to the interests and security of states, UNHCR is well-positioned to advocate for an international protection regime that reflects the dynamic of political and social reality.[131]

Initially concluded as an agreement between states on the treatment of refugees, the 1951 Convention has inspired both doctrine and practice in which the language of refugee rights is entirely appropriate. Something very similar has happened with statelessness and the rights of stateless people, and is now also evolving with regard to the protection of migrants in vulnerable situations.[132] UNHCR's long engagement in providing international protection has undoubtedly played a critical role in the progressive development of the law, both in the treaty field and in generating or "provoking" state practice in the sense of customary international law.[133] The global compacts on refugees and migration were adopted in December 2018,[134] and if they can be sufficiently "operationalized" through follow-up and oversight mechanisms, then the rights of the displaced and the unprotected will be assured of a continuing place on the international agenda. The United Nations and UNHCR may once again be well placed to build on practice and to strengthen protection through obligations recognized and accepted by member states.

[131] See Harold Honju Koh, "Transnational Legal Process" (1996) 75 Neb L Rev 181, 203: "In part, actors obey international law as a result of repeated interaction with other governmental and non-governmental actors in the international system."

[132] See Human Rights Council "Report of the Special Rapporteur on torture and other cruel, inhuman or degrading treatment or punishment. Note by the Secretariat" (26 February 2018) UN doc A/HRC/37/50; Human Rights Council "Principles and practical guidance on the protection of the human rights of migrants in vulnerable situations. Report of the United Nations High Commissioner for Human Rights" (3 January 2018) UN doc A/HCR/37/34; UNGA res 72/179 "Protection of migrants" (29 January 2018) UN doc A/RES/72/719; UNGA "Unlawful death of refugees and migrants. Note by the Secretary-General" (15 August 2017) UN doc A/72/335; UNGA "Follow-up to and review of the commitments of the New York Declaration. Report of the Secretary-General" (12 July 2017) UN doc A/71/978; Human Rights Council "Report of the Special Rapporteur on the human rights of migrants on a 2035 agenda for facilitating human mobility. Note by the Secretariat" (28 April 2017) UN doc A/HRC/35/25.

[133] Guy S Goodwin-Gill, "*Non-refoulement*, Temporary Refuge, and the 'New' Asylum Seekers," in David Cantor and Jean-François Durieux (eds), *Refuge from Inhumanity? War Refugees and International Humanitarian Law* (Brill Nijhoff 2014).

[134] UNGA res 73/151, "Office of the United Nations High Commissioner for Refugees", 17 December 2018 (181-2-3); UNGA res 73/195, "Global Compact for Safe, Orderly and Regular Migration", 19 December 2018 (152-5-12).

CHAPTER 23A

INTERNATIONAL CRIMINAL LAW AND UN TREATIES

SALVATORE ZAPPALÀ

THE punishment of individuals for "international crimes"[1] is a tool to strengthen the guarantees that certain fundamental rules be respected, intended to protect the relevant underlying fundamental values shared by all states.[2] Bringing certain violations under the umbrella of international criminal law (ICL) is the expression of a value judgment by the international community. It indicates that those rules are of such importance that their violation entails a common reaction of a somewhat extraordinary nature through *individual criminal* responsibility—both forms of responsibility, individual and criminal, being exceptional under international law.

This "criminal law mechanism" can be implemented either through what has been described as "indirect enforcement" (imposing on states the obligation to proscribe and criminalize certain conduct) or through "direct enforcement" (establishing international institutions implementing responsibility on behalf of the international community such as the International Criminal Court (ICC)).[3]

[1] The notion of international criminal law adopted for the purpose of this study is centered on the prevention and repression of the so-called "core crimes" listed in Article 5 of the Rome Statute of the International Criminal Court (ICC): war crimes, crimes against humanity, genocide, and aggression. This does not mean that broader notions of ICL are not appropriate in other contexts; see Antonio Cassese, *International Criminal Law* (3rd edn, OUP 2013), 18–21, who includes under ICL torture and terrorism as discrete offenses; and M Cherif Bassiouni, "The Penal Characteristics of Conventional International Criminal Law" (1983) 15 Case West Reserve JIL 27–28 (and the authors cited therein) suggesting a wider definition.

[2] See eg Santiago Villalpando, "The Legal Dimension of the International Community: How Community Interests Are Protected in International Law" (2010) 21 EJIL 387, 406. See also F Lattanzi, *Garanzie dei Diritti dell'Uomo nel Diritto Internazionale Generale* (Giuffrè, 1983) 351–418.

[3] For these categories cf. M Cherif Bassiouni, *Introduction to International Criminal Law* (2nd edn, Brill-Nijhoff 2013) 27–44.

While the first attempts to establish international criminal courts predate the creation of the United Nations,[4] the foundations of the international criminal justice system as we know it today share many of the values and principles of the UN. First of all is rejection of the illegal use of armed force, coupled with the need to respect some minimal rules even during armed conflicts, which in ICL translated into the criminalization of *aggression* and in provisions on *war crimes*—an aspect not directly addressed in UN treaties but successfully implemented through UN tribunals. Second is protection and promotion of human dignity and fundamental human rights, which led to the provisions on the prevention and repression of *crimes against humanity* and *genocide*. Third is the idea of an "enforcement mechanism" based on supranational authority, which ultimately allows the international community to step in when states do not act as required by international law.

For these reasons, it is not surprising that the UN has emerged as the main forum where most of the developments regarding ICL have taken place, including the ICC Statute—the most important ICL treaty today. This also explains why a number of processes linked to the ICC Statute system continue to take place at the UN and why some of the criticisms to the activities of the Court resonate in those rooms.

Nonetheless, although in recent years, some sore aspects have emerged in the interaction between the UN and the ICC (particularly between the Security Council and the Court), there can be little doubt that the two institutions are "partners of shared values."[5]

1 International Criminal Law at the UN

The UN started to work on ICL immediately after the establishment of the Organization, and in its very first years of operations some landmark instruments were adopted. Both the General Assembly (UNGA) and the Secretariat were actively involved in these processes. Initially, in 1946, the UNGA adopted resolutions on extradition and punishment of war criminals[6] and affirming the Nuremberg principles;[7] subsequently, in 1948, on the basis of a draft prepared by the Secretariat and negotiated in ECOSOC, it adopted

[4] A well-known example is the attempt, after the First World War, to bring to trial "William II of Hohenzollern, formerly German Emperor, for a supreme offence against international morality and the sanctity of treaties" as reflected in Article 227 of the Versailles Treaty.

[5] On the occasion of the day of international criminal justice in 2014 the UN Secretary General Ban Ki-moon stated that "[the] objectives of the Court and the United Nations are clearly aligned" <www.un.org/sg/en/content/sg/statement/2014-07-17/secretary-general-remarks-international-criminal-jusice-day> and the USG for Legal Affairs Miguel de Serpa Soares further emphasized that "we [the United Nations and the Court] are indeed partners with shared values"; see <legal.un.org/ola/media/info_from_lc/mss/speeches/MSS_Intl_Crim_Justice_Day_10th_anniv_UN-ICC-RA-17-July-2014.pdf> accessed January 24, 2019.

[6] UNGA Res 3(I) (13 February 1946).

[7] UNGA Res 95(I) (11 December 1946).

the Genocide Convention; in parallel, and to a certain extent in competition,[8] also in 1948, the Assembly also adopted the Universal Declaration on Human Rights (HR), which launched the era of UN HR treaties.

Moreover, the Assembly entrusted the International Law Commission (ILC)—the specialized body for the codification and progressive development of international law—with the preparation of a draft code of international crimes, including reflecting on the definition of the crime of aggression and on a draft statute for an international criminal court.

In these first stages of development, the focus was mainly on codifying substantive law on international crimes, while implementation was entirely left to domestic authorities.[9] Starting in the early 1950s, the Cold War and associated political tensions prevented any concrete progress,[10] in particular as far as the establishment of an international court was concerned. However, some treaties contained provisions that kept alive the principle of individual criminal responsibility, albeit without the activation of a system of direct enforcement.

It was only after the fall of the Berlin Wall that the process for the institutionalization of ICL was relaunched. After the breakthrough establishment by the Security Council of the International Criminal Tribunal for the former Yugoslavia (ICTY) in 1993 and of the International Criminal Tribunal for Rwanda (ICTR) in 1994, the final push for the creation of an international criminal court was given and, in 1998, with the adoption of the Rome Statute, the ICC was eventually established.

Thereafter, the UN has continued to be closely involved in institutional developments of ICL, including through treaties for the internationalized, mixed, and hybrid tribunals such as the Special Court for Sierra Leone and the Extraordinary Chambers in the Courts of Cambodia. Moreover, the UN was instrumental in the establishment of the Special Tribunal for Lebanon, on the basis of an agreement with the Lebanese government, which was subsequently endorsed and operationalized through Security Council resolution 1757 (2007). In the same period, UN territorial administrations created or contributed to the creation of special courts in East Timor, Bosnia, and Kosovo. More recently the UN has been involved in the Central African Republic (CAR) supporting the Special Criminal Chamber dealing with international crimes, as well as in South Sudan, where the UN is assisting the African Union to work with the government for the establishment of hybrid courts to deal with international crimes.

Last, although outside treaty processes, the UN has been the forum of innovative developments with the creation by the UNGA of the Independent Impartial Investigative

[8] Or at least this is how Rafael Lemkin (the man who invented the term "genocide") described it; see DL Frieze (ed), *Totally Unofficial: The Autobiography of Rafael Lemkin* (Yale University Press 2013) 157.

[9] See the work of the ILC 8th edition volume I, 2012, 98.

[10] Speech by Philippe Kirsch, President of the ICC, "*From Nuremberg to the Hague. The Nuremberg Heritage: A Series of Events Commemorating the Beginning of the Nuremberg Trials*," 4, <www.icc-cpi.int/NR/rdonlyres/08AB9F8F-53A2-4533-BCE0-887419726332/143894/PK_20051119_En.pdf> accessed January 24, 2019.

Mechanism for crimes committed in Syria since 2011,[11] and the more recent Security Council decision to establish an Investigative Team, with the purpose of securing the collection, preservation, and conservation of evidence of crimes committed by Daesh in Iraq.[12]

These ICL experiments based either on closer relationships with national authorities or on innovative measures to promote accountability for international crimes are the result of both the acknowledgment that the ICC alone cannot address all impunity concerns, but also of the fact that there still are several UN member states that are not parties to the ICC Statute. These developments confirm the central role the UN can play in further shaping ICL, even beyond the specific realm of UN treaty processes.

2 The Penal Provisions

2.1 The Laws of War

Leaving piracy aside, we note that the laws of war were the first area in which the idea of punishing individuals for violations of certain rules originated. War crimes provisions developed, some even before the League of Nations, due to a mix of humanitarian concerns and self-interest (the intention to avoid excessive brutality against one's own troops and population). Initial categories of war crimes were established in the 1899 and 1907 The Hague conventions and regulations.[13] They were subsequently codified after the Second World War with the adoption of the four 1949 Geneva Conventions, supplemented in 1977 by the additional protocols. International Humanitarian Law (IHL) provisions relating to war crimes impose on states the obligations: (1) to prohibit certain acts or omissions, (2) to prevent them, (3) to criminalize, as well as (4) to prosecute and punish the perpetrators. The punishment of perpetrators is ensured through trials at the national level (normally national or territorial states). In some cases, such as grave breaches of the 1949 Geneva Conventions, the possibility of bringing perpetrators to justice under the principle of universal jurisdiction has been established. IHL war crimes provisions entail individual criminal responsibility, but do not per se provide for resort to an international criminal court.

All these treaties developed outside the UN framework; however, the most powerful push for the consolidation of this body of law in terms of ICL came from the UN when, in the 1990s the UN Security Council decided on the establishment of the ad hoc Tribunals, the ICTY and ICTR, respectively by resolutions 827 (1993) and 955 (1994).[14] These Tribunals clarified the scope and meaning of most war crimes provisions, with

[11] UNGA Res 71/248 (21 December 2016). [12] UNSC Res 2379 (21 September 2017).

[13] See eg G Solis, *The Law of Armed Conflict* (CUP 2010) 3–27.

[14] cf M Sassoli, "Humanitarian Law and International Criminal Law," in Antonio Cassese et al (eds), *Oxford Companion to International Criminal Justice* (OUP 2009) 113, emphasizing that "IHL provisions on the prosecution of war crimes were largely ignored until 1990."

some of that language being codified in the ICC Statute.[15] One may therefore consider that UN engagement with this body of law, although not through UN treaties, was very influential. The Security Council resolutions gave real life to the existing penal provisions of IHL conventions. Not only the UN tribunals applied war crimes provisions and fleshed out their actual meaning translating abstract principles into concrete judgments, but they also proved that direct enforcement through an international tribunal was indeed possible, giving remarkable impulsion to the establishment of the ICC, discussed later on in the chapter.

2.2 Human Rights Law

The other area in which ICL developed is more closely connected to the activities of the United Nations: human rights. The process that led to the Nuremberg trials had shown that one of the key difficulties in addressing Nazi crimes was how to cover atrocities committed, particularly by state officials, against one's fellow nationals. The provisions on crimes against humanity addressed precisely this concern, even though to mitigate their innovative character in Nuremberg they were linked to the other crimes provided for under the Charter. However, the Copernican revolution[16] launched with Nuremberg was only completed with the adoption of provisions on the protection of human rights. This notion, which can be found in the UN Charter itself, was subsequently boosted through the Genocide Convention and the Universal Declaration on Human Rights, as well as the numerous human rights treaties concluded thereafter. On the basis of these treaties, states are subjected to an international rule of law in the treatment of all human beings, including their own nationals. ICL added the perspective that criminal law could be a mechanism through which human rights could receive additional protection, and a number of conventions included criminalization as a means to protect the rights provided for under the relevant treaty.[17]

The key convention in this area, which belongs to the foundational core of ICL, is the 1948 Convention on the Prevention and Punishment of the Crime of Genocide, adopted by the General Assembly through resolution 260 (III) A on December 9, 1948.[18]

[15] The ad hoc Tribunals contributed to a very large extent to clarify the interpretation of The Hague and Geneva laws and gave momentum to the final drafting of the provisions of the Rome Statute on war crimes; eg, in this regard see Antonio Cassese, "The Statute of the International Criminal Court: Some Preliminary Reflections" (1999) 10 EJIL 144; see also T Meron, "Convergence of International Humanitarian Law and Human Rights Law" (2000) 94 AJIL 239.

[16] R Maison, *Justice pénale internationale* (Puf 2017) 141 (and authors cited therein).

[17] Prior to the creation of the UN, for example, the 1926 Slavery Convention (concluded in the framework of the League of Nations) resorted to criminalization as a means to strengthen compliance.

[18] In general, see William Schabas, *Genocide in International Law* (CUP 2000); P Gaeta (ed), *The UN Genocide Convention. A Commentary* (OUP 2009); H Abtahi and P Webb, *The Genocide Convention. The Travaux Préparatoires* (Nijhoff-Brill, 2008). As highlighted by Schabas "the Genocide Convention was the first human rights treaty adopted by the General Assembly…" William A Schabas, "Convention on the Prevention and Punishment of the Crime of Genocide: Introductory Note" *UN Audiovisual Library of International Law* <legal.un.org/avl/ha/cppcg/cppcg.html> accessed January 24, 2019.

Despite the fact that the Nuremberg trials had just documented the magnitude of the extermination of Jews and other groups by the Nazis, there were several hurdles surrounding the negotiation of the Convention.[19] Some delegations seemed to see more disadvantages than advantages in concluding a Convention against genocide (even the term "genocide" created some "discomfort" and did not appear in the Nuremberg Charter or Judgment). Other difficulties were on the scope of the Convention, in particular the quarrel as to the inclusion within the scope of the Convention of so-called "political" and "cultural" genocide, as well as issues of jurisdiction. The idea that states should be able to exercise universal jurisdiction was discarded for a more limited "territorial" jurisdiction—a dubious move, since genocidal acts are typically committed by the authorities governing a given territory. Nonetheless, divisions eventually were set aside and the Convention adopted. It included a definition of genocide, criminalized the relevant conduct without any link to an armed conflict, imposed on states the obligation to adopt relevant provisions in their domestic legal systems, and provided for the jurisdiction of the state in which the crime is committed as well as for the establishment of an international criminal court.

With the adoption of the Convention the momentous process launched by the Nuremberg Charter achieved a moment of "closure." It seemed as if the crimes of WWII had been addressed and the international community could move on. This may also contribute to explain why, after the adoption of the Convention, further developments in the field of ICL were rather slow and attention shifted onto the negotiations of human rights treaties. The main ICL issues—the drafting of a code of crimes and of the statute of an international criminal court—were sent for further study to the International Law Commission, where they languished for several decades.

Nonetheless, during this time of slower ICL developments, some criminal law aspects did appear in UN human rights treaties: the 1956 Supplementary Convention on the Abolition of Slavery, the Slave Trade, and Institutions and Practices Similar to Slavery;[20] the 1965 International Convention on the Elimination of All Forms of Racial Discrimination;[21] the 1968 Convention on the Non-Applicability of Statutory Limitations to War Crimes and Crimes Against Humanity (which directly dealt with ICL issues);[22]

[19] The process originated from a proposal introduced by Cuba, India, and Panama, which led to resolution 96 (I) of 11 December 1946 by which the GA launched a process for the preparation of a draft convention on genocide. The Convention was prepared on the basis of inputs from the Secretariat, it was further negotiated in the framework of the ECOSOC and was subsequently brought to the GA for approval.

[20] Adopted by a Conference of Plenipotentiaries convened by ECOSOC resolution 608(XXI) of 30 April 1956 and done at Geneva on 7 September 1956.

[21] Adopted with GA resolution 2106 (XX) of 21 December 1965; entered into force 4 January 1969.

[22] On November 26, 1968, the GA adopted resolution 2391 (XXIII) with the convention as an annex. The resolution was adopted with a vote (58 in favor, 7 against, and 36 abstentions). The Convention was a useful reminder of some of the principles contained in the Nuremberg legacy, a recollection that individual criminal responsibility for international crimes continued to apply and a powerful statement that "time does not cancel" this responsibility. States, however, were divided on the adoption of the Convention, for during the drafting process additional elements had been added concerning the definitions of the crimes. In particular, reference to apartheid and broadening the notions of crimes against humanity and war crimes did not seem to some states to be coherent with the need to respect the principle

and the 1973 Convention on the Suppression and Punishment of the Crime of Apartheid. In particular, the issue of apartheid as an international crime entailing individual criminal responsibility and reservations relating to the principle of legality created divisions among member states in the negotiations of the 1968 and 1973 conventions, leading several states to not ratify them. The 1973 Convention indicated that apartheid was a crime and that the alleged perpetrators could be brought to justice by any state party that might have acquired jurisdiction; moreover, the Convention provided for the establishment of an international criminal court. In this framework, there was an attempt in 1980 to establish such a court, with jurisdiction over the crime of apartheid and other crimes. It did not prove successful.[23]

The work on these conventions clearly shows signs of the confrontational political climate of those times: during the Cold War it was widely believed that any initiative in the area of human rights and ICL could be politically "instrumentalized" by one side or the other.

In 1984, the UNGA adopted the Convention Against Torture and Other Cruel, Inhuman or Degrading Treatment or Punishment. The Convention provided for states other than the national or territorial state to exercise jurisdiction, though it did not provide for the establishment of an international court. The 2006 Convention of Enforced Disappearances is probably the latest HR treaty that contains ICL elements. That Convention affirms the criminalization of enforced disappearances and acknowledges the fact that enforced disappearance, in certain circumstances, may constitute a crime against humanity. It also established a Committee to monitor the implementation of the convention.

Most of the other HR conventions did not resort to criminal law. This was true, for example, of the major conventions such as the 1966 Covenants on Civil and Political Rights and Economic, Social, and Cultural Rights, as well as the 1979 Convention on the Elimination of all forms of Discrimination Against Women and the 1989 Convention on the Rights of the Child. Nonetheless, they share with ICL the fundamental notion that states are bound to respect some minimum rules in the treatment of all human beings, including their nationals, and do provide for some international monitoring mechanisms over the implementation of the treaty, which bear some elements of "enforcement" on behalf of the international community.

of legality; these states eventually opposed or abstained in the voting, and ultimately did not ratify the Convention. Some states considered too innovative the provisions of the Convention or that the language was imprecise; some raised concerns in terms of non-retroactivity; others challenged other provisions, such as article 3 on extradition. For the views of states see UN doc A/PV.1727 23rd session 26 November 1968, eg the UK (opposing adoption of the Convention) at paras 59–66, France (abstaining) at paras 71–73, Norway (abstaining as well) at paras 78–81.

[23] See UN doc E/CN.4/1426 Ad Hoc Working Group of Experts Draft Statute in M Cherif Bassiouni and DH Derby, "Final Report on the Establishment of an International Criminal Court for the Implementation of the Apartheid Convention and Other Relevant International Instrument" (1981) 9 Hofstra LR 523, 547–71.

2.3 Individual Responsibility

Both IHL and human rights conventions highlighted individual criminal responsibility as a tool to strengthen compliance—in some cases the treaties provide for an obligation to adopt legislation, and jurisdictional mechanisms that can ensure the prosecution of those responsible. States parties normally assume the *duty to criminalize* violations and, in some cases *to investigate and bring perpetrators to justice* before their municipal courts. Some of these conventions, notably those concerning genocide and apartheid, also allow for an international mechanism to accompany the obligation, although they do not themselves establish it.

These treaties contributed to the trend toward accountability for serious violations of human rights and IHL, in line with the Nuremberg legacy. Moreover, despite the fact that these conventions are largely based on an "indirect enforcement" system as far as their criminal law provisions are concerned, they do provide for some form of international control through the establishment of monitoring bodies (the "International Humanitarian Fact Finding Commission" for IHL and the various "expert committees" for human rights treaties),/and two of them referred to an international criminal court. However, until the creation of the ICC, at the end of the 1990s, the idea of ICL direct enforcement through an international court remained hypothetical.

3 The Statute of the International Criminal Court

3.1 From Nuremberg to Rome

The adoption of the Rome Statute of the ICC in 1998 was one of the defining moments in ICL. The process started with the Nuremberg and Tokyo Tribunals at the end of WWII.[24] Prior to the ICC Statute, resort to domestic authorities had been the only available mechanism, and this was not particularly satisfactory, for international crimes are generally committed either by the authorities enjoying territorial sovereignty or because these authorities are not in a position to prevent and punish such crimes. As noted by Georg Schwarzenberger, referring to the Genocide Convention (though it could be extended to ICL in general), in the absence of a direct enforcement mechanism, it is "unnecessary when applicable and inapplicable when necessary."[25] At the beginning of the 1990s, ICL was still lacking a credible and effective enforcement system.

[24] For a rich summary of the process leading to the ICC Statute see William Schabas, *The International Criminal Court: A Commentary on the Rome Statute* (OUP 2016) 1–27.

[25] Georg Schwarzenberger, *International Law* (3rd edn, Stevens and Sons 1957) vol 1, 143.

Despite the unfavorable political environment, advocacy for the establishment of an international criminal court had continued. Moreover, some possibilities of working on the issue were reopened when the General Assembly, in 1981, asked the ILC to resume work on the Draft Code of Crimes—work that had been interrupted in the mid-1950s.[26] In those years, however, the focus was still primarily on the offenses—the substantive law.[27] Things started to change at the end of 1989, when the General Assembly requested the ILC to work more actively on the idea of an international criminal court, after an initiative promoted by Trinidad and Tobago for an international court for drug trafficking crimes. The decisive push, however, came in connection with the tragic events of the Balkan wars (1992–1993) and the genocide in Rwanda (1994). With the establishment of the UN Ad Hoc Tribunals, the idea was concretely tested and the time was ripe for relaunching the project of an international criminal court.

In 1994, the ILC presented a draft Statute to the General Assembly; this draft was taken up by the UNGA, first, in an Ad Hoc Committee (1995) and subsequently through a Preparatory Committee (1996–1998);[28] over three years, with the help of the Secretariat, a draft Statute was finalized, and in the early summer of 1998 it was submitted to a UN Diplomatic Conference convened in Rome.

The draft Statute transmitted to the Conference contained over a thousand square brackets—diplomatic shorthand for provisions on which there is no agreement, sometimes containing various options. The Conference met in Rome from June 15 to July 17, 1998; it was attended by 160 states as well as various observers and a very large participation of NGOs. It turned out to be a success: the Conference adopted the Rome Statute of the ICC, an instrument consisting of a preamble and 128 articles, plus a final Act containing six resolutions. Such a result was a true historical achievement,[29] particularly, in light of the fact that at the eve of the closing of the Conference, there still were fundamental issues pending and the concrete risk of a postponement. It took an incredible effort by the Bureau of the Conference to prepare a package deal. On the last day it was presented to member states in an emotionally charged meeting of the Committee of the Whole, where voting took place twice to protect and push forward the text. Eventually it moved to the Plenary, where, in the middle of the night, a new vote was necessary for the treaty to be finally adopted. Crucial issues were addressed and solved during the

[26] The ILC worked for a decade with several reports by the Special Rapporteur, Doudou Thiam, together with the Secretariat, taking into account the comments of states.

[27] Some of the crimes listed in these drafts remained outside the scope of the ICC Statute or were drafted in a different way—for example the 1991 ILC draft Code included the following crimes: aggression; threat of aggression; intervention; colonial domination and other forms of alien domination; genocide; apartheid; systematic or mass violations of human rights; exceptionally serious war crimes; recruitment, use, financing and training of mercenaries; international terrorism; illicit traffic in narcotic drugs; and willful and severe damage to the environment.

[28] The ILC had worked on the issue of a code of crimes and a draft Statute since 1981 and until 1996.

[29] UN Secretary-General Kofi Annan at the ceremony held in Rome on July 18 stated this was "a giant step forward in the march towards universal human rights and the rule of law," see <www.un.org/press/en/1998/19980720.l2890.html> accessed January 24, 2019; in relevant legal literature see L Condorelli, "La Cour pénale international: un pas de géant..." (1999) 103 Revue générale de droit international public 7.

Diplomatic Conference, some of them in the very final hours. These comprised: the (1) scope of the jurisdiction of the Court, both *ratione personae* and *ratione materiae*, including the issue of aggression; as well as (2) the trigger mechanisms and the relationship with the Security Council.

On the first question, it was decided to limit the Court's jurisdiction to the "core crimes": war crimes, crimes against humanity, genocide, and aggression; work on other suggested crimes such as drug and arms trafficking, terrorism, and mercenarism was postponed to the future. The inclusion of the crime of aggression was agreed only in principle; it was one of the contentious issues until the very end, particularly in light of the relationship between the Security Council (SC) and the Court. Ultimately, no final agreement on aggression was reached in Rome, and both the definition and the modalities for the exercise of jurisdiction by the Court required further negotiations. On jurisdiction *ratione personae*, the compromise solution that prevailed granted the Court jurisdiction over individuals provided that the state of nationality or the territorial state were parties to the Statute, unless the SC activates the Court.

The second set of issues concerned the role of the UN Security Council in relation to ICC proceedings, both as far as the jurisdiction on aggression was concerned and the trigger mechanisms for international criminal proceedings more generally. Leaving it only to the Council to determine when investigations had to be opened would have meant entrusting a political body with the keys to international criminal justice. It would have entailed that the prosecution and punishment of the most serious violations of international law would have been left to political discretion. It was considered that the effectiveness of the Court as a tool for punishing very serious breaches of international law would have been seriously impaired if it had been systematically subject to a "veto," which would have allowed any permanent member of the Council to stop the opening of the investigation. On one point, however, even the states in favor of a broader investigative power for the prosecutor were in agreement: this power could not and should not be unconditional. Thus, in the Statute the power of the prosecutor to initiate investigations proprio motu was subjected to judicial scrutiny by the Pre-Trial Chamber (a panel composed of three judges). At the same time, in order to recognize the role of the SC as the guarantor of international peace and security, the power to request the suspension of proceedings for a renewable period of 12 months was recognized.[30] The crucial difference was that instead of any one permanent member being able to block an investigation, the Rome Statute required agreement on the part of the Council to delay an investigation for a year at a time.

In addition, the entire system hinged on a fundamental "guarantee" for state sovereignty: proceedings before the ICC are admissible only when domestic authorities are unable or unwilling to carry out genuine proceedings at a national level (principle of "complementarity").

[30] For a detailed analysis cf L Condorelli and S Villalpando, "Referral and Deferral by the Security Council" in Antonio Cassese, P Gaeta, and JRWD Jones (eds), *The Rome Statute of the International Criminal Court. A Commentary* (OUP 2002).

Interestingly enough, the Rome Conference, by establishing the power for the Prosecutor of the ICC to open investigations proprio motu, eventually agreed on a treaty that went far beyond the ILC Draft. This is contrary to what typically happens, with diplomatic negotiations watering down texts prepared by experts.

Massive participation in the Diplomatic Conference and the short time it took for many states to become parties to the treaty are important for two reasons. The first is obvious: since the system is treaty-based, and only state parties assume in full the obligations deriving from the treaty, broad participation is per se a positive element for the Court. The second is that widespread adherence to the Statute of the Court shows support for the provisions of the Statute, which are to a very large extent reflection of customary international law—thus binding also on states that do not ratify the Statute.

In sum: the establishment of the UN ad hoc Tribunals and their work, the studies by the ILC and its initial draft Statute, the lengthy negotiations in the GA framework, and ultimately the nearly miraculous Diplomatic Conference, lead to a result that is "revolutionary":[31] the establishment of an institution that can prosecute and punish the most serious crimes of concern to the international community as a whole—at last, the direct enforcement system, which had been lacking for so long, had been created.

However, activities on ICL at the UN, particularly in the framework of the ICC Statute system, did not finish once the treaty was adopted. On the basis of resolutions E and F, which were part of the Final Act of the Rome Conference, work resumed in the framework of the Preparatory Commission and, as far as aggression is concerned, it continued in the framework of the Special Working Group on the Crime of Aggression (SWGCA) established by the Assembly of States Parties in 2002, "open on equal footing to *all States Members of the United Nations* or members of specialized agencies or of the International Atomic Energy Agency."[32]

3.2 The Rome Statute System and the UN

The Rome Statute entered into force on July 1, 2002, after obtaining—surprisingly quickly—the 60 ratifications required. The entry into force of the Statute not only entailed the actual coming into life of the Court itself, but also meant the establishment, under Article 112 of the Statute, of an Assembly of States Parties (ASP) that would "meet at the seat of the Court or at the Headquarters of the United Nations once a year"[33] and be responsible for all the tasks listed in the Statute. Work in the Assembly started with sessions held in New York, in 2002 and 2003, to set in place all the requirements for the

[31] See Cassese (n 15) 145.

[32] cf op 2, resolution ICC-ASP/1/Res.1, Continuity of work in respect of the crime of aggression adopted at the 3rd plenary meeting, on 9 September 2002, see <asp.icc-cpi.int/iccdocs/asp_docs/Resolutions/ICC-ASP-ASP1-Res-01-ENG.pdf> accessed January 24, 2019. For an interesting stocktaking of the work on this item up to 2002, see M Politi and G Nesi (eds), *The International Criminal Court and the Crime of Aggression* (Ashgate, 2004).

[33] Rome Statute, Article 112(6).

concrete functioning of the Court from the election of the first judges and Prosecutor to the adoption of the budget. It also saw the transition from UN-driven activities in the Preparatory Commission to the work of the Assembly of States Parties, such as adoption of the Rules of Procedure and Elements of Crimes, and continued discussion of the crime of aggression.

Three main areas of work in the ASP bear relevance for our purposes: (1) the ICC relationship with the UN, (2) the negotiations over the crime of aggression, and (3) the quest for the universalization of the Statute. All these tasks were undertaken in the framework of the ASP since the very beginning. However, while the first "assignment" was completed rather quickly, with the adoption of the 2004 relationship agreement between the ICC and the UN (as envisaged in Article 2), work on the crime of aggression and the campaign for universalization required more time. Work on aggression has now been completed, with the decision on the activation of the Court's jurisdiction over this crime adopted in December 2017, taking effect on July 17, 2018. Universalization, on the other hand, is an ongoing task and presumably the biggest challenge for the ICC system.

Negotiations over the crime of aggression have been a long journey that took over 70 years to be completed and cannot be addressed in depth in this chapter.[34] Most of this process took place at the UN, even though in the final part within the more limited "circle" of the ASP.

As far as the quest for full universality is concerned, not only it would be important to increase the number of states parties, but also find ways to organize relationships with nonparties productively. This calls into question the ability of the ICC system to interact with the UN and its organs. The ICC system has been able to cooperate with the Secretariat and finds support in the General Assembly; it is also engaged with the Security Council, even though this relationship appears to be more problematic. In Rome, as mentioned, states did not want to leave the "keys" to the Court in the hands of the Council. This eventually led to lack of support by three of the five permanent members, which remain outside the Statute system. The United States and Russia have "unsigned" the Statute, while China never signed it. This creates an uneasy relationship between the Council and the Court. The need for a link with the UN, however, is not so much for effectiveness purposes, but rather to pursue full universalization. In reality, the Statute already possesses universal nature in its principles and rules, and by the very fact that the Security Council can activate the Court's jurisdiction in any situation. The Council confirmed it, by using its power to activate the Court on two occasions: in 2005, for the situation in Darfur (Sudan), with resolution 1593 (2005), and in 2011 for Libya, with resolution 1970 (2011). Council referrals, however, have not turned out to be blessings for the Court; on the contrary, they have made the Court the target of criticisms on double standards and selectivity: challenges that in theory should be more appropriately addressed to the Council.

[34] On this journey see C Kress and S Barriga, *The Crime of Aggression: A Commentary* (CUP 2016).

The General Assembly, on the other hand, could be the forum where more conducive work could be carried out, potentially including through further UN treaty processes.

4 New Areas for Developments

Before closing, it is worth noting four new areas in which there might be developments potentially leading to multilateral treaty processes.

First, the idea of a *draft treaty on crimes against humanity*. Of the four traditional categories of international crimes, crimes against humanity seemed to have remained the only one without a treaty that organizes and systematizes the category. Of course, the Rome Statute may have now made this idea obsolete; however, since not all UN member states are parties to the Statute, the project of such a convention might present some interest to revitalize the interest of all states for the fight against impunity. The project is currently at the ILC; a draft text with commentaries has been adopted on "first reading" and submitted to states for comments. Subsequently, there will be a second reading by the Commission; a new draft will be produced, and could be probably submitted to the GA by 2020. Preliminary reactions by states seem rather positive, and many see this as a potentially fruitful development in the area of ICL multilateral treaties.

Second, the issue of the *immunity of state officials from foreign criminal jurisdiction*. The ILC has been studying this topic since 2007. While there is broad agreement on immunities as a key component of international law, there seems to be divisions, both in the ILC and among member states, on their scope and on any exceptions for ICL crimes. Given the divide, it seems unlikely—at this stage—that the positions could be reconciled in the short term. Broadly speaking immunities and ICL do not coexist very well. A possible approach, should there be agreement on the fundamental rules governing immunities, could be to entrust any final decision in specific cases to an international institution. Naturally, this would require states to accept any such mechanism.

The third area is the work carried out in the Sixth Committee of the General Assembly on the *principle of universal jurisdiction*. This topic was originally introduced in 2009 at the request of Tanzania on behalf of the African group. The main concern at the time was the alleged abuse of universal jurisdiction by some states, particularly in Western Europe. The wording chosen for the agenda item in the end however was broader: "scope and application of the principle of universal jurisdiction," leaving ample room for discussion. Nearly 10 years of debates have highlighted many interesting aspects. All states seem to agree that at least in principle some cases of universal jurisdiction are admissible; there is also agreement that it should be exercised only under very exceptional circumstances. Yet the debates have not resulted yet in any concrete action. On the one hand, there seems to be disagreement as to the categories of crimes that fall under the universal jurisdiction principle; on the other, there are different ideas as to the consequences of the exercise of such jurisdiction and the appropriate mechanisms to address them. The diverging views have prevented any step forward so far. Several outcomes could be envisaged, including a draft convention. Such a convention could contain general principles; it could provide for specific rules addressing potential conflicts and should ultimately provide for a mechanism to solve conflicts of jurisdiction. However, since the main problem in the area of ICL so far remains the absence of exercise of jurisdiction, it would be ideal if such a convention would also include mechanisms to address "negative" conflicts of jurisdiction—that is, cases where impunity for international crimes prevails because no domestic authority is willing or able to investigate or prosecute. At this stage, however, any step in this direction seems premature.

Finally, another potential ICL development, although not embedded in any UN process, is the proposal by a group of states for a *treaty on mutual legal assistance on "core crimes."* At some point in the future, this project, mentioned on occasion at the UN by some of its proponents, could be brought into the realm of UN discussions. In the past, suggestions had been made that it could be developed in the framework of the Commission on Crime Prevention and Criminal Justice or in the UN GA Sixth Committee.[35] Unfortunately, the increasing polarization of international relations, and the fact that ICL issues tend to be divisive, makes it unlikely that any such draft convention will be adopted at the UN.[36]

All these initiatives show that the UN can be a relevant arena to discuss ICL developments. Clearly, the ICC system is bound to be the driving force of ICL, at the same time the UN remains the global forum where all states can engage with accountability issues.

5 Conclusion

As the embodiment of universal legitimacy, the UN is inextricably linked to ICL. This is reflected not only in numerous UN treaties, and above all the 1998 ICC Statute, but also in all UN activities that contribute to the larger effort to establish an "age of accountability."

The experience of the ad hoc and hybrid tribunals, as well as the first 15 years of operation of the Rome Statute system, have been a constant reminder that any ICL direct enforcement mechanism requires the constant support of states, including at the UN.

The ICC is designed to be a universal and permanent institution. The principles contained in the Statute are universal, and ratification by two-thirds of the UN member states is further evidence of the universality of the instrument. The Court is linked to the

[35] See W Ferdinandusse, "Improving Inter-state Cooperation for the National Prosecution of International Crimes: Towards a New Treaty?" (2014) 18 ASIL Insights 15.

[36] On recent developments relating to this treaty see <ilg2.org/2017/12/07/fighting-against-impunity-the-mutual-legal-assistance-initiative-for-domestic-prosecution-of-the-most-serious-crimes/> accessed January 24, 2019.

UN by the relationship agreement; the General Assembly adopts an annual resolution and the Secretariat cooperates with the Court in various areas. Under the Statute, the Security Council may activate the Court's jurisdiction and has done so twice (Darfur and Libya); moreover, the Council has recognized the work of the Court in other contexts (for example, CAR or Mali as reflected in relevant resolutions). Nonetheless, the Statute still lacks support in some quarters of the international community and several UN member states, for different reasons, remain outside the system.[37] This situation creates difficulties for a mechanism that oscillates between the universality of the values it defends and the treaty-based regime through which it operates.

The attacks against the ICC are mainly due to two reasons: (1) its relationship with the Security Council, and (2) the issue of immunity of state officials. Both aspects are evidence of a fundamental ICL conundrum: the relationship between justice and politics. Some problematic aspects of this relationship have emerged in tensions with certain African states and the AU over heads of states' immunity, as well as in the approach taken by some members of the Council. Nobody doubts the usefulness to allow room for political dialogue. However, the basic principle on which the Court is founded is that of independence and on the administration of justice in a fair and impartial manner. Attacks on the Court are mostly misplaced; however, serious and well substantiated criticism needs to be examined on its merits through dialogue. As far as states parties are concerned, this dialogue must occur in the ASP framework. It is precisely to this task that the first African president of the Assembly, Minister Sidiki Kaba of Senegal, devoted great efforts during his three years mandate (2014–2017). At the same time, however, dialogue must also take place at the UN and include in the discussion states that are not parties to the Statute.

The challenges ahead are linked to the ability of the UN and of the ICC system, in their respective spheres of competence, to continue to work together in addressing the fight against impunity. There are a number of areas of concern—deadlock in the proceedings concerning the situations referred by the Council, the financing of those referrals, or the inability of the Council to tackle accountability in other situations, such as the Syrian conflict or the Yemenite crisis. ICL (like the ICC) is a tool of last resort, kicking in when other mechanisms have failed; naturally, it could display more tangible preventive effects if accountability for international crimes were addressed more coherently. The fight against impunity should be a priority for all UN member states and it could be revived not only in Council action but also in the work of the General Assembly. In this regard, the prospective draft convention on crimes against humanity, as well as any discussions on a treaty on mutual legal assistance on core crimes, could prove useful tools to improve such commitment.

[37] Apart from China, Russia, and the United States, other countries outside the ICC system range from Algeria and Morocco to Egypt and Israel, from Lebanon and Saudi Arabia to India and Pakistan, from Indonesia and Singapore to Iran and Malaysia, from Cuba and Jamaica to Monaco and Turkey. Nonetheless should it decide so the Security Council could broaden the court's jurisdiction to nationals of these countries or their territories, irrespective of their not being contracting parties to the Statute.

The relationship between the UN and international criminal law is necessarily tempestuous: for ICL aims at justice, while the UN is the "house of politics." Politics and justice are bound to live in a certain tension.[38] Such tensions must be addressed through dialogue, and the UN provides the natural forum for such dialogue and, where appropriate, further incremental steps in the development of institutions to achieve their overlapping aims.

[38] A leading Italian scholar, in the nineteenth century, notoriously stated that "always and everywhere when politics enters through the gates of the temple, justice—scared—runs away from the window" and concluded that "politics and justice were not born sisters": F Carrara, *Programma del Corso di Diritto Criminale, parte speciale* (7th edn Casa Editrice Libraria "Fratelli Cammelli" 1898) 674–75.

CHAPTER 23B

INTERNATIONAL CRIMINAL LAW

practitioner reflection

HIRAD ABTAHI AND PHILIPPE KIRSCH, OC, QC*

By virtue of its longevity, territorial scope, mandate, and resources, the United Nations has played a crucial role in the development of international criminal justice. Specifically, in the wake of the trials of Nuremberg and Tokyo, the UN has been central in the creation of a range of courts with international components, aimed at dealing with the most serious crimes for which national systems were inadequately equipped. Absent any authoritative terminology to define these courts, this study, while acknowledging these debates, adopts an approach that is based not on the nature, strictly speaking, of those courts, but on the way in which the UN has contributed to their formation and/or functioning. Accordingly, this study will view them in two broad categories. On the one hand, there are the international criminal courts; that is to say those courts managed internationally in the form of international organizations or their subsidiary bodies. Hybrid courts, on the other hand, are those jurisdictions that are constituted by or function through a mix of national and international actors, and/or apply a mix of international and national elements.[1]

* Hirad Abtahi is the Legal Adviser, Head of the Legal and Enforcement Unit, Presidency, International Criminal Court. Judge Philippe Kirsch, OC, QC, was the first President of the International Criminal Court, from 2003 to 2009. The authors wish to thank Greemn Lim for the excellent research assistance she provided for the preparation of this chapter. The views expressed in this chapter are those of the authors alone and not necessarily those of the International Criminal Court.

[1] For a synthesis of how different commentators have used these terms, see SMH Nouwen, "'Hybrid Courts': The Hybrid Category of a New Type of International Crimes Courts" (2006) 2(2) Utrecht L Rev 192, 203. Commentators have adopted divergent approaches as to how certain hybrid courts are categorized. For instance, in one commentary, a distinction is made only between two subcategories of hybrid courts, namely: "domesticated internationalised courts" and "internationalised domestic courts," with the latter being set up to both prosecute international crimes and buttress the national judiciary and rule of law. See Ruth Mackenzie et al (eds), *The Manual on International Courts and Tribunals* (2nd edn, OUP 2010) 245–46.

As will be seen, the UN has played a polymorphous role in the development of these courts, ranging from the negotiation of their constitutive documents, and their actual establishment and functioning, through to their substantive law.

1 International Criminal Courts

The UN has been pivotal in the establishment of post-WWII's first international criminal courts. These have consisted of the treaty-based International Criminal Court (ICC) and the UN Charter Chapter VII-based ad hoc tribunals, such as the International Criminal Tribunal for the former Yugoslavia (ICTY) and the International Criminal Tribunal for Rwanda (ICTR), as well as East Timor's Special Panel for Serious Crimes (SPSC).

1.1 A Multilateral Treaty-Making Forum: The ICC

As a forum for the negotiation of complex multilateral treaties, the UN was instrumental in decades-long discussions and negotiations toward the establishment of the world's first permanent international criminal court, and finally in the adoption of the Rome Statute of the International Criminal Court (ICC Statute). The UN maintains a close link with the ICC through both its (1) creation, and (2) an interwoven relationship with it.

1.1.1 *The Creation of the ICC*

While not a part of the UN, the ICC was established under its auspices. Following the adoption of the 1948 Convention on the Prevention and Punishment of the Crime of Genocide (Genocide Convention), which foresaw the establishment of an international criminal court, UN General Assembly (UNGA) Resolution 260(III) invited the International Law Commission (ILC) to "study the desirability and possibility of establishing an international judicial organ for the trial of persons charged with genocide."[2] The ILC concluded that the establishment of a court to prosecute persons charged with genocide and crimes of similar gravity was desirable and possible. A special UNGA

[2] Convention on the Prevention and Punishment of the Crime of Genocide (adopted on 9 December 1948, entered into force on 12 January 1951) UN Doc A/RES/3/260. For an overview of the negotiation and drafting history of the ICC Statute, see also M Cherif Bassiouni, "Negotiating the Treaty of Rome on the Establishment of an International Criminal Court" (1998) 32 Cornell ILJ 443; Roy S Lee (ed), *The International Criminal Court: The Making of the Rome Statute Issues, Negotiations, Results* (Kluwer Law International 1999); John Washburn, "The Negotiation of the Rome Statute for the International Criminal Court and International Lawmaking in the 21st Century" (1999) 11 Pace ILR 361; Mahnoush H Arsanjani, "The Rome Statute of the International Criminal Court" (1999) 93 AJIL 18.

Committee prepared a draft statute and its revised version in 1951 and 1953.[3] The Cold War, however, blocked this path for the next 35 years.

In 1989, following a request by Trinidad and Tobago, the UNGA asked the ILC to resume its work and to elaborate a draft statute as a matter of priority.[4] In 1994, the ILC submitted the Draft Statute for an International Criminal Court to the UNGA.[5]

Therein, the ILC described the options for establishing the ICC. It could be a primary UN organ, such as the International Court of Justice (ICJ), but this would require the very complex task of amending the UN Charter.[6]

The ICC could also be established as a UNSC/UNGA subsidiary organ, under Chapter VII and Article 22 of the UN Charter respectively. Doubts were however expressed as to whether a UNGA resolution would constitute the proper legal basis, specifically for addressing individual criminal responsibility.[7] The ICC as a UN Security Council (UNSC) subsidiary organ would also be problematic as the UNSC could establish Chapter VII situation-specific ad hoc tribunals, which had to be distinguished from the authority to establish a permanent institution.[8] It was also suggested that the ICC be established as both a treaty body and a UNSC subsidiary organ through UNSC and UNGA concurrent resolutions, to be subsequently ratified by states, with the UNSC Chapter VII recourse before the entry into force of the ICC Statute.[9] No specific discussions ensued in this regard.

Eventually, it was the option of establishing the ICC through a treaty that prevailed.[10] In 1995, the UNGA convened the Ad Hoc Committee on the Establishment of an International Criminal Court[11] and the Preparatory Committee on the Establishment of an International Criminal Court (PrepCom),[12] mandated to produce a consolidated ICC draft statute. From June 15, 1998 to July 17, 1998, the UNGA convened the

[3] *See* ILC "Draft Statute for an International Criminal Court (1951)" in *Report of the Commission to the General Assembly on International Criminal Jurisdiction*, GAOR 7th Session Supp No 11 UN Doc A/2136; Revised Draft Statute for an International Criminal Court (Annex to the Report of the Committee on International Criminal Jurisdiction, 20 August 1953), GAOR 9th Session Supp No 12 at 21, UN Doc A/2645 (1954).

[4] UNGA Res 44/39 (4 December 1989) UN Doc A/RES/44/39. See also UNGA Res 45/41 (28 November 1990) UN Doc A/RES/45/41; 46/54 (9 December 1991) UN Doc A/RES/46/54; 47/33 (25 November 1992) UN Doc A/RES/47/33; 48/3 (19 December 1993); UN Doc A/RES/48/3.

[5] Report of the Commission to the General Assembly on the work of its forty-sixth session, UN Doc A/CN.4/SER.A/1994/Add.1 (Part 2), 1994.

[6] Report of the Commission to the General Assembly on the work of its forty-sixth session UN Doc A/CN.4/SER.A/1994/Add.1 (Part 2), 1994, p 22, para 51.

[7] Report of the Commission to the General Assembly on the work of its forty-sixth session UN Doc A/CN.4/SER.A/1994/Add.1 (Part 2), 1994, p 22, para 51.

[8] ibid, para 51.

[9] ibid para 52. Another option, not retained, was for the ICC to be an agency such as UNESCO or an independent entity established in association with the UN. See WA Schabas, Commentary to "Article 2," *The International Criminal Court: A Commentary on the Rome Statute* (OUP 2010) 63.

[10] UNGA Res. 50/46 (18 December 1995) UN Doc A/RES/50/46 and UNGA Res. 51/207 (17 December 1996) UN Doc A/RES/51/207.

[11] UNGA Res 49/53 (17 February 1995) UN Doc A/RES/49/53.

[12] UNGA Res 50/46 (11 December 1995) UN Doc A/RES/50/46.

UN Diplomatic Conference of Plenipotentiaries on the Establishment of an International Criminal Court (Rome Conference), a forum designed to negotiate the draft statute, building on efforts of the Ad Hoc Committee and the PrepCom with the participation of states, NGOs, and UN experts.[13] Eventually, there was consensus for a treaty-based ICC, independent from but brought into a relationship agreement with the UN.[14] The ICC Statute was adopted on July 17, 1998, by 120 states and entered into force on July 1, 2002.[15]

As shown by the many years needed to create the ICC, the very idea of such a court was controversial within the UN. The early 1990s' crimes committed in the former Yugoslavia and Rwanda, and the establishment of the ICTY and ICTR,[16] resulted however in a powerful momentum developed toward the strengthening of international criminal justice, while the end of the Cold War made progress politically possible. By the time the Rome Conference was convened, its goal was clear: create a permanent institution that would dispense with the need to establish a special tribunal every time genocide, war crimes, or crimes against humanity were committed. It was also broadly agreed that the ICC could only exercise its jurisdiction over a crime when states having their own jurisdiction over that crime were "unwilling or unable genuinely to carry out the investigation or prosecution."[17] This principle, called "complementarity," distinguishes the ICC from the Chapter-VII-based ad hoc tribunals, the latter having primacy over national systems.

Apart from that principle, states had very different ideas about key features of the system to be set up: particularly the powers of the Prosecutor, the role of the UNSC, and the conditions required for the exercise of the Court's jurisdiction over states.[18] The vast majority wanted a court that was fully independent and ready to intervene as required without too many constraints. They wanted a prosecutor who could trigger the jurisdiction of the Court, and a limited role for the UNSC. Many also favored a jurisdictional formula akin to universal jurisdiction for the court, and above all rejected any requirement that the state of the nationality of the accused could *alone* block the Court's jurisdiction. On the other hand, an influential minority wanted significant constraints over the exercise of jurisdiction and some form of political control, preferably the UNSC, accompanied by important limitations to the prosecutor's powers. A third, smaller but vocal group of states disliked both the prospect of an independent court *and* any UNSC role.[19] Those states clamored for protection of sovereignty and initially objected, for example, to the inclusion of crimes committed in internal conflicts within the jurisdiction of the court, even though such situations were in effect a primary reason for its creation.

[13] Bassiouni, "Negotiating the Treaty of Rome" (n 3); Washburn (n 2) 362ff.

[14] United Nations Diplomatic Conference of Plenipotentiaries on the Establishment of an International Criminal Court, Rome, 15 June–17 July 1998, (A/CONF.183/13 (vol II)) 2002.

[15] United Nations Diplomatic Conference of Plenipotentiaries on the Establishment of an International Criminal Court, Rome, 15 June–17 July 1998, (A/CONF.183/2 (vol I)) 2002.

[16] Lee (n 2)6. [17] ibid 27–28. [18] Arsanjani (n 2) 26–29.

[19] The different views held by states can be found in the United Nations Diplomatic Conference of Plenipotentiaries on the Establishment of an International Criminal Court, Rome, 15 June–17 July 1998, (A/CONF.183/13 (vol II)) 2002.

In the absence of effective negotiation on those issues, and given the need to finalize negotiations in Rome, the Bureau of the Committee of the Whole of the Conference proposed a text aimed at representing an acceptable balance among all those positions, that is, a system that would not automatically espouse the majority position but seek an equilibrium that would make the court viable through enough support from all sides.[20] Under that compromise, which ultimately was accepted by the Rome Conference, albeit with dissenting views, the ICC only exercises its jurisdiction with the consent of *either* the state of the territory where the crime was committed *or* the state of the nationality of the accused—the two classical and best accepted grounds for the exercise of criminal jurisdiction.[21] A UNSC referral is not required but is possible,[22] and the UNSC may request the ICC to defer proceedings in certain circumstances.[23] The Prosecutor is empowered to start an investigation in a situation that has not been referred to the Court either by a state or by the UNSC, but only with the authorization of a Pre-Trial Chamber.[24]

The inclusion of crimes to be subject to the ICC's jurisdiction within the three categories of "core crimes" (genocide, crimes against humanity, and war crimes) was difficult but more fruitfully negotiated than other jurisdictional issues. Nevertheless, persistent differences existed on some of the crimes proposed by states: most important the crime of aggression. Many considered it "the supreme crime" but could not agree either on its definition or on the conditions of exercise of the Court's jurisdiction over it, that is, what mechanism should be used for the determination that an *act* of aggression had been committed by a state before the ICC could undertake proceedings against an individual allegedly responsible for a related *crime* of aggression.[25] The latter issue generated considerable divisions. The UNSC permanent members and others argued for the exclusive responsibility of the UNSC in determining an act of aggression.[26] Other states felt that the UNSC tended to avoid making such determinations for political reasons even in clear cases of aggression, and favored alternative mechanisms in case of such inaction; for example, an ICJ advisory opinion, a UNGA resolution, or a decision of a Pre-Trial Chamber of the ICC.[27] In the absence of any agreement, the crime of aggression was included amongst the crimes listed in Article 5 of the ICC Statute, but the Court could only exercise its jurisdiction once pending issues were resolved. That was done

[20] Lee (n 2) 8–10; M Cherif Bassiouni, *The Legislative History of the International Criminal Court* (Transnational 2005) vol 1, 87–89.

[21] ICC Statute, art 12(2). [22] ICC Statute, art 13(b).

[23] ICC Statute, art 16. [24] ICC Statute, art 15.

[25] United Nations Diplomatic Conference of Plenipotentiaries on the Establishment of an International Criminal Court, Rome, 15 June–17 July 1998, (A/CONF.183/13 (vol II)) 2002; A/CONF. 183/C.1/SR.33, para 29. See also Arsanjani (n 2) 29.

[26] For example, Japan and the United States. *See* United Nations Diplomatic Conference of Plenipotentiaries on the Establishment of an International Criminal Court, Rome, 15 June–17 July 1998, (A/CONF.183/13 (vol. II)) 2002; A/CONF.183/C.1/SR.2, para 45; A/CONF.183/SR.9, paras 28–29.

[27] United Nations Diplomatic Conference of Plenipotentiaries on the Establishment of an International Criminal Court, Rome, 15 June–17 July 1998, (A/CONF.183/13 (vol II)) 2002; A/CONF.183/C.1/SR.18, para 141; A/CONF.183/C.1/SR.29, paras 22–26. See also Bassiouni, *Legislative History* (n 20) vol 2, 127–29.

through the adoption of complex provisions at a review conference held in 2010 in Kampala, Uganda.[28]

Difficult but constructive negotiations took place on the functioning of the Court. These were based on a principle that was not only generally accepted but deemed essential: the ICC had to be strictly judicial. There could be no risk that it might behave politically. This led to a detailed set of rules largely inspired by a basic objective: the unpredictability in the Court's exercise of its jurisdiction in unknown, future situations (retroactivity is excluded by the ICC Statute) should be balanced by high predictability in its behavior. As a result, the provisions of the ICC Statute—and the ICC Rules of Procedure and Evidence later prepared by states themselves in a Preparatory Commission set up in 1999—are considerably lengthier and more detailed than those of any other international and hybrid criminal court. The positive aspect of this approach is that states took ownership of the system and created certainty on the principles to be applied. The downside was the creation of a system that is complex and rigid, and even more difficult to change.

1.1.2 *An Interwoven Relationship*

While the ICC is an independent international organization, a web of institutional elements and substantive law link it to the UN.[29] While independent from each other, the UN and ICC entertain a multilayered relationship—institutionally and jurisdictionally. Elements of that relationship included cooperation and judicial assistance; dispute settlement provisions; attribution of treaty functions to the UN Secretary-General (UNSG) and links over budget and finance. Substantively, the range of crimes under the ICC jurisdiction largely coincides with those dealt with by other UN-created tribunals. Based initially on the ICC Statute, and then elaborated through the Negotiated Relationship Agreement between the International Criminal Court and the United Nations (the Relationship Agreement),[30] this relationship has also expanded in practice where, for example, the Assembly of States Parties (ASP) decided to comply with the UN's "common system of salaries, allowances and benefits."[31] These issues are developed later in this chapter.

Pursuant to Article 2 of the ICC Statute ("Relationship of the Court with the United Nations"), the ICC and UN concluded the Relationship Agreement, which entered into force in 2004.[32] The Relationship Agreement reaffirmed their shared objectives in preventing and responding to atrocity crimes—in conformity with the purposes/principles of the UN Charter. It provides that the ICC is invited to attend and participate

[28] *See* S Barriga & C Kreß (eds), *The Travaux Préparatoires of the Crime of Aggression* (CUP 2012).

[29] For detailed discussions on the relationship between the UN and the ICC, see R Higgins et al, "The International Criminal Court" in Rosalyn Higgins, Philippa Webb, Dapo Akande, Sandesh Sivakumaran, and James Sloan (eds), *Oppenheim's International Law: The United Nations* (OUP 2017) ch 31.

[30] Relationship Agreement between the United Nations and the International Criminal Court (20 August 2004) UN Doc A/RES/58/874.

[31] Resolution ICC-ASP/2/Res.2 (12 September 2003).

[32] Relationship Agreement between the United Nations and the International Criminal Court (20 August 2004) UN Doc A/RES/58/874.

in the work of the UNGA as an observer,[33] address the UNSC to assist on related activities of the Court,[34] and submit reports on its activities to the UN through the UNSG.[35] On cooperation and judicial assistance between the two organizations, the Relationship Agreement has served as an umbrella under which the UN and ICC have concluded agreements facilitating operations in situation countries.[36] Reference should be made to the UN-ICC Memorandum of Understanding (MOU) concerning cooperation between the United Nations Organization Stabilization Mission in the Democratic Republic of the Congo (MONUSCO) and the ICC.[37] Cooperation has also extended to the enforcement of sentences of imprisonment, where United Nations Office on Drugs and Crimes and the ICC have concluded a cooperation agreement.[38] Finally, the Relationship Agreement addresses the question of finances, including the conclusion of separate arrangements for funds provided to the ICC by decision of the UNGA, particularly regarding UNSC referral expenses.[39] The Relationship Agreement also foresees that the UN provide "advice on financial and fiscal questions of interest" to the ICC, upon the latter's request.[40] In 2003, following earlier discussions on staff pension and staff appointment, the ASP adopted the Staff Regulations and indicated that staff-related matters were in conformity with the UN common system. This has remained the case ever since.

Under the ICC Statute and the Relationship Agreement, the UNSG plays communication, representation, and convenor roles.[41] Specifically, the ICC Statute endows the UNSG with treaty functions. These include acting as the depository for the ICC Statute's signature, instruments of ratification, acceptance, approval or accession, and withdrawal.[42] The UNSG is also responsible for convening the ICC Statute review conference[43] and receiving, circulating, and depositing instruments of acceptance of ICC Statute amendment proposals.[44]

Importantly, where disputes between ICC states parties relating to the interpretation or application of the ICC Statute are to be referred to the ASP, the latter may make recommendations on further means of settlement of the dispute, including referral to the ICJ.[45]

[33] ibid art 4(1)–(2). [34] ibid art 4(3).

[35] ibid art 6. [36] ibid arts 15–20.

[37] Memorandum of understanding between the United Nations and the International Criminal Court concerning cooperation between the United Nations Organization Mission in the Democratic Republic of the Congo (MONUC) and the International Criminal Court (with annexes and exchange of letters), United Nations and the International Criminal Court, No. 1292, New York, 8 November 2005, https://treaties.un.org/doc/publication/unts/volume%202363/ii-1292.pdf.

[38] Memorandum of Understanding between the International Criminal Court and the United Nations, on Building the Capacity of States to Enforce, in accordance with International Standards on the Treatment of Prisoners, Sentences of Imprisonment Pronounced by the Court, 26 September 2014, ICC-PRES/15-02-14, https://www.icc-cpi.int/iccdocs/oj/26.09.2014-MOU_UNODC.pdf.

[39] UN Doc A/58/874 (20 August 2004) art 13; ICC Statute, art 115(b).

[40] UN Doc A/58/874 (20 August 2004) art 13(3).

[41] UN Doc A/58/874 (20 August 2004) art 4(1), 5–6.

[42] ICC Statute, arts 125–128. [43] ICC Statute, art 123. [44] ICC Statute, art 121(1) and (4).

[45] ICC Statute, art 119(2).

The ICC Statute mandates the ASP to hold its annual sessions at the UN Headquarters or at the seat of the Court.[46] Furthermore, the ICC has established a permanent liaison office in New York, close to the UN Headquarters.[47]

Regarding jurisdiction, the ICC Statute provides, inter alia, for the UNSC (acting under Chapter VII) to refer situations to the ICC and to defer investigations and prosecutions.[48] For UNSC referral situations, the ICC Statute foresees a reporting mechanism to the UNSC in case of state noncooperation.[49] The ICC Statute's crime of aggression also envisages a key role for the UNSC.[50] Substantively, the ICC Statute war crimes provision includes crimes against UN peacekeeping or humanitarian assistance operations or affecting the UN flag, uniform, or insignia.[51]

1.2 A Chapter VII Forum

As the first post-WWII international criminal tribunals, the ICTY and ICTR, as well as the entity mandated to carry out their residual functions, the Mechanism for International Criminal Tribunals (MICT), were directly established by the UNSC acting under Chapter VII. Two other jurisdictions, namely the East Timor's SPSC and the Kosovo Regulation 64 Panels were indirectly established as a Chapter VII measure, under the auspices of the UN.

1.2.1 *The Former Yugoslavia and Rwanda: The Ad Hoc Tribunals*

In the 1990s, serious violations of international humanitarian law (IHL) in both the former Yugoslavia and Rwanda prompted the UNSC to establish the: (1) ICTY, and (2) ICTR. The MICT was thereafter created to address their residual matters.

1.2.1.1 THE ICTY

In 1993, the UNSC decided through Resolution 808 to establish an international criminal tribunal to prosecute persons responsible for serious violations of IHL committed in the territory of the former Yugoslavia since 1991.[52] The UNSC requested the UNSG to prepare proposals for establishing such tribunal after consulting member states.[53] The UNSG consulted the UNSC-appointed Commission of Experts, member states, NGOs, and individual experts.[54] In his report, the UNSG indicated that such tribunal should

[46] ICC Statute, art 112(6). See also Rules of Procedure of the Assembly of States Parties, ch II. In practice, the ASP has done so by alternating the location of each session every year.

[47] Judge Philippe Kirsch, President of the International Criminal Court, Address to the United Nations General Assembly, 9 October 2006, p 4.

[48] ICC Statute, art 13(b) and 16.

[49] ICC Statute, art 87(5)(b) and 87(7).

[50] ICC Statute, art 13(b), 15 and 15 *ter*.

[51] ICC Statute, art 8(2)(b)(iii) and (viii); and art 8(2)(e)(iii).

[52] UNSC Res 808 (22 February 1993) UN Doc S/RES/808.

[53] ibid.

[54] Report of the Secretary General pursuant to paragraph 2 of UNSC Resolution 808 (1993) (3 May 1993) UN Doc S/25704, paras 13–15.

normally, for inclusiveness, be established by treaty.[55] However, given the urgency of the matter and having determined that the situation in the former Yugoslavia constituted a threat to international peace and security, the UNSG proposed that[56] the tribunal be established by the UNSC acting under Chapter VII.[57] The tribunal would thus be established as a subsidiary organ: an independent judicial institution not subject to UNSC control in performing its judicial functions.[58] Through Resolution 827 (1993), the UNSC approved the report, including the draft ICTY Statute, and requested the UNSG to urgently implement it.[59]

In terms of the ICTY composition, the judges would be elected by the UNGA from a list submitted by the UNSC, with the terms and conditions of service of the permanent judges being those of ICJ judges.[60] The Prosecutor would be appointed by the UNSC on nomination of the UNSG,[61] and the Registrar would be appointed by the UNSG after consulting the ICTY President.[62] Staff would be subject to the UN Convention on Privileges and Immunities,[63] and expenses would be UN-derived, per Article 17 of the UN Charter.[64] ICTY Statute amendments would be made through UNSC resolutions.[65] Regarding substantive law, the then-existing IHL was incorporated into the ICTY Statute.[66]

1.2.1.2 THE ICTR

In 1994, the UNSC requested the UNSG to make proposals for the investigations of serious violations of IHL in the 1994 Rwanda situation.[67] UNSC Resolution 918 (1994) determined that the situation in Rwanda constituted a threat to international peace and security and, inter alia, requested the UNSG to report on the situation.[68] Upon UNSC request,[69] the UNSG established the Commission of Experts to carry out investigations and examine possible jurisdictional matters.[70] Following a request from Rwanda,[71] the ICTR was established in 1994 as a UNSC Chapter VII measure through Resolution 955.[72]

[55] ibid para 19.

[56] ibid paras 24 and 27, citing Iraq and Kuwait as examples where subsidiary organs have been established.

[57] ibid paras 22–25, 30.

[58] ibid para 28.

[59] UNSC Res 827 (25 May 1993) UN Doc S/RES/827, p 2.

[60] Statute of the International Criminal Tribunal for the former Yugoslavia (ICTY Statute), art 13*bis*.

[61] ICTY Statute, art 16(4).

[62] ICTY Statute, art 17(3).

[63] ICTY Statute, art 30.

[64] ICTY Statute, art 32.

[65] *See* the Updated Statute of the ICTY of September 2009, reflecting amendments from 13 May 1998 by Resolution 827 through to amendments on 7 July 2009 by Resolution 1877.

[66] Report of the Secretary General pursuant to paragraph 2 of UNSC Resolution 808 (1993) (3 May 1993) UN Doc S/25704, para 29.

[67] Statement by the President of the Security Council on Rwanda, 30 April 1994, UN Doc S/PRST/1994/21, p 3.

[68] UNSC Res 918 (17 May 1994) UN Doc S/RES/918.

[69] UNSC Res 935 (1 July 1994) UN Doc S/RES/935.

[70] Report of the Secretary-General on the Establishment of the Commission of Experts Pursuant to Paragraph 1 of Security Council Resolution 935 (1994) UN Doc S/1994/879, paras 8–10.

[71] Letter dated 29 September 1994 from the Permanent Representative of Rwanda to the United Nations Addressed to the President of the Security Council (29 September 1994) UN Doc S/1994/1115.

[72] UN Doc S/RES/955 (1994).

Fully shaped by the UN,[73] the ICTR Statute mirrored the ICTY Statute. The modalities for composition, election, and terms and conditions of the judges, Prosecutor, and the Registrar are virtually identical to the ICTY.[74] In practice, the Prosecutor was common to both the ICTY and ICTR. The ICTR Statute was also identical to the ICTY Statute in terms of privileges and immunities for staff members,[75] expenses,[76] and statutory amendments.[77]

Regarding procedural law, the ICTR Statute adopted the ICTY Rules of Procedure and Evidence (ICTY Rules) with changes as deemed necessary.[78] On substantive law, IHL was incorporated into the ICTR applicable law.[79]

1.2.1.3 THE MICT

In 2010, anticipating the closure of the ICTY and ICTR, the UNSC established the MICT by Resolution 1966 under Chapter VII.[80]

Like the ICTY/ICTR, MICT is composed of international judges,[81] with terms and conditions of the MICT President and judges being the same as those of ICJ judges and ICJ ad hoc judges respectively.[82] The judges' election modalities are similar to those of the ICTY/ICTR, with preference for judge nominations from the ICTY/ICTR.[83] The UNSG appoints the MICT President after consulting the UNSC President.[84] The Prosecutor and Registrar are appointed in the same manner as the ICTY/ICTR.[85] In appointing MICT staff, preference is given to ICTY/ICTR staff members.[86] The MICT provision concerning expenses is the same as the ICTY/ICTR.[87] MICT would be operational initially for four years from the commencement date, with its renewal being subject to biennial reviews unless the UNSC decides otherwise.[88] The first years of work of the MICT imply temporal overlap with ICTR/ICTY.[89]

[73] Statute of the International Criminal Tribunal for Rwanda (ICTR Statute), adopted by Security Council Resolution 955 (1994) of 8 November 1994.

[74] ICTR Statute, Art 12*bis*, 12*ter*, 15, and 16.

[75] ICTR Statute, art 29.

[76] ICTR Statute, art 30.

[77] *See* Statute of the ICTR, as adopted by Resolution 955 (1994) on 8 November 1994 and as amended by Security Council resolutions from Resolution 1165 (1998) of 30 April 1998, through to Resolution 1901 (2009) of 16 December 2009.

[78] ICTR Statute, art 14.

[79] Mackenzie et al (n 1) 186–87.

[80] UNSC Res 1966 (22 December 2010) UN Doc S/RES/1966, with annexes: Annex 1: Statute of the International Residual Mechanism for Criminal Tribunals, and Annex 2: Transitional Arrangements. See also Statement by the President of the Security Council (19 December 2008) UN Doc S/PRST/2008/47, p 2.

[81] United Nations Mechanism for International Criminal Tribunals (MICT Statute), art 8(1).

[82] MICT Statute, art 8(4).

[83] MICT Statute, arts 10 and 14(4).

[84] MICT Statute, art 11.

[85] MICT Statute, arts 14(4) and 15(3).

[86] *See* MICT Statute, arts 10(1)(a), 14(5), 15(4). See also UNSC Res 1966 (22 December 2010) UN Doc S/RES/1966, Annex 2, art 7.

[87] MICT Statute, art 30. See also Statement by the President of the Security Council (19 December 2008) UN Doc S/PRST/2008/47, p 2.

[88] UNSC Res 1966 (22 December 2010) UN Doc S/RES/1966 (2010), para 17.

[89] "About the MICT" (*United Nations Mechanism for International Criminal Tribunals*) http://www.unmict.org/en/about accessed January 21, 2019.

1.2.1.4 AN INDIRECT CHAPTER VII FORUM

Two jurisdictions were established by the UNSC in an indirect fashion. These were the (1) SPSC, and the (2) Regulation 64 Panels, with their common denominator being the establishment, by the UNSC, of bodies that would in turn create these jurisdictions.

1.2.1.5 TIMOR-LESTE: THE SPECIAL PANELS FOR SERIOUS CRIMES

The SPSC[90] was established indirectly through Chapter VII in response to the serious violations of serious criminal offenses committed in the then-East Timor (Timor-Leste) during its independence from Indonesia.[91] In 1999, through Resolution 1272, the UNSC created under Chapter VII the UN Transitional Administration in East Timor (UNTAET), a transitional authority until 2001.[92] Absent any national government to contract with, UNTAET relied on this resolution as the legal basis for unilaterally establishing the SPSC within the District Court of Dili through Regulation No. 2000/15.[93] Through UNTAET's interpretation of Resolution 1272 leading to the establishment of the SPSC, Chapter VII indirectly generated its creation. Regulation No. 2000/16 established the Public Prosecution Service (PPS) and bestowed exclusive authority upon the East Timor's Office of the Prosecutor-General for Serious Crimes to supervise the investigation and prosecution of serious crimes.[94]

Regarding composition, the SPSC was composed of an internationally dominated panel of judges.[95] The PPS consisted of domestic and UN staff.[96] The SPSC and the PPS were funded through the UN.[97] Regarding substantive law, the core crimes of Regulation 2000/15 are virtually identical to the ICC Statute, specifically the definition of genocide,

[90] Described as a "hybrid tribunal" (C Reiger and M Wierda, "The Serious Crimes Process in Timor-Leste: In Retrospect" (March 2006) International Center for Transitional Justice); an "internationalised domestic tribunal," as well as a "strictly UN operation" (Suzannah Linton, "Cambodia, East Timor and Sierra Leone: Experiments in International Justice" (2000) 12 Crim L Forum 185, 205).

[91] UNTAET Regulation 2000/15 (6 June 2000).

[92] UNSC Res 1272 (25 October 1999) UN Doc S/RES/1272. See also UNTAET Regulation No. 1999/1 (27 November 1999), which recalls that Resolution 1272 (1999) in establishing UNTAET, endowed it with the overall legislative and executive authority, including the administration of justice.

[93] UNTAET Regulation No. 2000/15 (6 June 2000). *See* also M Pampalk, "Accountability for Serious Crimes and National Reconciliation in Timor-Leste: Progress or Wishful Thinking?" (2010) 3(1) ASEAS 13.

[94] UNTAET Regulation No. 2000/16 (6 June 2000), Section 14. See also Linton (n 90) 205.

[95] UNTAET Regulation No. 2000/15 (6 June 2000), Section 22.

[96] UNTAET Regulation No. 2000/16 (6 June 2000), Section 6.1. See also N Rosen, "Timor-Leste: Interaction between International and National Responses to the Mass Atrocities" (2011) DOMAC, 21–22.

[97] UNTAET Regulation No. 2000/11 (6 March 2000), Section 34 provides that "during the transitional period, UNTAET shall provide the necessary financial and technical support to the courts in East Timor." UNTAET Regulation No. 2000/16 (6 June 2000), Section 2, which provides that the funding of the PPS is provided by the Transitional Administrator of UNTAET. See also Linton (n 90) 205.

crimes against humanity, and war crimes.[98] Indonesian law continued to apply as the default subsidiary law.[99]

The SPSC functioned under East Timor's authority after its independence in 2002.[100] In 2004, the UNSC decided that the SPSC's proceedings had to end by 2005.[101] It also decided that the UN Mission of Support in Timor-Leste had to support local capacity building.[102] In May 2005, most UN infrastructure withdrew and the SPSC suspended operations indefinitely.[103]

1.2.1.6 KOSOVO: THE REGULATION 64 PANELS

Similarly, the Regulation 64 Panels were indirectly established in 1999 as a Chapter VII measure pursuant to Resolution 1244, in response to violence and repression in Kosovo by the Federal Republic of Yugoslavia.[104] Resolution 1244 established the UN Interim Administration in Kosovo (UNMIK),[105] which was responsible for governance and ensuring "conditions for a peaceful and normal life for all inhabitants in Kosovo."[106] Through its Regulation 2000/6, UNMIK, acting pursuant to the authority conferred on it by the UNSC through its founding resolution, promulgated that international judges and prosecutors could be appointed to strengthen the local judiciary.[107] In 2000, Regulation 2000/64 amended this by increasing the presence of international staff within the judiciary and designating an international prosecutor, international investigating judge, and two international judges, thus giving rise to the Regulation 64 Panels.[108] The rationale for this shift in composition was to ensure the "independence of the judiciary and the proper administration of justice."[109]

Regarding the applicable law, Regulation 64 Panels had the same jurisdiction as other Kosovar courts and applied domestic law with international standards, including UN human rights law treaties.[110] The UNSG Special Representative had an integral role in implementation, including clarifying how the Regulations 64 Panels were to function[111] as well approving or rejecting recommendations regarding the appointment of international

[98] See UNTAET Regulation No. 2000/15 (6 June 2000), Sections 4–6. See Linton (n 90) 206, 213; Reiger and Wierda (n 90) 23.

[99] See UNTAET Regulation No. 1999/1 (27 November 1999), Section 3.1; UNTAET Regulation No. 2000/15 (6 June 1000), Section 3. See also Reiger and Wierda (n 90) 24.

[100] "Special Panel for Serious Crimes (East Timor)" (*International Bar Association*) <http://www.ibanet.org/Committees/WCC_EastTimor.aspx> accessed January 21, 2019.

[101] UNSC Res 1543 (14 May 2004) UN Doc S/RES/1543, para 8.

[102] ibid para 3.

[103] "Special Panel for Serious Crimes (East Timor)" (*International Bar Association*) <http://www.ibanet.org/Committees/WCC_EastTimor.aspx> accessed January 21, 2019.

[104] UNSC Res 1244 (10 June 2009) UN Doc S/RES/1244, para 3.

[105] UNSC Res 1244 (10 June 2009) UN Doc S/RES/1244.

[106] UNSC Res. 1244 (10 June 2009) UN Doc S/RES/1244, Annex 2, para 5.

[107] UNMIK Regulation 2000/6 (27 May 2000), Sections 1 and 4.

[108] UNMIK Regulation 2000/64 (15 December 2000).

[109] UNMIK Regulation 2000.

[110] UNMIK Regulation 1999/24 (12 December 1999), Section 1.1.

[111] UNMIK Regulation 1999 (12 December 1999), Section 2.

staff. The UN presence in Kosovo, through UNMIK and the UNSG Special Representative, was gradually phased out and transitioned to local staff.[112]

2 Hybrid Criminal Courts

The UN has on multiple occasions served as a forum to assist in the establishment of hybrid criminal courts. This assistance has been facilitated by the UN through bilateral treaty making, as well as through ICTY rule 11*bis*. Whereas the former are triggered by a state request to the UN, under rule 11*bis*, courts respond to the ICTY's emphasis on strengthening competent national judicial systems.

2.1 A Bilateral Treaty-Making Forum

The UN has proven to be a decisive partner to member states in the establishment of hybrid criminal tribunals, based on an agreement between the UN and national authorities and involving a request from the member state in question. This has particularly been manifest in Cambodia with the: (1) Extraordinary Chambers in the Courts of Cambodia (ECCC), (2) Special Court for Sierra Leone (SCSL), and (3) Special Tribunal for Lebanon (STL).

2.1.1 *Cambodia*

The ECCC was established following lengthy and complex negotiations between Cambodia and the UN.[113] In June 1997, Cambodia requested UN assistance in the establishment of an accountability mechanism regarding serious crimes committed under the Khmer Rouge.[114] The report of the UNSG's Group of Experts[115] recommended that an ad hoc international tribunal be established by the UNSC or UNGA.[116]

In 1999, Cambodia created a task force to produce a draft law for the trial of senior Khmer Rouge leaders. The draft law received legal and technical contributions from national and UN experts. Upon review, the UN indicated its preference for a majority of

[112] T Perriello and M Wierda, "Lessons from the Deployment of International Judges and Prosecutors in Kosovo" (March 2006) International Center for Transitional Justice, 33–35.

[113] Described as an "internationalised domestic tribunal" (Linton (n 90) 188); as well as a "hybrid international-domestic tribunal" (MP Scharf, "The Iraqi High Tribunal: A Viable Experiment in International Justice" (2007) 5 J Intl Crim Just 259).

[114] Identical letters dated 23 June 1997 from the Secretary-General addressed to the President of the General Assembly and to the President of the Security Council, with Annex (24 June 1997) UN Doc A/51/930-S/1997/488.

[115] Established pursuant to UNGA Res 52/135 (1998).

[116] Report of the Group of Experts for Cambodia established pursuant to General Assembly Resolution 52/135 (15 March 1999) UN Doc A/53/850-S/1999/231 paras 129, 137.

foreign judges—the opposite of Cambodia's view. No consensus could emerge.[117] In 2000, faced with Cambodia's refusal to accept an international tribunal, the UN and Cambodia signed an MOU, agreeing to establish a tribunal under Cambodian law but with international participation.[118] In 2001, Cambodia passed the law on the establishment of the ECCC (ECCC Law),[119] which was subsequently signed into law by the king.[120] The law, however, failed to obtain UN approval.[121] Following the resumption of negotiations, Cambodia and the UN signed an agreement in 2003 "concerning the prosecution under Cambodian law" of crimes committed under the Democratic Kampuchea, to regulate UN-Cambodia cooperation.[122]

Regarding composition, the ECCC would consist of Cambodian (majority) and international judges (the latter being appointed by Cambodia upon nomination by the UNSG), and two investigative judges and two prosecutors (one international in each, both appointed similarly to the international judges).[123] ECCC staff would be domestic and international, the latter being nominated by the UNSG.[124] The UN would provide remuneration for the international elected officials and international personnel, defense counsel, witness transport, and safety and security arrangements, as well as other costs as agreed between Cambodia and the UN.[125] In practice, funding was borne by both Cambodia and the UN through a specially created trust fund comprising of voluntary contributions as well as member states' assistance.[126] Finally, if Cambodia changed the structure of the ECCC or caused it to function in a manner that would not conform to the agreement, the UN could "cease to provide assistance, financial or otherwise."[127]

[117] See also Report of the Group of Experts for Cambodia established pursuant to General Assembly Resolution 52/135 (15 March 1999) UN Doc A/53/850-S/1999/231, para 108; Linton (n 90) 189.

[118] Tribunal Memorandum of Understanding Between the United Nations and the Royal Government of Cambodia, Phnom Penh Post, No. 9/22, 27 October–9 November 2000, arts 1–2. See Linton (n 90) 189–90.

[119] Law on the Establishment of Extraordinary Chambers in the Courts of Cambodia for the Prosecution of Crimes Committed During the Period of Democratic Kampuchea, adopted by the National Assembly of the Kingdom of Cambodia on 2 January 2001. See David Scheffer et al., "The Extraordinary Chambers in the Courts of Cambodia" (abridgment of David Scheffer, "The Extraordinary Chambers in the Courts of Cambodia" in M Cherif Bassiouni (ed), *International Criminal Law* (3rd edn, Martinus Nijhoff 2008) 9.

[120] Signed on 10 August 2001. See Scheffer (n 119).

[121] D Jacobs, "Puzzling over Amnesties: Defragmenting the Debate for International Criminal Tribunals" in Lvd Herik and C Stahn (eds), *The Diversification and Fragmentation of International Criminal Law* (Martinus Nijhoff 2012) 321.

[122] Agreement between the United Nations and the Royal Government of Cambodia Concerning the Prosecution Under Cambodian law of Crimes Committed During the Period of Democratic Kampuchea, signed 6 June 2003. See also Report of the Secretary-General on the Khmer Rouge Trials (3 December 2003) UN Doc A/58/617.

[123] Agreement between the United Nations and the Royal Government of Cambodia Concerning the Prosecution Under Cambodian law of Crimes Committed During the Period of Democratic Kampuchea, signed 6 June 2003, arts 3(1), 5(5), and 6(5).

[124] ibid arts 3(5) and 6(5).

[125] ibid art 17.

[126] See "How Is the Court Financed?" (*Extraordinary Chambers in the Courts of Cambodia*, <https://www.eccc.gov.kh/en/faq/how-court-financed>; Linton (n 90) 190; and Scheffer (n 119).

[127] Agreement between the United Nations and the Royal Government of Cambodia Concerning the Prosecution under Cambodian law of Crimes Committed During the Period of Democratic Kampuchea, signed 6 June 2003, art 28.

The ECCC's procedure would follow Cambodian law. Where Cambodian law did not deal with particular issues, guidance may be sought from international law.[128] The ECCC would operate in accordance with international standards of justice, fairness, and due process.[129] The ECCC's subject-matter jurisdiction would, inter alia, include the crime of genocide as defined in the Genocide Convention and crimes against humanity, inspired by the ICC Statute.[130]

Following amendments to meet UN standards,[131] the Agreement entered into force in 2005[132] and the ECCC became operational in 2006.[133]

2.1.2 *Sierra Leone*

The UN was an instrumental partner to Sierra Leone through the establishment of both the (1) SCSL and the (2) Residual Special Court for Sierra Leone (RSCSL) for its civil war crimes.

2.1.3 *The SCSL*

In 2000,[134] Sierra Leone requested the UN's assistance for the establishment of a special court to address serious crimes committed during its civil war.[135] UNSC Resolution 1315 (2000) reiterated that the situation in Sierra Leone continued to constitute a threat to international peace and security, and requested the UNSG to negotiate an agreement with Sierra Leone to create an "independent special court."[136]

In his report to the UNSC, appended with a draft statute and UN-Sierra Leone agreement, the UNSG recommended the creation of a UN-Sierra Leone-administered internationalized domestic tribunal, separate from the national criminal justice system. The UNSG noted that the establishment of the SCSL via an agreement between the UN and Sierra Leone, would be "a treaty-based *sui generis* court of mixed jurisdiction and composition." The UNSG contrasted this with the ICTY and ICTR, which were established by the UNSC and constituted subsidiary organs of the UN.[137]

128 ibid art 12. 129 ibid art 12(2). 130 ibid art 9.

131 Law on the Establishment of the Extraordinary Chambers, with inclusion of amendments as promulgated on 27 October 2004 (NS/RKM/1004/006).

132 See also UNGA Res 57/228 (22 May 2003) UN Doc A/RES/57/228 B (approving draft ECCC Agreement); Report of the Secretary-General on Khmer Rouge trials (25 November 2005) UN Doc A/60/565), para 4.

133 See Report of the Secretary General on the Khmer Rouge trials (27 August 2007) UN Doc A/62/304.

134 The SCSL is described as an "internationalised domestic tribunal" (Linton (n 90) 186); as well as a "hybrid international-domestic tribunal" (Scharf (n 113) 259).

135 Letter dated 9 August 2000 from the Permanent Representative of Sierra Leone to the United Nations addressed to the President of the Security Council (10 August 2010) UN Doc S/2000/786, Annex: Agreement between the United Nations and the Government of Sierra Leone on the Establishment of a Special Court for Sierra Leone.

136 UNSC Res 1315 (14 August 2000) UN Doc S/RES/1315, paras 1 and 6.

137 Report of the Secretary-General on the establishment of a Special Court for Sierra Leone (4 October 2000) UN Doc S/2000/915, paras 9, 39.

In 2002, the UN-Sierra Leone Agreement on the Establishment of a Special Court for Sierra Leone was signed, annexed with the SCSL Statute.[138] The SCSL would comprise both domestic and international judges; the latter—as well as the Prosecutor—would be appointed by the UNSG.[139] The UNSG would also appoint the Registrar—a UN staff member—after consultation with the SCSL President.[140] SCSL expenses would be borne by the international community's voluntary contributions, led by the UNSG. Should those contributions not suffice, the UNSG and UNSC could explore alternative means.[141] Finally, the UN Mission in Sierra Leone would provide security to the SCSL premises and personnel, subject to appropriate UNSC mandate.[142]

On procedural law, the SCSL Statute required that the ICTR Rules at the time of the establishment of the SCSL "shall be applicable *mutatis mutandis*" before the SCSL.[143]

2.1.4 *The RSCSL*

The RSCSL was established in 2010 to carry out the SCSL's essential functions after its closure, pursuant to a UN-Sierra Leone agreement and its annexed RSCSL Statute.[144] Accordingly, the RSCSL continued the jurisdiction, functions, rights, and obligations of the SCSL.[145] Institutionally, among its domestic and international judges, the latter would be appointed to a roster by the UNSG taking into account the experience of former judges of SCSL, ICTY, ICTR, ECCC, ICC, and STL.[146] The Prosecutor would be appointed by the UNSG after consultation with Sierra Leone.[147] The RSCSL expenses would be borne by voluntary contributions.[148] Its staff were accorded the privileges and immunities afforded to UN officials.[149]

In 2011, the agreement was ratified in domestic law and signed into law in 2012.[150]

[138] Agreement between the United Nations and the Government of Sierra Leone on the Establishment of a Special Court for Sierra Leone (with Statute) (2002), United Nations, Treaty Series, vol 2178, no 38342, p 137. Some provisions in the Agreement (eg, expenses (art 6) and safety (art 16)) are not expressly covered in the SCSL Statute.

[139] Agreement between the United Nations and the Government of Sierra Leone on the Establishment of a Special Court for Sierra Leone (2002), United Nations, Treaty Series, vol 2178, no 38342, arts 2 and 3; and SCSL Statute, arts 12(1)(a) and 15(3).

[140] SCSL Statute, art 16(3).

[141] Agreement between the United Nations and the Government of Sierra Leone on the Establishment of a Special Court for Sierra Leone (2002), United Nations, Treaty Series, vol 2178, no 38342, art 6.

[142] ibid art 16. [143] SCSL Statute, art 14(1).

[144] Agreement between the United Nations and the Government of Sierra Leone on the Establishment of a Residual Special Court for Sierra Leone, 11 August 2010, Preamble; annexed with Statute of the Residual Special Court (RSCL Statute).

[145] ibid art 1(3). [146] RSCSL Statute, art 11(3).

[147] RSCSL Statute, art 14(1).

[148] Agreement between the United Nations and the Government of Sierra Leone on the Establishment of a Residual Special Court for Sierra Leone, 11 August 2010, art 3.

[149] ibid art 10.

[150] The Residual Special Court for Sierra Leone Agreement (Ratification) Act, Supplement to the Gazette Vol. CXLIII, No 6 of 9 February 2012.

2.1.5 *Lebanon*

Following the killing of former Lebanese prime minister Hariri and others,[151] the UNSC through Resolution 1595 (2005) established the UN International Independent Investigation Commission, to assist Lebanon in conducting investigations into the matter.[152] In December 2005, Lebanon requested the UN to establish a tribunal of an international character for the killings.[153] Pursuant to Resolution 1664 (2006), the UNSC requested the UNSG to "negotiate an agreement with [Lebanon] aimed at establishing a tribunal of international character based on the highest international standards of criminal justice."[154] Consultations were also held with former ICTY Presidents.[155]

In his 2006 report on "the establishment of a special tribunal," the UNSG explained that the legal basis for the establishment of the STL would be a UN-Lebanon agreement, which was annexed to the report together with the STL Statute. The STL would be a treaty-based entity—neither part of the UN nor the Lebanese judiciary.[156] Referring to it as a "United Nations-assisted" jurisdiction,[157] the UNSG explained that "the constitutive instruments of the [STL] in both form and substance evidence its international character," and that the STL Rules would be partially inspired by reference materials reflecting the highest standards of international criminal procedure.[158] In November 2006, the UNSC endorsed the UN-Lebanon agreement and STL Statute, and invited the UNSG and Lebanon to conclude the agreement.[159] Through Resolution 1757 (2007), the UNSC, acting under Chapter VII, decided that the agreement and STL Statute would enter into force on June 10, 2007.[160] The UNSC also requested the UNSG to coordinate with Lebanon to establish the STL.[161] The STL commenced work on March 1, 2009.[162] Thus, unlike the SPSC and the Regulation 64 Panels, which were set up unilaterally by

[151] The STL is described as a "a tribunal of international character" (UN Doc S/RES/1757 (30 May 2007)), as well as a "hybrid, or international court, which is composed of both Lebanese and international judges and staff" at "STL Close-up" (*Public Information and Communications Section of the Special Tribunal for Lebanon*) <http://www.stl-tsl.org/images/stories/About/STL_Close-up_EN.pdf> accessed January 11, 2019.

[152] See UNSC Res 1595 (17 April 2005) UN Doc S/RES/1595.

[153] Letter dated 13 December 2005 from the Chargé d'affaires ai of the Permanent Mission of Lebanon to the United Nations addressed to the Secretary-General (13 December 2005) UN Doc S/2005/783. See also UNSC Res 1644 (15 December 2005) UN Doc S/RES/1644.

[154] UNSC Res 1664 (29 March 2006) UN Doc S/RES/1664.

[155] Report of the Secretary-General on the establishment of a special tribunal for Lebanon (15 November 2006) UN Doc S/2006/893, para 3.

[156] Report of the Secretary-General on the establishment of a special tribunal for Lebanon (15 November 2006) UN Doc S/2006/893, para 6.

[157] Report of the Secretary-General on the establishment of a special tribunal for Lebanon (15 November 2006) UN Doc S/2006/893, para 9.

[158] Report of the Secretary-General on the establishment of a special tribunal for Lebanon (15 November 2006) UN Doc S/2006/893, para 7.

[159] Letter dated 21 November 2006 from the President of the Security Council addressed to the Secretary-General (24 November 2006) UN Doc S/2006/911.

[160] UNSC Res. 1757 (30 May 2007) UN Doc S/RES/1757, p 2.

[161] UNSC Res. 1757 (30 May 2007) UN Doc S/RES/1757, para 3.

[162] "STL Close-up" (*Public Information and Communications Section of the Special Tribunal for Lebanon*) <http://www.stl-tsl.org/images/stories/About/STL_Close-up_EN.pdf> accessed January 21, 2019.

Chapter VII bodies, the STL was conceived as a UN-Lebanon bilateral agreement, which was only subsequently entered into force through a UN Chapter VII resolution.

Regarding composition, the STL would consist of both Lebanese and international judges. The UNSG would appoint the international judges, Prosecutor, Registrar, and Head of Defence.[163] The STL expenses would be funded via Lebanon (49 percent) and voluntary state contributions (51 percent). Should the latter not suffice, the UNSG and the UNSC would explore alternate financing means.[164] The agreement also provided that after the STL's initial three years, should the UN and Lebanon—in consultation with the UNSC—determine that the STL activities have not been completed, the agreement would be extended for a period determined by the UNSG in consultation with Lebanon and UNSC.[165] On its procedural law, the STL Rules bore a close resemblance to the ICTY/ICTR Rules—combining elements of common/civil law.[166]

2.2 ICTY-Supported Criminal Courts

The ICTY, as a part of the UN, has also had an impact on the establishment of other criminal courts. This has been done by virtue of: (1) Rule 11 *bis* of the ICTY Rules (Rule 11*bis*), and (2) the Kosovo Specialist Chambers.

2.2.1 *Rule* 11*bis Criminal Courts*

A varied degree of international and UN involvement can be ascertained by virtue of Rule 11*bis*, which serves a dual purpose of fulfilling the ICTY Completion Strategy and enhancing national judicial capacity building to prosecute international crimes. Beyond the ad hoc tribunals, criminal proceedings relating to the former Yugoslavia's 1990s' atrocities also led to the establishment of the War Crimes Chambers (WCC) in: (1) Bosnia and Herzegovina (BiH), (2) Serbia, and (3) Croatia, which are brought into relationship with the ICTY through Rule 11*bis*.

2.2.1.1 BIH: THE WCC

A specialist chamber attached to the Criminal Law Division in the Court of BiH in 2002—the WCC[167]—was established under the auspices of the Office of the High Representative (OHR) and was subsequently assisted by ICTY.

[163] Report of the Secretary-General on the establishment of a special tribunal for Lebanon, UN Doc S/2006/893 (15 November 2006), Attachment: Statute of the Special Tribunal for Lebanon, arts 9 (referring to article 2 of the UN-Lebanon agreement), 11 (referring to article 3 of the UN-Lebanon agreement), 12–13.

[164] Report of the Secretary-General on the establishment of a special tribunal for Lebanon, UN Doc S/2006/893 (15 November 2006), Annex I: Agreement between the UN and the Lebanese Republic on the establishment of a Special Tribunal for Lebanon, art 5.

[165] Report of the Secretary-General on the establishment of a special tribunal for Lebanon, UN Doc S/2006/893 (15 November 2006), Annex I: Agreement between the UN and the Lebanese Republic on the establishment of a Special Tribunal for Lebanon, art 21.

[166] Mackenzie et al (n 1) 214.

[167] Described as being a "hybrid court" or "hybrid war crimes tribunal" established with strong international support and envisaged to become entirely national (B Ivanišević, "The War Crimes Chamber in

In 2002, the UNSG endorsed the ICTY Completion Strategy advising the UNSC that the WCC's creation was a prerequisite for the transfer of low-to-intermediate-level accused to BiH.[168] It recommended the creation of the WCC within the existing Court of BiH, initially composed of national and international judges,[169] as well legislative and judicial reforms with international support prior to the transfer of cases to BiH.[170]

In 2002, the BiH Parliament adopted the law establishing the Court of BiH, including the WCC.[171] The UNSC endorsed the ICTY Completion Strategy to enable the ICTY to complete all first instance trials by 2008.[172] In September 2002, Rule 11*bis* was amended to enable the transfer of ICTY cases to national jurisdictions.[173] In 2003, the Joint Conclusions of the OHR and ICTY also echoed the Completion Strategy recommendations.[174] While BiH laws would apply, it was recommended that the ICTY experiences be used as a basis for developing WCC Rules of Procedure and Evidence.[175]

The UNSC endorsed the ICTY's completion strategy in Resolution 1503 (2003), and, acting under Chapter VII, called on donor communities to support the OHR's work in creating the WCC.[176]

In 2004, BiH passed the Law on the Transfer of Cases from the ICTY to the Prosecutor's Office of BiH and the use of Evidence Collected by ICTY in Proceedings Before the Courts in Bosnia and Herzegovina.[177] This provided the legal framework for transferring ICTY cases to the WCC, pursuant to Rule 11*bis*. It provided for information

Bosnia and Herzegovina: From Hybrid to Domestic Court" (2008) International Center for Transitional Justice 1, 5); also described as an "internationalised domestic tribunal" (Scharf (n 113) 259).

168 Letter dated 17 June 2002 from the Secretary-General addressed to the President of the Security Council, UN Doc S/2002/678 (19 June 2002), with Enclosure: Report on the Judicial Status of the International Criminal Tribunal for the Former Yugoslavia and the Prospects for Referring Certain Cases to National Courts.

169 Letter dated 17 June 2002 from the Secretary-General addressed to the President of the Security Council (19 June 2002) UN Doc S/2002/678, with Enclosure: Report on the Judicial Status of the International Criminal Tribunal for the Former Yugoslavia and the Prospects for Referring Certain Cases to National Courts, pp 23–25, and para 85.

170 Letter dated 17 June 2002 from the Secretary-General addressed to the President of the Security Council (19 June 2002) UN Doc S/2002/678, Enclosure, paras 47–58.

171 Law on Court of Bosnia and Herzegovina, ("Official Gazette" of Bosnia and Herzegovina, 29/00, 16/02, 24/02, 3/03, 37/03, 42/03, 4/04, 9/04, 35/04, 61/04).

172 Statement by the President of the Security Council (23 July 2002) UN Doc S/PRST/2002/21.

173 ICTY Rules, Rule 11*bis*, adopted on 12 November 1997, revised on 30 September 2002, amended on 10 June 2004, 28 July 2004, 11 February 2005. See also UN Doc S/2006/898 (16 November 2006).

174 Similar to the ICTY Completion Strategy, the OHR-ICTY Joint Conclusions stated that the WCC should be established within the Court of BiH, operating under the laws of the state and that it should involve a temporary international component. *See* ICTY Press Release of 21 February 2003, OHR/P.I.S./731e.

175 ICTY Press Release, 21 February 2003, OHR/P.I.S./731e.

176 UNSC Res 1503 (28 August 2003) UN Doc S/RES/1503, pp 2–3.

177 Published in the "Official Gazette of Bosnia and Herzegovina," 61/04, as amended in 2006. See Law on the Amendment to the Law on Transfer of Cases from the ICTY to the Prosecutor's Office of BiH and the use of evidence collected by the ICTY in proceedings before the courts in BiH ("Official Gazette of Bosnia and Herzegovina," 53/06).

exchange, namely ICTY evidence and documents used by the WCC,[178] although the WCC would not be subject to the UNSC oversight.[179] In 2005, the WCC became operational with temporary international staff to support local capacity building and transition into a purely domestically operated Court.[180] International staff was phased out after five years and financial responsibility transferred to the national budget.[181] To foster mutual cooperation and support national prosecutions, a MOU between the ICTY and BiH was signed in September 2005 stipulating mutual cooperation, including for requests of assistance, and access to documents.[182]

2.2.1.2 SERBIA: THE WCC OF THE BELGRADE DISTRICT COURT[183]

In July 2003, the WCC of the Belgrade District Court was established after the Serbian Parliament passed a law enabling the national prosecution of war crimes.[184] This was the product of negotiations among the Organization for Security and Cooperation in Europe (OSCE), International Bar Association (IBA), United States, and Serbia, which was prompted through an OSCE visit in April 2003 during which Serbia declared its willingness to draft a new war crimes law establishing the WCC.[185] The first Serbian draft law was reviewed by the IBA, followed by consultations with Serbia, the United States, the OSCE, and NGOs.[186]

In October 2003, the OSCE Mission to Serbia and Montenegro devised a strategy to support national capacity building and launched a parallel Selected Trial Monitoring

[178] Law on the transfer of cases from the ICTY to the Prosecutor's Office of BiH and the use of evidence collected by the ICTY in proceedings before the courts in Bosnia and Herzegovina, ("Official Gazette of Bosnia and Herzegovina," 61/04), art 8.

[179] M Cherif Bassiouni, *Crimes against Humanity: Historical Evolution and Contemporary Application* (CUP 2011) 230.

[180] ibid 231; "Press Release: OHR-ICTY Working Group on Development of BiH Capacity for War-Crimes Trial Successfully Completed" (*United Nations Mechanism for International Criminal Tribunals*, 21 February 2003).

[181] Law on Court of BiH ("Official Gazette" of Bosnia and Herzegovina, 29/00, 16/02, 24/02, 3/03, 37/03, 42/03, 4/04, 9/04, 35/04, 61/04), art 65. See also Ivanišević (n 167) 23; M Fischer, "Transitional Justice: Lessons from the Western Balkans" (2016) Berghof Foundation, 5.

[182] Memorandum of Understanding between the Office of the Prosecutor of the International Criminal Tribunal for the Former Yugoslavia and the Special Department for War Crimes of the Prosecutor's Office of Bosnia and Herzegovina, 2 September 2005.

[183] Described as a "domestic war crimes tribunal," established with support and assistance from the international community, including the UN. *See* Bogdan Ivanisevic and Jennifer Than, "Justice at Risk: War Crimes Trials in Croatia, Bosnia and Herzegovina, and Serbia and Montenegro" (*Human Rights Watch*) 13 October 2004 <https://www.hrw.org/report/2004/10/13/justice-risk/war-crimes-trials-croatia-bosnia-and-herzegovina-and-serbia-and> accessed January 21, 2019; and "specialized structures" within the domestic legal system to deal with war crimes (B Ivanišević, "Against the Current: War Crimes Prosecutions in Serbia" (2007) International Center for Transitional Justice 1).

[184] Law on Organization and Jurisdiction of Government Authorities in Prosecuting Perpetrators of War Crimes (Official Gazette of the Republic of Serbia No 67/2003, 135/2004, 61/2005, 101/2007, and 104/2009). See also Ivanišević (n 183) 2.

[185] MS Ellis, "Coming to Terms with Its Past—Serbia's New Court for the Prosecution of War Crimes" (2004) 22 Berkeley Intl L 165, 168.

[186] ibid 167.

Project, with the ICTY playing an important role in this regard.[187] The WCC entered into a relationship with the ICTY pursuant to Rule 11*bis*.[188] The ICTY ensured the training of staff, judges, and prosecutors, and provided technical assistance and access to evidence.[189]

In 2004, the Serbian War Crimes law was amended to allow for the use of ICTY evidence in domestic criminal proceedings.[190] Although the WCC receives a significant portion of its funding from the international community, particularly the United States, it does not incorporate international judges or personnel even in an advisory capacity.[191]

2.2.1.3 CROATIA: THE WCCS IN ZAGREB, OSIJEK, RIJEKA, AND SPLIT

In October 2003,[192] Croatia passed its implementing legislation regarding the ICC, war crimes, and IHL crimes.[193] This law also established new war chambers in Zagreb, Osijek, Rijeka, and Split.[194] In terms of substantive law, the WCCs' jurisdiction would include the ICC Statute's core crimes.[195] The investigations would be carried out by special investigation departments composed of judges experienced in serious and complex crimes.[196] Croatia's law also does not affect the implementation of international regulations related to the work of the ICTY and any cooperation with it.[197]

The ICTY helped prepare the framework for transfer of its cases to Croatia as part of its Completion Strategy pursuant to Rule 11*bis*. The ICTY's Office of the Prosecution

[187] OSCE Mission to Serbia and Montenegro, "War Crimes before Domestic Courts: OSCE Monitoring and empowering of the domestic courts to deal with War Crimes" Belgrade, October 2003.

[188] Ivanišević (n 183) 26. See also Sarah Williams, *Hybrid and Internationalised Criminal Tribunals: Selected Jurisdictional Issues* (Hart 2012) 140, who points out that, as of 2012, only one case had been referred from the ICTY to the WCC (*Prosecutor v. Kovacevic* (Decision on Referral of Case Pursuant to Rule 11*bis)* ICTY-01-42/2-1 (17 November 2006)).

[189] Memorandum of Understanding on Access to Documents through the Electronic Disclosure Suite between the Office of the Prosecutor of the ICTY and the Office of the War Crimes Prosecutor of the Republic of Serbia, reprinted in Center for Transitional Processes (Belgrade), *Justice in Transition*, September 2006 (Special Edition), 152–53.

[190] Law Amending the Law on the Organization and Competences of the State Organs in the Proceedings against the Perpetrators of War Crimes, December 21, 2004, Official Gazette of the Republic of Serbia, no 135/04, art 7 (introduces art 14(a), para 4).

[191] Williams (n 188) 139–40.

[192] The WCCs in Zagreb, Osijek, Rijeka and Split are described as domestic war crimes chambers, established with support and assistance from the international community, including the UN. See Bogdan Ivanisevic and Jennifer Than, "Justice at Risk: War Crimes Trials in Croatia, Bosnia and Herzegovina, and Serbia and Montenegro" (*Human Rights Watch*) 13 October 2004 <https://www.hrw.org/report/2004/10/13/justice-risk/war-crimes-trials-croatia-bosnia-and-herzegovina-and-serbia-and> accessed January 21, 2019; "Development of the Local Judiciaries" (*United Nations Mechanism for International Criminal Tribunals*) <http://www.icty.org/en/outreach/capacity-building/development-local-judiciaries> accessed January 21, 2019.

[193] Law on the Application of the Statute of the International Criminal Court and the Prosecution of Criminal Acts against the International Law of War and International Humanitarian Law, 2003, art 1.

[194] ibid art 12(1). [195] ibid arts 1–2. [196] ibid art 13. [197] ibid art 46.

(OTP) cooperated with the Croatian County Courts by providing investigative materials for the local prosecution of war crimes cases.[198]

2.2.2 *Serbia and Kosovo: The KSC*

A far more remote relationship also exists between the UN and the Kosovo Specialist Chambers (KSC). In 2008, the ICTY Prosecutor made allegations of organ trafficking of ethnic Serbs in the 1999 Kosovo crisis,[199] which was followed by the Council of Europe's comprehensive report.[200] The KSC was established under the auspices of the European Union, within the framework of UNSC Resolution 1244.[201] In 2015, Kosovo passed Law No. 05/L-053 on the Specialist Chambers and Specialist Prosecutor's Office, which envisages a role for the ICTY in supporting the KSC work through information sharing, with ICTY evidence being admissible in KSC proceedings.[202] The law partly incorporates the ICC provision on war crimes—specifically those against UN peacekeeping or humanitarian assistance operations or affecting the UN flag, uniform, or insignia.[203] In terms of composition, the KSC is operated entirely by international staff although it may be characterized as an "internationalised domestic court" in matters of legal form, established by domestic law.[204]

3 Conclusion

As demonstrated, the UN has made a unique contribution to the development of international criminal justice. The UN's impact has in fact been mostly on the institutional level, particularly in terms of genesis, establishment, and functioning of international and hybrid criminal courts. But the UN has also shaped, varyingly, the procedural and substantive law of the aforementioned courts.

Starting with the first to be established—the ad hoc tribunals—the UNSC, acting under Chapter VII, adopted their statutes following the UNSG's submission of draft statutes as a result of his consultations with member states, IGOs, and experts. The UN's role here was unprecedented for two reasons. First, it set up the twentieth century's first *truly* international criminal tribunals (Nuremberg and Tokyo were military tribunals

[198] OSCE Mission to Croatia, "Background Report on Domestic War Crimes Prosecutions, Transfers of ICTY Proceedings and Missing Persons," 12 August 2005, p 1.

[199] *See* Marija Ristic, "From Kosovo's Organ-Harvesting Controversy to Special Court" (*Balkan Transitional Justice*, 21 January 2011) <http://www.balkaninsight.com/en/article/timeline-kosovo-organ-harvesting>.

[200] Council of Europe, Parliamentary Assembly, Committee on Legal Affairs and Human Rights: "Inhuman treatment of people and illicit trafficking in human organs in Kosovo," Report, Dick Marty, Doc 12462 (7 January 2011).

[201] UNSC Res 1244 (10 June 1999) UN Doc S/RES/1244.

[202] Law No 05/L-053 on Specialist Chambers and Specialist Prosecutor's Office (3 August 2015), art 37.

[203] ibid art 14(1)(b)(iii) (vii) and 14(1)(d)(iii).

[204] See: Robert Muharremi, "The Kosovo Specialist Chambers and Specialist Prosecutor's Office" (*ASIL Insights*, 26 May 2016).

set up by and composed of WWII victors). Secondly, the UN played a holistic and exhaustive role in drawing up and adopting the ICTY and ICTR Statutes, which included provisions on both their composition and jurisdiction. These tribunals were, further, fully managed by the UN. To a lesser extent, the same could be said of the SPSC.

Moving to the hybrid criminal courts, we see that the UNSC and the UNSG have proven pivotal in their creation. On the one hand, there are the ECCC, SCSL, and STL, where the UN served as a bilateral treaty-making forum for the negotiation and conclusion of UN-member states' agreements in response to national authorities' requests for assistance. Were it not for the UN's diplomatic gravitas, these courts would not have materialized as such. Since their substantive law has a strong national foundation, the UN's contribution has been more limited: relying, for the purpose of co-drafting their statute, mainly on its experience with the establishment of the ad hoc tribunals. On the other hand, there are those domestic courts internationalized through the UN for varying time periods to enhance national judicial capacity building to prosecute international crimes. The ICTY, through its completion strategy and rule 11*bis*, paved the way for the establishment of the WCCs, although the UN contribution has been limited to evidence and information exchange with those courts.

Last but not least, there is the ICC. Here, the UN served as the multilateral treaty-making body par excellence for half a century, starting with the 1948 Genocide Convention and continuing with the process leading to the adoption of the ICC Statute. First prepared by the ILC, then negotiated under UN auspices in the Ad Hoc Committee and the PrepCom in the 1990s by states, IGOS, and NGOs, and finally adopted at the 1998 Rome Conference, the ICC Statute created a complex institutional and jurisdictional relationship with the UN while remaining an independent permanent body. Institutionally, that relationship has consisted of cooperation and judicial assistance, dispute settlement functions, attribution of treaty functions to the UNSG, and links over budget and finance. Jurisdictionally, this has involved Chapter VII referrals and deferrals and jurisdiction over a range of crimes similar to those dealt with by other UN-created tribunals. Based initially on the ICC Statute, and then elaborated through the Relationship Agreement, the UN-ICC relationship has also gone as far as the ICC deciding to comply administratively with the UN common system.

These experiences have overlapped with each other—and relied on or inspired each other—as the creation of each institution required years of negotiations both intra-UN as well as between the UN and states. Either way, since the first reference to an international criminal court in the Genocide Convention, the role of the UN has remained pivotal in the creation of most international and hybrid criminal courts. While more recently a number of criminal courts have been—or are being—set up without any significant UN involvement,[205] the UN experience and its lessons learned will no doubt be of use to them.

[205] See eg the Extraordinary African Chambers, Senegal, regarding former Chadian president, Hissène Habré; the Iraqi Special Tribunal, regarding former Iraqi president Saddam Hussein and his military and civilian entourage; the International Crimes Division, Uganda; and the International Crimes Tribunal, Bangladesh, regarding the post-independence situation from Pakistan.

D. INTERNATIONAL LAW

CHAPTER 24A

LAW OF TREATIES

MALGOSIA FITZMAURICE

MUCH of the development of the law of treaties has taken place under the auspices of the United Nations International Law Commission (ILC). Its dual function is defined by Article 13 of the UN Charter, in which the General Assembly is given the task of encouraging "the progressive development of international law and its codification." Article 18 of the Statute of the ILC defines its role as being "to survey the whole field of international law with a view to selecting topics for codification." The ILC has a holistic vision of international law, which is indispensable in such an over-compassing work as the codification of the law of treaties in its entirety. It involves not only in-depth knowledge of the law of treaties but also international law in general.[1] The 34 members of the ILC represent various legal systems, which especially in the realm of the law of treaties, contribute to a better understanding of various approaches to the law of treaties. It is hard to imagine any other entity being able to draft a document such as the three Vienna Conventions on the law of treaties; this is in part due to its functions and its expertise, but also to the universal membership of the United Nations to which the ILC reports.

This chapter will deal with all law of treaties codifications that were completed within the International Law Commission, thus under the aegis of the United Nations.

[1] On November 21, 1947, the United Nations General Assembly passed Resolution 174, which provided for the creation of an "International Law Commission" in order to fulfil the obligations under Article 13 of the UN Charter. To the resolution was attached the statute of the Commission, which defined its purposes as being: promoting the codification of international law, and solving problems within both public and private international law. Article 15 of Statute of the ILC defines progressive development as meaning preparation of a draft convention on subjects that have not yet been regulated by international law or in regard to which the law has not been sufficiently developed in the practice of States. Codification is meant as a more precise formulation and systematization of rules of public international law where there has already been extensive states' practice, precedents, and doctrine. Its membership has increased from its original 15 members under to its present number of 34 under UNGA Resolution 36/39 of 18 November 1981 "to reflect the ever-widening range of States becoming members of the international community." Sir Arthur Watts, "Codification and Progressive Development of International Law" Max Planck Encyclopaedia of Public International Law <http://opil.ouplaw.com/view/10.1093/law:epil/9780199231690/law-9780199231690-e1380?prd=EPIL> accessed April 17, 2018.

This chapter will analyze the three Vienna Conventions—the 1969 Vienna Convention on the Law of Treaties (1969 VCLT), the 1986 Vienna Convention on the Law of Treaties between States and International Organizations or between International Organizations[2] (1986 VCLTIO), and the 1978 Vienna Convention on Succession of States in respect of Treaties (1978 VCSST)[3]—as well as the 2011 the Guide to Practice on Reservations to Treaties (Reservations Guide),[4] the Draft Articles on Effects of Armed Conflicts on Treaties[5], and Subsequent Agreements and Subsequent Practice in Relation to Treaty Interpretation.[6]

The Preamble to the Charter of the United Nations includes as one of the aims of the UN "to establish conditions under which justice and respect for the obligations arising from treaties and other sources of international law can be maintained." In the Declaration of the High-level Meeting on the Rule of Law, member states reaffirmed that states shall abide by all their obligations under international law (para. 37). The Legal (Sixth) Committee is the primary forum for the consideration of legal questions in the General Assembly. All of the United Nations member states are entitled to representation on the Sixth Committee as one of the main committees of the General Assembly. Through the work of the International Law Commission, the UN system supports the codification of international law and its progressive development (Article 13 of the Charter). The Commission was commended in the Declaration of the High-level Meeting on the Rule of Law (para. 33). The United Nations as a universal organization is the best forum to codify the law of treaties where states represent all legal systems of the world and can exchange views at the forum of the Sixth Committee. Political organs of the United Nations also contribute to development of the lawmaking. Dame Rosalyn Higgins, the former President of the ICJ, has said even 'the political bodies of international organizations are a relevant forum in which to search for acknowledged sources of law, namely treaties and customs; and further, that the United Nations provides a comparatively sharply focused forum for state practice by United Nations Members; and that United Nations organs, in their day-to-day work, necessarily contribute to the clarification and creation of law.[7]

[2] The 1986 Vienna Convention on the Law of Treaties between States and International Organizations or between International Organizations 25 ILM 543, not yet in force.

[3] The 1978 Vienna Convention on Succession of States in Respect of Treaties 1946 UNTS 3, entered into force 6 November 1996.

[4] The 2011 Guide to Practice on Reservations to Treaties, sixty-third session (26 April–3 June and 4 July–12 August 2011) General Assembly Official Records sixty-sixth Session Supplement No. 10, available at <http://legal.un.org/ilc/reports/2011/english/addendum.pdf> last accessed April 18, 2018.

[5] At its 3116th to 3117th meetings, held on August 2 and 3, 2011, the Commission adopted the commentaries to the aforementioned draft articles. First Special Rapporteur Sir Ian Brownlie; Second Special Rapporteur Professor Lucius Caflisch.

[6] At its 70th session, the ILC adopted 13 Draft Conclusions on Subsequent Agreements and Subsequent Practice in Relation to Treaty Interpretation. See Special Rapporteur Professor Georg Nolte, UN Doc A/CN.4/L917/Add.1 (2018).

[7] Rosalyn Higgins, "The United Nations and Lawmaking: The Political Organs" (1970) 64 ASIL Proceedings 37, 38.

1 The 1969 Vienna Convention on Treaties

The 1969 VCLT is generally thought of as the most important achievement of the ILC to date: its "prime" achievement.[8] The law of treaties was one of the topics selected by the ILC at its very first session in 1949 as being suitable for codification. Despite the well-entrenched rules of customary international law, there were certain areas that required clarification.[9] The ILC took approximately 15 years to complete the draft of the 1969 Convention. Brierly,[10] Lauterpacht,[11] Fitzmaurice,[12] and Waldock[13] were appointed by the ILC as Special Rapporteurs on the subject, with Waldock also serving as the Expert Consultant at the United Nations Vienna Conference on the Law of Treaties. Initially the ILC's approach was to codify the law of treaties in a form of an expository code, which in particular was the view of Fitzmaurice during his term as a Special Rapporteur. Such a code was conceived as primarily exhortatory or descriptive. This approach was due in in particular to the ILC's difficulty in embodying in a multilateral treaty a set of provisions on the law of treaties that was essentially part of customary international law, which would be the basis for the force and effect of such a multilateral treaty on the subject.[14] In 1961, the ILC changed its approach and decided to prepare a set of draft articles on the law of treaties that could serve as a basis for the convention.[15]

The ILC made the following statement to explain its new approach:

> First, an expository code, however well formulated, cannot in the nature of the things be so effective as a convention for consolidating the law; and the consolidation of the law of treaties is of particular importance at the present time when so many new States have recently become members of the international community. Secondly, the codification of the law of treaties through a multilateral convention would give all the new States the opportunity to participate directly in the formulation of law if they so wished; and their participation in the work of the codification appears to the Commission to be extremely desirable in order that the law of treaties may be placed upon the widest and more secure foundations.[16]

[8] Anthony Aust, "Vienna Convention on the Law of Treaties" Max Planck Encyclopaedia of Public International Law <http://opil.ouplaw.com/view/10.1093/law:epil/9780199231690/law-9780199231690-e1498> accessed April 17, 2017.

[9] ibid. [10] J Brierly Reports: 1950–1952.

[11] Lauterpacht Reports: 1953–1954. [12] Fitzmaurice Reports: 1956–1960.

[13] Waldock Reports: 1962–1966.

[14] Ybk ILC (11th session, 1959), vol II, p 91, para 18. Cited in Sir Arthur Watts, *The International Law Commission 1949–1998*, Volume Two: The Treaties, Part Two (first published 1999, OUP 2007) 611.

[15] Ybk ILC (13th session, 1961), vol I, pp 247–58 and vol II, p 128; see also Ybk ILC (14th session, 1962), vol II, p 160, para 17, cited in Watts (n 14) 611.

[16] Ybk ILC (14th session, 1962, vol II, p 160, para 17, cited in Watts (n 14) 611.

The new approach to drafting the law of treaties resulted in the ILC having been able to complete its draft article at its eighteenth session in 1966.[17] These articles were the basis for the UN conference held in Vienna in 1968 and 1969, convened on the basis of the December 1967 UN GA Resolution 2287 (XXII). The diplomatic conference adopted the 1969 VCLT based largely on the ILC Draft Articles. It is widely accepted that many of the provisions of the 1969 VCLT have been viewed as representing preexisting customary international law before the Convention's entry into force, in relation to states not formally bound by the Convention, or in relation to treaties concluded before its entry into force (not within the scope of the 1969 VCLT). It was also presumed that after the passage of time, the Convention's provisions will acquire the force of customary international law.[18] The entry into force of the 1969 Convention took quite a long time. There were various reasons for this. One such reason may have been the lack of the Convention's applicability to treaties concluded beforehand.[19]

The 1969 VCLT was not meant to encompass all issues pertaining to the law of treaties, and there are several treaties that have been excluded from its scope, such as:

(i) agreements with and between international organizations (The 1986 Vienna Convention on the Law of Treaties between States and International Organizations or between International Organizations);
(ii) oral or tacit agreements;
(iii) effects on treaties of succession (The 1978 Vienna Convention on Succession of States in Respect of Treaties);
(iv) effect on treaties of the outbreak of hostilities (Article 73 of the 1969 VCLT and 2011 Draft articles on the effects of armed conflicts on treaties, with commentaries 2011[20]);
(v) the question of state responsibility (Article 73 of the 1969 VCLT and 2001 Articles on Responsibility of States for Internationally Wrongful Acts 2001[21]);[22]
(viii) the application of treaties providing for obligations or rights to be performed or enjoyed by individuals; and
(ix) treaties that were concluded before the date of the entry into force of the 1969 VCLT (Article 4: no retrospective effect principle).

It was suggested that Articles that could be classified as "progressive development" concerned those relating to (1) the adoption of a treaty texts at international conferences

[17] Ybk ILC (18th session, 1966, vol II, p 177, reproduced in Watts (n 14) 619.

[18] Watts (n 13) 611–12. [19] Watts (n 14) 612.

[20] Adopted by the International Law Commission at its sixty-third session, in 2011, and submitted to the General Assembly as a part of the Commission's report covering the work of that session (UN Doc A/66/10). Ybk ILC 2011, vol II, part 2.

[21] Text adopted by the Commission at its fifty-third session, in 2001, and submitted to the General Assembly, formed a part of the Commission's report covering the whole work of that session. Ybk ILC 2001, vol II, part 2.

[22] Ybk ILC (16th session, 1964), vol II, p 176, para 21.

by a vote of two-thirds present and voting (Article 9 of the 1969 VCLT), (2) the obligation to refrain from frustrating the objects of a proposed treaty pending negotiations (Article 15 (a) of the ILC Draft Articles-rejected by the Diplomatic Conference), (3) the provisions on reservations (Articles 19–23 of the 1969 VCLT, which rejected the classical unanimity principle and followed the Advisory Opinions on Reservations to Genocide Convention flexible approach[23]), (4) the amendment and inter se modification of multilateral treaties (Article 40 and 41 of the 1969 VCLT), and (5) certain grounds of invalidity, termination, and suspension of the operation treaties (Part V of the 1969 VCLT), including the notion that the treaty is void if, when concluded, it conflicts with a norm of jus cogens. The concept of jus cogens (Article 53 of the 2969 VCLT) was the embodiment of the progressive development of international law contained in the 1969 VCLT.[24]

By Resolution 2287 (XXII) of 6 December 1967, the General Assembly convened the first session of the UN Conference on the Law of Treaties at Vienna in March 1968 in Vienna from March 26 to May 24 1968 with participation of representatives of 103 countries and observers from 13 specialized and intergovernmental agencies. The second session was held from April 9 to May 22, 1969, also at Vienna, and with the attendance of representatives of 110 countries and observers from 14 specialized and intergovernmental agencies. The subject matter of the first session of the Conference was primarily a consideration by a Committee of the Whole and by a Drafting Committee of the set of draft articles adopted by the ILC. The first part of the second session was focused on meetings of the Committee of the Whole and of the Drafting Committee, completing their consideration of articles left from the previous session. The remainder of the second session was conducted in 30 plenary meetings that considered the articles adopted by the Committee of the Whole and reviewed by the Drafting Committee.[25]

At present it may be said that substantive provisions of the 1969 VCLT are part and parcel of customary international law. International courts and tribunals, in particular the International Court of Justice (ICJ), frequently rely on the 1969 VCLT as codifying custom—a position endorsed by the ICJ itself.[26] The ICJ has relied on Article 62 (fundamental change of circumstances)[27] and Article 60 (material breach of a treaty);[28] in the *Gabcikovo-Nagymaros* case it analyzed Articles 60, 61, and 62. The approach of the

[23] *Reservations to the Convention on Genocide* (Advisory Opinion) [1951] ICJ Rep 15.

[24] Watts (n 14) 613; Sir Ian Sinclair, *The Vienna Convention on Treaties* (2nd edn, Manchester University Press 1984) 12–18.

[25] <http://legal.un.org/diplomaticconferences/lawoftreaties-1969/lawoftreaties-1969.html> accessed May 20, 2017.

[26] The best example is *Kasikili/Sedudu Islands Case (Botswana/Namibia)*, in which the ICJ interpreted and applied the Heligoland-Zanzibar Treaty of 1890 between the United Kingdom and Germany in accordance with the rules in Articles 31 and 32 VCLT, despite the Article 4 VCLT rule against retrospection. Most importantly neither of the states was a party to the 1969 VCLT [1999] ICJ Rep 1045 para 18.

[27] *Fisheries Jurisdiction case (Iceland v United Kingdom)* [1973] ICJ Rep 3, para 36.

[28] *Legal Consequences for States of the Continued Presence of South Africa in Namibia* (Advisory Opinion) [1971] ICJ Rep 9, para 94.

ICJ in respect of procedural provisions—whether they are declaratory of customary international law or still constitute progressive development—remains not fully clarified as in the 1997 *Gabcikovo-Nagymaros Project*, in which the ICJ stated that Articles 65 to 67 have been accepted as "at least generally reflect[ing] customary international law and contain[ing] procedural principles which are based on an obligation of to act in good faith."[29]

However, in the 2006 *Democratic Republic of Congo v Rwanda* case the ICJ stated that:

> Thus in the present case the rules contained in the Vienna Convention are not applicable, save in so far as they are declaratory of customary international law. The Court considers that the rules contained in Article 66 of the Vienna Convention are not of this character. Nor have the two Parties otherwise agreed to apply Article 66 between themselves.[30]

The question of an interplay between the substantive and procedural provisions of the 1969 VCLT was raised in the in the 2016 arbitration between Croatia and Slovenia.[31] In this case the material breach of a treaty (Article 60, substantive provision) was analyzed together with Articles 65(4) and 66 (procedural provisions). The parties to the dispute have not challenged the normative character of procedural rules and analyzed in particular the content of Article 65(4),[32] which was of a fundamental importance for the case as reliance on it permitted continuing jurisdiction of the Arbitral Tribunal (paras. 166–167).

The 1969 VCLT is a living instrument, and its succinct provisions have been developed and fleshed out by the judicial practice of international courts and tribunals. The example is the evolution of the definition of a treaty, which has been defined by the 1969 VCLT in the following manner

> '1. For the purposes of the present Convention:
>
> (a) "Treaty" means an international agreement concluded between States in written form and governed by international law, whether embodied in a single instrument or in two or more related instruments and whatever its particular designation' (Article 2 (a). It may be said that for an agreement to constitute a treaty, not only must international law (as opposed to any other legal system) be applicable to it, but international law must also designate the agreement as one that is legally binding on the parties (as opposed to an agreement which is morally binding or political in nature). Numerous courts and arbitral tribunals fleshed out further what constitutes

[29] *Gabcikovo-Nagymaros Project (Hungary v Slovakia)* [1997] ICJ Rep 7, para 99.

[30] *Armed Activities on the Territory of the Congo (New Application: 2002) (Democratic Republic of the Congo v Rwanda)* (Jurisdiction and Admissibility) (Judgment) [2006] ICJ Rep 6, para 125.

[31] *In the Matter of and Arbitration under the Arbitration Agreement between the Government of the Republic of Croatia and the Government of the3 Republic of Slovenia, signed on 4 November 2009* (Partial Award) 30 June 2016, <https://pcacases.com/web/sendAttach/1787> accessed April 18, 2017.

[32] Art 60(4): "nothing in in the foregoing paragraphs shall affect rights or obligations of the parties under nay provision in force binding the parties with regard to the settlement of disputes."

an international treaty from the points of its substance and form, and their findings have become an indispensable part of the definition of a treaty'.[33]

The 1969 VCLT was frequently relied upon by the Court of Justice of European Union (CJEU).[34] At first blush, the application of the 1969 VCLT may appear to follow closely its provisions. However, a detailed reading evidences that there are several deviations from the application of provisions of the 1969 VCLT by the CJEU.[35] There are several examples of the different practice of the CJEU, such as favoring the notion of the "object and purpose" of the treaty (teleological interpretation) in applying Article 31 1969 VCLT over other methods of treaty interpretation, such as subsequent practice.[36] Another example is the definition of a treaty. The CJEU approach is "broad and non-formalistic and is arguably wider than that under international law."[37] Such approach by the CJEU to the 1969 VCLT was criticized for a variety of reasons, such as undermining international law and contributing to the fragmentation of international law. It was suggested that the CJEU is entitled to develop an autonomous meaning of certain terms.

The 1969 VCLT is without doubt one of the greatest achievements of the ILC. The judicial practice and the practice of states evidence its lasting importance. Its flexibility and the largely residual character of its provisions contributed to its staying power. However, it must be also mentioned that there are views that the 1969 VCLT had its day and that it is "incapable of coping with the demands of the twenty-first century."[38] However, international practitioners, who approach the 1969 VCLT as their "Bible," do not adhere to this view and do not think that it needs any amendments.[39] One practitioner writes: "[i]t has proved itself to be a most adaptable tool, well able to deal with the challenges to treaty-making presented by the many changes in international life. In short, the VCLT is widely regarded by those who have to draft, negotiate, and otherwise deal with treaties, as a sensible and practical guide."[40]

[33] See eg *Aegean Sea Continental Shell* case (*Greece v Turkey*) (Jurisdiction) [1978] ICJ Rep 4, paras 101–108; *Maritime Delimitation and Territorial Questions between Qatar and Bahrain (Qatar v, Bahrain)* (Jurisdiction and Admissibility) [1994] ICJ Rep 112, paras 21–30; *Dispute concerning delimitation of the maritime boundary between Bangladesh and Myanmar in the Bay of Bengal (Bangladesh/Myanmar)* <https://www.itlos.org/en/cases/list-of-cases/case-no-16/>; *Case Concerning the Land and Maritime Boundary between Cameroon and Nigeria (Cameroon v Nigeria; Equatorial Guinea Intervening)* (Judgment) (10 October 2002), para 265; *Maritime Delimitation in the Indian Ocean (Somalia v Kenya)* (Preliminary Objections), (Judgment) 2 February 2017 <http://www.icj-cij.org/docket/files/161/19330.pdf> (paras 31–106) accessed April 18, 2018.

[34] Jed Odermatt, "The Use of International Treaty Law by the Court of Justice of the European Union" (2015) 17 Cambridge Ybk European Legal Studies 121–44. The Court has rejected the application of the 1969 VCLT to EU's founding treaties, due to their special character: *SP SpA et al v Commission, Joined Cases T-27/03, T-46/03, T-58/03, T79/03, T-80/03, T-97/03 and T-98/03, EU:T:2007*, para 78. The Court, however, has applied the provisions of the 1069 VCLT insofar as they reflect customary international law: *Brita v Hauptzollamt Hamburg Hafen, C-386/08 EU:C2010:91* para 42. Odermatt (n 34), 122.

[35] Odermatt (n 34) 122. [36] ibid 122. [37] ibid 126.

[38] Aust (n 7), para 5. [39] ibid. [40] ibid.

2 The 1979 Vienna Convention on the Succession of States in Respect of Treaties

This Convention forms part and parcel of a general subject matter of state succession.[41] It was noted that the geopolitical framework of the international community lacked stability. States disintegrate, new states emerge, states merge (one state replaces two or more states), and states lose territory to other states (resulting in the former state becoming smaller and the latter larger). The questions that result from these changes require responses as to whether and to what extent the applicability of original state(s)' rights and obligations continues, and whether (and to what extent) they are passed on a new state(s). This complex problem has been very difficult to deal with by international law due to the inherent complexity of the question of succession, which has to consider two sets of variables: the varied kinds of situations of succession that resulted from political circumstances, and the differing categories or rights and obligations that are influenced by these circumstances. As each and every situation has different legal features, it is difficult, if not impossible, to draw some general rules.[42]

There are several identified factors that contribute to the lack of certainty in the area of succession of states in respect of treaties. The questions of succession are highly political—whether a state is bound by legal obligations following succession depends to a large degree on the recognition of the position of a successor state by other states.[43] There is also a marked lack of the relevant practice. The most significant factor is, at least to a certain extent, the "ideology driven attempt at codifying the law"[44] that resulted in the 1979 VCSST.

The theories of succession of states in respect of treaties does not reflect the practice, which "yields a sampling of contradictions and inconsistencies, and underscores the unique complexity of the problems of state succession."[45]

The Convention is divided in seven parts: Part I, Articles 1–14 (general provisions); Part II, Article 15 (special category of succession in respect of part of territory); Part

[41] On state succession, see Giovanni Distefano, Aymeric Hêche, Oxford Bibliographies, <http://www.oxfordbibliographies.com/view/document/obo-9780199796953/obo-9780199796953-0045.xml> accessed April 18, 2018, which includes all publications on the subject. On the VCSST see in particular: Zidane Meriboute, *La Codification de la succession d'Etats aux traités—Décolonisation, sécession, unification* (Graduate Institute Geneva Publications, 1984); Gerhard Hafner and Gregor Novak, "State Succession in Respect of Treaties" in Duncan B Hollis (ed), *The Oxford Guide to Treaties* (OUP 2012) 396; Distefano (n10).

[42] Hafner and Novak (n 42) 396.

[43] Andreas Zimmermann and James G Devaney, "Succession to Treaties and the Inherent Limits of International Law" in Christian J Tams, Antonios Tzanakopoulos, and Andreas Zimmermann, with Anthea E Richford (eds), *Research Handbook on the Law of Treaties* (Edward Elgar 2014) 507.

[44] ibid 507.

[45] Matthew G Maloney, "Succession of States in Respect of Treaties: The Vienna Convention of 1978" (1979) 19 Virginia J Intl Law 885, 895.

III, Articles 16–24 (succession of newly independent states); Part IV, Articles 30–38 (uniting and separating of states); Part V, Articles 39–40 (miscellaneous provisions); Part VI, Articles 41–46 (procedures for settlement of disputes); Part VII, Articles 46–50 (final provisions).

Article 2(1)(b) of the VCSST defines succession as "the replacement of one state by another in the responsibility for the international relations of territory."

The ILC had decided that the best way is not to focus on the succession of the governments but rather that a priority should be accorded to the succession in respect of treaties.[46]

State succession in respect to treaties is one of the most contentious and complex areas of the law of treaties and state practice. It has to be said that the VCSST has not solved the legal questions relating to the succession to treaties. In 1967, the ILC had begun work on the subject of succession of states in respect of treaties. The second session of the United Nations Conference on Succession of States in respect of Treaties was held at Vienna from July 31 to August 23, 1978, and resulted in the adoption of the 1978 VCSST.[47]

The ILC has particularly focused on the succession in respect of treaties by newly independent states, as the end of the colonialism era peaked in the 1960s. This controversial decision resulted in diverting the ILC's work from the more general and universal aspects of succession to treaties. The delays of entry into force of the VCSST meant that the legal questions of the succession to treaties of the newly independent states were no longer of utmost importance or topicality. Article 7(2–4) introduced the right of a successor state to make an optional declaration, applicable on a reciprocal basis in relation to other states accepting the declaration, to the effect that the Convention applies in respect of its own succession of states occurring before the entry into force of the Convention (Article 7(2–4), Temporal Application of the Present Convention). This Article attempted "to ensure the fullest vitality of the Convention's principles," but it is considered to be the most controversial provision of this Convention.[48]

The ILC has acknowledged the existence of certain (not well-defined) general principles of succession. It identified three broad categories that required separate rules: succession in respect of territory, newly independent states (limited only to former dependent territories), and uniting and separating of states. The work of the ILC has proved to be very controversial; during diplomatic conferences, there were several legal questions as to which no agreement could be reached. The ILC admitted, however, that:

> a close examination of State practice afforded no convincing evidence of any general doctrine by reference to which the various problems of succession in respect treaties

[46] Watts (n 14) 988.

[47] "Succession of States and Governments" was included on the ILC's agenda initial provisional list of 14 topics suitable for codification in 1949, and it began work on the subject matter in 1962. See ILC Reports: Waldock: 1968–1971; Vallat: 1974; Final Draft Articles, 1974.

[48] Maloney (n46 905–906. It was approved by a very narrow margin of 8-4, with five abstentions.

> could find their appropriate solution... [which] is not [made] easier by the fact that a number of different theories of succession are to be found in writings of jurists.[49]

The legal character of sizeable parts of the Convention was a progressive development not the codification of existing law: "There were 15 articles referring to new independent states in the whole text of the Convention."

In relation to succession of treaties by newly independent states, the main principle adopted by the ILC is that of a "clean slate" (with some very carefully phrased exceptions, e.g., territorial regimes). The Convention deals with succession to multilateral treaties in three different contexts: those in force at the date of succession (Article 16), these not in force at the date of succession (Article 18), and those signed by the predecessor but subject to a constitutional procedure of ratification, acceptance, and approval (Article 19). Succession to bilateral treaties is much less complex and provides that a bilateral treaty continues when a successor state and the other party either expressly agree or, through their conduct, are considered to have so agreed (Article 24).

The succession of states in respect of treaties in relation to uniting or separating of state is based on the principle of ipso jure continuity, which is embodied in Article 31 of the VCST. Article 34 (succession of states in cases of separation of parts of territory) is based on the principle of universal succession. This Article provides that when two or more states unite to form a single successor state, any treaty in force at the date of succession remains in force for any of the predecessor unless parties agree otherwise or unless succession would be incompatible with the object and purpose of the treaty. The sole Article 15 deals with the situation when a territory is added to the existing one without involving a merger or a union. This phenomenon is termed "moving treaty frontiers." In relation to territorial regimes and boundaries (Articles 11 and 12), the VCSST has adopted the principle that succession does not affect them.

The VCST has been met with varied reactions from balanced to vehemently opposing it. It may be said that the most vociferous critique of the Convention was by O'Connell:

> State succession is a subject altogether unsuited to the processes of codification, let alone of progressive development, but this particular essay in refashioning the law was marred from its inception by a preoccupation with the special problem of decolonisation, around which myth and emotions have accumulated like mists in the marsh, so that the whole context became intellectually distorted; and, furthermore, it might be said that it has come too late to serve any practical purpose in that matter.[50]

O'Connell evaluated the Convention as totally insignificant, unsophisticated, lacking any doctrinal subtlety, and "intellectually debilitating."[51] In his view, the ILC fitted into a rather inflexible and oversimplistic framework a very complex and nuanced question of

[49] Ybk ILC (26th session, 1974), vol II, part 2, 168, para 51.

[50] DPO O'Connell, "Reflections on State Succession Convention" (1979) 39 ZaöRV 725, 726.

[51] ibid 727.

succession of states in respect to treaties. The theory of the "clean slate" have been used in cases of decolonization as a result of "pure rhetoric" and not for reasons of jurisprudence, with numerous examples that have run counter to the "clean slate" doctrine.[52]

A more measured approach was expressed by Yasseen (a member of the ILC).[53] He was of the view that:

> La Convention de Vienne sur la succession d'Etats en matière de traités reflète, en général, la pratique internationale. Les solutions qu'elle prévoit sont conçues dans le contexte du droit des traités, mais répondent toutefois aux exigences du phénomène de la succession d'Etats.
>
> Cette Convention est appelée à être le droit commun de la succession d'Etats en matière de traités. Elle aidera certes les Etats successeurs, dans une période de transition, qui peut être difficile, à connaître clairement la portée de leurs droits et de leurs obligations. Elle épargnera surtout aux Etats nouvellement indépendants des négociations compliquées, dans des circonstances qui, souvent, ne leur sont pas favorables.[54]

The VCSST's contribution is identification of various categories of succession in respect to treaties. However, it is an undisputed fact that the process of the codification of the VCSST was a politicized exercise. Being drafted in the specific context of newly independent states, its practical importance for cases such as the breakup of the former Yugoslavia and the USSR is insignificant. It may be said that the Convention is a product of its time.[55] On reflection, it may be said that the principle of universal succession contained in Article 34 was abided by in the cases of the dissolution of a state (Yugoslavia and CSFR); it was not uniformly applied in cases of separation, such as the USSR and Eritrea. As it argued: "This confirms that when it comes to instances of separation the codification effort undertaken in 1978 by the VCSST, already then not supported by state practice, has not significantly contributed to a further deployment of customary law."[56]

The greatest difference between the VCLT 1969 and the 1978 VCSST is that the first of these Conventions deals with the daily business of states, whereas the second is only of relevance in possible instances of a state succession. A view was expressed that "states may not appreciate the benefits of ratifying a treaty codifying rules pertaining to state succession."[57] The usefulness of rules on state succession may be doubted. State succession arises in fragile and political contexts; when the importance of rules of international law is limited.[58] It also appears that both successor and third states prefer ad hoc political solutions rather than rigid and fixed rules. However, such solutions lead to further uncertainties in relation to the legal aspects of succession in respect to treaties.[59]

[52] ibid 729.
[53] Mustafa Kamil Yasseen, "La Convention de Vienne sur la succession d'Etats en matière de traités' (1978) AFDI 24, 59–113.
[54] ibid 112. [55] Zimmermann and Devaney (n 43) 509. [56] ibid 530.
[57] ibid 538. [58] ibid 538–39. [59] ibid 539.

International courts and tribunals rarely rely on the VCSST. Usually, courts rely on its provisions that are established as customary international law. In the *Gabcikovo-Nagymaros* case the ICJ stated that Article 12 reflected customary international law (non-boundary territorial regimes), and that the rule was decisive in that case as the bilateral treaty between Hungary and Slovakia had established the territorial regime within the notion of Article 12 of the VCSST. The ICJ, however, declined to take a position vis-à-vis Article 34—whether or not it was a norm of customary international law.[60]

3 1986 Vienna Convention on Treaties between States and International Organizations or between International Organizations

Sir Arthur Watts[61] once noted that the ILC was very mindful about the increasing role of international organizations; as a result "no work on the law of treaties could be regarded as complete if it did not also deal with treaties to which international organizations were parties."[62] VCLTIO has not yet entered into force.

One of the most controversial and still debated issue in the law of treaties is the question of agreements with and between international organizations, and its relationship with the 1969 VCLT. As to the first of these issues, it was debated from the outset whether to extend the scope of the Convention to include international organizations. In Brierly's First Report,[63] followed by the Reports of Lauterpacht,[64] Fitzmaurice, and Waldock,[65]

60 *Gabcikovo-Nagymaros Project (Hungary v Slovakia)* [1997] ICJ Rep 7.

61 1986 Vienna Convention on Treaties between States and International Organizations of between International Organizations (1986) 25 ILM 543, not in force. Paul Reuter, Special Rapporteur. Reports: 1972–1982; Draft Articles Ybk ILC, (34th session, 1982), vol II, part 1, 17. Signed in Vienna on 21 March 1986. See generally Neri Syberma-Knol, "The New Law of treaties: The Codification of the Law of Treaties Concluded between States and International Organizations and International Organizations" (1985) 15 Georgia JICL 425; Gorgio Gaja, "A ' New' Vienna Convention on Treaties Between States and International Organizations or between International Organizations: A Critical Commentary" (1987) 58 British Ybk Intl L 255; Mary Footer, "International Organization and Treaties: Ratification and (Non)-Implementation of *Other* Vienna Convention on Treaties" in Alexander Orakhelashvili and Sarah Williams (eds), *40 Years of the Vienna Convention on the Law of Treaties* (BICL 2010) 183; Catherine Brölmann, "International Organizations and Treaties: Contractual Freedom and Institutional Restraint" in Jan Klabbers (ed), *Research Handbook on International Organizations* (Edward Elgar 2011) 293; Catherine Brölmann, *The Institutional Veil in Public International Law: International Organizations & the Law of Treaties* (Hart 2010).

62 Watts (n 14) 614.

63 JL Brierly, First Report on the Law of Treaties (Art 1(a)) 228.

64 Lauterpacht, First Report on the Law of Treaties (Art 1) 94.

65 G Fitzmaurice, First Report on the Law of Treaties (Art 1(3)) 117; CHM Waldock, First Report on the Law of Treaties (Art 1(a)) 32.

as well as at the Vienna Diplomatic Conference,[66] it was proposed that the VCLT should extend to include international organizations. In 1950, the ILC was in favor of extending the scope of the Convention to international organizations.[67]

However, in 1962, the ILC confirmed its decision to defer examination of treaties entered into by international organizations until it had made further progress with its draft on treaties concluded by states.[68] In 1965 the ILC finally decided to limit the scope of the Draft Articles to treaties concluded between states and inserted a new article expressly providing so.[69] In 1966 the ILC expressly reaffirmed its position that "the principles set out in the draft articles are to a large extent relevant also in the case of treaties concluded between states and other subjects of international law and between two or more such other subjects of international law." Following this statement, the ILC inserted a new provision that became VCLT Article 3(c), the purpose of which was to safeguard the legal force of such agreements.[70]

As is stated in VCLT Article 1, the VCLT relates only to treaties concluded between states. However, in light of the previous Article, the formulation of 1969 VCLT Article 3(c) is not very clear and rather confusing, stating that: "The fact that the present Convention does not apply to international agreements concluded between states and other subjects of international law or between such other subjects of international law, or to international agreements..., shall not affect:...the application of the Convention to the relations of states as between themselves under international agreements to which other subjects of international law are also parties."

This Article should be read in conjunction with Article 73 of the 1986 Vienna Convention on the Law of Treaties between States and International Organizations or between International Organizations ("[a]s between states parties to the [VCLT], the relations of those states under a treaty between two or more states and one or more international organizations shall be governed by [the VCLT]"), indicates that the 1969 VCLT applies also to some extent to relationships between states and international organizations. The scope of this applicability was, however, never clearly specified.[71]

66 See the proposals of the United States and Vietnam, The Vienna Diplomatic Conference, UN Doc A/Conf.39/ll/Add.2, at 110.

67 "Report of the International Law Commission to the General Assembly on the work of its second session" (1950) II Ybk ILC, UN Doc A/1316, para 162, at 381: "A majority of the Commission were also in favour of including in its study agreements to which international organizations are parties."

68 "Report of the International Law Commission to the General Assembly on the work of its fourteenth session" (1962) vol II Ybk ILC, UN Doc A/5209, para 21 of the Introduction, at 161.

69 "Report of the International Law Commission to the General Assembly on the work of the first part of its seventeenth session" (1965) vol II Ybk ILC, UN Doc A/6009, at 159.

70 "Report of the ILC to the General Assembly on the work of the second part of its seventeenth session" (1966) vol II Ybk ILC, UN Doc A/6309/Rev.I, at 190.

71 Art 73 of the 1986 Convention on "Relationship to the Vienna Convention on the law of treaties" provides that "[a]s between States parties to the Vienna Convention on the Law of Treaties of 1969, the relations of those States under a treaty between two or more States and one or more international organizations shall be governed by that Convention." See, eg, Gaja (n 61).

Therefore, it has been said that:

> the Vienna Convention, applying specifically to treaties between States, is limited to agreements governed by international law between subjects of international law. But how the codified law applies to subjects of international law which are not States (other than, now, international intergovernmental organizations), or even how those other subjects are to be identified, are issues left completely open.[72]

The 1986 Vienna Convention evolved from the Vienna Diplomatic Conference where a resolution was adopted to request the ILC to analyze the problem of treaties between states and international organizations, or between two or more organizations.

The VCLTIO is a very curious instrument, if not paradoxical: on one hand mirroring the 1969 VCLT, and on the other trying to accommodate particular features of international organizations, as the ILC was instructed to do. As described aptly, "the new Convention would have to design rules and principles for the declaredly special treaties of organizations, but it would also . . . have to incorporate these rules in the existing law of treaties."[73] Therefore, as it was observed, a "newly adopted text gives a reader a strong feeling of *déjà vu*."[74] There were two emerging trends concerning the discussion on the Draft Convention. One trend supported the growing capacity of international organizations (a question related to autonomous will of organizations—*volonté distincte*); the other emphasized the need to respect the will of states (expressed in the constituent instruments of organizations).[75] The ILC treated the VCLTIO as an extension of the VCLT 1969, with its articles mirroring the "mother" Convention.[76] However, as Brölmann observed, the VCLTIO introduced several terminological novelties in order to distinguish between states and international organizations as subjects of the law of treaties. Such an example is Article 2 (Use of terms) on the "rules of the organization"—an expression used throughout of the Convention. This is the only new added paragraph in relation to the formulation of the 1969 VCLT.[77] Article 6 recognizes the limited capacity of international organizations to conclude a treaty that is expressed in terms "governed by the rules of that organization." This formulation introduced uncertainty as to the extent of the organizations' treaty-making power by implying that the constitution of a particular international organization will be decisive on that matter. Gaja explains that the wording of Article 2(2j)[78] is not meant to be comprehensive in character nor is it reference to "established practice" intended to be "conditional on the constitutional instrument of the organization respected."[79]

[72] Shabtai Rosenne, *Developments in the Law of Treaties 1945–1986* (CUP 1989) 22.

[73] Brölmann, "International Organizations and Treaties" (n 61) 293.

[74] Gaja (n 61) 254 [75] Footer (n 61) 187. [76] ibid.

[77] Brölmann, *The Institutional Veil* (n 61) 293. On all differences between the VCLTIO and the 1969 VCLT see Olufemi Elias, "Who Can Make Treaties? International Organizations" in Hollis (n 41) 78.

[78] According to this Article under organizational rules is understood "in particular, the constitutive instruments, decisions and resolutions adopted in accordance with them, and established practice of the organization."

[79] Gaja (n 61)262.

In the end, the approach adopted by the ILC was to draft article-by-article, which followed as closely as possible the structure and terminology of the VCLT 1969 while at the same time accommodating to some extent special features of international organizations. This required the modification of the VCLT 1969:[80] an arduous task, not entirely successful, leading to certain anomalies[81] such as the abandonment of Article 36*bis*, which was supposed to regulate the relationship between an international organization and its member states in the law of treaties. This Article was meant to deal with the situation as to rights and obligations that would flow to the members under a treaty concluded by an international organization.[82] The Article was abandoned due to the legal confusion as to its content. The inconclusive debates in the ILC on this Article were eventually focused on whether the provision was only relevant to the situation in which the European Economic Community (EEC) will find itself or whether it was of a wider application. In the end, the ILC came to the conclusion that Article 36*bis* would be incompatible with the EEC treaty-making capacity.[83]

Therefore, it may be said that the VCLTIO "is perhaps more interesting for it does not, than for what it does contain."[84] Regarding its entry into force, organizations are placed on lesser footing than states. Article 85(1) as the entry into force of the Convention depends on a number of ratifications by states.[85]

It is fair to say that the 1986 VCLTIO will probably never enter into force. States were not quite convinced that there was a need for such a convention so closely linked to the VCLT 1969 (also in light of Articles 3(c) of 1969 VCLT and 73 VCLTIO).[86] The similarity of the provisions of both conventions, coupled with the failed attempt to fully accommodate peculiarities of treaty-making of international organizations, cast a shadow of doubt on the usefulness of this Convention. The failed Article 36*bis* clearly shows the difficulties in defining the powers of international organizations in relation to treaty-making. At any rate, the majority of the provisions of the VCLTIO have become part of customary international law, so it has acquired a parallel existence.[87]

[80] ibid 293. In the course of the drafting, the ILC eliminated several topics from the scope of the VCLTIO: the effect of the outbreak of hostilities on an existing treaty obligations, the recognition of states, state responsibility, the question of most favored nation clause, and the interpretation of the UN Charter provisions.

[81] Brölmann, *The Institutional Veil* (n 61).

[82] Footer (n 61) 192.

[83] See in-depth, Brölmann, *The Institutional Veil* (n 61) 212–25; Footer (n 61) 193–94; Ian Scobie, updating El-Erian's "International Organizations and International Relations" in R-J Dupuy (ed), *Manual sur les organizations internationales/*a *handbook of international organizations* (2nd edn, 1988) part 2, 877.

[84] Brölmann, "International Organizations" (n 61) 293.

[85] Footer (n 61) 192.

[86] Article 3(c) governs the relations between state parties to a treaty to which international organizations are also parties. Prima facie it would appear that according to Article 1 of the VCLTIO, this Convention governs all relations arising from the treaties including international organizations. However, Article 73 of the VCLTIO preserves the applicability of 1969 VCLT in relation to the states in question. "This provision reflects the desire of States to preserve the application of the 1969 Vienna Convention to agreements between States and international organizations which are within the scope of the 1986 Convention," Philippe Gautier, "Article 1," in Oliver Corten and Pierre Klein (eds), *The Vienna Convention on the Law of Treaties, Commentary* (OUP 2011) vol 1, 30.

[87] Anthony Aust, *Modern Treaty Law and Practice* (3rd edn, CUP 2013).

4 Filling the Gaps

This section deals with other topics on the codification of the law of treaties that have been completed by the ILC. A Topic that remains under consideration—provisional application of treaties—will not be included.

4.1 Guide to Practice on Reservations to Treaties

The 1969 and 1986 Vienna Conventions devote six provisions to reservations: Article 2(1)(d) gives a definition of reservations for the purpose of the conventions, and Articles 19 to 23 provide general indications as to their legal regime. Due to the very obscure character of reservations under the 1969 and 1986 Conventions and gaps in this regime (concerning lack of provisions on interpretative declarations, the legal consequences of invalid reservations, and the reservations to human rights treats), coupled with inconsistent practice of states in respect of reservations,[88] the ILC decided to include the topic of "the law and practice relating to reservations to treaties" on its agenda in 1993, and subsequently appointed Professor Alain Pellet as the Special Rapporteur in 1994. Professor Pellet has submitted 17 reports and completed the process with a 630-page document "Guide to Practice on Reservations to Treaties" (the Guide), including 179 guidelines adopted by the ILC in 2011 (the Guidelines).[89] The ILC decided to adopt a form of guide rather than convention to enable the widest possible dissemination.[90] The most delicate and controversial is Guideline 4.5.3, which deals with legal consequences of invalid reservations.[91]

The core concept of reservations under the Guidelines can be summarized as follows:

> First, according to the Guide, Article 19 VCLT should be regarded as laying down objective criteria for the validity of reservations. Secondly, Articles 20–23 VCLT deal with only those reservations which are objectively valid under Article 19; they do not mention or pertain to reservations which are in fact invalid (Section 3 of the Guide and commentary). Thirdly, while states may object to reservations that they consider invalid, this is merely persuasive evidence of invalidity (Guideline 4.5.2).

[88] The idea was to adopt a non-binding instrument whose aim would only be "filling the gaps and...removing the ambiguities in the existing rules, but without embarking on their amendment" 1st Report, on the Law and Practice Relating to Reservations to Treaties, UN Doc A/CN.4/470, Ybk ILC (1995), vol II, part 1, 153, para 166.

[89] Report of the ILC on the Work of its 63rd session, GA, Official Records, 66th Session, Supplement No 10, Addendum 1, UN Doc A/66/10/Add.1, hereinafter: "Guide to Practice" or "Guide"). On Pellet's Guide see in particular: Pellet, "The ILC Guide to Practice on Reservations to Treaties: A General Presentation by the Special Rapporteur" (2013) 24 EJIL 1061.

[90] Report of the ILC on the Work of its 63rd Session, Official Records of the GA, 66th Session, Supplement N. 10, UN Doc A/66/10, at 18, para 73.

[91] Pellet (n 89) 1092.

> In fact, objections have real legal effect only if they are made against reservations which are objectively valid; the objecting state may object for any reason whatsoever, simply because it does not want to accept the modified treaty bargain that the reserving state is offering (Guideline 4.3). Fourthly, while the VCLT does not say what the consequences of an invalid reservation are, the only sensible option is to accept that such a reservation is null and void (Guideline 4.5.1). Fifthly, however, saying that an invalid reservation is a nullity does not resolve the issue of the reserving state's status as a party to the treaty. That will depend on the intention of the reserving state, which has a choice—either stay on as a party to the treaty without the benefit of the invalid reservation, or say that it no longer considers itself bound by the treaty. In the absence of a clearly expressed position in this regard, there is a rebuttable presumption that the reserving state intends to remain a party (Guideline 4.5.3).[92]

Another special feature of the Guidelines is that the Special Rapporteur and the ILC could not at the inception of the drafting accept the argument that "human rights are special." However, the ensuing years resulted in an adoption of a compromise and an acceptable solution, which emerged on the basis of a so-called "reservations dialogue"[93] with monitoring bodies of human rights treaties. The inclusion of the interrogative declarations is yet another very commendable feature of the Guidelines.

The Guide was defined in the following words:

> The 50 years that have passed since have shown us just how far Vienna was from being a comprehensive regulatory framework for reservations. This is where the Guide steps in, as essentially a Vienna-plus; nominally a non-binding instrument interpreting and elaborating on the VCLT, but in fact developing it further, filling the gaps, and building upon the wealth of actual post-Vienna treaty practice.[94]

The most remarkable feature of the Guide is its approach to the invalidity of reservation and clarification of reservations to human rights treaties, without, however, accepting any idea of speciality.[95] The Guide has imposed a general regime applying to all treaties, "but it still moves from the inter-subjective approach in which state objections are paramount, it treats invalid reservations as a nullity, and it allows them to be severed."[96]

[92] Marko Milanovic and Linos-Alexander Sicilianos, "Reservations to Treaties: An Introduction" (2013) 24 EJIL 1055, 1058.

[93] It is not a term of art in international law. "[T]he term refers to the informal exchanges that may take place between the reserving state and a state or states that have concerns about a reservation or an interpretative declaration, and may be considering reacting either bilaterally or in a wider or institutional forum. The term seems to signal that such exchanges should be regarded not so much as a "dispute" as a constructive effort to resolve differences, a "pragmatic dialogue with the author of the reservation," as the seventh preambular paragraph of the conclusions puts it: Michael Wood, "Institutional Aspects of the Guide to Practice on Reservations" (2013) 24 EJIL 1099, 1107.

[94] Milanovic and Sicilanos (n 93) 1056. [95] ibid 1058. [96] ibid.

It must be stated, however, that the "the Guide is not, at present, entirely user friendly. To become familiar with it requires considerable effort. . . . "[97]

It is difficult to foresee how and whether states and international organizations will follow the ILC Guide. If they do, it certainly would clarify murky practice of states in respect of reservations. However, as Sir Michael Wood observed: "But the somewhat cavalier attitude of many states towards reservations does not give grounds for optimism."[98]

4.2 Draft Articles on the Effects of Armed Conflicts on Treaties

Article 1 of Draft Articles mentions Article 73 of the 1969 Vienna Convention on the Law of Treaties.

Article 1 of the Draft established their scope: "The present draft articles apply to the effects of armed conflict on the relations between states under a treaty." This wording indicates that the Articles in question also cover the position of states that are not parties to an armed conflict but parties to a treaty with a state involved in the conflict. Three aspects are considered: (1) treaty relations between two states engaged in an armed conflict, on opposite sides or on the same side; (2) treaty relations between a state involved in an armed conflict with another state, and a third state not party to the conflict; and (3) the impact of a non-international armed conflict within a state on the treaty relations of that state.[99] Relations arising under treaties between international organizations or between states and international organizations are excluded from these Articles.

The Articles cover internal as well as international armed conflicts. They also relate to situations involving no armed actions, such as occupation and blockade.

The armed conflict influences not only the law of treaties but also other areas of international law. Accordingly, Part Three (Miscellaneous) includes draft Articles 14 to 18, which deal with a number of miscellaneous issues with regard to such relationships through "without prejudice" "or saving clauses."[100] The framework of this chapter does now allow to analyze all points of the Draft Articles, such as an important departure from the VCLT 1969 in relation to termination, withdrawal, or suspension of treaty as a result of armed conflict as a matter not only of treaty interpretation but also of other factors external to a treaty (Article 6a).[101]

97 Wood (n 93)1102. 98 ibid 1108.

99 Lucius Caflisch, "Articles on the Effects of Armed Conflict on Treaties" United Nations Audiovisual Library of International Law <http://legal.un.org/avl/pdf/ha/aeact/aeact_e.pdf> accessed April 18, 2018.

100 "Draft articles on the effects of armed conflicts on treaties, with commentaries" <http://legal.un.org/ilc/texts/instruments/english/commentaries/1_10_2011.pdf> accessed April 17, 2017. See also Caflisch (n 99).

101 Yaël Ronen, "Treaties and Armed Conflict" in Tams et al (n 43) 547.

The Draft Articles were transmitted to the UN General Assembly with the recommendation to take note of them and to consider, at a later stage, the conclusion of a convention on the subject. This recommendation was accepted in General Assembly Resolution 66/99 of 9 December 2011. The General Assembly also decided to return to the topic in 2014 in order to decide on the form to be given to the Articles. In 2014, the General Assembly decided to return to the issue in 2017. At its 29th meeting, on 6 November 2017, the Committee adopted draft resolution A/C.6/72/L.15 without a vote. Under the terms of this draft resolution, the Assembly would express its appreciation to the International Law Commission for its continuing contribution to the codification and progressive development of international law; emphasize the value of the articles on the effects of armed conflicts on treaties in providing guidance to States and invite States to use the articles as a reference whenever appropriate; and decide to revert to the question of the effects of armed conflicts on treaties at an appropriate time.[102]

These Draft Articles are based on a core principle enshrined in Article 3—legal stability and continuity of treaties. It does not mean an outright presumption of continuity, as it might contradict the prevailing position under international law.[103] These Articles adopt a holistic approach. They also cover internal armed conflicts. They have left a number of open questions, such as the relationship between 1969 VCLT and the Draft Articles on grounds of termination and suspension, the role of armed conflict with respect to rules of state responsibility precluding wrongfulness (force majeure and necessity), the relationship between the laws of armed conflict and human law, and the exterritorial application of human rights obligations in situations of non-international conflict that take place across borders.[104]

4.3 Subsequent Agreements and Subsequent Practice in Relation to Interpretation of Treaties

In 2018, the ILC concluded the topic on a second reading. It adopted 13 draft Conclusions, together with Commentaries. Conclusions are based on the VCLT. Conclusion 1 (on scope) and Conclusion 2 (General Rule and means of treaty interpretation) posit subsequent agreements and subsequent practice within the rules of treaty interpretation, as enshrined in Articles 31 and 32 of the VCLT. The most challenging was the inclusion of the subsequent agreement and subsequent practice under both Article 31 para 3(a), which is defined as 'an agreement between the parties, reached after the conclusion of the treaty, regarding the interpretation of the treaty or the Application of its provisions. A subsequent practice as a supplementary means of interpretation under Article 32 'consists of conduct by one or more parties in the application of the treaty, after its conclusion. The most debated was Conclusion 13 on pronouncements of

102 Sixth Committee (Legal), 72nd session: Effects of armed conflicts on treaties (Agenda item 86) <http://www.un.org/en/ga/sixth/72/armed_conflicts.shtml> accessed January 16, 2019.

103 Caflisch (n 99). 104 Ronen (n 101) 563–54.

expert bodies. Such a body was defined as 'a body consisting of experts serving in their own personal capacity, which is established under a treaty and is not an organ of and international organization'.[105]

5 Conclusion

This chapter's purpose was to give an overview of the codification efforts of the ILC in respect of treaties. As this brief survey shows, those efforts cover an exceptional variety of issues and complex tasks. The ILC was often forward-looking; much of its work entailed progressive development of the law. The ILC is a uniquely qualified body to undertake such a task. The ILC's theoretical and practical approach to the law of treaties is at its best exemplified by the VCLT 1969. Most of its provisions have withstood the passage of time. It is really difficult to imagine international law without the 1969 VCLT.[106] It may be emphasized that the main principle underlying all codifications in the areas of treaty law is the stability of treaties.

It would be an exaggeration to claim that all conventions enjoy the same success as the VCLT 1969. Overall, however, the codification of the law of treaties is a unique and invaluable contribution of the ILC. Apart from its practical importance, they have become fertile ground for international courts and tribunals, which in turn further clarified the conventions' provisions. Finally, the debates within the ILC and all reports constitute an invaluable source of knowledge.

As it was mentioned in the introduction to this chapter, only such a unique forum as the United Nations, and in particular the ILC and the Sixth Committee, could codify and progressively develop the law of treaties in the Vienna Conventions and in other codification efforts in the area of the law of treaties. The universality of the forum of the UN provided the necessary framework for such treaties, which, in order to be effective, require global recognition by the community of states. It may be said without any doubt that the drafting of the Vienna Conventions would not have been possible without collaborative efforts of states, the ILC, and the Sixth Committee, which could only be possible within the UN.

[105] Draft Conclusions (n 6); Pavel Šturma, 'Customary International Law, Interpretation of Treaties and Other Topics at the 70th Session of the International Law Commission' (2018) 9 Czech YB of Public & Private Intl L 365, 370–372.

[106] It may be noted that there are many other several unresolved questions relating to the law of treaties, one of them being the so-called "federal state clauses" that limit the scope of the treaty's obligations to those that the federal government has the constitutional authority to assume. Such an example is Article 35 of the 2003 Convention of Safeguarding of the Intangible Cultural Heritage, Duncan Hollis, "Applying the Treaty" in Hollis (n 41) 719–20.

CHAPTER 24B

LAW OF TREATIES

practitioner reflection

LIONEL YEE*

ARTICLES 31 and 32 of the Vienna Convention on the Law of Treaties (VCLT)[1] set out the most significant customary international law rules governing the interpretation of treaties. While the starting point for interpretation is the text of the treaty itself, these articles refer to other materials to which the interpreter may have recourse.

Under Article 31(1), a treaty must be interpreted in good faith in accordance with the ordinary meaning to be given to its terms in their context and in the light of its object and purpose. Article 31(2) stipulates that, for the purpose of interpretation, the context consists of not just the treaty text in its entirety, but also: (1) any agreement relating to the treaty made between all the parties in connection with the treaty's conclusion, and (2) any instrument made by one or more parties in connection with the treaty's conclusion and accepted by the other parties as an instrument related to the treaty. Article 31(3) additionally allows the interpreter to take into account, inter alia, any subsequent agreement on interpretation or any subsequent practice between the parties that establishes such an agreement. Finally, Article 31(4) provides for the exceptional case where, notwithstanding the apparent meaning of a term in its context, the parties intended a special meaning to be applied.

Article 32 allows interpreters to have recourse to "supplementary means of interpretation." These include the preparatory work of the treaty—the *travaux preparatoires* or the "*travaux*"—and the circumstances of its conclusion. But such recourse is only for the purpose of either (1) confirming the meaning resulting from the application of Article 31, or (2) determining the meaning when interpretation according to Article 31 leads to an ambiguous, obscure, manifestly absurd, or unreasonable result.

* The views expressed in this reflection are the personal views of the author and do not represent the views of his government. The author acknowledges with gratitude the assistance he has received from Allison Phua, State Counsel, International Affairs Division, Attorney-General's Chambers, Singapore.

[1] Vienna Convention on the Law of Treaties (adopted 23 May 1969, entered into force 27 January 1980) 1155 UNTS 331.

As rules of interpretation, it is not surprising that the common perception of Articles 31 and 32 is that they come into play primarily *after* the relevant treaty has entered into force, when its provisions need to be given effect to, or when disputes arise as to their meaning (regardless of whether such disputes are referred to adjudication before courts or tribunals). What is less appreciated is the equally important ex ante role that these rules play during the stage of a treaty's creation in providing the practitioner or negotiator a set of tools to employ—either to safeguard interests or to bridge differences in order to arrive at an agreement among all the parties. In my experience, for the international law practitioners in governments whose work covers the drafting and negotiation of treaties, these ex ante roles of Articles 31 and 32 are as significant as their ex post facto roles.

1 Interpretive Materials during Negotiations

The ex ante use of the rules often takes the form of a deliberate creation by the negotiators of the interpretive materials set out in Articles 31 and 32 to articulate a particular interpretation that is not covered by, or which sometimes may not even be entirely consistent with, the text of the treaty itself. In many cases, the impetus for this is a need to retain or use a particular textual formulation in the treaty, even though the negotiating parties agree that that particular formulation is to be understood or applied in a manner that is either not apparent from the text itself, or that is peculiar to particular circumstances or even a particular party or set of parties. The reason for strict adherence to a particular textual formulation in the treaty ranges from the need to preserve certain optical effects (often for political reasons or to avoid overloading the formal treaty text with details),[2] to a reluctance to alter the overall balance of rights and duties for the majority of the state parties while providing a degree of accommodation for minority interests.

These interpretive materials may take a variety of forms.

First, negotiators may choose to insert *annexes or footnotes* in the text of the treaty to record the understanding of the parties on the interpretation of particular provisions. The United Nations Convention on Jurisdictional Immunities of States and Their Property,[3] for example, has an Annex articulating a series of shared "understandings" on the interpretation of specific articles, which, in accordance with Article 25 of the Convention, "forms an integral part of the Convention." This device was used in the negotiations to arrive at a consensus text for various reasons.[4] The understanding that

[2] Anthony Aust, *Modern Treaty Law and Practice* (CUP 2013), 211.

[3] United Nations Convention on Jurisdictional Immunities of States and Their Property (2 December 2004, not yet in force), UNGA Resolution 38, UN GAOR, 59th Session Supp 49, at 486 UN Doc A/59/49 (2004); 44 I.L.M. 803 (2005).

[4] Tullio Treves, "Some Peculiarities of the UN Convention on Jurisdictional Immunities of States and Their Property: A Footnote on the Codification Technique" in Isabelle Buffard, James Crawford, Alain Pellet and Stephan Wittich (eds), *International Law between Universalism and Fragmentation: Festschrift in Honour*

Article 10(3) does not preclude inter alia the piercing of the corporate veil addressed the concerns of some of the negotiating parties who needed a "savings clause,"[5] even though it was probably perceived by others as no more than comfort language and therefore not necessary to be included at all.[6] Another understanding in the Annex that the reference to "security interests" in Article 11(2d) of the Convention is "intended primarily to address... national security and the security of diplomatic missions and consular posts," uses a formulation ("primarily") that detracts from full legal effect[7] and would normally not be found in the text of a treaty.

In UN treaty practice, it would appear that footnotes in the treaty text are usually not used to record the agreement or understanding of the parties on the interpretation of treaty provisions. They are, however, more commonly used for this purpose in general treaty practice and may be deployed to record the agreed interpretation of specific provisions affecting the parties jointly[8] or even unilaterally.[9] In the latter case, they may even be used to create exceptions for a party from the provisions of the treaty.[10]

Second, *side agreements* that are not formally part of or incorporated into the treaty may be used to record the shared understanding of the parties as to how treaty provisions are to be interpreted.

In the context of bilateral treaties, these agreements or understandings that are on the "side-lines" of the treaty may take the form of letters exchanged between the parties in conjunction with the signing of the treaty. The texts of the letters to be exchanged are often negotiated together with the treaty text, and the exchange is usually initiated by the party with the interest in having that particular interpretation apply to the treaty writing to the other side to set out the relevant terms. The other side then responds to confirm its agreement. In the China-Australia Free Trade Agreement, while the parties entered into some side agreements which were annexed to and made an integral part of

of Gerhard Hafner (Martinus Nijhoff 2008) 503, 505; Roger O'Keefe and Christian J Tams, *The United Nations Convention on Jurisdictional Immunities of States and Their Property: A Commentary* (OUP 2013) 9.

[5] Treves (n 4) 504. [6] O'Keefe and Tams (n 4) 181. [7] Treves (n 4) 504.

[8] United States-Singapore Free Trade Agreement, 6 May 2003 <https://www.iesingapore.gov.sg/~/media/IE%20Singapore/Files/FTA/Existing%20FTA/US%20Singapore%20FTA/Legal%20Text/United20StatesSingapore20FTA20Legal20Text.pdf>accessed January 11, 2019, footnote 15-9, which subjects the interpretation of Article 15.6 on expropriation to inter alia an exchange of letters recording a common understanding between the parties on what constitutes expropriation, in particular indirect expropriation, of investments under the Agreement; see exchange of letters on expropriation dated May 6, 2003, between Robert B Zoellick, United States Trade Representative and George Yeo, Minister for Trade and Industry, Singapore, available at the above website. The footnote was likely to have been inserted by the parties in the light of inter alia some arbitral awards, eg *Metalclad Corporation v The United Mexican States* (ICSID Case No. ARB(AF)/97/1), which adopted a more expansive approach to when government regulatory measures constituted indirect expropriation.

[9] United States-Singapore Free Trade Agreement (n 8) footnote 4-1, which clarifies that the obligation under Article 4.4(1)(a) to ensure at least one level of independent review of determinations of customs authorities is met by Singapore when its customs authority's determinations are reviewed by the government ministry supervising the customs authority.

[10] ibid, footnote 9-3, which provides for exemptions for rural telephone companies of the United States from the obligations under Article 9.4 of the Agreement pertaining to nondiscriminatory treatment, competition, etc. for telecommunication service providers.

the Agreement,[11] there was also an exchange of side letters on cooperation in the field of traditional Chinese medicine,[12] which were neither annexed nor referred to in the Agreement, but which appear to elaborate upon its provisions regarding cooperation in this field.[13]

Third, the interpretive materials may also take the form of statements that record a *shared understanding* on interpretation of the treaty.

In the case of the United Nations Convention on Jurisdictional Immunities of States and Their Property, the General Assembly, in its resolution adopting the Convention by consensus, indicated that it "[a]grees with the general understanding reached in the Ad Hoc Committee that the United Nations Convention on Jurisdictional Immunities of States and Their Property does not cover criminal proceedings."[14] Unlike the "understandings" discussed earlier, this general understanding on criminal proceedings was neither incorporated nor referred to in the text of the Convention itself.

A similar approach was taken by the Conference, which adopted the Convention on the Conservation of Antarctic Marine Living Resources.[15] The Conference decided to include in its Final Act the text of a statement made by the Chairman on certain carveouts from the Convention's application to waters adjacent to the French territories of Kerguelen and Crozet, and on the fact that there were no objections to that statement.[16]

2 Legal Effect

Turning to the legal effect of the above three categories of interpretive documents, the position for those in the first category (*annexes and footnotes* to the treaty) is straightforward. Article 31(2) of the VCLT makes it clear that a treaty includes its preamble and annexes, and by logical extension its footnotes as well. Recourse to the annexes and footnotes does not even take one beyond the confines of interpretation of the terms of the treaty in their context in accordance with Article 31(1).[17]

[11] Free Trade Agreement between the Government of Australia and the Government of the People's Republic of China, 17 June 2015 <https://dfat.gov.au/trade/agreements/in-force/chafta/official-documents/Documents/chafta-agreement-text.pdf> accessed September 23, 2017, and <https://dfat.gov.au/trade/agreements/in-force/chafta/official-documents/Documents/chafta-annex-iv-side-letters.pdf> accessed October 1, 2017, Article 17.1 and Annex IV (containing side letters to the agreement).

[12] Letters dated June 17, 2015, between Andrew Robb, Minister for Trade and Investment, Australia and Gao Hucheng, Minister of Commerce, People's Republic of China, <https://dfat.gov.au/trade/agreements/in-force/chafta/official-documents/Documents/chafta-tcm-side-letters.pdf> accessed October 1, 2017.

[13] China-Australia Free Trade Agreement (n 11), Article 8.25, paras 2 and 3.

[14] UN Convention on Jurisdictional Immunities (n 3) operative para 2.

[15] Convention on the Conservation of Antarctic Marine Living Resources (20 May 1980) <https://www.ccamlr.org/en/organisation/camlr-convention-text> accessed October 1, 2017.

[16] Available at <https://www.ccamlr.org/en/system/files/Conference%20on%20the%20Conservation%20of%20Antarctic%20Marine%20Living%20Resources.pdf> accessed October 1, 2017.

[17] In relation to the understandings contained in the Annex to the Convention on Jurisdictional Immunities, see Hazel Fox and Philippa Webb, *The Law of State Immunity* (OUP 2013) 295.

The legal effect of the second category of documents, namely *side agreements*, is also straightforward. As long as the text is clear as to its intended interpretive effect, a side agreement of this nature is an agreement made in connection with the conclusion of the treaty (Article 31(2)(a)), or an instrument made in connection with the conclusion of the treaty and accepted by the parties as an instrument related to the treaty (Article 31(2)(b)). The effect of either classification is similar. If, on the other hand, the side agreement was entered into subsequently, it could also be an interpretive reference point by virtue of Article 31(3)(a).

What should be borne in mind, however, is the fact that some side agreements, especially those entered into bilaterally, may be confidential in nature and may not be registered under Article 102 of the Charter of the United Nations. This means that they cannot be invoked before a UN organ such as the International Court of Justice (ICJ). A state does not, however, appear to be precluded from waiting until it is about to commence proceedings to register the agreement for the purpose of such invocation before the ICJ.[18] Nevertheless, a separate issue may arise as to whether that state is in breach of an obligation of confidentiality to the other contracting state by doing so.

The legal effect of statements in the last category, namely statements recording a *shared understanding* on interpretation, is less clear-cut. This is because they can take diverse forms and be made in varying circumstances. In some cases, it is doubtful whether the statements in question can be regarded as articulating understandings that are shared by all the negotiating parties. Even if the statements can be so regarded, some may constitute agreements or instruments under Article 31(2) while others are no more than part of the *travaux*. The dividing lines are not always clear. The fact that the agreement or instrument predates or postdates the conclusion of the treaty does not preclude it from being an agreement or instrument for the purposes of Article 31(2). The International Law Commission, in proposing the draft of this article, did envisage the possibility of an agreement or instrument of this nature being entered into before the treaty itself.[19] However, proximity in time may be indicative of whether it is to be so regarded.[20]

More significantly, there is neither any requirement for the agreement or instrument to take a particular form nor a clear need for formal or express consent or acceptance by all for a statement to be considered an agreement or instrument under Article 31(2). The statement highlighted earlier by the Chairman in the Final Act of the Conference adopting the Convention on the Conservation of Antarctic Marine Living Resources on the scope of its application and on the fact that there was no objection to that statement has therefore been regarded as sufficient to constitute an agreement made in connection with the conclusion of a treaty under Article 31(2).[21]

[18] *Maritime Delimitation and Territorial Questions Between Qatar and Bahrain* (Jurisdiction and Admissibility) [1994] ICJ Rep 112, 122, paras 28–29.

[19] ILC, "Report of the International Law Commission on the work of its Eighteenth Session" GAOR 21st Session Supp 9, at 169, UN Doc A/6309/Rev.1 at 221, para 14.

[20] Robert Jennings and Arthur Watts, *Oppenheim's International Law* (Longman 1992) §632 at 1273–74.

[21] Aust (n 2) 211.

The fact that a statement is not directly attributable to the entire membership of the negotiating body also does not preclude it from being a statement recording a shared understanding if it reflects the consensus of those states that have a direct interest in the treaty provision in question. During the negotiations on the 1982 United Nations Convention on the Law of the Sea,[22] the coastal states and major user states of the Straits of Malacca and Singapore reached a shared understanding on specific circumstances in which the Convention's Article 233 conditions would be met for the coastal states to take enforcement measures against foreign vessels transiting the straits. This was set out in a statement attached to a letter to the President of the Third United Nations Conference on the Law of the Sea from a coastal state and in letters of confirmation or non-objection by the other coastal states and major user states.[23] The statement has been included in the official records of the Conference and is regarded as "an important interpretation of Article 233."[24]

Even the fact that some negotiating delegations have expressed reservations, though not outright opposition, to a statement on the interpretation of a treaty provision may not necessarily preclude the statement from being reflective of an agreement relating to the treaty under Article 31(2)(a). A case in point would be the "understandings" relating to Articles I, II, III, and IV of the 1976 Convention on the Prohibition of Military or Any Other Hostile Use of Environmental Modification Techniques,[25] which were included in the report transmitted by the Conference of the Committee on Disarmament to the General Assembly.[26]

As for the understanding, discussed earlier, that the United Nations Convention on Jurisdictional Immunities of States and Their Property does not cover criminal proceedings, the intent of the drafters appears to be for it to be treated as an instrument related to the Convention under Article 31(2)(b).[27] However, some have regarded it as an agreement under Article 31(2)(a),[28] while others consider it as being no more than part of the

[22] United Nations Convention on the Law of the Sea (10 December 1982) 1833 UNTS 3.

[23] Third United Nations Conference on the Law of the Sea Official Records, Vol. XVI, Eleventh Session, UN Doc A/CONF/62/L.145 (1982), Annex and Adds 1–8, 250–51 (Malaysia) and 251–53 (Indonesia, Singapore, France, United Kingdom, United States of America, Japan, Australia, and Federal Republic of Germany).

[24] Myron Nordquist, *United Nations Convention on the Law of the Sea 1982: A Commentary* (Martinus Nijhoff 1993) 388, para 233.8.

[25] Convention on the Prohibition of Military or Any Other Hostile Use of Environmental Modification Techniques (18 May 1977) 1329 UNTS 48.

[26] "Report of the Conference of the Committee on Disarmament" Volume 1, GAOR, 31st Session Supp 27, UN Doc. A/31/27 (1977), at 85, para 382 and at 93, para 9, recording the delegation of Brazil's reservations on the understanding relating to Article I. On treatment of the understandings as an agreement under Article 31(2)(a) of the Vienna Convention on the Law of Treaties, see Aust (n 2) 211.

[27] Writing in his personal capacity, the Chair of the Ad Hoc Committee on the Convention stated that General Assembly resolution 59/38, which adopted the Convention, "must... be considered as part of the context for the purposes of interpretation according to Article 31(2)(b) VCLT as it could be ranked among the instruments 'made by one or more parties in connection with the conclusion of the treaty and accepted by the other parties as an instrument related to the treaty'"; see Gerhard Hafner and Ulrike Kohler, *The United Nations Convention on Jurisdictional Immunities of States and Their Property* (2004) 35 Netherlands Ybk Intl L 3, 46.

[28] Aust (n 2) 211.

preparatory work of the Convention[29] and therefore merely a supplementary means of interpretation under Article 32.

A World Trade Organization dispute settlement panel has observed that an uncontested interpretation of a treaty provision given at a diplomatic conference by the chairman of its drafting committee may constitute an "agreement" under Article 31(2)(a), whereas interpretive or explanatory statements by members of a drafting committee in their personal capacity should be considered simply as part of the *travaux*.[30] Even in the former situation, it would appear that the legal effect is highly contextual. Others have noted that statements from the chair of a conference, even if they are in the conference records, may only be part of the *travaux*, although they may have a more persuasive effect.[31]

The distinction between (1) treatment as an agreement relating to or an instrument in connection with the conclusion of a treaty, and (2) treatment as *travaux* may be significant. While the former forms part of the context of the treaty and is therefore a primary means of interpretation, there can only be recourse to *travaux* either to confirm an Article 31 interpretation, or when the precondition that an interpretation according to Article 31 would result in ambiguity, manifest absurdity, and so on, is met.

With regard to the use of *travaux* in interpretation, assuming that the conditions for recourse to Article 32 are met, what needs to be considered next is whether that particular portion of the *travaux* can, in fact, be used to aid interpretation. Some key questions are whether what is being relied upon constitutes an accurate record of the negotiations, and whether the record shows that the negotiators had in fact intended a particular interpretation to be applied to the provision in question, bearing in mind that texts are often in a state of flux at this point and are different from the treaty provisions that eventually emerge.

3 Conclusion

The foregoing observations on legal efficacy should be borne in mind by negotiators in deciding on the form that an interpretation of a particular treaty provision agreed upon by the parties should take. It may not always be possible for agreement to be reached by all on a form with a clear-cut legal effect. In such circumstances, what is required is an assessment of whether the risks of adopting a less-than-ideal approach are acceptable.

However, it should also be noted that when no agreement has in fact been reached, individual negotiators may, from time to time, attempt to unilaterally have their preferred interpretation officially recorded. They may do so by, for example, making a formal statement containing such an interpretation in the hope that non-objection, or the

[29] Treves (n 4) 505.

[30] World Trade Organization Panel Report, United States – Section 110(5) of the US Copyright Act (WT/DS160/R), adopted 27 July 2000, DSR VIII, 3769, at para 6.46.

[31] Richard Gardiner, "Treaties and Treaty Materials: Role Relevance and Accessibility" (1997) 46(3) ICLQ 643, 653; Ian Sinclair, *The Vienna Convention on the Law of Treaties* (Manchester University Press 1984) 130.

absence of a record of any objection by the other negotiating parties, may be argued subsequently to indicate a tacit agreement or understanding on the interpretation proffered by them.

The legal efficacy of such attempts is uncertain. In the face of conduct by a state party, silence or inaction by other states parties is capable of constituting subsequent practice for a treaty in question.[32] There should therefore be no reason silence or inaction to an interpretive statement made by another state, in circumstances where a response was called for, cannot be likewise capable of constituting an agreement on or acceptance of a particular interpretation, or, in the case of *travaux*, evidence of a shared understanding by the negotiators to that effect. It is, however, likely that a court or tribunal, faced with statements of this nature, will approach the issue with caution and circumspection. There is a world of difference between, on the one hand, a record of negotiations adopted formally by all parties and explicitly articulating an agreement or understanding on the interpretation of a particular provision, and, on the other, a record that has not been the subject of assent by all the parties or that sets out nothing more than a unilateral statement made by one party at some point in the negotiation process. Nevertheless, in the light of the uncertainties highlighted earlier, treaty negotiators would do well to err on the side of caution when faced with attempts of this nature, and ensure that there is a formal record of their objection to, or at least a reservation of, their position in such circumstances.

[32] *Kasikili/Sedudu Island (Botswana/Namibia)* (Judgment) [1999] ICJ Rep 1045, 1094, para 74.

CHAPTER 25A

LAW OF THE SEA

YOSHIFUMI TANAKA

THIS chapter seeks to examine the role of the United Nations in treaty-making in the field of the law of the sea. The first intergovernmental attempt to codify the law of the sea was the 1930 Hague Conference for the Codification of International Law. The Hague Conference was instigated by the League of Nations between March 13 and April 12, 1930, and was attended by 47 governments and an observer (the USSR).[1] The Conference aimed to codify international law concerning three subjects: nationality, state responsibility, and territorial waters. Even though a majority of states agreed that the coastal state possessed territorial sovereignty over its territorial sea, opinions of states were sharply divided with regard to the breadth of the territorial sea. While maritime powers, such as Great Britain and the United States, claimed that the breadth of the territorial sea belt was 3 miles, some coastal states suggested various breadths beyond three miles, such as 4, 6, or 12 miles.[2] The positions of states were further complicated by the problem regarding the contiguous zone.[3] In light of the wide cleavage of opinion between states, no rule was formulated with regard to the breadth of the territorial sea, and the Hague Conference ended without the adoption of a convention on the territorial sea. However,

[1] Concerning the list of the participating Governments, see "Conference for the Codification of International Law Held at the Hague in March-April, 1930: Final Act" (1930) 24 AJIL Supplement 169. With regard to the Hague Conference, see Jesse S Reeves, "The Codification of the Law of Territorial Waters" (1930) 24 AJIL 486–99; Gilbert Gidel, *Le droit international public de la mer: le temps de paix, Tome III, La mer territoriale et la zone contiguë* (Duchemin 1981) 124–52; United Nations, "Documents on the Development and Codification of International Law: Historical Survey of Development of International Law and Its Codification by International Conferences" (1947) 41 AJIL Supplement 80–147; Constantin John Colombos, *The International Law of the Sea* (6th revised edn, 1967) 103–06; Lawrence Juda, *International Law and Ocean Use Management: The Evolution of Ocean Governance* (Routledge 1996) 62–67. Documents in the Conference were reproduced in Shabtai Rosenne (ed), *League of Nations Conference for the Codification of International Law 1930*, 4 vols (Oceana 1975).

[2] Juda (n 1) 62; Reeves (n 1) 492.

[3] Reeves (n 1) 492–93.

it is not suggested that the Hague Conference was without significance. Indeed, the Hague Conference produced valuable statements on important issues regarding the law of the sea, such as: the principle of freedom of navigation, territorial sovereignty over the territorial sea, and the right of innocent passage through the territorial sea.[4]

It was only after World War II when principal rules of the law of the sea were codified through a series of UN Conferences of the Law of the Sea. As will be discussed in this chapter, treaty-making under the auspices of the UN significantly contributed to the development of the law of the sea.[5] The UN treaty-making can be said to mirror changes of the function of the law of the sea. Traditionally, the primary function of the law was to reconcile various states interests by distributing jurisdiction of states in multiple jurisdictional zones. In addition to the traditional function, at present, the law of the sea performs an increasingly important role in the protection of the common interests of the international community or community interests at sea, such as preservation and protection of the marine environment, including marine living resources and biological diversity. If we reflect on the expansion of the role of the law of the sea, we see that the role of the UN treaty-making in this field may change over time.

Noting this point, first, this chapter reviews the First United Nations Conference on the Law of the Sea.[6] This chapter then analyzes the Third United Nations Conference on the Law of the Sea. Next it moves on to examine the treaty-making process of two implementation agreements, that is, the 1994 Implementation Agreement[7] and the 1995 Fish Stocks Agreement.[8] Finally, this chapter briefly discusses the ongoing process of treaty-making with regard to the conservation and sustainable use of marine biological diversity of areas beyond national jurisdiction, before offering concluding remarks.

[4] Yoshifumi Tanaka, The International Law of the Sea (2nd edn, CUP 2015) 20–21.

[5] In addition to the United Nations, other international institutions and judicial bodies also perform a valuable role in the development of the law of the sea. For instance, the role of the International Maritime Organization (IMO) is of particular importance in adopting treaties regulating vessel-source marine pollution and international shipping. Furthermore, the International Seabed Authority (ISA) performs a crucial role in lawmaking with regard to the regulation of seabed activities in the Area, that is, the seabed and ocean floor and subsoil thereof, beyond the limits of national jurisdiction. Moreover, the International Tribunal for the Law of the Sea and Annex VII arbitral tribunals also make an important contribution to the development of the law of the sea. Because of the limitations of space, this chapter focuses on treaty-making through the United Nations.

[6] This chapter also touches on the 1930 Hague Conference for the Codification of International Law and the Second United Nations Conference on the Law of the Sea.

[7] The full title is Agreement relating to the implementation of Part XI of the United Nations Convention on the Law of the Sea of 10 December 1982, 1836 UNTS 42, (1994) 33 ILM 1309, entered into force 28 July 1996. As at January 2019, 150 states have ratified the Agreement.

[8] The full title is United Nations Agreement for the Implementation of the Provisions of the United Nations Convention on the Law of the Sea of 10 December 1982 relating to the Conservation and Management of Straddling Fish Stocks and Highly Migratory Fish Stocks. Text in: 2167 UNTS 3, entered into force 11 December 2001. As of January 2019, 89 states have ratified the Agreement.

1 The First UN Conference on the Law of the Sea (1958)

After World War II, control of offshore natural resources emerged as a central issue in the law of the sea. In particular, the increasing demand for petrol prompted coastal states to extend their jurisdiction over natural resources on the continental shelf. At the same time, claims on these resources on the high seas were also increasingly advocated by the coastal states. Since the Truman Proclamations of September 28, 1945, regarding the continental shelf as well as the fisheries zone,[9] unilateral extension of coastal state jurisdiction toward the high seas has been a driving force of development in the law of the sea.

Against that background, the International Law Commission (ILC) came to wrestle with the codification of the law of the sea. The ILC commenced its work on the codification of the law of the sea at its first session in 1949, and J.P.A. François was appointed as the special rapporteur on the regime of the high seas. In its eighth session in 1956, the ILC submitted its final report on "Articles Concerning the Law of the Sea" to the United Nations.[10] This report provided the basis for the work at the First United Nations Conference on the Law of the Sea, which was convened in Geneva on February 24, 1958, with the participation of 68 states. The Conference successfully adopted four conventions and an optional protocol on dispute settlement:

(i) The Convention on the Territorial Sea and the Contiguous Zone;[11]
(ii) The Convention on the High Seas;[12]
(iii) The Convention on Fishing and Conservation of the Living Resources of the High Seas;[13]
(iv) The Convention on the Continental Shelf;[14] and
(v) The Optional Protocol of Signature Concerning the Compulsory Settlement of Disputes.[15]

In addition, the Conference adopted nine resolutions concerning nuclear tests on the high seas, pollution of the high seas by radioactive materials, fishery conservation,

[9] The full titles are: Proclamation by President Truman of September 28, 1945 on Policy of the United States with respect to the Natural Resources of the Subsoil and Sea Bed of the Continental Shelf, Proclamation by President Truman of September 28, 1945 on Policy of the United States with respect to Coastal Fisheries in Certain Areas of the High Seas.

[10] ILC, "Articles concerning the Law of the Sea with Commentaries" (1956) II Ybk ILC 265ff <http://legal.un.org/ilc/texts/instruments/english/commentaries/8_1_8_2_1956.pdf> accessed January 14, 2018.

[11] 516 UNTS 205. Entered into force 10 September 1964.

[12] 450 UNTS 11. Entered into force 30 September 1962.

[13] 559 UNTS 285. Entered into force 20 March 1966.

[14] 499 UNTS 311. Entered into force 10 June 1964.

[15] 450 UNTS 169. Entered into force 30 September 1962.

cooperation in conservation measures, human killing of marine life, coastal fisheries, historic waters, convening of a Second UN Conference on the Law of the Sea, and a tribute to the ILC.[16] Four points can be made with regard to the First UN Conference on the Law of the Sea.

A first point concerns the codification of the zonal management approach as *lex scripta*. Under this approach, the ocean is divided into multiple jurisdictional zones and, in principle, the law of the sea provides the rights and obligations of a coastal State and third States according to these jurisdictional zones. In this regard, Article 1 of the Convention on the High Seas stipulates that: "The term 'high seas' means all parts of the sea that are not included in the territorial sea or in the internal waters of a State." Under the Convention on the High Seas, the ocean was divided into marine spaces under the territorial sovereignty, that is, internal waters and the territorial sea, and marine space beyond the territorial sovereignty, that is, the high seas. Furthermore, the legal institution of the continental shelf was embodied in the Convention on the Continental Shelf. Moreover, the contiguous zone, which may not extend beyond 12 miles from the baseline, was provided in the Convention on the Territorial Sea and the Contiguous Zone.[17] Thus the Conference codified the zonal management approach as *lex scripta*.

A second point relates to the absence of an agreement with regard to the maximum limit of the territorial sea. In broad terms, the reconciliation of interests of states, in particular, interests of coastal states and those of maritime states, constituted a principal theme of the First Conference on the Law of the Sea. A hardcore issue in this regard concerned the maximum extent of the territorial sea. The spatial ambit of the territorial sea prima facie coincides with the monopoly of marine resources by the coastal state. Accordingly, it was not surprising that the breadth of the territorial seas was a matter of important concern for every state with fishery interests.[18] Owing to the sharp division of opinions among states on this issue,[19] the Conference failed to reach an agreement with respect to the breadth of the territorial sea. Unless the spatial ambit of coastal state jurisdiction is determined, the zonal management approach cannot properly function. The absence of the agreement on the maximum limit of the territorial sea signified that the zonal management approach under the Geneva Conventions contained a serious deficiency. Subsequently, on March 17, 1960, the Second UN Conference on the Law of the Sea was convened in Geneva in order to discuss the outer limit of the territorial sea as well as the fishery zone. Yet, the joint Canada-US proposal of six-mile territorial sea plus six-mile fishery zone was defeated by a single vote.[20] Thus the efforts to fix the maximum breadth of the territorial sea at the Second Conference proved once again in vain.

[16] UN Doc A/CONF.13/L.56. United Nations Conference on the Law of the Sea, Official Records, Vol II: Plenary Meetings (Geneva, 24 February–27 April 1958), 143–45.

[17] However, the contiguous zone is part of the high seas under Article 24 (1) of the 1958 Convention on the Territorial Sea and the Contiguous Zone. Thus, arguably the contiguous zone cannot be regarded a main category of marine spaces.

[18] Shigeru Oda, *International Control of Sea Resources* (Nijhoff 1989) 13.

[19] With respect to the discussion at the First UN Convention on this issue, see in particular ibid 97–111.

[20] ibid 104.

A third point pertains to the protection of community interests at sea. At the First UN Conference on the Law of the Sea, protection of community interests attracted little attention. In fact, the Convention on the Territorial Seas and the Contiguous Zone and the Convention on the Continental Shelf contained no provision dealing directly with the protection of the marine environment. The Convention on the High Seas covered only a few sources of marine pollution, namely the discharge of oil from ships, pipelines, the exploitation and exploration of the seabed and its subsoil,[21] and the dumping of radioactive waste.[22] As a consequence, subject only to the few limitations imposed by customary international law, states had a wide discretion to pollute the oceans. While an obligation to conserve marine living resources was, for the first time, enshrined in the Convention on Fishing and Conservation of the Living Resources of the High Seas, the Convention has been ratified by only 39 states and achieved only limited success.

Fourth, at the First UN Conference, a compulsory procedure of dispute settlement could be established only as a separate instrument owing to opposition by many states to the mechanism of settlement either by the International Court of Justice (ICJ) or through arbitration. To date, only 38 states have become parties to the Optional Protocol of Signature Concerning the Compulsory Settlement of Disputes. The absence of procedures of international dispute settlement as an integral part of the Geneva Conventions would undermine the effectiveness of rules provided in the Conventions.

2 The Third UN Conference on the Law of the Sea (1973–1982)

The legal order established by the 1958 Geneva Conventions very soon came to encounter serious challenges. Among various elements for demanding the revision of the legal order established in the Geneva Conventions,[23] particular attention must be paid to two contrasting factors.

The first factor relates to the demand for unilateral expansion of the coastal states jurisdiction toward the high seas. Growing demand for a supply of marine natural resources led the coastal states to further extend national jurisdiction toward the high seas. At that time, some 20 coastal states had already claimed exclusive fisheries jurisdiction beyond 12 nautical miles.[24] It was becoming apparent that the traditional dualism between the narrow territorial sea and the vast high seas was in need of serious reconsideration.

The second factor pertains to the emergence of the principle of the common heritage of mankind. In 1967, Maltese ambassador Dr. Arvid Pardo made a historic proposal that the seabed and its natural resources beyond the limits of national jurisdiction should be

[21] Article 24. [22] Article 25. [23] Tanaka (n 4) 24–25.

[24] Memorial submitted by the United Kingdom in the *Fishery Jurisdiction* case, 31 July 1973, vol 1, 353, para 245.

the common heritage of mankind.[25] The concept of the common heritage of mankind was innovative in the sense that it aimed to safeguard the interest of mankind, not individual states. In response to his proposal, UN General Assembly Resolution 2340 (XXII) of 18 December 1967 decided to establish the Ad Hoc Committee on the Peaceful Uses of the Sea-Bed and the Ocean Floor beyond the Limits of National Jurisdiction (the Seabed Committee), consisting of 35 members chosen to reflect equitable geographical representation. By UN General Assembly Resolution 2467A (XXIII) of 21 December 1968, this Committee was replaced by the permanent Committee on the Peaceful Uses of the Sea-Bed and Ocean Floor beyond the Limits of National Jurisdiction. Nonetheless, it became apparent that discussions would not be limited to mineral resources in the deep seabed. Eventually it was acknowledged that there was a great need to review the existing rules of the law of the sea as a whole because marine issues were closely interrelated. Thus, on December 17, 1970, UN General Assembly Resolution 2750 C (XXV) decided to convene the Third UN Conference on the Law of the Sea in order to adopt a comprehensive convention on the law of the sea.[26]

The first session of the Conference was held in New York on December 3–15, 1973, and a total of 11 sessions were convened from 1973 to 1982.[27] Unlike at the First and Second UN Conference on the Law of the Sea, the preparatory work was not assigned to the ILC. The primary reason was that in light of the political sensitivity of issues underlying the Conference, the ILC was regarded as inappropriate to deal with these questions. Developing states were also concerned that they were underrepresented in the ILC and that the ILC was too conservative in its approach.[28] It can be said that from the outset, the Conference was understood to be a political process.[29] It was characterized by three principal features.

The first noteworthy feature concerns the nature of the task with which the Conference was charged. The tasks of the Conference included not only the reconciliation of interests of individual states, but also the safeguarding of community interests reflected in, inter alia, the principle of common heritage of mankind and marine environmental protection. In this regard, the scope of the issues addressed at the Third UN Conference went

[25] *Note Verbale* of 17 August 1967 from Malta to UN Secretary-General (18 August 1967) UN Doc A/6695; reproduced in Edward D. Brown, *The International Law of the Sea* vol 2 (Dartmouth 1994) 333.

[26] UNGA Res 2750C (XXV) (17 December 1970).

[27] For an overview of the Third UN Conference on the Law of the Sea, see Bernard H Oxman, "The Third United Nations Conference on the Law of the Sea" in René-Jean Dupuy and Daniel Vignes (eds), *A Handbook on the New Law of the Sea* vol 1 (Nijhoff 1991) 163–244; Tommy Koh and Shanmugam Jayakumar, "The Negotiating Process of the Third United Nations Conference on the Law of the Sea" in Myron H Nordquist et al (eds), *United Nations Convention on the Law of the Sea 1982: A Commentary*, vol I (Nijhoff 1985) 29–134.

[28] This does not mean, however, that the role of international lawyers was minor in the Third UN Conference on the Law of the Sea. Most of the delegations in the Conference were international lawyers, and they played a key role in formulating acceptable draft rules. A Shibata, "International Law-Making Process in the United Nations: Comparative Analysis of UNCED and UNCLOS III" (1993) 24 California Western Intl LJ 17, 33–35.

[29] Alan Boyle and Christine Chinkin, *The Making of International Law* (OUP 2007) 144–45.

well beyond the issues discussed at the First and Second UN Conferences. It is important to note that protection of community interests became one of the crucial issues at the Third UN Conference on the Law of the Sea.

The second feature is the universality of the participants.[30] At the time of the First and Second UN Conferences, many developing states had not gained independence. Accordingly, participation of developing states was limited at the First UN Conference, and the claims of these states had little impact on the 1958 Geneva Conventions.[31] In contrast, the Third UN Conference participants comprised members of the UN, including developing states, specialized agencies of the UN and the International Atomic Energy Agency, and parties to the Statute of the International Court of Justice, as well as Guinea-Bissau and the Democratic Republic of Vietnam. The participants in the Conference also included a wide range of observers, such as intergovernmental and nongovernmental organizations, trust territories, associated states, the United Nations Council for Namibia, and national liberation movements recognized in their region by the Organization of African Unity or the League of Arab States. The universality of the participants can be considered as an important element securing the legitimacy of the process of international lawmaking.

The third feature concerns the long duration of the Conference. In fact, it took 10 years—from 1973 to 1982—to complete the work. Taking into account the preparatory work of the Seabed Committee, which commenced in 1967, it took nearly 16 years to successfully adopt the UN Convention on the Law of the Sea (UNCLOS).[32]

2.1 Procedure

To a significant degree, the success of the Third UN Conference on the Law of the Sea can be attributed to the particular methods and procedures for negotiations employed at the Conference.[33] Five methods and procedures merit being highlighted.[34]

The first noteworthy method employed at the Conference concerns the consensus procedure. This procedure refers to the method of obtaining the general agreement of all relevant actors in a conference or an organ through negotiations without vote.[35] The consensus procedure seeks to make every effort to reach an agreement on politically

[30] Participants at the sessions of the Conference were listed in the Final Act of the Third United Nations Conference on the Law of the Sea.

[31] Jens Evensen, "Working Methods and Procedures in the Third United Nations Conference on the Law of the Sea" (1986-IV) 199 Recueil des Cours de l'Académie de Droit International 415, 432.

[32] Adopted 10 December 1982, entered into force on 16 November 1994. 1833 *UNTS* 3.

[33] Boyle and Chinkin (n 29) 144. Further, see Evensen (n 31) 483ff.

[34] See also Practitioner's Reflection by Tommy Koh in chapter 25 this volume.

[35] The consensus procedure must be distinguished from unanimity. While adoption with unanimity means adoption by voting after all actors involved have agreed, the consensus procedure precludes voting.

sensitive issues. At the Conference, the consensus procedure was indirectly mentioned in the "Gentlemen's Agreement" of the Conference as follows:

> The Conference should make every effort to reach agreement on substantive matters by way of consensus and there should be no voting on such matters until all efforts at consensus have been exhausted.[36]

The Rules of Procedure for the Conference made no explicit reference to the consensus procedure. However, Paragraph 1 of Rule 37 stated that: "Before a matter of substance is put to the vote, a determination that all efforts at reaching general agreement have been exhausted shall be made" by the two-thirds majority specified in Rule 39(1). The consensus procedure worked successfully throughout the Conference even though it was abandoned when adopting UNCLOS at the end of the Conference.

The second noteworthy procedural technique used at the Conference is the package-deal approach. This is a comprehensive approach by which all key issues are addressed, with reasonable give and take between interested parties and groups. Under the package-deal approach, the final treaty is to be accepted in its entirety. This approach contributed to the adoption of a comprehensive convention, that is, UNCLOS, even though the package-deal approach has complicated the decision-making process at the Conference owing to trade-off tactics by certain states.

The third noteworthy method for negotiations at the Conference was the group approach. The Conference realized at an early stage that working groups would be more efficient than plenary meetings owing to the large number of participants and sensitive issues involved. As a consequence, negotiations were to a large extent carried out in smaller working or negotiating groups on the basis of interest in a particular issue, such as: the group of 77 consisting of developing countries, the coastal states group, the group of archipelagic states, the Oceania group, the landlocked and geographically disadvantaged states group, the territorialist group, the group of broad-shelf states, the straits states group, and the group of maritime states.[37]

The fourth innovative method relates to the single text approach. It has been considered that the only way for the Conference to extricate itself from the proliferation of individual proposals was to formulate a Single Negotiating Treaty Text as the basis for discussion. Therefore, the President of the Conference recommended that the Chairmen of the three Committees should each prepare a single negotiating text concerning the subjects entrusted to his Committee.[38] This was an important procedural innovation.

Finally, informality of negotiation merits particular notice. At the Conference, most substantive meetings were informal and without summary records. As a consequence, there is little in the way of formal records of debates and amendments by delegations at the Conference. Some of the most intractable issues of the Conference

[36] Declaration Incorporating the Gentlemen's Agreement made by the President and Endorsed by the Conference at its 19th Meeting on 27 June 1974. Reproduced in (1974) 13 ILM 1209.

[37] Concerning various groups, see, in particular, Koh and Jayakumar (n 27) 68–86.

[38] Third UN Conference on the Law of the Sea, Official Records, vol 4, 26, para 92. See also Evensen (n 31) 462–79.

were resolved in privately convened negotiating groups, such as the Evensen group and the Castañeda group.[39]

After several revisions of the texts, the Draft Convention on the Law of the Sea was adopted at the resumed 10th session on August 28, 1981.[40] At the 11th session, a number of changes and amendments were made to the final text of the Convention in order to accommodate the concerns of the United States. However, the United States did not support the adoption of the Convention by consensus or without a vote, requesting a recorded vote.[41] Consequently, the consensus procedure was abandoned in the final stage of the Conference. UNCLOS was finally adopted on April 30, 1982, by 130 in favor, 4 against, with 18 abstentions and 18 unrecorded.[42] The Convention was opened for signature on December 10, 1982. The adoption of UNCLOS marked the beginning of a new era in the international law of the sea.

2.2 Evaluation

A remarkable result of the Third UN Conference on the Law of the Sea was that it peacefully changed the legal order of the oceans. In this regard, two points can be made.

The first concerns the transformation of the legal order at sea from dualism to multilateralism. UNCLOS finally resolved the essential question relating to the breadth of territorial seas. As provided in Article 3 of UNCLOS, states had agreed on a maximum seaward limit of the territorial sea of 12 miles. It can be said that the zonal management approach was eventually established in UNCLOS in its true sense.[43] In this respect, it is important to note that the hard issue concerning the breadth of territorial seas could be concluded only by institutionalizing a new resource-oriented zone under the coastal state's jurisdiction: the 200-mile EEZ. In other words, states could reach agreement with respect to the breadth of the territorial sea only by diverging from the traditional principle of dualism that divides the sea into the territorial sea and the high seas. Consequently, the division of the sea was further promoted under UNCLOS, with the sea being divided into five basic categories: internal waters, the territorial sea, the EEZ, the high seas, and archipelagic waters.[44]

[39] Tommy Koh, "A Constitution for the Oceans" in United Nations, *The Law of the Sea: United Nations Convention on the Law of the Sea with Index and Final Act of the Third United Nations Conference on the Law of the Sea* (United Nations 1983) xxxvi.

[40] A/CONF.62/L.78 (28 August 1981). Third UN Conference on the Law of the Sea, Official Records, vol 15, 172. See also Oxman (n 27) 238–39.

[41] The United States changed its position after the victory of President Reagan in the 1980 presidential election. The new administration decided to re-evaluate the results of the Third UN Conference on the Law of the Sea as a whole. Evensen (n 31) 479–82; Oxman (n 27) 239–40.

[42] For the distribution of the votes, see ibid 243. Some documents recorded that 17 states abstained. However, it would seem that an abstention by Liberia, which was initially unrecorded, was not counted in the abstention number. By including Liberia's abstention, that number should be 18. As of January 2019, 168 states have ratified UNCLOS.

[43] Tanaka (n 4) 5.

[44] Where the coastal state has claimed its EEZ, the continental shelf is the seabed and subsoil of the EEZ. If not, the continental shelf is part of the seabed and subsoil of the high seas. International straits under Part III belong to the territorial sea of the coastal state.

The second point pertains to the creation of a deep seabed regime on the basis of the common-heritage-of-mankind principle. In this regard, Article 136 of the Convention declares that: "The Area and its resources are the common heritage of mankind." As provided in Article 140(1), activities in the Area are to be carried out for the benefit of mankind as a whole. To this end, a new international organization was established: the International Seabed Authority (ISA). Under Article 153(1), activities in the Area shall be organized, carried out, and controlled by the ISA on behalf of mankind as a whole. This means that mankind governs activities in the Area through its operational organ, that is, the ISA. This is an innovative institution in the sense that it may bring new viewpoints beyond the state-to-state perspective in the law of the sea.[45]

In summary, the Conference created the structural change of international spatial order in the oceans. It seems to suggest that treaty-making through international conference under the auspices of the UN may provide a democratic and institutionalized forum for peaceful change of the existing legal order.[46] Peaceful change of the existing rules through negotiations in international conferences can contribute to the prevention or settlement of dynamic disputes, that is, disputes arising from claims to alter the status quo.[47] In this regard, one can find the interlinkage between treaty-making under the auspices of the UN and peaceful settlement of international disputes. At the same time, it must be stressed that the effectiveness of the solution adopted by the Conference relied on the general acceptability by states. If the test of general acceptability were not met, the effectiveness of the solution would be dubious. Indeed, as will be discussed next, the deep seabed regime set out in UNCLOS came to encounter a considerable challenge.

3 The Role of the UN in the Adoption of the Two Implementation Agreements

3.1 The 1994 Implementation Agreement

The deep seabed regime under Part XI of UNCLOS was strongly opposed by some industrialized states, including the United States. Indeed, the United States voted against UNCLOS and did not sign it. Other industrialized states abstained and did not ratify the Convention. As a consequence, it became apparent that apart from Iceland, all states

45 Tanaka (n 4) 154.

46 Concerning the importance of international conferences, see Antônio Augusto Cançando Trindade, "International Law for Humankind: Towards a New Jus Gentium (II): General Course on Public International Law" (2005) 317 Recueil des Cours de l'Académie de Droit International 9, 247–68.

47 For the concept of dynamic disputes, see Josef L Kunz, "The Law of Nations, Static and Dynamic" (1933) 27 AJIL 630, 634–35; Yoshifumi Tanaka, *The Peaceful Settlement of International Disputes* (CUP 2018) 14ff.

parties to UNCLOS were developing states if the Convention would enter into force. Furthermore, major industrialized states, such as the United States (1980), the United Kingdom (1981), Federal Republic of Germany (1980, amended 1982), France (1981), Japan (1982), the USSR (1982), and Italy (1985), enacted unilateral domestic legislation in relation to deep seabed mining.[48] In 1984, eight industrialized states concluded the Provisional Understanding Regarding Deep Seabed Matters in order to avoid overlapping in deep seabed operations.[49] This situation ran the serious risk of damaging the unity and universality of the deep seabed regime established in Part XI and UNCLOS as a whole.

Against that background, in July 1990, UN Secretary-General Javier Pérez de Cuéllar took the initiative to convene informal consultations aimed at achieving universal participation.[50] In these consultations, he stressed the importance of securing general acceptance of UNCLOS.[51] At the same time, he noted political and economic changes of the situation surrounding the deep seabed regime. In fact, the delay in the commercial exploitation of deep seabed resources and economic shifted toward a more market-oriented economy. The Secretary-General also recognized the emergence of a new spirit of international cooperation in resolving outstanding problems of regional and global concern. These changes encouraged states to reconsider Part XI of UNCLOS. The informal consultations under the initiative of the UN Secretary-General took place from 1990 to 1994, and 15 meetings were convened.[52] The consultation process can be divided into two phases.

The first phase in 1990–1991 was devoted to the identification of issues of concern to some states, finding an approach to be taken, and searching for a solution. Specifically, nine issues were identified as areas of difficulty: (1) costs to state parties, (2) the Enterprise, (3) decision-making, (4) the Review Conference, (5) transfer of technology, (6) production limitation, (7) compensation fund, (8) financial terms of contract, and (9) environmental considerations. It was also agreed that there was a need to take an approach that enabled participants to examine all the outstanding issues with a view to resolving them and to decide how to deal with those that might remain unresolved.[53] According to the Report of the UN Secretary-General, issues were reviewed on the basis of information notes compiled by the Secretariat.[54] In the course of six informal consultations between 1990 and 1991, all the outstanding issues concerning the deep seabed mining provisions of UNCLOS were considered.[55]

48 Edward D Brown, "Neither Necessary nor Prudent at This Stage: The Regime of Seabed Mining and Its Impact on the Universality of the UN Convention on the Law of the Sea" (1993) 17 Marine Policy 93.

49 Entered into force 2 September 1984. The eight states are: Belgium, France, Federal Republic of Germany, Italy, Japan, the Netherlands, the United Kingdom, and the United States. For the text, see (1984) 23 ILM 1354–60.

50 Louis B Sohn, "International Law Implications of the 1994 Agreement" (1994) 88 AJIL 696.

51 Concerning the consultations process, see UNGA "Consultations of the Secretary-General on Outstanding Issues Relating to the Deep Seabed Mining Provisions of the United Nations Convention on the Law of the Sea, Report of the Secretary-General" UN Doc A/48/950 (9 June 1994) p 2 para 1 <http://www.un.org/depts/los/general_assembly/general_assembly_reports.htm> accessed January 14, 2018.

52 ibid para 4. 53 ibid 2–3, para 5. 54 ibid 3, para 6. 55 ibid 3, para 7.

At the second phase of the consultation process, which commenced in 1992, Mr Boutros Boutros-Ghali continued the informal consultations. The consultations were open to all delegations, and some 75 to 90 delegations attended these meetings.[56] At the informal consultations held in January 1993, it was generally agreed that the outcome must be of a legally binding nature and that a duality of regimes must be avoided.[57] During the course of the round consultations held in August 1993, a paper dated August 3, 1993, prepared by representatives of several developed and developing states, which was commonly known as the "Boat Paper," was circulated among delegations as a contribution to the process of the consultations. The "Boat Paper" was revised a few times and provided a useful basis for negotiation. In particular, in the second round of the informal consultations held in April 1994, an updated version of the "Boat Paper," entitled "Draft resolution and draft Agreement relating to the Implementation of Part XI of the 1982 United Nations Convention on the Law of the Sea," was submitted and participants undertook an article-by-article review of the draft Agreement.[58] The last meeting of the informal consultations was held in June 1994 and, on July 28, 1994, the UN General Assembly adopted the Agreement relating to the Implementation of Part XI of the United Nations Convention on the Law of the Sea of 10 December 1982, by a vote of 121 in favor, none against, and seven abstentions.[59]

An innovative feature of the treaty-making process of the 1994 Implementation Agreement was that the consultation process was developed under the initiative of the UN Secretary-General.[60] It is of particular interest to note that the UN Secretary-General's initiative was undertaken *before* entering into force of UNCLOS.

Under Article 2 of the Implementation Agreement:

> The provisions of this Agreement and Part XI shall be interpreted and applied together as a single instrument. In the event of any inconsistency between this Agreement and Part XI, the provisions of this Agreement shall prevail.

Furthermore, the Implementation Agreement was applied provisionally pending its entry into force in accordance with Article 7. As a consequence, the original deep seabed regime under Part XI of the Convention was modified by the Implementation Agreement, without using the amendment procedures of UNCLOS.[61] Notably, the modification was made *before* entering into force of UNCLOS. The modification of the Convention under the initiative of the UN Secretary-General can be considered as an innovative means in treaty-making.[62]

[56] ibid 3, para 9. [57] ibid 4, para 12. [58] ibid 5, paras 18–19.

[59] For an analysis of the Implementation Agreement, see for instance, Bernard H Oxman, "The 1994 Agreement Relating to the Implementation of Part XI of the UN Convention on the Law of the Sea" in Davor Vidas and Willy Østreng (eds), *Order for the Oceans at the Turn of the Century* (Kluwer 1999) 15.

[60] Boyle and Chinkin (n 29) 147.

[61] ibid. Amendments procedures are provided in Articles 312, 313, and 314 of UNCLOS. In particular, Article 314 provides procedures concerning amendments to the provisions of UNCLOS relating exclusively to activities in the Area.

[62] Boyle and Chinkin (n 29) 147.

At the same time, it must be stressed that the essential elements governing the Area, namely, the principle of the common heritage of mankind, the non-appropriation of the Area and its natural resources, the use exclusively for peaceful purposes, and the benefit of mankind as a whole, remained intact.[63] In fact, the Preamble of the Implementation Agreement reaffirmed that "the seabed and ocean floor and subsoil thereof, beyond the limits of national jurisdiction [...] as well as the resources of the Area, are the common heritage of mankind."[64] Overall, it can be said that the Implementation Agreement modified the manner of exploration and exploitation of mineral resources in the Area, while maintaining the cardinal principle governing the Area.

3.2 The 1995 Fish Stocks Agreement

Furthermore, the role of the UN in the adoption of the 1995 Fish Stocks Agreement must be examined.[65] Unlike the 1994 Implementation Agreement, the treaty-making of the 1995 Fish Stocks Agreement commenced under Canadian initiative. Many fish stocks in the Northwest Atlantic were known to be seriously depleted and the Canadian government was forced to totally close domestic fisheries for cod from 1992 to 1993.[66] In light of the grave situation that Newfoundland fishermen were facing in the Northwest Atlantic, Canada raised the question concerning conservation and management of high seas fisheries in 1990 when it commenced to prepare for the United Nations Conference on Environment and Development (UNCED).[67] Initially Canada and other cosponsors wanted their proposal reflected in Agenda 21. Since some of the elements in that proposal did not receive consensus support, however, they advanced the idea of convening a conference under the auspices of the UN to discuss high seas fisheries.[68] After international negotiations on this subject, at the UNCED at Rio de Janeiro in June 1992, it was agreed that states should convene an intergovernmental conference under UN auspices with a view to promoting effective implementation of UNCLOS on straddling fish stocks and highly migratory fish stocks.[69] The UN General Assembly thus decided, in its Resolution 47/192, to convene in 1993 an intergovernmental conference on straddling fish stocks and highly migratory fish stocks.[70]

63 Dolliver Nelson, "The New Deep Sea-Bed Mining Regime" (1995) 10 Intl J Marine & Coastal L 203.

64 See also section 4 of the Implementation Agreement; UNCLOS Article 311(6).

65 For a detailed analysis of the drafting process of the Agreement, see Moritaka Hayashi, "United Nations Conference on Straddling Fish Stocks and Highly Migratory Fish Stocks: An Analysis of the 193 Sessions" [1994] Ocean Ybk 20.

66 ibid 23. 67 ibid 26. 68 ibid 28.

69 UN Conference on Environment and Development, Rio de Janeiro, 3 to 14 June 1992, Agenda 21, para 17.49.

70 UNGA, "United Nations Conference on Straddling Fish Stocks and Highly Migratory Fish Stocks" (29 January 1993) UN Doc A/RES/47/192, para 1.

The UN Conference on Straddling Fish Stocks and Highly Migratory Fish Stocks was held at the UN Headquarters in New York between 1993 and 1995.[71] Its Rules of Procedure provided that the Conference should conduct its work on the basis of general agreement and that it may proceed to a vote in accordance with Rule 35 only after all efforts at achieving general agreement have been exhausted.[72] There was no basic proposal or document that formed the basis of discussion at the conference. Thus it decided to ask the Chairman to prepare a list of subjects and issues as guidance for its work, and the Chairman invited the conference participants to submit proposals containing these issues.[73] Accordingly, the Chairman prepared "A Guide to the Issues before the Conference" (the Chairman's Guide) at the first substantive session held in New York in July 1993.[74] While the conference focused on the Chairman's Guide, references were also made to a number of documents submitted by delegations. Furthermore, the Chairman conducted several informal consultations to discuss key issues on the basis of informal working papers prepared by the Chairman.[75] Subsequently the Chairman prepared for a new document, entitled "Negotiating Text," to provide the conference with a basic negotiation text.[76]

On August 4, 1995, the UN Conference adopted the Fish Stocks Agreement by consensus. As provided in Article 2 of the Agreement, "[t]he objective of this Agreement is to ensure the long-term conservation and sustainable use of straddling fish stocks and highly migratory fish stocks through effective implementation of the relevant provisions of the Convention." The Fish Stocks Agreement contains at least three crucial elements that are not explicitly provided in UNCLOS.

The first element is the concept of sustainable use. Article 5(a) requires coastal states and states fishing on the high seas to "adopt measures to ensure long-term sustainability of straddling fish stocks and highly migratory fish stocks and promote the objective of their optimum utilization." Furthermore, Article 5(h) places an obligation upon coastal states and states fishing on the high seas to "take measures to prevent or eliminate over-fishing and excess fishing capacity and to ensure that levels of fishing effort do not exceed those commensurate with the sustainable use of fishery resources."

The second crucial element concerns the precautionary approach. Article 6(1) of the Agreement places a clear obligation upon states to apply "the precautionary approach widely to conservation, management, and exploitation of straddling fish stocks and highly migratory fish stocks in order to protect the living marine resources and preserve the marine environment." Annex II of the Agreement provides Guidelines for the Application of Precautionary Reference Points in Conservation and Management of Straddling Fish Stocks and Highly Migratory Fish Stocks.

The third important element pertains to the ecosystem approach. The Preamble of the Agreement clearly notes "the need to avoid adverse impacts on the marine environment,

[71] "Final Act of the United Nations Conference on Straddling Fish Stocks and Highly Migratory Fish Stocks" (7 September 1995) UN Doc A/CONF.164/38, para 6.

[72] UNGA Rules of Procedure of the General Assembly, Rule 33 UN Doc A/CONF.164/6 (3 May 1993).

[73] Hayashi (n 65) 32.

[74] ibid; UN Document A/CONF.164/10 (24 June 1993).

[75] Hayashi (n 65) 33.

[76] ibid 34; UN Document A/CONF.164/13 (29 July 1993).

preserve biodiversity, maintain the integrity of marine ecosystems and minimize the risk of long-term or irreversible effects of fishing operations." Article 5(g) thus places an obligation upon coastal states and states fishing on the high seas to protect biodiversity in the marine environment.

The three elements are a prerequisite to promote sustainable management of marine living resources.[77] One can thus argue that the Fish Stocks Agreement further elaborates relevant rules of the Convention with regard to straddling and highly migratory fish stocks.[78] In so doing, the United Nations Conference on Straddling Fish Stocks and Highly Migratory Fish Stocks can be said to make a significant contribution to facilitating the implementation of UNCLOS.[79]

4 New Challenges

At present, the UN encounters a new challenge: development of a legally binding instrument with regard to the conservation and sustainable use of marine biological diversity in areas beyond national jurisdiction. Biological diversity is fundamental for human life because it provides essential services for the maintenance of the biosphere in a condition that supports human and other life. However, the decline of biological diversity, including marine biological diversity, is becoming a matter of more pressing concern in the world.[80] UNCLOS contains no explicit provision with regard to the conservation of marine biological diversity in the high seas and the Area. Thus, in 2004, the UN General Assembly established the Ad Hoc Open-ended Informal Working Group to study issues relating to the conservation and sustainable use of marine biological diversity beyond areas of national jurisdiction.[81] Since then, a series of meetings of the Working Group has been convened. To date, however, no legal framework has been established on this matter. Furthermore, marine genetic resources in areas beyond national jurisdiction are of growing scientific and commercial interest because of their potential for biotechnological, pharmaceutical, and cosmetic applications.[82] Yet, UNCLOS contains no specific provision with respect to these resources.

[77] See Tanaka (n 4) 248ff.

[78] See Moritaka Hayashi, "The 1995 UN Fish Stocks Agreement and the Law of the Sea" in Vidas and Østreng (n 59)37.

[79] ibid 52.

[80] According to the International Union for Conservation of Nature (IUCN), current extinction rates of threatened species are 50 to 500 times higher than extinction rates in the fossil record. Jonathan EM Baillie, Craig Hilton-Taylor, and Simon N Stuart (eds), *2004 IUCN Red List of Threatened Species. A Global Species Assessment* (IUCN 2004) xxi.

[81] UNGA Res, *"Oceans and the Law of the Sea" (17 November 2004)* UN Doc A/RES/59/24, 13–14, para 73.

[82] Convention on Biological Diversity, Decision VIII/21. *Marine and coastal biological diversity: conservation and sustainable use of deep seabed genetic resources beyond the limits of national jurisdiction*, UNEP/CBD/COP/DEC/VIII/21, 15 June 2006, 1, para 1; Iris Kirchner-Freis and Andree Kirchner,

Against that background, in 2015, the UN General Assembly decided to develop an international legally binding instrument under UNCLOS on the conservation and sustainable use of marine biological diversity of areas beyond national jurisdiction.[83] In its Resolution of 19 June 2015, the General Assembly stressed "the need for the comprehensive global regime to better address the conservation and sustainable use of marine biological diversity of areas beyond national jurisdiction, and having considered the feasibility of developing an international instrument under the Convention."[84] To this end, it decided to establish, prior to holding an intergovernmental conference, a preparatory committee—open to all members of the UN, members of the specialized agencies, and parties to the Convention, with others invited as observers in accordance with past practice of the UN—to make substantive recommendations to the General Assembly on the elements of a draft treaty under UNCLOS. The preparatory committee started its work in 2016, and it was required to report to the General Assembly on its progress by the end of 2017.[85] The report was adopted in July 2017.[86] The first session of the Intergovernmental Conference on this subject was convened in September 2018. The second and third sessions are to take place in 2019, and the fourth session is to take place in the first half of 2020.[87]

It is significant that the General Assembly decided to make a new treaty on this subject. At the same time, it cannot pass unnoticed that the spatial scope of the new treaty is limited to areas beyond national jurisdiction, even though the spatial scope of man-made jurisdictional zones does not always correspond to marine ecosystems.[88] In this regard, it appears that the compatibility of conservation measures between marine spaces under and beyond national jurisdiction should be one of the crucial issues that need further consideration.[89]

"Genetic Resources of the Sea" in David J Attard et al (eds), *The IMLO Manual on the International Maritime Law*, vol I (OUP 2014) 377. According to the Subsidiary Body on Scientific, Technical and Technological Advice of the Rio Convention, marine genetic resources are defined as "marine plants, animals and microorganisms, and parts thereof containing functional units of heredity that are of actual or potential value." Convention on Biological Diversity, Status and trends of, and threats to, deep seabed genetic resources beyond national jurisdiction, and identification of technical options for their conservation and sustainable use, UNEP/CBD/SBSTTA/11/11, 22 July 2005, 6, para 10. Generally on this issue, see in particular, David Leary, *International Law and the Genetic Resources of the Deep Sea* (Njihoff 2007).

[83] UNGA Res 69/292 (19 June 2015) UN Doc A/RES/69/292.

[84] ibid preamble.

[85] ibid para 1(a).

[86] *Report of the Preparatory Committee established by General Assembly resolution 69/292*, A/ AC. 287/2017/PC.4/2.

[87] See https://www.un.org/bbnj/content/sessions.

[88] This is an essential limitation of the zonal management approach. Tanaka (n 4) 453–454.

[89] In fact, the *Report of the Preparatory Committee* referred to this issue. *Report of the Preparatory Committee* (n 86) 11, para. 4.2. In this connection, it may be relevant to note that the Fish Stocks Agreement contains a provision to addresses this issue. See Article 7 of the Fish Stocks Agreement.

5 Conclusions

The above consideration reveals that the UN General Assembly made a significant contribution in treaty-making in the law of the sea by convening a series of international conferences. As shown by the adoption of the Implementation Agreement, the UN Secretary-General can also take an initiative in treaty-making. In this regard, it is important to note that the tasks of the conferences in the field of the law of the sea have changed over time.

At the First UN Conference on the Law of the Sea, its primary task was to establish a legal framework for coordinating interests of individual states according to multiple jurisdictional zones. Yet, little attention was paid to the safeguard of community interests, such as the protection of the marine environment. Furthermore, developing states could not affect the treaty-making process of the Geneva Conventions because of their limited participation. The same basically applied to the Second UN Conference on the Law of the Sea.

In contrast, the Third UN Conference on the Law of the Sea dealt not only with the reconciliation of competing state interests but also with the safeguard of community interests, such as the establishment of the deep seabed regime on the basis of the principle of common heritage of mankind and marine environmental protection. Thus, it is argued that the task of the Third UN Conference went well beyond the traditional scope of the reconciliation of interests of individual states. The Conference seems to signify the changing role of treaty-making conferences in the context of the law of the sea: the task of treaty-making conferences is no longer limited to the reconciliation of state interests. The safeguard and promotion of community interests should also be a subject of considerable importance in treaty-making conferences. This would be particularly true of the international conference for adopting an international legally binding instrument on the conservation and sustainable use of marine biological diversity of areas beyond national jurisdiction. It appears that the reconciliation between state interests and community interests should be a crucial issue in treaty-making in the international law of the sea.

CHAPTER 25B

NEGOTIATING THE UN CONVENTION ON THE LAW OF THE SEA

a practitioner's reflection

TOMMY KOH*

THE United Nations Convention on the Law of the Sea or UNCLOS is an extremely important treaty. It applies to 70 percent of the earth's surface. It is the embodiment of the modern law of the sea. It creates a legal order for the world's oceans. It promotes peace and cooperation. It supports the peaceful settlement of disputes and the rule of law.

The President of the Third UN Conference on the Law of the Sea (1973–1980) was Ambassador Shirley Hamilton Amerasinghe of Sri Lanka. He passed away in December 1980. In March 1981, I was elected to succeed him. In this chapter I will give a practitioner's account of the negotiating process that led to the adoption of UNCLOS.

1 PREPARING FOR THE CONFERENCE

The first point I wish to make is that the Third UN Conference on the Law of the Sea did not follow the negotiating process of the First (1958) and Second (1960) UN Conferences on the Law of the Sea. The preparatory work for the first two conferences was undertaken by the International Law Commission and, later, by a Group of Experts.

In the case of the Third Conference, the preparatory work was entrusted to the UN Seabed Committee. Inexplicably, the conference began in December 1973 without

* President, Third UN Conference on the Law of the Sea, 1981–1982.

a draft text. This is just one of the many unusual, if not unique features of the negotiating process of the Third Conference. I shall identify and discuss the most important of these features.

Second, the conference had an extremely broad agenda—covering almost every aspect of the oceans, its resources, and its uses. The agenda covered 25 very broad issues. This, plus the fact that the conference began without a draft text, accounted for the length of the conference. The whole process, beginning with the UN Seabed Committee, in 1968, took 14 years. The conference itself lasted 9 years.

Third, the conference agreed to work on the "package-deal" principle. The logic behind this principle is that many of the items on the agenda were interrelated. The ambition was to treat ocean space as an ecological whole. The second reason is that delegations were making trade-offs between their positions on different issues. They were willing to make a concession in one area in return for a gain in another area. The result was the consensus that delegations could not pick and choose. They had to accept the convention as a whole.

Fourth, the rules of procedure contained two unusual features. First, the rules discouraged the taking of decisions by voting. The objective was to adopt a convention that would command the widest support. Hence, it was felt that it was necessary to incorporate into the rules of procedure safeguards against hasty voting and providing for a cooling-off period. The second feature was the agreement to have special rules concerning the majority of votes required for the taking of decisions. During the cooling-off period, the President would make every effort to achieve consensus.

Fifth, in November 1973, a month before the commencement of the conference, the UN General Assembly adopted a resolution that included a so-called "Gentlemen's Agreement." The operational paragraph of this resolution states that "the conference shall make every effort to reach agreement on substantive matters by way of consensus and there should be no voting on such matters until all efforts at consensus have been exhausted." The agreement was observed in letter and spirit. No decision at the conference, on a substantive matter, was taken by vote except the vote on the adoption of the convention taken by the conference on April 30, 1982.

2 The Conference Begins

My sixth point is that the politics of the conference and the long duration of the negotiating process produced new groupings and alliances that both facilitated and hindered the negotiations. The usual UN regional groups existed in the conference but they were less influential than the interest groups that emerged at the conference. These interest groups cut across geographical regions, ideology, and development status. Some of the most influential groups were: the Coastal States Group, with 76 members; the Group of Landlocked and Geographically Disadvantaged States, with 55 members; the "Margineers Group" or Group of Broad-Shelf States, with 13 members; the Straits States Group; the Group of Archipelagic States; the Group of Maritime States; and the Great Maritime Powers.

Of the traditional groups, the most influential was the Group of 77, to which the developing countries belonged. This group played a major role in the negotiations on Part XI of the convention, which applies to the seabed and ocean floor beyond national jurisdiction. Of the regional groups, the one that was the most united and vocal was the Latin-American Group.

The emergence of the interest groups had a profound impact on the negotiations. The conference had to acknowledge their existence and allocate facilities for their meetings. On the positive side, they helped to identify and clarify the issues in dispute. On the negative side, the interest groups consumed a great deal of the conference's time and resources. Also, once a group had adopted a common position, it was often rigid in the negotiations.

Seventh, there were two parallel systems of negotiations. There was the official negotiating structure consisting of the plenary, the three main committees, and the subsidiary groups. There was an unofficial negotiating process consisting of the interest groups and the informal private negotiating groups.

The role of the informal private negotiating groups was a unique feature of the conference. They emerged to fulfill a need. The conference had 151 participating states. It was extremely difficult to negotiate in such a large body. It was difficult to reduce the size of the negotiating groups because no state was willing to be left out. The informal private negotiating groups emerged in order to fulfill the need for small but representative negotiating groups. The convenors of these groups were individuals who had stature at the conference. They could choose which delegations to invite to join their respective groups.

The remarkable story is that some of the most important provisions of the convention, for example, on the Exclusive Economic Zone, Straits Used for International Navigation, and the Legal Status of the Exclusive Economic Zone and Dispute Settlement, were the fruits of negotiations conducted in these informal private negotiating groups. The Group of Juridical Experts, convened and chaired by Jens Evensen of Norway, contributed many of the texts in the chapter on the Exclusive Economic Zone. The difficult issue of the status of the EEZ was resolved in the private negotiating group of 17 delegations, convened and chaired by Jorge Castaneda of Mexico. The chapter on Straits Used for International Navigation was negotiated in a private group of 13 delegations co-convened by Fiji and the United Kingdom. The text of chapter XV on Dispute Settlement emerged from a private group cochaired by Australia, El Salvador, and Kenya.

Eighth, the manner in which the single negotiating text came to be prepared was most unusual. The conference had begun in December 1973 without a negotiating text. At the third session of the conference in 1975, the delegation of Singapore proposed that it was time to prepare a single negotiating text. This was accepted by the conference and the task was entrusted to the chairman of the three main committees, namely, Ambassadors Paul Engo of Cameroon, Galindo Pohl of El Salvador, and Alexander Yankov of Bulgaria respectively. Ambassador Pohl had met with an accident and he delegated the task to his Rapporteur, Ambassador Satya Nandan of Fiji. It was extraordinary, to say the least, to entrust so much power and responsibility to three men. In retrospect, we can say that, fortunately for the conference, two of the three did their job well but one did not. The subsequent difficulties experienced by the conference in negotiating a balanced and acceptable text of Part XI of the convention could be traced back to this source.

Although President Amerasinghe had no mandate from the conference, he took it upon himself to offer a text on dispute settlement. He enlisted the help of Professor Louis Sohn of the US delegation and two members of the Secretariat, namely, Hugo Caminos and Gitakumar Chitty. The team relied heavily on the paper that had been prepared by the private group on dispute settlement. Professor Sohn had served as the rapporteur of that group.

Ninth, the conference leadership consisted of the President, the Chairman of the three main committees, the chairman of the drafting committee, and the Rapporteur-General. They constituted the collegium that played a pivotal role in the management of the Conference. When I succeeded Shirley Amerasinghe as the President, I consolidated the collegium and tried to inject it with a greater sense of unity and esprit de corps. The ability of the six principal officers of the conference to work as a team was important to the success of the conference because it provided it with leadership, good management, and direction.

Tenth, the Secretariat made an enormous contribution to the success of the conference. I entrusted the Head of the Secretariat, Under-Secretary General Bernardo Zuleta, on several occasions with the responsibility to undertake consultations on my behalf, on some procedural questions. Some members of the Secretariat helped the various chairmen of the main committees and negotiating groups with the preparation of texts. At its best, there was a symbiotic relationship between the conference leaders and the Secretariat.

Eleventh, the nongovernmental organizations played a very constructive role at the conference. In my tribute to them, I said that they had provided the conference with three valuable services. They brought independent experts to brief the delegates, especially on the highly technical issues. They helped the delegates of the developing countries to narrow the knowledge gap between them and their colleagues from the developed countries. They also provided the conference with opportunities to meet at informal settings and to brainstorm on some of the most difficult issues.

3 Conclusion

The negotiating process of the Third UN Conference on the Law of the Sea had several unique features. First, it was most unusual for a treaty-making conference to begin without a draft text. The subsequent decision to request the chairmen of the three main committees to prepare the single negotiating text was a leap of faith. The second unique feature was the role of the unofficial private negotiating groups. The third unique feature was the deep commitment to finding consensus on all substantive matters and to avoid voting.

The Third UN Conference on the Law of the Sea must be considered as one of the most important treaty-making conferences ever convened by the UN. The stakes for the member states of the UN and, indeed, for the entire global community were very high. Only the UN, with universal membership, could convene such a conference.

CHAPTER 26

PRIVILEGES AND IMMUNITIES OF THE UNITED NATIONS AND SPECIALIZED AGENCIES

DAVINIA AZIZ* AND ALISON SEE**

THIS chapter focuses on the very first instances of multilateral treaty-making undertaken under the auspices of the United Nations.[1] Months after the Charter was signed in June 1945, the General Assembly adopted the Convention on Privileges and Immunities of the United Nations ("the General Convention") at its first session in February 1946. At the same time, the General Assembly set in motion the process of elaborating the Convention on Privileges and Immunities of the Specialized Agencies ("the Specialized Agencies Convention"). By its second session in November 1947, the General Assembly had adopted the Specialized Agencies Convention. Together with Articles 104 and 105 of the Charter, as well as the equivalent provisions in the constituent instruments of the specialized agencies, the General Convention and the Specialized Agencies Convention remain cornerstones of the legal framework governing the privileges and immunities of the United Nations and its specialized agencies.

A singular feature of the legal framework governing the privileges and immunities of international organizations is that it is substantially treaty-based. In this regard, the provisions of the Conventions are further elaborated and supplemented, to fit the specificities of each arrangement in the territories of member states, through host state agreements,

* Senior State Counsel, International Affairs Division, Attorney-General's Chambers of Singapore and Adjunct Assistant Professor, Faculty of Law, National University of Singapore.

** Justices' Law Clerk, Supreme Court of Singapore; The views expressed in this chapter are those of the authors in their personal capacities, and do not necessarily reflect the views of the Singapore government.

[1] In this chapter, the term "United Nations" is used interchangeably with "the Organization," which also denotes the juridical entity, and with the abbreviation "UN."

ad hoc conference agreements, and other applicable bilateral agreements.[2] In the last 70 years, Convention language has featured numerous times before international courts and tribunals, national courts, and internal administrative tribunals,[3] as well as in the everyday practice of the legal adviser tasked to interpret the web of treaty obligations that constitute the privileges and immunities framework relevant to her brief.[4] In short, the enduring relevance of the Convention treaty regimes to the life of the UN family, and the relations between each organization in that family and respective member states, as well as other territories where each of these organizations may be present, cannot be overstated.

Comprehensive drafting histories of the two Conventions may be found elsewhere in the literature.[5] As such, in line with the focus of this *Handbook*, the present chapter analyzes the contribution of the United Nations, through its treaty-making, to the field of international organization privileges and immunities along the following thematic lines:

(*a*) the conceptual innovations of the two Conventions, including the key juridical shift from diplomatic to functional immunity, and the adoption of the multilateral format;

(*b*) key features of the treaty-making procedures followed in these first years of the Organization, some of which remain familiar to practitioners engaged in United Nations treaty-making today;

(*c*) the multiple roles of the Organization, as forum, subject (in the case of the General Convention), and active driver (in the case of the Specialized Agencies Convention) of the treaty-making process; and

(*d*) the role of the specialized agencies in operationalizing the Specialized Agencies Convention and its Annexes, including in the course of the Secretary-General's depositary practice relating to reservations.

The chapter concludes with a necessarily brief assessment of the Conventions' legacy for models of treaty practice, and for the modern law of international organizations.

[2] A compendium of such agreements concluded in the relevant calendar year is generally available in Chapter II of the UN Juridical Yearbook, available online for the years 1962 through 2013, <http://legal.un.org/unjuridicalyearbook/> accessed January 8, 2018).

[3] Decisions available to the UN Office of Legal Affairs are published in Chapters V, VII, and VIII of the UN Juridical Yearbook (n 2).

[4] Selected legal opinions of legal advisers to the secretariats of the UN and related intergovernmental organizations, including certain specialized agencies governed by the Specialized Agencies Convention, are published annually in Chapter VI of the UN Juridical Yearbook (n 2).

[5] See eg, for example, August Reinisch with Peter Bachmeyer (eds), *The Conventions on the Privileges and Immunities of the United Nations and its Specialized Agencies: A Commentary* (OUP 2016); Anthony J. Miller, "The Privileges and Immunities of the United Nations" (2009) 6 Intl Org. L. Rev. 7, 16–19 [hereinafter "Miller, 'United Nations'"]; Anthony J Miller, "The Privileges and Immunities of United Nations Officials" (2007) 4(2) Intl Org. L. Rev. 169, 180–83 [hereinafter "Miller, 'Officials'"]; Anthony J Miller, "United Nations Experts on Missions and Their Privileges and Immunities" (2007) 4(1) Intl Org L Rev 11, 17–19 [hereinafter "Miller, 'Experts'"]; "Review of the Multilateral Treaty-Making Process," UN Doc. ST/LEG/SER.B/21 (1985) [hereinafter "1985 Review"] at 314–16, 20–322.

1 1946 Convention on Privileges and Immunities of the United Nations

In the interwar decades, practical problems had arisen in operationalizing the status, immunities, and facilities accorded to the League of Nations and the International Labour Organization (ILO).[6] The Covenant of the League had provided in general terms for the entitlement of League Members' representatives and League officials to "diplomatic privileges and immunities," and for the inviolability of League premises.[7] Detailed legal arrangements governing the status of the League in Switzerland thus had to be worked out with the host state in a series of post-Covenant exchanges between the League and the Swiss Federal Council.[8] As for the ILO, the key issues were identified in a report submitted to the watershed May 1944 International Labour Conference in Philadelphia, and elaborated, together with legal arrangements already in place, in a January 1945 note from the International Labour Office to the Constitutional Committee of the ILO Governing Body.[9]

The following sections highlight how, in light of this context, delegates settled upon the essential scheme of the General Convention, as well as key aspects of the ensuing treaty-making process. This is a story that begins before the United Nations, in a technical committee of the San Francisco Conference, in the preparatory work for Articles 104 and 105 of the Charter. The subsequent lawmaking process to implement Articles 104 and 105 of the Charter can be traced from the Executive Committee of the United Nations Preparatory Commission, which convened in London over the summer and into the early autumn of 1945. This process continued in the Legal Committee (Committee 5) of the United Nations Preparatory Commission and subsequently the Sixth Committee of the General Assembly. The treaty-making process concluded in February 1946 with the General Assembly's adoption of the General Convention as part of a set of five resolutions on privileges and immunities.

[6] Scholarly writings contemporaneous with the treaty-making processes covered in this chapter outlined the main practical difficulties. See Martin Hill, *Immunities and Privileges of International Officials: The Experience of the League of Nations* (Carnegie Endowment for International Peace 1947), especially at 96–100; Josef L. Kunz, "Privileges and Immunities of International Organizations" (1947) 41(4) AJIL 828, especially at 844, 857, 860.

[7] *Covenant of the League of Nations*, 28 June 1919, 108 LNTS 188 (entered into force 10 January 1920), Article VII.

[8] Through *Modus Vivendi* of 1921 and 1926 with the Swiss Federal Council. The documentation is collected in Hill (n 6) Annex.

[9] International Labour Office, "General Note" (1945) 27(2) ILO Official Bulletin 197 [hereinafter "the ILO Memorandum"]. See also C Wilfred Jenks, *International Immunities* (Oceana Publications 1961).

1.1 The Multilateral Structure of United Nations Privileges and Immunities

There were two key conceptual innovations in the preparatory work for Articles 104 and 105 of the Charter. A key document of the San Francisco Conference that outlines the underlying policy thinking is the Report of the Rapporteur of Committee IV/2.[10] First, the drafters deliberately omitted the term "diplomatic," explaining that they had

> preferred to substitute a more appropriate standard, based, for the purposes of the Organization, on the necessity of realizing its purposes and, in the case of the representatives of its [M]embers and the officials of the Organization, on providing for the independent exercise of their functions.[11]

Second, at least two possible lawmaking scenarios were proposed in Article 105, paragraph 3. Not wishing to decide architecture for the General Assembly, the drafters thought that the Charter obligations might be operationalised through recommendations ("the General Assembly may make recommendations") or through conventions ("or may propose conventions to . . . Members"). Prescient as to the variegated nature of the current legal framework governing privileges and immunities, the drafters explained:

> Should it be appropriate, such recommendations could apply only to those [M]embers who, for instance, might have weightier obligations owing to the fact that the Organization or its organs happen to have establishments on their territory . . . Naturally the recommendations of the Assembly might differ according to the particular circumstances of the [S]tates to which they would be addressed. On the other hand, the possibility is not excluded of a general convention to be submitted to all the Members.[12]

Shortly thereafter, the Charter was signed on June 26, 1945.

Detailed explanation for the subsequent decision to adopt a multilateral treaty format as opposed to recommendations can be found in the later work done under the auspices of the Sixth Committee of the first General Assembly. Three main reasons for the multilateral treaty framework were adduced:

[10] United Nations Conference on International Organization, Committee IV/2, "Report of the Rapporteur of Committee IV/2" (1945) 13 Doc UN Conf on Int'l Org 703.

[11] Report of the Rapporteur of Committee IV/2 (n 10) 704.

[12] ibid. An earlier Canadian proposal had been to consider only a general convention as the way forward on treaty design: see United Nations Conference on International Organization, Documents for Meetings of Committee IV/2: Privileges and Immunities (1945) 13 Doc. U.N. Conf. on Intl Org. 727 at 727.

(*a*) the necessary immunities had to be specified "in a manner which was as precise as possible";

(*b*) a general convention "would be likely to lead to the greatest uniformity in application"; and

(*c*) a general convention would be the procedure that would "best... facilitate the passing by Members of the necessary domestic legislation."[13]

The following sections highlight three key features that characterized the methods deployed by delegates throughout the treaty-making process. It is possible to discern in these features the basic lines of treaty-making protocols used in later UN negotiations.

1.2 Legal Precedent and Policy Material

First, the General Convention was made in the context of legal and policy analyses relevant to the matters to be addressed through the new treaty.

By virtue of simple chronological fact, delegates did not have the benefit of draft articles or other prior work by the International Law Commission. Such work by the Commission would of course inform several significant lawmaking enterprises in the new Organization.[14]

However, delegates did not have to proceed from a blank slate. They had access to legal precedent, in terms of the Swiss *Modus Vivendi* with the League and other legal texts concerning the immunities of existing international agencies. In addition, delegates had access to assessments of these precedents, including the ILO Memorandum and a book manuscript by a League official.[15] These texts were not entered into the formal records, but their role is well-reported in contemporaneous and later literature.[16]

The Executive Committee to the United Nations Preparatory Commission synthesized learnings from these materials into a Study on Privileges and Immunities.[17]

[13] Sub-Committee on Privileges and Immunities, "First Report of the Sub-Committee on Privileges and Immunities," UNGAOR, 1946, UN Doc A/C.6/17 [hereinafter "First Report of the Sub-Committee"]; UNGAOR, 1st Year, 7th Mtg, UN Doc A/C.6/19 (1946) at 2.

[14] The Commission would not be established until November 1947 (UNGA Res 174 (21 November 1947)). For a summary of the Commission's output, see *Texts, Instruments and Final Reports*, online: International Law Commission <http://legal.un.org/ilc/texts/texts.shtml> accessed January 15, 2018.

[15] Hill (n 6) vi; *1985 Review* (n 5) 315; Miller, "Experts" (n 5) 27; *Applicability of Article VI, Section 22, of the Convention on the Privileges and Immunities of the United Nations*, "Written Statement Submitted on Behalf of the Secretary-General of the United Nations" (27 July 1989), online: International Court of Justice <http://www.icj-cij.org/files/case-related/81/9705.pdf> accessed January 9, 2018 [hereinafter "*Mazilu* Statement"] at 186.

[16] ibid.

[17] The Study is the Appendix to Part III, Chapter V of the Report by the Executive Committee to the Preparatory Commission of the United Nations, PC/EX/113/Rev.1 (12 November 1945) [hereinafter "Report by the Executive Committee"].

The Study did not at that stage incorporate draft treaty text. However, fulfilling a function that might today be filled by a first report of a Special Rapporteur or an initial study of the Secretariat of the Commission, the Study identified: (1) relevant legal provisions that applied to specialized agencies already in existence; (2) the need to coordinate the privileges and immunities of the United Nations with those of the specialized agencies, and to provide separately for the privileges and immunities of the new International Court of Justice; (3) the conceptual distinction between "diplomatic privileges and immunities," and the functional principle governing the privileges and immunities that the General Convention would prescribe; and (4) specific regulatory issues that the General Convention would address, being the creation of what eventually became the United Nations laissez-passer, and the taxation of United Nations officials in the state of which they are nationals.

1.3 Multistage Process and the Use of Small Groups

Second, the General Convention was made in a multistage process, reserving detailed work to small group settings. In the Preparatory Commission, following the consideration of the work by the Executive Committee, the work was remitted to Committee 5, which in turn established an 8-member Subcommittee.[18] In the Sixth Committee, a similar procedure was followed, but with a larger, 15-member Subcommittee.[19] In each case, final decisions were returned for formal action, including by vote, to larger groups more representative of the whole UN membership.[20]

The Subcommittees' reports to their parent bodies are part of the official records of the Preparatory Commission and the Sixth Committee. There are no formal records of Subcommittee discussions.[21] However, something of their work can be gleaned by comparing the draft texts that emerged from the Subcommittees. Such a comparison reveals significant changes seeded and ultimately retained.[22] For example, the Subcommittee at the Sixth Committee stage originated Article VI concerning

[18] Preparatory Commission of the United Nations, Committee 5, Summary Record of Meetings, 2d Mtg, Supp. No. 5, PC/LEG/10 (29 November 1945) (reporting that the topic needed more detailed study that could most suitably be done in subcommittees).

[19] UNGAOR, 1st Year, 6th Mtg, UN Doc SR/6 (1946) at 14.

[20] Committee 5 of the Preparatory Commission voted on an early draft of the General Convention on the understanding that delegations would be "at complete liberty to take up again various points at a later stage": see Preparatory Commission of the United Nations, Committee 5, Summary Record of Meetings, 10th Mtg, Supp. No. 5, PC/LEG/41 (17 December 1945). For the vote in the Sixth Committee, see UNGAOR, 1st Year, 11th Mtg, UN Doc A/C.6/37 (1946).

[21] The only reference in the official records to the character of the discussions that must have taken place is in the Second Report of the Sub-Committee on Privileges and Immunities to the Sixth Committee, in which it was stated that "[t]he draft General Convention on privileges and immunities was submitted to a most thorough discussion in the Sub-Committee": Sub-Committee on Privileges and Immunities, "Second Report of the Sub-Committee on Privileges and Immunities," UNGAOR, 1946, UN Doc A/C.6/31.

[22] The Subcommittee of the Preparatory Commission either made key drafting changes or introduced novel text in relation to:

experts on missions for the United Nations.[23] The comparison is also interesting for its disclosure of ideas articulated but not retained. For example, treaty text prescribing that the Secretary-General should ensure proper third-party motor car insurance coverage was jettisoned even though the proposal arose from an existing practical issue.[24] Several principles and textual proposals relating to the specialized agencies were cabined off for later work.[25]

The Subcommittees also coordinated laterally with the subcommittees tasked to work on legal arrangements between the Organization and its host state. At the Preparatory Commission stage, placeholders for such coordination were marked in respect of two issues: facilities in respect of communications, and freedom of travel to the seat of the United Nations for the press, representatives of nongovernmental organizations, and private individuals. The Subcommittee liaised with the juridical subcommittee of Committee 8 on these issues. Coordination was completed on the first issue when Article III (Facilities in Respect of Communications) was inserted into the text by the Subcommittee at the Sixth Committee stage.[26] As to the second issue, no text was ultimately incorporated into the General Convention.

(*a*) moving references to Articles 104 and 105 of the Charter, which had originally appeared in a first article entitled "Authority," into the preamble; the preamble appears in virtually the same terms in the final text of the General Convention;

(*b*) accession, the interaction between the General Convention and national laws of Members, and the depositary function of the Secretary-General;

(*c*) the scope of tax privileges of the United Nations;

(*d*) the scope of immunities to be accorded to representatives of members and UN officials, and specific categories of representatives and UN officials entitled to such immunities; and

(*e*) the principle that privileges and immunities are granted for the benefit of the United Nations, waiver of immunity, and alternative modes of dispute settlement.

[23] *Mazilu* Statement (n 15) 186. The original mandate of Committee 5 had included "international officials who may be appointed in an expert capacity by the organs of the United Nations": see Report by the Executive Committee (n 17) PC/EX/113/Rev. 1 at 134. Other significant changes were to:

(*a*) assign titles and section numbers to each Article;

(*b*) substitute the concept of the United Nations' undertaking, in place of a prohibition, not to claim certain forms of tax exemption from members, and, in general, refining the General Convention provisions concerning tax privileges; and

(*c*) design the mechanism by which the Secretary-General would specify the categories of United Nations officials entitled to privileges, immunities, and the use of the UN laissez-passer.

[24] The issue was subsequently dealt with as an instruction from members to the Secretary-General by way of a General Assembly resolution adopted alongside the resolution containing the text of the General Convention: see "Resolution relating to the insurance against third party risks of motor-cars of the Organization and of members of the staff," UNGAOR, 1st Sess, UN Doc A/RES/22(I) E (1946).

[25] For example, a New Zealand proposal to include a reference in the General Convention to its application to "comparable officials in the specialized agencies" was tabled thus at the request of the Chairperson of the Sixth Committee: see UN Doc A/C.6/37 (n 20) 30–31.

[26] Draft Recommendation from the Sixth Committee to the General Assembly, UNGAOR, 1st Sess, UN Doc A/C.6/28 (5 February 1946) at 4.

1.4 Key Delegations and Individuals

Third, the records disclose the outsize roles of Canada, and of the United Kingdom delegation member Eric Beckett—later Sir Eric Beckett, Foreign Office Legal Adviser.[27]

Notably, the Canadian delegation to the Philadelphia International Labour Conference in May 1944 had proposed a draft resolution catalyzing the work that resulted in the ILO Memorandum, though the official records do not support formal links.[28] In addition, it was the Canadian delegation that circulated the very first draft of the General Convention in Committee 5 of the Preparatory Commission.[29] While the Canadian draft was inevitably modified in the course of the treaty-making process, it remained influential, and one can still see its essential scheme in the General Convention.

Sir Eric Beckett chaired the Subcommittee on Privileges and Immunities in the Preparatory Commission. In that capacity, he personally undertook coordination with the subcommittee studying relations with the host state. Beckett also originated key provisions governing the legal standing of the United Nations vis-à-vis the General Convention and its states parties: Article VIII (section 30), including the role of the International Court of Justice in settling differences between the United Nations and members in the exercise of its advisory jurisdiction; and the Final Article (sections 35 and 36), including the drafting choice to frame the General Convention as "in force between the United Nations and every [acceding] Member." When the General Convention moved to the Sixth Committee, Beckett served as Rapporteur of its Subcommittee. In the absence of formal documentation, one can only surmise the precise extent of his contributions in subcommittee. What the official records do uncontrovertibly show is that Beckett's contributions inspired a unanimous vote of thanks in the Sixth Committee.[30]

[27] On the role of key delegations and individuals in other UN treaty-making processes, see eg Paul Szasz, "General Law-Making Processes," in Christopher Joyner (ed), *The United Nations and International Law* (CUP 1997) 27 at 35; Tommy TB Koh and Shunmugam Jayakumar, "The Negotiating Process of the Third United Nations Conference on the Law of the Sea," in Myron H. Nordquist (ed), *United Nations Convention on the Law of the Sea 1982: A Commentary*, vol 1 (Martinus Nijhoff 1985) 29; Fanny Benedetti et al, *Negotiating the International Criminal Court: New York to Rome, 1994–1998* (Martinus Nijhoff 2014).

[28] ILO Memorandum (n 9) 197.

[29] Preparatory Commission of the United Nations, Committee 5: Delegation of Canada, Draft Resolution concerning the Question of Immunities, Facilities and Privileges to the Organisation, to Representatives of the Members and to the Officials, PC/LEG/17 (30 November 1945). On the Canadian proposal concerning treaty design at the San Francisco Conference, see (n 12).

[30] See UN Doc A/C.6/37, *supra* (20) 31. Beckett was familiar with both codification in general, as well as the specific legal issues involved in drafting the General Convention, and its domestic implementation: see Geoffrey Marston, "The Origin of the Personality of International Organisations in United Kingdom Law" (1991) 40 ICLQ 403; GG Fitzmaurice and FA Vallat, "Sir (William) Eric Beckett, K.C.M.G., Q.C. (1896–1966): An Appreciation" (1968) 17 ICLQ 267, 280–81.

2 1947 Convention on Privileges and Immunities of the Specialized Agencies

In some respects, the Specialized Agencies Convention was made in much the same way as the General Convention. Elements of the treaty-making process had begun before the General Assembly conferred any formal mandate to negotiate.[31] Aspects of the ILO Memorandum continued to be influential, as in the concept of abuses of privileges in what eventually became Article VII.[32] Similar small group techniques were deployed for detailed work; key roles were filled by familiar individuals, such as Sir Eric Beckett, who served as Rapporteur of the Subcommittee established in the Sixth Committee for work on the Specialized Agencies Convention.

In other respects, the process was fundamentally different. First, the new Organization moved from passive forum and subject matter to active driver of the treaty-making process. This move was consequential to the structural maturation in the Organization by the time of the negotiation of the Specialized Agencies Convention, including the election of the first Secretary-General, who along with the Secretariat, played a key role in the treaty-making process. Second, the design of the Specialized Agencies Convention is unique, with its innovative two-part character set forth in Article X. The specialized agencies' participation is sustained today, including through their special role in United Nations treaty depositary practice on reservations.[33] The following sections therefore focus on these two aspects of the treaty-making process.

2.1 The United Nations as Active Driver of the Treaty-Making Process

The General Assembly adopted the General Convention on February 13, 1946.[34] In a companion resolution, the General Assembly "instruct[ed]" Trygve Lie, the United Nations' newly installed Secretary-General,[35] to "open negotiations with a view to the re-consideration…of the provisions under which the specialized agencies [then enjoyed] privileges and immunities."[36] By March 6, 1947, the Secretary-General and officials of

[31] See (n 25) and accompanying text. [32] See Section 4.2, *infra*.

[33] See Section 4.3.2, *infra*.

[34] Resolution relating to the adoption of the general convention on privileges and immunities of the United Nations, and text of the convention, UNGAOR, 1st Sess, UN Doc A/RES/22(I)A (1946).

[35] Secretary-General Lie was formally installed on February 2, 1946: UNGAOR, 1st Sess, 22d Plenary Mtg, UN Doc A/PV.22 at 323.

[36] Resolution on the Co-ordination of the Privileges and Immunities of the United Nations and the specialized agencies, UNGAOR, 1st Sess, UN Doc A/RES/22(I)D (1946) [hereinafter "Co-ordination Resolution"]

the specialized agencies were meeting to discuss an initial draft treaty text drawn up by the United Nations Secretariat.[37] The key document is the Secretary-General's report of 20 August 1947 to the General Assembly, which summarized the outcome of the consultations and annexed the Secretariat's draft of the Specialized Agencies Convention.[38]

The consultative process helmed by the Secretary-General and supported by his officials significantly influenced the final outcome in at least two fundamental ways. First, by supplying a draft of a single convention, the Secretariat expressed a preliminary choice on treaty design. The treaty text was modified and a further significant structural change was made in the Sixth Committee. However, there was no change in the essential multilateral character of the Secretariat's draft. In particular, 19 sections in the draft that eventually emerged from the Sixth Committee's Subcommittee remained "virtually identical to sections of the draft contained in the Secretary-General's report."[39] Second, the consultations allowed the specialized agencies to articulate and resolve particularities arising from their respective mandates.[40] Certain specialized agencies used the inter-sessional period between the March and July 1947 meetings to consult their own memberships on the Secretariat's draft.[41] In the case of the international financial institutions, the issues first articulated in the course of these consultations found final expression in Article X (section 40), which prescribes the interpretive rule that the Specialized Agencies Convention should not be read to diminish the content of the constituent instrument of the relevant specialized agency.[42]

2.2 "A Single Convention" in "Two Distinct Parts"

When the second session of the General Assembly opened in autumn 1947, the Sixth Committee again established a Subcommittee to consider the question of coordination of the privileges and immunities of the United Nations and the specialized agencies.[43] The key documents explaining the major structural change to the draft annexed to the

[37] Report of the Secretary-General, Co-ordination of the Privileges and Immunities of the United Nations and of the Specialized Agencies, UNGAOR, 2d Sess, UN Doc A/339 (20 August 1947) at 2 [hereinafter "Secretary-General's Report"].

[38] ibid. [39] 1985 Review, *supra* (n 5) at 322.

[40] This policy consideration concerning the privileges and immunities of the specialized agencies was recognized in the Report of the Executive Committee (n 17) 70 and repeated, virtually verbatim, in the operative language of the Co-ordination Resolution (n 36).

[41] Secretary-General's Report (n 37) 4.

[42] Secretary-General's Report (n 37) 3 (reporting the views of the IMF and IBRD representatives who, "while agreeing with the principle of having a single convention, were nevertheless anxious to make it clear that the privileges which had already been conferred upon them by their basic instruments must remain intact"); Behrouz Moradi, "Annexes and Application (Article X Sections 33–40 Specialized Agencies Convention)" in Reinisch and Bachmeyer (eds), *Commentary* (n 5) 609, 623.

[43] Memorandum by the Secretariat, "Proposed Plan of Work and Organization of the Committee," UNGAOR, 2d Sess, UN Doc A/C.6/136 (24 September 1947) at 1. The question of coordination was remitted to the Subcommittee with two related matters: the Headquarters Agreement with the United States, and the privileges and immunities of members' representatives.

Secretary-General's report are the Subcommittee's interim and final reports, made in September and November 1947 respectively. The Subcommittee's final report is also notable for its detailed commentary on several key provisions of the draft treaty text that was presented to the Sixth Committee, as well as the manner in which the Subcommittee worked by receiving assistance from advisers of certain specialized agencies in preparing the draft annexes to the Specialized Agencies Convention, instead of by convening a separate conference as originally envisaged.[44]

The treaty architecture chosen for the Specialized Agencies Convention had to "coordinate" the privileges and immunities of the specialized agencies with that of the United Nations. A single convention would achieve this objective. This method would also facilitate domestic implementation, as with the General Convention. However, the drafters' design brief was complicated by the recognition that not all specialized agencies would require the same list of privileges and immunities to carry out their functions.[45] Moreover, some extant specialized agencies already had constituent instruments prescribing certain privileges and immunities in terms different than those of the General Convention.

The chosen drafting solution appears today as Article X. As the Subcommittee explained, this approach entailed dividing the Specialized Agencies Convention into "two distinct parts." The first part would consist of "a general chapter defining the standard privileges and immunities of the Specialized Agencies" (now Articles II through IX). The second part would consist of "a number of annexes in which would be set out those divergences from the standard privileges and immunities in the case of each Specialized Agency which did not require all the standard privileges or which on account of the special nature of its functions require certain special privileges" (now Article X read with the Annexes).[46]

Article X is a rather complex provision consisting of eight sections (33 through 40). Its main outlines are:

(*a*) Section 33 marries the standard clauses with the annexes by stipulating that the standard clauses shall operate "subject to any modifications set forth in the final (or revised) text of the annex relating to that agency." Section 33 allows for "any modification" of the standard clauses in the annex relating to the particular specialized agencies. Thus, the Specialized Agencies Convention reserves a certain discretion to the specialized agencies to depart from the standard clauses.[47]

(*b*) Section 34 is an overarching teleological rule of treaty interpretation, linking the Specialized Agencies Convention to the constituent instrument of each specialized

[44] Final Report of Sub-Committee 1 of the Sixth Committee, "Co-ordination of the Privileges and Immunities of the United Nations and of the Specialized Agencies," UNGAOR, 2d Sess, UN Doc A/C.6/191 (15 November 1947) at 6–20.

[45] (n 40).

[46] Interim Report of the Sub-Committee No. 1 to the Sixth Committee, "Co-ordination of the Privileges and Immunities of the United Nations and of the Specialized Agencies," UNGAOR, 2d Sess, UN Doc A/C.6/148 at 2.

[47] Moradi (n 45) 609, 613.

agency. The result is that the Specialized Agencies Convention would be interpreted in relation to any specialized agency "in the light of the functions with which that agency is entrusted by its constitutional instrument."

(*c*) Article X incorporates treaty conflict provisions governing the relationship between the Specialized Agencies Convention and headquarters or other applicable supplemental agreements (section 39), as well as the relationship between the Specialized Agencies Convention and the constituent instrument of the specialized agency (section 40). In general, headquarters and other supplemental agreements, and the constituent instrument of the specialized agency are prioritized over the Specialized Agencies Convention.

(*d*) Finally, provisions were also included in the Specialized Agencies Convention that govern the procedure for the application of the Convention to each specialized agency (sections 36 and 40). These account for the internal rules of each specialized agency.

In this way, Article X was a practical legislative device that sought to reconcile the need for the privileges and immunities of the various specialized agencies to be set out in a single instrument with the corresponding need to accommodate the functional and constitutional particularities of each specialized agency.

3 Key Features of the Treaty Regimes Established by the General Convention and the Specialized Agencies Convention

3.1 The General Convention

Article I of the General Convention facilitates daily operations by granting the Organization the capacities enjoyed by the subjects of private law. In particular, the provision grants the Organization "juridical personality" and the capacity to (1) contract, (2) acquire and dispose of immovable and movable property, and (3) institute legal proceedings.

The fundamental immunity granted to the UN under the General Convention is the immunity, except in cases of waiver, from "every form of legal process," per Article II (section 2). Given the drafting of section 2, the precise scope of the immunity thus granted has become the broad focus of critical commentary centered on conceptions of UN accountability.[48] On one view, section 2 grants absolute immunity rather than

[48] See eg, Dame Rosalyn Higgins et al, *Oppenheim's International Law: United Nations* (OUP 2017) 566–67; José E. Alvarez, *The Impact of International Organizations on International Law* (Brill/Nijhoff

functional immunity. This is because section 2 does not reproduce the formulation found in the Charter's Article 105, paragraph 1: "necessary for the fulfilment of its purposes." Some national courts have interpreted this drafting to mean that the Organization's entitlement to immunity from legal process under the General Convention cannot be conditioned.[49] Another view is that section 2 does specify the general principle of immunity based on the Charter principle of "functional necessity,"[50] as evidenced by the General Convention's preamble and drafting history. On this basis, it is said that section 2 cannot be read as granting the Organization immunity that is any broader than what the Charter itself explicitly specifies.[51]

The potentially broad scope of immunity under Article II (section 2) of the General Convention is moderated in principle by Article VIII, pertaining to dispute settlement. Article VIII (section 29) obliges the UN to provide appropriate modes for the settlement of disputes of a private law character and disputes involving any official of the UN whose immunity has not been waived by the Secretary-General.[52] Article VIII (section 30) also provides that disputes arising out of the interpretation or application of the General Convention will be referred to the International Court of Justice, unless otherwise agreed.

Article II (section 3) provides for the inviolability of UN premises. UN property and assets are thus "immune from search, requisition, confiscation, expropriation and any other form of interference." Article II (section 7) provides fiscal privileges through tax and custom duty exemptions. Article III privileges the official communications of the Organization in the territory of each member.

2017) 407–08 and 416; August Reinisch, "Privileges and Immunities" in Jacob Katz Cogan et al (eds), *Oxford Handbook of International Organizations* (OUP 2016) 1055–56 (summarizing the main lines of debate); August Reinisch, "Immunities and Privileges, A Jurisdictional Immunity, Immunity of Property, Funds, and Assets (Article II Section 2 General Convention)" in Reinisch and Bachmeyer (eds), *Commentary* (n 5, 86–87) (summarizing the case law).

[49] High-profile examples of such decisions include the United States Court of Appeals for the Second Circuit decision in the case concerning a cholera outbreak in Haiti, *Georges et al v United Nations et al* 84 F. Supp. 3d 246 (2d Cir 2015) (following earlier Second Circuit authority affirming that "[a]s the [General Convention] makes clear, the United Nations enjoys absolute immunity from suit unless it has expressly waived its immunity") and the Dutch Supreme Court decision in the case related to the 1996 events in Srebrenica, *Mothers of Srebrenica v Netherlands and the United Nations*, Case No.10/04437 (13 April 2012).

[50] See Higgins et al (n 48) 559–64.

[51] Reinisch (n 5) 63. See also Miller (n 5) 38–40 (observing the "limited practical interest" of this "doctrinal debate" for the United Nations in practice given, among other reasons, the availability of arbitration for the settlement of disputes of a private law character pursuant to Article VIII (section 29, paragraph (*a*)) of the General Convention).

[52] Miller (n 5) 95–109; see also the discussion of section 29 in the context of *Georges et al v United Nations et al* and UN positions on the Haiti cholera outbreak in *Report of the Special Rapporteur on extreme poverty and human rights*, UNGAOR, 71st Sess, UN Doc A/71/367 (21 August 2016) at paras 28–37, *Letters on U.N.'s Response to Cholera in Haiti*, 24 October 2016, online: The New York Times <https://www.nytimes.com/interactive/2016/10/24/world/americas/document-United-Nations-Letters-on-Cholera.html> accessed January 11, 2018, and Report of the Secretary-General, "A new approach to cholera in Haiti," UN Doc A/71/620 (25 November 2016).

The General Convention also specifies privileges and immunities for three categories of individuals. Articles IV, V, and VI grant privileges and immunities to members' representatives, the Organization's officials, and experts on missions, respectively. At the same time, Article IV (section 14), Article V (section 20), and Article VI (section 23) specify that such privileges and immunities are granted "not for the personal benefit of the individuals themselves," but in the interests of the Organization. A member must waive the immunity of its representative where such immunity would "impede the course of justice" and such waiver would not prejudice the purpose for which immunity is accorded.[53] The Secretary-General bears the same duty with respect to the UN officials and experts on mission.[54] Sections 14, 20, and 23 are thus expressly aligned with the "functional necessity" principle set forth in the Charter's Article 105, paragraph 2.

3.2 The Specialized Agencies Convention

The term "specialized agency" is defined in a non-exhaustive manner since it encompasses "[a]ny other Agency in relationship with the United Nations in accordance with Articles 57 and 63 of the Charter."[55] As for the structure and substance of the standard clauses, these mostly correspond with the provisions of the General Convention and are thus not described here at length. The two key changes seen in the standard clauses of the Specialized Agencies Convention are: (1) the omission of a provision governing the status of experts on mission, and (2) the inclusion of an article on abuse of privileges or immunities.

As to experts on mission, the drafters considered that an equivalent of Article VI of the General Convention should not be included in the standard clauses because "it could not be said that every Specialized Agency required immunities of this character."[56] However, the drafters did not exclude the possibility that individual specialized agencies "might show good and sufficient causes" for the extension of immunities to experts, which could be provided for in the annexes.[57]

As to the provision on abuse, an initial proposal to grant states parties a right of denunciation upon abuse was rejected in favor of the concept of a right to withhold the benefit of privileges or immunities in cases of abuse. This aspect of the Specialized Agencies Convention shares broad conceptual roots with a similar proposal in the ILO Memorandum.[58] In its final form, however, the Convention text is more specific and conditions this right on procedural safeguards per Article VII (section 24), including a possible referral to the International Court of Justice. The safeguards are:

[53] General Convention, Article IV (section 14).
[54] General Convention, Article V (section 20), Article VI (section 23).
[55] Specialized Agencies Convention, Article I (section 1, paragraph (*ii*), sub-paragraph (*j*)).
[56] Final Report of Sub-Committee 1 of the Sixth Committee (n 44) 12.
[57] ibid. [58] ILO Memorandum (n 9) 219.

(*a*) consultations must first be held between the affected state and the specialized agency "to determine whether any such abuse has occurred and, if so, to attempt to ensure that no repetition occurs";

(*b*) if consultations yield no satisfactory result, "the question whether an abuse of a privilege or immunity has occurred shall be submitted" to the Court in accordance with Article IX (section 32);

(*c*) if the Court finds that an abuse has indeed occurred, the affected state must first notify the specialized agency concerned before exercising its right to "withhold…the benefits of the privilege or immunity so abused" from that specialized agency.

Moreover, Article VII (section 25) permits the expulsion of representatives of members and officials of specialized agencies present in a country to perform official functions in instances of abuse of privileges of residence "committed…in activities in that country outside his official functions." Again, the discretion to expel is conditioned by procedural safeguards, per Article VII (section 25, paragraph 2):

(*a*) the Government must use the diplomatic procedure applicable to accredited diplomatic envoys, if the person sought to be expelled is a representative of a member, or a person entitled to diplomatic immunity under Article VII (section 21);

(*b*) if the person sought to be expelled is an official of a specialized agency who is not entitled to diplomatic immunity under Article VII (section 21):

(*i*) the Foreign Minister must approve the order to leave the country;

(*ii*) such approval can only be given after consultation with the executive head of the specialized agency concerned; and

(*iii*) if expulsion proceedings are taken against the official, the executive head of the specialized agency concerned has the right to appear in those proceedings on behalf of the official against whom the proceedings are instituted.[59]

3.3 The Conventions in Practice

Even as the Conventions were being drafted, it was envisaged that future action would be required to operationalize the treaty regimes they established. Due to their multilateral character, the Conventions could absorb only a certain degree of granularity.[60] Moreover, certain treaty provisions prescribed specific post-treaty processes to facilitate participation and implementation, as in Article V (section 17) of the General Convention (on categories of UN officials), and Articles X and XI of the Specialized Agencies Convention (on approval and accession processes applicable to the specialized agencies and states parties respectively). The drafters recognized early that the Conventions

[59] Specialized Agencies Convention, Article VII (section 25, paragraph 2, sub-paragraph (II)). This provision was based on Article IV (section 13, paragraph (*b*), sub-paragraph (2)) of the UN-US Headquarters Agreement: see Final Report of Sub-Committee 1 to the Sixth Committee (n 44) 11–12.

[60] (n 24) and accompanying text.

would coexist with applicable bilateral agreements governing the presence of the UN and its specialized agencies in the territories of States.[61]

Today, the General Convention and the Specialized Agencies Convention remain the foundation of a large body of law regulating each set of relationships between entities forming part of the UN system and individual states.[62] The Organization itself now comprises not only the organs established by the Charter, but subsidiary organs as well as a variety of funds and programs. Moreover, the Specialized Agencies Convention now covers 17 specialized agencies.[63] The development of certain aspects of this law was specifically contemplated at the time of drafting, as described previously; other developments have had a more organic character. Without implying any particular normative hierarchy,[64] this law might be classified along the lines of the four-part typology described in the following sections.

3.3.1 *Implementing Decisions Specifically Contemplated by Convention Provisions*

This first category encompasses implementing decisions specifically contemplated in the Convention texts. Thus, the earlier examples cited of General Assembly resolutions instructing the Secretary-General on third-party motor car insurance, and approving the Secretary-General's prescription of categories of UN officials to whom Articles V and VII of the General Convention would apply, fall into this first category.

However, the Conventions also contemplate decisions of a judicial character within the framework of the dispute settlement mechanisms they either establish or require: namely, justice systems to provide for alternative modes of dispute settlement,[65] and decisions of the International Court of Justice.[66] On this last point, the Court has delivered two advisory opinions interpreting provisions of the General Convention, both of which concerned the status of mandate-holders appointed within the framework of the former Commission on Human Rights.[67] It is worth noting that only one—the

[61] (n 12) and accompanying text; General Convention, Final Article (section 36); Specialized Agencies Convention, Article X (section 39).

[62] See the description at *The UN System*, online: United Nations System Chief Executives Board for Coordination < https://www.unsceb.org/content/un-system> accessed January 11, 2018.

[63] Number derived from the list of final texts or revised texts of annexes transmitted to the Secretary-General at *Convention on the Privileges and Immunities of the Specialized Agencies*, online: United Nations Treaty Collection <https://treaties.un.org/Pages/ViewDetails.aspx?src=IND&mtdsg_no=III-2&chapter=3&lang=en> accessed January 11, 2018.

[64] Dinah Shelton, "Normative Hierarchy in International Law" (2006) 100(2) AJIL 291.

[65] General Convention, Article VIII (section 29, paragraph (*b*)); Specialized Agencies Convention, Article IX (section 31, paragraph (*b*)).

[66] General Convention, Article VIII (section 30); Specialized Agencies Convention, Article IX (section 32).

[67] *Applicability of Article VI, Section 22, of the Convention on the Privileges and Immunities of the United Nations*, Advisory Opinion [1989] ICJ Rep 177 [hereinafter "the *Mazilu* Advisory Opinion"]; *Difference Relating to Immunity from Legal Process of a Special Rapporteur of the Commission on Human Rights*, Advisory Opinion [1999] ICJ Rep 62 [hereinafter "the *Cumaraswamy* Advisory Opinion"].

so-called *Cumaraswamy* Advisory Opinion—was given expressly pursuant to the Court's role under the General Convention's Article VIII (section 30). In the case of the *Mazilu* Advisory Opinion, the referral to the Court was made by ECOSOC, due to the reservation that Romania had formulated against section 30. Nevertheless, the Court proceeded to answer the questions referred in substance.[68]

3.3.2 *Institutional Positions*

This second category encompasses formal statements of position by the Organization and the specialized agencies, including through high officials such as the legal adviser, as well as in the context of institutional practice that has developed around the treaty regimes, such as the practice of circulating new reservations formulated against the Specialized Agencies Convention to the heads of specialized agencies.

Formal statements of position are conveniently compiled in the UN Juridical Yearbook, and consist of selected legal opinions of the UN Office Legal Affairs as well as certain specialized agencies, and other significant material, such as the UN Legal Counsel's 1967 statement to the Sixth Committee. The 1967 statement exemplifies an Organizational position articulated at a high conceptual level, and is notable in that it discloses a formal view that the Organization stands in direct legal relationship with members under the General Convention. Consequently, it is the UN's position that members are obliged to accord the privileges and immunities specified in the General Convention as a matter of "the general international law governing the relations between States and the United Nations."[69]

However, there are numerous examples of statements on more quotidian issues. A review of the 2012 Yearbook alone reveals advice on matters ranging from certification in respect of IT equipment procured for a peacekeeping mission,[70] to a weight limitation on diplomatic bags used by the United Nations Development Programme[71]—all given on the basis of applicable Convention provisions.

One aspect of the Specialized Agencies Convention regime that remains understudied in the literature is the role accorded to the heads of the specialized agencies in pronouncing

[68] *Mazilu* Advisory Opinion (n 68) para 38 (drawing a distinction between a difference concerning the "applicability" of the Convention to the expert concerned, and a difference concerning the "application" of the Convention to the expert concerned).

[69] UN Legal Counsel, "Question of privileges and immunities of the United Nations, of representatives of Member States and of officials of the Organization" (1967) UN Juridical YB 311, 312 and 314. *Cf. Reparation for Injuries Suffered in the Service of the United Nations, Advisory Opinion* [1949] ICJ Rep. 174, 179 (stating that the General Convention "creates rights and duties between each of the signatories and the Organization").

[70] UN Office of Legal Affairs, "Letter to the Permanent Mission of a Member State to the United Nations, concerning certifications related to licenses for certain equipment" (2012) UN Juridical YB: Special Ed. 3.

[71] UN Office of Legal Affairs, "Note to the Ministry of Foreign Affairs of [State] regarding the introduction of a weight limitation on United Nations diplomatic bags used by the United Nations Development Programme" (2012) UN Juridical YB 453.

on new reservations.[72] Although this aspect of UN treaty depositary practice is premised on the institutional view that the specialized agencies "have the necessary juridical standing to object to reservations"—a role normally reserved to other contracting parties to the treaty[73]—the specialized agencies' participation in the Specialized Agencies Convention "reservations dialogue" has also been justified as follows:

> Irrespective of the question whether or not each agency may be described as a "party" to the Convention in the strict legal sense, each specialized agency has a direct interest in any proposal by an acceding State to alter in any way the terms of the Convention. It has therefore been the policy of the agencies not to accept reservations which would have the effect of introducing elements of difference in the treatment accorded by States to the specialized agencies under the Convention in matters of general concern; and the history of the Convention has consistently demonstrated a strong opposition by the specialized agencies to reservations in general.[74]

Accordingly, there is an established practice for the heads of the specialized agencies to be consulted, and express their views on, the compatibility of new reservations with the object and purpose of the Specialized Agencies Convention. The documentation is not generally available in the public domain.[75] However, the UN Office of Legal Affairs states that consultations with states seeking to formulate reservations that the specialized agencies assess as incompatible with the Convention "have usually resulted in the withdrawal of the reservations."[76]

[72] See the description of the practice in United Nations, *Summary of Practice of the Secretary-General as Depositary of Multilateral Treaties*, UN Doc ST/LEG/7/Rev.1 (1994) [hereinafter "*1994 Summary of Practice*"] 60–61. The process appears to have been inherited by the UN Chief Executives Board for Coordination: see *1947 Convention on the Privileges and Immunities of the Specialized Agencies*, UN Doc CEB/2008/HLCM/XVI/INF.4/Rev.1 (18 September 2008) paras 12–13. In the International Law Commission's Guide to Practice on Reservations to Treaties, depositary practice concerning the Specialized Agencies Convention is referenced only in two footnotes: first, under guideline 1.1.3 (Reservations relating to the territorial application of the treaty), noting the Secretary-General's "position of principle" on the treatment of "territorial reservations" formulated against both Conventions (footnote 75); and second, under guideline 2.1.5 (Communication of reservations), where the Commission simply states: "It is interesting to note that, while the specialized agencies of the United Nations are not, nor are they entitled to become, 'parties' to the 1947 Convention on the Privileges and Immunities of the Specialized Agencies, they do receive communications relating to the reservations formulated by some States with regard to its provisions" (footnote 534). The most comprehensive treatment of this practice in the literature appears to be in Christina Binder, "Final Provisions (Article XI Sections 41–49 Specialized Agencies Convention)," in Reinisch and Bachmeyer (eds), *Commentary*, (n 5) 662–63 (with accompanying footnotes).

[73] Vienna Convention on the Law of Treaties, 23 May 1969, 1155 UNTS 331 (entered into force 27 January 1980) and Vienna Convention on Treaties between States and International Organizations or between International Organizations, 21 March 1986 (1986) ILM 543 (not yet in force), Article 20, paragraph 3.

[74] *1994 Summary of Practice* (n 72) para 201.

[75] See references cited in Binder (n 72).

[76] *1994 Summary of Practice* (n 72) para. 203.

3.3.3 *Headquarters and Other Applicable Bilateral Agreements*

This third category comprises different types of bilateral agreements used to regulate legal relations between UN system entities or the specialized agencies, as the case may be, and the individual states where these organizations may operate. In line with the general principle of "functional necessity," the scope and content of these agreements vary with the extent and permanence of the organization's physical presence.[77] One consistent element is the centrality of Convention standards in drafting techniques used specifying applicable privileges and immunities;[78] where the state concerned is not party to the relevant Convention, the usual practice is to make the Convention standards applicable mutatis mutandis.[79] Further, these "downstream" agreements—thus termed for present purposes in that they specify, with higher levels of granularity, precisely how Convention standards should apply in individual states—are particularly noteworthy for the manner in which they operationalize the obligation of the organizations concerned to "make provision for" dispute settlement mechanisms with respect to disputes of a private law character.[80]

3.3.4 *National Positions*

A key characteristic of the treaty regimes established by the Conventions is that they give rise to legal obligations that directly engage core elements of the sovereign state, such as customs, fiscal, and security matters. Giving effect to the requisite status, facilities, privileges, and immunities under the Convention frameworks can involve adjustment to existing domestic measures, or the enactment of new ones.[81] Domestic legislation implementing the Conventions, such as in common law states following the UK model where Sir Eric Beckett was again influential,[82] tends to be modeled on the basic scheme of the privileges and immunities as set forth in the Convention texts.

[77] Generally collected under Chapter IV of the UN Juridical Yearbook: see *Chapter IV*, online: United Nations Juridical Yearbook <http://legal.un.org/unjuridicalyearbook/chapters/chapterIV/> accessed January 11, 2018.

[78] See eg the drafting formula used in Article XI (Privileges and immunities) of the Agreement between the United Nations and the Government of the Kingdom of Bahrain regarding arrangements for the 2013 United Nations Public Service Forum (2013) UN Juridical YB 16 at 19, which is broadly in line with that prescribed in the UN model agreement: United Nations Secretariat, "Administrative Instruction – Guidelines for the preparation of host government agreements falling under General Assembly resolution 40/243," UN Doc ST/AI/342 (8 May 1987), online: United Nations HR Portal <https://hr.un.org/handbook/source/administrative-instructions/date> accessed January 11, 2018 [hereinafter "UN Model Agreement"] at 14.

[79] UN Model Agreement (n 78) 14.

[80] General Convention, Article VIII (section 29); Specialized Agencies Convention, Article IX (section 31).

[81] Generally collected under Chapter I of the UN Juridical Yearbook, though the collection also includes domestic measures taken in relation to organizations not covered by the General Convention or the Specialized Agencies Convention: see *Chapter I*, online: United Nations Juridical Yearbook <http://legal.un.org/unjuridicalyearbook/chapters/chapterI/> accessed January 11, 2018.

[82] Marston (n 30); Fitzmaurice and Vallat (n 30).

In addition, notwithstanding the Convention provisions on alternative modes of dispute settlement,[83] and the consequential drafting techniques noted previously in Section 3.3.3, there is a wealth of national case law concerning the precise scope of privileges and immunities under the Convention treaty regimes, as well as their interaction with international legal obligations undertaken by states in other spheres, such as the European Convention on Human Rights guarantee of access to justice.[84] It is also the practice of certain host state governments to enter an appearance in national court proceedings concerning the organization seated in their respective territory, in order to state an official position concerning immunity from legal process.[85]

4 Conclusion

The United Nations' first forays into multilateral treaty-making were, and remain, fundamentally important in three key ways.

First, the working methods used between 1945 and 1947 can still be recognized in some of the treaty-making processes followed today. These methods demonstrate mimesis from other organizations, as seen in the influence of the ILO Memorandum, and an effort to overcome practical issues of the past, as seen in the movement away from the language of diplomatic law, and the innovation toward the multilateral structure of both Conventions. The use of small groups for detailed technical work remains a common conference device, and it is in the nature of multilateral work that key individuals continue to play important roles to advance treaty-making at United Nations fora.

Second, notwithstanding the primarily treaty-based nature of the immunity frameworks the Convention regimes create, the roles of the United Nations and the specialized agencies under these regimes potentially advance the general law of international organizations in several interesting respects. In terms of the capacity of international organizations to engage in treaty relations, the question of the Organization's formal status as regards the General Convention—in particular, whether the Organization is a mere beneficiary or also party—remains a point of scholarly debate.[86] Further, the active participation of the specialized agencies in depositary practice relating to the Specialized Agencies Convention appears to have no comparable analog in the law of treaties. Through this "reservations dialogue," the specialized agencies express substantive institutional positions about the compatibility of intended reservations with the Specialized Agencies Convention.

[83] General Convention, Article VIII (section 29); Specialized Agencies Convention, Article IX (section 31).

[84] August Reinisch, *International Organizations before National Courts* (CUP 2000); Karel Wellens, *Remedies against International Organizations* (CUP 2002).

[85] As was done, for example, in *Georges et al v. United Nations et al* (n 49).

[86] See eg Higgins et al (n 48) 548; Reinisch and Bachmeyer (eds), *Commentary* (n 5) 11–12; Miller (n 5) 172.

Third, the Convention frameworks remain paradigmatic treaty models for managing legal risk. The design of the General Convention functions as a practical baseline for new entities established under existing treaty regimes, such as the Seoul-based Green Climate Fund, established under the UN Framework Convention on Climate Change.[87] However, the baseline has also been used by organizations with nontraditional architecture. The Geneva-based Global Fund to Fight AIDS, Tuberculosis and Malaria, an organization with a global public health mandate established under Swiss private law, has drawn from Convention design to manage legal risk, including by undertaking advocacy efforts to secure conferrals of privileges and immunities in the territories of individual states.[88] The Convention regimes have thus inspired movement at the very frontier of the law of international organizations, including debate about the manner in which international organizations should be defined for the purpose of public international law.[89]

[87] Green Climate Fund, "Samoa Grants Privileges and Immunities Status to GCF" (December 13, 2016), online: Green Climate Fund <http://www.greenclimate.fund/-/samoa-grants-privileges-and-immunities-status-to-gcf> accessed January 15, 2018) ("The immunities granted are in line with those of other international organizations and those applied in the United Nations system.")

[88] Global Fund, *Privileges and Immunities*, GF/B34/19 (16–17 November 2015), online: Global Fund to Fight AIDS, Tuberculosis and Malaria <https://www.theglobalfund.org/media/4176/bm34_19-annualreportprivilegesandimmunities_report_en.pdf?u=636199576680000000> accessed January 15, 2018. See also Note verbale dated 14 July 2009 from the Permanent Mission of the United Republic of Tanzania to the United Nations addressed to the Secretary-General, "Observer status for the Global Fund to Fight AIDS, Tuberculosis and Malaria in the General Assembly," UN Doc A/64/144 (14 July 2009) at paras 21–5.

[89] See eg Singapore's statement at the 72nd Session of the General Assembly in the context of the Sixth Committee's debate on the agenda item *Responsibility of international organizations*, online: United Nations PaperSmart <https://papersmart.unmeetings.org/ga/sixth/72nd-session/statements/> accessed January 29, 2018, in which Singapore noted "interesting policy issues [arising] with the establishment of international organizations under national private law [with] sophisticated mixed membership structures and [which], in some cases, undertake mandates and operations comparable to those of intergovernmental organizations."

CHAPTER 27

DIPLOMATIC AND CONSULAR RELATIONS

SANDERIJN DUQUET AND JAN WOUTERS

THE United Nations (UN) is committed to a global order that values its member states' bilateral diplomatic exchanges. Ever since its inception, lawmaking by treaty has been the preferred way for the UN to advance legal rules that facilitate diplomatic and consular affairs. Measuring by the high degree of observance and their influence on the international and national legal orders, the 1961 Vienna Convention on Diplomatic Relations (VCDR)[1] and the 1963 Vienna Convention on Consular Relations (VCCR)[2] are among the most successful international instruments ever to be drawn up under the UN's auspices. The twin conventions provide a complete framework for the establishment, maintenance, and termination of permanent diplomatic and consular relations between sovereign states. The Vienna framework is supplemented by the 1973 UN Convention on the Prevention and Punishment of Crimes against Internationally Protected Persons, including Diplomatic Agents (Convention on the Protection of Diplomats; CPD), which

[1] Vienna Convention on Diplomatic Relations, signed in Vienna on 18 April 1961 and entered into force on 24 April 1964, 500 UNTS 95 (192 states parties). Two optional protocols were added to the Convention: the Optional Protocol to the Vienna Convention on Diplomatic Relations concerning Acquisition of Nationality, signed on 18 April 1961 and entered into force 2 May 1964, 500 UNTS 223 (51 states parties) and the Optional Protocol to the Vienna Convention on Diplomatic Relations concerning Compulsory Settlement of Disputes, signed on 18 April 1961 and entered into force 2 May 1964, 500 UNTS 241 (70 states parties).

[2] Vienna Convention on Consular Relations, signed in Vienna on 24 April 1963 and entered into force 19 March 1967, 596 UNTS 261 (179 States parties). Two optional protocols were added to the Convention: the Optional Protocol to the Vienna Convention on Consular Relations concerning Acquisition of Nationality, signed on 24 April 1963, entered into force 19 March 1967, 596 UNTS 469 (41 states parties) and the Optional Protocol to the Vienna Convention on Consular Relations concerning the Compulsory Settlement of Disputes, signed on 24 April 1963 and entered into force 19 March 1967, 596 UNTS 487 (51 states parties).

criminalizes attacks against the person or liberty of diplomatic and consular envoys.[3] With 192 (VCDR), 179 (VCCR), and 180 (CPD) states parties respectively, the Conventions' application is nearly global. Success stories were interspersed with lawmaking exercises that had far less resonance. In 1969, the UN sought to clarify the status, rights, and duties of missions performing specific tasks in the Convention on Special Missions (CSM).[4] In 1975, it aimed to catch up with multilateral realities of international relations in the Convention on the Representation of States in their Relations with International Organizations of a Universal Character (CRSIO).[5] The first Convention is poorly ratified; the second has not yet entered into force.

This chapter revisits the central contribution made by the UN to the law on diplomatic and consular relations by examining various factors that may have influenced the UN's performance in the field. A first section contends that the achievements and setbacks in treaty-making processes depended on the "ripeness" of a subject for codification and states' appreciation thereof (Section 2). Subsequently, we examine the different procedural steps and choices made by UN actors in the treaty-making process and (Section 3) go beyond treaty-making efforts to examine whether the UN has also contributed to states' compliance with the diplomatic and consular regimes (Section 4). In a final section, we highlight some remaining challenges for the UN in dealing with this subject area (Section 5).

1 The Diplomatic and Consular Domain

1.1 Diplomatic and Consular Relations: A Theme Worth Codifying?

As spelled out in Article 13 of the Charter of the United Nations (UN Charter), one of the organization's objectives is to encourage "the progressive development of international law and its codification." The UN took this objective to heart. During its first session in 1949, the International Law Commission (ILC) identified a list of topics suitable for

[3] Convention on the Prevention and Punishment of Crimes against Internationally Protected Persons, including Diplomatic Agents, signed in New York on 14 December 1973 and entered into force on 20 February 1977, 1035 UNTS 167 (180 states parties).

[4] Convention on Special Missions, signed in New York on 8 December 1969 and entered into force 21 June 1985, 1400 UNTS 231 (39 states parties). One Optional Protocol concerning the Compulsory Settlement of Disputes, signed on 8 December 1969 and entered into force on 21 June 1985, 1400 UNTS 339 (17 states parties) was added to the Convention.

[5] Convention on the Representation of States in their Relations with International Organizations of a Universal Character, signed in Vienna on 14 March 1975, 34 parties, not yet entered into force.

codification, among which were the rules on "diplomatic intercourse and immunities" and "consular intercourse and immunities."[6] Three years later, the UN General Assembly (UNGA) elevated the topics to a "priority status" after having accepted a draft resolution tabled by Yugoslavia, which was born out of discontent with incidents the country considered a serious violation of diplomatic custom by the Soviet Union.[7]

But even shorn of political preoccupations of the hour, states considered diplomatic and consular law to be a theme ripe for codification. A first reason relates to diplomacy's firm establishment in history. Diplomatic and consular intercourse has been at the core of international relations long before the UN was established. Diplomacy enables states to maintain mutual relations and to communicate both with nationals living or traveling abroad and with foreign audiences. In its earliest form, international relations were carried out by traveling missions representing the interests of rulers.[8] The first permanent representations made their appearance in the twelfth century, when trading nations and cities began appointing agents with representative tasks to one another's ports and commercial centers.[9] Since the time of the League of Nations, moreover, it had become common practice for member states and observer states (and later also third states) to send diplomats to an international organization to take part in multilateral discussions.[10]

A second explanation for the selection of diplomatic and consular law as a codification priority is the near-perfect match between the objectives of the five multilateral Conventions and those of the UN. Particularly the 1961 and 1963 Vienna Conventions benefited from a renewed postwar international engagement with principles of international cooperation, equality of states, peaceful coexistence, and the establishment of friendly relations—intents laid down in their preambles and in the UN Charter. At the same time, the Conventions are based on the principles of sovereignty, noninterference, and territorial jurisdiction, which were even agreeable to states in the midst of the Cold War. One can therefore conclude that the Vienna framework considers the international order to be a community of states necessitating a sufficient amount of interaction. Among the many functions of diplomacy, its contribution to the preservation of peaceful relations may be the most outspoken. The UN gave the concept of peace a broader meaning, matching diplomacy's preventive (conflict prevention) and corrective

[6] ILC, Report to the UNGA on the work of its first session, 1949 YBILC 280–81.

[7] See UNGA Res 685 (5 December 1952). Kai Bruns, *A Cornerstone of Modern Diplomacy: Britain and the Negotiation of the 1961 Vienna Convention on Diplomatic Relations* (Bloomsbury Academic 2014) 3.

[8] For an overview starting in the Ancient Near East, but also discussing Ancient Greek, Roman, Byzantine, and Venetian practices, consult: Ivor Roberts (ed), *Satow's Diplomatic Practice* (6th edn, OUP 2011) 5 et seq.

[9] Ernest Nys, *Les Origines de La Diplomatie et Le Droit D'ambassade Jusqu'à Grotius* (Librairie Européenne C Muquardt 1884).

[10] Pitman B Potter, "Permanent Delegations to the League of Nations" (1931) 25 Am Pol Sci Rev 21; Vittorio Mainetti, "The League of Nations and the Emergence of Privileges and Immunities of International Organizations" in Roberto Virzo and Ivan Ingravallo (eds), *Evolutions in the Law of International Organizations* (Brill Nijhoff 2015).

(conflict resolution, peaceful settlement of disputes) dimensions.[11] The International Court of Justice (ICJ) confirmed this when it stated that:[12]

> [t]he institution of diplomacy [...] proved to be an instrument essential for effective co-operation in the international community, and for enabling States, irrespective of their differing constitutional and social systems, to achieve mutual understanding and to resolve their differences by peaceful means.

Similar to the UN Charter's aim of developing "friendly relations among nations," diplomacy thus also promotes a more dynamic cooperation between states.[13]

A third given is that codification was pushed forward by states' self-centered goals in a field dominated by reciprocal exchanges. Diplomacy is an excellent means for states to protect their interests, as well as those of their citizens and businesses, around the world. Benefits from the exchange of representatives, moreover, can be mutually obtained by states acting as equals on a level playing field. This compatibility also triggers reciprocal behavior between states (being both sending and receiving states), which greatly facilitates the mutual respect for diplomatic and consular law and the immunities, inviolability, and privileges of diplomats and consuls. The transcription of these interests in the VCDR and VCCR was called for by UN member states. In contrast, the benefits resulting for states in ad hoc and multilateral diplomacy are less visible, less mutual, and of less direct concern. The act of one state sending an envoy on a special mission to another state for a short period of time to conduct political reporting or negotiations is by definition non-reciprocal. Likewise, a certain mismatch exists between the burden imposed on states hosting an international organization or conference and those states sending permanent representatives to that same forum. In ad hoc and multilateral diplomacy, states should find their motivation in the general interest of the cooperative world order in protecting those who serve for the greater good of the international office, rather than in a concrete tit-for-tat incentive. This complicates the finding of agreement, and may explain the difficulties experienced in drawing up and implementing the CRSIO and CSM compared to the VCDR, VCCR, and CPD.

1.2 The Codification of Diplomatic and Consular Law in Context

The legal and historical context in which codification took place also requires some reflection. UN efforts in the diplomatic and consular domain between 1961 and 1975

[11] Laurence Boisson de Chazournes, Marcelo G Kohen, and Jorge E Viñuales (eds), *Diplomatic and Judicial Means of Dispute Settlement* (Martinus Nijhoff 2013).

[12] *Case concerning United States Diplomatic and Consular Staff in Tehran (United States of America v Iran)* (Order) [1979] ICJ Rep 21, para 39.

[13] The League of Nations Covenant (Paris, 28 June 1919) only promoted "the prescription of open, just and honourable relations between nations."

cannot be disconnected from the changes that were ongoing in the world at the time. Among those global events are the rise of newly independent states, the Cold War confrontation between East and West, and the steady rise of international organizations and global governance. The shift toward a politically and culturally more diverse world order influenced the codification processes as well as the content of the actual rules adopted. We would argue however that the success of the codification exercises in 1961, 1963, and 1973 lies in the fact that negotiators were able to focus on legal-technical issues—avoiding debates on the political issues that otherwise preoccupied the world.[14] That same technique was less successful in other episodes of multilateral lawmaking, when agreement had to be found on a broader range of issues.

This argument is supported by the observation that, in the tumultuous early 1960s, reaching agreement was easier because the negotiations tackled areas where there was extensive state practice, precedent, and doctrine. Established—if not universally respected—rules of international law were present with regard to diplomatic exchanges. The VCDR codified customary rules on bilateral diplomatic relations between states[15] although it also carried an element of "progressive development."[16] Moreover, diplomatic law had already been the subject of smaller (for example, the 1815 *Règlement de Vienne* on precedence and protocol and the 1818 Aix-la-Chapelle Protocol on etiquette) and academic (for example the 1932 *Harvard Research Draft* on privileges and immunities) codification exercises. Contrary to its diplomatic counterpart, the VCCR was not considered, at the time of its adoption, to be a codification of customary international law.[17] It could however rely on other existing norms: the VCCR incorporated state practice as exemplified in bilateral consular conventions and/or national laws.[18]

The VCDR and VCCR show that the success or otherwise of a decision to proceed with the drafting and negotiating of a treaty is largely dependent on the prior recognition of the existence of a set of (customary) rules and practices in an area in which international action appears desirable. These elements were not present at the time of the "codification" of the rules on ad hoc diplomats and diplomats accredited to international organizations in the CSM and CRSIO. Unlike permanently established bilateral missions, special missions do not have a general right to represent the sending state vis-à-vis the receiving state for all aspects of foreign relations. Rather, ad hoc representations are, under customary international law, entitled only to perform specific tasks as agreed

[14] Bruns (n 7) 201.

[15] See *Case concerning United States Diplomatic and Consular Staff in Tehran (United States of America v Iran)* [1980] ICJ Rep 3, paras 45 and 62 in fine; *Case concerning the Arrest Warrant of 11 April 2000 (Democratic Republic of the Congo v. Belgium)* [2002] ICJ Rep 3, para 52.

[16] Geoff R Berridge, *Diplomacy: Theory and Practice* (5th edn, Palgrave Macmillan 2015) 109–10; Eileen Denza, *Diplomatic Law: Commentary on the Vienna Convention on Diplomatic Relations* (4th edn, OUP 2016) 2–5; Joe Verhoeven, *Droit International Public* (Larcier 2000) 106.

[17] Before the VCCR came into force, only the inviolability of consular archives and the immunity of consuls in regard of official acts were recognized as customary international law; William Eric Beckett, "Consular Immunities" (1944) 21 *Brit YBIL* 34; Roberts (n 8) 265–66.

[18] In the meantime, its main provisions have acquired customary status; Tehran Hostage Case (n 15) para 62; Luke T Lee and John B Quigley, *Consular Law and Practice* (3rd ed, OUP 2008) 21–23.

upon between the two states. The scope of immunities necessary to execute those functions and the categories of individuals who may enjoy them is traditionally defined by the same agreement. The protection offered will be limited in time—most often coinciding with the duration of the mission. While it was not at all unusual pre-1967 that a receiving state granted special missions a status that coincided with that of the permanent diplomatic agents it received on its territory, it was disputed whether they did so out of courtesy or out of a sense of legal obligation.[19]

Missions accredited to international organizations were a relatively new phenomenon, for which Article 105(2) UN Charter provided that they would "enjoy such privileges and immunities as are necessary for the independent exercise of their functions in connection with the Organization."[20] Yet this language, insofar as it entailed representations enjoying only functional privileges and immunities, did not correspond to the practices of host states.[21] Headquarters and host state agreements granted representatives of international organizations full diplomatic privileges and immunities, subject to certain variations.[22] The UN's attempt to catch up with the diplomatic realities of the multilateral world by introducing a common immunities regime for representatives at international organizations was considered excessive.[23] Significant controversy was caused, for instance, because the CRSIO does not grant the host state the power to declare a permanent representative to an international organization persona non grata—a right firmly established in bilateral diplomatic exchanges.[24] Therefore, the CSM and CRSIO did not appropriately reflect the common will of receiving and host states at the time. From those states' point of view, the most problematic was that the Conventions curbed their freedom.[25] Paradoxically, in the meantime it has become more widely accepted that certain basic CSM and CRSIO principles now reflect customary international law.[26]

[19] The records of the ILC show that the debate preoccupied the Commission: ILC, Fourth report of the Special Rapporteur, 1967-II YBILC, paras 138–141.

[20] See also: Convention on the Privileges and Immunities of the United Nations, done at New York, 13 February 1946, entry into force, 17 September 1946, 1 UNTS 15 (CPIUN).

[21] Chanaka Wickremasinghe, "Immunities Enjoyed by Officials of States and International Organizations" in Malcolm D Evans (ed), *International law* (4th edn, OUP 2014) 401–02.

[22] See the Agreement Between the United Nations and the United States regarding the Headquarters of the United Nations, signed on 26 June 1947, and approved by the UNGA on 31 October 1947, 11 UNTS 11. Under Section 15, the United States entitles principal resident representatives of such missions: "in the territory of the United States to the same privileges and immunities, subject to corresponding conditions and obligations, as it accords to diplomatic envoys accredited to it."

[23] See for a discussion on the differences: Alison Duxbury, "Intersections between Diplomatic Immunities and Immunities of International Organizations" in Paul Behrens (ed), *Diplomatic law in a New Millennium* (OUP 2017) 305. One minor difference is the absence of civil and administrative immunity from jurisdiction for accidents with motor vehicles for delegations to organs and to conferences (Part III), an exception that does not apply to permanent representations to IOs. Roberts (n 8) 308–09.

[24] JG Fennessy, "The 1975 Vienna Convention on the Representation of States in Their Relations with International Organizations of a Universal Character" (1976) 70 AJIL 62, 67.

[25] Anthony Aust, *Handbook of International Law* (CUP 2010) 141.

[26] The customary status has been accepted in German, but not in US courts; Malcolm N Shaw, *International Law* (CUP 2014) 563. In the Satow and Oppenheim handbooks, CIL status is denied: Roberts (n 8) 192; Robert Y Jennings and Arthur Watts (eds), *Oppenheim's International Law*, vol 1 (9th edn, Longman 1992) 553. In contrast, Hazel Fox and Philippa Webb (*The Law of State Immunity*

The 1973 CPD stands out among the other four UN Conventions because it was not designed to create a new system of law on diplomacy. Rather, the CPD was concluded as one of the many Conventions in a sequence of universal legal instruments elaborated by the UN on terrorism.[27] Following a sharp rise in politically motivated violence against official representatives of states in foreign countries in the late 1960s, UN member states wished to focus on the judicial dimension of the protection of diplomats. The result was a UN Convention supplementing the Vienna framework on this specific point. In the 1973 CPD, states parties commit to criminalize attacks against the person or liberty of envoys (including murder and kidnapping), as well as the threat with, attempt to, or participation in such an attack. States equally pledge to undertake to adapt internal laws to ensure jurisdiction and extradition. Receiving state obligations to protect foreign envoys are among the oldest rules of diplomatic and consular law.[28] The CPD thus draws on the strong basis of existing rules on diplomatic inviolability under customary international law, and the mutual and urgent interest of UN member states to secure the safety of envoys, as well as the existence of earlier UN Conventions criminalizing terrorism.

2 From the Idea of Codification to the Ratification of Five Multilateral Treaties

2.1 Preparatory Phase

Two UN bodies serve as the organization's engine in the codification and the progressive development of diplomatic and consular law. The UNGA's Sixth (Legal) Committee and the ILC frequently engaged in an institutional tango: the former (intergovernmental) body planned the lawmaking agenda and instituted legal dialogues; the latter (expert) body executed research on the topic, formulated recommendations, and developed drafts.[29] The law on permanent diplomatic representations was the first to be put at the front and center of UN lawmaking. In 1954, the ILC appointed its Swedish member Emil

(3rd edn, OUP 2013) 567) and James Crawford (*Brownlie's Principles of Public International Law* (OUP 2012) 414) argue that certain of the CSM's basic principles regarding inviolability and immunity reflect CIL. The same stance was defended by the American Law Institute, Third Restatement of US Foreign Relations Law (1986) 470. See in the UK practice: High Court of Justice, Divisional Court, *The Freedom and Justice Party* et al. *v Secretary of State* et al. [2016] EWHC 2010 (Admin).

[27] These tackled, among others, terrorism when occurring on board a ship (1988), aircraft (1963), in an airport (1971), or by means of explosives (2001) or nuclear weapons (2007), or more generally the financing of terrorism (1999).

[28] Upon codification in the VCDR and VCCR, personal inviolability was deemed so long established in CIL that negotiators barely engaged in a discussion on its scope or formulation; Denza (n 16) 214.

[29] Article 13 of the 1945 UN Charter assigns the codification duty to the UNGA; the 1947 ILC Statute allocates preparatory codification tasks to the ILC.

Sandström as Special Rapporteur. Sandström would formulate 28 draft articles that were debated at the UNGA's Sixth Committee and sent to all UN member states along with an invitation to submit comments. On the basis of the report that was the result of the survey, the ILC produced a set of revised draft articles that formed the point of departure at the UN Conference on Diplomatic Intercourse and Immunities convened by UNGA Resolution 1450 (XIV) of 7 December 1959. A similar methodology was applied to the codification of consular law. In 1955, the ILC appointed Jaroslav Zourek as Special Rapporteur, who prepared a series of provisional draft articles by 1957.[30] Governmental comments were received in 1960 and draft articles formulated in 1961. By UNGA Resolution 1685 (XVI) of 18 December 1961, a new Conference was convened at the Neue Hofburg in Vienna.

With the first two codification processes still underway, the ILC in 1958 ventured into the privileges and immunities of those serving in "multilateral diplomacy" and "ad hoc diplomacy."[31] The Commission's observation that these topics feature in special conventions rendering unnecessary an urgent codification was not to the satisfaction of the UN membership. That same year the UNGA adopted Resolution 1289(XIII) by recommendation of its Sixth Committee and based on a French proposal. The Resolution invited the ILC to study the relations between states and international organizations "at an appropriate time", meaning after the ILC would have concluded its work on permanent diplomatic and consular relations as well as on ad hoc diplomacy.[32]

Emil Sandström was nominated Special Rapporteur for Special Missions and his report—containing just three draft articles[33]—was transmitted to the Vienna Conference on Diplomatic Intercourse and Immunities, for it to be considered together with the ILC Draft Articles on permanent diplomatic missions.[34] In Vienna, however, a Conference subcommittee found that the draft articles were unsuitable for inclusion in the final treaty text. In 1961, the UNGA referred the matter back to the ILC, which produced a more detailed study under the leadership of Special Rapporteur Milan Bartoš. The outcome were new draft articles formulated by the Commission in 1967, following the VCDR's model.[35]

The immunities and privileges of delegations to international organizations were tackled after the 1961 and 1963 Vienna Conferences had taken place. The topic was

[30] "Report on consular intercourse and immunities," 1957-II YBILC 71–103.

[31] Report of the Commission on the work at its 10th session, 1960-II YBILC 89, paras 51–52.

[32] UNGA Res 1289(5 December 1958), "Relations between States and inter-governmental organizations."

[33] Sandström argued the Draft Articles that would later turn into the VCDR, applied to special missions: "turning now to the applicability of the provisions of Section II of the 1958 draft, dealing with diplomatic privileges and immunities, it has been suggested above . . . that this part of the draft would, in the main, be applicable to special missions. The activities of a special mission are part of what are usually functions of a permanent mission, and since privileges and immunities are granted in the interest of these functions and for promoting good relations between the States, it is natural that these advantages be granted also to special missions, unless they are based on circumstances which apply only to permanent missions"; "Report on Special Missions" 1960-II YBILC, para 23.

[34] Report of the ILC, 1960-II YBILC 179, paras 32–33.

[35] Report of the ILC on the work of its 19th session, 1967-II YBILC.

initially part of a broad ILC project on the status of international organizations, until in 1966, Special Rapporteur Abdullah El Erian of Egypt, suggested to the ILC that it should concentrate its work on the status, privileges, and immunities of states representatives.[36] The draft articles, largely modeled on the VCDR and inspired by the CSM, attracted comments by states hosting UN organs, bodies, programs, and specialized agencies.[37] Without significantly revising the Special Rapporteur's original conception, the ILC adopted draft articles in 1971, after which the UNGA convened a new Conference in Vienna in 1975.

2.2 Codification Phase

Vienna—host city to three UN multilateral conferences—plays a central role in the codification of diplomatic and consular law. Participants recall the good spirit and collaborative atmosphere at the first two Conferences in 1961 and 1963,[38] one reason being the emphasis on legal rather than political arguments.[39] Another reason can be found in the choice made by states to staff their delegations in 1961 with representatives that had followed the debates in the Sixth Committee and, again in 1963, with representatives that had attended the 1961 Conference.[40] The fact that the Conferences took place within two years after careful preparation by a group of people who had familiarized themselves with one another, and with the matter of substance, kept the wind in their sails. The Conferences furthermore followed the established pattern for codification conferences and had an organization and structure delegates were accustomed to.[41] Finally, participation was significant without being unmanageable: 81 states took part in the diplomatic Conference held from March 2 to April 14, 1961; 92 states participated in the consular Conference held from March 4 to April 22, 1963. In terms of modern treaty-making, the Conferences were fairly homogenous, lacking the involvement of nongovernmental organizations and with only a small number of specialized agencies and other international organizations attending as observers.[42] This should not be a surprise, as the texts

[36] Johan G Lammers, "Immunity of International Organizations" (2014) 10 Intl Org L Rev 276, 277.

[37] Fennessy (n 24) 63.

[38] Nelson Iriñiz Casás, "Views of a Delegate to the 1961 Vienna Conference" in Paul Behrens (ed), *Diplomatic law in a New Millennium* (OUP 2017); Eileen Young (Denza), "The Development of the Law of Diplomatic Relations" (1964) 40 British YBIL 141.

[39] Bruns (n 7) 201.

[40] States in 1961 preferred to appoint legal experts instead of experienced diplomats to their delegations in Vienna. This resulted in a continuation of the legal craftsmanship that had already taken place in the UNGA and ILC.

[41] Work was divided in different thematic committees that functioned alongside general, drafting, and accreditation committees. Delegates intensively reworked the ILC Draft Articles after which the Treaty text was adopted in the plenary meeting.

[42] In 1963, the International Labour Organization, the Food and Agriculture Organization, the International Atomic Energy Agency, and the Council of Europe attended.

being negotiated dealt with a domain in which states representatives themselves serve as experts par excellence.

A different story emerges from the 1975 Conference on Representation of States in their Relations with International Organizations, held in Vienna from February 4 to March 14, 1975. The Conference was the latest in a series of UN treaties in diplomatic and consular law, taking place 14 years after the first one. The institutional setting, organization, and the Conference duration (approximately six weeks) stayed the same, but other elements had changed. First, with the generational turnover in delegates and a decrease in attendance rate, there was a loss of experience and motivation.[43] Particularly noticeable are the reports of the less cooperative spirit that prevailed at the Conference.[44] Second, a large number of unresolved issues were brought to Vienna, where the divisions between sending states and host states only worsened. The result was the adoption of a largely unsupported treaty text for which it was clear during the negotiations that ratification would not happen swiftly. When submitted to a vote after weeks of debates, the text was adopted thanks to the sending states use of their majority in the face of opposition by host states.[45]

A different model of treaty-making was followed for the CSM and CDP. Instead of convening a multilateral conference, the conventions were discussed in a working group assembled by the Sixth Committee, with the agreed texts then adopted by the UNGA plenary upon its recommendation. Usually, this working mode is preferred for reasons of practicality and cost-effectiveness. In the case of the CSM, it was clear that the UNGA did not want to move the discussion back to Vienna after the 1961 Vienna Conference had refused to include rules on ad hoc diplomacy. On the basis of the draft adopted by the ILC, the UNGA placed the item "Draft convention on special missions" on its agenda in 1968 and again in 1969, entrusting its consideration to the Sixth Committee. By Resolution 2530 (XXIV) of 8 December 1969, the UNGA adopted the Convention on Special Missions. Likewise, convening a diplomatic conference of plenipotentiaries specifically to deal with the protection of envoys seemed somewhat exaggerated. The CPD was adopted as an UNGA Resolution 3166 (XXVIII) of 14 December 1973, within two years after discussions had commenced at the ILC, which was exceptionally fast by UN standards.[46]

[43] Out of all UN states, only 81 accepted the invitation to attend the Conference. Many of them were absent during the debates, as the voting record (usually containing 60–65 votes) shows.

[44] Fennessy (n 24) 71.

[45] Belgium (host state to many UN bureaus and liaison offices) voted against; abstentions were recorded by the US (UN headquarters); Switzerland (UN organs, ILO, WHO, UPU, etc.), Austria (IAEA and UNIDO), Canada (ICAO), France (UNESCO), and the UK (IMCO).

[46] Allen B Green, "Convention on the Prevention and Punishment of Crimes against Diplomatic Agents and Other Internationally Protected Persons: An Analysis" [1973] Virginia J of Intl L 703; Michael C Wood, "The Convention on the Prevention and Punishment of Crimes against Internationally Protected Persons, Including Diplomatic Agents" [1974] ICLQ 791.

2.3 Ratification Phase

The acceptance of new law by states can be measured by their willingness to ratify a newly negotiated treaty speedily. When looking at the five UN Conventions, significant differences arise. The VCDR and the CPD both entered into force three years after their conclusion, in 1964 and 1977 respectively.[47] Compared to these, the VCCR's and CSM's ratification processes were much slower. Although the VCCR entered into force in 1967 when the 35th state acceded to the Convention, quite a number of states were reluctant to ratify quickly in light of Cold War tensions.[48] The CSM only entered into force in 1985, and it currently counts a mere 39 states parties. At the time of writing, 34 states have ratified the CRSIO, which will enter into force following the accession or ratification of a 35th state party (article 89 CRSIO). The underwhelming numbers relating to these latter Conventions accurately reflect the opposition of many states to substantial parts of their texts, while also underlining the reluctance of states to submit to UN lawmaking efforts they consider to be imposed on them.

3 Compliance with the UN Conventions

Another indicator for a Convention's success is the level of compliance among its parties. The diplomatic and consular conventions encompass two models: enforcement is undertaken by the parties themselves (self-enforcement) and by the ICJ (enforcement by judicial means). A third, extra-conventional, way to make states comply with the rules of diplomatic and consular law is through the monitoring and discussion of incidents in the UNGA. To different extents, the UN is involved in all three mechanisms.

For centuries, compliance happened solely through the principle of reciprocity—a fundamental underlying principle of the diplomatic and consular system. Typically, reciprocity embodies states' desire to see the protection they offer to foreign diplomats and consuls in their territory equally accorded to their own diplomats accredited in another country.[49] In other words, reciprocity serves as the incentive for states exchanging envoys to apply the highest standards of protection: it is in their own and their agents' best interests to do so. Mutual commitments also serve the related function of a legal sanctioning mechanism, even though reciprocal reprisals are only allowed in the specific circumstances described in the nondiscrimination principle laid down in Articles 47 VCDR

[47] For both Conventions, this happened 30 days after they received their 22nd ratification (Art 51 VCDR; Art 17 CPD).

[48] Lee and Quigley (n 18) 24.

[49] Alain Plantey, *Principes de Diplomatie* (2nd edn, Pedone 2000) 207–208.

and 72 VCCR.[50] The success of the compliance system lies in the fact that the sanctions mechanism depends on states' motives of self-interest and brings about direct consequences (not in the least for state agents).

Historically, the legal field tended to favor self-enforcement. This may explain why the jurisdiction of the ICJ is a noncompulsory option, only installed for three conventions. Nevertheless, by acceding those optional protocols to the VCDR, VCCR, and CSM concerning the compulsory settlement of disputes, a good number of UN member states have now accepted the ICJ's jurisdiction to rule on disputes arising out of the application of these UN Conventions.[51] This allowed the Court to contribute to the interpretation of diplomatic and consular concepts, something which the ICJ has occasionally done since. In particular, the Court left its marks on the interpretation of the rules on diplomatic asylum, host state obligations, and a consul's right to assist nationals of the sending state in a receiving state (the so-called "right to consul").

A first landmark judgment predates the 1961 Vienna Convention. In the 1950 *Colombian-Peruvian Asylum* case, the ICJ explained that a decision to grant diplomatic asylum involves a derogation from the sovereignty of a receiving state.[52] The Court specified that a right of diplomatic asylum is not recognized under general international law and that Colombia had failed to establish the existence of a regional custom.[53] The case is particular because, a good decade later, the subject of diplomatic asylum was still considered not ready for codification in the VCDR. The case incited further lawmaking efforts in the UN: the UNGA and ILC studied the issue of diplomatic asylum at various sessions following the judgment and the coming into force of the VCDR, as of yet without reaching an agreement.[54]

Second, the legal rules on the protection of an embassy were tested during the infamous 1979 Iran hostage crisis, which gave rise to one of the most cited ICJ cases on diplomatic relations. On November 4, 1979, a militant group of Iranian students entered the US embassy in Tehran and overtook it, taking its 52 occupants hostage. In the 1980 *Tehran Hostages* judgment, the Court found the receiving state, Iran, in violation of the VCDR and VCCR.[55] Despite the fact that the hostage takers were not agents of the state, the Court concluded that Iran, which had proved itself unwilling to prevent the takeover

[50] In its 1958 Commentary to the Draft Articles on Diplomatic Intercourse and Immunities, the ILC submitted that "[f]ailure by a diplomatic agent to fulfil his obligations does not absolve the receiving State from its duty to respect the agent's immunity;" ILC, Draft Articles on Diplomatic Intercourse and Immunities with commentaries, 1958-II *YBILC* 104.

[51] See the references to these Protocols in footnotes 1, 2, and 4.

[52] ICJ, *Colombian-Peruvian Asylum Case (Colombia v Peru)* [1950] ICJ Rep 266, paras 274–275. See also: *Haya de la Torre Case (Colombia v Peru)* [1951] ICJ Rep 71.

[53] *Colombian-Peruvian Asylum Case* (n 52) para 277.

[54] UNGA Res 3497 (15 December 1975); ILC, Report to the UNGA, 1977-II YBILC 130, para 109.

[55] *Tehran Hostage Case* (n 15) para 61: "[b]y a number of provisions of the Vienna Conventions of 1961 and 1963, Iran was placed under the most categorical obligations, as a receiving State, to take appropriate steps to ensure the protection of the United States Embassy and Consulates, their staffs, their archives, their means of communication and the freedom of movement of the members of their staffs."

or to end it, was responsible for its inactions.[56] The *Tehran Hostages* case confirmed that the inviolability of diplomatic premises may in certain circumstances require the taking of preventive measures by the receiving state. In case the receiving state does not provide the appropriate protection against intrusion of diplomatic or consular premises or the occurrence of damage, this can trigger its international responsibility.[57]

A third topic concerns the right to consul as laid down in Article 36 VCCR. The ICJ addressed the topic on the merits in the 2001 *LaGrand*[58] and the 2004 *Avena and Other Mexican Nationals* judgments.[59] The first case concerned two German brothers sentenced to death in the United States. The ICJ noted that the language of Article 36(1)(*b*) VCCR does not leave room for misinterpretation where it stipulates that "[local] authorities shall inform the person concerned *without delay*[60] of his or her rights [to inform the consular post of the state of his or her nationality of a detention or arrest]."[61] The case contained the even more weighty finding of the Court that Article 36 provides a rare instance in which a treaty obligation affects the rights of the sending state and the individual rights of the national concerned.[62] These principles were confirmed in *Avena*, a case concerning 52 Mexican nationals who faced the death penalty in the United States and had been unable to communicate with the Mexican consulate, or not told that they could do so.[63] After the United States was found to be in violation of the VCCR, it withdrew from the Optional Protocol to the VCCR concerning the compulsory settlement of disputes.[64]

Finally, the UN is involved in fostering states' compliance with the Conventions on diplomatic and consular relations through the UNGA. The UNGA's agenda features a

[56] *Tehran Hostage Case* (n 15) para 67.

[57] *Tehran Hostage Case* (n 15) paras 63, 68, and 95. See more recently also the issuance of provisional measures by the ICJ calling on France to respect the inviolability of the premises presented by Equatorial Guinea as housing its diplomatic mission and grant appropriate protection pending a final decision in the case; *Immunities and Criminal Proceedings (Equatorial Guinea v. France)* (Order) [2016] ICJ Rep 163, para 92.

[58] *LaGrand (Germany v United States of America)* (Judgment) [2001] ICJ Rep 466.

[59] *Avena and Other Mexican Nationals (Mexico v United States of America)* [2004] ICJ Rep 12. In 1998, the ICJ had already issued provisional measures calling upon the United States not to execute a Paraguayan national, Angel Breard, who had not been made aware of rights to consular access. Although the US Supreme Court declined the ruling, Paraguay decided to dismiss the case after Breard was executed: *Case Concerning the Vienna Convention on Consular Relations* (*Paraguay v United States of America*), Order of 10 November 1998, [1998] ICJ Rep 426.

[60] *Avena Case* (n 59) para 63.

[61] J Fitzpatrick, "The Unreality of International Law in the United States and the LaGrand Case" (2002) 27 *Yale J of Intl L* 427, 428.

[62] See paras 77 and 125, *LaGrand Case* (n 58). For a more detailed assessment, see JB Quigley, "*LaGrand*: A Challenge to the US Judiciary" (2002) 27 *Yale J of Intl L* 435; Fitzpatrick (n 61).

[63] *Avena Case* (n 59) para 40; Request for Interpretation of the Judgment of 31 March 2004 in the same case dated 9 January 2009.

[64] On March 7, 2005, the UN Secretary-General received a communication from the US government notifying its withdrawal from the Optional Protocol, the exact consequences of which are debated in the lack of a denunciation clause in the Protocol; JB Quigley, "The United States' Withdrawal from International Court of Justice Jurisdiction in Consular Cases: Reasons and Consequences" (2008) 19 *Duke J of Comp and Intl L* 263.

recurrent item on the "consideration of effective measures to enhance the protection, security and safety of diplomatic and consular missions and representatives." The item was included following the dramatic events that resulted in the ICJ's *Tehran Hostages* judgment and has been considered annually, then biennially, by the UNGA in the framework of the Sixth Committee. In the context of this item, the Sixth Committee follows the state of ratification of the UN Conventions on diplomacy, as well as instances of breaches of the conventions, resulting in resolutions dedicated to the topic. Issues of diplomatic law are also discussed in the UNGA's subsidiary committee on Relations with the Host State. The range of issues the Committee deals with, though often practical in nature and targeted to the US government, sometimes surpass the relations with the host state to venture out to legal issues the diplomatic community at large faces. For example, in a 2014 resolution on bank accounts held by diplomatic missions,[65] the Committee mediated between the US government and permanent missions to the UN of countries that could no longer open bank accounts in the United States as a result of economic or personal sanctions.[66]

4 Challenges in the Further Development of Diplomatic and Consular Law

The final element of the lawmaking process concerns the maintenance of its relevance. There is a challenge in keeping diplomatic and consular law up to date and in line with state practice. Complex global problems have transformed a "strict foreign policy," traditionally including matters of trade and security, into a "broad foreign policy," which also includes environmental, social, and human rights concerns. This evolution has been matched by a change in the methods used by the diplomatic community to conduct its work, along with a broadening of its membership. A wide range of less traditional actors, including governmental and nongovernmental organizations, substate governments, parliaments, technical experts, and business representatives have become involved in diplomacy in the broader sense of the word.[67] The way in which diplomats handle information has also changed. Technological developments that allow for the fast and uncomplicated distribution of data have been introduced to diplomatic correspondence and negotiations, increasing both efficiency and vulnerability. Furthermore,

[65] UNGA Res 68/306 (9 September 2014), on the enhancement of the administration and financial functioning of the United Nations.

[66] Host State Committee discussions, 10 December 2014, UN Doc A/69/PV.68.

[67] Ronald P Barston, *Modern Diplomacy* (4th ed, Pearson 2013) 6; Kishore Mahbubani, "Multilateral Diplomacy" in Andrew F Cooper, Jorge Heine, and Ramesh Thakur (eds), *The Oxford Handbook of Modern Diplomacy* (OUP 2013).

the number of international organizations that accredit member and non-member states has multiplied.

Although it would appear that the exercise of diplomatic functions has become more demanding than when the Vienna framework was concluded over 50 years ago, this has not given rise to a desire amongst states to modify the legal framework as its stands. There are no apparent initiatives to renegotiate existing treaties or craft a broad, new multilateral framework for diplomatic and/or consular affairs. Rather, member states are collaborating to keep diplomatic and consular law up to date in other ways. Here too, the UN—in particular the ILC and UNGA—has made notable contributions. Continuing its work on diplomatic and consular law, the ILC identified state practice regarding the diplomatic and consular bag as an area in need of further consideration.[68] At the time of accession to the VCDR, several states had entered reservations regarding the protection of the diplomatic bag as defined by article 27 VCDR. These countries sought to limit the inviolability of the diplomatic bag, and tried to reserve the right to open or return a diplomatic bag in specific circumstances. Other states objected to these reservations, arguing inter alia that the reservations go against the object and purpose of the VCDR and as such are not valid. In its 1989 draft articles on the status of the diplomatic courier and the diplomatic bag, the Commission tried to codify state practice regarding the screening of a diplomatic pouch for the presence of explosives, metal, drugs, or nuclear substances without opening it, for example through scanning methods or sniffer dogs. Perhaps surprisingly, the draft articles confirm that the diplomatic bag is exempt from examination directly or through electronic or other technical devices. Airline authorities are however allowed to refuse their transport where a threat to aircraft safety is presumed (article 28). This is the prevailing practice at many airports, although diplomats and diplomatic couriers now oftentimes voluntarily agree to a scan of their personal baggage and the diplomatic bags. Yet the ILC's recommendation to the UNGA that it convene an international conference to study the draft articles to conclude a convention on the subject was referred to an undecided moment in the future when diverging views on article 28 will be reconciled.

Another challenge in the digital era is the growing number of accusations of state surveillance, the interception of diplomatic communications, and the use of diplomatic and consular missions as surveillance posts in host countries. This is one of the topics discussed in the framework of the UNGA recurrent item considering "effective measures to enhance the protection, security and safety of diplomatic and consular missions and representatives." One of the outcomes is UNGA Resolution 69/121. In the resolution, the international community reminds receiving states of the obligations of diplomatic law with regard to the protection of secrecy. Its innovative character lies in the confirmation of the modern definition of diplomatic documents and archives—giving a modern interpretation to the VCDR provision—to include electronic means.

[68] See for further reading: Jeffrey F Addicott, "The Status of the Diplomatic Bag: A Proposed United States Position" (1991) 13 Houston J of Intl L 221, 224–25; Wilfried Bolewski, "Diplomatischer Kurier: Völkerrechtliches Instrument Und Gefahren Seines Missbrauchs" (2005) 43 Archiv des Völkerrechts 537.

One final observation concerns the contribution of the UN Security Council (UNSC) to the law of diplomacy. The UNSC regularly defines the modalities of diplomatic and consular law. First, while the principle of consent is central to diplomatic and consular relations (article 2 VCDR; article 2 VCCR), it can be trumped by a binding UNSC resolution.[69] As a result, the exercise of states' rights to establish, suspend, or terminate diplomatic or consular relations or to open or close a mission may be (temporarily) limited by the UNSC when circumstances so demand. The Council has exercised this power on a few occasions, including in Resolution 217 (1965) of 20 November 1965 on the declaration of independence of Southern Rhodesia. In the resolution, the UNSC called

> upon all States not to recognize this illegal authority and not to entertain any diplomatic or other relations with it.

Second, the UNSC can restrict sending states' rights to determine the size of their missions in agreement with the receiving state, and limit the freedom of movement of diplomats as foreseen by article 26 VCDR. For example, in Resolution 748 (1992), the UNSC obliged states to[70]

> [s]ignificantly reduce the number and the level of the staff at Libyan diplomatic missions and consular posts and restrict or control the movement within their territory of all such staff who remain.

Third, the UNSC regularly reminds UN member states that diplomatic privileges and immunities must be respected. A case in point is the situation in the Democratic People's Republic of Korea (DPRK). In its 2016 and 2017 resolutions, the UNSC expressed concern that the DPRK is abusing the privileges and immunities accorded under the VCDR/VCCR and demanded that the country comply with its obligations under those Conventions.[71] At the same time, the UNSC prompts other member states to respect UN sanctions without prejudice to the activities of the DPRK's diplomatic missions pursuant to the Vienna Conventions.[72]

[69] Article 41 of the UN Charter is worded as follows: "[t]he Security Council may decide what measures not involving the use of armed force are to be employed to give effect to its decisions, and it may call upon the Members of the United Nations to apply such measures. These may include complete or partial interruption of economic relations and of rail, sea, air, postal, telegraphic, radio, and other means of communication, and the *severance of diplomatic relations*" [emphasis added].

[70] UNSC Res 748 (31 March 1992), para 6(a). See also Res 2321 (30 November 2016), para 14, in which the UNSC calls upon "all Member States to reduce the number of staff at DPRK diplomatic missions and consular posts."

[71] UNSC Res 2270 (2 March 2016), preamble; Res 2321 (2016), preamble and para 17–18; UNSC Res 2371 (5 August 2017), preamble and para 16.

[72] UNSC Res 2375 (11 September 2017), para 27. In UNSC Res 2371 (2017), para 26, the UNSC specifies that sanctions will not apply with respect to financial transactions with the DPRK Foreign Trade Bank or the Korea National Insurance Corporation "if such transactions are solely for the operation of diplomatic or consular missions in the DPRK." See in the same sense: UNSC Res 2270 (2016) paras 32 and 35. However, in UNSC Res 2371 (2016), paras 16 and 31, the Council decided that "all States shall take steps to limit the number of bank accounts to one per DPRK diplomatic mission and consular post, and one per accredited DPRK diplomat and consular officer, at banks in their territory."

5 Conclusion

Through its multilateral treaty-making activities, the UN has advanced the law on diplomatic and consular intercourse substantially, contributing to the quality as well as quantity of international interactions of and between member states. Yet the outcome of the UN's pursuit of the codification of the law on diplomatic and consular relations paints a mixed picture. Tremendous achievements (the 1961 and 1963 Vienna Conventions on permanent diplomatic and consular missions and the 1973 Convention on the protection of diplomats) have been followed by a worthwhile lawmaking exercise (1969 Convention on special missions), but also by an attempt at harmonization that straightforwardly failed to attain its goals (1975 Convention on permanent representations to international organizations). This chapter found a positive correlation between the willingness of sovereign states to ratify and implement Conventions and the UN's accommodation of their needs and desires. States proved ready to codify and/or develop diplomatic and consular rules when they felt a subject had been sufficiently established in customary international law (VCDR and CPD) or bilateral treaties (VCCR), political circumstances called for it (VCDR, CPD), and the law would be reciprocally beneficial (VCDR, VCCR, and CPD). When explaining the obstacles faced by the UN, we argued that the CSM and CRSIO also became the victim of the VCDR's success: many of its principles were too easily and quickly considered general law and transposed without having established broad support.

Although the UN facilitated the negotiation and drafting of treaties through the institution of conferences and meetings, its role cannot be reduced to that of just a convening power. Through the ILC and the UNGA—in particular its Sixth Committee—the UN also expedited legal craftsmanship and consensus-building. The ICJ settled disputes between states on the interpretation of diplomatic and consular law, enabling the continuation of the maintenance of friendly relations between states parties. In many ways, the efforts in this field also advanced the UN's own objectives. First, the development of (rules on) diplomacy allows for the realization of the principles of peaceful coexistence and the development of friendly relations. Second, the UN managed to improve and create coherence in the legal field. As a result, through its multilateral dynamics the UN has left a strong mark on the evolution of bilateral diplomatic and consular relations, international communication, and the finding of negotiated solutions.

CHAPTER 28

INTERNATIONAL COMMERCIAL ARBITRATION

CORINNE MONTINERI

ARBITRATION has long been deeply rooted in the ideals of a universal organization, going back to the Covenant of the League of Nations.[1] Article 33, paragraph 1, of the Charter of the United Nations specifically mentions "arbitration" as one of the peaceful means to resolve disputes. Peaceful settlement of disputes is a key dimension of the work of the United Nations, and remains an essential area of international trade law. An effective and constructive dispute settlement mechanism may help preserve long-term relationships and, depending on the scale of the dispute, economic stability. The certainty that it provides is a key factor in encouraging investment. In that context, international commercial arbitration[2] is of great benefit not only in economic terms but also to society in general.

The United Nations has contributed to the development of international commercial arbitration over the past decades. Within the United Nations system, the Commission on International Trade Law, UNCITRAL, established in 1966 as a subsidiary organ of the General Assembly with the mandate to "further the progressive unification and harmonization of international trade law,"[3] has made great strides in creating a favorable

[1] For instance, the Protocol on Arbitration Clauses (Geneva, 1923) and the Convention on the Execution of Foreign Arbitral Awards (Geneva, 1927).

[2] Commercial arbitration is understood here as covering arbitration between purely private entities as well as arbitration between a state or state-owned entity and an investor.

[3] UNGA Res 2205 (17 December 1966) para 8; for more information on the mandate for the progressive development of the law of international trade, see the Report of the Secretary-General, UN Doc A/6396 (1966); the Report of the Fifth Committee of the General Assembly at its twenty-first session, UN Doc (1966); and the relevant summary records of the proceedings of the Sixth Committee, which are contained in the Official Records of the General Assembly, twenty-first Session, Sixth Committee, 947th–955th meetings (UN Doc A/C.6/SR.947–955). In its sessions, UNCITRAL follows the rules of procedure of the General Assembly (see UNCITRAL rules of procedure and methods of work, Official Records of the General Assembly, sixty-second Session, Supplement No. 17 (UN Doc A/62/17 (Part I)),

environment for resolving disputes. More generally, UNCITRAL's efforts to contribute to the progressive development of international trade law have helped states to enhance the business environment, thereby contributing to sustainable development and growth.[4]

UNCITRAL is responsible for two treaties[5] concluded in the field of international arbitration: the Convention on the Recognition and Enforcement of Foreign Arbitral Awards (New York, 1958) ("New York Convention"),[6] and the United Nations Convention on Transparency in Treaty-based Investor-State Arbitration, also known as the Mauritius Convention on Transparency[7] ("Transparency Convention").[8] The latter was adopted more than 50 years after the former. When we consider these two instruments—their genesis, negotiation, adoption process, and the monitoring of their application—common elements may be identified that may be of interest in light of current projects and proposals for work by UNCITRAL in the fields of mediation and reform of the existing investor-state dispute settlement regime.[9]

Treaties often provide for a definition of key terms. It may be worth noting that commercial arbitration is not defined by any convention or soft law instrument.[10] Arbitration is one of many possible procedures for the settlement of disputes in respect to economic transactions. Although it is a voluntary procedure that depends on the agreement of the parties, once such agreement has been reached neither party can withdraw from it unilaterally. Consequently, the final and binding decision rendered by the arbitral tribunal in the form of an award must resolve the dispute. The 157 states that have become parties to the New York Convention have thereby committed themselves to enforcing foreign arbitral awards, albeit with limited exceptions. The newly adopted Transparency Convention deals with a specific type of arbitration, which finds its origin in bilateral and multilateral investment treaties, and involves a state or state-owned entity as a party.

paras 234–241; and UN Doc A/62/17 (Part II), paras 101–107. Notes by the Secretariat, UN Docs A/CN.9/638 and Add, and A/CN.9/653).

4 Address of the UN Secretary-General at the occasion of the ICCA Congress 2016 in Africa (Mauritius), available at <https://www.un.org/sg/en/content/sg/statement/2016-05-09/secretary-generals-address-international-council-commercial> accessed January 14, 2019.

5 Other treaties have been developed in the field of international arbitration: the Convention on the Settlement of Investment Disputes between States and Nationals of Other States (the ICSID Convention or the Convention) that established the International Centre for Settlement of Investment Disputes as one of the organizations of the World Bank Group; the 1975 Inter-American Convention on International Commercial Arbitration, called the "Panama Convention," modeled after the New York Convention; and the European Convention on International Commercial Arbitration of 1961.

6 330 UNTS 3.

7 The government of Mauritius made an offer to UNCITRAL at its 47th session in 2014 to host the signing ceremony of the Convention; see UNGA Res 69/116 (10 December 2014), which authorized the Ceremony and recommended that the Convention be known as the "Mauritius Convention on Transparency."

8 UN Doc A/69/17, chapter III and Annex I; UNGA Res 69/116 referred to previously.

9 UN Doc A/72/17, UNCITRAL work programme.

10 On the question of the definition of "commercial arbitration," see Report of the Working Group on International Contract Practices on the work of its third session, UN Doc A/CN.9/216 paras 15–18; Report of the Secretary-General, "Possible Features of a Model Law on International Commercial Arbitration," UN Doc A/CN.9/207 paras 29–30.

1 Genesis of the Conventions: The Role of the Business Community and Civil Society

1.1 New York Convention

The New York Convention has often been considered as one of the key pillars of the international system of justice. It establishes a framework for the recognition and enforcement of foreign arbitral awards, and arbitration agreements.

In a nutshell, the Convention obligates Contracting States to recognize arbitral awards meeting the requirements of the Convention as binding and to enforce them, if requested to do so, under the law of the state in which the action is brought (lex fori). Each Contracting State may determine the procedural mechanisms for doing so where the Convention does not prescribe any requirement.

The Convention defines five grounds upon which recognition and enforcement of an arbitral award may be refused at the request of the party against whom it is invoked. These grounds are: (1) the incapacity of the parties or invalidity of the arbitration agreement, (2) a violation of due process, (3) the fact that the award exceeds the scope of the arbitration agreement; (4) matters relating to the jurisdiction of the arbitral tribunal, and (5) the fact that the award was set aside or suspended in the country in which, or under the law of which, it was made. The Convention defines two additional grounds—arbitrability and public policy—upon which the court may, on its own motion, refuse recognition and enforcement of an award.

The goal of encouraging recognition and enforcement of awards is achieved through article VII (1) of the Convention, which allows the continued application of any national legislative provisions that give special or more favorable rights to a party seeking to enforce an award.

Due to the fact that enforcement of an award can be refused if the agreement upon which it is based is not recognized as valid, the Convention contains specific provisions on arbitration agreements. Article II provides that Contracting States shall recognize written arbitration agreements and give full effect to them. In that respect, UNCITRAL adopted, at its 39th session in 2006, a Recommendation that seeks to provide guidance to Contracting States on the interpretation of the requirement in article II (2) that an arbitration agreement shall be in writing. The Recommendation was drafted in recognition of the widening use of electronic communications and enactments of domestic legislation as well as case law, which are more favorable than the Convention in respect of the form requirement governing arbitration agreements.[11]

[11] UN Doc A/61/17), Annex II; (2006) 37 UNCITRAL YB, Part Three, Annex II. See also comments from states at the 41st session of UNCITRAL, UN Doc A/CN.9/661 and Add (2008).

In order to understand why and how the New York Convention was developed under the auspices of the United Nations, one should consider the historical context, which finds its origins at the beginning of the twentieth century. At that time, only a few national arbitration laws were in place. The call for the establishment of an international framework on arbitration came from the business community, in particular the International Chamber of Commerce (ICC), which advocated in the 1920s for a convention on arbitration. The main concerns were to ensure that arbitration agreements would be respected and arbitral awards enforced.

The Assembly of the League of Nations in Geneva adopted on September 24, 1923, the Protocol on Arbitration Clauses (ratified by 30 states), and on September 26, 1927, the Convention on the Execution of Foreign Arbitral Awards (ratified by 24 states), which supplemented and expanded the scope of the 1923 Protocol.

The ICC again in the 1950s carried out studies confirming that the two Geneva instruments did not satisfy the needs of international trade, and called for further reform of the legal framework. The main issues identified by the ICC were that: (1) Article 1(1) of the Geneva Convention required that awards should be rendered in the territory of one contracting state, and that the parties should be subject to the jurisdiction of one of the contracting states; (2) the party seeking enforcement had the burden of proving that the required conditions were fulfilled; and (3) the award had to be final in the country where it was made. This last requirement was referred to as the "double exequatur" requirement. A major breakthrough of the New York Convention was to replace the requirement that the award be final by the requirement that it be "binding," thereby removing the need for double exequatur, and placing the burden of proof on the party resisting enforcement.[12]

In so doing, the final text of the New York Convention complied with the wish initially expressed by the Committee on the Enforcement of Foreign Arbitral Awards, set up within the framework of the United Nations Conference on International Commercial Arbitration (New York, May 20–June 10, 1957), "that it would be desirable to establish a new convention which, while going further than the Geneva Convention in facilitating the enforcement of foreign arbitral awards, would at the same time maintain generally recognized principles of justice and respect the sovereign rights of States."[13]

In parallel to consideration of the question of recognition and enforcement of foreign arbitral awards, the United Nations Conference on International Commercial Arbitration, which worked on the preparation and adoption of the New York Convention from May 20 to June 10, 1958, underlined in its final Act the importance of other measures for increasing the effectiveness of arbitration in the resolution of private law disputes. The topics mentioned included collection and publication of information on existing

[12] Summary Records of the United Nations Conference on International Commercial Arbitration, UN Doc E/CONF.26/SR.17.

[13] Economic and Social Council, Report of the Committee on the Enforcement of International Arbitral Awards, UN Doc E/2704 E/AC.42/4/Rev.1, para 14.

arbitration law and facilities, technical assistance in the development of arbitral legislation and institutions, and preparation of model law on arbitration.[14]

When UNCITRAL was established, a few years after the adoption of the New York Convention, the topic of dispute resolution was included as a matter of priority on its agenda. The recommendations of the diplomatic Conference to strengthen the existing framework served as a roadmap for UNCITRAL. At its second session, in 1969, most representatives considered that UNCITRAL should not undertake to draft a new convention on international commercial arbitration since the preparation of an international convention "involved considerable difficulties and, to judge from the pace of the work which had led to the adoption of the existing conventions, was bound to be a long-term undertaking." The decision of UNCITRAL at its very first sessions was clear: efforts should be deployed to obtain the largest possible number of ratifications or accessions to the New York Convention, and UNCITRAL should concern itself with problems of practical application and interpretation of existing conventions, including the New York Convention, since those conventions were interpreted in various ways and it would be desirable to encourage a uniform interpretation as far as possible.[15]

Following this approach, the preferred avenue for establishing an international framework on arbitration has been the development of soft law instruments, such as the UNCITRAL Arbitration Rules,[16] a document of a contractual nature, established to assist parties to tailor the arbitration procedure to their needs; and the development of a model law on arbitration,[17] which would build upon the arbitration procedure found in the Rules, and on the provisions of the New York Convention, providing in its chapter VIII a possible model legislation implementing the New York Convention.[18]

More than 50 years after the adoption of the New York Convention, and after having successfully established soft law instruments that have been widely adopted and used, UNCITRAL undertook the preparation of a convention in the field of treaty-based investor-state arbitration with the aim of promoting the value of transparency in investment arbitration.

As shown in the previous sections, the initiative to develop the New York Convention originated from the private sector—based upon identified inadequacies of the

[14] Economic and Social Council, UN Docs A/Conf.26/6 (1 May 1957) and E/CONF.26/8Rev.1.

[15] UN Doc A/7618, paras 101–113.

[16] UNCITRAL Arbitration Rules (1976), UN Doc A/31/17, para 57, (1976) 7 UNCITRAL YB, Part one, Chap II, Sect A, para 57. UNCITRAL Arbitration Rules (as revised in 2010), UN Doc A/65/17, Annex I. The UNCITRAL Arbitration Rules (adopted initially in 1976, and revised in 2010 and 2013) have been used for the settlement of a broad range of disputes, including disputes between private commercial parties where no arbitral institution is involved, commercial disputes administered by arbitral institutions, investor-state disputes, and state-to-state disputes. The Rules are recognized as one of the most successful international instruments of a contractual nature in the field of arbitration.

[17] UN Doc A/40/17, Annex I, and United Nations publication, Sales No. E.95.V.18.

[18] The UNCITRAL Model Law on International Commercial Arbitration (1985, as amended in 2006) has been enacted in more than 90 jurisdictions (see status of the Model Law on the internet at: <http://www.uncitral.org/uncitral/en/uncitral_texts/arbitration/1985Model_arbitration_status.html> accessed January 14, 2019.

international legal framework and at a time where many jurisdictions were still hesitant about the right articulation between arbitration and the judiciary. By contrast, calls to undertake work on transparency originated mainly from representatives of civil society.

1.2 Transparency Convention

The leading institution in the field of investment arbitration is the International Centre for Settlement of Investment Disputes (ICSID), established as one of the organizations of the World Bank Group by the Washington Convention on the Settlement of Investment Disputes between States and Nationals of Other States, introduced by the World Bank in 1965. The ICSID Convention establishes a self-contained regime for resolving investment disputes and enforcing their outcomes. The UNCITRAL Arbitration Rules have been used alongside the ICSID Rules for resolving disputes arising out of investment treaties. When UNCITRAL started the revision of its Arbitration Rules, in 2006, ICSID had just completed the revision of its own rules, through which it had sought to provide for more transparency in the arbitration procedure. Not surprisingly, calls for aligning the UNCITRAL Arbitration Rules to these new transparency standards led UNCITRAL to undertake work in relation to investment arbitration, in contrast to its usual generic approach to arbitration procedure that did not differentiate between purely commercial and investment arbitration.

At a session of the UNCITRAL Working Group on Arbitration tasked with the revision of the UNCITRAL Arbitration Rules, in February 2008,[19] the Special Representative of the Secretary-General on Human Rights and Transnational Corporations and other Business Enterprises stated that "adequate transparency where human rights and other States responsibilities are concerned is essential if the public is to be aware of proceedings that might affect the public interest. Transparency lay at the very foundation of what the United Nations and other authoritative entities had been promulgating as the precept of good governance."[20] In his intervention, the Special Representative highlighted the benefits of such cross-UN discussions on how shared values, including human rights, could be embedded into institutional practices in the context of economic globalization. In addition, two nongovernmental organizations, the Center for International Environmental Law (CIEL) and the International Institute for Sustainable Development (IISD), made proposals at that same session for amendments to the UNCITRAL Arbitration Rules to ensure transparency in investment arbitration proceedings.[21]

[19] Report of the UNCITRAL Working Group on Arbitration and Conciliation on the work of its 48th session (February 2008), UN Doc A/CN.9/646, paras 54–69, and Annexes I, II and III.

[20] ibid, Annex I.

[21] Transparency in investment arbitration was not new when UNCITRAL started its work on the topic. In 2006, ICSID had revised its Rules to include provisions on transparency.

The matter was considered further at the annual session of UNCITRAL in July 2008,[22] where the government of Canada submitted observations, and concluded that "endorsement of secrecy in investor-state arbitration would be contrary to the fundamental principles of good governance and human rights upon which the United Nations is founded."[23] Disputes brought pursuant to investment treaties often involve regulations with public policy implications, such as tax laws, environmental laws, and health regulations. Further, the defense of any claim and the payment of any award ultimately come from public funds.[24]

UNCITRAL therefore decided that transparency in treaty-based investor-state arbitration should be addressed as a matter of priority, after completion of the revision of the UNCITRAL Arbitration Rules.[25]

When considering the genesis of the Transparency Convention, it is important to differentiate the work on substantive issues, which started in 2010 and was completed in 2013 with the adoption of the Transparency Rules;[26] and the work on the Convention itself, which was completed one year later, in 2014, and was meant to provide a means to apply the Transparency Rules to investment treaties concluded before adoption of the Rules. The content of the transparency standards was easier to agree on than the form of the instrument and its scope of application. The Transparency Rules, as adopted after long debates, provide for: (1) creating public knowledge of the initiation of an investor-state arbitration, (2) making the decisions and award of the tribunal public, (3) allowing third parties to make submissions, (4) allowing open hearings, and (5) preserving the existing power of an arbitral tribunal to allow closed proceedings and restrict access to documents, or portions thereof, when necessary to protect confidential business information and/or information that is privileged or otherwise protected from disclosure under the domestic law of the disputing state, or when required to protect the integrity of the proceedings.

The Transparency Rules apply to treaties concluded after the date of their entry into force; they may also apply to investment treaties concluded *before* that date, provided that the states parties to the investment treaty or the parties to the dispute agree to their application.[27]

[22] Report of the UNCITRAL Working Group on Arbitration and Conciliation on the work of its 48th session (February 2008), UN Doc A/CN.9/646, para 69. In its report, the Working Group stated that it will "seek[s] guidance from the Commission on whether, after completion of its current work on the Rules, the Working Group should consider in further depth the specificity of treaty-based arbitration and, if so, which form that work should take."

[23] Observation by the Government of Canada, Note by the Secretariat, UN Doc A/CN.9/662, para 20.

[24] ibid para 9.

[25] UN Doc A/63/17, para 314.

[26] UNCITRAL Rules on Transparency in Treaty-based Investor-State Arbitration, UN Doc A/68/17, para 128 and Annex I.

[27] The clear distinction regarding application of the Transparency Rules between treaties concluded before and after the coming into effect of such Rules is meant to avoid application of the Transparency Rules under existing investment treaties through a dynamic interpretation of such treaties (see UN Doc A/CN.9/717, paras 36–41; and UN Doc A/CN.9/741).

The need to provide for an efficient and flexible mechanism for recording the agreement of states parties to such investment treaties triggered the preparation of a convention. This was considered to be an important endeavor, insofar as more than 3,000 such treaties are currently in force. One of the main advantages of a convention would be to permit the application of the Transparency Rules to arbitration under existing investment treaties, without states having to amend those treaties through a bilateral process, which would be time-consuming, and unlikely to happen soon. UNCITRAL therefore decided to prepare a convention "that was intended to give those States that wished to make the Transparency Rules applicable to their existing investment treaties concluded before 1 April 2014 an efficient mechanism to do so, without creating any expectation that other States would use the mechanism offered by the convention."[28] That mandate provides an indication of the difference of views amongst states regarding application of transparency to disputes arising under existing investment treaties. Where some states supported its application as a matter of principle to all arbitration cases, others expressed preference for a case-by-case approach. It should also be noted that not all states have the same level of experience with investment arbitration, or the same approach to the topic. In order to take into account these nuances, the Transparency Convention provides for flexibility through the various reservations that states may make, such as excluding certain investment treaties from the application of the Convention.

The Convention does not include any provision on the substance of transparency. The substance is in the Rules. The Convention is an instrument by which parties to investment treaties concluded before April 1, 2014, express their consent to apply the Transparency Rules. So, its scope is limited. But the potential for reforms that it opens is vast.

In brief, the Convention supplements existing investment treaties with respect to transparency-related obligations. It determines when and how the Transparency Rules shall apply to investor-state arbitration within the scope of the Convention, providing for application when all states parties to the investment treaty are also party to the Transparency Convention, as well as when only the respondent state (and not the state of the investor-claimant) is a party to the Convention (unilateral offer of application). A party to the Convention has the flexibility to formulate reservations, thereby excluding from the application of the Convention a specific investment treaty or a specific set of arbitration rules other than the UNCITRAL Arbitration Rules. A party may also declare that it will not provide a unilateral offer of application. Last, in the event the Transparency Rules are revised, a party may also declare, within a limited period after such revision, that it will not apply that revised version. By defining specific timing for the formulation and withdrawal of reservations, the Convention provides the necessary level of flexibility, while ensuring that reservations cannot be used to defeat the purpose of the Convention. The Convention and any reservation thereto apply prospectively, that is to arbitral

[28] UN Doc A/68/17, para 127.

proceedings commenced after the entry into force of the Convention for the Party concerned. Together with the Transparency Rules, the Convention aims to balance the public interest in such arbitration and the interest of the parties in resolving disputes in a fair and efficient manner.

2 Negotiation and Adoption Processes: Government-Led, and Inclusive Process

Both the New York Convention and the Transparency Convention have been negotiated through a process within the United Nations. In both cases, delegations from states of different legal backgrounds and stages of economic development, as well as delegations from observer international organizations, whether intergovernmental or nongovernmental, took part in the preparation and adoption of the instrument. For the New York Convention, 45 states took part in the diplomatic conference, together with 2 intergovernmental organizations and 10 nongovernmental organizations.[29] More than 50 years later, with the development of international arbitration, and the growing interest in the matter, more than 90 state delegations took part in the preparation of the Transparency Convention, together with around 5 intergovernmental organizations and 45 nongovernmental organizations.

The New York Convention was prepared before the establishment of UNCITRAL, so the process involved the establishment of an ad hoc committee by the United Nations Economic and Social Council.[30] The ad hoc Committee was tasked with the review and analysis of the draft convention prepared by the ICC, and it produced a new draft text. This text was a compromise between the ICC draft, which favored a truly international arbitration framework, and the will of states to keep a role for the domestic framework. The Transparency Convention was prepared by UNCITRAL, on the basis of a draft proposed by the Secretariat at the request of states.

In both processes, states and international organizations were given the opportunity to submit written comments. In relation to the New York Convention,[31] comments touched on all provisions, including observations on the scope of application of the Convention, the articulation between matters to be covered by the Convention and those that should be left to be covered by national laws, how the notion of "foreign"

[29] Economic and Social Council, UN Doc E/CONF.26/8Rev.1.

[30] ECOSOC Res 520 (VII). See UN Doc E/2704 (28 March 1955).

[31] Comments by Governments and Organisations on the Draft Convention on the Recognition and Enforcement of Foreign Arbitral Awards: January 1956–March 1958; UN Doc E2822 and Add. See also UN Doc E/AC.42/1. Amendments to the Draft Convention Submitted by Governmental Delegations: 21–28 May 1958, UN Docs E/CONF.26/7, E/CONF.26/L7 to E/CONF.26/L34.

arbitral awards could be understood, the need for reservations limiting the scope of application of the Convention,[32] and whether the Convention ought to cover arbitration agreements.[33]

In the case of the Transparency Convention, only Israel, Japan and the European Union provided written comments in advance of the UNCITRAL session finalizing the draft convention in 2014. Decisions adopting and finalizing the texts were taken by consensus.[34] The Convention was then adopted in December of the same year by the General Assembly without further comment or modification. Since the preparation of the United Nations Convention on Assignment of Receivables in International Trade, in 2001,[35] it has been the practice at UNCITRAL when preparing a convention to ensure that the draft convention receives sufficient consideration and reaches the level of maturity for it to be generally acceptable to states. UNCITRAL then submits the draft convention as approved by UNCITRAL for adoption by the UN General Assembly.

At earlier stages of the preparation of the Transparency Rules, states provided comments on their experience with transparency in investment arbitration.[36] Comments were also submitted by states parties to the North American Free Trade Agreement (NAFTA) in order to share their experience with the implementation of transparency standards embodied in that agreement. It is noteworthy that ICSID made two submissions during the preparation of the standards on transparency: at an early stage of the process, ICSID provided information to UNCITRAL about the content and implementation of the transparency provisions of the ICSID Rules;[37] later in the process, ICSID, together with a number of other interested organizations, such as the Permanent Court of Arbitration, the ICC, the Arbitration Institute of the Stockholm Chamber of Commerce, the Cairo Arbitration Centre, and the London Court of International Arbitration, provided comments on the interplay between the Transparency Rules and their own arbitration Rules.[38]

Both the New York Convention and the Transparency Convention, prepared and adopted through a process involving all stakeholders, reflect a delicate balance between different principles.

The New York Convention aims at striking a balance between its main goal of facilitating international arbitration, and at the same time ensuring that the various

[32] The New York Convention contains two reservations in its article 1(3), usually referred to as the reciprocity reservation (application of the Convention only to recognition and enforcement of awards made in the territory of another Contracting State) and the commercial reservation (application of the Convention only to differences arising out of legal relationships, whether contractual or not, that are considered commercial under the national law).

[33] United Nations Conference on International Commercial Arbitration, Summary Record of the 16th Meeting, UN Doc E/CONF.26/SR.16.

[34] Decisions at UNCITRAL are made by consensus, which, in the context of UNCITRAL practices has been interpreted to mean not requiring unanimity, and is instead based on a widely prevailing majority and the absence of a formal objection that would trigger a request for a vote.

[35] UN Doc A/56/17 (2000), para 200.

[36] UN Doc A/CN.9/WG.II/WP.159 and Add.

[37] UN Doc A/CN.9/WG.II/WP.167.

[38] UN Doc A/CN.9/WG.II/WP.173. The Transparency Rules have been applied in one ICSID case by agreement of the disputing parties, BSG Resources Ltd against Republic of Guinea.

legal principles of different states are observed. A guiding principle was that "the extent of judicial control over the recognition and enforcement of arbitral awards must be defined with precision, so as to avoid the possibility that a losing party could invoke without adequate justification a multiplicity of possible grounds for objections in order to frustrate the enforcement of awards rendered against it."[39]

The Transparency Convention aims at providing a mechanism to apply the Transparency Rules, which aim at striking a balance between the public interest in being informed and parties' interest in an efficient resolution of their dispute, as well as between transparency and the need to protect confidentiality and the integrity of the arbitral process.

3 Implementation of the Texts: In Search of Creativity

Monitoring implementation of conventions is the next important step after successful preparation and adoption.

The Transparency Convention is a very recently adopted instrument, and there is for now little to report regarding challenges in its implementation. By contrast, the New York Convention, widely adopted and often applied, offers an interesting overview of implementation issues.

As an illustration of such issues, the New York Convention is silent on its application to arbitral awards or arbitration agreements in effect at the date on which a state becomes bound by the Convention, and any possible retroactive effect. That matter has therefore been dealt with in various manners by states. A vast majority of states remained silent on the temporal effect of the Convention when adopting it. In line with the pro-enforcement approach of the Convention, they considered that the Convention applies to valid arbitration agreements and enforceable arbitral awards made either before or after the coming into effect of the New York Convention. This is based on the assumption that parties enter voluntarily into arbitration agreements with the aim of complying with the final decisions of the arbitrators. Only in case of bad faith would parties enter into an arbitration agreement without the intention of complying with an enforceable award. So, in line with the spirit of the Convention, the Convention is to apply to all valid arbitration agreements and enforceable arbitral awards, whether such agreements or awards were made before or after the entry into force of the Convention. Some states have dealt with the matter in subsequent implementing legislation, by including a provision on whether the Convention applies retroactively or only prospectively to either arbitration agreements or arbitral awards, while others have left that matter for determination by the state courts.

[39] Nations, Economic and Social Council, UN Doc E/Conf.26/2, para 9.

A specific case is that of Yugoslavia, which made a declaration, when adopting the New York Convention, on the question of the retroactive effect of the Convention.[40] It did so for historical reasons: at the time of the negotiation of the New York Convention, Yugoslavia proposed that a provision be included in the Convention on that matter; that proposal was rejected. As a result, states from the former Yugoslavia continue to benefit from that declaration. This reservation, which is not contemplated by the Convention, raises the question of the effect of additional reservations under the New York Convention. By contrast, the Transparency convention provides that "No reservations are permitted except those expressly authorized (. . .)."

3.1 Case Law on UNICTRAL Texts (CLOUT) and the Guide on the New York Convention

Since 1988, UNCITRAL has established a reporting system for case law on UNCITRAL texts (CLOUT)[41] in order to assist judges, arbitrators, lawyers, and parties to business transactions. By making available decisions of courts and arbitral tribunals interpreting UNCITRAL texts (notably conventions and model laws), UNCITRAL seeks to further the uniform interpretation and application of those texts.

The New York Convention is one of the most important and successful UN treaties in the area of international trade law, and its promotion is an integral part of the work program of UNCITRAL.[42] UNCITRAL decided to undertake the preparation of a Guide on the New York Convention, as a project of its secretariat, in cooperation with experts,[43] on the basis of General Assembly resolution 62/65 of 6 December 2007. In that resolution, the General Assembly expressed its conviction that the New York Convention strengthens respect for binding commitments, inspires confidence in the rule of law, and ensures fair treatment in the resolution of disputes arising over contractual rights and obligations. It emphasized the necessity for further national efforts

[40] The former Yugoslavia had acceded to the Convention on February 26, 1982, with the following reservation:"1. The Convention is applied in regard to the Socialist Federal Republic of Yugoslavia only to those arbitral awards which were adopted after the coming of the Convention into effect." In a latter declaration dated June 28, 1982, the government of Yugoslavia had specified that the first reservation only constituted an affirmation of the legal principle of retroactivity. For more information, see United Nations Treaty collection, <https://treaties.un.org/>.

[41] Report of the United Nations Commission on International Trade Law on the work of its 21st session, 11–20 April 1988, UN Doc A/43/17, paras 98–109. CLOUT reports are published as UN Docs A/CN.9/SER.C/ABSTRACTS/1 to A/CN.9/SER.C/ABSTRACTS/168 (latest document available at the date of this Digest revision). The 168 CLOUT reports are also available on UNCITRAL's website at <https://uncitral.un.org/> accessed January 17, 2019.

[42] "Note by the Secretariat: further work in respect of international commercial arbitration," UN Doc A/CN.9/169)—Commission 1979.

[43] See UNCITRAL Secretariat Guide on the New York Convention, available at <http://newyorkconvention1958.org/> accessed January 17, 2019 and <https://uncitral.un.org/sites/uncitral.un.org/files/media-documents/uncitral/en/2016_guide_on_the_convention.pdf> accessed January 17, 2019>.

to achieve universal adherence to the Convention, together with its uniform interpretation and effective implementation.

This Guide serves as a reference tool that collates a wide range of decisions on the New York Convention and analyzes extensively how domestic courts interpret and apply its provisions. Its purpose is to assist in the dissemination of information on the Convention and further promote its adoption as well as its uniform interpretation and effective implementation. A website[44] has been established as a joint project[45] in order to make the information gathered in preparation of the Guide on the New York Convention publicly available. The site contains an electronic version of the Guide in all official languages of the United Nations, a significant corpus of judicial interpretation of the New York Convention by states parties, information on the ratification of the Convention, and the *travaux préparatoires*, as well as a bibliography, that is a comprehensive directory of publications relating to the application and interpretation of the Convention.[46]

3.2 The Transparency Registry

The Transparency Convention aims at making the Transparency Rules applicable to existing investment treaties, and would not fulfill its purpose without the Transparency Registry. The Registry is a central repository for the publication of information and documents in treaty-based investor-state arbitration. It is an essential feature of the Transparency Convention, and will be used for the publication of procedural documents issued as part of arbitral proceedings to which the transparency standards apply. Therefore, the Transparency Registry is different in nature from the tools developed for the application of the New York Convention.

4 Conclusion

The whole system of international commercial arbitration is based on the New York Convention. Without the Convention, international commercial arbitration could never have developed as it did so far. Indeed, the Convention has largely contributed to the status of international arbitration as today's normal means of resolving commercial

[44] <www.newyorkconvention1958.org> accessed January 17, 2019.

[45] The website has been established jointly by Shearman & Sterling LLP, the Columbia Law School and UNCITRAL.

[46] The search engine of the website allows a thorough search among the decisions, and enables searching the Guide, the *travaux préparatoires*, the case law, and the bibliography. In relation to each case, it contains the full text of the decision, and a translation of the decision in English where relevant, as well as a summary of the cases. It supplements the cases collected in the CLOUT (Case Law on UNCITRAL Texts) database and serves as a primary reference tool underlying the Guide on the New York Convention.

disputes. The United Nations has also further contributed to the standardization of procedures of international commercial arbitration with the adoption of the UNCITRAL Arbitration Rules and the Model Law on International Commercial Arbitration.

In its project on Investing Across Borders, the World Bank has developed indicators of foreign direct investment regulation and proceeded to an assessment of the strength of the legal framework for alternative dispute resolution and judicial support to arbitration using as a reference tool the instruments developed by UNCITRAL in the field of international commercial arbitration.[47] In a recent publication, the effect of signing the New York Convention has been evaluated in order to quantify the impact of international arbitration on foreign direct investments, and hence on development. The results of the study suggest that increasing access to international commercial arbitration has a positive effect on foreign direct investments.[48]

As indicated in the introductory remarks to the New York Convention Guide, despite the diversity of Contracting States' legal systems, interpretation and application of the Convention has been rather consistent and in conformity with the Convention's policy of favoring recognition and enforcement.[49]

The Transparency Convention is designed to bring greater efficiency and coherence to the dispute settlement system and, together with the Transparency rules, aims at encouraging investment in key economic sectors, particularly in energy and other basic-need areas, by increasing confidence in the investment arbitration process. Transparency, which permits meaningful and trustworthy public information, is a strong support to good governance. It also follows that transparency and accountability are enablers for inclusive and sustainable growth and development.

Both the New York Convention and the Transparency Convention have paved the way for possible future reform projects. Two of these recent projects may be mentioned here. The first concerns the preparation of a convention mirroring the New York Convention in relation to enforcement of settlement agreements resulting from mediation. In that respect, a proposal by the Delegation of the United States of America in 2014 suggested that UNCITRAL work on the development of a convention on the enforceability of international commercial settlement agreements reached through conciliation, with the goal of encouraging conciliation in the same way that the New York Convention facilitated the growth of arbitration.[50] The work on the topic resulted in the adoption of the Convention on International Settlement Agreements Resulting from Mediation (also known as the Singapore Convention on Mediation) by the UN General Assembly on 20 December 2018,[51] and a revision of the UNCITRAL Model Law on International Commercial Conciliation.[52]

[47] See The World Bank group, Investing Across Borders, Indicators of foreign Direct Investment Regulation, Arbitrating Commercial Disputes, available at <http://iab.worldbank.org/data/exploretopics/arbitrating-commercial-disputes> accessed January 17, 2019.

[48] Andrew Myburgh and Jordi Paniagua, "Does International Commercial Arbitration Promote FDS?," 59 JL and Econ 597–627.

[49] See New York Convention Guide, Introduction, paras 11–13.

[50] UN Doc A/CN.9/822.

[51] A/RES/73/198.

[52] UN Doc A/73/17, annex II and A/RES/73/199.

A separate project concerns the question of possible reform of the investor-state dispute settlement regime, and whether the Transparency Convention could be used as a model for implementing further broader reforms.[53] UNCITRAL commenced work on possible reform of investor-state dispute settlement in the fall of 2017, on the basis of a broad mandate. In discharging that mandate, UNCITRAL would ensure that the deliberations, while benefiting from the widest possible breadth of available expertise from all stakeholders, would be government-led, with high-level input from all governments, consensus-based and fully transparent. Consideration of a possible reform is meant to unfold following three steps: (1) first, identify and consider concerns regarding investor-state dispute settlement; (2) second, consider whether reform was desirable in the light of any identified concerns; and (3) third, if it were to be concluded that reform was desirable, develop any relevant solutions.

The legal analyses on whether the Transparency Convention could serve as a model to apply any wider reform of investor-state dispute settlement as studied in a research paper[54] highlight a number of issues, such as law of treaty questions including the relation of a new convention with the existing investment treaties and the ICSID Convention; the questions of application of a new convention by both the investor's home state and the host state, or by one of them only; and the possible reservations that would allow states to tailor their level of involvement in a reform. As concluded by the research paper, the challenges involved in broader reforms of the investor-state arbitration regime are substantially more complex than the introduction of a transparency standard in investment treaties. At the same time, it also shows that the Transparency Convention could provide a useful model if states wish to pursue such broader reform initiatives at a multilateral level.[55]

[53] UN Doc A/72/17. See also the report on whether the Convention on Transparency could be used as a model for further reforms to the investor-state dispute settlement regime, presented at the 49th session of UNCITRAL, in 2016, available at <https://uncitral.un.org/en/commission> accessed January 17, 2019. in particular document A/CN.9/890, the CIDS research paper on whether the Mauritius Convention can serve as a model for further reforms as well as the report of UNCITRAL on the work of its 49th session, UN Doc A/71/17, paras 187–195. See also UN Doc A/CN.9/917.

[54] See CIDS research paper on whether the Mauritius Convention can serve as a model for further reforms, available at <https://uncitral.un.org/en/commission> accessed January 17, 2019.

[55] ibid 4 (Executive summary) and paras 274–289 (Conclusive remarks).

CHAPTER 29

RESPONSIBILITY OF STATES AND INTERNATIONAL ORGANIZATIONS

PIERRE BODEAU-LIVINEC*

A series of paradoxes lies behind the consideration of issues relating to responsibility of states and international organizations as potential topics for UN treaties, that is, conventional instruments concluded under the auspices, or with a significant contribution, of the world organization. Quite obviously, classical issues relating to responsibility belong to the realm of hard law, at least in the sense that they essentially pertain to the international legal system. In the famous words used by Max Huber, "*la responsabilité est le corollaire nécessaire du droit*";[1] accordingly, it could very well be expected that, in parallel to the development of multilateral treaties covering an ever-wider field of social activities and issues, relevant aspects of legal responsibility would be expressly covered. However, one cannot fail to observe that, at least in the context of "UN treaties" broadly conceived, there only are very rare occurrences of the topic of responsibility in a conventional context.

The treaties governing activities in the exploration and use of outer space specifically refer to the matter,[2] although the main focus relates to "liability" rather than "responsibility"

* Professor of public law—University Paris Nanterre.

[1] *British Claims in the Spanish Zone of Morocco Case*, "Rapport sur les responsabilités de l'État dans les situations visées par les réclamations britanniques", 23 October 1924, reproduced in 2 RIAA 641. See also *Barcelona Traction, Light and Power Company, Limited* (Merits) [1970] ICJ Rep 36, para 33 ("Responsibility is a necessary corollary of a right").

[2] See the 1967 Treaty on Principles Governing the Activities of States in the Exploration and Use of Outer Space, including the Moon and Other Celestial Bodies (610 UNTS 206, esp. Arts. VI and VII); and the 1979 Agreement Governing the Activities of States on the Moon and Other Celestial Bodies (1363 UNTS 3, Art. 14(1)).

sensu stricto.[3] But, beyond these classical examples, conventions adopted under the auspices of the Organization or dealing with its own activities[4] infrequently address issues of responsibility. The principle that "[r]eparation is the indispensable complement of a failure to apply a convention and [thus] there is no necessity for this to be stated in the convention itself"[5] may provide a logical and classical explanation for that silence. However, with the growing complexity and variety of legal questions pertaining to responsibility,[6] such a cautious approach proves quite difficult to understand nowadays.

Here lies the second paradox of the legal treatment reserved to responsibility by or within the United Nations. While a whole set of well-known "Vienna Conventions," adopted on the basis of texts drafted by the International Law Commission (ILC), now covers some of the most significant aspects of international legal relations, the legal "fate" of responsibility remains outside the realm of treaty law.[7] The topic "State responsibility" was duly included in the initial list of 14 topics selected for codification by the ILC in 1949,[8] and the Commission spent more than 30 years studying it, from the first report on the topic by Roberto Ago in 1969 to the final adoption on second reading of the Articles on Responsibility of States for Internationally Wrongful Acts (ASR) in 2001.[9] Yet, since then, the status of this text has not significantly evolved: the ASR formally pertain to soft law and, quite likely, are the instrument of such kind which is the most heavily relied upon in international legal practice. Albeit less influential, the Articles on the Responsibility of International Organizations (ARIO) have followed a similar path since their adoption by the Commission in 2011,[10] with no perspective of a convention being concluded on their basis in the foreseeable future.

[3] See the 1972 *Convention on International Liability for Damage Caused by Space Objects* (961 UNTS 187). Article 304 of the United Nations Convention on the Law of the Sea also combines "responsibility and liability for damage" as a "without prejudice" clause preserving "the application of existing rules and the development of further rules regarding responsibility and liability under international law."

[4] Since the adoption of UNGA Res 52/247 (26 June 1998) on "Third-Party Liability: Temporal and financial Limitations," Status-of-Forces Agreements between the UN and countries hosting peacekeeping operations usually include a provision on the "limitation of liability of the United Nations"; see eg, the 2004 Agreement between the United Nations and the Government of Haiti Concerning the Status of the United Nations Operation in Haiti (2271 UNTS 235, Section 54). See also Article 9 of the Model Memorandum of Understanding between the United Nations and Troop-Contributing Countries (UN Doc A/C.5/63/18).

[5] Permanent Court of International Justice, *Case Concerning the Factory at Chorzów (Germany v Poland)* (Claim for indemnity) (Jurisdiction), PCIJ Rep Series A N° 9, at 21.

[6] See Pierre Bodeau-Livinec and Laurence Dubin, "La responsabilité des institutions internationales dans tous ses états", *in* Laurence Dubin and Marie-Clotilde Runavot (eds), *Le phénomène institutionnel international dans tous ses états* (Pedone 2014) 231–59.

[7] On this paradox, described upon the completion of the ASR, see David CARON, "The ILC Articles on State Responsibility: The Paradoxical Relationship between Form and Authority," (2002) 96 *AJIL* 857–73.

[8] See 1949 YBILC 281, para 16.

[9] The text of the Articles on Responsibility of States for Internationally Wrongful Acts is annexed to UNGA Res 56/83 (12 December 2001).

[10] The text of the Articles on Responsibility of International Organizations is annexed to UNGA Res 66/100 (9 December 2011).

How to reconcile the conceptual importance of these texts with the clear reluctance of states to crystallize them in treaty law? Assessing the current situation as far as issues of responsibility are concerned may prove instrumental in considering the potential added value of UN treaties in the formation and further development of contemporary international law in the field.

1 The Conventional Drafting of the Articles on State Responsibility and the Articles on Responsibility of International Organizations

One may reasonably assume that, even though it did not take any express decision in that respect when it began drafting the ASR, the International Law Commission may have considered that the result of its work would eventually be embodied in treaty form. However, that initial prospect progressively vanished, first in the ILC and later in the General Assembly.

1.1 The Elaboration of Draft (Conventional) Principles of Responsibility

After an initial failure to consider the topic in an appropriate manner, the ILC decided in 1963 to change substantially its approach and focus on "the definitions of the general rules governing the international responsibility of the State,"[11] leaving aside the responsibility of other subjects of international law and the identification of relevant primary rules, concerning in particular injuries to aliens and their property. Quite interestingly, however, the Commission did not actually undertake the study of the topic before it had completed its examination on the law of treaties, as if there was some logical sequence in its work on the major and general themes of international law, culminating with the consideration of state responsibility.[12]

On most of the previous topics considered at the time by the Commission, the texts adopted on second reading formed the basis of a treaty later negotiated among states. The series of "Vienna Conventions" provide the most obvious illustrations of that trend, albeit with variable success: some have gained almost universal participation

[11] 1963-II YBILC 224, para 52.

[12] In 1968, that is, almost immediately after the conclusion of the second reading of the draft articles on the law of treaties, the General Assembly urged the ILC to "make every effort to begin substantive work on State responsibility as from its next session" (UNGA Res 2400 (11 December 1968) para 4 (c)).

(on diplomatic and consular relations); some others, such as the Vienna Convention on the Law of Treaties, entered into force quite a long time after their adoption, and a few are not yet in force to date.[13] In order to complete the drafting of the main principles of the international legal system, it would have appeared only logical that a "Vienna Convention on Responsibility of States for Internationally Wrongful Acts" be eventually concluded on the basis of the work done by the Commission.

The ILC itself refrained from addressing the issue of the final form to be given to its draft articles when it started its study based on the annual reports of Roberto Ago.[14] However, it successfully combined, in the drafting of the ASR, the codification of fundamental principles of state responsibility (relying on an abundant and ancient practice, case law, and literature)—for example on issues of attribution and reparation—with elements of progressive development—for example aspects of the regime of countermeasures, violation of jus cogens obligations, invocation of responsibility by non-injured states, etc. This method, quite typical of the Commission, would naturally call for the elaboration of a treaty on the basis of the draft articles, so as to give those an identical legal regime.[15]

Moreover, the logical structure of the text adopted in 2001, especially with its final general provisions delineating the ambit of the text,[16] closely follows that of a conventional instrument. Some salient and controversial aspects of the draft articles as adopted on first reading, such as the mechanism of compulsory conciliation and arbitration supported by the then Special Rapporteur Gaetano Arangio-Ruiz, would clearly have required a treaty.[17] Those elements have not been retained on second reading, thus showing the will of the ILC to leave the question of the form of the ASR open until the final stages of its consideration of the topic.

In a resolution concomitant to its acknowledgment of the ASR, the General Assembly requested the ILC to begin its work on the topic "Responsibility of International Organizations."[18] Some formal parallelism was thus established between the consideration of the law of treaties (first in relation to states (1969 Vienna Convention) and, later, to states and international organizations (1986 Vienna Convention)) and the

[13] See for example the UN Convention on Jurisdictional Immunities of States and Their Property, in the UN Treaty Collection <https://treaties.un.org/Pages/ParticipationStatus.aspx?clang=_en> accessed January 28, 2019.

[14] See the future plan of work on the topic as described in 1969-II YBILC 233, paras 79–84.

[15] According to Article 15 of the ILC Statute, "the expression 'progressive development of international law' is used for convenience as meaning the preparation of draft conventions on subjects that have not yet been regulated by international law or in regard to which the law has not yet been sufficiently developed in the practice of states. Similarly, the expression 'codification of international law' is used for convenience as meaning the more precise formulation and systematization of rules of international law in fields where there already has been extensive State practice, precedent and doctrine" (see UNGA Res 174 (21 November 1947)).

[16] See in particular Arts. 55 (*Lex specialis*), 56 (Questions of State responsibility not regulated by these articles), and 59 (Charter of the United Nations).

[17] See Part Three ("Settlement of Disputes") of the Draft Articles on State Responsibility as adopted on first reading, in 1996-II(2) YBILC 64–65.

[18] See UNGA Res 56/82 (12 December 2001) para 8.

study of international responsibility. Substantial differences however exist, which would have certainly called for a more distinct treatment of the legal questions at stake. While issues pertaining to the law of treaties primarily relate to the legal regime of the instrument, making it quite easily possible to consider the case of international organizations in that respect by analogy with that of states, issues pertaining to responsibility vary significantly with the specific features of the responsible or injured person (e.g., as far as problems of attribution and reparation are concerned). Therefore, it is far from obvious that, even if a convention on state responsibility were eventually adopted, the ARIO would easily and necessarily follow a similar fate.

Nevertheless, and quite strangely, there is a close filiation between the ASR and the ARIO, both in terms of structure and content of the draft instruments. It is thus likely that no decision would be taken on the ARIO before the question of the form of the ASR is ultimately resolved. Since 2001, the issue has been central in the debates on international responsibility within the General Assembly's Sixth Committee.

1.2 Reconsidering the Possibility of a Convention on Responsibility

Once appointed Special Rapporteur on state responsibility, with the mandate to complete the second reading of the ILC's draft articles by 2001, James Crawford immediately addressed the most contentious issues of the text as it then stood, including that of the eventual form of the instrument.[19] Quite wisely, he recommended that the treatment of that question be deferred until the completion of the second reading:[20] once the substance of the provisions would be settled, the Commission would actually be in a better position to make a relevant recommendation as to the form of the text.

1.2.1 *The Final Debate and Recommendation of the ILC in* 2001

When the Commission resumed its discussion on the form to be given to its draft articles in 2001, a series of arguments were expressed in favor of, or against a convention. For some members, the adoption of the draft articles as a convention "would ensure their place, together with the 1969 Vienna Convention [on the Law of Treaties], as one of the fundamental pillars of public international law,"[21] and "would give them additional certainty, reliability and binding force,"[22] with a limited risk that states could, during the negotiation process, substantially endanger or change the balance reached by the Commission. Other members—including the Special Rapporteur[23]—conversely considered that it would be preferable for the General Assembly either to take note of the articles of the Commission or to adopt them as a non-binding declaration.

[19] See the First Report on State Responsibility by J. Crawford, UN Doc A/CN.4/490 and Add. 1–3 (1998).

[20] UN Doc A/CN.4/490 (24 April 1998) para 42.

[21] 2001-II(2) YBILC 24, para 62.

[22] ibid.

[23] See Fourth Report on State Responsibility, UN Doc A/CN.4/517 (2 April 2001) para 26.

They questioned the necessity of a treaty on responsibility and insisted on the risks associated with such a choice: in addition to the possibility of reservations and the potential discrepancies among states parties and others, it was argued that "an unratified convention containing significant elements of customary international law could result in 'reverse codification.' "[24]

The Commission eventually opted for a compromise, albeit clearly favoring a non-binding text in the short term.[25] It recommended to the General Assembly

> that it take note of the draft articles on responsibility of States for internationally wrongful acts in a resolution, and that it annex the draft articles to the resolution[;]
>
> [...]
>
> that the General Assembly consider, at a later stage, and in the light of the importance of the topic, the possibility of convening an international conference of plenipotentiaries to examine the draft articles on responsibility of States for internationally wrongful acts with a view to concluding a convention on the topic.[26]

The General Assembly, while formally following this balanced recommendation, adopted in fact an even more cautious approach.

1.2.2 *The Undecisive Debate within the GA*

In its resolution putting an end to the substantial work of the ILC on state responsibility, the General Assembly merely decided to

> take [...] note of the articles on responsibility of States for internationally wrongful acts, presented by the International Law Commission, the text of which is annexed to the present resolution, and commend[ed] them to the attention of Governments *without prejudice to the question of their future adoption or other appropriate action.*[27]

As appears clearly from such a wording, the General Assembly actually favored a more static stance as to the form of the articles than the position advocated by the Commission: it made no commitment whatsoever to consider at a later stage the adoption of a convention or, even, of a declaration embodying the text in a more formal manner than a mere product of the Commission. The articles were left on their own, duly taken note of by the international community of states without any blessing or, at least, official acknowledgment.

[24] 2001-II(2) YBILC 24, para 63. For a synthesis of the arguments discussed during the debate, see ibid., paras 61–67.

[25] Santiago Villalpando describes this phenomenon as a form of "codification light" ("Codification Light: A New Trend in the Codification of International Law at the United Nations" (2013) 8 *Anuário Brasileiro de Direito Internacional* 117, esp. at 140 ff).

[26] 2001-II(2) YBILC 25. A similar recommendation was made, in 2011, with respect to the ARIO (ILC Report on its 63rd Session, UN Doc A/66/10, at 53).

[27] UNGA Res 56/83 (12 December 2001) para 3 (emphasis added).

Quite strikingly, the situation has not significantly evolved since 2001, even though the General Assembly has maintained the topic on its agenda and continues considering it every three years. In 2004, member states were invited "to submit their written comments on any future action regarding the articles" and the Secretary General received the mandate "to prepare an initial compilation of decisions of international courts, tribunals and other bodies referring to the articles."[28] From 2007 onward, the General Assembly has created a working group within the Sixth Committee entrusted with the task of discussing "the question of a convention on responsibility of States for internationally wrongful acts or other appropriate action on the basis of the articles."[29] Although the working group has been reconvened since then "with a view to taking a decision,"[30] this status quo remains unaffected and resembles more and more a normative stalemate. Quite tellingly if one considers that the General Assembly may not want to keep indefinitely this item on its agenda, it now envisages to request the Secretary-General to provide "information on all procedural options regarding possible action on the basis of the articles";[31] this, however, will not happen before 2019 at best.

Obviously, the hesitation shown by the Assembly proceeds from the divergent opinions expressed by its member states on a matter of most legal significance. These views, as stated in 2007, may broadly be identified along the following lines.

For a first group of states, the articles should be embodied in a treaty: as strongly put by Portugal—urging other states not to be "over-cautious"—"the draft articles on State responsibility could and should constitute the third structuring pillar of the international legal order set up after the Second World War"[32] (together with the UN Charter and the 1969 Vienna Convention on the Law of Treaties). Achieving a Convention would have the additional benefit, at least for some states, of reopening "the option of including [...] principles for the settlement of disputes arising in relation to State responsibility."[33] It must however be noted that, even among this first group, reasons given in support of a convention may differ: France, for example, considers that, "in the light of the importance and novelty of some of the rules set forth in the articles, it is essential to invite States to examine the proposed rules at a conference where they could present their views";[34] in such a perspective, the ILC Articles would only offer "a good basis on which to work."[35]

For a second group of states, exemplified by the United Kingdom, "no further action [would be] necessary or desirable";[36] given the standing of the ASR as "an authoritative statement of international law" frequently relied upon in state and judicial practice,

[28] UNGA Res 59/35 (2 December 2004) paras 2–3.

[29] UNGA Res 62/61 (6 December 2007) para 4.

[30] UNGA Res 65/19 (6 December 2010) para 4; UNGA Res 68/104 (16 December 2013) para 5; UNGA Res 71/133 (13 December 2016) para 8.

[31] UNGA Res 71/133 (13 December 2016) para 5.

[32] UN Doc A/62/63, at 4. See also the comments by Brazil (UN Doc A/65/96, at 2), Lithuania (A/65/96, at 4), Mexico (A/65/96, at 4–5), Chile (considering the possibility of adopting a General Assembly declaration only as a "transitional measure" toward a Convention; UN Doc A/68/69, at 3).

[33] El Salvador (UN Doc A/65/96/Add.1, at 2).

[34] UN Doc A/65/96, at 3.

[35] ibid.

[36] UN Doc A/62/63, at 5.

the articles "should not be put at risk lightly" by a tentative of "crystallization [...] in a treaty text."[37] The conclusion follows unabated:

> there is a significant risk that a convention with a small number of participants may have a de-codifying effect, may serve to undermine the current status of the draft articles and may be a "limping" convention, with little or no practical effect.[38]

Finally, a third group of states favors an intermediary solution, with the ILC articles being formally endorsed as a resolution or declaration of the General Assembly. As explained by the Czech Republic, "[s]uch alternative would offer a greater chance for the document to become, in the view of the majority of States, acceptable as a proof of the existence of an *opinio juris* in the event of any future examination of the customary nature of these rules of international law."[39] However, these states do not seem to support a progressive evolution toward a treaty form: even the Nordic states, which had initially indicated that they favored, "in principle" "the idea of a future Convention,"[40] have later made it clear that the articles were "in the strongest possible position as an annex to a resolution."[41]

From this brief overview, one may reasonably conclude that, even though the arguments advanced in support of one option over the others may have evolved since 2001, states remain clearly divided on the issue, with no consensus progressively emerging in favor of a Convention. While the General Assembly seems keen to take a final stance on the topic, the current status quo clearly benefits those who consider that the Articles are better left within the realm of soft law, either as a mere Commission's text or as a declaration of the General Assembly.

Undoubtedly, the question of the form to be given to the ARIO appears less controversial. In 2011, the General Assembly had simply duplicated the wording used in respect of the ASR in 2001.[42] While a few states have expressed some readiness to consider the adoption of a convention,[43] most of them have emphasized the ARIO's distinct character and legal value, despite their formal resemblance with the ASR, to indicate that, in their view, "the time was not ripe"[44] for the elaboration of a convention on the responsibility of international organizations. The United Kingdom explained, for example, that

> there was as yet no pressing need for a convention on the topic of the responsibility of international organizations, nor was there a clear indication that there was sufficient

[37] ibid 6.

[38] ibid 7. See also the United States of America (UN Doc A/62/63/Add.1); Germany (UN Doc A/65/96, at 3); Australia (UN Doc A/71/79, at 2).

[39] UN Doc A/62/63, at 2.

[40] UN Doc A/62/63, at 4.

[41] UN Doc A/65/96, at 3. See the cautious approach of the Netherlands (ibid 5–6), Qatar (ibid 7), or Austria (questioning "whether the conditions for future work on a convention exist," UN Doc A/71/79, at 3).

[42] See UNGA Res. 66/100 (9 December 2011) para 3.

[43] See Russian Federation (UN Doc. A/C.6/69/SR.18 (23 October 2014), at 9, para 55); Cuba (ibid 9, para 58).

[44] Singapore (ibid 10, para 68). See also Denmark (ibid 8), Israel (ibid. 11), Greece (ibid 12, para 77), and the United States (ibid 12, para 80).

> consensus on the law in that area. It was also unlikely that negotiations, which inevitably would be a long and complex process, would result in a sufficient consensus for the adoption of a convention.[45]

Quite tellingly, even states that have been constantly supportive of the adoption on a treaty on state responsibility did not militate in favor of a similar exercise, at least until further developments on the ASR, as far as the ARIO are concerned.[46] In a significant move, 24 international organizations issued in 2017 a joint submission very critical of the ARIO and stating that "negotiating a treaty based on these articles would be premature."[47] Hence, there is no realistic prospect that a convention on the responsibility of international organizations will be drafted in the near future. The ongoing debate seems only relevant as far as state responsibility is concerned.

2 The Conventional Debate on the Articles on State Responsibility

In significant respects, the form to be given to the ASR does not appear as a substantial issue anymore or, at least, not one on which the international community would be likely to adopt a widely shared decision soon. However, while strong arguments support keeping the ASR in their current soft law form, the added value of a Convention should not be underestimated.

2.1 The Reluctance towards Engaging into a Conventional Exercise

As clearly summarized by James Crawford in its introduction to the ILC's Articles, a series of argumentative lines support the two-stage approach taken by the Commission regarding the eventual form of its text.[48] The former Special Rapporteur recalled that "[a] more realistic and potentially more effective option would be to rely on international courts and tribunals, on State practice and doctrine to adopt and apply the rules in the text."[49] More importantly, a diplomatic conference "could endanger the balance of the text"[50] found by the Commission. These arguments differ in nature: while the latter is based on an assessment of the intrinsic value of the Articles, the former

45 ibid 10, para 66. 46 See Portugal (ibid 12, para 76).

47 See UN Doc A/72/80 (26 April 2017) para 6. 48 See Section 1.2.1 of this chapter.

49 James Crawford, *The International Law Commission's Articles on State Responsibility—Introduction, Text and Commentaries* (CUP 2002)58–59.

50 ibid 59.

relates to their reception by international courts and tribunals and other relevant actors. On closer analysis, we see that both however retain some ambivalence and thus fail to be entirely conclusive.

In its 2004 resolution 59/35, the General Assembly requested the Secretary-General "to prepare an initial compilation of decisions of international courts, tribunals and other bodies referring to the articles"[51] on state responsibility. On the basis of that request, reiterated in each consideration of the topic since then,[52] the Secretary-General (in actual fact the Codification Division of the Office of Legal Affairs) has issued four substantive compilations, reproducing relevant extracts of international case law organized along the structure of the ASR.[53] The result is unquestionably impressive, both quantitatively and qualitatively. Taken all together, these documents show that, by 2016, almost 300 decisions—adopted by dozens of international and regional courts, arbitral tribunals, WTO panels and Appellate Body, human rights bodies or administrative tribunals of international organizations—had referred to, or expressly relied upon, the ASR. The variety of judicial institutions involved and the wide range of issues dealt with in terms of responsibility unequivocally demonstrate the importance which that soft law instrument has gained in international practice.

Judicial practice appears to confirm the internal "balance" of the text, advocated by those who support the status quo as to the form of the ASR. Courts and tribunals have indeed relied upon most of the provisions of the Articles, and all parts of the text, including the most progressive or debatable—such as the particular consequences of a serious breach of a jus cogens obligation,[54] the regime of countermeasures,[55] or the invocation of responsibility by a non-injured state[56]—have already found a significant echo in their practice. Accordingly, the complex process eventually leading to the adoption of a treaty based on the ASR could prove useless or, even, counterproductive.

Before we reach such a conclusion, however, a closer reading of relevant international case law may call for a measure of caution. Quite clearly, international courts and tribunals have sometimes developed diverging interpretations of key provisions of the text.[57] More surprisingly perhaps, some tribunals have sometimes gone as far as considering the ASR in toto as "a codification of the rules of customary international law,"[58]

[51] UNGA Res 59/35 (2 December 2004) para 3.

[52] See UNGA Res 62/61 (6 December 2007) para 3; UNGA Res 65/19 (6 December 2010) para 3; UNGA Res 68/104 (16 December 2013) para 4; UNGA Res 71/133 (13 December 2016) para 6.

[53] See UN Docs A/62/62 and Add.1 (2007), A/65/76 (2010), A/68/72 (2013), and A/71/80 (2016).

[54] See eg UN Doc A/68/72 para 137.

[55] See eg, UN Doc A/62/62 paras 126–133, UN Doc A/65/76 paras 45–53.

[56] See eg, UN Doc A/62/62 paras 124–125 and UN Doc A/68/72 para 138.

[57] The most obvious example of such divergences concerns Article 8 of the ASR on conduct directed or controlled by a state, which gave rise to conflicting arguments by the International Criminal Tribunal for Yugoslavia and the International Court of Justice (UN Doc A/62/62 paras 64–65 and UN Doc A/62/62/Add.1 para 3).

[58] International Centre for the Settlement of Investment Disputes *Biwater Gauff (Tanzania) Ltd. v. United Republic of Tanzania* (24 July 2009) paras 773 and 774. In a similar vein, the cases decided by ICSID tribunals, the Permanent Court of Arbitration, and the European Court of Human Rights, quoted in UN Doc A/71/80 paras 8–12.

while others—even within the same institution—have adopted opposing views as to their legal value.[59] These discrepancies, while certainly inescapable to some extent, might be reduced if states collectively purported to reconsider and refine the ASR, with a view to minimize confusion and provide a formal standing to the text. In such a perspective, entering into a conventional exercise may prove a useful, albeit risky, endeavor.

2.2 The Ways and Means of a UN Convention on Responsibility

Three main procedural options present themselves when one considers the potential future of the ASR. The first one—and the most likely to date if one considers the current stalemate on the topic[60]—would be for the General Assembly formally to acknowledge that the ASR will be left as such. The second option would consist in the endorsement of the ASR as a non-binding declaration by the General Assembly; while it would give more solemnity to the text, such a possibility would not add much (if anything) legally to its current standing. Finally, the Assembly could decide to initiate the process of drafting a treaty based on the ASR, either in the framework of a diplomatic conference or within a Special Committee of the Sixth Committee: such a choice could appear as the most classical, if one considers the history of Vienna Conventions on general issues of international law, but would also be the most demanding and uncertain one.

Strong arguments militate against such an adventurous exercise.[61] At best, the instrument could quite likely remain substantially similar to the 2001 text, as states are not expected to do significantly better than the Commission in reaching a balanced and informed result. If such an assumption prevails, the added value of the treaty-making process would clearly be questionable, all the more so that a convention on responsibility could run the risk of not attracting a sufficient figure of ratifications, thus creating a dual regime between states bound and those not bound by the instrument.

At worst, the treaty-making process could prove to have a "decodifying" effect, in the sense that states could be inclined to defuse or erase some of the most significant and innovative aspects of the current text—such as those on countermeasures. The risk associated with a conventional exercise should not be underestimated. One of its main theoretical advantages—that is, instituting a mechanism for settling disputes among states relating to responsibility—would most likely be difficult to achieve in practice: given the current structure of international relations, one fails to see how states could accept to submit the wide range of responsibility disputes to third-party settlement,

[59] See the positions adopted by a WTO panel and the Appellate Body in the *United States—Definitive Anti-Dumping and Countervailing Duties on Certain Products from China* case (2010–2011), in UN Doc A/68/72 paras 9–11 and 13–15.

[60] See Section 1.2.2 of this chapter.

[61] See, among others, Alain Pellet, "Les articles de la C.D.I. sur la responsabilité de l'État pour fait internationalement illicite. Suite – et fin?" (2002) 48 *Annuaire Français de Droit International* 1–2.

even via the device of a specific optional protocol. Besides, drafting a treaty would also have the effect of leaving aside the very substantive, and sometimes illuminating, commentaries attached to the ASR. In that sense, a Convention on state responsibility could be viewed as a depleted version of the text on which it would be based.

Does all this inevitably condemn engaging in a treaty-making negotiation as far as state responsibility is concerned? The answer may not be as straightforward as it seems.[62] The often-commended balance reached by the Commission in 2001 may assist in the success of a conventional process, as a reasonable anticipation of what an inter-state dialogue could eventually lead to. States will also be able to rely on an impressive body of law already applied and interpreted in practice. They may prioritize consensual aspects of the topic via an approach by clusters of provisions, leaving more controversial features to the end of the process as the Commission itself did during the second reading of the ASR.[63]

More generally, the risk of a "decodifying" effect of a treaty-making process, while unquestionable, should also be assessed as against the disadvantages of the current stalemate. Those are at least twofold. First, the function of the ILC—and its perception from the benches of the Sixth Committee—would be altered significantly if it is now endowed with the challenging task of drafting instruments deprived of any form of posterior international blessing. Much may be said in favor of confining the role of the ILC to its advisory capacity, against the temptation of entrusting it with the competences of legal diplomacy.[64] Second, and more importantly, leaving such a prominent text as the ASR in its current informal standing would also generate a phenomenon of "disownership" (*désappropriation*) of international law, insofar as states would be kept away from the collective management of major legal issues.[65]

Arguably, it belongs first and foremost to states to define the exact perimeters of their responsibility under international law. As is well known, despite a somewhat misleading title, the *Articles on Responsibility of States for Internationally Wrongful Acts* only deal with the relations between states, or between states and the international community as a whole, "without prejudice to any right, arising from the international responsibility of a State, which may accrue directly to any person other than a State."[66] Moreover, issues pertaining to the responsibility "of any State for the conduct of an international organization" are not covered by the text as it stands, even though they were later addressed in

[62] For an exhaustive plea in favor of a Convention on state responsibility, see Laurence T Pacht, "The Case for a Convention on State Responsibility" (2014) 83 *Nordic J of Intl L* 439–75, esp. at 462–71.

[63] See Pellet (n 61) 4.

[64] cf Michael Wood, "'Weighing' the Articles on Responsibility of International Organizations", in Maurizio Ragazzi (ed), *Responsibility of International Organizations. Essays in Memory of Sir Ian Brownlie* (Nijhoff 2013) 65.

[65] On the "limits of [the Commission's] legitimacy to state what the law is" and its "role of legislator," see respectively David Caron, "The ILC Articles on State Responsibility: The Paradoxical Relationship between Form and Authority" (2002) 96 *AJIL* 863–64, and Sean D. Murphy, "Codification, Progressive Development, or Scholarly Analysis? The Art of Packaging the ILC's Work Product," in Ragazzi (ed) (n 64) 35, 40.

[66] Article 33(2) of the ASR.

the ARIO.[67] As a consequence, the ASR fail to cover all potential cases of state responsibility, among which some of the most pressing instances of responsibility toward individuals or nonstate entities.

Filling such a gap would certainly prove quite complex, legally speaking. The ILC text has sufficiently stood the test of time, however, to provide a solid basis on which states could explore these largely unchartered territories. Doing so would also be politically sensitive. But, after all, dealing with such issues is what "United Nations treaties" should be all about. If states wish to regain ownership of the realm of responsibility, they may have to follow that path.

[67] See UNGA Res 66/100 (9 December 2011), Annex.

PART III

TECHNIQUE—INNOVATION IN TREATY-MAKING AT THE UNITED NATIONS

CHAPTER 30

THE NEGOTIATION OF MULTILATERAL TREATIES AT THE UNITED NATIONS

a negotiator's view

MICHAEL WOOD[1]

WHEN discussing negotiation, it is common to distinguish between negotiating a treaty and negotiating the settlement of a dispute, though disputes may sometimes be settled by a treaty.[2] Most studies have addressed negotiation as a method of dispute settlement, where it holds pride of place as the most common method, especially for the settlement of bilateral disputes.[3] The negotiation of multilateral treaties is a distinct matter.

[1] Barrister, 20 Essex Street, London; Member of the International Law Commission. The author thanks Alfredo Crosato Neumann for his invaluable assistance in preparing this contribution.

[2] Carl-August Fleischhauer, "Negotiation" in Rudolf Bernhardt (ed), *Encyclopedia of Public International Law*, vol III (North Holland 1981, add. 1995) 535–37; Kari Hakapää, "Negotiation," in Rudiger Wolfrum (ed), *Max Planck Encyclopedia of Public International* Law (OUP 2013). The 1999 UN Principles and Guidelines for International Negotiation (UNGA Res. 53/101) state, in their fourth preambular paragraph, "that international negotiations constitute a flexible and effective means for, among other things, the peaceful settlement of disputes among States and for the creation of new international norms of conduct."

[3] Negotiation is mentioned first in Article 33, para 1, of the UN Charter. The 1988 Manila Declaration on the Peaceful Settlement of International Disputes states that "States should bear in mind (...) that direct negotiations are a flexible and effective means of peaceful settlement of their disputes" (para 10). On negotiation as a method of dispute settlement, see *Handbook on the Peaceful Settlement of Disputes* (United Nations 1992) 9–24; JG Merrills, *International Dispute Settlement* (6th edn, CUP 2017) ch 1; John Collier and Vaughan Lowe, *The Settlement of Disputes in International Law: Institutions and Procedures* (OUP 2000); Fred Charles Iklé, *How Nations Negotiate* (Evanston 1964); John Kaufmann, *Effective Negotiation: Case Studies in Conference Diplomacy* (Martinus Nijhoff 1989); VD Pastuhov, *A Guide to the*

While multilateral treaties may in fact settle bilateral and other disputes (as, for example, the United Nations Convention on the Law of the Sea undoubtedly did[4]), that is not seen as their primary aim.

Since its creation, the United Nations (UN) has been at the heart of multilateral treaty-making, including as regards what are sometimes termed "law-making" treaties (that is, treaties that set out general rules of law potentially applicable to all states).[5] Over the last 70 years, a large number of treaties have been negotiated within or under the auspices of various UN organs,[6] and a variety of procedures have been employed.[7] This chapter reviews some of the options available for treaty-making at the UN,[8] and does so from the point of view of negotiating parties.[9] The role of the International Law Commission (ILC), a subsidiary organ of the UN General Assembly, is also highlighted.

The present chapter focuses on the negotiation of treaties within the UN itself, with examples taken from the practice of UN organs, especially in the "law-making" field. It does not address directly the great codification conferences, such as the first Law of the Sea Conference of 1958, the various Vienna Conferences, the Third UN Conference on the Law of the Sea (1973–1982), or the Rome Conference of 1998. Such conferences have already been the subject of useful writings, including recently.[10]

Practice of International Conferences (Carnegie Endowment for International Peace 1945); *Multilateral Environment Agreement: Negotiator's Handbook* (UN Environmental Programme 2007) at https://unfccc.int/resource/docs/publications/negotiators_handbook.pdf accessed January 15, 2019.

[4] As the tribunal in the *South Sea China Arbitration* noted, "[t]he Convention was a package deal that did not, and could not, fully reflect any State's prior understanding of its maritime rights. Accession to the Convention reflects a commitment to bring incompatible claims into alignment with its provisions, and its continued operation necessarily calls for compromise by those States with prior claims in excess of the Convention's limits" (*The Republic of the Philippines* v. *The People's Republic of China*, PCA Case N° 2013–19, Award of 12 July 2016, para 262).

[5] Modern treaty-making may be traced back at least to the Peace of Westphalia (1648) and the Congress of Vienna of 1814/1815. The Hague Peace Conferences of 1899 and 1907 marked an important stage. The League of Nations produced a number of important treaties, though its major codification exercise, culminating in the Codification Conference of 1930, is generally regarded as having been less than successful.

[6] The numbers increase considerably if one takes account of those adopted within the wider UN system, including the specialized agencies and the International Atomic Energy Agency. Regional and subregional organizations, such as the Council of Europe, the Organization of American States, the African Union and ASEAN, are also much involved in treaty-making.

[7] In 2016 the General Assembly referred to the possibility of requesting the Secretary-General to provide information on all procedural options regarding possible action on the basis of the articles on responsibility of states for internationally wrongful acts of 2001 (see: UNGA Res. 71/133 (19 December 2016)). Whether the articles should take the form of a treaty or not has been much debated by states since they were adopted, and the Secretariat's response will be of much interest.

[8] Similar considerations may also apply to negotiations within specialized agencies and regional organizations.

[9] For a view from the Secretariat, see chapter 3 by Stephen Mathias in this *Handbook*.

[10] Kirsten Schmalenbach, "Lawmaking by Treaty: Negotiation of Agreements and Adoption of Treaty Texts" in Catherine Brölmann and Yannick Radi (eds), *Research Handbook on the Theory and Practice of International Lawmaking* (Edward Elgar 2016) 87–110. It has been argued that "[m]any of the functions served by international conferences are nowadays equally capable of being performed either by a separate conference convened for a specific purpose or alternatively through the medium of a plenary gathering

1 The United Nations and the Techniques of Treaty-Making

The techniques of treaty-making remain largely uncodified and are inherently flexible.[11] While there are some common elements, each negotiation has its own special features and dynamics. To seek to reduce matters to tidy theories or to generalize is not particularly rewarding, or necessarily welcome to participants. Nonetheless, it is illuminating to look briefly at the different efforts of states and the UN to develop the techniques of treaty negotiation.

Early attempts to codify and develop rules concerning treaty negotiation were made at the time of the League of Nations. The Committee of Experts for the Progressive Development of International Law had the idea of codifying procedural rules for international conferences.[12] The goal of the Committee was to put at the disposal of states rules that they could apply or modify, without being overly prescriptive.[13]

The Committee of Experts established a subcommittee to deal with this question. The subcommittee issued a report noting that codification was possible, as long as the rules were broad enough to give states the necessary freedom to adapt them to specific circumstances.[14] The report also noted that some procedural rules may have a customary status.[15] However, the reactions of states to the report showed that they did not desire to see such rules codified, or considered that, were they to be codified, they should be simply *jus dipositivum* and broad.[16] No further action was taken by the Committee or the League in this matter.[17]

of the principal organ of an international organization" (*Satow's Diplomatic Practice* (OUP 2017) 586). This is perhaps so, but the characteristics of each forum may have an impact on the way those functions are carried out.

[11] George Korontzis, "Making the Treaty," in Duncan B. Hollis (ed), *The Oxford Guide to Treaties* (OUP 2014) 179.

[12] The Committee decided to analyze the following question: "S'il est possible de formuler des règles à recommander pour la procédure des conférences internationales, ainsi que pour la conclusion et rédaction des traités, et quelles pourraient être ces règles". See Comité d'experts pour la codification progressive du droit international, Rapport au Conseil de la Société des Nations sur les questions qui paraissent avoir obtenu le degré de maturité suffisant pour un règlement international (Questionnaires n° 1 et 7), adopté par le Comité à sa troisième session, tenue en mars-avril 1927, at 105. See Robbie Sabel, *Rules of Procedure at the UN and at Inter-Governmental Conferences* (3rd edn, CUP 2017) XX–XX.

[13] Comité d'experts pour la codification progressive du droit international, Comité d'experts (n 12) 105.

[14] ibid 106. [15] ibid 107.

[16] ibid, comments by Austria (at 138), United Kingdom (at 145), Chile (at 148), Denmark (at 151), United States (at 161), France (at 165), Norway (at 178), Romania (at 201), Sweden (at 238), Switzerland (at 251), and Egypt (at 259).

[17] Sabel (n 12) XX; *Satow's Diplomatic Practice* 595; Raymond Cohen and Paul Meerts, "The Evolution of International Negotiation Processes" (2008) 13 *Intl Negotiation* 149–56.

The question of developing procedural rules for treaty negotiation came up again decades later. In its work on the law of treaties, in 1962, the ILC adopted on first reading a draft article 5 entitled "Negotiation and drawing up of a treaty." The draft article read:

> A treaty is drawn up by a process of negotiation which may take place either through diplomatic or some other agreed channel, or at meetings of representatives or at an international conference. In the case of treaties negotiated under the auspices of an international organization, the treaty may be drawn up either at an international conference or in some organ of the organization itself.[18]

The commentary to this provision stated that, while the contents of the article were more descriptive than normative, the Commission decided to include it "since the process of drawing up the text is an essential preliminary to the legal act of the adoption of the text (...)."[19] In 1965, the Special Rapporteur for the law of treaties proposed, with little apparent enthusiasm, a new draft. There were divided views within the Commission on its usefulness, and it was referred to the drafting committee.[20] After consideration, the drafting committee proposed its deletion, and the Commission agreed.[21]

The Vienna Conference on the Law of Treaties (1968/1969) likewise did not include an article on negotiation. Nevertheless, as finally adopted, the Vienna Convention offers some basic guidance, referring (if only in a limited way) to the requirement of full powers (article 7) and to the adoption of the text of a treaty (article 9).

In the 1970s, upon an Australian initiative, the General Assembly considered an item entitled "Review of the multilateral treaty-making process." The item resulted in an interesting volume in the UN Legislative Series, which, as has been noted elsewhere, remains of substantial interest today.[22]

In 1998, upon a Mongolian initiative, the UN General Assembly adopted, without a vote, a resolution entitled "Principles and guidelines for international negotiations."[23] The preamble to the resolution recognized the importance of identifying principles and guidelines for purposes of negotiation, as they could "contribute to enhancing the predictability of negotiating parties, reducing uncertainty and promoting an atmosphere of trust at negotiations." Its first operative paragraph broadly restates the principles enshrined in the 1970 Declaration on Principles of International Law concerning Friendly Relations and Co-operation among States, and reaffirms that they are "of relevance to international negotiations." The second operative paragraph formulates seven guidelines. These include such statements of the obvious as "States should take due account of the importance of engaging, in an appropriate manner, in international

[18] (1962-II) YBILC 166. The text was proposed by Roberto Ago, who saw it as an essential preliminary to the draft articles that followed. There was, however, little support for this provision among members of the Commission, who did not see it as indispensable (see: (1962-I) YBILC 245).

[19] (1962-II) YBILC 166. [20] (1965-I) YBILC 40–43.

[21] ibid 255. See also Korontzis (n 11) 179.

[22] "Review of the Multilateral Treaty-Making Process" (1980) UN Doc ST/LEG/SER.B/21. See chapter 3 by Stephen Mathias in this *Handbook*.

[23] UNGA Res 53/101.

negotiations the States whose vital interests are directly affected by the matters in question" and "States should adhere to the mutually agreed framework for conducting negotiations." Those guidelines are in fact so broad that it is difficult to assess to what extent they are actually followed in practice. States must be assumed to negotiate in good faith and in full respect of international law, unless proven otherwise.

Perhaps unsurprisingly, no subsequent attempts have been made to establish general rules or principles concerning treaty negotiation at the UN. States seem to prefer to elaborate tailor-made rules for each negotiation. Nevertheless, such rules are not necessarily elaborated anew every time; experience does exist, and states and the UN have built upon it. The Rules of Procedure of the General Assembly, for example, are often used as a basis for negotiations.[24] They are well understood, and the result of long experience of multilateral diplomacy. Indeed, they were originally based largely on the rules of national parliamentary bodies. They aim to guarantee that proceedings are conducted fairly, while ensuring that progress cannot be unreasonably hampered and that business can be conducted efficiently.

2 Negotiating Multilateral Treaties within the UN: A Few Illustrations

This section provides some examples of negotiation of multilateral treaties within the UN. The aim is to indicate the variety of methods that may be employed by negotiators within the various organs of the UN, whether in New York, Geneva, Vienna, Nairobi, or elsewhere. As already mentioned, treaty negotiation is a flexible process, and new ways of negotiating treaties can always be envisaged.

2.1 Convention on the Prevention and Punishment of the Crime of Genocide (1948)

The negotiation of the Genocide Convention took place in the early days of the UN, between 1946 and 1948, at a time when the Organization had little experience of treaty-making, and before the ILC had commenced its work. The negotiation proceeded in a somewhat haphazard way, with the involvement of a range of bodies at various stages.[25]

[24] Sabel (n 12); Korontzis (n 11) 183.

[25] Hirad Abtahi and Philippa Webb, *The Genocide Convention. The Travaux Préparatoires* (Martinus Nijhoff 2008); Paola Gaeta (ed), *The UN Genocide Convention: A Commentary* (OUP 2009); William A Schabas, *Genocide in International Law* (CUP 2009) 59–90; Christian Tams, Lars Berster, and Björn Schiffbauer (eds), *Convention on the Prevention and Punishment of the Crime of Genocide: A Commentary* (CH Beck 2014) 35–38.

The negotiation began with a draft resolution proposed by Cuba, India, and Panama,[26] which was considered by a subcommittee of the General Assembly's Sixth (Legal) Committee. The subcommittee proposed early action with a view to the preparation of a draft convention on genocide and suggested that the General Assembly should request the Economic and Social Council (ECOSOC) to undertake the necessary studies and prepare the draft convention.[27]

On December 11, 1946, the General Assembly, upon the recommendation of the Sixth Committee, adopted resolution 96(I), requesting ECOSOC to undertake the necessary studies to draw up the draft convention. ECOSOC decided to entrust both the Commission on Human Rights and the Secretary-General with undertaking studies and preparing drafts.[28] The Secretariat prepared a study in 1947, which included a draft convention with commentaries.[29] This draft was prepared by the Secretariat with the assistance of the very distinguished legal experts: Pella, Lemkin, and Donnedieu de Vabres.

Later in 1948, ECOSOC established an ad hoc committee, which produced a second full draft convention.[30] This draft was sent to the General Assembly for further discussion.

It was during that year in the General Assembly, and particularly in the Sixth Committee, that the Convention started to "take shape."[31] A new draft was prepared, which was sent to a drafting committee. The latter presented a new text in late November 1948, which was further discussed and adopted by 30 votes to none.[32]

The final draft was submitted to the plenary of the General Assembly, which adopted the Convention on December 9, 1948.

The successful conclusion of this important convention, within the UN, might have been followed by similar action on other topics. In fact, however, for the next two decades (and with the exception of treaties in the field of human rights), the major "law-making" conventions were all negotiated at diplomatic conferences. These were held under the auspices of, but not within, the UN. The diplomatic conference had been the traditional forum for negotiating a multilateral convention, and was probably deemed more suitable for the concentrated and deliberate negotiation required for the adoption of a well-considered and well-drafted treaty text. It was not until 1968/1969 that another major convention was negotiated within the UN itself.

2.2 Convention on Special Missions (1969)

Earlier conventions on diplomatic law (the Vienna Conventions on Diplomatic and Consular Relations of 1961 and 1963 respectively), like the 1958 Geneva Conventions on the Law of the Sea, were adopted at diplomatic conferences convened by the General Assembly to negotiate on a specific topic, on the basis of draft articles drawn up by the

26 Abtahi and Webb (n 25) 3.

27 ibid 32. It was also suggested by some members of the subcommittee that the draft convention should be prepared by a small committee of jurists, but this was not taken forward.

28 ibid 43–60.

29 ibid 61.

30 ibid 1110.

31 Tams, Berster, and Schiffbauer (n 25) 11.

32 ibid 12.

ILC. The Convention on Special Missions, however, was drawn up and adopted by the UN General Assembly.[33] It was negotiated within the Sixth Committee, over two sessions in 1968 and 1969, on the basis of a draft that the ILC had prepared at the request of the General Assembly.

In many ways, the procedure within the Sixth Committee followed that of the diplomatic conferences. The Sixth Committee formed a working group (corresponding to the Committee of the Whole of a conference). After discussion of amendments, texts were referred to a drafting committee, where much of the negotiation of the text took place.[34]

2.3 Convention on the Prevention and Punishment of Crimes against Internationally Protected Persons, Including Diplomatic Agents (1973)

The Internationally Protected Persons Convention was drawn up rapidly, with a succession of terrorist attacks on diplomats no doubt instilling a sense of urgency among UN delegates.[35] Perhaps because it largely followed precedent in the antiterrorism field (The Hague and Montreal Conventions of 1970 and 1971 respectively), it was considered suitable for adoption within the Sixth Committee, without the need for a diplomatic conference. But that may have led to a certain politicization, since it was adopted by the same organ that was simultaneously dealing with the very controversial agenda item on "International terrorism."[36]

It was the ILC itself that, in 1971, indicated to the UN General Assembly that, if requested, it would prepare at its 1972 session a set of draft articles on the protection of diplomats.[37] Later in 1971, the Assembly requested the ILC to study as soon as possible the question of the protection of diplomatic agents, with a view to preparing draft articles.[38]

In the course of a single session in 1972, the ILC adopted a set of draft articles and submitted them to the General Assembly.[39] In doing so, it departed from its usual methods.

[33] See chapter 27 on diplomatic and consular relations by Duquet and Wouters in this *Handbook*. On the Convention on Special Missions, see Andrew Sanger and Michael Wood, "The Immunities of Members of Special Missions" in Tom Ruys, Nicolas Angelet, and Luca Ferro (eds), *Cambridge Handbook on Immunities and International Law* (CUP, 2019) 452–80.

[34] John W Young, "The United Kingdom and the Negotiation of the 1969 New York Convention on Special Missions" (2014) 36(1) The Intl History Rev 171–88.

[35] Michael Wood, "The Convention on the Prevention and Punishment of Crimes against Internationally Protected Persons, Including Diplomatic Agents" (1974) 23 ICLQ 791–817.

[36] An item entitled "Measures to prevent international terrorism which endangers or takes innocent human lives or jeopardizes fundamental freedoms, and study of the underlying causes of those forms of terrorism and acts of violence which lie in misery, frustration, grievance and despair and which cause some people to sacrifice human lives, including their own, in an attempt to effect radical changes" was included in the agenda of the General Assembly in 1972, in response to the attack by the Black September on Israeli athletes at the Munich Olympics.

[37] (1971-II(2)) YBILC 352, paras 133–134.

[38] UNGA Res 2780 (3 December 1971).

[39] (1972-II(2)) YBILC 309–323, paras 54–69.

It did not appoint a Special Rapporteur, but instead acted through a working group. That same year, the General Assembly considered the ILC's report, and decided to take up the matter in 1973 with a view to the elaboration of a convention by the Assembly.[40]

The Sixth Committee negotiated the text of a convention on the basis of the text prepared by the ILC, and the General Assembly adopted the Convention in December 1973.[41] Somewhat unusually, the resolution by which the Convention was adopted became an important part of the negotiation. The resolution included a hard-fought-over paragraph, recognizing that the Convention could not in any way prejudice the exercise of the legitimate right to self-determination and independence, in accordance with the purposes and principles of the Charter, and—uniquely, it is believed—decided that the resolution, "whose provisions are related to the annexed Convention, shall always be published together with it."[42] This shows the risk of politicization of negotiations with organs of the UN, which is perhaps greater in New York than at Geneva or Vienna conferences.[43]

2.4 Convention against Torture and Other Cruel, Inhuman or Degrading Treatment or Punishment (1984)

The UN Torture Convention of 1984 was negotiated within an informal working group of the Commission on Human Rights, over some six years.[44] It was largely in the hands of human rights specialists, not generalist international lawyers. This may account for some of its novel provisions.

In December 1977, the General Assembly requested the Commission on Human Rights to draft the text of a Convention,[45] based on the General Assembly's 1975 Declaration on Torture.[46] The Commission entrusted this task to an informal inter-sessional working group,[47] which received drafts from the International Association of Penal Law and the Swedish government, the latter being chosen by the Commission as the basis for deliberations.

[40] UNGA Res 2926 (28 November 1972). [41] UNGA Res 3166 (14 December 1973).

[42] As indeed it is, in UN publications, for example, in *The Work of the International Law Commission* (9th edn, United Nations 2017) 144.

[43] The controversies that arose when negotiating antiterrorism conventions and resolutions in the 1970s (terrorists/freedom fighters) foreshadowed the debate that has, since the year 2000, stalled the negotiations within the Sixth Committee of a comprehensive convention against terrorism (see chapter 8B by Rohan Perera in this *Handbook*).

[44] J Herman Burgers and Hans Danelius, *The United Nations Convention against Torture: Handbook on the Convention against Torture and Other Cruel, Inhuman or Degrading Treatment or Punishment* (Martinus Nijhoff 1988); Manfred Nowak and Elizabeth McArthur, *The United Nations Convention against Torture: A Commentary* (OUP 2008).

[45] UNGA Res 32/62 (8 December 1977).

[46] UNGA Res 3452 (9 December 1975), "Declaration on the Protection of All Persons from Being Subjected to Torture and Other Cruel, Inhuman or Degrading Treatment or Punishment."

[47] UNCHR Res 18 (7 March 1978).

Negotiations within the informal inter-sessional working group lasted some six years, from 1978 to 1984. Eventually the working group succeeded in completing a draft convention, which the Human Rights Commission transmitted to the General Assembly. Two controversial questions remained: the competence of the Committee against Torture to issue country-specific comments and suggestions under article 19; and the mandatory character of the inquiry procedure under article 20. Most states wanted to adopt the Convention quickly, and Western states in the Third Committee of the General Assembly gave in to certain demands of the socialist states (which resulted in articles 28 and 19(3) of the 1984 Convention).[48]

It will be seen that the Convention was negotiated entirely within the UN organs responsible for human rights: the Commission on Human Rights, an informal inter-sessional working group of the Commission, and the Third Committee of the UN General Assembly. As noted previously, that no doubt influenced the drafting of the convention.

2.5 United Nations Convention against Corruption (2003)

The UN Convention against Corruption of 2003 followed close on the heels of the UN Convention against Transnational Organized Crime of 2000, and the negotiating processes were similar.[49]

An open-ended intergovernmental ad hoc committee for the negotiation of a convention on corruption was established by General Assembly Resolution 55/61 on December 4, 2000. Its terms of reference were taken note of in Resolution 56/260 in 2002.[50] It followed the Rules of Procedure of subsidiary bodies of the General Assembly.[51]

An informal preparatory meeting took place in Buenos Aires in December 2001. Fifty-six states attended, and 26 proposals were submitted for consideration. This resulted in a consolidated draft text that was submitted to the ad hoc committee in Vienna.[52] The ad hoc committee started its work on January 21, 2002, and held seven sessions. It finalized its work on October 1, 2003, and submitted a draft convention to the General Assembly.[53] Negotiations took place in Vienna, at the headquarters of the United Nations Office on Drugs and Crime (UNODC).

A number of points may be noted concerning this negotiation. The participation of NGOs, for example, was important, as it is for the negotiation of other major conventions nowadays. The ad hoc committee in fact allowed NGOs without consultative

[48] Nowak and McArthur (n 44) 5.

[49] For a brief account of the negotiation process of the latter Convention, see: "Report of the Ad Hoc Committee on the Elaboration of a Convention against Transnational Organized Crime on the work of its first to eleventh sessions" UN Doc A/55/383 (2 November 2000).

[50] Travaux Préparatoires of the negotiations for the elaboration of the United Nations Convention against Corruption (United Nations 2010) vii. The terms of reference are available in UN Doc A/AC.260/2 (8 August 2001).

[51] "Report of the Ad Hoc Committee for the Negotiation of a Convention against Corruption on the work of its first to seventh sessions" UN Doc A/58/422 (7 October 2003), para 23.

[52] ibid, paras 19–20. [53] ibid.

status with ECOSOC to participate on a case-by-case basis.[54] There was also a technical workshop on asset recovery, with invited experts to provide the negotiators with technical information.[55] Additionally, the ad hoc committee established a "consistency group" to ensure the consistency of the draft convention in all UN languages.[56] The importance of ensuring that the different language versions correspond is sometimes overlooked in the rush to sign a convention, which can negatively impact the final outcome. It is necessary to factor in, at an appropriate (late) stage, some process for ensuring that the different language versions are correct.[57]

2.6 United Nations Convention on Jurisdictional Immunities of States and Their Property (2004)

The ILC recommended in 1977 to the General Assembly the selection of the topic *Jurisdictional immunities of States and their property* for codification and progressive development.[58] That same year, the General Assembly invited the Commission to commence work to this end.[59]

The drafting of the Convention was a protracted affair, and some consider its adoption as a "minor miracle":[60] there was a long lapse of time between the adoption of the final draft articles by the ILC in 1990 and the adoption of the Convention by the General Assembly in 2004. During this period, attention focused on five issues identified as most problematic, with the Sixth Committee referring the matters back to the ILC. This process was less than ideal, and some have suggested that it affected the coherence of the final text.[61] Be that as it may, the negotiation of the Convention also illustrates the variety of methods that can be employed within the UN for purposes of treaty-making, and how it can facilitate the conclusion of treaties that touch upon sensitive issues.

54 ibid, paras 24–26. 55 ibid, paras 36–43. 56 ibid, para 98.

57 The importance of ensuring the consistency between languages versions has been highlighted in the context of some of the other major conventions. With respect to the UN Conference on the Law of the Sea, for example: "The procedure adopted by the Drafting Committee for carrying out its task was novel. The Committee operated on three levels. On the first level there were the language groups of the Drafting Committee representing the six languages of the Conference (…) The language groups were open to all delegations whether members of the Drafting Committee or not (…) On the second level there were the co-ordinators of the six language groups who met under the direction of the Chairman of the Drafting Committee (…) Finally, on the third level was the Drafting Committee itself (…) The use of language groups by the Drafting Committee is a unique and particularly significant feature. They served an important technical function in that their existence enabled all language versions of the text to be examined more closely than would otherwise have been the case and in many cases by those who participated in the negotiations" (LDM Nelson, "The Drafting Committee of the Third United Nations Conference on the Law of the Sea: The Implications of Multilingual Texts" (1986) 57 British Ybk Intl L 171–74.

58 (1997-II(2)) YBILC130, para 110. 59 UNGA Res. 32/151 (19 December 1977).

60 Roger O'Keefe and Christian J. Tams (eds), *The United Nations Convention on Jurisdictional Immunities of States and Their Property: A Commentary* (OUP 2013) xxxviii.

61 ibid xxxix.

While in 1990 the ILC recommended to the General Assembly that it convene an international conference to examine the draft articles and conclude a convention, the timing was not good. But soon there were fundamental changes in international relations, some directly relevant to state immunity. Instead of convening a conference, the General Assembly established an open-ended working group of the Sixth Committee. The working group's mandate was to consider states' written comments and observations on the ILC's draft articles and the views expressed in the General Assembly in order to facilitate the adoption of a convention. It would also continue to examine the question of convening a conference.[62]

The working group held meetings in 1992 and 1993, but no agreement was reached with respect to several substantive issues.[63] The General Assembly subsequently decided that informal consultations should also take place,[64] but these did not result in progress. In 1994, the General Assembly decided to defer the consideration of the topic until 1997, inviting states to submit comments on the Sixth Committee's work in the interim.[65]

In 1998, the General Assembly once again decided to establish an open-ended working group of the Sixth Committee to consider the outstanding substantive issues related to the draft articles. This working group met in 1999 and 2000. It also invited the ILC to present any preliminary comments it may have on those outstanding issues.[66] The ILC established a working group to deal with this request, which submitted a report by 1999.

In 2000, the General Assembly established an Ad Hoc Committee on Jurisdictional Immunities of States and Their Property, which was to meet in 2002 for two weeks to further the work done, consolidate areas of agreement, and resolve outstanding issues.[67] The Ad Hoc Committee met in three annual sessions, from 2002 to 2004. It decided to establish a Working Group of the Whole[68] and, when necessary, informal consultative groups to deal with specific substantive issues.[69] The Committee adopted a final report and submitted it to the General Assembly in 2004.[70] Later that year, the General Assembly adopted the Convention.[71]

3 Lessons to Be Drawn

Before starting any treaty-making process, one should always ask two basic questions: Is a treaty really necessary to regulate the issue at hand, and, if so, what is the proper time to start negotiations? The answer to these questions will depend on many factors,

[62] UNGA Res 46/55 (9 December 1991).

[63] O'Keefe and Tams (n 60) 6. On the negotiation of the 2004 Convention, see also Arnold Pronto and Michael Wood, *The International Law Commission 1999–2009* vol. IV (OUP 2010) 13–20 (with bibliography).

[64] UNGA Res 48/413 (9 December 1993).

[65] UNGA Res 49/61 (9 December 1994).

[66] UNGA Res 53/98 (8 December 1998).

[67] UNGA Res 55/150 (12 December 2000).

[68] UN Doc. A/57/22, para 8.

[69] UN Doc. A/58/22, para 9.

[70] UN Doc A/59/22.

[71] UNGA Res 59/38 (2 December 2004). While it has not yet entered into force, the Convention has proven to be quite influential since many of the rules contained therein have been considered to reflect customary international law.

including the subject matter of the possible treaty and the political context in which negotiations would take place. Vision and knowledge of the law are needed to get the answers right, and doing so is crucial because the success or failure of negotiations may depend on it. It could be assumed that when negotiations are highly protracted or when a treaty has little adherence (some examples have been given previously), these questions may have not been addressed correctly.

Once the decision to move toward a treaty has been taken, good preparation in advance of negotiations ("pre-conference phase"[72]) is of vital importance. As experience shows, when a negotiation takes place within the UN itself, advance preparation will usually include the preparation (or selection) of a basic text. In contrast to negotiation in a conference, there is in principle no need to agree in advance on rules of procedure, arrange the venue, set up a secretariat, decide on the length and number of sessions, etc. Negotiating within the UN can be considered to be less costly in these aspects and others (political, accommodation, and security),[73] although, of course, actual costs will be allocated to the UN Secretariat. The services of the UN Secretariat, including translation services and the possibility to negotiate in all UN official languages, are an asset. The UN may furthermore be considered a neutral place to negotiate treaties.

A possible additional advantage of negotiating a treaty within the UN is that it is always possible to request UN expert bodies for contributions at any stage of the negotiation. This was the case, for example, when the General Assembly asked the ILC to present comments in 1998 in respect of the draft articles on jurisdictional immunities of states and their property.

The role of the ILC in the treaty-making process, and particularly at the preparatory stage, deserves special mention.[74] The ILC is a primary means by which the General Assembly implements its function under Article 13.1(a) of the UN Charter of "encouraging the progressive development of international law and its codification."[75] In 1979, the ILC recalled that "the preparation of draft articles by the International Law Commission, a primary task inherent in its functions, has become an undertaking frequently leading to the elaboration of multilateral treaties, constituting to that extent part and parcel of the

[72] Schmalenbach (n 10). [73] *Satow's Diplomatic Practice* (OUP 2017) 587.

[74] As shown in the previous section, other UN expert bodies, such as the Commission on Human Rights, can also play an important role at the preparatory stage of a negotiation. However, their role has not been as prominent as that of the ILC.

[75] Bruno Simma, "Article 13," in Bruno Simma et al (eds), *The Charter of the United Nations: A Commentary* (3rd edn, OUP 2012) 525–51; Rosalyn Higgins et al, *Oppenheim's International Law, United Nations* (OUP 2017), ch 25 (Promotion of International Law). While the Statute of the ILC distinguishes between progressive development and codification, providing for different procedures for each, the Commission has not in practice observed this distinction, adopting instead what it has termed "consolidated method and techniques of work." See: Observations of the International Law Commission on the review of the multilateral treaty-making process, submitted pursuant to UNGA Res 32/48 (UN Doc A/CN.4/325), ILC Report 1979, vol II, Part One, at 183; Donald McRae, "The Interrelationship of Codification and Progressive Development in the Work of the International Law Commission" (2013) 111 Kokusaihō gaikō zasshi 75; Michael Wood, "The UN International Law Commission and Customary International Law," Morelli Lecture, 27 May 2017, *Gaetano Morelli Lecture Series*, E. Cannizzaro (ed.), *Methodologies of International Law* (forthcoming 2019).

contemporary multilateral treaty-making process."[76] The ILC specified that "[i]t is not for the Commission to elaborate multilateral treaties or conventions, but rather to prepare drafts susceptible of providing a basis for the elaboration of such treaties or conventions by States, should the General Assembly decide to make a recommendation to that effect."[77] In the same report, the Commission set out its "methods and techniques of work... as applied in general to the preparation of draft articles," as well as "other methods and techniques employed by the Commission."[78]

It is not the role of the ILC to prepare final texts of treaties. Therefore, and bearing in mind the subtleties of the Commission's own working procedures, care should be taken not simply to adopt drafts submitted by it at face value without proper discussion once they reach the negotiation process, for example in the Sixth Committee. Doing so could undermine the acceptability of certain multilateral treaties, as may have happened with the Convention on Special Missions.[79]

When deciding to negotiate a treaty within the UN, the question of where exactly in the UN to negotiate (that is, in which organ) immediately comes up. As shown in the previous section, negotiations in the past have taken place within a range of organs: the General Assembly's Sixth and Third Committees, the ECOSOC, the former Commission on Human Rights, and so on. Negotiations can of course take place in other organs as well. There are thus many options, and states can benefit from the different institutional arrangements that can be set up to carry out negotiations, as well as from the expertise of the representatives in the different UN organs. For example, negotiations of the UN Conventions against Corruption and Transnational Organized Crime were greatly enhanced since they took place in Vienna with the support of the UNODC.

The working methods, practice, and atmosphere within each of the UN organs varies, though in principle they all follow similar Rules of Procedure. A most important consideration is that the representatives of the member states in the various organs have different backgrounds, knowledge, and skills. This can greatly affect the drafting of a text.

Each organ has a plenary where general (and sometimes politicized) exchanges of views take place, which enable the negotiators to assess where negotiations are heading. Drafting committees are also crucial. They are usually (and ideally) composed of a smaller number of people and deal not only with drafting but also, at times, substantive points that cannot be settled in plenary. A consideration to bear in mind in this context is the importance of having comprehensive *travaux préparatoires* as well as good and accessible records.

As experience shows, it is also common practice within the UN to establish ad hoc committees or working groups to carry out substantive negotiations, which allows work to be done in a more informal manner (without records, and often with only a very

[76] "Observations of the International Law Commission on the review of the multilateral treaty-making process, submitted pursuant to General Assembly resolution 32/48," UN Doc A/CN.4/325, in (1979-II(1)) YBILC 183, para 24.

[77] ibid, para 25. [78] ibid, paras 34–63. [79] Young (n 34) 184.

concise report). An atmosphere of confidentiality is sometimes important, especially when sensitive issues are being discussed.[80]

Choosing the right chairperson may be of the outmost importance, as the success of a negotiation may largely depend on his or her skills in guiding the discussions. For example, Gerhard Hafner's able chairmanship of the Ad Hoc Committee on Jurisdictional Immunities of States and Their Property between 2002 and 2004 was crucial in bringing the work on that topic to a successful conclusion. The role of the chair of the Drafting Committee may likewise be vital.[81] Other members of the bureau may play an important role. As suggested previously, having participants who are experienced in multilateral negotiations and are good at drafting, and in the main languages,[82] may prove highly beneficial.

Because the UN works on an annual cycle, states negotiating treaties in that forum usually have ample opportunity to carry out inter-sessional work. This is important because it gives states enough time to reflect on the debates and discussions, to prepare thoroughly, and to hold informal discussions among themselves. However, having too much time to do something is not necessarily a good thing: the lack of pressure and the feeling that work can always be done the next year can prolong negotiations unduly and may be counterproductive. A central question here is how urgent are the adoption and entry into force of the desired treaty.

The choice of decision-making procedure may be critical, as was seen in relation to the Arms Trade Treaty of 2013. This was negotiated at a conference convened by the General Assembly, the rules of procedure of which required consensus for all non-procedural decisions. Three States (Iran, the Democratic People's Republic of Korea, and Syria) voted against the text of the treaty on the last day of the conference (March 28, 2013). Just five days later, on April 2, 2013, the General Assembly proceeded to adopt the text by vote (154-3-23), and opened the Treaty for signature.[83] And the importance of the choice of procedure was seen again in relation to the 2017 Treaty on the Prohibition of Nuclear Weapons. When the UN disarmament bodies could not take things further (because they operate by consensus), the UN General Assembly, by Resolution 71/258 of 23 December 2016, decided to convene "a United Nations conference to negotiate a legally binding instrument to prohibit nuclear weapons, leading towards their total elimination," and further decided "that the conference shall convene in New York, under the rules of procedure of the General Assembly unless otherwise agreed by the conference."

[80] Many debates between delegates are not recorded officially, and there are limited documents that can serve as *travaux préparatoires*. Sometimes informal summaries of general exchanges of views are provided, but these are not intended to be official records of the discussions. See eg "Report of the Ad Hoc Committee established by General Assembly resolution 51/210 of 17 December 1996," UN Doc A/58/37 (2 April 2003), paras 9 and 13.

[81] Eg MK Yasseen at the Vienna Conference on the Law of Treaties.

[82] Anthony Aust, *Modern Treaty Law and Practice* (3rd edn, CUP 2013) 387–90.

[83] UNGA Res. 67/234B (2 April 2013). For a brief account of the negotiation, see Stuart Casey-Maslen, Andrew Clapham, Gilles Giacca, and Sarah Parker, *The Arms Trade Treaty: A Commentary* (OUP 2016) 9–13.

A Treaty on the Prohibition of Nuclear Weapons was adopted by the Conference on July 7, 2017, by a vote of 122:1 (Netherlands):1 (Singapore). Some 69 member states did not take part in the conference, including all of the nuclear-weapon States.

The choice of forum may determine the choice of procedure; for example, a subsidiary organ of the General Assembly is likely to follow the voting rules in the General Assembly's Rules of Procedure. In practice, however, many treaty negotiations proceed on the basis of consensus, at least until the very last stages (when it may be necessary to vote down a recalcitrant participant). A whole range of options are possible: consensus, unanimity, simple or two-thirds majority. The choice will have an important impact on how negotiations are carried out.[84] The advantages of working toward a package deal ("nothing is agreed until everything is agreed") should be considered.[85]

When it comes to the choice of forum, there are two main routes open to states: a diplomatic conference and negotiation within a principal or subsidiary organ of the UN.

One of the main differences between negotiating within the UN or in a conference is the atmosphere and the people involved in each one of these fora. It is one thing to negotiate a treaty in a conference, where the representatives of states (diplomats and experts in the relevant field) are sent from capitals to carry out one specific task in a limited period of time. They can be expected to be specially chosen for and focused on the task at hand and to participate actively. A completely different matter is negotiating within a UN organ, where states' representatives are usually diplomats (often generalists and not necessarily lawyers) serving their respective missions who have a great number of other issues to address besides negotiating a treaty. It can be expected that less effort will be put into the negotiating process. Of course, states can deploy experts to their missions when a treaty is being negotiated within a UN organ, but that is not usually the case. Also, as mentioned previously, because the UN works on an ongoing annual basis, there is often a feeling that things can always be delayed, and the lack of pressure may cause a loss of momentum.

These issues were considered by the ILC in the 1950s, in terms that are still relevant today, when it considered what recommendation to make under Article 23 of its Statute on how states should proceed with its draft articles on *Diplomatic intercourse and immunities*. In 1957, Fitzmaurice (who favored a code rather than a convention) pointed to the

[84] Hakapää (n. 2), para 10; Korontzis (n 11) 183–84. According to one very experienced author, states should first set out their goal in terms of participation in a treaty (is it desirable or indispensable that a certain number of or all states become parties to the treaty?), then decide on a provision on entry into force accordingly (how many ratifications are needed for the entry into force?), and finally agree on the rule on decision-making procedure ("consensus if possible" if universal participation is only desirable; if universal participation is indispensable then consensus is the only way): Guy De Lacharrière, "Suggestions pour Négocier Mieux un Droit International Plus Efficace," in Jerzy Makarczyk (ed), *Essays in International Law in Honour of Judge Manfred Lachs* (Martinus Nijhoff 1984) 149, 156–57.

[85] Robert Y Jennings, "Law Making and the Package Deal," in *Mélanges offerts à Paul Reuter* (Pedone 1981) 347–55; G. de Lothaire, "Aspects Juridiques de la Négociation sur un Package Deal à la Conférence des Nations Unies sur le Droit de la Mer," in *Essays in Honor of Erik Castren* (Finnish Branch of the International Law Association 1979) 30–45; Hakapää (n 2) para 10.

disadvantages that the examination of the draft articles by the General Assembly might have, as opposed to examination at a conference:

> It was most improbable either that the General Assembly would simply approve a draft convention in the form in which it was submitted by the Commission and open it for signature, or that it would convene a special conference to consider it, as it had done in the case of the draft articles on the law of the sea. It would be much more likely to examine it itself, *with far less time for careful study of it than the Commission had been able to afford; and in those circumstances, any changes it made might not be for the better.*[86]

A year later, the matter was still being discussed within the Commission. Mr. García Amador explained that:

> many conferences were held under the auspices of the United Nations. Some, such as the United Nations Conference on the Law of the Sea, had been very technical, but in the case of the draft articles before the Commission, no specialist knowledge was required. He therefore agreed with Mr. Alfaro; because of the need to reduce the number of conferences to a minimum, and because the subject was straightforward, the General Assembly might well, after discussion, submit the draft convention to Members for signature.[87]

The Secretary to the Commission (Mr. Liang), however, explained that:

> Except for the Convention on Genocide, he could recall no case in which the General Assembly had examined a draft convention in detail, article by article, and recommended it forthwith to States. He thought that it was unlikely that the General Assembly would itself examine the draft and commend it to Members for signature. The Assembly had a heavy agenda each year; furthermore many of the delegations did not contain more than a small number of lawyers.[88]

In the event, the ILC decided to recommend to the General Assembly that the draft articles should be recommended to member states with a view to the conclusion of a convention.[89]

The result of this decision was the highly successful Vienna Conference on Diplomatic Intercourse and Immunities, which was held over a single session in 1961. The high-level expert participation, and the fact that delegates were able to devote themselves full-time to the negotiations in Vienna, presumably contributed greatly to its success. Negotiation within an organ of the United Nations (such as the Sixth Committee) would be unlikely

[86] (1957-I) YBILC 88, para 67 (emphasis added). For an account of the debate, see Kai Bruns, "On the Road to Vienna: The Role of the International Law Commission in the Codification of Diplomatic Privileges and Immunities, 1949–1958," in Paul Behrens (ed), *Diplomatic Law in a New Millennium* (OUP 2017) 54–71.

[87] Yearbook of the International Law Commission, 1958, vol 1, at p 199, para 71.

[88] ibid, para. 76.

[89] Yearbook of the International Law Commission, 1958, vol 2, at p 89, para 50.

to have led to as satisfactory an outcome. On the other hand, there are cases, such as the 1973 Internationally Protected Persons Convention and other counterterrorism conventions, where the subject matter is such that negotiation within the UN itself is effective and efficient. The decision on the forum can be critical. It will be interesting to see what choice is made if the General Assembly ever decides to move toward a convention on the Responsibility of States for internationally wrongful acts.

4 Conclusions

While the brief account of the negotiation of a selection of multilateral treaties within the UN provided in Section 2 of this chapter indicates the great variety of negotiating procedures, it is also possible to draw some general lessons, as was done in Section 3. Some of these are particularly relevant to negotiating within the UN proper, taking into account its unique characteristics, while others apply to negotiations more generally, regardless of forum.

However, as indicated in Section 1, notwithstanding the wealth of treaty-making practice within the UN, there has been only limited attempts to gather the experience together and draw up general guidelines or best practices. Indeed, experience suggests that each negotiation is different and flexibility is of the essence. That is hardly a surprise. Indeed, perhaps the most important factor is the least predictable: the human element. Negotiations are hugely influenced by the quality and qualities of the individual negotiators, especially the officeholders, the chairperson, and bureau members. Among the qualities required are a profound knowledge of the subject, and its political background. And perhaps above all common sense and patience. The experience and abilities of key players are often more important than their nationality; although it can in fact be an advantage if the leaders of the negotiation come from a state that is less directly involved in the negotiations. The quality of the secretariat members involved is also often important.

CHAPTER 31

THE PARTICIPATION OF NONSTATE ACTORS IN THE MULTILATERAL TREATY PROCESS

PHILIPPA WEBB*

THE participation of nonstate actors (NSAs) in international lawmaking is long-standing.[1] What is relatively new is the increased level and visibility of participation of NSAs in UN treaty practice and the modalities for that participation to take place.[2] Shifting the locus of treaty negotiations from ad hoc conferences to international institutions such as the

* I thank the editors and the other contributors to this volume for their insightful comments and rich discussion. I specially thank Dorota Lost-Sieminska, head of the Legal Affairs Division of the International Maritime Organization, and Stephen Mathias, Assistant Secretary-General in the UN Office of Legal Affairs, for their guidance and provision of information on the approach of their respective organizations.

[1] Peace societies at The Hague Peace Conferences in 1899 and 1907 engaged in lobbying and mass publicity: Steve Charnovitz, "Two Centuries of Participation: NGOs and International Governance" (1996–1997) 18 Mich J Intl L 183, 196–97. Charnovitz explains how NGOs have participated in international lawmaking for two centuries, influencing international treaties on the laws of war, intellectual property, admiralty, prostitution, narcotics, labor, and protection of the environment (212). See also Kal Raustiala, "NGOs in International Treatymaking" in DB Hollis (ed), *The Oxford Guide to Treaties* (OUP 2012) 150, 150, 172.

[2] Peter J Spiro, "Accounting for NGOs" (2002) Chi J Intl L 161. There is an extensive literature on the role of NGOs in the making and implementation of treaties on the environment, human rights, and international criminal justice. See Tobias Böhmelt, Vally Koubi, and Thomas Bernauer, "Civil Society Participation in Global Governance: Insights from Climate Politics" (2014) 53 Eur J Polit Res 18; Mahnoush H Arsanjani. "The Rome Statute of the International Criminal Court" (1999) 93 AJIL 22, 23; Z Pearson, "Non-governmental Organizations and the International Criminal Court: Changing Landscapes of International Law" (2006) Cornell Intl LJ; Raustiala (n 1). There is also literature on the debate as to whether NSAs are "subjects" of international law, which goes beyond the scope of this chapter.

UN has increased the influence of NSAs.[3] The particular contribution of the UN as a forum for treaty-making is that it has facilitated the involvement of NGOs through accreditation and increased transparency.

This chapter will focus on contemporary UN practice that has until now received less attention in the literature. It defines NSAs as including and going beyond nongovernmental organizations (NGOs): interest groups, industry groups, corporations, business associations, individual experts, and scholarly societies.[4] Even the term "NGOs" encompasses a wide range of actors including internationalist, progressive bodies such as Greenpeace; conservative lobby groups such as the National Rifle Association; and bodies established by (usually authoritarian) governments.[5]

The diversity of NSAs is matched by the diversity of their different functions in the treaty-making process. A useful framework for understanding is the "seven decision functions" developed by Lasswell, McDougal, and Reisman with respect to the role of NGOs in general:[6]

i. Intelligence function: gathering, analysis and dissemination of information relevant to decision-making;
ii. Promotion function: advocacy of policy alternatives to authoritative decision-makers either directly or indirectly through a broader public;
iii. Prescription function: designation of policies and the communication and authority and control intention;
iv. Invocation function: characterization of behavior as deviating from prescribed policy and the assertion of control to abate the deviation;
v. Application function: giving effect to prescriptions in concrete disputes;
vi. Termination function: catalysts in pressing for putting an end to prescriptions that do not contribute to the common interest;
vii. Appraising function: evaluating the degree to which the policies of an international system are achieved in fact.

[3] Jose E Alvarez, "The New Treaty Makers" (2002) 25 BC Intl & Comp L Rev 213. But see the International Campaign to Ban Landmines that was critical to the making of the Ottawa Mine Ban Treaty and operated outside of the UN framework. Its mobilization efforts were recognized with the Nobel Peace Prize: Kenneth R Rutherford, "Implications of the Role of NGOs in Banning Antipersonnel Landmines" (2000) 53 Wld Pol 74. See chapters 7A by Barry Kellman and 7B by Daniel Prins in this *Handbook*.

[4] For the role of the UN Secretariat, see chapter 3 by Stephen Mathias, and for the role of international organizations, see chapter 32 by Jan Klabbers, both in this *Handbook*.

[5] Moises Naim, "What Is a GONGO?" *Foreign Policy* (18 April 2007) 96; Daniel B Baer, "Mind the GONGOs: How Government Organized NGOs Troll Europe's Largest Human Rights Conference" (30 September 2016) <https://osce.usmission.gov/mind-gongos-government-organized-ngos-troll-europes-largest-human-rights-conference/> accessed December 2, 2017.

[6] Myres S McDougal, Harold D Lasswell, and W Michael Reisman, "The World Constitutive Process of Authoritative Decision," in Myres S McDougal and W Michael Reisman (eds), *International Law Essays: A Supplement to International Law in Contemporary Practice* (Foundation Press 1981) 219, 221–22, 267–69.

These functions can map onto the five-stage process identified by Stephen Mathias in chapter 3 in this volume.

This chapter first considers the UN Charter framework for the participation of NSAs in the work of the Organization and the modalities that flow from that. It then examines the participation of NSAs in UN treaty-making from the most intense forms of participation to the least, from NSAs being at the negotiating table to being left out in the cold. It concludes with an evaluation of the contribution of the UN and NSAs to treaty-making.

1 The United Nations Framework for Participation of NSAs

1.1 Article 71 of the Charter

The starting point for the participation of NSAs in the activities of the UN, including multilateral treaty processes, is Article 71 of the Charter.[7] This provides that the Economic and Social Council (ECOSOC) shall "make suitable arrangements for consultation with nongovernmental organizations which are concerned with matters within its competence."

This was a compromise text to tread the line between those who advocated the participation of a particular NSA—NGOs—in UN work and those who opposed it.[8] It codified the custom of NGO participation in the ECOSOC, and gave NGOs "a hunting license" to pursue their involvement in the UN beyond ECOSOC.[9] At the same time, ECOSOC has made clear that NGOs with consultative status have lesser rights to participate than the right "to participate, without vote" in ECOSOC deliberations granted to states that are not members of the Council and representatives of specialized agencies.[10]

The arrangements for NGO participation in ECOSOC have undergone three transformations.[11] These adjustments have been driven by the recognition of the diversity of the NGOs, the breadth of their expertise and the capacity to support the work of the UN, and the emergence of numerous national and regional organizations.[12] The 1996 ECOSOC Resolution defines the current framework. For the purposes of treaty

[7] The Covenant of the League of Nations had lacked such a provision.

[8] Stephan Hobe, "Global Challenges to Statehood: The Increasingly Important Role of Nongovernmental Organizations" (1997) 5 Indiana J Glob Leg Stud 191, 201. Stephan Hobe, "Article 71" in Bruno Simma et al (eds), *The Charter of the United Nations: A Commentary* (3rd edn, OUP 2013).

[9] Charnovitz (n 1) 257–58.

[10] Articles 69 and 70 of the United Nations Charter; ECOSOC, "Review of Consultative Arrangements with Non-governmental Organizations," ESC Res 288(x) (27 February 1950), para 12.

[11] ECOSOC Res 288(x) (27 February 1950), superseded by ECOSOC Res 1296 (XLIV) (23 May 1968), and updated in ECOSOC Resolution 1996/31 (25 July 1996).

[12] Preamble to ECOSOC Resolution 1996/31 (25 July 1996). The resolution divides NGOs into three categories: general consultative status, special consultative status, and those on the Roster.

processes, the most relevant section is Part VII (Participation of Non-Governmental Organizations in International Conferences Convened by the United Nations and their Preparatory Process). In keeping with the "limited rights" approach that has defined consultative status, the Resolution states that the intergovernmental nature of conferences and preparatory meetings means that "active participation" of NGOs is "welcome" but does "not entail a negotiating role." NGOs may briefly address the committee or conference, at the discretion of the chairperson. They may make written presentations, but these will not be issued as official documents.[13]

Over 4,000 NGOs have some form of consultative status with ECOSOC.[14] But this does not capture the full picture of participation by NSAs. Under paragraph 4 of the 1996 ECOSOC resolution, "organization" is defined as "non-governmental organizations at the national, subregional, regional or international levels." Article 71 and the ECOSOC framework are not adapted to managing the participation of other types of NSAs in UN activities. The ECOSOC framework does not capture the modalities for access and participation granted by other departments or related UN bodies.

The International Maritime Organization (IMO), for example, has a stricter approach than ECOSOC to accreditation.[15] An NGO must be truly international in order to be accredited. NGOs with a regional focus are only accredited when that expertise is needed by the IMO for a particular area of work.[16] If an applicant NGO's expertise overlaps with that of an accredited NGO, it will not tend to be accepted.[17] For the 2015 and 2016 sessions, the IMO chose not to accredit any new NGOs. Unlike at ECOSOC,[18] at the IMO accreditation is reviewed every two years and includes an examination of whether that NGO attended meetings, submitted documents, and promoted the IMO in other fora.[19] A lack of participation may lead to a recommendation to remove the accreditation of the NGO. This is not an idle threat: two NGOs were removed from the accredited list in 2016.

1.2 Modalities for Participation by NSAs

When the General Assembly convenes a treaty-making conference, it passes a resolution that, in most cases, specifies the states and other entities that may participate in the conference concerned. In some instances, the General Assembly adopts an additional

13 ECOSOC Resolution 1996/31 (25 July 1996), paras 50–52.

14 ECOSOC "Note by Secretary-General: List of non-governmental organizations in consultative status with the Economic and Social Council as of 1 September 2014" (3 December 2014) UN Doc E/2014/INF/5.

15 In June 2017, 77 NGOs were accredited by the IMO.

16 IMO, Rules and Guidelines for Consultative Status of Non-governmental International Organizations with the International Maritime Organization, as amended 4 December 2013.

17 IMO Guidelines to Rule 3: "Consultative status should not be granted where each of two or more rival organizations purports to represent a particular interest to the exclusion of the others."

18 General and special status NGOs are required to submit a "quadrennial report" every four years, but in reality, accreditation is rarely removed.

19 The review is conducted by a group of eight IMO member states, but any member state may attend. The group makes a recommendation to the Council. Rule 10 and Guideline of the Rules and Guidelines on Consultative Status.

resolution that sets out the detailed modalities of the conference, including whether and how NSAs may participate in the conference.

With regard to the participation of NGOs in conferences mandated to draw up treaties, in the 1990s General Assembly resolutions tended to set out detailed arrangements concerning the participation of NGOs. In more recent years, such detailed arrangements have often been made by the relevant conference itself. A few examples illustrate the interaction among the General Assembly, the conference, and NGOs.

For the 1998 UN Diplomatic Conference of Plenipotentiaries on the Establishment of an International Criminal Court (Rome Conference), the General Assembly resolution convening the Conference set out a detailed arrangement on the participation of NGOs. The Assembly "request[ed] the Secretary-General to invite non-governmental organizations, accredited by the Preparatory Committee . . . to participate in the Conference, along the lines followed in the Preparatory Committee, on the understanding that participation means attending meetings of its plenary and, unless otherwise decided by the Conference in specific situations, formal meetings of its subsidiary bodies except the drafting group, receiving copies of the official documents, making available their materials to delegates and addressing, through a limited number of their representatives, its opening and/or closing sessions, as appropriate, in accordance with the rules of procedure to be adopted by the Conference."[20]

Similarly, for the 1993–1995 UN Conference on Straddling Fish Stocks and Highly Migratory Fish Stocks, the General Assembly invited "relevant non-governmental organizations from developed and developing countries to contribute to the conference, within the area of their competence and expertise, on the basis of procedures for the accreditation used for the United Nations Conference on Environment and Development, as recommended in paragraph 38.44 of Agenda 21."[21]

More recently, the General Assembly has specified that NGOs may participate in and contribute, but has left the modalities for the conference itself to decide. For the UN conference to negotiate a legally binding instrument to prohibit nuclear weapons, leading toward their total elimination, the General Assembly convened the conference by a resolution passed in December 2016,[22] and the Conference decided on the arrangements for NSA participation at its meeting in February 2017.[23] It gave NGOs with ECOSOC consultative status (and those that could show activity in areas relevant to the scope of the Conference) the right to participate in public meetings without the right to vote.

[20] UNGA, "Establishment of an international criminal court," UNGA Res 52/160 (15 December 1997) UN Doc. A/RES/52/160, para 8.

[21] UNGA Res 47/192 (22 December 1992) UN Doc A/RES/47/192.

[22] UNGA, "Taking forward multilateral nuclear disarmament negotiations," UNGA Res 71/258 (11 January 2017) UN Doc A/RES/71/258: "[d]ecide[d] that the conference shall convene in New York, under the rules of procedure of the General Assembly unless otherwise agreed by the conference, from 27 to 31 March and from 15 June to 7 July 2017, with the participation and contribution of international organizations and civil society representatives."

[23] UNGA "United Nations conference to negotiate a legally binding instrument to prohibit nuclear weapons, leading towards their total elimination: Participation of non-governmental organizations in the conference" (22 February 2017) UN Doc A/CONF.229/2017/4.

NGOs were also to be provided with documents related to the Conference on request and were able to submit written material that would be circulated in the original language.

For the 2012–2013 UN Conference on the Arms Trade Treaty, the General Assembly resolutions convening the Conference were silent on the participation of NGOs in the Conference.[24] The arrangements for participation were contained in rule 63 of the rules of procedure of the Conference.[25] Rule 63 allowed NGO representatives to address the Conference "during one meeting specifically allocated for this purpose" and this meeting would not coincide with other meetings of the Conference. If an NGO wanted to provide material to delegations, this was to be done at their own expense and outside the conference room. Interestingly, the Rule 63(f) noted "[a]rrangements concerning the accreditation and attendance of non-governmental organizations at the Conference shall in no way create a precedent for other United Nations conferences."

2 Levels of NSA Participation in UN Treaty-Making

2.1 Nonstate Actors with a Seat at the Table

Starting with the most intense form of participation, an NSA may be given a seat at the negotiating table for a multilateral treaty. The NSA may (1) form part of a national delegation to a treaty-making conference, (2) be invited as an expert to draft a treaty, (3) perform the role of secretariat to the conference,[26] or (4) have full voting rights on decisions at a conference.

The International Labour Organization (ILO) is well known for its tripartite structure according to which labor unions and business representatives are formal participants in its work, alongside member states.[27] National delegations to its conferences must include representatives of the government, employers, and workers "able to act in full independence of each other."[28] The minimum composition of delegations is two government delegates, one employers' delegate, and one workers' delegate.[29]

For the UN Convention on the Rights of Persons with Disabilities, delegations were not tripartite, but NSA representatives benefited from "formal equalisation" in that they

[24] UNGA Res 64/48 (12 January 2010) UN Doc A/RES/64/48 and 67/234 A (4 January 2013) UN Doc A/RES/67/234.

[25] UNGA "United Nations Conference on the Arms Trade Treaty: Provisional rules of procedure of the Conference" (7 March 2012) UN Doc A/CONF.217/L.1.

[26] See chapter 3 by Stephen Mathias in this *Handbook*.

[27] See chapter 11 by George P. Politakis in this *Handbook*.

[28] Submission of Credentials to the International Labour Conference 107th Session (28 May–8 June 2018) Explanatory note for national delegations, <http://www.ilo.org/wcmsp5/groups/public/@ed_norm/@relconf/documents/meetingdocument/wcms_213289.pdf>, section 3, accessed December 2, 2017.

[29] Article 3(1) ILO Constitution.

had the same speaking and voting rights as government representatives on the Ad Hoc Committee that drafted the Convention. It was the "most inclusive" process in the UN's history. [30] The Ad Hoc Committee included representatives of over 400 NGOs and disability people's organizations.[31] It is reported at least 80 percent of the final text comes from the International Disability Caucus.[32]

Although not technically a treaty, the drafting process for the UN Declaration on the Rights of Indigenous Peoples gave indigenous groups a seat at the table. The Chairperson of the UN Permanent Forum on Indigenous Issues expressed their contribution as follows:

> This Declaration has the distinction of being the only Declaration in the UN which was drafted with the rights-holders, themselves, the Indigenous Peoples. I hail the independent experts and representatives of States and NGOs who contributed actively to this process.[33]

2.2 Nonstate Actors on the Sidelines

The "limited rights," "consultative" vision of the 1996 ECOSOC Resolution on accreditation can be characterized as NSAs "on the sidelines" of treaty-making processes. But the word "sidelines" should not imply a lack of influence. Indeed, the critical decisions and turning points in multilateral treaty negotiations are often a result of "corridor diplomacy"[34] in which NSAs are heavily involved. As Raustiala observes, NGOs typically "receive negotiating documents, informally present proposals and are consulted by and lobby State delegations."[35] They hold parallel conferences or side-events during the conference. Some NSAs prefer a role on the margins because they want to be less visible to the actual delegates. For the Arms Trade Treaty, for example, National Rifle Association exerted their influence at the national parliament level, so they did not need to be at the international negotiating table.[36]

For the Paris Agreement on Climate Change, NSAs could attend some of the intergovernmental negotiations and at times make interventions. This was usually done through the UNFCCC's official constituencies that bring together civil society, business,

[30] Jochen von Bernstorff, "Non-State Actors in law-making and in the shaping of policy: On the legality and legitimacy of NGO participation in international law," Study for the preparation of the Konrad-Adenauer-Foundation's Conference on International Law 2007, 17–20, <http://www.kas.de/wf/doc/kas_12358-544-2-30.pdf?071119171748> accessed 1 April 2018.

[31] UNGA Res 56/168 (26 February 2002) UN Doc A/RES/56/168, established the Ad Hoc Committee on a Comprehensive and Integral International Convention to Promote and Protect the Rights and Dignity of Persons with Disabilities. See Gráinne de Burca, "The EU in the Negotiation of the UN Disability Convention" (2010) 35 EL Rev 174.

[32] Arlene S Kanter, "The Promise and Challenge of the United Nations Convention on the Rights of Persons with Disabilities" (2006–2007) 34 Syracuse Intl L & Com 287, 288–89, 294.

[33] UN Press Release (13 September 2007) <http://www.un.org/esa/socdev/unpfii/documents/2016/Docs-updates/Statement-Press-Release-IDWIP-2007.pdf> accessed December 3, 2017.

[34] Raustiala (n 1) 163?. [35] ibid. [36] See chapter 7B by Daniel Prins in this *Handbook*.

trade unions, indigenous peoples, and youth. Observer organizations were invited to submit information and views on items under negotiations.[37] NSAs perform a valuable role in tracking and reporting on conference negotiations through daily bulletins.[38] These documents may end up becoming a nonofficial but authoritative set of texts serving as *travaux prépartoires* of the resulting treaty.

The IMO has a well-developed model for including NSAs while not necessarily placing them at the negotiating table. The model is premised on the idea that NSAs perform important intelligence and promotion functions.[39] Rule 2 of the Rules on Consultative Status sets out the purposes of such status:

> (a) to enable the International Maritime Organization to obtain information or expert advice from non-governmental international organizations with special knowledge in a particular sector of the Organization's activities; and
>
> (b) to enable such non-governmental international organizations representing large groups whose activities have an important and direct bearing on the work of the International Maritime Organization, to express their points of view to the Organization.

Most NSAs that participate in the IMO have a technical orientation. For example, one of the most active and respected NSAs at the IMO is the International Association of Classification Societies (IACS), a not-for-profit membership organization of 12 societies that set minimum technical standards and requirements for ship design to enhance maritime safety and environmental protection.[40]

While the promotion function is understood by Lasswell, McDougal, and Reisman as "advocacy of *policy alternatives* to authoritative decision-makers,"[41] the IMO requires NSAs with consultative status to undertake "to support the activities of the International Maritime Organization and to promote the dissemination of its principles and work, bearing in mind the objectives and functions of the International Maritime Organization on the one hand, and the competence and activities of the non-governmental international organization on the other."[42] So any advocacy of alternatives by NSAs has to be undertaken in the context of a generally supportive attitude to the work of the IMO.

The legal basis for NSA participation at the IMO is Article 62 of the 1948 Convention on the IMO,[43] which provides that the IMO "may, on matters within its scope, make suitable

[37] Harro van Assel, "The Role of Non-state Actors in Reviewing Ambition, Implementation, and Compliance under the Paris Agreement" (2016) 6(1) Climate Law 4.

[38] See examples in Raustiala (n 1) 166.

[39] Lasswell, McDougal, and Reisman (n 6).

[40] The objective of ship classification is "to verify the structural strength and integrity of essential parts of the ship's hull and its appendages, and the reliability and function of the propulsion and steering systems, power generation and those other features and auxiliary systems which have been built into the ship in order to maintain essential services on board": IACS, "Classification Societies: Their Key Role," 4, <http://www.iacs.org.uk/media/3784/iacs-class-key-role.pdf> accessed December 5, 2017.

[41] Lasswell, McDougal, and Reisman (n 6) emphasis added.

[42] Rule 4 of the Rules and Guidelines on Consultative Status.

[43] Convention on the International Maritime Organization (adopted 6 March 1948, entered into force 17 March 1958) 289 UNTS 3.

arrangements for consultation and cooperation with non-governmental international organizations." The Rules and Guidelines on Consultative Status and the Rules of Procedure of each IMO organ provide more detailed arrangements.[44] In general, NSAs have the following rights of participation:[45]

i. The right to receive the provisional agenda for sessions;
ii. The right to submit documents on agenda items;
iii. The right to be represented by an observer at plenary meetings of the Assembly and, on the invitation of the Secretary-General, at other meetings "at which matters of special interest" to the NSA are to be considered;
iv. The right to receive the texts of resolutions, recommendations on matters of special interest to the NSA, and supporting documents.

With respect to the right to submit documents, NSAs cannot propose new treaties or amendments by themselves, but they can join or support a proposal sponsored by a member state. NSAs can be the driving force behind a treaty. Many of the IMO's conventions started in the Comité Maritime International (CMI),[46] an important association of maritime lawyers. Recently CMI developed a draft treaty on foreign judicial sales of ships and their recognition, but could not propose the treaty itself. It therefore found state sponsors (China and the Republic of Korea) in order to table the proposal before the IMO.[47] The proposal was ultimately rejected for not reaching IMO's high standard of a "compelling need" for a new treaty, but the CMI has been successful in proposing other treaties in the past, such as the liability conventions.[48]

With respect to the right to be represented at meetings, the NSA observer has no right to vote but may, on the invitation of the Chairman and with the approval of the body concerned, speak on any item of the agenda of special interest to the NSA.[49] NSAs are allowed to take the floor after member states, but in practice NSAs speak throughout the session, rather than in a block of time at the end.

[44] The IMO Assembly, the Council, the Maritime Safety Committee, the Legal Committee, the Marine Environment Protection Committee, the Technical Co-operation Committee, and the Facilitation Committee.

[45] Rule 6 of the Rules and Guidelines on Consultative Status.

[46] CMI is a nongovernmental not-for-profit international organization established in Antwerp in 1897. Its object is to contribute by all appropriate means and activities to the unification of maritime law in all its aspects, and to this end promotes the establishment of national associations of maritime law and cooperates with international organizations. Article 1, Constitution of the CMI, available at <http://comitemaritime.org/part-1-general/0,2736,13632,00.html> accessed December 5, 2017.

[47] IMO Doc LEG 103/11/3 (5 April 2016).

[48] Eg, the Convention Relating to Civil Liability in the Field of Maritime Carriage of Nuclear Material 1971; the International Convention on Limitation of Liability for Maritime Claims, 1976; 1969 International Convention on Civil Liability for Oil Pollution Damage and the 1976 SDR Protocol; 1971 International Convention on the Establishment of an International Fund for Compensation for Oil Pollution Damage, and the 1976 SDR Protocol. See CMI, *Handbook of Maritime Conventions* (LexisNexis 2004).

[49] Rule 7 of the Rules and Guidelines on Consultative Status.

The observer status of NSAs at the IMO means that they can and do participate in treaty-making and amendment at all stages. Proposals for new treaties or amendments tend to originate in a working group; NSAs may comment on proposed amendments.[50] The proposal will be considered by the plenary (at which NSAs may also speak) and, if accepted, NSAs can be observers in the drafting group that formulates the text. Usually an open invitation is issued in the plenary for those member states and NSAs that wish to join the drafting group. When the draft is ready, it is submitted to the IMO Council and the Assembly for approval. The Assembly will then recommend the draft to member states for adoption.[51]

Although the IMO does not place NSAs "at the table," their influence from the sidelines is significant and multifaceted. It does not adopt a tripartite structure like the ILO, but NSAs do form alliances with member states that may prove to be just as influential as regional or other groupings. Environmentalist NSAs tend to prefer cooperative working relations with Australia, Canada, New Zealand, and the Scandinavian countries. Shipping industry NSAs work closely with countries such as the Bahamas, Liberia, the Marshall Islands, and Panama.

2.3 Nonstate Actors behind the Scenes

NSAs may influence the dynamics of UN treaty-making behind the scenes. This may occur in several ways. NSAs may be present at preparatory meetings[52] for a conference, influencing the agenda and key issues for negotiators. NSAs may engage in substantial capacity building for developing country delegations that would not otherwise be able to participate due to a lack of resources or knowledge. NSAs may engage in such capacity building on a regional basis too.

In extreme cases, NSAs may represent or act as a close advisor to a state, often tiny and under-resourced, in treaty negotiations. The Permanent Mission of Palau to the United Nations is at times staffed by law students from New York University.[53] Independent Diplomat is a nonprofit organization that advises "the least wealthy" states on political, legal, and media strategy. It sees itself as remedying the "diplomatic deficit" by helping governments "put their views across effectively in bilateral and multilateral

[50] See, eg, IMO Doc MEPC 31/3/1 (27 April 2017), "Draft amendments to MARPOL Annex VI" submitted by the Institute of Marine Engineering, Science & Technology (IMarEST), an international professional body and learned society for marine professionals.

[51] The IMO Assembly will also take a decision with regard to convening a diplomatic conference. See Article 2, IMO Convention.

[52] In 1946 ECOSOC initiated preparatory meetings for UNCTAD with participants from the International Chamber of Commerce, the AFL, the WFTU, and the International Cooperative Alliance. The reports and statements of the ICC "had a direct influence on shaping provisions in the Charter" for the International Trade Organization: Charnovitz (n 1) 254.

[53] "Guarini Center and IILJ welcome President of Palau and Prime Minister of Grenada," *NYU Law News* (17 February 2012) <http://www.law.nyu.edu/news/climate_change_palau_grenada> accessed December 6, 2017.

negotiations."[54] A more thematic approach is taken by Islands First, a nonprofit that works with small island developing states to "amplify their voice" at the UN on climate change, oceans, and sustainable development.[55]

2.4 Nonstate Actors on the Outside

The final manner of NSA participation is where they are "on the outside" of UN treaty-making, but this does not necessarily mean that they do not have an influence. Indeed, the invocation, termination, and appraising functions of NSAs may be enhanced by their outsider status.

During the negotiations on developing a wide-ranging treaty on business and human rights based on the UN Guiding Principles on Business and Human Rights (also known as the Ruggie Principles), the "open-ended intergovernmental working group" has been debating whether business should have a voice in the discussions. The member states driving the idea of a treaty, Ecuador and South Africa, have welcomed the participation in public meetings of NGOs in consultative status with ECOSOC, but have not opened the door to business representatives. Business representatives have been told they "may be able to access the public gallery or side events during the session."[56] This attitude seems to make little sense given that the idea is to develop an instrument that intends to regulate or even bind businesses. Business representatives will be well placed to argue that any resulting treaty has not taken their views into account.

In another context, states have been resistant to *any* NSA participation despite a treaty norm that promotes such involvement. Article 13 of the UN Convention against Corruption (UNCAC) does not concern treaty-making as such, but defines the importance of transparency and participation of "society,"[57] not just "civil society," in fighting corruption as part of the treaty's object and purpose. Article 13(1) provides:

> Each State Party shall take appropriate measures, within its means and in accordance with fundamental principles of its domestic law, to promote the active participation of individuals and groups outside the public sector, such as civil society, non-governmental organizations and community-based organizations, in the prevention of and the fight against corruption and to raise public awareness regarding the existence, causes and gravity of and the threat posed by corruption.

[54] <https://independentdiplomat.org/support-our-work/> accessed December 6, 2017.

[55] <http://www.islandsfirst.org/what-we-do/> accessed December 6, 2017.

[56] Third session of the open-ended intergovernmental working group on transnational corporations and other business enterprises with respect to human rights, <http://www.ohchr.org/EN/HRBodies/HRC/WGTransCorp/Session3/Pages/Gallery.aspx> accessed December 7, 2017.

[57] The UNODC, *Technical Guide to the United Nations Convention against Corruption* (UN 2009) explains that "States parties should take a broad view of what comprises society and representative associations with whom they should engage," which include "NGOs, trade unions, mass media, faith-based organizations, etc." See further, Merryl Lawry-White, "Article 13," in Cecily Rose, Michael Kubiciel, and Oliver Landwehrl (eds), *Commentary to the UN Convention against Corruption* (OUP 2019).

Despite this normative obligation, the rights of NSAs to participate in the ongoing work of UNCAC have been controversial. The UNCAC Coalition, a NGO of 350 civil society organizations from over 100 countries,[58] has been advocating for the start of the Implementation Review process, as well as for increased transparency and participation of civil society in the process. The UNCAC Coalition claims that, contrary to Article 13, NSAs have been excluded from observing sessions of the Implementation Review Group (IRG) and meetings of other subsidiary bodies.[59] As of the fourth session, certain NSA representatives may attend an annual briefing on the side of the IRG session.[60] The exclusionary approach also appears to go against the spirit of Article 63 of UNCAC, which allows for information from accredited NSAs to be considered, and Rule 17 of the Rules of Procedure of the Conference of States Parties, which states ECOSOC-accredited NGOs should normally be granted observer status upon application.

Some states have expressed frustration with the resistance to NSA participation and failure to reach an agreement on modalities for their involvement. Finland has observed that the question of the participation of civil society in the meetings on the implementation of UNCAC has become a "politicized… question that is taking focus, time and resources away from useful work."[61]

Even in treaty conferences where NSAs have observer status, they are often placed on the outside in the final, critical stages of decision-making when delegates retreat into a "proliferation of working groups and informal meetings" to which NSAs do not have access.[62] As Raustiala observes, NSAs are welcomed by delegates for their ideas and resources (intelligence and promotion functions), but their access is restricted when it comes to hammering out the details of final positions or monitoring treaty implementation (involving the less welcome invocation, termination, and appraising functions of NSAs).[63]

NSAs can still perform an important role from the outside by alerting the press and the general public to problems of treaty negotiation or implementation. During the Paris Agreement negotiation, NSAs shamed laggard states by awarding "Fossil of the Day".[64]

3 Conclusion

The UN makes a distinctive contribution to treaty-making by providing a forum for the meaningful participation of NSAs. The increasing involvement of NSAs is facilitated by

[58] <http://uncaccoalition.org/en_US/about-us/about-the-coalition/> accessed December 6, 2017.

[59] <http://uncaccoalition.org/en_US/the-uncac-needs-civil-society-in-order-to-succeed/> accessed December 7, 2017.

[60] Letter submitted by the UNCAC Coalition, a nongovernmental organization not in consultative status with the Economic and Social Council, CAC/COSP/IRG/2015/NGO/2 (21 May 2015), para 6. See Lawry-White (n 57).

[61] <https://www.unodc.org/documents/treaties/UNCAC/COSP/session6/V1506751e.pdf> accessed December 7, 2017.

[62] Raustiala (n 1) 168–69.

[63] ibid.

[64] van Assel (n 37).

the UN's "entrenched norms of openness,"[65] though this differs according to the topic and range of actors involved.

The active participation of NSAs—by having them "at the table" or "on the sidelines"—can enhance the quality of information available to delegates and help set the corners of the negotiation. It increases the diversity of views in the room. There are genuine concerns about the representativeness and legitimacy of NSAs, but they are representative of interests that are different from governments.[66] We cannot expect them to be, first and foremost, democratic and representative. They represent specific issues and interests that may well be supported by only a minority of the population. Their role is not to fill a void left by fragile or nonparticipating states. If a treaty takes into account not just the views of States but also of "society" (see the discussion of UNCAC in Section 2.4 of this chapter), then NSAs have a definite contribution to make.

Using their intelligence and promotion functions, NSAs perhaps make the greatest contribution when new treaties are drafted,[67] which is when the demand for information and creative ideas is highest. NSAs can also bridge gaps in the ability of delegations to participate by engaging in capacity building. This can also increase continuity and institutional knowledge; diplomats change postings every three to four years, but NSAs may have year-on-year expertise that becomes vital to extended treaty negotiations or the monitoring of implementation.

At the same time, NSAs can have a negative effect on treaty-making. They may skew the issues under discussion to satisfy special interests at the expense of the trade-offs needed to reach consensus. The most active NSAs still tend to have a Western, liberal orientation and thus may entrench rather than counteract North-South asymmetry in the UN.[68] Questions about legitimacy of NSAs may have a knock-on effect on the reputation of the resulting treaty. NSAs may also undermine their own impact by splintering, infighting and forming factions. There is a wide range of professionalism in the NSA world. In the worst-case scenario, NSAs add to the cacophony of UN treaty-making rather than facilitate its transparency and effectiveness.

An under-explored aspect of NSA participation is the application function, defined by Lasswell, McDougal, and Reisman as giving effect to prescriptions in concrete disputes. Could this function encompass a role for NSAs in *legitimating* treaties by promoting the acceptance of their provisions as binding? The invocation and application of treaty norms by reputable NSAs can legitimate a treaty before it has achieved either the requisite number of ratifications to enter into force or the status of customary international law.

A particular challenge for UN treaty-making is how to deal with NSAs that are not NGOs, but represent industry or business. There is a fragmented approach to involving such representatives in negotiations. As mentioned previously, the open-ended working group on a treaty on business and human rights has so far excluded business participants.

[65] Raustiala (n 1) 152. [66] ibid 170.

[67] Steve Charnovitz, "Nongovernmental Organizations and International Law" (2006) 100 AJIL 349, 352.

[68] von Bernstorff (n 30): "[I]t became clear that charismatic single persons from partly small western special associations could influence the treaty text above average."

The IMO welcomes business associations for their expertise in technical maritime issues.[69] The World Intellectual Property Organization (WIPO) defines NGO as including "business entity." The World Health Organization (WHO) 2003 Framework Convention on Tobacco Control involved NSAs from health-related NGOs but did not allow tobacco industry representatives to participate directly. The resulting Convention states in Article 5(3) that "[i]n setting and implementing their public health policies with respect to tobacco control, Parties shall act to protect these policies from commercial and other vested interests of the tobacco industry in accordance with national law." The exclusion from the conference room did not however stop the tobacco lobby from having a voice behind the scenes.[70] And tobacco companies can have an influence on certain governments because, according to the interpretation of at least one tobacco company, "most national laws and practices require an inclusive consultation process during the development of regulation" under the Framework Convention.[71]

In 2016, WHO has adopted a detailed Framework of Engagement with Non-State Actors (FENSA), the first such policy in the UN System that divides NSAs into various categories: NGOs, private sector entities, philanthropic foundations, and academic institutions.[72] It provides a valuable insight into what UN bodies see as the risks[73] of engaging with NSAs as well as the benefits.[74] It expressly states that "WHO does not engage with the tobacco industry or non-State actors that work to further the interests of the tobacco industry. WHO also does not engage with the arms industry."[75] Excluding arms and tobacco industry representatives may protect negotiations from powerful

[69] The NGOs in consultative status with the IMO include: European Chemical Industry Council, the Community of European Shipyards' Associations, Cruise Lines International Association, the European Association of Internal Combustion Engine Manufacturers, the Federation of National Associations of Ship Brokers and Agents, the International Chamber of Commerce, the International Marine Council of Marine Industry Associations, and the International Association of Independent Tanker Owners.

[70] See chapter 17A by Allyn Taylor and chapter 17B by Gianluca Burci in this *Handbook*.

[71] <http://www.bat.com/group/sites/UK__9D9KCY.nsf/vwPagesWebLive/DO9EBF2Q> accessed December 6, 2017.

[72] WHO Doc WHA69.10 (May 2016) <http://www.who.int/about/collaborations/non-state-actors/A69_R10-FENSA-en.pdf?ua=1> accessed December 6, 2017.

[73] Para 7: "(a) conflicts of interest; (b) undue or improper influence exercised by a non-State actor on WHO's work, especially in, but not limited to, policies, norms and standard setting; (c) a negative impact on WHO's integrity, independence, credibility and reputation; and public health mandate; (d) the engagement being primarily used to serve the interests of the non-State actor concerned with limited or no benefits for WHO and public health; (e) the engagement conferring an endorsement of the non-State actor's name, brand, product, views or activity; (f) the whitewashing of a non-State actor's image through an engagement with WHO; (g) a competitive advantage for a non-State actor."

[74] Para 6: "(a) the contribution of non-State actors to the work of WHO Policies, norms and standard setting includes information gathering, preparation for, elaboration of and the decision on the normative text (b) the influence that WHO can have on non-State actors to enhance their impact on global public health or to influence the social, economic and environmental determinants of health, (c) the influence that WHO can have on non-State actors' compliance with WHO's policies, norms and standards; (d) the additional resources non-State actors can contribute to WHO's work; (e) the wider dissemination of and adherence by non-State actors to WHO's policies, norms and standards."

[75] WHO Doc WHA69.10 (n 72) para 44.

lobbying interests that threaten public health, but such exclusion does not necessarily neutralize such interests. It may even feed into a narrative of "unfair exclusion" that may empower such interests. It would be worth considering how to engage with such interests in a limited way to, for example, encourage some compliance with health standards and prevent children from having access to their products.

NSAs are not a monolith, and neither is their ability to contribute to UN treaty-making. They may exercise at least seven "functions" from intelligence-gathering to appraisal. They may be most useful in the generation of big ideas or the fine technicalities of drafting or the longer term on-the-ground work of implementation or monitoring. The UN has established practices for accreditation and participation that have facilitated the increasing contribution of NSAs. But there are challenges that remain, from risks to legitimacy to controversy over the involvement of industry and business interests. The sophisticated and nuanced approaches of the IMO, with its modalities for engaging NSAs according to the topic and phase of decision-making as well as the nature of the NSA, provides a potential model for continued improvement of NSA participation in UN treaty-making.

CHAPTER 32

PARTICIPATION OF INTERNATIONAL ORGANIZATIONS IN UN TREATIES

JAN KLABBERS*

WHEN international organizations were first set up, mostly in the latter third of the nineteenth century, little thought was given to how they might relate to each other. And little thought needed to be given: the working assumption was that each organization (then still typically referred to as "union") would be responsible for its own specific tasks, and that those tasks would rarely, if at all, need to be harmonized with each other. Each union had its own function, and was set up by member states precisely to give effect to that function.[1]

This picture is no longer tenable, if it ever was, and the topic of relations between international organizations inter se has come to generate its own research agenda. One particular manifestation of relations involving several international organizations is that certain organizations can participate in the activities of others or under auspices of others, including in practices of treaty-making. This applies, in general form, to what are sometimes referred to as "regional economic integration organizations"; in actual practice, there is really one entity that is generally considered to fit the bill, and that is the European Union (EU).

Treaty-making is not the only relevant arena, nor is it a particularly well-defined one. There is, for instance, much cooperation going on involving international organizations under headings as diffuse as standard-setting, or even enforcement: this too can generate

* Professor of International Law at the University of Helsinki.

[1] The underlying theory is often referred to as "functionalism." For a theoretical critique, see Jan Klabbers, "The EJIL Foreword: The Transformation of International Organizations Law," (2015) 26 Eur J of Intl L 9–82.

standards that may not formally amount to new treaty provisions, but may nonetheless exercise normative authority over international actors. The work of the Contact Group on Piracy off the Somali Coast, a loose network of international organizations, states, industry groups, and others, might be taken as an example.

This chapter is however largely devoted to a discussion of the legal issues provoked by the position of regional economic integration organizations with particular reference to the UN system, especially relating to the EU's participation in treaties concluded within the UN system.[2] For, the EU's special position raises a number of intriguing and potentially complicated legal issues, many of them masking (or sublimating), as so often, highly controversial political issues. Such issues manifest themselves both within the UN—as a matter of UN law, one might be tempted to say—and within the EU, as a matter of EU law. In what follows, I will briefly address the reason(s) these matters call for new techniques of lawmaking and procedure (Section 1) and sketch some conceptual issues (Section 2). Section 3 will discuss some of the issues this raises within the EU—the EU being effectively the only entity to which this applies. Section 4 will shift the focus to the UN and related organizations (such as the FAO), and aims to provide a discussion of the sort of questions this provokes and how these, generally, receive their answer. Section 5 concludes.

A search of the UN Treaty Series suggests that the EU, in its various incarnations (EEC, EC, EU, and including treaties to which also EU member states are parties) is a party to close to 1,000 treaties (974). That is a respectable number: a bit more than Haiti (754), but less than Canada, India, or the United States, all of whom are parties to more than 1,000 treaties.[3] Still excluded are treaties to which EU offspring are parties, such as those concluded by the European Investment Bank or the European Chemicals Agency. Moreover, the number does not reflect participation of the EU in practices that are held not to amount to formal treaties, nor in treaty practices that have not been registered with the UN.

1 The Logic

The EU is, thus far, the only generally recognized specimen of "regional economic integration organization." There is no single authoritative international definition available of the term,[4] but given that the EU is usually regarded as the only example, it is not

[2] Editorial note: I will steadfastly refer to the EU, also when addressing earlier incarnations (EEC, EC), unless the context demands differently. The Treaty on European Union shall be abbreviated as TEU, whereas TFEU stands for the more detailed (less "constitutional") Treaty on the Functioning of the European Union.

[3] See <https://treaties.un.org/pages/Home.aspx?clang=_en> accessed June 4, 2018. It seems that 1,000 is the maximum number of hits available when doing a search for treaty participants.

[4] Nor is it likely that there could be a single authoritative definition, given the uncertainty surrounding the concept of international organization generally. See Jan Klabbers, "Unity, Diversity, Accountability: The Ambivalent Concept of International Organization," (2013) 14 Melbourne J of Intl L 149–70.

unlikely that would-be regional economic integration organizations should take on some or all of the characteristics of the EU: set up by sovereign states, who have conferred sovereign authority and competences on common institutions in economic matters to take decisions or enter into agreements binding those same sovereign states.[5] In other words, one key element would seem to be the possibility of binding the member states, and this entails that few organizations qualify. It is not excluded, of course, that in the future other organizations take on similar characteristics, although with the emergence of trade wars and new protectionism in the first half of 2018, it is unlikely that this will happen any time soon.

Hence, while this contribution aims to address generally the position of international organizations, including regional economic integration organizations, the practical examples will be derived from the role and experiences of the EU. In this light, it may be useful briefly to sketch the EU setup: the EU experience is bound to be repeated or mimicked if other regional economic integration organizations will be created.

When the EU was originally established, in the 1950s, one of the ambitions behind what was at the time the European Economic Community (EEC) was that, after a transitional period of some 12 years, by 1970, certain competences would exclusively rest upon the EEC. This made instrumental sense: given the idea that the EEC should be a common market, it would need a common tariff at its external borders; such a common tariff, in turn, implied a common commercial policy; and this, in turn, implied that the six member states (as they were at the time) were expected to pool their resources and grant the EEC exclusive competences to engage in trade relations with the outside world. If the EEC treaty was explicit on external trade powers, similar reasoning was applied to other fields as well, even where the Treaty did not explicitly grant such powers to the EEC, at the exclusion of the member states.

Most famously this occurred in the field of transport, where the Court of Justice made clear that the power to legislate internally (i.e., with respect to the six member states) necessarily entailed the power also to act externally: *in foro interno, in foro externo*.[6] The precise setting in which the agreement at issue was concluded was not considered particularly relevant for purposes of internal EU consideration: the European Road Transport Agreement had been negotiated under the auspices of the UN's Economic Commission for Europe (UNECE), but this only affected the Court's reasoning in that the forum of UNECE triggered consideration of the provision of the EEC Treaty authorizing cooperation with and within international organizations but "only by common action" of the member states.[7]

After the entry into force of the Lisbon Treaty, and the most recent amendment of the EU treaties, it is clear that the EU has powers in external policy fields that are directly relevant to UN treaty-making, such as trade and investment as well as environmental

[5] These elements are present in the definition contained in a number of conventions: see example the 2000 Palermo Convention on Organized Crime, article 2(j), as well as in the way US antitrust law defines the regional economic integration organization: see 15 USCS § 6211.

[6] See Case 22/70, *Commission* v *Council* (European Road Transport Agreement), ECLI:EU:C:1971:32.

[7] ibid, paragraph 76.

protection; maritime matters as well as transport matters; development as well as agriculture. In addition, the EU is explicitly empowered to act within a number of international organizations, including the UN family, but also covering entities such as the Organization for Economic Co-operation and Development and the Council for Europe.[8]

It is undisputed that the EU has external powers (and can thus, for instance, conclude treaties), but the precise division of powers inevitably reflects power struggles along two axes, which may come into play in the framework of multilateral treaty-making.

On the one hand, there is the struggle between the Union and its member states: the latter may be reluctant to give up what they see as their sovereign prerogatives, whereas the Union may be keen to appropriate powers in order to do justice to what it holds to be its main raison d'être: ensure European integration.

In addition, though, there is a second axis of trouble: the Union's institutions do not always see eye to eye. The Commission is the executive organ and supposed to represent the EU's common interest. This, in turn, may diverge from the interest as conceived by the member states (as represented in the Council and variations thereon, such as the European Council) or the peoples of Europe, represented via direct elections in the European Parliament. And then there is the Court of Justice, which sees itself as representing the law: it is the guardian of legality in the EU. It is by no means uncommon for the Council and the Commission to have diverging opinions, or for other vectors of disagreement among institutions to arise.

Either way, the precise boundaries between its powers and those of its member states remain disputed. The reason for this seems obvious: a power granted to the EU is a power abdicated by the member states.[9] Put graphically, if the EU has an exclusive power to enter into fisheries conservation treaties with third states, this entails that France, or Germany, or any other of the (still) 28 member states of the EU, is barred from doing so—preempted, in Euro-jargon.

Hence, the scope of exclusive external powers is subject to a continuous struggle between the Union and its members: the EU is generally keen on centralization; the member states are generally keen on retaining their powers, even while realizing that pooling their resources may be more advantageous than going solo—acting as a single bloc prevents third parties (Russia, China, Japan, the United States) from entertaining "divide and rule" tactics. And this pattern is likely to repeat itself in other regional economic integration organizations, as our political imagination is limited and we usually resort to mimicry when setting up new entities.

Where powers are supposed to be shared between the EU and its member states (as is the case with environmental protection), the site for struggle becomes the precise distribution of competences. In case of a shared competence, for example, the question arises

[8] See Art 220 TFEU.

[9] This, at least, is the generally accepted narrative, treating powers as a zero-sum game. This seems rather too stylized though: it is possible for the EU to interfere with member state prerogatives while exercising its own proper powers, and vice versa. See further Jan Klabbers, "Restraints on the Treaty-Making Powers of Member States Deriving from EU Law," in Enzo Cannizzaro (ed.), *The European Union as an Actor in International Relations* (Kluwer 2002), 151–75.

which part (EU or member states) is responsible for which aspect of a treaty under negotiation. If the treaty aims at creating a comprehensive regime, for example, it may be the case that its putative provisions concerning one domain (e.g., on transboundary transportation of hazardous wastes) rests with the member states, whereas the provisions on another topic (say, conservation of marine resources) rests with the EU.

But even where it is clear that the EU's powers are exclusive, political struggle has not come to an end. The EU has exclusive powers in trade (including investment), fisheries conservation, and possibly antitrust matters, but how key terms are defined determines the precise scope of those exclusive powers. The factor time adds another complication: upon the EU assuming exclusive competence, the member states can no longer conclude their own bilateral agreements with third parties.[10]

2 Conceptual Matters

Like any other regional economic integration organization (but as noted, the EU is thus far the only recognized species of the genus), the EU can play a role in UN treaties (broadly conceived) in a variety of ways, and while the legal regimes may overlap, nonetheless it may be useful to distinguish various modes of participation.

First, there is *full membership* of the UN, or related organizations: the "UN family" consists of some 20 international organizations that have entered into a relationship with the UN. These include several organizations with tasks that overlap with those of the EU, and one of them has allowed the EU to join: the Food and Agricultural Organization (FAO). It bears emphasizing that the EU is the only international organization currently in existence that is a member of a UN-affiliated organization. Membership of the UN itself and quite a few of the other specialized agencies is for the time being out of reach for international organizations: most specify that they are only open for membership by states,[11] and not even the EU is a state in any recognized meaning of that term.[12] Full membership entails the full panoply of rights (and obligations), including the right to participate in treaty-making under auspices of the organization concerned. This raises questions about the division of tasks and rights between the EU and its members that are independent members of the same organization. With respect to the FAO, the basic principle is that when the EU participates in a vote, its member states do not,

[10] In some of the *Open Skies* cases (concerning bilateral air traffic agreements concluded between various member states and the United States), the Court of Justice rather quickly held that an amended treaty is to be regarded as a novel legal creation. See eg, case C-466/98, *Commission* v *United Kingdom*, ECLI:EU:C:2002:624.

[11] With respect to the UN the International Court of Justice confirmed as much in an early opinion, without however paying too much attention to the precise contours of the requirement of statehood. See *Conditions of Admission of a State to Membership in the United Nations (article 4 of the Charter)*, (Advisory Opinion) [1948] ICJ Rep 57.

[12] See Jan Klabbers, "*Sui Generis*? The EU as an International Organization," in Dennis Patterson and Anna Södersten (eds), *A Companion to European Union Law and International Law* (Wiley 2016), 3–15.

and if it is the EU participating, its amount of votes equals the number of its member states entitled to vote on the same issue. The matter is further governed by a "declaration of competence" issued by the EU upon joining the FAO, as required under the FAO Constitution.[13]

Second, in organizations that reserve their membership to states, international organizations may be given *observer status*. The EU holds observer status with the UN (its General Assembly) as well as with most of the "specialized agencies" (UN-related international organizations), including the most recent addition, the International Organization for Migration (IOM).

The precise details may differ from organization to organization, but generally, observers are allowed to participate in meetings and will be invited to attend diplomatic events both formal and informal (including cocktail parties), but may not table proposals or vote.[14] With respect to the relationship between the UN and the EU, as much is laid down in a General Assembly resolution adopted in 2011, sketching some rights for the EU, but also explicitly stating that the EU representatives shall not have the right to vote, to cosponsor resolutions or decisions, or to put forward candidates. The resolution was adopted with overwhelming support: 180 states in favor, with two abstentions (Syria and Zimbabwe) and some absentees. Nonetheless, Nauru voiced some (justifiable) concerns about how this helps to cement a privileged position for entities able to wield economic and political influence.[15] Be that as it may, often the EU will act on behalf of its member states during treaty negotiations, even where the EU itself only has observer status, and under EU law, the member states are under an obligation to coordinate their positions and represent the EU in other fora. This does not always work: sometimes political divisions between EU member states are simply too deep. But in order to harmonize positions treaty negotiations tend to be accompanied by EU "coordination meetings," where the EU's member states decide what position to adopt and how to approach the matter at hand. These typically take place before multilateral negotiations commence (sometimes starting many months earlier) and continue in the margins of multilateral treaty negotiations: early in the morning and during weekends.

The status of observers is often said to follow from functional needs: they are co-opted to the extent that they carry sufficient political weight to be instrumental in the solution or management of common issues. One curiosity about observer status is that in various organizations (including the International Maritime Organization and the World Intellectual Property Organization) observer status is held not by the EU but rather by

[13] For a brief overview, see Geert De Baere, "EU Status in Other International Organizations," in Robert Schütze and Takis Tridimas (eds), *Oxford Principles of European Union Law. Volume I: The European Union Legal Order* (OUP 2018), 1234–81, esp. 1255–58. See also below.

[14] The literature is in serious need of updating, with the most authoritative studies dating from the late 1970s and early 1980s. See Eric Suy, "The Status of Observers in International Organizations," (1978) 160 Recueil des Cours de l'Académie de Droit International 75–179; Neri Sybesma-Knol, *The Status of Observers in the United Nations* (Brussels Free University 1981).

[15] See UNGA Res 65/276 for the text of the resolution, while the debate is reported on at <http://www.un.org/press/en/2011/ga11079.doc.htm> accessed January 10, 2018.

one of its organs: the European Commission. This is curious because it would seem that the Commission lacks the required personality to be performing acts under international law, and consequently, the treaty partner would be the EU rather than its Commission.[16]

A third way of participation by international organizations, including the EU, in UN settings is to participate in *formal or informal groups, organizations, and networks* set up by the UN. Perhaps the most eye-catching example of recent years is the Contact Group on Piracy of the Coast of Somalia, mentioned previously. In addition, the EU sometimes concludes treaties with the UN or with UN programs or agencies: an example is the 2016 agreement with UNCTAD on cross-border trade in Central Africa.[17]

Fourth, where the EU is already a party to a multilateral treaty, it enjoys a relatively privileged position when it comes to the negotiation of further instruments or amendments. In particular, other international organizations willing and able to join still have a lengthy process to accomplish; they still need to fight for a seat at the table, where the EU is already seated. And being already seated implies that often the EU has a voice in who else gets to be seated.

Finally, it may be the case that international organizations participate in treaties concluded under auspices of the UN—it seems that this is, again, largely the sole preserve of the EU. Typically, the EU participates in environmental agreements and maritime agreements, as in these matters it has some generally recognized competences, while commodity agreements (which may, but need not be, negotiated under auspices of the UN or UNCTAD) would also affect the EU's competences.[18] Still, the EU has also joined other regimes set up by the UN or UN-related agencies: it is a party, for instance, to the 2000 Palermo Convention on Organized Crime and all its protocols, the WHO Framework Convention on Tobacco, and even to a human rights convention: the Convention on the Rights of Persons with Disabilities.

The policy rationale is usually that the multilateral treaty concerned touches upon some aspect of EU competence: for example, the WHO 2003 Framework Convention on Tobacco addresses, amongst other things, tobacco advertising, and this can have a bearing on the EU's internal market: different advertising rules across the EU's member states would potentially undermine the internal market. Likewise, treaties on cooperation in criminal matters, such as the 2003 Corruption Convention, will touch upon an EU competence: since the early 1990s the EU has the clear ambition of achieving cooperation and integration in the field of justice and cooperation in criminal matters. Much the same could be said for human rights treaties, but these tend to come with monitoring

[16] See case C-327/91, *France* v *Commission*, ECLI:EU:C:1994:305.

[17] As reported at <http://unctad.org/en/pages/newsdetails.aspx?OriginalVersionID=1356> accessed January 20, 2018.

[18] It has been reported that the "EU and its member States" have taken an active part in the negotiations leading to the Convention on the Rights of Persons with Disabilities, for instance, and that the EU has also become a party to this Convention. On the other hand, in the same breath is mentioned the Enforced Disappearances convention, which, however, is only open to member states of the UN. See Hadewych Hazelzet, "The EU's Human Rights Policy in the UN: An Example of Effective Multilateralism?," in Jan Wouters et al (eds.), *The United Nations and the European Union: An Ever Stronger Partnership* (TMC Asser Institute 2006), 183–94, at 187.

mechanisms that are often deemed incompatible with the role of the Court of Justice of the European Union as the ultimate guardian of legality within the EU. This perceived incompatibility has thwarted several attempts by the EU to join the European Convention on Human Rights,[19] but formed no obstacle to the EU joining the Convention on the Rights of Persons with Disabilities, as with respect to this convention the monitoring mechanism is provided in a separate protocol (to which the EU is not a party).

Hence, there are several possible forms in which the role of international organizations (in reality mostly the EU) within the UN and its family can play out. Adding the EU perspective, the picture becomes more complicated still. Partly this is because external agreements can relate to each of the three former pillars of the EU (economy, foreign policy, home affairs), which are subject to different procedures and dynamics, resulting from different sensitivities relating to sovereign prerogatives. In foreign policy, for example, initiatives should emanate from the High Representative rather than from the Commission, and the role of the Court of Justice of the European Union (CJEU) over foreign policy issues is seriously limited when compared to its general role.[20]

3 European Experiences

The main practical issue arising with respect to the EU is often colloquially referred to as "mixity," an intriguing technique for managing the coexistence of legal powers held by both the EU and its member states. Some have, somewhat charitably perhaps, heralded mixity as the EU's contribution to political theory—as its own, uniquely European, version of quasi-federal doctrine; and while charitable, there is some truth to this.[21]

At the core of mixity is the idea that where competences are shared, both "shareholders" ought to be involved. Agreements with third parties, in other words, ought to have "mixed" participation of both the member states and the EU itself. This sounds easy and rather obvious, but it is not: many treaties, for instance, are only to open for participation by states, and since the EU is not a state, it cannot always participate.

This came to the fore already in the early 1970s, once the external commerce power had been transferred to the EU. It turned out that this demanded collective action within the General Agreement on Tariffs and Trade, but GATT did not provide for membership by an entity such as the EU. The Court found a pragmatic solution in a theory of succession, launched in *International Fruit Company*.[22] It held that the EU was the successor to the rights and obligations of its member states under GATT, and posited three requirements

[19] Most recently in *Opinion 2/13*, ELI:EU:C:2014:2454.

[20] See Article 275 TFEU; see Panos Koutrakos, "Judicial Review in the EU's Common Foreign and Security Policy," (2018) 67 ICLQ 1–35.

[21] See JHH Weiler, "The External Legal Relations of Non-unitary Actors: Mixity and the Federal Principle," reproduced in JHH Weiler, *The Constitution of Europe* (CUP 1999), 130–87.

[22] See Cases 21–24/72, *International Fruit Company* v *Produktschap voor Groenten en Fruit*, ECLI:EU:C:1972:115.

for such a succession theory to apply. First, the member states must have *intended* to transfer powers to the EU; second, they must have *actually transferred* these powers; and third, their treaty partners (in this case the other GATT parties) must have *accepted* the transfer.[23]

The succession theory is less appropriate in those fields where there can be legitimate doubt whether member states have intended to transfer powers or have actually transferred powers (and have done so irrevocably). Surely, such an argument is much more compelling in the field of commerce than it is in, say, security, or even transport.[24] Note however that it was accepted, in the first instance, in a well-known case involving United Nations sanctions, although the succession doctrine did not survive the appeals stage of the same case.[25] The net result is that in some settings, the EU cannot join even if all its member states have joined an external regime; in such cases, the member states are under a strong duty of cooperation.[26]

The more common technique then is mixity, that is, the joint participation of both the EU and its member states.[27] The need to do so, as noted, arose when external agreements would cover topics that fell in part within the exclusive competence of the EU and in part within the exclusive competence of the member states, but this rationale has been expanded. Mixed treaties are concluded when competences are shared but not strictly delimited, and even when the subject matter falls solely within the powers of the EU.[28] In the latter case, the justification is a practical one: involving all the member states is bound to enhance the legitimacy of the external agreement in the eyes of those member states, and this will help in faithful implementation.[29]

Since the obvious question arises about which part is ultimately responsible for implementation of which part of any external agreement, often regional economic integration organizations such as the EU are required to issue a declaration on the division of competences. The EU tends to be reluctant to be overly specific, for the (understandable) reason that a clear declaration on division of competences may come to have the effect of freezing that particular division: if the EU declares that the power to do X rests

[23] The Court engaged in a narrative from which these three requirements can be deduced.

[24] See eg, Case 308/06, *Intertanko*, ECLI:EU:C:2008:312.

[25] The doctrine was upheld by the EU's Court of First Instance in Case T-315/01, *Kadi* v *Council and Commission*, ECLI:EU:T:2005:332, paras 193–203. On appeal, the CJEU effectively ignored the succession doctrine, reaching its conclusions via a different route. See Case C-402/05 P, *Kadi* v *Council and Commission*, ECLI:EU:C:2008:461.

[26] See Opinion 2/91 (*ILO*), ECLI:EU:C:1993:106.

[27] Seminal is Joni Heliskoski, *Mixed Agreements as a Technique for Organizing the International Relations of the European Community and Its Member States* (Martinus Nijhoff 2001); see also Christophe Hillion and Panos Koutrakos (eds), *Mixed Agreements Revisited: The EU and Its Member States in the World* (Hart 2010).

[28] Not always though: the EU is a party to some treaties, especially commodity agreements, in the exercise of its exclusive powers. Examples include the 2007 International Coffee Agreement and the 2010 International Cocoa Agreement (not in force, but provisionally applied).

[29] The EU may have a bureaucratic apparatus, but it lacks its own customs officials, police officers, prison wardens, etc.; hence, for the implementation of the agreements to which it is a party, the EU strongly depends on its member states, acting, one might say, as organs of the EU.

with the member states, it might preempt the possibility of the power to do X being transferred to the EU in the near future.[30] As a result, such declarations tend to include the caveat that the current division of powers should not be seen as final—an example is the declaration attached to the instrument of confirmation of the Convention on the Rights of Persons with Disabilities, which provides that the "scope and exercise" of Union competence are "by their nature, subject to continuous development...."[31]

Technically, mixed agreements give rise to sometimes complicated or awkward issues.[32] One relatively straightforward issue relates to the question of signature: Who gets to sign the treaty concerned? Obviously, in case both the EU and its member states are involved, all member states are expected to sign, as is the EU. The question remains though who is to sign on behalf of the EU. This depends on a Council decision, as the Council is authorized, under Article 216 TFEU (Treaty on the Functioning of the European Union), to decide on the issue. It may do so itself (mostly through the member state occupying the Presidency), or delegate it to the Commission or even, hypothetically, to yet another member state. Even so, for internal legality purposes, the Council must adopt a decision approving the agreement in question—the agreement cannot be considered approved without such a decision. As a corollary, when the validity of the agreement is later contested, all that can be done internally is that the Council decision approving it is invalidated—the EU cannot, on its own, declare an agreement concluded with third parties invalid.

In most cases, there is an additional complication in that the Council can approve external agreements only with the consent of the European Parliament, or having consulted the European Parliament. Parliament's consent is required for several classes of agreements, including association agreements or other agreements setting up an institutional framework, including those negotiated under UN auspices. In most other cases it needs to be consulted, with the exception of foreign policy agreements.[33]

Two additional issues stand out, neither of them seemingly spectacular or of great legal import but both of them of the utmost practical—and political—relevance. The first relates to the negotiating position: with a couple of interested institutions (Council, Commission, and Parliament) and 28 member states, it is by no means self-evident what position the EU shall take, and how it shall try to give effect to its position. The TFEU does not offer much guidance beyond suggesting that the matter of treaty negotiations is formally in the hands of the Council.[34] And yet, a number of practical issues need to be discussed beforehand, including the question of what kind of agreement will be negotiated. Typically, the Council will work on the basis of a recommendation stemming from the

[30] Obviously, the reverse applies as well, but is generally considered to be less of a concern, if only because powers are often considered to be revocable by the member states. The classic study is Daniela Obradovic, "Repatriation of Powers in the European Community," (1997) 34 *Common Market L Rev* 59–88.

[31] <https://treaties.un.org/Pages/ViewDetails.aspx?src=TREATY&mtdsg_no=IV-15&chapter=4&clang=_en> accessed October 3, 2017.

[32] Also, during the life of a treaty: think of the making of reservations, the authority to interpret, or the facility of proposing amendments.

[33] See Article 218 TFEU.

[34] A separate procedure relates to trade agreements, under Article 207 TFEU.

Commission (or, if the matter relates mostly to security, from the High Representative of the Union for Foreign Affairs and Security Policy), outlining why the topic is relevant, what the Union's interest is, and how it is best approached from an EU perspective. Once this is done, the Council can decide to allow the Commission to enter into negotiations, designate the Commission as the main negotiator, and present it with the negotiation directives.

All of this breaks down into a number of more detailed questions. To what extent is EU competence involved? Is the EU itself even allowed, under the rules of the relevant international organization, to participate in the negotiations, and if so, can it do so as a full participant or only as an observer? In the latter case, after all, it may not be allowed to vote (and thus needs to rely on its member states toeing the line), and may not even have a seat at the main negotiating table. More to the point, usually with mixed agreements issues within EU competence shall be left to the Commission, with the Council Presidency (which rotates among member states every six months) representing member state competences—it is thus convenient if the Commission and Presidency can be seated in close proximity.[35]

4 On the Receiving End

As a theoretical matter, international organizations can only act within other international organizations if and when they are allowed to act: third parties are under no obligation to recognize their existence, and are under no obligation to facilitate internal processes within some organization or other by collaborating in its external relations. It follows that, if and when treaties are only open for participation by states, organizations have no role to play unless the putative treaty partners allow this. This starting point seems to be generally accepted: it already underpinned the "succession theory" launched by the CJEU in *International Fruit Company*.

In this light, it is perhaps surprising how willing third parties, both within and without the UN, have been to accommodate the EU, even though functionally much of this makes sense. Clearly, since the EU exercises powers on a number of issues (sometimes excluding member state powers), there is a functional reason to facilitate cooperation with it.

In some cases, cooperation warrants amendment of constituent documents. The FAO, as is well known, changed its Constitution in order to allow the EU to join it. Originally only open to "nations,"[36] and allowing international organizations on the basis of an

[35] Much of this is culled from Hillion and Koutrakos (eds), *Mixed Agreements Revisited*; see also Pieter Jan Kuijper et al (eds), *The Law of EU External Relations: Cases, Materials, and Commentary on the EU as an International Legal Actor* (OUP 2013), esp. 69–75.

[36] Article II, paragraph 2 FAO. This is rare, and potentially risky, in that states and nations need not (indeed, often are not) identical. Some treaties are only open to "governments," which is also rare and perhaps a tad inaccurate, as governments tend to represent states. An example is the 1946 International Whaling Convention.

observer-type status but without the right to vote,[37] in the early 1990s the FAO constitution was amended so as to facilitate membership of regional economic integration organizations, meaning the EU. Several conditions must be met though: such an organization must be composed of states; a majority of its member states must also be members of the FAO, and it must have competence over matters within the purview of the FAO.[38]

This does not exhaust the matter, as the joint membership of both the EU and its member states raises a number of practical issues, ranging from speaking and voting rights and membership of subsidiary organs to such things as budgetary assessments. As mentioned, within the FAO, careful delimitations have been put in place. Article II FAO specifies, in paragraphs 5–7, that regional economic integration organizations need to submit declarations of competence of the sort discussed previously; that they shall announce changes in the division of competences; and that the default presumption is that competences are presumed to have been retained by member states unless otherwise notified or informed.

Membership rights, so paragraph 8 of Article II continues, shall be exercised on an "alternative basis" between the EU and its member states in their respective spheres of competence, and the EU can participate in meetings and organs of the FAO within its competences, except in organs of limited membership. Voting too relates to the division of competences: where the EU is competent, it can vote but then its member states cannot—and vice versa.[39] For the time being, the FAO is the only organization in the UN family of which the EU is a member, indeed, to which any international organization is a member.[40] Organizations play a role in other UN-related organizations, whether as observer or otherwise, but falling short of membership.

Other conventions have imagined different mechanisms to accommodate regional economic integration organizations. Such organizations are, for instance, allowed to become a party to the 1992 UN Framework Convention on Climate Change, but if they do and none of their member states also join, then they shall be bound by all the obligations under the Convention.[41] In other words, any possibly internally existing division of competences shall be ignored. This is, however, a highly unlikely scenario; the more likely scenario is that of joint or mixed membership, in which case the regional economic integration organization concerned shall issue a declaration on the division of competences, as discussed previously with respect to the EU.

Even when not formal members, international organizations may and do exercise influence on treaty-making processes,[42] and for good reason. After all, often enough

[37] Article II, paragraph 5 FAO (old).

[38] Article II, paragraph 4 FAO (as amended).

[39] Article II(10) FAO.

[40] The EU is a founding member of the World Trade Organization, but the WTO is not considered a member of the UN family.

[41] See article 22 UN Framework Convention on Climate Change.

[42] The EU proudly boasts that a 2017 IMO agreement to improve safety of passenger ships owes much to the work of the EU and its European Maritime Safety Agency: see <https://ec.europa.eu/transport/modes/maritime/news/2017-06-16-maritime-transport-commission-welcomes-international-agreement_en> accessed January 10, 2018.

international organizations possess a broad knowledge base, typically the sort of expertise that may be of assistance when negotiating a multilateral treaty on a particular topic associated with the common good, and it is typically on such topics that agreements are concluded under UN auspices. An example, still ongoing, relates to the conclusion of a convention on marine biodiversity in areas beyond national jurisdiction. Here, an informal working group laying much of the groundwork included "permanent observers" such as the EU, the Caribbean Community, the Asian-African Legal Consultative Organization, and the Pacific Islands Forum,[43] as well as a number of specialized agencies (FAO, WIPO, International Seabed Authority, and UNESCO) and other organizations with an ad hoc participant status, such as various regional fisheries commissions. Given the substance matter of the agreement under preparation (a convention addressing biodiversity in maritime areas beyond national jurisdiction, dealing with conservation but also with possible industrial applications of natural resources and the intellectual property implications thereof), all of these can be considered stakeholders in a relevant sense, boasting specific expertise or having a specific interest.[44]

While the precise prerogatives of such participating organizations may differ in different contexts, having a seat at the table well-nigh guarantees possibilities for exercising at least a modest degree of influence, both by means of taking the floor and (possibly of greater practical relevance) by lobbying the national delegations, bringing matters to their attention, and generally bringing their expertise to bear on the matter.

5 To Conclude

The position of international organizations within other organizations has thus far rarely been studied,[45] and practical examples are few and far between. Much the same applies to practices of treaty participation: it is generally acknowledged that the EU participates in treaties,[46] but with respect to other organizations, far less is known. It is sobering to realize perhaps that the leading study on the UN's treaty practice dates back to the 1950s,[47] and that there is no comprehensive study available of the legal aspects

[43] Also mentioned is the International Union for the Conservation of Nature, but it is unclear whether this qualifies as an intergovernmental organization.

[44] The composition can be found at <http://www.un.org/Depts/los/biodiversityworkinggroup/documents/participants_wg9.pdf> accessed January 20, 2018. Most of these are also participating in the work of the Preparatory Commission advising the General Assembly on elements of a convention: see <http://www.un.org/depts/los/biodiversity/prepcom_files/Final_List_of_Participants_BBNJ_IV_Jan_2018.pdf> accessed January 10, 2018.

[45] A pioneering monograph, now largely outdated, is Rachel Frid, *The Relations between the EC and International Organizations: Legal Theory and Practice* (Kluwer 1995).

[46] For an overview, see Delano Verwey, *The European Community, the European Union and the International Law of Treaties* (TMC Asser Instituut 2004).

[47] See Shabtai Rosenne, "United Nations Treaty Practice," (1954) 86 Recueil des Cours 275–444.

of treaty-making within the UN. The General Assembly reviewed the multilateral treaty-making process, but did so as long ago as the late 1970s and early 1980s.

The treaty practice of the EU, in all its diverse aspects, has inspired a number of in-depth studies over the years. By contrast, its membership of international organizations has been less popular as a research topic, and relations between international organizations generally inter se is only starting to be recognized as a proper topic for further study and reflection, and much the same applies to the position of the EU in UN-sponsored treaty negotiations. These are topics of great practical and political significance, not least with a view to the lessons any future regional economic integration may learn. They are also, however, of great theoretical relevance: the more organizations interact with each other, the more they must be seen as autonomously operating entities. And this, in turn, suggests they can no longer accurately be portrayed as merely exercising powers delegated by their member states. Any novel way of thinking about international organizations must probably reserve some role for delegation (this, after all, is how organizations come into being), but should not hesitate to look beyond delegation as well. This is a lesson the EU teaches us in its own right, and a lesson taught even more strongly when considering the relationship between the EU and the UN and the EU's role in UN treaty-making processes.

CHAPTER 33

THE ROLE OF THE UNITED NATIONS IN PROMOTING TRANSPARENCY IN THE INTERNATIONAL TREATY FRAMEWORK

a view through the registration and publication of treaties under article 102 of the charter of the united nations

JONATHAN AGAR AND CHRISTEL MOBECH*

THE promotion of transparency in the international treaty framework is one of the founding mandates of the United Nations Organization.

Indeed, it is striking to note that the only use of the term "treaty" within the operative sections of the Charter are found not in its Articles addressing peace and security or human rights, but in the far less heralded Article 102 on the registration and publication of treaties.

Through paragraph 1 of this Article, the principle of absolute transparency in the conclusion of treaties, and the role of the United Nations in achieving this goal, was enshrined in the Charter:

> Every treaty and every international agreement entered into by any Member of the United Nations after the present Charter comes into force shall as soon as possible be registered with the Secretariat and published by it.

In doing so, negotiating states underlined the central importance of open diplomacy for the future stability of international relations and recognized the United Nations as the

* The views expressed in this Chapter are the personal views of the authors and do not represent the views of the United Nations.

appropriate institutional framework for its realization. The registration of all treaties concluded by member states was to be the tool by which transparency in the international treaty framework would be achieved.[1]

Seventy-two years after the entry into force of the Charter, the Organization can reflect on significant success in this effort, with over 70,000 treaties, along with over 125,000 related treaty-actions (ratifications, accessions, withdrawals, etc.), having been registered with and published by the Secretariat of the United Nations. This process continues on a daily basis, with an average of 250 treaties and treaty actions submitted for registration with the Secretariat each month.

Through the United Nations Treaty Collection website[2] maintained by the Secretariat, the public has unprecedented access to information on all treaties and treaty actions registered since 1946. With an average of over 3,000,000-page views each year, the Treaty Collection provides a unique and in-depth picture of the global treaty-making landscape that would have been far beyond even the most ambitious hopes of those at the San Francisco conference.

Despite these real successes however, we remain a long way from the absolute transparency envisaged at the time of the conclusion of the Charter. A significant number of treaties remain unregistered, and a geographic imbalance in compliance with Article 102 is clear in the registration practice of member states.

This chapter will first explore the historical origins of Article 102 of the Charter, and consider the role played by the organs of the United Nations in the realization of its aim of absolute transparency in the international treaty framework. Drawing on the tens of thousands of treaties and treaty actions contained in the United Nations electronic treaty database, along with the practice of the Secretariat of the United Nations in exercising its functions under Article 102, the chapter will then consider the unique perspective it provides on the key trends and challenges in global treaty-making activity.

Finally, the chapter will consider the extent to which Article 102 has achieved its objective in securing openness and transparency in the conclusion of treaties, and reflect on what steps could be taken to further reinvigorate its implementation.

1 The Origins of Article 102 of the Charter: "Open Covenants of Peace, Openly Arrived At"

Following the discovery, both during and in the aftermath of the First World War, of a series of secret treaties between major powers, the international community resolved that open diplomacy would be a central pillar in the new global order. This principle was

[1] For an exploration of the promotion of transparency in treaty-making more broadly see Andrea Bianchi and Anne Peters (eds), *Transparency in International Law* (CUP 2013). See also chapter 31 of this *Handbook* on "The Participation of Nonstate Actors in the Multilateral Treaty Process."

[2] United Nations Treaty Collection, <https://treaties.un.org/> accessed January 25, 2019.

most clearly manifested in the first of United States president Woodrow Wilson's 14 points to be used for peace negotiations, presented to the United States Congress on January 8, 1918, under which he called for "[o]pen covenants of peace, openly arrived at, after which there shall be no private international understandings of any kind but diplomacy shall proceed always frankly and in the public view."[3]

This global commitment to transparency in treaty-making was reflected in article 18 of the Covenant of the League of Nations, establishing an unprecedented obligation for members of the League to register with the Secretariat "every treaty or international engagement entered into hereafter." Article 18 further provided the fearsome sanction that "[n]o such treaty or international engagement shall be binding until so registered." However, different interpretations of this sanction, and an unwillingness of the Permanent Court of International Justice to apply it in practice,[4] created confusion and led to difficulties in its implementation.[5]

Following the dissolution of the League of Nations, the principle of universal registration and publication was retained in Article 102 of the Charter of the United Nations, with some important changes. The wording of paragraph 1 was amended slightly to refer to "international agreement" rather than "international engagement," which had been seen as less definite.[6] In addition, in place of the Covenant's ultimately unworkable requirement that unregistered treaties be considered non-binding, Article 102 provides that no party to a treaty or agreement that has not been registered may invoke that treaty or agreement before any organ of the United Nations. Negotiating states considered that this sanction would give the efficacy desired, without causing the difficulties of application seen during the time of the League of Nations.[7]

2 The Implementation of Article 102: Toward Open Diplomacy?

Following the entry into force of the Charter, action has continually been taken by the organs of the United Nations, often in concert with one another, to convert the general obligation contained in Article 102 into a fully functioning system of treaty registration and publication. The General Assembly, the Secretariat, and the International Court of Justice in particular have played a central role.

[3] Appended to Robert Lansing, *The Peace Negotiations: A Personal Narrative* (Houghton Mifflin Company 1921), appendix IV, 314–16.

[4] See in particular the Court's judgement in *Interpretation of the Treaty of Neuilly*, [1924] PCIJ Rep., Series A, No 4.

[5] See The First Assembly of the League of Nations, vol IV, no1 (February 1921).

[6] See Report of Subcommittee IV/2/A (25 May 1945).

[7] See Report of Subcommittee IV/2/A/3 (25 May 1945).

2.1 The General Assembly of the United Nations: Operationalizing Article 102

At the first session of the General Assembly, member states recognized that significant steps were needed in order to facilitate the implementation of Article 102, and thus instructed the Secretary-General to circulate draft Regulations in this regard.[8] Following detailed consideration by the Sixth Committee, the Regulations to Give Effect to Article 102 of the Charter of the United Nations were adopted by the Assembly on December 14, 1946.[9] The Regulations, which served to clarify the scope and effect of the obligation contained in Article 102, therefore represent one of the first legal instruments adopted by member states to operationalize the provisions of the Charter.

The General Assembly has on three occasions returned to amend the Regulations in order to reflect changes in treaty-making practice and to increase the efficiency of the registration and publication process.

Through the first two sets of amendments, adopted in 1949 and 1950 respectively, the Assembly addressed the challenges identified early on in the life of the registration and publication system. Specifically, the Assembly recognized the nascent role of the Secretary-General in the international treaty framework by extending the registration obligation to him in his capacity as depositary of multilateral treaties,[10] and lightened the administrative burden of the Secretariat by reducing the number of languages in which the register is kept as well as removing the obligation to send a certificate of registration to all parties to a treaty upon registration, requiring instead that a certificate be sent only to the registering party.[11]

In 1978, through its third and most significant amendment to date, the Assembly sought to reduce the significant backlog that had developed in the publication of treaties by giving the Secretariat the discretion not to publish certain categories of bilateral treaties *in extensor.*[12] This discretion was later extended to multilateral treaties.[13]

During the 1980s and 1990s the Assembly intermittently re-engaged with the topic of the registration and publication of treaties. Stopping short of any formal amendments to the Regulations, the Assembly did however endorse the use of new technological tools in the registration and publication process, including the electronic treaty database and the UN Treaty Collection website.[14]

As considered in the conclusion to this chapter, the Assembly has recently shown a renewed interest in the registration and publication of treaties, presenting a possible opportunity for further modernization.

[8] UNGA Res 23 (10 February 1946). [9] UNGA Res 97 (14 December 1946).

[10] UNGA Res 364 (B) (1 December 1949). [11] UNGA Res 482 (12 December 1950).

[12] UNGA Res 33/141 A (19 December 1978). [13] UNGA Res 52/153 (15 December 1997).

[14] See, in particular, UNGA Res 51/158 (16 December 1996).

2.2 The Secretariat of the United Nations: Managing the Registration and Publication Process

The Secretariat of the United Nations is the central organ in the registration and publication process. In accordance with Article 102, it is *with* the Secretariat that member states must register treaties, following which it is then incumbent on the Secretariat to publish them. In exercising these functions, the Secretariat is guided by the legal framework established by the General Assembly in the form of the Regulations.

In practical terms, it is the Treaty Section of the UN Office of Legal Affairs that receives the copies of treaties submitted for registration along with relevant supporting documentation, inserts the relevant information into the electronic treaty database, analyzes the submissions, requests additional information where necessary, and then proceeds to formalize registration, including through transmission of the certificate of registration to the submitting entity. The Treaty Section sends over 230 pieces of correspondence to member states and relevant intergovernmental organizations each year with respect to the registration of treaties.

In fulfillment of its obligations with regard to the publication of treaties, the Secretariat produces the *United Nations Treaty Series*, which contains information on all treaties registered in accordance with Article 102, including the texts of the majority of those instruments. First published in 1946, the *United Nations Treaty Series* now comprises over 2,800 volumes. With treaties produced in over 100 languages it represents one of the most linguistically diverse publications of the Organization.

The role of the Secretariat in the registration and publication process is often described as administrative; this term can however obscure the significant substantive analysis it conducts, when assessing whether the instruments submitted for registration do in fact constitute treaties under international law. Section 4 of this chapter will consider in detail some of the key issues that the Secretariat must address when carrying out this work.

The Secretariat also seeks to support member states in fulfilling their obligations under Article 102 of the Charter through the provision of technical assistance and training activities. In recent times, the Treaty Section has delivered regional training seminars in Latin America, Southern Africa, and Eastern Africa, in addition to delivering training sessions for representatives of member states at UN headquarters. Following the delivery of these seminars, the Secretariat has often seen an increase in submissions from participating states.

2.3 The Role of the International Court of Justice: Considering the Legal Effect of (Non) Registration

The International Court of Justice, as the principal judicial organ of the Organization, has served as the key forum for consideration of two key issues concerning the legal impact of Article 102. First, the Court has on a number of occasions been confronted with the question of how strictly the sanction under Article 102 should be applied in practice, that is, whether a state should be prevented from invoking a treaty that has not been registered. Second, the Court has served as the setting for discussion on the legal effects of registration and its relevance to the views of the parties as to the legal status of a particular instrument.

With regard to the application of the sanction for non-registration, the Court has ultimately adopted a flexible approach, as exemplified in *Qatar v. Bahrain* (1994).[15] Here, the Court was required to consider a double exchange of letters relating to the maritime boundary dispute, which both parties noted had not been registered. Despite this, and even after directly referring to the sanction under Article 102 in its judgment, the Court did not consider itself prohibited from citing the instrument as a basis for its jurisdiction. A similar approach was adopted by the Court in *Nicaragua v. Honduras* (2007),[16] in which it felt able to consider the text of the Regional Central America-Dominican Republic Free Trade Agreement of 16 April 1998, despite the fact that the Agreement had not been registered.

Recent proceedings before the Court in the *Jadhav Case* demonstrated contrasting views amongst the parties as to the relevance of non-registration. Noting that an agreement on consular access concluded in 2008 between Pakistan and India had not been registered, India asserted that, consequently, "Pakistan cannot invoke this Agreement before this Court."[17] Perhaps aware of the Court's previous aversion toward enforcement of Article 102, Pakistan responded that it was unfortunate that "the Applicant State seeks to rely upon what can best be described as a technicality."[18] The Court proceeded to refer to the 2008 Agreement on a number of occasions in its order on provisional measures, and made no reference to the objections raised by India on the basis of non-registration.[19]

It should be noted, however, that the Court is not alone in appearing to take a flexible approach to the application of the sanction under Article 102. Both the General Assembly and the Security Council have permitted non-registered treaties to be considered and cited in relevant resolutions when of central importance to the issue under consideration.[20]

While the Court has largely ignored the sanction for non-registration, one can however identify within its proceedings a number of occasions in which registration has been considered as relevant to the legal status of an instrument under international law.[21]

15 *Maritime Delimitation and Territorial Questions* (*Qatar v Bahrain*), (Jurisdiction and Admissibility) [1994] ICJ Rep 112.

16 *Territorial and Maritime Dispute between Nicaragua and Honduras in the Caribbean Sea* (*Nicaragua v. Honduras*) (Judgement) [2007] ICJ Rep 726.

17 *Jadhav Case* (*India v Pakistan*) (Verbatim Record) [CR 2017/5] para 16, see also para 66(b).

18 *Jadhav Case* (*India v Pakistan*) (Verbatim Record) [CR 2017/6] p 11.

19 *Jadhav Case (India v Pakistan)* (Order on provisional measures) [2017] see paras 21, 25, 33, 41, and 43.

20 See the Agreement of 18 January 1974 between Egypt and Israel concerning disengagement of forces, which was reproduced as a Security Council document (S/11198 of 18 January 1974) prior to registration.

21 For a broader exploration of the legal effects of registration and non-registration see David N. Hutchinson, "The Significance of the Registration or Non-registration of an International Agreement in Determining Whether or Not It Is a Treaty" (1993) 46 Current Legal Problems 257.

In *Peru v. Chile* (2014)[22] the Court considered the status of the Santiago Declaration of 18 August 1952, which Chile contended established a maritime boundary between the two states. In its submission, Peru claimed that the instrument was originally "declarative" in character but accepted that "it later acquired the status of a treaty after being ratified by each signatory... and registered as such with the United Nations Secretariat." Consequently, the Court observed that it was no longer contested that the Santiago Declaration constituted a treaty. Most recently in *Kenya v, Somalia* (2017),[23] the Court noted, in concluding that a memorandum of understanding between the government of the Republic of Kenya and the Transitional Federal Government of the Somali Republic was a valid treaty, that "Kenya considered the MOU to be a treaty, having requested its registration in accordance with Article 102 of the Charter..., and Somalia did not protest that registration until almost five years thereafter."

By contrast, in the aforementioned case of *Qatar v. Bahrain*, the Court was explicit in rejecting the view that non-registration may indicate the absence of an intention to conclude a treaty. With respect to a set of agreed minutes between the parties, Bahrain argued that their subsequent conduct, in particular the fact that Qatar had waited for six months before registering the instrument and that Bahrain had subsequently objected to registration, showed that they never considered the agreement to be binding. The Court rejected this view, noting that "non-registration or late registration does not have any consequence for the actual validity of the agreement, which remains no less binding on the parties."

3 A View of the International Treaty Framework through Article 102 of the Charter

Through its role in exercising the registration and publication functions of the Secretariat, the Treaty Section of the UN Office of Legal Affairs has developed a unique view of global treaty-making practices. This section will attempt to share this perspective in two ways. First, drawing on the hundreds of thousands of data entries in the Treaty Section electronic treaty database, a statistical picture will be painted of some key treaty-making trends. Second, drawing on the Secretariat's work in analyzing and processing treaties submitted for registration, we will consider some of the central treaty-making challenges faced by states and international organizations.

3.1 Global Trends in Treaty-Making

A key identifiable trend with respect to the substantive focus of global treaty-making is the prominence of commercial matters. Chart A below indicates that there are almost

[22] *Maritime Dispute (Peru v. Chile)* (Judgement) [2014] ICJ Rep 24.

[23] *Maritime Delimitation in the Indian Ocean (Somalia v. Kenya)* (Preliminary Objections) [2017].

three times the number of treaties concluded in the field of trade and investment as there are in the next most common fields of military matters and taxation.

Chart A - Registered Multilateral Treaties

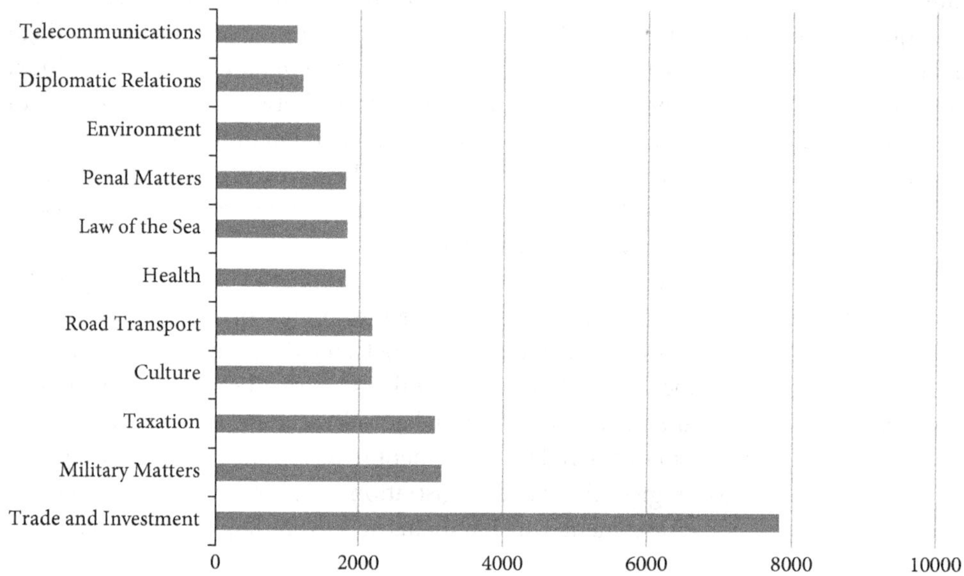

Mention should also be made here of less-heralded areas of treaty-making, such as culture and road transport, which, while not at the forefront of political or academic discussions, appear to represent a significant proportion of the day-to-day treaty-making activity of states. Of course, this graph encompasses only those treaties that have been registered, which may go some way to explain the absence of some thematic areas that we might expect to have seen figure more prominently.[24]

3.1.1 *A gradual decline in multilateral treaty-making?*

An apparent gradual decrease in the conclusion of multilateral treaties can also be identified.[25] Chart B indicates that the number of multilateral treaties concluded per year has been in decline since a peak of 121 treaties in 1967.

Three separate periods can be identified in this regard. Following an initial steep increase after the end of the Second World War, an average of 70 multilateral treaties concluded in the late 1940s to the early 1960s have been registered. Between 1962 and 1976 we then see a significant increase in multilateral treaty-making activity, reaching an

[24] This information is based on a thematic analysis of the "Subject Term' attributed to each treaty in the UN electronic treaty database.

[25] Multilateral treaty for the purposes of this Chart is defined as "a treaty between more than two subjects of international law."

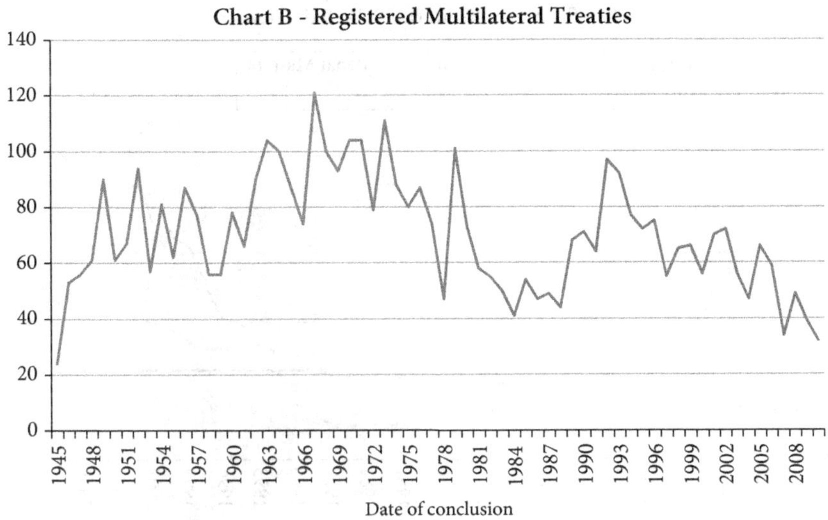

average of 95 registered multilateral treaties per year. Finally, following a somewhat erratic period in the mid-1980s,[26] we see an apparent steady decline from 1995 to 2010.

However, although the number of multilateral treaties concluded per year appears to have decreased, the overall participation of states in the international treaty framework is not necessarily on the decline. Based on the information held by the Treaty Section, the number of subsequent treaty actions (registrations, accessions etc.) effected each year in relation to registered multilateral treaties appears to have actually increased in the last 20 years.

3.1.2 *Multilateral and Bilateral Treaties: A mutually supportive relationship*

Perhaps one of the most interesting trends identifiable from the data is the connection between bilateral and multilateral treaty-making activity within thematic fields, with a complementary relationship emerging in a number of areas.

Chart C demonstrates the cumulative growth in the number of multilateral treaties deposited with the Secretary-General in selected thematic fields, providing an insight into the multilateral treaty-making priorities of member states since the establishment of the Organization.

We can see for example the rapid increase in treaty-making in the environmental field, in particular in the early 1990s following the Rio Summit at which the Convention on Biological Diversity, the UN Framework Convention on Climate Change, and the UN Convention to Combat Desertification were opened for signature. With respect to

[26] This apparent steep drop and recovery in treaty-making activity in the mid-1980s is more likely connected to an overall decrease in the number of treaties registered, itself related to funding challenges faced by the UN at the time.

Chart C - Multilateral Treaties deposited with the UN Secretary-General: Selected Themes

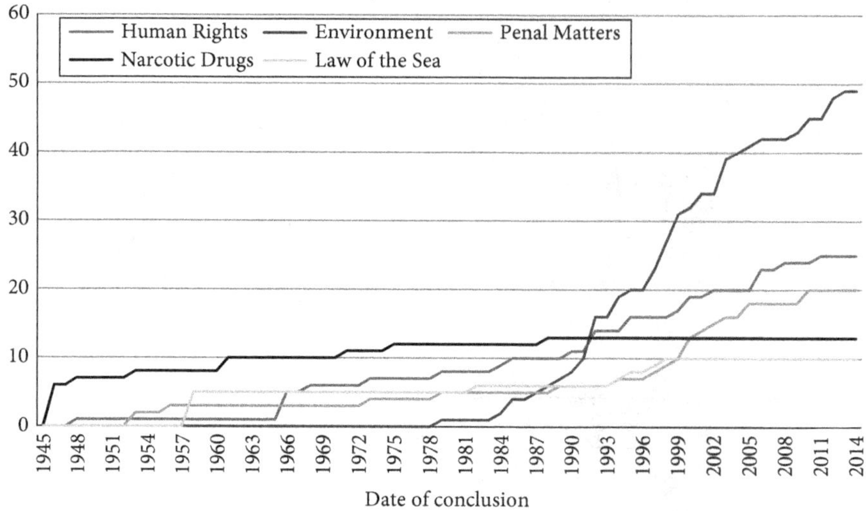

penal matters, we can similarly observe a rapid increase in the early 2000s with the adoption of the Rome Statute of the International Criminal Court in 1998, and the UN Convention against Transnational Organized Crime (UNTOC) and its three Protocols in 2000, followed by the UN Convention against Corruption (UNCAC) in 2003.

Chart D - Penal Matters

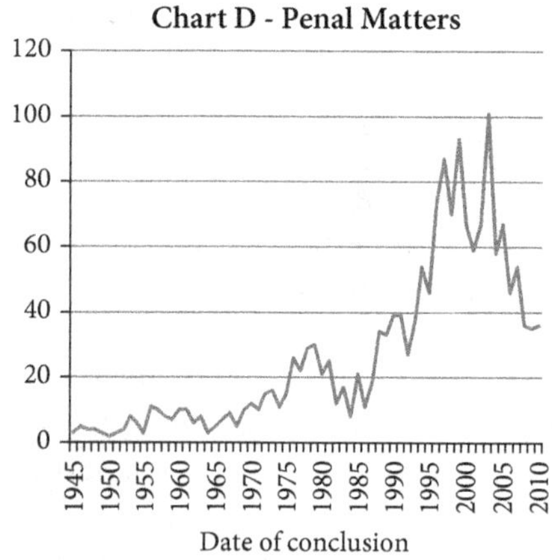

Chart E - Environment

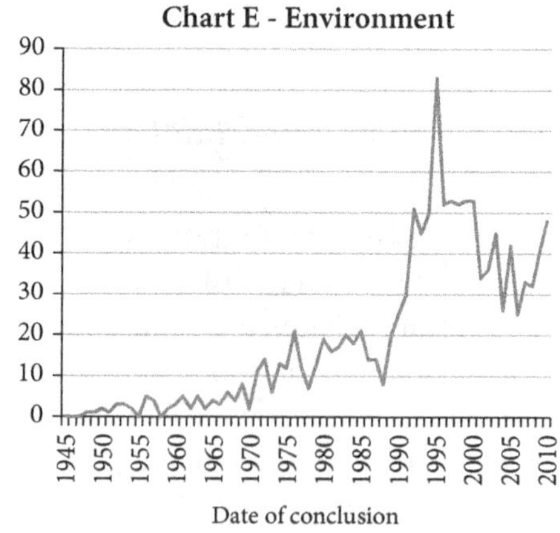

Charts D, E, F, and G provide a parallel view of the total number of treaties, both bilateral and multilateral, concluded in relation to a number of the thematic areas highlighted in Chart C. Strikingly, we can see something of a call-and-response relationship emerge between the bilateral and multilateral regimes.

In the field of penal matters, we see a rapid increase in bilateral treaty-making in the 1990s, leading up to the adoption of the key multilateral treaties highlighted previously.

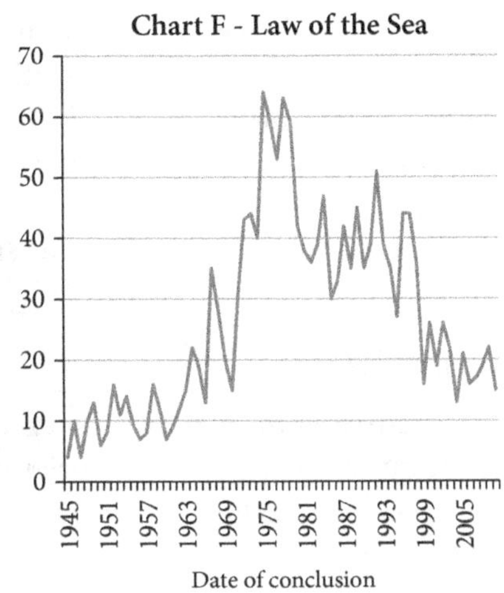

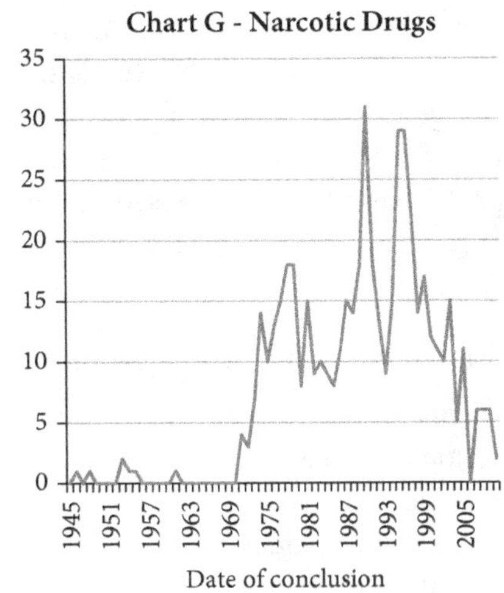

Indeed, the two peak years for overall treaty-making in that thematic area come, respectively, one year before the conclusion of the UNTOC, and on the same year as the conclusion of the UNCAC.

In the related field of narcotic drugs, we see a significant increase in bilateral treaty-making in the late 1980s and early 1990s, mirroring the multilateral treaty-making activities being undertaken within the UN at the time leading to the adoption of the UN Convention against Illicit Traffic in Narcotic Drugs and Psychotropic Substances in 1988. Similarly, we see a rapid increase in treaty-making related to the law of the sea in the 1970s at a time when the codification process ultimately leading to the adoption of the UN Convention on the Law of the Sea in 1982 was fully underway.

A slightly different relationship between bilateral and multilateral treaty-making emerges in the field of the environment, with a significant peak in bilateral activity three years after the opening for signature of the three Rio summit instruments. A substantive analysis of these treaties demonstrate that a large number relate to the provision of financing to developing countries to assist them in adhering to the requirements of the new multilateral instruments.

3.2 Key Challenges in Treaty-Making: Lessons from the Practice of the Secretariat

3.2.1 *A thematic analysis of treaty-making: The predominance of commercial matters*

As reflected in the Repertory of Practice of United Nations Organs, the Secretariat is often required, as part of its role in managing the registration process, to address central legal issues in the field of treaty law including the treaty-making capacity of certain entities and international organizations. In seeking to be consistent with regard to such questions, the Secretariat looks, as its key sources of guidance, to the provisions of article 102 and article 1 of the Regulations along with the position taken by other UN organs,[27] general principles of international law, and its own prior practice.[28]

The need for the Secretariat to consider such questions often stems from the fact that state practice is often far from settled. In this sense, the registration practice of member states provides a useful insight into the main questions of controversy in the field of treaty law.

3.2.2 *Treaty-Making Capacity of Territorial Entities*

Perhaps one of the most sensitive issues that the Secretariat must address in exercising its functions under Article 102 of the Charter is the question of which territorial entities should be accepted as being capable of validly concluding treaties. Unsurprisingly, the practice of states in the registration of treaties reflects their broader divergences of views regarding the legal status of specific territories.

One of the more contentious questions in this respect is the capacity of the territory of Palestine, and more recently the State of Palestine, to conclude treaties. In this regard, the Secretariat has consistently taken the view that agreements concluded prior to 2012 with the territory of Palestine or the Palestinian Liberation Organization cannot be registered. The practice of a number of a number of member states however indicates that they considered these entities to benefit from treaty-making capacity, with six states and two international organizations having submitted for registration a total of 21 agreements to which Palestine or the Palestinian Liberation Organization are a party. Following such submissions, the Secretariat consistently responds indicating that, as the capacity of Palestine or the Palestinian Liberation Organization to conclude agreements on the international plane had not been established, the relevant agreement is not registrable.

The Secretariat's practice differs significantly however with respect to agreements concluded with the State of Palestine after it was granted non-member observer state status within the United Nations through General Assembly Resolution 67/19, adopted on November 29, 2012.[29] As the State of Palestine has been recognized as a state within the United Nations, the Secretariat considers that it has treaty-making capacity as of November 29, 2012, and any treaty concluded between the State of Palestine and another state or international organization concluded after that date is registrable. Since the adoption of Resolution 67/19, the Secretariat has received and registered three bilateral agreements to which the State of Palestine is a party, with all three having being submitted by South Africa.

The Secretariat also has a well-established practice with respect to agreements concluded with Kosovo. As the competent organs of the United Nations have not yet clarified the status of Kosovo, the Secretariat will not register bilateral treaties to

[27] In particular the Sixth Committee of the General Assembly.

[28] *Repertory of Practice of the United Nations Organs, vol. V, Articles 92–111 of the Charter*, (United Nations publication), art 102, para 30.

[29] UNGA Res 67/19 (29 November 2012).

which Kosovo is a party or any subsequent actions effected by Kosovo in relation to multilateral treaties. This view reflects in particular the position adopted by the Security Council in its Resolution 1244 and the "status neutral" position taken by the Secretary-General since the unilateral declaration of independence of Kosovo. In its response to the submission of such agreements and treaty actions for registration, the Secretariat notes that, as it cannot determine whether agreements concluded with Kosovo meet the definition of a treaty under international law, registration will remain pending until clarification has been provided by the competent authorities of the United Nations.

A limited number of agreements concluded with the Sahawari Arab Democratic Republic (SADR) have also been submitted to the Secretariat for registration. However, in light of the status of Western Sahara as a Non-Self-Governing Territory under Chapter XI of the UN Charter, and given that the process for the holding of a referendum to determine the future of the territory continues to be administered by a UN peacekeeping force authorized by the Security Council, the Secretariat has adopted as its practice not to register bilateral treaties to which Western Sahara or the SADR is a party, until the question of Western Sahara's self-determination is resolved.

The question of the status of internal political entities under international treaty law has also arisen frequently in the registration practice of member states, particularly with respect to agreements concluded by the federated entities of Belgium. Following constitutional changes introduced in 1993, article 167 of the Belgian Constitution provides that community and regional governments may conclude treaties "regarding matters that fall within the competence of their Parliament."

Consequently, a number of member states appear to take the view that the federated regions of Belgium possess treaty-making capacity under international law, with nine agreements concluded with the Regions of Walloon and Flanders having been submitted for registration. In the context of an agreement relating to watercourses, one member state explicitly asserted the view in correspondence with the Secretariat that such federated entities can be parties to international treaties.[30] However, the Secretariat has consistently responded to such submissions by indicating that it is unable to proceed with registration of agreements with a federated entity as a party, as such an agreement does not constitute an international agreement within the purview of Article 102.

Similarly, a small number of member states have submitted agreements concluded with the government of Quebec for registration as treaties. Here also, the Secretariat has indicated to the submitting states that the relevant agreement cannot be registered as concluded with the government of Quebec as the latter does not possess treaty-making capacity under international law.

Member states have also submitted a significant number of agreements that prima facie appear to have been concluded directly with overseas territories of other states. In particular, the Secretariat receives a significant number of agreements each year

[30] See also in this regard André Alen and Patrick Peeters, "Federal Belgium within the International Legal Order: Theory and Practice," in *International Law: Theory and Practice. Essays in Honour of Eric Suy* (Martinus Nijhoff 1998) 123–43.

submitted by member states as concluded with the overseas territories of the United Kingdom of Great Britain and Northern Ireland. In such cases, the Secretariat has consistently indicated to submitting states that these agreements can only be considered as treaties for the purpose of Article 102 if it is possible to establish that the agreement concerned is formally binding on the state responsible for the conduct of the foreign relations of the dependent territory.[31]

3.2.3 *Treaty-Making Capacity of International Organizations*

The Secretariat is regularly faced with questions relating to the treaty-making capacity of international organizations. Indeed, it is perhaps the issue that most frequently gives rise to the need for the Secretariat to communicate concerns regarding the legal status of instruments submitted by member states for registration.

In 2016 alone, the Secretariat indicated to submitting states on seven occasions that the agreement they had submitted for registration had been filed for information as the Secretariat concluded that the organization concerned did not have treaty-making capacity, while the registration of a further three agreements was postponed pending clarification from the submitter as to the legal status and capacities of the organization concerned.

The Secretariat's practice when it comes to the capacity of international organizations to conclude treaties follows the 1986 Vienna Convention on the Law of Treaties between States and International Organizations or between International Organizations, which, while not yet in force, is generally considered as customary law in this area.[32] Its preamble notes that international organizations possess the capacity to conclude treaties that are necessary for the exercise of their functions and the fulfillment of their purposes, and that the practice of international organizations in concluding treaties with states or between themselves should be in accordance with their constituent instruments. The Convention further provides in its article 6 that the capacity of an international organization to conclude treaties is governed by the rules of that organization.

Underlying these provisions is the view that when states create an intergovernmental organization they decide which powers they want to provide it with, including if it should have treaty-making capacity, and the extent of that capacity. However, if treaty-making capacity is not expressly addressed in the constituent instrument, nor explicitly excluded, it may nevertheless still be implied, for instance if treaty-making power is necessarily required in order to give effect to other powers granted to the organization. The power to conclude a host-country agreement, for example, without which the organization would not be able to operate, would normally be implied as a necessary element of being an international organization.[33]

[31] *Repertory of Practice of the United Nations Organs, vol. V, Articles 92–111 of the Charter*, (United Nations publication), art 102, para 31 (d).

[32] Olufemi Elias, "Who Can Make Treaties? International Organizations" in Duncan B Hollis (ed.), *The Oxford Guide to Treaties* (OUP 2012) 77.

[33] Jan Klabbers, *Advanced Introduction to the Law of International Organizations* (Edward Elgar 2015).

Based on the above, the Secretariat has developed a clear practice when it comes to agreements between states and international organizations or between international organizations. The Secretariat first analyzes the organization's constituent instrument. If the constituent instrument provides the organization with international legal personality, does not contain explicit limitations relating to the ability to conclude treaties, and the type of treaty is essential for the work of the organization, this would normally constitute sufficient evidence for treaty-making capacity, and thus for the Secretariat to proceed with registration of the treaty.

However, if the organization does not have any external relations and lacks competence to engage in such relations, or the constitution denies it international legal personality, the Secretariat will normally conclude that it does not have treaty-making capacity, and will inform the submitter accordingly. Where an analysis of the constituent instrument does not provide clarity with regard to the relevant organization's treaty-making capacity, the Secretariat consults the submitter of the treaty, requesting further clarification on the status of the organization.

In perhaps one of its most significant early cases on this issue, the Secretariat took the position that the International Committee for the Red Cross (ICRC) was not an intergovernmental organization, and consequently declined to effect registration of two agreements between a member state and the ICRC.[34] Subsequently, a number of agreements between member states and the ICRC have been submitted for registration, in response to which the Secretariat has noted that they have been filed for information on the basis that the ICRC does not have treaty-making capacity.

The Secretariat is also on occasion required to consider the legal status of bodies within the broader UN institutional family. Most recently this issue has arisen with respect to agreements concluded by member states with the Secretariat of the United Nations Framework Convention on Climate Change. Due to a lack of clarity with regard to the legal status and treaty-making capacity of the UNFCCC Secretariat such agreements have been registered as concluded by the Secretariat on behalf of the Conference of the Parties to the UNFCCC, and this only when a decision by the Conference of the Parties explicitly requesting the Secretariat to conclude such an agreement has been adopted.

4 The Impact of Article 102 and Priorities for Reform

When assessing the overall success of the work of the United Nations in promoting transparency in the international treaty framework, note must first be taken of the hundreds of thousands of visitors to the United Nations On-line Treaty Collection each year

[34] *Repertory of Practice of the United Nations Organs, supplement no. 5, vol. V, articles 92–111 of the Charter,* (United Nations publication), art 102, para 6.

that are able to access information on over 72,000 registered treaties. This in itself represents at least partial fulfillment of the goal that states sought to achieve through the establishment of an absolute obligation in the Charter to register treaties.

Encouragingly, the rate of registration, as can be seen in Chart H, has increased significantly over time, with the 14,298 treaties registered in the last 10 years representing a 10 percent increase on the previous decade, and more than double the number of treaties registered in the 1950s. While recognizing that this growth in registration may also reflect a broader pattern of increased bilateral treaty-making activity and a significant expansion in the membership of the Organization, it nevertheless demonstrates a continued adherence to the registration obligation under Article 102 by many member states.

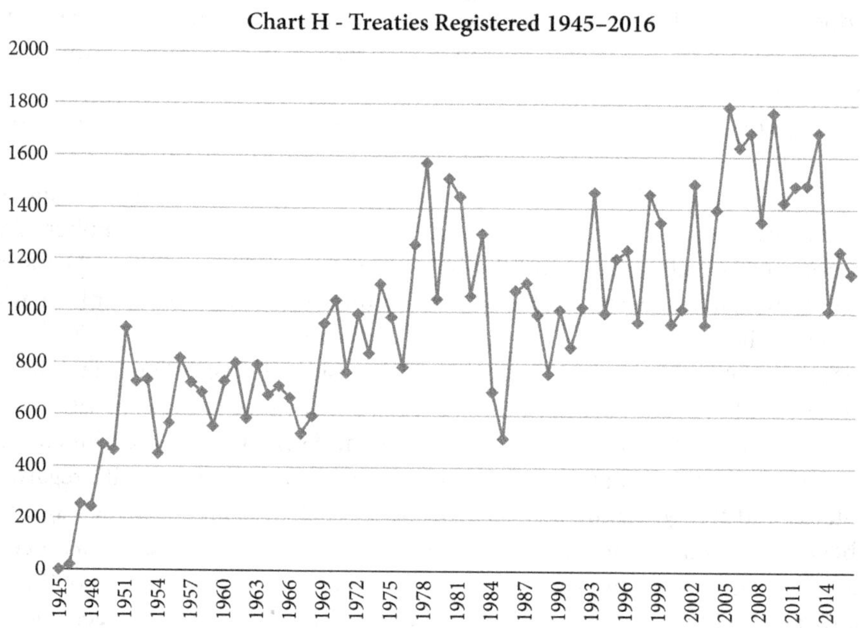

Any honest assessment would however recognize that further work is needed to fully meet the objectives of Article 102. Perhaps in part due to the flexible approach adopted by the Court and other UN organs with regard to the sanction under Article 102, the establishment of the obligation to register treaties under the Charter has not led to universal compliance. While it is not possible to ascertain the total number of existing treaties since 1945, it is clear that a significant number of treaties in force have not been registered.[35]

In this regard, a comparison of the number of bilateral investment treaties listed on the website of the United Nations Conference on Trade and Development and those

[35] See in this regard Paul Reuter, *Introduction aux Droit des Traités*, (2nd edn PUF 1985) 52; RB Lilich, "The Obligation to Register Treaties and International Agreements with the United Nations" (1971) 65 AJIL 771; and *UN Jur YB* (1979) 195–97.

registered under Article 102 is instructive, with the UNCTAD resource containing around three times the number of treaties registered with the Secretariat.[36]

Furthermore, registration of treaties by states is geographically imbalanced, with a small number of states registering the majority of treaties. As can be seen in Chart I, in the period from 2007 to 2016 states from the Western European and Others Group registered almost two-thirds of the total number of treaties registered in that period. While this can be explained to some extent by higher levels of treaty-making by certain states and the differing number of states in each regional group, it undoubtedly also reflects an imbalance in adherence to Article 102.

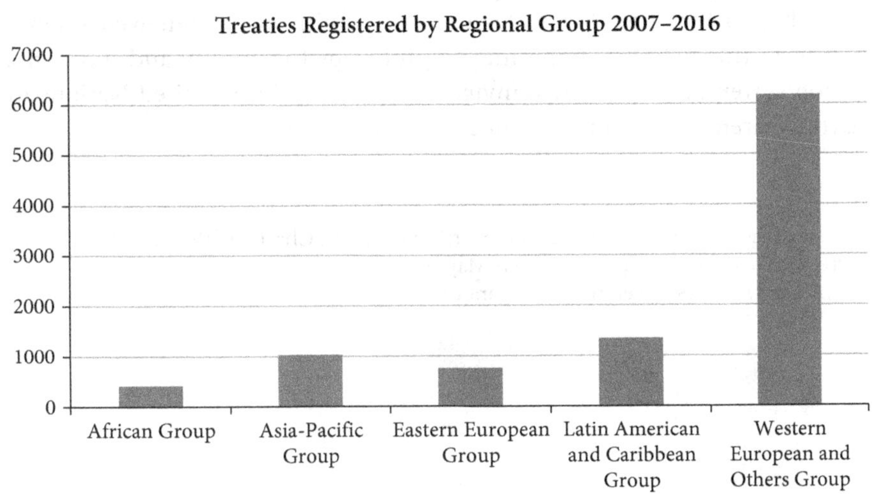

Beyond the negative impact that this "registration gap" has on the overarching objective of transparency, imbalance in registration practice can also have a particularly detrimental effect on those states that, due to a lack of capacity, awareness, or resources, fall short in the fulfillment of their obligations under Article 102. A failure to register deprives those states, in principle, from the ability to cite agreements they have concluded before any UN organ, while reducing awareness of such agreements in political, academic, and legal communities. Further work is therefore required to support all states to engage in the registration process.

It is in the context of these challenges that the General Assembly has recently returned to the topic of transparency in treaty-making as part of its work on the item "The rule of law at the national and international levels." In response to a request from the Assembly at its 71st session,[37] the Secretary-General produced a report identifying a series of potential amendments to the Regulations with the aim of ensuring that they reflect the current practice of the Secretariat, give useful guidance to member states on the fulfillment of their obligations under Article 102 and increase the efficiency of the registration

[36] UNCTAD Investment Policy Hub <http://investmentpolicyhub.unctad.org/IIA> accessed January 25, 2019.

[37] UNGA Res 71/148 (13 December 2016) para 24.

and publication process.[38] Key among these recommendations were the simplification of the procedural requirements for registration, the increased use of electronic resources in the registration process, and consideration as to whether the current publication policy, and in particular the requirement that all published treaties be translated into English and French, meets the needs of member states.

Having reviewed the Secretary-General's report, the Assembly at its 72nd session stressed that the Regulations should be useful and relevant to member states,[39] but declined to mandate any specific action on the basis of the Secretary-General's recommendations. However, in advance of its 73rd session, the General Assembly appears ready to address the registration and publication of treaties as a separate agenda item. It is to be hoped that member states can now build on the renewed interest and momentum in this field by taking meaningful steps to simplify and modernize the registration system, and thereby reinvigorate the role of the United Nations in promoting transparency in the international treaty framework.

[38] "Review of the regulations to give effect to Article 102 of the Charter of the United Nations," Report of the Secretary-General, UN Doc A/72/86 (11 May 2017).

[39] UNGA Res 72/119 (18 December 2017) para 10.

CHAPTER 34

THE ROLE OF THE SECRETARY-GENERAL OF THE UNITED NATIONS AS DEPOSITARY OF MULTILATERAL TREATIES

ARANCHA HINOJAL-OYARBIDE*

A depositary is someone to whom something is given in trust. The depositary of a treaty is a government, or an authority or organ of an international organization to which a treaty is entrusted.[1]

Traditionally, the duties of the depositary of a treaty, as codified in the Vienna Convention on the Law of Treaties (VCLT), are the custody of the original and of the instruments related to the treaty, the execution and recording of treaty procedures and formalities, and the dissemination to all states[2] of all acts relating to the life of the treaty. The depositary thus ensures that treaty formalities and procedures, such as the preparation of the original of the treaty and its certified true copies, the affixing of signatures, the deposit of instruments of ratification,[3] the determination of entry into force, etc., are properly executed and recorded, and that all states concerned are appropriately informed.

* The views expressed herein are those of the author and do not necessarily reflect the views of the United Nations.

[1] The term "treaty," as used in this chapter, means any international agreement binding under international law, including any subsequent international agreement, such as a protocol or an amendment.

[2] In this chapter, unless otherwise noted, the term "state" also means an international organization entitled to negotiate and become party to a treaty.

[3] When the term "ratification" is used in this chapter, it is intended to extend, unless otherwise noted, to other methods of expression of consent to be bound by a treaty, such as acceptance, approval, or accession.

Despite the vital role it plays in the life of a treaty, the depositary has often been perceived as an institution of limited relevance. But this perception has changed. The depositary has become an indispensable and widely recognized player in multilateral treaty-making, due to the growing number of actors and the widening scope and complexity of the treaties they conclude.

This chapter will elaborate on the unique role played by the Secretary-General of the United Nations ("the Secretary-General") in his capacity as depositary of multilateral treaties and describe how this role has evolved and gained relevance. The Secretary-General is the largest depositary in the world, with around 600 multilateral treaties of worldwide interest deposited with him. The Secretary-General delegates his depositary functions onto the Office of Legal Affairs of the Secretariat of the United Nations, which in turn assigns them to its Treaty Section.[4]

Important developments in the depositary practice of the Secretary-General have taken place since the late 1990s, when an innovative and proactive approach to the performance of his depositary duties started to develop. Using information technologies, the Treaty Section designed a sophisticated and highly customized treaty database—which integrates an electronic publication component—with the objective of gaining in efficiency and timeliness in the preparation and dissemination of treaties and treaty information through the United Nations Treaty Collection website ("the UN Treaty Collection").[5]

The Secretary-General has undertaken other innovative outreach activities, such as the organization of high-level signing ceremonies, capacity-building seminars, and the preparation of publications on treaty law and practice, which have broadened the traditional role played by the depositary.

The Secretary-General has also raised awareness on the important role the depositary plays within the UN treaty-making processes. In 2001, he issued a bulletin entitled "*Procedures to be followed by the departments, offices and regional commissions of the United Nations with regard to treaties and international agreements*" ("the 2001 Bulletin"), which sets forth procedural requirements with regard to treaties concluded by or under the auspices of the UN.[6] The 2001 Bulletin provides, inter alia, that the draft final clauses of treaties to be deposited with the Secretary-General must be submitted by the relevant UN office to the Treaty Section for review and comment prior to their finalization in treaty negotiations. This chapter will give special consideration to the contribution of the Secretary-General, in his depositary role, to the drafting of final clauses and their application and interpretation, showing how the depositary has influenced and shaped the final text of multilateral treaties and contributed to the evolution of treaty-making at the UN.

[4] The only exception is the deposit of charts and lists of geographical coordinates under the UN Convention on the Law of the Sea, which is effected by the Division for Ocean Affairs and the Law of the Sea of the Office of Legal Affairs.

[5] <https://treaties.un.org> accessed January 20, 2019.

[6] UN Doc ST/SGB/2001/7 (28 August 2001).

1 The Nature of the Role of the Secretary-General as Depositary

The functions of the depositary of a treaty are international in nature, which obliges the depositary to act with impartiality. This principle is codified in article 76 of the VCLT.

When the depositary is a state, a conflict may arise between the position of that state and the performance of the depositary functions, in which case the depositary is under the obligation to act independently and with detachment from such a conflicting position. International organizations performing depositary functions may also face differing positions with one or more of their member states, and must equally act independently. In the event of any difference appearing between a state and the depositary as to the performance of the depositary functions, the depositary must bring the question to the attention of all states concerned and, where appropriate, of the competent organ of the international organization.[7]

Treaties rarely designate more than one depositary. When they do so, it is often to avoid conflict[8] or to recognize the special contribution of certain states to the treaty-making process.[9] However, this practice may create complications and uncertainty resulting from possible differences in depositary practices. For that reason, the Secretary-General does not accept being a co-depositary nor does he delegate his depositary functions to any office other than the Office of Legal Affairs, to ensure the uniformity and harmonization of treaty-making practices at the UN.

The Secretary-General operates in a unique and complex political and legal environment. While his depositary functions must be performed in an objective, independent, and transparent manner, the discharge of such functions is inevitably influenced by the policies and rules of the political Organization in which his functions are discharged. As a result, the performance of the Secretary-General's depositary functions is not only guided by the law of treaties and his depositary practice, but also by resolutions, decisions, and other directives of the General Assembly and other UN organs. This is for example the case when sensitive issues arise with respect to the application of participation clauses to certain entities, territories, or states whose claims to becoming parties to a treaty raise questions for the UN or part of its membership. It is also the case when the Secretary-General declines depositary functions because the application of the treaty by the parties may be contrary to UN policies or to the parties' obligations under other treaties deposited with him.

[7] See VCLT, Art 77(2).

[8] In the 1960s, the United Kingdom, the United States, and the Soviet Union were designated as co-depositaries of certain treaties, such as for example the Treaty on the Non-Proliferation of Nuclear Weapons, to enable participation by states that had no universal recognition.

[9] For example, Canada and Hungary are co-depositaries of the Treaty on Open Skies of 24 March 1992, and the Organization for Economic Co-operation and Development and the Council of Europe are co-depositaries of the Convention on Mutual Administrative Assistance in Tax Matters.

Depositary functions are legal in nature, and must be distinguished from administrative functions (such as issuing invitations to conferences, circulating proposals of amendments, or keeping registries or lists of authorities), which are performed by treaty secretariats. In the past, in exceptional circumstances (most notably, when no substantive secretariat existed), the Treaty Section has performed administrative tasks assigned in the treaty to "the Secretary-General." However, more recently, the Treaty Section has started to transfer such administrative tasks to offices that have assumed secretariat functions. For example, in 2014, the UN Office on Drugs and Crime agreed to receive, record, and share information from states parties relating to the designation of central authorities and languages for mutual legal assistance under the United Nations Convention against Corruption and the United Nations Convention against Transnational Organized Crime, an administrative function that was previously discharged by the Treaty Section. Similarly, since 2014, the circulation of notifications under article 103 of the Rome Statute of the International Criminal Court ("the Rome Statute") is handled by the Legal and Enforcement Unit of the Presidency of the Court.

2 Depositary Functions and Recent Features of the Secretary-General's Depositary Practice

Apart from the substantive provisions that are the object of a treaty, treaties include provisions on procedural legal matters, such as signature, consent to be bound, entry into force, reservations, or withdrawal. These provisions are called final clauses or final provisions.

The Secretary-General's depositary functions start when he is consulted and provides advice on a treaty's final clauses before the adoption of the treaty intended to be deposited with him. While he has traditionally been consulted on treaty law matters, it is only following the issuance of the 2001 Bulletin that his advisory role has become increasingly sought after and recognized.

The main aspects of the Secretary-General's depositary practice are described in the *Summary of Practice of the Secretary-General as Depositary of Multilateral Treaties* ("the Summary of Practice," last updated in 1994[10]) and the *Final Clauses of Multilateral Treaties Handbook* (last updated in 2003).[11] The analysis later in this chapter will particularly highlight developments and recent practice not covered in these two publications.

[10] *Summary of Practice of the Secretary-General as Depositary of Multilateral Treaties* (United Nations 1994) UN Doc ST/LEG/7/Rev 1 at<https://treaties.un.org/doc/source/publications/practice/summary_english.pdf> accessed January 20, 2019.

[11] *Final Clauses of Multilateral Treaties: Handbook* (New York 2003) at <https://treaties.un.org/doc/source/publications/FC/English.pdf> accessed January 20, 2019.

2.1 Provision of Advice and Application and Interpretation of Final Clauses

The depositary's legal advice is guided by the provisions of the treaty; public international law, including customary international law as it may be deemed codified by the VCLT; the depositary practice developed over many years; and general principles flowing from relevant resolutions, decisions, and directives of the General Assembly and other UN organs. Nowadays, states and the secretariats involved in treaty negotiations consistently consult the Treaty Section along the negotiation process and acknowledge its role in facilitating the adoption of well-drafted procedural provisions.

2.1.1 *Designation of the Depositary and Assignment of Functions Other than Depositary Functions*

The Secretary-General is not obliged to accept the role of depositary for a treaty. His general policy is to accept treaties negotiated under the UN auspices, including UN regional bodies.[12] However, he can make exceptions to this policy and accept being depositary for multilateral treaties concluded outside the UN framework,[13] in which case he must first receive a request and must accept performing depositary functions.[14]

The treaty should clearly designate the Secretary-General as depositary in a separate provision. The depositary functions should not be specified unless they include functions other than those well established and codified in article 77 of the VCLT. Negotiating states are often reminded that the Treaty Section, which performs the depositary functions on behalf of the Secretary-General for a massive quantity of treaties, has neither the resources nor the technical expertise to effectively carry out functions that exceed the depositary ones.[15] For example, in 2015, during the negotiations of the Paris Agreement, the Treaty Section advised against the designation of the Secretary-General as the authority responsible for recording and maintaining a public registry of "nationally determined contributions" (NDCs). The Paris Agreement finally established that NDCs

[12] *Summary of Practice* paras 12–14.

[13] For example, in 2002, the Secretary-General accepted being the depositary of the Agreement on Succession Issues between the then five successor states of the former Yugoslavia but, in 2003, he declined to be the depositary of the Framework Agreement on the Sava River Basin and its Protocol on Navigation Regime, which were open to some of the successor states to the former Yugoslavia and, unlike the Agreement on Succession Issues, was of a very technical nature and negotiated without any involvement of the UN.

[14] This was the case of the Convention on the Prohibition of the Use, Stockpiling, Production and Transfer of Anti-Personnel Mines and on their Destruction.

[15] For example, in the case of the Agreement concerning the Establishing of Global Technical Regulations for Wheeled Vehicles, Equipment and Parts which can be fitted and/or be used on Wheeled Vehicles, as revised in 1995, the Secretary-General took the view that the notifications relating to the Compendium of Candidate Global Technical Regulations and the Registry of Global Technical Regulations created under the Agreement were administrative functions related to its implementation and not depositary functions and that, accordingly, they had to be performed by the UN Economic Commission for Europe (UNECE), in its capacity as secretariat for the Agreement.

were to be communicated to the climate change secretariat and recorded in a public registry maintained by it.[16]

The Treaty Section consistently advises that, if a treaty were to assign administrative tasks to the "Secretary-General of the United Nations," it would be understood that such tasks are to be performed by the substantive UN office concerned, which would then act on behalf of the Secretary-General as chief administrative officer.

2.1.2 *Authentic Languages*

In the past, the Secretary-General accepted depositary functions for a few treaties concluded in languages other than the official languages of the UN.[17] Following the release of the 2001 Bulletin, which provides in its section 4.3 that texts of treaties to be deposited with the Secretary-General should be concluded only in the six UN official languages, the Secretary-General only accepts depositary functions for treaties concluded in any or all UN official languages. This practice is justified by the fact that, without the expertise and resources to operate in non-UN official languages, the Secretary-General cannot duly fulfill his legal responsibilities, including the preparation of the original of the treaty.

Accordingly, in 2001, the Treaty Section advised against the adoption of the Budapest Convention on the Contract for the Carriage of Goods by Inland Waterway in Dutch and German.[18] In the cases of the International Agreement on Olive Oil and Table Olives, 2005, and the International Coffee Agreement, 2007, the Secretary-General declined depositary functions when Italian and Portuguese, respectively, were designated as authentic languages.[19]

The negotiating states are also advised of the need that the treaty be negotiated (or at least carefully drafted) in all its authentic languages, as they all have identical legal value when the meaning of its provisions needs to be determined. Following formal adoption, no further changes can be made to the texts, except through a cumbersome correction procedure. However, adopted texts very often contain errors that require corrections.

2.1.3 *Opening for Signature*

The treaty intended to be deposited with the Secretary-General may stipulate the date and place of the opening for signature. If the date is not indicated, the treaty will open for signature at the UN Headquarters in New York as soon as the original and the certified

[16] Article 4(12) of the Paris Agreement.

[17] The Secretary-General accepted depositary functions for the International Agreement on Olive Oil and Table Olives, 1986, which was concluded in Arabic, English, French, and Spanish, as well as Italian—a non-UN official language. Similarly, he was the depositary of the International Coffee Agreement, 2000, that was concluded in English, French, and Spanish, as well as Portuguese, a non-UN official language.

[18] This Convention was adopted in a diplomatic conference organized under the joint auspices of the UNECE, the Central Commission for the Navigation of the Rhine, and the Danube Commission, in Dutch, German, English, French, and Russian. It is deposited with the government of Hungary.

[19] The 2005 Agreement was then deposited with the government of Spain. Interestingly, the draft International Agreement on Olive Oil and Table Olives, 2015, maintained Italian as authentic language until it was removed to ensure that the Secretary-General would accept depositary functions, which he did.

true copies are prepared and made available. Negotiating states are advised not to open the treaty for signature immediately after adoption, since the preparation of the original and the production and circulation of certified true copies is a process that may take a few weeks. The depositary is also responsible for organizing and officiating in signing ceremonies, which sometimes attract many high-level signatories, and, for this reason, he needs to be consulted beforehand.[20]

2.1.4 *Participation Clauses: Signature and Consent to Be Bound*

Final provisions establish who can sign and become a party. Treaties may be open to participation by all states ("all States" formula), which is currently the general practice for treaties of universal scope, or only to certain states (for instance, treaties of a regional scope). Some older treaties used the so-called "Vienna formula" (or "Vienna clause"), which opens the treaty for participation by states members of the UN, any of its specialized agencies or the IAEA, parties to the Statute of the International Court of Justice, and states invited by the General Assembly. This formula was developed to overcome difficulties that arose during the Cold War relating to participation in treaties open to "all States" of entities that appeared otherwise to be states but could not be admitted to the UN due to the veto of a permanent member of the Security Council. That difficulty did not arise for membership in specialized agencies.[21] The Vienna formula became unnecessary when the General Assembly directed the Secretary-General as depositary to follow its practice whenever an "all States" formula was used in a treaty and, whenever advisable, request the opinion of the Assembly before receiving a signature or an instrument of ratification.[22] However, the application of participation clauses continued to raise complex legal and political issues.

For example, in 1992, the General Assembly, upon the recommendation of the UN Security Council, adopted a resolution that held that the Federal Republic of Yugoslavia (FRY) could not, as it had claimed, automatically continue the former Yugoslavia's membership in the UN, and instead had to apply for membership.[23] The Secretary-General considered that this resolution did not address the FRY's status regarding treaties deposited with him, and that he needed clear guidance in this respect. In the interim, he accepted treaty actions deposited by the FRY and listed them under the old short name "Yugoslavia."[24] When the General Assembly admitted the FRY to membership on November 1, 2000, after the latter renounced its claim to continue the legal personality

[20] For example, the ceremony for the opening for signature of the Paris Agreement attracted 175 signatures (and 15 ratifications) and the Convention on the Rights of Persons with Disabilities and its Optional Protocol 127 signatures and 1 ratification.

[21] See *Final Clauses Handbook* 11–16; *Summary of Practice* paras 79–81.

[22] See *Summary of Practice* paras 82–100.

[23] UN Doc A/47/485 (30 September 1992).

[24] "Status of the Federal Republic of Yugoslavia After General Assembly Resolution 47/1, Especially with Regard to the Publication 'Multilateral Treaties deposited with the Secretary- General'" (1994) UN Juridical YB 460–62.

of the former Yugoslavia, the FRY deposited a declaration of succession and the Secretary-General undertook a review of all actions previously recorded.[25]

In 2014, the Secretary-General accepted in deposit instruments of accession by Palestine to several treaties open to "all States," on the basis that General Assembly Resolution 67/19, by which Palestine was accorded "non-member observer State status in the United Nations", contained an unequivocal indication that the General Assembly considered Palestine to be a state. Canada, Israel, and the United States subsequently communicated their objection to such deposits.

The Secretary-General has also addressed the question of treaty participation of regional economic integration organizations (REIOs). This expression is interpreted as requiring an appropriate transfer of competences from their members, and the participation of certain international organizations that did not fulfill this condition has been declined on this basis.[26] The depositary recommends that participation clauses in a treaty precisely define the required characteristics of REIOs. The Convention on the Rights of Persons with Disabilities, which is a good example of careful consideration and thoughtful drafting of final clauses, uses the expression "regional integration organization" (without the word "economic") to restrict participation to international organizations with authority to bind their member states in relation to the Convention's matters. The European Union (EU) is today the only integration organizations with such competence in the relevant social areas covered by the Convention, such as health, justice, or employment.[27]

The EU has the ability, as an international organization with treaty-making capacity, to sign and become party to a treaty in its own behalf and as an individual party. However, the EU has not traditionally had the capacity to sign and ratify treaties or undertake other treaty actions on behalf of its member states. A novel decision pointing in that direction among the treaties deposited with the Secretary-General is reflected in the International Agreement on Olive Oil and Table Olives, 2015, which assigns to the EU only, and not to its member states, participation shares in the International Olive Council.

Some international entities have sought to participate in treaties deposited with the Secretary-General as international organizations. In 2006, the Secretary-General considered that the Iran-United States Claims Tribunal, which had submitted an instrument of accession to the Vienna Convention on the Law of Treaties between States and International Organizations or between International Organizations, did not appear to be an international organization with treaty-making capacity, and informed the Tribunal and the two states parties to its constituent treaty. While Iran supported accession, the United States considered that there was no intent to grant treaty-making capacity to the Tribunal. Accordingly, the Secretary-General did not accept the deposit of the instrument.

[25] See *Final Clauses Handbook* 17–20.

[26] Upon a 2009 request for advice from the African Union on the possibility of it acceding to the UN Framework Convention on Climate Change, the Secretary-General concluded that the African Union did not fulfill the requirements to participate as a REIO to this Convention.

[27] See Art 44 of the Convention.

2.1.5 *Entry into Force of the Treaty*

Issues have arisen with respect to the entry-into-force clauses.

Sometimes, the treaty is silent as to when it enters into force for those states that deposit their instruments of ratification between the date on which the conditions for entry into force are met (e.g., the deposit of the 50th instrument of ratification) and the date the treaty enters into force (e.g., 90 days following the deposit of the 50th instrument). When the issue arose with respect to the Arms Trade Treaty, the depositary followed its practice by which a state that deposits its instrument of ratification after the date on which the conditions for entry into force of the treaty are met but before the date of entry into force of the treaty, becomes a party on the date of entry into force of the treaty.[28]

In 2016, the issue of possibly counting the deposit by the EU of its instrument of ratification of the Paris Agreement as 28 parties (the number of its member states) arose, but the Secretary-General considered that it would not be in line with the participation clause of the Paris Agreement.

2.1.6 *Amendment Procedures and Entry into Force of Amendments*

Amendments to a treaty deposited with the Secretary-General are also deposited with him.

The circulation of proposals of amendment prior to their adoption is not a depositary function. Accordingly, modern treaties assign this task to their substantive secretariat. One exception are the proposals of amendment to most UNECE transport treaties, which are deemed adopted when the conditions for their entry into force are fulfilled. The Rome Statute and the Single Convention on Narcotic Drugs, 1961, as amended by the Protocol of 25 March 1972, provide that the Secretary-General must circulate proposals of amendment, but this is exceptional (and unnecessary as both treaties have secretariat bodies).

The depositary also determines the date of entry into force of amendments, which may raise difficulties. For example, where the treaty provides that an amendment shall enter into force after it has been ratified by three-fourths of the parties to the treaty, it is necessary to determine whether this means three-fourths of the parties at the time the amendment was adopted ("fixed-time" approach) or three-fourths of the parties counted at the time the depositary receives each ratification of the amendment ("current time" or "moving target" approach). Where the treaty is silent or ambiguous, the long-standing practice of the Secretary-General is to apply the current time approach, which was applied for instance to the amendments to the Charter of the UN.[29]

[28] See eg, the ratification by South Africa and Lithuania a few days before the entry into force of the Arms Trade Treaty (C.N.823.2014.TREATIES-XXVI.8, <https://treaties.un.org/doc/Publication/CN/2014/CN.823.2014-Eng.pdf> accessed January 20, 2019; C.N.813.2014.TREATIES-XXVI.8, <https://treaties.un.org/doc/Publication/CN/2014/CN.813.2014-Eng.pdf> accessed January 20, 2019.

[29] For example, the Secretary-General calculated the percentage of parties established in Article 108 of the UN Charter (two-thirds of UN members) for the entry into force of the Amendment to Article 61 based on the number of parties to the Charter as of September 24, 1973, and not as of December 10, 1971.

Only in two recent occasions, the parties have requested the depositary to apply the fixed-time approach.[30]

Difficulties also arise where the conferences of the parties make decisions that modify the amendment provisions of the treaty. For example, the five amendments to the Montreal Protocol on Substances that Deplete the Ozone Layer set out that they enter into force on a specific date, provided that at least 20 instruments of ratification are deposited. This contradicts article 9(5) of the Vienna Convention for the Protection of the Ozone Layer that requires ratification by at least two-thirds of the parties to the Protocol.

Similarly, in the case of the Kampala Amendment to the Rome Statue on the Crime of Aggression, the issue arose that article 121 provides for two different entry-into-force procedures, depending on which articles are being amended. The Kampala Amendment would have been subject to both procedures, which would have been unmanageable (and nonsensical). The Review Conference then decided that all the amendments on the crime of aggression would enter into force pursuant to the procedure set out in paragraph 5 of that provision.[31, 32]

Despite that, it is important to note that treaty provisions (including amendment provisions) can only be modified by agreement of the parties according to the procedure set out in the treaty or in accordance with international law. Article 39 of the VCLT provides that a treaty may be amended by "agreement between the parties... except insofar as the treaty may otherwise provide." Accordingly, when a treaty sets out rules for its amendment, those rules must be observed. At their meetings or conferences, the parties are competent to negotiate and agree on the text of an amendment and adopt it, but they are not entrusted to make the adopted amendment binding upon the parties without their consent to be bound. The only other manner the amendment provisions could be amended is by the consent of all parties to be bound by a different procedure, by virtue of the principle *lex posterior derogat priori* codified in article 30 of the VCLT.

There are amendments that necessarily require their entry into force for all parties. The Convention on the Rights of the Child expressly provides that an amendment enters into force when ratified by two-thirds of the parties but only for those that ratified the amendment. When an amendment to article 43 (2) of the Convention, which increased the number of members of the Committee on the Rights of the Child, entered into force, the Committee started to operate under the new composition for all parties to the

[30] In 2011, the Meeting of the Parties to the Convention on Environmental Impact Assessment in a Transboundary Context adopted a decision on the Amendments of 27 February 2001 and 4 June 2004, interpreting the Convention's provision on the calculation of the entry into force of amendments as referring to the parties at the time of their adoption (see Decision V/2). In the same year, the Conference of States Parties to the Basel Convention on the Control of Transboundary Movements of Hazardous Wastes and their Disposal agreed to apply the fixed-time approach to the entry into force of the 1995 Amendments to Convention (see Decision BC-10/3). The Conference later agreed that the calculation had to count those specific states that were parties to the Convention at the time of adoption of the 1995 Amendments (and not simply the number of states parties).

[31] See RC/Res.6 (11 June 2010) op para 1.

[32] C.N. 651.2010.TREATIES -8 at <https://treaties.un.org/doc/Publication/CN/2010/CN.651.2010-Eng.pdf> accessed January 20, 2019.

Convention (obviously). The depositary purposefully remained silent in his depositary notification to states on which parties were bound by the Amendment.[33]

2.1.7 *Withdrawal or Denunciation*

The question whether a state is entitled to withdraw from a treaty that does not contain a withdrawal provision has arisen several times in the depositary practice. In 1997, when he received the instrument of withdrawal from the International Covenant on Civil and Political Rights by the Democratic People's Republic of Korea (DPRK), the Secretary-General was of the view that the negotiators of the Covenant had taken the deliberate decision not to provide for withdrawal. Considering article 56 of the VCLT, he sustained that withdrawal from the Covenant would not appear possible unless all parties agreed with such withdrawal. He circulated to all states the instrument of withdrawal and an aide-memoire containing his position.[34] Several states supported this view and objected to the DPRK's withdrawal, which was not accepted in deposit.

On the other hand, when in 2005 the United States deposited its instrument of withdrawal from the Optional Protocol to the Vienna Convention on Consular Relations concerning the Compulsory Settlement of Disputes, the Secretary-General concluded that the possibility of withdrawal from the Protocol could be implied from the voluntary nature of the dispute settlement mechanism, which was the sole purpose of the Optional Protocol. The same rational applied to Colombia's withdrawal, in 2017, from the Optional Protocol of Signature concerning the Compulsory Settlement of Disputes.[35]

2.2 Other Depositary Functions

2.2.1 *Preparation of the Original of the Treaty and Certified True Copies*

Once a treaty is adopted, the Secretary-General prepares the original and issues copies that are certified as true and complete. These copies are circulated under the cover of a depositary notification and made available online. Simultaneously, another depositary notification informs states of the opening for signature of the treaty.

2.2.2 *Correction of Errors*

The original of a treaty and the certified true copies may need to be corrected because of errors in typing, printing, spelling, numbering, or discrepancies with the official records of the negotiations or between the different authentic languages. The correction procedure is the responsibility of the depositary and is regulated in article 79 of the VCLT and

[33] See C.N.1208.2002.TREATIES-17, <https://treaties.un.org/doc/Publication/CN/2002/CN.1208.2002-Eng.pdf> accessed January 20, 2019 or C.N.592.2017.TREATIES-IV.11.a, <https://treaties.un.org/doc/Publication/CN/2017/CN.592.2017-Eng.pdf> accessed January 20, 2019.

[34] See C.N.467.1997.TREATIES-10, <https://treaties.un.org/doc/Publication/CN/1997/CN.467.1997-Eng.pdf> accessed January 20, 2019.

[35] C.N.521.2017.TREATIES-XXI.5, <https://treaties.un.org/doc/Publication/CN/2017/CN.521.2017-Eng.pdf> accessed January 20, 2019.

described in the Summary of Practice. Correction procedures are frequent, tedious, and cumbersome, and demand enormous efforts and resources from the depositary, negotiating states, and secretariats. Such efforts could be avoided if more attention were paid to the careful drafting of texts in all authentic languages during the negotiation process.

Corrections take effect from the date of the adoption of the treaty. The Secretary-General's practice is not to incorporate the corrections into the original. Accordingly, once the corrections are accepted, the text of the treaty must be read together with the corrections circulated in separate depositary notifications.

2.2.3 *Acceptance of Signatures and Instruments, and Their Dissemination*

Part of the daily work of the depositary is receiving and reviewing full powers, instruments of ratification, and other treaty-related instruments, such as declarations or reservations. Following such review, the Secretary-General allows for signatures to be affixed to the treaty or instruments to be deposited.

In addition to keeping custody of these instruments, the Secretary-General has the function of disseminating the relevant information. This is done through the issuance of depositary notifications, which are today distributed exclusively by electronic means. The information contained in these notifications is also reflected in the *Status of Multilateral Treaties Deposited with the Secretary-General*, a publication that used to be annually printed and is today only available online in the UN Treaty Collection website and updated daily.[36]

A practice has developed by which the Secretary-General accepts to effect a deposit on the basis of a copy of the signed original instrument. In this case, the depositing state must ensure that the original will follow as soon as possible. This practice is useful to expedite the entry into force of treaties, for example, when a state needs to deposit its instrument by a certain date to be able to participate in a conference of the parties, or when the deposit of the instrument is subject to deadlines, such as in the case of objections to reservations.

2.2.4 *Reservations*

The Secretary-General's depositary practice with respect to reservations has evolved over the years and is described in the Summary of Practice.[37]

In the 1970s, the Secretary-General started to follow a practice on "late reservations," which deviates from the requirement of article 19 of the VCLT that reservations be formulated, at the latest, at the time of the deposit of the instrument of ratification. When the Secretary-General receives a late reservation, he notifies signatories and contracting states and gives them a period of time (initially 90 days but prolonged in 2000 to 12 months) to object to the reservation and/or its deposit. The Secretary-General considers the absence of objection as a tacit agreement by all states to its deposit. For the deposit to be declined, it suffices for one state to object. The same practice applies to the

[36] See <https://treaties.un.org/Pages/ParticipationStatus.aspx?clang=_en> accessed January 20, 2019.

[37] *Summary of Practice* paras 161 and 216.

modification of reservations.[38] More recently, a practice has developed by which, under certain conditions, late reservations are accepted without applying the 12-month objection procedure.[39]

2.3 Outreach Activities by the Depositary

The Secretary-General has developed several outreach activities beyond his customary depositary functions. In the late 1990s, as a part of UN celebrations for the new millennium, the Treaty Section proposed that the Secretary-General invite, in his capacity as depositary, heads of state and government to sign and ratify treaties deposited with him in a solemn high-level ceremony—called the "Treaty Event"—that was held in 2000, in the margins of the opening session of the General Assembly. Given the success of this initiative (273 treaty actions were undertaken at that ceremony), the Treaty Event has continued to be held yearly since then, resulting in over 2,000 treaty actions undertaken. This has proven to be an effective tool to promote participation in treaties and raise awareness of the importance of multilateral treaties as a primary source of international law.

In 2000, the Treaty Section also started to organize capacity-building seminars on treaty law and practice for legal experts from member states. Several seminars are held every year at the UN Headquarters and worldwide. The Treaty Section also issues several legal publications on treaty law and practice.

3 Conclusions

The developments highlighted in this chapter show that the Secretary-General is not—or at least not anymore—a mere custodian or broadcaster of depositary notifications. While adhering to the principles of impartiality and transparency that guide the performance of his international role, the Secretary-General expresses his own views as to the law and practice, and the legal consequences and viable solutions of matters bestowed on him. He inspires and guides other depositaries that consult him, particularly when complex legal developments that deserve careful thought arise. He advises numerous treaty secretariats that have proliferated in parallel to treaty-making. In sum, he influences and shapes the final text of treaties and contributes to the evolution of treaty-making at the UN while raising awareness of the importance of multilateral treaties as a primary source of international law.

[38] See note verbale of the Legal Counsel of the United Nations, 4 April 2000 (Ref. LA 41 TR/221 23-1), <https://treaties.un.org/doc/source/publications/nv/2000/4_04_00.pdf> accessed January 20, 2019.

[39] This applies when the reservation is expressly permitted by the treaty and has been deposited before the entry into force of the treaty for the reserving state. See eg C.N.78.2012.TREATIES-2, <https://treaties.un.org/doc/Publication/CN/2012/CN.78.2012-Eng.pdf> accessed January 20, 2019.

Index

Note: Tables are indicated by an italic *t* following the page number.

D

J

K

N

O

T

U